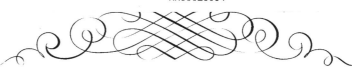

ISBN 978-0-282-85999-2
PIBN 10870007

AN ILLUSTRATED

HISTORY

OF

BAKER, GRANT, MALHEUR AND HARNEY

COUNTIES

WITH A BRIEF OUTLINE OF THE EARLY HISTORY OF THE

STATE OF OREGON.

WESTERN HISTORICAL PUBLISHING COMPANY
1902

DEDICATED

TO THE

Pioneers of Baker, Grant, Malheur and Harney Counties,

THE BRAVE MEN AND DEVOTED WOMEN,
THOSE WHO HAVE GONE AND
THOSE WHO REMAIN.

"YET NEVER A DOUBT, NAY, NEVER A FEAR
OF OLD, OR NOW, KNEW THE PIONEER."

PREFATORY.

IN offering this volume to the public, its publishers can hardly hope that it will in all respects meet the approval of those whose golden opinions are so ardently desired. The accuracy and completeness of such a work depends not alone on the conscientiousness and care of the compilers, but more especially upon the amount and quality of the materials which *happen* to have been preserved. For months the editorial force of the company has been searching with zeal and avidity for everything which could possibly throw light upon the past and present of Baker, Grant, Malheur and Harney counties. Their search has not been as successful as they could wish, but they have done the best they were able under the circumstances. It is thought that practically all printed matter which directly or indirectly related to the subject has been examined. Where no contemporaneous printed accounts could be found, the editors have been compelled to rely upon the testimony of pioneer settlers who took part in the events which they relate. In such cases they have, when possible, verified the statements of one man by those of another, knowing how treacherous and deceptive the memory frequently proves. But, with all vigilance, we cannot feel sure but that erroneous statements may have crept into the volume, and we feel constrained to invoke the kind charity of the reader to the faults he may discover.

The compilers have almost invariably been received with courtesy by those whom they have had occasion to approach, and to all who have in any way assisted, their sincere gratitude is hereby cordially extended. To make specific acknowledgements to everyone to whom they are due is impossible, but we must in a special way bear testimony to the kindly assistance rendered by the committees who have perused the manuscript histories of Baker and Grant counties, giving us the benefit of their ripe knowledge and experience. We are greatly indebted to the Bedrock Democrat, whose grand old files have preserved for us valuable information concerning events transpiring not alone in Baker county, but in all southeastern Oregon, also to the Grant County News, the Ontario Argus, the Times-Herald, of Burns, the Harney Valley Items, and the Harney County News, for the use of valuable files. The editors of these and other newspapers have shown us every courtesy, exposing their files for our use, and giving us such information and aid as they were able. In only one instance has a newspaper man met us with other than cordiality and kindness. We must not forget to give due credit to Isaac Hiatt, for the very great help which we received from his valuable little book entitled "Thirty-one Years in Baker County." Without its assistance it would have been impossible to give so complete a picture of the early days as is herewith presented. We are indebted also to the writings of Professor Waldemar Lindgren, of the United States Geological Survey, and Dr. Thomas Condon, of the Oregon State University, for information about the mines and geology of the region, and in an especial manner to Charles W. Parrish, Esq., for kindly giving us the results of his own extensive investigations made in his capacity as historian of the cabin of Oregon Native Sons, at Burns. The various sets of county officers are also entitled to due credit for having granted us access to the records under their care, cheerfully pointing out where the desired information could be most readily obtained.

ENDORSEMENTS.

We, the undersigned, pioneer settlers of Baker County, have listened to the reading of the major portion of the manuscript history of Baker county to be published by the Western Historical Publishing Company; we have called the attention of its authors to such errors and omissions as our knowledge of the facts has enabled us to detect and we believe that as prepared by them and corrected by us it presents an impartial record of events, accurate and comprehensive in its treatment of the subject.

Signed——W. C. HINDMAN,

MRS. I. A. PACKWOOD,

E. P. PERKINS.

Baker City, Ore., October 15, 1902.

We, the undersigned, pioneers of Grant county, having been chosen as a committee to pass judgment upon the merits of a county history soon to be published by the Western Historical Publishing Company, of Spokane, do affirm by our signatures that we have listened to the reading of the greater portion of said history of Grant County, and that in our judgment it chronicles the past and present events and conditions accurately and well and we commend it as a faithful, comprehensive and interesting story of the early struggles and later triumphs of our commonwealth.

Signed——G. I. HAZELTINE,

O. P. CRESAP,

W. S. SOUTHWORTH.

Canyon City, Ore., October 4, 1902.

TABLE OF CONTENTS.

EARLY OREGON HISTORY.

HISTORY OF BAKER COUNTY.

CHAPTER III.

1878 TO 1902.

CHAPTER IV.

POLITICAL.

CHAPTER V.

EDUCATIONAL.

CHAPTER VI.

BAKER CITY.

HISTORY OF GRANT COUNTY.

CHAPTER I.

CURRENT HISTORY, 1862 TO 1885.

CHAPTER II.

CURRENT HISTORY, 1885 TO THE PRESENT.

HISTORY OF MALHEUR COUNTY.

CHAPTER I,

SETTLEMENT AND PASSING-EVENTS.

Early Explorations—The Name "Malheur"—Immigration of 1845—Mormon Basin—Eldorado—Malheur City—Keeney's Cabin—Stock Ranches in Jordan Valley—Piutes and Bannocks—Indian Raids in 1868—Chinese Massacre—Settlements on Willow Creek—Beginning of the Stock Industry—Purchase of the Keeney Station by L. B. Rinehart—Names of Pioneer Settlers—Settlement on Bully Creek—Malheur Stock Ranges—

HISTORY OF HARNEY COUNTY.

CHAPTER I.

CURRENT HISTORY 1865 TO 1902.

CHAPTER II.

POLITICAL.

TABLE OF CONTENTS.   xv

CHAPTER III.

Towns of Harney County.

Burns—Platted in 1878—Nearest Postoffice at Camp Harney—First Business Established—Post office Removed
from Egan to Burns in 1888—Named in Honor of the Scottish Poet—Rapid Growth—Eastern Oregon Herald
Established in 1887—The United States Land Office—Incorporated in 1891—First City Officers—Center of a
Rich Agricultural and Stock District—Present Business Directory—Churches—Schools—Fraternal Orders—
Burns Business College—Harney—First Business Establishments—Trouble Over the Town Site—Absorption
of the Lower Town—Temporary County Seat—Business Men of the Town in 1888—Slow Growth—Present
Business—Lawen—Drewsey—Situation—General Merchandise Store Opened in 1883—Post Office Establish-
ed the Same Year—The Growth Slow until 1897—I. O. O. F. Hall Built in 1899—Healthy Development now
in Progress—Present Business Directory—Grist Mill.. 651

DESCRIPTIVE AND GENERAL.

CHAPTER I.

Topography, Resources, etc., of Baker, Grant, Malheur and Harney Counties.

Introduction—Baker County—Agricultural Resources—Area—Boundaries—Valley of the Powder River—Climatic and Other Conditions—Sumpter Valley—Elevation—Upper Burnt River Valley—Rye Valley—Valleys
of the Panhandle—Principal Agricultural Districts of the County—Stock in the County—Value of Live Stock
—Lumbering Interests—Grant County—Geology—John Day Valley—Valley of the South Fork—Valley
Region in the North—The Middle Fork—Long Creek Valley—Fox Valley—Haystack and Corncob Valleys
—Valley of the Silvies—Bear Valley—Murderer's Creek Valley—Contour of the County—Elevations—Physi-
cal Barriers—Stage Lines—Telephone Lines—A Ride over the Stage Lines—Mining Regions—Rocks and
Fossils of the John Day Valley—Mineral Springs—Forests—Live Stock—Soil—Cereals—Horticulture—Cli-
mate—Grant's Possibilities—Harney County—A Ride over the Ontario-Burns Stage Line—Area of Harney
Valley—Irrigation—Alfalfa—Elevation—The Cereals—Immense Cattle Farms—Wool Growing—Possibilities
of the Soil—The Small Valleys—Mountain Ranges—Sawmills—Lack of Transportation—Trout Creek Mining
Camp—Pueblo Mining District—Climate—Topography—Lakes—Malheur Cave—Cliff Dwellers' Ruins—
Malheur County—Area—Boundaries—Willow Creek—Bully Creek—Malheur River—Malheur Butte—
Owyhee River—Fossils and Ruins—Snake River—Soil—Climate—Irrigation and Production—Gas, Coal and
Oil—Conclusion... 717

CHAPTER II.

The Indian War of 1878.

Introduction—Causes of the War—Plan of the War—Sale of Fire-arms to the Indians—Payne's Ferry—Meeting
of the Bannocks and Piutes on Warm Springs Reservation—First Raid into Barren Valley—Skirmish at
White Horse Ranch—The Smith Massacre—Attack on French's Party in Happy Valley—Battle of Silver
Creek—Death of Buffalo Horn—Retreat of the Indians Northward—Preparations at Canyon City—Volunteer
Company Formed at Prairie City—Destruction of Property in the John Day Valley—The Fort at Long
Creek—Bannocks and Piutes Joined by Columbia River Indians—Baker County Escapes Hostilities—Baker
City Division Headquarters for the Army—Col. Parsons' Story of the War in Umatilla County—Death of
Egan—End of the War..:................. 743

CHAPTER III.

The Gold Fields of Eastern Oregon.

ntroduction—Four Gold-bearing Areas in Oregon—The Blue Mountain Field—Placer Mining—Quartz Mining
—Mormon Basin—Susanville—Virtue Mine—Connor Creek—La Belleview—Monumental—Cornucopia—
Cracker Creek District—Gold Production between 1880 and 1899—New Mining Districts—Minerals of East-
ern Oregon—The Elkhorn District—Pocahontas District—Minersville and Auburn Districts—Sumpter and

CHAPTER IV.

HISTORY OF THE PRESS.

CHAPTER V.

REMINISCENT.

GENERAL ILLUSTRATIONS.

INDEX.

BAKER COUNTY BIOGRAPHICAL.

xx

INDEX.

BAKER COUNTY PORTRAITS.

✓ GRANT COUNTY BIOGRAPHICAL.

GRANT COUNTY PORTRAITS.

MALHEUR COUNTY BIOGRAPHICAL.

MALHEUR COUNTY PORTRAITS.

HARNEY COUNTY BIOGRAPHICAL.

HARNEY COUNTY PORTRAITS.

BAKER, GRANT, MALHEUR AND HARNEY COUNTIES.

CHAPTER I.

EXPLORATIONS BY WATER.

The opening of a new century is a fitting time to cast a backward glance in our local history, reconstruct to the eye of the present the interesting and heroic events of the past, and by comparison between past and present forecast something of the future.

Old Oregon Territory, of which this county and this state were once parts, with its isolation, its pathos, its hospitality, has passed away. It had a strange history. It was the *ignis fatuus* of successive generations of explorers, luring them on with that indescribable fascination which seems always to have drawn men to the ever-receding circle of the "Westmost West," and yet for years and years veiling itself in the mists of uncertainty and misapprehension.

We do not usually realize how soon after the time of Columbus there began to be attempts to reach the western ocean and solve the mystery of the various passages, northwest, southwest and west, which were supposed to lead through the Americas to Asia. The old navigators had little conception of the breadth of this continent. They thought it to be but a few leagues across, and took for granted that some of the many arms of the

sea would lead them through to another ocean that would wash the Asiatic shores.

In 1500, only eight years after Columbus, Gasper Cortereal, the Portuguese, conceived the idea of entering what afterward became known as Hudson's Bay and proceeding thence westward through what he called the strait of Anian.

That mythical strait of Anian seems to have had a strange charm for the old navigators. One of them, Maldonado, a good many years later, gave a very connected and apparently veracious account of his journey through that strait, averring that through it he reached another ocean in latitude seventy-five degrees. But by means of Magellan's straits and the doubling of stormy Cape Horn, a connection between the two oceans was actually discovered in 1519.

In 1543 Ferrelo, a Spaniard, coasted along the shores of California, and was doubtless the first white man to gaze on the coast of Oregon, probably somewhere in the vicinity of the mouth of the Umpqua river.

In 1577 that boldest and most picturesque of all English sailors and freebooters, Francis Drake, started on the marvelous voyage by which he plundered the treasures of the Spanish main, cut the golden girdle of Manila, queen of the treasures of the Spanish orient, skirted the coast of California, Oregon, and Washington, and at last circumnavigated the globe.

But in 1592, just one hundred years after Columbus, comes the most picturesque of all those misty stories which enwrap the early history of Oregon. This is the story of Juan de Fuca, whose name is now preserved in our northwest boundary strait. According to this romantic tale of the seas, Juan de Fuca was a Greek of Cephalonia, whose real name was Apostolos Valerianos, and under commission of the king of Spain he sailed to find the strait of Anian, whose entrance the Spaniards wanted to fortify and guard so as to prevent ingress or egress by the English freebooters who were preying on their commerce. According to the account given by Michael Lock, "he followed his course, in that voyage, west and northwest in the South sea, all along the coast of Nova Spania and California and the Indies, now called North America (all which voyage he signified to me in a great map, and a sea-card of my own, which I laid before him), until he came to the latitude of forty-seven degrees; and that, there finding that the land trended north and northwest, with a broad inlet of sea, between forty-seven and forty-eight degrees of . latitude, he entered thereinto, sailing more than twenty days, and found that land still trending northwest, and northeast, and north, and also east and southeastward, and very much broader sea than it was at the said entrance, and that he passed by divers islands in that sailing; and that, at the entrance of the said strait, there is, on the northwest coast thereof, a great headland or island, with an exceeding high pinnacle or spired rock, like a pillar, thereupon. Also he said that he went on land in divers places, and that he saw some people on the land clad in beasts' skins; and that the land was very fruitful and rich of gold, silver and pearls and other things, like Nova Spania. Also he said that he being entered thus far into the said strait, and being come into the North sea already, and finding the sea wide enough everywhere, and to be about thirty or forty leagues wide in the mouth of the straits where he entered, he thought he had now well discharged his office; and that not being armed to resist the force of savage people that might happen, he therefore set sail and turned homeward again toward Nova Spania, where he arrived at Acapulco, anno 1592, hoping to be rewarded by the viceroy for this service done in the said voyage."

This curious bit of past record has been interpreted by some as pure myth, and by others as veritable history. It is at any rate a generally accurate outline description of the straits of Fuca, the Gulf of Georgia and the shores of Vancouver Island and the mainland adjoining. And whether or not the old Greek pilot did actually exist and first look on our "Mediterranean of the Pacific," it is pleasant to imagine that he did, and that his name fittingly preserves the memory of the grand old myth of Anian and the northwest passage.

There is one other more obviously mythical tale, concerning our northwest coast. It is said that in the year 1640 Admiral Pedro de Fonte, of the Spanish marine, made the journey from the Atlantic to the Pacific and return, through a system of rivers and straits, entering the coast at about latitude fifty-three degrees. Coming from Callao in April, 1640, and after having sailed for a long distance through an archipelago, he entered the mouth of a vast river, which he named Rio de Los Reyes. Ascending this for a long distance northeasterly he reached an immense lake, on whose shores he found a wealthy civilized nation, who had a capital city of great splendor called Conasset, and who welcomed the strangers with lavish hospitality. From this lake flowed another river easterly, and down this Fonte descended until he reached another great lake, from which a narrow strait led into the Atlantic ocean.

There is one curious thing about these legendary voyages, and that is the general accuracy of their description of the coast. Although these accounts are unquestionably mythical, it is not impossible that their authors had actually visited the coast or had seen those who had, and thus gathered the material from which they fabricated, with such an appearance of plausibility, their Munchausen tales.

We are briefly referring to these fascinating old legends, not for the purpose of discussing them here at any length, but rather to remind the reader of the long period of romance and myth which enveloped the early history of our state. Many years have passed after the age of myth before there were authentic voyages. During the seventeenth century practically nothing was done in the way of Pacific coast explorations. But in the eighteenth, as by common consent, all the nations of Europe became suddenly infatuated again with the thought that on the western shores of America might be found the gold and silver and gems and furs and precious woods for which they had been striving so desperately upon the eastern coast. English, French, Spanish, Portuguese, Dutch, Russian and American entered their bold and hardy sailors into the race for the possession of the land of the occident. The Russians were the first in the field. That gigantic power, which the genius of Peter the Great, like one of the fabled genii, had suddenly transformed from the proportions of a grain of sand to a figure overtopping the whole earth, had stretched its arms from the Baltic to the Aleutian archipelago, and had looked southward across the frozen seas of Siberia to the open Pacific as offering them another opportunity of expan-

sion. Many years passed, however, before Peter's designs could be executed. It was 1728 when Vitus Behring entered upon his marvelous life of exploration. Not until 1741, however, did he thread the thousand islands of Alaska and gaze upon the glaciated summit of Mt. Elias. And it was not until thirty years later that it was known that the Bay of Avatscha in Siberia was connected by open sea with China. In 1771 the first cargo of furs was taken directly from Avatscha, the chief port of eastern Siberia, to Canton. Then first Europe realized the vastness of the Pacific ocean. Then it understood that the same waters which frowned against the frozen bulwarks of Kamtchatka washed the tropic islands of the South seas and foamed against the storm-swept rocks of Cape Horn.

Meantime, while Russia was thus becoming established upon the shores of Alaska, Spain was getting entire possession of California. These two great nations began to overlap each other. Russians became established near San Francisco. To offset this movement of Russia, a group of Spanish explorers, Perez, Martinez, Heceta, Bodega and Maurelle, swarmed up the coast beyond the present site of Sitka.

England, in alarm at the progress made by Spain and Russia, sent out the Columbus of the eighteenth century, in the person of Captain James Cook, and he sailed up and down the coast of Alaska and of Washington, but failed to discover either the Columbia river or the straits of Fuca.

His labors, however, did more to establish true geographical notions than had the combined efforts of all the Spanish navigators who had preceded him. His voyages materially strengthened England's claim to Oregon, and added greatly to the luster of her name. The great captain, while temporarily on shore, was killed by Indians in 1778, and the command devolved upon Captain Clarke, who sailed northward, passing through Behring strait to the Arctic ocean. The new commander died before the expedition had proceded far on its return journey; Lieutenant Gore, a Virginian, assumed control and sailed to Canton, China, arriving late in the year.

` The main purposes of this expedition had been the discovery of a northern waterway between the two oceans and the extending of British territory, but, as is so often the case in human affairs, one of the most important results of the voyage was entirely unsuspected by the navigators and practically the outcome of an accident. It so happened that the two vessels of the expedition, the Revolution and the Discovery, took with them to China a small collection of furs from the northwest coast of America. These were purchased by the Chinese with great avidity, the people exhibiting a willingness to barter commodities of much value for them and endeavoring to secure them at almost any sacrifice. The sailors were not backward in communicating their discovery of a new and promising market for peltries, and the impetus imparted to the fur trade was almost immeasurable in its ultimate effects. An entirely new regime was inaugurated in Chinese and East India commerce. The northwest coast of America assumed a new importance in the eyes of Europeans, and especially of the British. The "struggle for possession" soon began to be foreshadowed.

One of the principal harbors resorted to by fur-trading vessels was Nootka, used as a rendezvous and principal port of departure. This port became the scene of a clash between Spanish authorities and certain British vessels, which greatly strained the friendly relations existing between the two governments represented. In 1779 the viceroy of Mexico sent two ships, the Princess and San Carlos, to convey Martinez and De Haro to the vicinity for the purpose of anticipating and preventing the occupancy of Nootka sound by fur-traders of other nations and that the Spanish title to the territory might be maintained and confirmed

Martinez was to base his claim upon the discovery by Perez in 1774. Courtesy was to be extended to foreign vessels, but the establishment of any claim prejudicial to the right of the Spanish crown was to be vigorously resisted.

Upon the arrival of Martinez in the harbor, it was discovered that the American vessel Columbia, and the Iphigenia, a British vessel, under a Portuguese flag, were lying in the harbor. Martinez at once demanded the papers of both vessels and an explanation of their presence, vigorously asserting the claim of Spain that the port and contiguous territory were hers. The captain of the Iphigenia pleaded stress of weather. On finding that the vessel's papers commanded the capture, under certain conditions, of Russian, Spanish or English vessels, Martinez seized the ship, but on being advised that the orders relating to captures were intended only to apply to the defense of the vessel, the Spaniard released the Iphigenia and her cargo. The Northwest America, another vessel of the same expedition, was, however, seized by Martinez a little later.

It should be remembered that these British vessels had in the inception of the enterprise divested themselves of their true national character and donned the insignia of Portugal, their reasons being: First, to defraud the Chinese government, which made special harbor rates to the Portuguese, and second, to defraud the East India Company, to whom had been granted the right of trading in furs in Northwest America to the exclusion of all other British subjects, except such as should obtain the permission of the company. To maintain their Portuguese nationality they had placed the expedition nominally under the control of Juan Cavalho, a Portuguese trader. Prior to the time of the trouble in Nootka, however, Cavalho had become a bankrupt and new arrangements had become necessary. The English traders were compelled to unite their interests with those of King George's Sound Company, a mercantile association operating under license from the South Sea and East India companies, the Portuguese colors had been laid aside and the true national character of the expedition assumed. Captain Colnutt was placed in command of the enterprise as constituted under the new regime, with instructions, among other things, "to establish a factory to be called Fort Pitt, for the purpose of permanent settlement, and as a center of trade around which other stations may be established."

One vessel of the expedition, the Princess Royal, entered Nootka harbor without molestation, but when the Argonaut, under command of Captain Colnutt, arrived, it was thought best by the master not to attempt an entrance to the bay lest his vessel should meet the same fate which had befallen the Iphigenia and the Northwest America. Later Colnutt called on Martinez and informed the Spanish governor of his intention to take possession of the country in the name of Great Britain and to erect a fort. The governor replied that possession had already been taken in the name of his Catholic Majesty and that such acts as he (Colnutt) contemplated could not be allowed. An altercation followed and the next day the Argonaut was seized and her captain and crew placed under arrest. The Princess Royal was also seized, though the American vessels in the harbor were in no way molested.

After an extended and at times heated controversy between Spain and Great Britain touching these seizures, the former government consented to make reparation and offered a suitable apology for the indignity to the honor of the flag. The feature of this correspondence of greatest import in the future history of the territory affected is that throughout the entire controversy and in all the royal messages and the debates of parliament, no word was spoken asserting a claim of Great Britain to any territorial rights or denying the claim of sovereignty so positively and persistently avowed by Spain, neither was Spanish sovereignty denied or in any way alienated by the treaty which followed. Certain real property was restored to British subjects, but a transfer of realty is not a transfer of sovereignty.

We pass over the voyage of the illustrious French navigator, La Perouse, as of more importance from a scientific than from a political standpoint; neither can we dwell upon the explorations of Captain Berkley, to whom belongs the honor of having ascertained the existence of the strait afterward denominated Juan de Fuca. Of somewhat greater moment in the later history of the northwest are the voyages of Meares, who entered and described the above mentioned strait, and who, in 1788, explored the coast at the point where the great Columbia mingles its crystal current with the waters of the sea. In the diplomatic battle of later days it was even claimed by some that he was the discoverer of that great "River of the West." Howbeit, nothing can be surer than that the existence of such a river was utterly unknown to him at the time. Indeed his conviction of its non-existence was thus stated in his own account of the voyage: "We can now with safety assert that there is no such river as the St. Roc (of the Spaniard, Heceta) exists, as laid down in the Spanish charts," and he gave a further unequivocal expression of his opinion by naming the bay in that vicinity Deception Bay and the promontory north of it Cape Disappointment. "Disappointed and deceived," remarks Evans facetiously, "he continued his cruise southward to latitude forty-five degrees north."

It is not without sentiments of patriotic pride that we now turn our attention to a period of discovery in which the vessels of our own nation played a prominent part. The northern mystery, which had been partially resolved by the Spanish, English, French and

Portuguese explorations, was now to be completely robbed of its mystic charm, speculation and myth must now give place to exact knowledge, the game of discovery must hereafter be played principally between the two branches of the Anglo-Saxon race, and Anglo-Saxon energy, thoroughness and zeal are henceforth to characterize operations on the shores of the Pacific northwest. The United States had but recently won their independence from the British crown and their energies were finding a fit field of activity in the titanic task of national organization. Before the constitution had become the supreme law of the land, however, the alert mind of the American had begun projecting voyages of discovery and trade to the northwest, and in September, 1788, two vessels with the stars and stripes at their mastheads arrived at Nootka sound. Their presence in the harbor while the events culminating in the Nootka treaty were transpiring has already been alluded to. The vessels were the ship Columbia, Captain John Kendrick, and the sloop Washington, Captain Robert Gray, and the honor of having sent them to our shores belongs to one Joseph Barrel, a prominent merchant of Boston, and a man of high social standing and great influence. While one of the impelling motives of this enterprise had been the desire of commercial profit, the element of patriotism was not wholly lacking, and the vessels were instructed to make what explorations and discoveries they might.

After remaining a time on the coast, Captain Kendrick transferred his ship's property to the Washington, with the intention of taking a cruise in that vessel. He placed Captain Gray in command of the Columbia with instructions to return to Boston by way of the Sandwich Islands and China. This commission was successfully carried out. The vessel arrived in Boston in September, 1790, was received with great eclat, refiitted by her owners and again despatched to the shores of the Pa-

cific with Captain Gray in command. In July, 1791, the Columbia, from Boston, and the Washington, from China, met not far from the spot where they had separated nearly two years before. They were not to remain long in company, however, for Captain Gray soon started on a cruise southward. On April 29, 1792, Gray met Vancouver just below Cape Flattery and an interesting colloquy took place. Vancouver communicated to the American skipper the fact that he had not yet made any important discoveries, and Gray, with equal frankness, gave the eminent British explorer an account of his past discoveries, "including," says Bancroft, "the fact that he had not sailed through Fuca strait in the Lady Washington, as had been supposed from Meares' narrative and map." He also informed Captain Vancouver that he had been "off the mouth of a river in latitude forty-six degrees, ten minutes, where the outset, or reflux, was so strong as to prevent his entering for nine days."

The important information conveyed by Gray seems to have greatly disturbed the equipoise of Vancouver's mind. The entries in his log show that he did not entirely credit the statement of the American, but that he was considerably perturbed is evinced by the fact that he tries to convince himself by argument that Gray's statement could not have been correct. The latitude assigned by the American was that of Cape Disappointment, and the existence of a river mouth there, though affirmed by Heceta, had been denied by Meares; Captain Cook also had failed to find it; besides, had he not himself passed that point two days before and had he not observed that "if any inlet or river should be found it must be a very intricate one, and inaccessible to vessels of our burden, owing to the reefs and broken water which then appeared in its neighborhood." With such reasoning, he dismissed the matter from his mind for the time being. He continued his journey northward, passed through the strait of Fuca, and engaged in a thorough and minute exploration of that mighty inland sea, to a portion of which he gave the name of Puget Sound.

Meanwhile Gray was proceeding southward "in the track of destiny and glory." On May 7th he entered the harbor which now bears his name and four days later he passed through the breakers over the bar, and his vessel's prow plowed the waters of that famous "River of the West," whose existence had been so long suspected. The storied "Oregon" for the first time heard other sound than "its own dashing."

Shortly afterward Vancouver came to Cape Disappointment to explore the Columbia, of which he had heard indirectly from Captain Gray. Lieutenant Broughton, of Vancouver's expedition, sailed over the bar, ascended the river a distance of more than one hundred miles to the site of the present Vancouver, and with a modesty truly remarkable, "takes possession of the river and the country in its vicinity in his Britannic Majesty's name, having every reason to believe that the subjects of no other civilized nation or state had ever entered it before." This, too, though he had received a salute of one gun from an American vessel, the Jennie, on his entrance to the bay. The lieutenant's claim was not to remain forever unchallenged, as will appear presently.

CHAPTER II.

EXPLORATION BY LAND.

With the exploration of Puget sound and the discovery of the Columbia, history-making maritime adventure practically ceased. But as the fabled strait of Anian had drawn explorers to the Pacific shores in quest of the mythical passage to the treasures of the Indian, so likewise did the fairy tales of La Hontan and others stimulate inland exploration. Furthermore, the mystic charm always possessed by a *terra incognita* was becoming irresistible to adventurous spirits, and the possibilities of discovering untold wealth in the vaults of its "shining mountains" and in the sands of its crystal rivers were exceedingly fascinating to the lover of gain.

The honor of pioneership in overland exploration belongs to one Verendrye, who, under authority of the governor-general of New France, in 1773 set out on an expedition to the Rocky mountains from Canada. This explorer and his brother and sons made many important explorations, but as they failed to find a pass through the Rocky mountains by which they could come to the Pacific side, their adventures do not fall within the purview of our volume. They are said to have reached the vicinity of the present city of Helena.

If, as seems highly probable, the events chronicled by La Page in his charming "Histoire de la Louisiane," published in 1758, should be taken as authentic, the first man to scale the Rocky mountains from the east and to make his way overland to the shores of the Pacific was a Yazoo Indian, Moncacht-ape or

Montcachabe by name. But "the first traveler to lead a party of civilized men through the territory of the Stony mountains to the South sea" was Alexander Mackenzie, who, in 1793, reached the coast at fifty-two degrees, twenty-four minutes, forty-eight seconds north, leaving as a memorial of his visit, inscribed on a rock with vermilion and grease the words, "Alexander Mackenzie, from Canada by land, July 22, 1793." His field of discovery was also without the scope of our purpose, being too far north to figure prominently in the international complications of later years.

Western exploration by land had, however, elicited the interest of one whose energy and force were sufficient to bring to a successful issue almost any undertaking worth the effort. While the other statesmen and legislators of his time were fully engaged with the problems of the moment, the great mind of Thomas Jefferson, endowed as it was with a wider range of vision and more comprehensive grasp of the true situation, was projecting exploring expeditions into the northwest. In 1786, while serving as minister to Paris, he had fallen in with the ardent Ledyard, who was on fire with the idea of opening a large and profitable fur trade in the north Pacific region. To this young man he had suggested the idea of journeying to Kamtchatka, then in a Russian vessel to Nootka sound, from which, as a starting point, he should make an exploring expedition easterly to the United States. Ledyard acted on the suggestion, but was arrested as a spy in the spring of 1787 by Russian officials, and so severely treated as to cause a failure of his health and a consequent failure of his enterprise.

The next effort of Jefferson was made in 1792, when he proposed to the American Philosophical Society that it should engage a competent scientist "to explore northwest America from the eastward by ascending the Missouri, crossing the Rocky mountains and descending the nearest river to the Pacific ocean." The

idea was favorably received. Captain Meriwether Lewis, who afterward distinguished himself as one of the leaders of the Lewis and Clarke expedition, offered his services, but for some reason Andre Michaux, a French botanist, was given the preference. Michaux proceeded as far as Kentucky, but there received an order from the French minister, to whom, it seems, he also owed obedience, that he should relinquish his appointment and engage upon the duties of another commission.

It was not until after the opening of the new century that another opportunity for furthering his favorite project presented itself to Jefferson. An act of congress, under which trading-houses had been established for facilitating commerce with the Indians, was about to expire by limitation, and President Jefferson, in recommending its continuance, seized the opportunity to urge upon congress the advisability of fitting out an expedition, the object of which should be "to explore the Missouri river and such principal streams of it as, by its course of communication with the waters of the Pacific ocean, whether the Columbia, Oregon, Colorado or any other river, may offer the most direct and practical water communication across the continent, for the purpose of commerce."

Congress voted an appropriation for the purpose, and the expedition was placed in charge of Captains Meriwether Lewis and William Clark (or Clarke). President Jefferson gave the explorers minute and particular instructions as to investigations to be made by them. They were to inform themselves should they reach the Pacific ocean "of the circumstances which may decide whether the furs of those parts may be collected as advantageously at the head of the Missouri (convenient as is supposed to the Colorado and Oregon or Columbia) as at Nootka sound or any other part of that coast; and the trade be constantly conducted through the Missouri and United States more beneficially than by the circumnavigation now practiced." In addition to the instructions already quoted, these explorers were directed to ascertain if possible on arriving at the seaboard if there were any ports within their reach frequented by the sea-vessels of any nation, and to send, if practicable, two of their most trusted people back by sea with copies of their notes. They were also, if they deemed a return by the way they had come imminently hazardous, to ship the entire party and return via Good Hope or Cape Horn, as they might be able.

A few days before the initial steps were taken in discharge of the instruction of President Jefferson, news reached the seat of government of a transaction which added materially to the significance of the enterprise. Negotiations had been successfully consummated for the purchase of Louisiana on April 30, 1803, but the authorities at Washington did not hear of the important transfer until the 1st of July. Of such transcendent import to the future of our country was this transaction and of such vital moment to the section with which our volume is primarily concerned, that we must here interrupt the trend of our narrative to give the reader an idea of the extent of territory involved and, if possible, to enable him to appreciate the influence of the purchase. France, by her land explorations and the establishment of trading posts and forts, first acquired title to the territory west of the Mississippi and east of the Rocky mountains, though Great Britain claimed the territory in accordance with her doctrine of continuity and contiguity, most of her colonial grants extending in express terms to the Pacific ocean. Spain also claimed the country by grant of Pope Alexander VI. A constant warfare had been waged between France and Great Britain for supremacy in America. The latter was the winner in the contest, and, in 1762, France, apparently discouraged, ceded to Spain the province of Louisiana. By the treaty of February 10, 1763, which gave Great Britain the

Canadas, it was agreed that the western boundary between English and Spanish possessions in America should be the Mississippi river, Great Britain renouncing all claim to the territory west of that boundary. In 1800 Spain retroceded Louisiana to France "with the same extent it has now in the hands of Spain, and which it had when France possessed it, and such as it should be according to the treaties subsequently made between Spain and other states."

The order for the formal delivery of the province to France was issued by the Spanish king on October 15, 1802, and, as above stated, the United States succeeded to the title by treaty of April 30, 1803.

When the treaty ceding Louisiana territory to the United States was negotiated the three ministers conducting the negotiations were Monroe and Livingston, representing the United States, and Barbe-Marbois, who had been selected by Napoleon to represent France. Marbois's relations with Napoleon at that time were close and confidential, and the current traditions of Napoleon's attitude throughout the negotiations is a more or less inaccurate version of the report made by Marbois in his "Histoire de la Louisiane," written after the Bourbon restoration and published in Paris by the Didots in 1829. The original edition, now rare in the United States, contains one of the earliest, if not the earliest, of the French maps of "the territory added to the United States by the treaty and its consequences," but interesting as this is, it scarcely compares in importance with the summary of the situation then existing as Marbois gives it, and with his report of Napoleon's conversations and speeches on the subject.

The second part of the work, which is devoted to the treaty and its effects on the destinies of the world—which he appreciated with surprising foresight—opens with a valuable summary of the attitude of the United States toward France and England. He shows that the defeated Federalists were taking advantage of Jefferson's well-known French sympathies to press against France and against the administration of the United States the dangerous questions which had been raised by the attitude of the West in demanding assurances of the free navigation of the Mississippi. "Although a very active faction in Congress," he writes, "worked secretly to force a declaration of war against France by the United States, the chiefs of the administration desired sincerely to preserve a good understanding. On its side the Consular government (Napoleon personally) seemed to wish to follow toward the republic a course opposed to that of the directory. War between France and England seemed inevitable, and the American Cabinet easily understood that in case it was declared the French consul would be under the necessity of postponing the occupation of Louisiana."

He then quotes from the message of December 18, 1802, in which Jefferson called the attention of Congress to the importance of the possible reoccupation of Louisiana by France, and details the circumstances under which Monroe was sent to France to re-enforce Livingston, who was already in Paris attempting to negotiate for the city of New Orleans and the territory which controlled the mouth of the Mississippi.

Marbois defines Livingston's mental state at this time as one of exasperation. He had been evaded and put off in what he considered a treacherous manner, until he was ready to square issues by making demands which no one thought France would consider—among others as Marbois records it—"for the whole of the vast territory north of the Arkansas." This seems to be the first presentation of the idea of the cession as a whole, and Marbois feels certain that Livingston's aggressiveness represented his own feelings rather than those of the American administration. To such an extent had this aggressiveness taken possession of Livingston—though he does not seem to

have expected to have the proposition for the cession of the country north of the Arkansas entertained, Marbois records with disapproval —that when Monroe landed in Paris, Livingston met him with a proposal "to take possession of New Orleans first and trade afterwards."

This sufficiently suggests Marbois's understanding of the attitude of the United States, an administration in power friendly to France, but urged against France by a powerful minority using the control of the Mississippi as a lever to such effect that the supporters of the administration were beginning to show signs of breaking away from control and forcing issues.

To understand the attitude of Napoleon it must be recalled that in becoming first consul he had announced himself as a pacificator of the world, and after attempting to conciliate the powers in the treaty of Amiens, had continued vigorously the attempt to reconstruct France in accordance with his own ideas. This he considered the object of paramount importance at the time, and whatever plans he had for extending the empire of France over Europe were to be postponed until he had firmly intrenched himself at home and reorganized France completely. In a great measure, he had carried out his plans for doing this, when he saw that England was once more about to take the aggressive against him—this just at a time when he was preparing to cease to be first consul and to become "Napoleon the First."

This is the situation which Marbois defines, and it explains the stimulus under which Napoleon's genius acted in reaching the decision that there must be a radical change in the attitude of France toward the United States. After the Revolutionary war France had hoped to hold the United States as a ward under an informal French protectorate and had co-operated with Spain to that end. To keep the United States surrounded by French and Spanish territory was part of this plan. When Monroe sailed for France Napoleon seems to have reached a decision, foreshadowed in a conversation in the Tuileries, to abandon once for all the idea of controlling the United States, and, by a sudden stroke, to set them loose as a first-class power against England. He announced this decision in a conference at which Marbois was present, just before Monroe landed.

Before calling this conference he had denounced the claims of England to be "mistress of the seas," and had said "to free the world from the commercial tyranny of England it is necessary to oppose to her a maritime power which will one day become her rival. It must be the United States. The English aspire to dispose of all the riches of the world. I will be useful to the entire universe if I can prevent them from dominating America as they dominate Asia."

It appears that after announcing at the Tuileries that the United States might be thrust forward as a rival for England, Napoleon brooded over the matter, as was his habit; and then, after he had really made up his mind, he called his advisers to him and addressed to them his request for advice in what was really a demand for their assent to his plans, "made with vehemence and passion," which did not invite argument. The first declaration of his purposes is thus given by Marbois:

"I know the worth of Louisiana, and I have wished to repair the error of the French negotiator who abandoned it in 1763. I have recovered it on paper through some lines in a treaty, but I have hardly done so when I am about to lose it again. But if it escapes me, it shall one day be at a dearer cost to those who force me to give it than the cost to those to whom I will surrender it. The English have successively taken from France Canada, the Isle Royal, Newfoundland, Acadia, and the richest territories of Asia. They are intriguing and disturbing in Santo Domingo. They shall not have the Mississippi, which they covet. Louisi-ana is nothing in comparison with their aggrandizement in all parts of the globe, but the jealousy they feel because of its return under the dominion of France warns me that they intend to seize it, and it is thus they will begin the war. They have already twenty vessels in the Gulf of Mexico—they swagger over those seas as sovereigns—and in Santo Domingo, since the death of Leclerc, our affairs are going from bad to worse. The conquest of Louisiana will be easy if they only take the trouble to descend upon it. I have not a moment to lose in putting it out of their power. I do not know but what they are there already. That is their usual way of doing things, and as for me, if I was in their place I certainly would not have waited. I wish to take away from them even the idea that they will ever be able to own this colony. I contemplate turning it over to the United States. I would hardly be able to say I had ceded it to them, for we are not yet even in possession of it. But even a short delay may leave me nothing but a vain title to transmit to these republicans, whose friendship I seek. They are asking me for but a single city of Louisiana, but I already consider the whole colony as lost, and it seems to me that in the hands of this rising power it will be more useful to the politics and even to the commerce of France than if I attempt to keep it."

"Tell me your opinion," said Napoleon, in conclusion, and his ministers made speeches, one for, the other against—the cession. He listened and asked questions. It was the next morning after this that he called them to him again and announced that England had broken faith in refusing to evacuate Malta, and that there was no time for further deliberation.

From the current translations of Napoleon's second speech preceding the negotiations with Monroe and Livingston, the opening and closing are generally omitted. As Marbois reports it, Napoleon, the day after he had listened to the arguments for and against the cession, called his counsellors together, told them that he had just received letters from his ambassador in London, and then proceeded:

"The English demand of me Lampedusa, which does not belong to me, and at the same time they wish to keep Malta for ten years. That island, where military genius has put forth its resources of defense to an extent which is incredible to those who have not seen it, would be another Gibraltar for them. To leave it to them would be to deliver to them the commerce of the Levant and to ruin my southeastern provinces. They wish to keep possession of it, and they demand that I evacuate Holland.

"There is no time for uncertainty and deliberation. I renounce Louisiana. It is not New Orleans only that I wish to cede; it is the whole colony, without reservation. I know the price of what I abandon, and I have already proved the value I set on the province, as my first diplomatic act with Spain had its recovery for its object. I renounce it with keen regret; but the obstinate determination to hold it would be folly. I empower you to negotiate with the envoys of Congress. Do not even await the arrival of Mr. Monroe. Open negotiations to-day with Mr. Livingston. But I need a great deal of money for this war, and I do not wish to begin it with fresh taxes. For a hundred years France and Spain have been making investments in improving the trade of Louisiana, for which it has not indemnified them. The sums which have been advanced to companies and to cultivators have never come back into the treasury. The repayment of all this is owed us. If I based my conditions on the importance of this vast territory to the United States, they would be unbounded. In consideration of the necessity under which I wish to sell I shall be moderate. But keep it in mind that I must have 50,000,000 francs and that I will not treat for less. I will rather make a desperate attempt to keep this beautiful country. To-morrow you shall have your full authority."

Napoleon paused here, but when one of his hearers, probably Marbois himself, spoke of the difficulties of selling "what the Germans call souls," he continued:

"There you go (voila!) with all of your perfection of ideology, 'of the rights of nature and of man.' But I need money to make war on a nation which has it in abundance. Send your doctrines to London. I am sure they will be the object of great admiration there, and that they will not pay the least attention to them when it is a question of seizing the best parts of Asia.

"Perhaps it may be objected," he went on, "that the Americans will be found too powerful for Europe in two or three centuries. But my foresight takes no account of terrors at a distance. Moreover, you can look to the future for dissensions in the bosom of the Union. The confederations which are called perpetual only endure until one of the parties to the contract finds reason to break it. It is against present dangers to which we are exposed by the colossal powers of England that I wish to provide a safeguard."

Marbois consulted with Livingston before Monroe's arrival, finding him full of suspicions and unable to believe it when told that the first consul would negotiate, not for New Orleans only, but for the cession of the entire territory. He thought this merely another French device to gain time, and when Marbois met Monroe and Livingston together for the first time, he found that both had doubts of his good faith. He soon removed them, however, and the negotiations proceeded without a hitch, except over the price and the boundaries. The jurisdiction of the ecclesiastical authorities at New Orleans had been claimed to the Pacific, but France was not willing to guarantee this, and the American envoys wished a definition of boundaries, because publicists had held invalid treaties in which such definitions were not clearly given. It was finally decided, however, to accept the French view, and it is intimated that there was an understanding that this would be to the advantage of the United States in proceeding against England for the occupation of the western Pacific territory. Indeed, the whole inference from Marbois's book is that, back of the purchase price, which was important at the time to give Napoleon money for war against England, there was a much more important, if even wholly undefined, understanding that the cession involved, on the part of the United States, the assumption of the aggressive against England in support of France. This is strongly brought out in Marbois's report of Livingston's speech, made at the signing of the treaty.

When the treaty had been actually signed, Marbois says that the three negotiators (Monroe, Livingston and himself) "felt a sentiment superior to glory. Never," he says, "had negotiators tasted a joy more pure than theirs." As soon as they had signed they rose, shook hands, and Livingston, expressing the satisfaction of all, said: "The treaty we have signed has not been brought about by finesse nor dictated by force.

"Equally advantageous to both the contract-ing parties, it will change vast solitudes into a flourishing country. To-day the United States take their place among the powers of the first rank. All exclusive influence in the affairs of the United States is lost to England forever. Thus is done away with one of the chief causes of European hatreds and rivalries. Moreover, if wars are inevitable, France will have in the New World a friend, increasing year by year in power, which cannot fail to become puissant and respected on all the seas of the world. It is by the United States that there will be re-established for all the peoples of the earth maritime rights which are now usurped by a single country. Thus treaties will become a guarantee of peace and good will between commercial states. The instrument we have signed will cause no tears to flow. It will prepare centuries of happiness for innumerable generations of the human race. The Mississippi and the Missouri will see them prosper and increase in the midst of equality, under just laws, freed from the errors of superstition, from the scourges of bad government, and truly worthy of the regard and the care of Providence."

It appears that in discussing the treaty the same "ideology" which Napoleon had so peremptorily disposed of was considered by Messrs. Marbois, Livingston and Monroe with courtesy, but with the same conclusion. Marbois says that when the question of buying and selling Louisiana without consulting its inhabitants was raised, "the three ministers expressed sincere regrets, but a preliminary of this nature was rendered impossible by circumstances." He adds in explantaion: "To defer the cession would have been to make Louisiana a colony of England, to render its power predominant in America, and to enfeeble for centuries all that which the whole world ought to wish to set wax and grow greater in that part of the globe. This insoluble difficulty was at once put aside."

Jefferson, when the same difficulty was presented to him, wrote to Senator Breckenridge, of Kentucky, that "the Executive in seizing the fugitive occurrence which so much advances the good of his country, has done an act beyond the Constitution." He wished to have the Constitution amended to cover the case, but his recommendation was put on file with the other "insoluble difficulties" to which M. Marbois refers.

In closing his review of Napoleon's action throughout the negotiations, Marbois says that "the following words (spoken when the signing of the treaty was announced) are enough to demonstrate what thought then dominated the first consul: 'This accession of territory,' said he, 'assures (affermit) forever the power of the United States, and I have given England a maritime rival which sooner or later will humble her pride.' "

Exact boundaries had not been established

at that time, but some idea of the extent of this purchase may be had when we remember that it extended from the present British line to the Gulf of Mexico and included what are now the states of Minnesota, North Dakota, Nebraska, Iowa, Kansas, Missouri, Arkansas and Louisiana, the territory of Oklahoma, Indian Territory, more than three-fourths of Montana and Wyoming, also parts of Colorado and New Mexico.

Thus an enterprise which had in its inception for its chief object to advance the commercial interests of the United States acquired a new purpose, namely, the extending of the geographical and scientific knowledge concerning *our own domain.* Upon Lewis and Clarke a further duty devolved, that of informing the natives that obedience was now due to a new great father.

The expedition of Lewis and Clarke excited a peculiar interest at the time of its occurrence, and has ever since occupied a unique place in our history.

To our colonial ancestors, caged between the sea and the domains of hostile natives and rival colonies, afterward absorbed in a death struggle with the mother country, all the vast interior was a sealed book. And when the successful issue of the Revolutionary war permitted them to turn around and see where they were, still more when the great purchase of Louisiana from France enabled them to look toward the tops of the "Shining mountains" with a sense of proprietorship, all the romance and enthusiasm and excitement of exploration, hitherto sternly denied them by their narrowing lot, seized and fascinated all classes.

The world-old wizard of "out west" stretched his wand over them, and under its magic sway they began, by mountain trail and river and open highway of the prairie, to follow it into the wilderness. The same impulse led them which drew the camel-drivers of Syria to the shores of the Mediterranean, which filled the sails of Roman galleys, which

beckoned the Norse Viking to the desolate grandeur of Greenland, and which lit a signal fire in the tropic verdure of the Bahamas for the far-reaching vision of Columbus. So our great-grandfathers were chasing toward the sunset the shadows of their own coming greatness, a shadow gigantic but always growing, crossing the great plains with seven-league boots and stepping across the ridge-pole of the continent like a Colossus.

It is not surprising that to minds just admitted to this atmosphere of boundless expectation, even this plain and common-place narrative of Lewis and Clark should have had the fascination of a novel.

This historic expedition had been projected and even partially fitted out by Jefferson before the purchase of Louisiana. But immediately upon the completion of that most sagacious investment, the lingering preparations were hastened, and on the 14th of May, 1804, the party left St. Louis by boat, upon the muddy current of the Missouri, to search for the unknown mountains and rivers between that point and the Pacific. Their plan was to ascend the Missouri to its source, cross the divide, strike the headwaters of the Columbia, and, descending it, reach the sea.

And what manner of men were undertaking this voyage, fraught with both interest and peril? Meriwether Lewis, the leader of the party, was a captain in the United States army, and in Jefferson's judgment was, by reason of endurance, boldness and energy, the fittest man within his knowledge for the responsible duties of commander. His whole life had been one of reckless adventure. It appears that at the tender age of eight he was already illustrious for successful midnight forays upon the festive coon and the meditative possum. He was lacking in scientific knowledge, but, when appointed captain of the expedition, had, with characteristic pluck, spent a few spare weeks in study of some of the branches most essential to his new work.

William Clark, second in command, was also a United States officer, and seems to have been equally fitted with Lewis for his work. The party consisted of fourteen United States regulars, nine Kentucky volunteers, two French voyagers, a hunter, an interpreter and a negro. To each of the common soldiers the government offered the munificent reward of retirement upon full pay with a recommendation for a soldier's grant of land. Special pains were taken to encourage the party to keep complete records of all they saw and heard and did. This was done with a vengeance, insomuch that seven journals besides those of the leaders were carefully kept, and in them was recorded nearly every event from the most important discoveries down to the ingredients of their meals and doses of medicine. They were abundantly provided with beads, mirrors, knives, etc., etc., wherewith to woo the savage hearts of the natives.

After an interesting and easy journey of five months they reached the country of the Mandans, and here they determined to winter. The winter having been profitably spent in making the acquaintance of the Indians and in collecting specimens of natural history of the plains—which they now sent back to the president with great care—they again embarked in a squadron of six canoes and two pirogues. On June 13th they reached the great falls of the Missouri.

A month was spent within sound of the thunder and in sight of the perpetual mist-cloud rising from the abyss, before they could accomplish the difficult portage of eighteen miles, make new canoes, mend their clothes and lay in a new stock of provisions. Of material for this last there was no end. The air was filled with migratory birds, and the party was almost in danger of being overrun by the enormous herds of buffalo.

The long, bright days, the tingling air of the mountains, the pleasant swish of the water as their canoes breasted the swift current the vast camp fires and the nightly buffalo roasts —all these must have made this the pleasantest section of their long journey.

The party seems to have pretty nearly exhausted its supply of names, and after having made heavy draughts on their own with various permutatory combinations, they were reduced to the extremity of loading innocent creeks with the ponderous names of Wisdom, Philosophy and Philanthropy. Succeeding generations have relieved the unjust pressure in two of these cases with the sounding appellations of Big Hole and Stinking Water.

On the 12th of August the explorers crossed the great divide, the birthplace of the mighty rivers, and descending the sunset slope found themselves in the land of the Shoshones. They had brought with them a Shoshone woman, rejoicing in the pleasant name of Sacajawea, for the express purpose of becoming acquainted with this tribe, through whom they hoped to get horses and valuable information as to their proper route to the ocean. But four days were consumed in enticing the suspicious savages near enough to hear the words of their own tongue proceeding from the camp of the strangers. When, however, the fair interpretress had been granted a hearing, she speedily won for the party the faithful allegiance of her kinsmen. They innocently accepted the rather general intimation of the explorers that this journey had for its primary object the happiness and prosperity of the Shoshone nation, and to these evidences of benevolence on the part of their newly adopted great father at Washington, they quickly responded by bringing plenty of horses and all the information in their poor power.

It appears that the expedition was at that time on the headwaters of the Salmon river, near where Fort Lemhi afterwards stood. With twenty-nine horses to carry their abundant burdens, they bade farewell to the friendly Shoshones on the last day of August, and committed themselves to the dreary and desolate solitudes to the westward. They soon became entangled in the savage ridges and defiles, already spotted with snow, of the Bitter Root mountains.

Having crossed several branches of the great river named in honor of Captain Clark, and becoming distressed at the increasing dangers and delays, they turned to the left, and, having punished a brawling creek for its inhospitality by inflicting on it the name Coltkilled, commemorative of their extremity for food, they came upon a wild and beautiful stream. Inquiring the name of this from the Indians, they received the answer, "Kooskooskie." This in reality meant simply that this was not the stream for which they were searching. But not understanding, they named the river Kooskooskie. This was afterward called the Clearwater, and is the most beautiful tributary of the Snake.

The country still frowned on them with the same forbidding rocky heights and blinding snowstorms as before. It began to seem as though famine would ere long stare them in the face, and the shaggy precipices were marked with almost daily accidents to men and beasts. Their only meat was the flesh of their precious horses.

Under these circumstances Clark decided to take six of the most active men and push ahead in search of game and a more hospitable country. A hard march of twenty miles rewarded him with a view of a vast open plain in front of the broken mountain chain across which they had been struggling. It was three days, however, before they fairly cleared the edge of the mountains and emerged on the great prairie north and east of where Lewiston now is. They found no game except a stray horse, which they speedily dispatched. Here the advance guard waited for the main body to come up, and then all together they went down to the Clearwater, where a large number of the Nez Perce Indians gathered to see and trade with them. Receiving from these Indians, who, like all that they had met, seemed very amicably disposed, the cheering news that the great river was not very distant, and seeing the Clearwater to be a fine, navigable stream, they determined to abandon the weary land march and make canoes. Five of these having been constructed, they laid in a stock of dog meat, and then committed themselves to the sweeping current with which all the tributaries of the Columbia hasten to their destined place. They left their horses with the Nez Perces, and it is worthy of special notice that these were remarkably faithful to their trust. Indeed, it may be safely asserted that the first explorers of this country almost uniformly met with the kindest reception. The cruelty and deceit afterward characteristic of the Indians were learned partly of the whites.

On the 10th of October, having traveled sixty miles on the Clearwater, its pellucid waters delivered them to the turbid, angry, sullen and lava-banked Snake. This great stream they called the Kimooenim, its Indian name. It was in its low season, and it seems from their account that it, as well as all the other streams, must have been uncommonly low that year.

Thus they say that on October 13th they descended a very bad rapid four miles in length, at the lower part of which the whole river was compressed into a channel only twenty-five yards wide. Immediately below they passed a large stream on the right, which they called Drewyer's river, from one of their men. This must have been the Palouse river, and certainly it is very rare that the mighty Snake becomes attenuated at that point to a width of twenty-five yards. Next day, as they were descending the worst rapid they had yet seen (probably the Monumental rapid), it repelled their effrontery by upsetting one of the boats. No lives were lost, but the cargo of the boat was badly wetted. For the purpose of drying it they stopped a day, and finding no other timber, they were compelled to use a very appropriate pile which some Indians had very carefully stored away and covered with stone. This trifling circumstance is noticed because of the explorers speaking in connection with it of their customary scrupulousness, in never taking any property of the Indians, and of their determination to repay the owner, if they could find him, on their return. If all explorers had been as particular, much is the distress and loss that would have been avoided.

They found almost continuous rapids from this point to the mouth of the Snake, which they reached on October 16th. Here they were met by a regular procession of nearly two hundred Indians. They had a grand pow-wow, and both parties displayed great affection for each other, the whites bestowing medals, shirts, trinkets, etc., in accordance with the rank of the recipient, and the Indians repaying the kindness with abundant and prolonged visits and accompanying gifts of wood and fish. On the next day they measured the rivers, finding the Columbia to be 960 yards wide and the Snake 575. They indulge in no poetic reveries as they stand by the river which had been one principal object of their search, but they seem to have seen pretty much everything of practical value. In the glimmering haze of the pleasant October morning they notice the vast bare prairie stretching southward until broken by the rounded summits of the Blue mountains. They find the Sohulks, who lived at the junction of the rivers, a mild and happy people, the men being content with one wife, whom they actually assist in the family work.

Captain Clark ascended the Columbia to the mouth of a large river coming from the west, which the Indians called the Tapteal. This was, of course, the Yakima. The people living at its mouth rejoiced in the liquid name of Chimnapum. Here Captain Clark shot what he called a prairie cock, the first he had seen. It was a sage hen, no doubt; a handsome bird, nearly as large as a turkey and very common along the river at the present time.

After two days' rest, being well supplied with fish, dog, roots, etc., and at peace with their own consciences and all the world, with satisfaction at the prospect of soon completing their journey, they re-embarked. Sixteen miles below the mouth of the Kimooenim, which they now began to call the Lewis river, they descried, cut clear against the dim horizon line of the southwest, a pyramidal mountain, covered with snow—their first view of Mount Hood.

The next day, being in the vicinity of Umatilla, they saw another snowy peak at a conjectured distance of one hundred and fifty miles. Near here Captain Clark, having landed, shot a crane and a duck. Some Indians near were almost paralyzed with terror, but at last they recovered enough to make the best possible use of their legs. Following them, Captain Clark found a little cluster of huts. Pushing aside the mat door of one of them, he entered, and in a bright light of the unroofed hut discovered thirty-two persons, all of whom were in the greatest terror, some wailing and wringing their hands.

Having by kind looks and gestures soothed their grief, he held up his burning glass to catch a stray sunbeam with which to light his pipe. Thereat the consternation of the Indians revived, and they refused to be comforted. But when the rest of the party arrived with the two Indian guides who had come with them from the Clearwater, terror gave way to curiosity and pleasure. These Pishquitpaws—such was their name—explained to the guides their fear of Captain Clark by saying that he came from the sky accompanied by a terrible noise, and they knew there was a bad medicine in it.

Being convinced now that he was a mortal after all, they became very affectionate, and having heard the music of two violins, they became so enamored of the strangers that they stayed up all night with them and collected to the number of two hundred to bid them good-bye in the morning. The principal business of these Indians seemed to be catching and curing salmon, which, in the clear water of the Columbia, the explorers could see swimming about in incredible numbers. Continuing with no extraordinary occurrence, they passed the river now called the John Day, to which they applied the name Lapage. Mount Hood was now almost constantly in view, and since the Indians told them it was near the great falls of the Columbia, they called it the Timm (this seems to be the Indian word for falls) mountain.

: On the next day they reached a large river on the left, which came thundering through a narrow channel into the equally turbulent Columbia. This river, which Captain Lewis judged to contain one-fourth as much water as the Columbia (an enormous overestimate), answered to the Indian name of Towahnahiooks. It afterward received from the French the name now used, Des Chutes.

They now perceived that they were near the place hinted at by nearly every Indian that they had talked with since crossing the divide —the great falls. And a weird, savage place it proved to be. Here the clenched hands of trachyte and basalt, thrust through the soil from the buried realm of the volcanoes, almost clutched the rushing river. Only here and there between the parted fingers can he make his escape.

After making several portages they reached that extraordinary place (now called The Dalles) where all the waters gathered from half a million square miles of earth are squeezed into a crack forty-five yards wide. The desolation on either side of this frightful chasm is a fitting margin. As one crawls to the edge and peeps over he sees the water to be of inky blackness. Streaks of foam gridiron the blackness. There is little noise compared with the shallow rapids above, but rather a dismal sough, as though the rocks below were rubbing their black sides together in the vain effort to close over the escaping river. The river here is "turned' on edge." In fact, its depth has not been found to this day. Some suppose that there was once a natural tunnel here through which the river flowed, and that in consequence of a volcanic convulsion the top of the tunnel fell in. If there be any truth in this, the width of the channel is no doubt much greater at the bottom than at the top. Lewis and Clark, finding that the roughness of the shore made it almost impossible to carry their boats over, and seeing no evidence of rocks in the channel, boldly steered right through this "witches' cauldron." Though no doubt whirled along with frightful rapidity and flung like foam flakes on the crests of the boiling surges, they reached the end of the "chute" without accident, to the amazement of the Indians who had collected on the bluff to witness the daring experiment. After two more portages the party safely entered the broad, still flood beginning where the town of The Dalles now stands. Here they paused for two days to hunt and caulk their boats. They here began to see evidences of the white traders below, in blankets, axes, brass kettles, and other articles of civilized manufacture. The Indians, too, were more inclined to be saucy and suspicious.

The dalles seemed to be a dividing line between the Indian tribes. Those living at the falls, where Celilo now is, called the Eneeshurs, understood and "fellowshipped" with all the up-river tribes. But at the narrows and thence to the dalles was a tribe called the Escheloots. These were alien to the Indians above, but on intimate terms with those below the cascades. Among the Escheloots the explorers first noticed the peculiar "cluck" in speech common to all down-river tribes. The flattening of the head, which above belónged to the females only, was now the common thing.

The place where Lewis and Clark camped while at The Dalles was just below Mill Creek (called by the natives Quenett), on a point of rocks near the present location of the car shops.

The next Indian tribe, extending apparently from the vicinity of Crate's point to the cascades, capped the climax of tongue-twisting names by calling themselves Chilluckittequaws.

Nothing of extraordinary character seems to have been encountered between the dalles and the cascades. But the explorers had their eyes wide open, and the calm majesty of the river and savage grandeur of its shores received due notice. They observed and named most of the streams on the route, the first of importance being the Cataract river (now the Klickitat), then Lableshe's river (Hood river), Canoe creek (White Salmon) and Crusatte's river. This last must have been Little White Salmon, though they were greatly deceived as to its size, stating it to be sixty yards wide. In this vicinity they were much struck with the sunken forest, which at that low stage of the water was very conspicuous. They correctly inferred that this indicated a damming up of the river at a very recent time. Indeed, they judged that it must have occurred within twenty years. It is well known, however, that submerged trees or piles, as indicated by remains of old Roman wharves in Britain, may remain intact for hundreds of years; but it is nevertheless evident that the closing of the river at the cascades was a very recent event. It is also evident from the sliding, sinking and grinding constantly seen there now that a similar event is liable to happen at any time.

The cascades having been reached more portages were required. Slow and tedious though they were, the explorers seemed to have endured them with unfailing patience.

They were cheered by the prospect of soon putting all the rapids behind and launching their canoes on the unobstructed vastness of the lower river. This was prosperously accomplished on the 2d of November. They were greatly delighted with the verdure which now robed the gaunt nakedness of the rocks. The island formed at the lower cascade by Columbia slough also pleased them greatly by its fertility and its dense growth of grass and strawberry vines. From this last circumstance they named it Strawberry island. At the lower part of that cluster of islands, that spired and turreted relic of the old feudal age of the river, when the volcano kings stormed each other's castles with earthquakes and spouts of lava, riveted their attention. They named it Beacon rock, but it is now called Castle rock. They estimated its height at eight hundred feet and its circumference at four hundred yards, the latter being only a fourth of the reality.

The tides were now noticeable. This fact must have struck a new chord of reflection in the minds of these hardy adventurers; this first-felt pulse beat of the dim vast of waters which grasps half the circumference of the earth. And so, as this mighty heart-throb of the ocean, rising and falling in harmony with all nature, celestial and terrestrial, pulsated through a hundred and eighty miles of river, it might have seemed one of the ocean's multiplied fingers outstretched to welcome them, the first organized expedition of the new republic to this westmost west. It might have betokened to them the harmony and unity of future nations, as exemplified in the vast extent, the liberty, the human sympathies, the diversified interests, industries, and purposes of that republic, whose motto yet remains, one from many.

The rest of their journey was a calm floating between meadows and islands from whose shallow ponds they obtained ducks and geese in great numbers. They thought the "quicksand river"—Sandy—to be a large and important stream. They noticed the Washougal creek, which from the great number of seals around its mouth they called Seal river. But strange to say they missed the Willamette entirely on their down trip. The Indians in this part of the river called themselves Skilloots. Dropping rapidly down the calm but misty stream, past a large river called by the Indians the Cowaliske—Cowlitz—through the country of the Wahkiacums, at last, on the 7th of November, the dense fog with which morning had enshrouded all objects, suddenly broke away, and they saw the bold mountainous shores on either side to vanish away in front, and through the parted headlands they looked into the infinite expanse of the ocean.

Overjoyed at the successful termination of their journey, they sought their first pleasant camping ground and made haste to land. The rain, which is sometimes even now observed to characterize that part of our fair state, greatly marred the joy of their first night's rest within sound of the Pacific's billows.

Six days passed in mouldy and dripping inactivity at a point a little above the present Chinook. They then spent nine much pleasanter days at Chinook Point. This, however, not proving what they wanted for a permanent camp, they devoted themselves to explorations with a view to discovering a more suitable location.

The party wintered in a log building at a point named by them Fort Clatsop. On the 23d of March, 1806, they turned their faces homeward, first, however, having given to the chiefs of the Clatsops and Chinooks certificates of hospitable treatment, and posted on the fort the following notice: "The object of this last is, that, through the medium of some civilized person who may see the same, it may be made known to the world that the party consisting of the persons whose names are hereunto annexed and who were sent out by the government of the United States to ex-

plore the interior of the continent of North America, did penetrate the same by way of the Missouri and Columbia rivers, to the discharge of the latter into the Pacific ocean, at which they arrived on the 14th day of November, 1805, and departed on their return to the United States by the same route which they had come."

Of this notice several copies were left among the Indians, one of which fell into the hands of Captain Hall, of the brig Lydia, and was conveyed to the United States.

The expedition made its way with no little difficulty up the Columbia river. They discovered on their return a large tributary of that river (the Willamette) which had escaped their notice on their outward journey, and made careful inquiry of the Indians concerning it, the results of which were embodied in their map of the expedition.

At the mouth of the John Day river their canoes were abandoned, their baggage was packed on the backs of a few horses they had purchased from the Indians, and traveling in this manner, they continued their homeward march, arriving at the mouth of the Walla Walla river on April 27th. The great chief Yellept was then the leader of the Walla Walla nation, and by him the explorers were received with such generous hospitality that they yielded to the temptation to linger a couple of days before undertaking further journeyings among the mountain fastnesses. Such was the treatment given them by these Indians that the journal of the expedition makes this appreciative notation concerning them: "We may indeed justly affirm that of all the Indians that we have seen since leaving the United States, the Walla Wallas were the most hospitable, honest and sincere."

Of the return journey for the next hundred and fifty miles, that venerable pioneer missionary, Dr. H. K. Hines, writes as follows: "Leaving these hospitable people on the 29th of April, the party passed eastward on the great 'Nez Perce trail.' This trail was the great highway of the Walla Wallas, Cayouses and Nez Perces eastward to the buffalo ranges, to which they annually resorted for game supplies. It passed up the valley of the Touchet, called by Lewis and Clark the 'White Stallion,' thence over the high prairie ridges and down the Alpowa to the crossing of the Snake river, then up the north bank of Clearwater to the village of Twisted Hair, where the exploring party had left their horses on the way down the previous autumn. It was worn deep and broad, and on many stretches on the open plains and over the smooth hills twenty horsemen could ride abreast in parallel paths worn by the constant rush of the Indian generations from time immemorial. The writer has often passed over it when it lay exactly as it did when the tribes of Yellept and Twisted Hair traced its sinuous courses, or when Lewis and Clark and their companions first marked it with the heel of civilization. But the plow has long since obliterated it, and where the monotonous song of the Indian march was droningly chanted for so many barbaric ages, the song of the reaper thrills the clear air as he comes to his garner bringing in the sheaves. A more delightful ride of a hundred and fifty miles than this that the company of Lewis and Clark made over the swelling prairie upland and along the crystal stream between Walla Walla and the village of Twisted Hair, in the soft May days of 1806, can scarcely be found anywhere on earth."

To trace the journeyings of these explorers further is not within the province of this work, but in order to convey a general idea of the labors and extent of the voyage we quote the brief summary made by Captain Lewis himself:

"The road by which we went out by the way of the Missouri to its head is 3,096 miles; thence by land by way of Lewis river over to Clark's river and down that to the entrance of Traveler's Rest creek, where all the roads from different routes meet; thence across the rugged part of the Rocky mountains to the navigable waters of the Columbia, 398 miles; thence down the river 640 miles to the Pacific ocean—making a total distance of 4,134 miles. On our return in 1806 we came from Traveler's Rest directly to the falls of the Missouri river, which shortens the distance about 579 miles, and is a much better route, reducing the distance from the Mississippi to the Pacific ocean to 3,555 miles. Of this distance 2,575 miles is up the Missouri to the falls of that river; thence passing through the plains and across the Rocky mountains to the navigable waters of the Kooskooskie river, a branch of the Columbia, 340 miles, 200 of which is good road, 140 miles over a tremendous mountain, steep and broken, sixty miles of which is covered several feet deep with snow, on which we passed on the last of June; from the navigable part of the Kooskooskie we descended that rapid river seventy-three miles to its entrance into Lewis river, and down that river 154 miles to the Columbia, and thence 413 miles to its entrance into the Pacific ocean. About 180 miles of this distance is tide water. We passed several bad rapids and narrows, and one considerable fall, 268 miles above the entrance of this river, thirty-seven feet eight inches; the total distance descending the Columbia waters 640 miles—making a total of 3,555 miles, on the most direct route from the Mississippi at the mouth of the Missouri to the Pacific ocean."

The safe return of the explorers to their homes in the United States naturally created a sensation throughout that country and the world. Leaders and men were suitably rewarded, and the fame of the former will live while the rivers to which their names have been given continue to pour their waters into the sea. President Jefferson, the great patron of the expedition, paying a tribute to Captain Lewis in 1813, said: "Never did a similar event excite more joy throughout the United

States. The humblest of its citizens have taken a lively interest in the issue of this journey, and looked with impatience for the information it would furnish. Nothing short of the official journals of this extraordinary and interesting journey will exhibit the importance of the service, the courage, devotion, zeal and perseverance under circumstances calculated to discourage, which animated this little band of heroes, throughout the long, dangerous and tedious travel."

CHAPTER III.

THE ASTOR EXPEDITION.

The limits of our volume must render this first or introductory part somewhat fragmentary. For a complete history of the extremely interesting and romantic period prior to the organization and permanent settlement of our state we can only refer the reader to the many more pretentious works already published. We must, however, in view of its effect upon subsequent history, revert briefly to those mammoth forces in the early annals of our northwest country,—the great fur companies. At the outset it is pertinent to inquire what were the motives which prompted the formation of those gigantic commercial organizations, whose plans were so bold, far-reaching and comprehensive, and whose theatre of action was as wide as the world.

The profits of the fur trade were such as might well entice daring and avarice to run the gauntlet of icebergs, of starvation, of ferocious savages and of stormy seas. The net returns from a single voyage might liquidate even the enormous cost of the outfit. For instance, Ross, one of the clerks of Astor's company and located at Okanogan, relates that one morning before breakfast he bought of Indians one hundred and ten beaver skins at the rate of five leaves of tobacco per skin.

Afterward a yard of cotton cloth worth say ten cents purchased twenty-five beaver skins, the value of which in the New York market was five dollars apiece. For four fathoms of blue beads, worth, perhaps, a dollar, Lewis and Clark obtained a sea otter skin, the market price of which varied from forty-five to sixty dollars. Ross notes in another place that for one hundred and sixty-five dollars in trinkets, cloth, etc., he purchased peltries valued in the Canton market at eleven thousand two hundred and fifty dollars. Indeed, even the ill-fated voyage of Mr. Astor's partners proved that a cargo worth twenty-five thousand dollars in New York might be replaced in two years by one worth a quarter of a million, a profit of a thousand per cent. We can not wonder then at the eager enterprise and fierce, sometimes bloody, competition of the fur traders.

The fur-producing animals of especial value in the old Oregon country were three in number. The first, the beaver, was found in great abundance in all the interior valleys, the Willamette country, as was discovered, being pre-eminent in this respect. The two others, the sea otter and seal, were found on the coast. The sea otter fur was the most valuable, its velvety smoothness and glossy blackness rendering it first in the markets of the world of all furs from the temperate zones of North America, and inferior only to the ermine and sable, and possibly to the fiery fox of the far north.

Such, then, was the prospect which prompted the formation of the Pacific Fur Company, which shall have the first place in our narrative as being the first to enter the Columbia river basin, though it was long antedated in organization by several other large fur-trading corporations. The soul and prime mover of this enterprise was that famed commercial genius, John Jacob Astor, a native of Heidelberg, who had come to America poor, and had amassed a large fortune in commercial transactions. In 1810 there was conceived in the brain of this man a scheme which for magnitude of design and careful arrangement of detail was truly masterful, and in every sense worthy of the great *entrepreneur*. Even the one grand mistake which wrecked the enterprise was the result of a trait of character which "leaned to virtue's side." Broadminded and liberal himself, he did not appreciate the danger of entrusting his undertaking to the hands of men whose national prejudices were bitterly anti-American and whose previous connection with a rival company might affect their loyalty to this one. He regarded the enterprise as a purely commercial one, and selected its *personnel* accordingly, hence the failure of the venture.

Mr. Astor's plan contemplated the prosecution of the fur trade in every unsettled territory of America claimed by the United States, the trade with China and the supply of the Russian settlements with trading stock and provisions, the goods to be paid for in peltries. A vessel was to be dispatched at regular intervals from New York, bearing supplies and goods to be traded to the Indians. This was to discharge her cargo at a depot of trade to be established at the mouth of the Columbia river, then trade along the coast with Indians and at the Russian settlements until another cargo had been in part secured, return to the mouth of the river, complete her lading there, sail thence to China, receive a return cargo of Canton silks, nankeen and tea, and back to New York. Two years would pass in completing this vast commercial "rounding up." An important part of the plan was the supply of the Russian posts, at New Archangel, the object being two-fold,—first to secure the profits accruing therefrom, and secondly, to shut off competition in Mr. Astor's own territory, through the semi-partnership with the Russians in furnishing them supplies. Careful arrangements had been made with the Russian government to prevent any possible clash between the vessels of the two companies engaged in the coast trade. "It was," says Brewerton, "a colossal scheme, and deserved to succeed; had it done so it would have advanced American settlement and actual occupancy on the northwest coast by at least a quarter of a century, giving employment to thousands and transferred the enormous profits of the Hudson Bay and Northwest British fur companies from English to American coffers."

Like a prudent business man, Mr. Astor anticipated that, though the Northwest Company had no trading posts in the region west of the Rocky mountains and south of fifty-two degrees north, its enmity and jealousy would be speedily aroused when a new competitor entered the field. He resolved to soften enmity by frankness, so wrote to the directors of the British company the details of his plan and generously offered them a third interest in the enterprise. This ingenuousness on his part found no response in the characters of the shrewd and unscrupulous men in whom he had so unwisely confided. Nobleness, in this instance, failed to enkindle nobleness. They met candor with duplicity, generosity with perfidy.

Playing for time, they pretended, Cæsar-like, to take the matter under advisement, and at once dispatched David Thompson, the astronomer and surveyor of their company, with instructions "to occupy the mouth of the Columbia, to explore the river to its head waters, and, above all, to watch the progress of Mr. Astor's enterprise." They then declined the proposal.

But Mr. Astor proceeded with his project energetically and skillfully. He associated with himself as partners in the enterprise (and here was his great mistake) Donald Mackenzie, Alexander Mackay, who had accompanied Alexander Mackenzie on his voyages of discovery, hence possessed invaluable experience, and Duncan MacDougal, all late of the Northwest Company, and though men of great skill and experience, schooled in the prejudices of the association with which they had so long maintained connection and able to see only through British eyes. To the partners already enumerated were subsequently added Wilson P. Hunt and Robert Maclellan, Americans, David and Robert Stuart and Ramsey Crooks, Scotchmen, and John Clarke, a Canadian, and others.

Wilson P. Hunt was given the post of chief agent on the Columbia, his term of office being five years, and when he was obliged to be absent temporarily a substitute was to be elected by the partners who happened to be present, to act in his place. Each partner obligated himself in the most solemn manner to go where sent and to faithfully execute the objects of the company, but before subscribing to this bond two of the British perfidiously communicated to the British minister, Mr. Jackson, temporarily in New York, the details of Mr. Astor's plan and inquired of him concerning their status as British subjects trading under the American flag in the event of war. They were given assurances that in case of war they would be protected as English subjects and merchants. Their scruples thus put at rest, they entered into the compact.

The larger part of the expedition was to go via Cape Horn and the Sandwich islands to the mouth of the Columbia, there to await the arrival of the Hunt party, which was sent out by land. To convey them thence the ship Tonquin, a vessel of two hundred and ninety tons burden, was fitted up for sea. She was commanded by Captain Thorne, a lieutenant of the United States navy on leave, and had on board Indian trading goods, the frame timbers for a coasting schooner, supplies of all kinds, and in fact everything essential to comfort.

Before the vessel had left the harbor Mr. Astor was apprised that a British war vessel was cruising off the coast for the purpose of intercepting the Tonquin and impressing the Canadians and British who were on board. This was a ruse of the Northwest Company to delay the expedition so that their emissary, Thompson, should arrive at the mouth of the Columbia first. But Mr. Astor secured as convoy the now famous United States frigate Constitution, commanded by the equally famous Captain Isaac Hull, and the Tonquin, thus protected, proceeded safely on her way. She arrived at her destination March 22, 1811, after a voyage the details of which must be sought in Irving's Astoria, Franchere's narrative, or in some of the publications based upon the latter work. On the 12th of the following month a part of the crew crossed the river in a launch and established at Fort George a settlement to which the name of Astoria was given in honor of the projector of the enterprise. They at once addressed themselves to the task of constructing the schooner, the framed materials for which had been brought with them in the Tonquin. An expedition also was made by Mr. Mackay to determine the truth or falsity of the rumor that a party of whites were establishing a post at the upper cascades of the river, but when the first rapids were reached the expedition had to be abandoned, the Indian crew positively refusing to proceed further.

On the 1st of June, the ill-fated Tonquin started north, Mr. Mackay accompanying. We must now pursue her fortunes to their terrible conclusion. Mr. Franchere, a Frenchman, one of Mr. Astor's clerks, is the chief authority for the story. With his account Irving seems to have taken some poetic license. According to that graceful writer, with a total force of twenty-three and an Indian of the Chehalis tribe called Lamazee, for interpreter, the Tonquin entered the harbor of Neweetee. Franchere calls the Indian Lamanse, and the harbor, he says, the Indians called Newity. We shall probably be safe in following Bancroft, who surmises that the place was Nootka sound, which has been referred to on a previous page as a bad place for traders. In 1803 the ship Boston and all her crew but two had been destroyed there.

But it is well worth noting that these Indians, like all others on the coast, were disposed at first to be friendly, and only the indignities and violence of the traders transformed their pacific disposition to one of sullen treachery. Captain Thorne had been repeatedly and urgently warned by Mr. Astor and his associates against trusting the Indians. One standing rule was that not more than four or five should be allowed on deck at once. But the choleric Thorne treated with equal contempt the suggestions of caution and the savage hucksters. A great quantity of the finest kind of sea otter skins had been brought on deck, and to all appearance a most lucrative and amicable trade was before them. But twenty years of traffic with the whites and a long course of instruction from the diplomatic and successful chief, Maquinna, had rendered the Nootka Indians less pliable and less innocent than Thorne expected. His small stock of patience was soon exhausted. At one cunning and leering old chief, who seemed to be urging the others to hold out for higher prices, the captain soon began to scowl with special rage. But the oily visage was scowl-proof, and the impatient sailor had the mortification to see that he was likely to be out-Jewed by one of those dirty and despised redskins. He could stand it no longer. In his most impressive and naval manner he bids the Indians to leave. But the obnoxious chieftain stands motionless, a perfect statue of savage impudence. All sense and judgment vanished from the captain's mind. Seizing him by the hair, he propelled him rapidly toward the ship's ladder. Then, with a convenient bundle of furs, snatched up furiously, he emphasized the chieftain's exit. Nor is it likely that he spared a liberal application of boot leather to the most accessible part of the savage trader's anatomy. Instantly, as if by magic, the Indians left the ship. In place of the babel of jabbering traffickers were only the hair-brained captain and his astonished and silent crew.

Mr. Mackay, the partner on board, was very indignant when, on returning from a short trip ashore, he learned of the untimely cessation of trade. He assured Captain Thorne that he had not only spoiled their business, but had endangered all their lives. He therefore urged making sail from the place at once. The Chehalis Indian, Lamanse, also enforced Mackay's wish, asserting that further intercourse with the Indians could only result in disaster. But the stubborn captain would listen to no advice. So long as he had a knife or a handspike they needn't scare him into running before a lot of naked redskins. The night passed in quiet. Early the next morning a number of Indians, demure and peaceable as can be imagined, paddled alongside. Bundles of furs held aloft signified their wish to trade. In great triumph Captain Thorne pointed out to Mackay the successful issue of his discipline. "That is the way to treat them," he said; "just show them that you are not afraid and they will behave themselves." The Indians were very respectful and exchanged their furs for whatever was offered.

Pretty soon another large boat-load, well supplied with the choicest peltries, asked permission to go aboard. The now good-natured and self-satisfied skipper gladly complied. Then another canoe, and a fourth, and a fifth, disgorged a perfect horde on board. But some of the more watchful sailors noticed with alarm that, contrary to custom, no women left the canoes, and that certain of the fur bundles the savages would not sell at any price, while as to others they were perfectly indifferent. Pretty soon it was noticed that, moving as if by accident, the Indians had somehow become massed at all the assailable points of the vessel.

Even Captain Thorne was startled when this fact became unmistakable. But putting a bold front upon his sudden fear, he gave the order to up anchor and man the top-mast, preparatory to sailing. He then ordered the Indians to return to their boats. With a scarce perceptible flush darkening their listless faces, they picked up their remaining bundles and started for the ladder. As they went, their cat-like tread scarcely audible even in the oppressive stillness, their knotted fingers stole into their bundles. Out again like a flash and in them long knives and cruel bludgeons.

In an instant the wild war-yell broke the awful silence. And then the peaceful Tonquin's deck saw a slaughter grim and pitiless. Lewis, the clerk, and Mackay were almost instantly dispatched. Then a crowd with fiendish triumph set upon the captain, bent on evening up at once the old score. The brawny frame and iron will of the brave, though foolhardy old salt made him a dangerous object to attack, and not until a half dozen of his assailants had measured their bleeding lengths on the slippery deck did he succumb. Then he was hacked to pieces with savage glee. Meanwhile four sailors, the only survivors besides the interpreter, Lamanse, by whom the story is told, having gained access to the hold, began firing on the triumphant Indians; and with such effect did they work that the whole throng left the ship in haste and sought the shore. Lamanse, meanwhile was spared, but held in captivity for two years. The next day the four surviving sailors attempted to put to sea in a small boat, but were pursued and probably murdered by the Indians. And then like a band of buzzards circling around a carcass, the Indian canoes began to cluster around the deserted ship.

The night had been spent in savage mirth, and now in prospect of the rifling of an entire ship their joys knew no bounds. All was silent. The hideous tumult of the day before was succeeded by an equally hideous calm. Cautiously at first, and then emboldened by the utter lifelessness, in throngs the Indians clambered to the deck. Their instinctive fears of stratagem were soon lost in gloating over the disfigured forms of their vanquished foes, and in rifling the storehouses of the ship. Arrayed in gaudy blankets and adorned with multiplied strands of beads, they strutted proudly over the deck. Five hundred men, women and children now swarmed the ship.

Suddenly with an awful crack, crash and boom, the luckless Tonquin, with all its load of living and dead, is flung in fragments around the sea. Her powder magazine had imitated Samson among the Philistines, and she had made one common ruin of herself and her enemies in the very scene of their triumph. Dismembered bodies, fragments of legs and arms, and spattered brains, stained and darkened the peaceful waters far and wide. According to Lamanse, as quoted by Franchere, two hundred Indians were thus destroyed. Franchere also said that no one knows who blew up the ship, though he thinks it most likely that the four sailors left a slow train on board when they abandoned her. Irving most thrillingly describes Lewis as having been wounded, and remaining on board after the four survivors had gone for the purpose of enticing the savages on board and then letting off the train so as to destroy himself and them in one final and awful retribution. Bancroft, however, finding no warrant for this in the narrative of Franchere, the only known authority, does not hesitate to accuse Irving of fabricating it.

Whatever may have been the details, the general fact, with its horrible results to both whites and natives, rapidly spread abroad. Ere long it began to be whispered with bated breath among the Chinooks around Astoria. Then it reached the ears of the traders there. At first entirely disbelieved, it began to be painfully sure, after the lapse of months, and no Tonquin in sight, that there must be something in it. The floating fragments of story finally assumed an accepted form, though not until the reappearance of Lamanse, two years after the event, was it fully understood.

On July 15, 1811, David Thompson, with eight white men, arrived at Astoria. His expedition had been long delayed on the eastern side of the Rocky mountains, in the search for a pass. Desertions among his crew also impeded his progress, and the final result was that he had to return to the nearest post and remain over winter. In the early spring he hurried forward. The party distributed many small flags among the Indians along the Columbia, built huts at the forks of the river and took formal possession of the country drained by the Columbia and its tributaries in the name of the King of Great Britain, and for the company which sent them out. But the main object of the expedition was not realized. They were unable to occupy the mouth of the Columbia, and the perfidy of the Northwest Company failed of its reward. Hostile though the expedition was, it was received at Astoria with open-handed cordiality, MacDougal furnishing Thompson with supplies for the return journey against the urgent remonstrance of David Stuart. Such generosity to one's commercial enemy is, to say the least, a little unusual, but the magnanimity displayed has for some reason failed to call forth the plaudits of historians.

At the time of Mr. Thompson's arrival David Stuart was about to start for the Spokane country to establish a post, and he delayed his departure for a short time, that his and Mr. Thompson's parties might travel together. At the confluence of the Columbia and Okanogan rivers Mr. Stuart erected Fort Okanogan, the first interior post west of the Rocky mountains within the limits of the present state of Washington.

On January 8, 1812, a part of the Hunt expedition reached Astoria, in a pitable condition. We must here take a backward step, chronologically, to pursue the fortunes of this ill-fated party of adventurers. While the Tonquin was making her exit from New York harbor under convoy of the Constitution and was pressing forward to her destination in the west, the second partner in the enterprise, Wilson Price Hunt, was organizing at St. Louis a land party, which was to cross the plains and co-operate with the division by sea. Hunt had been merchandising for some years at St. Louis. His principal trade being with trappers and Indians, he had become very familiar with the requirements of the business. In addition to this primary requisite he possessed a character, native and acquired, worthy of more frequent mention in our early annals and of more frequent emulation by his associates and successors. Brave, humane, cheerful and resolute, he has risen from the mists of history and reminiscence as the highest type of the Jasons who vied with those of ancient story in their search for the fleeces (this time seal and beaver fleeces instead of golden ones) of the far west. To a powerful physique and iron nerve, Hunt added a refinement and culture rare indeed among the bold, free spirits of the frontier.

In company with Hunt from the outset was another partner, Donald Mackenzie by name. He was a man insensible of fear, inured by years of hardship to the ups and downs of a trapper's life, and renowned even on the border for his marvelous accuracy with the rifle. The first thing for them was to get their men. To do this all the tact and patience of Hunt were brought into full play. For a proper understanding of his position it will be necessary to describe briefly the classes from whom he was obliged to fill his ranks.

There were at this time two great classes of trappers. The first and most numerous were the Canadian voyageurs. These men were mainly of French descent. Many of them were half-breeds. They were the legacy of the old French domination over Canada. Cradled in the canoe or batteau, their earliest remembrance being the cold blue lake or foaming river, almost amphibious by nature and training, gay and amiable in disposition, with true French vivacity and ingenuity, gilding every harsh and bitter experience with laugh and song, with their quick sympathies and humane instincts easily getting on the best side of the savages, not broad in designing but patient, courageous and indomitable in executing, these French voyageurs were the main dependence of traffic in the wilderness.

The second class were free trappers,— Booshaways they were sometimes called. These men were mainly Americans. Virginia and Kentucky were the original homes of many of them. They were the perfect antipodes of the voyageurs. Often with gigantic frames built up on prairie dew and mountain breeze, with buffalo steak and wild birds' flesh wrought into their iron sinews; with nerves of steel on which it seemed might harmlessly play even the lightnings of Missouri storms, the drifting snows of winter but a downy coverlet to them, and the furnace blasts of summer but balmy zephyrs; gorging themselves in the midst of plenty, but mocking the power

of hunger and thirst when in want; mighty braggarts, yet quick as lightning to make good their boasts; patient and indefatigable in their work of trapping, but when on their annual trips to the towns given to wild dissipations and savage revelings, "sudden and rash in quarrel," careless of each other's sympathy or company; harsh and cruel to the Indians when in power over them, but bold and recklessly defiant when weaker than they; seizing without compunction the prettiest Indian women and the best horses as their rightful booty; with blood always in their eyes, thunder in their voices, and pistols in their hands, yet underneath it all many of them having hearts as big as those of buffaloes, could they but be reached—this now vanished race of Booshaways has gone to a place in history beside the old Spartans, whose greatest boast it was that their city had no wall, their army being the wall and every man therein a brick, or beside the Spanish conquerors of Mexico and Peru, like Orellano, who descended the Amazon on a raft and then put to sea with such a climax of audacity that even the stormy Atlantic was frightened into acquiescence and let him pass in safety.

This old streak of brutality and tyranny, originally cast into the Anglo-Saxon nature and manifested in its best form in the savage grandeur of the Norse Valhalla, and in the overpowering energy of the Vikings, and at every emergency breaking with volcanic fury through the thin crust of modern culture, has shown itself in no way more notably than in the whole Indian management of the American government.

These free trappers executed with a vengeance the unspoken, but not less real, policy of our government. Humanity, and even shrewd policy, have little place in the thoughts and actions of most of them. The Indians were simply to be stamped on like so many rattlesnakes. In the trappers' code, for an Indian to look longingly at a white man's horse, or even to be seen in the vicinity of a beaver trap, was sufficient warrant to send a rifle ball boring its way through his heart.

The Gallic gentleness which enabled the Canadian voyageurs to go almost anywhere unharmed among the Indians found no counterpart in the sterner composition of the great majority of American trappers and traders.

Such were the men from whom Hunt had to make up his little army, and a vexatious job it was, too. The rivalries of opposing companies were the opportunity of the trappers. Big wages were demanded. Old whisky bills had to be paid off. Worst of all, Hunt found at nearly every station where he tried to engage men that the agents of the Missouri Fur Company, chief of whom was a Spaniard named Manuel Lisa, were neutralizing his efforts by representing dangers from the hostile tribes and barren wastes intervening between the Missouri plains and the Pacific. But Hunt's patience and perseverance, backed by Astor's unstinted purse, overcame all obstacles, and in April, 1811, the winter rendezvous at the mouth of the Nedowa (four hundred and eighty miles above St. Louis) was abandoned, and in four boats, one of large size and mounting a swivel and two howitzers, the party of sixty set forth up the almost untraveled Missouri. Of the party five were partners, Hunt, Crooks, Mackenzie, Miller and Maclellan. One was a clerk, Reed by name. There were two English naturalists, Bradbury and Nuttall. Forty of the party were Canadian voyageurs. These latter were to do the rowing, transporting, carrying, cooking and all the drudgery in general. The remainder were American hunters and trappers. These were the fellows to hunt and fight and plan and explore, and, when the proper place was reached, to cast themselves upon the mercy of the savages and wild beasts, endure hunger and thirst, and despite every difficulty establish trading posts The chief of these hunters was a Virginian named John Day. We shall meet

him frequently. The party was in all respects most bountifully equipped. They designed following as nearly as possible the route of Lewis and Clark.

Many interesting and some thrilling and exciting scenes were encountered on the passage up the Missouri, especially on their way through the country of the Sioux Tetons. But they met with no serious hindrance, and on the 11th of June they reached a large village of the Arickaras, fourteen hundred and thirty miles above the mouth of the Missouri. It had been determined before this, on the advice of several hunters who joined the party in the wilderness, after they had left the Nedowa, to abandon their canoes at this point and, securing horses, strike across the country south of Lewis and Clark's route, so as to avoid the dreadful Blackfeet, who, alike the terror of the other Indians and of the whites, dominated all the region of the upper Missouri. So with eighty-two horses heavily loaded—the partners only, together with the family of Pierre Dorion, being mounted—on the 18th of July they set out hopefully, despite the many gloomy prognostications from trappers remaining at the Arickara village, on their march across the Great American Desert and through the volcanic defiles of the great divide.

On the wide monotony of the sky-bordered prairie they seemed to make no progress. Day succeeded day, and every morning's sun arose hot and dry, on apparently the very landscape of the day before. They did not seem, in fact, though taking a more direct route, to make so good time as did Lewis and Clarke. Guided by the Crow Indians, they penetrated range after range of the stepping stones to the final ridge, supposing each to be the last, only to find when it was surmounted that one yet higher succeeded, and at last on the 15th of September—the summer already gone—they mounted a lofty peak whence the boundless wilderness over which they had come as well as that which they must yet traverse lay like a map at their feet. Gazing attentively westward, their guide finally pointed out three shining peaks ridging the western sky, whose bases he assured them were washed by a tributary of the Columbia. These peaks are now known as the Tetons from their peculiar shape. A hundred miles evidently lay between the weary travelers and that .goal. When there, they felt that they would be almost at the end of their journey, little realizing the character of the thousand miles of travel yet awaiting them.

Passing the green banks of Spanish river, a tributary of the Colorado, they laid in a large stock of the plentiful buffalo, gave their horses five days' rest and grazing on the abundant grass, and on the 24th of September, crossing a narrow ridge, found themselves on the banks of a turbulent stream, recognized by their guide as one of the sources of the Snake. From the name of the guide the stream was called Hoback's river. Down the rugged promontories which flanked this stream the party descended, often in danger of fatal falls, to its junction with a much larger one, which so much exceeded the first in fury of current as to receive the name of Mad river. This seemed to issue from the midst of the Tetons whose glacial and snowy immensity overtopped the camp of the travelers at the junction of the two streams. The all-important question now arose, should they abandon the horses and make canoes with which to descend the river. It was evident that, though containing abundant water for large boats, it was so impetuous as to render navigation a dangerous business. But the Canadians insisted on making the attempt. Weary of the toilsome and rocky footpaths of the mountains, and having all confidence in their well-tried ability in handling boats in any kind of water, 'they longed to betake themselves once more to their favorite element, and, paddle in hand, their gay French songs beating time to the music of the paddles, they would be ready to shoot another Niagara

if it came in their way. The partners finally gave their consent to make canoes. Forthwith the voyageurs repaired with joyful hearts to the adjacent woods, which soon began to yield up its best timber for the projected boats. Meanwhile a party of three, of whom the redoubtable John Day was one, went down Mad river on a two days' journey. They returned declaring that neither in boats nor with horses along the banks could the party possibly go.

Disappointed in this plan, they now took the advice of Hoback to go to a trapping post which had been established the year before by Mr. Henry, of the Missouri Fur Company. This post Hoback knew to be on one of the upper waters of the Snake and he thought that it could not be far distant. A violent storm of sleet, arising in the midst of their deliberations, admonished them that winter was near at hand and that they must hasten one way or the other. The Snake Indians who had come to their camp before the storm and professed to know the location of Henry's post now agreed to guide them thither. Accordingly on the 4th of October, the hills all around being spotted with snow, they resumed their horseback march. Four days of cold and difficult journeying took them to a cluster of deserted log huts. This had been Henry's trading station, but was now entirely abandoned. Beside the huts flowed a beautiful river a hundred yards wide. It was to all appearance a fine navigable stream. Two weeks of industrious work provided fifteen canoes, and in these, hastily embarking, they pushed out into the stream. Their horses were left in charge of the two Snake Indians. Nine men also, including Mr. Miller, one of the partners, had been detached from the party at points between Mad river and Henry's river, as the new stream was called. These men were to divide up into squads and trap on the streams thereabout. Well provided with traps, clothes, horses and ammunition, they set out cheerfully into the unknown and wintry recesses of the mountains, expecting to issue thence in spring with a great stock of valuable peltries. With these they could make their best way to Astoria.

With the rapid current aiding the skillful paddles of the voyageurs, whose spirits arose to an unwonted height, even for them, as soon as they found themselves on the water, the canoes swept swiftly on toward the sunset. They soon came to the mouth of a stream which they took to be their old friend Mad river. They now considered themselves fairly embarked on the main body of the Snake, and already, in imagination, they began to toss on the vast current of the Columbia, and even to smell the salt breeze of the mild Pacific. Occasional rocky points abutting on the river made rapids which alternated with calm stretches of water, whose banks, shallow and grassy, were enlivened with perfect clouds of wild geese and ducks. For nine days they swept gaily on, with comparatively slight interruptions, making over three hundred miles from the place where they had first embarked.

Then they met with a most lamentable disaster. In the second canoe of the squadron were Mr. Crooks as bowman and Antoine Clappine as steersman. The first canoe having safely passed a dangerous rapid, the second essayed to follow. With a sudden lurch she missed her course and the next instant split upon a rock. Crooks and three of his companions succeeded, after a hard struggle, in reaching the land, but Clappine, one of the most popular and useful men in the company, was lost amid the boiling surges. They had now arrived at an unboatable chain of rapids and frightful bluffs, among which neither boats nor horses, nothing. in short, but wings, were of use. At the beginning of this strait was one of those volcanic cracks peculiar to the rivers of this coast, in which the whole volume of the Snake is squeezed into a place thirty feet wide. This miniature maelstrom received

from the disheartened voyagers the name "Cauldron Linn."

The whole squadron now came to a halt. It was evident that a portage at least would be needed. And from the craggy volcanic appearance about and below them, they had great fear that the obstructions extended a long distance. This fear was realized when, after a forty-mile tramp down the river, Mr. Hunt discovered no prospect of successful navigation. Returning to the main body, therefore, and discovering that they had but five days' food and no prospect of getting more, he determined to divide the party into four parts, hoping that some of them might find abundant game and a way out of the lifeless, volcanic waste in which they were. One party, under Maclellan, was to descend the river; another under Crooks was to ascend it, hoping to find game or Indian guides on the way, but, if not, to keep on to the place where they had left their horses. Still another detachment, under Mackenzie, struck northward across the plains, having in view to reach the main Columbia.

Mr. Hunt, left in charge of the main body, proceeded at once to cache a large part of their goods. Nine caches having been made to hold the large deposit, they took careful notice of the land marks of the neighborhood for future return, and then got themselves in readiness to move just as soon as the word should come from any of the scouting parties. Within three days Crooks and his party returned. Despairing of success on their doleful, retrograde march, they had determined to share with their companions whatever might await them on their onward trip. Five days later, the party meanwhile beginning to see the ghastly face of famine staring at them, two of Maclellan's party returned, bidding them abandon all thought of descending the river. For many miles the river ran through volcanic sluice-ways, roaring and raging, at many places almost lost from sight underneath impending crags, generally inaccessible from its desert bank, so that, though within sound of its angry ravings, they had often laid down to their insufficient rest with parched and swollen tongues.

To manifest their anger at the hateful stream they named this long volcanic chute the "Devil's Scuttle Hole." What now remained? Nothing, evidently, but to hasten with all speed, their lives being at issue, to some more hospitable place. The party was, therefore, divided in two. One division, under Hunt, went down the north side of the river, and the other, under Crooks, took the opposite side. This was done in order to increase the chances of finding food and of meeting Indians. It was on the 9th of November that they started on this dismal and heartsickening march. Until December they urged on their course, cold, hungry, often near starvation. At occasional wretched Indian camps they managed to secure dogs for food, and once they got a few horses. These were loaded down with their baggage, but, through scarcity of food, began soon to be too weak to be of much service, and so their attenuated carcasses one by one were devoted to appeasing the hunger of the famished explorers.

The country through which they were passing presented an almost unvarying aspect of volcanic and snowy desolation. The few frightened and half-starved Snake Indians that they encountered could give no information as to the route. They signified, however, that the great river was yet a long way off. Hunt estimated that they had now put about four hundred and seventy miles between them and Cauldron Linn. They were evidently approaching something, for gigantic snowy mountains, lifeless and almost treeless, seemed to bar their future way. Nevertheless they persisted with the energy of despair and clambered painfully up the snowy heights until at a sufficient elevation to command a vast

view. Then, with a waste of mountains in front and bitter winds whirling the snow and sleet in their faces, they first began to despair of forcing their way. The short winter's day shut in upon their despair, and they were compelled to camp in the snow. Timber was found in sufficient quantity to prevent freezing, but during the night another snow storm burst on them furiously, and daylight, sluggishly stealing through the snow-clogged atmosphere, found them in a perfect cloud. The roaring river far below them was their only guide to further progress. Down the slippery and wind-swept mountain side they picked their way to the river bank. Here the temperature was much milder. Having devoured one of their skin-and-bone horses, they crept a few miles along the rocky brink of the brawling flood and made a cheerless camp. On the following morning (December 6) they were startled by seeing on the opposite bank of the stream a party of white men more forlorn and desolate than themselves. A little observation convinced Hunt that these men were Crooks and party. Shouting across the stream at last he made himself heard above the raging river, and as soon as the men discovered him they screamed for food. From the skin of the horse killed the night before Mr. Hunt at once constructed a canoe, and in this crazy craft one of the Canadians daringly and successfully crossed the fearful-looking river, taking with him a part of the horse and bringing back with him Crooks and Le Clerc.

Appalled at the wasted forms and despondent looks of these two men, and still further disheartened at the account they gave of the unsurmountable obstacles to continuing down the river, Hunt determined to retrace his steps to the last Indian camp they had passed, there to make a more determined effort to obtain guides and horses. With dismal forebodings, therefore, on the following morning they took the back track. Crooks and Le Clere were so weak as to greatly retard the rest of the party. In this extremity the men besought Hunt to leave those two to their fate while they hastened on to the Indian camp, but Hunt resolutely refused to abandon his weakened partner. The men gradually began to push ahead until by night but five remained to bear him company. No provisions were left them except four beaver skins. After a night of freezing coldness, one of the men being badly frost-bitten, Hunt, finding Crooks entirely unable to travel, concluded that his duty to the main company demanded his presence among them. Accordingly, having made the exhausted men as comfortable as possible and leaving two of the men and all but one of the beaver skins with them, Hunt and the remaining three men hastened on. A day and night of famine and freezing brought them up with their companions. The pangs of hunger were beginning to tell in vacant looks and tottering steps. Some of them had not eaten for three days. Toward evening of that distressing day they saw with surprise and profound gratitude a lodge of Shoshones with a number of horses around it.

Necessity knew no law. They descended on the camp, and seizing five horses, at once dispatched one of them. After a ravenous meal had satisfied their immediate necessities, they bethought themselves of their deserted companions. A man was at once sent on horseback to carry food to them and to aid them in coming up. In the morning Crooks and the remaining three men made their appearance. Food must now be got to the men on the opposite bank, but a superstitious terror seemed to have seized their companions as they looked across the sullen river at them. Ghastly and haggard the poor wretches beckoning across with bony fingers, looked more like spectres than men. Unable to get any of the Canadians, overwhelmed as they were with ghostly fancies, to cross, one of the Kentucky hunters at last ventured the dangerous undertaking. ·Putting forth all his strength he at

3

last succeeded in landing a large piece of horse meat, and, encouraged by this, one of the Canadians also ventured over.

One of the starving crew, frantic by his long deprivations, insisted on returning in the canoe. Before they had got across, the pleasant savor of the boiling meat so inspired him that he leaped to his feet and began to sing and dance. In the midst of this untimely festivity the canoe was overturned and the poor fellow was swept away in the icy current and lost.

John Day, considered when they started the strongest man in the company, also crossed the river. His cavernous eyes and meager frame showed well how intense had been the suffering of the detachment on the west bank of the river. Often the wild cherries, dried on the trees, together with their moccasins, were their only food.

The mountains which thus turned back this adventurous band were no doubt that desolate and rather unnecessary range bordering the Wallowa country and the mouth of Salmon river. The detachments under Mackenzie and Maclellan, having reached these mountains before the heavy snows, and having found each other there, had stuck to that route until they had conquered it. After twenty-one days of extreme suffering and peril they reached the Snake at a point apparently not far from the site of Lewiston, and building canoes there, descended the river with no great trouble, reaching Astoria about the middle of January.

Hunt and his men, saved from starvation by the discovery of the horses, hastened on to find Indian guides. But first Hunt, with his usual honesty, left at the lodge (for the occupants had fled at their coming) an amount of trinkets sufficient to pay for the horses he had taken. A few days later they reached a small village of Snake Indians. This, the largest village that they had seen on this side of the mountains, they had observed on their down trip, but had not been able to get any assistance from the inhabitants. Now, however, with a persistance born of their necessities, they insisted on a guide. The Indians demurred, representing that the distance to the river was so great as to require from seventeen to twenty-one days of hard travel. They said that the snow was waist deep and that they would freeze. They very hospitably urged the party to stay with them. But as they also said that on the west side of the mountains was a large and wealthy tribe called the Sciatogas, from whom they might get food and horses, Hunt determined to push on, if he could find a single Indian to accompany him. By a most bountiful offer this desideratum was finally obtained. They were informed that they must cross to the west bank of the river and enter the mountains to the west. With infinite tact and patience Hunt sustained the drooping spirits of the party. Many of them wanted to cast their lot for the winter with the vagabond troupe of Snakes. They shrunk from crossing the chilly flood of Snake river with its huge ice blocks grinding each other with a dismal sound. Then to commit themselves again to the mountains inspired them with terror. In fact, four of the Canadians, together with Crooks and John Day, were unable to go at all. But at last, in spite of doubt and weakness, everything was got together (though they were obliged to desert their six sick companions), and in the bitter cold of the early evening (December 23d) they crossed the river and at once struck for the mountains. They could make only about fourteen miles a day. Their five jaded horses floundered painfully through the snow. Their only food was one meal of horse meat daily. On the fourth day of their journey the mountains gave way to a beautiful valley, across which they journeyed twenty miles. This must have been Powder river valley. Leaving this valley and turning again into the mountains, a short but toilsome march brought them to a lofty height whence they looked down into a fair and snowless prairie, basking in the sunlight and looking to the winter-worn travelers like a dream of summer. Soon, best of all, they discerned six lodges of Shoshones, well supplied with horses and dogs. Thither hastening eagerly, their hungry mouths were soon filled with roasted dog. This valley, which looked so much like a paradise, must have been the Grande Ronde. Beautiful at all times, it must have seemed trebly so to these ragged and famished wanderers. The next morning the new year (1812) burst in upon them, bright and cheerful, as if to make amends for the relentless severity of its predecessor. The Canadians must now have their holiday. Not even famine and death could rob them of their festivals. So with dance and song and dog meat roasted, boiled, fried and fricaseed, they met the friendly overtures of the newly-crowned potentate of time. Rested and refreshed, they now addressed themselves to what their guides assured them was to be but a three-days' journey to the plains of the great river. The time was multiplied by two, however, ere the cloudy canopy, which so enswathed the snowy waste as to hide both earth and sky from sight, parted itself before a genial breath from some warmer clime. And then, wide below their snowy eyrie, lay stretched the limitless and sunny plains of the Columbia. Not more gladly did Cortez and his steel-clad veterans look from their post of observation upon the glittering halls of the Montezumas. They swiftly descended the slopes of the mountains and emerged upon that diamond of the Pacific coast, the Umatilla plains.

Here a tribe of Sciatogas (Cayuses) or Tushepaws (Umatillas) were camped, thirty-four lodges and two hundred horses strong. Well clad, active and hospitable, these Indians thawed out, almost as would have a civilized community, the well-nigh frozen energies of the strangers. Rejoiced above all was Mr. Hunt to see in the lodges axes, kettles, etc., indicating that these Indians were in communication with the whites below. In answer to his eager questionings the Indians said that the great river was only two days distant and that a party of white men had just descended it. Concluding that these were Mackenzie and party, Hunt felt relieved of one great anxiety.

After a thorough rest the now joyful wayfarers set forth across the fertile plains, and after a pleasant ride of two days on the horses obtained of the Tushepaws, lifting their eyes they beheld a mighty stream, a mile wide, deep, blue, majestic, sweeping through the treeless plain—the Columbia. The hard and dangerous part of the journey was now at an end. In the absence of timber, however, and because of the unwillingness of any Indians that they met to sell canoes, they were obliged to wait till reaching the Dalles before launching upon the stream. In the vicinity of the present Rockland (they had come from Umatilla on the north bank of the river) they had a "hyas wa wa" with the redoubtable Wishram Indians. Sharpened by their location at the confluence of all the ways down stream, these Indians had clearly grasped the fundamental doctrine of civilized trade, to-wit: Get the greatest possible return with the least possible outlay. To this end they levied a heavy toll on all unwary passers. These levies were usually collected while the eyes of the taxed were otherwise engaged. In short, these Wishram Indians were professional thieves.

Endeavoring first to frighten Mr. Hunt into a liberal "potlatch" then to beg of him by representing their great services in protecting him from the rapacity of other Indians, but finding no recognition of their claims except abundant whiffs at the pipe of peace, they gave up in disgust and contented themselves with picking up whatever little articles might be lying around handy. After considerable haggling several finely-made canoes were procured of these people and in these the last stage of the journey was begun. Nothing extraordi-

nary marked the two-hundred-mile boat ride down the river.

On the 15th of February, rounding the bluffs of Tongue Point, they beheld with full hearts the stars and stripes floating over the first civilized abode this side of St. Louis. Right beyond the parted headlands and the water-bordering horizon they recognized the gateway to the illimitable ocean. As they drew near the shore the whole population of Astoria came pouring down to the cove (near the modern site of Dad's sawmill, now wharved over) to meet them. First in the crowd came the party of Mackenzie and Maclellan, who, having no hope that Hunt and his men could escape from the winter and the famine, were the more rejoiced to see them. Their joy in re-uniting was proportioned to the darkness of death which had so long enshrouded them. The Canadians, with French abandon, rushed into each other's arms, crying and hugging like so many schoolgirls. And even the hard-visaged Scotchmen and nonchalant Americans gave themselves up to the unstinted gladness of the occasion. The next day was devoted to feasting and story telling. No doubt, like the feasting mariners of the Aeneid, they discussed with prolonged speech the *"amissos socios."* These, as the reader will remember, were Crooks and John Day, with four Canadians, who had been left sick on the banks of the Snake. Little hope was entertained of ever seeing them again. But as their story is a natural sequel to that just ended, it shall be given now.

The next summer a party under Stuart and Maclellan, on their way from Okanogan to Astoria, saw wandering on the river bank near Umatilla two wretched beings naked and haggard. Stopping their canoes to investigate, they discovered to their glad surprise that these beings were Day and Crooks.

Their forlorn plight was quickly relieved with abundant food and clothes, and while the canoes went flying down stream with speed accelerated in the joy of deliverance, the two men related their pitiful tale. Left in destitution of food and clothing, they had sustained life by an occasional beaver or a piece of horse meat given by the Indians, who, seeming possessed of superstitious fear, dared not molest them. With rare heroism and self-abnegation, Crooks remained by the side of John Day until he was sufficiently recuperated to travel. Then, abandoned by three of the Canadians, they had plodded on amid Blue mountain snows, subsisting on roots and skins. On the last of March, having left the other Canadian exhausted at a Shoshone lodge, Crooks and Day pressed on through a last mountain ridge and found themselves in the fair and fertile plains of the Walla Wallas.

Here they were received with the kindness which marked the intercourse of those Indians with the whites. Fed and clothed, they continued down the river with lightened hearts, only to find at the Dalles that there are differences in Indians as well as whites, for there the Eneeshurs, or Wishrams, as Irving calls them, first disarming suspicion by a friendly exterior, perfidiously robbed them of the faithful rifles which thus far in all their distress they had never yet lost sight of, and stripping them drove them out.

More wretched than ever they now turned toward friendly Walla Walla. And just as they were striking inland they saw the rescuing boats. So with added gratitude they all paddled away for Astoria. But poor Day never recovered. In an insane frenzy he tried to kill himself. Prevented from this, he soon pined away and died. The barren and bluffy shores of John Day river possess an added interest as we recall the melancholy story of the brave hunter who first explored them. The four Canadians were afterward found alive, though destitute, among the Shoshones.

On the 5th of May, 1812, the Beaver, another of Astor's vessels, reached Astoria.

Among those on board was Ross Cox, author of "Adventures on the Columbia River," a work of great historical value. About this time, also, Robert Stuart, while bearing dispatches by land to Mr. Astor, discovered the South Pass through the Rocky mountains, which in later years became the great gateway to the Pacific for immigrant trains.

Pity it is that the historian must record the failure of an enterprise so wisely planned as that of Astor, so generously supported and in the execution of which so much devoted self-abnegation was displayed, so many lives sacrificed. But the clouds were now beginning to darken above the little colony on the shores of the Pacific. On August 4th the Beaver sailed northward for Sitka, with Mr. Hunt aboard. While an agreement was entered into between that gentleman and the Russian governor, Baranoff, the gist of which was that the Russian and American companies were to forbear interference with each other's territory and to operate as allies in expelling trespassers on the rights of either. The Beaver had been instructed to return to Astoria before sailing to Canton, but instead she sailed direct, so Mr. Hunt was carried to Oahu, there to await a vessel expected from New York, on which he should obtain passage to Astoria. But he did not arrive until too late to avert the calamity which befell the Pacific Fur Company. War was declared between Great Britain and the United States. Mr. Astor learned that the Northwest Company was preparing a ship mounting twenty guns, the Isaac Todd, wherewith to capture Astoria. He appealed to the United States for aid, but his efforts were unavailing. Discouragements were thickening around the American settlement. Mackenzie was unsuccessful at his post on the Shahaptan river, and had determined to press for a new post. He visited Clarke, and while the two were together, John George MacTavish, of the Northwest Company paid them a visit and vauntingly informed them of the sailing of the

Isaac Todd and of her mission, the capture or destruction of Astoria. Mackenzie returned at once to his post on the Shahaptan, broke up camp, cached his provisions, and set out in haste for Astoria, at which point he arrived January 16, 1813. MacDougal was agent-in-chief at Astoria in the absence of Hunt. It was resolved by him and Mackenzie that they should abandon Astoria in the spring and re-cross the mountains. Mackenzie at once set off to recover his cached provisions and to trade them for horses for the journey. He also carried dispatches to Messrs. Clarke and David Stuart, advising them of the intention to abandon Astoria and directing them to make preparations accordingly. Mackenzie met a party of the Northwest Company, with Mac-Tavish as one of the leaders, and the parties camped, as Irving says, "mingled together as united by a common interest instead of belonging to rival companies trading under hostile flags."

On reaching his destination Mackenzie found his cache had been robbed by Indians. He and Clarke and Stuart met at Walla Walla as per arrangement and together descended the Columbia, reaching Astoria June 12th.

Stuart and Clarke refused to break up their posts and to provide horses or make other preparations for leaving the country. Furthermore, Mackenzie's disappointment in finding his cache broken into and its contents stolen made it necessary that the departure should be delayed beyond July 1st, the date set by Mac-Dougal for dissolution of the company. Treason was to have time and opportunity to do its worst. MacTavish, who was camped at the fort, began negotiations for the purchase of trading goods, and it was proposed by Mac-Dougal to trade him the post on the Spokane for horses to be delivered the next spring, which proposition was eventually accepted. An agreement for the dissolution of the company to take effect the next June was signed by the four partners, Clarke and Stuart yield-

ing to the pressure much against their wills. Hunt, who arrived on the 20th of August, also reluctantly yielded, the discouraging circumstances having been pictured to him by Mac-Dougal, who pretended to be animated by a desire to save Mr. Astor's interests before the place should fall into the hands of the British, whose war vessels were on their way to effect its capture. Hunt then sailed to secure a vessel to convey the property to the Russian settlements for safe-keeping while the war lasted, first arranging that MacDougal should be placed in full charge of the establishment after January 1st should he fail to return.

While en route to advise Messrs. Clarke and Stuart of the new arrangement, Mr. Mackenzie and party met MacTavish and J. Stuart with a company of men descending the river to meet the Phoebe and the Isaac Todd. Clarke had been advised of the situation and was accompanying them to Astoria. Mackenzie decided to return also to the fort, and with Clarke attempted to slip away in the night and so reach Astoria before the members of the North-west Company arrived, but was discovered and followed by two of MacTavish's canoes. Both MacTavish and Mackenzie reached their objective point on October 7th, and the party of the former camped at the fort. Next day Mac-Dougal, by way of preparation for his final coupe, read a letter announcing the sailing of the Phoebe and the Isaac Todd with orders "to take and destroy everything American on the northwest coast."

"This dramatic scene," says Evans, "was followed by a proposition of MacTavish to purchase the interests, stocks, establishments, etc., of the Pacific Fur Company. MacDougal then assumed sole control and agency because of the non-arrival of Hunt, and after repeated conference with MacTavish, in which the presence of the other partners was ignored, the sale was concluded at certain rates. A few days later J. Stuart arrived with the remainder of the Northwest party. He objected to MacTavish's prices, and lowered the rates materially. Mr. Stuart's offer was accepted by MacDougal and the agreement of transfer was signed October 16th. By it Duncan MacDougal, for and on behalf of himself, Donald Mackenzie, David Stuart and John Clarke, partners of the Pacific Fur Company, dissolved July 1st, pretended to sell to his British *confreres* and co-conspirators of the Northwest Company 'the whole of the establishments, furs and present stock on hand, on the Columbia and Thompson's rivers.' " Speaking of the transaction in a letter to John Quincy Adams, Secretary of State, Mr. Astor himself says:

"MacDougal transferred all of my property to the Northest Company, who were in possession of it by sale, as he called it, for the sum of fifty-eight thousand dollars, of which he retained fourteen thousand dollars as wages said to be due to some of the men. From the price obtained for the goods, etc., and he having himself become interested in the purchase and made a partner of the Northwest Company, some idea may be formed as to this man's correctness of dealing. He sold to the Northwest Company eighteen thousand one hundred and seventy pounds of beaver at two dollars, which was at that time selling in Canton at five and six dollars per skin. I estimate the whole property to be worth nearer two hundred thousand dollars than forty thousand dollars, about the sum I received in bills on Montreal."

Charitably disposed persons may suggest that MacDougal's actions were in a measure justifiable; that a British force was actually en route to capture Astoria, and that the post, being without adequate means of defense, must surely fall; that it was better to save a pittance than that all should be lost. MacDougal's conduct subsequent to the transfer of Mr. Astor's property was, however, "in studied and consistent obedience to the interest of the Northwest Company." On his return on February 28, 1814, in the brig Pedler, which he purchased to convey Mr. Astor's property to a

place of safety, Mr. Hunt found his old partner whom he had left in charge of the fort still presiding over it, but now a dignitary in the camp of the enemy. There was no other course open to him than to digest the venom of his chagrin as best he could, take his diminutive drafts on Montreal, and set sail in the Pedler for New York. MacDougal had been given a full partnership in the Northwest Company. What was the consideration?

It is needless to add that on the arrival of the British vessels Astoria became a British possession. The formal change of sovereignty and raising of the Union Jack took place on December 12, and as if to obliterate all trace of Mr. Astor's operations, the name of Astoria was changed to Fort George. The arrival of the Isaac Todd the following spring with a cargo of trading goods and supplies enabled the Northwest Company to enter vigorously into the prosecution of their trade in the territory of their wronged and outraged rival. "Thus disgracefully failed," says Evans, "a magnificent enterprise, which merited success for sagacity displayed in its conception, its details, its objects; for the liberality and munificence of its projector in furnishing means adequate for its thorough execution; for the results it had aimed to produce. It was inaugurated purely for commercial purposes. Had it not been transferred to its enemies, it would have pioneered the colonization of the northwest coast by citizens of the United States; it would have furnished the natural and peaceful solution of the question of the right to the territory drained by the Columbia and its tributaries.

*   *   *   *   *   *   *

The scheme was grand in its aim, magnificent in its breadth of purpose and area of operation. Its results were naturally feasible, not over-anticipated. They were but the logical and necessary sequence of the pursuit of the plan. Mr. Astor made no miscalculation, no omission; neither did he permit a sanguine hope to lead him into any wild or imaginary venture. He was practical, generous, broad. He executed what Sir Alexander Mackenzie urged should be adopted as the policy of British capital and enterprise. That one American citizen should have individually undertaken what two mammoth British companies had not the courage to try was but an additional cause which had intensified national prejudice into embittered jealousy on the part of his British rivals, the Northwest Company."

By the first article of the Treaty of Ghent entered into between Great Britain and the United States, December 14, 1814, it was agreed "that all territory, places and possessions whatsoever taken by either party from the other, during or after the war, should be restored." Astoria, therefore, again became the possession of the United States, and in September, 1817, the government sent the sloop-of-war Ontario "to assert the claim of the United States to the sovereignty of the adjacent country, and especially to reoccupy Astoria or Fort George." The formal surrender of the fort is dated October 6, 1818.

Mr. Astor had urged the United States to repossess Astoria, and intended fully to resume operations in the basin of the Columbia, but the Pacific Fur Company was never reorganized, and never again did the great captain of industry engage in trade on the shores of the Pacific.

CHAPTER IV.

THE NORTHWEST AND HUDSON'S BAY COMPANIES.

It is pertinent to now enquire somewhat more particularly into the fortunes and antecedent history of the Northwest and Hudson's Bay Companies, which are each in turn to operate exclusively in the territory with which our volume is concerned. By the Joint-Occupancy Treaty of October 20, 1818, between the United States and Great Britain, it was mutually covenanted "That any country which may be claimed by either party on the northwest coast of America, westward of the Stony mountains, shall, together with its harbors, bays and creeks, and the navigation of all rivers within the same, be free and open, for the term of ten years from the date of the signature of the present convention, to the vessels, citizens and subjects of the two powers; it being well understood that this agreement is not to be construed to the prejudice of any claim which either of the two high contracting parties may have to any part of the said country; nor shall it be taken to affect the claims of any other power or state to any part of said country; the only object of the high contracting parties in this respect being to prevent disputes and differences among themselves."

The Northwest Company, whose members were, of course, British subjects, was, therefore, permitted to operate freely in all disputed territory, and it made good use of its privileges. Its operations extended far and wide in all directions; its emissaries were sent wherever there was a prospect of profitable trade; it respected no rights of territory, it scrupled at no trickery or dissimulation. When it learned of the expedition of Lewis and Clarke it sent Daniel W. Harmon with a party, instructing him to reach the mouth of the Columbia in advance of the Americans. The poor health of the leader prevented this consummation. Of its efforts to circumvent Mr. Astor's occupancy of the mouth of the Columbia we have already spoken.

It showed also its animus to confirm and strengthen British title to all territories adversely claimed, and wherever a post was established the territory contiguous thereto was ceremoniously taken possession of "in the name of the king of Great Britain, for the Northwest Company." Its establishments and possessions afterward constituted the substantial basis of Great Britain's claim to the territory.

Although organized in 1774, the Northwest Company did not attain to high prestige until the dawn of the nineteenth century. Then, however, it seemed to take on new life, and before the first half decade was passed it had become the successful rival of the Hudson's Bay Company for the fur trade of the interior of North America. The Hudson's Bay Company when originally chartered in 1670 was granted in a general way the right to traffic in Hudson's Bay and the territory contiguous thereto, and the Northwest Company began to insist that the grant should be more strictly construed. The boundaries of Prince Rupert's land, as the Hudson's Bay territory was named, had never been definitely determined and there had long been contention in those regions which were claimed by that company but denied to it by the other fur-traders. Beyond the recognized area of the Hudson's Bay territory, the old Northwest Company (a French corporation which had fallen, at the time of the fall of Canada, into the possession of the British) had been a competitor of the Hudson's Bay Company. When this French association went out of existence the contest was kept up by private merchants,

but without lasting success. The new Northwest Company, of Montreal, united and cemented into one organization all these individuals for the better discharge of the common purpose. It is interesting to note the theory of trade of this association as contrasted with that of the Hudson's Bay Company.

From established posts as centers of operations, the Montreal association dispatched parties in all directions to visit the villages and haunts of the natives and secure furs from every source possible. It went to the natives for their goods, while the rival company so arranged its posts that these were convenient to the whole Indian population, then depended upon the aborigines to bring in their peltries and exchange the same for such articles as might supply their wants or gratify their fancies. Consequently the one company required many employes, the other comparatively few. The clerks or traders of the Montreal association were required to serve an apprenticeship of seven years at small wages. That term successfully completed, the stipend was doubled. Skill and special aptitude in trading brought speedy promotions, and the chance to become a partner in the business was an unfailing incentive to strenuous effort. The Hudson's Bay Company, on the other hand, had established fixed grades of compensation. Promotion was slow, coming periodically rather than as a reward for specially meritorious service, and though faithfulness to duty was required, no incentive was offered for special endeavor. The Hudson's Bay Company based its territorial title upon a specific grant from the crown, while the rival association sought no other title than such as priority of occupancy and pre-emption afforded. It claimed as its field of operation all unoccupied territory wherever located.

Such, in general, were the methods of the two companies whose bitter rivalry was carried to such an extent that both were brought to the verge of bankruptcy, and that civil strife was at one point actually precipitated. In 1811 Lord Selkirk, a Scotch nobleman of wealth, who had become the owner of a controlling interest in the Hudson's Bay Company, attempted a grand colonization scheme. His project was to send out agricultural colonies to the basin of the Red River of the North. The enmity of the Northwest Company was at once aroused. They fully realized that Selkirk's scheme was inimical to their business, especially so because his grant lay directly across their pathway between Montreal and the interior. Its effect would be to "cut their communication, interposing a hostile territory between their posts and the center of operations." They protested that the grant was illegal, that it was corruptly secured, and urged that suit be instituted to test Lord Selkirk's title. But the government favored the project and refused to interfere. A colony was established at Assinaboia. Its governor prohibited the killing of animals within the territory, and the agents of the Northwest Company treated his proclamation with contempt. Matters grew worse and worse until hostilities broke out which ended in a decisive victory for the Northwest Company, in a pitched battle fought June 19, 1816, twenty-two of the colonists being killed. Numerous arrests of Northwesters engaged in the conflict followed, but all were acquitted in the Canadian courts. The British cabinet ordered that the governor-general of Canada should "require the restitution of all captured posts, buildings and trading stations, with the property they contained, to the proper owners, and the removal of any blockade or any interruption to the free passage of all traders and British subjects with their merchandise, furs, provisions and effects through the lakes, rivers, roads and every route of communication used for the purpose of the fur trade in the interior of North America, and the full and free permission of all persons to pursue their usual and accustomed trade without hindrance or molestation."

But the competition between the companies continued. Both were reduced to the verge of bankruptcy. Something had to be done. The governor-general of Canada appointed a commission to investigate conditions, and that commission recommended a union of the two companies. Nothing, however, of material benefit resulted. Eventually, in the winter of 1819-20, Lord Bathurst, British secretary of state for the colonies, took up the matter and through his mediation a union was finally effected. On March 20, 1821, it was mutually agreed that both companies should operate under the charter of the Hudson's Bay Company, furnishing equal amounts of capital and sharing equally the profits, the arrangement to continue in force for twenty-one years. By "An act for regulating the fur trade and establishing a criminal and civil jurisdiction in certain parts of North America," passed in the British parliament July 2, 1821, the crown was empowered to issue a license to the combined companies for exclusive trade "as well over the country to the east as beyond the Rocky mountains, and extending to the Pacific ocean, saving the rights of the Hudson's Bay Company over this territory." "That is to say," explains Evans, "in the territory granted to the Hudson's Bay Company by their charter, this license did not operate. The company in the Hudson's Bay territory already enjoyed exclusive privileges; and this license recognized that territory as a province, excepting it as a British province from the operation of this license."

Agreeably to the provisions of the statute just referred to, a license was granted to the Hudson's Bay Company and to William and Simon McGillivray and Edward Ellice, as representatives of the shareholders of the Northwest Company. The license was one of exclusive trade as far as all other British subjects were concerned, and was to be in force for a period of twenty-one years. It was to extend to all "parts of North America to the northward and westward of the lands and territories belonging to the United States or to any European government, state or power, reserving no rent.".

Of the grantees a bond was required conditioned upon the due execution of civil process where the matter in controversy exceeded two hundred pounds, and upon the delivery for trial in the Canadian courts of all persons charged with crime. Thus it will be seen that Americans operating in the Oregon territory (which was, by the act of the British parliament and the license issued under it, treated as being outside of "any legally defined civil government of the United States,") were subject to be taken, when accused of crime, to Canada for trial. How did that comport with the treaty of 1818, one provision of which was that neither power should assert rights of sovereignty against the other? The fact that the British government required and the company agreed to enforce British law in the "territory westward of the Stony mountains" shows clearly the animus of the ever earth-hungry British lion to circumvent the treaty of 1818, and make Oregon in fact and verity a British possession.

By 1824 all the rights and interests of the stockholders late of the Northwest Company had passed into the hands of the Hudson's Bay Company. The absorption of the one corporation by the other was complete. The treacherous and perfidious treatment of Mr. Astor and the demoralization of his partners availed the greedy Northwesters but little, for they were soon after conquered and subdued and forever deprived of their identity as a company by their powerful rival and enemy.

The Hudson's Bay Company now became the sole owner and proprietor of the trade west of the Rocky mountains, and of all the rights accruing under the license of trade of December 5, 1821. An extended narration of the methods and rules of this corporation would be very interesting, but, mindful of our as-

signed limits and province, we must be brief. The company has been aptly characterized by Evans as an "imperium in imperio," and such it was, for it was in possession of well-nigh absolute power over its employes and the native races with whom it traded. It was constituted "The true and absolute lords and proprietors of the territories, limits and places, save always the faith, allegiance and sovereign dominion due to us (the crown), our heirs and successors, for the same, to hold as tenants in fee and common soccage, and not by knight's service, reserving, as a yearly rent, two elks and two black beavers." Power was granted, should occasion arise, to "send ships of war, men or ammunition to any fort, post or place for the defense thereof; to raise military companies, and appoint their officers; to make war or conclude peace with any people (not Christian), in any of their territories," also "to seize the goods, estate or people of those countries for damage to the company's interest, or for the interruption of trade; to erect and build forts, garrisons, towns, villages; to establish colonies, and to support such establishments by expeditions fitted out in Great Britain; to seize all British subjects not connected with the company, or employed by them, or in such territory by their license, and send them to England." Should one of its factors, traders or other employes "contemn or disobey an order, he was liable to be punished by the president or council, who were authorized to prescribe the manner and measure of punishment. The offender had the right to appeal to the company in England, or he might be turned over for trial by the courts. For the better discovery of abuses and injuries by the servants, the governor and company, and their respective president, chief agent or governor in any of the territories, were authorized to examine upon oath all factors, masters, pursers, supercargoes, commanders of castles, forts, fortifications, plantations, or colonies, or other persons, touching or concerning any matter or thing sought to be investigated." To further strengthen the hands of the company, the charter concludes with a royal mandate to all "admirals, vice-admirals, justices, mayors, sheriffs, constables, bailiffs, and all and singular other our officers, ministers, liegemen, subjects whatsoever, to aid, favor, help and assist the said governor and company to enjoy, as well on land as on the seas, all the premises in said charter contained, whensoever required."

"Endowed with an empire over which the company exercised absolute dominion, subject only to fealty to the crown, its membership, powerful nobles and citizens of wealth residing near and at the court jealously guarding its every interest, and securing for it a representation in the government itself, is it to be wondered," asks Evans, "that this *imperium in imperio* triumphantly asserted and firmly established British supremacy in every region in which it operated?"

Something of the *modus operandi* of the company must now be given. The chief factors and chief traders were paid no salaries, but in lieu thereof were given forty per cent of the profits, divided among them on some basis deemed equitable by the company. The clerks received salaries varying from twenty to one hundred pounds per annum. Below these again were the servants, whose term of enlistment (for such in effect it was) was for five years, and whose pay was seventeen pounds per annum without clothing. The servant was bound by indentures to devote his whole time and labor to the company's interests; to yield obedience to superior officers; to defend the company's property; to faithfully obey the laws, orders, etc.; to defend officers and agents to the extent of his ability; to serve in the capacity of a soldier whenever called upon so to do; to attend military drill; and never to engage or be interested in any trade or occupation except in accordance with the company's orders and for its benefit. In addition to the pittance paid him, the servant was entitled,

should he desire to remain in the country after the expiration of his term of enlistment, to fifty acres of land, for which he was to render twenty-eight days' service per annum for seven years. If dismissed before the expiration of his term, the servant, it was agreed, should be transported to his European home free of charge. Desertion or neglect might be punished by the forfeiture of even the wretched pittance he was to receive. It was, furthermore, the policy of the company to encourage marriage with the Indian women, their purpose being to create family ties which should bind the poor slave to the soil. By the time the servant's term of enlistment had expired, there was, therefore, usually no choice left him but to re-enlist or accept the grant of land. "In times of peace, laborers and operatives were ever on hand at mere nominal wages; in times of outbreak they were at once transformed into soldiers amenable to military usage and discipline."

The system was certainly a fine one, viewed from the standpoint of the company, but while it may command admiration for its ingenuity, it is certainly not to be commended for magnanimity. Its design and purpose was to turn the wealth of the country into the coffers of the English noblemen who owned Hudson's Bay stock, even though this should be done at the expense of the manhood, the self-respect and the independence of the poor sons of toil who foolishly or from necessity bound themselves to its service.

The Indian policy of the company was no less politic than its treatment of its employes, but it had much more in it that was truly commendable. Its purpose did not bring its employes into conflict with the Indian, nor require his expulsion, neither was there danger of the lands of the savage being appropriated or the graves of their people disturbed. The sale of intoxicants was positively and successfully prohibited. Conciliation was the wisest policy for the company, and it governed itself accordingly; but when punishment was merited, it was administered with promptness and severity. When depredations were committed the tribe to which the malefactor belonged was pursued by an armed force and compelled to deliver up the guilty to his fate. A certain amount of civilization was introduced, and with it came an increase of wants, which wants could only be supplied at the company's forts. Indians were sent on hunting and trapping expeditions in all directions, so that concentration of tribes became difficult, and if attempted, easily perceived in time to circumvent it and prevent trouble. Thus the company secured an influence over the savage and a place in his affections, from which it could not easily be dislodged.

In its treatment of missionaries, civil and military officers and others from the United States, the company's factors and agents were uniformly courteous and kind. Their hospitality was in the highest degree commendable, meriting the gratitude of the earliest visitors and settlers. The poor and unfortunate never asked assistance in vain. But woe to the American who attempted to trade with the Indian, to trap, hunt or do anything which brought him into competition with the British corporation. All the resources of a company supplied with an abundance of cheap labor, supported by the friendship and affection of the aboriginal peoples, backed by almost unlimited capital, and fortified by the favor of one of the wealthiest and most powerful nations of the earth, were at once turned to crush him. Counter-establishments were formed in his vicinity, and he was hampered in every way possible and pursued with the relentlessness of an evil fate until compelled to retire from the field.

Such being the conditions, there was not much encouragement for American enterprise in the basin of the Columbia. It is not, however, in the American character to yield a promising prospect without a struggle, and several times efforts were made at competition

in the Oregon territory. Of some of these we must speak briefly. The operations of William H. Ashley west of the Rocky mountains did not extend to the Oregon country and are of importance to our purpose only because in one of his expeditions, fitted out in 1826, he brought a six-pounder, drawn by mules, across the Rocky mountains, thereby demonstrating the feasibility of a wagon road. In 1826, Jedediah S. Smith, of the Rocky Mountain Fur Company, encouraged by some previous successes in the Snake River district, set out for the country west of the Great Salt Lake. He proceeded so far westward that no recourse was left him but to push onward to the Pacific, his stock of provisions being so reduced and his horses so exhausted as to render an attempt to return unwise. He went south to San Diego for horses and supplies, and experienced no little difficulty on account of the suspicions of the native Californians, who were jealous of all strangers, especially those from the United States. Eventually, however, he was able to proceed northward to the Rogue river, thence along the shore to the Umpqua, in which vicinity serious difficulty with Indians was experienced. Fifteen of the nineteen who constituted the party were massacred, indeed all who happened to be in camp at the time except one were killed. This man, aided by friendly Indians, reached Fort Vancouver, and told his story to the magnanimous chief factor of the Hudson's Bay Company, Dr. John McLoughlin, who offered the Indians a liberal reward for the safe return of Smith and his two companions. A party of forty men was equipped at once to go to the Umpqua country, but before they got started Smith and the men arrived. McLoughlin took steps to secure the property stolen from Smith, and so successfully did he manage the affair that peltries to the value of over three thousand dollars were recovered, and the murderers were severely punished by other Indians. Smith was conquered by kindness and at his solicitation, the Rocky Mountain Fur Company retired from the territory of the Hudson's Bay Company.

Of various other expeditions by Americans into the Oregon country and of the attempts by American vessels to trade along the coast, we cannot speak. Some reference must, however, be made to the work of Captain B. L. E. Bonneville, who in 1831, applied for a two years' leave of absence from the United States army that he might "explore the country to the Rocky mountains and beyond, with a view to ascertaining the nature and character of the several tribes of Indians inhabiting those regions; the trade which might profitably be carried on with them; quality of soil, productions, minerals, natural history, climate, geography, topography, as well as geology of the various parts of the country within the limits of the territories of the United States between our frontier and the Pacific. The request was granted. While Bonneville was informed that the government would be to no expense in fitting up the expedition, he was instructed that he must provide himself with suitable instruments and maps, and that he was to "note particularly the number of warriors that may be in each tribe of natives that may be met with, their alliances with other tribes, and their relative position as to state of peace or war; their manner of making war, mode of subsisting themselves during a state of war and a state of peace; the arms and the effect of them; whether they act on foot or on horseback; in short, every information useful to the government." It would seem that a government which asked such important services ought to have been willing to make some financial return, at least to pay the expenses. But Captain Bonneville had to secure financial aid elsewhere. During the winter an association was formed in New York which furnished the necessary means, and on May 1, 1832, the expedition set out, the party numbering one hundred and ten men. They took with them in wagons a large quantity of trading goods to be used in traffic with the Indians in the basins of the Colorado and Columbia rivers. Bonneville himself went as far west as Fort Walla Walla. Members of his expedition entered the valleys of the Humboldt, Sacramento and Colorado rivers, but they were unable to compete with the experienced Hudson's Bay and Missouri companies and the enterprise proved a financial failure. The expedition derives its chief importance from the fact that it forms the basis of one of Irving's most fascinating works, which "in language more thrilling and varied than romance, has pictured the trapper's life, its dangers, its exciting pleasures, the bitter rivalry of competing traders, the hostility of the savages," presenting a picture of the fur trade, which will preserve to latest posterity something of the charm and fascination of that wild, weird traffic.

Captain Nathaniel J. Wyeth, of Massachusetts, projected in 1832, an enterprise of curious interest and some historical importance. His plan was to establish salmon fisheries on the Columbia river, to be operated as an adjunct to and in connection with the fur and Indian trade. He crossed overland to Oregon, dispatching a vessel with trading goods via Cape Horn, but his vessel was never again heard from, so the enterprise met defeat. The next year Captain Wyeth returned to Boston, leaving, however, most of his party in the country. Many of the men settled in the Willamette valley, and one of them found employment as an Indian teacher for the Hudson's Bay Company.

Not to be discouraged by one failure, Captain Wyeth, in 1834, fitted out another land expedition and dispatched to the Columbia another vessel, the May Dacre, laden with trading goods. On reaching the confluence of the Snake and Port Neuf rivers, Wyeth erected a trading post there to which he gave the name of Fort Hall. Having sent out his hunting and trapping parties, and made arrangements for the season's operations, he proceeded to Fort Vancouver, where, about the same time, the May Dacre arrived. He established a trading house and salmon fishery on Wapato (now Sauvie's) island, which became known as Fort William. The fishery proved a failure and the trading and trapping industry could not stand the competition and harassing tactics of the Hudson's Bay Company, and the constant hostility of the Indians. George B. Roberts, who came to Oregon in 1831, as an employe of the Hudson's Bay Company, is quoted as having accounted for the trouble with the red men in this way. He said "that the island was thickly inhabited by Indians until 1830, when they were nearly exterminated by congestive chills and fever. There were at the time three villages on the island. So fatal were the effects of the disease, that Dr. McLoughlin sent a party to rescue and bring away the few that were left, and to burn the village. The Indians attributed the introduction of the fever and ague to an American vessel that had visited the river a year or two previously. It is not therefore a matter of surprise to any who understood Indian character and their views as to death resulting from such diseases, that Wyeth's attempted establishment on Wapato island was subject to continued hostility. He was of a race to whom they attributed the cause of the destruction of their people; and his employes were but the lawful compensation according to their code for the affliction they had suffered."

Wyeth eventually returned to Massachusetts disheartened. Fort Hall ultimately passed into the hands of the Hudson's Bay Company, and with its acquisition by them, practically ended American fur trade west of the Rocky mountains. But though Wyeth's enterprise failed so signally, his account of it, published by order of congress, attracted the attention of Americans to Oregon, and did much to stimulate its settlement. Paradoxical though it may sound, the Hudson's Bay Com-

pany's success in this instance was its failure.

It will readily be seen, then, that whatever advantage the establishment of fur trading enterprises might give in the final settlement of the Oregon question was with the British. We shall attempt a brief and succinct account of the "struggle for possession" in a later chapter, but it will here be our task to determine in some measure what the political mission of the Hudson's Bay Company might be and what part that association was playing in international affairs. In 1837 the company applied to the home government for a new license, granting enlarged privileges. In enforcing its request, it pointed boastfully to its efficient services in successfully crushing out American enterprise, and in strengthening the British title to the territory, contrary to the spirit and letter of the Joint-Occupancy treaties of 1818 and 1827.

In presenting the petition, the company's chief representative in England, Sir John Henry Pelly, called the attention of the lords to the service rendered in securing to the mother country a branch of trade, wrested from subjects of Russia and the United States of America; to the six permanent establishments it had on the coast, and the sixteen in the interior, besides the migratory and hunting parties; to its marine of six armed vessels; to its large pasture and grain farms, affording every species of agricultural produce and maintaining large herds of stock. He further averred that it was the intention of the company to still further extend and increase its farms, and to establish an export trade in wool, hides, tallow and other produce of the herd and the cultivated field, also to encourage the settlement of its retired servants and other emigrants under its protection. Referring to the soil, climate and other circumstances of the country, he said they were such as to make it "as much adapted to agricultural pursuits as any other spot in America; and," said he, "with care and protection the British dominion may not only be preserved in this country, which it has been so much the wish of Russia and America to occupy to the exclusion of British subjects, but British interest and British influence may be maintained as paramount in this interesting part of the coast of the Pacific."

Sir George Simpson, who was in charge of the Hudson's Bay Company's affairs in America, in making his plea for the renewal of the license, referred to the international import of the company's operations in this language: "The possession of that country to Great Britain may be an object of very great importance; and we are strengthening that claim to it (independent of the claims of prior discovery and occupation for the purpose of Indian trade) by forming the nucleus of a colony through the establishment of farms, and the settlement of some of our retired officers and servants as agriculturists."

One might almost expect that Great Britain would utter some word of reproof to a company which could have the audacity to boast of violating her treaty compacts with a friendly power. Not so, however. She was a party to the breach of faith. Instead of administering merited reproof, she rewards the wrong-doer by the prompt issuing of a new license to extend and be in force for a period of twenty-one years. This renewed license, the date of which is May 31, 1838, granted to the company "the exclusive privilege of trading with the Indians in all such parts of North America, to the northward and westward of the islands and territories belonging to the United States of America, as shall not form part of any of our (British) provinces in North America, or of any lands or territories belonging to the said United States of America, or to any European government, state, or power. Without rent for the first five years, and afterward the yearly rent of five shillings, payable on the 1st of June." The company was again required to furnish a bond conditioned on their executing by their authority over the persons in their employ, "all civil and criminal process by the officers or persons legally empowered to execute such process within in all territories included in the grant, and for the producing or delivering into custody, for the purpose of trial, all persons in their employ or acting under their authority within the said territories, who shall be charged with any criminal offences." The license, however, prohibited the company "from claiming or exercising any trade with the Indians on the northwest coast of America westward of the Rocky mountains to the prejudice or exclusion of any of the subjects of any foreign state, who, under or by force of any convention for the time being between Great Britain and such foreign states, may be entitled to and shall be engaged in such trade." But no provision could be framed, nor was it the wish of the grantors to frame any, which should prevent the Hudson's Bay Company from driving out by harassing tactics and fierce competition, any American who might enter the Oregon territory as a trader.

One of the strangest ruses of this wonderfully shrewd and resourceful company must now receive due notice. It was not in the power of the British government to convey lands in the Oregon country, neither could the Hudson's Bay Company in any way acquire legal title to realty. It therefore determined upon a bold artifice. A co-partnership was formed on the joint stock principle, the personnel of the company being made up largely of Hudson's Bay Company stockholders. The name adopted for it was the Puget Sound Agricultural Company. The idea which animated this association was to acquire a possessory right to large tracts of rich tillable and grazing lands, use these for agricultural purposes and pasturage until the Oregon controversy was settled, then, should the British be successful in that controversy, apply at once for articles of incorporation and a grant. It was, of course, the purpose of the promoters, from motives of self-interest as well as of patriotism, to strengthen the claim of the mother country in every possible way. Great Britain never acquired title to the lands in question; the Puget Sound Agricultural Company never gained a corporate existence; it never had anything more than a bare possessory right to any lands, a right terminating on the death or withdrawal from the company of the person seized therewith. Logically, then, we should expect the absolute failure of the scheme. But it did not fail. So forceful was this legal figment and the Hudson's Bay Company behind it, that they had the power to demand as one of the conditions upon which peace might be maintained between the two governments chiefly concerned in the Oregon controversy, that "the farms, lands and other property of every description belonging to the Puget Sound Agricultural Company, on the North side of the Columbia river, shall be confirmed to the said company. In case, however, the situation of those lands and farms should be considered by the United States to be of public and political importance, and the United States government should signify a desire to obtain possession of the whole or a part thereof, the prop-

erty so required shall be transferred to the government, at a proper valuation, to be agreed upon between the parties."

The Puget Sound Company laid claim under the treaty to two tracts, the tract of the Nisqually, containing two hundred and sixty-one square miles and the Cowlitz farm, containing three thousand, five hundred and seventy-two acres. When the matter came up for settlement, the company asked five millions of dollars in liquidation of its claims. So the United States was forced, in the interests of peace and humanity, into an illogical agreement to purchase lands, the claim to which was established in open violation of the Joint Occupancy treaties of 1818 and 1827. She was forced by a provision of the treaty of 1846, to obligate herself to purchase lands which the same treaty conceded as belonging to her. More humiliating still, she was compelled to reward a company for its acts of hostility to her interests in keeping out her citizens and breaking up their establishments. But the sacrifice was made in the interests of peace and civilization, and who shall say that in conserving these it lacked an abundant justification?

CHAPTER V.

MISSIONS OF OREGON AND THE WHITMAN MASSACRE.

With Wyeth's overland expedition, previously mentioned, were Dr. Nuttall, a naturalist, and J. K. Townsend, an ornithologist, both sent out by a Boston scientific society; also Rev. Jason Lee and his nephew, Rev. Daniel Lee, Cyrus Shepherd, Courtney M. Walker and P. L. Edwards, a missionary party sent out by the Methodist Missionary Board of the United States. The five men last named were destined to exert a tremendous influence upon the imperial Hudson's Bay Company and the British struggle for mastery in Oregon. The scientific men and the missionary party left Wyeth, who was delayed in the construction of Fort Hall, and were guided the rest of the way by A. R. McLeod and Thomas McKay, Hudson's Bay men, to old Fort Walla Walla, which they reached September 1st, and thence down the Columbia to Vancouver, where they arrived two weeks later. Little did these staunch and devoted servants of the great British fur monopoly dream that the plain and unassuming missionary party, which they so kindly piloted from Fort Hall to Vancouver, was but another Trojan horse within whose apparently guileless exterior was confined a hostile force, which would, within a decade of years, throw wide open the gates of exclusive privilege and introduce within the jealously guarded walls a host of foes, to the utter destruction of intrenched monopoly and the final overthrow of British dominion and pretension on the Pacific coast!

Well might Governor McLoughlin, the autocrat of the Pacific northwest, when he welcomed this modest party of meek Methodists, and assigned them lands near Salem, have recalled the misgivings of the Trojan prophetess: *Timeo Danaos, et dona ferentes*—I distrust the Greeks when they offer gifts. "The American missionary was the advance agent of Yankee invasion." In sight of the field where Jason Lee's plow first stabbed the primeval sod, three score and six years ago, reigns the beautiful city of Salem, with its ten thousand busy and prosperous inhabitants, proud capital of a mighty commonwealth, while from the lofty golden dome of its state-house, the fierce glare of Jove's bolts, chained for the service of mortals, makes bright the places where once lurked savage beasts, and still more savage men; within gunshot of Fort Vancouver, inside whose uncouth stockade McLoughlin received the missionaries, with knightly hospitality, imperial Portland, metropolis of the great northwest, takes its rise, spreads over Willamette's broad plain, crowns the lofty hills, spans the broad river, and with its ten times ten thousand citizens, abides a noble monument to the brave men who risked their fortunes and their lives in the almost hopeless attempt to wrest the Oregon country from the relentless grasp of the British; while Oregon, Washington, Idaho, Montana and California, great sister commonwealths, by their very existence, pay rich trib-

4

ute of gratitude to the courage, foresight and patriotism of these heroes.

About the time Wyeth's main party arrived at Vancouver, his ship, the May Dacre, on board which were his goods for the fur trade, together with the furniture and supplies of the missionary party, arrived at Vancouver. On October 6th the missionaries' goods were landed at Wheatland, as they called the place where the mission was to be established. By November 3d a log house was sufficiently advanced for occupation, but before the roof was completed Indian children were admited as pupils, and December 14th Jason Lee bapized twenty-one persons, of whom seventeen were children, at Vancouver. As evidence of the good will of the people at the fort, he received a gift of twenty dollars from them in aid of his work. This was a humble beginning, but it was the foundation stone of the evangelization and Americanization of the Oregon country. That this generous treatment of the missionaries by McLoughlin's people was not exceptional, appears by the following letter accompanying a donation of one hundred and fifty dollars sent to Mr. Lee by Dr. McLoughlin and other employes of the Hudson's Bay Company, of Vancouver, at a subsequent date:

Fort Vancouver, 1st March, 1836.
The Rev. Jason Lee,
DEAR SIR: I do myself the pleasure to hand you the enclosed subscription, which the gentlemen who have signed it request you will do them the favor to accept for the use of the mission; and they pray our Heavenly Father, without whose assistance we can do nothing, that of His infinite mercy He will vouchsafe to bless and prosper your pious endeavors, and believe me to be, with esteem and regard, your sincere well-wisher and humble servant,   JOHN McLOUGHLIN.

All previous efforts of Americans, and the enterprise of Wyeth, which was then under way, met with crushing and ruinous opposition from the all-powerful British monopoly, but the missionaries were assisted and encouraged in every way. Bonneville, Wyeth and the other American adventurers had come to Oregon to compete with the British traders or to colonize against British interests. Jason Lee and his party were there to Christianize the pagan inhabitants, to instruct the ignorant, to minister to the sick and the dying and to set a godly example to the irreligious, reckless and semi-barbarous employed and ex-servants of the corporation. Hence the difference in their reception.

It is not our province, at this time, to give a detailed account of the early struggles, trials, sufferings, misfortunes and final triumph of the missionaries and first settlers, but it is necessary, in order to appreciate and rightly value the men like Dr. William C. McKay, Major Narcisse A. Cornoyer, Captain William Martin and their comrades, who fought with savage foes for the possession of the Inland Empire, that we should briefly recite the romantic story of the overthrow of British dominion and the subjugation of the aborigines in Oregon.

The advent of the American missionaries in the Willamette valley, as before suggested, was the turning point in the history of the Pacific coast. The story of the causes of their undertaking is one of the most romantic character. It is a tale which fitly illustrates how apparently trivial affairs will influence, and sometimes dominate, the most momentous human events—how Divine Providence "moves in a mysterious way his wonders to perform."

Far up in the mountains of Montana, in one of the many valleys which sparkle like emeralds on the western slope of the "Stony" range, a handful of natives, whom the whites called by the now inappropriate name of "Flatheads," met to ponder over the unique tale repeated by some passing mountaineer of a magic Book possessed by the white man, which assured its owners of peace and comfort in this life and eternal bliss in the world beyond the grave. The Flatheads were a weak and unwarlike people; they were sorely beset by the fierce Blackfeet, their hereditary foes, through whose terrible incursions the Flatheads had been reduced in numbers and harrassed so continuously that their state was most pitiable. To this remnant of a once proud race the trapper's story was a rainbow of promise; the chiefs resolved to seek this Book, and possess themselves of the white man's treasure. They chose an embassy of four of their wisest and bravest men, and sent them trustfully on the tribe's errand. The quest of the "Three Kings of Orient," who, two thousand years ago, started on their holy pilgrimage to the lowly manger of the Babe of Bethlehem, was not more weird, nor was search of the knights of King Arthur's round table for the Holy Grail more picturesque and seemingly hopeless. Though they knew that there were men of the pale-face race on the lower waters of the Columbia, and one of these doubtless had told them of the Book, they knew that these uncouth trappers, hunters and fishers were ungodly men in the main and not custodians of the precious volume for which their souls so ardently longed. These were not like the fishers of old by the sea of Galilee, who received the gospel "gladly," and, following the footsteps of the Master, themselves became fishers of men, but were scoffers, swearers and contemners of holy things. So the Indians, like the ancient wise men, turned their faces to the east.

They threaded their toilsome way by stealth through the dreaded Blackfoot country, scaled the perilous "Stony" mountains, descending the eastern slope, followed the tributaries of the Missouri through the dreaded country of the Dakotas, and then pursued the windings of the Missouri till they struck the Father of Waters, arriving at St. Louis in the summer of 1832. Indians were no rarity in this outpost of civilization, and the friendless and forlorn Flatheads soon discovered that the white trappers, hunters, flatboatmen, traders, teamsters and riff-raff of a bustling young city were about the last people in the world to supply Indians, who had no furs to sell, with either spiritual or material solace. The embassy was not only without money, but its members could not even speak the language of the pale-faces. Nor was any one found who could serve as interpreter. It would have been easy enough to have obtained a Bible, if they could have met with a stray colporteur, but none was in evidence, and the average denizen of St. Louis was better provided with cartridge belts and guns than with literature of any sort. In despair they applied to Governor Clark, the official head of the territory, whose headquarters were in the town— the same William Clark who, with Captain Meriwether Lewis, had led the expedition to the mouth of the Columbia nearly thirty years before. It is possible that they may have heard of Clark by reason of his travels through their country a generation previous. By means of signs and such few words of jargon as they could muster, they attempted to explain to Governor Clark the purpose of their visit, but it is evident that they succeeded none too well. In response to their prayer for spiritual food he bestowed on them blankets, beads and tobacco —the routine gifts to importunate redskins— and the discouraged Flatheads abandoned their illusive quest for the magic Book. Before leaving for home the Indians made a farewell call on General Clark, during which they, or one of them, made a speech. Just what the speaker said, or tried to say, may be a matter of doubt, but the report made of it, and given to the press, is a marvel of simple eloquence. It is as follows:

"We came to you over a trail of many moons from the setting sun. You were the friend of our fathers, who have all gone the long way. We came with our eyes partly opened for more light for our people who sit in darkness. We go back with our eyes closed. How can we go back blind to our blind people? We made our way to you with strong arms, through many enemies and strange lands, that we might carry back much to them. We go back with both arms broken and empty. The two fathers who came with us—the braves of many winters and wars—we leave here asleep by your great water and wigwam. They were tired with their journey of many moons, and their moccasins were worn out.

"Our people sent us to get the white man's Book of Heaven. You took us where they worship the Great Spirit with candles, but the Book was not there. You showed us the images of good spirits, and pictures of the good land beyond, but the Book was not among them to tell us the way. You made our feet heavy with burdens of gifts, and our moccasins will grow old with carrying them, but the Book is not among them. We are going back the long, sad trail to our people. When we tell them, after one more snow, in the big counsel, that we did not bring the Book, no word will be spoken by our old men, nor by our young braves. One by one they will rise up and go out in silence. Our people will die in darkness, and they will go on the long path to the other hunting grounds. No white man will go with them, and no Book of Heaven to make the way plain. We have no more words."

The story of the Flathead embassy and their unique quest subsequently reached George Catlin, through the medium of Governor Clark. Catlin was an artist who had made a special study of Indian types and dress, and had painted with great ability and fidelity many portraits of noted chiefs. In the National Museum, at Washington, D. C., may be seen a very extensive collection of his Indian paintings, supplemented with almost innumerable recent photographs, among which are those of Chief Joseph, the great Nez Perce warrior, and the Umatilla reservation chieftains, Homli, Peo and Paul Showeway. Mr. Catlin was not only a portrait painter, but a gifted writer. He converted the plain, unvarnished tale of Governor Clark, concerning the Flatheads, into an epic poem of thrilling interest, and gave it to the press. Its publication in the religious journals created a great sensation, and steps were immediately taken to answer the Macedonian cry of the Flat-

heads. The sending of Jason Lee and his party to Oregon was a result.

The quest of the Flatheads, the sad deaths of all their embassy save one on the journey, and the temporary failure of their project, seemed a hopeless defeat, but they "builded wiser than they knew," for the very fact of their mission stirred mightily the hearts of the church people and through that instrumentality the attention of Americans was sharply directed to the enormous value of the Pacific northwest. The interest thus excited was timely—another decade of supine lethargy on the part of the narrow provincialism which then dominated American diplomacy, and the entire Pacific coast, from Mexico to the Russian possessions, on the north, would have passed irretrievably under British control.

The Flatheads' search for the magic Book was to all appearance an ignominious failure, but their plaintive cry, feeble though it was, stirred the mountain heights, and precipitated the irresistible avalanche of American enterprise into the valley of the Columbia, overwhelming the Hudson's Bay Company with its swelling volume of Yankee immigration and hurling British "Joint Occupation" aside as a thing of naught.

In a lesser way, also, their mission succeeded, though success was long on the road. The western movement of white population engulfed the hated Blackfeet, thinned their numbers till they were no longer formidable, even to the Flatheads, confined them within the narrow limits of a reservation in northern Montana, where they were ordered about by a consequential Indian agent, and collared and thrust into the agency jail for any trifling misdemeanor, by the agency police; while the one-time harrassed and outraged Flathead roams unvexed through his emerald vales, pursues without fear, to its uttermost retreat in the Rockies, the lordly elk or the elusive deer, tempts the wily trout from the darkest pool of the sequestered mountain torrent with the seductive fly, or lazily floats on the surface of some placid lake, which mirrors the evergreen slopes of the environing hills, peacefully withdrawing, now and again, the appetizing salmon-trout from its cool and transparent depths, to be transferred presently, in exchange for gleaming silver, to some thrifty pale-faced housewife, or some unctious Chinese cook, for a tenderfoot tourist's dinner—forgetful all and fearless of Blackfoot ambush or deadly foray. Of a verity, the child-like quest for the magic Book was not without its compensation to the posterity of the Flathead ambassadors!

In the year 1835 the American Board sent Dr. Marcus Whitman, of Rushville, New York, and Dr. Samuel Parker, of Ithaca, New York, to examine the Oregon field and report on the conditions for missionary work. Having reached Green river, the general rendezvous of the trappers, it was decided that Dr. Parker should continue his journey to the Pacific and Dr. Whitman should return east and make ready to come back and locate somewhere in Oregon Territory. Accordingly, in the early spring of 1836, in company with his newly-made bride, Narcissa (Prentice) Whitman, and Rev. H. H. Spalding and wife, Dr. Whitman started across the plains. From the Loup fork of Platte river to Green River the missionary party traveled with the fur company's annual detachment, but at the latter point they committed their fortunes and lives to a body of Nez Perce Indians who had come to meet them. The letters and journals of Mrs. Whitman and Mrs. Spalding give us some conception of the heroic fortitude with which they met the hardships and dangers of that unprecedented bridal journey of three thousand miles across the American wilderness. Reaching Fort Walla Walla, now Wallula, on September 1, 1836, and being in the general vicinity of the region where they had expected to labor, it became apparent that they would need to establish friendly relations with the Hudson's Bay Company, the great auto-

crats of the Columbia valley. Accordingly they made the additional journey by boat to Vancouver, where Dr. McLoughlin, a true-born king of men, received them with the kindly courtesy which always characterized his treatment of those who came to him. By his advice Whitman was established at Waiilatpu, six miles west of the present Walla Walla.

We must pass rapidly over the events of the next few years. Suffice it to say that they were years of great activity on the part of the missionaries. Travelers who visited the station expressed their wonder at the amount accomplished by Dr. Whitman.

He had brought over two hundred acres of land under cultivation, had built several large buildings, had put into running order a small grist mill, operated by water power from Mill creek, had also a small saw-mill on Mill creek, about fourteen miles above the present site of Walla Walla, had gathered together a large number of Indian children for instruction, and with all this, was acting as physician to all the whites in the country, and to many of the Indians.

He was a keen observer of the international politics which gathered about Oregon, and could not fail to see that his plans were necessarily antagonistic to those of the great English fur company, whose Briarean arms reached to all parts of the land, and whose evident and, in fact, necessary purpose was to keep the country in a state of savagery. Although the personal relations between Dr. Whitman and Dr. McLoughlin were of the pleasantest sort, each was keen enough to see that success for the one meant defeat for the other.

Busy as Whitman was with the multifarious duties which he had loaded upon himself, he became more and more absorbed in the vital question as to who was going to own this country. Among a number of Americans coming to Oregon in 1842 was A. L. Lovejoy, a man of intelligence and force, who informed

Whitman of the pending Webster-Ashburton treaty between England and this country, the effect of which many Americans thought would be detrimental to their country.

The more Whitman thought of it the more he became possessed of the idea that it was his patriotic duty to go to Washington and inform the authorities of the nature of this country and its value, and assist the emigrants of the next year to cross the plains and mountains on their way to Oregon. That was one idea of that great winter ride of 1842-3, made by Whitman, Lovejoy accompanying as far as Fort Bent. The details of that grand, heroic ride, with the momentous results hinging upon it, and the magnificent success achieved, have been many times narrated, have been discussed, hotly disputed, exaggerated and belittled, and yet out of the general turmoil certain historical facts may be regarded as definitely established. First, it is now conceded by all that Whitman's idea was "to save Oregon to the United States."

Many writers have questioned this in the past. One writer (we are glad to say but one), has the unenviable distinction of having attributed low and sordid motives to the hero, believing that his object mainly was to secure the continuance of the mission as a source of profit to himself. She even, at one time, went so far as to suggest a doubt whether Whitman was ever in Washington at all. Although those to whom Whitman had related his experiences, as well as men who actually recalled seeing him in Washington, had given their testimony, yet these persistent efforts to depreciate him had produced a good deal of effect in the public mind. It was therefore a matter of profound interest when, in 1891, there was made in the archives of the War department an extraordinary discovery. This was a letter from Dr. Whitman himself to the department, proposing a bill for the establishment of a line of forts from the Kansas river to the Willamette. This entire letter

and proposed bill appeared in the Walla Walla Union-Journal of August 15, 1891. A perusal of it will convince any one that Whitman's aim in his tremendous exertions was political, as well as that he had all the essential elements of statesmanship. We incorporate here the beginning and closing of this letter.

To the Hon. James M. Porter, Secretary of War:

SIR:—In compliance with the request you did me the honor to make last winter while at Washington, I herewith transmit to you the synopsis of a bill, which, if it could be adopted, would, according to my experience and observation, prove highly conducive to the best interests of the United States generally; to Oregon, where I have resided for more than seven years as a missionary, and to the Indian tribes that inhabit the intermediate country.

The government will now doubtless for the first time be apprised through you, and by means of this communication, of the immense migration of families to Oregon, which has taken place this year. I have, since our interview, been instrumental in piloting across the route described in the accompanying bill, and which is the only eligible wagon road, no less than ———— families, consisting of one thousand persons of both sexes, with their wagons, amounting in all to more than one hundred and twenty, six hundred and ninety-four oxen, and seven hundred and seventy-three loose cattle.
* * * * *

Your familiarity with the government policy, duties and interests, render it unnecessary for me to more than hint at the several objects intended by the enclosed bill, and any enlargement upon the topics here suggested as inducements to its adoption would be quite superfluous, if not impertinent. The very existence of such a system as the one above recommended suggests the utility of post offices and mail arrangements, which it is the wish of all who now live in Oregon to have granted them, and I need only add that contracts for this purpose will be readily taken at reasonable rates for transporting the mail across from Missouri to the mouth of the Columbia in forty days, with fresh horses at each of the contemplated posts. The ruling policy proposed, regards the Indians as the police of the country, who are to be relied upon to keep the peace, not only for themselves, but to repel lawless white men and prevent banditti, under the solitary guidance of the superintendent of the several posts, aided by a well-directed system to induce the punishment of crime. It will only be after the failure of these means to procure the delivery or punishment of violent, lawless and savage acts of aggression, that a band or tribe should be regarded as conspirators against the peace, or punished accordingly by force of arms.

Hoping that these suggestions may meet your approbation, and conduce to the future interests of our growing country, I have the honor to be, Honorable Sir, your obedient servant, MARCUS WHITMAN.

The second fact established in regard to Whitman's work is that he did produce a profound influence on the minds of President Tyler and Secretary Webster and others in authority, and as a result, other influences, perhaps, also reaching them, our government took an entirely new stand and began to raise the demand of "Fifty-four forty."

A third fact is that he published broadcast in the spring of 1843, his intention to return and pilot the train across the mountains. It is also true that many immigrants, though by no means all, were induced to come by his presence and representations.

A fourth fact is that he succeeded in conducting a thousand people, with wagons and cattle, to the promised land of Oregon.

A fifth fact may be added to the effect that Whitman's station on the Walla Walla became the rallying point for Americans, with all their interests, between the Rocky mountains and

the Cascades. Waiilatpu was the eastern frontier of American settlement in Oregon. For though the mission posts of Lapwai and Tchimakain were actually farther east, they had no bearing on the political question of the time.

Such briefly summarizes the acknowledged facts in regard to Dr. Whitman and his work. As to the comparative value of his services, as to the controverted questions of what some have styled the "Whitman Myth," this is not the place to speak. Suffice it to say that by the uniform testimony of his contemporaries as well as of the students of history, Whitman was one of the heroes of America.

But Whitman's destiny was not yet fulfilled. Missionary, patriot, statesman and hero, he must now become a martyr.

THE WHITMAN MASSACRE.

After Whitman's return in 1843 the Indians had become restive and ugly. They could form no conception of the exalted sentiments which actuated the missionaries. They began to see in a rude way the logic of American occupation. It meant a change in their whole method of life. It implied farming, cattle-raising, houses, fixed and narrowed domains, instead of the hunting and wild life of their ancestral habits. They saw also the antagonism between the Americans and the British, and inasmuch as the latter were the more disposed to maintain the existing condition of savagery, the Indians generally inclined to sympathize with them. Dr. Whitman perceived the danger, and during the summer of 1847 he had in contemplation a removal to The Dalles. He had arranged to purchase the Methodist mission there and was planning to remove thither in the spring. In the meantime sinister influences were gathering around his devoted head, all unknown to him. His two principal enemies were Tamsuky, a Cayuse chief, and Joe Lewis, a renegade half-breed who had wandered to the mission, had been

befriended by Whitman, and then with the in-
iquity which seemed to be inherent in his de-
testable nature, become a prime mover in the
murderous plot.

During the summer of 1847, measles, introduced by immigrants, became epidemic
among the Cayuses. Their native method of
treating anything of a feverous nature was to
enter into a sweat house, stripped of clothing,
and remain there until thoroughly steamed, and
then plunge naked and perspiring into a cold
stream. Death was the almost inevitable result. Whitman was faithful and unremitting
in his ministrations, but many died. At this
critical moment the wretch Lewis perceived
that his opportunity had come. He made the
Indians think that Whitman was poisoning
them. He went so far as to affirm that he had
heard a conversation between Spalding and
Whitman as to what they would do when they
had got possession of the country.

The Indians determined to make a test case
of a sick woman, giving her some of Whitman's medicine, and agreeing that if she died
they would kill the missionaries. The woman
died, and the plot came to a focus.

Istickus of Umatilla, who had always been
a warm friend of Whitman, had felt some ink-
ling of the plot, and suggested to him his danger. He had never realized it before, but with
his daring spirit had laughed off thoughts of
harm. At the warning of Istickus, Mrs. Whitman, noble, intrepid soul that she was, felt the
darkening of the approaching tragedy, and was
found by the children in tears for the only time
since the death of her beloved little girl eight
years before. The doctor told her that if possible he would arrange to remove down the river
at once.

But the next day, the fatal 29th of November, 1847, dawned. Great numbers of Tamsuky's adherents were in the vicinity. Survivors of the massacre say that on the day before, the little hill on which the monument is
now situated, was black with Indians looking

down upon the scene. Their presence and their
unfriendly looks added to the alarm felt by
Mrs. Whitman.

At about one o'clock on the 29th, as Dr.
Whitman was sitting reading, a number of Indians entered, and having attracted his attention by the accustomed request for medicine,
one of them, said afterwards by the Indians
to have been Tamchas, drew forth a hatchet
and buried it in the head of his benefactor. Another, named Telaukait, who had
received many favors from Whitman, then
came up and proceeded to beat and hack
the noble face that had never expressed any
sentiment but kindness toward those children of darkness. The work of murder,
thus begun, was followed with fiendish energy.
None of the white men, scattered and unsus-
pecting, could offer any effective resistance.
They were quickly shot down, with the exception of such as were in places sufficiently remote
to elude observation and glide away at night.
Five men in that manner escaped, and after
incredible suffering, reached places of safety.
Mrs. Whitman was the only woman who suffered death. The other women were shamefully outraged, and the children, both boys and
girls, were held in captivity several days.

On the day after the massacre at Waiilatpu
William McBean, in charge of the Hudson's
Bay Company's fort at Walla Walla, and who
was the father of John McBean, recently the
interpreter at the Umatilla Indian reservation
in this county, sent a messenger to Fort Vancouver to apprise the chief factor, James Douglas, of what had transpired. The messenger
stopped at the Dalles and procured a boat from
Mr. Alanson Hinman, missionary at that place,
with which to continue his journey. He neglected to inform Mr. Hinman of the massacre
and the danger in which they were. The messenger reached Vancouver on December 4th,
and Chief Factor Douglas sent, on the morning of the second day thereafter, a letter to
Governor Abernethy at Oregon City, inform-

ing him of what had taken place at the Whitman mission. On December 7th Peter Skeen Ogden, of the Hudson's Bay Company, started from Vancouver with a force of men to the scene of the tragedy, and, on leaving The Dalles, advised the Americans at that place to abandon the mission · and seek safety in the Willamette valley, which they did.

The next day Governor Abernethy informed the legislature of the catastrophe, and called for volunteers to rescue the prisoners and punish the Indians. A company of soldiers was immediately organized and sent to The Dalles, as an outpost in case the Indians had · hostile intentions against the Willamette settlements.

The legislature pledged the credit of .the provisional government to pay the expenses of the outfit for · the company, and appointed a committee to visit Vancouver and negotiate for the same from the Hudson's Bay Company; but they were compelled to become personally responsible for the amount involved. On December 10th the company reached Vancouver, received their supplies,. and pushed on to The Dalles, where they arrived on the 21st of December.

In the meantime the legislature entered with great energy on a series of resolutions and enactments, with a view to organizing a sufficient military force to punish the Indians; and the citizens, by private subscriptions and enlistments, warmly seconded the efforts of the provisional government. Many of the more ardent were pushing forward into the Indian country at once, with a formidable force; but more prudent counsels prevailed, and nothing was done likely to prevent the Indians from surrendering their captives to Mr. Ogden, of the Hudson's Bay Company, who had gone among them for that purpose.

Ogden reached Fort Walla Walla December 19th, called a council of the chiefs at the Catholic mission on the Umatilla river, just above Pendleton, in which the Indians signed the following declaration of their wishes:

First—That the Americans may not go to war with the Cayuses.

Second—That they may forget the lately committed murders, as the Cayuses will forget the murder of the son of the great chief of Walla Walla, committed in California.

Third—That two or three great men may come up to conclude peace.

Fourth—That as soon as these great men have arrived and concluded peace, they may take with them all the women and children.

Fifth—They give assurance that they will not harm the Americans before the arrival of these two or three great men.

Sixth—They ask that Americans may not travel any more through their country, as their young men might do them harm.

This document was signed, "Place of Tawatowe, Youmatilla, twentieth of December, 1847.   (Signed,)

Tilokaikt,
Camaspelo,
Tawatowe,
Achekaia."

On the 23d of December the chiefs assembled at the fort to hear what the Hudson's Bay factor had to say to them, and the following speeches by Factor Ogden and three of the Indian chiefs, made on that occasion, explain the situation:

"I regret," said Mr. Ogden, "to observe that all the chiefs whom I asked for are not present—two being absent. . I expect the words I am about to address to you to be repeated to them and your young men on your return to your camps. It is now thirty years since we have been among you. During this long period we have never had any instance of blood being spilt, until the inhuman massacre, which has so recently taken place. We are traders, and a different nation from the Americans. But recollect, we supply you with ammunition not to kill the Americans. They are of the same color as ourselves, speak the same language, are children of the same God, and humanity makes our hearts bleed when we behold you using them so cruelly. Besides this revolting butchery, have not the Indians pillaged, ill treated the Americans, and insulted their women, when peacefully making their way to the Willamette? As chiefs, ought you to have connived at such conduct on the part of your young men? You tell me your young men committed the deeds without your knowledge. Why do we make you chiefs, if you have no control over your young men? You are a set of hermaphrodites, and unworthy of the appelation of men as chiefs. You young, hotheaded men, I know that you pride yourselves upon your bravery, and think no one can match ou. Do not deceive yourselves. If you get the Americans to commence once, you will repent it, and war will not end until every one of you are cut off from the face of the earth. I am aware that a good many of your friends and relatives have died through sickness. The Indians of other places have shared the same fate. It is not Dr. Whitman that poisoned them, but God has commanded that they should die. We are weak mortals and must submit, and I trust you will avail yourselves of the opportunity. By so doing it may be advantageous to you, but at the same time remember that you alone will be responsible for the consequences. It is merely advice that I give you. We have nothing to do with it. I have not come here to make promises or hold out assistance. We have nothing to do with your quarrels; we remain neutral. On my return, if you wish it, I shall do all I can for you, but I do not promise you to prevent war.

"If you deliver me up all the prisoners, I shall pay you for them on their being delivered, but let it not be said among you afterward that I deceived you. I and Mr. Douglas represent the company, but I tell you once more we promise you nothing. We sympa-

thize with these poor people, and wish to return them to their friends and relations by paying you for them. My request in behalf of the families concerns you; so decide for the best."

The young chief (Tawatue) replied: "I arise to thank you for your words. You white chiefs command obedience with those that have to do with you. It is not so with us. Our young men are strong headed and foolish. Formerly we had experienced, good chiefs. These are laid in the dust. The descendants of my father were the only good chiefs. Though we made war with the other tribes, yet we always looked and ever will look upon the whites as our brothers. Our blood is mixed with yours. My heart bleeds for so many good chiefs I had known. For the demand made by you, the old chief Teloquoit is here. Speak to him. As regards myself, I am willing to give up the families."

Teloquoit then said: "I have listened to your words. Young men do not forget them. As for war, we have seen little of it. We know the whites to be our best friends, who have all along prevented us from killing each other. That is the reason why we avoid getting into war with them, and why we do not wish to be separated from them. Besides the tie of blood, the whites have shown us a convincing proof of their attachment to us by burying their dead 'longside with ours. Chief, your words are weighty. Your hairs are gray. We have known you a long time. You have had an unpleasant trip to this place. I cannot, therefore, keep these families back. I make them over to you, which I would not do to another younger than yourself."

Serpent-Jaune (Peo-peo-mox-mox) followed, stating that: "I have nothing to say. I know the Americans to be changeable; still I am of the opinion as the young chief. The whites are our friends and we follow your advice. I consent to your taking the families."

Mr. Ogden then addressed two Nez Perce chiefs at length, in behalf of the Rev. H. H.

Spalding and party, promising he would pay for their safe delivery to him. The result was that both chiefs, James and Itimimipelp, promised to bring them, provided they were willing to come, and immediately started to Clearwater with that purpose, bearing a letter from Chief Factor Ogden to Mr. Spalding.

The result of that conference was the delivery, on the 29th of December, to Mr. Ogden (for which he paid to the Cayuse Indians five blankets, fifty shirts, ten fathoms of tobacco, ten handkerchiefs, ten guns and one hundred rounds of ammunition), the following captives:

Missionary children adopted by Dr. Whitman—Miss Mary A. Bridger; Catherine Sager, aged thirteen years; Elizabeth Sager, ten; Martha J. Sager, eight; Henrietta N. Sager, four; Hannah L. Sager; Helen M. Meek.

From Du Page county, Illinois—Mr. Joseph Smith; Mrs. Hannah Smith; Mary Smith, aged fifteen years; Edwin Smith, thirteen; Charles Smith, eleven; Nelson Smith, six; Mortimer Smith, four.

From Fulton county, Illinois—Mrs. Eliza Hall; Jane Hall, aged ten years; Mary C. Hall, eight; Ann E. Hall, six; Rebecca Hall, three; Rachel M. Hall, one.

From Osage county, Mississippi—Mr. Elam Young; Mrs. Irene Young; Daniel Young, aged twenty-one years; John Young, nineteen.

From La Porte county, Indiana—Mrs. Harriet Kimball; Susan M. Kimball, aged sixteen years; Nathan M. Kimball, thirteen; Byron M. Kimball, eight; Sarah S. Kimball, six; Mince A. Kimball, one.

From Iowa—Mrs. Mary Sanders; Helen M. Sanders, aged fourteen years; Phebe L. Sanders, ten; Alfred W. Sanders, six; Nancy L. Sanders, four; Mary A. Sanders, two; Mrs. Sally A. Canfield; Ellen Canfield, sixteen; Oscar Canfield, nine; Clarissa Canfield, seven; Sylvia A. Canfield, five; Albert Canfield, three.

From Illinois—Mrs. Rebecca Hays; Henry C. Hays, aged four years; also Eliza Spalding, Nancy E. Marsh, Lorrinda Bewley.

On New Year's Day, 1848, Rev. H. H. Spalding, with ten others, being all the Americans from his mission, arrived at Walla Walla fort under escort of fifty Nez Perce Indians, to whom Mr. Ogden paid for their safe delivery twelve blankets, twelve shirts, twelve handkerchiefs, five fathoms of tobacco, two guns, two hundred pounds of ammunition and some knives.

Three days later Mr. Ogden started to Fort Vancouver with the captives in boats. Shortly after he had left the fort at Walla Walla, fifty Cayuse warriors dashed up to the place and demanded the surrender of Mr. Spalding, to be killed, as word had reached them of the arrival of American soldiers at The Dalles, to make war upon them, and they held him responsible for that fact.

On January 10th, the rescued captives arrived safely at Oregon City.

The killed in the Whitman massacre were: Dr. Marcus Whitman, Mrs. Narcissa Whitman, John Sager, Francis Sager, Mr. Crockett Bewley, Mr. Rogers, assistant missionary, Mr. Kimball, Mr. Sales, Mr. Marsh, Mr. Saunders, James Young, Jr., Mr. Hoffman, Mr. Isaac Gillen.

THE CAYUSE WAR.

The ransomed missionaries from Waiilatpu, Lapwai and Tchimakain, reached the Willamette valley in safety. Concerning those from Lapwai and Tchimakain, it may be said here to the credit of the Indians that though one band, the Cayuses were murderers, two bands, the Nez Perces and Spokanes, were saviors. Few things more thrilling ever came under the observation of the writer than the narration by Fathers Eells and Walker of the council of the Spokanes at Tchimakain to decide whether or not to join the Cayuses. The lives of the missionaries hung on the decision. Imagine their emotions as they waited with bated breath in their mission-house to know the result. After hours of excited discussion with the Cayuse emissaries, the Spokanes announced their conclusion: "Go and tell the Cayuses that the missionaries are our friends and we will defend them with our lives." The Nez Perces made the same decision. Bold though those Cayuses were—the fiercest warriors of the inland empire,—their hearts must have sunk within them, as they saw that the Umatillas, the Nez Perces and the Spokanes, and even the Hudson's Bay Company, were all against them and that they must meet the infuriated whites from the Willamette. For as soon as tidings reached the Willamette the provincial government at once entered upon the work of equipping fourteen companies of volunteers by an act of December 9. These volunteers mainly provided their own horses, arms and ammunition, without a thought of pecuniary gain or even reimbursement.

Cornelius Gilliam, father of W. S. Gilliam, of Walla Walla, was chosen colonel of the regiment, and with great energy pushing all necessary arrangements, he set forth from the rendezvous at The Dalles on February 27, 1848. Several battles occurred on the way, the most severe being at Sand Hollows, in the Umatilla country.

The battle of Sand Hollows began on a plain where depressions in the sand made convenient natural rifle pits. These were occupied by the Indians in force. The baggage train, protected by the company of Captain Lawrence Hall, formed the center of the white forces. The left flank, consisting of the companies of Captain Philip F. Thompson and of Captain H. J. G. Maxon, were on the north side of the road, and the companies of Captain Levi N. English and Captain Thomas McKay constituted the right of the command. The first onset of the Indians fell upon McKay's company which was at the extreme right.

The forces of the Indians were composed of Umatilla, Cayuse and Walla Walla braves, who were in arms, not so much for the protection of the Whitman murderers as for the defense of their country from a general white invasion. They feared, and with reason, that if they permitted a regiment of white soldiers to invade their territory severe reprisals would be made, and the innocent suffer with the guilty. Their principal leaders were Five Crows, the general chief of all three tribes and a recent Protestant convert, and War Eagle, also a Cayuse. These chiefs had assured their followers that the white soldiers should never reach the Umatilla river because they were both "big medicine" men. Five Crows asserted that no ball from a white man's gun could kill him, for he was a wizard, thereby calling forth the inference that his recent conversion had been neither deep nor abiding. War Eagle claimed that he was not only invulnerable to bullets, but that he could catch between his teeth and swallow all the balls from all the guns of the white army if they were fired at him.

As the troops approached the Umatilla river the two chiefs rushed from under cover, galloped up to the white line of battle, to prove their powers and ability as wizards, and—*horrible dictu*—shot a small dog belonging to one of the soldiers which had run out to bark at them. The troops had been ordered not to fire first on the Indians, as the desire of Colonel Gilliam, in command, was to avoid hostilities if possible, but when gallant Tom McKay saw the chiefs charging fiercely toward the lines and saw the flash of their guns, he was not to be restrained any longer, so, taking careful aim at War Eagle, the nearest, he shot him, killing him instantly. First Lieutenant Charles McKay, brother to the captain, followed his example, and, firing hastily, wounded Five Crows so seriously that he was compelled to give up his command to another chief. This unexpected disaster, and the accompanying disillusion of the Indians as to their chiefs' invulnerability, operated as a wet blanket on the ardor of the Indians, though they contested the advance of the troops stubbornly till evening put an end to the engagement. Once during the afternoon Captain Maxon's company advanced beyond supporting distance, and, being surrounded, was extricated with great difficulty, eight of his men being wounded. Eleven soldiers were wounded in the battle, but no one was killed. The Indian loss was severe, though, as usual, they carried off most of their dead and wounded. The next day the troops continued their advance, reaching the Whitman mission the third day after the engagement.

They paused several days to recuperate and give a reverent burial to the remains of the martyrs, which had been hastily covered with earth when Ogden ransomed the captives, but were afterward partially exhumed by coyotes.

The Indians had now fallen back to Snake river. Following them thither, the whites were somewhat outgeneraled. They surprised and captured a camp of Indians, among whom were, as was afterward discovered, some of the murderers themselves. But the wily Cayuses professed great friendship, and pointing to a large band of horses on the hill, said that the hostiles had abandoned them and crossed the river. Completely deluded, the whites surrendered the camp, and rounding up the horses, started on the return. And now the released captives, mounting at once, began a furious attack, which proved so harrassing that the volunteers were obliged to retreat to the Touchet, and finally, although they repelled the Indians, they let loose the captured horses. These the Indians seized, vanishing with them over the plains.

In the struggle on the Touchet, when the retiring volunteers reached its banks, William Taylor was fatally shot by an Indian who sprang up in the bushes near by. Nathan Olney, who was afterward agent of the Umatilla Indian reservation, avenged the deed by rushing upon Taylor's assailant, snatching from his hand a war club in which was fastened a piece of iron, and dealing him such a blow on the head as to cause the iron to split the club, and yet without killing him. In the hand-to-hand struggle which then ensued Olney finally succeeded in finishing the Indian with a knife.

But the Indians in general had no wish to fight, and finding that the whites insisted on a surrender of the murderers, the tribe scattered in various directions; Tamsuky with his friends going to the head waters of the John Day. There they remained for two years. In 1850 a band of Umatillas undertook to capture them and after a fierce fight killed Tamsuky and captured a number. Of the captives five were hanged at Oregon City on June 3, 1850. Just previous to their execution they signed the following declaration of innocence:

Kilokite—"I am innocent of the crime of which I am charged. Those who committed it are dead, some killed, some died; there were ten, two were my sons; they were killed by the Cayuses. Tamsuky, before the massacre, came to my lodge; he told me they were going to hold a council to kill Dr. Whitman. I told him not to do so, that it was bad. One night seven Indians died near the house of Dr. Whitman, to whom he had given medicines. Tamsuky's family were sick; he gave them roots and leaves; they got well. Other Indians died. Tamsuky came often. I talked to him, but his ears were shut; he would not hear; he and others went away. After a while some children came into my lodge and told me what was going on. I had told Tamsuky over and over to let them alone; my talk was nothing; I shut my mouth. When I left my people the young chief told me to come and talk with the big white chief and tell him who it was that did kill Dr. Whitman and others. My heart was big; 'tis small now. The priest tells me I must die to-morrow. I know not for what. They tell me that I have made a confession to the marshal that I struck Dr. Whitman. 'Tis false. You ask me if the priests did not encourage us to kill Dr. Whitman? I answer no, no. I am innocent, but my heart is weak since I have been in chains, but since I must die I forgive them all. Those who brought me here and take care of me, I take them all in my arms; my heart is opened."

Quiahmarsum (Panther Skin)—"I was up the river at the time of the massacre, and did not arrive until the next day. I was riding on horseback; a white woman came running from the house. She held out her hand and told me not to kill her. I put my hand upon her head and told her not to be afraid. There were plenty of Indians all about. She, with the other women and children, went to Walla Walla to Mr. Ogden's. I was not present at the murder, nor was I in any way concerned in it. I am innocent. It hurts me to talk about dying for nothing. Our chief told us to come down and tell all about it. Those who committed the murder are killed and dead. The priest says I must die to-morrow. If they kill me, I am innocent. I was sent here by my chief to declare who the guilty persons were; the white chief would then shake hands with me; the young chief would come after me; we would have a good heart. My young chief told me I was to come here to tell what I know concerning the murderers. I did not come as one of the murderers, for I am innocent. I never made any declarations to any one that I was guilty. This is the last time that I may speak."

Kloakamus—"I was there at the time; I lived there, but I had no hand in the murder. I saw them when they were killed, but did not touch or strike any one. I looked on. There were plenty of Indians. My heart was sorry. Our chief told us to come down and tell who the murderers were. There were ten; they are all killed. They say I am guilty, but it is not so; I am innocent. The people do not understand me. I can't talk to them. They tell me I must die by being hung by the neck. If they do kill me I am innocent, and God will give

me a big heart. I have no reason to die for things I did not do. My time is short. I tell the truth. I know that I am close to the grave; but my heart is open, and I tell the truth. I love every one in this world. I know that God will give me a big heart. I never confessed to the marshal that I was guilty, or to any other person; I am innocent. The priests did not tell us to do what the Indians have done. This is my last talk."

Siahsaluchus (Wet Wolf)—"I say the same as the others; the murderers are killed, some by the whites, some by the Cayuses, and some by others. They were ten in number. I have nothing more to say; I think of God. I forgive all men; I love them. The priest did not tell us to do this."

Tamahas—"I did not know that I came here to die. Our chief told us to come and see the white chief and tell him all about it. The white chief would then tell us all what was right and what was wrong; learn us how to live when we returned home. Why should I have a bad heart, after I am showed and taught how to live? My eyes were shut when I came here. I did not see, but now they are opened. I have been taught; I have been showed what was good and what was bad. I do not want to die; I know now that we are all brothers. They tell me the same Spirit made us all. Tamahas joined with Kilokite. My heart cries my brother was guilty, but he is dead. I am innocent. I know I am going to die for things I am not guilty of, but I forgive them. I love all men now. My hope, the priest tells me, is in Christ. My heart shall be big with good."

The Cayuse Indians, however, admit that one of those condemned was really guilty, namely, Tamahas, who struck Dr. Whitman the first blow. Their claim that the others were innocent is very likely true, and if so, is but another instance of the lamentable failure to apply either punishment or mercy accurately, which has characterized all Indian wars on both sides. The innocent have borne the sins of the guilt in more ways than one.

Many men afterward famous in Oregon and Washington history took part in the Cayuse wars. Among them we may name James W. Nesmith, afterward United States senator from Oregon, and father of the wife of Levi Ankeny, president of the First National Bank of Pendleton; Joel Palmer, later speaker of the house of representatives of Oregon; Captain William Martin, who was sheriff and county judge of Umatilla county for sixteen years, and who died full of years and honors, at Pendleton, in 1899; Captain Thomas McKay, First Lieutenant Charles McKay and Second Lieutenant Alexander McKay, all of whom were conspicuous for their valor and important services during the campaign. The three last named were the sturdy sons of that Alexander McKay, partner of Astor, who was murdered on the ill-fated ship Tonquin, in 1812. As before related, when Jason Lee crossed the continent, in 1834, he traveled from Fort Hall with Thomas McKay and his band of hunters. The two men became close friends, and when Lee returned to the states, in 1838, he was accompanied by McKay as far as Bear river, where the latter's infant son, Donald, was baptized by Mr. Lee. This infant was the same Donald McKay who afterward gained fame as an Indian scout, and was, at the time of his death, several years ago, the government interpreter on the Umatilla reservation. As Thomas McKay was unable to go all the way east, he turned three of his sons over to Mr. Lee to take to the States to be educated. Mr. Lee entered the boys in the Wesleyan Academy at Wilbraham, Massachusetts. One of them, the late Dr. William C. McKay, of Pendleton, afterward finished his studies at the Wesleyan University, at Middletown, Connecticut. As Dr. H. K. Hines well says in his Missionary History: "Many about the old Wesleyan Academy, at Wilbraham, and the University at Middletown have called to mind the intelligent half-caste, William C. McKay, who became an educated

physician and an important personal force in the history of Oregon from the time of his return as an educated American to his native place until his death as an honored citizen, in 1894. It was Mr. Lee's influence that led Mr. McKay at the first to send his sons to an American school instead of to an English or a Canadian. It was an important act, as showing the commanding influence that Mr. Lee had gained over one of the most forceful elements of the mixed society of Oregon at that time; as Mr. McKay was very intimately associated with Dr. McLoughlin, the ruling power of the Hudson's Bay Company on the Pacific coast."

Colonel Gilliam, who had shown himself a brave and capable commander, was accidentally killed on the return trip, a most melancholy end of a career which was full of promise to this section of the country.

In taking our leave of this great epoch we can only say in the way of reflection, that grievous as the end of Whitman's career was, it no doubt will ultimately be seen to have produced greater results for this region and the world than if he had survived to enjoy a well merited rest; for the subsequent development of this section, the founding of Whitman College, and the whole train of circumstances arising from American occupation may be seen in some measure to have grown out of the tragedy of Waiilatpu. Here, as elsewhere, martyrdom seems a necessary accompaniment of the profoundest progress.

While the offences of the Indians cannot be condoned, yet charity compels the admission that the poor creatures were hardly more responsible than the wild beasts who also disputed the ground with civilized men, and though the progress of the world demanded the removal of both as obstacles, yet the disposition of many people to indiscriminate hate and to hold the savages to a higher standard of responsibility than we would allow even for the best of ourselves, does little credit to our boasted civilization and Christianity.

CHAPTER VI.

THE OREGON CONTROVERSY.

The reader is now in possession of such facts as will enable him to intelligently approach the contemplation of the great diplomatic war of the century, the Oregon controversy. It may safely be asserted that never before in the history of nations did diplomacy triumph over such wide differences of opinion and sentiment and effect a peaceable adjustment of such divergent international interests. Twice actual conflict of arms seemed imminent, but the spirit of compromise and mutual forbearance ultimately won, a fact which shows that the leaven of civilization was working on both sides of the Atlantic, and gives reason to hope that the day when the swords of the nations shall be beaten into plowshares and their spears into pruning hooks may not be as far in the future as some suppose.

We need not attempt to trace all the conflicting claims which were at any time set up by different nations to parts or the whole of the old Oregon territory, nor to go into the controversy in all its multiform complications, but will confine our inquiry mainly to the negotiations after Great Britain and the United States became the sole claimants. France early established some right to what was denominated "the western part of Louisiana," which, in 1762, she conveyed to Spain. This was retroceded to France some thirty-eight years later, and in 1803 was by that nation conveyed with the rest of Louisiana to the United States. So France was left out of the contest. In 1819, by the treaty of Florida, Spain ceded to the United States all right and title whatsoever which she might have to the territory on the Pacific, north of the forty-second parallel.

What then were the claims of the United States to this vast domain? Naturally they were of a three-fold character. Our government claimed first in its own right. The Columbia river was discovered by a citizen of the United States and named by him. The river had been subsequently explored from its sources to its mouth by a government expedition under Lewis and Clark. This had been followed and its effect strengthened by American settlements upon the banks of the river. While Astoria, the American settlement, had been captured in the war of 1812-15, it had been restored in accordance with the treaty of Ghent, one provision of which was that "all territory, places and possessions whatsoever, taken by either party from the other during the war, or which may be taken after the signing of this treaty, shall be restored without delay."

It was a well-established and universally recognized principle of international law that the discovery of a river, followed within a reasonable time by acts of occupancy, conveyed the right to the territory drained by the river and its tributary streams. This, it was contended, would make the territory between

forty-two degrees and fifty-one degrees north
latitude the rightful possession of the United
States.

The Americans claimed secondly as the successors of France. By the treaty of Utrecht,
the date whereof was 1713, the north line of
the Louisiana territory was established as a
dividing line between the Hudson's Bay territory and the French provinces in Canada.
For centuries it had been a recognized principle
of international law that "continuity" was a
strong element of territorial claim. All European powers, when colonizing the Atlantic seaboard, construed their colonial grants to extend, whether expressly so stated or otherwise,
entirely across the continent to the Pacific
ocean, and most of these grants conveyed in
express terms a strip of territory bounded north
and south by stated parallels of latitude and
east and west by the oceans. Great Britain
herself had stoutly maintained this principle,
even going so far as to wage with France for
its integrity, the war which was ended by the
treaty of 1763. By that England acquired
Canada and renounced to France all territory
west of the Mississippi river. It was therefore contended on the part of the United States
that England's claim by continuity passed to
France and from France by assignment to this
nation. This claim, of course, was subject
to any rights which might prove to belong to
Spain.

Thirdly, the United States claimed as the
successor of Spain, all the rights which that
nation might have acquired by prior discovery
or otherwise having accrued to the United
States by the treaty of Florida.

In the negotiations between Great Britain
and the United States, which terminated in
the Joint-Occupancy treaty of 1818, the latter
nation pressed the former for a final quit claim
of all territory west of the Rocky mountains.
In so doing it asserted its intention "to be without reference or prejudice to the claims of any
other power," but it was contended on the
5

part of the American negotiators, Gallatin and
Rush, that the discovery of the Columbia by
Gray, its exploration by Lewis and Clarke, and
the American settlement at Astoria rendered
the claim of the United States "at least good
against Great Britain to the country through
which such river flowed, though they did not
assert that the United States had a perfect
right to the country."

When, however, the United States succeeded to Spain, it was thought that all clouds
upon its title were completely dispelled, and
thereafter it was the contention of this government that its right to sole occupancy was perfect and indisputable. Great Britain, however,
did not claim that her title amounted to one
of sovereignty or exclusive possession, but
simply that it was at least as good as any other.
Her theory was that she had a right of occupancy in conjunction with other claimants,
which by settlement and otherwise might be
so strengthened in a part or the whole of the
territory as to ultimately secure for her the
right to be clothed with sovereignty.

In the discussion of the issue, the earliest
explorations had to be largely left out of the
case, as they were attended with too much
vagueness and uncertainty to bear any great
weight. The second epoch of exploration was,
therefore, lifted to a position of prominence it
could not otherwise have enjoyed. Perez
and Heceta, for the Spaniards, the former in 1774,
the latter a year later, had explored the northwest coast to the fifty-fifth parallel and beyond,
Heceta discovering the mouth of the Columbia
river. To offset whatever rights might accrue
from these explorations, England had only
the more thorough but less extensive survey
of Captain James Cook, made in 1778. The
advantage in point of prior discovery would,
therefore, seem to be with the United States
as assignee of Spain.

After the Joint-Occupancy treaty of 1818
had been signed, negotiations on the subject
were not re-opened until 1824. In that year,

obedient to the masterly instructions addressed to him on July 22, 1823, by John Quincy Adams, secretary of state, Richard Rush, minister to England, entered into negotiations with the British ministers Canning and Huskisson for the adjustment of the boundary. Mr. Rush was instructed to offer the forty-ninth parallel to the sea, "should it be earnestly insisted upon by Great Britain." He endeavored with great persistency to fulfill his mission, but his propositions were rejected. The British negotiators offered the forty-ninth parallel to the Columbia, then the middle of that river to the sea, with perpetual rights to both nations of navigating the harbor at the mouth of the river. This proposal Mr. Rush rejected, so nothing was accomplished. By treaty concluded in February, 1825, an agreement was entered into between Great Britain and Russia, whereby the line of fifty-four degrees, forty minutes, was fixed as the boundary between the territorial claims of the two nations, a fact which explains the cry of "Fifty-four, forty or fight" that in later days became the slogan of the Democratic party.

In 1826-7 another attempt was made to settle the question at issue between Great Britain and the United States. Albert Gallatin then represented this country, receiving his instructions from Henry Clay, secretary of state, who said: "It is not thought necessary to add much to the argument advanced on this point in the instructions given to Mr. Rush, and that which was employed by him in the course of the negotiation to support our title as derived from prior discovery and settlement at the mouth of the Columbia river, and from the treaty which Spain concluded on the 22d of February, 1819. That argument is believed to have conclusively established our title on both grounds. Nor is it conceived that Great Britain has or can make out even a colorless title to any portion of the northern coast." Referring to the offer of the forty-ninth parallel in a dispatch dated February 24, 1827,

Mr. Clay said: "It is conceived in a genuine spirit of concession and conciliation, and it is our ultimatum and you may so announce it." In order to save the case of his country from being prejudiced in future negotiations by the liberality of offers made and rejected, Mr. Clay instructed Gallatin to declare "that the American government does not hold itself bound hereafter, in consequence of any proposal which it has heretofore made, to agree to a line which has been so proposed and rejected, but will consider itself at liberty to contend for the full measure of our just claims; which declaration you must have recorded in the protocol of one of your conferences; and to give it more weight, *have it stated that it has been done by the express direction of the president.*"

Mr. Gallatin sustained the claim of the United States in this negotiation so powerfully that the British plenipotentiaries, Huskisson, Grant and Addington, were forced to the position that Great Britain did not assert any *title* to the country. They contented themselves with the contention that her *claim* was sufficiently well founded as to give her the right to occupy the country in common with other nations, such concessions having been made to her by the Nootka treaty. The British negotiators complained of the recommendation of President Monroe in his message of December 7, 1824, to establish a military post at the mouth of the Columbia river and of the passage of a bill in the House providing for the occupancy of the Oregon river. To this the American replied by calling attention to the act of the British parliament of 1821, entitled "An act for regulating the fur trade and establishing a criminal and civil jurisdiction in certain parts of North America." He contended with great ability and force that the recommendation and bill complained of did not interfere with the treaty of 1818, and that neither a territorial government nor a fort at the mouth of the river could rightly be complained of by a government which had granted such wide privileges and comprehensive powers to the Hudson's Bay Company.

Before the conclusion of these negotiations, Mr. Gallatin had offered not alone the forty-ninth parallel but that "the navigation of the Columbia river shall be perpetually free to subjects of Great Britain in common with citizens of the United States, provided that the said line should strike the northeastermost or any other branch of that river at a point at which it was navigable for boats." The British, on their part, again offered the Columbia river, together with a large tract of land between Admiralty Inlet and the coast, protesting that this concession was made in the spirit of sacrifice for conciliation and not as one of right. The proposition was rejected and the negotiations ended in the treaty of August 6, 1827, which continued the Joint-Occupancy treaty of 1818 indefinitely, with the proviso that it might be abrogated by either party on giving the other a year's notice.

"There can be no doubt," says Evans, "that, during the continuance of these two treaties, British foothold was strengthened and the difficulty of the adjustment of boundaries materially enhanced. Nor does this reflect in the slightest degree upon those great publicists who managed the claim of the United States in those negotiations. Matchless ability and earnest patriotism, firm defense of the United States' claim, and withal a disposition to compromise to avoid rupture with any other nation, mark these negotiations in every line. The language and intention of these treaties are clear and unmistakable. Neither government was to attempt any act in the derogation of the other's claim; nor could any advantage inure to either; during their continuance the territory should be free and open to citizens and subjects of both nations. Such is their plain purport; such the only construction which their language will warrant. Yet it cannot be controverted that the United States had thereby precluded itself from the sole enjoyment of the territory which it claimed in sovereignty; nor that Great Britain acquired a peaceable, recognized and uninterrupted tenancy-in-common in regions where her title was so imperfect that she herself admitted that she could not successfully maintain, nor did she even *assert* it. She could well afford to wait. Hers was indeed the policy later in the controversy styled masterly inactivity: 'Leave the title in abeyance, the settlement of the country will ultimately settle the sovereignty.' In no event could her colorless title lose color; while an immediate adjustment of the boundary would have abridged the area of territory in which, through her subjects, she already exercised exclusive possession, and had secured the entire enjoyment of its wealth and resources. The Hudson's Bay Company, by virtue of its license of trade excluding all other British subjects from the territory, was Great Britain's trustee in possession—an empire company, omnipotent to supplant enterprises projected by citizens of the United States. Indeed, the territory had been appropriated by a wealthy, all-powerful monopoly, with whom it was ruinous to attempt to compete. Such is a true exhibit of the then condition of Oregon, produced by causes extrinsic to the treaty, which the United States government could neither counteract nor avoid. The United States had saved the right for its citizens to enter the territory, had protested likewise that no act or omission on the part of the government or its citizens, or any act of commission or omission by the British government or her subjects during such joint-occupancy treaties, should affect in any way the United States' claim to the territory.

*   *   *   *   *   *   *

"The treaties of 1818 and 1827 have passed into history as conventions for joint occupancy. Practically they operated as *grants* of possession to Great Britain, or rather to her representative, the Hudson's Bay Company, who, after the merger with the Northwest Company, had become sole occupant of the territory. The situation may be briefly summed up: The United States claimed title to the territory. Great Britain, through its empire-trading company, occupied it,—enjoyed all the wealth and resources derivable from it."

But while joint occupation was in reality non-occupation by any but the British, it must not be supposed that the case of the United States was allowed to go entirely by default during the regime of the so-called joint occupancy. In congress the advisability of occupying Oregon was frequently and vehemently discussed. Ignorance and misconception with regard to the real nature of Oregon, its climate, soil, products and healthfulness, were being dispelled. The representations of the Hudson's Bay Company that it was a "miasmatic wilderness, uninhabitable except by wild beasts and more savage men," were being found to be false. In 1821 Dr. John Floyd, a representative in congress from Virginia, and Senator Thomas H. Benton, of Missouri, had interviews at Washington with Ramsey Crooks and Russel Farnham, who had belonged to Astor's party. From these gentlemen they learned something of the value of Oregon, its features of interest and its commercial and strategic importance. This information Dr. Floyd made public in 1822, in a speech in support of a bill "to authorize the occupation of the Columbia river, and to regulate trade and intercourse with the Indians therein." On December 29, 1823, a committee was appointed to inquire as to the wisdom of occupying the mouth of the Columbia and the committee's report, submitted on April 15 of the following year, embodied a communication from General Thomas S. Jesup, which asserted that the military occupancy of the Columbia was a necessity for protecting trade and securing the frontier. It recommended "the dispatch of a force of two hundred men across the conti-

nent to establish a fort at the mouth of the Columbia river; that at the same time two vessels, with arms, ordnance and supplies, be sent thither by sea. He further proposed the establishment of a line of posts across the continent to afford protection to our traders; and on the expiration of the privilege granted to British subjects to trade on the waters of the Columbia, to enable us to remove them from our territory, and secure the whole to our citizens. Those posts would also assure the preservation of peace among the Indians in the event of a foreign war and command their neutrality or assistance as we might think most advisable." The letter exposed Great Britain's reasons for her policy of masterly inactivity, and urged that some action be taken by the United States to balance or offset the accretion of British title and for preserving and perfecting its own. "History," says Evans, "will generously award credit to the sagacious Jesup for indicating in 1823 the unerring way to preserve the American title to Oregon territory. Nor will it fail to commend the earnest devotion of that little Oregon party in congress for placing on record why the government should assert exclusive jurisdiction within its own territory." In the next congress the subject was again discussed with energy and ability. In 1831 formal negotiations with Great Britain were resumed.

All this discussion had a tendency to dispel the idea, promulgated, as we have seen, by the Hudson's Bay Company, that the territory was worthless and uninhabitable, also to excite interest in the mystic region beyond the mountains.

The United States claimed theoretically that it was the possessor of a vested right to absolute sovereignty over the entire Oregon territory, and in all the negotiations after the signing of the treaty of Florida, its embassadors claimed that the title of their country was clearly established. The fact, however, that joint occupancy was agreed to at all after 1828 could hardly be construed in any other light than as a confession of weakness in our title, notwithstanding the unequivocal stipulations that neither party should attempt anything in derogation of the other's claims, and that the controversy should be determined on its merits as they existed prior to 1818. If the United States came into possession of an absolute title in 1819, why should it afterward permit occupation by British subjects and the enforcement of British law in its domain?

The United States' title, as before stated, rested upon three foundation stones,—its own discoveries and explorations, the discoveries and explorations of the Spaniards, and the purchase of Louisiana. While it was not contended that any one of these conveyed exclusive right, the position of our country was that each supplemented the other; that, though while vested in different nations they were antagonistic when held by the same nation, they, taken together, amounted to a complete title. The title was, therefore, cumulative in its nature and had in it the weakness which is inherent under such conditions. It was impossible to determine with definiteness how many partial titles, the value of each being a matter of uncertainty, would cumulatively amount to one complete title. And however clear the right of the United States might seem to its own statesmen, it is evident that conviction must be produced in the minds of the British also if war was to be avoided.

These facts early came to be appreciated by a clear-visioned, well-informed and determined little band in congress. The debates in that body, as well as numerous publications sent out among the people, stimulated a few daring spirits to brave the dangers of Rocky mountain travel and to see for themselves the truth with regard to Oregon. Reports from these reacted upon congress, enabling it to reason and judge from premises more nearly in accordance with fact. Gradually interest in Oregon became intensified and the determination to hold it for the United States deepened.

While the country never receded from its conviction of the existence of an absolute right of sovereignty in itself, the people resolved to establish a title which even the British could not question, to win Oregon from Great Britain even in accordance with the tenets of her own theory. They determined to settle and Americanize the territory. In 1836 an element of civilization was introduced of a vastly higher nature than any which accompanied the inroads of the Hudson's Bay Company employes and of trappers and traders. We refer to the American missionaries spoken of in the preceding chapter. The part which these, and especially that great missionary hero, Dr. Marcus Whitman, had in stimulating this resolution of the American people have been sufficiently treated heretofore. The results of Whitman's midwinter ride and labors and of the numerous other forces at work among the people were crystallized into action in 1843, when a great swelling tide of humanity, pulsating with the restless energy and native daring so characteristic of the American, pushed across the desert plains of the continent, through the fastnesses of the Rocky mountains and into the heart of the disputed territory. Other immigrations followed, and there was introduced into the Oregon question a new feature, the vital force and import of which could not be denied by the adverse claimant. At the same time the American government was placed under an increased obligation to maintain its rights to the valley of the Columbia.

But we must return now to the diplomatic history of the controversy, resuming the same with the negotiations of 1831. Martin Van Buren was then minister at London. He received instructions relative to the controversy from Edward Livingston, secretary of state, the tenor of which indicated that the United States was not averse to the presence of the British in the territory. While they asserted confidence in the American title to the entire

Oregon territory, they said: "This subject, then, is open for discussion, and, until the rights of the parties can be settled by negotiations, ours can suffer nothing by delay." Under these rather lukewarm instructions, naturally nothing was accomplished.

In 1842 efforts to adjust the boundary west of the Rocky mountains were again resumed, this time on motion of Great Britain. That power requested on October 18th of the year mentioned that the United States minister at London should be furnished with instructions and authority to renew negotiations, giving assurance of its willingness to proceed to the consideration of the boundary subject "in a perfect spirit of fairness, and to adjust it on a basis of equitable compromise." On November 25th Daniel Webster, then secretary of state, replied: "That the president concurred entirely in the expediency of making the question respecting the Oregon territory a subject of immediate attention and negotiation between the two governments. He had already formed the purpose of expressing this opinion in his message to congress, and, at no distant day, a communication will be made to the minister of the United States in London."

Negotiations were not, however, renewed until October, 1843, when Secretary Upshur sent instructions to Edward Everett, American minister to London, again offering the forty-ninth parallel, together with the right of navigating the Columbia river upon equitable terms. In February of the ensuing year, Hon. Richard Packenham, British plenipotentiary, came to the American capital with instructions to negotiate concerning the Oregon territory. No sooner had discussion fairly begun than a melancholy event happened, Secretary Upshur being killed on the United States vessel Princeton by the explosion of a gun. A few months later his successor, John C. Calhoun, continued the negotiations. The arguments were in a large measure a repetition of those already advanced, but a greater aggressiveness on the part of the British and persistency in denying the claims of the United States were noticeable. As in former negotiations, the privileges accorded by the Nootka convention were greatly relied upon by Great Britain, as proving that no absolute title was retained by Spain after the signing of that treaty, hence none could be assigned. One striking statement in Lord Packenham's correspondence was to the effect that "he did not feel authorized to enter into discussion respecting the territory north of the forty-ninth parallel of latitude, which was understood by the British government to form the basis of negotiations on the side of the United States, as the line of the Columbia formed that of Great Britain." He thus showed all too plainly the animus of his government to take advantage of the spirit of compromise which prompted the offer of that line and to construe such offer as an abandonment of the United States' claim to an absolute title to all the Oregon territory. It is hard to harmonize her action in this matter with the "perfect spirit of fairness" professed in the note of Lord Aberdeen to Mr. Webster asking for a renewal of negotiations. No agreement was reached.

During the sessions of congress of 1843-4 memorials, resolutions and petitions from all parts of the union came in in a perfect flood. The people were thoroughly aroused. In the presidential election which occurred at that time the Oregon question was a leading issue. "Fifty-four Forty or Fight" became the rallying cry of the Democratic party. The platform framed in the Democratic national convention declared: "Our title to the whole of Oregon is clear and unquestionable. No portion of the same ought to be ceded to England or any other power; and the reoccupation of Oregon at the earliest practical period is a great American measure." The position of the Whig party was milder and less arrogant, but equally emphatic in its assertion of belief in the validity of the United States' title. The fact that the Democrats carried in the election, despite the warlike tone of their platform and campaign, is conclusive evidence that the people were determined to hold their territory on the Pacific regardless of cost. "Never was a government more signally advised by the voice of a united people. The popular pulse had been felt, and it beat strongly in favor of prompt and decisive measures to secure the immediate reoccupation of Oregon. It equally proclaimed that 'no portion thereof ought to be ceded to Great Britain.'" In January, 1845, Sir Richard Packenham, the British minister, proposed that the matter in dispute be left to arbitration, which proposal was respectfully declined. So the administration of President Tyler terminated without adjustment of the Oregon difficulty.

Notwithstanding the unequivocal voice of the people in demand of the whole of Oregon, James Buchanan, secretary of state under President Polk, in a communication to Sir Richard Packenham, dated July 12, 1845, again offered the forty-ninth parallel, explaining at the same time that he could not have consented to do so had he not found himself embarrassed if not committed by the acts of his predecessors. Packenham rejected the offer. Buchanan informed him that he was "instructed by the president to say that he owes it to his country, and a just appreciation of her title to the Oregon territory, to withdraw the proposition to the British government which has been made under his direction; and it is hereby accordingly withdrawn." This formal withdrawal of previous offers of compromise on the forty-ninth parallel, justified as it was by Great Britain's repeated rejections, left the Polk administration free and untrammeled. Appearances indicated that it was now ready to give execution to the popular verdict of 1844. The message of the president recommended that the year's notice, required by the treaty of 1827, be immediately given, that measures be adopted for maintaining the rights of the United

States to the whole of Oregon, and that such legislation be enacted as would afford security and protection to American settlers.

In harmony with these recommendations, a resolution was adopted April 27, 1846, authorizing the president "at his discretion to give to the government of Great Britain the notice required by the second article of the said convention of the sixth of August, eighteen hundred and twenty-seven, for the abrogation of the same."

Acting in accordance with the resolution, President Polk the next day sent notice of the determination of the United States "that, at the end of twelve months from and after the delivery of these presents by the envoy extraordinary and minister plenipotentiary of the United States at London, to her Britannic Majesty, or to her majesty's principal secretary of state for foreign affairs, the said convention shall be entirely annulled and abrogated."

On the 27th of December, 1845, Sir Richard Packenham had submitted another proposal to arbitrate the matter at issue between the two governments. The proposal was declined on the ground that to submit the proposition in the form stated would preclude the United States from making a claim to the whole of the territory. On January 17th of the following year, a modified proposal was made to refer "the question of title in either government to the whole territory to be decided; and if neither were found to possess a complete title to the whole, it was to be divided between them according to a just appreciation of the claims of each." The answer of Mr. Buchanan was clear and its language calculated to preclude any more arbitration proposals. He said: "If the governments should consent to an arbitration upon such terms, this would be construed into an intimation, if not a direct invitation to the arbitrator to divide the territory between the two parties. Were it possible for this government, under any circumstances, to refer the question to arbitration, the title and the title alone, detached from every other consideration, ought to be the only question submitted. The title of the United States, which the president regards clear and unquestionable, can never be placed in jeopardy by referring it to the decision of any individual, whether sovereign, citizen or subject. Nor does he believe the territorial rights of this nation are a proper subject of arbitration."

But the British government seems now to have become determined that the question should be settled without further delay. The rejected arbitration proposal was followed on the 6th of June, 1846, by a draft of a proposed treaty submitted by Sir Richard Packenham to Secretary of State Buchanan. The provisions of this were to the effect that the boundary should be continued along the forty-ninth parallel "to the middle of the channel which separates the continent from Vancouver Island; and thence southerly through the middle of said channel and of Fuca's strait to the Pacific ocean." It stipulated that the navigation of the Columbia river should remain free and open to the Hudson's Bay Company and to all British subjects trading with the same; that the possessory right of that company and of all British subjects south of the forty-ninth parallel should be respected, and that "the farms, lands and other property of every description belonging to the Puget Sound Agricultural Company shall be confirmed to said company. In case, however, the situation of these farms and lands should be considered by the United States to be of public importance, and the United States government should signify a desire to obtain possession of the whole, or any part thereof, the property so required shall be transferred to the said government at a proper valuation, to be agreed between the parties."

Upon receipt of the important communication embodying this draft, the president asked in advance the advice of the senate, a very unusual, though not unprecedented procedure.

Though the request of the president was dated June 10, and the consideration of the resolution to accept the British proposal was not begun until June 12th, on June 13th it was "resolved (two-thirds of the senators present consenting), that the president of the United States be, and he is hereby, advised to accept the proposal of the British government, accompanying his message to the senate, dated June 10, 1846, for a convention to settle the boundaries, etc., between the United States and Great Britain, west of the Rocky or Stony mountains." The advice was, however, "given under the conviction that, by the true construction of the second article of the project, the right of the Hudson's Bay Company to navigate the Columbia would expire with the termination of their present license of trade with the Indians, etc., on the northwest coast of America, on the 30th day of May, 1859."

The wonderful alacrity with which this advice was given and with which five degrees and forty minutes of territory were surrendered to Great Britain, is accounted for by some historians (and no doubt they are correct) by supposing that the "cession" was made in the interests of slavery. The friends of that institution were unwilling to risk a war with Great Britain which would interfere with the war with Mexico and the annexation of Texas. Their play was to acquire as much territory from which slave states could be formed as possible, and they were not overscrupulous about sacrificing territory which must ultimately develop into free states. But for unfortunate diplomacy, "it is quite probable that British Columbia would be to-day, what many would deem desirable in view of its growing importance, a part of the United States."

Notwithstanding the great sacrifice made by the United States for the sake of peace, it was not long until war clouds were again darkening our national skies. The determining of the line after it reached the Pacific ocean soon became a matter of dispute. Hardly had the ratifications been exchanged when Captain Prevost, for the British government, set up the claim that Rosario was the channel intended in the treaty. The claim was, of course, denied by Mr. Campbell, who was representing the United States in making the survey line. It was contended by him that the Canal de Haro was the channel mentioned in the treaty. Lord Russell, conscious, no doubt, of the weakness of his case, proposed as a compromise President's channel, between Rosario and de Haro straits. The generosity of this proposal is obvious when we remember that San Juan island, the principal bone of contention, would be on the British side of this line. Indeed, Lord Lyons, the British diplomatic representative in the United States, was expressly instructed that no line would be accepted which did not give San Juan to the British. The position of the United States was stated by Secretary of State Lewis Cass, with equal clearness and decisiveness. Efforts to settle the matter geographically proved unavailing and diplomacy again had to undergo a severe test.

For a number of years the matter remained in abeyance. Then the pioneer resolved to try the plan he had before resorted to in the settlement of the main question. He pushed into the country with wife and family. The Hudson's Bay Company representatives were already there and the danger of a clash of arms between the subjects of the queen and the citizens of the United States, resident in the disputed territory, soon became imminent. Such a collision would undoubtedly involve the two countries in war.

In the session of the Oregon territorial legislature of 1852-'3, the archipelago to which San Juan island belongs was organized into a county. Taxes were in due time imposed on Hudson's Bay Company property, and when payment was refused, the sheriff promptly sold sheep enough to satisfy the levy. Recriminations followed as a matter of course and local excitement ran high. General Harney, com-

mander of the Department of the Pacific, inaugurated somewhat summary proceedings. He landed over four hundred and fifty troops on the island, and instructed Captain Pickett to protect American citizens there at all costs. English naval forces of considerable power gathered about the island. Their commander protested against military occupancy. Pickett replied that he could not, under his orders, permit any joint occupancy. General Harney, however, had acted without instructions from the seat of government, and the president did not approve his measures officially, though it was plainly evident that the administration was not averse to having the matter forced to an issue.

At this juncture, the noted General Scott was sent to the scene of the difficulty, under instructions to permit joint occupancy until the matter in dispute could be settled. Harney was withdrawn from command entirely. Finally, an agreement was reached between General Scott and the British governor at Vancouver that each party should police the territory with one hundred armed men.

Diplomacy was again tried. Great Britain proposed that the question at issue be submitted to arbitration and she suggested as arbiter the president of the Swiss council or the King of Sweden and Norway or the King of the Netherlands. The proposition was declined by the United States. For ten years longer the dispute remained unsettled. Eventually on May 8, 1871, it was mutually agreed to submit the question, without appeal, to the arbitrament of Emperor William of Germany. George Bancroft, the well-known historian, was chosen to present the case of the United States, and it is said that "his memorial of one hundred and twenty octavo pages is one of the most finished and unanswerable diplomatic arguments ever produced." The British also presented a memorial. These were interchanged and replies were prepared by each contestant. The emperor gave the matter careful and deliberate attention, calling to his assistance three eminent jurists. His award was as follows: "Most in accordance with the true interpretation of the treaty concluded on the 15th of June, 1856, between the governments of her Britannic Majesty and the United States of America, is the claim of the government of the United States, that the boundary line between the territories of her Britannic Majesty and the United States should be drawn through the Haro channel. Authenticated by our autograph signature and the impression of the Imperial Great Seal. Given at Berlin, October 21, 1872." This brief and unequivocal decree ended forever the vexatious controversy which for so many years had disturbed friendly feelings and endangered the peace of the two great Anglo-Saxon peoples. No shot was fired; no blood was shed; diplomacy had triumphed.

CHAPTER VII.

THE INDIAN WARS OF THE '50s.

We have seen in the previous chapter the struggle for possession with England. America won. Her home-builders outmatched the fur traders. But there was, as there always has been in our national history, another inevitable struggle for possession. This was with the Indians. The so-called Christian nations have never stopped to consider much the rights of the native claimants of the land. This, too, though accompanied by needless cruelty, deceit and treachery, is one of the necessary though seemingly hard and bitter laws of life. The thing greatly to be deplored in all Indian wars, however, has been the general practice on both sides of inflicting punishment upon any innocent persons that might happen along. Some drunken and ferocious savages, as devoid of humanity as the wild beasts about them, would plunder, outrage and kill some family of immigrants or settlers, and forthwith, a band of the brave, manly, yet harsh and intolerant frontiersmen who have made our early history, would rush forth impetuously and kill some poor Indian wretches who had never heard of the outrage and had not the remotest conception of having committed any offense. In like manner, when some avaricious white had swindled the ignorant Indians out of land or some other valuable property, or some lustful and conscienceless white desperado had outraged Indian women or murdered unoffending braves, a band of Indians, inflamed with whisky purchased of some post-trader, and armed with weapons from the same source, would go on the war path and torture, mutilate and murder some innocent, helpless women and children, who had never had a thought of injuring a living thing. No one who has ever lived on the frontier can wonder at the bitter and intolerant hatred of the whites for the Indians. But if we, the civilized and the victors, could put ourselves in the place of the natives and view life with their eyes, none of us would wonder that they had hated us with the fury and frenzy of wild beasts. For it is safe to say that for every pang suffered by whites, a score have been suffered by Indians. And we, the higher race, must admit that we know better than they, and have less excuse for inhumanity and intolerance.

Yet in the final summary there can be no other conclusion than that the extermination of the majority of the Indians and the total destruction of their claims as owners of this country was "writ down in the book of fate." It was simply part of the irrepressible conflict of life. Moreover by reason of the necessities of existence the early settlers could not wait to argue abstract questions of rights. They had obeyed the fundamental law to subdue and replenish the earth, and in pursuance of that condition of all progress they could not stop to philosophize on the principles of human brotherhood. They had to live, and with a tomahawk just leveled over their heads they had to repel. And if the right to repel existed, the right to counter attack followed as a matter of course; and extermination of their enemies was, generally speaking, the only effectual means of repelling. It was sad but inevitable. And though we have lived a "Century of Dishonor," it is much easier now to condemn than it would have been then to improve.

By reason of the conditions just noted, we find the history of our Indian wars the subject of bitter controversy. Hardly any two writers or witnesses give the same version of supposed facts. One has a bias in favor of the pioneers and makes his facts conform to his opinions, and hence represents the pioneers as always justifiable and the Indians as always to blame. Another gives the reverse impression. Nor are pioneers generally much disposed to blame. or smooth either their opinions or expressions. It is all one thing or all the other with them. The other fellow is a fool or a liar and that ends it. Compromise does not flourish in pioneer conditions. All are angels on one side and all devils on the other.

We shall use our best endeavor in these pages to present the facts without bias, acknowledging the probable impossibility of satisfying all readers, but believing that at this distance from the time, though not far from the scenes of the struggle, we can calmly view it and clearly see that its good or evil are not to be found exclusively on one side or the other, but as with all human affairs, the texture of each is of a mingled warp and woof.

After the Cayuse war had ended in 1850, by the execution of the supposed murderers of Dr. Whitman, there was a lull along the bunch-grass plains and sage-brush banks of the Columbia and Snake rivers, and a few adventurous explorers and ranchers began to seek locations on the streams hallowed by martyrdoms. The most considerable settlement was at Frenchtown, ten miles below Walla Walla, According to the best information obtainable, there were eighty-five persons, the men entirely of French origin and former Hudson's Bay Company employes, with Indian wives and a good stock of half-breed children, living there and in the vicinity. There were a few men at what is now Wallula. There were some fifteen men living at various separated points. Among them were Henry M. Chase, well-known for many years in Walla Walla, and Dr. W. C. McKay, the most famous man of mixed white and Indian blood that ever lived in Oregon. There were three men, Brooke, Bamford and Noble, at Whitman station.

On the 3d of March, 1853, Washington became a separate territory. Major Isaac I. Stevens was appointed governor, and in the following summer he set out for his domain. Gold had been discovered in the Colville country and there were many adventurers moving across the plains in that direction. The Indians were very restive. These explorations they regarded with well grounded suspicion as the entering wedge of the establishment of white sovereignty.

There were at that time two remarkable Indian chiefs, chiefs who belong to that line of remarkable red men of which Philip, Pontiac,

Red Jacket and Tecumseh were more illustrious specimens; whose qualities of mind and character contain a hint of what Indians might have been had they had any wide or long continued opportunity. These two Columbia valley chiefs were Kamiakin, of the Yakimas, and Peopeomoxmox, of the Walla Wallas. Like all the Indian chiefs, they perceived the handwriting on the wall revealed by the entrance of the whites, and they determined to make a desperate effort to burst their tightening bonds while there was yet a chance of success.

There was a general outburst of all the tribes of Oregon and Washington in 1853 and '54 which led into the great war centering in Walla Walla in 1855. This series of troubles began in the summer of 1853 in the Rogue river valley in southern Oregon. The usual bitter controversy raged as to who was to blame for this. It looks as though whites and Indians were equally so. In 1854 occurred the horrible "Snake River Massacre," in which a number of immigrants who had offered no provocation whatever, were butchered in the most brutal manner. Norman Ward, of Pendleton, then a boy of thirteen, was the only survivor. That massacre occurred on the Boise a few miles above Fort Boise. Great excitement ensued in the Willamette valley when this atrocity was known, and Major Haller was sent by General Wool, then commanding the Department of the Pacific, to the scene. Having partially punished the supposed perpetrators of the outrage, the command returned to The Dalles. All these things with many smouldering causes of discontent, prepared the Indians for war.

The great war of 1855 had three fields of operation. One was southern Oregon, another Puget Sound, a third Yakima and Walla Walla valleys. In all there were probably four thousand Indians under arms, and many have believed that nothing but lack of intelligent co-operation among these, prevented the annihilation of all the smaller settlements. But the various petty feuds and conflicting purposes,

always characteristic of barbaric wars, prevented such co-operation. Indian fought against Indian, and whites profited thereby.

In May, 1855, Governor Stevens and General Joel Palmer met the representatives of seventeen tribes at Walla Walla, to endeavor to make treaties for the cession of their lands. The council ground was on and around the identical place now occupied by Whitman College. The immemorial council ground of the Walla Walla and other tribes of this country lay between the college brook and the one north of it, and around the place now known as Council Grove. A fair, entrancing spot it must have been in its primeval luxury and wildness. The tents of the great chiefs were pitched, as nearly as can be ascertained, on the spot now occupied by the house of Mrs. E. H. Baker.

JOURNAL OF COUNCIL AT WALLA WALLA, MAY AND JUNE, 1855.

Below is given the journal of Col. Lawrence Kip, U. S. A., which graphically describes his trip from Astoria to Walla Walla, showing the situation of affairs along the route, and giving the actual proceedings of the great council, which established the white race in full possession of Eastern Oregon and Umatilla county. It is contemporaneous with the events it records, and no one can read it without being charmed by the writer's style, and deeply impressed with the magnitude of the issues involved in the controversy.

It was about ten o'clock on a morning in the beginning of May, that our good steamer crossed the bar at the mouth of the Columbia river, from its shifting shoals the most dangerous navigation on the whole Pacific coast. Our passage of six days from San Francisco had been remarkably stormy, and probably there were none on board more delighted than myself at the prospect of once more standing on terra firma. "Life on the ocean wave" has some very pretty poetical ideas connected with it, but I prefer to have got through with all my rocking in my babyhood, and now sympathize with the conservative party in wishing all things to be firm and stable. I am unfortunately one of those "Whose soul does sicken o'er the heaving wave." At noon we reached the village of Astoria, rendered classical ground by Washington Irving. An old trapper still living, who belonged to Mr. Astor's first party, says he has often seen 1,000 Indian canoes collected on the beach in front of the fort. When the Hudson Bay Company took charge of it, they removed their establishment up the river to Vancouver, and allowed the fort to fall into decay, till not a vestige of it now remains. A few houses like the beginning of a village are scattered along the banks which slope down to the river, wooded to the edge with pines. Opposite to this we anchored for a few hours to land freight, and then continuing our course up the river, night found us still "on our winding way."

At daylight I was awakened by the ceasing of the monotonous stroke of the engine and found we were opposite Fort Vancouver. The sun was just rising when I came on deck, so that I had the whol_ scene before me. Near the river are low meadow grounds, on which stands the post of the Hudson's Bay Company—a picketed enclosure of about three hundred yards square, composed of roughly split pine logs. Within this are the buildings of the establishment, where once much of its immense fur trade was carried on. From these headquarters, their companies of trappers, hunters and voyageurs, generally Canadians, were sent out to thread the rivers in pursuit of the beaver. Alone they traversed vast plains, or passed months in the heart of the mountains, far north to the Russian possessions, or south to the borders of California, returning in one or two years with the furs to barter at the Fort. Then came generally a short time of the wildest revelry, until everything was dissipated or perhaps gambled away, when with a new outfit they set forth on another expedition. From Vancouver the company sent their cargoes of furs and peltries to England, and thence they received by sea their yearly supplies. They possessed an influence over the Indians which was wonderful, and which the perfect system of their operations enabled them for years to maintain. But the transfer of the country to the Americans and the progress of civilization around them, driving out the Indians and beaver, has forced them to remove much of their business to other posts.

Some distance back the ground rises, and on the ridge stand the buildings of Fort Vancouver, one of the frontier posts of the United States Army, marked by the American flag waving on the parade ground in front. Far in the distance, like a cone of silver, on which the first rays of the sun was glancing, rose the snow-capped point of Mount Hood.

Among our passengers were one hundred and fifty recruits for the Fourth Infantry, in charge of Captain Anger, with whom I landed about six o'clock, and was. soon at the hospital quarters of Captain Wallen.

Fort Vancouver was at this time under command of Lieutenant-Colonel Bonneville, whose "Adventures" for three years in the adjoining Indian country will always live and be read in the fascinating pages of Irving. Two. companies of the Fourth Infantry and one of the Third. Artillery were stationel there. Altogether, it is probably the most pleasant of our posts on the Pacific coast. The place is healthy, the scenery around beautiful, furnishing opportunities of fishing, hunting and riding, while its nearness to Portland and Oregon City prevents the young officers from being, as at many other Western posts, deprived of the refining influence of female society. Many are the occasions on which they find it necessary to drop down to these places. Deserters are supposed to be lurking there, garrison stores. are to be provided, or some other of Uncle Sam's interests are to be looked after. Then, these visits must be returned, for the inhabitants of these places have an equal care for the welfare of their neighbors at the fort. Numerous, therefore, are the parties of pleasure which come from these towns to enliven the solitude of the garrison. On these occasions they are welcomed by balls, night after night the Regimental Band is heard. floating over the waters of the Columbia river and the brilliant glare of lights from the fort shows that tattoo. is not the signal for all within its walls to retire.

Here, a few days passed pleasantly, in the way garrison life always does. In such places there is but little change. "One day telleth another." Guard mounting— the morning ride—the drill—the long talk over the dinner table—the evening parade—the still longer talk at night with reminiscences of West Point days—and then. to bed. At this time Lieutenant Hodges (Fourth Infantry) was ordered to the post at The Dalles, about ninety miles distant, to conduct thither a company of recruits, and I, having no definite object in view, except to see as much of the country as possible, determined to accompany him.

We left Vancouver about six A. M., in a small steamer, "The Belle," which runs up the Columbia river about fifty miles, as far as the Cascades. The scenery of the river is in all parts beautiful but very varied in its character. The pine forests stretch down to the. banks, enlivened here and there by a cultivated spot which some settler has cleared, whose axe awakened new and strange echoes as it rang through the primeval woods. On the margin of the shore, and particularly on one of the islands, we noticed the dead houses of the Indians, rudely constructed of logs. Within, the bodies of the deceased are placed for a time, attired in their best array, until the building becomes filled. Then, the oldest occupants are removed and placed on the shore, . till the tide launches them off on their last voyage and' they are swept down to the ocean, which to the "untutored savage," as to his more cultivated brethren, symbolizes Eternity.

About noon, after a morning of almost incessant rain, we reached the Cascades, the head of navigation. Here, a *portage* has been made as the river for more than two miles flows over rocks, whirling and boiling in a succession of rapids, similar to those in the river St. Lawrence. Here is the great salmon fishery of the Columbia river, the season for which commences in this month, when the fish ascend the river in incredible numbers. The banks are inhabited by the remains of some of the Indian tribes, who display their skill in catching the salmon, which they dry for exportation. As we passed up, we found them scattered along the shore employed in this work. Little bridges are thrown out over the rocks, on which the Indians post themselves, with nets and hoops, to which long handles are attached. With these they scoop up the fish and throw them on the shore. They are then pounded fine between two stones, cured and tightly packed in bales of grass matting lined with dried fish skin, in which state they will keep for years. The process is precisely the same as it was described by Lewis and Clark. The aboriginal village of Wish-ram, at the head of the narrows, which they mention as being the place of resort for the tribes from the interior to barter for fish, is yet in existence. We still notice, too, the difference which the early explorers observed, between these Indians and those of the plains. The latter living on horseback, are finely developed, and look like warriors; the former, engaged only in their canoes or stooping over the banks, are low in stature and seem to have been dwarfed out of all manhood. In everything noble they are many degrees below the wild tribes of the plains.

We walked for about five miles, until we had passed the Cascades, and then took another little steamer which was to carry us to The Dalles. The scenery above is similar to that which we had already passed. In one place the mountains seem to come down to the river, ending in a huge rock perfectly steep, which has received the name of Cape Horn. Above, the precipices are covered with fir and white cedar; two small cascades, like silver lines, leap from point to point for a distance of 150 feet, while below, in the deep shadows the water seems to sweep around the rocks with a sullen sound. At ten at night we reached the end of our journey.

The post at The Dalles possesses none of the outward attractions of scenery which distinguish that of Vancouver. Its principal recommendation is its healthiness. The buildings are badly arranged, having been planned and erected some years ago by the Mounted Rifles, when they were stationed in Oregon. The officers' quarters are on the top of a hill, and the barracks for the men some distance further down, as if the officers intended to get as far from them as possible. There is a want of compactness, as there is no stockade—nothing

in the shape of a fortification: in case of an outbreak by any of the hostile tribes of Indians, the post might easily be surprised. At this time, two companies of the Fourth Infantry were stationed there under command of Major Rains.

Here I spent a week very much as I had done at Vancouver. During this time we were enlivened by a visit from Governor Stevens, the Governor of Washington Territory. He was on his way to the interior of the Indian country—to Walla Walla—in connection with the Indian Commissioners, to hold a grand council, to which he had summoned the tribes far and near. For some time they had been restless, numerous murders of emigrants crossing the plains had occurred, and it is deemed necessary by the Government to remove some of the tribes to reservations which have been selected for them. The object of this council was therefore to propose to them the purchase of their territory—a proposition which it was expected (as it afterwards proved) would be received by some tribes with violent opposition. Governor Stevens had therefore stopped to request a small body of troops to be sent on to meet him at the council ground, to act as escort to the commissioners, and also to guard the presents which were to be forwarded for distribution among the Indians.

A lieutenant and about forty men were therefore detailed by Major Rains for this duty, to which were added two half-breeds to act as packers, and a Cayuse Indian, who was to officiate as guide. This worthy from having been shot in the mouth in a fight with the Snake Indians, rejoiced in the *sobriquet* of Cutmouth John. Wounds are said to be honorable, particularly when received in front, but this was certainly not ornamental, for it had given him a dreadful distortion of visage.

On invitation of the young commander of the expedition I agreed to accompany it. The choice of this officer indeed held out every promise of a pleasant time, Lieutenant Archibald Gracie, in addition to his high qualifications as a soldier and gentleman—traits which he shared in common with the other officers of the post —had for my purpose the advantage of our cadet life together for a while at West Point, which gave us a common topic and ground of interest in the past. Many an evening, therefore, have we spent lying before our camp fire, out on the still plains or by rushing waters waters of the Umatilla, talking over these recollections or discussing the probable fortunes of those who were with us in the House of Bondage.

Our preparations were soon made, for army expeditions do not allow much time for packing trunks. The command was mounted, some fifteen pack mules added to carry the camp equipage, and about noon, May 18th, we bid farewell to the officers and rode away from The Dalles. Our course during the afternoon was through the Des Chutes Valley, an admirable grazing country, as the temperature is such that cattle can be kept out for the whole year and always find sub-sistence. It was formerly the place where the Hud-son's Bay Company raised all the best horses they used. The country appears, however, from the absence of timber, to be waste and desolate, though the soil is said to be rich and admirably adapted to agriculture. After passing the little river of Des Chutes, we found some springs near the Columbia river and encamped, having advanced about twenty miles.

Our arrangements for sleeping were soon made. We carried no tents, so that a buffalo robe and a blanket formed our bedroom furniture. This did well enough on pleasant nights, but when it rained, it required some skill to take refuge under the buffalo robe in such a way as to keep dry, and not wake up finding one's self lying in a pool of water. As soon as we encamped, fires were made by the soldiers and the cooking commenced. Our suppers, indeed, were not very sumptuous, the invariable bill of fare being bacon, hard biscuit and a cup of coffee. Yet, a long day's ride would supply the appetite, and after the horses were picketed and we were sitting cosily by the fire or were lying down watching the stars above us, with no sound on the wide plain but the measured tread of our sentinel, there was a degree of freedom about it far more pleasant than the conventional life of cities.

Saturday, May 19th. We were up early this morn-ing with the intention of making a long march, but were disappointed, as some of our animals had strayed off. There being no Indians in the neighborhood, they had been turned loose. Men had to be sent out to hunt them up, and it was near eleven o'clock before the com-mand was ready to march. However, we improved on the previous day, going twenty-five miles. During this morning, we reached John Day's river. This is so called from a hunter who was one of the original mem-bers of Mr. Astor's enterprise. It took us some time to cross, as the water was high, and all the pack mules had to be unloaded and their packs taken across in a canoe. We went into camp about 5 o'clock.

Sunday, May 20th. This was anything but a day of rest, for our march was the most severe one we have had, being more than forty miles, with the sun, hot as the tropics, beating down upon our heads. There was nothing, too, in the appearance of the country to afford any relief. Far as the eye could reach was only a wide sunburnt plain, perfectly lifeless, for the summer's sun, by burning up the herbage, had driven the game to seek refuge by the rivers. The prairie was covered with only a miserable crop of salt weed and wormwood, and our animals drooped as we pushed on to find some rest-ing place. Added to this was the want of water, for often in these regions we are obliged to march from twenty to twenty-five miles before we can reach a spring or water course. We were forced in this case to ride the whole day without stopping, until towards evening we reached Wells' Springs, a desolate looking

place, at the foot of a range of hills. Here, however, we had water, and therefore encamped. Night, too, was at hand, so that we were relieved from the intoler-able glare and heat, and in addition one of the corpor-als had the good fortune to shoot a couple of ducks that were lingering about the neighborhood of the spring, so that our evening fare was quite luxurious.

Monday, May 21st. To-day we made a shorter march, of thirty miles, and went into camp at 3 o'clock. Three miles from our camping ground we passed the Indian agency, a house erected by the Government at an expense of six thousand dollars, for the residence of the agent. He is, however, seldom here, making his home at The Dalles, and when we passed the place it was unoccupied. In the evening a party of Indians, whom we found to be Walla Wallas, rode into camp. After a little pow-wow they left us, but having some suspicions of our visitors our little camp was arranged with extra care. The horses were carefully picketed, lest they should be run off, and Lieutenant Gracie directed the guard in walking their rounds to examine that their muskets were ready for immediate use.

In the course of the night the rain had commenced and Lieutenant Gracie and I were striving to keep dry and sleep under the little tent of pack-covers we had hastily erected, when we were startled from our first slumbers by a terrific yell. It may be imagined that it did not take us many seconds to be on our feet, with our pistols ready for, what we supposed, was an attack. Looking out, however, in the dark night, everything seemed quiet on the prairie. The animals were grazing around, and not an Indian to be seen. Upon inquiry we discovered that the disturbance had been caused by one of the soldiers finding a large snake in bed with him. The reptile probably did not like the rain, and therefore crawled under the soldier's blanket for warmth. What species it was he did not learn, for the snake, disgusted with his inhospitable reception; glided away, and the soldier did not detain him to make any inquiries about his parentage.

Tuesday, May 22d. Our course this morning was through the same desolate country, until we struck the Umatilla, a beautiful stream fringed with trees. About 10 o'clock we came upon a party of ten soldiers of the Fourth Infantry, who were encamped by the river. They had been sent out from The Dalles a week before, under the command of a corporal, in pursuit of some Indian murderers, in finding whom, however, they had been unsuccessful. As Lieutenant Gracie had been directed, in event of meeting them, to add them to his command, their camp was broken up and they marched on with us, making the number of soldiers forty-seven. Towards evening our guide announced that we were but a few miles from the valley which was the resi-dence of the Cayuse tribe. Lieutenant Gracie, there-fore, sent on the soldiers under command of a sergeant to find a camping place for the night, while we, under the guidance of Mr. Cut-mouth John, struck across country to visit his countrymen. We found their lodges in a beautiful, well-watered valley, which I am not surprised they are unwilling to give up. They are, however, much diminished in numbers, and did not seem to amount to more than two hundred. We went into several of their lodges, and although they are notoriously the most unfriendly tribe to the whites among all the Indians in this region, of which we afterwards had some strong evidences, yet on this occasion they received us well and showed no feelings but those of cordiality. After leaving them, we returned to the trail, and riding on about five miles, found our party encamped by the Umatilla.

Wednesday, May 23d. At 2 o'clock P. M. we arrived at the ground selected for the council, having made the march in six days. It was in one of the most beautiful spots of the Walla Walla valley, well wooded and with plenty of water. Ten miles distant is seen the range of the Blue Mountains, forming the southeast boundary of the great plains along the Columbia, whose waters it divides from those of the Lewis river. It stretches away along the horizon until it is lost in the dim distance where the chain unites with the Snake river mountains.

Here we found General Palmer, the Superintendent of Indian Affairs for Oregon, and Governor Stevens, with their party, who had already pitched their tents. With the latter we dined. As was proper for the highest dignitary on the ground, he had a dining room separate from his tent. An arbor had been erected near it, in which was placed a table, hastily constructed from split pine logs, smoothed off, but not very smooth. Our preparations were made for a more permanent encampment than we have as yet had. A tent was procured for Lieutenant Gracie and myself, while the men erected for themselves huts of boughs, spreading over them pack covers.

Thursday, May 24th. This has been an exceedingly interesting day, as about twenty-five hundred of the Nez Perce tribe have arrived. It was our first specimen of this prairie chivalry, and it certainly realized all our conceptions of these wild warriors of the plains. Their coming was announced about 10 o'clock, and going out on the plain to where a flag staff had been erected, we saw them approaching on horseback in one long line. They were almost entirely naked, gaudily painted and decorated with their wild trappings. Their plumes fluttered about them, while below, skins and trinkets of all kinds of fantastic embellishments flaunted in the sunshine. Trained from early childhood almost to live upon horseback, they sat upon their fine animals as if they were centaurs. Their horses, too, were arrayed in the most glaring finery. They were painted with such colors as formed the greatest contrast; the white being smeared with crimson in fantastic figures, and the dark colored streaked with white clay. Beads and fringes

of gaudy colors were hanging from the bridles, while the plumes of eagle feathers interwoven with the mane and tail, fluttered as the breeze swept over them, and completed their wild and fantastic appearance.

When about a mile distant they halted, and half a dozen chiefs rode forward and were introduced to Governor Stevens and General Palmer, in order of their rank. Then on came the rest of the wild horsemen in single file clashing their shields, singing and beating their drums as they marched past us. Then they formed a circle and dashed around us, while our little group stood there, the center of their wild evolutions. They would gallop up as if about to make a charge, then wheel round and round, sounding their loud whoops until they had apparently worked themselves up into an intense excitement. Then some score or two dismounted, and forming a ring danced for about twenty minutes, while those surrounding them beat time on their drums. After these performances, more than twenty of the chiefs went over to the tent of Governor Stevens, where they sat for some time, smoking the "pipe of peace," in token of good fellowship, and then returned to their camping ground.

The Nez Perces, or pierced-nose Indians, received their name from the early traders and trappers, but they call themselves by the name of Chipunish. While they are the most friendly to the whites of any tribe in this region, they are at the same time one of the most numerous and powerful, roaming over the whole Rocky mountains; along the streams to the west, and across the almost limitless plains to the east, until they reach the hunting grounds of the tribes of the Missouri. They hunt the elk, the bear, the mountain sheep and the buffalo, while they trap the beaver to sell the skin to the whites. They are celebrated for their droves of horses, which, after being branded, are turned loose to roam upon the fertile plains till needed by their owners; when this is the case, it requires but a few days to break them sufficiently to answer the purpose of their bold riders.

About seventy women are seen among the warriors, for their presence is necessary when the tribe is to be encamped for any length of time. They perform all the menial offices, arranging the lodges, cooking and bringing wood, for it would be a disgrace to their lords to be seen engaged in these things. It would procure for them the title of *squaws*. Everything but the perils of war and the chase are beneath their attention. When at home and not occupied in preparing their arms, or in feats of horsemanship, they are gambling, lounging in groups on the mounds of the prairie, or listening to some story-teller, who recounts the exploits of the old warriors of the tribe. The Walla Wallas, another of the principal tribes present, is one much reduced in numbers and importance since the pioneer trappers first came among them. They range through the valley for thirty miles, to old Fort Walla Walla, once a central trading post of the Hudson's Bay Company, on the left bank of the Columbia river near where the Walla Walla empties into it.

In the afternoon, I visited the lodge of an old chief of the Nez Perces, named Lawyer. He showed us a wound in his side from which he was yet suffering, although several years had elapsed since it was received. It had been inflicted in a fight with their old hereditary enemies, the Blackfeet Indians. These are the most dangerous banditti among all the tribes—perfect Ishmaelites—who, while they are at war with all the neighboring savages, have nourished the most implacable hatred toward the whites, since they first met them in the days of Lewis and Clark. War is their employment, and the booty they gain by it, their support. They are admirable horsemen and as much distinguished for their treachery as for their headlong courage. Their hunting grounds extend from the Yellow Stone and Missouri rivers to the Rocky mountains. He showed us also some locks of their hair which he wore about him —not as a love token, or presented willingly by the former owners, but rather the reverse, as I presume they are the remains of scalps he had taken.

To-day Governor Stevens and Mr. Doty, one of his party, dined with us. It was the first dinner party we had given in the wilderness. Yet think not, O ye who dine your friends at Delmonico's that our entertainment was at all like yours! In the center of a tent a buffalo robe was laid on the ground (the luxury of a table being confined to the governor), on which were placed tin plates which were our only dishes, for china is not adapted to mule traveling on the plains. About this we reclined rather in Oriental style. At one end of the table (I mean the buffalo skin) was a beef steak from one of the cattle daily killed at the camp, and at the other end a portion of the same unfortunate animal's liver. One side-dish was a plate of potatoes—the other a plate of bread of leaden heaviness. The second course was—coffee, likewise served in tin cups. Yet we gathered about this feast with appetites which could not be found among the strollers in Broadway, and which it required no French sauces to provoke.

Friday, May 25th. We awoke this morning to hear the rain pattering about us, and to be thankful that we were encamped, and not obliged to resume our march. At about noon it cleared up, when we procured our horses and rode over to the Indian camp to pay another visit to our friend Lawyer. We found the old chief surrounded by his family and reading a portion of the New Testament, while a German soldier of Governor Stevens' party was engaged taking his portrait in crayon. He afterwards presented me with a copy, which I keep as memento of these pleasant days in the wilderness.

In the evening he came to our tent to return our visit. We feasted him to the best of our ability, not omitting the indispensable pipe, and he seemed exceedingly gratified with his entertainment. A discussion had

6

taken place some time before as to the hospitality of the Indians, and Lieutenant Gracie determined on this occasion to test the question; so, when the old chief's heart seemed to be warmed up with our good cheer, he enquired, "Whether Lawyer would be glad to see him if he came to his country to make a short visit?" To this rather direct hint no reply was for some time given, and the old man evidently endeavored to change the subject. At last finding it pressed upon him, he said "That Mr. Craig (an American) had a very good house not far from his lodge." The nearest to an invitation that he would give, was to answer in reply to Lieutenant Gracie's question, "Perhaps so."

Saturday, May 26. I spent the morning on horseback exploring the country. In the course of my ride I met an Indian boy with a prairie chicken he had just killed, and which he was delighted to exchange for an old silk handkerchief. There are three peculiarities for which this region of country has been remarked—its gorgeous sunsets, the rapidity with which the waters in its streams rise and fall, and the contrast between its hot days and cool nights.

Towards evening the Cayuse tribe arrived, numbering about three hundred. They came in whooping and singing in the Indian fashion, and after circling round the camp of the Nez Perces two or three times, they retired to form their own at some little distance. In a short time some of the principal chiefs paid their respects to Governor Stevens and then came to look at our camp. It was not, as we had reason to believe afterwards, a friendly visit, but rather a reconnoisance to learn our numbers and estimate our powers of resistance. In the evening I again visited Lawyer and also a number of his tribe. Some of them we found singing sacred music to prepare for to-morrow, which is Sunday.

Sunday, May 27th. The rain this morning when we woke, was not pattering upon our tent, but fairly splashing around it, so that we were content to keep within its covering till noon, when the returning sunshine invited us forth. After riding over to Governor Stevens' to lunch, we went to the Nez Perces' camp, where we found they were holding service in one of the largest lodges; two of the chiefs were officiating, one of them delivering an address (taking the Ten Commandments for his text), and at the end of each sentence the other chief would repeat it in a louder tone of voice. This is their invariable custom with all their speeches. Everything was conducted with the greatest propriety, and the singing, in which they all joined, had an exceedingly musical effect. There is an odd mixture of this world and the next in some of the Nez Perces',—an equal love for fighting and devotion, the wildest Indian traits with a strictness in some religious rites which might shame those "who profess and call themselves Christians." They have prayers in their lodges every mornin gand evening—service several times on Sunday

—and nothing will induce them on that day to engage in any trading.

At an early day the Roman Catholic missionaries went among them, and as this tribe seemed blessed with a more tractable disposition than most of their brethren, the labors of the Fathers appear to have met with considerable success. A kind of Christianity was introduced among them, strangely altered, indeed, in many respects, to make it harmonize with Indian thoughts and actions, yet still retaining many of the great truths of the faith. It exerted, too, a very perceptible influence over their system of morality.* The Methodists, I believe, have more recently added their teaching; so that if the theological creed of the Nez Perces was now investigated, it would probably be an odd system, which would startle an ordinary D. D.

After service we rode through the Cayuse camp, but saw no evidence of Sunday there. The young warriors were lounging about their lodges, preparing their arms or taking care of their horses, to be ready for the evening races. The Christianity among these Indians, we suspect, is confined to the Nez Perces.

Monday, May 28th. At noon to-day I rode out about five miles from camp to visit some gentlemen who resided on the site of one of the old missions. It was once the residence of the Methodist missionaries, who seem to have succeeded the Roman Catholic priests in some parts of the country. For what reason, I know not, they appear to have abandoned their ground, and when the old *adobe* buildings stood vacant, being well situated, with timber around, they were taken by these gentlemen who were endeavoring to raise stock, to sell to emigrants crossing the plains, or settlers who will soon be locating themselves through these valleys. They have since abandoned it and moved fifty miles farther into the interior to a claim of their own. About a stone's throw from the house are the graves of Dr. Whitman and his family (seven in number), who were murdered in 1847, by a band of Cayuses. He was, I believe, physician to the mission.† We spent the afternoon at the Nez Perce camp, where a band of some thirty young warriors were engaged in dancing and singing. Their musical instruments are few in number and of the rudest kind. The singing is very harsh, and to us, who listened to it only as a collection of sounds seemed utterly discordant. The songs are almost entirely extemporaneous, like the improvisatore recitations of the Italians, a narrative of some past events, or perhaps suggested by the sight of persons present, or by

*Lieutenant Kip was misinformed in regard to the Catholics being first among the Nez Perces; also, the first missionaries were Congregationalists instead of Methodists.—ED.

. †Dr. Whitman was a missionary instead of a physician to the mission, although a regular physician.—ED.

trifling circumstances known to the audience. We never saw the women dancing and believe they rarely do, and never with the men. During the dancing we had a little interlude in the shape of a speech. A young chief delivered it, and at the end of each sentence it was repeated in a louder voice by one of the old men. This repetition is their invariable custom, and a crier seems to be a necessary accompaniment to all their villages.

To-day, leading chiefs belonging to some of the most distant tribes, attended by their followers, have been coming into camp, and most of those for which the commissioners have been waiting are now represented. Their encampment and lodges are scattered over the valley for more than a mile, presenting a wild and fantastic appearance. The council will probably open to-morrow. According to the original orders received by Lieutenant Gracie, this was to have been our last day here, but foreseeing this delay, Governor Stevens had some time ago sent an express to The Dalles, stating the necessity for the soldiers' remaining. To-day the express returned, bringing instructions from Major Haller to Lieutenant Gracie, authorizing him to remain on the council-ground until the treaty was concluded, and informing him that provisions had been sent to the escort for seven days more.

Tuesday, May 29th. To-day the council was to have met at 12, but it was 2 o'clock before they came together. About eight tribes were represented. Nothing, however, was done but to organize the council and swear in the interpreters. Governor Stevens then made a short address. All this occupied two hours, then it began to rain and the council adjourned to meet again at 10 o'clock to-morrow morning if the weather should be pleasant; otherwise on the first pleasant day. A fine prospect for the extension of our stay in the valley! There are about five thousand Indians, including squaws and children, on the ground.

We had another of our recherche dinner parties this evening, entertaining one of the gentlemen residing at the Mission, and another attached to Governor Stevens' party. We received news to-day of the inspection visit of General Wool to Fort Vancouver and his order for an expedition to set out on the 20th of June, from Fort Dalles, fro the Snake Indian country, the force to be commanded by Major Haller.

Wednesday, May 30th. At 1 o'clock this afternoon the council met, and business seems to be really commencing. It was a striking scene. Directly in front of Governor Stevens' tent, a small arbor had been erected, in which, at a table, sat several of his party taking notes of everything said. In front of the arbor on a bench sat Governor Stevens and General Palmer, and before them, in the open air, in concentric semi-circles, were ranged the Indians, the chiefs in the front ranks, in order of their dignity, while the background was filled with women and children. The Indians sat on the ground (in their own words), "reposing on the bosom of their Great Mother." There were probably one thousand present at a time. After smoking for half an hour (a ceremony which with them precedes all business), the council was opened by a short address by General Palmer. Governor Stevens then rose and made a long speech, setting forth the object of the council and what was desired of them. As he finished each sentence, the interpreter repeated it to two of the Indians who announced it in a loud voice to the rest—one in the Nez Perce and the other in the Walla Walla language. This process necessarily causes business to move slowly. Many of the Indians have been to our camp to visit us to-day; among them, Stickus, an old chief of the Cayuses.

Thursday, May 31. On arriving at Governor Stevens' tent, I found that the council had already met. After the usual preamble of smoking, Governor Stevens and General Palmer, in succession, made long speeches to them, explaining the benefits they would receive from signing this treaty, and the advantages which would result to them from their removal to the new lands offered in exchange for their present hunting grounds. The council lasted until 3 o'clock

This evening we went, as usual, to the Nez Perce camp. There was a foot race, but the great events of the evening were horse races. Each of the tribes now here possesses large numbers of horses, so that wherever they are, the prairies are covered with these animals, roaming at large till they are wanted by their masters. Part of these are derived from the wild horses of the prairies, while some, from the marks with which they are branded, show that they have been stolen from the Spaniards in upper Mexico. To capture horses is esteemed next in honor to laurels gained in actual war, and they will follow the party of a hostile tribe for weeks, watching an opportunity to run off their horses. It is for this, too, that they are hovering around the emigrants on the plains, who sometimes by a stampede or a single bold dash lose in a single night all their animals, and are left helpless on the plains, as a ship at sea without sails. Living as they do on horseback, racing forms one of their greatest amusements. They will ride for miles, often having heavy bets depending on the results. On this occasion we saw nearly thirty Indians start at once and dash over the plains like the winds, sweeping round in a circle of several miles.

Friday, June 1. The council did not meet this morning, as the Indians wished to consider the proposals made to them during the past few days. We learned that two or three of the half-civilized Nez Perces, who could write, were keeping a minute account of all that transpired at these meetings.

At the races this evening a serious accident took place, and which had nearly proved fatal. The Indians, as usual, were dashing about on horseback, some going up and others down, when two of them came in colli-

sion, knocking down both horses and leaving the riders senseless. No bones happened to be broken; the "medicine men" took charge of them, and it is supposed they will recover.

To-day has been the warmest we have had; there has not been a breath of air stirring, and the valley seemed like an extensive oven. At evening, however, the skies darkened, and for two hours we had the most tremendous thunder storm I ever witnessed. It was worthy of the tropics.

Saturday, June 2. Just before I was up this morning, we had a call from some of the Indians, who pay little regard to visiting hours. After breakfast I rode over to see the gentlemen at the old Mission, and on my return to camp, found that the council was already assembled, having met at 12 o'clock. The Indian chiefs had at length begun to reply, so that another step has been gained. After Governor Stevens' opening speech, several of them followed in short addresses. I arrived there just in time to hear the last one, made by one of the Cayuse chiefs. He did not commit himself as to what they would do, but the whole tenor of his address was unfavorable to the reception of the treaty. After a few words in conclusion from Governor Stevens, the council adjourned till 10 o'clock on Monday.

Then came part of my daily routine of amusement, to ride out and see Lieutenant Gracie practice the soldiers at target firing. He has been gradually lengthening the distance, and some of the men are now able to make very admirable shots. At the Indian camp to-night, there was a great foot race between about a dozen competitors, who ran over two miles. It was a good test of the long-winded endurance of the young warriors. As they raced off over the plain, parties of Indians, and those of us who were on horseback, rode on each side of them, the friends of the competitors encouraging them and taunting those who flagged.

Sunday, June 3. A quiet day, most of it was spent in reading in my tent. In the afternoon rode over to the Mission, and on my return dined with Governor Stevens. This evening the pack mules from Fort Dalles with seven days' provisions arrived at the Mission, and are to be brought over early to-morrow morning by some soldiers.

Monday, June 4. Breakfast at the fashionable hour of 10, as I was waiting for Lieutenant Gracie, who was obliged to go early to the Mission to see about the pack mules. An express came in this morning from The Dalles, giving him orders to join Major Haller's command, forty-five miles below this place, as soon as the council breaks up.

The diplomatists met to-day at 1:30 o'clock. After Governor Stevens' address, the old chief Lawyer spoke, which was the first time anything had been heard from the Nez Perces. Several of the other chiefs followed, and the council finally adjourned at 5 o'clock, without having made any sensible progress. The maxim "that time is money," which prevails so extensively among the Anglo-Saxons, has not yet penetrated into the wilderness to be received as a motive in any way influencing the conduct. With the Indians, "the next moon" will answer just as well as this month, for any business that is to be transacted. I should think, however, the commissioners would have their patience utterly exhausted.

Until a late hour we heard from the Indian camps the sound of their singing and the beating of their drums, and could see the figures flit before the fires as the dancing went on.

Tuesday, June 4. Another visit before breakfast from some of our Indian friends. Early this morning Lieutenant Gracie sent off an express to The Dalles to report progress. Then came the same routine of the council; Governor Stevens, at the opening, gave them the most elaborate address he has yet made, explaining to the chiefs most definitely, what lands he wished to give up, and what their "Great Father" (the President) would give them in return, together with the benefits they would derive from the exchange. General Palmer afterwards made a speech an hour long, in which he endeavored to illustrate to his audience the many advantages resulting from their being brought into contact with civilization. His reasoning at one time led him to give an account of the railroad and telegraph. It was sufficiently amusing to listen to this scientific lecture (as Julian Avenel says of Warden's homily in the Monastery), "quaintly conceived and curiously pronounced, and to a well chosen congregation," but it probably would have been much more diverting could we have known the precise impressions left upon the minds of his audience, or have heard them talk it over afterwards in their lodges. After he had finished, Stickus, the old Cayuse chief, made a short speech, and then Governor Stevens adjourned them until to-morrow.

There is evidently a more hostile feeling towards the whites getting up among some of the tribes, of which we had to-night a very unmistakable proof. The Cayuses, we have known, have never been friendly, but hitherto they have disguised their feelings. To-night, as Lieutenant Gracie and I attempted, as usual, to enter their camp, they showed a decided opposition; we were motioned back, and the young warriors threw themselves in our way to obstruct our advance. To yield to this, however, or show any signs of being intimidated, would have been ruinous with the Indians, so we were obliged to carry out our original intentions. We placed our horses abreast, riding round the Indians, where it was possible, and at other times forcing our way through, believing that they would not dare to resort to actual violence. If, however, this hostile feeling at the council increases, how long will it be before we have an actual outbreak?

Wednesday, June 6th. To-day the Indians again determined not to meet in council, as they wished to consult among themselves; so there is another day lost.

After my ride up the valley to the Mission, I found on my return to dinner an old trapper and Indian trader had come in to visit us, and was to be our guest. We had, however, a sumptuous repast, for he brought with him a buffalo tongue, a great luxury on the plains, and one which anywhere might tempt the epicure.

The races to-night were the most exciting we have seen, as the Indians had bet some sixteen or eighteen blankets (a great stake for them) on the result, and all the passions of the savage natures were called into play. There was visible none of that Mohawk stoicism of manner which Fenimore Cooper describes. After the races were finished, Lieutenant Gracie and I concluded to ride into the camp of our amiable friends, the Cayuses, to see how they felt this evening. There was no attempt to exclude us, though if savage and scowling looks could have killed, we should both have ended our mortal career this evening in this valley of Walla Walla.

Thursday, June 7th. Mr. M'Kay took breakfast with us. He is the son of the old Indian hunter so often mentioned in Irving's 'Astoria,' and whose name is identified with pioneer life in this region.

The council met to-day at 12, and I went into the arbor, and taking my seat at the reporters' table, wrote some of the speeches delivered. There is, of course, in those of the Indians, too much repetition to give them fully, but a few extracts may show the manner in which these wearisome meetings were conducted day after day.

Governor Stevens.—"My brothers! we expect to have your hearts to-day. Let us have your hearts straight out."

Lawyer, the old Nez Perce chief.—The first part of his speech was historical, relating to the discovery of this country by the Spaniards, which is a favorite topic with the Indian orators. In course of it, he thus narrated the story of Columbus and the egg, which he had heard from some of the missionaries:

"One of the head of the court said, 'I knew there was such a country.' Columbus, who had discovered it, said, 'Can you make an egg stand on its end?' He tried to make the egg stand, but could not do it. He did not understand how. It fell over. Columbus then showed them all that he could make it stand. He sat it down and it stood. He knew how, and after they saw it done, they could do it."

He thus described the manner in which the tribes at the east receded at the approach of the whites:

"The red man traveled away farther, and from that time they kept traveling away further, as the white people came up with them. And this man's people (pointing to a Delaware Indian, who was one of the interpreters) are from that people. They have come on from the Great Lake where the sun rises, until they are near us now, at the setting sun. And from that country, somewhere from the center, came Lewis and Clark, and that is the way the white people traveled and came on here to my forefathers. They passed through our country, they became acquainted with our country and all our streams, and our forefathers used them well, as well as they could, and from the time of Columbus, from the time of Lewis and Clark, we have known you, my friends; we poor people have known you as brothers."

He concluded by expressing his approval of the treaty, only urging that the whites should act toward them in good faith.

Governor Stevens.—"We have now the hearts of the Nez Perces through their chief. Their hearts and our hearts are one. We want the hearts of the other tribes through their chiefs."

Young Chief, of the Cayuse.—(He was evidently opposed to the treaty, but grounded his objections on two arguments. The first was, they had no right to sell the ground which God had given for their support unless for some good reasons.)—"I wonder if the ground has anything to say? I wonder if the ground is listening to what is said? I wonder if the ground would come alive and what is on it? Though I hear what the ground says, 'It is the Great Spirit that placed me here. The Great Spirit tells me to take care of the Indians, to feed them aright. The Great Spirit appointed the roots to feed the Indians on.' The water says the same thing. 'The Great Spirit directs me. Feed the Indians well.' The grass says the same thing. 'Feed the horses and cattle.' The ground, water and grass say, 'the Great Spirit has given us our names. We have these names and hold these names. Neither the Indians or whites have a right to change these names." The ground says, 'The Great Spirit has placed me here to produce all that grows on me, trees and fruit.' The same way the ground says, 'It was from me man was made.' The Great Spirit, in placing men on the earth, desired them to take good care of the ground and to do each other no harm. The Great Spirit said, 'You Indians who take care of certain portions of the country should not trade it off except you get a fair price.' "

The other argument was, that he could not understand clearly what they were to receive.

"The Indians are blind. This is the reason we do not see the country well. Lawyer sees clear. This is the reason why I don't know anything about this country. I do not see the offer you have made to us yet. If I had the money in my hand I should see. I am, as it were, blind. I am blind and ignorant. I have a heart, but cannot say much. This is the reason why the chiefs do not understand each other right, and stand apart. Although I see your offer before me, I do not understand it and I do not yet take it. I walk as it were in the dark, and cannot therefore take hold of what I do not see. Lawyer sees and he takes hold. When I come to understand your propositions, I will take hold. I do not know when. This is all I have to say."

Five Crows, of the Walla Wallas.—"I will speak a few words. My heart is the same as Young Chief's."

General Palmer.—"We know no chief among the Walla Wallas but Peo-peo-mox-mox. If he has anything to say, we will be pleased to hear it."

Peo-peo-mox-mox.—"I do not know what is straight. I do not see the offer you have made to the Indians. I never saw these things which are offered by my Great Father. My heart cried when you first spoke to me. I felt as if I was blown away like a feather. Let your heart be, to separate as we are and appoint some other time. We shall have no bad minds. Stop the whites from coming up here until we have this talk. Let them not bring their axes with them. The whites may travel in all directions through our country, we will have nothing to say to them, provided they do not build houses on our lands. Now I wish to speak about Lawyer. I think he has given his land. That is what I think from his words. I request another meeting. It is not in one meeting only that we can come to a decision. If you come again with a friendly message from our Great Father, I shall see you again at this place. To-morrow I shall see you again, and to-morrow evening I shall go home. This is all I have to say."

General Palmer.—"I want to say a few words to these people, but before I do so, if Kamiakin wants to speak, I would be glad to hear him."

Kamiakin, Yakima Chief.—"I have nothing to say."

General Palmer.—"I would enquire whether Peo-peo-mox-mox or Young Chief has spoken for the Umatillas? I wish to know farther, whether the Umatillas are of the same heart?"

Owhi, Umatilla Chief.—"We are together and the Great Spirit hears all that we say to-day. The Great Spirit gave us the land and measured the land to us, this is the reason I am afraid to say anything about the land. I am afraid of the laws of the Great Spirit. This is the reason of my heart being sad. This is the reason I cannot give you an answer. I am afraid of the Great Spirit. Shall I steal this land and sell it? or what shall I do? This is the reason why my heart is sad. The Great Spirit made our friends, but the Great Spirit made our bodies from the earth, as if they were different from the whites. What shall I do? Shall I give the land which is a part of my body and leave myself poor and destitute? Shall I say I will give you my land? I cannot say so. I am afraid of the Great Spirit. I love my life. The reason why I do not give my land away is, I am afraid I will be sent to hell. I love my friends. I love my life. This is the reason why I do not give my land away. I have one word more to say. My people are far away. They do not know your words. This is the reason I cannot give you an answer. I show you my heart. This is all I have to say."

Governor Stevens.—"How will Kamiakin or Schoom speak?"

Kamiakin.—"What have I to be talking about?"

General Palmer.—"We have listened and heard our chiefs speak. The hearts of the Nez Perces and ours are one. The Cayuses, the Walla Wallas, and the other tribes say they do not understand us. We were in hopes we should have but one heart. Why should we have more than one heart? Young Chief says he does not know what we propose to him. Peo-peo-mox-mox says the same. Can we bring these sawmills and these gristmills on our backs to show these people? Can we bring these blacksmith shops, these wagons and tents on our backs to show them at this time? Can we cause fields of wheat and corn to spring up in a day that we may see them? Can we build these school-houses and these dwellings in a day? Can we bring all the money that these things will cost, that they may see it? It would be more than all the horses of any one of these tribes could carry. It takes time to do these things. We come first to see you and make a bargain. We brought but few goods with us. But whatever we promise to give you, you will get.

"How long will these people remain blind? We come to try and open their eyes. They refuse the light. I have a wife and children. My brother here has the same. I have a good house, fields of wheat, potatoes, and peas. Why should I wish to leave them and come so far to see you? It was to try and do you good, but you throw it away. Why is it that you do so? We all sometimes do wrong. Sometimes because our hearts are bad, and sometimes because we have bad counsel. Your people have sometimes done wrong. Our hearts have cried. Our hearts still cry. But if you will try to do right, we will try to forget it. How long will you listen to this bad counsel and refuse to receive the light? I, too, like the ground where I was born. I left it because it was for my good. I have come a long way. We ask you to go but a short distance. We do not come to steal your land. We pay you more than it is worth. There is the Umatilla valley that affords a little good land between two streams and all around it is a parched up plain. What is it worth to you? What is it worth to us? Not half what we have offered you for it. Why do we offer so much? Because our Great Father told us to take care of his red people. We come to you with his message to try and do you good," etc., etc.

These extracts will give a specimen of the kind of "talk" which went on day after day. All but the Nez Perces were evidently disinclined to the treaty, and it was melancholy to see their reluctance to abandon the old hunting grounds of their fathers and their impotent struggle against the overpowering influences of the whites. The meeting closed to-day with an effective speech by Governor Stevens, addressed to the chiefs who had argued against the treaty. I give it in part:

"I must say a few words. My Brother and I have talked straight. Have all of you talked straight? Lawyer has and his people have, and their business will be finished to-morrow. Young Chief says he is blind and does not understand. What is it that he wants? Stickus says his heart is in one of these places—the Grand Ronde, the Tuche, and the Tucanon. Where is the heart of Young Chief? Peo-peo-mox-mox cannot be wafted off like a feather. Does he prefer the Yakima to the Nez Perce reservation? We have asked him before. We ask him now. Where is his heart? Kamiakin, the great chief of the Yakimas, has not spoken at all, his people have no voice here to-day. He is not ashamed to speak? He is not afraid to speak? Then speak out. Owhi is afraid to, lest God be angry at his selling his land. Owhi, my brother! I do not think God will be angry with you if you do your best for yourself and your children. Ask yourself this question to-night. Will not God be angry with me if I neglect this opportunity to do them good? But Owhi says his people are not here. Why then did he tell us, come hear our talk? I do not want to be ashamed of him. Owhi has the heart of his people. We expect him to speak out. We expect to hear from Kamiakin and from Schoom. The treaty will have to be drawn up to-night. You can see it to-morrow. The Nez Perces must not be put off any longer. This business must be dispatched. I hope that all the other hearts and our hearts will agree. They have asked us to speak straight. We have spoken straight. We have asked you to speak straight; but we have yet to hear from you."

The Council then adjourned until six o'clock. In the evening I rode over as usual to the Nez Perces camp and found many of them playing cards in their lodges. They are the most inveterate gamblers, and a warrior will sometimes stake on successive games, his arms, and horses, and even his wives, so that in a single night he is reduced to a state of primitive poverty and obliged to trust to charity to be remounted for a hunt. In the other camps everything seemed to be in violent confusion. The Cayuse and other tribes were very much incensed against the Nez Perces for agreeing to the terms of the treaty, but fortunately for them, and probably for us, the Nez Perces are as numerous as the others united.

Friday, June 8th. As the Council does not open until noon, our morning passes in the same way. Lieutenant Gracie and I practice pistol shooting, read, and ride about the country visiting Governor Stevens' party and at the mission.

To-day it was nearly three o'clock before they met. After a few remarks by Governor Stevens, General Palmer made a long speech addressed to those chiefs who refused yesterday to accede to the treaty. He told them, as they do not wish to go on the Nez Perces reservation (the tribes never having been friendly to each other) he would offer them another reservation, which would embrace part of the lands on which they were now living. After this offer had been clearly explained to them and considered, all acceded to it, except one tribe, the Yakimas.

It seemed as if we were getting on charmingly and the end of all difficulties was at hand, when suddenly a new explosive element dropped into this little political caldron. Just before the Council adjourned an Indian runner arrived with the news that Looking Glass, the war chief of the Nez Perces, was coming. Half an hour afterward he, with another chief and about twenty warriors, came in. They had just returned from an incursion into the Blackfoot country, where there had been some fighting, and they had brought with them as a trophy one scalp, which was dangling from a pole. Governor Stevens and General Palmer went out to meet them and mutual introductions were made. Looking Glass then, without dismounting from his horse, made a short and very violent speech, which I afterward learned was, as I suspected, an expression of his indignation at their selling the country. The Council then adjourned.

At the races this evening in the Nez Perces camp we found ten of the young braves who came in that afternoon, basking in the enjoyment of their laurels. Dressed in buffalo skins, painted and decorated in the most fantastic style, they stood in a line on one side of the race ground, exhibiting themselves as much as possible and singing songs in honor of their exploits. After the races we rode through the Cayuse camp. They seemed to be in commotion, apparently making preparation to depart.

Saturday, June 9th. This morning the old chief Lawyer came down and took breakfast with us. The Council did not meet till three o'clock and matters seemed to have reached their crisis. The treaty must either soon be accepted, or the tribes will separate in hopeless bad feeling. On the strength of the assent yesterday given by all the tribes, except the Yakimas, the papers were drawn up and brought into the Council to be signed by the principal chiefs. Governor Stevens once more—for Looking Glass' benefit—explained the principal points in the treaty, and among other things told them there would be three reservations—the Cayuses, the Walla Wallas and the Umatillas, to be placed upon one—the Nez Perces on another—and the Yakimas on the third, and that they were not to be removed to these reservations for two or three years. Looking Glass then arose and made a strong speech against the treaty, which had such an effect that not only the Nez Perces, but all the other tribes, refused to sign it. Looking Glass, although nominally only the second chief, has more influence than Lawyer, and is in reality the chief of the different Nez Perce tribes. Governor Stevens and General Palmer made several speeches to induce him to change his decision, for, should he do so, the other chiefs would follow his example; but in

vain, and the Council was obliged to adjourn until Monday. In the meanwhile, it is supposed the commissioners will bring some cogent arguments to bear upon Looking Glass and induce him to accede to the treaty.

Near the race ground this evening we found the women collected in circles on the ground, gambling with the most intense earnestness. Like the men, they will spend hours around the lodge fires, staking everything they have on the changes and chances of the game. Near them stood, as on last evening, the returned warriors, exhibiting their fantastic finery and apparently thus challenging the applause of the softer sex. We supposed yesterday that we would have started this evening for the Umatilla, but the prospect now is that we shall be delayed several days longer.

Sunday, June 10th. We understand there has been great excitement through the Indian camps to-day. The Nez Perces have been all day long holding a council among themselves, and it is represented, the proposition has been made to appoint Looking Glass head chief over Lawyer. Yesterday, while Looking Glass was speaking Lawyer left the Council without saying anything; which many of them are disposed to regard as the surrender of his place. Should this proposition be carried into effect it would give a quietus to the treaty.

Monday, June 11th. Before breakfast we had a visit from Lawyer with some other Indians. At ten o'clock the Council met. Governor Stevens opened it with a short speech, at the close of which he asked the chiefs to come forward and sign the papers. This they all did without the least opposition. What he has been doing with Looking Glass since last Saturday we cannot imagine, but we suppose savage nature in the wilderness is the same as civilized nature was in New England in Walpole's day, and "every man has his price." After this was over the presents which General Palmer had brought with him were distributed, and the Council, like other legislative bodies, adjourned *sine die*.

As soon as the business was finished, we at once struck our tents and began our march toward Umatilla. On our way Lieutenant Gracie and I made our parting visit at the mission, and then proceeded about fifteen miles before we encamped for the night. Just before we started an express arrived from The Dalles bringing us letters and papers.

We have now ended our connection with the Council and bid adieu to our Indian friends. It is therefore an appropriate place to say that we subsequently discovered we had been all the while unconsciously treading on a mine. Some of the friendly Indians afterward disclosed to the traders that during the whole meeting of the Council active negotiations were on foot to cut off the whites. This plot originated with the Cayuses, in their indignation at the prospect of being deprived of their lands. Their program was, first to massacre the escort, which could *have been easily* done. Fifty soldiers against 3,000 Indian warriors, out on the open plains, made rather too great odds. We should have had time, like Lieutenant Gratton at Fort Laramie last season, to have delivered one fire and then the contest would have been over. Their next move was to surprise the post at The Dalles, which they could also have easily done, as most of the troops were withdrawn, and the Indians in the neighborhood had recently united with them. This would have been the beginning of their war of extermination upon the settlers. The only thing which prevented the execution of this scheme was the refusal of the Nez Perces to accede to it, and as they were more powerful than the others united, it was impossible to make the outbreak without their consent. Constant negotiations were going on between the tribes, but without effect, nor was it discovered by the whites until after the Council had separated.

Tuesday, June 12th. We were up bright and early this morning, expecting by sunrise to have been on our march. But some of our horses had strayed away during the night and it was eight o'clock before they could be collected to enable us to set out. After riding thirty miles we reached the Umatilla. Here we found a sergeant of the Fourth Infantry and five men encamped, who had been sent to meet us with provisions. Just then a pour of rain began, and we were glad to make our preparations for the night.

Wednesday, June 13th. I awoke to find it still raining in torrents and the wind blowing a beautiful accompaniment, as it swept through the trees which line the bank of the river. Fortunately the sergeant had brought with him a tent, which had turned over to us, and we remained tolerably comfortable. In the midst of the storm, however, a visitor arrived. He was a Mr. Whitney, who lived about a mile from our encampment, with Mr. McKay, on a claim he is cultivating, belonging to the latter. He invited Lieutenant Gracie and myself to take tea with him. About three o'clock it cleared up and we rode over to his residence, where for the first time in several weeks we had the satisfaction of seeing something which looked like domestic comfort. Mr. Whitney had his wife and child with him, and he took us over his garden and showed us his crops. At six o'clock we had tea, after the manner of civilized people, which was a great luxury to us after our camp fire in the wilderness. Just as we were bidding them good-night three of our acquaintances arrived from the Council ground on their way to The Dalles. We learned from them that the Indians celebrated a great scalp dance the night before, in which one hundred and fifty of the women took part. The tribes then broke up their lodges and returned to their own hunting grounds.

Thursday, June 14th. The place where we now are is an old camping ground, well known to all western hunters, being a central spot where several trails diverge. The emigrant trail passes by it and stretches to the Blue mountains, leading to Fort Boise. Here Lieutenant

Gracie had orders to remain until the arrival of the rest of the command, which starts from The Dalles on the 20th to enter the Snake country. He has been, therefore, making arrangements to-day for a more permanent encampment, as he may be delayed here for a couple of weeks. The tents have been regularly arranged, our own a little in advance, and those of the men built of boughs and pack covers, so as to protect them from the weather. A log house has been erected at one end of the camp, to hold the provisions, and to-day the men have been employed in constructing a corral, or enclosure to secure the horses. This evening our Indian guide came in. He had been left at the Council grounds to hunt up some stray horses.

Friday, June 15th. Early this morning Lieutenant Gracie sent off the Indian guide to The Dalles, as he had no further use for him. Mr. Cut-mouth John has apparently served us faithfully, though being a Cayuse, we cannot tell how deeply he has been implicated in the plotting of his countrymen this summer, or what part he would have taken had their projected outbreak ripened into action. To-day Lieutenant Gracie began to have his drills for the men, one before breakfast and the other after supper. At the early drill they are exercised in shooting at a target. This evening, at Mr. McKay's, we met the old chief Stickus, who had stopped there on an expedition after some missing cattle. He seemed quite pleased to see us. While there General Palmer and his party also arrived from the Council ground.

Saturday, June 16th. After drill we rode over to Mr. McKay's and found General Palmer's party still encamped there, as he was taken ill this morning. He probably needs rest of both body and mind, and on the plains this is the great prescription, as the remedies which the hunters can give are comprised in a list of very few simples. Nature is generally expected to perform the cure. Had his illness come on at the Council he could have had the "medicine men" of our friends, the Nez Perces, to prescribe for him. Their prescriptions, however, are always the same, whatever may be the disease, whether ague or fever, or small-pox. The patient is shut up in a small close lodge, called a "sweat-house," where he is subjected, until almost stifled, to a vapor bath produced by water slowly pouring over red-hot stones.

Sunday, June 17th. My last Sunday on the plains, and it is passed quietly enough. After Lieutenant Gracie had finished inspection and we had taken our usual bath in the river, we rode over to General Palmer's encampment to enquire about his health. We found him still too unwell to travel. The rest of the day was spent in reading, for we have found a small supply of books at Mr. McKay's, which proved quite a treasure in the wilderness.

Monday, June 18th. Lieutenant Gracie has commenced practicing the men at skirmish drill for an hour a day, and is thus preparing them for their Snake country expedition. It has become too hot, except in the morning and evening, to move about with comfort, and after drill, our ride over to Mr. McKay's, and our bath in the Umatilla, we are content to spend the remainder of the day in lounging and reading under the shelter of our tent. In an encampment on the plains, during the dead silence of a sultry noon, with no conventional restraints of civilization about us, we realize more fully than in any other place the truth of the Neapolitan maxim—*"Dolce far niente."*

We had to-day a visit from five of the Cayuse Indians, two of whom had been accustomed to visit us at Walla Walla.

Tuesday, June 19th. Before we were up we had an arrival of another party of the Cayuse tribe. Their lodges are in a valley about eight miles from the camp. They smoked the "pipe of peace," and probably this time with sincerity, as they knew we had force enough with us to defeat any attempt they might make. The principal chief of the Umatillas also came into our camp and some strange Indians we had never before seen.

As Lieutenant Gracie is obliged to remain at this camping ground, and it may be some days before the command arrives from the Dalles, I had myself determined to proceed on to that post to-morrow in company with Mr. McKay. I therefore this evening rode over to his place and made my arrangements for setting off the next morning.

Wednesday, June 20th. This morning a messenger arrived from The Dalles with papers and the latest news—the latter having been almost forgotten by this time in the settlements.

After drill I took my final leave of the camp. Lieutenant Gracie rode with me over to Mr. McKay's, where I left my horse, as he belonged to the command, transferring my saddle and bridle to one of Mr. McKay's, which I am to ride. And here Lieutenant Gracie and I parted. We had been companions for weeks by day and night, and in this his first independent command (in many incidents which I could not relate in this brief journal) he has established, with those at the Council who were accustomed to military expeditions in the Indian country, a character for decision and energy which gives the promise of distinction in much wider and more responsible scenes of action in the future.

We set off about half-past nine o'clock—Mr. McKay and myself with two boys, whose business it was to drive the pack mules. Our traveling arrangements were made in the old Spanish-California style, still common in those parts of the country where horses are plenty. Besides those we rode were seven or eight which ran loose and were driven by the boys, to be used when our own began to fag.

We crossed the Umatilla at once, and on the opposite side striking a trail on which we had gone into the interior, commenced our return westward. After riding twenty miles we reached the Indian agency. Here two of our horses were caught, our saddles and bridles transferred to them and the tired ones turned loose to follow with the rest. Then on we went until five in the evening, when we encamped for the night at Well's Springs, having traveled during the day fifty-five miles.

Thursday, June 21st. We were on our way this morning by five o'clock, on the trail we passed every little while solitary graves, the last resting places of some unfortunate emigrants. The road from Missouri to the Rocky Mountains can almost be traced by these sad memorials, and no human language can convey an idea of the sorrow and suffering which has taken place on the plains, caused by this rush to the land of gold. About ten miles on our way we met a portion of the Fourth Infantry and Third Artillery under Lieutenants Day, Hodges and Mendell. At noon we halted at Willow creek (seventeen miles from Well's Springs), for several hours to rest our horses. We then pushed on until eight o'clock in the evening, when we reached John Day's river, where a refreshing bath recompensed us for the long and hot ride. We had ridden to-day about forty-five miles.

Friday, June 22d. We left John Day's river about seven o'clock, and after riding twelve miles met Major Haller (commander of the expedition) and Captain Russell, Fourth Infantry, with their escorts, with whom we stopped for a short time. Soon afterward we met another detachment of troops, with two or three wagons, each drawn by six mules. About noon we struck the Columbia river, whose solitary banks were quite enlivened by the long trains of wagons containing the provisions of the detachment. We counted twenty-four, half of which were on one side of the river and half on the other. The different detachments and wagons will all meet at the camping ground on the Umatilla where we left Lieutenant Gracie. There will be about one hundred and fifty mounted men besides the packers and wagons. After resting for a couple of hours on the Columbia we set out for The Dalles, where we arrived at five o'clock. Here we found Lieutenant Dryer, who is to set out to-morrow morning and join the command as quartermaster.

And thus ended my expedition into the wilderness. It has shown me the rough side of army life, and yet the time has passed pleasantly from the very novelty and freshness of everything. And now, amid all the refinements of civilization, I cannot but look back with something like regret to the freedom of our little camp on the quiet plains, where no sound was heard to break our slumbers but the steady tread of our sentinel or the rippling of the Umatilla.

The treaties negotiated at Walla Walla, June 12, 1855 (though dated June 9th), provided for the surrender by the Yakimas of the vast area of twenty-nine thousand square miles, being substantially Chelan, Yakima, Kittitas, Franklin, Adams, and the most of Douglas and Klickitat counties. From that cession was to be excepted the princely domain, one of the finest bodies of land in the world, now known as the Yakima reservation. The Yakimas, it may be said, constituted a "nation" composed of fourteen tribes, extending from the Cascade summits to the Palouse river. The Nez Perces agreed to relinquish almost as large an area, embracing what is now a good part of Whitman, Garfield, Columbia and Asotin counties in Washington; Union and Wallowa counties in Oregon; and Washington, Idaho and Nez Perce counties in Idaho. A very large reservation was provided by the treaty for the Nez Perces; being, in addition to that now embraced in the Nez Perce reservation, large tracts between the Alpowa and Snake rivers and the Wallowa valley. The retention of the Wallowa was insisted on by Chief Joseph, and seems to have been the key to the ratification of the entire plan; and it is the more to be deplored that the modification of the treaty in 1863, afterward precipitated the Nez Perce war of 1877. That change in 1863 involved the surrender of the Wallowa and the reduction of the Nez Perce reservation to what it was prior to its recent opening. But few Indians seem to have been consulted, and young Joseph, son of the Joseph who took part in the treaty of 1855, insisted on their claim to the country, and the difficulty led to the memorable war of 1877. This is not the place to discuss the event, but we refer to it here in order to illustrate the lamentable results which follow a failure to adhere to a given agreement from one administration to another. The treaty of 1855 should have been faithfully observed unless abrogated by the clear and general agreement of both parties. And there was the deeper obligation on the part of the government to do it in the case of the Nez Perces, for to them Governor Stevens and his party owed their

lives, and the settlers owed a debt of thankfulness not to be computed. Instead of remembering this, the land-grabbers goaded those steadfast friends of the whites into a cruel and causeless war. In connection with this Wallowa matter, an interesting reminiscence was given the writer by John McBean, son of the Hudson's Bay employe of that name. Young McBean was at that time a boy of twelve, and being a half-breed and knowing the Indian language perfectly, could pass at any time for an Indian. He related that while acting as a spy on the grounds, he heard the discussion about the treaties, and the whole matter depended upon whether the Nez Perces would accept it. This they finally did on the distinct agreement that Joseph and his band should have permanent possession of the Wallowa. That point assured, the Nez Perces agreed. The others followed. That settled the whole matter. Otherwise the treaties would never have been accepted. Yet eight years after, without general agreement by the tribe, the vital point was violated and the cherished Wallowa valley left out of the reservation to be demanded in later years by white settlers. It should be added that those immediate settlers were in no way personally guilty. Government was to blame. That is a sample of one kind of reason for Indian wars. So much for the Nez Perce part of the agreement.

The Umatillas, Cayuses and Walla Wallas, under the terms of this treaty, relinquished their right to another magnificent territory, embraced substantially in the present limits of Walla Walla county in Washington, and Umatilla, Morrow, and part of Union and Gilliam counties in Oregon. Their reservation was essentially that now known as the Umatilla reservation. Which of these three superb domains was the best would puzzle a good judge to decide. Any one of them is larger than most of the Atlantic states, and in point of opulence of natural resources surpasses equal areas in most parts of the world.

For their concessions the Indians were to receive what seems a just and even liberal compensation, though to the mind of civilized man, ridiculously small; for the whole vast area of probably thirty million acres outside of reservations, was relinquished for about six hundred and fifty thousand dollars; in all, perhaps, roughly estimated, two cents per acre. It is probably worth to-day, with its improvements, nearly a quarter of a billion dollars.

The compensation of the Yakima nation was two hundred thousand dollars, paid in annuities, with salaries for the head chiefs of five hundred dollars for twenty years, also some special agreement in regard to houses, tools, etc. The compensation of the Nez Perces was the same. The Umatillas, Cayuses and Walla Wallas were to receive one hundred thousand dollars; each of the head chiefs to have an annuity of five hundred dollars for twenty years, and also to have the usual special donations for houses, tools, etc. Peopeomoxmox, whose favor was especially courted, was granted the unique privilege of beginning to draw his salary at once, without waiting for the formal ratification of congress. His remaining son was to receive an annuity of one hundred dollars a year, a house, and five acres of land, plowed and enclosed. Peopeomoxmox was also to be given three yoke of oxen, three yokes and chains, one wagon, two plows, twelve hoes, twelve axes, two shovels, a saddle and bridle, a set of wagon harness and one set of plow harness.

Having completed this great work, Governor Stevens passed on to the north and east to continue the same line of negotiations with the Indians there. We may say in brief, that he succeeded in making a treaty with the Blackfeet, but was unsuccessful with the Spokanes. Meanwhile, during his absence, the great Walla Walla and Yakima war had burst with the suddenness of a cyclone upon the Columbia plains. And not only here but throughout the Sound country the storm of war had burst on all sides.

That the outbreak of hostilities should have occurred almost simultaneously at places so remote from each other as Walla Walla, Puget sound and Rogue river, has led many to suppose that there was a definite and widespread conspiracy. Others have believed that there was simply an identity of causes, and that these produced like results at like times. While it is altogether likely that there may have been hints of outbreak in the air which spread from tribe to tribe, it is likely that the second is the true solution.

Kamiakin, the Yakima chief, and Peopeomoxmox, the Walla Walla chief, were the animating force of the movement on this side of the mountains. Kamiakin was a natural general and diplomat. He seems to have signed the treaty at Walla Walla only under great pressure, and with the mental reservation that he would break it at the first opportunity. Hardly had the ink dried on the treaty when he was rounding up the warriors over the wide domain of the Yakima nation. These chiefs seem to have seen, as did Philip and Pontiac, that the coming of the whites, if not checked, meant the destruction of Indian rule. If they struggled against fate at all they must do it then. From their standpoint they were adopting the only possible policy. As some of the Nez Perces told Governor Stevens, they were not afraid of explorers, or trappers, or soldiers, but they were afraid of men with wagons and axes. They had now been watching for fifteen years a steady stream of immigrants passing down to the Willamette. Steamboats were running on the Columbia and Willamette rivers. Towns were springing up. It was now or never for them. One Indian only, and that was Lawyer, the Nez Perce, perceived the impossibility of the Indians ever coping with the whites, and that, therefore, the only wise course for them was to yield to the inevitable as easily as possible and adopt the white man's mode of life and live on terms of amity with him. Though Looking Glass and Eagle-from-the-Light had dissented very strongly from the first, they had finally yielded to Lawyer's powerful influence and the treaty had resulted. Now in the midst of the fury of war they remained true to their agreement.

Kamiakin had gathered together a great council of the disaffected at a point north of Snake river. The fierce and intractable Cayuses were the most active in the movement of any except Kamiakin himself and his immediate friends. Young Chief and Five Crows were the Cayuse chiefs leading the war, Stechus alone, with a very small following, holding aloof.

The war broke out rather prematurely in September by the murder of miners who were traversing the Yakima valley. Agent Bolon, having gone courageously into the valley to investigate the matter, was murdered and burned to ashes on September 23d. It is said that Quelchen, son of Owhi and nephew of Kamiakin, committed this crime.

Tidings of the outbreak of hostilities having reached The Dalles, Major Haller with a hundred men started north at once and Lieutenant Slaughter went from Steilacoom across the Natchez pass to the Yakima to co-operate with Haller. But on October 6th the Indians burst upon Haller with such energy that he was obliged to retreat with the loss of a fourth of his men, besides his howitzer and baggage. At this stage of affairs Peopeomoxmox fell upon old Fort Walla Walla, now Wallula, and though it had no garrison the Indians plundered the fort of a considerable quantity of stores. The Walla Walla valley was swept of settlers. The regions bordering Puget sound were also ravaged by the Indians. At this time General Wool was the commander of the Department of the Pacific. It is not possible here to enter into any examination of the bitter and rancorous dispute that has arisen as to General Wool's conduct of this war. It was intensely unsatisfactory to the settlers. Wool seems to have decided that the whites in southern Oregon were more to blame than the Indians, and he felt disposed in consequence to let them meet the results of their own acts.

Discovering from experience that there was little to be hoped for from the regulars, Governor Curry and the Oregon legislature speedily equipped a strong force under Colonel J. W. Nesmith. Colonel Nesmith having gone to the Yakima country with four companies under general charge of Major Raines, of the regulars, on what proved to be a fruitless expedition, Lieutenant-Colonel J. K. Kelly, in command of five hundred men, marched to Walla Walla.

There occurred the famous battle of the Walla Walla, on the 7th, 8th, 9th and 10th of December, 1855. The force of Oregon volunteers having reached Wallula on December 2d, found that the Indians whom they had hoped to meet there had eluded them, leaving the fort in ruins. Setting forth in two divisions on December 5th, the volunteers proceeded up the Walla Walla river to the Touchet. Turning up the latter stream, they had gone about ten miles when there suddenly appeared with a flag of truce no less a personage than Peopeomoxmox himself. Captain Cornoyer, who was in the vanguard, entered into a parley with the Walla Walla chieftain, in which the chief stated that he and his people were anxious to make peace. He told Nathan Olney, the Indian agent with whom he conversed, that he had at first intended to make war on the whites, but on reflection had decided that it would not be good policy.

While the conference was in progress the troops, as well as the Indians, had gradually gathered around in considerable numbers and finally passed on in the direction of an Indian village near at hand.

Seeing that they were approaching a dangerous canyon, Colonel Kelly became suspicious that the Indians were meditating treachery, and he determined to return a short distance back upon the trail and camp without supper for the night. It was a cold, wretched night. Snow began to fall. Colonel Kelly, in his anxiety to make a forced march, had given orders to travel light and they were so very light that they had no supplies.

Much difference of opinion developed as to the wisdom of pausing and camping on the trail. Captain Cornoyer held the opinion, which he afterwards stated to Colonel Gilbert, that Peopeomoxmox was acting in good faith and that if the army had gone on with him, he being entirely in their power, they would have reached the village in safety and would have found plenty of food, passed a comfortable night, and that the war would have ended then and there. Colonel Kelly believed otherwise and has left on record the following reasons for his opinion:

Colonel Kelly writes that Peopeomoxmox "stated that he did not wish to fight and that on the following day he would come and have a talk and make a treaty of peace. On consultation with Hon. Nathan Olney, Indian agent, we concluded that this was simply a ruse to gain time for removing his village and preparing for battle. I stated to him that we had come to chastise him for the wrongs he had done to our people, and that we would not defer making an attack on his people unless he and his five followers would consent to accompany and remain with us until all difficulties were settled. I told him that he might go away under his flag of truce if he chose, but that if he did so we would forthwith attack his village. The alternative was distinctly made known to him, and to save his people he chose to remain with us, a hostage for the fulfillment of his promises, as did also those who accompanied him. He at the same time said that on the following day he would accompany us to his village; that he would then assemble his people and make them deliver up their arms and ammunition, restore the property which had been taken from the white settlers, or pay the full value of that which could not be restored, and that he would furnish fresh horses to remount my command and cattle to supply them with provisions to enable us to wage war against other hostile tribes who were leagued with him. Having made these promises, we refrained from making the attack, thinking we had him in our power, that on the next day his promises would be fulfilled. I also permitted him to send one of the men who accompanied him to his village to apprise the tribes of the terms of the expected treaty, so that they might be prepared to fulfill it.

"I have since learned from a Nez Perce boy who was taken at the same time with Peopeomoxmox, that instead of sending word to his people to make a treaty of peace he sent an order for them to remove their women and children and prepare for battle. From all I have since learned, I am well persuaded that he was acting with duplicity and that he expected to entrap my command in the deep ravine in which his camp was situated, and make his escape from us."

We will not now undertake to say who was correct, but all seem to have agreed in one thing, and that is that the men had a most wretched night and became exceedingly impatient, and rather blindly feeling that Peopeomoxmox was to blame for all their discomfort, they were in the mood for the tragedy that followed.

This move of the "Yellow Serpent" was hard to explain in any way. It seemed very strange that he would have put himself right in the hands of his enemies unless he really meant to act in good faith. Moreover, it is not easy to see how he could have expected to gain anything by leading the whites to his village, so long as his own life was sure to be the instant forfeit of any treachery. But on the other hand, it is very strange that if he was perfectly honest the Indians should have made the attack on the next day. However it may have been, it was plain that things were not going just according to program, for during the night Indians had gathered in great numbers about on the hills, and were evidently watching in great anxiety to see what might be the fate of Peopeomoxmox.

The subsequent events made it seem likely that the Indians had made a change of policy during the night. They shouted words in the Cayuse language evidently intended for the captive chief alone.

When morning of that bleak December day dawned, Peopeomoxmox was very anxious to get some stay of proceedings: He said that his people needed time to prepare provisions, etc., in order to give the whites a fitting reception. It was nearly noon before the cold, hungry, disgusted command got started, and after passing through the canyon in safety they reached the Indian village, but alas, no warmth of food or welcome awaited them. The village was deserted. Scouts were seen on the surrounding hills, and finally, after much shouting and gesticulating, one Indian was induced to come to the camp. He proved to be the son of Peopeomoxmox. Having entered into conversation with his son, the old chief finally directed him to notify the people to come in and make peace. The son told him that they were only awaiting the arrival of Five Crows to do so. But they waited a long time and the famished and exhausted volunteers saw that they must return to the mouth of the Touchet to join those that were left with provisions and baggage. Doing so, night found them at the Touchet.

In the morning early the force was under way with baggage and all available resources, moving toward Whitman mission, where Colonel Kelly planned to make a winter camp. Peopeomoxmox, with several companions, was still with them. Soon after the volunteers had

crossed the Touchet the ball opened. Who fired first is still a matter of dispute. Gilbert quotes A. P. Woodward as asserting that the whites fired first, a member of Company B named Jont being the one that fired the first shot. A running fight up the Walla Walla valley ensued. At the mouth of Dry creek, near the present Loudon place, the Indians made a brief stand, but being forced from their position, they broke again and pressed on hastily toward Frenchtown. There, spreading across the valley, they made a determined stand. Here Lieutenant J. M. Burrows, of Company H, was killed and a number of men were wounded. Giving way again, the savages retreated to the location of the Tillier ranch, and there, near the present site of the Frenchtown church the fight was renewed. There Captain Bennett, of Company F, and Private Kelso, of Company A, were killed.

The soldiers had found an abandoned howitzer at Wallula, and this, under charge of Captain Wilson, was now brought to bear on the enemy. At the fourth discharge the piece burst, severely wounding Captain Wilson. But the Indians now broke again and fled. The fight was over for the time and the soldiers camped that night on the field of battle. The spot where the severest contest occurred was marked a few years ago by a gathering with appropriate exercises and the raising of a flag provided by Mrs. Levi Ankeny,—a deeply interesting occasion, in which veterans of that war took great joy. Prominent among those were General McAuliff, William Painter, Lewis McMorris and A. G. Lloyd.

During the first day's battle, at about the hottest part of the action, occurred a very unfortunate event, concerning which there has been much discussion. Peopeomoxmox and his companions in captivity were, with one exception, killed by the guards and volunteers surrounding them, and whether this action was justifiable from the fact that the prisoners

attempted to escape or was wholly unwar-
ranted, will never be ascertained with certainty. The eyewitnesses of the affair are not
in accord as to the facts; indeed it is quite
probable that no one of them is able to give
an absolutely correct and detailed statement
of all that transpired, such was the confusion
and excitement prevailing at the time. Of this
affair Gilbert says: "The following is an account of it as given to the writer by Lewis Mc-
Morris, who was present at the time and saw
what he narrated. The hospital supplies were
packed on mules in charge of McMorris, and
had just reached the LaRocque cabin, where
the first engagement had taken place. The
surgeon in charge had decided to use it as a
hospital in which to place those wounded in
the battle and McMorris was unpacking the
mules. Near it the unfortunate J. M. Burrows lay dead, and several wounded were being attended to. The combatants had passed
on up the valley, and the distant detonations
of their guns could be heard. The flag of
truce prisoners were there under guard, and
everyone seemed electrified with suppressed
excitement. A wounded man came in with
his shattered arm dangling at his side and
reported Captain Bennett killed at the front.
This added to the excitement, and the attention of all was more or less attracted to the
wounded man, when some one said: 'Look
out, or the Indians will get away!' At this
seemingly every one yelled, 'Shoot 'em! Shoot
'em!' and on the instant there was a rattle of
musketry on all sides.

"What followed was so quick, and there
were so many acting, that McMorris could
not see it in detail, though all was transpiring
within a few yards of and around him. It
was over in a minute, and three of the five
prisoners were dead another was wounded,
knocked senseless and supposed to be dead,
who afterwards recovered consciousness, and
was shot to put him out of his misery, while
the fifth was spared because he was a Nez

Perce. McMorris remembers some of the
events that marked the tragedy, however, such
as an impression on his mind of an attempt
by the prisoners to escape, that started the
shooting; that everybody was firing because
they were excited and the target was an Indian; that he saw no evidence of an attempt
to escape, except from being murdered; that
they were killed while surrounded by and
mingled among the whites; and that but one
Indian offered to defend his life. The prisoner offering resistence was a powerful Willamette Indian called 'Jim' or 'Wolfskin,' who,
having a knife secreted upon his person, drew
it and fought desperately. 'I could hear that
knife whistle in the air,' said McMorris, 'as
he brandished it, or struck at the soldier with
whom he was struggling.' It lasted but a
moment, when another soldier, approaching
from behind, dealt him a blow on the head
with a gun that broke his skull and stretched
him apparently lifeless upon the ground. All
were scalped in a few minutes, and later the
body of Yellow Bird, the great Walla Walla
chief, was mutilated in a way that should entitle those who did it to a prominent niche in
the ghoulish temple erected to commemorate
the infamous acts of soulless men."

Gilbert also states that McMorris' account
was confirmed by G. W. Miller and William
Nixon, both of whom were present.

A. P. Woodward, now living at Athena,
and who was nearby when the chief was
killed, tells us that the facts were briefly these:
When asked what should be done with the
prisoners, Colonel Kelly had told the guard
he "didn't care a damn." The prisoners were
neither tied nor in any way confined, but
were mingled with the volunteers. When the
firing became warm, and several wounded had
been brought back to where the guard and
prisoners were, some of the troops became
badly excited and called out, "Shoot the
damned Indians and kill them!" Several
shots were fired, and two or three of the In-

dians fell, though they were not attempting to escape. Then Peopeomoxmox sprang off his horse, and walking toward those who were firing, said: "You don't need to kill me,—I am not Jesus Christ," and with these words he fell. The biting sarcasm of the dying words of Peopeomoxmox, if these were his words, can only be appreciated when we remember that they were uttered by a savage who could not be made to understand why the white men had, according to their own account, killed their own God. It should be stated, however, that in answer to a direct question as to whether any such language was used, Samuel Warfield, the slayer of Peopeomoxmox, stated that the only foundation for the story was something that occurred on the evening previous. Wolfskin, he says, attempted to escape. He was immediately recaptured and while being tied to prevent a repetition of this attempt, he said: "That's as much as could be expected of you. Christ died for his people and I can die for mine," whereupon one of the volunteers rejoined, "Christ did not run," raising a general 'laugh.

It is but fair to add the account of the killing given by Mr. Warfield, the man who actually took the life of the Walla Walla chieftain. At the request of the writer he furnished the following statement: "Amos Underwood and I were guards over the six Indian prisoners, Peopeomoxmox, Klickitat Jimmy, or Wolfskin, Nez Perce Billy and three others. About 4 o'clock in the evening there were a number of soldiers around the guard and prisoners. Word was sent two or three times for those soldiers to come to the front; but they did not go. Finally Colonel Kelly came and ordered them to the front. I said to the colonel, 'I want to go to the front. What will we do with these prisoners?' He replied, 'Tie them and put them in the house, if they will submit to you, if not, put them in anyhow. Major Miller was there present among the wounded, having

been shot in the arm. Just at that time Wolfskin pulled his knife from his legging and struck at Major Miller, cutting his arm as it was thrown up to ward off the blow. In an instant some one broke a musket over the Indian's head, killing him. Then the fight began. Five of the Indian prisoners were killed, being either shot or struck over the head with the guns, Peopeomoxmox being the last one. I showed him to cross his hands so that I could tie him and put him in the house as the colonel had told us, when he grabbed my gun and tried to wrench it around so as to shoot me. I jumped back and grabbed him by the collar and threw him down, still keeping hold of my gun. I also shot at him but missed, he being too close. He caught me by the breeches leg and tried to regain his feet. I again jumped back from him as he tried to get up, struck him over the head with my gun, settling him for all time."

This account of Mr. Warfield's is probably substantially correct as far as it goes, but it leaves open the question as to what incited Wolfskin to draw his knife. One of the volunteers confessed to the writer that he became so excited by the fact that the whites at the front were being hard pressed and that some of them were killed and wounded that he completely lost his head and rushed back, shouting, "Shoot the Indians and kill them!" This and the attempted tying of their hands inspired the Indians with a belief that they would certainly be murdered, causing them to offer resistance, with the melancholy results above given. If this surmise is correct neither the Indians nor their guards could be very much blamed, the real cause of the tragedy being the hare-brained man, whose wild shoutings alarmed the Indian prisoners. It is hard to understand how the officers could justify their conduct in retaining the Indians at all any longer than they wished to stay. They came under flag of truce, and if Colonel Kelly's report is true, remained voluntarily as hostages, and when they were no longer willing to stay they should have been set at liberty. Nathan Olney, the Indian agent, is quoted as having said: "If you let Peopeomoxmox escape our hides will not hold shucks." Whether this was true or not, the whites were not justified in retaining any advantage gained by disrespect of a flag of truce and the honors of war, and the officers cannot therefore escape censure as being ultimately responsible for the massacre of the Indians.

While speaking of Peopeomoxmox it is but fair to that heroic character to give him the benefit of a correct translation of his Indian name. Major Lee Moorhouse, of Pendleton, who has given much attention to the history of the aborigines of this region, informs the writer that the name Peopeomoxmox (as it should be spelled in English) means Yellow Bird and not Yellow Serpent, as a malicious French half-breed interpreter, who had a grudge against the chief, translated it to the whites.

A. P. Woodward describes the chief as a man of middle age, six feet two inches tall, straight as an arrow, with piercing eyes and a nose like a hawk—hence his name of Yellow Bird, or Hawk.

On the next day the battle was renewed. Colonel Kelly thus describes the events of the next two days, and inasmuch as his official report thus embraces the essential features of the case, we quote it at length.

Early on the morning of the 8th, the Indians appeared with increased forces, amounting to fully six hundred warriors. They were posted as usual in the thick brush by the river—among the sage bushes and sand knolls, and on the surrounding hills. This day Lieutenant Pillow, with Company A, and Lieutenant Hannon with Company H, were ordered to take and hold the brush skirting the river and the sage bushes on the plain. Lieutenant Fellows with Company F, was directed to take and keep possession of the point at the foot of the hill. Lieutenant Jeffries with Company B, Lieutenant Hand with Company I, and Captain Cornoyer with Company K, were posted on three several points on the hills, with orders to maintain them and to assail the enemy on other points of the same hills. As usual the Indians

7

were driven from their position, although they fought with skill and bravery.

On the ninth they did not make their appearance until about ten o'clock in the morning and then in somewhat diminished numbers. As I had sent to Fort Henrietta for Companies D and E, and expected them on on the tenth, I thought it best to act on the defensive and hold our positions which were the same as on the eighth, until we could get an accession to our forces sufficient to enable us to assail their rear and cut off their retreat. An attack was made during the day on Companies A and H, in the brushwood, and upon B on the hill, both of which were repulsed with great gallantry by those companies with considerable loss to the enemy. Companies F, I and K also did great honor to themselves in repelling all approaches to their positions, although in doing so one man in Company F and one in Company I were severely wounded. Darkness as usual closed the combat, by the enemy withdrawing from the field. Owing to the inclemency of the night, the companies on the hill were withdrawn from their several positions Company B abandoning its rifle pits which were made by the men of that company for its protection. At early dawn of the next day the Indians were observed from our camp to be in possession of all points held by us on the preceding day. Upon seeing them, Lieutenant McAuliff of Company B, gallantly observed that his company had dug those holes, and after breakfast they would have them again; and well was his declaration fulfilled, for in less than an hour the enemy was driven from the pits and fled to an adjoining hill which they had occupied the day before. This position was at once assailed, Captain Cornoyer with Company K and a portion of Company I, being mounted, gallantly charged the enemy on his right flank, while Lieutenant McAuliff with Company B dismounted, rushed up the hill in face of a heavy fire and scattered them in all directions. They at once fled to return to this battle field no more, and thus ended our long contested fight.

In making my report I cannot say too much in praise of the conduct of the officers of the several companies and most of the soldiers under their command. They did their duty bravely and well during those four trying days of battle. To Second Major Chinn, who took charge of the companies in the bush by the river, credit is due for bravery and skill; also to Assistant Adjutant Monroe Atkinson, for his efficiency and zeal as well in the field as in the camp. And here while giving to the officers and men of the regiment the praise that is justly due, I cannot omit the name of Hon. Nathan Olney, although he is not one of the Volunteers. Having accompanied me in the capacity of Indian agent, I requested him to act as my aid on account of his admitted skill in Indian warfare; and to his wisdom in council and daring courage on the battle field, I am much indebted and I shall ever appreciate his worth.

Companies D and E having arrived from Fort Henrietta on the evening of the tenth, the next morning I followed with all the available troops along the Nez

Perce's trail in pursuit of the Indians. On Mill creek, about twelve miles from here, we passed through their village, numbering one hundred and nintey-six fires, which had been deserted the night before. Much of their provisions were scattered by the wayside, indicating that they had fled in great haste to the north. We pursued them until it was too dark to follow the track of their horses, when we camped on Coppei creek. On the twelfth we continued the pursuit until we passed some distance beyond the stations of Brooke, Noble and Bumford on the Touchet, when we found the chase in vain as many of our horses were completely broken down and the men on foot. We therefore returned and arrived in camp on yesterday evening with about one hundred head of cattle which the Indians left scattered along the trail in their flight.

On the eleventh, while in pursuit of the enemy, I received a letter from Narcisse Raymond by the hand of Tintinmetzy, a friendly chief (which I enclose), asking our protection of the French and friendly Indians under his charge.

On the morning of the twelfth I dispatched Captain Cornoyer with his command to their relief. Mr. Olney, who accompanied them, returned to camp this evening, and reports that Captain Cornoyer will return to-morrow with Mr. Raymond and his people, who now feel greatly relieved from their critical situation. Mr. Olney learned from these friendly Indians what before we strongly believed, the Palouses, Walla Wallas, Umatillas, Cayuses, and Stock Whitley's band of Des Chutes Indians were all engaged in the battle on the Walla Walla. These Indians also informed Mr. Olney that after the battles the Palouses, Walla Wallas and Umatillas have gone partly to the Grande Ronde and partly to the country of the Nez Perces; and Stock Whitley, disgusted with the manner in which the Cayuses fought in the battle, has abandoned them and gone to the Yakima country to join his forces with those of Kamiakin. We have now the undisputed possession of the country south of Snake river, and I would suggest the propriety of retaining this possession until such time as it can be occupied by the regular troops. The Indians have left much of their stock behind, which will doubtless be lost to us if we go away. The troops here will not be in a situation for some time to go to the Palouse country, as our horses at present are too much jaded to endure the journey, and we have no boats to cross Snake river, no timber to make them nearer than this place; but I would suggest the propriety of following up the Indians with all possible speed, now that their hopes are blighted and their spirits broken. Unless this is done they will perhaps rally again.

Today (December 14, 1855) I received a letter from Governor Stevens, dated yesterday, which I enclose. You will perceive that he is in favor of a vigorous prosecution of the war. With his views I fully concur.

I must earnestly ask that supplies be sent forward to us without delay. For the last three days none of the volunteers, except the two companies from Fort Henrietta, have had any flour. None is here and but little at that post. We are now living on beef and potatoes, which are found *en cache*, and the men are becoming much discontented with this mode of living. Clothing for the men s much needed as the winter approaches. To-morrow we will remove to a more suitable point, where grass can be obtained in greater abundance for our worn-out horses. A place has been selected about two miles above Whitman station, on the same (north) side of the Walla Walla, consequently I will abandon this fort, named in honor of Captain Bennett of Company F, who now sleeps beneath its stockade, and whose career of usefulness and bravery was here so sadly but nobly closed.

Very respectfully your obedient servant,

JAMES K. KELLY,
Lieutenant Colonel Commanding Left Column
W. H. FARRAR,
Adjutant of Regiment, O. M. V.

The winter following the battle of the Walla Walla was one of the coldest and most trying ever known in this country. The veterans among the volunteers have left on record accounts of the sufferings, which show that war in an Indian country was not a picnic in those times. The writer has heard the late W. C. Painter describe vividly the experience of sleeping, or trying to, with scarcely any covering and the mercury at twenty below zero.

Meantime, while these events were occurring in the Walla Walla and Yakima countries, what was Governor Stevens doing? As already noted, after having negotiated the treaty at Walla Walla in June, 1855, he passed on to the Blackfoot country, where he also negotiated a successful treaty. Having reached Hellgate, in the present Montana, on his return, he was met by a detachment of Nez Perce Indians, who informed him of the war and of the fact that he was thus cut off from any direct communication with his government. His own official report to the secretary of war gives so clear and vivid an account of what followed that we reproduce it here:

"The result of our conference was most satisfactory. The whole party, numbering fourteen men, among whom were Spotted

Eagle, Looking Glass and Three Feathers, principal chiefs among the Nez Perces, expressed their determination to accompany me and share any danger to be encountered. They expressed a desire that after crossing the mountains I should go to their country, where a large force of their young men would accompany me to The Dalles and protect us with their lives against any enemy.

"Having replenished my train with all the animals to be had, on November 14th we pushed forward, crossed the Bitter Root mountains the 20th, in snow two and a half to three feet deep, and reached the Coeur d'Alene mission the 25th, taking the Coeur d'Alenes entirely by surprise. They had not thought it possible that we could cross the mountains so late in the season. ·

"With the Coeur d'Alenes I held a council, and found them much excited, on a balance for peace or war, and a chance word might turn them either way. Rumors of all kinds met us here: that the troops had fought a battle with the Yakimas and drove them across the Columbia towards the Spokane, and that the Walla Wallas, Cayuses and Umatillas were in arms, and that they had been joined by a party of Nez Perces. The accounts were of so contradictory a nature that nothing certain could be ascertained from them, excepting that the several tribes below were in arms, blocking up our road, and had threatened to cut off my party in any event. However, I determined to push to the Spokane.

"The Spokanes were even more surprised than the Coeur d'Alenes on seeing us. Three hours before my arrival they had heard that I was going to the settlements by way of New York. I immediately called a council; sent to Fort Colville for Mr. McDonald, in charge of that post of the Hudson's Bay Company; sent also for the Jesuit fathers at that point. They arrived. A council was held, at which the whole Spokane nation was represented.

The Coeur d'Alenes and Colville Indians also were present. .

"The Spokanes and Colville Indians evinced extreme hospitality of feeling; spoke of the war below; wanted it stopped; said the whites were wrong. The belief was current that Peupeumoxmox would cut off my party, as he had repeatedly threatened. They had not joined in the war, but yet would make no promise to remain neutral. If the Indians now at war were driven into their country they would not answer for the consequences; probably many of the Spokanes would join them. After a stormy council of several days, the Spokanes, Coeur d'Alenes and Colvilles were entirely conciliated, and promised they would reject all overtures of the hostile Indians and continue the firm friends of the whites. .

"Having added to my party and organized, etc., we thence made a forced march to the Nez Perce country. Mr. Craig had received letters which informed me that the whole Walla Walla valley was blocked up with hostile Indians, and the Nez Perces said it would be impossible to go through.

"I called a council and proposed to them that one hundred and fifty of their young men should accompany me to The Dalles. Without hesitation they agreed to go. Whilst in the council making arrangements for our movements, news came that a force of gallant Oregon volunteers, four hundred strong, had met the Indians in the Walla Walla valley and after four days' hard fighting, having a number of officers and men killed and wounded, had completely routed the enemy, driving them across Snake river and toward the Nez Perce country. The next day I pushed forward, accompanied by sixty-nine Nez Perces, well armed, and reached Walla Walla without encountering any hostile Indians. They had all been driven across Snake river below us by the Oregon troops.

"It is now proper to inquire what would have been the condition of my party had not the Oregon troops vigorously pushed into the field and gallantly defeated the enemy.

"The country between the Blue mountains and the Columbia was overrun with Indians, numbering one thousand to twelve hundred warriors, including the force at Priest Rapids under Kamaiakun, who 'had sworn to cut me off; it was completely blocked up. One effect of the campaign of the regulars and volunteers in the Yakima country under Brigadier General Raines was to drive Kamaiakun and his people on our side of the Columbia river, and thus endanger our movement from the Spokane to the Nez Perce country. Thus we had been 'hemmed in by a body of hostile Indians through whom we could have only forced our way with extreme difficulty and at great loss of life. We might all have been sacrificed in the attempt. For the opening of the way to my party I am solely indebted to the Oregon volunteers. Peupeumoxmox, the celebrated chief of the Walla Wallas, entertained an extreme hostility toward myself and party, owing to imaginary wrongs he supposed to have been inflicted upon him in the treaty concluded with the Cayuses and Walla Wallas last June, and had been known repeatedly to threaten that I never should reach The Dalles. He was the first to commence hostilities by plundering Fort Walla Walla and destroying a large amount of property belonging to the United States Indian Department.

    *   *   *   *   *   *   *

"At Walla Walla I found some twenty-five settlers—the remainder having fled to The Dalles for protection. With these were one hundred friendly Indians. Special Indian Agent B. F. Shaw, colonel in the Washington Territory militia, was on the ground, and I at once organized the district, placed him in command and directed him, if necessary, to fortify, at all events, to maintain his ground should the Oregon troops be disbanded before

another force could take the field. The Nez Perce auxiliaries were disbanded and returned home.

"Thus we had reached a place of safety unaided, excepting by the fortunate movements of the Oregon troops. Not a single man had been pushed forward to meet us, although it was well known we should cross the mountains about a certain time, and arrive at Walla Walla about the time we did. Why was this? Arrangements had been made with Major Raines by Acting Governor Mason to push forward a force under Colonel Shaw to meet me at Spokane about the time of my arrival there. A company had been enlisted, organized and marched to Fort Vancouver to obtain equipments, rations and transportation, which Major Raines had promised both Governor Mason and Colonel Shaw should be promptly furnished them. Some little delay ensued, and in the meantime Major General Wool arrived, who immediately declined equipping the company, as promised by Major Raines, and stated that he could not in any manner recognize volunteers or furnish them equipments or transportation, and declined to supply their places with regular troops, of whom, at Vancouver alone, were some three hundred and fifty men."

Following this description of his journey, Governor Stevens went on to prefer charges of gross negligence on the part of General Wool. All history abounds in instances of intense personal feuds and disagreements, but our Pacific coast history seems to have been especially fruitful in them. That between General Wool with some of the officers who echoed his opinions, the regulars, in short, on one side, and Governor Stevens, supported by the volunteers and the nearly united people of the territory on the other, was peculiarly acrimonious. We insert the following extract from the report by Governor Stevens to the secretary of war:

"When remonstrated with by Captain

William McKay, in command of the company, to push forward to my assistance, when informed of the object for which the company was enlisted, and that if it was not pushed forward at once, or if some other force was not sent, Governor Stevens and his party would be in the most imminent danger, the general replied that in his opinion the danger was greatly exaggerated; that probably Governor Stevens would be able to protect himself, but if he could not, then Governor Stevens could obtain an escort from General Harney.

"What a reply was that! A moiety of the Indians now in arms had defeated a detachment of one hundred United States regulars, Major Raines had placed on record his opinion that an insufficient force would be defeated by these Indians, and my party was supposed to number no more than twenty-five men. Yet Major General Wool very coolly says, 'Governor Stevens can take care of himself.' So, too, in the remark that I could obtain aid from General Harney. Did General Wool know that the distance from Fort Benton to the supposed position of General Harney was greater than the distance from Fort Benton to The Dalles and that to obtain aid from him would require not less than six months, and that an express to reach him must pass through the entire breadth of the Sioux? Such ignorance shows great incapacity and is inexcusable.

"Mr. Secretary, Major General Wool, commanding the Pacific Division, neglected and refused to send a force to the relief of myself and party when known to be in imminent danger, and believed by those who were less capable of judging, to be coming on to certain death, and this, when he had at his command an efficient force of regular troops. He refused to sanction the agreement made between Governor Mason and Major Raines for troops to be sent to my assistance, and ordered them to disband. It was reserved for the Oregon troops to rescue us.

"The only demonstration made by Major Raines resulted in showing his utter incapacity to command in the field. As has heretofore been said, his expedition against the Yakimas effected nothing but driving the Indians into the very country through which I must pass to reach the settlements.

"I therefore prefer charges against General Wool. I accuse him of utter and signal incapacity, of criminal neglect of my safety. I ask for an investigation into the matter and for his removal from command."

CHAPTER VIII.

INDIAN WARS OF THE '50s—Continued.

Governor Stevens reached Olympia early in January, 1856, and found that the storm of war was in full blast from east to west. The Sound Indians, aided by Yakimas, had ranged over the greater part of the region adjacent to the sound and had killed many settlers. Governor Stevens, full of courage and resources, roused the disheartened settlers and set on foot measures for saving the territory by the equipment of an army of one thousand volunteers, organizing forces of friendly Indians, issuing scrip for meeting expenses, seizing necessary stores and implements, inducing the settlers to get back again upon their farms and plant their crops, and sending Secretary Mason to Washington to acquaint the government with their plight and needs. In the very midst of his appeal, the Indians, by a sudden attack, seized Seattle and destroyed the most of it. Nevertheless the brave words and acts of the governor roused the faint-hearted and the territory speedily got itself into a better posture of defense and finally of attack. The Washington volunteers were equipped and the second regiment under command of Colonel B. F. Shaw, started in the summer of 1856 for Walla Walla.

Meanwhile the Oregon volunteers had been spending that dismal winter and spring at Walla Walla and vicinity. The first American fort of the regular army at Walla Walla was laid out on the location of McBride's stable, one of the old buildings, remaining there until a few years ago. The volunteers camped at a later time higher up the creek near the present location of the ranch of Patrick Lyons.

During the spring Colonel Kelly returned to Portland, leaving Colonel T. R. Cornelius in command. The detachment set forth from their camp on Mill creek on March 10th and proceeded to the Yakima country, meeting and dispersing the Indians whom they met there and then, passing on to the Columbia, they returned to Oregon and disbanded. They had rendered signal service, having broken up the Indian forces of both the Walla Walla and Yakima countries.

While they were doing this one of the most daring blows struck by any of the Indians fell upon the settlers up and down the Columbia near the Cascades. The famous old block house there is a souvenir of that epoch. Associated with it also is the memory of the fact that Phil Sheridan fought there one of his first battles, distinguished, as he later was, for dare-devil courage and impetuosity. That Cascades disaster was one of the most cruel and severe that the settlements had suffered.

The United States troops at that time made The Dalles their chief headquarters, and the force there had their hands full with wars and rumors of wars from Walla Walla, Yakima and the Cascades. The officers more especially concerned with the campaign on the east side of the mountains were Colonel Wright, Colonel Steptoe and Major Raines. It is to be remembered that there were three distinct forces operating in the country, viz.: United States regulars, Oregon volunteers and

Washington volunteers. Governor Curry, of Oregon, and Governor Stevens, of Washington, were in entire harmony, believing alike in a vigorous prosecution of the war, but the United States forces were entirely aloof from them in sympathy of aim and action.

We have already outlined the achievements of the Oregon volunteers. In May, Colonel Wright moved from The Dalles to Yakima. There he found a force of twelve hundred or more defiant Indians, whose evident strength seems to have led Colonel Wright to crave peace without a battle. He shaped his policies in the direction of acceding to the demand of the Indians that he withdraw from the country and exclude settlers therefrom.

In July the second regiment of Washington volunteers, under Colonel B. F. Shaw, moved up the river and on July 8th camped on the place now owned by the heirs of Alfred Thomas, about two miles above Walla Walla. Learning that the hostiles were in force in the Grande Ronde valley, Colonel Shaw determined to move thither and strike. Pushing rapidly over the mountains, he encountered the savages on July 17th, and in the most decisive battle thus far fought he scattered them in all directions. The excellent Life of Governor Stevens, by his son, Hazard Stevens, contains a picturesque account of how Colonel Shaw, with his long, red beard and hair streaming in the wind, swept down like a hurricane upon the foe and drove them fifteen miles clear across the valley. Colonel Shaw's own version is so clear and vivid that we believe our readers will enjoy its perusal. More clearly than any present description could, this account preserves the flavor of the time in which it happened; that time which, though only forty-five years ago, seems so remote from our own.

BATTTLE OF GRANDE RONDE, JULY 17, 1856.

"We arrived in the Grande Ronde valley on the evening of the 16th, and camped on a branch of the Grande Ronde river in the timber, sending spies in advance, who returned and reported no fresh sign. On the morning of the 17th, leaving Major Blankenship, of the Central, and Captain Miller, of the Southern battalions, assisted by Captain De-Lacy, to take up the line of march for the main valley, I proceeded ahead to reconnoitre, accompanied by Major Maxon, Michael Marchmean, Captain John and Dr. Burns. After proceeding about five miles we ascended a knoll in the valley, from which we discovered dust rising along the timber of the river. I immediately sent Major Maxon and Captain John forward to reconnoitre and returned to hurry up the command, which was not far distant. The command was instantly formed in order; Captain Miller's company in advance, supported by Maxon, Henness and Powell's companies, leaving the pack train in charge of the guard under Lieutenant Goodwin, with a detachment of Goff's company, under Lieutenant Wait, and Lieutenant Williams' company in reserve with orders to follow on after the command.

"The whole command moved on quietly to this order until within half a mile of the Indian village, when we discovered that the pack train had moved to the left, down the Grande Ronde river. At this moment a large body of warriors came forward singing and whooping, and one of them waving a white man's scalp on a pole. One of them signified a desire to speak, whereupon I sent Captain John to meet him and formed the command in line of battle. When Captain John came up to the Indians they cried out to one another to shoot him, when he retreated to the command and I ordered the four companies to charge.

"The design of the enemy evidently was to draw us into the brush along the river, where from our exposed position they would have the advantage, they no doubt having placed an ambush there. To avoid this I charged down the river toward the pack train. The warriors then split, part going across the river and part down toward the pack train. These were soon overtaken and engaged. The charge was vigorous and so well sustained that they were broken, dispersed and slain before us. After a short time I sent Captain Miller to the left and Major Maxon to the right; the latter to cross the stream and cut them off from a point near which a large body of warriors had collected, apparently to fight, while I moved forward with the commands of Captain Henness and Lieutenant Powell to attack them in front. The Major could not cross the river, and on our moving forward the enemy fled after firing a few guns, part taking to the left and part continuing forward.

"Those who took to the left fell in with Captain Miller's company, who killed five on the spot, and the rest were not less successful in the pursuit, which was continued to the crossing of the river, where the enemy had taken a stand to defend the ford. Being here rejoined by Captain Miller and by Lieutenant Curtis with part of Maxon's company, we fired a volley and I ordered a charge across the river, which was gallantly executed. In doing this Private Shirley, ensign of Henness company, who was in front, was wounded in the face. Several of the enemy were killed at this point. We continued the pursuit until the enemy had reached the rocky canyons leading toward Powder river, and commenced scattering in every direction, when, finding that I had but five men with me, and the rest of the command scattered in the rear, most of the horses being completely exhausted, I called a halt and fell back, calculating to remount the men on the captured horses and continue the pursuit after night.

"I found the pack train, guard and reserve encamped on a small creek not far from the crossing, as I had previously ordered them to do, and learned that a body of the enemy had followed them up all day and annoyed them but had inflicted no damage beyond capturing many of the animals which we had taken in charge and left behind.

"I learned also that Major Maxon had crossed the river with a small party and was engaged with the enemy and wanted assistance. I immediately dispatched a detachment under Lieutenants Williams and Wait, sending the man who brought the information back with them as a guide. They returned after dark without finding the Major, but brought in one of his men whom they found in the brush, and who stated that one of the Major's men was killed and that the last he saw of them they were fighting with the Indians. At daylight I sent out Captain Miller with seventy men, who scouted around the whole valley without finding him, but who unfortunately had one man killed and another wounded whilst pursuing some Indians. I resolved to remove camp the next day to the head of the valley, where the emigrant trail crosses it, and continue the search until we became certain of their fate. The same evening I took sixty men, under Captain Henness, and struck upon the mountains and crossed the heads of the canyons to see if I could not strike his trail. Finding no sign, I returned to the place where the Major had last been seen, and there made search in different directions and finally found the body of one of his men (Tooley) and where the major had encamped in the brush. From other signs it became evident to me that the Major had returned to this post by the same trail by which we first entered the valley.

"Being nearly out of provisions, and unable to follow the Indians from this delay, I concluded to return to camp, recruit for another expedition in conjunction with Captain Goff, who had, I presumed, returned from his expedition to the John Day's river.

"I should have mentioned previously that in the charge the command captured and afterward destroyed about one hundred and fifty horse loads of lacamas, dried beef, tents, some flour, coffee, sugar and about one hundred pounds of ammunition and a great quantity of tools and kitchen furniture. We took also about two hundred horses, most of which were shot, there being about one hundred serviceable animals.

"There were present on the ground from what I saw, and from information received from two squaws taken prisoners, about three hundred warriors of the Cayuse, Walla Walla, Umatilla, Tyh, John Day and Des Chutes tribes, commanded by the following chiefs: Stock Whitley and Simmistastas, Des Chutes and Tyh; Chickiah, Plyon, Wicecai, Watahstuartih, Winimiswoot, Cayuses; Tahkin, Cayuse, the son of Peupeumoxmox; Walla Walla and other chiefs of less note.

"The whole command, officers and men, behaved well. The enemy was run on the gallop fifteen miles, and most of those who fell were shot with the revolver. It is impossible to state how many of the enemy were killed. Twenty-seven bodies were counted by one individual, and many others were known to have fallen and been left, but were so scattered about that it was impossible to get count of them. When to these we add those killed by Major Maxon's command on the other side of the river, we may safely conclude that at least forty of the enemy were slain and many went off wounded. When we left the valley there was not an Indian in it, and all the signs went to show that they had gone a great distance from it.

"On the 21st instant we left the valley by the emigrant road and commenced our return to camp. During the night Lieutenant Hunter, of the Washington Territory volunteers, came into camp with an express from Captain Goff. I learned to my surprise that the captain and Major Layton had seen Indians on John Day's river, had followed them over to Burnt river and had a fight with them, in which Lieutenant Eustus and one private were killed, and some seven Indians. They were

shaping their course for the Grande Ronde valley and had sent for provisions and fresh horses. I immediately sent Lieutenant Williams back with all my spare provisions and horses and continued my march. On Wild Horse creek I came across Mr. Fites, a pack master who had been left in camp, who informed me, to my extreme satisfaction, that Major Maxon and his command had arrived safe in camp and were then near us with provisions and ammunition. These I sent on immeditely to Captain Goff.

"I learned that Major Maxon had been attacked in the valley by a large force of Indians on the day of the fight; had gained the brush and killed many of them; that at night he tried to find our camp, and hearing a noise like a child crying, probably one of the captured squaws, had concluded that my command had gone on to Powder river and that the Indians had returned to the valley by another canyon. He moved his position that night and the next day saw the scout looking for him, but in the distance thought that it was a band of Indians hunting his trail. Conceiving himself cut off from the command, he thought it best to return to this camp, thinking that we would be on our way back to Grande Ronde with provisions and ammunition."

While Shaw was winning this very important victory, Governor Stevens was making every effort to sustain the friendly faction of the Nez Perces under Lawyer, aided by William Craig, a white man who had been adopted by the Nez Perce tribe and who had been one of the greatest factors in sustaining Governor Stevens. To hold the Walla Walla country seemed to the governor the key of the situation, because thus only could he come in touch with these faithful Nez Perces. The moral effect of Shaw's victory proved so great that the governor decided to go in person to Walla Walla to hold another great council of the friendly and neutral tribes and to get as many as possible of the hostiles to attend the same.

He seems to have had the double aim of giving the hostiles every reasonable chance to
make peace and also of refuting the slanderous
charges of Wool to the effect that he was treating the hostiles cruelly and dishonestly. On
August 3d he urgently advised Colonel Wright
to establish a permanent garrison in the Walla
Walla valley and requested also that he meet
him in conference at The Dalles on September
14th. He also called out two hundred more
volunteers to take the place of Shaw's force,
whose term had expired.

And so Governor Stevens set forth again
on another of those harrassing, exhaustive and
dangerous expeditions to which fate seemed to
have appointed him. Reaching Vancouver on
August 13th, he met Colonel Wright, who informed him that he could not attend the proposed council, but would dispatch Lieutenant
Colonel Steptoe with four companies of regulars to reach Walla Walla in season for the
meeting.

Ascending the river to The Dalles in company with Colonel Wright, and while there
meeting the chief officers of the command, Governor Stevens, with the ardor and enthusiasm
of his nature, and with his personal ascendency
over men, so influenced them that for the time
being he seemed to have won them over entirely to hearty co-operation with him in his
plans. In reality, however, they were at that
very time under orders from General Wool to
disband the volunteers and expel them from
the country and to forbid white settlers to remain anywhere in the upper country, and to
allow the Hudson's Bay people only to occupy
it. Wool's idea was to make the Cascade
mountains the eastern frontier of American
settlement. Wright and Steptoe were almost
guilty of dishonesty in allowing the gallant
governor to proceed into the heart of the Indian
country with such an erroneous impression of
their real orders. Leaving The Dalles on August 19th, the indefatigable little governor
pushed on ahead of Steptoe, attended only by

Pearson, a trusty scout, and with no escort except the "bull-punchers" of his ox train, he
reached Shaw's camp, two miles above Walla
Walla, on the 23d. On September 5th, Steptoe
reached Walla Walla and established himself
at a point four miles below Shaw's camp, said
by Lewis McMorris to have been at the present
garrison. The next day came Lawyer with a
large force of Nez Perces, faithful still.

Governor Stevens was exceedingly anxious
to have perfect harmony of action with the
regulars and thereby present a united front to
the enemy, many of whom had drawn the conclusion that the regulars and volunteers were
entirely different sets of people. He therefore
requested Steptoe to move camp to a point near
his own. On the next morning Steptoe got
under way and paused at the governor's tent,
who supposed, of course, that he was going to
make camp there. He was dumfounded, as
he well may have been, to discover that Steptoe
was passing on from sight up the valley. This
was the more startling, for on account of a report that volunteers below were being attacked, Shaw had gone down, leaving Stevens
with but ten men. However, it had now become necessary for Shaw and his force to leave
permanently, and with this in view, the governor requested Steptoe to return to his near
vicinity. Incredible as it may seem, Steptoe
declined to do so, alleging that General Wool's
orders did not authorize him to make any such
arrangements. The governor, though it must
have made his hot blood boil, had to retain a
detachment of sixty-nine men and left Steptoe
to his own devices, at a camp which was on
the island on the present Gilkerson place.

And now opens

THE SECOND GREAT WALLA WALLA COUNCIL.

Space does not permit us to give the details
of this remarkable meeting, fully as remarkable as the one of the year before. The Nez
Perces were in large force at first, and the fac-

tion under Lawyer was fully committed to the support of the whites. But a large number, even of the Nez Perces, led by Looking Glass, Speaking Owl, Joseph, Red Wolf, and Eagle-from-the-Light, were plainly on the verge of outbreak. Kamiakin, the redoubtable chief of the Yakimas, was coming out with a strong force. The scowling Cayuses and the brawny Umatillas came whooping, yelling and firing the prairie grass. Murder was in the air. Governor Stevens sent an urgent request to Steptoe to come to the council with at least one company. Steptoe returned in answer to the effect that if the Indians were really meditating an outbreak, he had not enough force to defend both camps, and therefore he deemed it necessary for Stevens to move to him, instead of he to Stevens. The heart of the fiery governor was almost broken at this humiliation, but he had to yield to necessity, and he adjourned the council to Steptoe's camp. On the march Kamiakin and Owhi, with one hundred and five warriors under the immediate command of Qualchen, the murderer of Bolon, met them. The fierce and threatening looks of these Yakima braves did not reassure the little force, and things looked exceedingly squally. On every day of the council but the first, Indians, armed to the teeth, took places near the governor, with the evident design of murdering him and then attacking the force, but the nerve and vigilance of the governor and those around him prevented. The faithful Nez Perces kept their drums beating all night and maintained a guard around Stevens' camp. As remarked before, the debt of gratitude to these Nez Perces is beyond computation. One of the remarkable features of the last days of the council was the speech of Spotted Eagle, a Nez Perce, and one of the warm adherents of the whites. Governor Stevens mentioned this speech as one which, for feeling, courage and truth, he had never seen surpassed.

And now the council was ended, and what had been accomplished? Nothing. They stood just where they were at first. Half the Nez Perces were determined to stand by the treaty, the other half not. All the other tribes were hostile. The governor repeated to them the terms of peace alone possible: "They must throw aside their guns and submit to the justice and mercy of the government, but as they were invited under safe conduct they were safe in coming, safe in council, and safe in going."

Governor Stevens naturally felt disappointed at the failure of his hopes, but having done all that man could do, he had no cause to reproach himself. Whatever impediments had fallen in his way were due to the position of General Wool and the officers who felt compelled to echo his opinions. It may be very properly said here that Wright and Steptoe discovered their errors soon and modified their policy. Wool never did, and in the early part of 1857 he was relieved of his command, and was succeeded by General N. G. Clarke, who gave, as we shall learn later, a "new deal" to the impatient pioneers of the Inland Empire.

And now the governor and his retinue must move again westward. It must needs be that another battle be fought. Governor Stevens' own official report is the best summary of his return, and of this last battle in Walla Walla:

"So satisfied was I that the Indians would carry into effect their determination avowed in the councils in their own camps for several nights previously, to attack me, that, in starting, I formed my whole party and moved in order of battle. I moved on under fire one mile to water, when, forming a corral of the wagons and holding the adjacent hills and the brush on the stream by pickets, I made my arrangements to defend my position and fight the Indians. Our position in a low open basin five or six hundred yards across (he was attacked on what is now known as Charles Russell's ranch) was good, and with the aid of our corral, we could defend ourselves against a vastly superior force of the enemy.

"The fight continued till late in the night:

Two charges were made to disperse the Indians, the last led by Lieutenant-Colonel Shaw in person with twenty-four men; but, whilst driving before him some one hundred and fifty Indians, an equal number pushed into his rear, and he was compelled to cut his way through them towards camp, when drawing up his men, and, aided by the teamsters and pickets who gallantly sprang forward, he drove the Indians back in full charge upon the corral. Just before the charge the friendly Nez Perces, fifty in number, who had been assigned to hold the ridge on the south side of the corral, were told by the enemy they came not to fight the Nez Perces but the whites. 'Go to your camp,' said they, 'or we will wipe it out.' Their camp, with the women and children, was on a stream about a mile distant, and I directed them to retire as I did not require their assistance and was fearful that my men might not be able to distinguish them from hostiles, and thus friendly Indians be killed.

"Towards night I notified Lieutenant-Colonel Steptoe that I was fighting the Indians; that I should move the next morning, and expressed the opinion that a company of his troops would be of service. In his reply he stated that the Indians had burned up his grass and suggested that I should return to his camp, and place at his disposal my wagons, in order that he might move his whole command and his supplies to the Umatilla or some other point, where sustenance could be found for his animals. To this arrangement I assented and Lieutenant-Colonel Steptoe sent to my camp Lientenant Davidson, with detachments from the companies of dragoons and artillery with a mounted howitzer. They reached my camp about two o'clock in the morning, everything in good order and most of the men at the corral asleep. A picket had been driven in by the enemy an hour and a half before that on the hill south of the corral, but the enemy was immediately dislodged, and, ground pits being dug, all the points were held. The howitzer having been fired on the way out, it was believed nothing would be gained by waiting till morning and the whole force immediately returned to Lieutenant-Colonel Steptoe's camp.

"Soon after sunrise the enemy attacked the camp but was soon dislodged by the howitzer and a charge by detachment from Steptoe's command. On my arrival at the camp, I urged Lieutenant-Colonel Steptoe to build a block house immediately; to leave one company to defend it with all his supplies, then to march below and return with an additional force and additional supplies, and by a vigorous winter campaign to whip the Indians into submission. I placed at his disposal for the building, my teams and Indian employes. The block house and stockade were built in a little more than ten days. My Indian storeroom was rebuilt at one corner of the stockade.

"On the 23d day of September, we started for The Dalles, which we reached on the 2d of October. Nothing of interest occurred on the road.

"In the action of the 19th, my whole force consisted of Goff's company of sixty-nine, rank and file, the teamsters, herders, and Indian employes numbering about fifty men. Our train consisted of about five hundred animals, not one of which was captured by the enemy. We fought four hundred and fifty Indans and had one man mortally, one dangerously, and two slightly wounded. We killed and wounded thirteen Indians. One-half of the Nez Perces, one hundred and twenty warriors; all of the Yakimas and Palouses, two hundred warriors; the great bulk of the Cayuses and Umatillas, and an unknown number of the Walla Wallas and Indians from other bands were in the fight. The principal war chiefs were the son of Ouhi, Isle de Pere and Chief Quoltomee; the latter of whom had two horses shot under him, and who showed me a letter from Colonel Wright, acknowledging his valuable services in bringing about the peace of the Yakimas.

"I have failed, therefore, in making the desired arrangements with the Indians in the Walla Walla, and the failure, to be attributed in part to the want of co-operation with me as superintendent of Indian affairs on the part of the regular troops, has its causes also in the whole plan of operations of the troops since Colonel Wright assumed command.

"The Nez Perces, entirely friendly last December and January, became first disaffected in consequence of the then chief of the Cayuses, Ume-howlish, and the friendly Cayuses going into the Nez Perce country contrary to my positive orders. I refused to allow them to go there in December last, saying to them: 'I have ordered the Nez Perces to keep hostiles out of the country. If you go there your friends in the war party will come; they cannot be kept out. Through them disaffection will spread among a portion of the Nez Perces.' Ume-howlish, my prisoner, was sent into the Nez Perce country by Colonel Wright, and from the time of his arrival there all the efforts made by Agent Craig to prevent the spread of disaffection were abortive. What I apprehended and predicted had already come to pass. Looking Glass, the prominent man of the lower Nez Perces, endeavored to betray me on the Spokane as I was coming in from the Blackfoot council, and I was satisfied from that time that he was only awaiting a favorable moment to join bands with Kamaiakun in a war upon the whites, and Colonel Wright's management of affairs in the Yakima furnished the opportunity.

"The war was commenced in the Yakima on our part in consequence of the attempt first to seize the murderers of the agent, Bolon, and the miners who had passed through their country; and, second, to punish the tribe for making common cause with them and driving Major Haller out of the country. It is greatly to be deplored that Colonel Wright had not first severely chastised the Indians, and insisted not only upon the rendition of the murderers, but upon the absolute and unconditional submission of the whole tribe to the justice and mercy of the government. The long delays which occurred in the Yakimas, the talking and not fighting, this attempt to pacify the Indians and not reducing them to submission, thus giving safe conduct to murderers and assassins, and not seizing them for summary and exemplary punishment, gave to Kamaiakun the whole field of the interior, and by threats, lies and promises, he has brought into the combination one-half of the Nez Perce nation, and the least thing may cause the Spokanes, Coeur d'Alenes, Colvilles and Okanogans to join them.

"I state boldly that the cause of the Nez Perces becoming disaffected and finally going into war, is the operations of Colonel Wright east of the Cascades—operations so feeble, so procrastinating, so entirely unequal to the emergency, that not only has a most severe blow been struck at the credit of the government and the prosperity and character of this remote section of the country, but the impression has been made upon the Indians that the people and the soldiers were a different people. I repeat to you officially that when the Indians attacked me they expected Colonel Steptoe would not assist me, and when they awoke from their delusion Kamaiakun said, 'I will now let these people know who Kamaiakun is.' One of the good effects of the fight is, that the Indians have learned that we are one people, a fact which had not previously been made apparent to them by the operations of the regular troops.

"Is, Sir, the army sent here to protect our people and punish Indian tribes, who, without cause and in cold blood, and in spite of solemn treaties, murder our people, burn our houses and wipe out entire settlements? Is it the duty of General Wool and his officers to refuse to co-operate with me in my appropriate duties as superintendent of Indian affairs, and thus practically to assume those duties themselves? Is-it the duty of General Wool, in his schemes of pacifying the Indians, to trample down the laws of congress; to issue edicts prohibiting settlers returning to their claims, and thus for at least one county, the Walla Walla, make himself dictator of the country?"

And now that we have allowed the governor to tell his own story of the final struggle in the Walla Walla, every reader asks, "And how did it come out?" Gilbert pronounces that the Indians got all they wanted, and that so the great Walla Walla war of '55 and '56 must go down in history as an Indian victory. After Stevens had reached The Dalles, Wright went back again for a short time to Walla Walla, with a force increased by one company. But having reached the scene of the council and the farewell fight, he held an amicable meeting with the hostile chiefs and assured them that "The bloody cloth shall be washed, past differences thrown behind us, and perpetual peace must exist between us." He even went so far as to recommend that the Walla Walla treaties should never be confirmed. Steptoe, by Wool's orders, issued a proclamation that no whites should return to Walla Walla, except Hudson's Bay people and missionaries. Wool, in general orders of October 19th, expresses the hope that Wright, "warned by what has occurred, will be on his guard against the whites, and prevent trouble by keeping the whites out of the Indian country." But Steptoe had got his eyes partly open by the events of the season, and a little later he ventured to suggest that a good, industrious colony be permitted to settle in the Walla Walla valley. Wool promptly stepped on the suggestion by declaring that "the Cascade range formed, if not an impassible barrier, an excellent line of defense, a most excellent line of separation between two races always at war when in contact. To permit settlers to pass The Dalles and occupy the natural reserve is to give up this advantage, throw down the wall, and advance the frontier hun-

dreds of miles to the east, and add to the protective labor of the army."

Governor Stevens did not mince matters in summarizing this war and its results. His letters, both to Wool directly and to the War Department might, without putting too fine a point on it, be styled "vitriolic." To the frontiersmen of the country it seemed shameful surrender. After the bitter struggle of those frigid winters, after all the tedious traversing of dusty plains and snowy precipitous mountains, after the lives lost and the many wounds received, and especially after the brilliant and well-deserved victories won, then to have the regulars step in and rob them of all the fruits of victory by a practical capitulation to the hostilities,—that was a pretty hard dose for Stevens and his constituents. We need not blame the governor for some rather strong talk.

Thus at the close of 1856 the Walla Walla valley was, by military order, remanded to barbarism. In 1857 the present Fort Walla Walla was established, and there a force in charge of Lieutenant-Colonel Steptoe lay inactive.

One thing interesting to note in connection with the mustering out of the volunteers is that the horses which they had captured on the Grande Ronde were sold at such a good price as to pay the entire cost of the expedition. Sales were for scrip issued by the territory, which depreciated but little. The total amount of scrip issued was $1,481,475.45, and the entire number of volunteers was 1,896. The general testimony of witnesses of those times is that there was a remarkably high morale on the part of all the volunteer forces, and that this was due very largely to the character, ability and magnetic influence of Washington's first governor, certainly the greatest man in the official history of those times. And so there was "quiet in the land by the space of a year." In 1858 the Yakimas became so troublesome that Wright began to conclude 'that they were not such desirable citizens after all. Major Garnett was accordingly sent into their country with a strong force, and he seized and executed a number of their chiefs and braves, killed seven hundred of their ponies and secured quiet at last in the land of the sage-brush.

And now, though no battle was to be fought again on Walla Walla soil, it was the outfitting point for the most remarkable disaster in the history of the territory, one which, if it had not been for the ever-faithful Nez Perces, would probably have anticipated the Custer massacre in completeness and horror. This was the

STEPTOE DEFEAT OF 1858.

Colonel E. J. Steptoe set out in May, 1858, to go with two hundred cavalry to the Spokane country, though those powerful and independent Indians had warned troops to keep out, alleging that they were neutral and would not allow either Yakimas or whites in their country. Steptoe, or, more strictly speaking, his subordinates, committed a most egregious and incomprehensible blunder in starting from Walla Walla. On account of the great weight of provisions and baggage, a brilliant quartermaster conceived the idea of *leaving behind the greater part of the ammunition,* by way of lightening the load. As Joseph McEvoy expresses it, the force was beaten before it left Walla Walla.

The expedition was made in May. The wild torrent of Snake river was running bankfull from the floods of summer as the command crossed. Timothy, a chief of the Nez Perces, with a few followers, was living then at the mouth of the Alpowa, and by his efficient aid the soldiers crossed the wicked-looking stream in good order and good time, and continued on their way, the brave old chief accompanying them.

On May 16th the force reached a place which George F. Canis, on the authority of Thomas B. Beall, chief government packer of the expedition, describes as low and marshy, with big swales and thickets of quaking asp abounding, and surrounded by hills without timber. Mr. Beall locates the place as near the present town of Spangle. There is, however, much difference of opinion among the survivors as to where all this happened. But wherever it was, there the Indians gathered with hostile intention. Steptoe, realizing the dangerous odds, decided to return.

On the next day as the soldiers were descending a canyon to Pine creek, not far from where Rosalia is now located, Salteese, subchief of the Coeur d'Alenes, came up with an interpreter for a conference with Steptoe. The chief was making great professions of friendship, when one of the friendly Nez Perces struck him over the head with a whip, nearly knocking him from his horse. "What do you mean by speaking with a forked tongue to the white chief?" demanded the Nez Perce brave. Salteese, very angry, rode away in defiant mood. No sooner were the retreating forces well in the canyon than the attack was made. Second Lieutenant William Gaston's forces were the first to draw the fire of the enemy. Steptoe ordered Gaston to hold fire. When again asked for orders he gave the same command; but Gaston disobeyed and soon the firing became general. Gaston and Captain O. H. P. Taylor were in command of the rear guard, and, with amazing courage and devotion, kept the line intact, foiling all efforts of the Indians to rush through. They sent word to Steptoe to halt the line and give them a chance to load. But Steptoe deemed it safer to make no pause, and soon after those gallant heroes fell. A fierce fight raged for possession of their bodies. The Indians secured that of Gaston, but a small band of heroes, fighting like demons, got the body of the noble Taylor. One notable figure in this death grapple was De May, a Frenchman, who had been trained in the Crimea and in Algeria, and who made havoc among the savages with his gun-barrel used as a sabre. But at last he, too, went down before numbers, crying, "Oh, my God, for a sabre!"

At nightfall they had reached a point said to be somewhere on the flanks of Steptoe butte, though there is difference of opinion as to the exact location. Here the disorganized and suffering force made camp, threw out a picket line for defense, and buried such dead as they had not been forced to leave. In order to divert the Indians they determined, having buried their howitzers, to leave the balance of their stores. They hoped that if the Indians made an attack in the night they might succeed in stealing away. The Indians, however, feeling sure that they had the soldiers at their mercy, made no effort at a night attack. But it is stated that Kamiakin, head chief of the Yakimas, urged them to do so. Had he carried his point, the night of May 17, 1858, would have been one of melancholy memory. Another massacre would have been added to the series of frontier outrages which have darkened our earlier annals.

There was but one chance of salvation, and this was by means of a difficult trail which the Indians had left unguarded, as the Nez Perce Chief Timothy discovered by reconnoitreing; the savages rightly supposing it to be entirely unknown to the whites. But by the good favor of fortune or providence Timothy knew this pass. But for him, the next day would doubtless have witnessed a grim and ghastly massacre. During the dark and cloudy night the soldiers, mounted and in silence, followed Timothy over the wretched trail. Michael Kinney, a well-known resident of Walla Walla, was in charge of the rear guard, and is our chief authority for some portions of this narrative.

The horrors of that night retreat were probably never surpassed in the history of Indian warfare in the northwest. Several of the

wounded were lashed to pack animals, and were thus led away on that dreadful ride. Their sufferings were intense, and two of them, McCrossen and Williams, suffered so unendurably that they writhed themselves loose from their lashings and fell to the ground, begging their comrades to leave some weapon with which they might kill themselves. But the poor wretches were left lying there in the darkness. During the night the troops followed, generally at a gallop, the faithful Timothy, on whose keen eyes and mind their lives depended. The wounded and few whose horses gave out were scattered at intervals along the trail. Some of these finally reappeared, but most were lost. After twenty-four hours they found that they had ridden sixty miles or more, for the yellow flood of Snake river suddenly broke before them between its desolate banks. Here the unwearied Timothy threw out his own people as guards against the pursuing enemy and set the women of his tribe to ferrying the force across the turbulent river. This was safely accomplished, and thus the greater portion of the command reached Walla Walla from that ill-starred expedition in safety.

A dramatic incident which occurred on the evening of May 20th merits a brief narration. While the horses were being picketed and preparations were in progress for the night, the guards noticed a cloud of dust in the distance. In a short time a band of mounted Indians, approaching at full gallop, came into view, and the clattering of the hoofs of their horses and the thick dust enveloping them gave the impression that the little band of soldiers, which had had such trying experiences and now seemed within reach of safety, was to be literally wiped from the face of the earth. Excitement ran high. The soldiers became greatly agitated, and orders to prepare for battle were about to be issued when the standard-bearer of the oncoming horde, noting the confusion and mistrusting its cause, flung the stars and stripes to the breeze in token of friendly intentions. When the Indians swarmed into camp it was found that the banner was borne by none other than the ever-faithful Chief Lawyer. In the party were some of the sub-chiefs from Kamiah and noted members of the Nez Perce tribe. Steptoe declined to return to the conflict with the hostiles, much to the disappointment of Lawyer, who clearly pointed out how Indian allies could be secured and an easy victory won over the confident and exulting Indians of the Palouse country. The Nez Perces had, no doubt, learned of the defeat of Steptoe by means of the wonderful system of signaling in vogue among the aborigines.

Individual narratives of experiences on that expedition have been given by men long after living in Walla Walla and elsewhere. Among these was John Singleton, Sr., now deceased, who told Professor Lyman that, being without a horse, he crawled on his hands and knees during the greater part of two days, running at night, until he at last reached Snake river and was put across the stream by the Nez Perces. His knees and hands were worn to the bones. A soldier named Snickster reported that he and Williams, riding one horse, had reached the Snake river and were preparing to cross, when the Indians overtook them and in a spirit of grim pleasantry told them that if they could swim the river they might escape. Plunging into the turbid flood with their horse, they soon found the Indian bullets boiling around them. Williams and the horse were almost immediately killed, and Snickster, with an arm already broken, swam the rest of the way across Snake river. This story is told in several ways. George F. Canis, the correctness of whose account is vouched for by the chief government packer of the expedition, Thomas B. Beall, tells the story substantially as above, except that he says Snickster and Williams were set adrift in a canoe by the Indians, who practiced marksmanship upon them.

According to this account, Williams was shot and Snickster escaped by swimming, though his arm was broken. Michael Kinney considers the entire tale a fabrication. Mr. Singleton, however, told Professor Lyman he believed it true. Joseph McEvoy regards it as true in part, though he claims that Williams was killed in battle. The story was generally credited in early times, but it is hard to believe that anyone, even under the most favorable circumstances, could swim the Snake river in flood time with a broken arm.

Relative to the controverted question as to where the battle between Steptoe and the Indians took place, the writer cannot undertake to discuss the matter in detail. The evidences seem quite good, however, that the fight began in the vicinity of the present town of Rosalia. In the spring of 1899, while plowing some three miles north of that town, J. B. Wells unearthed three old Colt's army revolvers, such as were in use in 1858. These weapons, as well as a cannon ball, cannon tire and stirrup, discovered near Rosalia, are now the property of Mrs. Mattie L. Anderson, they having been purchased by her deceased husband. It is related also that Indian Louis, also known as "Wild Coyote," who called to see the relics, told Messrs. Ralston McCaig and Charles Thompson, of Rosalia, in an interview with these gentlemen, that there were "lots and lots" of Indians engaged; that he saw fifteen bodies of whites on the field; that three of the whites were killed on Little creek, three miles away (and he pointed toward the place where the revolvers were found); that he nearly killed two whites and was preparing to take the scalp of the second victim, who was wounded by an arrow from his bow, when the soldier raised up and shot him with a revolver, severely wounding him. Asked at what points the dead whites were seen by him, he said, "Three up there," (pointing to the Little creek above referred to) "one at the bridge" (directing attention to a place about a mile north of Rosalia) "and six over there" (pointing to the hill south of the town).

The sequel of Steptoe's defeat furnishes a more creditable chapter in the history of our Indian warfare. General Clarke at once ordered Colonel Wright to equip a force of six hundred men, proceed to the Spokane country and castigate the Indians with sufficient severity to settle the question of sovereignty forever. On August 15th Colonel Wright left Walla Walla on his northern campaign. In the battle of Four Lakes, fought on September 1st, and in the battle of Spokane Plains, September 5th, Colonel Wright broke forever the spirits and power of the northern Indians. Lieutenant Kipp's description of the former fight is so picturesque that we cannot resist the temptation to reproduce it. He says:

"On the plain below us we saw the enemy. Every spot seemed alive with the wild warriors we had come so far to meet. They were in the pines at the edge of the lakes, in the ravines and gullies, on the opposite hillsides and swarming over the plain. They seemed to cover the country for two miles. Mounted on their fleet, hardy horses, the crowd swept back and forth, brandishing their weapons, shouting their war-cries and keeping up a song of defiance. Most of them were armed with Hudson's Bay muskets, while others had bows and arrows and long lances. They were in all the bravery of their war array, gaudily painted and decorated with their wild trappings. Their plumes fluttered above them, while beneath skins and trinkets and all kinds of fantastic embelishments flaunted in the sunshine. Their horses, too, were arrayed in the most gorgeous finery. Some of them were even painted with colors to form the greatest contrast, the white being smeared with crimson in fantastic figures, and the dark-colored streaked with white clay. Beads and fringes of gaudy colors were hanging from their bridles, while the plumes of eagle's feathers,

interwoven with the mane and tail, fluttered as the breeze floated over them, and completed their wild and fantastic appearance.

"'By heavens! it was a glorious sight to see
The gay array of their wild chivalry.'

"As ordered, the troops moved down the hill toward the plain. As the line of advance came within range of the minie rifles, now for the first time used in Indian warfare, the firing began. The firing grew heavier as the line advanced, and, astonished at the range and effectiveness of the fire, the entire array of dusky warriors broke and fled toward the plain. The dragoons were now ordered to charge, and rode through the company at intervals to the front, and then dashed down upon the foe with headlong speed. Taylor's and Gaston's companies were there and soon they reaped a red revenge for their slain heroes. The flying warriors streamed out of the glens and ravines and over the open plains until they could find a refuge from the flashing sabres of the dragoons. When they had found the refuge of the wooded hills the line of foot once more passed the dragoons and renewed the fire, driving the Indians over the hills for about two miles, where a halt was called, as the troops were nearly exhausted. The Indians had almost all disappeared, only a small group remaining, apparently to watch the whites. A shell sent from the howitzer, bursting over their heads, sent them also to the shelter of the ravines. Thus the battle ended."

In the battle four days later at Spokans Plains quite a number of Indians were killed, and Kamiakin, the war-chief of the Yakimas, was wounded. After resting a day the forces moved on up the river and encamped above the falls. While there they were visited by Chief Gearry, a fairly well educated, rather bright Indian, who professed to be against the war. There is reason to doubt the sincerity of these representations, however. Colonel Wright talked plainly to him, saying that if he and the other Indians wanted peace they could have it by complete and unconditional surrender. On the 8th the march was resumed. About ten miles east of Spokane Indians were seen in the act of driving their horses to the mountains. The horses were captured and shot, with the exception of one hundred and thirty picked ones, which were kept for the use of the troops. Defeat in battle, the loss of their horses and the execution of a few Indians who had participated in murders completely humiliated the hostile tribes. Councils were held by Colonel Wright at the Coeur d'Alene mission and with the Spokanes, at which it was found that the Indians were prepared to enter a treaty of entire submission to the whites. Thus ended the era of Indian wars in eastern Washington and Oregon.

CHAPTER IX.

OREGON, ITS LOCATION, AREA AND PHYSICAL FEATURES.

Previous to the admission of Washington as a state Oregon was the most northwesterly state of the Union. On the north side it is bounded by Washington, on the east by Idaho, on the south by Nevada and California, and on the west by the Pacific ocean. With the Columbia forming the northern, and the Snake river most of the eastern boundary, and the waters of the Pacific washing its entire west coast, Oregon is almost surrounded by navigable waters. The average width of the state, from east to west, is 350 miles, and from north to south 275 miles. Its area is 95,274 square miles, or nearly 64,000,000 acres. It is as large as all the New England states, with Indiana added, and larger than New York and Pennsylvania combined. To more fully impress the reader with the liberal proportions of Oregon, it may be added that it is half as large as France, nearly twice as large as England, five times as large as Switzerland, and seven times the size of Holland. Oregon has a population of over 300,000. Were it as closely settled as Switzerland, it would have 12,000,000 people; as France, about 17,000,000; as Holland, about 25,000,-000; or as England, at least 40,000,000. In its proportion of productive to waste land, it will compare well with the average of the foreign countries named. In soil or climate or other conditions affecting the growth of vegetation or commercial interests, the comparison would be vastly in favor of Oregon. Situated between the parallels of 42 degrees and 46 degrees and 18 minutes north latitude, this state is not unlike, in climate and physical characteristics, Virginia or Tennessee.

The Cascade mountains divide Oregon into two unequal parts differing widely from each other in topography, soil and climate, and to some extent in productions. Along its western border the Coast Range also traverses it from north to south, while along its eastern boundary the Blue Mountain range, with its various spurs, covers probably a fifth of the total area of the state. Other lesser ranges, generally spurs of those named, jut into the intermediate regions, lending to the entire country an extraordinary diversity of feature. Fruitful valleys of varying extent, each of which is traversed by a more or less important stream, are numerous. The valleys of its western third have an average elevation of only a few score feet above the sea-level. The eastern part, embracing fully two-thirds of the superficial area of the state, is much higher, from 1,500 to 5,000 feet above the ocean. The general divisions of the country, including scores of districts, are three. That part of Oregon lying west of the Cascade mountains and north of the Rogue River mountains (which range runs east and west, about one hundred miles from the southern boundary) is known as western Oregon. That part of the state lying east of the Cascade mountains, excepting two counties on the southern border, is called eastern Oregon. The country lying south of the Rogue River mountains, with the two countries further east above referred to, is called southern Oregon.

The western division is about one-fourth of the state, but it contains at least one-half of the arable land, including the matchless valley of the Willamette, which is one hundred and forty by fifty miles in extent. Scarcely less important than the Willamette valley is the coast district of western Oregon, which borders the ocean for about one hundred and fifty miles. Between these arable districts lie broad ranges of forest, affording a supply of timber practically inexhaustible. No country in the world is more bountifully watered than western Oregon. It is a land of rivers. Clear and pure water gushes from every hillside, and it is rare that a square mile is found through which a crystal stream does not flow.

What is called southern Oregon includes about one-fifth of the superficial area of the state. A small portion of this, lying next to the ocean, has physical characteristics and climate similar to western Oregon, while the remainder, compassed about with mountains, and being more elevated, has a climate of its own, drier than western Oregon, yet not so dry as the climate of eastern Oregon. In sum-

mer these districts lie under a warmer sun than their northerly neighbors. Being in the elevated country, east of the Cascade mountains, they suffer, if not extreme cold, lower temperatures than are ever experienced west of that great ridge.

Eastern Oregon is a general designation given to all that part of the state east of the Cascade mountains, excepting the much smaller southern portion last above described. This division embraces two-thirds of the area of the state. In its general characteristics this region may be described as high and dry, warm in summer, cool in winter, rich in soil, and fairly well supplied with timber. In a country so vast there are many local variations from this general statement. The average elevation of eastern Oregon is about 2,500 feet. The southwestern portion of this section, notably all that lying south of Malheur river, is so dry as to require irrigation for the maturing of almost all crops. The northern central portion of this eastern Oregon country is much broken by minor ranges of mountains, which afford fine pasturage; and here and there are narrow valleys, unsurpassed for fertility. The southern central section is known as the Harney Lake region, which has long been celebrated as the main grazing region of the state. This may be described as a vast, rolling tableland, interspersed with valleys of considerable extent, which are natural meadows of luxuriant and nutritious grasses.

RIVERS, WATER-COURSES AND SPRINGS.

Oregon probably has no equal in our Union for the number, size and economical disposition of its water-courses. The Columbia ranks with the greatest rivers of the world. From its birth, among the most magnificent scenes of the earth, in the far north and in the heart of Yellowstone National Park, down through its 2,500 miles of irresistible sweep to the western sea, it is an avenue of wealth and wonder.

Inland for three hundred miles from the Pacific, it averages about two miles in breadth, reaching over six miles near its mouth. Engineers estimate that it carries off a volume of water but little, if any, less than does the Mississippi. Its immense drainage of 395,000 square miles can be imagined from the fact that during the melting of the snows in the northwestern mountain ranges, its daily increase, for days at a time, has been equal to the entire volume of the Hudson. It is the only river in our great republic which is navigable for deep sea-going vessels 120 miles into the interior, or for a river steamer 1,000 miles inland. The Willamette river is next in size and may be navigated by the largest ocean steamships and sailing vessels as far as Portland, 112 miles from the sea, and by river steamers a distance of 138 miles beyond. It gathers up the waters of forty-two streams, some of which are navigable for light-draft steamers. The Snake river is next in importance, being in fact the main fork of the Columbia. It has been navigated by light-draft steamers to a point within 125 miles of Salt Lake City, almost under the shadows of the Wahsatch range.

Among other navigable streams are Rogue river and Umpqua river in southwestern Oregon. Flowing from south to north in central Oregon and emptying into the Columbia are the Des Chutes and John Day rivers, each about three hundred miles long. In southeastern Oregon are the Owyhee and Malheur rivers, the former rising five hundred miles southward, in Nevada, and emptying into the Snake where the latter stream strikes the eastern Oregon boundary line. In northeastern Oregon are the Powder, Grande Ronde and Umatilla rivers, all swift, strong streams, watering large areas of fertile valley lands.

The mountain tributaries of these rivers are almost innumerable. Rising among the eternal snows of the higher ranges, or bursting forth from thousands of crystal springs, they are among the greatest of Oregon's attractions, both on account of their value in the development of many material interests, and for their varied charms for the sportsman and tourist. The government has appropriated large sums of money for the improvement of the Columbia river at its passage through the Cascade range. When the work contemplated is completed, this stream with its tributaries will be the artery of almost unbounded commerce with a vast domain north and east of Portland, the metropolis of the state. Work is also progressing on the improvements of the other navigable streams, all of which, when completed, will greatly accelerate the development of the regions they drain.

There is unlimited and unrivaled water-power at many points along these rivers and streams. There are falls almost innumerable, ranging from 25 to 500 feet in height, some of which are already being utilized, as will appear under the head of "Manufacturing," in succeeding pages.

There are several commodious harbors for vessels of light draft on the coast line, exclusive of those found at the mouths of the several rivers. At these places a thriving business is carried on in lumbering, coal-mining, fishing, oystering, dairying and agricultural products.

As will be gathered from the foregoing, Oregon abounds in springs, large and small. These are found everywhere, from the seashore to the most elevated mountain peaks. Some are so large and deep as to almost arrive at the dignity of lakes, and the waters they throw forth at once make respectable creeks. This is especially the case in the Harney Lake region and in western and southern Oregon.

CLIMATOLOGY AND HEALTHFULNESS:

Each of the three natural divisions of Oregon has a climate peculiar to itself. The climate of western Oregon is mild and equable. The average spring temperature is 52 degrees;

summer, 67 degrees; autumn, 53 degree; winter, 39 degrees; or an average of 52.75 degrees for the whole year. The thermometer seldom rises above 90 degrees in the hottest days in the summer, and rarely falls below 20 degrees in the winter; so that out-door labor may be performed at all times of the year, and at all hours of the day. Considering the thermometer's limited range during the four seasons, and the other conditions peculiar to the locality, a year would more properly be divided into two seasons—the wet and dry, the former lasting from the middle of November until May, during which period the rainfall is copious and regular, insuring certain crops and good pasture. In the Willamette valley the annual rainfall is forty-four inches—about the same as at Davenport, Memphis and Philadelphia, while in all other valleys it is sufficient to prevent any drouth. The rain never comes in torrents, but gently and without atmospheric disturbance. Thunder storms are rare.

CHAPTER X.

SETTLEMENT OF OREGON.

In our endeavor to properly lay the foundations for our county annals we have already extended these introductory chapters far beyond the limits contemplated in our original plan, but it is yet necessary that we trace briefly the inception of civil government in Oregon that we may understand the source of civil institutions in the counties with whose history we are primarily concerned. Already, we trust, we have conveyed to the mind of the reader as vivid an impression as our limitations would permit of the first feeble knockings of civilization's standard bearers upon our western shores, of some of the expeditions by which the land so long a *terra incognita* was robbed of its mystery and the overland route to it discovered, of the regime of the fur trader and the trapper, of the diplomatic negotiations by which our title to sovereignty was established, of missionary occupancy and the advent of the pioneer settler and of that second struggle for possession which cost so much hardship and sacrifice on the part of both the white and the red races and has left so tragic a stain on our earlier annals.

We shall, however, go back a few years chronologically to get a clearer idea of the first settlement of old Oregon Territory. Of those Americans who came to Oregon with the early expeditions three in 1832 and twenty-two in 1834 became permanent settlers. The names of these are preserved by W. H. Gray, as follows:

"With Jason Lee's party, besides himself, were Daniel Lee, Cyrus Shepard, P. L. Edwards and Courtney M. Walker. From Captain Wyeth's party of 1832 there remained S. H. Smith, Sergeant, and Tibbets, a stone cutter, and from his party of 1834, James O'Neil and T. J. Hubbard. From the wreck of the William and Ann, a survivor named Felix Hathaway remained. With Ewing Young from California in 1834, a party came who remained in Oregon, consisting of Joseph Gale, who died in Union county, that state, in 1882, John McCarty, Carmichael, John Hauxhurst, John Howard, Kilborn, Brandywine and a colored man named George Winslow. An English sailor named Richard McCary reached the Willamette from the Rocky mountains that year as did also Captain J. H. Crouch, G. W. Le Breton, John McCaddan and William Johnson from the brig Maryland. This made twenty-five residents at the close of 1834, who were not in any way connected with the Hudson's Bay Company, all of whom were here for other than transient purposes. There were no arrivals in 1835."

The year 1836, however, was, as may be gleaned from previous pages, an important one for Oregon. While, as Gray states, there were no permanent residences established in Oregon in 1835, that was the year in which Rev. Samuel Parker and Dr. Marcus Whitman were sent out by the American Board to explore the country and report upon it as a field for missionary labors. These gentlemen were met at the trappers' rendezvous on Green river by the noted Chief Lawyer, by whom they were persuaded into the plan of establishing their proposed mission among his people, the Nez Perces. When this conclusion was reached Dr. Whitman started back to the east, accompanied by two Nez Perce boys, Mr. Parker continuing his journey westward to the shores of the Pacific. It was agreed that Parker should seek out a suitable location among the Nez Perces for the mission, while Dr. Whitman should make arrangements for the westward journey of a sufficient force and for the establishment and outfitting of the post. The result of Mr. Parker's journeyings are embodied in a work of great historic value from his own pen, entitled "Parker's Exploring Tour Beyond the Rocky Mountains." From information conveyed by this volume, Gilbert summarizes the conditions in Oregon in 1835 as follows:

"Fort Vancouver on the Columbia, under charge of Dr. John McLoughlin, was estab-lished in 1824, and consisted of an inclosure by stockade, thirty-seven rods long by eighteen wide, that faced the south. About one hundred persons were employed at the place, some three hundred Indians lived in the immediate vicinity. There were eight substantial buildings within the stockade, and a large number of small ones on the outside. There were 459 cattle, 100 horses, 200 sheep, 40 goats and 300 hogs belonging to the company at this place; and during the season of 1835 the crops produced in that vicinity amounted to 5,000 bushels of wheat, 1,300 bushels of potatoes, 1,000 bushels of barley, 1,000 bushels of oats, 2,000 bushels of peas, and garden vegetables in proportion. The garden, containing five acres, besides its vegetable products, included apples, peaches, grapes and strawberries. A grist mill, with machinery propelled by oxen, was kept in constant use, while some six miles up the Columbia was a sawmill containing several saws, which supplied lumber for the Hudson's Bay Company. Within the fort was a bakery employing three men, also shops for blacksmith, joiners, carpenters and a tinner.

"Fort Williams, erected by N. J. Wyeth at the mouth of the Willamette, was nearly deserted, Mr. Townsend, the ornithologist, being about the only occupant at that time. Wyeth had gone to his Fort Hall in the interior. Of Astoria at the mouth of the Columbia but two log houses and a garden remained, where two white men dragged out a dull existence, to maintain possession of the historic ground. Its ancient, romantic grandeur had departed from its walls, when dismantled to assist in the construction and defenses of its rival, Fort Vancouver. Up the Willamette river was the Methodist mission, in the condition already noted, while between it and the present site of Oregon City, was the Hudson's Bay Company's French settlements of Gervais and McKay, containing some twenty families whose children were being taught by young Americans. In one of these settlements a grist mill had been just completed. East of the Cascade mountains Fort Walla Walla was situated at the mouth of a river by that name. It was 'built of logs and was internally arranged to answer the purposes of trade and domestic comfort, and externally for defense, having two bastions, and was surrounded by a stockade.' It was accidentally burned in 1841 and rebuilt of adobe within a year. At this point the company had 'horses, cows, hogs, fowls, and they cultivated corn, potatoes, and a variety of garden vegetables.' This fort was used for a trading post, where goods were stored for traffic with the Indians. Fort Colville, on the Columbia a little above Kettle falls, near the present line of Washington Territory, a strongly stockaded post, was occupied by a half-dozen men with Indian families, and Mr. McDonald was in charge. Fort Okinagan, at the mouth of the river of that name, established by David Stewart in 1811, was, in the absence of Mr. Ogden, in charge of a single white man. Concerning Fort Hall nothing is said; but it fell into the hands of the Hudson's Bay Company in 1836. It was then a stockaded fort, but was rebuilt with adobes in 1838. Mr. Parker is also silent in regard to Fort Boise, which was constructed on Snake river from poles in 1834 as a rival establishment to Fort Hall; was occupied in 1835 by the Hudson's Bay Company, and later was more substantially constructed from adobe. If there were other establishments in 1835, west of the Rocky mountains, between the forty-second and forty-ninth parallels, the writer has failed to obtain evidences of them."

Meanwhile Whitman was working with his characteristic energy in the east, and he succeeded in raising funds and securing associates for two missions in Oregon. The results of his labors and their sudden and sad ending have been previously adverted to, but the matter which now concerns us is that the American population of Oregon was in 1836

thereby increased by five persons, namely, Dr. Marcus Whitman, Narcissa Whitman, Rev. H. H. Spalding and wife and W. H. Gray. The ladies mentioned gained the distinction of having been the first white women whose feet pressed the soil of old Oregon and whose blue and dark eyes looked into the dusky, mystic orbs of the daughters of the Columbia basin. A few months later the Methodist mission was also blessed by the purifying presence of noble womanhood, but the laurels of pioneership have ever rested upon the worthy brows of Mrs. Whitman and Mrs. Spalding, and so far as we know no fair hand has ever been raised to pluck them thence. The missionary party brought with them eight mules, twelve horses and sixteen cows, also three wagons laden with farming utensils, blacksmith and carpenter's tools, clothing, seeds, etc., etc., to make it possible for them to support themselves without an entire dependence upon the Hudson's Bay Company for supplies. Two of the wagons were abandoned at Fort Laramie and heavy pressure was brought upon Dr. Whitman to leave the third at the rendezvous on Green river but he refused so to do. He succeeded in getting it to Fort Hall intact, then reduced it to a two-wheeled cart, which he brought on to Fort Boise, thus demonstrating the feasibility of a wagon road over the Rocky mountains.

Although a reinforcement for the Methodist mission sailed from Boston in July, 1836, it failed to reach its destination on the Willamette until May of the following year, so that the American population at the close of 1836 numbered not to exceed thirty persons, including the two ladies.

Prior to 1837 there were no cattle in the country except those owned by the Hudson's Bay Conmpany and those brought from the east by the Whitman party. The Hudson's Bay Company wished to continue this condition as long as possible, well knowing that the introduction of cattle or any other avenue of wealth production among the American population would have a natural tendency to render the people that much more nearly independent. When, therefore, it was proposed by Ewing Young and Jason Lee that a party should be sent to California for stock, the idea at once met with opposition from the autocratic Columbia river monopoly. Thanks largely to the assistance of William A. Slocum, of the United States navy, by whom money was advanced and a free passage to California furnished to the company's emissaries, the projectors of this enterprise were rendered independent of the Hudson's Bay Company. Ewing Young was captain of the expedition; P. L. Edwards, of the Willamette mission, was also one of its leading spirits. The men purchased seven hundred head of cattle at three dollars per head and set out upon the return journey. They succeeded in getting about six hundred head to the Willamette country, notwithstanding the bitter hostility of the Indians. Gilbert quotes from the diary of P. L. Edwards, which he says, was shown him by the latter's daughter in California, to prove that the trouble with the Indians was caused by the wanton and cold-blooded murder by members of the party of a friendly Indian who was following the band. The Indian hostilities were not incited by the Hudson's Bay Company, but may properly be laid at the doors of the men who committed this barbarous outrage in revenge for wrongs suffered by a party to which they belonged two years before,—another instance of the innocent suffering for the sins of the guilty.

The arrival of neat cattle in the Willamette country provided practically the first means of acquiring wealth independent of the Hudson's Bay Company. "This success in opposition to that interest," says Gilbert, "was a discovery by the settlers, both American and ex-employes that they possessed the strength to rend the bars that held them captives under a species of peonage. With this one blow, directed by missionaries and dealt by ex-American hunters, an independent maintenance in Oregon had been rendered possible for immigrants."

As before stated the reinforcements for the Methodist mission arrived in May, 1837. By it the American population was increased by eight persons, namely; Elijah White and wife, Alanson Beers and wife, W. H. Willson, the Misses Annie M. Pitman, Susan Downing and Elvina Johnson. In the fall came another reinforcement, the personnel of which was the Rev. David Leslie, wife and three daughters, the Rev. W. H. K. Perkins and Miss Margaret Smith. Add to these Dr. J. Bailey, an English physician, George Gay and John Turner, who also arrived this year, and the thirty or thirty-one persons who settled previously, and we have the population of Oregon independent of the Hudson's Bay Company's direct or indirect control in the year 1837.

In January of that year W. H. Gray, of the American Board's missions, set out overland to the east for reinforcements to the missionary force of which he was a member. His journey was not an uneventful one, as will appear from the following narrative, clothed in his own words, which casts so vivid a light upon transcontinental travel during the early days that we feel constrained to quote it. He says:

"Our sketches, perhaps, would not lose in interest by giving a short account of a fight which our Flathead Indians had at this place with a war party of the Blackfeet. It occurred near the present location of Helena, in Montana. As was the custom with the Flathead Indians in traveling in the buffalo country, their hunters and warriors were in advance of the main camp. A party of twenty-five Blackfeet warriors was discovered by some twelve of our Flatheads. To see each other was to fight, especially parties prowling about in this manner; and at it they went. The first fire of the Flatheads brought five of the Blackfeet to the ground and wounded five more. This was more than they expected, and the Blackfeet made little effort to recover their dead, which were duly scalped, and their bodies left for food for the wolves and the scalps borne in triumph into the camp. There were but two of the Flatheads wounded: one had a flesh wound in the thigh, and the other had his right arm broken by a Blackfoot ball.

"The victory was complete, and the rejoicing in camp corresponded to the number of scalps taken. Five days and nights the usual scalp dance was performed. At the appointed time the big war-drum was sounded, when the warriors and braves made their appearance at the appointed place in the open air, painted as warriors. Those who had taken the scalps from the heads of their enemies bore them in their hands upon the ramrods of their guns.

"They entered the circle, and the war-song, drums, rattles and noises all commenced. The scalp-bearers stood for a moment (as if to catch the time), and then commenced hopping, jumping and yelling in concert with the music. This continued for a time, when some old painted woman took the scalps and continued to dance. The performance was gone through with as many nights as there were scalps taken.

"Seven days after the scalps were taken, a messenger arrived bearing a white flag, and a proposition to make peace for the purpose of trade. After the preliminaries had all been completed, in which the Hudson's Bay Company trader had the principal part to perform, the time was fixed for a meeting of the two tribes. The Flatheads, however, were all careful to dig their war-pits, make their corrals and breastworks, and, in short, fortify their camp as much as if they expected a fight instead of peace. Ermatinger, the company's leader, remarked that he would sooner take his chances of a fight off-hand than endure the anxiety and suspense of the two days we waited for the Blackfeet to arrive. Our scouts and warriors were all ready, and all on the watch for peace or war, the latter of which, from the recent fight they had had, was ex-

pected most. At length the Blackfeet arrived, bearing a red flag with H. B. C. in white letters upon it, and advancing to within a short distance of the camp were met by Ermatinger and a few Flathead chiefs, shook hands and were conducted to the trader's lodge—the largest one in the camp—and the principal chiefs of both tribes, seated upon buffalo and bear skins, all went through with the ceremony of smoking a big pipe, having a long handle or stem trimmed with horse-hair and porcupine quills. The pipe was filled with the traders' tobacco and the Indians' killikinick. The war-chiefs of each tribe took a puff each of the pipe, passed it to his right-hand man, and so around till all the circle had smoked the big medicine pipe, or pipe of peace, which on this occasion was made by the Indians from a soft stone which they find in abundance in their country, having no extra ornamental work upon it. The principal chief in command, or great medicine man, went through the ceremony, puffed four times, blowing his smoke in four directions. This was considered a sign of peace to all around him, which doubtless included all he knew anything about. The Blackfeet, as a tribe, are a tall, well-formed, slim-built and active people. They travel principally on foot, and are considered very treacherous.

"The peace made with so much formality was broken two days afterward by killing two of the Flatheads when caught not far from the main camp.

"It was from this Flathead tribe that the first Indian delegation was sent to ask for teachers. Three of their number volunteered to go with Gray to the States in 1837 to urge their claim for teachers to come among them. The party reached Ash Hollow, where they were attacked by about three hundred Sioux warriors, and, after fighting for three hours, killed some fifteen of them, when the Sioux, by means of a French trader then among them, obtained a parley with Gray and his traveling companions,—two young men that had started to go to the States with him. While the Frenchman was in conversation with Gray, the treacherous Sioux made a rush upon the three Flatheads, one Snake and one Iroquois Indian belonging to the party, and killed them. The Frenchman then turned to Gray and told him and his companions they were prisoners, and must go to the Sioux camp, first attempting to get possession of their guns. Gray informed them at once: 'You have killed our Indians in a cowardly manner, and you shall not have our guns,' at the same time telling the young men to watch the first motion of the Indians to take their lives, and if we must die to take as many Indians with us as we could. The Sioux had found in the contest thus far that, notwithstanding they had conquered and killed five, they had lost fifteen, among them one of their war chiefs, besides several severely wounded. The party was not further molested till they reached the camp, containing between one and two hundred lodges. A full explanation was had of the whole affair. Gray had two horses killed under him and two balls passed through his hat, both inflicting slight wounds. The party were feasted, and smoked the pipe of peace over the dead body of the chief's son; next day they were allowed to proceed with nine of their horses; the balance, with the property of the Indians, the Sioux claimed as part pay for their losses, doubtless calculating to waylay and take the balance of the horses. Be that as it may, Gray and his young men reached Council Bluffs in twenty-one days, traveling nights and during storms to avoid the Indians on the plains."

Gray proceeded east and with the energy and courage which ever characterized him set about the task of securing the needed reinforcements. He succeeded in enlisting Rev. Cushing Eells, Rev. E. Walker and Rev. A. B. Smith with their wives, also a young man named Cornelius Rogers. He also succeeded in inducing a young woman to become his own bride and to share with him the dangers and tedium of a transcontinental westward journey and whatever of weal or woe the new land might have in store for them. Mention should likewise be made of the noted John A. Sutter, an ex-captain of the Swiss guard, who accompanied this expedition and who afterward became an important character in the early history of California.

Two priests, Revs. F. N. Blanchet and Modest Demers, also came during this year, so that the seeds of sectarian strife, which did so much to neutralize the efforts and work of the Protestant missionaries, then began to be sown. The population of Oregon independent of the Hudson's Bay Company must have been about sixty at the close of the year 1838.

In the fall of 1839 came Rev. J. S. Griffin and Mr. Munger with their wives, Ben Wright, Lawson, Keiser and Geiger, also T. H. Farnham, author of "Early Days in California," Sidney Smith, Blair and Robert Shortess. W. H. Gray in his history of Oregon estimates the population as follows: "Protestant missionaries, 10; Roman priests, 2; physicians, 2; laymen, 6; women, 13; children, 10; settlers, 20; settlers under Hudson's Bay control with American tendencies, 10; total, 83."

In 1838 Jason Lee made a journey overland to the States for the purpose of procuring a force wherewith to greatly extend his missionary operations. His wife died during his absence and the sad news was forwarded to him by Dr. McLoughlin, Dr. Whitman was hired by Gray. In June, 1840, Lee returned with a party of forty-eight, of whom eight were clergymen, one was a physician, fifteen were children and nineteen were ladies, five of them unmarried. Their names are included in Gray's list of arrivals for 1840, which is as follows:

"In 1840 Mrs. Lee, second wife of Rev. Jason Lee; Rev. J. H. Frost and wife; Rev. A. F. Waller, wife and two children; Rev. W.

W. Kone and wife; Rev. G. Hines, wife and sister; Rev. L. H. Judson, wife and two children; Rev. J. L. Parish, wife and three children; Rev. G. P. Richards, wife and three children; Rev. A. P. Olley and wife. Laymen—Mr. George Abernethy, wife and two children; Mr. H. Campbell, wife and one child; Mr. W. W. Raymond and wife; Mr. H. B. Brewer and wife; Dr. J. L. Babcock, wife and one child; Rev. Mrs. Daniel Lee; Mrs. David Carter; Mrs. Joseph Holman; Miss E. Phillips. Methodist Episcopal Protestant mission—Robert Moore, James Cook and James Fletcher, settlers. Jesuit priests—P. J. De Smet, Flathead mission.

"Rocky mountain men; with native wives: William Craig, Robert or Dr. Newell, J. L. Meek, George Ebbetts, William M. Dougherty, John Larison, George Wilkinson, a Mr. Nicholson, Mr. Algear and William Johnson, author of 'Leni Leoti'; or the Prairie Flower.'" Mr. Gray sums up the population of all the old Oregon territory, not including Hudson's Bay operatives, as about two hundred.

In 1841 eight young men built and equipped a vessel, named the Star of Oregon, in which they made a trip to San Francisco. Joseph Gale served as captain of the doughty little craft, of which Felix Hathaway had been master builder. The vessel was exchanged at Yerba Buena (San Francisco) for three hundred and fifty cows. Gale remained in the Golden state through the winter, then set out overland to Oregon with a party of forty-two immigrants, who brought with them, as J. W. Nesmith informs us, 1,250 head of cattle, 600 head of mares, colts, horses and mules and three thousand sheep. The incident forms the theme of one of Mrs. Eva E. Dye's most charming descriptions, but its strategic importance in helping to Americanize Oregon and break up the cattle monopoly seems to have been overlooked by many other writers.

The Joseph Gale who figured so prominently in this undertaking was afterward a

member of the first triumvirate executive committee of the provisional government. He is affectionately remembered in eastern Oregon, where he passed the closing years of his eventful life, and particularly in Umatilla county, where his aged widow resides. Like nearly all the other early trappers who turned settlers, Gale married an Indian woman, though few were so happy as he in their choice. Although now about ninety years old and totally blind, his widow is still bright and lively. She lives on the Umatilla reservation with her daughter, Mrs. Edwin Simpson, and no doubt rejoices in the splendid standing which her progeny have won for themselves in the various communities in which they live. Some of her children and grandchildren are among the most worthy and highly esteemed of the citizens of the Inland Empire.

By the close of the year 1841 the independent population of Oregon had reached 253; thirty-five of whom are classed as settlers. In 1842 came an immigration of 111 persons, two of whom, A. L. Lovejoy and A. M. Hastings, were lawyers. In this year, also, came the Red River immigration of English and Scotch and of French-Canadian half-breeds to the Puget sound country. This immigration was inspired by the Hudson's Bay Company, which designed it as an offset to the growing American power in the Oregon country. It had, however, very little political effect, as many of its members drifted southward into the Willamette and became members of the provisional government. 1842 is also memorable for the famous winter-ride of Dr. Whitman.

In 1843 came the largest immigration the Oregon country had yet known, piloted across the plains and over the mountains by Whitman himself. Its 875 persons, with their wagons and thirteen hundred head of cattle, settled forever the question of the national character of Oregon. J. W. Nesmith has preserved for us the names of all the male members of this expedition over sixteen years of age, as also of those remaining from the immigration of the year previous. In 1844 came eight hundred more Americans, and in 1845 a much larger number, estimated by some at three thousand. 1846 added another thousand to Oregon's American population. In that year the ownership of the country was definitely settled by treaty with Great Britain, and the famous world problem was solved.

It is unnecessary to trace the settlement of Oregon further. From this time forth its subjugation was assured and the man of prevision might foresee its importance as an integral part of the great American commonwealth. The reader will naturally inquire what sort of government existed among these people so far from the seat of federal authority, and as the inception of civil institutions in Oregon is an important and interesting subject it shall receive brief treatment in our next chapter. It is of interest at this juncture, however, to give some description of the inner life of the Oregon pioneer, and this can be done in no way better than by reproducing some portions of an address delivered by Colonel J. W. Nesmith, that well known and influential pioneer of the state, before the Oregon Pioneer Association. He says:

"The business of the country was conducted entirely by barter. The Hudson's Bay Company imported and sold many articles of prime necessity to those who were able to purchase. Wheat or beaver skins would buy anything the company had for sale. But poor waywern emigrants, just arriving in the country, were as destitute of wheat and beaver as they were of coin. The skins purchased by the company were annually shipped in their own vessels to London, while the wheat was shipped to the Russian possessions on the north, and to California, to fill a contract that the Hudson's Bay Company had with the Russian Fur Company. A small trade in lumber, salt, salmon, shingles and hooppoles gradually grew up with the Sandwich Islands, and brought in

return a limited supply of black and dirty sugar in grass sacks, together with some salt and, coffee.

"There being no duty collected upon importations into Oregon previous to 1849, foreign goods were comparatively cheap, though the supply was always limited; nor had the people means to purchase beyond the pure necessities. Iron, steel, salt, sugar, coffee, tea, tobacco, powder and lead, and a little ready-made clothing and some calico and domestics were the principal articles purchased by the settlers. The Hudson's Bay Company in their long intercourse with the Indians, had, from prudential motives, adopted the plan in their trade of passing articles called for out through a hole in the wall or partition. Persons were not allowed inside among the goods to make selections, and the purchaser had to be content with what was passed out to him through the aperture. Thus, in buying a suit of clothes, there was often an odd medley of color and size. The settlers used to say that Dr. McLoughlin, who was a very large man, had sent his measure to London, and all of the clothing was made to fit him. The hickory shirts we used to buy came down to our heels, and the wrist-bands protruded a foot beyond the hands; and as Sancho Panza said of sleep, 'they covered one all over like a mantle. They were no such 'Cutty sark' affairs of 'Paisley ham' as befuddled Tam O'Shanter saw when peeping in upon the dancing warlocks of 'Alloway's auld haunted kirk.' A small sized settler purchasing one could, by reasonable curtailment of the extremities, have sufficient material to, clothe one of the children.

*   *   *   *   *   *   *

"The pioneer home was a log cabin with a puncheon floor and mud chimney, all constructed without sawed lumber, glass or nails, the boards being secured upon the roof by heavy weight poles. Sugar, coffee, tea and even salt were not every day luxuries, and in many cabins were entirely unknown. Mocassins made of deer or elk skins and soled with rawhide made a substitute for shoes, and were worn by both sexes. Buckskin was the material from which the greater portion of the male attire was manufactured, while the cheapest kind of coarse cotton goods furnished the remainder. A white or boiled shirt was rarely seen and was a sure indication of great wealth and aristocratic pretension. Meat was obtained in some quantities from the wild game of the forests or the wild fowl with which the country abounded at certain seasons, until such time as cattle or swine became sufficiently numerous to be slaughtered for food. The hides of both wild and domestic animals were utilized in many ways. Clothing, moccasins, saddles and their rigging, bridles, ropes, harness and other necessary articles were made from them. A pair of buckskin pants, moccasins, a hickory shirt and some sort of cheaply extemporized hat rendered a man comfortable as well as presentable in the best society, the whole outfit not costing one-tenth part of the price of the essential gewgaws that some of our exquisite sons now sport at the ends of their watch-chains, on their shirt-fronts or dainty fingers. Buckskin clothing answered wonderfully well for rough and tumble wear, particularly in dry weather, but I have known them after exposure to a hard day's rain to contract in a single night by a warm fire a foot in longitude, and after being subjected to a webfoot winter or two, and a succeeding dry summer, they would assume grotesque and unfashionable shapes, generally leaving from six inches to a foot of nude and arid skin between the top of the moccasins and the lower end of the breeches; the knees protruded in front, while the rear started off in the opposite direction, so that when the wearer stood up the breeches were in a constant struggle to sit down and vica versa.

"The pioneers brought garden seeds with them, and much attention was paid to the production of vegetables, which, with milk, game and fish, went a long way toward the support of the family. Reaping machines, threshers, headers, mowing machines, pleasure carriages, silks, satins, laces, kid gloves, plug hats, high-heeled boots, crinaline, bustles, false hair, hair dye, jewelry, patent medicines, railroad tickets, postage stamps, telegrams, pianos and organs, together with the thousand and one articles to purchase which the country is now drained of millions of dollars annually, were then unknown and consequently not wanted. A higher civilization has introduced us to all these modern improvements, and apparently made them necessaries, together with the rum-mill, the jail, the insane asylum, the poor house, the penitentiary and the gallows."

Of the people who lived in Oregon during the period of which we are writing, Judge Burnett in his book entitled "Recollections of an Old Pioneer," says: "Among the men who came to Oregon the year I did, some were idle, worthless young men, too lazy to work at home and too genteel to steal, while some were gamblers and others reputed thieves. But when we arrived in Oregon they were compelled to work or starve. It was a dire necessity. There was there no able relative or indulgent friend upon whom the idle could quarter themselves, and there was little or nothing for the rogues to steal. There was no ready way by which they could escape into another country, and they could not conceal themselves in Oregon. I never knew so fine a population, as a whole community, as I saw in Oregon most of the time I was there. They were all honest because there was nothing to steal; they were all sober because there was no liquor to drink; there were no misers because there was nothing to hoard; they were all industrious because it was work or starve."

CHAPTER XI.

EVOLUTION OF GOVERNMENT.

Such was the general character of the early pioneer as depicted to us by men who knew whereof they spoke. The discussion of the subject now under consideration will bring to light another characteristic of the early Oregonian—his political capabilities. His environments and isolation from the rest of the world compelled him to work out for himself many novel and intricate economic promlems; the uncertany as to the ownership of Oregon, and the diverse national prejudices and sympathies of its settlers made the formation of a government reasonably satisfactory to the whole population an exceedingly difficult task. There were, however, men in the new community determined to make the effort, and the reader will be able to judge how well they succeeded from what follows.

As early as 1838 some of the functions of government were exercised by members of the Methodist mission. Persons were chosen by that body to officiate as magistrates and judges and their findings were generally acquiesced in by persons independent of the Hudson's Bay Company because of the unorganized condition of the community, though there was doubtless a strong sentiment among the independent settlers in favor of trusting to the general morality and disposition to do right rather than to any political organization. The most important act of the mission officers was the trial of T. J. Hubbard for the killing of a man who attempted to enter his house at night with criminal and burglarious intent. Rev. David Leslie presided as judge during this noteworthy judicial proceeding, which resulted in the acquittal of the defendant on the ground that his act was justifiable.

In 1840 a petition was drafted, signed by David Leslie and others, and forwarded to Congress. It is not entirely free from misstatements and inaccuracies, but is nevertheless an able and important state paper. It reads as follows:

To the Honorable, the Senate and House of Representatives of the United States of America in Congress Assembled:

Your petitioners represent unto your honorable bodies, that they are residents in the Oregon Territory, and citizens of the United States, or persons desirous of becoming such.

They further represent to your honorable bodies, that they have settled themselves in said territory, under the belief that it was a portion of the public domain of said states, and that they might rely upon the government thereof for the blessings of free institutions, and the protection of its arms.

But your petitioners further represent, that they are uninformed of any acts of said government by which its institutions and protection are extended to them; in consequence whereof, themselves and families are exposed to be destroyed by the savages around them, and OTHERS THAT WOULD DO THEM HARM.

And your petitioners would further represent, that they have no means of protecting their own and the lives of their families, other than self-constituted tribunals, originated and sustained by the power of an ill-constructed public opinion, and the resort to force and arms.

And your petitioners represent these means of safety to be an insufficient safeguard of life and property, and that the crimes of *theft, murder, infanticide, etc.,* are increasing among them to an alarming extent; and your petitioners declare themselves unable to arrest this progress of crime, and its terrible consequences without the aid of the law and tribunals to administer it.

Your petitioners therefore pray the Congress of the United States of America to establish, as soon as may be, a territorial government in the Oregon Territory.

And if reasons other than those above presented were needed to induce your honorable bodies to grant the prayer of the undersigned, your petitioners, they would be found in the value of this territory to the nation, and the alarming circumstances that portend its loss.

Your petitioners, in view of these last considerations, would represent that the English government has had a surveying squadron on the Oregon coast for the last two years, employed in making accurate surveys of all its rivers, bays and harbors; and that, recently, the said government is said to have made a grant to the Hudson's Bay Company of all lands lying between the Columbia river and Puget Sound; and that said company is actually exercising unequivocal acts of ownership over said lands thus granted, and opening extensive farms upon the same.

And your petitioners represent that these circumstances, connected with other acts of said company to the same effect, and *their*

declarations that the English government own and will hold, as its own soil, that portion of Oregon Territory situated north of the Columbia river, together with the important fact that the said company are cutting and sawing into lumber, and shipping to foreign ports, vast quantities of the finest pine-trees upon the navigable waters of the Columbia, have led your petitioners to apprehend that the English government do intend, at all events, to hold that portion of this territory lying north of the Columbia river.

And your petitioners represent, that the said territory, north of the Columbia, is an invaluable possession to the American Union; that in and about Puget Sound are the only harbors of easy access, and commodious and safe, upon the whole coast of the territory; and that a great part of this said northern portion of the Oregon Territory is rich in timber, waterpower, and valuable minerals. For these and other reasons, your petitioners pray that Congress will establish its sovereignty over said territory.

Your petitioners would further represent, that the country south of the Columbia river, and north of the Mexican line, and extending from the Pacific ocean one hundred and twenty miles into the interior, is of unequalled beauty and fertility. Its mountains, covered with perpetual snow, pouring into the prairies around their bases transparent streams of the purest water; the white and black oak, pine, cedar and fir forests that divide the prairies into sections convenient for farming purposes; the rich mines of coal in its hills; the salt springs in its valleys; its quarries of limestone, standstone, chalk and marble; the salmon of its rivers, and the various blessings of the delightful and healthy climate, are known to us, and impress your petitioners with the belief that this is one of the most favored portions of the globe.

Indeed the deserts of the interior have their wealth of pasturage; and their lakes, evaporating in summer, leave in their basins hundreds of bushels of the purest soda. Many other circumstances could be named, showing the importance of the territory in a national, commercial and agricultural point of view. And although your petitioners would not undervalue considerations of this kind, yet they beg leave especially to call the attention of Congress to their own condition as an infant colony, without military force or civil institutions to protect their lives and property and children, sanctuaries and tombs, from the hands of uncivilized and merciless savages around them. We respectfully ask for the civil institutions of the American Republic. We pray for the high privilege of American citizenship; the peaceful enjoyment of life; the right of acquiring, possessing and using property; and the universal, unrestrained pursuit of rational happiness. And for this your petitioners will ever pray.

DAVID LESLIE (and others).

(Senate document, Twenty-sixth Congress, first session. No. 514.)

Inasmuch as the population of Oregon including children did not exceed two hundred at this time, the prayer of the petitioners, it need hardly be said, was not granted. But it must not be supposed that the document was therefore without effect. It did its part toward opening the eyes of the people of the east and of congress to the importance and value of Oregon and toward directing public attention to the domain west of the Rocky mountains.

Notwithstanding the paucity of the white people of Oregon, the various motives which impelled them thither had divided them into four classes, the Hudson's Bay Company, the Catholic clergy and their following, the Methodist missions and the settlers. The Catholics and the Company were practically a unit politically. The settlers favored the missions only in so far as they served the purpose of helping to settle the country, caring little

9

about their religious influence and opposing their ambitions.

The would-be organizers of a government found their opportunity in the conditions presented by the death of Ewing Young. This audacious pioneer left considerable property and no legal representatives, and the question was what should be done with his belongings. Had he been a Hudson's Bay man or a Catholic, the company or the church would have taken care of the property. Had he been a missionary his coadjutors might have administered, but being a plain American citizen there was no functionary possessed of even a colorable right to exercise jurisdiction over his estate. In the face of this emergency, the occasion of Young's funeral, which occurred February 17th, was seized upon for attempting the organization of some kind of a government. At an impromptu meeting it was decided that a committee should perform the legislative functions and that the other officers of the new government should be a governor, a supreme judge with probate jurisdiction, three justices of the peace, three constables, three road commissioners, an attorney general, a clerk of the court and public recorder, a treasurer and two overseers of the poor. Nominations were made for all these offices and the meeting adjourned until next day, when, it was hoped, a large representation of the citizens of the valley would assemble at the mission house.

The time specified saw the various factions in full force at the place of meeting. A legislative committee was appointed as follows: Revs. F. N. Blanchet, Jason Lee, Gustavus Hines and Josiah L. Parish, also Messrs. D. Donpierre, M. Charlevo, Robert Moore, E. Lucier and William Johnson. No governor was chosen; the Methodists secured the judgeship and the Catholics the clerk and recorder. Had the friends of the organization been more fortunate in their choice of a chairman of the legislative committee the result of the movement might have been different, but Rev. Blanchet never called a meeting of his committee and the people who assembled on June 1st to hear and vote upon proposed laws found their congregating had been in vain. Blanchet resigned; Dr. Bailey was chosen to fill the vacancy and the meeting adjourned until October. First, however, it ordered the committee to confer with Commodore Wilkes of the American squadron and John McLoughlin, chief factor of the Hudson's Bay Company, with regard to forming a constitution and code of laws. Wilkes considered it unnecessary and impolitic to organize a government at that time, giving as his reasons:

"First—On account of their want of right, as those wishing for laws were, in fact, a small minority of the settlers.

"Second—That these were not yet necessary even by their own account.

"Third—That any laws they might establish would be a poor substitute for the moral code they all now followed, and that evildoers would not be disposed to settle near a community entirely opposed to their practices.

"Fourth—The great difficulty they would have in enforcing any laws, and defining the limits over which they had control, and the discord this might occasion in their small community.

"Fifth—They not being the majority, and the larger portion of the population Catholics, the latter would elect officers of their party, and they would thus place themselves entirely under the control of others.

"Sixth—The unfavorable impressions it would produce at home, from the belief that the missionaries had admitted that in a community brought together by themselves they had not enough of moral force to control it and prevent crime, and therefore must have recourse to a criminal code."

The friends of the movement could not deny the cogency of this reasoning, and, it appears, concluded to let the matter drop. The

October meeting was never held and thus the first attempt at forming a government ended. However, the judge elected made a satisfactory disposition of the Young estate.

But the question of forming an independent or provisional government continued to agitate the public mind. During the winter of 1842-3 a lyceum was organized at Willamette Falls, now Oregon City, at which the propriety of taking steps in that direction was warmly debated. On one evening the subject for discussion was "Resolved, That it is expedient for the settlers on this coast to establish an independent government." McLoughlin favored the resolution and it carried. Mr. Abernethy, defeated in this debate, skillfully saved the day by introducing as the topic of the next discussion, "Resolved, That if the United States extends its jurisdiction over this country within four years, it will not be expedient to form an independent government." This resolution was also carried after a spirited discussion, destroying the effect of the first resolution.

Meanwhile the settlers in the vicinity of the Oregon Institute were skillfully working out a plan whereby a provisional government might be formed. They knew the sentiment of their confreres at the Falls, the result of the deliberations at that place having been reported to them by Mr. Le Breton; they knew also that their designs would meet with opposition from both the Hudson's Bay Company and the mission people. The problem to be solved was how to accomplish their ends without stirring up an opposition which would overwhelm them at the very outset. Their solution of this problem is a lasting testimony to their astuteness and finesse.

As a result of the formation of the Willamette Cattle Company and its success in importing stock from California, almost every settler was the owner of at least a few head, and, of course, the Hudson's Bay Company and the missions also had their herds. The fact that wolves, bears and panthers were destructive to the cattle of all alike furnished one bond of common interest uniting the diverse population of Oregon, and this circumstance furnished the conspirators their opportunity. Their idea was that having got an object before the people upon which all could unite, they might advance from the ostensible object, protection for domestic animals, to the more important, though hidden, object, "preservation both for property and person." The "wolf meeting," as it is called' convened on the 2d of February and was fully attended. It was feared that Dr. I. L. Babcock, the chairman, might suspect the main object, but in this instance he was even less astute than some others. The utmost harmony prevailed. It was moved that a committee of six should be appointed by the chair to devise a plan and report at a future meeting, to' convene, it was decided, on the first Monday in March next, at 10 o'clock A. M.

After the meeting pursuant to adjournment had completed its business by organizing a campaign against wolves, bears and panthers, and adopting rules and regulations for the government of all in their united warfare upon pests, one gentleman arose and addressed the assembly, complimenting it upon the justice and propriety of the action taken for the protection of domestic animals, but "How is it, fellow citizens," said he, "with you and me and our children and wives? Have we any organization upon which we can rely for mutual protection? Is there any power or influence in the country sufficient to protect us and all we hold dear on earth from the worse than wild beasts that threaten and occasionally destroy our cattle? Who in our midst is authorized at this moment to call us together to protect our own and the lives of our families? True, the alarm may be given, as in a recent case, and we may run who feel alarmed, and shoot off our guns, while our enemy may be robbing our property, ravishing our wives and burning the houses over our defenceless fam-

ilies. Common sense, prudence and justice to ourselves demand that we act consistent with the principles we have commenced. We have mutually and unitedly agreed to defend and protect our cattle and domestic animals; now, fellow citizens, I submit and move the adoption of the two following resolutions, that we may have protection for our persons and lives, as well as our cattle and herds.

" 'Resolved, That a committee be appointed to take into consideration the propriety of taking measures for the civil and military protection of this colony.

" 'Resolved, That said committee consist of twelve persons.' "

If an oratorical effort is to be judged by the effect produced upon the audience, this one deserves a place among the world's masterpieces. The resolutions carried unanimously. The committee appointed consisted of I. L. Babcock, Elijah White, James A. O'Neil, Robert Shortess, Robert Newell, Etienne Lucier, Joseph Gervais, Thomas Hubbard, C. McRoy, W. H. Gray, Sidney Smith and George Gay. Its first meeting was held before a month had elapsed, the place being Willamette Falls. Jason Lee and George Abernethy appeared and argued vehemently against the movement as premature. When the office of governor was stricken from the list the committee unanimously decided to call another meeting on the ensuing 2d of May. W. H. Gray, in his history of Oregon, describes this decisive occasion with such graphic power that it would be a wrong to the reader not to give it in his own language. He says:

"The 2d of May, the day fixed by the committee of twelve to organize a settlers' government, was close at hand. The Indians had all learned that the 'Bostons' were going to have a big meeting, and they also knew that the English and French were going to meet with them to oppose what the 'Bostons' were going to do. The Hudson's Bay Company had drilled and trained their voters for the oc casion, under the Rev. F. N. Blanchet and his priests, and they were promptly on the ground in an open field near a small house, and, to the amusement of every American present, trained to vote 'No' to every motion put; no matter if to carry their point they should have voted 'Yes' it was 'No.' Le Breton had informed the committee, and the Americans generally, that this would be the course pursued, according to instructions, hence our motions were made to test their knowledge of what they were doing, and we found just what we expected was the case. The priest was not prepared for our manner of meeting them, and, as the record shows, 'considerable confusion was existing in consequence.' By this time we had counted votes. Says Le Breton, 'We can risk it; let us divide and count.' 'I second the motion,' says Gray. 'Who's for a divide?' sang out old Joe Meek, as he stepped out; 'all for the report of the committee and an organization, follow me.' This was so sudden and unexpected that the priest and his voters did not know what to do, but every American was soon in line. Le Breton and Gray passed the line and counted fifty-two Americans and but fifty French and Hudson's Bay men. They announced the count—'fifty-two for, and fifty against.' 'Three cheers for our side!' sang out old Joe Meek. Not one of those old veteran mountain voices was lacking in that shout for *liberty*. They were given with a will, and in a few seconds the chairman, Judge I. L. Babcock, called the meeting to order, when the priest and his band slunk away into the corners of the fences, and in a short time mounted their horses and left."

After the withdrawal of the opponents of this measure, the meeting became harmonious, of course. Its minutes show that A. E. Wilson was chosen supreme judge; G. W. Le Breton, clerk of the court and recorder; J. L. Meek, sheriff; W. H. Willson, treasurer; Messrs. Hill, Shortess, Newell, Beers, Hubbard, Gray,

O'Neil, Moore and Dougherty, legislative committee; and that constables, a major and captains were also chosen. The salary of the legislative committee was fixed at $1.25 per day, and it was instructed to prepare a code of laws to be submitted to the people at Champoeg on the 5th day of July.

On the day preceding this date, the anniversary of America's birth was duly celebrated, Rev. Gustavus Hines delivering the oration. Quite a number who had opposed organization at the previous meeting were present on the 5th and announced their determination to acquiesce in the acts of the majority and yield obedience to any government which might be formed, but representatives of the Hudson's Bay Company even went so far in their opposition as to address a letter to the leaders of the movement asserting their ability to defend both themselves and their political rights.

A review of the "organic laws" adopted at this meeting would be interesting, but such is beyond the scope of our volume. Suffice it to say that they were so liberal and just, so complete and comprehensive that it has been a source of surprise to students ever since that untrained mountaineers and settlers, without experience in legislative halls, could conceive a system so well adapted to the needs and conditions of the country. The preamble runs: "We, the people of Oregon Territory, for purposes of mutual protection, and to secure peace and prosperity among ourselves, agree to adopt the following laws and regulations, until such time as the United States of America extend their jurisdiction over us." The two weaknesses, which were soonest felt, were the result of the opposition to the creation of the office of governor and to the levying of taxes. The former difficulty was overcome by substituting, in 1844, a gubernatorial executive for the triumvirate which had theretofore discharged the executive functions, and the latter by raising the necessary funds by popular subscription. In 1844 also a legislature was substituted for the legislative committee.

Inasmuch as the first election resulted favorably to some who owed allegiance to the British government as well as to others who were citizens of the United States, the oath of office was indited as follows: "I do solemnly swear that I will support the organic laws of the provisional government of Oregon, so far as the said organic laws are consistent with my duties as a citizen of the United States, or a subject of Great Britain, and faithfully demean myself in office. So help me God."

Notwithstanding the opposition to the provisional government, the diverse peoples over whom it exercised authority, and the weaknesses in it resulting from the spirit of compromise of its authors, it continued to exist and discharge all the necessary functions of sovereignty until, on August 14, 1848, in answer to the numerous memorials and petitions and the urgent appeals of Messrs. Thornton and Meek, Congress at last decided to give to Oregon a territorial form of government with all the rights and privileges usually accorded to territories of the United States. Joseph Lane, of Indiana, whose subsequent career presents so many brilliant and so many sad chapters, was appointed territorial governor.

The limits and province of our work preclude further narration of the history of Oregon in general. By the act of March 3, 1853, the country north of the Columbia was organized into a separate territory, bearing the name of the great father of his country. At later dates the area of Oregon was further curtailed by the formation of Montana and Idaho territories, but in 1859, notwithstanding this curtailment, the country had so far advanced in population and general development as to gain admission to the Union.

The provisional system had originally divided the territory governed by its provisions into three districts. The development and settlement of the country necessitated an increase in the number from time to time and soon the name county was substituted for district. When eastern Oregon became sufficiently populous to gain recognition in the councils of the state it was organized into Wasco county, with its seat of local government at The Dalles. The discovery of gold in eastern Oregon and Idaho soon populated the wilderness to such an extent that the inconvenience of this ponderous and unwieldy empire county began to be oppressive, and in 1862 two new counties, Umatilla and Baker, were organized. With the further history and development of one of these two older children of Wasco, the mother of eastern Oregon counties, our work will concern itself in future chapters.

BAKER COUNTY

A MINING SCENE.

PINE VALLEY.

HISTORY OF BAKER COUNTY.

CHAPTER I.

SETTLEMENT TO 1863.

When we consider the various types and shades of character to be found among men, the diverse motives which impel them to action and the fact that each is practically free to think and do as he pleases to pursue happiness of the kind which most appeals to his fancy and in a way of his own choosing, it seems almost impossible that there should be such a thinig as a philosophy of history. A superficial survey of the past annals of the race reveals a vast seething ocean of human life, lashed into fury by the passions of the hour, the waves apparently receding always as far as they advance. King contends with king, nation with nation, and principle with principle. Men are elevated to the highest honors in the gift of nations only to be cast down into the lowest depths of degradation and disgrace. Today the masses shout "down with royalty" and to-morrow they crown a new king with enthusiastic bursts of applause and obsequious assurances of their loyalty and support. But a' more extended study of conditions reveals the existence of method in all this seeming madness, and the flight of centuries discloses the fact that of chaos, cosmos is being evolved, and that this apparent confusion is working out for each race and nation its own "manifest destiny." The truth is that while individuals differ materially in thought and purposes, so much so that a science of human nature never has been and never can be developed, yet there are certain passions which move all men alike, certain basic principles embedded in the constitution of the race, which, when appealed to, cause simultaneous movements to take place among large numbers and shape the current of history.

As the love of personal and religious liberty populated New England, and the aristocratic proclivities of the southern people inclined them to favor the institution of slavery, so the acquisitiveness inherent in humanity impelled it across the wide prairies and through the fastnesses of the Rocky mountains until it poured its all subduing tide upon the shores of the boundless Pacific. The desire of wealth may be considered the dominating factor in the development of the west and one particular manifestation of this passion, the love of gold, has contributed immensely to the subjugation of its natural resources. The presence of this metal in any locality has meant the speedy settlement and development of that locality and when once gold has been discovered no matter where, no danger from aboriginal inhabitants, no remoteness from a base of supplies, and no toils and hardships of the journey could keep the doughty pioneer from repairing thither, bringing with him the elements of civilization and progress.

The trail of the westward moving army of civilization passed through Powder river valley, but notwithstanding the beauty of the Blue mountains and the abundance of ever green timber upon their sides, and crests, there was nothing here of sufficient interest to stay the weary emigrant, obedient as he was to the impulse which was bidding him follow the star of empire as far toward the occident as possible. The agricultural possibilities of these sagebrush and bunchgrass plains were unknown and unsuspected; the presence of the red men would prove a constant menace to the settler and the distance from a base of supplies was an obstacle not easily overcome, even if a sufficient inducement for settlement were known to exist. When, however, gold was discovered in this section, these obstacles were soon shown to be not insurmountable and the seeds of future development at once began to be planted.

The chain of events leading to the discovery of gold in eastern Oregon reaches back to the immigration of 1845, mention of which has been made previously. No notice, however, was taken in former chapters of a very strange occurrence connected with that expedition, an occurrence which is to form the first link in the concatenation of causes, the ultimate effect of which was the settlement of Baker county. Identified with the Methodist Mission in the Willamette valley was one Dr. Elijah White, whose character has been bitterly attacked by some writers, and who certainly seems to have been a self-seeking, ambitious and not overly scrupulous man. His connection with the mission was cut short on this account, but he figured in Oregon affairs afterward as sub-Indian agent and in other capacities. In 1845 he set out for Washington, D. C., his purpose being, as has been supposed, to get himself appointed governor of Oregon, should it be organized into a territory according to the general expectation.

What his connection with the events we are about to narrate may have been is not conclusively established, but that he was mainly responsible for the sufferings endured by a portion of the immigration of 1845 is generally believed. When not far from Fort Boise he met a company of immigrants. Bancroft says there can be but little doubt of his having induced about two hundred of these families to leave the established road down Snake river, taking instead an abandoned trail up the Malheur. His idea probably was that they would be almost certain to find a pass through the Cascades and that eventually the credit of having made a most important discovery would be given to him.

It appears that shortly before he left Oregon City, some one had sent word east that a new and better route had been discovered over the Cascades to the Willamette, and if fortune should favor Dr. White, and the expedition he had directed should discover a pass the honor would most surely be his. "It cannot be reasonably supposed," says Mr. Hiatt in his Thirty-One Years in Baker County, "that he would have urged a company of immigrants to try a new and unknown route if he had anticipated the suffering which they were doomed to endure. Doubtless he had perfect faith in the feasibility of the enterprise, for at that time there was nothing known of the character of all that country lying between Snake river and the Cascade mountains, and it would be but reasonable to suppose that the Malheur and Burnt rivers had their source in the Cascade mountains and, judging from the size of those streams, the distance to the summit could not be so very great. The existence of the lake basin and desert plains between the heads of those streams and the Cascade mountains was not then known. But whatever may have been White's motives, and whether or not he did induce a company to leave the emigrant road and follow the trail up the Malheur river, certain it is that they did try that route with Stephen H. L. Meek for a guide. He was a brother of Joe Meek, who, it has been erroneously stated, induced the company to make the unfortunate attempt, himself acting as guide."

What Stephen Meek's private reasons might be for undertaking to lead a party through a country utterly unknown to himself will probably always remain one of the unsolved problems in Oregon history. It is likely that he had heard enough of the country from trappers and adventurers to create in his mind a sanguine faith in his ability to successfully accomplish what he undertook. It is certain that he had no designs to do the emigrants harm, for he went with them, sharing all their hardships and in every way acting the part of a true and honorable man. While the company were following the banks of the Malheur river all went well, but as soon as they entered the alkali lake region they began to murmur against their guide, who showed signs of knowing little more about the country than did the people themselves. Their sufferings became intense, and some of them died from having drunk of the poisonous alkali water. As they proceeded their discontent heightened into anger and they began to make threats against the life of their guide. They turned into the dry country between the Des Chutes and John Day rivers and here their patience was sorely tried. Little or no water was to be had. Their resentment against Meek became so bitter that it was considered unsafe for him to longer remain with them and he acted upon the advice of some of the more moderate members of the party and separated from the expedition. His friends went on in advance of the main body to explore the way, and by keeping in touch with them he reached in safety a suitable place for crossing the Des Chutes river. He thought that he there might await the arrival of the train, inasmuch as the company had fared much better for a few days past, having succeeded in obtaining water by dropping a bucket at the end of a rope two hundred feet long, down the precipitous canyon side and into the Des Chutes. But when the foremost of the advancing column came up, he was informed that one man had vowed to shoot him on sight, in revenge for the death of two members of his family.

Meek therefore pushed on down the river and across it, eventually reaching The Dalles. Upon his arrival there he showed a willingness to atone for whatever wrong he may have committed by sending a man with pack animals loaded with provisions to the relief of the families, who in due time reached that town without further casualties.

The incident of this trying adventure which in later years directly affected our section of the country is yet to be related. While somewhere near the head waters of the Malheur river, members of the expedition discovered nuggets of a curious yellow metal, undoubtedly gold, but not being experienced in mining and having never seen the precious mineral in its natural state, no thought of the value of the discovery entered their heads. A probably correct account of this discovery was given by S. D. Clarke of Salem, in the Portland Daily Bee, and quoted by Bancroft as follows:

"The first gold discovery in Oregon made by an American was near the head of the Malheur river, on a small creek divided from the Malheur by a ridge. This stream ran southwest and was supposed to be a branch of the Malheur, an error that caused much trouble and disappointment to prospectors eight or ten years later. Daniel Herron, a cousin of W. J. Herron, of Salem, was looking for lost cattle while the company were in camp here, and picked up a piece of shining metal on the rocky bed of the creek and carried it to camp as a curiosity. No one. could tell what the metal was, and no one thought of its being gold. Another nugget was found and brought to Mr. Martin's wagon, who tested it by hammering it out on his wagon tire, but not being able to tell its nature, it was thrown into the tool chest and forgotten and ultimately lost. After the gold discovery in California, these incidents were remembered, and many parties went in search of the spot where the emigrants said this gold was found, but were misled by being told it was on a tributary of the Malheur."

However true or false this story may be, its narration had the effect of inducing several expeditions in search of the "Blue Bucket" diggings, as they were called on acount of the statement that a blue bucket had been left near the site of the discovery, or some say because such a vessel had been filled with nuggets. The most important of these expeditions set out from Portland in August, 1861. Its history is strangely analogous to that of the emigrant party of 1845. It appears that a man named Adams was one day relating the story of the lost diggings on the streets of Portland when some California miners who were temporarily in that city en route to the Oro Fino mines, chanced to join the company of listeners. Being somewhat undecided as to the advisabilty of going on to Oro Fino owing to discouraging reports from that region, these adventurous men were in the proper frame of mind for any new and promising undertaking, and curiosity soon gave place to intense interest. They eagerly questioned Mr. Adams as to his knowledge of the locality, and were informed that he had seen the gulch in which the gold had been found, that he could find it again without difficulty and that he was more than willing, if a company could be formed sufficiently large to insure safety against possibly hostile Indians, to guide such company to the land where fortunes could be picked up on the surface of the

ground. As the statements of Adams were corroborated by three young men who also claimed to have been present at the place in 1845, and to have seen the diggings, they readily gained credence, and soon a company of men, including the four Californians, were equipped for the expeditions. With Adams for guide, they set out through the Cascades by the Barlow route and reached the Des Chutes at the point where it was eventually crossed by The Dalles and Canyon City wagon road, the same point at which the emigrants effected a crossing in 1845. Proceeding thence to Crooked river, a tributary of the Des Chutes, they ascended that stream to its head waters. Their further progress led them into a dry region, and soon they began to suffer for water as had the company of emigrants some sixteen years before. History repeated itself. Suspicions of the veracity of their guide, whose knowledge of the country was evidently not very extensive, were soon aroused. When threatened in an angry manner, the three young men who had confirmed Adams's story in Portland weakened, admitting that they had prevaricated and that they were not with Adams in 1845 and had never seen the so-called Blue Bucket diggings. Adams, however, still persisted in asserting that his story was true and that he could lead the party to the spot where gold had been found. Notwithstanding the shock which their faith in Adams had received, the company continued to follow him until the region of poisonous alkali water was again entered by a party of white men. Here the men refused to follow their guide further and turning to the northward, proceeded to the banks of the Malheur and thence toward the head waters of the Burnt river.

Although they had varied from the course in which Adams would have led them, they still insisted upon his finding the diggings, threatening him with death in case of failure.

Indeed more than once a pistol had been drawn and it seemed that his last hour had come. Things assumed such a serious aspect that once Mr. Adams endeavored to effect his escape, but failing in this he was given one more day in which to find the diggings. Many of the men had left growing crops in the Willamette valley, feeling certain from the positive assertions of Adams that they would be more than recompensed for any pecuniary loss they might sustain in consequence. Now they had not only allowed their crops to go to waste, but had endured incredible hardships and personal suffering, and all apparently for nothing. However, a considerable portion of the party, including the Californians, had no such aggravated personal motives for hostility, and being perhaps better used to the disappointments of mining life, they did not share the extremely bitter feeling which animated the majority. When the evening of the day of grace arrived, with the diggings yet undiscovered, the extremists were strongly in favor of the immediate execution of Adams, but the minority succeeded in gaining him a respite till morning, though he was guarded the entire night. About ten o'clock the next day, it was decided to put him upon his trial. A jury was selected and all the outward forms in vogue in legally constituted tribunals were observed, except that naturally much incompetent testimony was admitted. After a trial of a day's duration, the case was given to the jury in the evening. Next morning the jurors announced their verdict to be that the defendant was guilty and that he should be deprived of all his property, including arms, ammunition, provision, etc., in fact everything but the clothing he had on, and that in this impoverished condition he should separate himself from the rest of the company, each member of which should be privileged to shoot the culprit should he be discovered anywhere in sight. He was also humiliated by being required to sign a confession of perjury.

It may be that some members of the jury favored this procedure rather than a sentence to immediate death, in the hope that they might later devise a plan by which the guide's life might be saved. At any rate there were those in the company who did not purpose to allow Adams to perish in such a barbarous and inhuman manner. They planned to supply the wants of the condemned, keeping him concealed from the majority of their comrades until a point was reached at which the party had agreed to divide, the major portion returning via the route over which they had come and the minority striking out in a northeasterly direction to the old emigrant road, over which they purposed to return to Portland. The plan worked and Adams's life was saved.

What the true explanation of this man's conduct may be is another unsolved problem of Oregon history. Hiatt suggests that he may have heard of the Blue Bucket diggings so many times that the imaginary scene became so vivid as to cause belief that it was an actual experience. Such a supposition seems hardly consistent with sanity, but then Adams may have been slightly deranged. It is likely that he had so much faith in his ability to find the diggings that he overstated the facts for the purpose of inspiring like faith in the minds of others and thus insuring the formation of a company and the equipping of the expedition. To this view it may be objected that if Adams was a member of the emigration of 1845 he ought to have profited by Meek's experience. On the other hand it is a well known fact that not all men are wise enough to avoid the pitfalls into which others may have fallen to their knowledge.

With the party which returned by the route over which they had made the outward journey

we have here no further concern. The other
party prospected along their route, finding colors on China creek and elsewhere, but discovering no pay dirt until on the evening of October 23, 1861, in the gulch which has ever
since borne his name, Henry Griffin sank a
hole about three feet deep, striking bedrock
and a good prospect. Twenty-two more
claims were staked off, each of one hundred
feet, and the choice among these was determined by lot. Elk creek was not far distant
from the head of the gulch and a site for a
ditch tapping it was at once surveyed out, the
first requisite, of course, being water wherewith to work the claims. This survey completed, the party broke up camp and set out
for Walla Walla. From that point the main
company proceeded on to the Willamette, but
Griffin, Stafford, Littlefield and Schriver returned with provisions, intending to spend the
winter at the mines. November found the
four indomitable pioneers last mentioned again
encamped on Griffin's gulch, where they built
a cabin and prepared to pass the winter. It
will be remembered that this first winter spent
by white men in Baker county was one of considerable severity, as though the elements
themselves were determined to prove the metal
of the advance agents of civilization, jealous
that none unworthy should be allowed to remain. The four miners were not unworthy.
No sooner had they completed their cabin than
snow fell to a depth of three feet, but early
in the following month a five days' rain converted all this snow, as well as that accumulated in the mountains, into floods of water. The
result was that all of Powder river valley became a vast, shallow lake.

No sooner had the snow disappeared than
the miners began operations upon their claims.
So plentiful was the water, however, that the
necessity of gum-boots became painfully apparent and the men perceived that another trip
to Walla Walla must be made. Accordingly,
about the middle of December two of them,

Littlefield and Schriver, set out upon this arduous journey, taking with them more than one
hundred dollars' worth of gold dust. A very
interesting and, to the present generation,
strange incident of this expedition took place
in Ladd canyon, as it is now called, on the edge
of Grande Ronde valley. One night Mr. Littlefield awoke from slumber to find facing him
at no great distance what afterwards proved to
be a large gray wolf. Awaking his companion
and concomitantly drawing his revolver, he
attempted to shoot the intruder but the powder had become damp and the gun missed fire.
Schriver then tried with the same result for
a while, but eventually he succeeded in discharging his weapon. The animal was hit.
He gave vent to his feelings in howls of pain
and forthwith a chorus of howls rose on all
sides. The unwounded members of the pack
fell upon their stricken companion and devoured him ravenously. The men built a
fire for protection, beside which they kept vigil
until morning, when the wolves skulked away.

It must have given our adventurers great
pleasure to find at the farther side of the
Grande Ronde valley and near the site of the
present Island City, a considerable settlement
of white persons. With these they spent
Christmas day and as Mr. Hiatt informs us,
"witnessed one of those freaks in the affairs
of life which are to be seen only in new and
unorganized settlements. A married couple
had learned, after thirty or forty years' experience, that they could not live together agreeably, but found it equally difficult to separate
on account of a disagreement about the division of their property. For the purpose of
settling the affair and preventing more serious
trouble which it seemed probable might follow,
the settlers organized a court and took the case
up and divorced them, and divided the property betwixt them, making a settlement that
answered all purposes as well as if it had been
done legally."

Having reached Walla Walla, disposed of

their gold dust and purchased their rubber boots and other supplies, Messrs Littlefield and Schriver set out upon the return journey. They had with them one pack animal. Upon the Blue mountains they found the snow ·so deep that their horse could get, as they supposed, nothing to eat, but they resolved to give him a fair chance for his life, so unpacked him and turned him loose, taking the load upon their own shoulders. Thus relieved, the horse managed to subsist upon twigs and the bark of trees. He followed them all the way across the mountains, and was doubtless pressed into service again on reaching the lower levels. Before January was over, they were again with their companions in Griffin's gulch. The snow fall during the winter, according to measurements made by one of the miners, aggregated fourteen feet.

The horses belonging to the company were turned out upon Powder river valley to subsist by pawing for grass and to shelter themselves from storms as best they could. Most of them fell victims to the rapacious packs of wolves which that winter infested the valley. The mode of attack of these ravenous animals was to skulk around until they found a horse separated from the rest of the band, then to fall upon him enmasse. The five horses which did survive until spring owed their lives to intelligent co-operation. When any one of their number was attacked all would quickly assemble together and turning their flanks toward a common center, present a solid front in every direction, fighting off the common enemy with their fore feet. Mr. Hiatt tells us that it was very seldom a gray wolf was seen after the first winter, though some three or four years later a pack was known to cross Powder river above Auburn.

In April, 1862, two of the miners, while prospecting at a point commanding a view of the Powder river valley, were greatly surprised and startled to see a large band of horses near the edge of the valley. Had the owners of this band been hostile Indians, as was at first supposed, the situation of the miners would have been indeed precarious, but on reconnoitering a little, they found that the party consisted of about fifty white men. The coming of these to the valley was a result of a strange trait in the character of the early western people and indeed in human nature generally, leading some to frabricate wild, romantic tales upon a relatively unimportant basis of facts and others to give at least sufficient credence to such tales to incite them to action. It appears that the gold dust taken by Messrs. Littlefield and Schriver to Walla Walla was purchased by Mr. Humason of The Dalles and sent by him to Portland, where it was placed on exhibition in a show case. It remained as a proof of all the tales that might be spun by the romancer, much the same kind of proof, to be sure, as that offered by Mark Twain in support of his story about a notorious horse which bucked so hard he threw the saddle sixty feet in the air. "If you don't believe it," says the famous humorist, "I will show you the saddle."

The hardy pioneers of Griffin's gulch must have been inspired with a new sense of their importance when they learned that notwithstanding the absorbing interest centering in the great Civil war, their humble efforts were attracting so much and such wide-spread attention. One would think also that the newcomers who had traveled so many miles expecting to find a spot where men filled gum boots with nuggets and realized as high as $150 per pan of dirt would suffer a corresponding depression of spirits when they learned the real truth, but if so they bore their disappointment philosophically. They immediately set out in search of prospects and before many days made discoveries in numerous gulches and creek beds in the vicinity.

The party of men whose work we have just been describing were not many days in advance of another party. However, the membership

of the second expedition was made up mostly
of stuff less stern.   When this company were
well on their way, they met a number of persons who informed them that the reports about
the mines were utterly without foundation, as-
cribing them to hirelings of the Oregon Steam
Navigation Company, who, they said, had been
employed to spend the winter on Powder river
and initiate stories calculated to cause a rush.
These statements induced the major portion to
return to their homes breathing forth impre-
cations upon innocent heads of the company
and its supposed accomplices in the wrong.
Four or five who continued their journey
reached Griffin's gulch in safety, saw for themselves the evidences that gold had been found
and proceeded to hunt claims of their own.
During the entire summer following men
roamed over this section of the country in all
directions, exploring every river and creek and
locating claims wherever good prospects could
be found.   Traveling parties came from Nevada, California and other western states,
many of them en route to the celebrated Salmon river mines, determined to try their fortunes in this region.   Among the members of
these parties some have ever since remained,
assisting in the establishing and upbuilding of
civil institutions and the development of the
country's resources.

Hardin Estes and Fred Dill were leading
members of a Nevada expedition numbering
about twenty which has always been known as
the White Horse company, from the color of
the steeds most of them brought.   These men
and their companions might have been lost to
Baker and Grant counties were it not for the
high water of the spring of 1862, which for
a time prevented their crossing Powder river
and the valley through which it flows.   While
reconnoitering for a place to cross near the
mouth of North Powder they were informed
of the impossibility of their so doing by John
Hibbard, who was on his way to Walla Walla.
They returned some distance and camped in a

canyon, but Mr. Estes went still further up the
river, discovering a mining camp on its opposite side and also a place at the mouth of Blue
canyon where a bridge might be constructed.
Bringing the remainder of the company to this
site he and his companions built a rude bridge
of trees and brush covered with mud, the first
bridge that ever spanned the crystal waters of
Powder river.   About half of the company remained in this vicinity and the other half went
to the John Day mines; Mr. Estes eventually
settled in Washington gulch, taking on the
16th day of June, 1862, the first land claim
ever filed upon in the Powder river valley.

A little later in the season than the White
Horse company came John B. Bowen and some
forty-eight others from California, likewise
enroute to the celebrated Salmon river mines.
While reconnoitering for a way across the river
and valley they struck the Estes trail, which of
course led them to the bridge, but upon arriving there they found a man in charge who
demanded a dollar a horse toll for crossing.
The company protested but finally paid the
exorbitant charge and went on to the mines,
where they met a man from the Salmon river
country.   By his reports they were discouraged from going on, so the population of the
Powder river district was further augmented.
When Mr. Estes learned that another had tak-
en possession of his bridge, he repaired to the
spot and sold the man the bridge, stipulating,
however, that the toll should forthwith be reduced to fifty cents per head for horses.

It must not be supposed that the companies above mentioned constituted the entire immigration into the country during the spring
and summer of 1862.   On the contrary there
were numerous other arrivals from California,
Nevada and the Willamette valley, many of
whom became permanent residents and leading
citizens of Baker county.   Nor were these intrepid pioneers all men.   Mrs. Love had the
honor of having been the first lady to enter the
district, but she was not to be long without

the companionship of her own sex, for Mrs. Lovell, Mrs. and Miss Rackerby and others came almost immediately afterwards.

The development of an agricultural and stock-raising section is necessarily slow, but owing to the peculiar fascination and excitement attending mining operations, localities where gold is found are usually settled with a rush. The population, however, is less stable and a new excitement in some other section is liable to cause the camp to be totally or partially depopulated as speedily as it had been settled. Although the population of this mining district in the fall and winter of 1861 consisted of just four white men, the spring of 1862 brought a numerous and varied population, and as early as May or June the propriety of founding a town began to be canvassed. This agitation crystalized into a definite movement on the thirteenth of the latter month, when, at a meeting called by William H. Packwood and others, it was decided to lay out a town. Why they named this town Auburn the writer does not know, but in the light of its subsequent history one might almost infer that its founders had some prophetic intuition of the time when like the "sweet Auburn" of the poet, it should be a "deserted village." June 14th saw a street laid out from Freezeout gulch to Blue canyon, on each side of which lots were quickly taken. Cabins sprang up like mushrooms and the town speedily assumed the aspect familiar to all who have ever visited primitive western mining camps.

Of course the methods in vogue among the pioneer placer mines of Baker county were necessarily of the crudest character at first. There is something, however, so exciting and energizing about the search for gold that obstacles which would deter for an indefinite period a less progressive people are speedily overcome by the mining classes. Patient in his search for a good prospect, reckless of danger and hardship when they lie in his uncertain

10

pathway to sudden wealth, the miner naturally is not lacking in the energy to push development work, when sure that he has a good thing. Had Griffin's gulch been an agricultural district and settled by an agricultural people, requiring water for irrigation purposes, the probabilities are that the farmers would have struggled along for years before arrangements could be perfected and a ditch secured. But since the water was to be used for washing out the yellow metal, no halting conservatism prevented the immediate construction of the ditch surveyed by Griffin and companions in the winter of 1861 and by the 20th of May, 1862, it was pouring the waters of Elk creek into the sluices of the Griffin's gulch miners.

But during the summer of 1862 it became apparent that much more water must be obtained, if work on the placer mines was to be carried on to any great extent and projects were soon talked of for bringing the water from Powder river into the district. It may not be possible to determine to whom the honor of originating the plan for an extensive ditch rightfully belongs, but there is no doubt that Mr. Packwood was the man who made the first definite move toward putting that plan into operation. He entered into negotiations with A. C. Goodrich, who was a surveyor and possessed an invaluable experience in the construction of ditches, inducing Mr. Goodrich to make the preliminary survey. The report being favorable, Mr. Packwood then called together those who were interested in the enterprise. As a result, a company was at once organized, stock being subscribed the first day as follows: G. W. Abbott, five thousand dollars; Henry Fuller, five thousand dollars; Ira Ward, three thousand dollars; Benjamin Chateau, five hundred dollars, George Berry, five hundred dollars; W. H. Packwood, two thousand five hundred dollars; A. C. Goodrich, one thousand dollars; J. J. Williams, two thousand five hundred dollars, and Isaac Smith, one thousand dollars. · The constitution and by-laws adopted provided among other things that the name of the association should be the Auburn Water Company; that the capital stock should be fifty thousand dollars, consisting of one hundred shares of five hundred dollars each, each share being entitled to one vote; that the officers of the company should consist of a board of three trustees, a secretary, a treasurer, and a superintendent, all of whom should be stockholders, and should be elected annually, and that stock should be forfeited for non-payment of assessments, with reserved privilege to the delinquent of redeeming forfeited stock at any time within sixty days. It was ordered that the ditch should be four feet wide at the bottom, seven at the top and two feet deep. The work was laid off in sections of forty rods each, and an estimate was made of the cost of constructing each separate section. Instead of giving the entire contract to one man, the company awarded the work to several different contractors.

Before the work was completed a proposition was made by a man named Crane to purchase the right, title and interest of the Auburn Water Company and in reply that company agreed to "sell, convey and quit-claim" thirty-six shares in the ditch for "twenty-five per cent. premium upon all the cost of constructing said ditch and upon all expenses incurred therein by said company in the prosecution of and completion of said water ditch as far as may be contracted for at this time." All allowances made or that it might be necessary to make to contractors and others for labor were to be confirmed and complied with by the purchaser, and the water ditch was to be pushed to completion in time to be ready for use early the next spring. .

By January 17, 1863, the Auburn Water Company had expended over twenty-five thousand dollars in the promotion of this enterprise, though its existence had been of only about four and a half months' duration. On that date it assigned all its rights and privileges to the Auburn Canal Company.

The doings of this private corporation have been related somewhat at length because, as Mr. Hiatt points out, the assistance their enterprise was destined to render in the permanent settlement and development of the country was more important than could be guessed by its projectors. · The beneficial effect which this expenditure of money had indirectly upon the business prospects of the community was far more important than the direct benefits accruing to contractors, and their employes. The various interests needed this stimulus to tide them over a trying period, and the water itself was necessary to permit the working of the mines, making it possible for the population of the place to remain. "How many men," says Hiatt, "were inspired with confidence and · stimulated to exertion by the example of the water company cannot be estimated, nor can the number of those be known who were enabled to remain in the country by reason of the work of ditch construction being done at that time. Only a portion of the mining ground in and about Auburn could have been worked, and that portion could have had but a small supply of water for a limited time in the spring and early summer. Without that ditch, Auburn as it was in 1863-4-5-6, would never have been; nine-tenths of the people would have had to seek employment elsewhere; the farmers in the valley who were struggling to make their business a success would not have had the aid of the Auburn market, and that alone would have been no slight loss, for a market for garden vegetables was a matter of prime necessity to many of them.

"In the fall of 1862 thousands of immigrants came to the country and many of them were dependent upon their daily labor for subsistence. But very few of them could have found employment, had it not been for the opportunity offered by the water company and by individuals who were led to build houses and engage in business through hopes for the future which the company's enterprise had inspired. The number of people in and about, Auburn in the fall and forepart of the winter is estimated at five to six thousand. Probably not one half of them had supplies for the winter nor the means of obtaining them, and leaving the work of ditch construction out of the count, there could have been no inducement for merchants to bring in the amount of goods which the necessities of the people required. The systematic way in which the company organized for the work, and the energy with which it was prosecuted in the face of all the difficulties in the way are worthy of admiration."

The rapidity with which mining development was pushed in 1862 is truly astonishing, but while the mineral wealth of the locality was the main factor in its population, other industries were not overlooked. The miners must needs have supplies, clothing, tools, etc., opening an opportunity for the merchant, the farmer and the freighter. Roads and bridges had to be constructed to make the importation of necessaries possible and expeditious. Ferries must be built and put in operation and little by little all the complex activities of civilized society must follow in turn. It is a well known fact that however rich a mining region may be, it cannot furnish a claim to every man which will pay from the start, and if the would-be-miner is not possessed of sufficient means to support him while his ditches are being dug and sluices put in, assuming that he has been fortunate enough to strike a claim at all, he must turn temporarily to something furnishing more speedy returns for his labor. It is related of William Baldock, who came to the valley in the fall of 1862, that, noticing the tall bunchgrass in its primitive luxuriance, he conceived the idea that perhaps it might be cut and cured for hay. Going to Auburn he ascertained that a ready market might there be found for all he could bring, so he procured a scythe and snath and proceded with his hay making, handling the mown product with forked sticks for pitchforks. The hay sold for from fifty to sixty dollars per ton, enabling him to support his family and to accumulate before spring four hundred dollars in cash. To Joseph Kenison, whose advent to the valley dates back to July, 1862, belongs the honor of pioneership in agriculture. He it was who plowed the first furrow, planted the first potatoes and corn and sowed the first oats in what is now the limits of Baker county. His experiments in this industry were made early in the spring of 1863. It seemed first that they were destined to end in failure, for early in June a frost occurred seemingly of sufficient severity to destroy all growing vegetables. But time proved that his crop was little injured and that fall he realized nearly four thousand dollars from his forty-acre tract.

Of some of the other men who introduced agriculture into Baker county, that esteemed pioneer and interesting writer, Mr. Hiatt, gives us the following account:

"Mr. Hibbard and family from the Umpqua valley settled at the foot of the mountains on a claim adjoining Mr. Morrison's, and Messrs. Worley, Spillman, Creighbaum and others took claims in the vicinity. Strother Ison took up a claim on Pine creek, where he continued to reside until his death, which occurred in the year 1889. Jerry Shea took up a claim south of Ison's, which he afterwards sold to Hardin Perkins, who has lived upon it ever since. About the same time, James Akers located the claim upon which he still resides (1893). George Ebell settled near the foot of the mountains, where he has made one of the best farms in the valley. Mr. Campbell settled on Powder river, near where Baker City now stands, and resided there until his death in 1889. Thomas McMurren took up a claim near Pocahontas, and other claims were located in different parts of the valley. Express ranch and Miller's ranch on Burnt river were taken in the fall of 1862."

We have spoken of the encouraging effect which the labors of the Auburn Water Company had upon the community in the development of various industries. The benficial influence of its construction continued after the plant passed into the hands of the Auburn Canal Company, which extended the ditch southward beyond Auburn, building above that town a reservoir from which distributing ditches were constructed to the various gulches. The disbursements of the company and its predecessor during the early years of the history of this section, aggregated something like $225,000. One very important service performed by this company was the importation during the spring of 1863 of more than $70,000 worth of provisions, thereby saving the community from actual suffering through want of the necessities of life. Even as it was, provisions were very scarce at that time.

The political history of the county will form the theme of a future chapter, but it is necessary to the current of our narrative that the inception of government in the community be here given. The reader will have guessed that so large an aggregation of people could hardly have gotten together without the presence of some who would not duly respect the tenets of morality and the rights of others, and hence the necessity for law and punishment and prison walls must soon arrive. Indeed a new mining camp is always a center toward which confidence men and thieves and outlaws invariably gravitate and Powder river valley was not without its share. It will be remembered that the great Civil war was in progress at this time, exerting the demoralizing influence attendant upon so much contention and bloodshed, its issues furnishing the themes for disputes too frequently ending in personal en-

counters and tragedies. Neither is it in the American people, accustomed as they are to the organization of government, to fail to rise to the occasion when conditions demand some kind of civil institutions. When the pioneers of 1861 made their way into this valley, it was a part of Wasco county and of course subject to the laws of the state. But the county seat was at The Dalles, two hundred and seventy-five miles distant, making it next to impossible to convict and punish offenders against the law. An example of this was furnished early in June 1862, when a man named Griffin was killed in his tent by his mining partner. The affair was consummated so quietly that, though several persons were near by at the time, no one heard a sound, yet the slayer justified his act on the ground that it was done in self-defense. After some deliberation among the crowd which gathered around the body of the deceased, two of the men offered to deliver the guilty party to the proper authorities at The Dalles. This proposition was accepted and fifty dollars were subscribed to defray the expenses of the journey. Neither the prisoner nor his guards ever reached The Dalles, and it was reported that all three were subsequently seen mining on Salmon river.

Some three or four months later another and still more atrocious homicide took place in the settlement. The two victims lived together in a tent in Auburn, the temporary character of their abode being due to their recent arrival from Colorado. One morning at breakfast one of them was taken with violent convulsions, and his partner hastily summoned Dr. Rackerby, the pioneer physician, who immediately diagnosed the case as one of strychnine poisoning. The doctor speedily dispatched Mr. Littlefield and two or three others, who had been attracted to the scene by the afflicted man's cries of pain, to a spring at which the messenger, who had summoned the physician had stopped to drink. They found him in convulsions and lying in the spring run. He was carried to the tent and to him and the other man antidotes were administered but without avail in the case of the one first attacked. The messenger recovered. A piece of the bread they had been eating was given to a dog, and soon after devouring it he too was thrown into convulsions and died.

An examination of the miners' flour revealed small crystals of the deadly drug and it was evident to all that the poison had been put there with homocidal intent. A Frenchman who had been their companion on the journey from Colorado was at once suspected. He had quarreled with the other men and had sworn to be revenged upon them for real or fancied wrongs. He was forthwith arrested and the question that presented itself for immediate solution was what should be done with him. With the distance to be traversed by the guards, the prisoner and the witnesses and the lack of transportation facilities in his favor, the chances were excellent for the defendant's escaping all punishment should he be taken to The Dalles. Why not organize a court and try him at Auburn? It was noticeable during the discussion of this matter that the hitherto lawless element at once became solicitous for the sanctity of the law, Matt. Bledsoe, their leader, displaying especially great concern that no violence should be offered to its authority. The reason for this sudden conversion is plainly discernable. He was opposed to the institution of a citizens' court, well knowing that if he should ever be arraigned before such a tribunal, as he was liable to be at any time, his chances of escaping merited punishment would be few. Notwithstandng the strenuous opposition of this worthy advocate of submission to legally constituted authority, the citizens eventually organized a court of their own and proceeded to try the accused. All the forms of law were observed. Sydney Abell was ap-

pointed judge, James McBride and W. H. Packwood, associate justices; George Hall, sheriff; Shaw & Kelly, attorneys for the plaintiff, and Pierce & Grey for the defendant. A jury was impaneled, which listened patiently to the evidence in the case, the arguments of counsel, etc., and after due deliberation, found the defendant guilty of murder in the first degree. Judgment was passed accordingly and the condemned was executed.

Referring to this event, Mr. Hiatt says: "The ability and integrity of the court and officers could not be questioned. The whole business from first to last was conducted with a deliberation, dignity and fairness worthy of any tribunal organized in a strictly legal form. Had the same men been selected for their several positions by the same constituency at a regular election and all the formalities of the law been observed throughout, their action in the matter could not have been different, and had there been a legally constituted government with officers at hand to enforce the law, they would have been the last men in the community to attempt to assume charge of the affair in any manner in the least infringing upon the prerogative of the proper officers."

Long before this event happened the miners had exercised some other functions of government, it being mutually understood that all should abide by the result and the minority yield to the will of the majority. Thus it is related that about the 20th of June, 1862, a meeting was held for the purpose of electing a recorder of claims for the Blue canyon district. There were two candidates for the office, both first-class men. Naturally no attention was paid to the political opinions of either, but the rivalry between Oregonians and Californians furnished a basis of division. A president was elected, who assigned the Oregon candidate, William H. Packwood, to stand on a log, and his opponent, E. C. Brainard, to a position on another near by. When the candidates had taken their respective positions, he said "Now boys, all of you who are in favor of Packwood for recorder, go over there and all who are in favor of Brainard for recorder, go over to him." An Oregonian started for Packwood, saying "Come on all you Webfooters. Here's our Webfoot candidate!" And a Californian led the opposing faction, saying "Come on all you Tarheads. Here's a Tarhead candidate!" The Californians won the count and Brainard was elected. It is of interest to note that by May 6, 1863, he had recorded 1,291 claims.

But though the citizens of Auburn and vicinity might exercise legislative or judicial functions whenever necessity should arise, yet they early began to feel the need of a duly organized local government. Monday, June 6, 1862, was election day in the state of Oregon. Probably for the sake of calling attention to their needs the people met on that day on Union flat, organized an election board, cast more than one hundred votes for the different candidates and certified their vote to the secretary of state as "election returns of Baker county." Of course the votes were not counted, but the authorities at Salem had a premonition of efforts to be made in future for the organization of a new county.

The people followed this suggestion up a few months later by sending O. H. Kirkpatrick to the state capital with instructions to gain admission to the house of representatives as a member if possible, otherwise to bring unofficially whatever influence he could to bear upon the legislature for the benefit of this section. He secured the passage of a bill incorporating Auburn, and doubtless had some influence in obtaining the erection of Baker county, which was created by an act passed at that session of the legislature. Its original territory included what are now Union, Wallowa and Malheur counties, as well as the present Baker county.

While the citizens, as we have seen, invariably acted with prudence and moderation before they had the advantages of a local government, exercising such deliberation and good judgment in the only illegal execution occurring as to take from it all the heinousness of an ordinary lynching, strange to say they allowed the mob spirit to become rampant among them when an excuse for it no longer existed, thus staining the otherwise fair record of their early activities. In November, 1862, two men were fatally stabbed by a man known to history as Spanish Tom. The murderer and his victims were all gamblers and the homicide was the result of a row over a game. To terminate the quarrel the two men afterward murdered had withdrawn from the scene, but the Spaniard followed, stabbed both of them fatally and fled. He was afterward captured at Mormon basin and delivered into the custody of Sheriff Hall, who put the prisoner into a room and placed him under guard. The citizens who would have insisted upon allowing the law to take its course paid little attention to the matter, though they knew of the movement on foot to lynch Spanish Tom, thinking he was beyond harm's reach; but the conspirators worked away zealously, perfecting their plans in secret. When the preliminary hearing before Justice Abell was about to be held, the mob came in numbers and demanded that the examination be held outside the building that all might see and hear. The officers so far acceded to the demand as to move to a shed on the hillside. They did not certainly know that any violence was meditated, but they had a guard of forty armed men to provide against any possible attempt to seize their prisoner. The mob was led by one Captain Johnson, who covered himself with infamy by the part he that day played.

While the prisoner was en route to the shed, surrounded by the guard, Johnson gave the word of command and immediately the sheriff, prisoner and guard found themselves in the center of a mob which vigorously demanded the surrender of the Spaniard. Mr. Kirkpatrick mounted a stump and addressed the assembly, urging that the officers be allowed to do their duty; Johnson mounted another stump and made a noisy plea for the seizure of the prisoner. About half the guard deserted and later half of the remainder followed their perfidious example. It appears that a chain had been fastened to one of the prisoner's ankles, the remainder of its length being allowed to drag on the ground, and in their eagerness to capture their victim, the crowd pressed up so closely that one of their number was enabled to seize the loose end of this manacle. A tug of war ensued the mob pulling on the chain and the sheriff with his men holding firmly to the Spaniard. Even Tom himself realized the hopelessness of the struggle and told the sheriff to let go. The guard thereupon relaxed their hold; the prisoner was hastily dragged to a street below, where a rope was fastened around his neck. He called to some Mexican friends to shoot him and in response a few shots were fired, slightly wounding one man, but failing of their mark. Crowds of excited men seized the rope and with it rushed madly down the street. At one point in this mad race, the head of the doomed man struck a log, the blow no doubt proving instantly fatal, but the mob never stopped until they reached a convenient tree, upon which they hanged the Spaniard's lifeless body.

Justice Abell's official record of this horrible affair reads as follows:

The People of the State of Oregon } MURDER.
vs.
Spanish Tom.

Complaint filed the 21st day of November, 1862. Warrant issued of same date. The defendant brought into court the 22d day of November, 1862. Kelly appointed for prosecution and McLaughlin for defendant. Witnesses sworn and testified—Mob seized the defendant—Dragged him through the street and hung his lifeless body on a tree.

S. ABELL,
Justice of the Peace.

The above account of this affair is substantially that given by Mr. Hiatt. It must be remembered, however, that all the details are recorded only in the memories of men, and as is almost universally true in such cases the witnesses are not in perfect accord. In a letter to W. H. Packwood, written in 1893, Samuel Clarke speaks of the affair as follows:

"Soon after I returned to Auburn, Tom, the Greaser, killed Desmond and his partner over a game of cards. Squire Abell came to me and asked me to help examine the witnesses, as I wrote rapidly and could administer an oath. We met at the head of Blue canyon in an open field with at least two thousand very excited men looking on. I sat at a table under the shed with the sheriff's posse at my left and Johnson's vigilantes massed on my right and Squire Abell, white haired and venerable, in part interrogating the witnesses. This had gone on quite a while and I had taken down evidence, though every little while Johnson's crowd would rush in and try to capture the prisoner. They were run off by the sheriff's men each time. But the third time they were so bad I stood up in the melee and Johnson jumped on my chair and on the table and commenced haranguing the crowd, when some one showed me that he had knocked my ink over on the table, and I knocked him off the table before I knew it. While he was picking himself up his furious men had their guns and pistols shoved in my face and Sheriff Hall's men had their guns shoved past my ears the other way. It was decidedly a risky situation. One fellow hissed at me that he would kill me. I have always felt ashamed of having said to them 'Shoot you ———— if you want to!'

But I was too angry to be polite just then I probably was not afraid because the sheriff's posse was, 'on hand like a thousand of brick.' Anyway they didn't shoot, because I was so angry I forgot to be frightened. I got a local reputation that was valuable to me those rough times.

"When the rumpus was over and the vigilantes driven back, judge what our consternation was when good old Squire Abell turned up missing. Here was a situation. Hardly knowing what I did I jumped on to the table and waved my hand to the crowd, and for a wonder silence fell upon them. I appealed to them to do the thing with regard to the reputation of the camp. 'We are a long way from courts, but organize your own courts and select your own jury. Let me finish taking the evidence and read it to the jury and let them decide if the man is guilty. Give him a show. The Squire is gone, but I am an officer and will help you in this.' Mr. Kirkpatrick took the same position. In an instant a shout went up, 'Bully for Clarke.'

"The jury was selected and took their place and the taking of the evidence went on. It was a November day and nearly noon, but every witness was examined and testimony written toward sunset. I took the manuscript and read it to the jury, who stood in a row outside the shed. All was done in perfect order. The sheriff's men were still there to maintain order and Johnson's crowd had to accept it as 'a square deal.' The jury said 'guilty' and as the sunset grew red the whiz of a lariat came from the outside. Some one picked up the noose and threw it over Tom's head and a hundred seized the rope and started down the gulch. The coolest man in the crowd was Tom. From my standpoint I saw it all, and in a moment, when his head struck a stump, I felt relieved because I knew the poor fellow's troubles were over."

As in the trial of the Frenchman, so in this affair Matt Bledsoe was much in evidence, making loud threats against them all, but when the lynchers gained the advantage he concluded it was safest to make good his escape from so uncongenial a crowd. Horrible, though this affair was, we are informed that it had a most salutary effect in Auburn, for the lawless element left the town forthwith, going, to Idaho and Montana.

In the letter referred to above, Mr. Clarke also tells of another criminal case that occurred sometime in the summer of 1862. The offender, a boy named Jim, whose father was a cousin of James K. Polk, was a member of a company of Tennesseeans, all of whom were secessionists except Jim. They were mining on Powder river and the Confederate sympathizers taunted the boy incessantly. One day Jim suddenly concluded that forbearance had ceased to be a virtue, so grabbed the knife in the sheath of his latest tormentor and stabbed him with it. Jim was arrested and kept for awhile, but eventually Mr. Clarke, who was preparing to go to The Dalles, was requested to take him to Squire Ninevah Ford for examination. He was committed for trial and Ford requested of Clarke that he should take the prisoner on to The Dalles. Mr. Clarke says he had met Jim in a friendly way and felt kindly to him, so told Jim that if he would give his word that he would not try to escape he should not be ironed. Mr. Clarke told the boy he would certainly be convicted of manslaughter and sentenced for life, but promised to have him pardoned in four years. Jim kept faith, assisting in herding horses and about the camp. In due time he was tried and convicted. Clarke saw him in prison and renewed his promise of securing a pardon. "Four years after," says Mr. Clarke, "he called to thank me and my wife for having pardoned him and went forth a free man and I think a good one."

CHAPTER II.

1863 TO 1878.

The year 1863 was not as crowded with events of great moment in the history of Baker county as its predecessor had been, though men still continued to strive zealously for the yellow metal and to push actively all forms of material development. Excitement had brought thousands of people into the country, and excitement was taking thousands of them out again. All who failed to realize satisfactory returns for their labor were ready to resume the line of march. In the fall of 1862 the tide began to set in toward the Boise mines and before winter had passed this movement swelled to great proportions. So hopeful was the gold seeker that often he left wife and family but poorly provided for and not infrequently he failed to secure and send back the needed means, so that many times the Auburn miners were called upon that winter to help the destitute families. It is stated that their responses to such appeals were invariably hearty and liberal.

The year 1863 saw another expedition in search of the Blue Bucket diggings. A number of men set out from Clark's Canyon and Auburn determined to find the famous spot and when they reached Canyon City, they were joined by about as many more adventurers. The expedition found the old emigrant trail and followed it to a point near the head of a stream, but whether this stream was tributary to the Malheur or the Silvies river, they were unable to determine. At any rate the place answered the general description given by the emigrant of 1845 of the locality in which they had found their yellow metal. Some old wagon tires were to be seen also, two graves, but no trace of any nuggets could be discovered far or near. To add to their disappointment and discomfiture, the Indians stole their horses, making it necessary for them to return on foot and to leave behind so much of their equipments as they were unable to carry.

During the fall of this year a man named Philip Waggy and his companion in a hunt for horses discovered some floats of gold-bearing quartz about eight miles in a northeasterly direction from Baker City. This circumstance induced Messrs. Rockafellow and Wills to prospect for a ledge in that locality in the spring of 1864, and their efforts were rewarded by the discovery of a ledge which has since achieved great fame as an ore producer. This discovery induced the erection at Baker City of the Ruckel quartz mill, a water power plant, which, though not very capacious, was yet equal to the task of reducing the output from this first discovered quartz mine of Baker county. The mine has long been known as the Virtue.

Indians seem to have quite generally refrained from depredations in Baker county prior to the spring of 1863, but during the years following not a few people were killed by them and robberies were frequent. Baker county was never the home of the red man, though its territories were held as neutral grounds by all the Indians of eastern Oregon. Every Indian considered himself free to hunt and fish in the forests and streams of this section and to roam at will over its broad levels; but upon the approach of winter, he would return with his share of the booty to his home in the north, east or south according as he belonged to the Umatilla or Cayuse tribes, the Bannocks or the Piutes.

After the Indian wars of the 'fifties, there were no more organized hostilities with the aboriginal tribes in eastern Oregon until 1878, though the war of 1877 in northern Idaho was occasioned by a disagreement between the Indians and the United States government about territory in this part of the state. The Indians, however, were quite troublesome for several years subsequent to 1863, stealing horses and frequently firing upon solitary white men or small companies. Their nefarious operations extended from the source of Powder river to the shores of the Snake and it has been supposed that they were directed and encouraged by white marauders who shared the booty. There were also many white horse thieves who plied their contemptible vocation independently of the Indians. The red men commenced their depredations by attacking a packer named Porter while crossing Powder river en route to Clark's creek. His horses were driven away and he himself was shot through the neck, but eluded the Indians and eventually reached Auburn. He recovered.

It is related also that during a term of the circuit court in Auburn the Indians made a successful raid upon a corall on Poker flat, capturing horses belonging to the judge and several of the attorneys as well as to different citizens of the town. The animals were taken from the possession of a man named Thompson, and were probably never recovered by their owners. Indeed, no effort was made to recapture stolen property at first, but so frequent did these raids become that the people

were eventually compelled to do something in self-defense.

While the mining region contiguous to Powder river valley was being settled and developed, similar causes were producing similar effects in other parts of the vast domain then constituting Baker county. In all this western country there is not a fairer spot than Grande Ronde valley. Its broad expanse of grass clad prairies, its rippling streams coursing downward from the mountain heights and the mountains themselves, of nature's deepest blue and beautiful beyond description, did not fail to attract the attention of emigrant trains as they hastened toward the ever alluring "westmost west." At first, however, its distance from a base of supplies and its unprotected condition made settlement impossible, but with the discovery of gold in Idaho and eastern Oregon and with the consequent development of the Powder river valley on the south and of the valley of the Umatilla on the north, these difficulties gradually disappeared. Its agricultural lands were therefore eagerly appropriated and before 1864 two towns had been started and a very considerable settlement effected. Though the creation of Baker county had greatly bettered the condition of the people in southeastern Oregon, the territory constituting this political division was so extensive that many of the people were necessarily inconveniently far from the seat of government and its progress of events must result in the formation of new counties. By 1864 the Grande Ronde valley settlements and settlements contiguous thereto considered themselves strong enough to bear the burdens of independent county organization and in the fall of that year the legislature created Union county out of the northern portion of the original county of Baker.

The creation of this new county necessitated some changes in the personnel of Baker county's quota of officers which will be noticed

NORTH POWDER LAKE, ELEVATION 6,000 FEET.

PLACER MINING ON DEER CREEK.

in the chapter on political history. In the light of subsequent developments, it has been considered that a mistake was made in giving to Union county the territory now known as the Panhandle country, extending from the Blue mountains west of North Powder river to the Wallowa county line, and by recent legislation this section has been returned to Baker county.

Prior to the year 1865, a large immigration had come to Baker county from Missouri and Iowa. These people became permanent settlers, have ever supported the best interests of the county and are to-day among its most prominent and influential citizens. During the years 1865 and 1866 the people who were working out the material and social development of Baker county pursued the even tenor of their course, with nothing happening to excite unusual interest except the difficulties with the Indian tribes, and the sensational quarrels between rival ferrymen on the rivers. The former year witnessed the establishment of a mail route between Baker City and Auburn, also a change in the route of the old Dalles-Kelton stage line from the emigrant road to Place's toll road and via Baker City; the year 1866 saw a similar route established to Canyon City, with Baker City as its eastern terminus.

The month of June, 1866, will be remembered as the date of an important Indian raid upon the horses in the vicinity of Washington ranch, and a determined effort to recover the stolen property. The pursuing party consisted of twelve men. They followed the trail of the horses to the head waters of Elk creek, thence to Powder river, from that to Burnt river on the other side of the divide and into the Willow creek country. Here half of the party turned back, but the other half, the personnel of which is given by Mr. Hiatt as John Hibbard, Hardin Estes, Frank Johnson, Hiram Kinnison, Joe Hodgeons and Curtis, continued the pursuit. Indians, being well acquainted with the country, knew how to keep in stony soil so that

their tracks could not easily be followed by a pursuing party, if any should give them chase. When the whites came to places where it was impossible to follow the impression of the horses' hoofs, their usual procedure was to divide and one company going to the right and the other to the left, to keep to the outer edge of the hard ground, watching for the place where the Indians had emerged. Though hampered by these difficulties the white men gained steadily upon the thievish red skins and late in the afternoon of the tenth day they saw from a high bluff in the basin of the south fork of the Malheur, the horses and mules for which they had journeyed so far. They could count six tepees and supposing those to contain all the Indians there were, they resolved in their hasty consultation to attack the camp, hoping to stampede the Indians and recover the horses. But on coming into a better view they found that the Indians were in considerable numbers. To attack them would be folly, so they returned to Powder river valley to recruit reinforcements. They soon succeeded in organizing a company of fifty with Hardin Estes as captain. These might have been successful in the expedition upon which they at once set out, had it not been for the treason of one man, who insisted upon joining them at Auburn, representing himself as a recent arrival from Canyon City. When the company crossed Burnt river, this man made an excuse to separate from them, promising to rejoin his companions shortly, but he was never seen again. The company on reaching the place where the party of six had seen the Indians, found that the red skins had hastily departed shortly before, and they became convinced that their Canyon City man was a spy for the Indians and had warned them of the approach of the whites. Of course they proceeded, following the trail of the retreating Indians. On a fork of the Malheur, they sighted a camp, but could not tell at first whether the encamped were Indians or white men. Reconnoisance proved them to be soldiers, and one detachment of the volunteers, advancing too recklessly, came near being fired upon, but when the soldiers found who the strangers were they welcomed them warmly. Most of the soldiers were away from camp in pursuit of the same band of Indians which Mr. Estes' party were following, and that day they had a brush with the red skins, resulting in the death of Corporal William B. Lord, a Civil war veteran.

Next day volunteers and soldiers continued in pursuit. They followed until all hope of recovering the horses was lost, then the volunteers, except four, returned to their homes. The four continued in the company of the soldiers for many days but finally they too gave up the chase after a hard and bootless campaign of five weeks' duration. The Indians owed their escape to one or two fortunate accidents, causing delay to the soldiers and volunteers.

The story of the troubles between rival ferry owners on the rivers between the Columbia and the Boise mines is a long one and is not deemed of sufficient importance to merit narration here. The line of travel was beset by rough, lawless characters, who made themselves disagreeable on more than one occasion to farmers and others along the stage lines. Sometimes they paid for their insolence with their lives.

E. S. McComas, formerly of the La Grande Chronicle, tells the experience with these roughs of George Walker, who in the spring of 1864 took a claim on the Owyhee river and started a ferry. At this time the "Plummer Rustlers," a gang of outlaws were roaming over the country and robbing stages as well as all individuals they might meet whom they considered worth the trouble. Two of these characters came to the ferry and found Mr. Walker in possession of an old boot well filled with coin, the proceeds of a profitable day's work. Of this they took charge, but not satisfied, they notified the ferryman that he was oc-

cupying their claim and must vacate forthwith. Walker ran to the house for his revolver. He was hotly pursued and a battle royal took place, resulting in defeat for the desperadoes, one of whom was killed and the other wounded. But the wounded man reached his horse and mounting, rode away, telling Walker he would be back again with the sheriff. The ferryman knew what this meant and not having faith in his ability to successfully give battle to a whole gang, he saddled his horse and set out for Salt Lake City. He returned thence to Iowa, but soon afterward moved to southern Kansas, where he died in 1887.

The Washoe ferry on Snake river is said to have ben a sort of rendezvous for desperate characters. Early in the year 1865 a party of men from Idaho crossed the river at this point, captured three of the desperadoes and took them over to the Idaho side of the river, intending to hang them the next day for alleged horse stealing. They imprisoned their captives in a house some ten miles up the river, placing a guard over them, but during the night the prisoners pried open the door, eluded the guard and escaped. At the ferry they armed themselves with repeating rifles, expecting that they would be pursued. In this they were not mistaken. They had gone a number of miles, however, before footfalls were heard behind them, and when at length their pursuers were seen to be approaching, the fugitives concealed themselves in as safe a place as could be found and awaited the coming of their enemies. A conference was soon arranged which ended in the pursuing party's agreeing to return without molesting the horse thieves in consideration of the latters' agreement to leave the country. The men thus compelled to seek other climes were part owners in the Washoe ferry. They were not given time to dispose of their interests, but fortunately one of them met Mr. Packwood in the Blue mountains and negotiated a sale to him of his own interests and those of his companions, so that Mr. Packwood became principal owner of the ferry. Thus this important aid to travel passed into the hands of an honest and enterprising pioneer, one of the leading men of the early days, and of course soon lost its unsavory reputation. At a later date Mr. Packwood united his interests with the Burnt river toll road and the Olds ferry, forming a corporation, the official name of which was the Burnt River Toll Road, Bridge and Ferry Company. This firm made many improvements in the primeval highway of transportation. They continued to do a large business for several years, inasmuch as all the supplies for southern Idaho had in early days to come over the roads and ferries. It is said that their income sometimes aggregated one thousand dollars per day. But when the Union Pacific Railway Company completed their track to the Salt Lake valley, supplies were brought in from that direction and the business of the road, bridge and ferry company rapidly declined. To this result, also, the agricultural development of the country contributed not a little, the markets being supplied in part with home products.

In 1867 there was a revival of interest in the Burnt river ditch, which had been surveyed from the river whose name it bore to the Clark's creek mines, and upon which some work had been done as early as 1863. The activities upon this project in 1867 were stimulated by a desire to convey water to the Shasta mining district. Eleven miles of the ditch were made that year and during the next two years thirty-six miles more were completed. In 1870 the ditch was constructed as far as the Shasta mines, the cost of all operations up to that time aggregating $150,000. The year 1867, like its predecessors, brought its share of Indian troubles. The red men renewed their raids with each returning season. This year two of them stole one horse too many and paid for their crime with their lives. C. C. Davis, a daring Indian scout, set out in pursuit with two companions and in due time came upon the Indians

in their camp, between Dixie creek and Burnt river. Upon coming near, Mr. Davis directed the two men to go one to his right and the other to the left while he himself should proceed directly to the camp. The Indians, as soon as they saw Davis, grabbed their bows and arrows, but the white man was too quick for them and they being in line were killed with one shot. They had slaughtered the horse and were drying the meat.

The most noted Indian massacre of the year was that of a man named Scott and his wife while returning to their home on Burnt river from a dance in Rye valley. The affair occurred on September 1st. As Mr. Scott was approaching the river with his wife and children in the wagon, the sharp crack of the savages' rifles rang out upon the still air. Scott fell backward at the first fire. His wife, too, was mortally wounded but she seized the lines and drove down the road to Burnt river as fast as frightened horses could run. The Indians were so close behind that one actually grasped the wagon, but he was unable to hang on. Notwithstanding the steep and rough character of the road, the team pulled up at the farm yard gate without further casualties. Scott lived only a short time afterward and Mrs. Scott survived him but a few hours. Mr. and Mrs. Packwood had been invited to accompany the Scotts to the Rye valley dance, but were compelled to decline through pressure of business, and to this, perhaps, they owe their lives.

About the same time a company of Indians attacked from ambush a man named Folger while he was journeying from Mormon Basin to the ferry at Farewell Bend on Snake river. He was twice wounded, one ball striking the hip and the other the thigh bone, but he nevertheless held on to his horse, which ran three miles down the gulch before it could be gotten under control. As soon as the animal quieted, he got off its back and crawled to water. He was not equal to the task of mounting, however, so had to lie there the remainder of the day and all that night. The next day he again attempted to gain a seat in the saddle, but though he tried many times, not until evening did he succeed. A ride of two miles brought him to the ferry, where Mr. and Mrs. Packwood cared for him until he died some six weeks later.

So imminent was the danger from nomadic Indians at all times, that it was thought necessary by Mr. Packwood to build and equip a small fire-proof fort near his ferry for defense in case of attack. Similar fortifications were also maintained in other places. Mr. Hiatt tells us that: "In those days it was no unusual thing for persons who were)traversing the country from Burnt river southward to the head waters of the Owyhee, to find the remains of men who had doubtless been killed by Indians. Notwithstanding the well known danger, men would go through the country, sometimes one alone, sometimes in small parties, and in all probability, but few of those who perished left any trace that has ever been discovered to tell their fate."

There seems to have been no unprovoked attacks upon Indians during the early days in Baker county, at least the writer has never seen any account of whites having assumed the offensive in any of the troubles or committed wanton depredations upon Indians, yet the eastern people and even those occupying high official positions in Washington were prone to consider every outbreak among Indians as attributable to land grabbers and "border ruffians." This false notion provoked in 1873 an eloquent defense of the pioneer peoples of Oregon and Washington by the Hon. J. G. Wilson, in which he shows that the aspersers of Oregonians knew nothing of the real character of the Indian, their ideas of him being formed solely by the romance writer. "It has become," says Mr. Wilson, "a custom in the east to call every Indian war or disturbance on the Pacific Coast an act caused by the dishonesty of Ore-

gonians for the purpose of speculation, and to speak freely of their usual cruelty and inhumanity toward the red man. In the formation of this custom officials at Washington have lent their aid, until now the people of that western coast can be branded as 'border ruffians' and destitute of instinct and feeling, by official speakers before Washington audiences, and without any reason therefor other than the complaint of a Digger Indian or the scribbling of an irresponsible correspondent. Twenty years of life in Oregon and an acquaintance with probably three-fourths of its citizens, enable me to claim them the peers of any in their peaceful and law-abiding character and true humanity." Mr. Wilson then proceeds to attack the feeble, unjust, vacillating and utterly incompetent "Quaker policy," in an article forceful in its presentation and unanswerable in its reasoning. While it may be admitted that the Indian history of the Pacific coast does present instances of the whites having outraged and wronged the red man, it must be borne in mind that it also presents innumerable instances of robberies, murders and other outrages committed by savages without provocation and without other reason than to gratify their love of bloodshed and desire to enjoy the rewards of labor without enduring its sacrifices.

In 1867 an effort was made to organize the whole country for co-operation against white and Indian horse thieves, but some of those whose neighborhood had never suffered took little interest in the matter. An organization was effected, however, which soon found work to do. Louis Carey and Anthony Sicord, while engaged in hauling lumber, were halted by six masked men who tied them, took their personal effects and their mules and horses except two, and then departed, telling them someone would be along shortly and untie them. The outraged men managed to untie themselves and mounting the two horses left by the robbers rode to Powder river valley for assistance. A company was formed consisting of four men, one of whom was Sheriff Virtue, and these were overtaken later by C. C. Davis and three others, who were also in pursuit of the robbers. The party were then upon the track of the thieves and following it up the creek they came to a camp, recently deserted, but whether it had been occupied by whites or Indians they could not determine. Following the trail of the robbers to a point twenty miles beyond Canyon City, they came upon them not far from the timber's edge. The desperadoes opened fire from the brush. Crossing the gulch in which the robbers were, the pursuers got between their men and the timber to cut off the retreat, then opened fire with their repeating rifles, being guided in their aim by the moving bushes. The robbers soon retreated to open ground and surrendered. One of them was slightly wounded in four places. Only four of the six were captured, the other two being away at the time, and of these four only two suffered punishment. They all escaped from jail, but Judd and Alexander were retaken, tried, convicted and sentenced to eight years' imprisonment.

During the three years from 1867 to 1870 there was comparatively little activity in the mines owing to the scarcity of water. A miner writing of the period gives a rather gloomy picture of affairs generally, saying that the towns were in a delapidated condition, most of the fine stores, saloon and other business buildings being empty. The general progress of the county up to this time, however, was sufficient to give token of permanency of settlement and future greatness. True, the population had not increased. On the contrary it numbered, perhaps, less than half what it was in the fall of 1862. A census taken in 1870 shows the number of dwellings in the county, 877; the number of families, 777; the number of male whites, 1,457; of female whites, 523; the number of colored males, 665, and of colored females, 18; total population, 2,663. The population of Auburn alone in the winter of 1862-

3 was estimated as being between four and six thousand. It must be remembered, however, that many of the people who first came to the county were adventurers brought here by a boom, while the census rolls of 1870 show only bona fide settlers, whose permanent homes were established in the county and whose interests were identified with it. Some very important improvements had been made by this time and in the course of the mining development, comprehensive enterprises had been projected and completed or carried well on toward completion. Conspicuous among these were the Auburn canal and the Burnt river ditch, the latter of which was then fifty-seven miles long. There were also many miles of smaller ditches. The pioneer town of Auburn had greatly declined in importance, but in its stead had grown up that prosperous mining center, Baker City, which had become the seat of local government in 1868. Settlements were made all along the principal streams, also in Mormon basin, Eagle valley, Rye valley, Sumpter valley, on Connor creek and in numerous other places. The seeds of civilization and development had been scattered widely over the county and had become deeply rooted.

After a lull in mining operations lasting about three years, activities were, in 1870, resumed in good earnest. The Bedrock Democrat, the pioneer paper of the county, was started on May 11th of this year, and in its review of the mining situation, it predicted that the gold output of the twelve months would exceed the combined production of the last three years. It states that in the Shasta district, which embraced Malheur, Eldorado and a portion of Willow creek, the outlook was bright; that on Clark's creek water was abundant, the miners were jubilant and the merchants happy; that in the Easton district, including Cash, Discovery, Resevoir and number of other very rich gulches, mining was progressing finely and that in Rye valley some claims were being worked night and day. Work was also in progress at

Auburn and under favorable circumstances, the canal furnishing abundance of water. The false notions about the unproductiveness of the alkali soil had been dispelled by this time and not a few farms had been brought under cultivation. The possibility of agricultural development was, however, quite circumscribed during this period owing to lack of transportation facilities, and though the first agriculturists of the county received rich rewards for their labors, the market was easily glutted by an overproduction of any one article. Thus, in 1864 so many rutabagas were grown that their abundance and comparative worthlessness became a standing joke and the farming communities were nick-named "rutabaga districts." Naturally the rearing of horses and stock early became an important industry. However, there was an abundance of excellent pasture all over eastern Oregon at that time, so that prices were lower than they are to-day. Furthermore, the profusion of thieves and rustlers, of both the white and red races, was a standing menace to the industry.

In 1871 Baker and Grant counties were made the victims of one of those inexcusable governmental blunders which have at different times retarded the growth of various sections of the west and disturbed their peoples. The United States officials have never covered themselves with glory in managing Indian affairs. Their policies seem to be framed in abject ignorance of the character of the Indians, the conditions in frontier territories and the genius of the west. In the spring of this year Hon. A. B. Meacham received a letter from the Indian department, which we produce here, as follows:

WASHINGTON, D. C. March 10, 1871.
To Hon. A. B. Meacham:
    SIR:—You are hereby informed that, upon report of this office and recommendation of the Hon. Secretary of the Interior, an executive order has issued, dated the 14th instant, directing that that portion of the state of Oregon lying between the forty-second and forty-fourth parallels of north latitude, and the one hundred and seventeenth and one hundred and twentieth degrees of west longitude (excepting so much thereof as may have been or hereafter may be granted for military or wagon road purposes) be withdrawn from market as public lands for the space of eighteen months with a view to the selection of a reservation upon which to collect all the Indians in that state east of the Cascade mountains, except those who may select lands in severalty upon the reservations on which they are located.
    You are hereby instructed to proceed to select such reservations without unnecessary delay.
                    E. S. PARKER, Commissioner.

Of course this order excited much opposition in Baker and surrounding sections. The proposed reservation comprised about one hundred miles square of the southern portion of Baker and Grant counties. It embraced some good placer gold mines, partly developed, also a portion of the country through which ran the Burnt river ditch. Canyon City and vicinity were within the district which the government proposed to remand to barbarism. Some portions of this vast area were populated by busy miners, and an attempt to remove them, reckless as they were, would doubtless result in bloodshed. Of course, the order was never carried into full effect, but it hung for months like a dark cloud over the section affected, retarding in a measure the settlement and development of the country.

Under the caption, "Then and Now," comparing Baker county as it was in 1872 with the county as he first saw it in 1862, the editor of the Bedrock Democrat says:

"In the summer of 1862 the valley and the mountain sides were one vast sea of as fine bunchgrass as ever grew. At that time a large portion of the valley was swamp and overflowed lands and the travel passed at or near the foothills. The settlement made by the emigrants of 1862 was the starting point of the present prosperity of Powder river valley. The settlers were poor and toil worn; now they are wealthy and comfortable. A view of Powder river valley now presents to the eye a homelike and civilized appearance, with towns, villages, farms and farm houses interspersed over its whole extent. The swamp and overflowed lands have in a large degree been reclaimed and made to yield bountiful harvests to repay the hardy and industrious pioneer husbandman. Churches and school houses now occupy the places where, but a short time since, the war-whoop of the savage was the only indication that a human being had an abiding place in this beautiful valley. We can now stand in our office door and view vast herds of cattle and sheep feeding upon the rich and luxuriant grasses of the valley and the surrounding foot-hills, a better range than which can not be found on the Pacific slope, which embraces the best and most extensive grazing lands in the world. The valley is surrounded by moun-tains, in which are found rich deposits of gold, silver and copper, which are being taken out by hardy and enterprising miners. The mining camps surrounding the valley supply a home market for the surplus produce of our farm-ers.

"The pioneer of 1862, in passing over the valley, looks with astonishment at the change and the improvements that have been made in so short a time and it is only by some inde-structible landmark that he can recognize his exact locality."

THE PIONEERS' DANCE.

"On with the dance! Let joy be unconfined."

In 1872 the settlers in Baker county, south of Malheur City, could almost have been count-ed on one's fingers, so few were there in this imperial region. At Malheur City there was quite a settlement of miners. The Eatons, Logans, Prices, McDowells, Turners, Coles, Imblers, Phillips's, Moretons and Thomsons were living on Willow creek, a few ranchmen had located in Jordan valley, William Emison lived on Snake river between the Malheur and Owyhee, and L. B. Rinehart had recently pur-chased the Keeney road station, situated where the old emigrant road crossed the Malheur river. In the fall of 1872 he erected here a commodious stone house, quite a pretentious

11

structure for those days. The builders finished their work during December and just before the new year dawned, the Rineharts issued in-vitations for a New Year's ball and supper to be given in honor of the opening of the stone house. There were few social events in Baker county in those days, particularly in this sec-tion, so that it was only natural that the settlers for fifty miles around prepared to participate in the celebration.

All day long, the day before the event, the settlers arrived at the stone house. Some came from as far as Dixie Slough and Middle-ton, settlements near Boise City, others came from the Payette valley and the remainder from Malheur City, Willow creek and other isolated settlements in this county. They came by wagon and they came in the good old pioneer fashion, on horseback. By nightfall forty-one numbers had been sold, each num-ber selling for five dollars. A few were dec-orated for this gala occasion with what little finery they were fortunate enough to possess; some wore the simple but striking and pictur-esque dress of the mountain and plain, while a larger number had relegated the matter of dress to a place of insignificant importance and were attired in their work-a-day clothes, those in which they felt the most comfortable. All were happy. The upper story of the house had been left unpartitioned purposely and here in this spacious ballroom, decorated with a few green sprigs and brightly-colored draperies, at early candlelight the company assembled. In one corner of the room a low platform had been built and here the musicians, two Owyhee fid-dlers, took their stations. Time has but made the memories of that event more vivid.

At last they are all assembled on the floor, renewing old friendships and forming new ac-quaintances. Suddenly there is a flurry on the musicians' platform and unusual stir and move-ment among all. Then, to the shrill notes of the bobbing violins and the deep, loud tones of the caller, the merry dancers bow, first to the left and then to the right, the nervousness of expectancy written on their smiling faces and displayed in their movements. A second ringing command. The bowing, scraping dancers move with a mighty swish and swirl, the figures melt into one indistinct mass of rotating color, the floor creaks and groans with joyous sympathy, and the dance is on. How swiftly the scene changes! Now there is dignity in the step and courtesy, now the figures are pretty and graceful and now there seems to be a mad scramble and frolic and out of the confusion order again appears. There is a rythym and swing to it all that is exhilarating. Terpsichore reigns supreme and for the time being all are her blind disciples, forgetful of worldly cares and sorrows and intent only on mastering the intricate figures and mazes of the dance and drinking deep of pleasure's cup. The shadows fall deeper upon the outside world, the coyote slinks away from the scene of confusion and noise to which his curiosity has drawn him, the rabbits and other wild animals, disturbed in their slumbers, steal hastily away into the blacker darkness, a few twinkling stars pierce the blue vault of the heavens, then a whole legion of jewels set earth's blue canopy a-sparkle in the glory of the Master Jeweler. The moon, a slender silver crescent appears in the western world. The revelry in the house only increases.

At midnight the music ceased and the room was cleared of the dancers. Then two long wooden tables, loaded heavily with choice viands and delicacies, appeared as if by magic and for the time being the dancers became banqueters, and the new year was ushered in amidst the joyous acclaim of all. After the inner man had been satisfied, the tables disappeared by the same subtle magic which caused their appearance.

Again the room is thronged, again the violins cry in their anguish and then suddenly burst into laughing sounds of delight, and again the revelers wind through the dreamy

mazes of the waltz, the quick step of the polka, the stately reel and schottische, or the difficult, rollicking figures of the square dance or lancers.

And thus the night was spent and ere the weary dancers tired or the dozing fiddlers finally dropped off into slumber during some familiar measure, the bright tints in the eastern horizon and the fading stars heralded the near approach of dawn. It was an event to be long remembered and the joys and pleasures of that pioneer New Year's ball, given in the dreary wilderness of southern Oregon, are among the pleasantest memories treasured by the early settlers of Malheur county.

During 1872 and the year following, activity in the mining region continued, especially along the course of the Eldorado or Big ditch, as the Burnt river ditch had come to be named. This mammoth artificial waterway was then ninety-seven miles long, eight and a half feet wide at the top and six feet wide at the bottom and three feet deep. In 1869 J. H. Johnson had become interested in the project of extending the Carter-Packwood ditch and had gone back east for the purpose of interesting capital in it. He succeeded in inducing Mr. Buford, of Rock Island, to come out and examine the country, and that gentleman was so pleased with the result of his investigation that he bought almost the entire stock of the Carter-Packwood, or Burnt river ditch, organizing the "Malheur and Burnt River Consolidated Ditch and Mining Company," with a capital stock of a million dollars.

At this time there was but one flouring mill in Baker county and its capacity did not exceed twenty barrels per day, so that notwithstanding the capabilities of the soil, flour had to be imported by teams from Union county and from Walla Walla valley, causing a continuous outflow of the precious metal, and consequent hard times. No doubt, too, the general depression throughout the United States made itself felt in Baker county and for a few years subsequent to 1873 this section seems to have been rather quiet.

In 1875 the Nevada and Northern telegraph line, between Walla Walla and Silver City was built through the Powder river valley, touching Baker City and other towns in this section. Its advent occasioned considerable rejoicing, not alone for its own sake, but because it was considered a forerunner and prophecy of the coming of the much-needed iron horse.

In March, 1877, a Baker County Agricultural Society was organized with a capital stock of $2,500 and the Baker City race track and grounds were purchased by it. The first fair held in the county was held during the six days commencing on the tenth of September following the date of organization of this society. A splendid display of fine stock, fruits, vegetables, cereals, fancy work, etc., was collected and arranged, and an excellent program of running and trotting events carried out. The attendance was large, notwithstanding the inclemency of the weather.

During this year there were two things to deeply agitate the public mind. One was the Nez Perce outbreak in northern Idaho and the other railroad agitation. In 1855 the United States government, by Governor I. I. Stevens, for Washington, and Joel Palmer, for Oregon, negotiated a treaty with the various tribes of Indians in eastern Oregon and Washington by which three reservations were formed, the Umatilla, the Yakima and the Nez Perce. As a condition precedent to the ratification of this important treaty, Chief Joseph insisted that the Wallowa valley should be confirmed to him and his band. Only when the commissioners agreed to this did he throw the weight of his influence in favor of the treaty, an influence without which it would never have been ratified. The confirming of the Wallowa valley to Joseph was the *sine qua non* of the whole negotiation. But notwithstanding all this the government some eight years later, concluded

another and supplementary treaty with the Nez Perces, to which Joseph and his band refused their consent, ceding to the United States for a consideration the cherished Wallowa valley. The theory of the United States in this as in all other Indian negotiations was that, as Indian lands are held in common, the action of a majority of the chiefs and embassadors in council disposing of them binds the whole tribe. While from a legal point of view this theory may be both necessary and just, the injustice of it in this particular case must be apparent to any unprejudiced mind. Technically the Wallowa valley was the property of the whole Nez Perce tribe and as such might be ceded to the government by consent of a clear majority of the chiefs; but it was understood by both the Indians and the representatives of the government in 1855 to be the special property of Joseph and his band. While, then, the treaty of 1863 was legally binding upon Joseph, in justice and good morals it ought to be considered of no validity, as it practically amounted to a sale, by certain Nez Perce chiefs, of land which did not equitably belong to them. Realizing the force of these facts and considerations, the government in the spring of 1873 directed that the Nez Perce Indians be permitted to occupy the Wallowa valley at such times as the weather would allow and that an appraisement should be made of the improvements of white settlers for the purpose of securing an appropriation by Congress wherewith to purchase the same and extinguish their rights. This was only a case of righting one wrong by the enactment of a greater one. The settlers had gone into the Wallowa valley by invitation of the United States, had endured the hardships and privations of pioneer life there, and had at great sacrifice built up the country, acquiring inchoate rights for which they could not be equitably recompensed by mere payment for improvements. A man might have nothing upon his homestead but a pioneer shanty, a fenced yard and a few acres of cultivated land, yet he might have an incipient right to a home which in a few years would be worth thousands of dollars. To take this from him by merely paying for the shanty, the fence and the plowing, even though the appraisers should deal with him most liberally, to set him and his family again adrift in the world, to send them in search of another opportunity to build a home and undergo the privations incident to the first few years of life on a new farm, that, too, after other men had been, during all the time he had spent in his Wallowa valley home, taking their choice of the remaining locations—the injustice of such a proposition is plainly manifest.

After disbursing some public money in making appraisements and keeping the settlers in suspense for months, naturally retarding the development and settlement of the country, the Indian department finally abandoned their project of returning the valley to Joseph's band. The Joseph of 1855 had died, but he was succeeded by a son, also named Joseph, who dared maintain what he conceived to be his hereditary rights. The outcome of the whole matter was the Nez Perce war of 1877. Though this war was fought out on Idaho soil, it elicited much interest in various parts of eastern Oregon and Washington. No one could certainly prophecy into what part the belligerent Indians might come or be driven, and in some places forts were built and other means of defense provided. Baker county was considered to be in no danger, yet to make security doubly secure, the Baker City Home Guards were organized. It consisted of about sixty men, of whom R. C. George was captain, J H. Parker, first lieutenant, and A. A. Houston, second lieutenant. No great alarm was felt here at any time, yet a lively interest was taken in the progress of the war, and some of the settlers in the remoter and wilder parts of the county moved to the towns for a time. But not once during the entire war did a hostile

Indian set foot in Baker county or even in the Walowa valley.

Although the county was now about fifteen years old it was still suffering for want of adequate transportation facilities and related conveniences. The general progress of events had brought some amelioration of conditions in this respect, but the great business of transportation was still in the hands of freighters, stage companies, etc. We are told by pioneers that in 1862 and during a part of 1863, all letters and newspapers had to be brought by expressmen from Walla Walla; and that the price for conveying the letters was one dollar each and the price at which newspapers sold was a dollar a copy. On August 1, 1862, J. H. Shepherd engaged in the business of transporting express packages and mail between Walla Walla and Auburn. He reduced the charge for carying letters to fifty cents each and made a like reduction in the price of newspapers. Mr. Shepherd won deserved success in the express business, frequently proving more alert and active than his competitors. In 1863 he extended his operations to the Boise mines and his business grew until it required twenty-six horses. He sold out in the fall of 1863 to the Wells Fargo Express Company, which made arrangements to carry letters and packages to all the principal points in the upper country.

During the early years the Northwestern Stage Company was a power in the land. Its mammoth operations extended over a route 860 miles long and it handled all the mail and express between The Dalles, Oregon, and Kelton, Utah, besides transporting passengers and their luggage. But little complaint was made of this company. Indeed, they seem to have transacted all business entrusted to them with fidelity and dispatch, but any such company, however well organized and equipped, was but a poor substitute for the huge gladiator of steel upon its iron track. It goes without saying that the people of eastern Oregon were from the earliest times deeply interested in all projects which seemed likely to give them a railroad. Hardly could they take a drive on any important road without being compelled to go down into their pocket-books for toll. Almost none of the principal streams and rivers could be crossed without paying high tribute to some ferryman. All articles of importation were likewise levied upon and the added cost was of course paid by the consumer. It speaks volumes for the productiveness of the mines that they were equal to the task of supporting their operators under such circumstances and it tells well for the enterprise and push of the early citizens that they have accomplished so much while their energies were fettered by such an incubus.

These being the conditions, it was natural that great interest should be excited in this and neighboring counties by Senator Mitchell's railroad bill, looking to the construction of the proposed Portland, Dalles and Salt Lake railway. The bill was introduced into the forty-fifth Congress in response to a monster petition signed by several thousand citizens of Oregon. Its main provisions were that the time for the completion of the Northern Pacific railroad down the Columbia river should be extended eight years; that the railroad should be built on the south, or Oregon side of the river, and that the company should, within six months after the passage of this bill, commence the construction of the road, beginning either at Portland or at Umatilla, and that at least forty miles should be constructed each year until the whole should be completed; that the lands granted the Northern Pacific to aid in constructing the above mentioned road should be surveyed and sold by the general government to actual settlers at $2.50 per acre, the proceds to be used in paying the interest bearing bonds of the company; that should the Northern Pacific fail to build the road known as the Northern or Snoqualmie Pass road within the time already prescribed by law, an equal num-

ber of acres should be granted to any company that would build a road on the route of the proposed Portland, Dalles and Salt Lake railroad, and that the track from Portland to Umatilla might then be used as common property upon such terms as should be fixed by arbitration of a commission.

Naturally the measure was opposed by the Northern Pacific Railroad Company and rather unnaturally, as it would seem, it was also opposed by the Oregonian and the Portland Board of Trade. Portland's opposition no doubt arose from the fact that many of the prominent citizens of that city were stockholders in the Northern Pacific Company, but there was a disposition manifested even before this on the part of west side residents to oppose measures for the advancement of eastern Oregon. Of course the development of this section might act as a temporary drawback to the west by attracting emigrants who would otherwise go on to the coast, but one can hardly account for the failure to foresee that Portland's ultimate greatness could only result from the development of all Oregon, and that her true policy must be to promote the interests of the entire state, as far as lay in her power. The Oregonian must, in 1877, have been less ambitious than it now is to be a true exponent of the interests of the whole people of Oregon without reference to merely local and temporary considerations.

But if the bill was opposed in western Oregon it was sustained with more than equal earnestness in the counties east of the Cascades. Mass meetings were held at Baker City, Union and elsewhere in this section, at which resolutions were unanimously passed, warmly commending Senator Mitchell's bill. We transcribe those passed at Baker City, as follows:

"*Resolved,* That the route and the means proposed by our United States Senator, John H. Mitchell, for the construction of the Northern Pacific and Portland, Salt Lake and South Pass railroads are, in our judgment, feasible and that we endorse the bill of Senator Mitchell and urge its passage.

"*Resolved,* That the constructing of such a means of transportation would be conducive to the best material, commercial and political interests of Baker county and every portion of eastern Oregon and of the great northwestern country generally.

"*Resolved,* That we sincerely believe that in encouraging and assisting that enterprise we express the sentiment of all who are building or expect to build their homes in a country so rich and boundless in resources as ours, inhabited by a class of people who are anxious to engage in all the industrial pursuits of life and who, as it were, with one stentorian voice ask the promotion of this enterprise to accelerate their advance in the arts, civilization and peace.

"*Resolved,* That a copy of these resolutions be forwarded to each of our Senators and Representatives in Congress.

"*Resolved,* That a copy of these resolutions be furnished the Bedrock Democrat with a request on behalf of this meeting, that the same be published.

"GEORGE J. BOWMAN,
"D. D. STEPHENSON,
"J. M. SHEPHERD,
"*Committee.*"

As may be imagined the discussion upon the proposed bill waxed warm in the press and on the platform. Both sides contended with great energy and enthusiasm, but the influence of the Northern Pacific Railroad Company in Congress was too great to be overcome and the measure met defeat. The outlook for help from the northern road now seemed rather gloomy, as that company already controlled the navigation of the Columbia and it was in no hurry to itself build a road down that river, neither would it willingly permit any other company to do so. But the people of eastern Oregon did not lose courage. They clearly foresaw that the Union Pacific must have a feeder from the Pacific coast over which no rival should exercise control. The Union Pacific had already built one hundred miles of road in furtherance of a scheme to start two lines, one to Montana and one to Boise City. The latter road could easily be completed through to Baker City, tapping the eastern Oregon mining region, thence to the farming and stock raising Grande Ronde valley and beyond. Furthermore the advantage to be gained by making this extension would be far more than proportionate to the cost, and the hope of eastern Oregon that it was soon to have a railroad certainly rested upon a firm foundation. Then, too, it is a well known fact that when trade once establishes a certain channel for itself, it is not easily diverted therefrom, and it was deemed possible that Portland, realizing this, would build a road to Baker City and thus be the first to secure the vast and rapidly increasing trade of eastern Oregon. The era of railroad building in the inland empire was plainly about to dawn. But before the advent of the iron horse with its impetus to industrial development, must come another temporary setback in the form of a second Indian war. A full account of that struggle will be found later in this volume.

An Indian war is always a deplorable thing, not alone for the loss of life and destruction of property it occasions, but more especially on account of the great check it gives to immigration and settlement. The Oregonian made the war of 1878 the subject of an article representing eastern Oregon as wild and unsafe and urging newcomers to the country to continue their journeys until securely domiciled in the western part of the state. A desire to keep the balance of political power on the Pacific side of the Cascades and a narrow localism occasioned these continued attempts to depreciate the inland country, but despite all this the railroad prospects were too bright and an era of progress too plainly discernable in the future to permit any great depression at this time.

The years 1879 and 1880 were not characterized by any events of a sensational kind, but the entire country progressed with a steady pace. The mines, the herds and the cultivated fields all poured forth their wealth to reward the labor of the delver and the husbandman, both of whom no doubt wrought with renewed courage, being assured that the day of stage coaches and freight teams must soon be ushered out and the day of railroads and telepraphs, with their closer bonds of trade affinities and higher civilization, be ushered in.

A census of Baker county, taken in 1880, shows the entire population and its distribution, as follows: District No. 1, Baker City and Pocahontas, 1,807; district No. 2, Sumpter, Auburn, Virtue, Burnt River and Clark's Creek, 1,165; district No. 3, Eldorado, Rye Valley, Humboldt Basin, Connor Creek, Quartz Gulch, Upper Burnt River and Stone, 949; district No. 4, Clover Creek, Pleasant Valley and Malheur agency, 235; district No. 5, Wingville and North Powder, 468; total, 4,624. The population of Baker City, including Chinese, numbered 815.

The winter of 1880-81 was very severe and cattle perished in great numbers throughout the entire inland empire. Early in February the loss was estimated at seventy per cent. of cattle and sheep, though some men lost their entire herds. The ranges, we are informed, were covered with carcasses. The heaviest blow fell upon Wasco county, Benjamin Snipes, the stock king of that section, losing eighty per cent. of his herds. The vicinity of Prineville escaped disaster, but it had sustained heavy losses during the previous winter and the number of cattle on hand was not large. It became evident to all stockmen that a change must be made in the manner of conducting their business, and that the only safe way in the future would be to prepare for feeding their animals during the winter months. When the cattle industry was in its incipiency in eastern Oregon, the bunch grass grew so tall and luxuriantly that only a very deep snow could cover it and the cold alone, even in a severe winter, was never extreme enough to cause serious loss. But for a decade herds had been multiplying until some men were rich in cattle, who were poor in every other kind of property. The result was that the bunchgrass was pastured down until a very shallow snow would cover it and when a winter came in which snow lay on the ground to a considerable depth for a long time, cattle must perish by the thousands. The result of this experience was to make the stockraiser more prudent in the matter of procuring winter feed. But while the loss of stock was a severe blow upon many individuals, its effect upon the county generally was not what one might expect.

By a strange compensation the same snow which brings disaster to the stockman almost invariably brings bountiful harvests to the farmer, and this was true of Baker county at the time of which we are writing. The spring of 1881 opened with bright prospects for large developments in the business world. As the Walla Walla Statesman informs us, "the building of the Northern Pacific in the columns of the newspapers" was of the past. Real active and practical work had begun in earnest. A call had been issued by the company, through General Sprague, for twenty million ties, three hundred and fifty thousand of which were to be delivered on the Yakima river or its tributaries on or before August 1, 1881. It looked, therefore, very much as though something would be done by the Northern Pacific Company which would relieve, in a measure, the urgent necessity for transportation facilities in eastern Oregon and Washington. Furthermore, the immediate construction of a road from Portland to The Dalles was assured and that completed, active work was to be begun on the gap between The Dalles and Walla Walla and there was the possibility that a start would be made on the proposed road through eastern Oregon to Salt Lake City. Thus the outlook for the country was most encourag-

ing and enterprise of all kinds was stimulated in Baker and adjoining counties.

In July, 1881, William Parker, John Austin and Thomas McEwen filed articles of incorporation organizing the "Powder River, Burnt River and Summit Wagon Road and Bridge Company," with a capital stock of $50,-000, their object to build a road from Prairie City to Auburn, a distance of forty miles. The construction of this road was of great value to Baker county, as it served to deflect the trade of the John Day valley from The Dalles to Baker City. It was also of incalculable benefit to the citizens of Grant county, enabling them to procure supplies at about a quarter of the distance they had formerly traveled.

In mining circles there was much activity. The spring of 1881 witnessed another attempt to discover the famous Blue Bucket diggings, but though the searchers kept their own counsels and refused to state whether or not they had been successful in their quest, time has proven that they were not. Notwithstanding the infancy of quartz mining at that time, it was estimated by J. W. Virtue, a man generally considered authority on mining matters, that eight million dollars had been produced from this source and that the annual product of the ledges was then $650,000. Mr. Virtue gave a list of mills in operation, as follows: Connor Creek, twenty stamps; Gold Hill, ten stamps; Moore & Estabrooks, two stamps; New England & Oregon Mining Company, five stamps, operating in silver ore; Virtue Gold and Silver Mining Company, twenty stamps, with steam hoisting and pumping works; Mammoth, five stamps; Tom Payne, two stamps. There were also about thirty arastre in operation. At this time Grant county had about forty stamps in the different mills, the largest of which was the Monumental, with fifteen stamps and all modern improvements.

That the settlement of the country during 1881 and 1882 was very rapid is evinced by the fact that a flour famine was threatened. There were only a few mills in this region and these were of small capacity, and even so, they could not get enough wheat to keep them in operation. We are informed that the price of flour in Baker City in November, 1882, was $12 per barrel, and that in some of the outlying districts of Oregon and Idaho, it could not be procured at any price.

But to return to our railroad history,—for fifteen years or more the people of eastern Oregon had been using their utmost endeavors to direct the attention of railway magnates this way, apparently without avail. When, however, the railway world at last awoke to the importance of the great inland empire, there was stir among almost all the companies operating in the west and a simultaneous rush for the prize, the value of which none of them had formerly seemed to realize. A company was incorporated at Seattle, known as the Seattle, Walla Walla and Baker Railroad Company, with a capital stock of $3,000,000. Its purpose was to build, equip and operate a narrow gauge road from Seattle, via Walla Walla, to Baker City. But it soon came to be seen that the laurels of victory would go to either the O. R. & N. Company or the Oregon Short Line, as the proposed road from Granger, Wyoming, into this region was called. As the building of these two roads progressed, the one working from the west eastward and the other in the opposite direction, a battle royal developed over the possession of the Burnt river canyon, between Baker City and Huntington. It was of great importance to the Union Pacific that it should get into eastern Oregon, so as to have an open route to the Pacific, and it was likewise of much moment to the O. R. & N. that it should secure a share of the business of southern Idaho. The Short Line was at Shoshone, Idaho, and the O. R. & N. was building from Pendleton, over the Blue mountains, to Baker City. The only feasible route for the Short

Line to reach the Pacific was through Burnt river canyon and this route was likewise necessary to the O. R. & N., if it was to secure the coveted southern Idaho business. The latter company was first to make its preliminary survey and file the necessary papers with the secretary of the interior. To further strengthen its claim it sent a force of men forward to the coveted pass early in the fall of 1882, and these were busily at work on the grade. The Short Line, also, had a surveying party in the canyon during the closing days of the year 1882, running a line near that of the O. R. & N. But as the canyon was so narrow and of such contour that the O. R. & N.'s road, as surveyed, would cross the river forty-four times in a distance of twenty miles, it was plain that both roads could not well occupy the pass. The difficulty was amicably settled at a joint meeting of the stockholders of the two companies, held in March, 1883, at New York City. The agreement there reached was that the O. R. & N. should complete its extension from Baker City to the Snake river and that the Oregon Short Line should connect with it at Huntington. Through traffic rates were arranged, schedules talked over and other details of the arrangement adjusted, and December 31, 1883, was fixed as the date for effecting the junction.

Both companies increased their forces many fold in order to insure the completion of the work in the time specified. They did not succeed, however, for it was twelve months later before the final spike was driven. On the train bringing the O. R. & N. officials to take part in this ceremony were H. S. Rowe, superintendent; P. T. Keene, private secretary; C. H. Prescott, senior manager; H. B. Thielson; R. M. Steele; G. R. Shaw, roadmaster; also Mr. Smeed, a Union Pacific engineer; J. Brandt, superintendent of the O. & C. road; Tony Noltner, of the Portland Standard; J. N. Steele, of the Portland News; Senator Slater; J. B. Fithian; J. S. Wilson, station agent at Baker City; and Thomas Merry, of the Oregonian. Two hundred people witnessed the ceremony, which consisted in placing the four rails in position and spiking them down, this necessary preliminary being followed by the driving of a highly polished steel spike. This was started by H. B. Thieson, after whom the various officials and guests each gave the spike a blow and when it had reached its final resting place, the two railroads were officially united.

The impetus given to industry by the anticipation of a railroad did not cease to exert its influence after the whistle of the locomotive had awakened the echoes with its unwonted sound. Every industry rapidly accommodated itself to the new regime and many of them assumed larger proportions, owing to the encouraging effect of cheaper and speedier transportation. The farmer was no longer dependent upon the local market alone and before the railroad was many months in existence, we find that he began shipping his products to outside cities, the first exportation being about fifteen cars of barley. Large numbers of cattle were also shipped. In June, 1885, the Oregon Horse and Land Company, which operated principally in Baker county, imported from France one hundred and nine Percheron horses, forty-seven males and sixty-two females, the average cost of each being one thousand dollars. By this venture the company added to its already very enviable prestige, for it was, prior to the purchase of these thoroughbreds, the largest horse raising association on the American continent, perhaps in the world. It is stated that in 1884 it branded over 8,000 horses and in 1885, a still larger number, probably 11,000.

The presence of these and other valuable horses in the county naturally drew to this vicinity a large number of thugs and desperadoes, and the loss of horses as a result of their ravages was a thing of almost daily occurrence. Not a few of these characters terminated their earthly pilgrimage at the end of a hempen cord, suspended from a tree, but they seemed to prefer risking such punishment to honest endeavor, though the opportunities for such teemed on every side. The most notorious character of the period was a boy of less than twenty years; his name was Fred Inkleman. He had been a criminal from life's early morning, but no doubt insanity was the cause of his most atrocious crimes. In the spring of 1885 he went to work for a man named Busby, and soon he had a disagreement with his employer concerning wages. One morning he departed without ceremony, taking ten head of fine horses with him. No doubt he intended to drive these to his former home at Lakeview and there sell them, but when near Sumpter, he met two of Baker county's most esteemed citizens, Rivers and Allen. It is supposed that he mistook them for officers; at any rate he killed both. Three days later he was captured. When arraigned before the circuit court in October he pleaded guilty and was sentenced to life imprisonment.

While awaiting trial, young Inkleman was accused of having added five more homicides to his load of guilt, by setting on fire the jail in which he was confined, hoping thereby to escape. He was the only prisoner who survived that terrible holocaust. There is, however, some doubt of his guilt in this instance. Twice while in the Baker county jail and twice in the penitentiary he attempted to take his own life. He was eventually transferred to the insane asylum, where he died of gangrene, at the age of nineteen years.

In July of the year 1886 a destructive wind and hail storm visited Sumpter valley, the most severe ever known in Baker county. Trees were uprooted, cabins razed to the ground, stock killed and several people seriously injured. At the Huckleberry mine a cabin was destroyed in which were three men at the time. Three large trees fell upon it almost simultaneously, but strange to say, all the men escaped without injury.

As affording to the reader a basis from which to estimate the material wealth of Baker county at this time, we quote the summary of assessments for the year 1886: 132,506 acres land, value $365,834; town lots, $286,710; improvements, $784,942; merchandise and implements, $297,971; money, notes, accounts, mortgages, $295,760; household furniture, $46,830; 15,605 horses, value, $392,510; 44,716 cattle, value, $635,517; 67,078 sheep, value, $97,901; 2,013 swine, value, $4,690; gross value of property, $3,208,665; indebtedness, $684,309; exemptions, $174,700; total taxable property in Baker county, $2,349,255.

The population of the county in 1886 was estimated at from fifteen to eighteen thousand, and though this may have been above the actual, yet it is certain that an enormous gain had been made as a result of the railroad's advent. The prices for staple commodities at this period, as given by C. M. Thorndyke & Company's published report were: Oats, 1 cent per pound; barley, 90 cents per hundred pounds; wheat, 50 cents per bushel; flour, $3.74 per hundred pounds; potatoes, 80 cents per hundred pounds; onions, $1.50 per hundred pounds; cabbage, the same; bacon, 8½ cents per pound; chickens, $2.50 per dozen; wood, $3 per cord; beef hides, $1 to $3.50; deer skins, 15 cents to 25 cents; sheep pelts, 15 cents to 25 cents; bear skins, $3 to $8; beaver skins, $2 to $4.50; otter skins, $3 to $7; fisher skins, $2.50 to $10; martin skins, 75 cents to $2; coyote skins, 25 cents to $1; red fox skins, $1 to $1.50.

At the Mechanics' fair, held in Portland in the fall of the year 1886, Baker county was especially well represented, its exhibit being one of the finest ever seen in the northwest. To the energy and good taste of J. W. Virtue, its manager, the excellence of this exhibit was mainly attributable, though no one man could have gotten together such a diverse and representative collection of the county's products. This could only be accomplished by public-spirited co-operation on the part of all the leading citizens. "One feature of the collection," says the Portland News, "is especially noteworthy. A map of a farm six miles from Baker City shows the various portions on which were raised wheat, barley, oats, potatoes, etc., also the orchard and the mountainous section. Around the map of the farm are magnificent specimens of wheat, barley, oats, timothy, potatoes and fruit raised thereon, and in a plate is over $50.00 worth of gold dust, gathered from the gulches of this same farm."

In the spring of 1887 an important reduction was made in the territorial extent of Baker county by the formation out of its southern portion of Malheur county, which, according to the law creating it, was to be organized April 1st. The boundaries of the new county were fixed by territorial enactment, as follows: "Beginning at a point on the boundary line between the states of Oregon and Nevada, which is at the southeast corner of Grant county, thence north on the line between Grant county and Baker county, to the first angle corner in the east line of said Grant county; thence north on range line between ranges 36 and 37 east, to the summit of the Burnt river mountains, in township 15 south, of range 36 east; thence easterly and following the summit of said Burnt river mountains, to the intersection of south boundary line of township 14 south, of range 43 east; thence east on said south boundary line of township 14 to the middle channel of Snake river, between the state of Oregon and the Territory of Idaho; thence up the meanderings of said Snake river, on the line between Oregon and Idaho, to the mouth of the Owyhee river on said line; thence south on the line between Oregon and Idaho, to the north line of the state of Nevada; thence west on the north line of Nevada to the place of beginning."

By this act Baker county lost about half its territory (ten of its twenty-seven voting precincts), and suffered a decrease in the total valuation of its taxable property of $859,624.

Of course the new political division assumed its share, amounting to $30,000, of the indebtedness of the old county.

This year is memorable also for the fact that in it the first shipment of lumber was made out of Baker county or this section of the state, an event which gave prophecy of an important industry to be developed. The shipment consisted of thirteen cars, consigned to Bernard White, Ogden, Utah. The consignors were McMurren, Crabill & Company, a firm of local capitalists.

In 1888 a new and important mining district came into prominence in Baker county, adding its stores to the mineral wealth of the region. Some time during the previous year a prospector, on one of his gold seeking expeditions, discovered a rich ledge in a narrow gulch known as Cracker creek. He immediately sold to a miner named Bourne, who, in partnership with Col. S. H. Knowles, worked it for about ten months. The result of this labor was to prove the mines among the richest in the world, and in 1888 they were sold to a St. Louis syndicate, the Oregon Mining Company, for one million dollars. By this corporation they were named the Eureka and Excelsior, and as such have become known to the world. Cracker City was laid out in July on a site seven miles northeast of Sumpter. Its name was later changed to Cleveland and still later to Bourne. There are mines all around it at present, but among the earliest discovered in the vicinity were the Columbia, Appotomax, Golconda, Wide West, Amazon and North Pole.

The extent of commercial operations in Baker county during the year 1888 is shown by the following statistics, compiled by the Oregonian and substantiated later by the investigation of M. S. Tichner, who was appointed by the board of trade to prepare a report of the county's commercial progress: Actual gross value of Baker county property, exclusive of mines, $15,000,000; wool produced in 1888,

1,250,000 pounds; hides, 30,000 pounds; pelts, 10,000 pounds; ore shipped to Denver, 500,-000 tons; sheep shipped, 150 carloads; cattle, 200 carloads; horses, 50 carloads; increase of shipping over previous year, 25 per cent.

The board of trade report for 1889 names as among the most important mining corporations operating in Baker county: Connor Creek Mining Company, Connor Creek, 35 stamps; Eureka & Excelsior, Cracker Creek, 20 stamps; Gold Ridge, 10 stamps; Bonanza, 10 stamps; Virtue, 20 stamps; White Star, 10 stamps; Elkhorn, 10 stamps; Cleveland, 10 stamps; Oregon Gold Mining Company, Cornucopia, 20 stamps; Auburn Mining Company, Auburn, 5 stamps; Miner, 10 stamps; Elkhorn Extension, 10 stamps; La Bellevue, 20 stamps; Monumental (silver), 20 stamps; Golden Monarch, 10 stamps; Baker City, 10 stamps; Worley, 10 stamps; Phoenix, 10 stamps; Evening Star, 10 stamps.

The death roll of pioneers this year includes the names of two prominent men in county affairs. Luther B. Ison, who served as a school teacher in this county during early days, as county clerk three terms, and finally as judge of the sixth judicial district, passed away on August 2, aged seventy-eight. He had been a resident of the county since 1862. A few days later occurred the demise of Hon. James H. Shinn, also a pioneer of 1862. He was elected sheriff in 1870 and served four years and in 1882 was summoned by the franchises of the people to the office of county judge, which he also retained four years.

The year 1890 was a remarkably lively one in Baker county. The first important movement was made early in the spring and consisted of an effort on the part of the Oregon Lumber Company to interest the citizens of Baker City and vicinity in the construction of a proposed Sumpter Valley railway, to connect Sumpter valley with the seat of local government. C. W. Nibley, president of the lumber company, at a citizens' meeting held in the

First National Bank, stated his firm had investigated thoroughly the large tracts of timber lying between Sumpter and Baker City, and had concluded to build a road to tap this belt, also to construct mills in the latter place for the reduction of this timber wealth to lumber. The whole undertaking, however, was contingent upon the company's receiving substantial encouragement from the citizens. Mr. Nibley's proposal was that if local capitalists would take fifty thousand dollars' worth of the two hundred and fifty thousand dollars stock deemed necessary for the building of the road, then the company would proceed at once to its construction and would have it in operation as soon as men could build it. A committee was forthwith appointed to solicit subscriptions. The work was done principally by Edwin Hardy and B. W. Levens, and by the middle of August the required fifty thousand dollars were subscribed. The officers of this company named in the articles of incorporation were: David Eckles, of Ogden, president; Joseph A. West, secretary and chief engineer; C. W. Nibley, John Stoddard, James Nibley and Ellis Salisbury, board of directors.

About this time the Baker Valley Irrigation Company, incorporated for the purpose of supplying this valley with water for irrigation purposes, made its preliminary surveys and located a site for an immense reservoir at the head of Powder river canyon. As this would obstruct the route by which the Sumpter Valley Railway proposed to enter the Sumpter country, and indeed the only feasible route, it seemed for a time that the two corporations were in danger of becoming involved in litigation, and that the beneficent designs of one or both would be thwarted. At length, however, it was arranged that the railway might cross the dam on a bridge, and other mutual concessions were made which led to an amicable adjustment of all differences.

Then the railway company announced that the fifty thousand dollars, demanded as a condition precedent to the building of the road, would not be called for, but that the company would build the entire line with its own capital, asking only for ten acres of land in Baker City on which to build depots, and for the right of way. By July it had already completed nineteen miles. Its engineers concluded that McEwen's station, twenty-two miles out from Baker City on the Canyon City stage route, should be the terminus. As this point was already a center where three stage lines convened and was now to become an important railway point, McEwen's farm and the territory adjacent were laid out into lots, and the town of McEwensville was started. The first carload of logs was hauled over this road on August first.

The spring of 1891 brought another business revival in Baker City and county, the result of the Seven Devils boom, for Baker City was the nearest railway point to that famous camp. The section also realized the benefit from the development of the lumbering industry incident to the construction of the Sumpter Valley Railway and the fact that the rich mining districts around Sumpter were made directly tributary to it. In the spring of 1892, an industry of very great importance to the mining interests of the county was established in Baker City, namely, the Baker City Sampling Works. The value of this plant to mining men generally is obvious when it is remembered that it enabled all ore producers to thoroughly test their products at home, whereas formerly this could not be done nearer than Denver or Butte.

In March, 1893, a Baker County Pioneer Association was organized for the purpose of collecting interesting stories of early days, photographs of pioneers, historical data, etc. In order to preserve as complete a list as possible of those who laid the foundation of the county's development, making the sacrifice without which civilized and enlightened society never could have had existence here, we reproduce the list of charter members as follows: Pioneer of 1844, William B. Perkins; pioneers of 1862, A. H. Brown, John J. Dooley, I. B. Bowen, Mrs. John Dooley, C. M. Foster, J. P. Bowen, Thomas Smith, Truman F. Smith, George Chandler, Mrs. J. A. Ison, John Cramblit, Isaac Hiatt, W. H. Packwood, Sr., Jere J. Dooley, D. S. Littlefield, Mrs. I. B. Bowen, F. Dill, James Rea, J. M. Shepherd, George W. Campbell, L. O. Ison, Mrs. A. G. Chandler, S. Osborn, Martin D. Flemming, Mary A. Littlefield; pioneers of 1863, John A. Payton, William A. Hamm, A. J. Vincent, Ned Blake, Daniel H. Slam, L. S. Jenkins, Thomas J. Denny, W. C. Hindman, John Bruner, Mrs. A. F. Cramblit, W. C. Miller, Richard Garrett; pioneers of 1864, F. M. Alfred, John Bulger, Hardin Z. Perkins, John Blize, Sara A. Hamm, R. C. George, James D. Young, J. M. Lachner, Carlos Perkins, F. W. Thompson, J. A. Reid, W. H. Killing; pioneers of 1865, P. R. Bishop, George Ebell, William Bentley, John I. Sturgill, Sarah P. Caviness, V. Pfeiffenberger, John McMillan, Mrs. M. E. Alfred, F. H. Henrizi, Alfred Caviness, Thomas Huffman. Only those who were residents of eastern Oregon prior to January 1, 1866, and residents of Baker county at the time of applying for admission to the society, were eligible for membership therein. The first officers of the association were: president, W. H. Packwood, Sr.; vice-president, A. H. Brown; second vice-president, Thomas Smith; secretary, C. M. Foster; treasurer, William Brown.

It is hardly necessary to remind the reader that 1893 was the year upon which 'was ushered in the era of financial stringency, panic and distress. Banks in Spokane, Portland, Tacoma, Boise and almost all the principal cities and in the smaller towns of the west were compelled to close their doors. A huge impenetrable black cloud overcast the financial sky, obscuring the sun of prosperity, which had hitherto shone in splendor. It might be sup-posed that Baker county must share in the general depression, must feel the weight of the incubus which was fettering the wheels of industry in other parts of the Union, but such was not to be, at least not at first. There is something so vitalizing about a mining boom that it draws out the latent energies and resources of the people, casting aside every hindrance as a thing of no importance. It so happened that a most opportune discovery was made in Baker county in the spring of 1893, which brought crowds of gold hunters to the section, neutralizing the effect which the panic might otherwise have had. Early in May James Baisley, who had been prospecting for weeks in the vicinity of the White Swan mine, walked into the Citizens' National Bank, and placed on exhibition a large piece of quartz, carrying heavy values. He had found it about three miles southwest of the White Swan mine, in a locality that had been prospected over many times. A rush was made to the new Eldorado. Every man who could possibly get away shouldered a pick and shovel and started for the latest Mecca. Counters were deserted. Salaries could no longer hold men. It became impossible to procure help of any kind in Baker City and regular business enterprises were necessarily neglected. Outsiders flocked to Baker City from the country surrounding, making trade for the merchant and demand for the produce of the farmer. The entire summer of 1893 was a lively one, but though the newly discovered district was indeed a rich one, the excitement gradually subsided and things resumed their former condition.

The mining men of Baker county and eastern Oregon generally, true to their accustomed public spirit and enterprise, made good use of the World's Fair at Chicago to advertise the mineral wealth of this section of the world. The work of collecting minerals in this part was assigned to assistant superintendent of the state exhibit, F. H. Rowe, and with the help of J. W. Virtue, C. M. Donaldson, G. B. Moulton and others, he made one of the most complete collections of the mining products of Baker county ever before gotten together. Each mine was requested to furnish a sample of its ore or dirt, to consist of not less than one hundred or more than five hundred pounds of the former or two or three sacks of the latter. The result was that minerals filling four cars were collected, most of which came from Baker county mines, though a portion was from other parts of southeastern Oregon. Among the minerals displayed as the products of this section were gold, silver, copper, lead, nickel, galena, iron and coal. Various building stones, granite, marble, sandstone and slate were included in the collection.

While, as we have said, local causes prevented the coming of hard times to Baker county as soon as to the northwest generally, they could not wholly overcome the effect of the outside depression and the years 1894 and 1895 were not productive of much advancement in any line. The passage of Coxey's tatterdemalion army through the county in May, 1894, gave ocular demonstration of the sad condition obtaining in some parts of the west, but it is safe to assert that the army received few, if any, recruits from Baker county.

A mining community, especially a gold producing community, seldom feels financial depression as do manufacturing and agricultural sections. Many persons, disappointed in their efforts to secure wealth in other walks of life, turn, at such times, to the search for the treasure supposed to be hidden in the secret vaults of earth, bringing with them a measure of prosperity to the mining centers. Many of them fail in their quest but a certain proportion are always successful. This causes revival of interests in mines, a greatly increased output of the precious metals and the gradual return of prosperity. There can be little doubt that the mining revival, caused by the financial stringency of 1893–6, was itself the chief factor in curing that stringency.

It is stated that the wealth production in this county, outside of minerals, in 1894, was approximated as follows: wheat, 77,835 bushels; oats, 94,131 bushels; barley, 78,330 bushels; potatoes, 40,081 bushels; apples 7,596 bushels; hay, 28,594 tons; wool, 81,704 pounds; butter, 660,090 pounds; corn, 176 bushels; tobacco, 1,070 pounds.

The new year brought a considerable business revival. A number of old mines changed hands and some pioneer placer claims that had been abandoned because they would not pay the wages prevailing in good times were relocated and worked. Reviewing the year, in the Oregonian, John C. Young summarizes conditions in substance as follows:

Considering the general depression in the whole northwest and eastern Oregon, Baker county probably fared as well, in 1895, as any of her sister counties. While there was but little, if any, development in an industrial line, the people were generally less oppressed by unfavorable conditions than they were the previous year, 1894, owing to the practice of more strict economy. The farmers made their old wagons, harnesses and machinery do; stockmen made no new hazards, as the upward spurt in the price of beef the year previous had been short lived, owing to the free importation of beef from Mexico; and while the mines were progressing favorably, but little new capital was invested in this branch of industry in 1895. Had it not been for the fact that debts, contracted in flush times, remained fixed in terms and that taxes are seldom reduced to correspond with the universal fall in prices, the people of this county would have speedily readjusted their affairs to changed conditions.

The farmers who depended on irrigation to raise crops reaped light harvests of grain and hay, owing to the drouth that followed the light snowfall in the mountains, although the lowlands produced abundantly. The hay crop was light in consequence of the drouth, though superior in quality. Hay brought from $3 to

$6 in the stack. The low price of grain, in 1894 resulted in a somewhat large "hog crop" in 1895, which in turn resulted in large shipments of hogs, bringing about 2½ cents per pound, live weight. The grain market was also affected by this overproduction, wheat bringing only half a cent per pound. Plenty of beef was marketed at a low figure. Three-year-olds brought in the neighborhood of $21 per head, while the pick of range cattle were sacrificed at $8 to $12 per head, by the herd.

The fruit crop of Eagle valley and the Burnt river fruit district was most abundant and of unexcelled quality, but the market being limited the prices realized were extremely low. Some young peach orchards on the Snake river came into bearing and produced fruit of high grade.

The lumber industry of eastern Oregon, being chiefly represented by the Oregon Lumber Company, entered the new year with a record of prosperity. The Oregon Company, owning the Sumpter Valley railroad, purposed to extend the line through to Sumpter and had already commenced grading. Directly and indirectly, the company furnished employment to nearly two hundred persons and the wages so distributed in this section, each year, could not but have a good effect on the community at large. The concern has lumber yards in all of the principal towns of Utah and in some of the towns along the Union Pacific in Wyoming and Idaho, besides its yards in Oregon, and has recently established yards at Walla Walla and other Washington towns.

The scarcity of water during the summer of 1895 had its effect on the products of the placer mines, which were greatly diminished. In the Cornucopia district, a little new capital was invested during 1895, one Utah company and one Montana company each putting in a milling plant in their quartz mines. In the Virtue district, several new discoveries were made of free gold quartz lodes, but new developments were insufficient to give that district a boom such as it had in 1892-93. The Virtue mine

constantly employed eighty men and was yielding in the neighborhood of $18,000 per month. The last strike of two small pockets turned out $44,000. The base ore mines of the Elkhorn district were not operated with very great vigor and financially the season was not a prosperous one. At Cracker Creek, the Longmaids, experienced mining men, had the E. & E. mine under lease and bond and were concentrating their ores for shipment to the Tacoma smelter. Their shipments averaged two carloads a week of concentrates, of the average value of $135 per ton. About forty men were employed and preparations were being made for the installation of twenty more stamps. At Cable Cove a Utah company was developing a group of claims under bond and the following June were to determine whether they would go on and erect a 30-ton concentrator or not.

The good year 1896, the year in which the financial cloud began to clear away, was marked in Baker county by a most lamentable catastrophe. On the night of June 15th the water of the Goodrich creek reservoir refused to be longer restrained within its accustomed bounds and breaking away rushed madly down the mountain side, wresting huge boulders from their places, tearing out trees by the roots and bearing huge quantities of debris before it. Had there been a village in its path, the Johnstown horror would have been repeated. As it was, the only family residing below the reservoir, consisting of C. S. French, wife and five children, perished utterly and without warning, for their remains when found, were clad in night attire. The reservoir was a large one, covering about forty acres. It was constructed by Zero Snow, in 1873, for irrigation purposes. In 1894 its headgate showed signs of decay. In 1895 it was not in use but the following year it was repaired and again pressed into service. The work done upon it was not sufficiently extensive and thorough, however, as the result proved.

During this year, the Sumpter Valley rail-

PLACER TAILINGS NEAR SUMPTER.

EAGLE VALLEY.

road was extended to Sumpter, an event which was celebrated, October 3d, by an excursion to that city and by appropriate exercises.

The report of the First National Bank of Baker City and many other indications make it manifest that prosperity had returned to this region, but it was not until 1897 that the last vestiges of distress were cleared away and the country took up the forward march with its wonted vigor. In the spring of 1897 the talk of building a railroad to tap the wonderfully rich Seven Devils copper camp of Idaho was resumed. Baker City business men have long felt that the trade of this great mining region ought to be secured by them. The expectation, this year, was that the Sumpter Valley railroad would be extended into the celebrated mining camp, tapping on its way the thriving Pine and Eagle valleys. This plan did not material- ize, but residents of Baker City have never ceased to hope and expect that their town will be connected with the copper mines. A road has already been built from Weiser part way to the region, but it is expected at this writing, that work will be commenced, within a short time, upon another from Baker City. The road if constructed will tap the gold mines of the Eagle mountains, and open a country rich in agricultural possibilities, minerel wealth and timber. It cannot fail to augment immensely the growth and commercial importance of Baker City.

Notwithstanding the Klondyke boom, which had a natural tendency to draw some mining men from the eastern Oregon region, the year 1898 was a productive one in mineral wealth, as its predecessor had also been. In- deed the Klondyke excitement had a whole- some effect in advertising the country and not a few of the eastern men, who started for Alaska, were so pleased with the prospects of this region that they remained here. The rapid development of Baker City since is evidence of this fact. Agriculture also received quite an

uplift in 1898, adding materially to the gross wealth production of the county. The wood shipments of the year brought about $100,000 as returns; 34,000 head of sheep were sold at an average price of $2.50 each; about 30,000 cattle at $30 per head; and eight hundred horses at $5 each. The cereal crops were also good and commanded a fair price. The year was one of unprecedented prosperity through- out the entire state. At the Trans-Mississippi exposition, Oregon was the only Pacific state represented and it is said that her mineral dis- play won thirty-seven gold medals and di- plomas and her entire exhibit three more gold medals than that of any other state.

The chief topic of interest during 1899 was the proposed Seven Devils railroad. Though it was not built, a wagon road was, as was also a road from Sumpter to Bourne. Some of the people of what was known as the "Pan- handle" of Union county had long been de- sirous of severing their connection with the political division of which their section formed a part, and uniting their fortunes with Baker county. During this year they began working energetically to this end but their exertions re- mained unrewarded until the beginning of the year 1901.

For the sake of record we reproduce the statistics of Baker county's population, pre- pared from the census of 1900 by William C. Hunt, as follows: Alder, 283; Baker City, First ward, 1,729, Second ward, 789, Third ward, 2,280, Fourth ward, 1,865; Baker pre- cinct, No. 1, 270; Bourne, 592; Bridgeport, 172; Cleary, 279; Connor Creek, 150; Depot, 69; Express, 417; Haines, 323; Huntington precinct, including the town of Huntington, 1,014; Huntington town, 821; McEwen, 292; North Powder, 162; North Sumpter precinct, including part of Sumpter town, 678; Parker, 538; Pocahontas, 330; Rock Creek, 447; Rye Valley, 142; South Baker, 506; South Sump- ter precinct, including part of Sumpter town,

12

1,179; Sumpter town, part of, 131; Unity, 257; Virtue, 317; Weatherby, 145; Willows, 185; Wingville, 187; total population, 15,597.

As just stated, a bill was enacted in February, 1901, giving to Baker county a large section of territory which had formerly belonged to Union county. The bill passed the lower house on the 21st, and the senate the following day, and became a law without the governor's signature. We quote a portion of this law as follows:

"Be it enacted by the Legislative Assembly of the State of Oregon:

"Section 1. That all that portion of the state of Oregon embraced within the following boundary lines and heretofore a part of Union county be and the same is hereby made a part of Baker county, to-wit: Commencing at the intersection of the township line between townships six (6) and seven (7) south, range forty (40) east, with Powder river, thence east on said township line to the center of range forty-two (42) east, thence north to the township line between townships five (5) and six (6) south, thence east on said township line between townships five (5) and six (6) to the Wallowa county line, thence easterly along the Wallowa county line to Snake river, thence up and along Snake river to the mouth of Powder river, thence up and along Powder river to the place of beginning.

"Section 2. That the territory embraced within said boundary lines shall hereafter be exempt from all laws, regulations, civil and military jurisdiction of said Union county, and shall be subject to the laws, regulations, civil and military jurisdiction of said Baker county.

"Section 3. The county clerk of Union county shall, within thirty days after this act shall have gone into operation, make out and deliver to the county clerk of Baker county a transcript of all taxes assessed upon all persons and property within said bounden territory, and all taxes which shall remain unpaid upon the day this act shall become a law shall be paid to

the proper officer of Baker county. The said clerk of said Union county shall also make out and deliver to the clerk of said Baker county, within the time above limited, a transcript of all cases in the circuit and county courts of said Union county in which the defendant resides in said above bounden territory and a transcript of all matters, probate or otherwise, in which the moving party or the property involved is within said bounden territory, and file said transcripts in the clerk's office of said Union county, and transfer all the original papers in said cases or matters to Baker county for further proceedings therein."

By this act the assessable property of Baker county received an increment of about $440,000 and was required to assume the proportionate part of Union county's indebtedness fairly chargeable against the section of country transferred, which amounted to $30,751.35.

Perhaps partly for the purpose of testing the validity of this act, George W. Benson, the county clerk of Union county, refused to furnish to Baker county the transcripts required by its provisions, whereupon Baker county applied to Judge W. R. Ellis for a writ of mandamus compelling Benson to comply with the law. The court granted the writ; the case was appealed on several grounds, one being that the bill was unconstitutional. By a decision, rendered December 2, 1901, the supreme court of Oregon affirmed that of Judge Ellis and the case was decided in Baker county's favor.

On Sunday, June 2, 1901, the Sumpter Valley railway fifteen-mile extension was formally opened to the public. This road furnished an outlet for the vast quantities of timber surrounding Whitney and provided for the utilization of a valuable source of wealth production.

At the Pan-American exposition of this year the mining men of Oregon, as is their usual custom, took the trouble to have their industry fairly represented. The mineral exhibit of the state was a fine one and inspired

Mrs. Harriet Connor Brown to write for the columns of the New York Engineering and Mining Journal a very flattering descriptive article. She said, in part:

"That the state of Oregon has stores of mineral wealth which are being rapidly developed is shown by its exhibits in the Mines building at the Pan-American exposition. The exhibit is in two parts. A general display of Oregon minerals is made by A. W. Miller, of Portland, who, as superintendent of Oregon's mineral exhibits at the Chicago and Omaha expositions, has done so much to make the resources of the state known to the world. A collection of specimens from the gold-ribbed mountains of eastern Oregon is exhibited by Fred R. Mellis, of Baker City, whose fine museum of mineral wonders is well known in his own locality. This joint Oregon display is attractively installed in a conspicuous position on the floor of the Mines building, and receives the favorable comment of all visitors. It is made under the auspices of the state, Mr. Miller and Mr. Mellis each having received a certain amount of the state appropriation to aid them in their work.

"Mr. Miller's collection includes a great variety of specimens and covers Oregon's mineral wealth very thoroughly from gold and copper to pebbles and mineral waters. Specimens of free gold and gold in various combinations are shown, some of them representing ore worth as much as $12,521 per ton. A few specimens of silver ore are exhibited, but they are not many or important.

"The varied riches of other sections of the state sink into comparative insignificance beside the golden treasures of eastern Oregon. Specimens of ore from that mineral belt, which includes all of Baker county and parts of Grant and Union counties, and embraces 14,000 square miles, are the chief pride of Mr. Mellis' collection. The specimens are most of them large in size, showing that they have been taken from developed mines by the aid of modern machinery."

The current of our narrative has brought us out of the realm of history and into that of the present. At this writing, prosperity continues her benign rule; the mineral output of the old established mines of the country is on the increase; new discoveries and prospects are being developed; railroad enterprises are being projected to facilitate the movement of ores; and confidence in the future everywhere lends buoyancy to the spirits of the citizens, inspiring and energyzing industrial operations. The ultimate destiny of the county cannot be even dimly foreseen, but its undeveloped resources of agriculture and timber give earnest of great things yet to be, while the variety, diversity and wide distribution of its mines lead to the belief that past achievements in this industry are but a trifle compared with the greater developments which the future will bring forth.

CHAPTER IV.

POLITICAL.

The circumstances which led to the organization of Baker county have been adverted to in former chapters. The officers appointed to perform the various official functions until such time as they could be succeeded by duly elected officers, were:

County judge, Hon. John Q. Wilson; sheriff, George W. Hall; clerk, Samuel A. Clarke; treasurer, William F. McCrary; assessor, W. D. Quigley; school superintendent, William H. Packwood.

These officers, or at least a part of them, entered upon their duties on the 3d day of November, 1862. Their first item in the journal of the county court read as follows:

County Court of Baker County, Oregon, met pursuant to law, November 3, 1862. Present, the Hon. John Q. Wilson, county judge; I. H. Wickersham, under sheriff; William Waldo, deputy county clerk.

It appears that the first attorneys to practice before this court were Grey and the firm of Heed & Pierce. Of these Mr. Grey was attorney for the plaintiff and Heed & Pierce for the defendant, in the case of A. B. Roberts vs. Thomas Allison, who have the distinction of being the first litigants to submit their cause to the adjudication of this court.

The first jury trial to come before this court, and probably the first jury trial before any legally organized tribunal in the county, was that of Thomas Allison vs. David Love, D. H. Belknap and A. B. Roberts, for damages.

The personnel of the jury in this trial is given by the records as follows: J. J. Blake, B. C. White, John A. Johns, William M. Powers, W. C. Wills, foreman, and I. Coleman. It appear that the jury awarded to the plaintiff damages in the sum of $140. The case was appealed but ultimately settled by agreement of the parties.

Having organized the county government, some of the appointed officers seemed to think that their mission was fulfilled and resigned. Thus it appears from the journal that at the term of county court commencing May 4, 1863, W. R. Park appeared as sheriff, vice George W. Hall resigned, and that on the 7th of July of the same year, James M. Pyle assumed the official position of Mr. Wilson, who had also resigned. Mr. Quigley also failed to serve out his full term as assessor and in November, 1863, John S. Rice assumed the duties of that office.

The first session of the circuit court to be held within the limits of Baker county convened at Auburn on June 15, 1863, the Hon. Joseph G. Wilson, who was circuit judge for the fifth judicial district, comprising Wasco, Umatilla, Baker and Grant counties, presiding.

Not even with the kindly assistance and aid of the very accommodating county officials were we able to find complete records of the early elections, the names of candidates, majorities, etc., but from the records it may be gleaned that at the first general election, which took place on the first Monday in June, 1864, the following were elected:

Joseph G. Wilson, circuit judge; James H. Slater, prosecuting attorney; James M. Pyle, state senator; Samuel Colt, representative; Neill Johnson, county judge; C. M. Foster, clerk; John Lovell, sheriff; A. Witherell and A. Morrison, county commissioners; W. F. McCrary, treasurer; John D. Rice, assessor; N. J. Snaver, coroner.

The creation of Union county necessitated the resignation of some of these men, for they were resident within the limits of the new political division. For this reason, Mr. Witherell resigned the office of county commissioner and in his stead was appointed B. K. Koontz, who declined. Valentine Grey was then appointed. With regard to the school superintendency, which was also left vacant by the formation of Union county, we find the following notation in the county court's journal under date of November 14, 1864:

"It appearing to the board of commissioners that J. R. Ellison, superintendent of common schools of Baker county, is no longer a resident of said county and that he has been appointed superintendent of common schools of Union county by the state legislature, it is therefore ordered by the county court that said office of superintendent be declared vacant and that the board of commissioners appoint Jesse B. Stump superintendent of common schools, vice J. R. Ellison, removed."

Mr. Stump resigned in 1865 and C. M. Foster finished the term. A vacancy in the shrievalty of Baker county was created in the fall of 1864 by the removal to Idaho of Jonathan Lovell, and John H. Ingraham, formerly deputy sheriff, was appointed to the office. John S. Rice having resigned as county assessor in May, 1865, Sheriff Ingraham performed the duties of that office also until the following January, when he, too, relieved himself of the burdens of public office. Hiram

Huffman served as sheriff the remainder of the term. At the December term, 1864, of the county court, Jonathan Keeney was granted a license, upon the payment of $100, to operate the Boise ferry across the Snake river, and George Walker and C. D. Bacheler license to operate a ferry on the Owyhee river "at a point within one mile of the present crossing of the Owyhee and Red Bluff roads," their license to be $50. Following were the rates fixed for both ferries: Each footman, 25 cents; each pack animal, 50 cents; each loose animal, 25 cents; each wagon, one ton freight and pair animals, $2; each additional ton freight, $1; each additional pair animals, 50 cents; and each sheep or hog, 10 cents.

At the March term of 1865 a license was granted to John Partin to operate the Washoe and Central ferries, and to R. P. Olds to operate one at Farewell Bend on the Snake river. August Trunk was also granted a license to operate a ferry on Burnt river, at the mouth of Clark's creek.

Naturally much attention was given, during the early days, to the formation of county roads. It would seem from the records, though they do not specifically so state, that the first county road established was from Auburn to Monohin's ranch in the Powder river valley. At the July session, 1864, a petition was presented and read, praying the commissioners to lay out and establish a county road commencing at A. Morrison's house in the Powder river valley and extending, via the Ladd canyon and LaGrande, to Fox's mill in the Grande Ronde valley.

The election in Baker county, held June 4, 1866, resulted as follows: For Congress, R. Mallory, 286, J. D. Fay, 294; for governor, G. L. Woods, 283, J. K. Kelley, 299; for secretary of state, S. E. May, 288, L. F. Lane, 292; for state treasurer, E. N. Cook, 285, J. C. Bell, 294; for state printer, W. A. McPherson, 288, J. O. Meara, 286; for district attorney, C. R. Meigs, 253, J. H. Slater, 287; for state

senator, L. W. Getchell, 243, S. Ison, 261; for
representative, William Corcoran, 242, A. C.
Loring, 263; for county commissioners, T. Mc-
Murren, 235, J. J. Jarvis, 237, J. M. Rea, 255,
J. C. Humphrey, 259; for joint representative,
William C. Wills, 243, W. C. Hindman, 261;
for sheriff, M. F. Colt, 230, J. W. Virtue, 262;
for clerk, C. M. Foster, 237, J. H. Shinn, 252;
for assessor, R. E. Brown, 232, P. R. William,
258; for treasurer, George Brattain, 248, L.
Pfeiffenberger, 243; for surveyor, I. B. Bowen,
237, M. T. Hindman, 258; for superintendent
public schools, J. M. Boyd, 237, L. Critton,
259; for coroner, M. C. Farrar, 234, O. Dean,
257.

In September, 1866, Neill Johnson resigned
the county judgeship and A. F. Johnson was
appointed to fill the unexpired term.

We have been unable to find any record of
the election returns for the year 1868, but Mr.
Hiatt gives the names of the successful candi-
dates as follows: Member of Congress, Joseph
Smith; member of the legislature, Ransom
Beers; county judge, L. L. McArthur; sheriff,
James W. Virtue; clerk, Joseph Shinn; treas-
urer, Joseph Beck; assessor, Hiram Osborn;
commissioners, John P. Bowen and A. J.
Weatherby.

The result of the election of state, county
and district offices in Baker county, for the year
1870, was: For Congress, Slate, Democrat,
561, Wilson, Republican, 414; for governor,
Grover, Democrat, 579, Palmer, Republican,
402; for secretary of state, Chadwick, Democrat, 582, Elkins, Republican, 401; for treasurer, Fleischner, Democrat, 577, Kincaid, Republican, 405; for district judge, McArthur,
Democrat, 591, Whitten, Republican, 363; for
district attorney, Lasswell, Democrat, 569,
Lichtenthaler, Republican, 372; for state senator, Brown, Democrat 486, Foster, Republican, 364; for representative, Porter, Democrat,
488, Olds, Republican, 366; for joint representative, McLean, Democrat, 510, Bentley, Republican, 356; for county judge, McFarland,

Democrat, 490, no opposition candidate; for
sheriff, Shinn, Democrat, 427, Littig, Republi-
can, 408; for clerk, Ison, Democrat, 488,
Webber, Republican, 355; for commissioners,
Schofield and Gardner, Democrats, 486 and
485 respectively, Brown and Boswell, Repub-
licans, 369 and 327 respectively; for treasurer,
Parker, Democrat, 477, Logan, Republican,
375; for assessor, Richardson, Democrat, 508,
Cole, Republican, 329; for surveyor, Johnson,
Democrat, 495, Crabill, Republican, 357; for
school superintendent, Foster, Democrat, 498,
Hiatt, Republican, 351; for coroner, Snow,
Democrat, 495, Cleaver, Republican, 351.

L. L. McArthur, who was elected county
judge in 1868, resigned before the expiration
of his term and L. O. Sterns was appointed in
his place. In 1870, as above stated, J. D. Mc-
Farland was elected county judge without opposition. A dispute arose as to who should have
the office, Mr. Sterns claiming that he should
hold it under his appointment until McArthur's
term should have expired, that is until 1872.
Mr. McFarland claimed the office in virtue of
his having been elected by the people and having been furnished a certificate of election.
Mr. Sterns held the office until the fifth of
September, when the county commissioners,
Judge McFarland and several substantial citizens insisted that he should vacate the seat in
favor of McFarland, holding that a certificate
of election was of more force than an appointment by the governor.

In 1872 the Democratic party of Baker
county, at its convention held February 26th,
nominated the following county officers: For
sheriff, James H. Shinn; for clerk, L. B. Ison;
for the legislature, J. B. Onstien; for county
treasurer, G. W. Parker; for county assessor,
William Quinn; for commissioners, H. W.
Estes and D. B. Schofield; for surveyor, John
Brattain; for coroner, Dr. T. N. Snow; for
school superintendent, J. W. Wisdom.

The Republicans held their convention on
the 4th of March and named as their candidates

the following persons: For sheriff, Walter Fernald; for clerk, Daniel Dwight; for treasurer, O. H. Clement; for assessor, D. S. Moomaw; for county commissioners, John Wade and William Baldock; for superintendent of schools, E. H. Bunnell; for county surveyor, J. E. Meacham; for coroner, Dr. J. M. Boyd; for representative, H. M. McKinney.

The result of the election following may be summarized as follows: J. B. Onstien, Democratic candidate for representative received 558 votes; H. M. McKinney, Republican, 326; Dunham Wright, Democratic candidate for joint representative, 554, S. S. White. Republican, 336; for county commissioners, H. W. Estes and D. B. Schofield, Democrats, received 521 and 432 votes respectively; W. Baldock and John Wade, Republicans, 356 and 423 respectively; for sheriff, James H. Shinn, the Democratic nominee, received 526 votes and W. Fernald, Republican, 342, while E. W. Reynolds, the independent candidate, received two votes. The popular choice for clerk was Luther B. Ison; for treasurer, G. W. Parker; for assessor, W. Quinn; for superintendent of schools, J. W. Wisdom; for coroner, Dr. T. N. Snow, all Democrats.

The Democratic convention of the year 1874 was held in the court house in Baker City, on the 23d of February. The nominees of this party for the various county offices were: For state senator, John W. Wisdom; for representatives, C. G. Chandler and J. C. Wilson; for sheriff, James H. Shinn; for county clerk, Luther B. Ison; for county judge, D. B. Schofield; for county commissioners, M. Kelley and W. Fuqua; for treasurer, George W. Parker; for assessor, William H. Hull; for surveyor, John Brattain; for school superintendent, W. F. Payton; for coroner, Dr. T. N. Snow.

The Republican convention held on the 17th of March, 1874, named the following ticket: for senator, Samuel Colt; for representatives, Thomas Littig and William Chambers; for sheriff, Dr. J. M. Boyd; for commissioners,

E. H. Bunnell and E. Imbler; for surveyor, Cy. Brattain; for coroner, Dr. J. T. Atwood. This convention endorsed D. B. Schofield, Democratic candidate for the office of county judge.

The election in Baker county resulted as follows: Representatives, Chandler and Wilson, Democrats, 452 and 437 votes respectively, Chambers and Lawrence, Republicans, 351 and 155 respectively; for state senator, Wisdom, Democrat, 434, Colt, Republican, 334; Sterns, 30; for sheriff, Shinn, Democrat, 379, Boyd, Republican, 436; for county judge, D. B. Schofield, the nominee on both tickets, 821; for county clerk, Ison, Democrat, 427, Webber, Republican, 395; for county treasurer, Parker, Democrat, 509, Grier, Republican, 325; for superintendent schools, Payton, Democrat, 445; McClelland, Republican, 376; for county surveyor, John Brattain, 478, J. C. Brattain, 334; assessor, William H. Hull, Democrat, 520, Pritchard, Republican, 291; for coroner, Snow, Democrat, 480; Atwood, Republican, 345; county commissioners, Fuqua and Kelley, Democrats, 466 and 549 respectively, Imbler and Bunnell, Republicans, 286 and 303 respectively.

The campaign of 1876 was an extremely strenuous, even virulent one. The Democrats held their county convention March 6th, and placed the following ticket in the field: For representatives, I. D. Haines and A. J. Lawrence; sheriff, R. C. George; clerk, George W. Parker; county treasurer, S. Ottenheimer; assessor, L. B. Rinehart; commissioners, William Glenn and Strother Ison; surveyor, C. L. Means; superintendent schools, S. H. Small; coroner, Dr. J. B. Hulsey.

On April 12th, the date set for the Republican convention, delegates representing the different precincts of the city and county met and placed a "Taxpayers'" ticket in nomination. This ticket was the first fusion ticket ever placed in the Baker county political field, the delegates being Republicans and Democrats not satisfied with their regular party organ-ization. The nominees were: For representa-tives, Dr. J. M. Boyd and David Littlefield; for sheriff, William Brown; clerk, T. J. Brow-er; treasurer, John P. Ross; assessor,—Ed-wards; county commissioners, William Cham-bers and Anse Loennig; superintendent coun-ty schools, P. Crabill; surveyor, Stephen Os-born; coroner, no nomination.

A few days later a call was issued, signed "Many True Republicans," for a county con-vention to be held April 24th, and relating that: "Whereas the delegates to the county conven-tion held on the 12th inst., false to the trust reposed in them by the Republican primaries which elected them, fused with the disap-pointed Democracy, to place in the field a so-called Taxpayers' ticket, thus completely ignor-ing the Republican organization and subordin-ating the public good and the party discipline to the requirements of private ambition and in-dividual chicanery; that the Republican party stands without representation or recognition in the political field and that all true Republicans be and they are hereby requested to meet in convention April 24th." On this date, "many true Republicans" assembled and having or-ganized themselves, adopted the following res-olution, contrary to the intent of the signed call:

"Resolved, That as true Republicans, hav-ing the best interests of the party and county at heart, we feel it our duty, aside from politi-cal issues, to endorse the 'Taxpayers' ' ticket, and we would appeal to every voter of the county to do the same."

The result of the election in June was as follows: For representatives, Haines and Lawrence, Democrats, received 563 and 465 votes respectively, Boyd and Littlefield, Fu-sionists, 387 and 381 votes respectively; for sheriff, George, Democrat, 481 votes, and Brown, Fusionist, 427 votes; for clerk, Park-er, Democrat, received 481 votes and Brower, Fusionist, 438 votes; for treasurer, Ottenheim-

er, Democrat, received 495 votes and Ross, Fusionist, 402 votes; for assessor, Rinehart, Democrat, 503 votes, Edwards, Fusionist, 392 votes; for commissioners, Glenn and Ison, Democrats, received 493 and 490 votes respec-tively and the Fusionist candidates, Chambers and Loennig, 419 and 416 votes respectively; for superintendent county schools, Small, Dem-ocrat, received 485 votes and Crabill, Fusion-ist, 411 votes; for surveyor, Means, Demo-crat, received 506 votes and Osborn, Fusion-ist, 406 votes; Dr. Hulsey, the Democratic nominee for coroner received 628 votes, there being no opposition. Judge McArthur, the only candidate for the county judgeship, re-ceived 666 votes.

The year 1878 found the two leading polit-ical parties rent by factional strife. The Dem-ocratic party in Baker county was said to be dominated by a ring, subservient to the inter-ests of a state ring at Salem. The Republi-cans had not yet forgotten their troubles in 1876 and the total disorganization of their party in this county that year. Then, too, county affairs were in a bad way financially. The exact condition of the treasury could not be ascertained, as the books were in such a muddled condition that the grand jury had em-ployed expert accountants to examine them, and these accountants had not yet reported when election day arrived. The Bedrock Democrat, the exponent of the Democratic party of this county and section of the state, was but lukewarm in support of that party's candidates, and was in open revolt against the Democratic leaders at Salem. On the whole, the situation was hazy and none could fore-tell results.

The Republican state convention met at Salem, April 17th, and placed in nomination the following ticket: governor, C. C. Beek-man; Congress, Rev. H. K. Hines; secretary of state, R. P. Earhart; state treasurer, Ed-ward Hirsch; state printer, W. B. Carter; su-perintendent public instruction, L. J. Powell;

district attorney, C. W. Parrish. At the county convention held April 3d, the Republicans chose the following as their standard bearers in county politics: State senator, J. P. Atwood; representatives, A. C. Goodrich and L. W. Nelson; clerk, A. C. McClelland; sheriff, Charles Kellogg; treasurer, A. P. Weller; county judge, A. B. Elmer; county commissioners, C. T. Lacy and John F. Stevens; assessor, William Morfitt; superintendent of schools, H. N. McKinney; surveyor, William Chambers; coroner, Thomas Smith.

The Democratic state nominees for 1878, nominated at Portland, April 11th, were: Governor, W. W. Thayer; Congress, Hon. John Whiteaker; secretary of state, T. G. Reames; state treasurer, A. H. Brown; state printer, A. Noltner; superintendent public instruction, T. G. Stites; district attorney, Luther B. Ison. The Democratic county convention was held March 25th, and nominated candidates as follows: state senator, I. D. Haines; representatives, C. G. Chandler and W. R. Curtis; sheriff, R. C. George; clerk, G. W. Parker; treasurer, S. Ottenheimer; county judge, W. J. Leatherwood; county commissioners, Hiram Osborn and R. P. Yantis; assessor, David Rankin; superintendent schools, L. C. Bare; surveyor, C. L. Means; coroner, Dr. G. W. Biggers.

The election was closely contested and for the first time in several years, the Republicans secured a fair share of the offices. The result in Baker county was as follows: Congress, Whiteaker, Democrat, 562, Hines, Republican, 334; governor, Thayer, Democrat, 543, Beekman, Republican, 366; secretary of state, Reames, Democrat, 533, Earhart, Republican, 372; state treasurer, Brown, Democrat, 409, Hirsch, Republican, 443; state printer, Noltner, Democrat, 474, Carter, Republican, 398; superintendent public instruction, Stites, Democrat, 540, Powell, Republican, 367; district attorney, Ison, Democrat, 407, Parrish, Republican, 480; state senator Haines, Democrat, 453, Atwood, Republican 424; representatives, Chandler and Curtis, Democrats, received 536 and 447 votes respectively and Goodrich and Nelson, Republicans, 445 and 325 votes respectively; sheriff, George, Democrat, 443, Kellogg, Republican, 424; county judge, Leatherwood, Democrat, 392, Elmer, Republican, 458; treasurer, Ottenheimer, Democrat, 352, Weller, Republican, 503; clerk, Parker, Democrat, 467, McClelland, Republican, 411; county commissioners, Yantis and Osborn, Democrats, 478 and 424 votes respectively, and Stevens and Lacy, Republicans, 452 and 371 votes respectively; assessor, Rankin, Democrat, 499, Morfitt, Republican, 366; surveyor, Means, Democrat, 465, Chambers, Republican, 364; superintendent public schools, Bare, Democrat, 407, McKinney, Republican, 450; coroner, Biggers, Democrat, 431, Smith, Republican, 408.

The spring election of the year that saw Garfield chosen president, 1880, was as lively as those preceding, and resulted in a Democratic victory. The Democrats were first in the field with their county convention, having held it March 15th, with the following result: Representatives, A. J. Lawrence and L. B. Rinehart; sheriff, Wallace W. Travillion; clerk, Thomas D. Parker; treasurer, H. C. Paige; assessor, David A. Rankin; superintendent county schools, John A. Payton; county commissioners, George Chandler and W. S. Glenn; surveyor, C. L. Means; coroner, H. C. Durkee. At the state convention held at Albany, Hon. John Whiteaker was a second time nominated for Congress. P. P. Prim, J. K. Kelly and John Burnett were nominated as justices of the state supreme court, and L. L. McArthur as district judge and D. W. Bailey as prosecuting attorney for the fifth judicial district. Besides these the regular number of presidential electors were named.

The Republicans held their county convention late in March and placed the following ticket before the electors of Baker county: Representatives, J. P. Atwood and Jere J. Dooley; sheriff, A. P. Weller; clerk, C. L. Palmer; treasurer, C. M. Kellogg; county commissioners, J. M. Swift and W. K. Stark; assessor, A. McPherson; superintendent county schools, H. N. McKinney; surveyor, C. M. Foster; coroner, C. W. Durkee. At Portland the Republicans placed M. C. George in nomination for Congress; John Waldo, W. P. Lord and E. B. Watson in nomination for supreme court judges; and M. L. Olmstead as district judge and Robert Eakin as prosecuting attorney for the fifth judicial district.

George, Republican, was elected to Congres over his Democratic opponent, Whiteaker, and McArthur defeated Olmstead for circuit judge. The county Democratic ticket went into office with a victory unmarred by the defeat of a single candidate.

Garfield and Arthur carried the state by a majority of 423 at the election in November. In Baker county the official returns gave Hancock and English 629 votes and Garfield and Arthur, 446 votes, thus making Baker county Democratic by a majority of 183.

The campaign of 1882 was as closely contested as that of 1878, the county electing a full set of Democratic officers with the exception of assessor, which went to the Republicans by a majority of 10 votes, and coroner. The Republicans waged their battle more on national issues than local, one phase being especially interesting to the west, the proposed passage by a Republican Congress of the Chinese Exclusion act. The Democrats sought to give first place to local issues and claimed among other reasons why their cause was the just one, that the state was in the hands of a federal ring. The campaign ranks as one of the bitterest of the county's early campaigns. The state gave the Republican ticket a majority of about 1500.

The roster of the Democratic nominees read as follows: For Congress, W. D. Fenton; for governor, Joseph S. Smith; for supreme judge, E. D. Shattuck; for secretary of state, J. K. Weatherford; for state treasurer, Hiram Abraham; superintendent public instruction, C. L. Worthington; state printer, Wilbur F. Cornell; prosecuting attorney, T. C. Hyde; for representatives, L. B. Ison and W. R. Curtis; for state senator, I. D. Haines; for county judge, James H. Shinn; for county commissioners, E. P. Perkins and J. T. Tillson; sheriff, W. W. Travillion; for clerk, T. D. Parker; assessor, R. Lineberger; for treasurer, R. D. McCord; for superintendent public schools, John Payton; for surveyor, M. D. Abbott; for coroner, J. W. Cleaver. The county convention was held April 27th.

The Republican county convention met in Baker City May 3d, and nominated the following ticket: For state senator, A. C. Goodrich; for representatives, S. T. Stacy and David L. Moomaw; for county judge, P. Crabill; for county commissioners, Henry Rust and ——— Caldwell; for sheriff, William Brown; for clerk, W. J. Estabrook; for treasurer, Peter Basche; for assessor, ——— Thompson; for superintendent public schools, ——— Reynolds; for surveyor, Charles Foster; for coroner, Julius Bamberger.

Baker county's official vote was as follows: Congress, Fenton, Democrat, 612, George, Republican, 491; governor, Smith, Democrat, 621, Moody, Republican, 484; secretary of state, Weatherford, Democrat, 612, Earhart, Republican, 489; state treasurer, Abraham, Democrat, 606, Hirsch, Republican, 498; state printer, Cornell, Democrat, 615, Byars, Republican, 490; superintendent public instruction, Worthington, Democrat, 618; McElroy, Republican, 487; supreme judge, Shattuck, Democrat, 627, Lord, Republican, 478; prosecuting attorney, Fifth district, Hyde, Democrat, 629, Leasures, Republican, 467; state senator, Haines, Democrat, 602, Goodrich, Republican, 478; representatives, Ison and Curtis, Democrats, 659 and 600 respectively, Stacy and Moomaw, Republicans, 449 and

373 respectively; county judge, Shinn, Democrat, 564, Crabill, Republican, 491; county commissioners, Perkins and Tillson, Democrats, 744 and 501 respectively, Caldwell and Rust, Republicans, 519 and 350 respectively; sheriff, Travillion, Democrat, 588, Brown, Republican, 483; clerk, Parker, Democrat 599, Estabrook, Republican, 469; treasurer, Mc-Cord, Democrat, 551, Basche, Republican, 522; assessor, Lineberger, Democrat, 532, Thompson, Republican, 542; superintendent county schools, Payton, Democrat, 673, Reynolds, Republican, 363; surveyor, Abbott, Democrat, 578, Foster, Republican, 496; coroner, Cleaver, Democrat, 504, Bamberger, Republican, 545.

The Republican county convention for 1884 was called for April 16th. On that day the convention nominated, as representatives of that party at the polls in June, the following: For representatives, William Morfitt and Lon Cleaver; sheriff, T. E. Hoffman; clerk, W. H. Packwood; treasurer, Walter Fernald; assessor, Dan Cavana; commissioners, B. F. Kendall and J. P. Faull; superintendent of schools, M. Alexander; surveyor, A. J. Newman; coroner, Charles Littlefield. The state ticket was led by Binger Hermann, candidate for Congress. D. Flinn was nominated for supreme judge; and M. L. Olmstead for circuit judge and C. W. Parrish for prosecuting attorney, of this judicial district. Besides these, three presidential electors were named.

The Democrats placed C. G. Chandler and R. A. Lockett in nomination for state representatives; J. T. Dealey for sheriff; M. D. Wisdom for clerk; P. Campbell for treasurer; F. Divens for assessor; A. J. Wetherby and E. P. Perkins for county commissioners; John A. Payton for superintendent public schools; C. L. Means for surveyor; and J. W. Cleaver for coroner. This convention was held April 7th. The Democratic state convention was held at The Dalles ten days later, at which the following state ticket was placed in the field:

Congress, John Meyers; supreme judge, W. W. Thayer; circuit judge, G. W. Walker; prosecuting attorney, M. D. Clifford; and presidential electors. Eastern Oregon was represented on the state ticket, this year, by a presidential elector, Luther B. Ison.

It was at this election that the woman suffrage question first manifested itself, a petition being circulated and signed by the women of Baker county to the number of 150, pledging themselves to vote, if granted that privilege. Their labors then, as now, were in vain.

State honors were about equally divided at the June election, Hermann, Republican candidate for Congress, leading Meyers, his opponent, and Thayer, Democratic candidate for supreme judge, being elected. The county went Democratic, as usual, by between 200 and 300, but one Republican receiving an office, namely, B. F. Kendall, who defeated A. J. Weatherby for county commissioner by four votes. Olmstead, Republican candidate for the district judgeship was elected and after a close fight, Clifford, the Democratic nominee for the attorneyship, defeated Parrish, Republican.

The vote in Baker county follows: Congress, Meyers, Democrat, 944, Hermann, Republican, 724; supreme judge, Thayer, Democrat, 980, Flinn, Republican, 694; district judge, Walker, Democrat, 894, Olmstead, Republican, 776; district attorney, Clifford, Democrat, 895, Parrish, Republican, 770; representatives, Chandler and Lockett, Democrats, 917 and 912 respectively, Cleaver and Morfitt, Republicans, 671 and 757 respectively; sheriff, Dealy, Democrat, 896, Hoffman, Republican, 732; clerk, Wisdom, Democrat, 916, Packwood, Republican, 713; treasurer, Campbell, Democrat, 841, Fernald, Republican, 787; county commissioners, Weatherby and Perkins, Democrats, 789 and 931 respectively, Faull and Kendall, Republicans, 739 and 793 respectively; assessor, Divens, Democrat, 998,

Cavana, Republican, 624; superintendent public schools, Payton, Democrat, 973, Alexander, Republican, 653; surveyor, Means, Democrat, 904, Newman, Republican, 695: coroner, Cleaver, Democrat, 842, Littlefield, Republican, 752.

Baker county added its small contribution to Cleveland's popular vote in the November election.

Without going into the small details which surround political campaigns in general, we give the following as the result of the campaign in Baker county, in 1886:

For Congress, Binger Herman, Republican, received 832 votes, N. L. Butler, Democrat, 1029, G. M. Miller, Prohibitionist, 41; for governor, T. R. Cornelius, Republican, 786, Sylvester Pennoyer, Democrat, 1,077, J. E. Houston, Prohibitionist, 42; for secretary of state, George W. McBride, Republican, 828, R. F. Gibbons, Democrat, 1011, A. C. Kinney, Prohibitionist, 45; for state treasurer, H. S. Marston, Republican, 814, George Webb, Democrat, 1042, John Long, Prohibitionist, 46; for state printer, F. C. Baker, Republican, 879, Charles Nickell, Democrat, 980, J. R. Shepard, Prohibitionist, 45;   for superintendent of public instruction, E. B. McElroy, Republican, 776, Napoleon Davis, Democrat, 1008, W. D. Lyman, Prohibitionist, 43; judge of supreme court, John B. Waldo, Republican, 803, R. S. Strahan, Democrat, 977; district judge, M. L. Olmstead, Republican, 824, L. B. Ison, Democrat, 1037; district attorney, G. O. Holman, Republican, 672, M. D. Clifford, Democrat, 1276; state senator, J. B. Huntington, Republican 783, George Chandler, Democrat, 976; for representatives, I. H. Holland and S. P. Williams, Republicans, received 919 and 805 votes respectively, and R. A. Lockett and H. Elms, Democrats, received 1000 and 856 votes respectively; for county judge, W. H. Packwood, Republican, received 744 votes and G. W. Parker, Democrat, 1043 votes; for commissioners, George E. Thompson and William

McMurren, Republicans, received 902 and 1051 votes respectively and Joseph Whitely and J. S. Locke, Democratic candidates, 892 and 709 respectively; for sheriff, J. I. Hinshaw, Republican, received 925 votes and J. T. Dealy, Democrat, 846; for clerk, E. H. Mix, Republican, received 924 votes and M. D. Wisdom, Democrat, 874; for treasurer, Charles St. Louis, Republican, 783 votes and S. B. McCord, Democrat, 1007; for assessor, J. H. Boyd, Republican, 786 votes and J. J. Sturgill, Democrat, 995; for superintendent of county schools, J. S. Bingham, Republican, 830 votes and L. B. Baker, Democrat, 965; for surveyor, C. M. Foster, Republican, 856, C. L. Means, Democrat, 918; for coroner, Charles Cleaver, Republican, 881 votes and J. M. Shepherd, Democrat, 889; J. S. Bingham, Independent, 1.

The Prohibitionists made their first official appearance in Baker county politics in the year 1888, nominating a full county ticket as follows: Representative, William Brown; sheriff, Simon L. Helms; clerk, G. G. Rigdon; treasurer, W. J. James; assessor, D. L. Wyatt; superintendent of schools, G. W. Kennedy; surveyor, John Fosnott; coroner, D. W. Yocum; prosecuting attorney, 6th district, D. D. Stephenson.

The Democratic county convention met March 26th, but did not finish its labors until the evening of the 29th, being three days in session. The occasion for this unusually lengthy session is to be found in the fact that a majority of the delegates could not agree upon the shrievalty nomination, causing a deadlock. Finally on the 22d ballot, W. H. Kilburn secured the coveted majority and was declared the nominee of the convention. I. D. Haines and W. C. Hindman were nominated for representatives; D. B. Jett for clerk; S. B. McCord for treasurer; E. J. Stevens for assessor; L. B. Baker for superintendent of schools; C. L. Means for surveyor; and R. T. Parker for coroner. Pendleton entertained the state convention, which met April 3d, and nominated the following: John M. Gearin for Congress; John Burnett for supreme judge; William Ramsey for circuit judge of the 6th district, and M. D. Clifford for prosecuting attorney. The lawful number of presidential electors were also nominated, this being a presidential year.

The Republican convention met early in April. The result of its deliberations follows: For representatives, G. O. Holman and N. C. Haskell; sheriff, I. S. Hinshaw; clerk, E. H. Mix; treasurer, Harry Twiss; assessor, George Borman; commissioners, George Thompson and William McMurren; superintendent of schools, C. H. Whitney; surveyor, C. M. Foster; coroner, J. H. Boyd. At the state convention, held at Portland April 11th, Binger Hermann was renominated for Congress; W. P. Lord was nominated for supreme judge; J. A. Fee, of Pendleton, for circuit judge of this district and J. L. Rand, of Baker City, for district attorney; besides the presidential electors.

A change in the law at this time, re-apportioning Baker county's representation in the legislature, necessitated the withdrawal of one of each party's nominees for representatives. Accordingly, W. C. Hindman withdrew his name from the Democratic ticket and G. O. Holman withdrew from the Republican ticket.

The official vote in Baker county was as follows: For Congress, Hermann, Republican, 800, Gearin, Democrat, 733, Miller, Prohibitionist, 20; for supreme judge, Lord, Republican, 783, Burnett, Democrat, 861; for district judge, Fee, Republican, 764, Ramsey, Democrat, 749; district attorney, Rand, Republican, 812, Crawford, Democrat, 700, Stephenson, Prohibitionist, 13; representatives, Haskell, Rpublican, 808, Haines, Democrat, 535, Hindman, 84; sheriff, Hinshaw, Republican, 848, Kilburn, Democrat, 644, Helms, Prohibitionist, 6; commissioners, McMurren and Thompson, Republicans, 867 and 763 votes respectively and Hutchinson and McClure, Democrats,

720 and 623 votes respectively; clerk, Mix, Republican, 875, Jett, Democrat, 609, Rigdon, Prohibitionist, 9; treasurer, Twiss, Republican, 666, McCord, Democrat, 820, James, Prohibitionist, 11; superintendent of schools, Whitney, Republican, 832, Baker, Democrat, 650, Kennedy, Prohibitionist, 10; assessor, Borman, Republican, 914, Stevens, Democrat,. 570, Wyatt, Prohibitionist 11; surveyor, Foster, Republican, 813, Means, Democrat, 662, Fosnott, Prohibitionist 11; coroner Boyd, Republican, 771, Parker, Democrat, 708, Yocum, Prohibitionist, 2.

In this year, 1888, an effort was made toward the establishment of a more comfortable and commodious home for the unfortunate poor of the county. A contract was entered into with Mr. Eugene Smith, of the Old Express ranch in the southern part of the county, which in effect was to convert the place into a poor farm. Previously a small building in Baker City did service as poorhouse, but this had long ago become inadequate.

The Republicans convened early in April, 1890, and placed their ticket in the field as follows: representative, Charles Duncan; county judge, William McMurren; commissioner, J. M. Duffy; sheriff, Deck Smith; clerk, Joseph McKay; treasurer, J. A. Geddes; recorder, George Borman; assessor, John H. Bacon; superintendent of schools, C. H. Whitney; surveyor, C. M. Foster; coroner, W. J. Patterson. The Portland convention on April 20th, naminated the following ticket: Congress, second district, Binger Hermann; governor; D. P. Thompson; supreme judge, R. S. Bean; secretary of state, G. W. McBride; state treasurer, Phil Metschan; state printer, Frank C. Baker; superintendent public instruction, E. B. McElroy; district judge, R. Eakin, and prosecuting attorney, J. L. Rand; joint senator, Baker and Malheur counties, O. M. Dodson.

April 17th was the date of the county Democratic convention which nominated a ticket headed by Edwin Hardy for representative. P. Conde secured the nomination for sheriff; H. H. Hindman for clerk; S. B. McCord was re-nominated for treasurer; B. W. Levens for re-corder; John B. Griffin for assessor; Patrick Campjbell for county judge; J. J. Sturgill for superintendent of schools; Emil Voigt for surveyor; and J. M. Shepherd for coroner. The state convention nominated R. A. Miller for Congress. Sylvester Pennoyer led the state ticket. The other nominees were: secretary of state, William M. Townsend; state treasurer, G. W. Webb; supreme judge, B. F. Bonham; state printer, John O'Brien; superintendent public instruction, A. LeRoy; district judge, Morton D. Clifford and district attorney, Charles F. Hyde; joint senator, Baker and Malheur counties, George Chandler.

The June election resulted in a sweeping Democratic state victory and also the defeat of the Republican candidates for district offices and the legislature. Interest in the election in Baker county was largely absorbed by the boom, then at its climax in Baker City, though on election day an unusually large vote was polled. Honors were about evenly divided in county politics as will be seen from the following official figures: Congress, Hermann, Republican, 959, Miller, Democrat, 900; supreme judge, Bean, Republican, 925, Bonham, Democrat, 931; governor, Thompson, Republican, 842; Pennoyer, Democrat, 1032; secretary of state, McBride, Republican, 954, Townsend, Democrat, 915; state treasurer, Metschan, Republican, 971, Webb, Democrat, 913; superintendent of public instruction, McElroy, Republican, 925, LeRoy, Democrat, 941; state printer, Baker, Republican, 937, O'Brien, Democrat, 938; circuit judge, Eakin, Republican, 682, Clifford, Democrat, 1166; prosecuting attorney, Rand, Republican, 954, Hyde, Democrat, 864; joint senator, Dodson, Republican 907, Chandler, Democrat, 909; representative, Duncan, Republican, 886, Hardy, Democrat, 919; for county judge, Mc-

Murren, Republican, defeated Campbell, Democrat; commissioner, Duffy, Republican, 931, Eyfer, Democrat, 874; sheriff, Smith, Republican 865, Conde, Democrat, 953; clerk, McKay, Republican, 1077, Hindman, Democrat, 707'; recorder Borman, Republican, 1090, Levens, Democrat, 738; treasurer, Geddes, Republican, 857, McCord, Democrat, 959; assessor, Bacon, Republican, 854, Griffin, Democrat, 960; superintendent of schools, Whitney, Republican, 1000; surveyor, Foster, Republican, 1012, Voigt, Democrat, 762; coroner, Patterson, Republican, 920, Shepherd, Democrat, 879.

The year 1892 marked the dawn of a new epoch in American politics. Certain forces had been at work for years crystallizing and organizing those who favored monetary and other reforms and the result was the formation of the People's party, which this year for the first time became a considerable factor in the old parties favored silver, and in mining com-stand them, were based upon the theory that the fiat of government is all that is necessary to give value to money. They therefore favored an irredeemable paper currency. While free coinage of silver was not all they wished, they considered it a step in the right direction, so were willing to join heartily with others of different political faiths who were advocating the 16 to 1 theory. Many members of both the old parties favored silver and in mining communities the movement was especially popular.

In Baker county especially were conditions favorable for the success of the Silver movement, as the placing of the white metal on an equal footing with gold would open up the silver mines in the western part of Baker county and those in Grant county and tributary to Baker City. Thus it was that on May 1st, the "First Free Coinage Silver Club of Oregon" was organized by about forty prominent citizens of this county, including bankers, merchants, ranchmen, mining men, miners, and representatives ·of other industries. Its principles were stated as follows: "Our motto—Equal rights for gold and silver, free coinage for both; our object—To use every. legitimate means to secure the free coinage of silver."* J. H. Parker, cashier of the First National Bank, was president of the club and J. C. Young was its first secretary. Its members were composed of Democrats, Republicans, Prohibitionists and independents alike.

The People's party, later to be known as the Populist party, was organized in this county at a county convention held March 9, 1892. Its beginnings were not auspicious but ere long it developed a strength which threatened seriously to render it the superior of the older parties. The campaign cry of the People's party in 1892 was "Anti-extravagance and anti-mismanagement." For the purpose of recording its principles we reproduce the platform adopted by the Baker City convention:

"Wheras, the people seeing the financial condition of Baker county, the public debt having grown in a few years to the enormous sum of nearly $200,000, and

"Whereas, the rate of taxation has been and now is enormously high, unequal and unjust, and

"Whereas, the public debt of Baker county is being increased at the annual rate of from $5,000 to $37,000, and

"Whereas, there has been a lavish expenditure of the people's money by the officers of Baker county, and

"Whereas, such officials' misconduct and high taxation has become and now is an unbearable burden, and

"Whereas, crime of every kind goes unwhipped of the law and gambling dives and other vices are openly conducted under the eyes and with full knowledge of the officials elected by the people, and whose sworn duty it is to diligently prosecute offenders against the law, and

"Whereas, large amounts of county orders

have been and are now issued for illegal purposes, now, therefore, be it

"Resolved, that we, the people, by and through this assembly, do protest against the extravagance and malfeasance of the present officers, and pledge ourselves to rectify the abuses by placing in nomination, clean, honest and capable men for the offices to be filled at the June election of 1892, of Baker county."

The county ticket placed in nomination by the People's party was: representative, H. H. Angell; commissioner, George Ebell; sheriff, Jerry Waggy; clerk, Arthur Smith; treasurer, W. J. James; recorder, W. H. Hull; assessor, B. W. Yoakum; superintendent schools, W. W. Lovelace; surveyor, Isaac Williamson; coroner, G. B. Sturgill.

The Republicans held their convention early in March wth the following result: for representative, C. H. Duncan; for sheriff, I. S. Hinshaw; for clerk, Joseph McKay; for recorder, W. S. Bowers; for treasurer, L. W. Place; for county comissioner, H. K. Fisher; for assessor, William Boyd; for superintendent of schools, M. Alexander; for surveyor, C. M. Foster; for coroner, W. J. Patterson. The state convention was held at Portland the first Wednesday in April and nominated as congressman from the second district, W. R. Ellis; F. A. Moore for supreme judge; L. R. Webster for attorney general; Harrison Kelly for circuit judge and Charles H. Finn for district attorney, 6th district; besides the regular presidential electors.

It was late in March when the Democrats met and chose their candidates for county political honors. The convention pledged itself to stand by any platform the state convention might adopt on the money question and in the state platform a lukewarm free silver plank was placed. However, it was but a secondary issue in the campaign of 1892, and was not destined to move men's passions to fiery heat until four years later. For representative, the Democrats chose William Smith; for sheriff,

P. A. Conde; for recorder, H. E. Freelove; for treasurer, S. B. McCord; for clerk, John A. Payton; for assessor, J. F. Dooley; for commissioner, J. H. Hutchinson; for superintendent of schools, W. R. Privett; for surveyor, B. Gale; for coroner, Dr. T. N. Snow. The state convention nominated as follows: congressman, second district, James H. Slater; supreme judge, A. S. Bennett; attorney general, George E. Chamberlain; circuit judge, M. D. Clifford and district attorney, Charles F. Hyde.

The June election sent Hermann and Ellis, Republicans to Congress, while in state and district offices, honors were about even. The vote in Baker county follows: supreme judge, Bennett, Democrat, 869, Moore, Republican, 738, Walker, Populist, 240; Welch, 42; attorney general, Chamberland, Democrat, 1006, Webster, Republican, 874; Congress, Ellis, Republican, 669, Slater, Democrat, 752, Luce, Populist, 468, Bright, 29; circuit judge, Clifford, Democrat, 1075, Kelly, 640, Green, Populist, 229; district attorney, Finn, Republican, 742, Hyde, Democrat, 898, Griffin, Populist, 299; board of equalization, Hunter, Democrat, 946, Morfitt, Republican, 972; representative, Duncan, Republican, 978, Smith, Democrat, 651, Angell, Populist, 307; sheriff, Conde, Democrat, 837, Hinshaw, Republican, 808, Waggy, Populist, 319; clerk, McKay, Republican, 1047, Payton, Democrat, 776, Smith, Populist, 123; recorder, Bowers, Republican, 1036, Freelove, Democrat, 673, Hull, Populist 242; treasurer, McCord, Democrat, 844, Place, Republican, 824, James, Populist, 262; commissioner, Ebell, Populist, 372, Fisher, Republican, 761, Hutchinson, Democrat, 798; assessor, Yoakum, Populist, 775, Boyd, Republican, 593, Dooley, Democrat, 563; superintendent of schools, Privett, Democrat, 1070, Alexander, Republican, 599, Lovelace, Populist 252; surveyor, Foster, Republican, 1132, Gale, Democrat, 480, Wilkinson, Populist, 303; coroner,

Snow, Democrat, 836, Patterson, Republican, 655, Sturgill, Populist, 346.

The office of sheriff was contested by Hinshaw and taken to the courts, where a decision was rendered by Judge Bradshaw in favor of Conde, giving him a majority, by corrected count, of 42.

By 1894 the silver element in Baker county had grown so strong that the Republican party incorporated a free silver declaration in its platform at the county convention held April 7th. At this convention, the following ticket was placed in nomination: Representative, J. Myrick; county judge, George E. Thompson; commissioner, W. W. Webber; sheriff, J. K. Fisher; clerk, Fred Eppinger; recorder, W. S. Bowers; treasurer, George H. H. Tracy; assessor, William Leitner; superintendent of county schools, J. A. Churchill; surveyor, L. L. Foster; coroner, Dr. T. N. Snow. W. P. Lord was nominated for governor at the state convention, held April 2d; H. R. Kincaid was nominated for secretary of state; Philip Metschan for state treasurer; C. E. Wolverton for supreme judge; C. M. Idleman for attorney general; G. M. Irwin for superintendent of public instruction; W. H. Leeds for state printer; W. R. Ellis for Congress from the second district; James A. Fee for judge and John L. Rand for prosecuting attorney in the sixth judicial district; and C. A. Johns for joint senator from Baker and Malheur counties. This convention did not come out openly for a gold standard neither did it declare itself opposed to the free coinage of silver.

The Democrats met on April 14th and placed their ticket in the field as follows: Representative, J. B. Messick; sheriff, J. L. Baisley; clerk, A. C. Shinn; treasurer, R. D. Carter; recorder, I. H. McCord; county judge, W. W. Travillion; commissioner, Thomas B. Moore; assessor, A. A. Kniss; coroner, J. M. Shepherd. The nomination for surveyor was left vacant. A week later the state convention met and nominated as follows: governor, William Galloway; attorney general, W. H. Holmes; secretary of state, Charles Nickell; state treasurer, T. L. Davidson; supreme judge, A. S. Bennett; superintendent public instruction, D. V. S. Reid; state printer, John O'Brien; Congress, second district, J. H. Raley. James A. Fee, the Republican nominee for the district judgship, was indorsed and J. M. Carroll, of Union, nominated for prosecuting attorney. E. H. Test received the nomination for joint senator to represent Baker and Malheur counties.

The Populists, who were to elect seven of the twelve county officers at the June election, met March 11th and agreed upon the following standard bearers: representative, J. C. Young; sheriff, W. H. Kilburn; clerk, H. B. Lowman; recorder, J. B. Taylor; treasurer, J. H. Jett; county judge, G. B. Moulton; commissioner, William Brown; assessor, D. W. Yoakum; superintendent of schools, W. R. Privett; surveyor, Arthur Philbrick; coroner, W. J. James. The state convention was held at Oregon City, March 16th, and resulted as follows: Governor, Nathan Pierce; secretary of state, Ira Wakefield; state treasurer, R. Campbell; supreme judge, R. P. Boise; attorney general, M. L. Olmstead; state printer, George M. Orton; superintendent of public instruction, T. C. Jory; congressman, second district, Joseph Waldrop; circuit judge, sixth district, Nat Hudson; prosecuting attorney, sixth district, Colonel William Parsons; joint senator, Baker and Malheur counties, William R. King.

E. H. Test, the Democratic nominee for state senator, did not accept the nomination tendered him, leaving the field to the Populists and the Republicans. The campaign was a lively one and fought mostly on local issues. The Populist party, in this county but two years off age, came out victorious, as will be gleaned from the following official figures: governor, Pierce, Populist, 874, Lord, Republican, 825, Galloway, Democrat, 603, Kennedy, Prohibitionist 32; supreme judge, Wolverton, Republican, 819, Boise, Populist, 758, Bennett, Democrat, 702, Hackleman, Prohibitionist 33; secretary of state, Wakefield, Populist, 892, Kincaid, Republican, 839, Nickell, Democrat, 536, McKercher, Prohibitionist, 36; state treasurer, Metschan, Republican, 889, Caldwell, Populist, 784, Davidson, Democrat, 433, Richardson, Prohibitionist, 94; attorney general, Olmstead, Populist, 1029, Idleman, Republican, 724, Holmes, Democrat, 500, Bright, Prohibitionist, 52; superintendent public instruction, Reid, Democrat, 860, Jory, Populist, 684, Irwin, Republican, 675, Harford, Prohibitionist, 79; state printer, Orton, Populist, 859, Leeds, Republican, 858, O'Brein, Democrat, 527, McKibben, prohibitionist, 49; congressman, Waldrop, Populist, 834, Ellis, Republican, 754, Raley, Democrat, 710, Miller, Prohibitionist, 24; circuit judge, Fee, Republican-Democrat, 1390, Hudson Populist, 834; district attorney, Rand, Republican, 1044, Parsons, Populist, 796, Carroll, Democrat, 458; joint senator, King, Populist, 1253, Johns, Republican, 986; representative, Young, Populist, 1000, Foster, Republican, 800, Messick, Democrat, 475; sheriff, Kilburn, Populist, 1030, Fisher, Republican, 667, Baisley, Democrat, 608; clerk, Eppinger, Republican, 973, Lowman, Populist, 692, Shinn, Democrat, 626; recorder, Bowers, Republican, 941, McCord, Democrat, 800, Taylor, Populist, 564; county judge, Travillion, Democrat, 990, Moulton, Populist, 716, Thompson, Republican, 581; treasurer, Jett, Populist, 919, Tracy, Republican, 762, Carter, Democrat, 613; commissioner, Brown, populist, 1002, Webber, Republican, 776, Moore, Democrat, 508; assessor, Yoakum, Populist, 1082, Leitner, Republican, 850, Kniss, Democrat, 354; surveyor, Foster, Republican, 1294, Philbrick, Populist, 923; superintendent of schools, Privett, Populist, 1432, Churchill, Republican, 809; coroner, Snow, Republican, 978, James, Populist, 681,

13

Shepherd, Democrat, 607. The state went Republican in this election by substantial majorities.

The campaign of 1896, one of the greatest and most important in the history of our republic, was a memorable one in Baker county as well as elsewhere, and was not lacking in the intense earnestness, the supreme effort on the part of the different contending forces, and the brilliancy which give the campaign distinction above all others. The fire of enthusiasm for the white metal kindled at the Chicago convention by William Jennings Bryan, swept westward with the rapidity of lightning, and burned in eastern Oregon with consuming fierceness. Baker county gained the distinction of being the banner silver county of the state. The disciples of Bryan argued the evil results of a single money standard, the humiliation and degredation of the laboring man, the despotic power of capital, and the misrule and ruinous policy of the Republican party; the supporters of McKinley were just as ardent in exposing the worthlessness and impracticability of a silver standard, in their belief that the American laborer would be elevated to a higher and more dignified plane by protecting his work from the competition of cheap labor, and in pointing out the commercial stagnation, and as a result the general demoralization, that would follow the introduction of the Democrats into office. The largest vote ever polled in Baker county, up to that time, was polled in that November day, 2827 ballots being cast, of which Bryan received 1870 and McKinley 957, or a majority for Bryan of 913. Baker county's large majority for the Democratic ticket, as has been said above, entitled this county to the distinction of being the banner Democratic county of Oregon. Eastern and southern Oregon, the mining sections of the state, gave Bryan a sufficiently large vote to cut the Republican majority in the entire state down to 2037.

The June election being more of local interest and conducted largely on local issues, was not so much disturbed by national politics and then, too, it was early in the presidential campaign. The Populists, now at the height of their power, were first in the field, placing in nomination, at a convention held March 14th, the following ticket: for representative, D. W. Yoakum; for sheriff, W. H. Kilburn; for clerk, M. E. Swan; for recorder, John G. Foster; for treasurer, J. H. Jett; for assessor, Wayman Miller; for commissioner, G. B. Moulton; superintendent of schools, W. R. Privett; surveyor, D. S. Littlefield; coroner, J. W. Roland. The state convention was held at Salem on the 26th of March, and resulted thus: For Congress, second district, Martin Quinn; supreme judge, Joseph Gaston; district judge, sixth district, R. J. Slater; prosecuting attorney, sixth district, H. E. Courtney; member state board of equalization, O. P. Goodall; and the presidential electors.

The Republicans held their county convention the last of March and selected their candidates as follows: representative, C. W. Nibley; sheriff, Thomas McEwen; clerk, F. W. Eppinger; recorder, J. W. Goodman; treasurer A. B. Elmer; assessor, A. G. Hempel; commissioner, W. W. Webber; superintendent of schools, C. H. Whitney; surveyor, C. M. Foster; coroner, Dr. T. N. Snow. At this convention, as might have been expected in such an important mining community, resolutions were passed favoring the free and unlimited coinage of silver at the ratio of 16 to 1. The state convention, held April 8, nominated as follows: congressman, second district, W. R. Ellis; supreme judge, R. S. Bean; district judge and prosecuting attorney, sixth judicial district, Robert Eakin and J. W. Knowles; member state board of equalization, W. T. Wright. Ellis, however, was nominated as a silver candidate by the second congressional district convention.

Immediately after the adjournment of this convention, the dissenting Republicans of this district, opposed to free silver, met and placed Judge Henry Northrup, of Portland, in nomination as their candidate for Congress. No other nominations were made.

W. F. Butcher, candidate for representative, led the Democratic county ticket nominated April 3d. George Whited was nominated for sheriff; I. H. McCord for recorder; W. W. Parker for clerk; J. M. Lachner for treasurer; J. H. Hutchinson for commissioner; J. A. Payton for assessor; Mrs. M. C. Byam, for superintendent of schools (the first woman to receive such a nomination in this county); Charles D. Brown for surveyor; J. M. Shepherd for coroner. The state convention made nominations as follows: For Congress, second district, A. S. Bennett; supreme judge, John Burnett; district judge, Thomas H. Crawford; district attorney, Samuel White; member of board of equalization, A. C. Craig. Both conventions adopted resolutions favoring the free and unlimited coinage of silver.

The result of this scattering of the silver forces was a state victory for the gold standard party, though in local politics the Populists greatly cut down Republican majorities. Ellis was elected to Congress by a very small majority. In Baker county the Democrats secured but two offices. The official figures are as follows: Congress, Quinn, Populist, 847 Ellis, Republican, 784, Bennett, Democrat, 541, Northrup, Independent Sound Money, 178, McKercher, Prohibitionist, 29; supreme judge, Bean, Republican, 898, Gaston, Populist, 734, Burnett, Democrat, 532; district judge, Eakin, Republican, 1389, Slater, Populist, 702, Crawford, Democrat, 449; district attorney, Courtney, Populist, 992, White, Democrat, 922, Knowles, Republican, 618; member state board of equalization, Wright, Republican, 1030, Goodall, Populist, 868, Craig, Democrat, 713; representative, Yoakum, Populist, 882, Butch-

er, Democrat, 797, Nibley, Republican, 787; sheriff, Kilburn, Populist, 1296, McEwen, Republican, 1111, Whited, Democrat, 150; clerk, Swan, Populist, 1113, Eppinger, Republican, 1099, Parker, Democrat, 261; recorder, McCord, Democrat, 1087, Foster, Populist, 808, Goodman, Republican, 532; treasurer, Jett, Populist, 1253, Lachner, Democrat, 701, Elmer, Republican, 540; assessor, Payton, Democrat, 1125, Hempel, Republican, 815, Miller, Populist, 581; commissioner, Moulton, Populist, 981, Webber, Republican, 804, Hutchinson, Democrat, 644; superintendent of schools, Privett, Populist, 1364, Whitney, Republican, 1022; surveyor, Foster, Republican, 1268, Littlefield, Populist, 665, Brown, Democrat, 413; coroner, Snow, Republican, 1309, Shepherd, Democrat, 588, Roland, Populist, 586.

The Populist star, which came upon the political horizon in 1892 and which had attained such brilliancy in 1896, was already growing dim when the year 1898 arrived, and before the nineteenth century dawned was destined to become a scarcely discernible point of light. The silver question had given a new lease of life to the Democracy and between the two older and stronger parties, Populism was swallowed completely. Democrats, Populists and Silver Republicans combined their interests and in a joint convention held at Portland, March 26th, nominated the following state ticket: For governor, W. R. King, Populist; for secretary of state, H. R. Kincaid, Silver Republican; supreme judge, W. A. Ramsey, Democrat; attorney general, J. L. Storey, Populist; state printer, J. O. Booth, Democrat; state printer, C. A. Fitch, Populist; superintendent public instruction, H. S. Lyman, Populist; congressman, C. M. Donaldson, Silver Republican. In district convention the following nominations were made: prosecuting attorney, Samuel White, Democrat; joint senator, Baker and Malheur counties, William Smith. At this state convention, a portion of the Populist delegates, afterwards known by the appellation "Middle-of-the-Roaders," refused to fuse with the Union party, formed of the silver elements of the Democratic, Republican and People's parties, and placed another state ticket in the field. In Baker county this fragmentary party attempted to reorganize the old People's party but it was too late. Several candidates were nominated, but the result on election day showed the uselessness of the nominations.

The Union party held its first county convention April 2d, and nominated the following ticket: representative, W. E. Grace; sheriff, W. H. Kilburn; clerk, M. E. Swan; recorder, I. H. McCord; county judge, W. W. Travillion; treasurer, A. C. McClelland; county commissioner, William Brown; assessor, J. A. Payton; surveyor, Arthur Philbrick; coroner, Dr. H. E. Currey.

The Republicans held their county convention April 8th, at which the following ticket was selected: representative, N. C. Haskell; county judge, P. Crabill; sheriff, A. H. Huntington; clerk, Frank Geddes; treasurer, T. W. Downing; assessor, George Tetrau; recorder, O. C. Stern; commissioner; C. M. Cartmille; superintendent of county schools, M. Alexander; surveyor, C. M. Foster; coroner, Dr. T. N. Snow. The state convention was held at Astoria, where the following ticket was placed in nomination: for governor, T. T. Geer; supreme judge, F. A. Moore; state treasurer, C. S. Moore; secretary of state, F. I. Dunbar; state printer, W. H. Leeds; attorney general, D. N. Blackburn; superintendent public instruction, J. H. Ackerman; Congress, second district, Malcolm Moody; circuit judge, C. W. Parrish; and prosecuting attorney, W. J. Lachner; joint senator, Baker and Malheur counties, J. H. Aitkin.

The campaign was waged on the same issues as was that of 1896 except of course, that in local elections local issues were also taken into account. The Republican state ticket was elected by a substantial majority, as were also both Republican congressmen, William Smith, Unionist, was elected joint representative and Crawford and White were also elected to the circuit judgeship and prosecuting attorneyship respectively. The following figures show the result in Baker county: governor, King, Union, 1436, Geer, Republican, 1191, Luce, Populist, 115, Clinton, Prohibitionist, 51; secretary of state, Kincaid, Union, 1398, Dunbar, Republican, 1091, Wakefield, Populist, 157, Davis, Prohibitionist, 75; state treasurer, Booth, Union, 1336, Moore, Republican, 1139, Sears, Populist, 205, Votaw, Prohibitionist, 51; Congress, Donaldson, Union, 1217, Moody, Republican, 1008, Courtney, Populist, 420, Ingalls, Prohibitionist, 61; supreme judge, Ramsey, Union, 1425, Moore, Republican, 1179, Hackelman, Prohibitionist, 95; superintendent public instruction, Lyman, Union, 1313, Ackerman, Republican, 1104, Hosmer, Populist, 148, Emerick, Prohibitionist, 71; state printer, Fitch, Union, 1178, Leeds, Republican, 1061, Grace, Populist, 322, McDaniel, Prohibitionist, 77; attorney general, Story, Union, 1385, Blackburn, Republican, 1140, Bright, Prohibitionist, 115; district attorney, White, Union, 1347, Lachner, Republican, 1285; joint senator, Smith, Union, 1435, Aitkin, Republican, 1171; representative, Grace, Union, 1595, Haskell, Republican, 939, Young, Populist 178; sheriff, Kilburn, Union, 1373, Huntington, Republican, 1405; clerk, Swan, Union, 1365, Geddes, Republican, 1366; assessor, Payton, Union, 1865, Tetrau, Republican, 852; recorder, McCord, Union, 1849, Stern, Republican, 874; superintendent schools, Privett, Union, 1621, Alexander, Republican, 1145; treasurer, McClelland, Union, 1026, Downing, Republican, 1009, Jett, Populist, 610; county judge, Travillion, Union, 1427, Crabill, Republican, 954, Sparks, Populist, 262; commissioner, Brown, Union, 1316, Cartmille, Republican, 1071,

Thomason, Populist, 271; surveyor, Philbrick, Union, 1103, Foster, Republican, 1507; coroner, Currey, Union, 1206, Snow, Republican, 1160, Lew, Populist, 292.

The campaign of 1900 was fought principally on issues growing out of the Spanish-American war, though the silver question and the general prosperity of the country under a Republican administration, each came in for a good share of attention. Compared to the previous presidential election, that of 1900 was less strenuous, though by no means apathetic. Oregon elected Republican congressmen, the justice of the supreme court, the dairy commissioner, and four Republican presidential electors. Samuel White, the Democratic candidate for the district attorneyship, defeated Cockran, his Republican opponent and in Baker county the officers were about equally divided.

The following resolution adopted by the Populists, in convention, marked the official demise of this meteoric party in Baker county: "Resolved, That we unite with the new Democracy; that we continue to urge the principles which made us; that as members and adherents of the new Democracy, we accept its good fellowship and will ever vie with our friends in the support of those grand principles which work for our common good." The "Middle-of-the-Road" Populists, who withdrew from the state convention in 1898, when the Union party was formed, made an attempt again this year to resurrect the People's party but met with even poorer success than in 1898.

The new Democracy met in county convention April 17th, and proceeded to nominate a ticket as follows: for representative, W. E. Grace; for sheriff, W. W. Looney; for clerk, George H. Foster; for recorder, C. W. James; for commissioner, W. H. Gleason; for assessor, G. W. Jett; for treasurer, A. C. McClelland; for superintendent of schools, W. R. Privett; for surveyor, John Hagel; for coroner,

Dr. E. B. McDaniel. W. M. Ramsey was nominated as chief justice of the supreme court and William Schulmerich as dairy commissioner, at the state convention. At this convention, also, William Smith was accorded the nomination for congressman from the second district and Samuel White was selected as the convention's choice for prosecuting attorney for this district.

At the Republican county convention held March 31st, the following ticket was placed in the field: For representative, John T. English; for sheriff, A. H. Huntington; for clerk, Frank Geddes; for recorder, Daniel C. Robbins; for assessor, Hiram Holcomb; for commissioner, H. Fieldew; for treasurer, Robert Palmer; for superintendent of schools, H. Hyde Stalker; for surveyor, C. M. Foster; for coroner, Dr. T. N. Snow. The state convention nominated M. A. Moody for Congress; C. E. Cockran for district attorney; Charles E. Wolverton for justice of the supreme court; and J. W. Bailey for dairy commissioner.

The Independent Democrats placed J. E. Simmons in nomination for congressman from this district, the Populists, Leslie Butler for the same office, and as before mentioned, a state ticket and candidates for several county offices. But as will be seen from the official vote, the influence of these independents was hardly felt.

Official returns of the June election: Congress, Smith, Democrat-Populist, 1454, Moody, Republican, 1438, J. E. Simmons, Independent Democrat, 197, Butler, Populist, 104; supreme judge, Wolverton, Republican, 1569, Greene, Democrat, 1535, Bright, Populist, 118; dairy commissioner, Bailey, Republican, 1497, Schulmerich, Democrat-Populist, 1283, Kenady, Populist, 152; district attorney, White, Democrat-Populist, 1704, Cockran, Republican 1314; representative, Grace, Democrat, 1693, English, Republican, 1463, Harbin, Populist, 98; for sheriff, Huntington, Republican, 1666, Looney, Democrat, 1475, Oliver, Populist, 56; county clerk, Foster, Democrat, 1569, Geddes, Republican, 1644, Finch, Populist, 54; recorder, James, Democrat, 1728, Robbins, Republican, 1396, Meisner, Populist, 99; assessor, Jett, Democrat, 1690, Holcomb, Republican, 1515; treasurer, Palmer, Republican, 1677, McClelland, Democrat, 1364; commissioner, Glason, Democrat, 1570, Fieldew, Republican, 1249, Estes, Populist, 198; superintendent of schools, Privett, Democrat, 1486, Stalker, Republican, 1469; surveyor, Foster, Republican, 1892, Hagel, Democrat, 1124; coroner, Snow, Republican, 2213.

At the presidential election in November, Baker county's vote was more evenly divided than in the election four years previous, standing as follows: McKinley, 1458; Bryan, 1615; People's party, regular, 6; Weaver, Prohibitionist, 40; Social Democrat, 44.

The Republican county convention for 1902 was held March 26th, at which the following ticket was named: for representative, George H. Chandler; for county judge, Charles Duncan; for sheriff, Harvey Brown; for clerk, James Chord; recorder, Robert Henry; for treasurer, Robert Palmer; for assessor, R. W. Fame; for commissioner, John R. Gilkinson; for surveyor, Charles M. Foster; for coroner, Dr. T. N. Snow. At the state convention held in Portland, April 2d, after an exciting contest, W. J. Furnish, of Pendleton, captured the gubernatorial nomination. R. S. Bean received the nomination for supreme judge; F. I. Dunbar for secretary of state; C. S. Moore for state treasurer; A. M. Crawford for attorney general; J. R. Whitney, for state printer; and J. H. Ackerman for superintendent of public instruction. At the district convention, J. L. Rand was nominated for joint senator from Baker, Malheur and Harney counties, and T. N. Williamson for congressman from this district.

The Democratic county convention was held April 3d and resulted as follows: representative, J. H. Robbins; county judge, W. W. Travillion; for sheriff, Thomas Profitt; clerk, A. G. Combs; recorder, C. W. James; treasurer, E. P. McDaniels; assessor, G. W. Jett; commissioner, J. C. Brooks; surveyor, John Hegle; coroner, Dr. Claude M. Pearce. The labors of the state convention which met at Portland April 11th, resulted as follows: for governor, George E. Chamberlain; for supreme judge, B. F. Bonham; for secretary of state, D. W. Sears; for state treasurer, Henry Blackman; for attorney general, J. H. Raley; for state printer, J. E. Godfrey; for superintendent of public instruction, W. A. Wann; Congress, second district, W. F. Butcher, Baker City; joint senator, Baker, Harney and Malheur counties, William Smith, Baker City.

CHAPTER V.

EDUCATIONAL.

"History repeats itself," is a well known maxim, yet perhaps few realize how completely the development of any section of country is a re-enactment in miniature of the history of the race. Enlightened humanity is the product of long continued and very gradual progress from a primitive condition of savagery. As the intellect of man became slowly developed, tribal relations were formed, then federations of tribes, then absolute monarchies, which were followed, as the masses advanced in the scale of civilization, by partially representative governments and last of all by republics. The beast of burden was early pressed into the service of man. As the wants of humanity multiplied the need of a servant more efficient for many purposes was felt and steam was harnessed. This in turn became inadequate to all the requirements of the advancing race and the lightnings were chained to turn man's wheels and flash his messages from place to place. So by gradual evolution came all the complex machinery of civilized life, factories to elaborate the products of the earth, railways to transport them to parts where needed, newspapers to tell men what their fellows are doing and thinking, telegraphs to keep the newspapers in touch with distant lands, churches, schools, colleges and universities to train men for the responsibilities of life.

When a new section is to be developed, the men and women who undertake the task do not go back to a condition of savagery, but they lay aside almost all the conveniences of this advanced age. They dispense with the railway, the telegraph, the telephone, the schools, churches and society, substituting the saddle horse for the palace car, the pack mule for the freight train, the rude cabin for the convenient modern dwelling. Then commences the process of development which gradually brings to the region all these conveniences and luxuries, repeating in general the process by which they first came into use among men.

The pioneer families whose destiny it was to lay the foundation of things in eastern Oregon early began the upbuilding of an educational system. The passion for gold brought them here, but even the love of the yellow metal never took such complete possession of them as to cause forgetfulness of the educational needs of their children. The inception of the public school system of the county is, however, not capable of being traced at this time consecutively or in much detail. The history of a county is analogous to the history of the race in another respect besides those just given, namely, in that it has its unauthentic period preceding the era when events are recorded in a permanent form. The old pioneers were not much given to the use of the pen. The printing press was unknown in their midst, and Mnemosyne often deceptive and uncertain, was practically the only annalist of the early days.

The story of the heroism and sacrifice upon

which the public school system was built may never be fully told, could not be even though the records had been kept in the most approved manner. It takes but a slight effort of the imagination, however, to picture the conditions under which the first rude schools were built and the work in them conducted. Certainly few luxuries had place in the pioneer temple of learning. The house was of logs, the furniture of home manufacture, the course of study such as the teacher herself might construct, and the textbooks those which could be found in the trunks and boxes which the people had brought with them on their long westward journey. It is a singular fact, however, that many of the boys and girls who took their first steps in the pursuit of knowledge under these circumstances acquired an intellectual grasp and a power of thought which served them well in the stern battles of later years.

The first settlement of Baker county was made in 1861, and less than a year later, the first school was opened. Miss O'Brien, now Mrs. W. H. Packwood, has the honor of having given inception to this pioneer educational institution. No sooner had she arrived in Auburn than she began raising money for the purpose of building a schoolhouse. A sufficient sum was speedily subscribed; the school was built and its doors opened for the reception of pupils. About fifty availed themselves of its privileges.

Miss O'Brien taught about six weeks, then gave her school to a Mrs. Stafford, who died sometime in the winter. Mrs. Stafford was the first public school teacher employed in the county, her predecessor, Miss O'Brien, having maintained a subscription school. Mr. Hiatt tells us that a school was also taught near Pocahontas during this same fall and winter by a Miss Chandler.

The first school superintendent was William H. Packwood, who divided the county into five districts. As this and Union were then one political division, the territorial extent of these districts was naturally great and the children in remote parts of each would have had long walks to school had there been any children living in the remote parts. We are told that Mr. Packwood granted four certificates, but of the first schools at Auburn and Pocahontas and of other schools taught during the early sixties we have no official account.

The oldest record of any kind in the county superintendent's office at present is a report by Thomas Smith as clerk of district No. 1, dated March, 1865, by which it is shown that the number of legal voters was 233, of pupils 85, thirty-seven of whom were enrolled; number of terms during which school was maintained, three; amount paid teacher, by subscription, $180; Mrs. C. Calberth, teacher. There is, however, a report nearly as old, submitted by William Chambers, clerk of district No. 2 (Pocahontas), which gives the number of pupils as 115, only eighteen of whom were enrolled. J. Wisdom, teacher:

During a portion at least of the year 1865, C. M. Foster served as county superintendent, and he it was who established district No. 5, (Baker City). The names of those whose qualifications to teach were certified by him are recorded as Mrs. J. Kilburn, Joseph H. Shinn, J. H. Johnson, Mrs. Adeline Buchanan and Mrs. Rachael Vincent.

Districts 7 and 8 were established by Superintendent J. H. Shinn, in 1866 and 1867 respectively. Then there were no more districts formed until 1870, when J. B. Foster organized Rye valley into district No. 9. An epitome of Superintendent Foster's report for the year ending April 1, 1871, shows eight districts in this county; the number of persons between the ages of four and twenty, 397; the amount paid in teachers' salaries for the year, $2,582.

During the administration of C. S. Means and W. F. Payton, districts 10, 11 and

12 were formed and nearly forty teachers' certificates were granted, but the amount of public funds disbursed seemed to decline steadily. We have no information as to the average length of term for which school was maintained in the different districts, but it is probable that the public fund was swelled considerably by private subscription and that most of the schools remained in session at least three months.

In a full report published in the Bedrock Democrat in January, 1879, Superintendent H. N. McKinney gives us a good insight into the condition of the public schools at that time. He states that with two exceptions, the Malheur district and No. 18, in Jordan valley, all the schools were or had been in session. The two exceptions were schools in sparsely settled communities of what is now Malheur county. Mr. McKinney states that rude schoolhouses housed most of the pupils, and as in all frontier settlements, school was irregularly held. Not much attention was generally paid to rules and discipline and considerable apathy was manifest among the settlers. The teachers, however, were for the most part earnest and tireless workers and in some instances were accomplishing great good, despite unfavorable circumstances. At this time diphtheria and other juvenile diseases were interfering with the work to an unusual extent. The recent Indian war, also, had upset conditions and on the whole the picture of the school system was of rather sombre coloring.

The tendency toward betterment of the system was steadily operative during the next few years, however, and superintendent John A. Payton's report for the year ending March 3, 1884, shows that the number of districts in the county had increased to twenty-nine, the number of children of school age to 1,600 and the enrollment to 919. It shows twenty-one active teachers in the county, receiving average stipends of $45 per month for males and

$35 for females. These salaries were so small in proportion to the cost of living and the average terms so short that teachers must necessarily have other occupations in order to live. This in itself was a great disadvantage, making teaching an avocation rather than a profession to which one's whole time and talent should be devoted. The financial showing is a very favorable one compared with those of earlier reports. The estimated value of school property was $6,535; the total amount of school funds received by the different school districts, $7,981.97, of which $6,948.76 had been expended in the maintenance of schools, leaving a balance on hand of $1,033.21.

The progress of the public schools during the next four years was quite marked, as will appear from a comparison of the figures above given with those in a resume of Superintendent L. B. Baker's report for the year ending March 5, 1888, which shows the population of the county between the ages of four and twenty as 1,765, of whom 897 were enrolled in the different schools. The total receipts for school purposes this year were $18,791.96 and the disbursements $10,594.28, leaving a healthy balance in the treasury. The average school term had been lengthened to five and a half months and the average wages of teachers had increased to $53.25 for males and $41.50 for females. The estimated value of furniture and apparatus was placed at $1,127. The number of school districts in the county had been reduced to twenty-nine, by the creation of Malheur county, and of these only twenty-three had school houses.

Prior to 1888 the county superintendents were not provided with suitable books for keeping records, nor with an office, but C. H. Whitney, who was elected to the superintendency in that year, introduced some radical reforms. He succeeded in getting a room in the court house suitable for an office, modern record books in which to keep statistics, and other needed equipments. His skill as a book-keeper was just what the superintendency required. Later superintendents have followed his example, so that any item in the affairs of the districts may now be easily discovered.

At a special election held in September, 1887, in Baker City school district, the taxpayers, by a vote of 71 to 61, authorized the bonding of the city in the sum of $30,000 for the purpose of building a school house, and during the following year a fine brick building was erected. This structure occupies a sightly location on a block of ground which was donated by the state to be used for school purposes. It had been given to the state in 1870 by J. M. Boyd as a site for an academy and for years had been occupied by the old Baker City institution.

Mr. Whitney's first report, that for the year ending March 4, 1889, shows that the amount of money on hand at the beginning of the year was $6,382.21; the amount received from district taxes, $9,420.05; from the county school fund, $8,992.45; from the state school fund, $2,206.25; from all other sources, $21,663.10, of which $20,698.22 belonged to district No. 5 (Baker City), procured no doubt by the sale of bonds; total, $48,561.14. Of this sum $8,503.80 were paid to teachers and $24,094.40 for buildings and sites. The value of school houses and grounds was estimated at $50,720; of school furniture, $3,830; of apparatus, $342.50. The census report showed 962 males and 982 females of school age in the county. There were twenty-three first grade, twenty-two second grade, and eight third grade certificates in force and five permits were issued.

It is not thought necessary to abstract the later reports year by year. An examination of them discloses some very encouraging tendencies in the public school system. There has been a steady and constant increase in the number of children of school age in the county, the last census showing a juvenile population of 2,104 males and 2,083 females; total, 4,187. The ratio between the children of school age and the enrollment varies considerably from year to year, but the percentage of enrollment is always too small, considering that there are so few private schools in the county. Last year a little less than seventy per cent. of the children had their names on the teachers' registers and when it is remembered that a considerable proportion of those who enroll in country schools withdraw after a brief attendance, it becomes evident that not a few children are reaping little or no benefit from the public schools. The reasons for this are not far to seek, but there should be a united effort on the part of school officers and parents to overcome obstacles in the way of children's attendance at school, so as to give them the benefit of an intellectual discipline which will be even more valuable in the future than it has been in the past. The primitive log school houses have been replaced by more commodious frame and brick ones. The value of school furniture and apparatus has steadily increased, showing a commendable disposition on the part of the patrons to provide the pupils with comforts and the teachers with needed facilities. One encouraging showing of the report is the average standing of the teaching profession. Of the thirty-three men and sixty-eight women employed in the schools during 1901, three men and thirteen women held state certificates or diplomas; twenty men and twenty-eight women, first grade county certificates; four men and thirteen women, second grade; and only three men and eleven women, third grade. Six teachers were granted temporary permits. To one familiar with the requirements for high grade certificates, these figures speak volumes for the professional training and liberal education of the teachers, and proclaim them the peers of any other profession in breadth of general culture. Ac-

BAKER CITY HIGH SCHOOL.

cording to the report the average salary paid to males was $53.07 a month and to females $44 a month. Though these stipends may seem small in proportion to the amount of money the same attainments and skill would bring in other walks of life, they are relatively good and furnish at least a measure of encouragement to the teacher to strive for professional success.

On the whole, the public schools of the county may be considered in a healthy condition. The taxpayer in general shows a readiness to part with his hard earned dollars, whenever they are needed for the purpose of extending a school term, erecting a new building or purchasing needed furniture and apparatus. The teachers are animated by an *esprit de corps* seldom found in the devotees of other professions. Parents are awake to the importance of giving their children the best possible intellectual training. All classes working together have built up a system of public instruction in the county fully equal in efficiency to any to be found in like communities in the west and the same forces are yet operative to remedy such defects as may still exist.

Baker City's schools naturally stand at the head of the system in the county, and its citizens are justly proud of the success which has rewarded their labors in sustaining and supporting the cause of popular education in their midst. At the Trans-Mississippi Exposition at Omaha, the schools of this city were granted a diploma and a gold medal as excelling all others in the state of Oregon, not excepting Portland schools, for excellence in maps, drawings and other evidences of efficient grade work.

The most inspiring scene of its kind which it ever was the good fortune of the writer to witness was the arbor day celebration of 1902 in Baker City. A more brilliant pageant could not well be imagined than that presented by the long line of beautifully costumed children of all grades, from the urchin just taking his first steps in the pathway to knowledge to the youths and maids of the high school, as they marched in perfect time through the principal thoroughfares of the town. Upon arriving at the scene of the day's exercises, they executed a program whose numbers included beautiful flag drills, soul stirring, patriotic music and a masterly oration by one of the high school boys. No supporter of the Baker City schools could see and hear the exercises of that day without feeling repaid for any personal sacrifice the schools may have cost him; while the man who has contributed in any way to the educational system of the county might there see the fruition of past planting and the hope of the future.

ST. FRANCIS ACADEMY.

St. Francis Academy is one of the pioneer educational institutions of eastern Oregon. The original school was known as Notre Dame Academy and to the Rev. Father DeRoo is given the credit of having originated the idea of founding this seminary. Certain it is that this learned and highly esteemed clergyman, who was one of Baker City's first settlers, early foresaw the need of such an institution for the education and training of the young men and women in this rough section, and having established a church, at once began the collection of funds for the erection of the school. He was so successful in his efforts that early in the year 1874 work was commenced on the structure, which was completed and opened to the public in July of the following year. The Sisters of the Holy Name, who were conducting similar institutions all over the United States, were placed in charge of this academy also.

Sister Superior Mary Justin and Sisters Leocadia, Stephen and Mary Henry had arrived in April, and while awaiting the completion of the building, conducted a school in a small house. Four pupils formed the nucleus of what was afterwards to be one of the largest and most influential schools in this portion of the country. In June, 1880, the first class, consisting of Mollie Packwood, Mary Stack and Rosa Hoffstater, was graduated from Notre Dame Academy. The year following showed an enrollment of seventy pupils. Between 1881 and 1885 Sister Perpetua assumed the position of Sister Superior.

In August of this year, 1885, control of the school passed into the hands of the Sisters of St. Francis, ten of whom, under Sister Superior Mary Cupertino, had come from Philadelphia to assume the management. With their advent, the name of the institution was changed from Notre Dame to St. Francis Academy, which title it now bears. Under their direction, the seminary has acquired a high standing among the educational institutions of the northwest and the number of its scholars has increased so rapidly that two hundred pupils, including thirty-five boarders, now receive instruction from its teachers. The scholastic year, divided into four quarters of ten weeks each, commences on the first Monday in September and continues until the middle of June. The course of studies embraces those common to the public schools, a col-

legiate course, degrees from which entitle the holders to entrance into examination for a state diploma, and special courses in music and art. Both sexes are admitted to the enjoyment of its privileges.

The old building, now occupied as St. Luke's Hospital, having become too small, in 1892 the grounds and residence formerly owned by James W. Virtue were purchased and the house remodeled to accommodate the school, which was removed to its new home in September. An addition built later did not furnish sufficient room for this rapidly growing school and in the spring of 1900, plans were matured for the erection of a modern stone and brick edifice, to cost between $70,000 and $80,000. Work was immediately begun, but after the completion of the foundation, was suspended for lack of funds. The necessary financial aid has now been secured and it is hoped that the new academy will be ready for occupancy by the first of next year. When finished this structure wil be one of the most commodious and imposing in the state. It will be thoroughly equipped with all modern conveniences and apparatus, the corps of instructors will be enlarged and with the advantages of a beautiful and healthful location, the future success of this worthy institution is assured.

CHAPTER VI.

BAKER CITY.

Not a little interest attaches to the history of the development of any thriving city or town from its earliest inception, the day of small things, until it becomes a substantial, firmly established trade center. Much faith is required of the men who would be the founders of a metropolis, much determination, no small amount of discernment as to the most likely location, eternal vigilance, a broad minded, liberal public spirit and a disposition to sacrifice, if need be, for the general well-being and the good of the town. It would seem that all these qualities must have been present in the men who laid the foundations of Baker City and planned its development during its infant days. Even with the limited knowledge of the tributary country's resources in the early '60s, and though many mines, which have since produced millions, were then hidden from the ken of man, it was not difficult to foresee that somewhere in Baker county must spring up a town of considerable importance. To tell where that town would be was a matter of greater difficulty.

Auburn, the pioneer town of this great section of country, had assumed much importance before the end of the year 1862 and for a few years thereafter it continued to thrive, but it was the result of a mining excitement and lacked the essential elements of permanence. About the time it started to decline, Baker City was platted, and as Auburn decayed, its more substantial rival grew. How

much the new town owed to the designs and planning of its founders and how much was fortuitous or attributable to circumstances over which none had any control may be not easy to determine at this time, but certain it is that even in the light of all the later developments, the location of the metropolis of the southeast must be considered a felicitous one. Baker City is so situated that it need have no fear of a powerful rival ever springing up in its portion of Oregon and a site more nearly central to the eastern Oregon mining country could not be found. With plenty of room to grow in every direction over a level area, with a rich, fertile soil capable of producing, with irrigation, every tree or shrub or grass which could lend beauty to street or yard, with ever beautiful snow-capped mountain ranges on all sides adding a charm to the scene, and above all with a wealth of pasturage and agriculture and timber and minerals in the hills and valleys for many miles around, Baker City must be considered a most favored spot. Its status as a substantial, permanent city has long been established beyond any doubt and the future may have much greater things in store for it, when all its mineral wealth has been discovered and is in process of reduction to the uses of man.

The plat of the original Baker City covered the southeast quarter of the southeast quarter of section 17, township 9 south, range 40 east of the Williamette meridian. It was made by R. A. Pierce, who claimed the land and was endeavoring to obtain title to it from the state. For some reasons, however, the state of Oregon did not act upon the matter until some three years later, allowing another man to establish a prior claim and so get the land from Mr. Pierce. Mr. Pierce named the town Baker, but Baker City seemed to sound better to the general ear so that came to be the universally accepted appellation. . The growth of the town was slow at first. The pioneer building, except the homes of Mr. Pierce and men who afterwards platted additions to the town, was a box saloon on the site now occupied by John Bowen's stone structure. Next came a boarding house built by Samuel Barger near the spot on which the Arlington Hotel was afterwards erected. Then S. and A. McMurren built a hotel and Robert McCord started a blacksmith shop. The Ruckel quartz mill, already alluded to as having been constructed in 1864, was also in the town.

A pioneer, writing anonymously in the Baker City High School Nugget, paints so vivid a picture of the town as he saw it in the fall of this year, and gives us so clear an insight into the forces which were leading people westward at this time, that we feel constrained to quote a few paragraphs of his narrative. He says:

"The western craze struck the town in which I was living in western Illinois with a force that few were able to withstand, especially the younger men, strong and healthy, eager for adventure and hungry for wealth.

"How much that word 'gold' implied to us as we talked over the possibilities awaiting us! Every one, we imagined, could make a fortune in a day. We would not go to the land flowing with milk and honey, but rather to the land flowing with gold and prosperity. We would return in a few months laden with riches. The stories of our experiences with the Indians in that fearful west would command respect of our hearers for our bravery.

"There, with five of my companions, I started for Portland, Oregon. When we arrived there the novelty was almost gone and the golden sun of anticipation was fast setting in the west, with only a few rays left to light us around. But the heart of youth is strong and discouragement does not baffle it. However, my companions found employment in the Indian service and I was left face to face with destiny.

"I started out horseback for Auburn in eastern Oregon, where the gold fields were, and in the evening of November 19, 1865, I arrived in Baker City, a new camp about ten miles from Auburn. I left my horse in the only livery stable of the village, then just completed and owned by Sylvester Grier and John Furman. Upon inquiry I was directed to the hotel across the street, built by S. and A. McMurren, as the Western Hotel, built by Reid and Fletcher, was not yet finished.

"After my supper, for which I paid seventy-five cents in gold dust, I asked the proprietor for a room. After looking me carefully over, he said, 'I guess you can get a bed, but it is customary to pay in advance,' to which I replied by paying fifty cents, this time in coin, as my supply of gold dust was limited, owing to my having just arrived, and I retired for the night.

"I arose about six o'clock next morning and after breakfast, which consisted of bread, coffee and bacon, I started to walk out and see what things of interest I could find. Walking down to Powder river I found Mr. Charles E. Place, the first settler of Baker City, as he came in the spring of '63 and built the log house on the bank of the river where he was living, this being the first house. He kept a toll gate at the foot of what is now known as the Reservoir hill. Around the foot of the hill, to my right, I saw a quartz mill and learned that it had been built by Colonel Ruckel in '64 for the Virtue mine, which property he owned.

"There were two daily stages running between Salt Lake and The Dalles one each way. Mr. A. H. Brown was keeping the only store in town, at the corner of First and Valley avenue, but the streets were not named at that time and in fact there was but one, Front street.

"First a saloon was built on Front street and stood where J. P. Bowen's stone building now stands. 'The Village Blacksmith' was Robert McCord and he struck his anvil at the present site of Wisdom's drug store. Upon walking farther down the street, I saw a boarding house built by Samuel Rogers. R. A. Pierce, Fisher, Place, Campbell and John Stewart owned the land which in after years the town was to occupy."

To James Virtue belongs the honor of having erected the first stone structure in the town, and to the Catholic priest, Rev. P. De-Roo, who has since distinguished himself by his historical researches and writings, that of having built the first brick building, the Arlington Hotel. This did not long antedate the brick mercantile house of S. A. Heilner & Company, on what is now the northwest corner of Front and Court streets. In 1867 L. W. Nelson opened a stove and tinware store, and so the business of the place continued to expand and the town to take on an air of permanence and stability.

Of course the necessity for schools, churches, etc., was felt here as elsewhere, and no sooner was the town well started than a public school was opened in a little pioneer building, with Mrs. Calbreath as teacher. The difficulties to be overcome by this estimable lady may well be imagined. With thirty-five or forty pupils, each supplied with such books as he or she might be able to muster (and there can be no doubt of the variety of texts, for

most of the books had been brought across the plains from the different eastern states), with insufficient room, with hand-made furniture and without apparatus, Mrs. Calbreath bravely assumed the responsibility of laying the corner stone of the public school system of southeastern Oregon's future metropolis. For three terms she toiled on, frequently remaining at her post an extra hour that all might receive due attention. Each term opened in a different building, her last school being held in her own home on First street between Auburn and Valley avenues. Her successor, a Mr. Miller, enjoyed the advantage of better quarters in which to instruct his pupils, for in 1867 the first regular school building in Baker City was erected. Its site is now occupied by the Warshauer block. The Baker City Academy was established some time in the late 'sixties with Prof. Frank Grubbs and his wife as its first corps of instructors.

The Romish clergy were the first to hold services in any part of Baker county and no doubt Baker City was visited by itinerant priests from its inception. At any rate the Catholics have the honor of pioneership in the matter of church building in Baker City. The first Protestant clergyman who visited the town for the purpose of preaching the gospel was a Methodist minister, Rev. John Flynn. He was a resident of Walla Walla, but several times each year he crossed the mountains into Powder river valley in the performance of his duty as presiding elder in the church. His first visit is said to have been in 1864. His successor, Rev. J. G. Deardorff, also visited this part of Oregon occasionally, as did the Rev. William Roberts, also Rev. I. D. Driver, who traveled in the interest of the American Bible Society, preaching in Baker City at intervals. So the people of the town enjoyed the blessings of both school and churches from its earliest days.

At the session of the legislature of the

year 1866, a bill was introduced. by Hon. W. C. Hindman, and passed, directly affecting Baker City, the language of which is as follows:

"An act to change the location of the county seat of Baker county.

"Sec. 1. Be it enacted by the legislative assembly· of the state; of Oregon, that at the next general election held in the county of Baker and state of Oregon, it shall be the duty of the county clerk of said county of Baker, to put in nomination the town of Baker, to be voted upon at said election for the county seat of said county.

"Sec. 2. The votes cast for and against said place shall be kept and counted as in other cases of election. And if it be found that said town of Baker receives the majority of all the votes cast, then said town shall be declared the county seat of said county.

"Approved October 24, 1866."

In accordance with the provisions of this act, the matter of relocating the county seat was voted upon in the county election of 1868 and resulted favorably to Baker City. Accordingly the records were brought over from Auburn that year.

On May 11, 1870, was issued the first newspaper ever published in Baker City or within the limits of this county. Its advertising columns contain the names of J. W. Virtue, broker; R. A. Pierce, L. O. Sterns and I. D. Haines, attorneys; Dr. T. N. Snow, physician and surgeon; Reid, of the Western Hotel; Reynolds & Ferguson, of the Express store; McCord Brothers, blacksmiths; McCrary & Tracy, variety store; J. W. Wisdom, druggist; Dr. Snow, City Drug store. In the issue of May 25th we find the following market report: Wheat, per bushel, $1.80; oats, per pound, 2¾ cents; barley, per pound, 3 cents; flour, per barrel, $13; bacon, per pound, 30 cents; butter, 50 cents; chickens, per dozen, $6; hay, baled, per ton, $15; loose, $10.

We have stated that the claim of R. A. Pierce to the land upon which the original Baker City was located was never carried into a. perfect title. His application to have the land selected by the state as a part of its grant from the national government remained without action, and in 1868 J. M. Boyd filed a preemption claim upon it. As the contest which ensued was one of great importance to the people of Baker·City at the time and elicited much interest we quote here the decision of the United States land commissioner, which briefly reviews the facts in the case:

WASHINGTON, D. C., August 4, 1871.
Register and Receiver, La Grande, Oregon:

GENTLEMEN: This office has examined the testimony and other papers in the contested case of the "State of Oregon *vs.* J. M. Boyd and the town-site of Baker City," involving the right to the SE ¼ Sec. 17, Tp. 9 S., Range 40 East, and find as follows:

It is shown by our records that under date of April 10, 1868, Mr. Boyd filed D. S. No. 860 for the West ½ and N. E. ¼ of said S. E. ¼, Sec. 17, alleging settlement same day, and that on July 13, 1868, he proved up and entered said 120 acre tract, per pre-emption cash entry, No. 18.

It also appears, that on April 16, 1868, the acting governor of the state filed in the local land office his application to select said quarter section as a part of the 50,000 acre grant, under the act of September 4, 1841, and that said application was rejected by the register, and not reported to this officer, on account of the prior filing of Boyd made six days previously.

It appears from the testimony in the case, that Mr. Boyd actually settled on his pre-emption claim, at the date alleged in his D. S.; and that he continued to reside upon and cultivate the same until the date of hearing; and from that time to the date of hearing, June 15, 1870.

R. A. Pierce, the party claiming under the state selection, shows that in 1865, he applied to the state authorities to purchase said S. E. ¼ of Sec. 17; and a certificate from the secretary of the state of Oregon, dated May 13, 1865, is produced setting forth the fact.

It is also shown that Mr. Pierce, under the impression that he had a valid claim to the land in question, settled upon and improved a portion thereof; and in 1865 laid off the S. E. ¼ of the said quarter section into blocks and lots, and disposed of a portion of the lots to different parties.

The settlers upon these lots, fearing that Pierce could not give them a good title, made application to enter their respective claims under the town site acts of 1864 and 1865; and a number of their entries have been allowed and reported to this office.

This office holds that, in case of this character, the right of the state does not attach prior to the filing of the application to selections made by the proper officer, at the local land office; and that the mere date of the selection, April 16, 1868, at the office of the governor, in Salem, gives the state no superior claim.

As Mr. Boyd has initiated a valid pre-emption claim to the 120 acre tract, above described, six days before the application to select was made, it held that his cash entry embracing the same, should be carried into patent: and that the entries already made by the claimants of lots, in Baker City should remain intact, and the remainder of the lots be subject to the entry of actual settlers, as stipulated in the acts referred to.

You will advise the parties in interest of this ruling; and allow sixty days from your notice for appeal—the parties appealing to indicate particularly the points of exception to this decision.

WILLIS DRUMMOND
Commissioner.

On appeal, the decision of the commissioner was affirmed and Mr. Boyd, having secured his title; proceeded to lay out the land as an addition to the city.

The Pacific Coast Directory for the year 1871, has this to say about Baker City:

"Baker City, Baker county, postoffice and county seat, is a thriving town on the south fork of the Powder river, in the fertile valley of the same, and enjoys considerable trade with the neighboring mining and agricultural districts. It is a new town and the center of a section which ten years ago was an untenanted and unbroken wilderness. Now a pretty town exists, with numerous hotels, schools, dwellings and business houses of various character. A good road leads to The Dalles and to the mining districts of Idaho, over which runs a daily stage conveying the United States mail and express. The Powder river valley, of which Baker City is the business center, possesses a large area of excellent arable land which invites the settler from every land to take possession of and to create, through the bounty of nature and our free government, homes of comfort and independence. The two forks of Powder river take their rise in the Blue Mountains, and the south fork, the larger of the two, after a northeast course of seventy-five miles, is joined by the lesser branch, when continuing their course upward of one hundred miles further, they empty into the Snake river. Burnt river is separated from it by a spur of the Blue mountains. A writer from the locality says: 'From the summit of the spur of the Blue mountains

14

that divide these two rivers, the scenery, for beauty and grandeur, cannot be surpassed. To the south can be seen the Burnt river valley, above Clark's creek, stretching away in a westerly direction in one unbroken line of verdant beauty—its smooth, green surface presenting a strong contrast to the undulating upland, alternating between grass-crowned hills and forests of gigantic pine. Turning to the north, the valley of the Powder river lying in full view, far more extensive and equally as beautiful, can scarcely fail to strike the eye of the beholder with awe and admiration and beget the wish for the mechanic, day laborer and landless poor of the old countries to apply the magic touch of civilization to those rich gifts of nature and convert those extensive wilds into happy homes.'"

Old residents of Baker City will remember that in 1872 their town was considerably shaken up by a seismic disturbance of from two three minutes duration. The earthquake began at 10:21 o'clock on the night of December 14th, and is described as consisting of one severe shock followed by trembling, then another severe shock, after which the disturbance was at an end. The earth appeared to roll from east of south to west of north. The shock was felt at Lagrande and at other places in the Inland Empire.

Baker City continued to grow with a healthy though slow development, and in 1874, its population was estimated at between 1,000 and 1,200 people. It was thought that the time had come when the town should be clothed with corporate powers and accordingly an effort was made to secure the passage of an incorporating act. As a result, the Oregon legislature at its 1874 session, passed an act providing that "The inhabitants of the town of Baker City, within the limits hereinafter described, shall be and they are hereby constituted a body politic and corporate in fact and in law, by the name and style of 'Baker City,' and by that name they and their successors shall be known in law and have perpetual succession, sue and be sued, plead and be impleaded, defend and be defended, in all courts of law and in all actions whatever," etc. The corporate area was to include all of the southwest quarter of section 17, and all of that portion of the southwest quarter of section 16 that lies west of Powder river; also the northeast quarter of the northeast quarter of section 20, and all of that portion of the northwest quarter of the northwest quarter of section 21 that lies west of Powder river, all being in township 9 south, range 40 east. The officers of the town were to be a board of five trustees, a recorder, a marshal, and a treasurer, to hold office for one year, elections to be held on the first Monday in November.

In accordance with the provisions of this act an election was held at which S. B. McCord, J. A. Reid, S. Grier, J. H. Parker, and G. J. Bowman were elected trustees. R. H. Cardwell was the first recorder and William M. Constable the first city marshal.

Notwithstanding the lack of transportation facilities, Baker City was in a thriving condition at this time. It was the depot of supplies for a large section of country and goods from its mercantile houses found their way into mining camps fifty to seventy-five miles distant. Numerous heavy freight teams arrived and departed daily, importing and exporting all varieties of merchandise. The town was even at that time stimulated by the hope that the proposed Portland, Dalles & Salt Lake Railroad would soon be here and that the transportation difficulty would shortly be removed. The Bedrock Democrat tells us that in 1875 travelers passing through saw more life in Baker City than in any other town between Portland and the Union Pacific Railroad, and that the city was beginning to draw citizens, mechanics, business men and capital from other towns. It was the staging center

of eastern Oregon, having daily service east and west, bi-weekly service to and from Canyon City, Connor Creek, Gem City and Sparta and tri-weekly service to and from Clarksville, Eldorado and Malheur City. Building operations were in progress on every hand.

Some time in 1875 the board of trustees of the town purchased a fire engine and on August 5th a meeting was held for the purpose of organizing an engine company. Of this first association of fire fighters the charter membership was as follows:

J. M. Shepherd, Charles H. Schellworth, W. G. Umberger, S. R. Ross, T. M. Britten, James Stephenson, J. T. Dealy, Peter Mann, J. W. Cleaver, S. H. Small, H. N. McKinney, William P. Brewer, John P. Ross, W. W. Coe, James Fletcher, Charles H. Littlefield, T. C. Hyde, Harry C. Shepherd, William W. Parker and H. C. Durkee.

Notwithstanding the development of business and the continued extending of the town's wholesale trade, Baker City did not increase much in population during the first few years of its existence as a municipal corporation, if the estimates made in 1874 were correct, for the population in 1879 was found to number 1,197, of whom 166 were Chinamen. There must have been many bachelors in those days, for the number of females, according to the census, was only 143. It is probable that the early estimates of population were much higher than the facts, for visitors did notice decided improvement during this period. Mrs. Duniway writing in the New Northwest in 1880, says:

"Baker City has almost outgrown our former conception of it during the five years that have elapsed since our last visit. Quite a number of new and substantial stone and brick houses adorn the main street, exhibiting the confidence of the proprietors in the future prosperity of the place. There are excellent farms in the valley and seemingly inexhaustible stock ranges on the mountains and hills. But the chief attraction is the mines, whose resources are scarcely yet imagined and certainly not developed."

The Fourth of July, 1883, was the first celebrated in Baker City in seven years and in honor of the event, the Bedrock Democrat of that week made its appearance in red and blue colors. It is said that about four thousand people participated in the celebration. During this year it became necessary to organize a new fire company, the pioneer organization and that of 1882 having passed away. This company was officered as follows: president, T. Williams; chief A. K. Holman; foreman, William Parker; secretary, R. C. Lawrence; treasurer, C. L. Palmer.

Another notable event of this year was the erection of a Chinese Joss house costing $10,-000. The building was of brick, fire-proof, two stories high, twenty feet by forty-five feet in dimensions and finished inside with hardwood. It is one of the few buildings erected by Chinamen in the city which are not wretched shacks.

On the morning of October 8, 1884, Baker City was aroused at about 5 o'clock by an alarm of fire and it was found that the city jail was being consumed by the flames. The horror of the occurrence was that a young German, named Charles Myres, had been confined there about three hours previous for drunkenness and creating a disturbance in a saloon, and all efforts to rescue him proved unavailing. Policeman Clark, who had imprisoned the man, was the first to notice the fire. With another man, he rushed to the building, unlocked the door and by heroic efforts reached the cell and opened it. He then had to retreat, however, and the prisoner did not escape. His charred remains were found when the fire had died down sufficiently to permit search. A new jail was erected at once.

Tuesday, August 19th of this year, was perhaps the most memorable day in the history of Baker City, rendered so by the arrival of the iron horse, which ever after was to convey goods and passengers to and from the town for a small fraction of the sums theretofore expended for such transportation, and in a smaller fraction of the time. In anticipation of this day, the pioneer had wrought out the development of the section to a high degree, enduring the privations of isolation, suffering the inconveniences of long freight hauls and long costly journeys by stage, ever buoyed up by the hope that there was a better day coming. Now faithfulness and courage were to have their reward. The joy of certainty that his labor in establishing a new community had not been in vain, was glowing in the breast of the pioneer. That a substantial and beautiful superstructure was to be reared upon his foundation, was now established beyond doubt. Naturally there was rejoicing in Baker City that day and naturally the unwonted whistle of the locomotive had a music for the ears of the pioneer people, which would not be detected by the residents of a more favored community. In the throngs which gathered at the depot to welcome the iron monster of strength and marvel of beauty as it toiled along with its load of ties, rails, telegraph poles, etc., were many who had never seen a locomotive before, and the quickness and exactness with which the rails were laid elicited many exclamations of delighted surprise. The train did not remain long at the depot, but pushed onward in its task of making connections which should place Baker City in direct communication with the Atlantic seaboard and the world.

In December of this year, in response to a general demand, the trustees of Baker City framed a new charter, the provisions of the incorporating act of 1874 having become entirely inadequate to the needs of the town in its more advanced age and development. This was presented to the legislature at its next regular session and the result was that in 1884 Baker City had a charter more suited to its necessities.

From the West Shore of February, 1885, we learn that the population at that time was estimated at 1,500 and that there were then fifteen large two-story brick or stone business blocks. The business of the town is summarized as follows: "There are four large stores of general merchandise and one clothing store, five provision and grocery stores, two bakeries, two drug stores, three livery stables, five hotels, one book store, three blacksmith shops, one wagon shop, two butcher shops, two millinery stores, one hide and fur store, one national bank, one private bank, nine lawyers, five physicians, two saddle and harness shops, three hardware stores, three jewelers, three shoemakers, two planing mills, one sawmill, one grist mill, four newspapers, two express offices, one tailor, three breweries, one surveyor, fourteen saloons, a large number of carpenters and blacksmiths, three painters, two barber shops, four hardware implement stores, two large Chinese stores, two cigar stores, three laundries, two dentists, one brickmaker, one undertaker, two furniture stores. There are seven secret societies, also six religious denominations represented, four of which have good church edifices. There is an excellent public school, employing three teachers; also a school for boys and one for girls, under the auspices of the Roman Catholics. The boys' school occupies a large three-story brick building and has four instructors. The enterprise and intelligence of the city is shown by the number and character of its newspapers. The Daily Sage Brush is a sprightly little sheet, while the Bedrock Democrat, Reveille and Tribune are well conducted and influential weeklies, giving much attention to home matters and working for the interests of the county."

We have mentioned the organization of two or three fire companies, also the purchase of a fire engine, yet when the fire fiend paid Baker City a visit, as it does sooner or later to almost all towns built largely of wood, it caught the people totally unprepared. In the fall of 1886, about noon one Sunday, flames began leaping from the rear of Mansfield's billiard hall, on Main street, and in a short space of time the entire block was in ruins. All the buildings were frame structures and burned so rapidly that but few goods could be saved. That a general conflagration did not ensue was owing to the fact that an almost dead calm prevailed at the time. The loss, according to the Bedrock Democrat, was distributed as follows: J. T. Wisdom, $3,000; Mrs. S. H. Small, $1,200; Mr. Boreman, $2,000; Louis Mansfield, $1,000; Rogers & Heyde, $100; O. H. P. McCord, $18,000; M. Mitchell, $500; J. H. McDonald, $6,000, with $2,000 insurance; Weller & Henry, $2,000; Oscar Trevalle, $500; A. B. Elmer, $2,000; J. M. Lachner, $5,000; Robert Pabst, $1,500.

This hint of danger passed unheeded by the people, as did another about a year later, when the Griffin residence on First street was destroyed, also a boarding house occupied by Mrs. L. E. Miller (the first frame structure erected in Baker City), Basche & Company's warehouse, the dwelling house of J. B. Gardner and three other frame buildings.

The result was that when a serious fire broke out on Wednesday morning, September 5, 1888, it found the people with no equipments wherewith to give it battle, but a few water buckets. This was by far the most disastrous fire that has ever occurred in the history of Baker City. On that eventful morning Ed Flanner, an officer, discovered a small blaze in an unoccupied building on the corner of First and Court streets. He endeavored to extinguish the fire, but seeing it was impossible to do so, gave the alarm. The cry of fire was not very promptly responded to, but the peals of the fire bell eventually aroused the people. They could offer but a feeble resistance, however. Soon the flames spread to the surrounding buildings and the wind, blowing in a southeasterly direction, carried the flames to the stone and brick structures on the east side. Though considered fireproof, these buildings soon fell, but J. B. Bowen's stone building on the southeast corner of the block, which had a tin roof and iron doors and shutters, easily withstood the flames, saving also all the business blocks to the east and south of it. The losses in this fire were: P. Basche & Company, largest hardware house in eastern Oregon, $50,000, insurance, $10,000; Baer & Bloch, stock and building, $75,000, insurance, $40,000; M. Weil & Company, $50,000, insurance, $20,000; A. Haussman & Company, $2,500, insurance, $1,000; James Richardson, $2,500, no insurance; H. Bamberger, building, $8,000, insurance, $4,000; George Hahn, building, $6,000, insurance, $4,000; W. J. VanSchuyver & Company, building, $15,000, insurance, $6,000; A. F. & A. M. hall, $4,000, no insurance; S. Ottenheimer, building, $2,500, no insurance; L. B. Ison, building, $1,000, no insurance; Basche & Parker, two buildings, $10,000, insurance, $4,000. .

This fire thoroughly aroused the people and in the election following the citizens voted to bond the city for the purpose of constructing water works. Bonds were placed on sale and by January 12, 1889, all were disposed of. The system thereupon constructed and installed was what is known as the direct pumping system, water being pumped from deep wells into a reservoir on the hill above town and carried thence into pipes to wherever needed. Though this plant cost $60,000, it did not

prove adequate and a new system was installed at a later date.

In January, 1889, the first building and loan association was instituted in Baker City, with a capital stock of $165,000, its officers and directors being leading men of the city. Its organization was a matter of no little importance in Baker City's future progress, enabling the erection of many homes, which could not be built without its aid. The same month also witnessed the first use of gas in the town. In February a new charter was asked of the legislature, making the following changes in the old one:

The city was divided into four wards, with two councilmen for each ward, to be elected one every year and hold office for two years. The limit of city indebtedness was extended from $20,000 to $60,000. The maximum license for the retail sale of liquors was increased from $300 to $1,000. Definite salaries were to be paid to the city treasurer, the city attorney and the police judge. The city council was to meet at least once per month.

In the fall of this year a franchise was granted to J. E. Kirk, of Arlington, Oregon, A. P. Campbell, of Denver, Colorado, T. F. Campbell, L. M. Robinson, E. H. Blake and Samuel White, to construct and operate a street railway in Baker City, extending from Auburn street along Front to Court, Washington or Center streets, and along one of these to the O. R. & N. depot. The railway was to be completed and in operation by June 1, 1890.

As the result of an act passed by the legislature providing for the organization of the First Eastern Oregon District Agricultural Society, comprising the counties of Baker, Malheur, Grant, Union and Wallowa, for the purpose of holding annual fairs and exhibitions, the initial district exhibit was held in Baker City in October, 1889. Products of the counties concerned were well represented, large crowds attended and much interest was manifested in this first fair held by the assistance of the state.

It will be seen from the foregoing that the year 1889 was one of unusual activity in Baker City. During its closing days, the three-story Heilner block was receiving its finishing touches, the Hotel Warshauer was being rapidly constructed and the brick work on the First National Bank was just completed. The report of M. L. Tichner, appointed by the board of trade to investigate the commercial standing in December, called attention to the fact that a municipal system of water works had been constructed; that a gas and electric light company had instituted a plant; that a telephone system had been inaugurated; a creamery started; the construction of a street railway begun; two national bank buildings erected; and other improvements made, both public and private. The estimated value of all the improvements of the year was $250,000.

In January, 1890, a great snow storm of two or three days' duration, resulted in cutting off communication with all points west of Baker City. The principal blockade was in Pyle's canyon, a deep gorge a few miles north of town, the snow being so deep at this point that nine days were required to clear it away. Meanwhile, trains from the east were pouring hundreds of people into Baker City. These were taken care of by the company and royally entertained by the citizens, who did all in their power to make the stay of the travelers as pleasant and comfortable as possible.

Early next spring the Interior Land and Improvement Company began operations in Baker City. They secured a bond on two thousand acres of land and began advertising the city and county extensively, but how much credit or blame is to be given them for the boom which followed is naturally a matter of opinion. Great financial prosperity was and for some time had been the portion of this entire section, so the time was opportune for a sudden inflation of values. The cause of these financial disturbances, so disastrous in their reactions, is a matter for the sociologist to determine, but certain it is that more than one western town has felt their wonderful temporary uplift and suffered the depression and demoralization which follows. So sudden was the advent of the boom to Baker City that between the first and fourth of May, many parcels of real estate doubled in value. Property changed hands so rapidly that not a quarter of the deeds could be recorded. Large sums of money passed from man to man in the streets daily. The country for several miles around was platted into town lots, and so great was the fever of speculation that many of them were sold for prices far in excess of their reasonable value. It is related that a ranchman, who owned three lots in the suburbs of Baker City, was met on his way to town and offered $80 each for his lots. Not being aware of the boom, he immediately accepted and while the purchaser was in the bank drawing the money wherewith to make good his offer, he was tendered $300 each for the lots. The Interior Land and Improvement Company sold $110,000 worth of lots in one week. On May 21, a party of three hundred came by special train from Portland and it is estimated that during the few days of their stay at the "Denver of Oregon," they invested $75,000 in realty. Of course the fever heat of this boom soon passed, but the mania lasted long enough to rob the election of June 6th of practically all its interest.

May 8th of this year will be remembered as the date of President Harrison's visit to Baker City. His train arrived at 10:45 p. m., remaining until 11 o'clock, and during the fifteen minute interim speeches were made by the President, Postmaster-General Wanamaker and by local speakers. At the conclusion of these brief addresses a miniature gold brick was presented to the president, upon which were inscribed the words "To Baby McKee." About two thousand people participated in this ovation to President Harrison.

Among the new enterprises inaugurated in 1890 was what was known as the Giroux Amalgamator Works. To secure this plant some of the people of Baker City subscribed stock, upon Giroux's representations that he intended to put in a large amount of machinery and institute a plant which would be of inestimable value to the mining interests of town and county. The plant actually constructed was a relatively small and unimportant affair, so the local stock subscribers refused to pay for their stock and the result was that the matter was taken into the courts. While the case was in litigation the plant burned down, entailing a loss of ten thousand dollars, six thousand of which was covered by insurance. Though successful in court, Mr. Giroux was morally in the wrong and subsequent developments proved him to be a man of questionable integrity.

The year of 1892 was one of steady development in Baker City, the most important establishment of the year being the sampling works before referred to. As heretofore stated, Baker City did not share the general depression of the panic of 1893, but on the contrary it was unusually lively, owing to the excitement caused by the Baisley brothers' rich discoveries in the White Swan mining district. The panic in Portland caused one business failure in Baker City in 1893, that of E. M. VanSlyck's drug store, which was compelled to close because it could not liquidate, on short notice, its indebtedness to a Portland drug firm.

In July, 1894, however, the Baker City National Bank was compelled to close its doors, not through any fault of its management or because of any local depression, but through the unfair action of its New York correspond-

ent, the Chase National Bank, which appropriated the deposit balance of the Baker City National to its own uses without notice, causing drafts against this deposit to be protested. Consequently there was a loss of confidence in the local bank, the result of which was heavy withdrawals of deposits.

The general feeling of panic and distrust caused another business failure or two during the year, resulting from a disposition on the part of creditors to force immediate settlements, rather than from any actual condition of insolvency. During such times it is impossible for any town to forge ahead at a rapid pace, but Baker City was unusually fortunate and while progress was out of the question, no such distress was experienced here as in other towns.

The depression was not such as to cause a suspension of smelter agitation. In 1895 it looked as if steps toward the securing of this desideratum would be taken forthwith. O. R. & N. officials and prominent mining men of the east met the leading men of Baker City in a conference, in which the project of putting in a $75,000 plant was thoroughly discussed. The plan failed to materialize, however, but the matter has been agitated at different times since and a smelter at Baker City is still considered as among the developments which the future shall bring forth.

The year 1896 brought a considerable revival of business activities in Baker City and the surrounding country, though times continued dull in other localities until the next year. It is stated that there was four times as much building within the limits of the town in 1896 as in 1895, the number of new structures put up being between fifty and sixty. It is said also that labor was very generally employed and at good wages.

The spring of 1897 was a disastrous one in Baker City. Early in April the weather turned off warm, rapidly melting the accumulated snow of a rather long winter. The residents along the banks of Powder river ex-. pected a flood, but it came so rapidly that they had not time to prepare for it. The ordinarily peaceful Powder river soon became a roaring torrent, rushing madly downward to the Snake, and bearing upon its bosom bridges, timber and debris of many kinds. On the 17th of April it overleaped its banks, causing much damage to city property. The roadbed of the Sumpter Valley Railroad, contiguous to the river, was completely washed out, entailing a loss of several thousand dollars. The railway necessarily discontinued operations and once again the stage was called into requisition. During the ensuing twenty-four hours every bridge on the river, within the city limits, was washed out, with one exception. When the Auburn avenue bridge went out not a little excitement was occasioned, for it was reported that a number of persons had gone down with it, and as a matter of fact several people did narrowly escape. On Tuesday, April 20th, the weather cooled, the river began to recede, and in due time it returned to its old channel, after having washed out acres of valuable real estate and done damage to the extent of several thousand dollars. An issue of the Bedrock Democrat, which appeared a few days after the river first overflowed, says: "The entire span of the river at the block bridge is filled with timbers and debris of every description and the main part of the river is running through a channel at the east of the bridge and circles over to the George Campbell residence. The water before coming to the bridge and near the rear of the Weil and Dilsheimer residences, runs straight and is inclined to force its way through the grade of the west side of the bridge and on through the Jenkins property. If another rise of the river occurs this channel will be cut and the loss of the Weil and Dilsheimer residences is certain, and perhaps the Jenkins place also. The only preventive is to clear the bridge of debris or take it out altogether.

"All over the north part of the city the ravages of the angry torrent of a day or so ago are plainly to be seen and the sight causes an expression of sympathy for the people who have been the victims of the flood. The damage done will take a long time and the expenditure of much money to repair.

"The Griffin residence on Auburn avenue will probably be saved from destruction, but the danger is not yet over. A heavy crib has been anchored along the bank and the current turned, but more or less washing out of the banks continues. The ice house, near the Griffin property, washed away Wednesday morning together with considerable ice."

In October following this flood a number of the leading property holders of East Baker constructed a levee five hundred feet long, to prevent future overflows. Large piles were driven into the earth at intervals, to which three inch boards were spiked, constructing a bulkhead about ten feet high. Against this earth was thrown, forming a solid embankment, the whole costing about $2,000.

Notwithstanding its unpropitious opening the year 1897 was a prosperous one in Baker City, as it was throughout the northwest generally. The expenditures for new homes and business buildings during the year were estimated at $200,000, some of the principal structures erected or begun being the Haskell block, the Faull building, the Geddes-Pollman block, the Hotel Sagamore, the Baker City Electric Lighting plant, the Waterman & Schmitz block, the Small & Donnelly block, St. Elizabeth's Hospital, the Sherman, the Grace and the Geiser-Pollman buildings. In the fall of the year Receiver Beard of the Baker City National Bank, which closed its doors in 1895, made the sixth and last payment to depositors, who received, in all, seventy-eight per cent. of their deposits. A few preferred depositors and creditors fared better, the officers of the bank having hypothecated some of the best securities to them before closing its doors.

On August 1, 1897, the Canyon City Telephone Company commenced operations in Baker City, giving the town a new local system and long distance connection with Sumpter, Bourne and the Columbia, Bonanza and Clifford mines, also promising communication, in the near future, with Canyon City, and, through affiliated lines, with LaGrande, Union, Heppner, Enterprise, and other points.

When in the spring of 1898 the wave of patriotic fervor inspired by the declaration of war with Spain, swept over our land in mighty force, Baker City was deluged as deeply as any other town, east or west. The news that Congress had passed belligerent resolutions caused greater excitement than would the discovery of a mountain of gold and from almost every business house and many residences the beautiful banner of the free was flung to the loyal breezes. Never before, since the close of the Civil war, was such a martial spirit abroad in the land. Even before the country was electrified by the news of Dewey's victory, sixty-four young men of Baker City and vicinity had offered their services to the United States, sending their names to Governor Lord with a request that they be organized into a militia company at once. As Oregon's first regiment could be fully made up of militiamen already organized and equipped, and as Baker City's old company had been allowed to decline and become practically disbanded, none of the boys from this section, except possibly a few who may have enlisted from other points, had opportunity to enroll in answer to McKinley's first call. By the time the second call issued, however, the young men of Baker City and county were ready to respond, and of the four hundred asked from Oregon, sixty-eight were furnished from this city.

Dewey's Manila victory caused a tremendous outburst of applause here, but unfortunately a little later an accident happened which put a quietus upon future demonstrations. It was known that on the evening of May 19th two trains from Boise, bearing a volunteer regiment of 800 men would pass through Baker City, and in order to give them a cordial greeting about two thousand people gathered at the O. R. & N. depot. A three-hundred-pound iron cannon was brought into requisition to salute the soldiers, which, by some miscalculation, was overcharged, and on being fired burst into fragments. Curtis Spencer, an eight-year-old boy, was struck on the head by a piece of the flying metal and died a few hours later. Another 70-pound fragment was hurled into the dense mass of humanity, knocking down three men and slightly injuring another man and a woman. Ernest Warswick's left leg was fractured.

The names of the sixty-eight who volunteered in response to the second call and were accepted, are here given, for reference, as follows:

Lieutenant Alliene Case, James B. Layton, Edward D. Trumbull, Daniel A. Rinard, Harlan U. Beatty, Charles A. Gagen, William H. Hutchinson, Charles W. Johnson, Arthur J. Lowell, Joseph R. Spearman, Ernst Ruoff, H. B. Barker, Wilbur M. Guile, Edward J. Gannon, Charles E. Snow, Sylvester L. Kellogg, Carleton W. Faull, Walter L. West, Anton Klause, Harold G. Sammons, Walter A. Nittle, James R. Gaskle, Michael Smelzer, Sebastian E. Hamilton, Brigham W. Young, Wallace G. Grill, Francis J. Muller, Van R. Roselle, Charles D. Abbel, John G. Saxton, John H. Wagner, Frank D. Dwight, George W. Rankin, Edward C. Rea, Herbert L. Whitehead, Frank D. Wheeler, Edward Dougherty, Edward T. Bowers, Robert Neuhaus, Michael Flemming, Mathias E. Garner, Hyland H. Corey, Henry H. Schroeder, Frank G. Jewett, Clement O. McWilliams, Harvey Flaugher,

Charles D. Albee, Don A. Roberts, William G. Small, Louis Weadman, Thomas P. Manus, Paschal M. Saunders, Angel Calcari, John J. Miller, Emery Case, John McKinnon, Thomas E. Hackett, Joseph E. Harrison, Frederick N. Fisher, Peter Peterson, Addison E. Coats, Lewis E. Case, Benjamin F. Evans, James P. Emerson, William H. Fairchild, Charles Hardman, Arthur Allison, Wayne E. Ewing and Clarence McConnell.

They were mustered into service Thursday, July 22, by Captain Kendall, and together with the Salem volunteers, manned Battery B, Oregon Volunteer Artillery, stationed at Ft. Vancouver, Portland. On October 22d, they were mustered out of service, without having enjoyed an opportunity to prove their mettle in the battle's front. Upon their return the Baker City contingent permanently organized themselves into a company of the Oregon National Guards.

During 1898 Baker City experienced two serious losses by fire. In August the Baker City Iron Works was burned to the ground, entailing a loss of ten thousand dollars, and a few days later the McCord block, Rust's opera house and two other frame buildings fell victims to the flames. Of the twenty-seven thousand dollars lost in this latter fire fifteen thousand was covered by insurance.

These fires no doubt inspired the reorganization of the fire department, which consisted of one hook and ladder and five hose cart companies.

On April 2, 1899, the old Commercial Club was dissolved and in its stead was organized the Baker City Chamber of Commerce, its object being, of course, to conserve the business interests of the city.

In its efforts in this direction and in all things looking toward progress it has the support of a united and energetic people alert to perceive opportunities to promote the general welfare and ever ready to lend a helping hand to any worthy project. Public spirit has enabled them to develop the mining wealth in their vicinity, to draw to themselves a fair share of the trade of the surrounding country and by utilizing the forces so abundant in their vicinity to build up a wealthy, substantial city. The same public spirit is still theirs. It is now and will ever continue to be operative in encouraging mining, promoting railway construction, inducing internal improvements and drawing to itself the means of growth and affluence. No rival attempts to compete with it for first place among the towns of this section and from the nature of the case it must always remain the metropolis of southeastern Oregon.

CHAPTER VII.

OTHER TOWNS OF BAKER COUNTY.

SUMPTER.

The visitor to the thriving little city of Sumpter is impressed as soon as he alights from the train by the spirit of progress which everywhere pervades the place. Hardly will he have reached the nearest hotel before he will have mentally observed how thoroughly the people believe in their town; at least such was the experience of the writer. No sooner had he entered the hotel door than he was handed a glass of water with the injunction: "Sample this water; you have no such water as that in Baker City." The genial host then called attention to his healthy looking person, supplied with an abundance of adipose tissue, remarking that he felt ten years younger than he did four years ago when he first came to Sumpter and attributed this remarkable rejuvenation to the purity of the air and water and the general salubrity of the climate. Sumpter certainly has pure water and a healthy climate; it also has a beautiful location at the head of the fine mountain valley whose name it bears, while the mineral wealth of the surrounding country gives earnest of the continuance of its material prosperity and forms the foundation of its present hopefulness and courage.

The town is old and yet new. The first settlement in its vicinity, we are told, was made by a party of five southerners in the fall of 1862. They named the primitive cabin which they built in a gulch near by, Fort Sumpter, to manifest their pleasure at the fall of the famous stronghold of that name in South Carolina. From this circumstance the valley and the little city which later sprang into existence came to be known by the names they now bear.

Though Sumpter began to be several decades ago, it remained for many years a mere hamlet, containing, perhaps, not more than a dozen houses. The timber in its vicinity could not be utilized owing to the lack of transportation facilities. Only a very vague idea of the mineral wealth hidden in the depths of the Blue mountains contiguous to the town existed in the minds of men, and there was nothing to keep it up but the placer mines, which, after the first few years, were worked only by Chinese. Chinamen may yet be seen in large numbers during the mining season on a hillside near town, industriously digging for the precious metal, but no estimate can be made of the amount of gold which rewards their labors, as inquiry into this delicate matter of private business invariably elicits the same reply: "Some days belly well, some days no good at all."

Gold bearing quartz ledges were discovered in Sumpter district before the close of the 'sixties, and even at that early date some few local miners had a general idea of the existence of mineral wealth, but time alone and the general development which it brings could render this wealth available. In 1896 came the much needed railroad, the Sumpter Valley narrow gauge being that year extended from McEwen. Naturally the advent of modern means of transportation infused new life into the town, but it was not until 1898 that it began to forge ahead at a rapid rate. Four years ago last January, the town consisted of two small general merchandise stores, a blacksmith shop, two hotels, a meat market, a small hardware store and a few other business establishments, a public school and a limited number of residences. It covered an area of about thirty acres, had a population of a few hundreds and improvements worth perhaps twenty-five or thirty thousand dollars.

Such was Sumpter when the boom came. In 1901, according to the Blue Mountain American, it covered an area of fourteen hundred acres, had eighty-one business houses with stocks of goods aggregating $420,000 in value; improvements worth in the vicinity of $500,000, eight brick buildings with a combined frontage of 351 feet, all the brick and lumber for which were manufactured at Sumpter; a fine gravity system of water works, the reservoir having a capacity of 1,200,000 gallons and the mains measuring five and a half miles; a thirty-thousand-dollar electric light plant; an efficient fire department, equipped with two hose carts, a drying tower, a well equipped hook and ladder truck, a three-hundred-dollar fire bell and tower, rubber coats, rubber boots, service hats, etc.; 1,850 feet of graded and paved streets; five and a half miles of sidewalk; twelve and a half miles of local telephone wire, and ten long distance telephones; an efficient city government, and almost everything else that an up-to-date town of more than three thousand inhabitants might be expected to have.

While the boom is now over no demoralizing reaction has yet come to the town, but progress continues and the evidences of commercial health are everywhere to be seen.

Though the marks of Sumpter's rapid growth are plainly visible, and the vices which go wherever prosperity reigns are well represented, the forces which make for morality, culture and the highest enlightenment are also here. The churchman may have his choice of four denominations, the Methodist Episcopal, Protestant Episcopal, Presbyterian or Catholic. Of these, one society, the Presbyterian, already has a neat church building, and the Methodists and Catholics have taken the initial steps toward erecting suitable temples of worship. It is expected that the last-mentioned' denomination will also build a school and a hospital. The town has a fine public school building, in which four teachers are at work, but it is not large enough to accommodate all who seek its benefits, so another room has to be rented and a fifth teacher employed. Among the educational forces of the community, the newspapers may also be classed. Of these there are three, the Blue Mountain American, the Sumpter Miner and the Sumpter Reporter, the last named being a daily. The papers are in an unusually healthy financial condition, and are surprisingly well equipped with machinery, presses, type and everything needful to well regulated modern plants. Editorially they are conducted on broad, liberal principles, and no effort is spared to make them faithfully portray the life of the community. The fraternal organizations are quite generally represented in the town.

To give a full and complete resume of all the business establishments of Sumpter would not be an easy task, but so far as could be learned in a brief space of time, the principle ones are as follows: Five general merchandise stores, one large hardware, two meat markets, two groceries, a racket store, two bakeries, one candy and cigar store, fourteen or fifteen saloons, four or five general blacksmith and repair shops, two millinery and

BURNT RIVER CANYON.

HUNTINGTON PUBLIC SCHOOL.

SNAKE RIVER NEAR THE OLD "OLDS FERRY."

fancy goods stores, two banks, four hotels, two restaurants, a large number of boarding and lodging houses, a large saw and planing mill, several mining offices, two assayers, three newspapers, three warehouses, two feed stores, two clothing stores, carrying shoes, etc., two plumbing establishments, four barber shops, two tailor shops, a photograph gallery, a second hand store, a dance hall, an opera house, three physicians and four lawyers.

Such is the Sumpter of to-day. Of its future it is not the province of the historian to speak, but all will readily see that it depends almost entirely upon the development of the mining region contiguous. Lumbering is still an industry of great importance and hay raising and some other forms of the hardier farming are carried on successfully in the valley, but these are subsidiary to mining and without the main source of wealth production would not support the town. The future of the mining district is, of course, more or less uncertain, but all indications point toward an indefinite development both in the number of properties and the average output. The opinions of some noted experts have been obtained and they are all to the effect that, if the experiences of mineralogists in California and elsewhere are to be confirmed here, the district must long continue one of the largest producers in the world. If the best mining science of the present is to prove trustworthy in Sumpter district, the future of the active, energetic little city which forms its central gem must be a bright one indeed.

HUNTINGTON.

On a small, level valley, girt round with towering, sage-clad hills, in the eastern part of Baker county, is Huntington, well known in railroad circles on account of its being the point of junction between the Oregon Short Line and the O. R. & N. railroads. Long before the advent of the iron horse or the inception of the town, Miller's Station on the overland route had been established in the valley, and had become well known to all who traveled in pioneer days. The land, however, was secured from the government by the Huntington Brothers, whose inchoate title was carried to patent about the time the railroad was built.

During the years 1883-4 these men maintained a small trading post on their land. In 1884, with the advent of the railroad, came J. T. Fifer, who had been selling general merchandise to the construction crews, moving his goods from town to town as the work progressed. Shortly after Mr. Fifer arrived the Huntingtons closed up, leaving him alone in the general merchandise business. He was not permitted to enjoy this monopoly long, however, for that fall came the Oregon Construction Company, consisting of R. M. Steele & Son and D. P. Thompson, with a stock of general merchandise. About the same time was opened the first blacksmith shop, that of E. Macri, and in 1885 the the Pacific Hotel was erected. The business establishments at the close of that year may be outlined as follows: Two general merchandise stores, a blacksmith shop, a good hotel and several boarding houses and restaurants, and a number of saloons. The town then stopped growing rapidly, though in 1886 a drug store was added by J. M. Duffey.

In 1888 J. H. Aitkin came to Huntington to assume charge of the O. C. Company's general merchandise business. He built a warehouse and began, by soliciting the attention of trade of points far to the south, to build up the forwarding trade of the town. He succeeded in drawing patronage and shipping business from places as far remote as Stein's mountain, in southern Harney county. The next year the state appropriated $10,000 for the construction of a road down the Snake river to Connor creek. The road encouraged farmers and miners to come to Huntington for supplies and to ship their products, also encouraged the people of Mineral City, a mining camp in Washington county, Idaho, to do their trading there. For years Huntington was practically the sole shipping point for the great cattle country to the south, but in recent years Ontario has been drawing a share of this business.

The growth of Huntington has been slow, but steady and substantial. No destructive general conflagrations have come to give it a setback and no boom periods to cause inflation of its realty value, followed by depression and business demoralization. In February, 1891, it became for the first time the home of a county newspaper. In that year also it acquired corporate existence, and installed its first corps of officers. In 1898 the Northwest Railway Company, promoted by Isaac E. Blake, began operations to connect Huntington with the people of Seven Devils by a standard gauge railroad. The company expended much money in developing the Iron Dyke copper mine, which also belongs to them, and several hundred thousand dollars in grading, but before their projects were carried to a successful issue they became embarrassed financially and both the mine and the road went into the hands of a receiver. Last winter the affairs of the company were satisfactorily settled and the project of building the road is being revived. It is stated that the company has recently been reorganized and capitalized at $4,000,000, their purpose being to resume work on the road in the near future. Though the mine is immensely rich in copper it is of no value without transportation and the people of Huntington are therefore hopeful that a road will be built that will not only develop the Iron Dyke and bring its trade to their city, but will also attract the trade of the Seven Devils copper camp beyond.

Huntington gains a very considerable advantage from its being the terminus of two railroads and the presence in it of their repair shops. The success of the Northwest Company scheme would greatly augment its importance as a shipping point and make it a very considerable railway center.

The business establishments of Huntington consist at this writing of the general merchandise stores of the O. C. Company, Shirk, Graham & Company, and J. T. Fifer; drug stores belonging to W. M. McClure and the estate of J. M. Duffey; the shoe store of F. M. Stubblefield; the Pacific Hotel, owned by the O. R. & N. Company, the Gate City Hotel, owned by Mr. Kruse; the Central Hotel, by Chinamen; the private boarding house of Mrs. Tirrill; the livery stables of L. Tirrill and the Brown Brothers; the blacksmith shop of F. Macri; the meat market of Cole & Insenhoffer; the millinery store of Mrs. M. B. Stephens; the jewelry and notion store of Mrs. W. A. Young; the barber shops of William J. Moore and A. C. Degel; the fruit, cigar and confectionery store of Abbott Brothers; the commission and forwarding business of the Frame Forwarding Company; the Bank of Huntington, J. H. Aitkin, president, A. W. Sutherland, cashier; the harness shop of J. W. Gray; the coal and wood business of L. Tirrill; the real estate and mining agency of Woods & Laman; the bowling alley of E. H. Griswold; and three saloons. The legal profession is not represented in the town, but there are two physicians there, Drs. W. O. Spencer and J. B. White. The town also has a local and long distance telephone exchange.

A water main, conveying water furnished by the railroad companies, extends around several of the principal business blocks, giving adequate protection against fire. This means of safety is rendered effective by an efficient volunteer company.

Huntington is possessed of all the conveniences and social privileges usually found in a town of this size. It has an excellent six-thousand-dollar brick schoolhouse, in which three teachers labor assiduously for the intellectual development of the young during about nine months of each year. Three denominations of Christians are represented, the Congregational, Catholic and Methodist Episcopal, the first of which have commodious edifices. At present the Methodists meet in the Odd Fellows' Hall. The Protestant church societies are both supplied with resident pastors, but no priest resides in Huntington at this time. Several fraternities maintain organizations in the town, among them the I. O. O. F., the A. O. U. W., M. W. A., W. of W. and G. A. R., with the corresponding ladies' auxiliaries.

With its substantial development already achieved, with its established social institutions, its excellent and extensive tributary territory, the promise of the mining districts in its vicinity and its railway prospects, Huntington faces the future with confidence, assured that in the onward march of the county it will bear its full part and receive its share of the reward of industry.

OTHER TOWNS OF BAKER COUNTY.

Besides Baker City, Sumpter and Huntington, there are a number of other very considerable towns in Baker county, deserving of a more extended description than we have space and opportunity to give them. Among these is Haines, situated in a prosperous farming country. It was shown by the census of 1900 to have a population of 147 and it has all the business houses, shops, etc., usually found in a town of that size. It is situated on the O. R. & N. line, ten miles north of Baker City. Bourne, in the northwestern part of the county, is a mining center of importance, credited by the census with a population of 75. Whitney, about the center of western Baker county, is the terminus of the Sumpter Valley Railroad. It is experiencing a very rapid growth at present. Durkee is a considerable town twenty miles west of Huntington on the O. R. & N. It is in the center of a good farming country and the mining district contiguous to it is promising. At this writing the town has two general stores, two hotels, barber shop, blacksmith shop, saloon and a local telephone exchange connecting a number of farmers in the neighborhood. Sanger, Cornucopia and Sparta are important mining centers in the Panhandle country credited by the census of 1900 with population of 24, 176 and 58, respectively. The volume of business transacted in them is doubtless much in excess of what one would suppose from their size. Hereford, Unity, Bridgeport, Weatherby, Eagleton, Keating, Halfway, Carson, Homestead, Pine, Newbridge, Richland, Pleasant Valley, Wingville and McEwen are small villages and settlements in various parts of the county, many of them remote from railroads.

WILLIAM C. HINDMAN.

BIOGRAPHICAL.

WILLIAM C. HINDMAN.—The worthy pioneer and noble veteran of many a struggle in life's battles whose name is at the head of this article, is one of the most familiar figures in Baker county, having been here from the earliest days and continued in the prosecution of the same enterprise constantly since, wherein he has displayed the commendable qualities of keen foresight and wise business management coupled with the most exacting uprightness and moral worth, while his public service and efforts for the advancement of the interests of the county and section in general have been untiring and eminently successful.

Mr. Hindman was born in Pennsylvania on April 30, 1821, being the son of Samuel and Sarah (Manning) Hindman. His father was a native of Pennsylvania, where his ancestors settled prior to the Revolutionary war, in which struggle they participated, while his father fought in the war of 1812. He was a millwright and followed his trade in the summer and taught school in the winter. Our subject's mother was a native of Baltimore, Maryland, and her ancestors came over with Lord Baltimore and settled in that city. Her father was a soldier in the Revolutionary war and was present at the memorable time when Cornwallis surrendered at Yorktown. She was born three years before Washington was elected for the first time.

Our subject received his primary education in the public schools, and after he was twenty-one years of age wrought his way through a good academy. His parents came to Ohio when he was but a child and from that state he went to Iowa and farmed near Council Bluffs for a time, and then came overland with ox and horse teams to Baker county, in 1863. For two years subsequent to his arrival he freighted and then embarked in cattle raising, taking a homestead and buying enough more land for this enterprise, and to the successful prosecution of this business he has devoted his entire energies, with the result of almost unbounded success. He is also interested in mining and owns some valuable city property. In 1867 he was called from private life by the ballots of his fellows and charged with the responsible duties of representing Baker and Union counties in the state legislature, which he did with display of ability and rigid faithfulness to the interests of his constituents.

The marriage of Mr. Hindman and Miss Sarah Kyle was celebrated in Iowa in 1853; she was a native of New Brunswick, but reared in Ohio. They became the parents of seven children: Clara; Phila; Agnes, deceased; Homer; Grace; Frank; Willard. His sons, Frank and Homer, have charge of his cattle. In 1883 Mrs. Hindman was called from the duties of her position on earth to the regions beyond.

On November 25, 1897, Mr. Hindman was married a second time, on this occasion Mrs. Tollie Mounts Douthitt became his wife. Mr. Hindman was brought up under the teachings of the Presbyterian church, but he has never united with any denomination, although his life is one of the strictest integrity and exemplification of the principles of truth.

* * *

GEORGE R. HODGINS.—One of the leading mechanics of the county and one whose skill and energy have placed him forward in the manipulation of the arts of his trade, the

15

subject of this sketch is here accorded a representation in this volume, since his real worth and commendable qualities justly entitle him to such, as well as his success in the enterprises that he has followed since coming to the county.

Across the waters, in the little Emerald Isle, that has been the home of some of the greatest men that have graced the human race, we find the birth place of Mr. Hodgins, and the memorable 1849 is the year of his nativity. While still a child he was brought by his parents to London, Canada, where he received his educational discipline and where he also learned the prince of all trades, the blacksmith's, having completed it when he was seventeen years of age, thus demonstrating both his ability and his energy. His first move was to Michigan, where he followed his trade for three years, then he came to Boise City in 1869 and there continued in the same occupation until he came to Baker county in 1876. One year later he migrated to Arizona and wrought in Phoenix and Prescott until 1881, then returned to Wingville, opened there a shop and beat the anvil to the time of honest industry until 1887. At that date he entered into partnership with John M. Rohner and opened a butcher shop and grocery store in Wingville, which business they prosecuted together until the fall of 1893, when they sold it out and took up stock raising and farming together. They own about four hundred acres of land, which is well improved and operated to the best advantage. Mr. Hodgins is road supervisor in his district at the present time and has held the responsible position of justice of the peace and in all these public positons he has shown both ability and integrity.

On November 1, 1881, Mr. Hodgins married Miss Trena, daughter of Jacob and Anna Rodner, who came here with her parents from Switzerland. They have become the parents of one child that died in infancy. Mr. Hodgins is a member of the I. O. O. F., Wingville Lodge, No. 69, and also of the W. of W., as well as of the Encampment No. 8. In religious affairs he is affiliated with the Methodist church, South, and has been very active in church work all the years of his life. At the present time he is superintendent of the Sunday-school and has been for fifteen years, having given much time to this work and making a fine success in his endeavors. Mr. Hodgins is associated with the Democratic party in political matters and takes an active interest in county and state affairs.

◆◆◆

JOHN ROHNER.—From every portion of the globe come those who make up the citizenship of this great land, and it is frequently the case that those born in foreign countries have a keener appreciation of our free institutions than those who are native born. Among that worthy class who have grown sturdy in the famous little republic of the Alpine region are many that have sought larger fields and greater chances in this utopia of the west and one of their number well known here for his enterprise and faithfulness, as well as his ability in the affairs of the land, is the prominent citizen and gentleman whose name appears at the head of this article.

On April 26, 1865, near the eternal snows of the world famous Alps, was born the subject of this sketch and there he spent the first eight years of his earthly life, at the end of which time he was brought by his parents to southern Utah, where they remained for two years and then removed to southern Nevada, in which place they resided until 1881. At that date they brought horses to Wingville, this county, and soon our subject settled where we now find him, about eight miles northwest from Baker City. Here, in partnership with his brother-in-law, G. R. Hodgins, mention of whom is made in the sketch immediately preceding, is engaged in farming and stock raising. During the interim from 1887 to 1893, our subject was engaged with Mr. Hodgins in the butcher and grocery business in Wingville, but at the last date they sold this business and engaged as has been said. Thrift and industry are manifest in all the affairs of Mr. Rohner and his skill and wisdom displayed in the art of tilling the soil is quite commendable. He is at the present time discharging the duties of justice of the peace of his district, the same being done with ability and straightforwardness. He has also been for a good many years clerk of the school board, as well as holding other positions of trust.

The marriage of Mr. Rohner and Miss Fannie R., daughter of William and Lydia B.

Ward, was solemnized in Skamokawa, Washington, on November 18, 1888, and to them have been born four children: William H., aged ten years; Anna P., seven years old; Charles F., four years of age; Archie, who has passed three years in this life. Mr. Rohner is a member of the I. O. O. F., Wingville Lodge, No. 68, and also of the W. of W., Lodge, No. 68, and also affiliates with the Methodist church, South, and demonstrates, both by precept and practice, his interest in his faith.

Mr. Rohner's father died while en route to this county, but his mother still resides at Wingville. The family consists of the following children: Trena, wife of J. R. Hodgins; Jacob, Jr.; John; Louisa, now Mrs. William Hindman; August; Emil; Freda, wife of Charles Haskill; Godfrey.

ELIJAH B. WOODWORTH.—Among those who have wrought for the development of this region for one-third of a century and whose skill and sturdy strength have added materially to the substantial progress of the county is the gentleman whose name initiates this paragraph and who has been a real pioneer in the fullest sense of that expressive word, having followed that most pioneer of all industries, mining, during a long and eventful life.

Mr. Woodworth was born in Warwick county, Indiana, on October 3, 1835, being the son of Benjamin and Mary Woodworth. When two years of age he was taken by his parents to Massac county, Illinois. His education was received in the schools of Cincinnati, and as early as 1854 he became desirous of viewing for himself the undiscovered regions of the boundless west and accordingly engaged with a freight outfit to Salt Lake and then made his way from there to California, where he embarked at once in mining, continuing thereat for eleven years, at the end of which time he had gathered a fortune, principally on the Feather river. But, as is so often the case in this occupation, he invested in another section and lost his hard earned dust. During the excitement on the Salmon river he started thither but stopped at Granite and later went to Canyon City, where he was again favored

with success in mining. Two years later he migrated to Idaho City, where he spent five years in the search for nature's vaults of treasure and then went to the Grand Ronde valley and from there he came to this county, where he has been for thirty years constantly following his chosen occupation. In the last few years he retired from the more arduous activities of the mines and settled on a farm seven miles west from Baker City, where, engaged in the pleasant duties of the basic art of agriculture, we find him at the present time.

The marriage of Mr. Woodworth and Miss Frances Mitchell was solemnized in 1864, in Idaho City, and to them have been born the following children: Eliza; Daisy; Molly; Bessie, married to Jack Chadd; and Minnie.

Mr. Woodworth is a man of sterling principles and possessed of fine abilities, which have rendered him great service as an exemplary member of society and a stanch and faithful citizen, while his demeanor has been such that he has won for himself the confidence and esteem of the people.

HANER W. LEE.—It is now our pleasure to give in epitome the salient points of the career of one of the leading stockmen and most substantial citizens of his section, whose life of marked ability and wise financiering, coupled with stanch integrity, has been a power for good and advancement in this county, while in his private business achievements he has been crowned with that success that comes to the wise manipulation of the resources that were so richly displayed in this favored section.

Mr. Lee was born in Michigan on July 22, 1859, being the son of Daniel and Betsey (Weatheruax) Lee, the latter having died when he was a child, and his father in 1890. He received his education in Jackson, his native state, and in 1872 came with his father to this county. In 1890 he took a homestead, where he now lives, in the Lower Powder river valley, fifteen miles northeast from Baker City. Here he devotes his attention to farming and raising blooded stock, mostly Short Horn Durham. He also buys and sells stock a great deal and operates a creamery, all of which occupies him continuously; but in each particular line he manifests commendable skill and every detail is cared for with such promptness and all is supervised with such wisdom that success is constantly on his portion to enjoy. In addition to these duties he finds time to give the attention demanded of every wide awake citizen to the affairs of state and government, and especially is he active in educational matters, having given good service on the school boards for a number of years.

The marriage of Mr. Lee and Miss Olive, daughter of Samuel and Jane (Moore) Colwell, was solemnized on January 1, 1888. They have one daughter, Minnie P., and they have also adopted a child, Owen M.

Mr. Lee's father was distinguished by his service in the Indian wars in an early day in Michigan and adjacent regions, while in p litical matters he was no less prominent, having been sheriff of Eaton county, in Michigan, for several terms, and also rendering other commendable service of a public nature. Our subject affiliated himself with the I. O. O. F., Union Lodge, No. 39, of Union county in 1884, and he is also a member of the Modern Woodmen of America, Lodge No. 5326, of Baker City, and of the Fraternal Union of America. In all of these social relations Mr. Lee is pleasantly distinguished and very popular among his fellows, while his whole life is fraught with kindness and industrious action and commendable achievements.

EDWARD B. McDANIEL, M. D.— Prominent among those who minister to the sick in Baker City and county is the learned and skillful physician whose name gives caption to this review, and though he has not been a resident of the political division with which our volume is concerned as long as many of those whose names appear herein, his high standing and prominence as a professional man and citizen render it fitting that due representation should be accorded him in this portion of our work.

Our subject is a native of the great commonwealth in which he is now living, the town of his birth being Cove, Union county, and the date March 19, 1873. He grew to early manhood there, acquiring his preliminary education in the public schools and in Leighton Academy. In the fall of 1889 he started to the

Beaumont Medical College, of St. Louis, Missouri, from which institution he graduated in 1892. His medical education was further augmented during the summer following by hospital practice and in the fall he entered Jefferson Medical College, of Philadelphia, and from this institution he also received a degree in the spring of 1893. A year was then spent in study in various eastern hospitals, after which our subject returned to his native town and began practice. Shortly afterward he went to Portland, where he practiced with Dr. A. C. Smith until 1897, which year is the date of his advent to Baker City. His skill and ability, the natural result of careful and long continued training, were speedily recognized, and he now has one of the most extensive practices enjoyed in the city. During the first years of his residence here he served as county physician, and at the present time he is chief physician and surgeon of the St. Elizabeth hospital of Baker City. He maintains an active membership in both the State and the American Medical Societies.

Our subject is also a very enthusiastic worker in the Masonic fraternity, belonging to the Consistory, the Temple, the Shrine and in fact all the branches of Masonry. Several times he represented the subordinate bodies to which he belongs in the grand lodge. Dr. McDaniel is also exalted ruler of the local organization of the B. P. O. E. He examines for the Massachusetts Mutual, the New York Mutual, the Pacific Mutual and other insurance companies.

EDWARD T. BORMAN.—It is with pleasure that we are enabled to present here a brief review of the life record of the successful mining man whose name appears above, for we are fully persuaded that the man who adds to the world's wealth in a way which brings no sorrow is to be honored as a benefactor of his race.

Mr. Borman is a native of Saxony, Germany, born August 15, 1831, the son of Fred and Augusta (Linzenbard) Borman. He received the public school training usually given to the German youth, then turned his attention to printing, a handicraft which he followed much of the time for the half decade succeeding his sixteenth year. When twenty-

EDWARD B. McDANIEL, M. D.

one years of age he put into execution a determination to enjoy the advantages of the new world, so emigrated to the United States. Locating first in the city of Boston, he there learned the trade of the shoemaker, a handicraft which he afterward followed for three years in Chicago. In 1857 he moved to Kansas City, Missouri. He took a claim in Shawnee county, Kansas, where he was during the John Brown raid and the other slavery difficulties. He was himself a pronounced free state man, but being peaceably disposed, he preferred to emigrate rather than take part in the troubles, so set out with ox teams for California. At Red Bluffs he followed his trade for a period of six years, and at the time of the mining excitement in Idaho in 1864, he came north to Silver City, where for another period of six years he busied himself in shoemaking. He then devoted a half decade to the hotel business and mining, thereafter coming to Baker City, where he has mined almost continuously since, though for a time he was in the general merchandise business at Virtue. He has a fine home and eighty acres of land, one mile southeast from Baker City, where his home now is, and where he is spending the remainder of his days in peace and quiet, though he is still active in mining ventures.

Mr. Borman has been in the Masonic order since 1867. His marriage was solemnized in 1853, when Miss Christina, daughter of William Dupel, became his wife, and they have had three children, namely: Clara E., deceased, Edward W., of Baker City, and George W., who married Miss Maggie Rea, also a resident of Baker City.

JUDGE M. L. OLMSTED.—Few men exert a great influence upon the country, and especially upon the communities during their early formative periods, than the legal fraternity, and among these the most influential and those destined to leave their impress upon the plastic embryonic body politic are the heads of the judiciary departments. As one of the leading representatives of those who have done faithful service upon the bench in Baker county and in eastern Oregon, stands the estimable gentleman whose name initiates this paragraph, and whose interesting career of worthy

achievement it is now our pleasant task to epitomize.

On September 29, 1842, our subject first saw the light in Tullahoma, Tennessee, where he remained until he was four years of age. He was still in his school work when the call came for volunteers to defend the nation, and with the promptness born of true patriotism and praiseworthy valor, he immediately responded for three months' service, which extended itself to the end of the war, during all of which time he rendered valiant service under the banner that he bore, the flag of freedom. His enlistments were in the Seventy-eighth and One Hundred and Second New York. Following the war he served some in various Indian conflicts in all parts of the frontier. He reached the rank of brevet lieutenant colonel in the Civil war and was commander of a company of volunteers in the Bannock war. After the close of that war he was elected to the position of judge of the sixth judicial district, which at that time included the greater portion of eastern Oregon. He discharged the duties thus incumbent upon him with display of acumen and probity and impartiality that commended him to the people in a very satisfactory manner. Since that time he has been devoting his energies to the practice of law in the various courts of his state, wherein he has achieved a very gratifying success, while in political matters he is very active and influential, having been nominated as one of the Bryan electors. He is interested in mining and handling timber products. Fraternally he is affiliated with the A. O. U. W., and has been for twenty-four years, also with the Woodmen of the World and the Fraternal Union.

The marriage of Judge Olmsted and Miss Celia E. East, a member of one of the pioneer families of Iowa, was solemnized in Iowa on November 5, 1867, and to them have been born two sons, Percy N. and Harland H. The elder one is now a lieutenant in the navy, having inherited the military spirit and valor of his father, and is serving on the Brooklyn. He was the acting flag lieutenant of the south Atlantic squadron, from which post he was assigned to duty with Sampson's fleet during the Spanish war. He was in charge of the eight-inch battery on the Indiana during the great naval conflict off Santiago and received honorable mention in the details of the battle. One of his home papers in Baker City spoke as follows: "Leslie's Weekly of July, 25 contains a picture of the gallant eight-inch gun crew of the Indiana as they appeared just after the sinking of Cervera's fleet, July 3. At the head of the line stands our Oregon boy, easily recognizable by his old time friends of Baker City." The May number of the Century, also, in an article headed "The Story of the Captains" mentions the lieutenant in honorable action. That day's work is history and written by a thousand pens, the best the world affords, and all are familiar with it. Following this brilliant day he was assigned to the flagship, Brooklyn, at Cavite, Philippine Islands, later the vessel went to Taku, China, and is at the present time at Nagasaki, Japan, he having been in continuous service on it. His parents in Baker City have a fine collection that he has sent to them, which consists of relics, arms, pictures, uniforms, coins of gold and silver melted and run together on the Spanish ships, and many other rare and interesting things. P. N. Olmsted was appointed by Congressman Binger Hermann to the U. S. Navy Academy at Annapolis in 1887, and on June 2, 1893, he was graduated with credit from that institution, being commander of the second Cadet Corps. Following this he was for two years on the protected cruiser, Philadelphia, in Honolulu, then assigned to the navy yard at New York as instructor, then sent with the South American squadron in 1896, holding the position of acting flag lieutenant. In December, 1897, he was recalled from Montevideo and assigned as artillery officer on the Iowa, and on February 15, 1898, he was given the position of division officer on the Indiana. Subsequent to this followed the brilliant service, as described above, which was attended with items of bravery and acts of commendable skill that would far exceed the space we are allowed, and which it is a matter of regret that we can not further detail. The second son of Judge Olmsted is being instructed at Hill's Military Academy in Portland and is giving promise of doing honor to the ancestors whose name he bears.

The Judge has been dentified with the history of eastern Oregon from an early day, having migrated to Canyon City in 1872, and to Baker City in 1886. He is esteemed by al'

that know his name, having ever been an exemplification of those principles of uprightness, truth and integrity that make the substantial citizen and worthy man.

FRANK GEDDES.—It is a source of gratification and deserving of worthy commendation to see the descendants of the early pioneers rising to take the places of those gone before and to push forward the work of development and upbuilding, the foundations of which were so skillfully and deeply laid by that praiseworthy band that first broke the sod in this favored region. Not least among this rising class is the gentleman whose name is mentioned above and whose career of usefulness and commendable achievement has demonstrated the excellent capabilities and fine principles with which he is possessed.

A product of this county, being born here on December 2, 1871, to Joseph A. and Eva M. (Freligh) Geddes, the subject of this sketch is proving himself to be a man of whom his native county may be proud and one worthy of the entire confidence and esteem of its population. His birthplace was within four miles of the site of Baker City, his parents having settled there the year previous. He was educated in the schools of the county, finishing that important part of a man's fitting for life in the Monmouth Normal, where he graduated from the commercial department and took one additional year in post-graduate studies. Following this he returned to Baker City and took part in assisting his father in his business until 1898. At that time the people of the county called him from this occupation and installed him as clerk of the county. So faithfully and with such efficiency did he discharge the functions thus devolving upon him that he was a second time elected to assume the same trust, and serving in this capacity with his characteristic virtues and talent, we find him at the present time. Since his majority and even before he has always evinced a great interest in the affairs of the county and the nation and is one of the prominent figures in his party, the Republican, where his counsels are received with credit, since his foresight and wisdom are becoming manifest to all.

The marriage of Mr. Geddes and Miss

Lulu M., daughter of George and Elizabeth Ebbert, was solemnized in Monmouth on April 5, 1899, and to them has been born one child, Otto Ebbert. Mr. Geddes owns a nice home at 2345 Grove street, besides other property. He is a member of the K. of P., Gauntlet Lodge, No. 8, and he has been a delegate to the grand lodge for the past two sessions. He is also a member of the Fraternal Union, and of the Elks, Baker City Lodge, No. 338. Mr. Geddes is possessed of that happy geniality and well rounded balance that wins and retains many friends and his popularity is very flattering, and it is pleasant to state that commensurate therewith is a very acceptable manifestation of wisdom that is sure to lead. free from the rocks in his onward journey.

LEE STEWART.—The enterprising and industrious young agriculturist whose name heads this article is a product of this county, being born in Baker City on March 5, 1871, and here he has wrought out the abundant success that is his to enjoy at the present time, gaining the same by his wisely directed efforts and careful business principles, which have the requisite aggressiveness, but tempered with a keen and wholesome foresight and proper conservatism, while his uprightness and excellent moral principles are quite commensurate therewith.

Our subject is the son of John and Barbara A. Stewart, who came to this country across the plains in 1864, making the entire journey with ox teams from Sioux City, Iowa. In Stewart's second addition to Baker City, Mr. L. Stewart first saw the light and there he lived until 1890, receiving meanwhile a good education in the public schools of the city, being a graduate of the high school. He first embarked in raising cattle and in 1894 sold his entire interests in that business and commenced his present occupation, farming and threshing. He owns in partnership with his brother twelve hundred acres of hay and grain land and in addition to the proper operation of this they are running a fine threshing outfit. He is one of the leading young men of the county and has displayed commendable energy and ability in his operations, demonstrating himself a native son in which his county may justly take

pride. He is affiliated with the I. O. O. F., Baker City Lodge, No. 25, and with the W. of W., Wingville Camp, No. 343.

The marriage of Mr. Stewart and Miss Edith, daughter of Henry and Sophia Lammert, and a native of Nebraska, occurred on June 24, 1900.

WILLIS W. CREWS.—What more pleasurable task could be alloted to one than to follow the career of a successful and capable man who has manifested fine principles and stanch integrity throughout, coupled with wisdom and enterprise that bring their own crown of success? An exemplification of which capabilities and virtues is the subject of this sketch, who is well known throughout the county both for his intrinsic worth and the successful prosecution of the enterprises that have culminated so pleasantly and profitably under his skillful management.

Mr. Crews was born in Illinois on December 6, 1833, being the son of James and Nancy (Little) Crews, natives of Tennessee and Illinois, respectively. In his native state he received his educational discipline and remained there until he had attained manhood's years and then migrated to Kansas and commenced operations on life's battlefield for himself. For four years he remained in that place and then went to Missouri, where he was engaged in farming for eight years and then in 1880 came to this county. He operated the first lime kiln in the county and furnished the lime for the first building in Baker City and transported some to Boise City. He reaped a good financial return from this enterprise and then sold out and located on his present place in the Lower Powder river valley, where he started an apiary on a small scale, getting his first queen from Italy direct. By skillful management and careful attention to business Mr. Crews has increased his business until he now handles one hundred and twenty-five stands of bees and markets every year five thousand pounds of honey. His is the most extensive apiary in the county. In addition to this enterprise he also has two fine fish ponds well stocked with carp, which he obtained from the Grande Ronde river, this having been stocked by the United States commissioner some fifteen years before. Mr. Crews handles some fine full blooded chickens, mostly of the Plymouth Rock kind, which he obtained from New York and Ohio. He was formerly connected with the Sparta mine, in addition to his other business matters. For four years he has been justice of the peace and was also nominated on the Populist ticket of Union county when that county embraced Baker county, for representative to the state legislature, but refused to run. At the present time he is notary public.

The marriage of Mr. Crews and Miss Mariah, daughter of Joshua and Nancy (Pollock) Cushman was celebrated in 1862 and to them have been born the following children: Grace, wife of W. H. Wellington; William S.; May, wife of H. Deboys, of Sparta; Maggie, wife of Avon S. Love; Tecumseh; Ada, living with Mrs. Love. Mrs. Crews' father was one of the earliest settlers near Cincinnati and was county judge of his county for a long period. Mrs. Crews died March 5, 1899, and is buried in Brown's graveyard on Goose creek. It is of interest that Mr. Crews' father served in the Blackhawk war when A. Lincoln was lieutenant.

GEORGE W. MOODY.—In the person whose name heads this article we have one of the prominent and substantial citizens of Baker county, who has spent about forty years within its precincts and has ever been in the front ranks of those who are working for its development and for the advancement of its interests, maintaining meanwhile a high standard of honor and uprightness and displaying faithfulness, ability and integrity in all of his dealings both public and private.

The parents of our subject, Michael and Mary (Mercer) Moody, were natives of North Carolina and Kentucky respectively, and in 1842 they removed to Missouri, where their home was until the time of their death. At the beginning of the war, our subject enlisted in Company A, Fifty-ninth Missouri Volunteer Infantry, and did faithful service there for ninety days, when he was discharged, being disabled by rheumatism. In 1863 he fitted up ox teams and crossed the plains settling first in the Burnt river valley, for one year, and then removed to Auburn, where he was engaged in mining for six years. Following

this period he repaired to Eagle valley and took land on Sage Brush flat, September 16, 1874, being the date of his settlement. In this place we find him at the present time engaged in farming and stockraising, having wrought for himself a marked success, for his holdings amount to eight hundred acres of fine land besides a great many head of thoroughbred Short Horn cattle and much other stock, in addition to the improvements of value upon his estate. He is also superintendent of three irrigating companies, where he does excellent service. He is a man that has always taken an active interest in the affairs of state and is always on hand at the conventions and primaries, displaying the part of a good citizen that is interested in the welfare of his county. He has been chosen as a delegate to every convention of the county since he has resided in his present place.

The marriage of Mr. Moody to Miss Auphenia, daughter of Peter and Mary (Knowles) Grier, was solemnized in 1860, and they have become the parents of the following children: Otis C., died when he was an infant; Lottie, died in 1880; Willard, married; Henry, married; George M.; Laura, wife of Mr. W. N. Young; Fannie, wife of Mr. William Cole. Mrs. Moody died in 1880, beloved and mourned by all.

Mr. Moody contracted a second marriage and the lady that became his wife was Polly Young, daughter of Mitchell and Rosa (Daniels) Young.

Our subject is one of the leading men of his vicinity and of the county and has always so demeaned himself that he has won the esteem and confidence of all who may have the pleasure of his acquaintance.

His is doubtless the finest place in the valley and his elegant residence is equal to any in the county. He manages his estate with wisdom, and neatness and thrift are manifested in every detail. It is of note that during the Indian war of 1878, the settlers made his yard a stockade and Mr. Moody volunteered to go to Union after night to obtain arms. He was able to secure ten guns and some ammunition only by giving a bond for one thousand dollars. The items that Mr. Moody gives in reference to the value of real estate in the valley are highly interesting. Land that to-day is bringing on the market seventy-five dollars

GEORGE W. MOODY.

per acre, could be bought in 1874 for as many cents per acre and a common cayuse could easily be traded for forty acres. Then the best crops were eighteen bushels of oats per acre and the same land now under irrigation produces one hundred bushels annually.

---◆◆◆---

WILLIAM JENKINS, deceased.—The ranks of the noble men and women who toiled through the arduous undertakings of opening a new and far distant country to civilization are thinning fast by the ruthless ravages of time and the silvered locks tell eloquently of the toil and endeavor of the days gone by forever. Prominent among this worthy class and well known throughout the county as one of the earliest of its settlers, was the stanch and faithful man whose memory we now pay tribute to in this memorial, wherein we endeavor to present the salient points of his interesting career.

The birth of our subject was in that most famous of modern countries, the Emerald Isle, on May 15, 1820, where he remained until 1839, at which date he became enamored of freedom's land and made his way hither. His first settlement was in St. Louis, where he remained until 1849, and then removed to Illinois. He was engaged there in tilling the soil until 1864, and then came to the west via the plains, using ox and horse teams for the journey. In the same year he landed on the present site of Baker City and soon selected land eight miles northeast, where he gained title to five hundred and twenty acres adjoining the stage road. Here he settled and devoted his entire attention to the rearing of cattle and horses, gaining the success that is the inevitable result of care and skill, coupled with industry, all of which were displayed in his career with exceptional excellence. For twenty-three years he toiled on this place and then removed with his family to Baker City, where he had a very comfortable home and resided for thirteen years. But on the 24th day of March, 1897, he was called to leave the land where he had wrought so faithfully and had manifested forth the light of a worthy and noble Christian life, and come to the world where there will be death no more and where the proper reward of faithful service will be

his for the enduring ages. He was a member of the Methodist church, south, and a consistent Christian during his long life, which was fraught with kind deeds and generous sympathy. His demise was mourned by all and the funeral was a time of expression of genuine sorrow at the loss, not only to his family, but to the entire community.

The marriage of Mr. Jenkins and Miss Elizabeth A. Maxfield took place in St. Louis in 1845, and to them were born the following children: Sarna J.; N. Emaline; Thomas H., deceased; William; Mary A.; John Edward; George W.; Francis M. Mrs. Jenkins still survives, having passed about fifty-seven years of married life, and is active in the management of the fine estate left by her husband. She is in good health and passes the golden years with the calm assurance of contemplating a life well spent and buoyed by a bright hope for the future.

---◆◆◆---

GEORGE RIZOR.—It is with pleasure that we are enabled to incorporate in this portion of our volume a brief resume of the very useful career of the honored pioneer agriculturist and stockman whose name appears above. A public spirited citizen, a gentleman of integrity and worth and a genial friend and neighbor, he enjoys the good will and confidence of the community in which he lives, and his standing is in all respects an enviable one,

Our subject was born in Holmes county, Ohio, September 3, 1837, his parents being Michael and Sarah Rizor. He received such educational advantages as the public schools of the place and period afforded, but it must be confessed that these were painfully meager. At the age of fifteen he removed to Jefferson county, Iowa, where he lived for several years, thereafter going to Pawnee county, Nebraska, his business in all these places being farming mostly.

In 1875 he emigrated to Baker county, Oregon, and in due time he located on a farm on Alder creek, six miles west of Express, where we now find him. In 1878 he was absent from his home for a while with General Howard in his pursuit of Chief Joseph.

Mr. Rizor is the owner of a fine, rich, well improved farm and is achieving a very enviable success in his pursuit of the basic art of agriculture and in stock raising. He is one of the thrifty· and successful farmers of his neighborhood, as he is one of its most esteemed citizens. He takes some interest in mining and has some properties of great promise.

Public spirited and actively interested in all matters of general concern, Mr. Rizor is especially solicitous that the cause of education be promoted in his neighborhood, and this solicitude has found expression in his serving for the past decade and a half as director of his district.

The marriage of our subject was solemnized in Jefferson county, Iowa, September 1, 1861, Miss Sarah Batten becoming his wife at that time, and to this union nine children have been born, namely: Michael, of Baker City; Benjamin C., living near home; John, of North Powder River; Wesley, of Geiser, Oregon; Anna, deceased; Lewis, deceased; H. J., at home; Ella, deceased; and Nellie, at home.

M. S. WARREN.—In a work of the character of the history of Baker county, there would be sad incompleteness were there omission to chronicle the interesting and eventful career of the worthy pioneer and estimable citizen whose name appears above and who has faithfully done his part in this region for nearly forty years, manifesting those substantial qualities which are the major exemplifications in those men who form the boast and pride of any well regulated community.

The birth of Mr. Warren occurred on July 3, 1837, in Somerset, Pulaski county, Kentucky, being the son of William and Elizabeth Warren, and in his native place he spent the first eighteen years of his life, being but poorly favored with school advantages, which lack, however, he has well made up by careful and continuous reading since. In 1855 he came to Grundy county, Missouri, and there engaged in farming until 1864, when he joined the stream of immigration to the pacific coast and with ox teams made the weary and dangerous journey from Missouri to his present ranch, consuming six months on the road. He immediately set himself to the task of development and improvement of his western home, and his efforts were soon apparent in the thrifty appearance and substantial returns that he re-

ceived from his land. In 1877 he went to Union county and for twenty years he labored and gained success there and then he came back to his old homestead and is there now, spending the golden years that begin to draw on apace, comfortably established on the land where he first broke the sod in the wild scenes of the west. Mr. Warren has passed the days of the years of his stay here in most commendable manifestations of unswerving integrity and real moral worth of the highest type.

The marriage of Mr. Warren and Miss Mary A., daughter of Hiram and Drusilla Osborn, and a native of Franklin county, Missouri, was solemnized on June 20, 1860, and they have become the parents of the following children: William; Lora; Leah; Tyra, wife of Pearl Cornell, and living in Union; Hiram.

PATRICK H. MILES.—To the esteemed gentleman and prominent citizen, whose name appears at the head of this article, is accorded a representation in this volume, both because of his prominence in the affairs of the county and his own intrinsic worth and stanch principles of uprightness, which during a long period from the earliest pioneer days until the present time he has exemplified in honest industry and wise and faithful demeanor in both public and private walk.

The son of James and Bridget (Doolen), natives of Ireland, our subject first saw the light in that famous little isle on December 29, 1841, and amid the rural scenes of his native land he passed the first six years of his life. 1847 was the year that the family tore themselves from the home land and sought their fortunes in America, settling first in Ontario county, New York, whence, two years later, they removed to Lockport, Illinois, where the father and mother passed to the other world, and at eighteen Patrick H. found himself on his own resources in this new land. He was possessed of strength and a dauntless spirit, coupled with consummate courage and pluck, and his energy at once caused him to try the west, his first venture being to Pike's Peak, where he mined and freighted for two years and then at the very beginning of the war enlisted in the Second Colorado Cavalry and did faithful military service for his chosen country in the army of the frontier in Missouri, Kansas, Colorado and New Mexico until the war closed. Soon after this time he was married to Miss Mary Crimmons, a native of Illinois, and together they migrated to Oregon, settling first in Union county, near the town of Union, and in 1869 he took land on Big creek in the same county, where he remained for twenty years, devoting his attention to the cultivation of the soil and stock raising. Following this period, he removed to his present place of one hundred and twenty acres in the Lower Powder river valley, fifteen miles from Baker City, where he is dividing his attention between agriculture and placer mining, which latter is prosecuted on Eagle creek. He is also interested in the recent oil finds in Malheur and Crook counties, this state, his son being the first discoverer of the same. In political matters he is a Republican and has frequently been called by his fellows to discharge the duties of public office, which has been done with faithfulness and the manifestation of ability.

To Mr. and Mrs. Miles have been born the following children: David A., James D., John D., Charles H., Ellen A., wife of W. Davis, of Eagle valley, Roland G.

CHARLES M. FOSTER.—It now becomes our pleasant task to outline in brief the career of the faithful pioneer, distinguished citizen and eminent gentleman whose name heads this article, and whose life of continued devotion to his profession in this county since its inception as a political division, has manifested rare capabilities and principles of honor and moral worth that are as refreshing as they are beautiful in exemplification.

The birth of Mr. Foster occurred in Caledonia county, Vermont, on October 3, 1835, and there he passed the years of his minority, gaining in the public schools the primary educational training and later taking a degree from the Barre academy, near Montpelier, the same institution from which Admiral Dewey graduated about that time. Following his graduation he took up a special course that thoroughly fitted him for his profession, that of civil engineering. Having received his degree, he engaged for a time with different rail-

road companies in the capacity of civil engineer, but in 1859 he crossed the plains to Pike's Peak and later to California, being transported by ox teams. The train was very small, having but three wagons, and although those preceding and following had much difficulty with the Indians, the company of Mr. Foster was unmolested. For one year he mined in the Golden state, then came to Portland in 1861 and served as clerk to the superintendent of Indian affairs, Edward R. Geary, there for a time, following which he went to Walla Walla and opened a mercantile establishment for six months and then went to Florence during the gold excitement in 1862. Succeeding this he removed to Auburn in Baker county and followed mining for a time, and then was elected clerk of Baker county, being the first incumbent of that office elected. After his term of two years in this service he gave his attention to his profession and this has occupied him since. In 1868 he was elected county surveyor, and excepting about eight years he has served in that capacity since, which continued term of faithful discharge of public trusts is in itself a most convincing proof both of ability and sound principles. In addition to this he has also served as city councilman and city surveyor and has always given entire satisfaction. He is possessed of an elegant residence at 1524 Dewey avenue, besides much other property, as houses and lots, farms and mines. He is also a member of the I. O. O. F. in Baker City.

The marriage of Mr. Foster and Miss Alice Erland took place in Auburn in 1869 and they have become the parents of three children: Leo L., married and living at the Bonanza mine, where he is bookkeeper; Harry E., bookkeeper at the Elkhorn mine; Calleen E. Mrs. Foster is a member of the First Presbyterian church and active in the interests of her faith.

ALBERT HINDMAN.—This honored pioneer and esteemed citizen of Express was born in Council Bluff, Iowa, on May 14, 1855. When nine years old he accompanied the remainder of the family to Baker country, Oregon, where they again engaged in farming, their location being four miles west of Baker City. Our subject received only a very limited education, the largest portion of his time and energy being devoted to the development and improvement of the parental homestead, upon which he wrought until he became twenty-three years of age.

Mr. Hindman then took a homestead about fifteen miles east of Baker City, and engaged for himself in the business of farming and rearing cattle, apparently achieving excellent success therein, for he is now the owner of eight hundred and forty acres of land. A part of this has been laid out into town lots, streets, alleys, etc., and upon it the town of Express is springing up. Our subject is the owner of quite a herd of cattle and horses, including some very choice Shorthorn and Hereford males and a Percheron stallion.

Mr. Hindman is one of the leading farmers and stockmen in the county, thrifty, energetic and progressive, while as a man and citizen his standing is one of which he has every reason to be proud. His benevolence was manifested in his having donated the ground for a union church in Express, and in his liberally contributing to the same, but it has also found expression in many other ways. A public spirited man, he takes an active interest in all affairs of general concern in town, county, and state, though he has never displayed any special ambition for political preferment or personal aggrandisement.

Our subject married, at Baker City, Oregon, on December 10, 1882, Miss Addie, daughter of E. R. and Annie Powers, and the issue of their union is five children, Claude O., Elmer C., Fannie E., Edgar I. and Amy E.

—◆◆◆—

OLIVER C. STERN.—Mr. Stern was born in Shellsburgh, Benton county, Iowa, on June 3, 1850, being the son of David M. and Mary (Heitchew) Stern, natives of Pennsylvania. He was educated in his native state and also received the invigorating exercise of assisting to till his father's farm until he was sixteen years of age, when he embarked on life's arena for himself, his first venture being to learn telegraphy, following the same in the employ of the B. C. R. & N. Railroad Company until 1874. Finding that it was necessary to satisfy his desire for more active life, at that time he embarked in contracting, a knowledge

of which important industry he had gained before. For two years in Iowa and one in Nebraska he prosecuted this business and then in 1880 determined to verify the experiences of that most unique of all undertakings, crossing the plains by team. He journeyed to Baker City and immediately upon arriving began operations in his contract work and building, which he followed continuously until 1884 when he was appointed to the position of superintendent of the water works system of Baker City, and to the discharge of the duties there incumbent upon him he has given his time and attention continuously since. This long term of service in caring for this department of the city's government and interests in itself speaks convincingly of his ability and trustworthiness. He is a member of the Maccabees lodge in this city and very popular in this relation.

The marriage of Mr. Stern and Miss Sadie E., daughter of John H. and Harriet Mitchell, was solemnized in Baker City on December 7, 1884, and to them have been born two children: Virginia M. and Frank C.

—◆◆◆—

EDMUND P. PERKINS. A veritable pioneer of the pioneers, a citizen of rare ability and stanch principles, manifesting ever that unswerving stability and uncompromising integrity that characterize a noble type of our race, the man whose name initiates this paragraph is one of the most familiar figures in our county and one of the most respected and beloved, whose life is exemplary and worthy of emulation by those who value virtue and genuine worth and his achievements are commensurate with his sterling qualities and manifested wisdom, which have given him a most enviable and gratifying success in the financial world.

Born and reared in Kentucky, he inherited from the time of his advent into this world, which occurred on January 23, 1832, the valor and chivalry of the sons of the old Blue Grass state and has demonstrated them with acceptability ever since. In 1850, he came with the rest of the family to Grundy county, Missouri, being a pioneer of that section, where he remained until 1862 occupied in the art of agriculture, and in the mercantile business in

Trenton. On May 4, of the year last mentioned, he "pulled up stakes" and, with his earthly goods in a wagon train drawn by oxen, grappled with the weary task of crossing the plains, and on September of the same year he landed in Baker county. He soon entered land and devoted his entire energies to the development of his farm and to raising stock, which kindred occupations have employed him continuously since, which together with his indomitable continuity in the care of detail and partinacity in prosecuting his enterprises have won for him a success that is a proper crowning. He still owns the old homestead and one half section in addition, part being northwest near Wingville and the other tract six miles north of Baker City. He and his son own four hundred head of cattle and their herds are among the finest in the state of Oregon. He also owns the entire block where his handsome residence is in the city of Baker.

His marriage occurred in Grundy county, Missouri, in 1853, February 15, when Miss Mary A. Henry, a native of that state, became his wife. They have become the parents of five children; Madella, wife of W. O. Reynolds; Brent, living twenty miles below on Powder river; Gustavus, in the cattle business with his father; Platt, a farmer; Myrtle. Mrs. Perkin's people were among the early settlers of Missouri. Mr. Perkins crossed the plains back to Missouri in 1866, using ox teams for the journey and then returned over the same route with mule teams. He is a member of the I. O. O. F., and has been since 1855, having his affiliation now in Lodge No. 25, of Baker City. He is also a member of the Methodist church, South, and is a powerful supporter of his faith, both in example of life and skillful presentation of precept.

HARLIN Z. PERKINS.—It is with especial pleasure that we devote space in this work for an epitome of the life of the leading agriculturist and stockman whose name is at the head of this article and who has manifested during the long years in which he has dwelt in this county a most commendable thrift and enterprise and wisdom in his private life and in the prosecution of his business, having continued, through bad years and good

years, to quietly and steadily pursue the same vocation, and the excellent success that is his now to enjoy is not the result of "luck," as some would vainly remark, but the natural outcome and the legitimate result of the wise effort put forth.

Mr. Perkins first saw the light in Garrard county, in the old Blue Grass state, being the son of Joseph D. and Mary E. Perkins. When he was twelve years of age, he came with his parents to Grundy county, Missouri, and there he was occupied on a farm until 1864, at which time he was seized with the fire of adventure, and the broad and unexplored west presented the finest of opportunities, accordingly he embarked on the trip across the plains with ox teams and was occupied for six months in the journey. He first settled where he is now living, about nine miles northwest from Baker City, and here he has remained continuously since, with the gratifying result that he has now perhaps the richest farm in all Baker county and its generous proportions extend to the limits of eleven hundred acres. As a sample of his customary farming we append the following: Last year he harvested from twenty-two acres two thousand one hundred and fifty-eight bushels of oats which went forty-two pounds to the bushel and brought in the market one and one-fourth cents per pound. The farm is improved in the most skillful and tasty manner, being also supplied with an abundance of running water, while all the heavy work, as wood sawing and feed cutting, is done by steam power. One item to be noticed in the success of Mr. Perkins is the excellent order observed in everything about the premises, even down to the smallest detail, everything having a place and being invariably found in that place. To the wise agriculturist this matter speaks volumes, and while his execution is so noticeable in these details, his ability is no less to be observed in the breadth of wisdom manifested in plans and general purposes.

The marriage of Mr. Perkins and Miss Elizabeth, daughter of Dr. C. B. and Sallie Fleece, was solemnized at Trenton, Missouri, on June 9, 1862, and to them have been born the following children: D. C., who is married to Letta Masters and is living one-half mile south from his father's place; Flavins, married to Alda Hannah and living one-half mile west from his father's place; Joseph, married to Maggie Osmet and living at Cottage Grove, this state; Lora, wife of Ed Jarman living at Haines; Irl, at home. Mrs. Perkins' father was one of the prominent doctors of Trenton and an eminent professional gentleman. Mr. Perkins is a member of the I. O. O. F., Wingville Lodge, No. 69, and he also affiliates with the Methodist church, South, where he is an exemplary member and his life of faithful manifestation of the principles of the One Whom he follows has made him a light in the community, where he is respected and esteemed by all.

JOHN A. TUCKER.—One of the earliest pioners of this section, and one that has constantly since his arrival in this region devoted himself to the substantial development and material progress of the county, wherein he has been a prominent figure and has demonstrated that ability and keenness of perception that characterize a man of success in public affairs as well as in private enterprise, in both of which he has achieved a worthy share, and coupled with this has demonstrated his fitness for the confidence of his fellows, which has been so generously bestowed, by the manifestation of sterling qualities of worth and unswerving integrity, the subject of this sketch is eminently entitled to representation in this volume.

Mr. Tucker was born in Virginia, near Petersburg, on December 31, 1834, being the son of William and Nancy (Stone) Tucker, natives of Virginia, and passed his boyhood days near Mobile, Alabama, residing by the Tombigbee river. In his native city, our subject received his educational training and then engaged with the Mobile and Ohio R. R., for three years after which time he joined the regular army, Company K, First Mounted Riflemen, where he served until just previous to the breaking out of the war. He enlisted at Mobile, Alabama, going from there to New Orleans, then across the Gulf of Mexico, by way of Galveston, to Powderhorn, and thence to San Antonio, where he rejoined his regiment. After this he entered the employ of the government as wagon master in New Mexico and in 1862, he came to Union county

and settled near Wingville. Three years later he removed to Bedrock creek and there was occupied with sheep raising and farming until 1895, when he bought the farm where he now resides and is engaged in farming and stock raising.

The marriage of Mr. Tucker and Miss Adelia, daughter of John and Irene (Morrow) Daily, was solemnized on May 31, 1862, in Denver, Colorado, and they then came west. Mrs. Tucker's parents were natives of Kentucky and after their marriage removed to Missouri, where she was born, then they went to New Mexico in 1858, and thence came to Baker county. The parents removed from here to California, and since both have died there. Mr. Tucker was the first justice of the peace in Bedrock precinct and has been clerk of the Erwin district for a number of years. He is a member of the Masonic fraternity. Mr. Tucker participated in the Seminole Indian war and also in many other famous frontier struggles from the Atlantic to the Pacific. In addition to his other interests, he has a share in the copper mines of his vicinity and also in other mining enterprises.

To Mr. and Mrs. Tucker the following children have been born: William A., deceased; Nancy, wife of C. Herring on Goose creek; Irene, married; John T., married; James B., deceased; Louiza, married; Phillip, married; Mary, married; Harry, at home; Maud, married; Grover C., at home; Laura, at home.

JOHN J. CHUTE.—Among the leading business men and miners of Baker county is he whose name gives caption to this review, and it is with pleasure that we accord him representation in this portion of our volume as one of the public spirited citizen and influential men of the section. He was born in Fairmount, Surry county, Virginia, July 28, 1862, his parents being John J. and Mary E. (Morris) Chute. He was reared on a farm, and received his elementary educational discipline in the village school, but when he became about twenty years of age he went to the medical college at Ann Arbor, Michigan, from which he graduated in due course. For seven years after receiving his degree he practiced medicine in various places, but he thereupon engaged in mining. He sought earth's treasures in Georgetown, Colorado, for about two years, then continued the search in Utah and Idaho for a number of years, eventually, in 1896, coming to Baker county, Oregon.

For two years after his arrival in this section, our subject followed mining continuously and assiduously, but apparently becoming tired of the pursuit, he then launched out into the merchandise business in Express, opening a general store there and also a pharmacy. He has the honor of being the pioneer merchant of the place.

Fraternally our subject is affiliated with the M. W. A. and the K. of P., in both of which lodges he takes quite an active interest. He is one of those who are raising the money for and pushing the construction of the union church in Express, and in numerous other ways is he manifesting an enlightened public spirit and a desire to do his share for the good of town and county. While not a politician, he takes the interest every good citizen should in the public affairs of his locality and state.

Mr. Chute married Miss Mary E., daughter of William and Mary Anderson, of Detroit, Michigan, on the 25th of May, 1887, and to their union have been born three children, Marguerite May, Kenneth E. and Avis V.

P. J. BROWN.—It is with pleasure that we incorporate in this volume an epitome of the interesting career of the esteemed gentleman and eminently successful stock raiser whose name appears above and whose efforts for the promotion of the welfare of this section and for its material and substantial progress and advancement have become well known and are deserving of great credit.

He was born in Iowa, on April 1, 1854, and lived there until he was ten years of age, when he came across the plains with ox teams, his parents, A. J. and Martha J. (Harp) Brown at that time migrating to Oregon. His father still lives in Baker City, but his mother died in 1874. The first settlement was made in Eagle Valley, Union county, where our subject received the major portion of his educational discipline in the public schools, after completing which he went to work on a farm for wages until 1875, when he assisted to drive

some cattle to Nevada, remaining there for two years teaming. Subsequent to this he returned to Eagle Valley and purchased a farm and to the cultivation of this and teaming he devoted himself for two years, and on New Year's day, 1880, he was married to Miss Zona E., daughter of W. N. and Nancy A. (Sublette) Young. His wife is a native of Illinois, her family being pioneers to this region in 1876 and her father still lives in Baker City, but her mother died on July 30, 1900. To our subject have been born the following children; S. Ella; William J., deceased; Roscoe P.; Chester J., deceased; June C.; Sylvester W. After the marriage Mr. Brown continued on his farm until 1897, when he moved with his entire family into Baker City. He still owns the farm of one hundred acres and an elegant home in Baker City, besides eight hundred head of cattle. In addition to this he holds in partnership with Tom Phrophet two ranches, one on Powder river of five hundred and sixty acres and another of three hundred and twenty acres near Sparta.

In fraternal affiliations he is with the A. O. U. W., and with the K. of P. In political matters he has always been active and prominent and frequently has been called upon by the people to discharge the duties of public office. In 1892 he was chosen commissioner of Union county and was later offered the office again, also the office of representative to the state legislature, but he was constrained by the pressure of business affairs to refuse both. He was clerk of his home school board for ten years and was director, when he succeeded in securing the erection of the finest house for school purposes in Eagle Valley. Mr. Brown is a man who has the genuine qualities of worth that command the respect and win the confidence of his fellows, which he enjoys to the fullest extent.

O. L. MILLER.—Among the leading men who have in later years been attracted to the opulent region adjacent to Baker City and who have become prominent in the affairs of the city and county, especial mention must be made of the gentleman whose name initiates this paragraph, and to whom we are constrained by force of right to accord a place in this volume of the chronicles of Baker county.

Mr. Miller is a native of Iowa, being born on January 15, 1859, and in that state he received his educational discipline, taking a degree from one of its leading institutions. Soon after completing his education he took up the work of the instructor and in 1889 he established the Denver City Business College in Denver and one year later relinquished the management of this institution, soon taking the superintendency of the Healds Business College in San Francisco, and also serving as manager of the San Francisco Business College. In 1897 he was admitted to the practice of law at Olympia, Washington, and soon after that came to Baker City, where he formed a partnership with Judge Olmsted, in which capacity he has continued since. At the establishment of the Chamber of Commerce in Baker City he was chosen secretary and has filled that position continuously subsequently thereto. He is also interested in some mining properties. In political affairs he takes an active interest and has served for one term as city councilman, where he did much to commend his ability and integrity. He was very active in retrenchment as to expense of city government; proposed the plan of the city owning her own light plant; knocked out the fifty year franchise of the electric light company; let the contract of city water at a much reduced rate; and also did several other important matters during this term.

The marriage of Mr. Miller and Miss Ropena Graves, a native of Iowa, was consummated on May 22, 1886, and to them has been born one child, Mary B. Mr. Miller is one of the leading attorneys of eastern Oregon and although he has spent but a few years in the practice in this locality he enjoys a lucrative patronage and his clientage is constantly and rapidly increasing, as is also his popularity wherever he is known.

———◆◆◆———

ARNST LOENNIG.—Among the most esteemed and prominent pioneers of the county, and a gentleman that has been a leader in various capacities since his settlement here until the present time, we mention him whose name initiates this paragraph, and whose worthy achievements have been patent in all his activities, wherein he has ever been dominated by wisdom and skill, paramount to which are his energy and industry, the substantial proof of which is evidenced in the broad fields that he has acquired, and the property that has been brought forth as the result of his enterprise.

Across the storm-tossed ocean must we go to seek the birthplace of Mr. Loennig, the spot being in the province of Saxony, Germany, the date being June 21, 1833. For twenty years he remained in that place and then sought his fortune in the new world, landing in New York on July 18, 1853. From there he migrated to Pennsylvania and engaged for wages on a farm, continuing in that capacity for one and one-half years. Following this he went to Cincinnati and then by boat down the Ohio and up the Mississippi to St. Paul and then returned on the same boat to Keokuk, Iowa, and the following year he went to Illinois. In Adams and Hancock counties, he remained until 1863, and then on March 13, fitted out an ox team conveyance and started for the Pacific coast. Baker county's attractions led him to remain here and on May 3, 1864, he settled where he now lives on Willow creek about four miles northwest from Haines. He held by squatter's right three hundred and twenty acres and secured the title to the same in 1873. He now owns six hundred acres of land of good quality in one body.

Mr. Loennig was first married in Adams county, Illinois, on June 28, 1857, Mrs. Mary Zeigler, a native of Bavaria, becoming his wife at that time and to them were born five children; Henry, married to Celestine Relling, now living on Rock creek; Elizabeth, deceased; Mary, wife of William Shoemaker, who is operating a flour mill on Rock creek; Frank, married to Emma Lang and living on Muddy creek. Mrs. Loennig had by a former marriage, two children, Cecelia and Johanna, both being small at the time of her marriage with Mr. Loennig. Cecelia and Mr. Loennig's oldest child died about two years later with membranous croup. Johanna is now married to Jake Ensminger, and they live on Muddy creek. Mr. Loennig gave as dowry to his daughter Mary, two hundred and eighty acres of land and to his son Frank he gave three hundred and twenty acres. Mrs. Loennig, died on August 26, 1876, being beloved and esteemed by all.

ARNST LOENNIG.

On April 2, 1877, Mr. Loennig contracted a second marriage at Warsaw, Illinois, Barbara George, a native of Bavaria, Lower Frontier, becoming his wife at that time. By this marriage he has no children. Mr. Loennig has always been active in the affairs of the county and especially in educational matters, having furnished money to build the first schoolhouse on Rock Creek and buying the furniture entirely out of his own means, for which he has received but little remuneration, and he has served as director for twelve consecutive years in his home district, No. 7. He has ever been faithful in all of his public and private service and has won the confidence of all who have the pleasure to know him.

GEORGE W. JETT.—One of the leading business men of the county, prominent in public life and active in business operations, the subject of this sketch holds distinguished position among those who have wrought faithfully and well for the upbuilding and material progress and welfare of the county and its interests, while in all of his interesting career he has manifested a devotion to business and sound principles that place him as one of the most substantial citizens of the entire county.

The birth of Mr. Jett occurred in Grundy county, Missouri, in May 31, 1854, being the son of William E. and Elizabeth (Miller) Jett, natives respectively of Virginia and Kentucky. In his native state, our subject passed his boyhood days and there received his educational training in the Ellis academy at Chillicothe. In 1871 he turned toward the west, landing first at Kelton, Utah. From that point the stage fare to Baker City was seventy-five dollars, and he and his brother, John H., walked the entire distance, believing that they could make good wages thereby. For the first year after arriving here, he was engaged in mining at the old Virtue mine, then he entered the grocery business in 1881 and for one decade prosecuted it with very gratifying success. In 1891 he sold this business and moved to McEwen, then the terminus of the Sumpter Valley railroad, and opened a general merchandise establishment, also taking charge of the railroad office and in this capacity he continued for four years. Later he removed to

Sumpter on his homestead and a part of the time acted as agent for the railroad and also as deputy county assessor for a number of years, until he proved up on the homestead. In the spring of 1900 he was elected on the Democratic ticket to fill the office of county assessor, and assiduously and faithfully laboring in the fulfillment of the duties devolving on him in this capacity we find him at the present time. He has acted as school clerk for many years and was in that office when the first brick structure for school purposes was erected and he was forced to give at that time a bond for sixty thousand dollars. He has ever manifested a very commendable interest in school and political affairs and whatever was for the benefit of the county.

The marriage of Mr. Jett and Mrs. Rhoda E. Sheppard, daughter of W. F., and Miranda Levens, was solemnized in May, 1882, and to them have been born two children; Lula May, assistant county assessor; George L. Mrs. Jett was the widow of Harry C. Sheppard, by whom she had one child, Harry C. Sheppard. Mr. Jett is a member of Gauntlet Lodge, No. 8, K. of P., in Baker City. He has acted as grand chancellor of the state and attended the supreme lodge at Washington, D. C., in 1894 and Cleveland, Ohio, in 1896 as supreme representative. He has been instrumental in organizing many lodges and initiating many candidates. He also affiliates with the A. O. U. W. and is past master of that order. The career of Mr. Jett has been fraught with enterprise and achievement in the industrial and business world and in public capacity, and throughout he has manifested unswerving integrity and excellent ability.

STEPHEN OSBORN. — Among the prominent men of this county, mention must be made of the esteemed citizen and substantial agriculturist and stockman of whom we now have the pleasure to speak, and whose commendable career here has been fraught with wisdom and manifestation of keen foresight and thoroughness of execution in all his private business matters that have placed him as one of the leading property owners of our county, and he is everywhere known as one in whom confidence may well be placed and upon whom one may rely.

The birth of Mr. Osborn was on January 8, 1847, near Milan, Sullivan county, Missouri, his parents being Hiram and Drusilla Osborn. One year after his birth he was taken by his parents to Grundy county in the same state and there he remained until he was fifteen years of age, receiving meanwhile his educational training in the public schools of that county. When he had arrived to that interesting age of fifteen years he accompanied his father across the plains, making the entire journey with ox teams and the following year, 1863, he settled on the place where we find him at the present time, eight miles west from Baker City; the remainder of the family, the father and son, followed in 1864. His farm is well improved with substantial buildings, and thrift and taste are manifested throughout; while in addition to this place he owns about twelve hundred acres of hay and farming land, which also is well improved and tilled. He feeds every winter about five hundred head of cattle, being one of the leading stockmen of the county. He affiliates with the I. O. O. F., Wingville Lodge, No. 69, and is also a member of the Methodist Episcopal church, South, where he is well esteemed and a prominent figure, being an ardent supporter of his faith both by precept and practical exemplification of the principles of Christianity.

Mr. Osborn and Miss Lettie, daughter of John W. and Mary Coleman, were married in Wingville on March 2, 1871, and the fruit of this union is nine children, six of whom are at home, their names being as follows: Orin, Pearl, Beulah, Jessie, Rowena, Louis. The three eldest, George, Homer and John, died with the diphtheria.

ROYAL A. PIERCE, JR.—We are pleased to have the privilege of epitomizing the career of the industrious and enterprising stock raiser and farmer whose name initiates this paragraph, and who is a native of this section, having been born beneath the stars of the occident, where he has already wrought for himself a place in the affairs of men, quite commensurate with the ability that he has manifested.

Our subject is the son of Royal and Eliza-

beth (Turk) Pierce, natives respectively of Vermont and Sussex, England. The father came to this county in 1862 and four years later was admitted to the practice of law and in 1879 went to Idaho, where he resides now, being one of the leading practitioners of the entire county. The mother came to this country in 1850, and settled in Wisconsin, where on December 18, 1853, she married Mr. Royal Pierce. They came to this county, crossing the plains with horse teams. In 1885 she took a homestead where Royal, Jr. is now living. She also owns property in other places and a residence on East street, in Baker City, where she now lives. To her and her husband have been born the following children: Lila, buried in Wisconsin; Augustus, also buried there; James A., buried in Baker City; Abel J., lives at Pocatello, Idaho; Martha H., wife of S. D. Sturgle; Nellie H., wife of J. A. Wilson; W. D., single, at Cornucopia; Mary E., wife of T. B. Perkins; Royal A., Jr., single. Our subject has demonstrated his ability as an agriculturist and stock raiser and takes rank among the leaders in that industry in this section. His faithfulness and integrity and real moral worth have won for him the esteem and confidence of the entire community and his life of unsullied character and uprightness has fully deserved these encomiums.

JOHN H. JETT.—Prominent among the leading men of the county, and one who has constantly wrought for the advancement of the interests of this section must be mentioned the gentleman whose name initiates this paragraph and whose faithful service in public capacity and excellent achievement in private business stamp him as a man of a high sense of honor and dominated by a characteristic wisdom and integrity that are refreshing and exemplary.

Mr. Jett is the son of William E. and Elizabeth (Miller) Jett, natives of Virginia and Kentucky, respectively, and was born in Grundy county, Missouri, near Trenton, on October 4, 1851. His father died in a northern prison for soldiers in 1862, and his mother with her children moved to Chillicothe, Missouri, where the subject of this sketch received his education in the public schools and also learned his trade of stone cutting. In 1871, in company with his brother, G. W., mention of whom is made in another part of this work, he started to the west to work out his destiny. They went by rail to Salt Lake and as the stage fare from there to Baker City was very high and their exchequer was lean, they decided to cover the distance on foot, which they did in fifteen days. Having no blankets they were often obliged to walk before daylight to keep warm. This unique trip served to demonstrate the pluck and perseverance with which Mr. Jett is so richly endowed, as well as his capability for completing a hard task. Upon his arrival here he at once commenced to operate in a placer mine on the Burnt river near Baker City and followed this industry until 1882, when he embarked in the grocery business with his brother. For four years he followed this business and then sold out to engage in stone cutting, and he at once founded the Baker City Marble Works, where he has been operating without intermission since. He runs a feed store and grocery store in connection with the monumental work and has just completed a fine two story stone structure at the corner of First and Valley streets. He also owns a fine residence at the corner of Valley and Fifth streets. Mr. Jett has been active in political affairs and in 1894 he was called by the people, his name appearing on the People's party ticket, to act in the responsible and exacting position of treasurer of the county and so faithfully and efficiently did he perform the duties of that office that he was elected to succeed himself. In fraternal affiliations he is with the I. O. O. F., W. of W. and the I. O. R. M.

The marriage of Mr. Jett and Miss Dora S., daughter of James and Angeline (Shinn) Tracy, took place in this county on December 27, 1883, and they have become the parents of two children, Jesse W. and Bessie F. Mr. Jett and family are members of the First Baptist church and he is an ardent promulgator and supporter of his faith both by precept and practical exemplification of the teachings of the same as well as in other substantial ways.

- - -

LEWIS J. SISLEY.—It is with pleasure that we are enabled to present here a brief epitome of the career of the venerable pioneer whose name forms the caption hereof. In him are developed many of the characteristics which render famous the class to which he belongs, courage, resourcefulness, stamina, and he also possesses the virtues which win one friends and esteem in civilized communities, a public spirited interest in the general welfare, and sterling integrity of character. With this brief preliminary estimate, we shall pass to the specific history of his life.

Mr. Sisley was born near Meadville, Mercer county, Pennsylvania, on December 5, 1828, the son of Lewis and Catherine Sisley. He resided on a farm in his native state until about fifteen years old, attending school off and on as he had opportunity, then moved to Cedar county, Iowa, where he passed the remaining years of his minority. As soon as he became twenty-one, however, he set out across the plains with ox-teams to the west, spending five months on the journey, and several times experiencing troubles with the Indians. At one time the train lost all their stock, but fortunately the animals were afterward recovered.

Arriving at last, after an eventful and danger-fraught journey, he settled in Jackson county, Oregon, and engaged in farming and mining. He was there for twelve years, at the end of which extended period he came to Baker county, locating first on Burnt river, and in 1872 removed to Snake river. In 1885 he moved to a place one mile southeast of Express, where he has ever since lived. He now has a fine, well improved farm, supplied with good buildings and equipments, and he is spending the evening of his life in peace and abundance. Furthermore he enjoys the pleasant consciousness that he is secure in the esteem of all who knew him in early days and of those who have made his acquaintance since.

It is of interest to note that our subject set out, at Weatherby, in 1865, the first orchard ever planted in this county.

As might be supposed, one who came to the county as early as did Mr. Sisley could hardly escape having some trouble with Indians, and we find on inquiry that such happy fortune was not his, for twice he participated in severe battles with them.

On Christmas day, 1856, in Phœnix, Jackson county, Oregon, Mr. Sisley married Martha Ann Culver, and to them the following children were born; Frank, deceased; Donna, residing in Jackson county; Lotta, wife of Loomis Near; Eugene, a resident of Burnt River; Ettie, wife of W. C. Lane, of Boise valley, Idaho; and Mattie, wife of James Coleman, of Jackson county.

Mr. Sisley's first wife died in 1868, and in February, 1872, he married Lottie O'Blenis, by whom he has one son, Archie, at home. In 1864 Mr. Sisley built the road down Burnt river to Weatherby, thus opening the country for settlement.

SYLVESTER GRIER.—Among the very oldest of those now living in Baker county, who came here in earliest days, is the gentleman whose name appears above and to whom we are constrained by force of right to accord a representation in this volume of chronicles of our county, both because of his worthy achievements for the advancement of the welfare of the county and his successful endeavors in replenishing his own exchequer, as well as for the exemplary life of integrity and uprightness that has been shown by him during all these years wherein he has wrought.

Crawford county, Pennsylvania, is his native place and July 5, 1830, the date of his birth. Until about ten years of age he remained there and then accompanied his stepfather to Illinois, in which state he received his education in the public schools, and remained assisting his step-father on his farm until April, 1852, at which date he turned toward the "regions beyond" and sought for a home in the territory of Oregon. October 4, of the same year, was the date in which he landed in Linn county and from that time until 1861 he was engaged in work for wages. Then he went to Florence, Idaho, searching for proper diggings but soon returned to the Willamette valley, whence later he again came to this region and prospected in various parts until May, 1864, when he came to Auburn and bought into a livery business and the following spring he came to Baker City and built a feed corrall, where he now owns what is known as the Grier and Kellogg stables. In 1871 he sold a half interest to Mr. Kellogg. They remained together for fifteen years in successful operation of the ever increasing business and then Mr. Grier bought the partner out and operated the stables alone until 1896, at which

time he rented them, desiring to retire from active business to secure more leisure for the ripening years of his life. He also bought the interest of Mr. Kellogg in a ranch which they had purchased together in 1872, and he now owns five hundred and forty acres, which is also rented. He owns a herd of seventy-five cattle and a number of horses.

The marriage of Mr. Grier and Miss Matikta Clark was solemnized in Linn county, Oregon, on October 29, 1865. She crossed the plains from Iowa in 1851 with her parents, A. F. and Christie Ann Clark. To our subject have been born eight children; Dollie, deceased; Lillie, wife of J. W. Daly; Clara Edith; Bird, deceased; Minnie, deceased; Oscar, deceased; Pearl; Vesta. Mr. Grier is a member of the I. O. O. F. In the spring of 1866 he volunteered for service in the Cayuse war and while he did not get called into active battle he assisted to drive the Indians across the Columbia and did service at Pendleton, Walla Walla and on the Snake river.

MOSES CARPENTER.—The prominent mining man whose name gives caption to this review deserves rank among the benefactors of his county, state, and nation, if one who increases the material wealth of the world may be considered as belonging to that class. The miner's gold is clean. It is never wrung from the horny hands of toil, nor does it come to the purse of its possessor wet with widow's tears. It is of the kind which brings to the world an unalloyed blessing. The man, therefore, who adds to the wealth and comfort of his race by discovering it and digging it out of its hiding place should be given due credit for having produced an amelioration of conditions. It is therefore with pleasure that we are enabled to say some word of appreciation of the work which our subject and many others like him in Baker county have done for their section, their state, and for humanity.

Inquiry into the life history of Mr. Carpenter brings to light the fact that he is a native of the famed old Bluegrass state, born near Mannsville, on September 28, 1845. His parents, Joseph and Annie (Hogan) Carpenter, died when he was a mere boy, and he became the ward of his uncle, Asa Mann, who

MOSES CARPENTER.

in 1855, took him to the vicinity of St. Joe, Missouri. When he became seventeen years old, he enlisted in the Confederate army and was assigned to General Joseph Shelby's cavalry brigade. He participated in several severe engagements during his service in the army, among them those at Kane Hill, Prairie Grove, the second battle of Springfield, Missouri, the battle at Helena, Arkansas, and the battle of Jenkin's Ferry. At Cedar Glade he was very seriously wounded in the head by a rifle ball and left on the field for dead. If his comrades had had time they would have buried him, but notwithstanding the severity of his wound he eventually regained his health and rejoined his regiment.

At the close of hostilities, Mr. Carpenter went to Mexico in company with his former commander, General Shelby, and in 1865 he came to the Pacific coast of that country, where he remained two years. He then removed to Baker county and engaged in mining in partnership with Judge Ison; who had been an old friend of his in Mexico, and whose school in eastern Oregon he attended for a while in the endeavor to retrieve the loss of educational advantages occasioned by the war.

At a later date our subject bought out Judge Ison. He has been engaged in mining continuously since, and naturally has had interests at different times in some very excellent properties. Besides his quartz prospects he has some very excellent placer ground in the county. He and his partner, J. T. Jones, own together forty acres of rich placer ground on the Upper Salmon creek, but they are giving the greater part of their attention now to the Carpenter-Jones of Never Sweat mine and the Nelson placer eight miles west of Baker City.

Mr. Carpenter is a public spirited citizen and has ever manifested a lively and intelligent interest in the affairs of his county and state, though he seems to be devoid of ambition for personal aggrandizement or political preferment. Fraternally he is affiliated with the well known brotherhood, the I. O. O. F., Wingville Lodge, No. 69.

On October 10, 1877, in Clackamas county, Oregon, our subject married Miss Glendora Thompson, daughter of Joseph R. and Minerva A. Thompson, pioneers of 1875. Their marriage has been blessed by the advent of five children, namely, Joseph E., Moses, Jr., Thomas W., Lamar, and Oates.

SOCRATES C. MANN.—It now becomes the pleasant task for us to outline in brief the salient points of the career of the estimable gentleman whose name initiates this paragraph and who takes rank as one of the prominent men of the county and is one of its most substantial citizens, having spent here many years of his life, and here he has accumulated the generous amount of property with which he is at present possessed, it being the material witness of his skill, energy, and wisdom which have been so patiently displayed.

The birth of Mr. Mann was on December 13, 1856, in Plainfield, Vermont, being the son of Abel and Lucia Mann, and in his native place he remained until he was nineteen years of age, receiving a good education in the Barre Academy, which was in the town of the same name. Upon the completion of the course in that institution he sought his fortune in the west and ultimately landed in Baker county in 1877, where he soon commenced operations as a farmer and stockman, which he has followed since with such enterprise and skill that he has accumulated eight hundred and forty acres of land, three hundred of which is timber land, besides other valuable property interests, as well as considerable personal property and stock. He affiliates with the Fraternal Union.

Mr. Mann was married to Miss Ellen E., daughter of William B. and Adaline Powers, and a native of Baker county, Oregon, on December 25, 1884, the ceremony taking place at North Powder. The fruit of this union is three children: Dora E., Leo L., Charles S. Mr. Mann has so demeaned himself in all his affairs and walk that he has won the entire confidence of his fellows and is esteemed by all who may have the pleasure of his acquaintance.

JUDGE WALLACE W. TRAVILLION.—It is necessary in a compilation of this character to make mention of the leading and prominent gentleman whose name initiates this article and whose well known ability and enterprise have wrought so faithfully for the material welfare and substantial progress of this region, while his unsullied reputation and characteristic manifestation of stanch principles of truth and uprightness have placed him in a position of great prestige in our county.

The subject of this sketch was born in Cooper county, Missouri, on January 24, 1849, being the son of Thomas and Anna E. (William) Travillion, natives of Virginia and Missouri, respectively. His mother was a granddaughter of Richard Brannin, who in 1822 was sent by President Monroe as Indian agent of the Osage Indians located where Kansas City is now situated. In his native state, our subject was educated and there passed the years of his minority. In the year 1870 he located in Baker City and gave his attention to the prosecution of mining for six years. At the expiration of these years, he was appointed deputy sheriff and in 1880 was elected as county sheriff, the responsible duties of which office he discharged with manifest ability and care to the satisfaction of his constituency for two terms. In 1894 he was again called by the people to public office, this time to the prominent position of judge of Baker county and continuously since that time he has filled this office, displaying his characteristic faithfulness and acumen coupled with probity and impartiality. The Judge owns a fine estate near the city.

The marriage of Mr. Travillion and Miss C. C. Sonna, a native of Denmark, was solemnized in Baker City in 1883 and they have become the parents of two sons, Clair E. and William W., Jr. The Judge is a member of the I. O. O. F. Lodge, No. 25, of Baker City, and is also affiliated with the Encampment, No. 7, in which order he has passed all of the chairs.

HON. JOHN W. WISDOM.—This distinguished and influential gentleman has the distinction of being the oldest business man in Baker City, having arrived in September, 1862, when the handiwork of man was not to be seen, and is one of the earliest pioneers of the county, having spent the major portion of his life within its precincts, where he has ever shown that rare business ability and stanch integrity that combine in the typical citizen, mak-

ing him one of the most esteemed and respected men of our county, while his worthy achievements are bright examples for the rising men in the hurrying business ranks of today.

Mr. Wisdom was born in Randolph county, Missouri, on March 15, 1840, being the son of Thomas Barnes and Lucinda (Guess) Wisdom, who came to Baker City in 1863; the mother died here two years after her arrival and his father passed away in 1893, at the age of seventy-five. Our subject was educated in the log schoolhouse in his native county and in 1856 removed to Grundy county, in the same state, where he was occupied in tilling the soil until 1861, when he removed to Boone county and in the following spring started across the plains to this country, being with a train of sixty wagons. The first winter he hauled the supplies from The Dalles. He was occupied in a blacksmith shop and on a canal for a time near Baker and then went to Idaho in the mines, following which he commenced to farm on a squatter's claim in this county; and on the night of June 21, 1864, his entire crop was destroyed by freezing. He divided his attention between farming and freighting until 1866, when he sold his teams and engaged in the drug business, where we find him to-day, continuing in the same stand, having never made a move during all these years. His is the pioneer business of the city and his faithfulness and care in his business has given him a gratifying success. He owns a stock farm of three hundred and sixty-seven acres and is interested in breeding blooded horses. He raised and owned Challenger Chief, a horse with a good record, and many other good ones. In political matters he has shown marked interest and has been the recipient of honors from the people, among which positions he has been called to fill by popular vote may be mentioned that of state senator in 1874, serving that year and all of the two following years, treasurer of Baker City five years; president of the board of school directors when the high school was built; and also he was delegate to the national Democratic convention that nominated Hancock and English.

The marriage of Mr. Wisdom and Miss Mary E. Sturgill, a native of Sullivan county, Missouri, occurred near Wingville, on June 14, 1868, and they have become the parents of the following children: Ada, deceased; Frank, deceased; Frances W., wife of E. H. Blake, of Kansas City, Missouri; Marguerite, deceased; Vesper, deceased; Loys Winter; Mable Gertrude; Glenn Albert; John W., Jr. Those who have passed away are all lying buried in the cemetery at Baker City.

Mr. Wisdom is a member of the I. O. O. F. and also of the Masons, being the oldest material member in Baker City Lodge, No. 25. He has so demeaned himself that his reputation is untarnished and geniality has won him hosts of friends throughout the entire county.

· LOUIS H. HULICK.—To the esteemed pioneer and representative citizen whose name initiates this paragraph, whose faithful labors for so many years were manifested in this region and whose upright life and unsullied character shone here in every walk of life that he was called to grace, we are pleased to accord this memorial, since in a work of this character there would be serious incompleteness if there were omission to chronicle the salient points of his career.

Louis H. Hulick was born in Indiana in 1845, where he grew to manhood and received his early educational training. In the state of Iowa he was joined in the bands of matrimony to Miss Margaret A. Gable, a native of Washington county that state. In 1864 they crossed the plains with ox teams, completing the perilous and arduous journey in good time. After the close of this unique pilgrimage they came to a halt in the Grande Ronde valley and there took up the related occupations of stock raising and farming, prosecuting the same with vigor that brought success. They removed to Big Creek in Baker county, where Mr. Hulick died, and then later went to the lower Powder river valley and settled on a quarter section, obtaining title thereto by purchase, and for twenty years this place has been the family home. In December, 1870, Mr. Hulick, after a faithful life of industry and enterprise, was called to depart from the scenes of this earth and enter upon the realities of another world. He left to mourn his sad demise a widow and the following children: George W.; John D.; Harriet J.; Tunis died

in 1898 at the age of thirty-one years; Franklin S.; Della A.; L. Edgar, and Willard. Mrs. Hulick has assumed the cares and responsibilities of directing the estate and is in a commendable manner discharging all the duties incumbent upon her in this trying position, while she is rounding out a well spent and bright life of faithful service and manifestation of noble and upright principles.

FRANK H. GRABNER.—The enterprising and successful farmer and stock raiser whose career it is now our task to outline was born in Waterloo, Iowa, on April 10, 1858, the son of George P. and Ermina Grabner. When a child he was taken by his parents to Austin, Nevada, whence in 1862 the family moved to Virginia City. Here our subject spent the ensuing eighteen years of his life, attending school during its sessions until he became sixteen years old, when he entered upon an apprenticeship to the trade of an iron molder. For a while after completing his apprenticeship he worked as a miner, but eventually he came via San Francisco and Portland to Baker county, Oregon, where he has since made his home.

In due time he acquired two hundred and forty acres of excellent land one and a half miles southeast of Express, and to the cultivation and improvement of this he has given himself with diligence and assiduity with the result that it has long since been brought to a high state of cultivation and made to yield the rich harvests of which it is capable. Mr. Grabner raises about three hundred tons of hay each year, which he feeds to his own stock. He is justly considered one of the most energetic and prosperous agriculturists in his section, and as a man and citizen his standing is an enviable one.

The marriage of our subject was duly solemnized on April 22, 1883, when Miss Georgia A., daughter of Joseph and Justina Prescott, and a native of Iowa, became his wife. The issue of their union is three children, Martin A., deceased; Abbie Gertrude, and Jennie Edna, both attending the public school. Mr. Grabner is a charter member of the K. of P., Triumph Lodge, No. 80, being also vice chancellor of the order.

PROF. JOHN A. PAYTON.—If it may be said that the members of any profession have more than those of another to do in the elevating of the people, the development of the latent powers of the masses, the bringing to a higher standard and better tone the community, and the advancement of the commonwealth to a more exalted plane of intelligence and to the aspirations for nobler ideals and more perfect exemplifications of the principles of pure political economy, that distinction belongs to the devotees of the educator's calling. As a leader in that profession in eastern Oregon for many years, stands the gentleman whose name initiates this paragraph, and whose worthy achievements in this and adjacent counties are so well known that we are treading familiar ground in attempting to epitomize his career; however, a volume of the character of the history of Baker county would be sadly incomplete were there failure to incorporate therein the salient points of this eventful and highly useful life.

The birth of our subject occurred in Missouri on January 27, 1850, being the son of William F. and Mary Payton, who crossed the dreary plains with their young son to where Baker City now stands, in the early days of 1863. They located on Powder river about seven miles from the site of Baker City and there in assisting to till his father's farm and acquiring the primary educational training possible to be had in the public schools of that day, our subject passed the years of his minority until he matriculated in the Agricultural College at Corvallis, in which institution he received his education. Immediately succeeding this he engaged in teaching and followed it for many years in this and adjacent sections, having the distinction of holding one position for nine consecutive years. In 1880 the people recognizing his ability and faithfulness, rewarded the same by electing him to the position of superintendent of the schools of the county. With such faithfulness and efficiency did he discharge the duties there incumbent upon him that he was re-elected and at the close of his second term he was called for a third time to assume the duties of that office. Then he retired to private life again, and in 1896 was called by the franchises of his fellows to the position of county assessor, and after the expiration of his first term of serv-

ice he was elected as his own successor. In the spring of 1901 he was appointed to fill the unexpired portion of the term of county superintendent, made vacant by the death of W. R. Privett, and in this capacity we find him at the present time. Prof. Payton has also accumulated a fine portion of the wealth of this world, having an estate of one thousand acres in the valley, well improved and stocked. He is also a prominent member of the I. O. O. F., has served as delegate to the grand lodge and as district deputy, and is a member of the Encampment and of the W. of W.

The marriage of Mr. Payton and Miss Rosa Pitney, a native of the plains, having been born at Soda Springs while her parents were en route to this country, was solemnized in Lane county, in February, 1873, and to them have been born the following children: William; Raleigh; Otis and Osie, twins; Alma; Elizabeth, deceased. Prof. Payton is one of the most highly respected and esteemed men of the county, having ever demeaned himself in such a commendable manner and with the manifestation of such integrity and stanch principles of moral worth that he has won the confidence of all who have the pleasure of his acquaintance.

HARDIN W. ESTES.—A veritable pioneer of the pioneers, the gentleman of whom we now speak has spent most of his eventful career upon the frontier of this great country, in preparing the way for the industries and people to follow, while in this county particularly he has wrought with an energy and wisdom that have brought to him the proper emoluments as well as to the county material progress, constantly displaying a broad public spirit and exemplifying the virtues and principles of a faithful Christian life.

Mr. Estes was born on a farm in Clay county, Missouri, on November 2, 1828, being the son of Joel and Martha (Stollins) Estes. He had but scanty opportunity to gain an education from the subscription schools of his locality, the buildings being of logs and the floors of puncheons and the teachers not of the best. At eighteen years of age he entered the commissary department of the United States army at Fort Leavenworth and served for one year there, then went with Colonel

HARDIN W. ESTES.

Childs and five hundred volunteers to establish posts from the Missouri river to The Dalles, and was given charge of the artillery, and in the fall of 1848 he assisted in his capacity of officer in the commissary to equip Joe Meek and Joe Lane, the former a noted man of this region and the latter the first governor of Oregon territory, for their journey across the plains. In 1849 he came to California with ox teams via the Truckee route, consuming about four and one-half months on the trip, and sometimes they suffered much from lack of water, losing about one-third of their stock, and again they crossed the Truckee river twenty-eight times in twenty miles. He mined for one year at Nevada City, California, then left in 1850 for San Francisco, whence he returned by water to his eastern home. In his mining he was abundantly successful, taking out as much as nine hundred and ninety-two dollars of dust in one day. In the spring of 1853 he crossed the plains again by ox teams and settled in Linn county and took up a donation claim of three hundred acres, giving his attention to its cultivation until 1857, then sold out and returned to Missouri again by the water route. The following year he entered the employ of the government as wagon master and came to Oregon again, this time with General Johnson, and by way of Salt Lake, where he helped to establish camp Floy City. He settled for a year in Linn county, then went to California and to Nevada and teamed for a time around Virginia City, then constructed the stage stations from Carson City to Salt Lake, using for material "doby" and rock, the owner of the stage being the well known Ben Halloday. In the spring of 1862, he started for the Salmon river mines but stopped in this county and located a ranch on Washington Gulch, the first one taken in the county, and he owns the place still and produces one hundred tons of fruit on it annually. In the early days he raised garden truck and sold it to the miners at good prices, thus making a handsome income. He took an active and prominent part in the organization of the county and has since continued one of the most effectual workers for its advancement and development. He filled at that time the important office of county commissioner for four years and helped by his wisdom and ability to

get things in running shape. He now owns a fine hay ranch of six hundred and forty acres, four miles north from Baker City and also two hundred acres of land suitable for other crops near by, and a one-third interest in five hundred lots in McCrary addition to Baker City, also a fine home and four lots where he lives at 2446 Church street.

The marriage of Mr. Estes and Miss Mahali Ring was solemnized in April, 1851, while he was in Missouri, and they have three children: Dr. Logan, deceased; Kate, wife of W. W. Boughton, of Skagway, Alaska; Lutitia, deceased.

The second marriage of Mr. Estes occurred in Baker City, on November 14, 1867, Mrs. Pearlina (Hackleman) Smith becoming his wife at that time and they have become the parents of four children: Rosa L., wife of Harry Bowen of Baker City; Amy, wife of Victor C. Lewis of Manilla; Mabel, wife of Robert Donald of Baker City; Meda. Mr. Estes and wife are members of the First Baptist church and very active in the exemplification of the teachings of their faith and in its promulgation.

BYRON T. POTTER.—In executing a compilation of this character, serious criticism would be brought upon us did we fail to mention the leading business man and prominent citizen whose name initiates this article and who has demonstrated in the arena of life's struggles his fitness for the distinction that he enjoys, proving himself a worthy descendant of the noted line of ancestry that precedes him, being a direct lineal descendant of the famous potter family that broke away from the thralldom of the established church in England in 1600 and assisted to found the world famous Quaker colonies in the United States, his mother also coming from one of the oldest families in the United States.

The birth of our subject occurred in Buffalo, New York, on July 26, 1854, his parents being Abram and Mary A. (Tucker) Potter, natives of the Empire state. In his native city he was educated, and when twenty years of age, he went to Chicago and embarked upon his business career, his initial effort being in the commission industry. After two years in this business he repaired to Fort Dodge, Iowa, and took up insurance and handling sewing machines until 1881, when he came west as a member of the engineers' corps for the Oregon Short Line, continuing in that capacity until 1884. The following year he came to Union county and took up general merchandising in the Cornucopia mining district, where he was favored with very gratifying prosperity. In 1890 he came to Baker City, following the same business for seven years, when he was asked to accept the position of postmaster for Baker City, and in this capacity he has been serving since, with the display of ability and faithfulness that have won for him commendations from all of the patrons of the office. He is considered a most conscientious and efficient officer. He has acted as chairman of the Republican county central committee and is very prominent in his party, where his counsels are prized. He was deputy sheriff in Union county from 1887 to 1889, and he always manifests a commendable interest in the affairs of the county, city and nation.

The marriage of Mr. Potter and Miss Eda L., daughter of James B. and Mary (Huion) Sisson, took place in Iowa on January 1, 1886. Mr. Potter is a member of the Masonic lodge, the A. O. U. W., and the K. of P. He is a stockholder in the Baker City National Bank and has a fine residence on Sixth and Church streets, besides considerable other property.

WILLIAM N. THOMPSON.—It is fitting that in a work of the character of the history of Baker county that mention should be made of the gentleman whose name is at the head of this article, and whose career of uprightness and enterprising effort and commendable walk and achievements are well known to all and to him have been entrusted some of the most trying and responsible duties of a public nature that the county has to bestow.

William N. was born in Leasburgh, Caswell county, North Carolina, on April 17, 1858, to Joseph R. and Minerva Thompson, who removed with their son to Dallas county, Arkansas, while he was still an infant. In that place he remained until he was sixteen years of age, gaining meanwhile a good common school education. At the age mentioned he was led to make the adventurous journey across the plains, using mule teams, and settled in Oregon City, remaining there for six years and then he came to this county. His first occupation here was mining for Carpenter and Jones on their placer properties for eight years, after which time he engaged in farming, meeting with good success, and five years ago he was called to take charge of the county poor farm. In this capacity he has been constantly occupied since and it is with great credit to himself, for in every respect he has given entire satisfaction, having demeaned himself in a very exemplary manner in all of this arduous service.

The marriage of Mr. Thompson and Miss Eva, daughter of James and Mary Hutton, and a native of Iowa, was solemnized on November 14, 1883, in this county. The fruit of this union is as follows: Clifford; Sydney, who died at the age of eight years; Roy; William. Mr. Thompson affiliates with the I. O. O. F., Wingville Lodge, No. 69, and also with the Encampment, No. 7, at Baker City, and with the W. of W. Lodge No. 343. He is a member of the Methodist church, south, and displays activity in the interests of his faith that manifests a genuine spirit of true Christianity, while his life has been such that he is highly esteemed by all who know him.

ANDREW J. BROWN.—In the person of the estimable gentleman whose name heads this article we have before us one of the intrepid and sturdy pioneers, not only of this section, but also of all of the Pacific states, where in various capacities he has wrought with the energy and enterprise born of true manhood and a noble spirit of advancement and interest in the welfare of others, as well as his own. His efforts in this and adjacent counties have been fraught with a wisdom and assiduity and breadth of public spirit that characterize him in all of his relations and have made him highly respected and beloved by all who have the pleasure of his acquaintance.

Andrew J. was born in Sumner county, Tennessee, on January 29, 1824, and at seven years of age he went to Illinois with the family and later to Iowa, in which two states he was educated in the public schools. He continued on his father's farm until he had reached his majority, and in 1850 gathered all together and commenced the weary journey to California with ox teams; and on September 1 of that year he reached Placerville and engaged in mining. Three years later he returned to the states via the Isthmus and farmed there until 1864, at which date he migrated to Montana and spent two years in getting timber for the mines. In 1867 he came to the Grande Ronde valley and homesteaded a quarter section in the lower Powder country. He continued in the stock business here and in this section until recently he sold his herds on account of the desire to retire from active enterprise and spend the golden years of a well spent life in more seclusion, enjoying the fruits of his labor. He owns three lots and a comfortable home in Baker City, besides other property.

Mr. Brown was married in Iowa on November 23, 1847, to Miss Martha A. Harp, a native of Illinois. To them have been born thirteen children: George W.; Mary Ellen; Pleasant J.; Hannah Rebecca; Rosella Alice; Ada Ann; Elosia, deceased; Andrew Jackson, deceased; Martha J.; Cornelia; Almina; Cora May, and one infant not named. On February 20, 1874, Mrs. Brown was called to lay down the burdens of this life and take her place in the scenes beyond. Mr. Brown is well advanced in years, but is enjoying good health and is the recipient of the good wishes and esteem of his wide circle of acquaintances, and his years are being passed in quiet enjoyment of the portion his toil justly accumulated.

WILLIAM R. STURGILL.—Among those who came to this county in the early years of its existence and who have wrought faithfully during all of the years that have followed for its material welfare and substantial progress, ever standing for the principles and ways that work for the good of all, especial mention must be made of the gentleman whose career it is now our pleasant task to outline and whose life is well known to all in this region, where his energy, industry and wisdom have also carved for himself a place in the world of property and wealth.

The birth of Mr. Sturgill occurred in Sullivan county, Missouri, near the city of Milan, on May 31, 1843, and there he remained until he had passed the first score years of his life

and gained a good education in the common schools. His first venture was a trip to Virginia City, Montana, where he spent eight months in the mines as laborer and then went to Denver and from there he later went back to his early home. In that place he was engaged in farming until 1868, when he made the trip across the plains to Baker county, using mules as teams. Here he first settled at Wingville, where he remained until 1899, and then removed to his present place, thirteen miles northwest from Baker City, where he owns a magnificent estate of six hundred and forty acres, all under the highest cultivation and excellently improved. Here he is engaged in farming, stock raising and the culture of fruit, having an orchard of four hundred trees.

The marriage of Mr. Sturgill and Miss Virginia A., daughter of William and Rachel Talley, was solemnized on March 4, 1866, at Milan, Missouri. They have become the parents of the following children: Elsie, deceased; Blanche; Fred H.; Susie; Benton; Cecil R. Mr. Sturgill is affiliated fraternally with the W. of W., Lodge No. 100, in Baker City. He is also a member of the Baptist church and is an exemplary Christian, a loyal citizen and a highly esteemed neighbor.

CHARLES F. HYDE.—The legal profession of Baker county is not wanting in men of large caliber and rare capabilities in comparison with the bar in other portions of the state, and prominent among the fraternity in this city, as well as among the legal lights of the state, stands the gentleman whose name initiates this paragraph and whose life has been spent in this section since his admission to the bar, in continuous practice of the law, in which he has manifested an ability second to none of the region and a keenness of perception and fearlessness of execution so essential to the successful practice of his profession; and in connection with this there has been displayed unswerving integrity and a depth of research and information and acumen that are highly commendable.

He is a native of the occident, being born in California on October 29, 1857. His father, Henry H., a native of New York, came to Oregon in 1843, and thence to California in

1849, the family removing to Grant county in 1869, locating at Canyon City. There the father opened a general merchandise establishment, being the first in Grant county, and he continued in the prosecution of this business until his death in 1877. Two years later the mother died and our subject removed to Forest Grove, this state, where he received a collegiate course, following which he spent five years in reading law with Whalley & Fechheimer, of Portland, his admission to the bar occurring in 1881. The following year he came to Baker City and has continued here ever since in the practice of his profession, and to-day he has a very lucrative and large practice. For five years he has been city attorney of Baker City, and for four years he was district attorney of the sixth judicial district, which includes seven counties. In all these public relations he has served with faithfulness and efficiency. He is a leader in politics and very active in the interests of good government. He is the owner of much valuable city property, besides other holdings.

His marriage occurred in Baker City on September 22, 1886, Miss Mary E. Packwood becoming his wife at that time. To them have been born six children: Edith Whalley, William H., Eleanor M., Loring C., Gilberta P., Marion. Mrs. Hyde is a native of Auburn, this county, being the first white child born there. Mr. Hyde is fraternally affiliated with the F. & A. M., the B. P. O. E., the W. of W., and the I. O. R. M., in all of which orders he is a very popular member.

DAVID S. LITTLEFIELD.—Of all the men who have helped to lay the foundation of Baker county's institutions none has a better right to receive credit at the hands of the historian than he whose name gives caption to this review. Mr. Littlefield is certainly the pioneer and pathfinder of the region or one of them, for though the soil of the country may have been pressed before his advent by the feet of advancing armies of colonization and enlightenment, to him belongs the honor of having discovered the metal which drew permanent settlers hither and made the region a place of happy homes and one lighted by the

lamps of civilization. Rightly may our subject be denominated the father of Baker county, for he it was, with his few associates, who not only first settled in the section, but who took the initial steps toward the organization of a local government. With truth it may be said that the history of Mr. Littlefield and his coadjutors is the history of Baker county during the first few years of its existence.

Mr. Littlefield is a son of Rufus and Sarah (Batchelor) Littlefield, his mother being of the good old Puritan stock. Born in Prospect, Waldo county, Maine, he spent the initial twelve years of his life there, receiving a somewhat meager common school education. The dauntless spirit of the lad then manifested itself, and he went to sea, and from that time until 1850, his home was on the deep. He then came by water to California, where he was engaged in placer mining until 1859, going then to the Fraser river country, in which he sought for treasure during one season. He washed out about one thousand dollars worth of gold dust, and with this returned to California. In 1861, he came to Portland, Oregon, intending to go to Oro Fino, but he was there dissuaded by other California miners who had been disappointed in that section. He informs us that Portland at that time consisted of one wooden hotel building and a few shacks, and that the people had a goodly supply of fruit but little else. Mr. Littlefield was one of those who made an expedition in search of the mythical "Blue Bucket" diggings, and after his return from this disappointing trip, he set out with Henry Griffin to the eastern Oregon country, and they discovered gold in the canyon since known as Griffin's gulch. At that time there was not a white man, except the members of the party, this side of the Blue mountains. During the winter of 1861, the little mining party ran short of provisions, so a trip to Walla Walla became necessary. They, of course, told of their good luck and the stories were greatly exaggerated and widely circulated, resulting in a great excitement and a rush the following spring. The merchants with whom they dealt deliberately exaggerated their reports, their object being to create a rush and augment their trade. When in April the advance guard reached Mr. Littlefield's mining camp the people therein thought for a

DAVID S. LITTLEFIELD.

time that the Indians were coming, but of course soon discovered their mistake.

Some of those who were in the first rush discovered gold on the site of the present Auburn, and thither our subject went, obtaining a claim. Gold was also discovered in numerous other places and excitement ran high. It should be remembered that at this time all of eastern Oregon constituted Wasco county, of which The Dalles was the county seat. The necessity for a smaller division and a seat of government nearer home soon began to be felt, so the miners organized and took the initial steps toward securing the erection of Baker county. In response to their petition, the governor appointed two executive officers, a county judge and a county sheriff to maintain order. The men named were respectively Wilson and Gray. It should be recorded that after the initial election held within the limits of the present Baker county, a man named Griffin was killed by his partner, one Herrington, in a most dastardly manner. The murderer was captured and taken to Auburn, where it was decided by vote to send him to The Dalles for trial and punishment. Two men were given fifty dollars to take him there. Letters to the sheriff at The Dalles failed to elicit any information concerning the prisoner and it was at length discovered that he and his two custodians were mining on Salmon river and enjoying excellent fortune. The miners determined they would try the next man charged with crime themselves.

Space forbids the tracing of Mr. Littlefield's very useful career further in detail. He still retains some of his mining properties, but latterly has given much attention to farming and the rearing of cattle and horses on his farm near Auburn. He has been quite as successful in the raising of horses as he was formerly in mining, and his stock have found their ways into all the principal marts of the United States.

In Auburn, on December 13, 1872, our subject married Mrs. Mary A., widow of Dr. Grant, a pioneer of 1862, and proprietor of the first drug store in the county, as also of the first pharmacy in Baker City. To them were born two children, Charles Grant, a resident of Baker City, and Isophine, wife of Prof. Alexander of this county. By a later marriage Mr.

Littlefield has three children: Rufus W., engaged in the stock business at Auburn; Eva, wife of Oliver Holloway, of Baker City; and Grace, wife of Wallace Holloway, engaged in the coal and ice business in Baker City.

HERBERT B. CRANSTON.—This leading stockman and agriculturist is a son of the occident and beneath its stars he has wrought out already a measure of success that is commendable and gratifying to all connected with this eminent sculptor of his own destiny. His parents, Edward P. and Anna (Connaughty) Cranston, were married in 1860 in Idaho City, being the first couple that entered the matrimonial state in that place. They were natives, respectively, of Ohio and New York. This elder Mr. Cranston struck out into the world for himself when he was twenty-three years of age and from that time to the present he has prosecuted a life of vigorous activity and enterprise. His first venture was in the mercantile world at Walla Walla, Washington, where he continued for one year; he then removed to Auburn in this county and operated there and also maintained a branch store in Idaho City, and one at Clarksville, until 1879. At that date he sold his entire mercantile interests and went to Salem and opened the same business which was later sold and he returned to Baker City, where he purchased the stock of goods of a Mr. A. H. Brown, and in connection with this establishment he operated a branch store at Sparta, this state. He finally sold the entire business and bought a ranch of three hundred and thirty acres, where he is at the present time engaged in raising stock and tilling the soil. He handles thoroughbred cattle and sheep, having traded cattle for sheep in 1887. The following children have been born to this worthy couple: Herbert B.; Walter B. died January 5, 1895; Edward T., married to Lena Sturgill; Earl F., married Maggie White; Anna E., wife of W. Moeller; Maude, at home.

Returning to the subject of our sketch, Herbert B. Cranston, we note that he was born on December 21, 1864, and in the various places that have been mentioned where his father did business he received his educational training and learned the ways of business by practical contact with the commercial world and the problems of the day. On March 5, 1889, he was married to Miss Laura Saunders, and to them were born the following children: Herbert C., Florence L., George A. On September 13, 1899, Mrs. Cranston was called from the duties of this life to enter the scenes beyond and left a mourning husband and her three children motherless.

At the present time Mr. Cranston is living about twenty miles from Baker City in the lower Powder river valley and operating his mammoth estate of six hundred and twenty acres, producing the fruits of the soil and raising stock. He is also discharging the duties of postmaster at the office called Keating, which is done with dispatch and faithfulness and acceptability to all the patrons. His demeanor is fraught with the display of uprightness and candor and genuine principles of truth and probity, which have gained for him the esteem and confidence of all who may have the pleasure of his acquaintance.

JAMES A. PANTING.—Of all the men who in recent years have made their home in Baker county, none come with a better record for past achievement, energy and progressiveness than he whose career we must now essay to epitomize. His has been, in a commercial and intellectual sense at least, a conquering life, and to him is due a large measure of the honor always instinctively bestowed upon those who prove themselves heroes in the fight.

Mr. Panting is a native of Gloucester, England, born April 1, 1861. His ancestry is one of which he may justly be proud, the Panting family being an old and distinguished one, and the home from which he came being likewise notable, hoary with age, but without the decrepitude usually attendant thereon. His parents were Alfred A. and Anne (Addis) Panting, natives, respectively of Wales and of England.

Our subject attended the common schools of his native land, showing great aptitude in his studies and early graduating from one of the higher schools. In 1877 he crossed the ocean to Grand Rapids, Michigan, where he graduated in Swensberg College, receiving a diploma as an expert accountant and mathematician, and attracted much notice, he being the youngest graduate the institution ever produced. His diploma was endorsed by the president of the G. R. & I. R. R. Co., also by the lieutenant governor of the state and by all the bank presidents of Grand Rapids.

Upon retiring from school he entered the service of his wealthy uncle, William Addis, for a while, then spent two years in learning the lumber business from the woods to the market. In 1881 he became manager for the firm of Copely, Marthinson & White, also of the Amoskeag mills near Eastman, Georgia. In time he followed the lumbering industry into Cuba and then to Central America, where he became interested in one of the rebellions. He was very successful in his business and in fact in everything he undertook. From Central America he came north to Mexico, thence to Seattle, Washington, where, during the boom, he became one of the largest real estate and mine owners in the city. He was at that time manager for the Huron Lumber Company.

Going to Cincinnati in 1893 he became a lumber broker there, and to that business he continued to devote himself with zeal and assiduity until 1896, when he came to Baker county, locating upon Gold Hill, five miles east of Express. He is extensively engaged in farming, stockraising and mining, and spends large sums of money in developing properties and in the employment of labor. He is also procuring water rights and farming lands for the companies he represents, and in numerous other ways is contributing a lion's share toward the development of his community and the county. He is and will continue to be a great benefactor of the entire section, and it is to be hoped that the example he sets of progressiveness and thrift will inspire others to greater activity and nerve them to nobler efforts. Mr. Panting's family consists of himself and wife and one child.

ALFRED M. BROWN.—A public spirited, benevolent man, worthy citizen and a good thrifty agriculturist and stock raiser, the man whose name appears as the caption of this article, is deserving of rank among those who have contributed to the well-being and progress of Baker county, and it gives us pleasure to be able to accord some slight recognition of his services and integrity. Mr. Brown, son of Samuel and Charlotte (Smith) Brown, was born near Centerville, Appanoose county, Iowa, on October 23, 1856. He was reared on a farm, and had but poor early opportunity to secure an education, attending school only during short intervals of time. When he became seventeen years old, however, he moved to Centerville, where for three years he attended high school. During the next few years he farmed, but eventually he engaged in the flouring mill business in company with his father. He followed this line of commercial activity for two years, but finding that it did not agree with his health he then sold out his interests and emigrated to Baker county, Oregon. He taught school for a while after his arrival, but as soon as possible he embarked in the stock raising industry, procuring a tract of land for the purpose, and to this he has devoted himself ever since. His farm, situated two and a half miles southeast of Express has been improved by the erection of a comfortable residence, a fine, commodious barn and other buildings, and with a beautiful, well chosen orchard. He keeps quite a large herd of cattle.

Our subject was married in Centerville, Iowa, on September 27, 1883, to Miss Linda, daughter of Jacob and Elizabeth Mishler, and to them have been born six children, namely: Theron C., Laurel L., Golda W., Minnie P., Opal A. and Athel M. Mr. Brown is also interested in mining and owns some good properties.

HON. LUTHER B. ISON, deceased.— Among the men who have wrought in Baker county from the time when the first pioneers settled upon its fertile territory until the later years, none have been more prominently distinguished and influential than was the gentleman whose name initiates this paragraph, and to whom we are pleased to accord this memorial, only regretting that we are not able to more fittingly portray his virtues and worthy efforts in our midst, where at least in two leading professions he gained marked distinction, while his entire life was fraught with

deeds of generosity and kindness and his career manifested that rare ability and uncompromising integrity and strict morality and exemplification of Christian principles that characterize the true Christian, the typical man and the noble citizen.

Luther B. Ison was born in Garrard county, Kentucky, on October 19, 1841, being the son of Strother and Judith Ison, who brought him in 1849 to Grundy county, Missouri, where he received his primary education in the public schools and then took a degree from Central College at Fayette, in the same state. During his college days he was converted and joined the Methodist church and from that time until the day of his departure he showed forth the teachings of the Saviour of men, both in precept and by practical example of an upright Christian life. In 1866 he came to Baker county to join his parents, who had preceded him, and there he settled and began to work out his destiny in the new land, where he was afterward to play so prominent a part. For a time he gave his energies to mining, but soon turned to the more important work of instruction and in this profession he soon rose to the highest ranks and was considered in his time the leading educator in eastern Oregon. He taught in the city schools of Baker and was elected to the position of superintendent of the county schools, ever displaying rare talent and consummate faithfulness in all his efforts. Many positions were offered to him, but he chose one in which he could fit himself for more extended usefulness and exert a wider influence for the benefit of his fellows and the promotion of the interests of the commonwealth, namely, the profession of law. In 1870 he allowed his name to be used on the Democratic ticket as candidate for county clerk, and was promptly elected and at the expiration of his term was re-elected with even a larger majority. During these years he devoted his spare moments to industriously perusing the lore of Blackstone and Kent under the direction of R. A. Pierce and in October, 1876, he was admitted to the bar and to the successful practice of law he bent his entire energies with the most gratifying success. His ability was immediately recognized and he was elected district attorney of the fifth judicial district and at the close of a term of most faithful and efficient service, he was re-elected to fill the position again. He built up a large and lucrative practice and in political matters he was a power in his party, the Democratic, and one of the most influential men in political circles in the state. In 1882 he was elected to represent his district in the legislature and few men have ever displayed in the state halls of Oregon such powerful forensic oratory as it was his pleasure to deliver. In 1884 he was chosen president of the electors of this state and his campaigning was noted for rich eloquence, convincing argument and untiring efforts. Two years later he was called by an appreciative constituency to accept the responsible position of judge of the fifth judicial district and in the impartial exercise of the exacting duties of this office he was engaged at the time of his death.

None have been more generally mourned and deeply lamented than the late Judge Ison, but he had fought a good fight and he went to accept the crown that was waiting him.

The marriage of Mr. Ison and Miss Josephine, daughter of Spencer and Phoebe (Cunningham) Cates, was solemnized on September 12, 1870, at the bride's home in Union, Oregon, and to them have been born three children: Bertha, deceased; Edna B., married to Mr. McDougall; Virgil S., attending Columbia Medical College, of New York City. Mrs. Ison is spending the years of her widowhood in the quiet retreat of her own home, awaiting the hour of greatest triumph of all true followers of the lowly Nazarene. She is a woman of gracious personality and well known for her deeds of loving kindness and charity.

WILLIAM H. GLEASON.—Hardly could the charge of inconsistency and incompleteness be successfully rebutted were there failure to incorporate in this part of our work an epitome of the life of the esteemed citizen and prominent political leader whose name gives caption to this article. More than once has he been entrusted with positions of trust and emolument, and when so honored he has never failed to prove faithful and efficient. It is therefore a pleasure to accord him such representation as we can and to give some feeble expression of our appreciation of his services and intrinsic worth.

Mr. Gleason was born in Canaan, Maine, on June 28, 1852, the son of Moses and Lydia (Fowler) Gleason, scions of old colonial families. He grew to manhood in his native town, receiving a common school training, but when he arrived at the age of twenty, he went to Michigan and engaged in the lumber business as an employee. He busied himself thus for about two years, then went back to Maine, where he lived for the ensuing seven years, his means of gaining a livelihood being agriculture. Going then to Wisconsin, he spent three more years in the lumbering industry, after which he came out to Oregon. He settled in Union county, on the Grande Ronde river, and resumed the line of activity he had before followed in Michigan and Wisconsin, continuing in the same until 1893. In that year, however, he removed to Sumpter and embarked in the meat market business, and in that he busied himself until 1899, since which year he has been practically out of all lines of activity except mining. He has interests in the Greenhorn district, on Cracker creek and on Deer creek, all of which are famous mining districts.

When the town of Sumpter was first incorporated, our subject was honored by being accorded a seat in its council chambers, and at the first general election he was the choice of the people for the mayoralty, the duties of which office were discharged by him with great faithfulness and with ability and good judgment. After serving as mayor of the town for two years, he was elected county commissioner on the Democratic ticket, and that office is still his. Mr. Gleason is a thoroughly public spirited man and always has the interests of his town and county near his heart.

Fraternally our subject is affiliated with the time-honored order of Masons, in which he has attained to the Scottish Rite, his membership in this degree being in Portland. His marriage was solemnized in Baker City, on October 23, 1895, when Mrs. F. D. Farnham, of Maine, became his wife.

ROBERT R. PALMER.—We are pleased to accord to the prominent young business man and capable and efficient public officer whose name initiates this paragraph, a representation

WILLIAM H. GLEASON.

WILLIAM H. GLEASON.

in this volume, since by force of right he stands among the leading men of the county, both because of his excellent abilities and sound principles and integrity, while in the years that he has been before the public in business relations, he has demonstrated his ability as a business man and has wrought for himself a very gratifying success in building up a very extensive trade and in reaping proper financial remuneration.

A son of the occident, being born in La Grande, this state, on October 9, 1868, he has passed his life in eastern Oregon, receiving here his education and business training and made here his success in life, being a product to which the institutions of Baker county can refer with pride. After completing the school course in the city he went to Portland for a course in the business college of that city, taking his degree from that institution in 1888. He came with his parents to Baker City first in 1877, and here he has remained since. Immediately succeeding his graduation he opened up a harness and saddle store in Baker City in partnership with Mr. Denham, the firm being known as Palmer & Denham, and in the prosecution of this business he has been found constantly, with the gratifying result that he has a patronage that comes from many miles in every direction. Their store is on Front street and they carry a large stock of goods, the harness and saddles being of their own make. In June, 1900, the people asked him to assume the duties and responsibilities of the important office of county treasurer, and with entire satisfaction to his constituency he has discharged the same since, displaying the same tireless energy and faithfulness that are characteristic of him in his own private business. He affiliates with the Republican party in political matters and is a prominent member of the same. He was city treasurer in La Grande for one term previous. In addition to his other large business interests he is handling considerable stock in this county.

Mr. Palmer was married to Miss Maud S., daughter of N. H. and Ada Starbird, from Minnesota, on October 1, 1894, in La Grande. To them has been born one child, Ruth M. Mr. Palmer's parents are John and Almira (States) Palmer. Our subject has ever demeaned himself in such an acceptable and upright manner that he has won the confidence and admiration

17

and esteem of all who have the pleasure of his acquaintance, and the same wisdom and indomitable effort that have wrought out his brilliant career to the present time will doubtless be further manifested with as gratifying results in the days to come.

◆◆◆

TULLE B. PERKINS.—It is always with gratification that one is enabled to view the products of his own land and it is with especial pleasure that we are permitted to chronicle the salient points in the career of the prominent stockman and representative citizen whose name is at the head of this article, and who first was brought into being in this county and since has become one of its ablest developers and most enterprising sons.

Our subject is the son of Edward and Mary (Henry) Perkins, who were among the very first settlers in this region, having drawn up their train on Sunday, September 4, 1862, within the boundaries of the county, where since they have lived and wrought for the welfare of the county's interests and its development, while they have prosecuted with success their own private business. On April 16, 1865, Tulle B. was born at Wingville, and there he passed the years of his minority with the exception of the time which was spent in Portland, where he was acquiring his education, after completing which he commenced at the age of eighteen the battles of life for himself, his first venture being to rent his father's place and embark in stock raising. The measure of success that crowned his efforts may be reckoned when we discover that after four years of this work he was enabled to purchase a farm for himself. He selected a quarter section in the lower valley of the Powder river and there we find him to-day engaged in farming and raising stock. His ability and faithfulness have been recognized by his fellows, for they have kept him in public office almost continuously since his settlement in that vicinity, and the school interests of the district have profited by his wisdom for many terms. He lives in the Keating district, No. 36.

The marriage of Mr. Perkins and Miss Mary, daughter of Royal and Elizabeth (Turk) Pierce, was celebrated on January 1, 1888. This union has been blessed by the advent of one child, Bernice. Mr. Perkins is highly esteemed by his fellows and his integrity and intrinsic moral worth are deserving of all the enconiums that he has received. Mr. Perkins has a beautiful and comfortable home and his farm is one of the most fertile in that favored region.

JOHN P. ROSS.—It is without doubt a fact that everyone of the far eastern commonwealths of the United States are represented by their children in the cosmopolitan population of Oregon, and the old Keystone state has not been backward in sending her full quota of children to these occidental regions, as we perceive by the stanch citizens who were brought up under the benign influence of the William Penn regime, but now form a considerable portion of our wide-awake and progressive inhabitants. Among this worthy class is the gentleman whose name heads this paragraph and whose enterprising career and commendable achievements have been largely wrought out in our midst, having come to this section in 1866, being actively engaged in business here since. His birth was in Allegheny county, Pennsylvania, on January 30, 1832, being the son of Samuel H. and Sarah (Livingston) Ross, both natives of the same state, and of Scotch extraction. In 1841 he removed with his parents to Iowa territory, settling near Mount Pleasant, where he remained until 1850, when he became desirous of satisfying his adventurous spirit by actual experience in the western regions and accordingly set out with ox teams for the Golden state, where he engaged in mining and freighting until 1866, at which time he came to Baker City and at once settled. At that time twelve houses and thirty-one people constituted the village and from that embryonic stage until the present, Mr. Ross has been one of the foremost men in the active promotion of the interests of the town and country adjacent. In 1863 he had passed through this place, but did not stop at that time. From the beginning he was very active in the organization of the city government and a very prominent factor in the establishment of her present commendable institutions. He was a member of the first city council and continued in that capacity for a number of years,

held other important positions and has always been a liberal supporter of the churches and other institutions of the city. In 1868 he engaged in business and continuously wrought therein until 1890, when he retired from more active operations to enjoy the rest and competence which his industry and enterprise had earned and entitled him to. He has a fine home on Resort street and considerable other city property and holdings also in other places.

He was married to Miss Martha A., daughter of Levi and Matilda Smith, in Mount Pleasant, Iowa, on September 27, 1869, and to them have been born two children: William A., in business in Baker City, and John M., in business in Union, Oregon. Mr. Ross is a member of the I. O. O. F., Baker Lodge, No. 25, of the Encampment, No. 7, and the Rebekah Degree, No. 8, all in this city. In his trip across the plains the Indians attacked the train at the Humboldt river, but none of the immigrants were injured.

SAMUEL WHITE.—Distinguished in the legal fraternity as a man far above the average in ability, fortified by deep research and extensive experience, the subject of this sketch is a gentleman to whom one may safely refer as a leader in his profession, having displayed distinct talents and commanding eloquence, coupled with unswerving integrity and intrinsic worth.

Mr. White is a native of Griffin, Georgia, being born on September 15, 1860, and the son of John Haywood and Jane Rebecca (Johnstone) White, natives, respectively, of Tennessee and Georgia. His father was captain of the Griffin Light Guards during the Rebellion, and after the war returned to his native town, where he resided until March, 1898, the time of his death. His mother is still living in that city. Our subject received his primary education in the public schools of his native town and then attended the University of Tennessee, after which he took up the study of law under the tuition of Frank L. Harralson, state librarian at Atlanta, Georgia, where he was admitted to the bar on October 6, 1881. He immediately began the practice of law in Atlanta, continuing the same until 1885, when he came to Oregon, locating at

Grant's Pass for two years, then removed to eastern Oregon, choosing Baker City as his home, and here he has since continued in the practice of his profession with an ever increasing patronage and brilliant success. In the political school he is allied with the Democrats and is a prominent leader in that party, being chairman of the state Democratic central committee, where his keenness and wise political foresight is much valued. He is also captain of Company A, Oregon National Guards and in 1898 was elected district attorney and in 1900 was elected as his own successor. Thus is shown the appreciation of his constituency in his ability and faithfulness, which in every way is justly merited. In fraternal affiliations he is associated with the B. P. O. E., the A. O. U. W. and the W. of W.

The marriage of Mr. White and Miss Ida Lawrence was solemnized in Baker City on October 8, 1890, and they became the parents of two children: John Haywood and Johnstone Lawrence. Mrs. White was the daughter of Judge A. J. Lawrence and a native of the Sandwich Islands, being born while her father was supreme judge in Honolulu. She died in 1892.

Mr. White was married the second time, February 17, 1896, Mrs. Frances E. Wisdom becoming his wife at that time. Mrs. White is the eldest daughter of Albert H. Brown, who was formerly treasurer of the state of Oregon. He came to the coast in 1849 and to Baker City in 1862. She was born in Yreka, California, on July 2, 1861. Her father now resides in Portland. Mr. White was a resident of Pendleton for a time previous to locating in Baker City, and while there he was city attorney at the time W. F. Matlock was mayor. It is but right that we should say that Mr. White is possessed of rare capabilities and has manifested integrity and moral worth that stamp him as a man in whom implicit confidence may be placed and this he has gained in unstinted measure from his fellows.

J. C. CHRISTENSEN.—The successful and enterprising business man, agriculturist and stockman of whom we now have the pleasure to speak, is one of the leading figures in his section, having demonstrated his ability

and good financiering in his investments and in the operation of his varied interests in this county from a very early day, himself being one of the worthy number who are denominated by that prince of all English words, pioneer, while his walk and life have ever been of that character which calls for the encomiums of his fellows and the respect of all.

The little kingdom of Denmark is the native land of our subject and the date of his birth was September 8, 1848, and for nineteen years he remained in the northern part of that land near the fiords of the sea, gaining a good education and learning the arts of honest toil. The confines of the diminutive land could hold his adventurous spirit no longer than until he arrived at manhood's estate, for he then sought out the new world and there began the struggle for his fortune that has resulted so successfully. For two years after arriving here he worked on the Union Pacific railroad and then in 1869 settled in Baker county. He bought land and commenced to raise horses and also engaged in mining for eleven years, after which time he devoted his whole attention to farming and raising stock until 1895. At that time he opened a general merchandise store in Haines, occupying a building that he had erected in 1888. In this capacity he has been blessed with his usual success and he has a large and lucrative trade, and in addition to superintending that he also gives attention to handling fine stock on his large farm of three hundred and ninety acres. He owns nearly one hundred head of fine well bred Short-horn cattle, besides other stock. In fraternal affiliations he is associated with the I. O. O. F., Lodge No. 112, and the A. O. U. W., Lodge No. 110. The people have frequently called him to serve on the school board and in other public capacities.

Mr. Christensen and Miss Clara Dwinell were married at Wingville in 1881, but in January, 1883, Mrs. Christensen died.

On April 26, 1884, at Pocahontas, this county, Mr. Christensen was married to Miss Elizabeth, daughter of James and Eliza Engram, and a native of Arkansas. They have become the parents of seven children: Mary; Thomas, attending school in Baker City; Nellie, John, Annie, George, William, all being at home except Thomas. Mr. Christensen is a man of great activity and fortunately possessed of great adaptability and he is making a fine success in each line of his varied activities, and it was he who in company with Mr. Toney opened the first butcher shop in Haines in connection with his other business.

———◆◆◆———

CASPER J. DURBIN.—It is with no little pleasure that we essay the task of outlining the career of the venerable Pacific coast pioneer and the successful farmer and stockraiser whose name appears as the caption of this review. He is one of the most thrifty and progressive of the agriculturists in the vicinity of Huntington, and his premises and environs bear eloquent testimony to his industry and good management. Though apparently not particularly ambitious for leadership among his fellows and never a candidate for any office, he takes the interest every good citizen should in the general welfare of his community and county, and ever manifests a willingness to contribute his share towards any enterprise of public concern.

Our subject was born near Belleville, Richland county, Ohio, on April 26, 1822, his parents being John and Sarah (Fitting) Durbin. He worked on a farm, attending school a few months out of each year, until about nineteen years old, then accompanied his parents to Clinton county, Missouri, remaining a period of two years. He then returned to Ohio, but the year 1845 found him again in Missouri. His parents crossed the plains that year to Polk county, Oregon, finally locating in Marion county.

In 1853 our subject also crossed the plains with ox-teams, rejoining the remainder of the family at Salem, Oregon, where he became a partner of his brother in the hotel and livery business. In 1855 he engaged in farming in the vicinity, and in 1862 he removed to Auburn, Baker county. He ran a feed stable at that place until 1864, then entered a homestead about a mile northwest of Huntington, where his home has ever since been. As may be supposed from the length of time spent in this one spot and the progressive character of Mr. Durbin, his place has been improved by the erection of a comfortable house, a fine large barn, all needful fences and everything which goes to make rural life attractive, and has been brought to an excellent state of cultivation. It produces an abundance of hay and fine fruit of many varieties, as well as other crops of different kinds.

Mr. Durbin once returned to his old home in Ohio, intending to find a location there and dispose of his property in the west, but like most of those who go east with similar intentions, he soon concluded that he would not exchange his occidental home for any farm in the east, if one condition should be that he should live there.

On March 1, 1849, our subject married Miss Julia Anne, daughter of William and Betsey Draper, a native of Canada, and to their union were born nine children only two of whom are living, John B., living at the head of Durbin creek, and Alice B., at home. Mrs. Durbin died March 28, 1884.

Our subject's father died at Salem, Oregon, at the age of one hundred and three, and his mother at ninety-eight. The latter was a first cousin to the late President William McKinley. It is of interest also to record that Mr. Durbin cast his first vote for William Henry Harrison, in 1844, and has supported the Republican ticket ever since. Mr. Durbin was in the employment of the United States government for five years and helped build the first house in Grand Island, Nebraska, it being built for the government, and he also was one of the first at Fort Laramie, Wyoming, being in the quartermaster's department.

———◆◆◆———

GEORGE B. STURGILL.—Among the sturdy pioneers that braved the dangers and hardships of that weariest of all journeys on this continent, crossing the plains in the earlier days with ox teams, mention must be made of the esteemed and prominent citizen whose name is at the head of this paragraph, and whose life of activity and enterprise is well known to the dwellers in this county.

Francis H. Sturgill and his wife, Caroline (Richmond), parents of our subject, and natives, respectively, of Alabama and North Carolina, and who were married in Virginia, Lee county, came to Missouri in 1841, settling in Sullivan county, where they remained until

CASPER J. DURBIN.

1865. At the last date mentioned they, in company with their children, undertook the trip across the plains to Oregon, and on August 29, while en route, the mother was taken from them by death. She was descended from a very prominent Virginia family, the Richmonds. Mr. Sturgill first settled at Wingville and took up a homestead, where he devoted his time and energy to agriculture until 1877, and then came to the lower valley of the Powder river. One day, while Mr. Sturgill was mowing, he stopped to remove the sickle and having completed that job leaned the sickle against a tree in the rear of the machine. The horses became frightened and backed so quickly that they caught his arm against the blade of the sickle, severing an artery, from which he bled to death. He was esteemed by all who knew him and his death was mourned by the entire community. He was in his sixty-second year at the time of his death, and his funeral was taken charge of by the Masons and in their cemetery in Baker City he lies buried. Mr. Sturgill had been very prominent in the politics of the county and had held several public offices, among them county assessor in 1870 to 1872. He was the father of the following children: George B., the subject of this sketch; W. R., whose wife is Miss Virginia Talley; Benjamin F.; Joel M.; Louis, married to Carrie Jones; Easter C.; John I., married to Mary Stevenson; Mary E., wife of Mr. Abbott; Steven D., married to Martha Pierce; Rachel, Rebecca. Robert, Henry, the last four deceased.

Returning to our immediate subject, George B. Sturgill was born December 8, 1841, in Sullivan county, Missouri, and there received his education and remained until the trip across the plains, above mentioned, on which occasion he acted as captain, being eminently fitted for the responsible position since he had been across the plains to Montana the year previous, and had spent the summer of 1864 in mining in the famous Alder gulch of Montana. In 1868 he commenced to buy and sell stock and for six years thereafter he resided in Union county, then returned to Wingville, where he remained until 1893, when he bought his present place in the lower valley of the Powder river, where he is at present engaged in farming and raising stock, being one of the most prosperous and substantial settlers of that community.

The marriage of Mr. Sturgill and Miss Lida A. White was solemnized in Missouri in October, 1861. Mrs. Sturgill's parents, Madison and Elizabeth (Abbott) White, were natives of Virginia and Ohio, respectively, and her mother died on June 1, 1850, and is buried in the Williams graveyard, near Milan, Missouri. To our subject and his wife have been born the following children: Jonathan J., married to Barbara Duckworth; Eliza B., wife of James Osborn; Lena C., wife of E. Cranston; May, wife of R. R. Sparks; Effie L., wife of James York; Joel C., married to Mintie Kase; Madison W., clerk at Baker City; Thornton, in Baker City. Mr. Sturgill is a member of I. O. O. F., Lodge No. 69, at Wingville, also of the Modern Woodmen, Lodge No. 48, of the same place. He is prominent in politics, having chosen the Populist party to affiliate with and frequently he is nominated for important office, in 1892 running for coroner. At the present time he is a member of the school board and is efficient and faithful in the discharge of public duties.

◆◆◆

WILLIAM A. GOSSETT.—It is ever a pleasure to chronicle the life history of one who has wrought energetically and faithfully, and one who has so prosecuted his own private business that in building up the same he has likewise contributed toward the general welfare. Such a man is he whose name gives caption to this article. Mr. Gossett is one of the most broadly enterprising citizens of the county, in which he ever manifests a vital and public spirited interest, and he has earned a place in the esteem of the people such as few enjoy.

Our subject is a son of Eli H. and Elizabeth (Briton) Gossett, born near Half Rock, Grundy county, Missouri, October 29, 1860. While yet an infant he was taken by his father to Mount Pleasant, Iowa, but soon after their removal thither, the older Mr. Gossett was killed in the battle of Shiloh, he having enlisted in the Fourteenth Iowa Infantry for service in the Civil war. When five years old our subject was placed in the orphans' home at Davenport, Iowa, where he remained, attending school, until thirteen years old. He then entered the high school at Mount Pleasant, graduating from the same two years later. Afterward he learned the trade of a barber, but he seems not to have followed his handicraft much in Iowa, for soon afterward we find him in Trenton, Missouri, whence in 1885 he came to Baker county, Oregon. For a time after his arrival he worked at the barber trade in Baker City, but soon misfortune overtook him, and for several years he was compelled by sickness to retire from active participation in any line of endeavor. When at length he recovered sufficiently he engaged in contracting and building and in the manufacture of lime. His kiln is located six miles east of Baker City, near the O. R. & N. track, and has a capacity of about one hundred and sixty barrels. Its production is of the very finest quality, less than three per cent. of the limestone being left as dross after a burning.

Mr. Gossett has a fine herd of about thirty thoroughbred Angora goats, in which he takes a pardonable pride. His energy and taste are further manifested in his having turned to good account the ponds near his place created by the overflow from springs in the vicinity. In these at present are about twenty thousand fish, mostly trout, and our subject will never be content until he has increased that number to one hundred thousand.

In fraternal affiliatons Mr. Gossett belongs to the Woodmen of the World, and his wife and two oldest daughter are members of the circle. On March 5, 1881, in Baker county, Oregon, our subject married Miss Mary M., daughter of Philip and Rosana Lenz, and to their union have been born six children: Rosa E., a photographer in Baker City; Katie L., Charles D., Pauline A., Bertha J. and Philip C.

WILLIAM E. WOOD.—Among the men who have come out to the Pacific coast at an early date, and have borne the brunt of the battle, as a result of which the darkness of barbarism has been dispelled and the bright day of civilization ushered in, must be counted the venerable pioneer whose name appears above. It is with no feigned pleasure that we accord him representation in our volume as one of the founders and builders of Baker county, some of whose most renowned mining properties were discovered by him and his partner, Mr. Eastabrooks.

Our subject was born in Westchester county, state of New York, on September 27, 1827: He worked on a farm and attended the public schools until about seventeen years old, then went to New York City, where he clerked in a store for a few years. Eventually he embarked at New Bedford, Massachusetts, on a whaling vessel, and while out visited Argentime Republic, cruised along the west coast of Africa to St. Helena, passed the Falkland islands, going thence to the Azores and on to the Cape Verde islands, returning in about two years to the port of departure with a vessel laden with sperm oil. This venture proved a decided success for him.

Mr. Wood then embarked in the merchandise business at Katonah, New York, but in 1853 he pulled up stakes and set out by the Panama route for Shasta county, California, where he for the first time engaged in mining. In the year 1866 he entered into partnership with Mr. Eastabrooks and they have been together ever since. They came to Baker county together and have been together interested in the Connor creek and Gold Hill mines and in other valuable properties, as they are in the prospects they now have and in their pleasant little farm near Weatherby.

While in California Mr. Wood joined a company organized by Captain Walker in 1854 and going down into Lower California, was there engaged for a time in fighting outlaws and Indians.

GEORGE J. BOWMAN.—After an extended career of activity and usefulness the esteemed citizen and thrifty western pioneer whose name forms the caption of this review has retired from the active pursuits of life, though he still maintains interest in public affairs, which has ever characterized him.

Like many other thrifty and successful men in various parts of the United States, Mr. Bowman is a native of Germany. He was born in that empire not far from the French border on January 1, 1829. He received a good public school education in his fatherland and shortly after leaving the school room entered upon an apprenticeship to the trade of wagon maker. In 1848 he came to the United States, and settling in Kentucky, there engaged in the pursuit of his handicraft. In

1852 he removed to Dover, Missouri, where he followed wagon making uninterruptedly until 1873, in which year he put into execution a determination to try his fortune in Baker county. He worked at his trade in Baker City for half a decade, at the end of which period he moved to Wallowa county and engaged in farming and stockraising. However, when he first came to Baker City he purchased property where the Gieser Grand hotel now is, and his property interests necessitated his being in this city a considerable portion of his time. Though he still owns his farm in Wallowa county, he has now become a permanent resident of Baker City, his tasteful and comfortable new home being on the corner of Third and Estes streets.

Mr. Bowman has always been a leader in the communities in which he has lived. He is enthusiastic in the promotion of the cause of education and has served on numerous school boards in different places, among them the board which inaugurated the first graded school in Baker City. He also has the distinction of having served four years as chairman of his home city's first council. He is, moreover, a very active worker in the First Presbyterian church, in which he has served as elder longer than any other person.

The marriage of our subject was solemnized in the state of Missouri on November 9, 1854, when Miss Elizabeth, daughter of David and Rachael Twoodie, became his wife. They have seven living children, namely: Mrs. Kate M. Palmer, of Baker City; Bettie, wife of J. P. Halle; Frank G., who married Miss Alice Shelton and is living in Eagle Valley; John T., married to Miss Mollie Poe and living in Eagle Valley; Robert B., living on his father's farm in Wallowa county; Beulah, a teacher in one of the Baker City schools; and Myrtle, a graduate of the Monmouth Normal school, wife of J. W. Campbell, of Wheeler county, Oregon.

————◆◆◆————

ELI CHANDLER.—In at least two lines of industry the gentleman whose name initiates this paragraph has achieved a commendable success, and it is with pleasure that we accord to him space for an epitome of his career, since it is the purport of this compilation to grant a representation to the leading and prominent citizens of the county, and to those that have been instrumental in the advancement of the material welfare and the substantial progress of this political division.

Hamilton county, Indiana, is the native place of our subject and the date of his birth was 1851, he being the son of Enoch and Sidney (Wright) Chandler, who were natives of the Buckeye state, but whose home was in Indiana until the time of their demise. At the age of twenty-two Mr. Chandler started out for himself, crossing the plains by railroad and stage to Jimtown, which is now Sparta, in Baker county, and in December, 1872, he settled in Eagle valley, where he devoted himself to farming and stock raising. He sold portions of his estate, until he has but fifty acres left, turning his attention, meanwhile, to the commercial world. Eighteen hundred and eighty-eight was the date when he first opened a store in Newbridge, and in 1899 he removed it to Richland, and since that time he has continuously prosecuted this enterprise and he has to-day a fine stock of general merchandise and his patrons are numbered by hundreds, while his trade is constantly increasing. His fine capabilities and uniform geniality and upright business principles are instrumental in making him the most popular merchant in his section.

Fraternally he is affiliated with the I. O. O. F., Lodge No. 123, in Eagle Valley.

The marriage of Mr. Chandler and Miss Susie B., daughter of William Rich, a native of Kentucky, was celebrated in 1899. It is pleasant to state that Mr. Chandler is one of the most highly respected members of society in the valley and is considered a leading property owner and substantial citizen, who is dominated by wisdom and skill of a high order in his business enterprises.

————◆◆◆————

ELLIS BEGGS.—A representative of a class of men now fast vanishing before the ever extending network of iron rails, and a splendid specimen of the type of bold, sturdy manhood developed by adventurous and dangerous undertakings in a new and but partly civilized country, the man whose name gives caption to this review is to be congratulated upon having escaped uninjured or with but a slight wound in many hazardous conflicts with the footpads who beset the routes of the stage driver, rendering his honest business exceedingly precarious. He is also to be congratulated upon the success which has attended his efforts in the commercial world since retiring from his former adventurous pursuits and upon the enviable standing he has acquired as a representative citizen of Baker county.

Mr. Beggs was born in Chickasaw county, Iowa, near Bradford on June 12, 1858. He resided there until twelve years old, then accompanied his parents to California and thence to Jacksonville, Oregon. At the age of fourteen he began driving stage on the route between Oregon and California, and in 1878 he came to Baker county, and drove between Kelton and Umatilla Landing. He continued in stage driving until 1895, making his trips over many different routes in Washington, Oregon and California, and in his extensive experience, he has been in no fewer than fourteen holdups. He was eight times overtaken by highwaymen on the Mendocino and Cloverdale route, escaping each time without injury, but on what is known as the Red Hill route, in 1891, he was shot through the wrist, though he succeeded in making good his retreat in a running fight.

In 1895, when our subject retired from stage driving, he engaged in freighting around Red Rock and Virginia City, Montana, and he still oversees the operations of his three sixhorse freight outfits in Baker county, though he gives most of his own time now to the livery business, he having a year and a half ago purchased an interest in the livery stable of his brother, Milo Beggs, in Baker City. The firm has an outfit of about forty single and double rigs and keeps in all about seventy-five head of horses.

◆◆◆

CAPT. CHARLES H. CRAIG.—This enterprising sheep man and farmer, of Eagle Valley, has the honor of being not alone a very early pioneer of the county and a veteran of the early Indian wars, but also of being one of those who in the dark days when the demons of disruption and disunion raised their heads rallied to the support of freedom and correct governmental principles. The public spirit which led him to take the risk, when the cause of his

country demanded it, has remained with him throughout all after life, rendering him a good, patriotic citizen, ever interested in the promotion of the general welfare.

Mr. Craig is a native of Morgan county, Illinois, born in 1836, the son of Joseph and Susan A. (Grady) Craig, natives respectively of Kentucky and Virginia. When he became nineteen, our subject gave inception to his independent career by engaging in farming in Missouri, and this was his business until 1862, when the call of patriotism summoned him to sterner duties. In February of that year, he enlisted in Company F, Second Missouri Cavalry, and for the ensuing thirty-seven months he followed the fortunes of war, his rank at the time of his discharge being duty sergeant. He participated in many engagements and skirmishes, and in the battle of Chalk Bluff, Arkansas, was shot through the hand.

At the close of hostilities, Mr. Craig resumed his farming in Missouri, but in 1869, he sold out his holdings and came to Baker county, Oregon, locating at Auburn. He mined there until 1872, then at Sparta until 1875, eventually coming to Eagle valley, where he filed on a homestead of one hundred and sixty acres. He now owns two hundred acres, and is engaged in general farming and in the sheep business, in both of which industries he is achieving an enviable success.

At the time of the Indian outbreak in 1878, our subject organized a company of volunteers in Eagle valley, of which he was captain, Tom Pearce being second lieutenant and Joseph Beck, first lieutenant. The most important engagement in which it participated was that at Lookout mountain, in which it suffered no casualties but killed a number of Indians.

At present, Mr. Craig is commander of Phil Kearny Post, No. 66, G. A. R. of Pine valley. His marriage was solemnized in October, 1861, the lady being Catherine, daughter of Peter B. and Mary Ann (Noell) Greier, natives of Virginia, and to this union, two children have been born, Richard Franklin, who married Rebecca E., and Clara, widow of Orley Moody, deceased.

Captain Craig and William Ainsworth are the discoverers of Lewis lake, which was named after a boy who caught incredible numbers of trout in its waters.

CAPT. CHARLES H. CRAIG.

Mrs. Craig had a narrow escape from the paws of a bear one 4th of July day. The family and J. Holcomb, while traveling on horseback, discovered a steer that had recently fallen a victim to the savage beast, and while they were looking at the carcass, Bruin put in an appearance. Several shots were fired at him, and soon he appeared to be dead. Dismounting, Mrs. Craig ran to him that she might be the first to touch him. To her surprise and dismay he soon proved to be very much alive, and it was only by presence of mind and agility that she was enabled to escape uninjured.

ELTON SISLEY.—Though not among the very earliest pioneers, the man whose career we must now attempt to trace in outline, is an old settler of the county with which our volume is concerned, and it is right to state that in the years of his residence here he has ever so ordered his life in its relations with his fellows as to secure their confidence and render him esteemed. He is an energetic, thrifty and successful agriculturist and stockraiser and in this line of activity is contributing to the wealth and advancing the material development of Baker county.

Our subject was born near Cedar Rapids, Linn county, Iowa, on August 6, 1852, the son of Simon S. and Rebecca (Coleman) Sisley. He attended the common schools until fourteen years old, then ran the parental farm, his father having died in 1862, until 1877, which year is the date of his and his mother's advent to Baker county. They located on a farm about two and a half miles below Weatherby, on Burnt river, where our subject is still to be found when at home, but his mother died on April 15, 1900, in Baker City. He has a fine farm, well improved and a very comfortable home, also a splendid herd of cattle on the range near his place.

Mr. Sisley was married March 26, 1885, the lady being Lucy I., daughter of Andrew J. and Sarah J. (Bashaw) Weatherby. They have no children of their own, but are rearing Laura Clarke, a daughter of Mrs. Sisley's deceased sister.

Mrs. Sisley's father, a prominent citizen of Weatherby, where he served as justice of the peace and postmaster, died January 11, 1890,

and her mother June 29, 1901. Of the demise of our subject's father, mention has already been made. It should be added, however, that he came to his death as a result of diseases contracted in the war of the Rebellion, he having enlisted in 1861 in Company D, Second Iowa Cavalry. He participated in the battles of Corinth and Pittsburg Landing and in numerous others until the illness of which he died compelled him to leave his regiment.

JOHN LEW, deceased.—On November 27, 1891, the community in which he lived, and in fact all of Baker county, was called upon to mourn the loss of the venerable pioneer and worthy citizen whose name appears above. His many good qualities as a man had rendered him endeared to those with whom he was by circumstances thrown in contact, while all recognized the benefits which had accrued to the community in consequence of his efforts and enterprise. It is but fitting, therefore, that a brief review of his eminently useful career be here given.

Our subject was born in Knox county, Canada, on August 9, 1836, and there he grew to man's estate and received his educational discipline. At the early age of sixteen he started in life for himself, going to Rochester, New York, where he learned the carpenter trade. He worked at that handicraft until 1856, then came via the Isthmus to California, where he followed placer mining until 1861. He then came to the Salmon river mines in Idaho. He was one of a party of nine men who prospected the Boise basin for six weeks when the Indians were very hostile and during that time he had many narrow escapes. In 1862 he came to Auburn in Baker county and engaged in mining there. He was one of six men who located the first mines where Sumpter now stands, and it is interesting to note that they named the place Sumpter from the fact that Fort Sumpter had fallen about that time. Our subject remained in that vicinity for two years, then moved to Granite, where the ensuing six years were spent in the effort to discover earth's hidden treasures and win them from her. About 1870 he moved onto a farm about six miles west of the present Baker City and engaged in the dual occupation of mining and farming. This he was enabled to do from the fact that a part of the farm, was fine placer ground, as is attested by the fact that he gathered four thousand five hundred dollars worth of gold dust the first year. At one time J. W. Virtue took a selection of fruit and a number of nuggets to a fair at Portland, both of which were from Mr. Lew's farm, and it is recorded that this singular exhibit attracted much attention. During the last few years of our subject's life he devoted his energies entirely to farming. He will long be remembered as one of the most enterprising and public spirited of Baker county's early settlers and one who assisted much in its development and its preparation for the purposes of civilized man.

In fraternal affiliations our subject was identified with the A. O. U. W. and the W. of W. His marriage was solemnized at Auburn on December 9, 1868, on which date he became the husband of Mrs. Elizabeth Hedges, nee Jones, who had crossed the plains with ox teams in 1863 from Iowa. The following children were born to them, namely: John H.; George; Harney, deceased; Albert F.; Katie M.; Bertha E., and C. Bertie, deceased; Ralph, deceased; Frank R. The children all live at home with their mother. They have an excellent farm of four hundred and eighty acres, improved with a fine house, a good barn and other substantial buildings, also eighty acres of valuable timber land.

JAMES BURRELL.—The prosperous farmer and stockraiser whose name appears above is a native of England, born in Essex county on January 15, 1835, the son of Richard and Nancy Burrell. He remained in his native country until twenty-two years old, acquiring his education in the public schools, and afterward engaging in farming. In 1857 he came out to Illinois, in Boone county of which state he lived for the ensuing two years, after which he crossed the plains to California, making the trip with horses. He worked at mining for about four years, then purchased a drove of cattle and came with them to the Bannock basin in Idaho. Coming to Baker county in 1867 he engaged in placer mining on Rock creek and on Muddy creek, in which business

he busied himself for about six years. He then bought some cattle and again engaged in the stock business, but three years later, in Elko, Nevada, he sold his herds. Returning to Baker county in 1876 he purchased a place a mile west of Haines postoffice, where he has ever since lived. He now has three hundred and eighty-seven acres of well improved farming land and is very comfortably situated, reaping a rich reward for his toil and industry. He is to be ranked among Baker county's most enterprising agriculturists, as he is one of its most highly esteemed citizens.

Fraternally our subject is affiliated with Haines Lodge, No. 112, I. O. O. F. In Pocahontas, Baker county, on November 27, 1877, he married Mrs. Nancy A. Clark, daughter of William and Nellie Goodman. They have one adopted daughter, Eva J., born May 27, 1897. Mrs. Burrell is a native of Tennessee, born in 1846, and came with her mother and the family to Baker county in 1877. The father died in Tennessee before the family came here and the mother died in this county May 10, 1900.

ERWIN P. HOWARD, M. D.—Among the various professions that conserve the interests of the human race, there is none that gives a wider range for the manifestation, both of skill and genuine expression of kindness to one's fellows, together with the power to assist in promoting the happiness of the members of the race, than does the practice of medicine, and dependent upon the powers of the surgeon or the skillful practitioner are the issues of life, hence it is that to the true and faithful doctor there is ever a debt of gratitude to be paid by the people, and as the subject of this sketch is one of the leading devotees of the healing art in the county and is held in high esteem by his fellows, both for his skill and his manifestation of kindness, we are bound to grant him representation in this volume.

Erwin P. was born in the Empire state on September 19, 1852, being the son of Alanson D. and Mary E. (Payne) Howard, natives, respectively, of Massachusetts and New York. When our subject was two years of age he was taken by his parents to Sturgis, Michigan, where they remained until the death of the father, which occurred on January 9, 1900. At the age of fourteen the son commenced the activities of life for himself, operating first as a clerk in a mercantile establishment in his home town. Four years later he began the study of medicine, taking up the profession wherein his father had won laurels. He took a course in the Bennett Medical College in Chicago and after the first year became enamoured with the reports from the gold fields of the Pacific slope and came there and took up mining in California. After some time at this captivating work he turned again to the study of medicine and took his degree. He was then engaged by the Union Pacific Railroad Company as surgeon, where he operated for a few years, giving entire satisfaction, and then he again turned to mining, having purchased some promising properties. While engaged in this he built a quartz mill and operated the same at the Cornucopia mines in this county. Later this property was destroyed by a snow slide and then he turned to the practice of medicine again, settling in the town of Richland, where he has been signally successful in the prosecution of his profession. Lately he has started a drug store in connection with his practice and he is also proprietor of a grocery store. Fraternally the Doctor is associated with the I. O. O. F., Lodge No. 123, in Eagle Valley, and also with the Modern Woodmen of America. Politically he affiliates with the Democratic party, being decided in his views, and since he is one of the leaders in the county he is a prominent figure at the conventions.

In 1876 the marriage of Dr. Howard and Miss Eliza B., daughter of Samuel and Mary (Spencer) Gill, was celebrated and they have become the parents of two children: Guyello, handling stock in Idaho; May Belle, holding the chair of music and elocution in the Salina Military Academy, at Salina, Kansas.

COL. WILLIAM W. KIRBY.—To the stanch veteran of the Civil and Indian wars, the stirring business man, estimable citizen and intrepid and doughty frontiersman and stockman whose name initiates this paragraph, we are pleased to accord space for an epitome of the career that has been fraught with enter-

prise and interest from incipiency until the present time. And it is matter of regret that, to one who interposed himself willingly in the breach of danger to stand and die, if need so demand, rather than see the flag of our glory trampled under treason's feet, it is matter of regret, I repeat, that space forbids a full account of deeds of bravery and a life teeming with stirring incident.

Mr. Kirby is the son of Wade H. and Emily (Blew) Kirby, natives of Kentucky, and he was born in Schuyler county, Missouri, in 1842. His mother's father, Richard Blew, fought for the independence of the colonies under General George Washington, and the military career of his grandson but adds luster to the brightness of the family record. In his native county our subject received his education and at the breaking out of the war enlisted in Company E, Twenty-second Missouri Volunteers, being but seventeen years of age, and his regiment was assigned to western duties. For three years he fought for the stars and stripes and after the expiration of his term he enlisted again to repel the savages from the frontier. Following this he engaged to the government as wagon master, and at the end of his services he was ranked as colonel, while he entered as private. In 1866 he settled down to farming and operating a mercantile establishment in Barry county, Missouri. Later he gave up the mercantile part and confined his efforts to stockraising and farming alone.

In 1886 he came to Eagle Valley, this county, and bought the farm where he is at present residing, and here he is devoting himself to tilling the soil and stock raising; however, he frequently is found in the mountains searching for the key to nature's hidden vaults of treasure and so successful has he been that at the present time he owns a fine property on the Snake river, consisting of fourteen claims. The mineral is copper and it is considered one of the finest properties in this section.

The marriage of Mr. Kirby and Miss Mary, daughter of William and Winifred (Buck) McClintock, natives of Ohio, was solemnized in 1864 and they are the parents of the following children: James A., married to Florence Wood; Maggie, wife of Mr. W. W. Chandler; Richard B., married to Miss Augustus; Cora E., wife of Mr. Samonis; William

L., married to Miss Samonis; Maud A., wife of Mr. Frasier. Mr. Kirby is affiliated with the G. A. R., where he is a prominent member, and he is also very active in politics, being associated with the Republican party, where he does good work and is known to ever stand for those principles and policies that are for the best interest of all concerned.

By way of reminiscence, it is of interest to state that Mr. Kirby was in the battle of Corinth, his regiment being attached to the Tenth Missouri, and after the charge he was among the number sent to Island Number Ten and later, with his company, was captured. He lay for a time in prison, and then with a man named Felix Cornelius, he made his escape, having some thrilling adventures and hair breadth escapes, meanwhile enduring all sorts of hardship from exposure, hunger and fatigue, swimming streams and other weary toils. At last they reached the Federal lines at Thomasville, Missouri, and he was assigned to duty with the First Missouri Cavalry, where he served out his time.

When the colonel was crossing the plains he was chosen train master and some exciting times were experienced with the Indians. On one occasion, near Julesburg, Colorado, a battle occurred with the redskins and one of them was killed, and a little further above, a part of the train went ahead, and they were attacked and killed by the Indians in plain view of the others, before assistance could be given.

JOEL B. WOOD.—This progressive and successful agriculturist and stockraiser of the vicinity of Pine is among the earliest pioneers of Baker county, and during all the years of his residence here he has shown himself a man worthy of respect and esteem, ever acting with integrity in his relations with his fellows. Forceful and industrious, he has contributed not a little toward the general progress, and he deserves rank among those who have in some measure proved a blessing to the neighborhood in which they have lived.

Born in Barre, Washington county, Vermont, on May 13, 1843, our subject grew to manhood there, remaining at home with his parents until twenty years old, working on the farm most of the time, but attending school at least a portion of each year. When twenty-three years of age, he put into execution a project, previously formed, of trying his fortunes in the wild west, crossing the plains with mule teams, and finally coming to a halt in Eagle valley, Baker county. He remained there most of the time during the first three years of his stay in the occident, then spent a half decade in the Sparta mines, eventually coming to Pine valley, where he homesteaded one hundred and sixty acres of land. Before the time arrived for making final proof, however, he sold his improvements, and purchased a quarter section a half mile east of where Pine postoffice now is, upon which he has ever since lived, engaged in general farming and raising cattle and horses.

Mr. Wood takes quite an active interest in political matters, supporting the tenets of the Republican party. In this connection it is of interest to record that his father, Ezekiel, who lived and died in Vermont, cast his first vote for William Henry Harrison, Whig candidate for president, and his last for Benjamin Harrison. He died at the old homestead in Barre in 1889 at the age of eighty-four. Our subject's mother, Emily (Foss) Wood, likewise a native of Vermont, died in the Green Mountain state at the age of sixty-six. Mr. Wood handles a goodly number of fine sheep, in addition to his other enterprises.

EUGENE SISLEY.—The son of respected pioneer parents and himself a native of Baker county, the young man whose name appears above has by his industry and thrift, and the courage with which he has thus far fought the battles of life, reflected credit both upon his parentage and his birthplace. An industrious man and a good citizen, he has by his integrity and worth won a place in the confidence of the people with whom he has been thrown in contact and he enjoys a very enviable standing in the community where his home now is.

Our subject was born in Baker City on May 27, 1867, the son of Lewis J. and Marthat (Calner) Sisley. His early life was spent on the parental homestead, and though his physical powers received their fullest development in the invigorating tussle with nature's opposing forces, his educational advantages were rather limited. At the early age of six-

JOEL B. WOOD.

teen he began the battle of life on his own account, following farming and stock raising and giving some attention to mining enterprises. About five years ago he removed to his present place of abode and there he now has a very good quarter section of land, which he is improving as rapidly as possible, and compelling to yield the abundant harvests of which it is capable.

The marriage of our subject was solemnized on June 15, 1887, Miss Minnie M., a daughter of Martin and Mary H. Hill, and a native of Indiana, then becoming his wife. They have had six children, Gladdys E., Hazel G., Maxwell E., deceased, Lettie H., Frank and Goldie.

JOEL P. KINNISON.—Few men within the confines of the county with which our volume is concerned have lived here longer and seen more of the development and progress of eastern Oregon than has he whose career it is now our task to present in epitome. He tells us that he has ridden all over the site of the present Baker City when he could not see a track even of a cow or a horse and that he has watched its growth from the time its first cabin was erected until the present date. He also has the honor of having broken the first sod, planted the first potatoes, sowed the first oats and operated the first mower in Baker county. During all the years of his residence in this important and wealthy political division he has been engaged in enterprises which have added to its prosperity, and his active public spirit has led him to take a vital interest in all its concerns and to promote its welfare whenever opportunity offered. What then can be more fitting than that his important services should receive due recognition in a work of this character?

Our subject was born in Perry county, Missouri, on the Mississippi river on March 11, 1838. His parents, J. P. and Harriette (Finch) Kinnison, natives of Virginia, died when he was quite young, so he early had to shoulder life's responsibilities alone. In 1853 he accompanied an uncle across the plains to California, making the journey with ox-teams in six months and four days. During the first two years after his arrival he worked for his uncle in the stock business and farming, then he and his

brother, H. A., bought a band of cattle and engaged in the industry on their own account. In 1862 they drove their herds through to Baker county, Oregon, and located on a place seven miles west of Baker City, where our subject now lives. They purchased a half section from the state of Oregon, and upon this they renewed their stock raising business.

It is of interest to note that for about one hundred beef cattle which they drove from California into the mining town of Placerville, Idaho, they received as high as twenty-five cents per pound dressed. They had quite an interesting experience with Captain Jack and his band of Indians while driving to Idaho. This doughty red skin surrounded the company and their cattle and demanded pay for the privilege of grazing stock on the range. The whites refused and, getting their guns, prepared for battle. The Indians seeing that their would-be enemies were in earnest, decided to compromise by accepting as pay a crippled cow.

In 1863 Mr. Kinnison raised fourteen acres of potatoes, for which he received ten cents per pound, also a patch of corn, the product of which sold for one dollar per dozen roasting ears. The same year he raised some five or six thousand pounds of oats more than were needed for their own consumption, and these sold for from sixteen to twenty cents per pound. In the spring of 1876 he and his brother drove one thousand head of cattle into Wyoming, realizing twenty thousand dollars upon the transaction. Verily these were the times to accumulate fortunes.

At present Mr. Kinnison has a fine farm of six hundred and forty acres, all in one parcel and well improved. He is also the owner of some valuable city property.

Our subject is a member of Wingville Lodge, I. O. O. F. He has been twice married. On January 18, 1865, in Baker county, Oregon, he married Miss Mary, a daughter of Charles and Rachael Chandler, and a pioneer of 1862. The had five children, Charles G., engaged in mining in Cripple Creek, Colorado; J. W.; Hiram B., residing in Baker county; Lawrence O., deceased; Joel P., Jr., at home. Mrs. Kinnison died in 1883, and her remains lie buried in Wingville cemetery. On December 28, 1884, Mr. Kinnison again married, the lady being Mrs. Mary Hanna, widow of Samuel Hanna, who came to Union county in 1862. She had two children by her former marriage, Ada, wife of Flavius Perkins, of this county; Anna, who was queen of the carnival in 1901; and she and Mr. Kinnison are parnets of two children, Mabel H. and Myrtle.

HENRY RUST.—There are few tasks more pleasant than to recount the items in the career of one who has given himself to the defense of his country and risked all, that he might preserve to posterity the institutions of freedom that are so dear to the human heart. Among the army of gallant and intrepid men who promptly responded to the first call of the president for men to follow the flag against rebellion's attacks was the estimable gentleman and loyal citizen whose name initiates this paragraph, and whose career it is now our privilege to epitomize.

We have to cross the waters to that substantial land whence come so many of our best citizens—Germany—to find the native place of our subject, his birth having occurred in Bavaria on September 25, 1835. In his native country he received a thorough education, taking a degree from the excellent universities of that land. After the completion of his education he entered the commercial life and continued therein until 1858, the time of his immigration to this land. His first occupation here was with a nursery firm in Monroe county, New York, where he acted as commercial salesman until April 16, 1861, when he demonstrated his loyalty to and love for the land of his choice by enlisting in Company C of the New York Infantry. His company was put in the first corps of the army of the Potomac, where he served until 1862, when he was wounded while on a transport, the wound being inflicted while they were taking new recruits between Baltimore and Washington. He was given his discharge on account of this disability, but three months later he was received in the commissary department, where he rendered excellent service until the close of the war. He was with Sherman's army and on the staff of General Milroy, with headquarters in Tennessee. In this service he was ordered to Nashville, then sent on the sea, to Georgia to meet Sherman, which he accomplished by

steamer from New York, and then he was dispatched to Morehead, North Carolina, where he was at the time of Lee's surrender. From here he went to Washington and continued until the main part of winding up the commissary affairs was completed, when he went to Montana in company with two other army officers and took up mining. In this enterprise he was sometimes successful and sometimes otherwise. The following year, 1866, he came to Oregon and bought the brewery at Clarksville and operated it for nearly two years and then went to Peru, Chili, and Bolivia, spending nearly a year in this trip. It was in 1874 that he established the brewery in Baker City, and he has devoted his energies to the successful operation of this since. He has a plant with a capacity of ten thousand barrels, and enjoys an excellent patronage. He also owns a fine estate in the country, which is leased. In the political field he has been an active participant and has served as president of the city council and also in other official capacities. He is director of the Soldiers' Home at Roseburg, and commander of the Grand Post at Huntington, while he is a member of the G. A. R. in Baker City. He affiliates with the Elks and is a very popular member of their ranks. In view of the excellent services that he rendered for the government and the wounds that he sustained in that service, he draws a pension from the public bounty.

In 1872 he was married to Miss Liza Kessler, a native of Germany, the nuptials occurring in Baker City. Mr. Rust is one of the most popular and esteemed citizens of the county and his stanch principles and unswerving integrity have won for him the confidence of all, which is richly merited.

EDWIN A. WHITTIER.—While the subject of this sketch has not been in the county as long as some, he has manifested such thrift and wisdom and enterprise in his achievements while here that he takes high rank among the leading stockmen and agriculturists of this section. From the rock-bound coast and distant region of Maine he has traversed a continent to settle in the snug little valley that composes a part of the fertile and rich Baker county.

The parents of Mr. Whittier were Newman and Sarah (Hill), both natives of the Pine Tree state, where the father died, but the mother is still living in Huntington, this state, and our subject was born in Augusta in 1855. When he had reached the age of nineteen years he left the parental roof and began life's activities for himself, engaging first as a hand on a ranch, and then shortly afterward we find him in Salem, this state. In the vicinity of that city he worked and practiced economy until in 1880, when he had sufficient funds to warrant him purchasing a ranch, which was done, the selection being where he now resides in Eagle valley. Here in partnership with his brother, he operates a sheep ranch and they are having very flattering success in the manipulation of the same. The favorite breeds raised by them being Delaino and Merino. It is with pleasure that we are able to announce that everything around the premises of these stockmen manifests them to be up to date and enterprising in every particular and they are reaping the proper reward of such care and thrift.

The marriage of Mr. Whittier and Miss Alice Shelton was solemnized in 1888, and to them has been born one child, Edna. Mr. Whittier is held in high esteem by all of his acquaintances and he has won the confidence of the entire community.

———◆◆———

ROBERT D. CARTER.——In chronicling the history of Baker county it is eminently fitting that especial mention should be made of the gentleman whose name heads this article, since his rare ability and stanch integrity and strict adherence to the principles of truth and uprightness have made him a potent factor in the municipal affairs of the county seat, as well as throughout the county in general, while his prominence as a distinguished citizen is well attested by all. Being a descendant of one of the worthy patriots who accompanied William Penn to this continent, his father's and mother's ancestors both participating in the Revolutionary war, we would expect to find exemplification of these same rare virtues in their son, which is abundantly verified throughout his entire career.

Mr. Carter was born in Cecil county, Maryland, on August 26, 1856, being the son of Daniel and Martha (Hanna) Carter. His education was received in his native county, where he remained until 1875, then came west to Colorado, Wyoming and Idaho. Two years were spent in these states and then he came to Baker City and engaged with J. M. Swift in the stock business, continuing therein for four and one-half years. The two years next succeeding this period he was in the employ of the O. R. & N. Company in the engineering department. After this he engaged in the butcher business, in which capacity he has continued uninterruptedly until the present time. He is in partnership with Mr. Miller, the firm being known as Carter & Miller, and they do a general butchering and packing business, besides operating a stock farm of eight hundred acres. Mr. Carter is also owner of considerable valuable real estate in Baker City and elsewhere and is also interested in mining, and is considered one of the leading business men of eastern Oregon. He was a member of the city council and also a member of the water committee when the Baker City water system was originally adopted. For a number of years he has served as chairman of the Democratic central committee, and is a valued man in that capacity. From 1894 to 1898 he served as councilman and in 1900 he was called by the people to fill the chair of chief executive of Baker City, and in this position we find him at the present time. It is refreshing to note that in all of this lengthy and arduous public service Mr. Carter has received the honors without the slightest solicitation on his part, believing that honor will come to whom honor is due, thus manifesting the grand example of the proper demeanor of an officer in a republic.

The marriage of Mr. Carter and Miss Clara M. Sprague, a native of Canada, was solemnized in Anacortes, Washington, and to them have been born two children: Roberta and Sprague H. Mr. Carter is a member of the F. & A. M.

———◆◆———

WILLIAM A. HAMM.—That sister country to the United States, Canada, has sent many of her sons to enjoy the fuller freedom and benefits of our democratic institutions, who rent asunder the ties that bound them to the native soil and accepted the responsiblities with the privileges that were conferred by the foster country, and no more loyal class of citizens exists in the bounds of the states than this same number of which we speak; and a leading figure of that class in this section is the man whose name initiates this paragraph and whose life of honest industry and wise operations has been fraught with much interest during the years spent in our midst, as well as in those of former days.

The birth of Mr. Hamm occurred in New Brunswick, near St. John, on January 1, 1830, being the son of William A. and Ann (Hardin) Hamm and of German descent. His educational discipline was received in his native land and there he remained until 1850 and then transferred his citizenship to the United States, stopping the first thirteen years in California, where he devoted his time and energies to mining. In 1863 he came to Oregon, locating first in Canyon City and engaging in placer mining. Success attended his efforts but later an unfortunate investment on Olive creek stripped him from all of his accumulations. Eighteen hundred and seventy was the date when he first saw Baker City, and freighting the occupation to which he devoted himself, transferring goods to the Cornucopia mines and to other places. This, with various other industries, was followed by him until 1898, when he was called by the people of Baker City to act in the capacity of street commissioner, and to the discharge of the duties devolving upon him in this incumbency he has devoted his entire energies continuously since, giving complete satisfaction to his constituency, and to him is due much credit for the advancement of the city's interests in the care and improvement of her highways. He has ever taken the proper part of a stanch citizen in the affairs of the city, county and nation. He owns a handsome residence at the corner of Fourth and Madison streets, besides other property in various places.

The marriage of Mr. Hamm and Miss Sarah, daughter of Dr. Riley, was celebrated on June 6, 1864, in California, and they are the parents of four children: William G., a miner; Ulysses S.; Abbie, wife of Samuel Coleman, of Baker City; Ida, wife of J. R. Coleman, of Hope, Idaho. It is a matter of note that when Mr. Hamm first came to this section it was in Grant county and The Dalles was the coun-

ty seat. He has labored faithfully and assiduously for the advancement of the country and city of his choice and has always displayed that unswerving integrity and public spirit, coupled with enterprise and wisdom that command the commendation and praise and admiration of all.

* * *

JAMES FLEETWOOD.—It is with pleasure that we are permitted to outline the career of the esteemed citizen and enterprising stockman and agriculturist whose name is at the head of this article and whose labors have been instrumental in developing the resources of the county of his choice and advancing the interests of civilization in the regions that were once the home only of the savage. His life has been well filled with commendable achievement and interesting incident and adventure and it is a matter of regret that more space cannot be granted to detail the same.

James Fleetwood was born to John and Sarah (Todd) Fleetwood, Jackson county, Indiana, on January 28, 1846. His early life was spent on the farm and he acquired his educational discipline from the district schools of his native place. At the age of fourteen he went to the American bottom in Illinois, twenty-five miles down the Mississippi from St. Louis, and in 1860 he went to Memphis, Missouri, whence three years later he started across the plains with mule team, arriving in Napa valley, California, in due time after a successful journey without serious accident. The following spring, he came to Canyon City, Oregon, and soon after went to Union, following farming there until 1867. At that date he went to Clarksville, on Clark's creek, and engaged in dairying, whence, two years later he came to his present place, two miles east of Hereford, where he owns five hundred acres of fertile soil, well watered and producing bountifully in hay. He has added many improvements that make his home comfortable and add charm to the life in the rural regions and make the estate one of value. He has abundant herds of cattle and horses, and also owns a residence in the county seat, where he frequently spends the winters for the school advantages for his children.

On September 30, 1865, was celebrated the

JAMES FLEETWOOD.

marriage of Mr. Fleetwood and Miss Marguerite, daughter of Aaron and Sarah Dunn. To them were born the following children: Jeremiah, married to Mattie Eblin and living in Baker City; Sarah A., wife of George Tetreau of Baker City; Mary M., wife of Bert Ware, living near Hereford; Ira Fulton, married to Miss Virginia M. Murry; George W., married to Barbara Hardman; Elizabeth, wife of Bert Lew; Justina, deceased; Augusta A.; bookkeeper in a store in Baker City; Edith, attending school in Baker City. Mrs. Fleetwood was called from the duties of life to the rewards of another world in December, 1898, while living at their residence in Baker City.

Mr. Fleetwood and Mary Evaline, daughter of Lambert and Emily Merrick, of Memphis, Missouri, were married in Baker City on November 12, 1899, and to them has been born one child, Janie Marguerite. Mrs. Fleetwood's grandfather was one of the first settlers of Keokuk, Iowa, and her father was the first white child born there. Her mother's father came from England and was a relative of Lord Chamberlain.

WALTER S. LOVE.—In a work that purports to give due representation to the leading citizens of this county there must be especial mention of the gentleman of whom we now have the pleasure to speak, since not only has he the distinction of being among the very first white children born in this section, but also he is to be mentioned from the fact that he has labored assiduously for the material progress of the county since an early day and has demonstrated his ability to work out worthy achievements for himself in private business and has also demonstrated the solution of one of the most important questions that concern the entire lower valley of the Powder river, where he is living at the present time. We refer to the fact that Mr. Love has demonstrated that it is possible to irrigate the valuable parts of the valley by the construction of reservoirs for the retention of the snow water. When he was putting forth that idea it was opposed by friend and foe alike, who demonstrated that it was not feasible, but the genius and perseverance of our subject were equal to the occasion and he has constructed a reservoir that has met the re-

18

quirements and is in successful operation at the present time. Thus have all the questions of value been brought out, and we look upon Mr. Love as a real benefactor of his fellows.

The birth of Mr. Love was near Eugene, Oregon, on January 15, 1858, being the son of David S. and Helen (Stewart) Love, natives of Pennsylvania, and as early as 1853 they made their way across the plains to this region. At the age of twenty-two our subject began the conflict of life for himself, undertaking at first the raising of sheep and to this industry he has devoted himself continuously since with the proper reward of his endeavors and his perseverance in abundant success. He is considered one of the most skillful and prosperous stockmen of the entire vicinity. He took a homestead and eighty acres of desert land and forty acres of school land in the lower Powder river valley and here he is residing at the present time, about twenty-two miles from Baker City.

The marriage of Mr. Love and Miss Rosa, daughter of Ellis and Mary (Dill) Bennett, was celebrated in 1879. Mrs. Love's parents were natives of Illinois and her father lies buried in Walla Walla, while her mother is still living in Alberta province, Canada. Mr. Love is affiliated with Queen City Camp of W. of W., in Baker City, and is very popular in these relations, as well as in all the walks of life, where he has ever demeaned himself with wisdom and faithfulness and uprightness. To our subject and his wife have been born the following children: Gertrude, wife of Rufus Bunch, of Powder river; Clarence E.; Helen; Edna; Mary; David S. died in 1895; R. Walter; Lourene died in 1897.

L. O. ISON.—The prosperous farmer and stock raiser whose life history we must now attempt to epitomize, was born in Garrard county, Kentucky, near the town of Danville, on April 10, 1848. When but an infant he was taken by his parents to Trenton, Missouri, and there he resided until 1862, when he came across the plains with the rest of the family to the vicinity of Wingville, Baker county. He assisted his father in farming and stock raising until 1869, then went to the state agricultural college at Corvallis, where he remained four years, graduating in the class of 1873. Upon receiving his degree he engaged in teaching, and for the ensuing decade and a half he followed this profession, having charge at different times of the schools at Wingville, Rye valley, Malheur City and in the vicinity of Boise, Idaho. In 1890 he located on a quarter section of land twelve miles northwest of Baker City, and he now has a very comfortable home and a fine, well improved farm, supplied with abundance of stock and with all kinds of buildings, farm machinery, implements, etc. He is among the most industrious and energetic agriculturists of his neighborhood, and one of its most esteemed citizens, his integrity and neighborly qualities rendering him popular with all. At present Mr. Ison is supervising the Nelson Mining Company irrigating ditch, in addition to managing his farm.

The marriage of our subject was solemnized on October 31, 1877, the lady who then became his wife being Miss Mollie A., daughter of Price and Abigal (King) Fuller, and a native of Oregon. Their union has been blessed by the advent of one son, Grover Cleveland, now seventeen years old, at home with his parents. Mr. Ison is interested in mining and owns three quartz claims. He gives a portion of each year to this industry and with a little more development he will have some fine producing properties. He is a charter member of the Queen City Camp, W. of W., of Baker City. Mrs. Ison's parents were natives of Ohio and crossed the plains in 1844 and located in Benton county, this state. When a small girl her mother died and she was raised by her uncle, A. W. King, who now resides in Portland. He is owner of the street railway of that city and one of its wealthiest men, being rated at over one million dollars.

DAVID CARTWRIGHT.—To the esteemed pioneer citizen of Baker county whose name appears as the caption hereof, belongs the honor, always a great one, of having rendered distinguished service in the cause of national union during the dark days when civil strife wrought its work of desolation and destruction in our land. A hero in war, he has likewise proved a man of force and energy in the blood-

less battles which have been fought since, and he deserves recognition as one of the potential factors in Baker county's development.

Mr. Cartwright is a son of George and Judith (Newman) Cartwright, and was born near Franklin, Venango county, Pennsylvania, on November 5, 1840. When quite young he was taken by his parents to Newcastle, Lawrence county, Pennsylvania, where he was reared on a farm, attending the common school at short intervals as he had opportunity. Before the time had arrived for him to inaugurate independent action, the Civil war broke out, and his initiation into the pursuits of life proved a very stern one. Enlisting in Company K, One Hundred and Third Pennsylvania Volunteers, he soon so far distinguished himself as to win a promotion to the second lieutenancy, but this he resigned shortly that he might be free to organize a company. This he did. The company was known as Company H, Eighty-seventh Pennsylvania Volunteers, of which he was the first lieutenant. While our subject participated in many hard-fought battles, he seems to have borne a charmed life, for never once was he even wounded.

On receiving his honorable discharge, our subject returned to his old home, but not to remain, for soon we find him engaged in coal mining in the Cumberland mountains. He served as foreman for the Nashville & Cumberland Coal Mining Company for a number of years, afterward going to Brazil, Indiana, thence to Danville, Illinois, thence several years later to Kansas and thence to Missouri, from which state he came direct to Baker county, arriving in his present place of abode, Rye valley, on the second day of August, 1882.

Ever since his arrival here, our subject has wrought with the energy and progressiveness which have always characterized him, following mining, stock-raising and farming. In 1894 he bought the Rye valley placer mines, which he has been operating successfully ever since. He is also the owner of quite a large amount of real property in the valley, including both agricultural and mineral lands, and all this he is utilizing to the best advantage possible under the circumstances.

In fraternal connection, our subject is a Knight of Pythias, and a past chancellor of his lodge. His marriage was solemnized December 16, 1868, when Sarah E., daughter of

Isaac O. Anderson, of Reelsville, Indiana, became his wife. Seven children were born of this marriage, namely: Mattie, deceased; Richard A., of Rye valley; David L., also of Rye valley; Janette, wife of Francis M. Powell; Roy, deceased; Annie, wife of Christopher Armbruster; George W., attending school at home. Mrs. Cartwright died on January 14, 1890, at the present home of the family.

———◆◆———

JOHN A. REID.—It is with an especial pleasure that we are enabled to present here a few of the salient points in the highly interesting career of the worthy pioneer and estimable gentleman and prominent citizen whose name appears above and whose life of activity and faithfulness has been passed for nearly forty years in this place, during which long period there has emanated from him an exemplary manifestation of those virtues and abilities that are the component part of the typical man.

Scotland is the place and April 19, 1834, the date of his birth, his eyes first opening to the light near the bounds of old ocean's realm and amid its thundering roar. Two years later he was transported to the United States by his parents, John and Margaret (Bennett) Reid, who located in Philadelphia, where they remained for a number of years, then removed to Michigan, where his father was engaged in ship-building, and then later they went to Canada. In that country and in Detroit our subject received his education and in 1861 he sailed from New York to encounter the adventures of and seek his fortune in the wild scenes of the Pacific coast. He had previously made himself master of the ship carpenter trade and to this he devoted himself on the "old Herman" until he reached Washington territory, when he went to the Cariboo mines in British Columbia, where he operated for two years, and then paid a visit to his brother in Elk City, Idaho. He spent one summer with his brother in work on the latter's claim, then repaired to The Dalles and engaged with the O. S. & N. Company until the following spring and then came to Baker county with a pack train, where he and his partner, James Fletcher, engaged in mining and carpentering. He gained possession of two very valuable mines,

the Gordon and the Collateral, which he afterwards sold. In 1866 he built the old Western house in Baker City and operated it for a number of years, also taking charge of the stage company's business at the same time. He was a member of the first city council and has always been very active and prominent in the upbuilding of the town. He now owns the whole block where he lives and has just completed an elegant residence at the corner of Fourth street and Auburn avenue, still owning the old Western hotel property, and considerable other city property and also valuable interests in Michigan.

The marriage of Mr. Reid and Miss Annie, daughter of Captain Duncan and Sarah (Coutts) McEachen, was celebrated in Canada, September 25, 1871, and it is of note that they started for their western home on the day of the beginning of the great Chicago fire, October 8, 1871. They have become the parents of six children: J. Gordon, married and living in Chicago; Pearl L., teacher in the public schools; William E.; Andrew D.; Sarah V. and Robert A. Mr. Reid is an active member of the First Presbyterian church and has ever been prominent in the advancement of the interests of all that was for the welfare of the people. He is the fourth in a family of eight children and seven of them are still living. It is of note that he is a relative of the well-known Gordon Bennett of New York.

———◆◆———

LEANDER FERGASON.—There are few among the sturdy pioneers of this section that have shown more perseverance and faithfulness in the prosecution of the duties of life and in the endeavors to promote the welfare and progress of the interests of the county, than the worthy subject of this sketch, while he has ever manifested those substantial qualities of integrity and genuine worth that make the typical man in any community.

The parents of our subject, Alexander and Elizabeth (Baker) Fergason, natives of Canada, came soon after their marriage to this country and settled first in New York, whence they came to Oregon in 1866, settling first here in the Grande Ronde valley. Later they removed to Eagle valley and in that place they both departed from the labors of this life, the mother at the age of sixty-five years and the father at the age of ninety years.

Our subject was born in New York in the year 1830, and he continuously remained with his parents until the time of their death, serving faithfully and exemplifying in a commendable manner that beautiful word of command, "Honor thy father and thy mother." After their demise, he removed from the old place to his present home on Goose creek in the lower valley of the Powder river, where he owns a quarter section and follows general farming and stock raising. His residence is twenty-one miles northeast from Baker City. In Mr. Fergason we have one of those men who admire the principles of the grand old Jeffersonian Democracy and stand by it with the fervor and energy that produce conviction that its principles are sound and its teachings are deep and trustworthy. In political matters he has always shown a marked activity and is careful to maintain the part of a good citizen in the attention paid to the same.

Mr. Fergason has never chosen a partner to share the joys and shades of life's way, preferring to remain with the joys of the single state. He is now passing the golden years of his life in the quiet prosecution of the affairs connected with his estate and is respected and esteemed by all that have the pleasure of his acquaintance.

━━━◆◆◆━━━

WILLIAM BROWN.—The energetic and successful stock raiser, fruit grower, and general farmer, whose name gives caption to this review, is a native of the north of Ireland, born March 1, 1841. When about three years old he accompanied his parents to the vicinity of Mineral Point, in Iowa county, Wisconsin, where he grew to manhood, his intellectual powers receiving their discipline in the public schools and his physical forces being developed in the effort to make the parental homestead yield up its wealth.

In 1862 our subject set out across the plains with horse teams to the section now known as Baker county, arriving here in August, the same year, and that winter was passed in the town of Auburn. The ensuing spring he went to the Boise basin, where for three years he mined, the scene of his principal operations be-

ing Placerville. Returning in 1865 to Baker county, in 1867 he settled on a quarter section of land about eight miles northwest of Baker City, and there he has resided continuously since. He now has a fine farm of two hundred and forty acres, which has been reduced by his industry and toil to an excellent state of cultivation, and which has been improved by the erection of needed buildings, fences, etc. He is one of the leading and most thrifty farmers of his vicinity.

Fraternally Mr. Brown is affiliated with the Masonic order, and in religious persuasion he is a Methodist. He takes a lively interest in political matters, and for seven years has been a member of the board of county commissioners. His marriage was solemnized on January 31, 1869, Miss Julia A., a daughter of O. R. and Sarah Dean, and a native of Mississippi, then becoming his wife. The issue of their union is four children: Lily, wife of W. B. Landreth, residing in Baker City; H. K.; Abbie, wife of W. A. Payton, a resident of this valley; Ella, now Mrs. M. S. Osborn, living in the valley.

━━━◆◆◆━━━

JAMES O. MAXWELL.—The worthy gentleman whose career it is now our task to present in outline is one of the best and most extensive farmers in Baker county, and it is a pleasure to accord him representation in this portion of our volume as one who has added and is yearly adding to the wealth of the community. He is an esteemed and honored citizen of the county, public spirited, and ever ready to do what lies in his power for the advancement of the general well-being and the promotion of every worthy public enterprise.

Mr. Maxwell was born near Rocheport, Boone county, Missouri, on November 24, 1853, his parents being Wallace and Anne Maxwell. He remained in his native state until about twenty-two years of age, coming then to California, where he wrought for wages during a full quadrennium, thereupon coming to Baker county. He purchased three hundred and twenty acres four miles northwest of Haines, and set assiduously and zealously about the task of improving and cultivating the same. Conserving the rewards of his thrift and enterprise, he was enabled to add

MRS. JAMES O. MAXWELL.

JAMES O. MAXWELL.

to his original realty holdings from time to time until he is now the owner of eight hundred acres, and has control of about a thousand acres in all. His place is perhaps as well improved as any in Baker county, and is stocked with about two hundred head of fine, graded Shorthorn cattle, thirty of which are dairy cows. Mr. Maxwell has also many hogs and horses, and a very choice family orchard.

In religion, Mr. Maxwell is a Baptist, his membership at present being in the church of that denomination at Haines. In Baker county, on January 23, 1887, he married Miss Nancy A., a native of Illinois, and a daughter of James and Elizabeth Hand, and to their union have been born seven children, all of whom are at home, namely, Lena A., J. Wallace, Myrtle E., John E., Rosa A., Charles Dewey and Omer O. In addition to the excellent improvements that adorn and enhance the value of the agricultural portion of Mr. Maxwell's estate, he has one of the most beautiful and comfortably and tastily furnished residences in the county, in which good cheer abounds and joy adds its grace to the material comforts of competence.

PHILIP R. BISHOP.—One of the leading mine owners of the county at the present time and a member of that estimable band of pioneers that made their way through the wilderness to this region in the early sixties and subdued the barriers to the development of this fertile section, is the gentleman whose name heads this article and who has been prominently identified with the progress and development of the county ever since, displaying an integrity and ability that have placed him in the ranks of the distinguished men of this part of the state.

Mr. Bishop is the son of Philip R. and Jane (Long) Bishop and a native of London, England, where he received his education and remained until he had attained the years of his majority. His educational discipline was quite extensive, being completed in some of the excellent colleges of his native country. Following the completion of this he embarked for Victoria, British Columbia, via Cape Horn and for one hundred and forty-seven days he was out of sight of land. The immediate object of this journey was to locate a brother, which he did later in New Zealand. He engaged in mining exclusively until 1864, when he came to this county and located at Auburn, buying and locating a group of claims. Afterwards he removed to Mormon Basin and followed mining there for a time and then gave his attention to stock raising for ten years; after which he sold out and again embarked in his favorite occupation, mining. At this time he located a number of quartz claims, among which was the famous Climax claims, and the opening up of the Climax group of mines in the Cracker creek district, which consisted in bringing this famous property to the producing point from a mere prospect, represents the climax of all his work.

The marriage of Mr. Bishop and Miss Sarah N. Dickenson, a native of Vermont, occurred in that state. Some time after he had brought his wife to his western home, he was called to mourn her death.

Again Mr. Bishop was married, this time Mrs. Samantha A. Tribulet, nee Reed, became his wife, the ceremony being solemnized in Wyandot county, Ohio, of which state she was a native. Mrs. Bishop is a niece of Mr. J. F. Burkett, supreme judge of Ohio. She has three daughters by her first husband. Mr. Bishop is a man of broad public spirit and has ever wrought with skill and energy for the advancement of those principles that are for the welfare of all, while he has displayed characteristics of real worth and virtue that have commended him to the confidence and esteem of his fellows wherever he is acquainted.

JOSEPH M. MASTERS.—It is with pleasure that we incorporate here a brief review of the life history of the thrifty and industrious farmer whose name forms the caption of this review. He was born in Overton county, Tennessee, on the 7th of April, 1844, and resided there, except while serving as a soldier, until 1880, engaging in agricultural pursuits as soon as he had completed his education and become old enough.

In 1862 he enlisted in the Eighth Tennessee Cavalry, Company F, determined to do what lay in his power for the cause he deemed to be right. His captain's name was Bilberry, his colonel's, Deverill, and his regiment was a part of General Forrest's cavalry command.

Our subject served as regimental color sergeant. He participated in the battle of Murfreesboro, and those around Nashville, and was taken prisoner in the battle of Parker's Cross Roads. He was confined for a period of about six months in Camp Douglas at Chicago, then exchanged and from that time until the close of the war he remained with his regiment, serving the cause of the Confederacy with faithfulness, and sharing the bravery which won the southern soldiers admiration even from their northern foes.

At the close of the war he resumed his business, farming and stock raising, continuing therein until 1880, when he sold and removed to San Juan county, Utah. He lived there three years, coming then to Baker county. He farmed a rented place here for a while, but as soon as he was able he purchased a quarter section for himself five miles west of Baker City, unto which he has added at times until he now has a fine farm of three hundred and sixty acres, where he handles about two hundred head of cattle. During the first few years of his residence here he was engaged a part of his time in selling meat throughout the country, and in 1900 in partnership with his son, he embarked in the meat market business in Baker City, but this establishment they sold before the year was over.

Fraternally, our subject is an Odd Fellow, and in religious persuasion he is an adherent of the Methodist church, South, although he was raised a Presbyterian. On September 11, 1864, he married Mary J., a daughter of Charles and Nancy Maxwell, also a native of Tennessee, and they have had six children, Simeon M., Cornelius W., Lettie L., wife of D. C. Perkins; James B. and William T. attending school in Baker City; and Mary Lee, deceased.

WILLIAM W. WEBBER.—Among the prominent men of Rye valley, is the venerable pioneer whose name gives caption to this article, and it affords us pleasure to incorporate here a summary review of his life, for we believe his achievemenes during the long term of his residence here have been such as to render it fitting that he should be given place among the leading citizens and builders of Baker county. Active in politics and in what-

ever he conceived to be for the highest general good, he has ever contributed his share of time and energy toward the general welfare, and has won a place in the esteem and confidence of the people such as can only be secured by those who generously and benevolently expend their energies for the public good.

Mr. Webber was born near Plymouth, Richland county, Ohio, the son of David B. and Lucy (Conklin) Webber. He was reared on a farm in his native state and received very good educational advantages. During his early manhood he followed teaching some, spending a few years in Iowa and Kansas, and being a resident of the latter state during the famous John Brown raid. Eventually he returned to his native community, remaining there until 1858, when he emigrated via the Panama route to San Francisco. He came thence by stage to Phœnix, Oregon, where he again engaged for a time in the teaching profession. Soon, however, he returned to California, but not to remain, for a few months later we find him again in Oregon, this time engaged in mining. For several years he sought mineral wealth in various parts of the country, eventually, in 1864, making his way to Baker county, where he has made his home ever since. Locating on a farm in Rye valley, he engaged in farming and stock raising, though he never lost his interest in mining ventures, and still owns some properties.

Fraternally, Mr. Webber is affiliated with the Masonic order, with the Woodmen of the World, and with the Order of Washington, his name being on the charter of the last-named society. His marriage was solemnized August 8, 1888, when Mrs. Mary Rancor, daughter of James and Eliza (Sheldon) Tony, became his wife, and to their union one child has been born, namely, Effie Alice, attending the home school.

Mr. Webber's father died in Ohio, at the old home place, in the year 1875, being then seventy-five years old, and his mother died on June 23, 1897, at the age of ninety-two years.

HON. N. C. HASKELL.—The business ability, keen foresight and good financiering displayed by the subject of this sketch are well known to all in this section, and it is by common consent that he is placed among the foremost men of the entire county, having demonstrated his capabilities in the arena of active enterprise, while he has ever displayed sterling qualities in all his operations.

Mr. Haskell is the son of Enoch and Esther (Mendenhall) Haskell, being born on March 17, 1850, in Oxford, Ohio, where he also received his educational training and remained until he was eighteen years of age. At that age he went to Montana and the next year continued his journey to Nevada, where he engaged in mining for one year, and then repaired to California, and embarked in the printing business and soon took the position of editor of the Yuba City Banner, which he made a journal of distinct merit and vitality, then resigned his position and came to this county in 1874. He was engaged with the Marysville mining company and in 1877 was installed as manager of all their properties here, continuing in this capacity with the manifestation of practical wisdom and marked executive ability for twelve years. Succeeding this he formed a partnership with H. W. Sloan, and engaged in hydraulic mining on Elk creek in the Susanville mining district until 1899, when he sold his entire interests there and has since devoted himself to the care of his large properties in and adjacent to Baker City as well as in other parts. He owns a handsome residence at 1441 Washington street and a fine brick business block on Front street, two-story and fifty feet front, a one story brick building with a frontage of eighty feet on Court street and a large frame building near the Republican office, an interest in the Haskell's addition to Baker City and much other property both here and elsewhere. He owns stock in the Baker Opera House Association and is one of its directors, has also stock in the Natatorium and is secretary of that association. In political matters he is ever active and has been of great worth to his party, the Republican, in advancing those principles for which it stands. He is now serving as school director in Baker City and in 1889 he was selected by the people to represent this county in the state legislature, which he did with ability and integrity.

The marriage of Mr. Haskell and Miss Florence J. Pennington was solemnized in California in March, 1877, and to them were born four children: John C., married and living in Susanville, Grant county; Francis E., machinist in Pocatello, Idaho, who served in Company G, First Idaho Volunteer Infantry during the Spanish war and also in the uprising in the Philippines; Florence E.; Clinton R. In 1891, on October 3, Mrs. Florence J. Haskell was called from a mourning family and devoted husband to the realms of another world and her remains were laid to rest in the city cemetery in Baker City.

In 1893 Mr. Haskell was again married and this time to Miss Elizabeth, daughter of Edward and Elizabeth Kimbell, of Newburyport, Massachusetts, and the nuptial ceremonies occured on February 14. Mrs. Haskell is a member of the First Presbyterian church in Baker City.

MICHAEL O'HARA.—From every quarter of the globe have come the stanch and energetic citizens of Baker county, and not least among these members are those who have been cradled among the Shamrocks of the Emerald Isle, whence have come some of the noble giants of the world. As a worthy representative of his enterprising race and a candid, stanch and prominent citizen of our county we are constrained to mention the gentleman whose life's career is now to be traced in epitome, and it is with pleasure that we are enabled to add his name to the list of distinguished citizens of Baker county.

On August 8, 1843, there was born to Michael and Helen O'Hara the subject of this sketch, the birth place being Ireland, and the parents of that nationality. About 1846 Mr. O'Hara, with his family and earthly belongings, bade farewell to friends and native scenes and embarked for the new world, where he arrived in due time without accident, and he immediately settled in New York state and there the subject of this sketch was reared and educated. When the call came for men to defend the Union, though a youth not yet twenty, he and his brother responded, enlisting in Company K, Thirteenth New York Heavy Artillery, the year being 1863, and there they did faithful service until hostilities ceased. They were detailed to serve on the army gunboat Reno, and participated in numerous skirmishes and did faithful and heavy military duty until their honorable discharge at the close of the war, the date of the laying down of arms for his company being July, 1865. Immediately following this he went to the great lakes and shipped as a sailor, where he soon rose to rank of captain, having command of a vessel in 1872-3, which was the schooner Cascade, and in 1876, of the schooner, Napoleon. In 1877 he left the waters and went to Texas, whence in 1882 he crossed the plains with teams and visited the northeastern part of Oregon, settling for a time near Milton. In 1884 he came to Baker county and here he has been since, numbered as one of the thrifty and progressive miners of the county. His home is near Weatherby and his time has been spent principally in the active operations of the search for nature's treasure vaults, with the gratifying result that he has to-day some of the valuable claims of the county, which promise to become rich producers soon. Politically Mr. O'Hara is a Republican and prominent in his community and is always active in the interests of good government and law and order. He is serving the second term as justice of the peace, where he has been placed by an appreciative and discriminating people. Fraternally he is associated with the G. A. R., U. S. Grant Post, No. 17, of Huntington, being past commander and now adjutant; with the I. O. O. F., Burnt River Lodge, No. 86; with the Eastern Gate Lodge, No. 40, Daughters of Rebekah, of which last he is a charter member. Mr. O'Hara is highly respected in the community where he lives and in the entire circle where he is known, being a man of capabilities and integrity, and is dominated by a wisdom and principles of truth that are commendable. Recently he has been selected to fill the office of postmaster at Weatherby and in this capacity he is giving entire satisfaction.

JAMES B. STODDARD.—One of the giants of local industrial achievement whose career we must now essay to outline, is a native of Utah, born January 15, 1857, the son of John and Emily (Kershaw) Stoddard. He grew to man's estate in the commonwealth of his nativity, receiving such educational advantages as the public schools afford, also a complete course in the college at Logan, Utah,

and another in Salt Lake City. Upon retiring from college, he accepted a position as principal of the high school at Wellsville, but later he engaged in the lumber business with his father and brothers in Wyoming, Utah, and Idaho, with them, supplying the lumber for the Utah Northern Railway and for the Union Pacific. In 1884, he went to Ogden, from which point as a center, he operated saw mills in various places, all of these being the property of his father and himself and brothers. He was afterwards with the Ogden Lumber & Building Company and the Rocky Mountain Lumber Company, both of Ogden, Utah.

After an active experience in the lumber business in Utah, covering a period of fourteen years, our subject sold out his interests, came to Baker City, Oregon, and before a year had passed was again in the lumbering industry in Sumpter, his partner in this venture being Thomas McEwen. Later Mr. McEwen sold to A. W. Ellis, who in turn sold to George Stoddard. A year later this last partner also withdrew, and Mr. Stoddard has conducted the business alone since. His mill has a capacity of twenty thousand feet per day, and furnishes practically all the trade of Sumpter and all the mines except those that have their own mills. Most of the materials out of which the town was built were manufactured by the plant of which our subject is the owner. He also ships large quantities of his product as far east as Wyoming and into southern Utah and Idaho.

Mr. Stoddard is extensively interested in Sumpter realty, being the owner of the hospital located there, a large share in the new hotel now being constructed, the Sumpter laundry and other property of high value, including a fine home at the foot of Main street, consisting of six acres of land and the handsomest residence in the town.

Mr. Stoddard is a past consul commander in the W. of W., of the local camp, of which he was an organizer. His marriage was duly solemnized in Utah, on January 6, 1881, Miss Esther, daughter of James A. and Catherine (Thomas) Leishman, then becoming his wife. The issue of their union is five children, Leon B., bookkeeper in his father's office; Carmen E., attending the Baker City high school; Milton A., Bessie K., and Sophia G.

It is but fair to add that our subject is as

JAMES B. STODDARD.

active in promoting the public good whenever opportunity offers as he is in building up his own business. He has ever manifested a public spirited interest in town, county, and state, himself serving as a member of the city council. He was active in securing the organization of the town, and was a candidate for the mayoralty thereof in its first election.

Of Mr. Stoddard's father we must say a word. The old gentleman and David Eccles established the Oregon Lumber Company, which has since spread out over the whole of Oregon and Utah, putting in many branch establishments, and building numerous mills. The older Mr. Stoddard built the large mill at Baker City, also the one at Hood River, and was one of the incorporators of the Sumpter Valley Railway. It is safe to say that he did more for the development of the lumber business in eastern Oregon than any other one man. He died in Utah in August, 1894, aged fifty-eight years.

JOHN SWISHER.—It is befitting that one who has braved the terrors of the unknown west in the early days and fought his way into the regions that are now the productive parts of this county, maintaining himself against all sorts of hardships and the savage raids of the cruel red men and continuing until the present time in the front ranks of those who sought for the development and advancement of this section, it is befitting, we repeat, that an epitome of his deeds be preserved, that generations who follow may read the accounts and learn what it costs to open this grand country for them to reap from. Among the very earliest settlers that turned the virgin sod of Baker county stands prominently this man whose name initiates this paragraph, and to whom we grant space for the salient points of his career in this volume.

Mr. Swisher was born in October, 1835, in the state of Pennsylvania, being the son of Jacob and Mary (Hunter) Swisher, both natives of the Keystone state, and there, also, they lie buried at the present time. In 1860 our subject stepped forth from the parental nest and began the duties and conflicts of life for himself. His first trip was the memorable one that so many of the worthy pioneers of

this region participated in, crossing the plains with ox teams. As early as 1860 was this trip made by Mr. Swisher and the Golden state was his destination, but two years later he sought out this land and settled here until 1867. Then he returned to the states and the following year again came to this region and took a squatter's claim in Eagle valley, and there devoted his energies to the improvement of the same until 1885, when he removed to his present place. During his residence in this valley he has had much trouble with the Indians, but they have ever been overmatched by the doughty and intrepid man of courage that settled here to stay, and the badge of his victory is the fact that he is here to-day spending the golden years of his life in quietness in the valley where savage cunning was so often displayed to drive him hence.

In 1872 occurred the marriage of Mr. Swisher and Miss Sarah, daughter of Thomas and Sarah Counsan. Seven years later, on November 27, Mrs. Swisher was called from the duties of life and her husband with two infants was left to do battle on the frontier alone. The two children mentioned were Anna, now wife of H. P. Swisher; and Jennie, wife of O. Potuine. Mr. Swisher did nobly and persevered through all of these hardships and troubles. To-day he owns a fine farm and is engaged in its culture and in stock raising, and his life has been such that he is greatly esteemed by his fellows, and beloved by all.

WILLIAM G. AYRE.—The citizens of Baker county have reason to be proud of the number of men who have risen from their ranks to places of distinction in the commercial and business world. Prominent among those who have found here the opportunity to achieve remarkable success in material things is he whose name forms the caption of this article. Mr. Ayre is a scion of a well known English family, and that he possesses a goodly share of the commercial spirit which has made his race a power in the world is proved by the fact that he is now reputed to be one of the wealthiest men in a county noted for its rich men. In epitomizing his life history, therefore, we enjoy such pleasure as is always ours when contemplating the battles and successes of one who has distinguished himself by the magnitude of his achievement in any line of human endeavor.

Mr. Ayre was born at Tiverton, Devonshire, England, on April 29, 1856, his parents being Thomas and Mary E. Apperley (Garnsey) Ayre, the former a native of Devonshire and the latter of Somerset. Tiverton is very notable on account of its having been for many years represented in the house of parliament by Viscount Palmerston, the eminent English statesman, and from its being the location of the celebrated Blundell's grammar school.

Our subject attended this institution seven or eight years, then went to a higher institution of learning and became a thorough Latin and Greek scholar. In 1884 he crossed the ocean to America, but instead of trying to utilize his education, he engaged in the very lucrative wool growing industry, with the result that he is now the most extensive sheep man in the county, and one of the largest in the state of Oregon. His residence and center of operations is located one mile west of Express, where he has a very elegant home. He is president of the Express Telegraph and Telephone Company.

In politics Mr. Ayre is a very strong Republican and a firm believer in protection, but he is too independent a man to be firmly tied to any party and always claims the right for himself to think independently on every proposition affecting the public weal.

The father of our subject is dead, but his mother still lives near the old home in England, which has been established for some centuries.

--- ◆◆◆ ---

JOHN H. AITKIN.—No compilation of the character of these chronicles of Baker county would be complete without a prominent place granted to the subject of this sketch, who stands to-day as one of the leading business men, not only of Baker county, but of this portion of the northwest. Fine natural capabilities, reinforced with a careful and valuable training in the commercial world, guided and controlled by a will that brooks no defeat nor pines at any obstacle, dominated by a sagacity that is keen and far-seeing, while his executive ability is in no whit behind his other excellent qualifications and with ability for handling the financial problems of the day in a safe, yet progressive manner, we have reason to expect from John H. Aitkin achievements of a substantial and mammoth character, and the results of his life's labors up to this present moment have in no way disappointed these expectations.

On August 15, 1858, in Michigan, the subject of this sketch was born to William and Elizabeth (Harley) Aitkin, both natives of Scotland, and this last fact gives us much clue to the stability and integrity that are manifest in their son. In Michigan John H. grew to manhood and received a good education from the schools, and commenced at the age of fifteen years the training that has made him so successful in his work. He first worked in a store as clerk at fifteen dollars per month and this was constantly continued until he was twenty-one years of age. At that time he went on the road as salesman and for seven years he continued in that excellent training and then started for himself in the mercantile world in Michigan. For one year he was occupied in that line and then perceiving the possibilities of the west, in 1888 he came to Baker county and located at the "Gate City," Huntington. He first took stock in the Oregon Construction Company, which operated a store at Huntington, and became manager of the store, and in that capacity he has continued since, and since 1896 he has also been president. In 1888 the old company was succeeded by the Oregon Commercial Company. His skill and ability soon became manifest and it was evident that, coupled to this, his uprightness and deferential treatment of all patrons would bring the patronage which makes success, and the facts of the years have borne this out in every respect. The Oregon Commercial Company is one of the largest mercantile establishments in the northwest and entirely exceeds any other concern in Baker county. In 1900 they sold two hundred and eleven cars of general merchandise and they were the first concern that ever shipped a train load of goods at one time to the northwest. They have ample room, having four large warehouses in addition to their salesrooms, and they do both a retail and wholesale business. In 1897 Mr. Aitkin organized the Bank of Huntington and has been its president since that time. He also organized the Huntington Lumber Company and is president of that corporation and was the first treasurer of the North West Railway Company. In addition to the houses in Huntington, the company also has a branch establishment at Durkee, and the patronage of these houses is extended far and near. The breadth of grasp, firm execution and unwearied care of detail put forth by the president and manager of these concerns, have made them the unbounded success that they are to-day. In addition to these cares and heavy responsibilities Mr. Aitkin finds time for the fraternal associations, and is prominent in the Knights of Pythias, being grand chancellor for the state of Oregon; he is also aide on the staff of Major General Carnahan, U. R. K. of P. In the Masonic fraternity Mr. Aitkin is a Knight Templar and is also a member of the A. O. U. W. and the W. of W. He served as city mayor for two years, being the oldest living mayor of the city; for three years he was treasurer of the city, holding these positions for five consecutive years, and is now chairman of the school board. In church matters Mr. Aitkin is active and besides all of his other weighty and pressing duties he gives attention to superintending the Sunday-school of the Congregational church, the institution where are his church relations. In politics Mr. Aitkin is a Republican and is frequently called on for counsel in the political matters of the county.

Mr. Aitkin and Miss Harriett M. Pike, a native of LeClaire, Iowa, were joined in the holy bands of wedlock on September 26, 1892, and the fruit of this union has been two children, J. Harold and F. Harley. It is pleasant to add that in supplementing the unbounded success that has attended the wise operations of Mr. Aitkin, there should be mentioned that he is held in high esteem by his fellows and in the business world and is respected and admired by all, having been faithful, kind and upright in all of his dealings and varied relations.

———◆◆◆———

J. D. HUNSTOCK.—The enterprising and progressive farmer and stock raiser whose career it is now our task to present in brief outline was born at East Baton Rouge, Louisiana, on November 24, 1834, being the son of William Henry and Eliza W. (Holmes) Hunstock, natives of Hamburg, Germany, and Vir-

ginia, respectively. He received a common school education, then engaged in farming, an enterprise in which he continued to seek his livelihood until 1856, when he went to clerking. He busied himself in this line of activity until the outbreak of the Civil war, then enlisted in Company B, First Louisiana Regiment, John Scott's Cavalry, and participated in many hard-fought battles and campaigns, among them Murfreesborough, Chickamauga and Richmond. At the close of hostilities he again engaged in farming at Baton Rouge, but in 1869 he sold and came out to Baker City, Oregon, making the journey to Kelton, Utah, by train and the remainder by stage.

For a year after his arrival he clerked in the store of his brother-in-law, A. H. Brown, and for the two years ensuing he worked in a quartz mill. In 1871 he purchased the place he now owns, but rented it for the first six years, he himself living upon and farming Mr. Brown's place. In 1879 he moved onto his own land, four miles west of the present Haines, where he has ever since lived, engaged in farming and stock raising. He is, as above intimated, an industrous, thrifty man and a good, progressive farmer.

On March 11, 1884, at Baton Rouge, Louisiana, Mr. Hunstock married Miss Mary, daughter of George and Caroline Cooper, and they have had four children, three of whom are still living, namely: Joseph D., Jr., Mable C. and Flavia G. Mrs. Hunstock's father was a relative of the Coopers of Revolutionary fame.

———◆◆◆———

JOHN H. TONEY.—This prosperous farmer, stockraiser and horticulturist was born in Jefferson county, Illinois, on October 4, 1858, and there he resided until seven years old, coming then across the plains with his uncle, Alfred Toney. His parents were John and Martha (Hudson) Toney and the mother died in Illinois in 1863, and the father died at the home of our subject on December 25, 1900. His father and brother had already crossed the continent to Baker county, and he joined them here, remaining with them until 1872, which year is the date of inception of his independent career. Though only fourteen years old his self-reliance was such that he feared not to face the stern battle of life, and for the ensuing twelve years he sought for mineral wealth in the mining regions of Arizona, Nevada, Idaho and Oregon. In 1886, however, he desisted from the search that he might join his brother, A. J., in dealing in and shipping horses. For more than half a decade they continued in this with fair success, but in 1890 our subject resolved upon a change of occupation, so purchased a farm five miles northwest of Haines. He now has two hundred and forty acres, having recently purchased a well improved tract adjoining his original home, upon which he now lives. He is regarded as one of the thriftiest and most progressive farmers in his neighborhood, while his life in all its relations with his fellows has been so ordered as to win for him their esteem and confidence.

Fraternally Mr. Toney affiliates with Wingville Lodge, No. 343, W. of W., and in religious persuasion he is a Methodist, his membership at present being in the First M. E. church at Haines. He was married in Weiser, Idaho, on April 9, 1881, to Victoria, a daughter of James and Lida Toney, and a native of Illinois. They have one son, Fred A.

JOHN H. RICHMOND.—Among the agriculturists and stockraisers of Baker county, the man whose name forms the caption of this article must be given a prominent and leading place. Though not one of the most extensive tillers of the soil he is one of the most thrifty, industrious, and progressive, his plan being intensive rather than otherwise, and his crops diversified rather than confined to one particular thing. As a man and citizen, also, his standing is a very enviable one.

The birthplace of our subject is Quebec, Canada, and the date of his advent into life July 11th, 1855. He lived with his parents, George and Mary Richmond, until 1879, engaged in farming while not attending school, then determined to inaugurate independent action. He worked in the woods of Minnesota and farmed in the Dakotas until 1893, when he came out to Baker county. Until two years ago, he was engaged in farming rented land, but he then bought a fine farm five miles west of Haines, and to the cultivation and improve-

ment of this he has devoted himself with assiduity and zeal ever since, the natural result being that he has excellent improvements and is very comfortably situated. He raises cattle, fruit, and various other kinds of farm products, ever studying to anticipate the market and supply that for which there is greatest demand.

In religious persuasion, Mr. Richmond is a Baptist, his membership at present being at Haines. On June 13, 1897, he married Mrs. Sarah E. Coles, widow of the late B. C. Coles, a pioneer, and daughter of August and Emma E. George, who were also very early settlers, and now reside at Haines. Mrs. Richmond had, by her former marriage, five children: Edward, who married Miss Ollie Taylor, living near Haines; Walter; Cleveland; Florence, wife of Elmer Hill, of Portland; Lulu, who died August 11, 1899. Mr. and Mrs. Richmond have one adopted daughter residing with them at present.

JOSEPH BECK.—A veritable pioneer of the pioneers and one that has ever wrought faithfully in that most commendable undertaking, opening up the frontier for the settlements from the east, a man that has served in public office, as well as energetically prosecuted private endeavor, always displaying that efficiency and unswerving integrity that commend to the confidence and esteem of his fellows, the subject of this sketch is accorded a place in these abiding records of Baker county with pleasure, and it is surely fitting that such as he should be held in honorable remembrance by the generations to follow.

Mr. Beck is the son of Christian and Elizabeth (Stamm) Beck, natives of Pennsylvania and Virginia, respectively, and he was born on March 29, 1826. In 1850 he traversed the plains with the ox team of the day and came to Hangtown, California, and engaged in mining, and in 1863 to Auburn, where he mined, after which he removed to Sparta, where he followed the same industry until the centennial year, when he settled in the Eagle valley, taking as a homestead the place where he now resides. Eighty acres of this place is devoted to fruit and grain and he has attained great success in the culture of the former, having taken prizes at the exposition at Philadelphia, among which was first prize on tomatoes.

RESIDENCE OF JOHN H. RICHMOND.

In political matters he has ever been very prominent, affiliating with the Democratic party. For two years he was elected to the position of treasurer of Baker county and has also served in several other public capacities. Mr. Beck is a veteran of the Mexican war, having served in Company A, First Illinois, for thirteen months, during which time he participated in much fighting, notably in the battle of Buena Vista.

The marriage of Mr. Beck and Miss Mary, daughter of William and Gernevia (Jackson) Lindsey, was solemnized on November 9, 1848. To them were born the following children: George A., Margaret E., William C., Anna, Joseph H., John Rolland, John Rice, all of whom have died. While Mrs. Beck was on a visit to the east, she was stricken with sickness and passed away. Thus has our subject been called to pass through an almost incredible amount of sadness and sorrow, but he has borne up well and is to-day pressing onward in the race of life with vigor.

Mr. Beck was married a second time, the lady that became his wife was Miss Mirandia, daughter of Pardon and Elizabeth (Pyburn) Williams. Our subject is a member of the Masonic fraternity, being one of the charter member of Baker City Lodge, No. 47.

JOHN J. DOOLEY.—One of the most influential and widely known men in this part of Oregon, and one of that class of men and women whose praiseworthy efforts opened this section for the advancement of civilization, the gentleman whose name iniates this paragraph is deserving of especial mention in a work of this character, since he has been intimately identified with the development and advancement of this region from a very early day until the present time.

John J. Dooley was born in Utica, Oneida county, New York, on March 14, 1838, and there passed the first sixteen years of his life. Then he came to Chicago and learned the machinist's trade and engaged as an engineer on the Galena & Chicago Union Railroad, now the Northwestern, where he remained for nine years. In 1862 he crossed the plains with ox and horse teams, settling in Auburn, then the county seat of Baker county, and a town of two thousand and five hundred inhabitants, in

August, the time of his arrival; but before the winter set in the number of people had increased to five thousand. Here he took up mining for six years and then was appointed collector of internal revenue for Idaho, and, during his incumbency in this office, two years, he resided in Idaho City. Following this he built the toll road over the mountains known as the Dooley toll road, and to the operation of this he devoted his time and energies for twenty years. It was one of the leading industries of the county and it facilitated communication with the surrounding country and was of inestimable benefit. After this work he removed to Baker City and engaged in raising sheep until six years ago, when he retired from active participation in business and sought more quiet for the golden years of his career, while he enjoys the fruit of his industry. He owns a handsome residence at 2043 Grove street in the city, where he dwells at the present time. Mr. Dooley has taken an active interest in the affairs of his county and state and city, being always allied with the Republican party. He is a member of the A. O. U. W. and has served as deputy grand master for a number of years. His interest in the welfare of this order is unflagging and he has done much to promote its advancement. He also affiliates with the I. O. O. F. When he crossed the plains there was much fighting with the Indians, but with no loss of life to the immigrants.

The marriage of Mr. Dooley and Miss Phoeba, daughter of Asa and Philura Knapp, old pioneers of Illinois, was solemnized in Chicago on December 25, 1861, and they have become the parents of the following children: Lilah, wife of Porter S. Colt of Mormon basin and it is said that she is the first white child born in Baker county, her birth being on November 3, 1862; Albert G., deceased; John F. married and in the mercantile business in Baker City; Emma, deceased; Frank R., clerking for Weil & Company of this city; Nora M., preparing for a professional nurse; Asa Knapp; Margaret A.

Mr. Dooley served as deputy sheriff in the fall of 1862 of this county and in that as in all his other public service, as well as private walk, he has ever demeaned himself with such wisdom, integrity and uprightness that he has won the confidence and esteem of all who may have the pleasure of his acquaintance.

JAMES N. HOLCOMB.—From Nimrod's day until the present there has been a certain attraction in the hunter's business that has called many men like Daniel Boone and the worthy subject of this sketch into the wilds of nature's frontiers, where they have become exceedingly expert in the chase and in opening the regions for other and slower feet to follow. In addition to this expertness acquired by our subject as a sleuth of the forest he has also gained a reputation as an expert and intrepid fighter of the savages that infested this region in the days gone by and were such a menace to civilization's progress.

Mr. Holcomb was born at Ionia, Michigan, in 1845, being the son of Gideon and Nancy (Houseman) Holcomb, natives of New York and Ohio, respectively, who also crossed the plains and took part in the development of this section till they were called to pass away, the father dying in Eagle valley and the mother in Prairie City. At the age of twenty our subject enlisted in Company A, Twenty-first Michigan Infantry, and for twenty-two months did valiant service for his country, being wounded in the arm by buckshot and in the leg with a minie ball. In 1867 he came by water to the coast and settled first in Canyon City and two years later returned to the states for his folks. In 1870 he settled in Eagle Valley and began to raise fruit, and although when he was fifty-two years old he won the gold medal for accurate shooting, he has won fully as great commendation for his efforts in the quieter field of husbandry and as an orchardist, having at the present time over four thousand bearing peach trees, besides much small fruit. He is also interested in apiarian pursuits, having two hundred colonies of the little honey gatherers. Mr. Holcomb has a fine farm, where he resides, besides other property. He is interested in political matters and has held several county offices. He is also affiliated with the G. A. R., of Pine Valley.

In 1866 Mr. Holcomb and Miss Marchy Bowen celebrated their marriage and one child, W. A. Holcomb, was the fruit of the union. At the early age of twenty-two years Mrs. Holcomb died, leaving one child and her husband to mourn her untimely demise.

The second marriage of Mr. Holcomb was with Miss Eliza Kenney, and to them were born six children: Gideon; Sarah, deceased; Maud; James, deceased; Newton, deceased; Marcy, deceased.

A third time he went to the nuptial altar, this time with Carrie Gale, daughter of ex-Governor Gale; and one child graced this union, Hazel, deceased.

Mr. Holcomb celebrated his fourth marriage when Miss Emma Kiersey became his bride and to them have been born three children: Earl, Ralph, Emily.

FREDERICK L. SHAW.—This energetic farmer and stock raiser and esteemed citizen of the county is, like many others who have achieved success in this country and won for themselves a place in the hearts of its people, a native of England, indeed, his mother belongs to one of the oldest and proudest families of Lincolnshire, the surname of which is East. Our subject was born in Nottingham on December 24, 1863. He attended the preparatory school there until ten years old; then entered Mintholm College, from which he graduated six years later, receiving his diploma at the remarkably early age of sixteen years. When eighteen he put into execution a desire long cherished of trying his fortune in the new world, and came to the United States. Locating in Nance county, Nebraska, he followed farming and stock raising there for nineteen years, at the end of which extended period of time, he came out to his present place of abode, half a mile south of Express. Immediately upon his arrival here he resumed his former occupation, farming and stock raising; and we now find him very energetically engaged in building a home for himself and family in his new location. Though his residence here has been of such short duration, he is already manifesting a public spirited interest in the local concerns, and doing what he can for the upbuilding of the new town of Express. He is the owner of a third interest in the telephone exchange there established, and is vice-president of the company.

On April 30, 1883, Mr. Shaw married Miss Grace Bennet, a native of England, and two children graced the union, Ruby, attending the Normal school at Weston, and Clare L., attending the high school at Express.

Mr. Shaw married a second time on December 29, 1893; Miss Kate Beagle, formerly of New York state, then becoming his wife; and two children have been born to them, namely: Phyllis and L. Kay.

Fraternally our subject affiliates with the Woodmen of the World and the Knights of Pythias, of the latter of which orders he is a past chancellor commander. Mr. Shaw was one of the leading spirits in building the Union church at Express, and he is a stanch supporter of the faith.

BERNARDINO J. MOURA.—Among the thriftiest and most prosperous farmers residing in the vicinity of Express is to be numbered the esteemed and trusted gentleman whose career we must now essay to epitomize. Mr. Moura is a native of the Azores Islands, born at Santa Maria, September 13, 1854, the son of Antonia and Antonia Moura, both of whom are still residents of the old home in the Azores. He continued to reside in his native town during all the years of his minority, acquiring a public school education and afterward devoting himself to the cultivation and improvement of the parental farm.

When twenty-one years of age, however, our subject emigrated to the United States, landing in Boston, Massachusetts, where he remained a short time. His next move was to Red Bluff, Shasta county, California, where he resided until 1879, coming then to Canyon City, the county seat of Grant county, Oregon. He went thence to his European home on a visit, and when he returned located half a mile south of Express, where we now find him. He has acquired three hundred and twenty acres of as desirable farm land, perhaps, as can be found anywhere in the county, and a water right that is certainly unsurpassable, Burnt river passing through the place, upon which also are numerous springs. Mr. Moura is to be congratulated on his good fortune in securing so enviable a location. He raises alfalfa hay, grain and other farm products, and has the comfortable consciousness that his land will produce almost anything, so that he can gauge his crops to suit the variations of the market.

Our subject is an active participant in political affairs, his party affiliations being with the Republicans. Fraternally he is identified with the Baker City organization of the A. O. U. W. and with Express Lodge, No. 80, K. of P. In Baker county, Oregon, Mr. Moura married Francisca M. Silver and to their union have been born four children: Antonio, Mary, Anna and Jessie, all of whom are still at home.

JOSEPH A. GEDDES.—'Tis a trait of human nature to admire those who through adversity and in spite of early difficulties and disadvantages have wrought their way to success in any line of human endeavor. It is therefore not without pleasure that we take under review the life history of him whose name appears above for he certainly has had to contend with obstacles such as beset the pathway of but few men and as certainly has he won a signal triumph.

Mr. Geddes is a native of Canal Dover, Tuscarawas county, Ohio, born November 2, 1850, his parents being Joseph and Catherine (Moore) Geddes. In 1854 the family removed to Williams county, in the subscription and public schools of which he received a meager education. When he was nine years old, his father died, leaving a family of twelve children, so youthful though he was, he had to begin life's battle on his own account. He worked on the farms in his neighborhood at whatever he could get to do. Though his earning capacity increased, of course, as he grew older, he continued in the same line of activity, namely, farm work, until he reached his majority, then he came west by railroad to Kelton, Utah, thence by stage to Baker City, Oregon. For the first two years after his arrival he sought his fortune in mining, but he then determined to try the surer business of farming and stock raising, so he purchased two hundred and forty acres of land about four miles north of town. He followed these kindred industries until 1889, in which year he left his farm in other hands and himself engaged in the meat market business in the town. Two years later William Pollman bought in with him, forming the firm of Geddes & Pollman. Mr. Geddes still owns the old home place and the firm to which he belongs has title to about twelve hundred acres in the county, upon which mammoth domain a large number of cattle find pasture. The firm is also the owner of considerable city property.

Thus it will be seen that from a very humble beginning Mr. Geddes has wrought his way until he has gained a place of no little prominence and power in the commercial world. It must not be supposed, however, that business success is the only form of achievement which has been his. He has ever been quite a potent factor in the progress and development of his section, taking a lively interest in the affairs of county and state, and for a number of years he has served as a member of the city council.

Fratrnally our subject is affiliated with the local lodges of the I. O. O. F. and the A. O. U. W. His marriage was solemnized in the state of Indiana on February 19, 1871, on which date Miss Eva J. Freligh became his wife. Their union has been blessed by the advent of six children: Frank A., county clerk of Baker county; Ora H., William E., J. Logan, deceased; Eva M.; Josephine, deceased.

TAYLOR N. SNOW, M. D.—This distinguished gentleman needs no introduction to the people of Baker county and no words of ours could in any measure enhance the esteem in which he is held by the people nor serve to commend the ability and skill and integrity that are already well known and appreciated by all who have the privilege to know him.

Dr. Snow is the county physician and coroner and holds his offices in the Crabill building. He was born in Portland, Indiana, on July 4, 1835, being the son of James and Susan A. Snow. His father was born in Boston in 1754 and served through the Revolution and the war of 1812. His mother died when he was born and his father, when he was eight years of age, and he early began a life of roving adventure traveling by stage coach to most of the important cities of the United States and by working his way on board ships made the tour of the principal seaports of the world. In 1851 he settled down to the study of theology, intending to enter the ministry of the Methodist Episcopal church, and to this end he entered Asbury University. Later he relinquished this purpose and commenced the study of medicine in the medical college of Louisville, Kentucky, but completing the course before he was twenty-one was refused his de-

gree, still he entered on the practice of his profession before he had reached his majority. From 1856 to 1858 he lectured on physiology and phrenology in addition to his practice. In 1859 he started on foot from Des Moines, Iowa, to California, and in due time he landed at Santa Rosa in the Golden state. During the toilsome journey he experienced many perilous adventures, encountered hostile Indians, met Horace Greeley, General Albert Sydney Johnston, and other historical characters. From 1860-4, he practiced medicine in San Francisco, and at the same time conducted a drug store. For about two years, he was assistant surgeon in the city and county hospital. In 1861-2 he attended two courses of lectures at the Cooper Medical College of San Francisco and at the time of the gold excitement in Idaho in 1864 he went thither and was appointed county coroner and physician of Alturas county in that territory, but he soon returned to California to take a further course of lectures at the state university, following which he repaired to Corvallis, Oregon, and practiced medicine during 1865-6 and then came to Baker City the next year. From that time until 1876, he held the offices of county coroner and physician of Baker county and at the same time he also acted as surgeon for the Idaho and Oregon Stage Company. He then practiced medicine for a brief period in Susanville, California, and then again attended a course of lectures at the Cooper Medical College, taking a degree from that instition on November 2, 1876. On July 2, 1876, the Eclectic Medical Society of California awarded him a certificate of honor upon examination and a similar token of merit was awarded him by the state board of medical examiners on March 21, 1877, and the Doctor also holds certificates from the state medical boards of Colorado and Oregon dated respectively 1881 and 1892. From his work at the Cooper Medical College he went to Reno, Nevada, and there practiced medicine until 1880, following which he gave himself to his profession in Gennison, Colorado, for one year, where also he was surgeon for the Barlow and Sanderson Stage Company, and medical officer with the rank of major on the staff of Brigadier-General Curtis. He also practiced in Bellevue, Idaho, where he was health officer

Taylor N. Snow,

of the city, and now for nearly twenty years he has been well known and highly appreciated as a leading physician in this city. Since 1882 he has been examining surgeon for the government and in 1887 he was appointed examining surgeon with the rank of lieutenant-colonel, in the Oregon State Militia on the staff of General Comston and here he served for eight years. He is also surgeon for the U. P. Railroad, chief surgeon for the S. V. R. R. Company, and the S. V. L. Company and chief medical examiner of the N. Y. Equitable Life Insurance Company. He has been elected county coroner and physician a number of times. He enjoys a very lucrative practice and has performed some of the most difficult and delicate surgical operations known to the profession.

The Doctor is a charter member and organizer of the A. O. U. W. and has twice represented the local organization in the grand lodge. He joined the I. O. O. F. twenty-six years ago in Baker City and also belongs to the Rebekah degree. He was a charter member and the first presiding officer of the Queen City Camp, No. 48, W. of W., and a charter member of the auxiliary of this order. He also belongs to the Foresters of America, the M. W. A., the Royal Neighbors, Order of Pendo, and American Order of Protection. He is medical examiner, physician and surgeon for the Court of Foresters and medical examiner for the A. O. U. W., the W. of W., the M. W. A., the Order of Pendo, the American Order of Protection, the Ladies Maccabees, and the Royal Neighbors of America. He owns a pleasant home in the city and many property interests in various places.

The marriage of Dr. Snow and Miss Susan A., daughter of Hon. Charles Chandler, was solemnized in this city and they have become the parents of three children: Dr. Charles V., deceased; Dr. Frederick, deceased; Jesse B., with his father in the office.

ARTHUR T. MERWIN.—The bushaway, the *courrier de bois*, and the voyageur live now only in history. The prospector with his "grub stake," his roll of blankets and his pony, has well nigh completed his work in this

country, and the stage driver and freighter have given place to the gladiators of steel and iron which swiftly draw their tons of burden over the paths of steel. Interesting, indeed, are the accounts furnished us of the age of poetry and romance preceding this age of railroads, telegraphs and telephones and it is ever a pleasure to meet with one who has outlived his generation and who brings into the present personal recollections of the wild, romantic past. Such a man is he whose name forms the caption of this article.

Mr. Merwin is a typical frontiersman and knight of the plains and in him have been developed in a high degree the best traits of character to be found in the honored pioneer. He was born in Morgan county, Ohio, on a farm near McConnelsville on June 24, 1840, his parents being Edwin and Susan (Jenkins) Merwin, natives of the Buckeye state. When twelve years old he accompanied the remainder of the family to Illinois, and four years later he moved with them to the vicinity of Lawrence, Kansas, where his home was until he arrived at the age of nineteen. Farm life developed his physical powers and spirit of manly independence, but of intellectual discipline he received little. His education had to be acquired afterward in the stern battle of life.

In 1859 he gave inception to his career of adventure by accepting employment as a teamster on the plains. After two years he was promoted to a position as wagon master and at the same time he became part owner in a train of freight wagons. Twenty-six wagons, he tells us, three hundred and twelve head of cattle and five mules constituted a train or full outfit. During the nine years ensuing he busied himself in freighting from Fort Leavenworth to Santa Fe, New Mexico; Denver, Colorado; Camp Douglas, Utah, Fort Laramie, Wyoming; and other points, and during all the years of this service except, perhaps, one or two, the Indians were hostile. He and his men had many serious adventures with the red skins and at one time our subject was the only man in the train who effected his escape. Mr. Merwin was a personal friend of the noted Kit Carson and was quite intimately acquainted with many other famous western scouts. He was present at Carson's death in 1867.

In 1868 our subject sold his teaming outfit

and came across the plains with mule teams
to Oregon. He located on the lower Powder
river, of the valley of which he is the first settler, taking as a homestead one hundred and
sixty acres of land. Later he purchased anotl.-
er quarter section adjoining and upon this,
his original home in the far west, he resided uninterruptedly until March of the present year
(1901), engaged for the most part in stock
raising. Then, however, he moved to 2305
Third street, Baker City, and retired from the
active pursuits of life.

A leader in the ushering in of civilization in
the west Mr. Merwin has been very active also
in public affairs since the country has been
organized and government fully established.
He served on a school board in Union county
consecutively for fourteen years and three times
afterward he was elected but refused to qualify. He has helped in numerous other ways
to established a good public school system, especially by assisting in the erection of school
houses. For four years he was deputy county
assessor in Union county, and he now holds a
like position here.

Fraternally our subject is affiliated with
Baker City Lodge, No. 25, I. O. O. F. He
was married at Lawrence, Kansas, April 6,
1866, the lady being Miss Celestia P. Wait, a
native of New York. They have had three
children, but two of them, Eugene and Charles
C., died in infancy. The third, Helen M., is
at home with her parents. She is a graduate
of the Baker City high school and is now engaged in teaching in Baker county.

THOMAS ROACH.—It is with pleasure
that we are enabled to chronicle here the life
record of the successful farmer and merchant
whose name appears above. While he is not,
so far as we are informed, one of those who
are especially ambitious for leadership and
great personal influence among his fellow men,
his integrity and inherent worth have won for
him the confidence and esteem of his neighbors
generally, and his standing in the community
is a very enviable one. With this brief pre-
view we shall address ourselves to the task of
epitomizing his career.

Mr. Roach was born on January 5, 1867,
near the town of Chilton, Calumet county, Wis-

consin, his parents being Edmund and Bridget
(Lynch) Roach. He continued to reside under
the parental roof until twenty years old, attending school most of the time until his fifteenth year had been completed. About the
year 1887 he moved to the northern part of
the state and engaged in the lumbering industry there, continuing in the same for two
years, after which he went to Santa Clara valley, in California. Conditions there seem to
have been not exactly to his liking for soon
he moved north to Puget sound, and thence to
Baker county, where he arrived in the spring
of 1890. Since his arrival here he has followed
mining some, but has given the major part of
his attention to farming and merchandising.
At the present time he is proprietor of a fine.
well stocked mercantile establishment at Weatherby, where he also has a good two-hundred-
and-forty-acre farm, a part, at least, of which
has been brought to a high state of cultivation
and has been well improved, its products being
fruit, hay and vegetables. Mr. Roach is justly
regarded as one of the leading and most progressive and enterprising citizens of Wetherby.

On March 28, 1892, our subject married
Miss Henrietta, daughter of E. F. and Mary
E. (Neymeyer) Foersterling, and they have
three children, Emmett, Ralph and Lenora.
For the seven years prior to the spring of 1901
Mrs. Roach served as postmistress in her
neighborhood.

GEORGE H. FOSTER.—It is with pleasure that we incorporate here a brief review of
one who can lay claim to sonship of the wild
and varied west and who has grown up to a
manhood which reflects credit upon the section in whose institutions his character was
formed and developed. Our subject's eyes first
looked out upon the light of day in the vicinity
of Florence, Nez Perce county, Idaho, he being, of course, the son of pioneer parents. His
father, James B., had crossed the plains in
1847, and his mother Elizabeth Foster, nee
Henderson, had made her way over the same
toilsome journey sometime in the early fifties.
Their birthplaces were respectively the states
of Iowa and Missouri.

Our subject was born January 6, 1866. In
1870 he was brought by his parents to Baker

county, of which his father, a Baptist minister, was elected the first school superintendent. The family owned and occupied what is now the county poor farm. After a residence of about five years here, they returned to Idaho, locating in Boise, where Mr. Foster received the major part of his ducational discipline. After leaving the Boise high school he served an apprenticeship in the handicraft of the printer, but he seems to have cared but little for that business, for soon we find him engaged in the railway mail service. To this six years of his life were devoted then he received an appointment as postmaster at Baker City, and for the ensuing three years he served as such with great faithfulness and efficiency. The next two years were given to the bakery business, he being proprietor of the City bakery, but in 1895 he was summoned by the franchises of the people to the office of city treasurer, where he is still efficiently serving. In 1898 he accepted the post of deputy county recorder, the duties of which are now being discharged by him in conjunction with the city treasurership. Mr. Foster brings to the work in which he is now engaged the same conscientiousness and painstaking thoroughness which have ever characterized him in both public and private life, and which have won him confidence and esteem from all who have known him intimately.

In that excellent fraternal organization, the I. O. O. F., our subject is a very active worker. He has passed through all the chairs in the subordinate lodge, and once was elected to an office in the grand body, to which he has many times been a delegate. Like most residents in a rich mining region, Mr. Foster is personally interested in the search for mineral wealth and in the process of its production. He owns some valuable properties in the Granite country.

GEORGE MOORE.—A worthy representative of that noble class, the pioneers, that pushed their way into these regions and subdued the savages and overcame the obstacles and difficulties that beset the path, Mr. Moore deserves mention in this work, and also because he has wrought here with a faithfulness and energy that have been instrumental in aiding very materially in the development of the county and the adjacent country.

George Moore was born in Trumbull county, Ohio, on July 26, 1834, being the son of Harvey and Phoebe Moore. His early life was spent on a farm and in attending common school during portions of each year until he was eighteen years of age, and then the adventurous spirit aroused by the tidings from the golden west determined him to try his fortune in these regions, and accordingly he came to California with an ox train, consuming six months in the trip. He landed in Vulcan mining camp and immediately began what proved to be his life's work, mining. In the early 'sixties he went to the camps about Florence and Elk City, Idaho, then returned to California and went to Virginia City, later to Diamond City, Montana, then in 1868 came to Baker county. Here he has made his home since and has constantly been occupied in mining. He has owned some valuable claims and has been a leader in his line for many years, having both the energy and the experience with the ability required for this position. At the present time he is still actively interested in mining and working some claims in the county. Fraternally Mr. Moore is affiliated with the I. O. O. F., Lodge No. 26, of Baker City, and he enjoys the honor of being past grand. Mr. Moore has so demeaned himself that he has won the entire regard and confidence of the people and is held in high esteem, while the golden years of his life are being spent in the associations of many friends.

ALFRED CAVINESS.—It is with pleasure that we are enabled to incorporate here a brief review of the honored pioneer and esteemed citizen whose name gives caption to this article. He has long been regarded as a man of integrity and worth, and in all his relations with his fellow men during the many years of his residence in Baker county, his life has been in every respect so ordered as to entitle him to the confidence of the people and to secure him their esteem.

Mr. Caviness is a native of Indiana, born October 12, 1840, being the son of John and Susan (Poe) Caviness, natives of North Carolina, and Indiana was his home until fourteen years old. He then accompanied the remainder of the family to Henry county,

Iowa, where he farmed until 1865. He then crossed the plains to Baker county, making the journey with oxen, as the custom of the time was, and settled on a spot within sight of his present place of abode, six miles west of Baker City. During the first two years of his residence in the west, he followed freighting from Umatilla Landing to the various mining camps, then he farmed in the Powder river valley for about three years, after which he engaged in placer mining in McCord's gulch. For several years he devoted his energies to this, but in 1897 he purchased eighty acres, where he now resides and engages in farming and stock raising. He follows the diversified plan, believing it better to till intensively a small tract rather than to farm superficially a large area.

In religious persuasion Mr. Caviness is a Methodist, his membership at present being in the M. E. church at Pocahontas. He was married August 3, 1862, in Henry county, Iowa, to Sarah P. Elliot, the daughter of George and Dorcas Elliot, and to their union eight children have been born, namely: George, a resident of Pleasant Valley; John, residing in Baker City; Bert, living on Burnt river; Sidney, a resident of Baker City; Frank, working in the Elkhorn mine; Fred, at home; Pink; Annie, attending high school at Baker City.

WARREN H. TOBIN.—It is with especial pride and pleasure that we are enabled to chronicle the career of the intrepid frontiersman and valiant defender of the early settlements whose name appears at the head of this paragraph, since his life of uprightness and faithfulness has placed him as an object of confidence and esteem from his fellows and also since he has been one of the men that opened this section to the settlement of the white men, having been one of those characters that are ever in the lead.

His parents were John and Eliza (McNealy) Tobin, natives of Kentucky, who moved to Platte county, Missouri, where they remained until the day of their death. At the early age of seventeen our subject left the shelter of the parental tree and met the battles of life alone. He first crossed the plains with ox teams to Hangtown, in California, where he

gave his attention to mining, meeting with much trouble from the Indians at a place called Ash Hollow and also at another point, named Soda Springs. In 1861 he came to Florence, a mining district two hundred miles northeast from Eagle valley. From there he came to Eagle valley and he enjoys the honor of being the first white man that traversed its rich fields, where he soon after settled. Here he married the daughter of the esteemed and beloved Governor Gale. This governor was the first man to organize civil government in the state and his wise methods and faithfulness in administering justice won him friends from all law abiding citizens, while to those that were not law abiding his name was a terror. He married an Indian woman by the name of Eliza, and it is recorded that she is still living on the Umatilla Indian reservation, and her descendants are among the leading people of the land, lawyers, bankers and law-makers being among the number, and it is recorded that one of her granddaughters was regarded in Washington society as one of the handsomest women in that great city.

Our subject is the owner of the well known mines, Alpine No. 1, and Alpine No. 2, which are properties of merit. He is a man of ability and stanch principles, and is regarded by all as one of the most substantial citizens of the county. And true it is that to these worthy pioneers that are all too soon passing away, we owe a debt of gratitude that time is too short to repay, since it is to their masterful efforts and wisdom and daring that we are indebted for the grand country that we now possess in this rich county.

ASA L. BROWN.—The prosperous farmer and esteemed citizen whose name forms the caption of this review, has the distinction of being a native of Baker county, and by his industry and thrift he is reflecting credit upon the section which witnessed his birth. He was born in Auburn, April 16, 1864, his father being A. H. Brown, the distinguished statesman who for several years represented Baker county in the upper and lower houses of the state legislature.

Our subject lived in Baker county until 1874, then accompanied the remainder of the family to Salem, whither his father went in consequence of his having been elected state treasurer. This gave Mr. Brown an excellent opportunity to complete his education in the well known Willamette University, in which he continued to study until 1879. Returning then to the parental farm, five miles west of Haines, he has lived there continuously since, except for two years, during which time he was handling stock in Wallowa county, where he took a homestead. He now has a very excellent farm in the vicinity of Haines, well improved, and abundantly supplied with buildings and equipment. He follows the diversified plan, rearing cattle, hay and whatever products he believes the market will most demand. It is no exaggeration to say that he is one of the most thrifty and progressive farmers in the county, of which he is also a representative and leading citizen. Public spirited and benevolently disposed, he takes a vital interest in political matters and in everything for the promotion of the general welfare, his interest in the cause of education finding manifestation in the faithfulness with which he discharges his duties as chairman of the board of trustees of his home district.

At Wingville, on March 25, 1890, our subject married Miss Catherine, a daughter of Levi and Catherine Benson, and they have four children, all at home, namely: Albert Lee, Cornelius J., Francis R. and Routherford A.

FREDERICK A. BOHNA.—This energetic and successful miner and fruit raiser, residing on Sisley creek, three miles north of Weatherby, is a son of Christian and Mary Bohna, born on March 14, 1844, in Hempstead county, Arkansas. When he was a very small child the family removed to Missouri, but shortly afterward they returned to Arkansas, where our subject passed his early youth and acquired his educational discipline, the same consisting of such as was to be obtained by attending the local public school during a few months of each year. In the year 1859 our subject, accompanied by his father, made the long journey across the plains to Bakersville, California, traveling, as was the custom in those days, with ox teams. There he followed farming and mining. In 1862 the father came north to Canyon City, Oregon, thence

to Auburn, in Baker county, where he was joined by our subject two years later.

From Auburn Mr. Bohna went to the Boise basin, but returning soon afterward to Baker City, he there established himself in the bakery business, a line of activity in which he continued for about seven years. Coming then to his present place of abode he secured a very desirable tract of land, and engaged in fruit raising, and he now has a fine, large orchard, producing an abundance of apples, peaches, pears and other varieties of fruit. He still retains his old enthusiasm for mining and is the owner of some promising properties.

A public spirited citizen, our subject has ever manifested an active interest in the political welfare of his county and state, supporting the tenets of the Democratic party. His solicitude for the maintenance of a good school in his neighborhood has found an unmistakable manifestation in his having served with faithfulness for twelve years as director of his district. In fraternal affiliations he is a Mason.

In 1875 our subject married Miss Martha A., a daughter of James A. and Sarah Dorsett, and to them have been born seven children, namely: Henry L., deceased; Birdie L., William F., Maggie L., Minnie A., Sadie, deceased and Elsie, deceased.

A. G. WALDRON.—It has been said that the mingling of all the races under the sun has produced the American nation, the leading type of humanity on the face of the earth to-day. True it is, that the Americans lead to-day, and true it is that there are within the borders of the United States representatives from every nation under the sun, but whether the admixture has caused the development of the race, or the free institutions founded here by stanch men of wisdom have brought out the latent talents of those privileged to exist under their benign influence, is a question; but it is a pleasure to find in every walk of life noble men, of fine ability and unbounded energy as the subject of this sketch, who trace their ancestry to the other side of the ocean, but who are the very substantial supporters and organizers of our excellent institutions.

Mr. Waldron was born in Butte county, California, in 1858, being the son of Charles and Levinia (Balsam) Waldron, natives, respectively, of England and France. The father came to the Golden state around Cape Horn and engaged in mining through that section and also over Idaho and Oregon, being a typical pioneer and frontiersman. At Sparta, this state, he was called to leave the scenes of his labors and enter upon his rewards. The mother died in Washington. Our subject was early forced to try the hardships of life, even at the age of nine years commencing for himself. He worked first in the salmon canneries, then followed mining for a time and finally gave himself to the blacksmith trade. In 1874 he came to Sparta and there mined for a time, and 1890 was the date that he settled in Eagle Valley, opening a blacksmith shop near Newbridge postoffice, where he is now beating the anvil to the time of honest industry.

Mr. Waldron and Miss Clara, daughter of Joseph Bowlby, a native of Iowa, were married in 1889 and they have become the parents of three children, Latteen, Francis, Lucille, all at home. Mr. Waldron is fraternally affiliated with the I. O. O. F., Eagle Valley Lodge, No. 123, and with the K. of P., Lodge No. 79. He is a man of broad public spirit and actively interested in all that is for the welfare of the community and county.

＊＊＊

BYRON GALE.—The energetic and successful wool grower and esteemed citizen of Baker county whose life history it is now our pleasant task to present in brief review, was born in Windsor, Canada, just across the line from Detroit, Michigan, on May 8, 1859. His parents, Benjamin and Caroline (Thornton) Gale, who are natives, respectively, of Canada and the state of Pennsylvania, moved to Michigan, Oakland county, in 1869, and he accompanied them. The family resided on a farm near the village of Rochester for a few years, then lived at Caseville on Saginaw Bay until 1877, in which year they moved to Texas and engaged in farming. To this basic industry they devoted their energies until 1883, when they crossed the plains to Baker county, Oregon.

Our subject, however, remained in Texas until 1885, employed during a portion of this time at least on the stock ranch of General Talbot. In early youth he had learned the trade of a cigar maker and had worked at it some, but the skill which proved most valuable to him in after life was that which resulted from his study of music. He was an expert cornetist and his services were frequently called into requisition by theatres in large cities.

In 1885 Mr. Gale came out to Baker county and turned his attention to the wool growing industry. He took on shares a band of sheep belonging to Mr. Swift, but this first venture proved disastrous and he was compelled, in consequence of losses sustained, to engage in work for wages. In 1888, in company with his father and his brother Albion, he purchased a band of six hundred sheep, and his interest in these formed the entering wedge into a business which has proven very profitable. At present Mr. Gale is the owner of about two thousand head. He resides in a fine home at 2533 Tenth street, Baker City, consisting of a comfortable, commodious and tastefully furnished house and three town lots. His standing in the community in which he lives is one of which he has reason to be proud. The confidence and esteem of his neighbors are manifested in many ways, but find more particular expression in their having elected him councilman from his ward. Active and public spirited, he has ever manifested a deep interest in the political affairs of city and county and a disposition to do what he could for the promotion of the general welfare.

The marriage of our subject was duly solemnized in Baker City, on October 3, 1894, Miss Minnie J. McAulay then becoming his wife. They have one child, Henry C. Mrs. Gale is a member of the Methodist church of Baker City. Her parents, Arthur K. and Nancy McAulay, natives of Michigan, are also residents of this city.

＊＊＊

JOHN S. LIVINGSTON.—Few men enjoy the good will of the community in which they live to a greater extent than does he whose career it is now our task to present in brief and necessarily incomplete resume. Our subject is a native of Union Star, De Kalb county, Missouri, born April 19, 1858, the son of DeWitt C. and Mary E. (Landers) Livingston. He worked on his father's farm until grown, enjoying the advantage of the local public school for a short interval out of each year, and when the time arrived for him to inaugurate independent action and to begin for himself the battle of life, he engaged in farming on the place adjoining the parental homestead. He continued to busy himself thus until 1889, in which year he emigrated to Baker county, Oregon, located in the vicinity of Express, and resumed his farming and stock raising. In 1890 he sold his farm, moved into town and engaged in the business in which we now find him, namely, that of a cigar and liquor merchant.

Mr. Livingston was married at Union Star, Missouri, on August 30, 1887, the lady of his choice being Miss Lizzie, daughter of Meredith B. and Elizabeth (Larkin) Taylor and to their union one child has been born, Alice May, at present attending school in Express.

Mrs. Livingston's father was a "forty-niner" in California, but after searching for gold there for several years, and finding some, he returned to his home in Missouri, where her mother still lives.

IRA B. BOWEN, deceased.—It is now our pleasant task to outline in brief the very useful and active career of one of Baker county's pioneer citizens and one who, during the years of his residence therein, has actively engaged in numerous enterprises, the effect of which was to increase its wealth and promote its material prosperity. While Mr. Bowen was not one to seek for personal aggrandizement or political preferment he belonged to that large army of progressive, industrious men who form the real strength of the great commonwealth of Oregon, toiling unostentatiously in various fields of endeavor and contributing toward the general progress in a degree of which they themselves, perhaps, have little conception.

Our subject was born in the vicinity of Ypsylanti, Michigan, May 28, 1825, his parents being Zolvia and Ann (Matthews) Bowen, natives of the Empire state. He was early taken to New York state, in the public schools of which he received his educational discipline. When he reached the age of eighteen he became second engineer on the steamer Edith, which

plied between Buffalo, New York and Chicago. After two years' service he was promoted to the post of first engineer, and he served as such until, some three or four years later, when his vessel was wrecked, sinking so rapidly that her crew had but three or four minutes in which to effect their escape.

Our subject then accepted a position as locomotive engineer on the Galena & Chicago Union Railway, now the Northwestern, and after three years had been spent in that he was made master mechanic. He continued to discharge the duties of this responsible position until 1862, when he resigned that he might be free to come west and try his fortunes in Baker county, Oregon. He crossed the plains in a train made up of both ox and horse teams and consisting largely of his own relatives. They were very fortunate in crossing the wide prairies and traversing the mountain passes in that they had no trouble with the Indians, though the trains just ahead of them lost heavily in conflicts with the reds.

Upon reaching his destination Mr. Bowen located at Auburn, where, the same year, in company with a Mr. Leveridge, he purchased a sawmill. This was the first mill of its kind operated by steam which was ever imported into the country. They ran it at Auburn until May, 1863, then removed it to Idaho City, where they kept it in operation both at night and day steadily for about fifteen months. At the end of that period Mr. Bowen sold his interest and returned to Auburn, where he embarked in the mercantile business in company with E. P. Cranston. The firm later established a branch store at Clark's creek. Having sold his interest in 1868, he moved with his family to Salem, where he was engaged in a like business for the ensuing three years. Returning then to Baker City he established here a mercantile business, putting in a store also at Sparta and purchasing, as a species of side issue, the Eagle Canal Company's water ditch. In 1880 he sold out and invested a portion of the proceeds in the Arlington hotel, of which he was proprietor until the date of his death, May 11, 1881.

Mr. Bowen always manifested a vital interest in the political and general welfare of his town and county, and to him belonged the honor of having been chairman of the first city council. He was married in Chicago, January

2, 1850, the lady being Miss Anna Dooley, daughter of Mark and Anora (Seymour) Dooley, and to their union the following children have been born, namely: Lilah, wife of E. P. Cranston, of Baker county; Catherine A., wife of Judge Miller; Amelia, wife of J. W. Virtue; Mary, deceased; Francis A., in Portland; Ira B., Jr., editor of the Morning Democrat; J. Frederick, deceased; Ned; Edward C.; Harry S.; Clinton; deceased; Edith E.; Ella A., wife of J. T. Anderson, of Boise, Idaho; and J. Clifford. Mrs. Bowen has a very pleasant home at 1667 Washington street and some other city property, also a fine farm of four hundred and forty acres about three miles south of Baker City.

JAMES H. BUTTERFIELD.—The gentleman whose name heads this article, is one of those men who has spent his life in the vanguard of civilization, laboring for the development and opening up of the regions where his lot has been cast, ever operating with a skill and energy and faithfulness that have placed him as one of the substantial leaders of his fellows.

The birth of Mr. Butterfield was in 1831, in the state of New York, being the son of Zimeny and Fillitta- (Powell) Butterfield, natives, respectively, of New Hampshire and Pennsylvania. They came to Illinois in an early day and settled on a farm that is now embraced in the city of Chicago. At the age of seventeen years our subject went to the Wisconsin river lumber region and operated as a lumberman for a number of years, then he returned to Chicago and remained there until 1859, when he made the weary journey from there to California across the plains with horse teams. Hangtown, in the Golden state, was the first point at which he arrived and there he commenced mining and at that industry he has continuously been engaged since. In 1881 he came to Eagle valley and since that time his home has been there. He is the owner of some valuable properties in Maiden gulch near the Powder river, where he has done considerable work. To one unaccustomed to mining, the work that is necessary to open up a vein in nature's vaults might seem inconsiderable, but to the initiated. it speaks volumes that one

has opened a mine and put a property on the producing list by the labor of his own hands, and to whom, more than to these same hardy and intrepid prospectors and developers do we owe that in Baker county have been opened some of the most valuable mines in the world? Surely the tribute that is generally paid to these doughty and faithful men is all too small, for had it not been for their herculean labors the vaults of nature would be as securely locked to-day as ever since the time that the glittering mineral was first placed there for our use. As a real leader among this class stands the subject of this sketch, and his faithfulness is recognized by all and he enjoys the confidence of his fellows in an unlimited measure.

Mr. Butterfield has become the father of two children: Chauncy J. and Lila M.

AVON S. LOVE.—Among the representative men of his section mention must be made of the worthy gentleman and stanch man of principle and loyal citizen whose name initiates this paragraph, since he is one of the foremost men of this region and one of the heaviest property owners, having acquired his holdings by his energy, industry and wise management of the resources of the time, being a fair specimen of the sons of the west, having been born in Eagle valley, and there he has wrought out the success that is so justly his.

Avon S. Love was born in 1866, being the son of David S. and Marion (Stewart) Love, and in Eagle valley he received the education that fitted him for the battles of life and as soon as he had finished this training, and in fact while he was going to school, he began to take part in the affairs of the farm and the management of the stock with such display of energy and wisdom that it was evident that success would very soon crown his efforts. His parents were natives of Pennsylvania and in 1852 they started across the plains with ox teams, but long before their arrival to the longed-for haven their oxen nearly all died and most of the immigrants were forced to walk and they also suffered greatly from lack of food. Finally they reached Eugene and settled in that section and gave their attention to farming until 1861, when they removed to

AVON S. LOVE.

Auburn in this county and commenced to operate in the mines. Later they removed to Eagle valley and took up government land, having the enviable distinction of being the first settlers in this favored spot. The father was a man of sound principles and well informed and active in political matters, and during the heated times of the Civil War he with one other was prominent by being the only ones that held for the Union. At such a time as this he was theatened with hanging if he did not remove from the country. He was not to be so easily frightened and it is pleasant to note that he remained until he died a natural death at a good ripe age, on November 9, 1895. The mother died on August 2, 1872, both remaining in the Lower Powder valley until the time of their departure, having come there in 1871. Our subject remained with his parents until their demise and then bought his present mammoth estate of nine hundred and twenty acres, where he devotes his entire attention to farming and stock raising. Mr. Love has just completed an elegant residence on his home place and the other improvements are commensurate therewith, an air of thrift and enterprise pervading the whole premises. He also owns the old homestead of two hundred and eighty acres in Lower Powder valley. In fraternal affiliations, Mr. Love is associated with the Masons, Woodmen of the World, and A. O. U. W., all of Baker City.

The marriage of Mr. Love and Miss Margaret, daughter of W. W. and Mariah (Cushman) Crews, was solemnized in 1889, and the fruit of the union is as follows: Clyde C., Jennette, Vernon C.

Mr. Love is esteemed by all who know him and his life has been fraught with such wisdom and faithfulness that he has the confidence of the entire community, which is manifested by the fact that he is almost constantly kept in public office.

CHARLES L. LOW.—Among the sons of Baker county who are reflecting credit upon the place of their birth and the institutions that molded their characters is the enterprising and thrifty farmer and stock raiser whose name forms the caption of this review, and it is with pleasure that we are enabled to accord him representation here as one who has, by his past achievement, given promise of a career of honor and usefulness.

Mr. Low was born on the parental homestead, seven miles west and a little north of Express, on September 7, 1871, being the son of Leonard and Malinda V. (Moss) Low. He attended the local public schools and for a time enjoyed the advantages of the graded schools in Baker City, then worked at home, acquiring a knowledge of farming and stock raising, of inestimable value to him in after life. For about a decade he has been engaged in this dual occupation on his own account, achieving a very enviable success. He now has a very well improved place, supplied with all needed buildings, fences and other equipments and stocked with quite a herd of cattle and some horses. His energy and good judgment, coupled with an intimate knowledge of his business, have enabled him to win success in his calling, and his integrity and many other good qualities as a man have gained him the confidence and good will of those who know him.

On August 17, 1898, in Baker county, Oregon, our subject married Miss Lyda, daughter of William and Ann C. Stewart, of Marshalltown, Iowa, and to their union has been born one child, Frederick C.

Mr. Low's father was a very early pioneer of Oregon, having emigrated from the state of Maine in 1859. Eighteen hundred and sixty-two is the date of his location in Baker county, and here his home was until May 20, 1893, when he passed to the great beyond. Our subject's mother is living in Baker City at present.

MILO BEGGS.—This enterprising and industrious young man has the distinction of being a son of Oregon, his birthplace being Jacksonville, Jackson county, and the date December 13, 1873. When eleven years old he accompanied his parents to California, but two years later the entire family returned to Jacksonville, where the ensuing quadrennium was passed. Coming then to Baker county, he went to work at stage driving, continuing to busy himself thus for the ensuing seven years. About four years ago he purchased the livery business of J. H. Parker & Son, and about a year and a half ago he admitted his brother, Ellis, to partnership therein. They are now enjoying a very extensive patronage, using in their business about seventy-five horses and about forty excellent single and double rigs. Mr. Beggs is also a stock raiser and deals quite extensively in horses. He is a very energetic and worthy young man, and enjoys the respect and good will of his community and city.

CALVIN EASTABROOKS.—This venerable pioneer of the Pacific coast is deserving of rank among the greatest benefactors of Baker county, many of whose most famous mines were discovered and developed by him. In the course of his long career he has had some exciting experiences with the red men, in one foray receiving a wound in the ankle, from which he never fully recovered. Notwithstanding his many discoveries of gold mines and his distinguished services in the development of this section, he is not rich in worldly treasure, but he is rich in the consciousness of having been a blessing to his race and is held in lasting honor by those who know him as one who has ever "stood foursquare to every wind," always acting with integrity and uprightness in the varied relations of life.

Our subject was born in Hamilton county, Ohio, on April 21, 1822, the son of John and Lucy Eastabrooks. He was reared on a farm, attending school during short intervals yearly, and when he became old enough farming became his settled occupation. In 1850 he crossed the plains with ox teams to California, consuming about six months in making the journey, and several times having unpleasant experiences with the aborigines. In one fight the company lost four men and had quite a number of cattle stolen. This was on the Humboldt river.

Arriving at last in Georgetown mining camp, California, Mr. Eastabrooks mined there and in the surrounding country until 1859, continuously except when engaged in Indian wars. In 1851 the Indians became very hostile in Placer county and a company was formed under Captain Tracy to assist in giving them battle, and in this our subject en-

listed. He served until the fall of 1852, or until the Indians were completely subdued. In the Humboldt war of 1859 he also saw some severe service, and it was in this that he received the wound in the ankle referred to above.

In 1859 our subject returned via the Panama route to his home in Ohio, remaining until 1862, when he crossed the plains a second time, coming to Baker county. He has had several skirmishes with the Indians since coming to Oregon, and has lost quite a number of cattle as the result of their ravages.

In company with his present partner, Mr. Wood, Mr. Eastabrooks located the Connor creek mine, and worked it for about five years, then discovered the celebrated Gold Hill mine and erected a mill on the same. He and his partner have owned and developed a number of other properties and at the present time are interested in some very promising gold and copper prospects. They are engaged now in farming also, their home place being about two and a half miles up Burnt river from Weatherby.

JOHN FRASER.—To the prominent citizen and substantial stockman and agriculturist whose name initiates this paragraph we are bound by force of right to grant a representation in this volume, since for some years he has been a leader in the region where he is at present domiciled and because he has ever manifested those principles and qualities that are praiseworthy and commendable.

Mr. Fraser was born in Scotland, whence come so many of our best and most industrious citizens, in 1842, being the son of Duncan and Mary Jane (Campbell) Fraser, natives of the same famous land, where also they passed the entire time of their pilgrimage in the scenes of earth. Our subject left the "banks and braes and streams" of his native land when he was twenty-five years of age and sought his fortune in the "home of the free." He first settled in Ohio and engaged in farming for a time, and then migrated to Umatilla county, where he took up sheep raising. About two years later he came to the Eagle valley and here he has lived continuously since. At first he embarked in the sheep business here, but soon disposed of these animals and devoted his attention to raising cattle and tilling the soil, adding also the culture of fruit. He owns at the present time a quarter section of land and his industry and thrift are manifested in the high state of culture which is shown in his farm. For a number of years previous to the change in the territory of the county he was a stock inspector of Union county, and in this trying position he rendered valuable and satisfactory service. At the present time he is discharging the duties of justice of the peace, having been re-elected to his third term, thus displaying the confidence that is reposed in him by the people of his precinct. In fraternal affiliation he is associated with the K. of P. Lodge No. 86, in Eagle valley.

The marriage of Mr. Fraser and Miss Flora, daughter of Peter and Mary (Monroe) Grant, who were farmers in Scotland, was solemnized twenty-six years ago, and to them have been born the following children: Fred A., Duncan P., Mary J., and Flora, who died two years ago, aged nine years, and her remains lie buried in Eagle valley. Mr. Fraser is a man that commands the respect and has won the confidence of all that know him.

HON WILLIAM R. USHER.—This gentleman has been one of the potent factors in the advancement of civilization in the frontier places where his lot has been cast, and especially so in this county, since here and in an adjoining state he has been a real leader in the fullest sense of the term, while his life has been fraught with both commendable labor and the display of unswerving integrity and upright principles, and his worth is manifest in that since the days of the Mexican war, of which struggle he has the honor of being a veteran, until the present, he has shown forth intrepidity, probity and fine ability.

Mr. Usher was born on the rolling deep while his parents, William R. and Elizabeth (Malsbury) Usher, were en route from England, their native land, to the United States, on June 21, 1832. While he was but a child his parents returned to England, where they both died, and at the age of eleven he went to steamboating on the Ohio. When he had reached the age of fifteen he entered the Mexican war, learning there the hardships of a

military career. In 1851 he started for San Francisco, and the next year landed in that city, and in that state he followed mining until 1861. Then he went to Nevada, and five years later to Idaho, and in 1864 he was in the famous Silver City mining camp. Five years later he removed to Utah, and in 1878 we find him again in Nevada, and in 1880 he came to Eagle valley, where he has since resided. He was one of the enterprising prospectors that discovered the well known Cornucopia mines and named them. He also laid out and named the town of Richland, which is situated on a portion of his homestead. While in Idaho he was called by the people to serve in the sixth session of the state legislature, and since then he has held numerous other offices, both in that state and here, being deputy sheriff of Union county for a term of years, and his name has frequently been before the conventions of the county. He is affiliated with the I. O. O. F. in Tuscarora, Nevada, and with the K. of P., Blue Mountain Lodge, No. 28, at Union.

The marriage of Mr. Usher and Miss Virginia, daughter of Dangerfield and Ellen (Randall) Carpenter, natives respectively of Virginia and Kentucky, was solemnized in 1865, and to them has been born one child, W. R., who died in Silver City in 1868. Mr. Usher is a notary public at the present time and is doing business for the Pennsylvania Fire Insurance Company.

ISREAL N. YOUNG.—Those men who form the bone and sinew, as it were, of any thrifty community are such as steadily and continuously meet the changing scenes of life with their freight of responsibility or adversity of success with the same uprightness, candor and unflinching determination to make the best of everything and then take hold and work out that end; such a man is the one whose name introduces this paragraph, and such has been his record from the time that he was thrown on the world at an early date until the present time.

Mr. Young was born in Ashmore, Illinois, on November 27, 1843, being the son of William and Nancy (Nicols) Young, natives respectively of Tennessee and Illinois. In this latter state the parents resided until the time of their death. When very young our subject was forced to live with strangers on account of the death of his parents, but when his eldest brother was married he made his home with his family and in company with them came to northern Missouri in 1856. Here they remained until 1863, when they toiled through the arduous journey from that point to the Grande Ronde valley, in this state. Here the elder brother took a homestead and our subject engaged in freighting until 1867, when he settled on a farm in the Grande Ronde valley, and four years later he went to Eagle valley, where he is at the present time engaged in farming and stock raising. He has bought and sold considerable land in the valley, but he still retains his old homestead. In political matters he allies himself with the Democratic party and is generally one of the delegates to the county conventions, while in school matters he is active, and is useful in advancing the interests of education in serving on the school board of his home district. Fraternally he is affiliated with the I. O. O. F., Lodge 123, Eagle valley.

The marriage of Mr. Young and Miss Adaline, daughter of Alex and Elizabeth (Baker) Furgason, was solemnized in 1867, and they have become the parents of the following children: Valentine; Effie; Edith; an infant, that died in 1874; Harley, who died in 1875; Lillian; Bertha; Lena. Mrs. Young's parents were natives of New York and agriculturists there, but in 1866 they came across the plains to the valley where the daughter now lives, and in this place they lie buried. While en route to Oregon their train was attacked by Indians, who secured all of the stock. Search was made and the stock recovered, but in the fight one of the Indians was killed, and when they came to examine his body they found that he was a white renegade, and evidences pointed to the belief that the other members of the band were also white. This occurred near the Black Hills.

◆─◆─◆

WILLIAM H. COLTON.—It is with pleasure that we incorporate here a brief review of the career of the enterprising and successful farmer and wool grower whose name forms the caption hereof, for to him belongs the honor and respect due to those who succeed in spite of difficulties and discourageing circumstances. Our subject is a native of Juneau county, Wisconsin, born near Mauston on January 1, 1855, his parents being Dr. John and Alice (Lever) Colton, natives respectively of Ireland and England. He grew to early manhood in the county of his birth, receiving there such educational discipline as the local public schools afforded. In 1875 he came west to Red Bluff, California, where for four years he was engaged in the lumbering business. At the end of that period of time he came to Umatilla county, Oregon, purchased the old Vanaernam saw mill and engaged in the lumbering industry on his own behalf. Later he purchased an interest also in the Eagle saw mill. He continued to busy himself in the manufacture of lumber, pursuing the business with energy and success for the ensuing eight years, eventually selling out and investing the proceeds or a portion thereof in a band of sheep. The scab got among them and wrought considerable havoc, and during the first winter, which proved a very severe one, he lost quite heavily, though owing to great care and diligence, his losses were not as heavy as those sustained by other sheep men. His flocks, however, were in a poor condition the next spring and he sold out for just what he had put into the business.

Coming then to a part of Union county which has since been transferred to the political division with which our volume is primarily concerned, he started again in the sheep business with one hundred and eighty-two ewes. Fortune favored him this time and his flocks continued to increase until he had six thousand head, of which he disposed in the spring of 1898. At the present time he is the owner of about four thousand head, though he expects in the near future, to run about ten thousand sheep. He is the owner also of about four hundred acres of excellent hay land under the ditch, upon which he raises three crops of alfalfa per year. Thus it will be seen that from a very humble beginning Mr. Colton has, by energy and faithful attention to business, acquired a very neat fortune, and his experience should be an inspiration to all young men who are similarly situated, showing them what steadfastness and a progressive, thrifty disposition will accomplish.

On November 7, 1881, our subject married Miss Caroline, a daughter of Joel M. and Mary J. Thrasher, natives of Missouri. They have eight children: George W., and Charles H., both in the sheep business in Baker county; Caroline M., Alice M., John J., Elizabeth, William M. and Nellie. Mr. Colton's father was a physician and surgeon in the Civil war. He was with General Custer in his first expedition from Fort Lincoln to the mouth of the Powder river.

CHARLES M. WATTERBURY.—Who can tell the amount of suffering and hardships endured, the sorrow and grief borne and the deprivations and self denial undergone by the early settlers that opened this vast region for their children to enjoy? Pen and paper cannot express it, nor words fittingly convey to our minds at this remote period the keenness and vividness of these scenes of half a century since, when the intrepid and dauntless persons threaded the dreary waste of sand and sage brush, arid plain and rocky mountain, to gain a home in these valleys. In the hateful deception known as Meeks cut off, Mrs. Watterbury, the mother of our subject, was lost with the train, and for days and weeks they were on the verge of starvation, and the stock was slain to keep life in their bodies, while hunting parties sent for help were never found again. From this living trap they finally emerged, what were left of them, and in due time found a resting place from their weary journey in the Willamette valley.

The immediate subject of this sketch, the son of worthy pioneers, was born in Portland, in 1865, thus becoming a native of this rugged promised land so sought after in the time of his parents, and here he has wrought out his destiny, never swerving from the constant conviction that the occidental stars were the ones that would finally smile the success to him that his enterprising and energetic achievements made him so manifestly worthy of. At the early age of fifteen years he commenced the struggle of life, embarking first in the stock business. Eight years later he took a homestead in Eagle valley, where he lives at the present time, and is now, as he has been, continuously since his first visit here, engaged in raising stock and tilling the soil.

The marriage of Mr. Watterbury and Miss Mamie Gibson, a native of Boise, Idaho, and daughter of Robert and Mary (Newman) Gibson, natives respectively of Wisconsin and Germany, was celebrated in 1890 and they have the following children: Christie; Llna; Dewey, who died at the age of two weeks and is buried in the Eagle valley cemetery; Viola, died at the age of two months and is buried in the same cemetery. Mr. Watterbury has been a prominent figure in the educational affairs of the county and has served in the capacity of school clerk for a number of years, where he has given faithful and efficient service. In social affiliations he is with the Fraternal Union of America and is a popular and highly esteemed member.

WILLIAM D. ADAMS.—A veteran of the Civil war, a respected pioneer of Baker county, and an energetic, forceful and highly respected citizen, the man whose name gives caption to this review is certainly deserving of mention in this part of our volume, and it affords us pleasure to grant him representation here.

Our subject was born in Natchez, Mississippi, on June 6, 1823. His father died when he was an infant and his mother with her children later removed to Kentucky, where he received his education in the public schools. When the time came for him to initiate independent action he engaged in the business his parents had previously followed, namely, farming. When the war broke out he enlisted in the Missouri home guards (he had moved to that state in 1855), and he continued to contribute his part toward the cause of the Union until the last disloyal gun had been silenced. He then took up farming again, following that branch of human activity there until 1881, when he and his family came out to Baker county, Oregon. They purchased a place near Wingville, five miles west of Baker City, and upon this our subject resided, engaged in farming and stock raising, until death claimed him for its victim, on February 14, 1901. He was one of the most thrifty and successful farmers of the county and had accumulated quite a large amount of valuable real estate. He was also quite active in the political affairs of the county and state, though he appears to have had little ambition for personal preferment.

Fraternally Mr. Adams was affiliated with the Masonic fraternity, an order in which he had taken great interest for a period of forty years. His marriage was solemnized in Trenton, Missouri, on April 16, 1857, when Miss Barbara A., daughter of Amos and Hulda Bailsey, natives of Pennsylvania, became his wife, and they had twelve children, seven of whom are still living, namely: Elizabeth, wife of James Worley, of Sumpter valley, this county.; Clarissa, wife of Frank Gardner, of Baker county; Amos O. L. and S. L. Dow, twins; George W.; Sydney L. and Thomas B. The family are member of the Christian church. Mrs. Adams resides in a fine home at 2130 First street, and is the owner of three farms, containing about nine hundred acres in all.

WILLIAM ASHWOOD.—This prosperous and progressive farmer and stock raiser is a native of the vicinity of Mineral Point, Iowa county, Wisconsin, born June 17, 1854. He grew to manhood there, receiving a public school education. In the year 1876 he crossed the plains with horses to the west and the same year he settled in Harlan county, Nebraska, near Orleans, where he farmed during the ensuing six years. He then came to Baker county, purchased a farm three and a half miles west of Haines, and again engaged in agricultural pursuits and stock raising. He is now the owner of a fine farm of four hundred acres, all well improved, and everywhere reflecting credit upon the industry and progressiveness of the man whose labor brought it to its present state. A very energetic and successful farmer and stock raiser, Mr. Ashwood is also a deserving citizen, possessed of a broad-minded public spirit and taking a very vital interest in everything which concerns the general welfare. His interest in the cause of education is manifested by his having consented to serve for six years as director of his school district.

Fraternally Mr. Ashwood is affiliated with Haines Lodge, No. 11, A. O. U. W., and in religious persuasion he is a Methodist, his membership at present being in the church of that denomination at Haines. On December 24, 1878, in Harlan county, Nebraska, our subject married Miss Kiturah, a daughter of Martin and Jane Marzolf, and a native of Mineral Point, Wisconsin. Their union has been blessed by the advent of four children: James, Mary, Millie and Minnie. Mr. Ashwood is interested in a company composed of twelve neighbors, which owns a threshing outfit for the use of each one on his farm. He is also stockholder in an irrigating company that has built a reservoir in the mountains for the purpose of furnishing water for irrigating the farms of the neighborhood. When Mr Ashwood took the farm where he now lives it was covered with sage brush and every one prophesied that he would be obliged to abandon it. However, he has gone forward, attended with the success that his wisdom and skill deserve, and is to-day possessed of as fine a farm as lies in the precincts of Baker county. Thus do wisdom, foresight and pluck overcome seemingly insurmountable obstacles, make the desert blossom as the rose and attach civilization's joys and comforts to the once barren land of the savage.

EMIL F. FOERSTERLING.—This public spirited citizen and enterprising blacksmith, farmer, and stockraiser of the neighborhood on Sisley creek, northeast of Weatherby, is a native of Prussia, born August 9, 1841. When eight years old he accompanied his parents across the ocean to America, and his first home in the new world was in Louisville, Kentucky. He attended school there for half a decade, then went to Jacksonville, Illinois, where he worked on a farm for a time and afterwards learned the trade of a blacksmith. In April, 1861, the even tenor of his life was somewhat rudely interrupted by the necessity of his obeying the call of patriotism. He enlisted in the Tenth Illinois Infantry, and served three months, and in the following April, he again enlisted, this time in the First Missouri Cavalry. He participated in several severe engagements, and once was captured by the rebels, being afterwards exchanged, but escaped without even a wound. His war record was a very honorable one and one of which he and his family have cause for pardonable pride.

After the last disloyal gun had been silenced, Mr. Foersterling worked at his handicraft in Dwight, Illinois, for a number of years, but in 1886, he emigrated to Baker county, and located on the place on which we now find him. He has a good farm, a comfortable home, an orchard of choice varieties of fruit-trees, and quite a herd of stock on the ranch.

Mr. Foersterling takes a very active interest in the cause of education, as he does in all other things which have for their object the amelioration of conditions and the promotion of the public good. He has served either as school director or as clerk for the past twelve years, ever discharging his duties with faithfulness and good judgment.

On May 25, 1865, our subject married Miss Mary E., daughter of William and Christina Niemeyer, and to their union thirteen children have been born, of whom eight are still living, namely, Edward C., Henrietta B., now Mrs. Thomas Roach, of Weatherby; Leonora L., Jesse W., Willis H., Mildred J., Meta E., and Frederick L. Mr. Foersterling is a prominent member of the G. A. R., U. S. Grant post at Huntington, and is also affiliated with the I. O. O. F.

◆◆◆

EDWARD W. COLES.—Among the sons of Baker county who have grown up to reflect credit, by their industry and ability in commercial pursuits, or in other walks of life, upon the place of their birth must be numbered the enterprising young stock man whose name appears above. His past achievements give promise of much greater successes to be realized in the future and we may be pardoned in expecting that time will make Mr. Coles one of the stock kings of the county.

As already implied, our subject is a native of the political division with which our volume primarily concerns itself, and the date of his advent into life is October 11, 1878. He is the son of Fred C. Coles, one of the early settlers of this section, who died at the family home a half mile north of Haines in 1895, and his mother, now Mrs. Richmond, is the daughter of Augustus George, another pioneer of an

early date. Mr. Coles acquired his education in the local public schools, in the high school at Baker City and in the Portland Business College, which latter institution he left in 1894, being called away by his father's illness. Since that time he has been in charge of the Coles stock ranch constantly. He keeps about two hundred head of graded Shorthorn and Hereford cattle also about two hundred head of Poland China hogs, many of which are registered. Our subject takes especial pride in these latter, and deals quite extensively in registered Poland-Chinas, buying and selling.

Fraternally, Mr. Coles is affiliated with Haines Lodge, No. 11, A. O. U. W., and with No. 144, W. of W., of the same place. At the home of her mother five miles west of Haines, on November 3, 1897, he married Miss Ollie, a daughter of James and Annie Taylor and a native of Missouri. Their union has been blest by the advent of one daughter, Leatha L.

◆◆◆

FREDERICK AND MARY J. SIMONIS. —To these worthy and faithful pioneers and substantial citizens of this county we are pleased to accord a representation in this volume, since their labors have been instrumental in developing this region and they have been in the lead in promoting the welfare of the county's interest in the long years in which they have been domiciled within its borders.

Mr. Simonis was born in New Jersey, being the son of Matthias and Mary (Grouse) Simonis, natives of Germany. Mrs. Simonis is the daughter of Alexander and Elizabeth (Baker) Furgason, natives of Canada, who came to the United States and settled in Eagle valley, where they are both buried now. The marriage of our subjects occurred in 1863, and then they set out on one of the most unique wedding journeys that is in the history of our country, namely crossing the plains from the central states to the Pacific coast with ox teams. Youth and energy were potent to keep their spirits bright as they steadily pursued their course toward the setting sun in search of a home for the days to come. Without special incident, they landed in this state and industriously set about carving out for themselves a home and fortune in its boundless resources. In 1874 they came to Eagle valley and settled where the widow is residing to-day. At the age of forty-eight, on May 6, 1889, the beloved husband was called to depart this life and in sorrow the widow took up the burdens that fell upon her. Mr. Simonis was very prominent in the county affairs and had served the people very acceptably as surveyor for the county for a number of years. He had also given of his time and talent to the promotion of good schools, serving as director for a long time.

The children of this worthy couple are as follows: Mary, who died at the age of twenty; Frederick, married; Matthias, married; Louis, married; James, at home; Joseph, still on the home farm; Leander, at home; Edward, at home; Anna, married; Ella, married; John, who died at the age of sixteen; Alexander, at home; Leo, who died at the age of thirteen. At the present time Mrs. Simonis is carrying on the affairs of the old homestead and is highly esteemed by all who know her as a faithful and exemplary Christian and wise woman.

DAVIS WILCOX.—It is always pleasant to trace the career of a successful man, and especially so when we see one that has wrought out by his own skill, energy and industry, a place for himself in the business world, having started at the bottom of the ladder and made his way to the top by genuine worth and ability, such as has the prominent citizen and estimable gentleman whose name appears at the head of this article, who came to this section as a saleman and is now the proprietor of one of the leading mercantile establishments of the entire county.

Mr. Wilcox was born on April 13, 1859, near Sharon, Walworth county, Wisconsin, being the son of David and Sarah Wilcox. His father was a tiller of the soil, and our subject received the invigorating exercise in assisting to carry on the farm until 1872, when they all removed to Washington county, Oregon. For seven years he remained there and then came to Umatilla and engaged in the mercantile establishment of John R. Foster & Company, as salesman for three and one-half years. From there he went to North Powder and operated in the same capacity for Kellogg,

Funch & Company until 1887, when he came to Haines and established a branch house for the firm. A little later, he bought out the establishment and is now engaged in the operation of one of the largest general merchandise concerns of the county, carrying everything that is needed by his large and ever-increasing patronage, and to dispense the goods that come from his shelves and warerooms seven salesmen are kept busy, while his time is ever occupied in the oversight of his mammoth business.

The marriage of Mr. Wilcox and Mrs. Mattie Hill, daughter of John Ferguson, was solemnized in 1892. He is fraternally affiliated with the A. O. U. W. Lodge No. 11, also with the W. of W., Lodge No. 341, both of Haines. Mr. Wilcox is a man that takes an active interest in the political and educational matters of his county and is of a broad public spirit and ever in the lead for the advancement of the interests of all, having manifested a very commendable spirit and rare ability during the years of his stay in this county, as well as throughout his entire business course and is highly esteemed by his fellows and respected by all. In addition to his large business interests he has been called to take charge of the postoffice at Haines and in the discharge of these particular duties he has given perfect satisfaction.

JOHN ERWIN.—It is with especial pleasure that we are allotted the pleasant task of outlining in brief the career of the well known pioneer and prominent citizen whose name introduces this article, since he has played a prominent part in the development of this region, has ever wrought with energy and wisdom, has maintained an unsullied life and has proved on the field of battle his devotion to his country and his love for its free institutions. And to whom, more than to the noble men, when fratricidal strife lowered and raged through this fair land, that laid aside the affairs of personal interest and went to the front to lift again into its place the banner that had so ignominiously been torn from the standard of freedom, should we delight to do honor by mentioning their lives of faithful devotion?

DAVIS WILCOX.

JOHN ERWIN.

FRANK LOENNIG.

MRS. FRANK LOENNIG.

John Erwin is the son of David and Elenor (Arnott), natives respectively of Ireland and Scotland, who came to this land and were married in New York state, where they settled in Genesee county. In that place, on September 20, 1839, our subject was born and there he recived his educational training. He had scarcely reached his majority when the call came for troops and he responded at once, enlisting in the One Hundred and Fourth Infantry, and in that capacity he remained until July 12, 1865, when he was discharged with the rank of sergeant major. He participated in all of the battles in Virginia and was in active service from the start to finish. On December 13, 1862, he received a bayonet wound at Fredericksburg, and on July 4, at Gettysburg, he was wounded by a sharpshooter and several other times his body stopped rebel lead, but from all these he recovered. Returning to his native state he engaged in general merchandising at Linden, and one year later all was lost by fire, following which he repaired to Oakland, Michigan, whence two years later he went to Baker county, 1868, being the date when he first landed here. For over twenty years he engaged in mining and raising cattle, being in company with J. C. Powers & Co., and at one time owned over one thousand head of cattle on the range. In 1892 he bought the farm where he now resides in Lower Powder river valley, and here he has devoted his entire attention to tilling the soil and stock raising and buying and selling stock. He has some fine thoroughbred Short Horn Durham cattle and some excellent horses. In political matters he has always been prominent in the Republican party and the county has profited much by his service in office. He was county commissioner of Union county for some time and justice of the peace for four years and for sixteen years he has been a school officer in Erwin district.

On January 23, 1881, Mr. Erwin and Miss Ada, daughter of A. J. and Martha (Harp) Brown, natives of Tennessee, were married and to them have been born the following children: Belle, wife of H. C. Easterbrook; James G.; Ethel O.; John P.; Ada E.; Jackson O.; Edith V.; Walter G.; all of whom, except the married daughter, reside at home. Mr. Erwin has made a number of trips to Michigan

20

for the purpose of selling horses. And during the early days it is to be recorded that he was very active in participating in the Indian wars of this region. He was one of the number that chased the notorious Indian chieftain, Egan, and has been to the front whenever there was danger to the settlers.

———◆◆◆———

FRANK LOENNIG.—This prosperous young farmer and stockraiser of the neighborhood situated about six miles west of Haines postoffice has the distinction of being a native of the county he is now helping to develop, having been born on Willow creek, four miles northwest of the present Haines, on November 5, 1867. His parents, Arnst and Marie Loennig, were pioneers of the county of the year 1863. Our subject lived with them until 1894, then purchased the place on which he now lives, three hundred and twenty acres. To the cultivation and improvement of this he has devoted himself energetically since, with the result that he has some very excellent improvements, and that an air of thrift is everywhere perceptible about the premises. Mr. Loennig is one of the substantial citizens of the county, belonging to that class which though not ambitions for personal aggrandizement or political preferment, or for leadership of any kind, are yet the real strength of any community, the earnest of its future progress.

On June 8, 1897, at his father's home on Willow creek, our subject married Miss Emma E., a native of Kansas, and daughter of Philip P. and Wilamina Lang, and to their union three children have been born, namely, Erna June and Franklin Lang, and an infant.

———◆◆◆———

CONRAD J. LANG.—The thrifty and progressive farmer and stock-raiser whose career it is now our task to present in epitome, was born near Sandy Hill, Steuben county, New York, on the twenty-fifth of January, 1860. When four years old he was taken by his parents to the vicinity of Appleton, Wisconsin, and there he took his initial steps in the pursuit of knowledge. In 1869, the family removed to Crawford county, Kansas, but after a residence of seventeen years duration there, the father died and the mother and her children returned to New York, where she also departed this life.

In 1882 our subject emigrated to Baker county, Oregon, and he has resided within its limits ever since, though his home has been located in various places at different times. In 1890 he settled upon a tract of land about three miles northeast of Weatherby, on Sisley creek, where he has ever since resided, and where he now has a very comfortable home, and a farm well improved and equipped with all necessary buildings, machinery, etc. His premises bear eloquent testimony to his thrift and industry.

On February 15, 1881, in Osage Mission, Kansas, Mr. Lang married Miss Sarah M., daughter of John and Susana (Sideling) Leibold, and to them have been born eight children: Joseph V., Edward W., Francis J., deceased, Regina, Mary R., Conrad M., Lewis G. and Arthur, all at home.

Fraternally, Mr. Lang is affiliated with the A. O. U. W., of Baker City.

———◆◆◆———

JOSEPH S. JETT.—Among the leading farmers of Baker county, must be mentioned the man whose name gives caption to this review. He likewise takes a vital interest in political matters and exhibits broad-minded public spirit and a willingness to do what lies in his power for the upbuilding of his community and county and the advancement of the general welfare. As a man and member of society, his standing is an enviable one, and it affords us pleasure to be able to accord him representation here as one of the county's leading men.

Mr. Jett is a native of Franklin county, Missouri, born May 12, 1844, his parents being William E. and Elizabeth Jett. In 1848 he accompanied his parents to Grundy county, same state, where he attended the district school during its sessions and worked on a farm the remainder of the time, until 1864. He then crossed the plains to Baker county, Oregon, locating first in the Powder river valley, near Baker City, where he lived until 1869. He then settled on the old Scott place, seven miles northwest of Huntington, on Burnt river, the original owners of which, Mr. and Mrs. Scott

were shot by Indians in 1867. To the cultivation and improvement of this tract, he has devoted himself zealously since, with the natural result that it has long since been brought to such a state of cultivation as to produce abundant crops of alfalfa and other farm products, including fruit of various kinds. Mr. Jett also has a large band of cattle on the range.

As before implied, our subject is a leader in political matters, his party affiliations being with the Democrats. He was married on December 11, 1881, to Henrietta Christenson, a native of Des Moines, Iowa, and they are now parents of eight children, Augusta M., Lizzie, deceased, Ida P., Clara, Ruth C., Joseph B., Hattie D., and Dorman E., all at home.

———◆◆◆———

WILLIAM D. EMELE.—This honored pioneer and successful farmer and stockman of the Powder river valley was born in Illinois, near the city of Quincy, on February 11, 1839. His father, William, was a native of Germany, and his mother, Evaline, of Illinois. The father died when he was quite young and the family moved to Iowa, settling near Burlington, in Des Moines county. Our subject received a good common school education, and with this for his only equipment, he set out at the age of twenty to try his fortunes in the wild and rugged west, crossing the plains in the primitive fashion of the times, namely, with ox-teams. His objective point was the Golden state, where he farmed for a period of two years. thereupon coming to Oregon. After arriving here he settled first in the Big Creek country, but soon he filed on a quarter section of government land in the Panhandle country, sixteen miles northeast of Baker City, where he now lives. For many years he has devoted himself assiduously and exclusively to the basic art and he now has a very excellent and well improved place all under irrigation. He keeps about forty head of well graded cattle, and in addition to his fine farm with its stock and equipments, he is the owner of some valuable city property at the county seat. The marriage of our subject and Miss Elizabeth Bowman was duly solemnized in the state of Missouri, on April 15, 1871, and they now have five children, namely, Elmer, living on Big

Creek, six miles north; Estella wife of J. M. Dean, a resident of the valley; Eveline, wife of R. J. Jameson, of Baker county; Benjamin, and Elizabeth.

WILLIAM C. NICHOLSON.—This energetic and successful farmer and fruit raiser, residing eight miles west of Haines, is deserving of representation in any work whose province is similar to that of our volume, he being not alone a leader in his line of activity but also an esteemed and highly respected citizen of his community and county, public spirited and a potent factor in the promotion of the general welfare. He was born in Hayward county, Tennessee, on March 19, 1842, and there he resided until sixteen years old, acquiring his educational discipline in the local private schools. In the year mentioned he accompanied the remainder of the family to Jackson county, Arkansas, where his home was until about 1867.

Our subject was not privileged to remain with his parents much after 1862, however, for the cause he believed to be right was summoning him to sterner duties, and in that year he enlisted in Colonel Matlock's cavalry regiment. He participated in the battle of Prairie Grove, where Colonel Young was killed and Hicks became colonel of the regiment, and in the battle at Helena, where he was wounded in the right chest and taken prisoner. Upon being exchanged in the fall of 1863, he joined Grider's battalion, and then under Colonel Mc-Gee, ranking as orderly sergeant, he participated in Price's campaign in Missouri, taking part in the battles of Bridgeport, Pilot Knob and in numerous other engagements and skirmishes.

In 1867 our subject moved to northern Arkansas and two years later came thence across the plains to Baker county, making the trip with ox-teams. For about eight years he farmed at Wingville, and two were passed in like employment in the Grande Ronde valley. He also followed agricultural pursuits in various other parts of the county until 1883, when he pre-empted a quarter section eight miles west of the present Haines, upon which he has since lived. He now has three hundred and twenty acres of fine land, most of which has been brought by industry and skill to a high state of cultivation, also a good house, and all needful outbuildings, fences, etc. His premises are an unmistakable monument to his industry and thrift.

Fraternally, Mr. Nicholson is a charter member of Haines Lodge No. 112, I. O. O. F., and of Haines Lodge No. 11, A. O. U. W. He is also a leading member and a deacon in the Baptist church. Twice our subject has been married. In Arkansas in the year 1865, he wedded Miss Sarah Miller, and to their union were born three daughters: Mary, now Mrs. Skaw, operating a boarding house at North Powder; Nancy, wife of Grant Hoburg, living at Baker City; Naomi, residing at Sumpter. His second marriage was solemnized on January 4, 1880, the lady being Mrs. Martha Burke, daughter of Reuben and Elizabeth T. (Baker) Haines and a native of Ohio. Mrs. Nicholson has one living son by her former marriage, James Burke.

SAMUEL F. GOVER.—It is ever gratifying to see exemplified that excellent quality of continuity and perseverance, and especially so when it is accompanied by other equally as fine and worthy talents, as is the case in the leading stockman and prominent citizen whose name heads this article, having been in the stock business here almost continuously for over a quarter of a century, gaining meanwhile a very marked and gratifying success in this enterprise.

Mr. Gover is the son of David and Jane (Shadowen) Gover, natives of Kentucky, in which state the father passed out of this life, and the mother died later in Missouri. At the age of eighteen, September, 1868, he left the Blue Grass state and landed in Missouri, near Marshall, where he worked on a farm for three years, after which he came to the Pacific coast, landing in Baker City in about 1872. He immediately went to the lower Powder river valley and engaged on a farm for wages, where he continued for four years. After this time, he went to driving cattle between this county and Rock Creek, Wyoming. He was one of the first men that contracted cattle to Seawright Brothers to go east. He has continued in the cattle business uninterruptedly since with the exception of a short time he was in Nebraska. About eight years ago he bought a ranch in Eagle valley and his wife also has one in the same valley. At Sturgill creek, Washington county, Idaho, he has a homestead, where the family reside at the present time.

The marriage of Mr. Gover and Miss Mattie, daughter of Henry and Vina Cundiff, was celebrated in 1891, on February 5. He made a trip to Somerset, Kentucky, to claim his bride, and together they came to their western home. They have two children, Walter C., and Vina, at his Idaho residence. Mr. Gover is one of the most experienced stockmen of this section and is looked up to by all, both for his wisdom and for his integrity, which is ever manifested in a becoming manner.

JACOB B. WHITE, M. D.—Upon no class of men are the issues of life and death so dependent as upon the physicians and thus it is that popular sentiment calls that they be men of great ability and stanch integrity and thorough training, that they may the more successfully cope with the dread enemies, disease and suffering. Baker county may well be proud of her quota of medical residents and well toward the head of this distinguished number must be placed the name of the prominent and skillful young doctor whose name initiates this paragraph and to whom we are pleased to accord a representation in this volume.

Doctor White is the son of Calvin G. and Emily (Thompson) White, being born on July 12, 1871, at Fremont, Nebraska. His father was a chaplain in the Civil war and after the close continued in the ministry in the Methodist Episcopal church and for a term of years was presiding elder of the Omaha and Lincoln districts. During his time in that state he was captain of Company C, of the Nebraska Home Guards and did some hard fighting in the Sioux Indian outbreak. After a long life of faithful and distinguished service in the cause of his Divine Master, he fell asleep on November 23, 1883. His widow also departed this life on June 30, 1900, in Kansas City. The immediate subject of this sketch was taken by his parents to Lincoln, in his native state and there attended the public schools until fifteen years of age and then entered the State University,

from which he took with honor the degree of B. S. in 1892. Immediately following this, he matriculated at the University of Michigan and graduated from that institution in 1895 with the degree of Doctor of Medicine and Surgery. In 1896 he came to Huntington in Baker county, and located and since that date he has given himself to the practice of medicine with a manifestation of skill and depth of erudition that have speedily and permanently won for him not only a large and lucrative practice but have also given him a high place in the esteem and affection of the people. Among his confreres he is held in high repute, having gained the distinction and encomiums that his real worth merits. The Doctor has displayed marked financial ability and keen foresight in his business life, and the meed of this worthy action is shown in that he is one of the heavy mine owners of his town. He owns and controls the Amyl group of mines in the southeastern part of the county, also the Eldorado group of placer mines near Malheur city; he is also largely interested in the Eldorado Oil Company in Malheur county and is a heavy shareholder in the Huntington Light and Artesian Water Company.

Among the first to detect the indications of oil in the recently discovered oil-belt of Idaho and Oregon, he gave all of his leisure hours for months to a thorough and exhaustive study of the geological formation there existing; from April to August in the year just past, the work proceeded quietly, with frequent pauses during the press of professional duties. During the month of August, the work of other investigators drew public attention to the task in hand and then in a few weeks was inaugurated the first stage of either the greatest oil-boom or one of the most laughable location crazes in modern times. The calm serenity of the Doctor's researches in geological lore soon changed to a hasty effort to secure for himself and friends the fruits of his labor. The whole country was overrun with locators of all descriptions from every walk of life. The hills and valleys fairly bristled with posts topped with location notices, many of the latter being fearfully and wonderfully made. Returning surveyors became more or less gratuitous instruments for the spread of the infection, and generally succeeded in augmenting the excitement. From the general chaos resulting the Doctor succeeded in locating several thousand acres of the choicest portions of the oil lands in the interest of a company of western capitalists who later incorporated under the name of the "Inter-State Petroleum Oil Company." This company, of which the Doctor was elected secretary, is now proceeding with the thorough exploiting of their property in the field, having in view the permanent growth and rational development of the same. Though too early to predict with certainty the outcome of the present undertaking of this and other companies, it is safe to say that no stone will be left unturned to tap nature's reservoir of crude petroleum, and secure for this portion of the state, if possible, an era of prosperity unprecedented in size and permanence.

The marriage of Doctor White and Miss Jessie M., daughter of Joseph M. and Ella M. (Smith) Duffy, was solemnized on June 21, 1899. Mr. Duffy was one of the most prominent men of the county in his time and his death occurred in the spring of 1896, while his widow is still living in Huntington. Doctor White is fraternally affiliated with the I. O. O. F. Burnt River Lodge, No. 86, and at the present time holds the position of noble grand in that lodge, also is a member of the Rebekahs, Eastern Gate, No. 40, and of the Modern Woodmen and the Woodmen of the World.

WILLIAM MILES.—To the man whose life record it is now our task to epitomize belongs the distinguished honor of being one of those who rallied to the support of the Union and the flag in the dark days when civil strife threatened to rend our land in twain. Like most of his comrades, also, Mr. Miles has sustained the good record of his military service in the severe battle of life which had to be fought before and since, and has contributed his share toward the progress and upbuilding of his part of the country he fought so valiantly to save. In peace and in war he has ever stood "four square to every wind" and he deserves and receives the good will and esteem of all who know him.

Inquiry into the past life of Mr. Miles develops the fact that his native country is Ireland, and that he was born January 8, 1839,

near Dublin. When about eight years old he was brought by his parents to America, and for the ensuing six years his home was in Ontario county, New York. In 1855 the family moved to Chicago and two years later to Joliet, Illinois, where our subject lived until 1862. In that year the even tenor of his life was somewhat rudely interrupted in consequence of the Civil war and the duty he felt it entailed of giving his support to the cause of national union. He enlisted, obedient to the call of patriotism, in Company C, Ninetieth Illinois, and from that time until the close of hostilities, he followed the fortunes of war. He participated in the struggles at Missionary Ridge, Jacksonville, Fort McAllister and other places, receiving a severe wound in the right arm at the point last named. His military record was one of which he and his family have reason to feel proud.

When hostilities ceased and he received his honorable discharge, he came out to Boise, Idaho, where he remained for three years, thereupon returning to Joliet. He was employed there for the ensuing fourteen years as foreman in the rolling mills of the town, but at the end of that extended period, he again came out to the west, locating this time in Baker county, where he took a homestead and where he has ever since lived. He is one of the thrifty and prosperous agriculturist of his locality and one of its leading citizens. At present he is serving as postmaster at Miles, which was named for him.

In fraternal affiliations our subject is identified with Bartleson Post, No. 6, G. A. R., of Joliet, Illinois. He married on November 2, 1872, Miss Annie E. daughter of John and Mary Harbison, of Odell, Illinois, and to them have been born eight children, Mary L.; Nellie, wife of Milton Martin; James, John, William, Agnes, Katie and Neal.

DR. MADISON B. MORRIS.—Few have had the privilege of passing through a more checkered career and meeting with more stirring scenes of interest than the subject of this sketch, whose life's opitome it is now our pleasant task to chronicle.

Madison B. Morris, familiarly known as Dr. Morris, was born in Henry county, Ten-

nessee, in 1824, being the son of Lemuel and
Martha (Estes) Morris, the father being
buried in Salem, Arkansas, and the mother in
Santa Anna, California. When twenty-seven
years of age, our subject commenced the study
of medicine and after finishing his course, he
at once commenced the practice and almost
constantly until within the past ten years he
has been engaged in that profession, although
owing to his stirring nature and love of activity he has frequently been engaged in other
enterprises in addition to the practice of medicine. He practiced in Bassville, Arkansas,
from 1848 to 1853, and then came to The
Dalles, Oregon, where he followed his
profession for four years, thence to the Cascades, where he also practiced and engaged in
supplying the steamboats with wood and also
took up a ranch opposite Dead Island in the
Columbia river. In 1865 we find him following his profession in Walla Walla and for fifteen years he was in that city; after which he
spent four years in Weston, and seven years
in Somerville and in 1882 came to Eagle valley,
where he now owns a quarter section of land
and is engaged in fruit culture and general
farming.

The marriage of Dr. Morris and Miss
Elizabeth Lillybridge was celebrated in 1867
and to them have been born the following
children: James, Lily, Lemuel, Della, Clyde,
deceased, Charley, deceased, Sadie. Mrs.
Morris' parents came across the plains with
ox teams in 1865 and many exciting and thrilling experiences were theirs to pass through
while en route. At one time the stock were
stampeded by the stage appearing suddenly
and at another time the Indians stampeded and
stole the cattle. Fortunately, they were enabled in the morning to recover all of their cattle so that they could proceed. The doctor met
this train on the Cascades, and then later followed the happy marriage we have mentioned
above. While the doctor was superintending
a train across the plains in 1853, he came across
a man that had been abandoned by the train
that preceded his, the poor unfortunate being
left to die. The doctor, like the Good Samari-
tan, picked up this helpless man and nursed
him to life, using his medical skill to restore
him. His train was stampeded on the Snake
river and many of their horses were never
recovered. When he was below the Cascades,

he barely escaped being murdered by the Indians in 1856, the date of a terrible massacre
in that section. At one time, the doctor had
the misfortune to fall through a poorly constructed bridge in Portland. He landed twenty-
six and one-half feet below and it was supposed that he was dead, for for three days
and nights he lay speechless, but he was enabled finally to pull through, although to-day
he is suffering from the effects of this same
fall, however, he has received no remuneration
from the city for their failure.

WILLIAM B. POWERS.—It is with
pleasure that we are enabled to accord representation in this portion of our volume to the
esteemed pioneer and thrifty, industrious agriculturist whose name appears as the caption
of this article. He was one of the earliest
settlers in the community in which he lives
and in Baker county, and during the nearly
three decades of his residence here his life has
been in all respects so ordered as to win him
the fullest confidence and most unfeigned and
hearty good will of those with whom he has
been thrown in contact. He is possessed of a
broad-minded public spirit, and has ever shown
himself a potent factor in the promotion of the
general well-being and the development of the
country.

Mr. Powers is a native of the vicinity of
Flemingburg, Fleming county, Kentucky, born
March 4, 1825. When he was still quite
young, he was taken by his parents, Edward
H. and Mary Powers, to Pike county, Missouri,
whence he accompanied them a few years later
to Lincoln county, and thence to Warsaw, Benton county, where for a number of years the
father had charge of a ferry. Our subject
farmed there until 1850, then set out across the
plains to California, making the trip with oxen:
He mined at Bear river, Auburn, Georgetown
and other places for a biennium, then returned
to Missouri via the isthmus of Panama, the
oceans and New York. He resumed his farming in Benton county, but after having seen
the west he could be contented there no longer,
and in 1864 he again set out across the plains,
his objective point this time being Baker county. He settled six miles west of the present
North Powder, taking a homestead. He has

purchased and disposed of much land since, but at present is possessed of two hundred and twenty acres, a part of which is the original home place. His realty is all fine farming land, and it has been improved by judicious cultivation and by the erection of fences and fine buildings, until it is one of the best farms in that section of the county. Mr. Powers has a fine orchard but gives his attention mainly to stock-raising and general farming, achieving in his efforts in this direction a very enviable success.

Our subject was married in Boone county, Missouri, in December, 1849, to Miss Adeline Barclay, who died in 1869, leaving seven children, namely: William, a miner in Idaho; Mary, wife of James Hutchinson, a resident of Union; John H., living at Salem; Ellenora, deceased; Ada, wife of R. L. Turner, living at Bourne, Oregon; Ellen, wife of S. C. Mann, a prominent farmer of the county; Laura, now Mrs. J. L. Dodson, living on the home place.

JOSEPH M. DUFFY, deceased.—As a slight tribute to the memory of the departed patriot, pioneer and distinguished citizen of Baker county, we are constrained to add this memorial to the name of the late Joseph M. Duffy, whose demise was lamented by all and whose memory is cherished by every one that had the pleasure of his acquaintance.

On August 6, 1849, Joseph M. was born in the town of Marshall, West Virginia, and in that place he passed the years of his minority, excepting what time was spent in the service of his country, to which he gave himself while yet in the tender years of boyhood that he might assist in saving to the generations to come the Union and retrieve from insult and ignominy the banner of the free that had been disgracefully attacked by treason's minions. He enlisted in Company D, Seventh West Virginia Cavalry, and was with General McClellan in the army of the Potomac, where he did faithful service and manifested intrepidity and stanch qualities that distinguished his tender years, and at the close of the war he was honorably discharged to take up the duties of civil life. In 1866 he went to Pike's Peak and later to the Black Hills and then to Georgetown, Colorado, in search for nature's gold; how suc-

cessful he was in this enterprise is not stated; but afterward we find him in the less adventurous walks of life. In 1875 he was in Macon, Missouri, and nine years later came to the Owyhee valley in this state. In 1886 he settled in Huntington, and was the first mayor of the city, and later held the office of county commissioner of Baker county from 1890 to 1894, ever faithfully discharging the trusts imposed upon him with discretion and ability.

The marriage of Mr. Duffy and Miss Ella M. Smith was celebrated in Macon, Missouri, in 1875, and to them have been born the following children: Harry A., mention of whom is made in another portion of this work; Jessie M., wife of Dr. Jacob B. White, of Huntington; Joseph M., Jr., deceased. Mr. Duffy was affiliated with the Masonic lodge at Baker City, with the I. O. O. F., Burnt River Lodge, No. 86, in Huntington. In political preference he was associated with the Republican party, and his ability and integrity were manifested so that he held a foremost position among the men of the county, being reckoned one of its leaders. On April 2, 1896, in the city of Huntington, death claimed him as a victim and he passed to the rewards of another realm, where his faithful service shall receive due meed in those things that fade not away. His demise was the cause of general mourning, and with proper and appropriate ceremonies he was consigned to his last resting place, to await the day when his eyes shall behold and his ears hear the Master whom he served here below. Mrs. Duffy survives her husband and resides in Huntington.

JAMES M. DEAN.—This prosperous farmer and stock raiser of the lower Powder river valley is a native of the great commonwealth in which he now lives, having been born in Washington county, near Oregon City, on April 6, 1857. His parents, Francis M. and Mary J. (Roberts) Dean, natives respectively of Tennessee and Missouri, were both pioneers of 1852. Our subject resided in the county of his nativity until 1870, then accompanied his parents to the Grande Ronde valley, whence, in 1871, he moved to a point not far distant from his present place of abode. His parents took the quarter section of land now known as the Turner place. Though he had attended school in Washington county, he had not finished his education at the time of his arrival here, so for some time he was a pupil in the Big Creek school, though it is situated six miles away.

As soon as our subject reached man's estate he engaged in the lumber business on Coos Bay, and to that his energies were devoted for a couple of years, at the end of which time he returned to Baker county and engaged in farming and the stock business, purchasing for the purpose the quarter section on which we find him at present. He now owns a beautiful farm of two hundred acres, all good, rich land under irrigation, and he formerly kept as high as four hundred head of cattle in partnership with one N. C. Love, but during recent years he has reduced his herd to about eighty. In 1899 he purchased a part interest in the saw mill of Jameson & Company, situated about eight miles northeast of his place, but he has since sold out the same, deeming it best to give his undivided attention to farming.

Mr. Dean is vitally interested in the cause of education, a fact which is manifested by his having served faithfully for twelve consecutive years as director of his district. Fraternally he is a member of the Modern Woodmen of America, Baker City Camp, No. 5326. On September 9, 1891, in the Powder river valley, he married Miss Estella I., a daughter of W. David and Elizabeth (Bowman) Emele, pioneers of this county. They have three children: Oval A., Marvin B. and Burl D.

GEORGE N. REED.—This honored pioneer of the state of Oregon is a native of Ypsilanti, Michigan, born in 1840, the son of Calvin and Alvira (Round) Reed. He crossed the plains with them ten years later, coming to Clackimas county, and making the trip by ox-teams. When twenty years old he struck out for himself, going into the cattle business and farming, and in 1864 he emigrated to the Palouse country. Two months later he went to Snake river and thence three months afterward to Walla Walla, from which point he journeyed to Helena, all this time with a band of horses. After having spent the summer in Montana's capital, he returned to Walla Walla,

and from that city he came to Eagle valley. In 1877 he took a homestead in Eagle valley, where he has ever since lived. He has a fine home, well improved and abundantly supplied with buildings, fences and other equipments.

In 1872 our subject married Miss Sarah, daughter of Abraham and Edith (Fairman) Swisher, natives of Pennsylvania, and to their union seven children have been born: Harriet, now Mrs. Samuel Sloan; Valeria, wife of Clarence Spaugh; Abraham, married to Ida Maley; Anna, Calvin, Donnie, and Gladys, at home.

Mrs. Reed's parents crossed the plains to Mexico in 1864, but soon returned to Pennsylvania, whence, in 1868, they came to Oregon, again crossing the plains with ox-teams. On the latter trip they had several casualties. In the North Platte river they upset, losing everything, so they had to send to Fort Laramie for aid. They experienced many difficulties with the Indians, and sometimes had to part their train to allow stampeding buffaloes to pass by.

GARRET W. VANDERWALL.—A splendid representative of the unconquerable Saxon race to which he belongs, Mr. Vanderwall possesses an abundant measure of the thrift and energy which has rendered the Dutch race famous and has made the sons of Holland who have found their way to America such desirable citizens.

Our subject is a native of the province of Friesland, born July 10, 1857. He resided in the land of his nativity until twenty-three years of age, acquiring a public-school education and such invigorating physical discipline as the farm affords. In 1880 he came to California, where for a period of four years he worked as a wage earner, saving his earnings that he might some day be privileged to engage in the more independent life of a farmer. The year 1884 found him in Baker county, Oregon, and in possession of a fine farm five miles west of Haines, where he has ever since lived. He is now the owner of two hundred and forty acres, well improved and abundantly supplied with all needed buildings, fences, etc., etc. Mr. Vanderwall is a general farmer, raising such products as he thinks will be most demanded by the market and keeping on the average about fifteen fine dairy cows.

Fraternally our subject affiliates with Haines Lodge, No. 11, A. O. U. W. His marriage was solemnized in Goshen, Indiana, on the 24th of April, 1884, Miss Anna Fisher, a native of Indiana, then becoming his wife. Their union has been blessed by the advent of three children, Sylvia, Leona and Roy.

WILLIAM POLLMAN. — Among the successful business men who have come to Baker county and have found here the "tide which taken at the flood leads on to fortune," must be counted the man whose career we must here essay to outline. Coming to this community with but very little money in his pocket, he has by dint of diligence, thrift and business ability wrought his way to at least moderate fortune and a very enviable position of power in the commercial world. We shall now attempt to present the specific history of his life.

Mr. Pollman was born in Quincy, Illinois, on the 24th of August, 1867, his parents being F. W. and Amelia Pollman, natives of Germany. When but two and a half years old he was taken to Lacygne, Kansas, where his father was engaged in the meat market and stock business. There our subject received his public school training, which was supplemented by a course in the Gem City Business College, of Quincy, Illinois, from which he received his diploma when twenty years of age. He had also attended previously the normal school at Fort Scott.

His experience in the meat business began while he was still a child. In 1889 he determined to try his fortune in the west, so came to Portland, Oregon, but apparently not finding the conditions obtaining there exactly to his liking, he returned that same fall to Baker City, where he was employed by Geddes and John Kraft for a short time, when he formed a partnership with Mr. Geddes, Mr. Kraft having sold his interest in the business, and together they continued in the meat business. Fortune has favored them, and at present they have large herds of stock in different parts of the county and ranches aggregating about twelve hundred acres. Mr. Pollman has valuable business and residence property in Baker City and is also interested in the Gas and Electric Company, of Baker City, of which he is president, and he owns a beautiful residence at No. 1615 Washington street. He is a public-spirited man and takes the interest every good citizen should in the general welfare of his town, county and state, though he is not personally ambitious for political preferment.

Fraternally our subject is affiliated with the K. of P., the I. O. O. F. and the B. P. O. E. His marriage was solemnized on February 5, 1896, when Miss Emma Geiser, daughter of John and Eliza Geiser, became his wife. They have two children, Louisa E. and Edna G.

HARRY A. DUFFY.—It is with pleasure that we are allowed the privilege of making mention in this volume of the prominent young business man and distinguished citizen whose name initiates this article and whose life has largely been spent in the county of Baker and with that uprightness and manifestation of ability and integrity that have won the esteem and confidence of all and where he has already carved for himself a place of enviable distinction both in the social and business world, being at the present time manager and part owner of the second oldest drug business in the county, the Duffy drug store.

The birth of Mr. Duffy took place in Macon, Macon county, Missouri, on February 29, 1876, being the son of Joseph M. and Ella M. (Smith) Duffy, especial mention of the father being made in another part of this work. When eight years of age the parents removed to Owyhee valley in this state, and two years later they repaired to this county, settling first in Huntington. Here our subject attended the graded schools, and graduated therefrom in 1897. The training acquired in this way was by no means all that he gained, for much of his time was spent in practical service in the drug business, and when he finished his schooling he was ready to go before the state board of pharmacy, and there he passed with honor the trying examinations to be undergone by those who would become registered pharmacists. He gained this distinction readily and at once entered business for himself and is at the present time enjoying a large and lucrative patronage, being well and favorably known throughout all the section adjacent to his home town, as well as through the county at large.

Fraternally Mr. Duffy is affiliated with the Burnt River Lodge, No. 86, I. O. O. F., also with the A. F. & A. M., Baker City Lodge, No. 47. He is a member of the Congregational church and is active in its support and in general church work. He has served as mayor of the city and is at the present time city councilman, and in all of this public work he has manifested the same sagacity and keen foresight that is characteristic of him in his private business enterprises. In political matters he is active and interested, and allies himself with the Republican party.

WILLIAM D. NASH, one of the public-spirited citizens and enterprising farmers and stockmen of Eagle valley, was born in Statesville, North Carolina, in 1854. When about fifteen months old he was brought by his parents, William M. and Elizabeth (Knox) Nash, to Missouri, and in 1869 he accompanied them to California. Though his home was with his parents until he became twenty-three years old, he began life's battles on his own account some nine years earlier. He herded sheep for a stockman in the Golden state, and eventually got to be foreman for his employer, then leased a band of sheep and embarked in the industry on his own account. During his wage-earning days he traveled over the entire state of California, and it was by working on the Sacramento river and vicinity that he got his start, and there he took his first place. In 1878 he settled in Lassen county, California, and there he remained until 1886, when he came to Eagle valley, Oregon. Purchasing a tract of one hundred acres on Eagle creek, he established a home there, while he utilized the ranges for pasturing his sheep and cattle. During the first sixteen years of his residence here he frequently made trips with his flocks as far as Montana.

Our subject takes the interest which becomes a good citizen in politics and matters of general concern. He belongs to the Odd Fellows and was one of the organizers of the subordinate lodge in Eagle valley.

Our subject married Miss Dora, daughter of Thomas and Rebecca (Cumings) Summers, and they have had six children: Carl, deceased and buried near Big Valley, California;

Lorena, wife of Frank Sultz; Zella, Bessie, Ruper J. and Odeta, at home; and one that died in infancy.

It is of interest to note that Nashville, Tennessee, was named after our subject's paternal uncle.

JAMES C. BROOKS.—The good, substantial citizen and prosperous farmer whose name appears above is a native of Newcastle, Delaware, born in 1843, his parents being Josiah and Mariah (Long) Brooks, likewise natives of Delaware. He was educated at Newcastle, where the school was maintained by funds bequeathed to it by William Penn, for the purpose of educating its youth. In 1868 he accompanied the remainder of the family to Kansas, in which state his father died, the date being 1872. He then assumed the management of the paternal estate, removing shortly with his mother and the other children to the Grande Ronde valley, Oregon, where they remained between the years 1875 and 1877. In the latter year they removed to Pine valley, located on a homestead of one hundred and sixty acres, two and a quarter miles northeast of Halfway postoffice, and engaged in cattle raising and general farming. He has a fine place and is comfortably situated, but has never been married and since the death of his mother, on July 13, 1888, has been without the cares and without the pleasures of domesticity. The remains of his mother were laid to rest in Halfway cemetery, after she had trodden the course of the pilgrim for one more year than the allotted three score and ten.

Mr. Brooks owns nearly two hundred head of cattle, and thirty horses, being a skillful handler of stock. He is one of the earliest settlers of this valley and deserves great credit for his labors here.

ISAAC N. PANCAKE, a veteran of the great Civil war, and an honored citizen of Baker county, in the development of which he has materially aided, was born in Noble county, Indiana, in 1838. His parents, Abraham and Mary (Choup) Pancake, natives of Ohio, were among the first settlers of northern Indiana, where they followed farming until death claimed them. Our subject remained under the parental roof until the outbreak of the Civ-

JAMES C. BROOKS.

ISAAC N. PANCAKE.

O. P. ISON.

ALFRED H. HUNTINGTON.

il war, then enlisted as a non-commissioned officer. He served three years and one month, participating in many hard-fought engagements and skirmishes, one of his superior officers for a part at least of the time being the famed General Lawton, who perished in the Philippine war. At the close of his service our subject was discharged as a color sergeant. Returning home, he remained with his parents about two years, then went to Linn county, Kansas, and engaged in farming, an occupation which continued to engage his energies until 1877, which year is the date of his advent to Pine valley. Arriving in September, he purchased a place two and a half miles north of the present Halfway postoffice, and again under new conditions and surroundings, began farming and stockraising, a business which he has followed energetically and successfully ever since. Thus has he demonstrated that the same conquering force of character which made him a good soldier in war times could enable him to win success in the less dangerous, but sometimes no less arduous, battles of civil life.

Mr. Pancake was married in Indiana in February, 1865, to Miss Nancy, daughter of Robert and Nancy (Cutler) Curtis, natives of Vermont, and to their union seven children were born, Bruce; Lena, wife of William Mills; Vertie, deceased; one that died in infancy; May, wife of Fred Painter; and two others who died in infancy.

Mr. Pancake's father was a leader in Ohio politics, having been twice representative of his district, also one of the first board of county commissioners of his county.

Our subject himself is vitally interested in matters of public concern, especially in the cause of education, which he has promoted by efficiently serving as trustee both in Kansas and where he now lives. Fraternally, he is affiliated with Phil Kearny Post, No. 66, G. A. R.

O. P. ISON.—Among the very first ones that came to this section and remained, honorable mention should be made of the gentleman whose name initiates this paragraph, who for nearly forty years has wrought here for the material welfare and substantial development of this county, while his fine business ability and keen foresight have given him the proper rewards of a good competence among the people who have bestowed in him their confidence and esteem, which have been richly merited, in every respect.

Mr. Ison was born in Garrard county, in the old Blue Grass state, on June 11, 1846. When but three years of age, he was removed by his parents to Trenton, Missouri, and there wrought on a farm until 1862, when the entire family made the trip across the plains with ox teams, settling near Wingville, and engaging in farming and stockraising. Our subject has given his attention to these related industries almost continuously since, and he is known as one of the most prosperous and experienced stockmen in eastern Oregon. His residence is one mile west of Baker City, but his hay farm, which consists of one half section of fine hay producing soil, is situated eight miles north from Baker City. He has at the present time over three hundred head of fine graded Short Horn and Hereford cattle, besides some fine specimens of thoroughbreds.

The marriage of Mr. Ison and Miss Martha J., daughter of Thomas B. and Mary J. Vernon, was celebrated on January 11, 1871, and to them have been born the following children: Orenea, wife of John G. Foster, of Baker City; Carrie Lee, wife of H. B. Kinniston, living near Wingville: Lilith B. Mrs. Ison is a native of Iowa and her father was the first blacksmith in Auburn, having come to that place from the Hawkeye state. Mr. Ison is fraternally affiliated with the Wingville Lodge, No. 69, I. O. O. F., where he holds a very popular position among his fellows. He is also a member of the school board of Baker City, district No. 5, and has ever manifested a spirit of public interest and especially in educational affairs, where his service is with wisdom and integrity, while his life shows forth those principles of worth and intrinsic moral qualities that are commendable in a high degree.

ALFRED H. HUNTINGTON.—Few men, perhaps, have added more to the wealth of Baker county and vicinity than he whose name gives caption to this paragraph and few have a better right to be classed as benefactors of the section. An active man in mining ventures and in various other lines of material and commercial activity, a leader also in the local government and politics of the county with which our volume is concerned, the subject of this review is certainly deserving of due representation herein and we should hardly escape the charge of incompleteness were there failure to accord him such.

Mr. Huntington is a son of C. A. and Lucretia A. (Watterman) Huntington, born in Rockford, Illinois, September 1, 1856. His mother was a daughter of the famed Judge Thomas A. Watterman, of Vermont. Of his father it is fitting that brief mention should be made, inasmuch as he was a pioneer of note and a man of much ability and force of character. He came via the isthmus route to Olympia, Washington, in 1863, as chief clerk in the office of William Watterman, superintendent of Indian affairs. In 1873 he became Indian agent at Neah Bay and in that capacity he served until 1879, when he removed to Eureka, California, to accept the pastorate of the Congregational church of that city. He had been ordained in 1868. His services as a minister of the Gospel continued until 1887, when he retired. He still lives in Eureka, and enjoys remarkably good health for a man over ninety years old.

Our subject received his educational discipline at Pacific University, where he took a two years' course. In 1875 he went to North Yakima, Washington, and engaged with his brother, J. B., in the cattle business. Fortune smiled upon their venture and by the fall of 1880 they found themselves in possession of six thousand head. The following winter, however, proved an unusually severe one, and before spring their herds were reduced in numbers to six hundred and eighty. With this remnant they removed to Baker county, Oregon, locating at the site of Huntington, where they purchased the Miller ranch and stage station. They were the ones who platted the town, and from them it takes its name. In 1883 they suffered some heavy losses and were compelled to make an assignment, which closed out the remnant of a one hundred and fifty thousand dollar estate.

In the spring of 1885 our subject stuck the first stakes which marked the Cornucopia mines, he being one of the original discoverers. In the fall of that year he sold his one-fourth interest, realizing only three thousand dollars therefor. The mine is now valued at about one hundred and forty thousand dollars. Later he became owner of some very valuable properties in the Cable Cove district, among them being the Herculean and the Eagle group, but, like most of the original discoverers of mines, he realized but litttle out of them. In 1895 he went to Burnt river and bought a farm where the town of Whitney now stands, and upon this he resided until 1898, when he was summoned by the franchises of the people to the office of county sheriff, so he disposed of his interests at Whitney. The excellence of his service as sheriff of the county is attested by the fact that in 1900 he was re-elected, and it is but fair to say that he has ever proved himself a conscientious and eminently efficient officer. His public service and his private life have both been such as to win him the esteem and respect of the people of his county, and his standing is indeed an enviable one.

In fraternal affiliation Mr. Huntington is identified with the time-honored A. F. & A. M., also with the W. of W., the Maccabees and the A. O. U. W. On January 26, 1897, in Eureka, California, he married Miss Inze Albee, and they have two children, Alfred H., Jr., and Lucius A.

In 1865 he was one of the two passengers on the stage from Burlington to Johnson, Virginia, which carried the news of Lee's surrender to Grant.

❖❖❖

ANDREW J. HARTUNG.—Among the progressive forces of Baker county must be numbered the prosperous and enterprising agriculturist whose name appears above. Not content with occupying a place among the foremost farmers of the section, and contributing to the general progress in that way, he is also interested in numerous mining properties in this and adjoining counties, and while developing these is at the same time contributing immeasurably to the development of the sections in which they are located. Truly he is deserving of rank among the benefactors of Baker county, and it is with pleasure that we accord him representation as such in this portion of our volume.

Mr. Hartung was born in Jasper county, Illinois, on February 19, 1859, his parents being Alexander and Lucinda Hartung. In 1865 the family went to Germany, intending to locate there, but after a residence of about six months in Europe they returned to the United States, locating in Plymouth, Wayne county, Michigan, where our subject completed his education. In 1874 they moved to Texas, and in 1877 they came thence with wagons and horses through Indian territory, Kansas, Colorado, Wyoming, Utah and Idaho to Baker county, in which they found themselves early in the year 1878.

Locating on Muddy creek, eight miles northwest of Haines, they there engaged in the basic art of agriculture, and there our subject has ever since lived. He is now the owner of a fine, well improved farm of two hundred and eighty acres, upon which he is raising almost every variety of product suited to the soil and climate and quite a number of horses and cattle. His premises proclaim him a careful, thrifty man, industrious, progressive and skillful. Mr. Hartung has interests in several quartz mines in Lacede district, Union county, also in Numbers 1 and 2, Copperwonder group, in Baker county. He is an organizer of the Killimacue Lake Reservoir and Rockcreek Irrigating Company and serves acceptably as one of the Muddy creek high school trustees.

In his fraternal affiliations our subject is identified with Haines Lodge, No. 11, A. O. U. W., while in religious persuasion he is a Seventh Day Adventist, his membership being in the church at Baker City. His marriage was solemnized in Paris, Illinois, on January 7, 1890, the lady being Miss Sadie Kirkpatrick, daughter of David and Mary, and a native of Kentucky. They have two adopted children, Ollivene and Alaric.

BERT W. GRAHAM.—Some one said that the pulse of a nation's prosperity is felt by knowing its commercial status, and equally true is it that the tradesman of any stated place is a standing index to both the financial condition and the enterprise and intelligence of the surrounding territory, and it is eminently fitting that in Baker county we find a most thrifty and stanch commercial element, especially progressive yet manifesting a due conservatism in the transactions of business; and distinguished among this number is the firm of Sherk & Graham Company, wholesale and retail general merchants of Huntington, of which company the gentleman mentioned at the head of this article is one partner.

The birth of Mr. Graham was in Croswell, Michigan, the date being February 24, 1873, and his parents, Robert and Laura (Wixon) Graham. He was reared on a farm and attended the common schools of that section until he was sixteen years of age, when he commenced teaching, and then took a course in the Cleary Business College of Ypsilanti, Michigan, after which he became editor and proprietor of a newspaper for four years. It was in 1899 that he came to the town of Huntington, and there in company with G. W. Sherk opened their present large and attractive establishment, where they have built up a fine patronage. While in the east Mr. Graham always took an active part in politics, supporting the Republican party, but since coming to the west, while he maintains the interest proper to good citizenship, he has given himself mostly to the prosecution of his business. He affiliates with the I. O. O. F., Burnt River Lodge, No. 86, and also with the Maccabees. His father was taken away by death in May, 1900, at the home place, but his mother is still living there.

The marriage of Mr. Graham and Miss Ida E., daughter of William and Charlotte Courtney, was celebrated in Carsonville, Michigan, on June 11, 1896.

GUSTAVUS T. PERRY.—The popular hotel man and prosperous farmer and stockraiser whose career it is now our task to outline in brief, was born in Green county, Illinois, in 1835, the son of William and Mary (Cooper) Perry, natives respectively of Virginia and Kentucky. In 1836 he was taken by parents to Missouri, where he grew to manhood and where he lived for a number of years after man's estate had been reached. He was connected with his father in the management and cultivation of a three-hundred-acre ranch until he became thirty-three years of age, then he engaged in farming on his own account, continuing to employ himself thus until 1886, when he crossed the continent to Eagle valley, in Baker county. For a time after his arrival he farmed in company with his brother-in-law, J. B. Feniel, in the upper part of the valley near where Newbridge postoffice now is, but in 1890 he bought sixty acres within the townsite of Richland, where we now find him. He has been engaged principally in farming and stock-raising since this last change of residence, as he was before, but for the last six years he has maintained a hotel in connection with his other enterprises, known as the Perry house.

Mention should be made of the fact that our subject was a soldier in the Confederate army during the war of the Rebellion, and served for two years as a member of Sterling's and Price's escorts, then on General Shelby's escort, the time of his entire service aggregating four years and one month, or about the entire time during which hostilities lasted. He was faithful and efficient in support of the cause which seemed to him to be right, and possessed, no doubt, his full share of the dash, daring and vigor which characterized the southern armies.

In 1870 our subject married Miss Susan, daughter of Zacariah and Sarah (Odeneal) Feniel, natives of North Carolina, and to this union seven children have been born: Ida, deceased; Waldo, a resident of Union county; Charles, at home; Edgar, at home; John, at home; Bessie, deceased; and Eula, at home. Mr. Perry handles about one hundred head of fine cattle.

---◆◆◆---

HARRY P. SWISHER.—One of the earliest pioneers of Baker county and one of those who have been forceful factors in the development of the country and in effecting its transformation from a state of barbarism and savagery to civilization, the man whose name appears as the caption of this paragraph is certainly worthy of recognition herein as one of the founders and builders of eastern Oregon.

Mr. Swisher was born in the great Keystone state, near Danville, Columbia county, on

September 13, 1852, his parents being Abraham and Edith (Fairman) Swisher, also natives of Pennsylvania. When sixteen years old he accompanied the remainder of the family on the long journey over the wide expanse of prairie and through the mountain fastnesses to Baker county, making the trip from St. Joe, Missouri, with ox-teams. The party experienced some difficulty with Indians at Rock creek, and were robbed of quite a number of their cattle, and on the north fork of Platte river, where North Platte is now located, they were overturned in the effort to effect a crossing and lost all their valuables, including several hundred dollars in greenbacks.

Arriving at last in Eagle valley, despite the exigencies of the journey, the parents settled on the spot where the nest was found from which the place received its name and at once engaged in farming and stock-raising. Our subject, who had not yet completed his education, attended school in Baker City for a time. When he arrived at the age of legal majority he took as a homestead a quarter section adjoining the parental farm and joined his brother in the stock-raising industry. They habitually kept on hand during those early days between five and six hundred head of neat cattle. On August 16, 1881, the mother of our subject departed this life, and on the 2d of December, 1898, his father also died. Mr. Swisher has succeeded them in interest, and in addition to the land bequeathed to him and that secured from the United States government, he is now the owner also of a quarter section acquired by purchase. In 1898 he moved to 2467 Madison street, Baker City, where he has since resided, directing the affairs of his farm from his urban home.

Fraternally our subject is affiliated with the Fraternal Union of Baker City, he having been a charter member of that order in Eagle Valley. His marriage was solemnized in Baker City, on March 20, 1895, Miss Annie Swisher, a daughter of John and Sarah (Corsen) Swisher, then becoming his wife. They have one child, Hayman.

We should not neglect to add the interesting reminiscence of Mr. Swisher's experience with the Indians during the Bannock war. He and other Eagle valley settlers were forted up at Mr. Moody's place for a while during the year 1877, and in 1878 the settlers again fortified, this time on the old Love place, but when the second stockade was built our subject and his father-in-law were in Umatilla Landing after a load of freight, or, in other words, they were on a journey which required forty-nine days for its completion. When at Cayuse Station, a few miles this side of Pendleton, they were met by Indians, who fired upon them, so they turned and retraced their steps to Pendleton. There they lay in the bushes all night, not knowing at what moment their hiding place might be discovered, for they could hear the red skins driving cattle the live-long night.

GEORGE W. SHERK.—In the large firm of Sherk, Graham Company, incorporated, we have one of the leading wholesale and retail mercantile establishments in eastern Oregon, and its successful establishment and prosperous continuance in the arena of business is largely due to the fine ability both executive and financial, coupled with excellent foresight of the senior partner in the concern, whose name heads this article and to whom we are endeavoring to grant a representation in this volume commensurate with his prominence and his stanch integrity.

. George W. Sherk, son of Henry and Blinda (Walker) Sherk, was born August 4, 1852, in Springfield, Ontario, Canada, and there received from the most excellent schools of that province his education, remaining also until he had attained manhood's estate and gained a commendable business training. In 1881 he came to Croswell, Michigan, and began a business career that demonstrated him to be possessed of marked ability, which brought to him the rewards that are dependent upon sagacity and probity. For eighteen years he was at the head of one of the most successful and powerful mercantile establishments in his section, known as the Sherk Brothers mercantile institution. In addition to the arduous duties devolving upon him in the capacity of directing such a concern, he was also director of the State Bank in his town, president of the Sans Pariel Roller Mill Company, director of the Rice and Allen Company, secretary of the Electric Light Company, besides being one year member of the town council, three years clerk of that body, and one term president of

the same. In January, 1900, he turned from the scenes of his many and successful labors and sought out Huntington, where he established, in connection with the junior member of the firm, B. W. Graham, who is specifically mentioned in another part of this work, the present large business house mentioned above. From the beginning there has been a large trade, which, augmented by the strict business principles maintained and the affableness of the proprietors, has grown to mammoth proportions. Mr. Sherk is president of this incorporation and has invested heavily in its establishment, but it is evident that again he was guided by sound financial wisdom, for the returns are already all that could be wished.

Mr. Sherk and Miss Phoebe H. Barton were married in Springfield, Ontario, February 24, 1881, and to them have been born the following children: Dafoe H., attending the University at Eugene, Oregon; H. Everett, attending the graded school in Huntington; Beatrice; George Barton. Mr. Sherk affiliates with the I. O. O. F., Burnt River Lodge, No. 86, with the Masons, Foresters, Maccabees, and Knights of the Legal Guard. Together with his wife, he is also a member of the Eastern Star and the Daughters of Rebekah.

THOMAS M. PEARCE.—One of the earliest settlers in Baker county, of which he has ever been a public-spirited and progressive citizen, the subject of this review has in all respects so ordered his life as to win and retain the good will and confidence of those with whom he has been thrown in contact, and his record since he has been in the section not alone for potency in promoting the general advance but as a worthy man and honorable member of society is one of which he has no reason to be ashamed. It is therefore with pleasure that we are enabled to accord him representation in this part of our volume.

Mr. Pearce is a native of Boone county, Illinois, born October 4, 1842. When ten years old he accompanied his parents on the long and dangerous journey across plain and mountain to the west, and in 1853 the family settled near Roseburg, in Douglas county. After a residence there of fourteen years' duration, they removed to California, where our subject's mother died.   1

The father, L. M. Pearce, moved back to Oregon, after this sad event, settling in Coos county, where he remained until the time of his death, which occurred in 1889.

In 1862, Mr. Pearce crossed the Cascades to Baker county, coming here during the big rush caused by the discovery of gold in Griffin's gulch, and for about three years after his arrival, he was engaged in packing to Boise and to other mining towns. About 1865, he engaged in the cattle raising industry in Umatilla county, which lucrative business was his for the ensuing six or seven years, whereupon he moved onto a place in Eagle Valley, where he now lives. He devoted his energies assiduously to cattle raising until about three years ago, when he sold out most of his neat stock and turned his attention to the sheep industry. That has been his line of activity ever since.

In politics, our subject is a Democrat. He was married near Pilot Rock in Umatilla county, on October 6, 1874, the lady being Laura M., daughter of John and Eliza Carter, the latter of whom is still living at Tillamook. Their union has been blessed by the advent of six children: Claud M., at Sumpter; Elsie M., at home; Pery R., F. R., Winnie D., likewise at home, and Elberten, deceased.

Mr. Pearce has two sisters, Mrs. Florence Buell, Mrs. Matilda A. Masters, both living in Coos county, Oregon.

GEORGE W. HACKER, who has the distinction of being an old and honored pioneer of the west, and who has contributed not a little to the development of Baker county, was born February 8, 1830. He lived with his parents, Eli and Scena (Smith) Hacker, until twenty-six years old, crossing the plains with them in 1854. Their objective point was Sacramento, California, but they soon moved thence to Marysville, where the father and mother died. For three years following 1859, our subject followed teaming, then he passed a couple of years in Ureka, coming thence in 1861 to The Dalles, Oregon, where he remained about a year and a half, driving stage between that point and Sylila. Selling out then he engaged in freighting to Boise.

In the sixties our subject enlisted at Salem, Oregon, in Company C, First Oregon Infantry, and from that date until the last disloyal gun was forever silenced he followed the fortunes of war, his term of service being of eleven months' duration. Upon receiving his discharge, he returned to Oregon, locating this time at Baker City, and again engaging in teaming. To this he has given himself almost continuously since until about three years ago, when he homesteaded a quarter section of land near Sparta and engaged in raising horses. For many years, also, he gave a portion of his attention to mining. He is an energetic man and a good, thrifty citizen.

ANDREW ELLIOTT is doubtless one of the earliest as well as one of the most intrepid and sturdy pioneers of the region with which our volume is concerned, and it is quite fitting that a review of his interesting career be embodied here, since his life has been spent in the worthy and commendable efforts that have resulted not only in giving him a good competence for the journey of life, but also in bringing about the development of the country that he loves so well and has aided to materially.

He was born in Orleans county, New York, to John and Nancy White Elliott, on October 15, 1842, where he spent the earlier years of his life on a farm with his father and sometime in the pursuit of knowledge in the public schools of his day. At the age of fourteen he started with his older brother to the country where Minneapolis now stands, and later took a trip down the Mississippi river, but when the hostilities of the Civil war broke out he returned to Dubuque, Iowa, in 1862, where he found the train which he joined and with which he crossed the plains, using horse teams. The journey was made without special adventure, save that at one ferry on the Snake river, instead of paying the exorbitant price asked, they went farther round and came through the section where Baker City now stands. The only white men in that region were John Bowen, Hiram and Joseph Kinnisson. Our subject, with some others, turned aside into the Powder river valley and there put up hay for the stock. The following spring, 1863, he started with a pack train from Auburn to Boise City, and thence to

ANDREW ELLIOTT.

THOMAS McEWEN.

WILLIAM P. ARBLE.

JOHN S. LOCKE.

Boise Basin, and engaged in mining, also worked at the Rock Bar, and in 1865, in company with two others, came to Walla Walla. This journey was attended with much danger on account of some desperate fellows that were bent on robbing them. Thence they went on the old Mullen road to Bear Gulch, where they wintered. From Walla Walla they took a pack train of tea and tobacco to the mines, which was sold at good figures, the tea bringing four dollars and the tobacco ten dollars per pound. From this time until 1868 he was in the various mining camps of the region adjacent to 'Missoula and Helena and then came over the famous Lo-Lo trail to Lewiston, where they outfitted and went into the Wallowa valley, the Grande Ronde valley, and the Edmunds mining camp, and later in the fall arrived in Sumpter. This he made headquarters and has been following mining, both quartz and placer, since in the various camps adjacent. His life has been one of hardship and arduous undertakings that are incident to pioneering and mining on the frontier. He has owned some very valuable claims, among which was the Wide West, on the Mother Lode, and sold to Mr. English for a good sum. In addition to this he has sold other properties and still owns some that are considered very fine. He also has a comfortable home in Sumpter.

Mr. Elliott is a member of the A. F. & A. M., having taken the master's degree, and is also affiliated with the Royal Arch Chapter. He was one of the committee of three appointed by Judge Schofield in 1871 to view the route for the road from Auburn to Sumpter. It is with pleasure that we are able to state that none are held in higher esteem by the people than is Mr. Elliott, and it is evident that none are more deserving of the confidence of his fellows, and also their encomiums, than is this worthy pioneer who has wrought with such energy and wisdom since the early days when he blazed the way into this favored region.

THOMAS McEWEN.— Among the thrifty sons of Scotland who have contributed to the development of Baker county he whose name gives caption to this article is certainly to be ranked one of the chiefest. He has

been assiduously engaged in numerous lines of activity during all the years of his residence here and success in abundant measure has crowned his efforts in practically everything he has undertaken. A leader in the councils of the Republican party, he has been frequently honored by that organization with preferment, and whenever it has fallen to his lot to perform public duties the same have been discharged with a faithfulness and integrity which have won him esteem and augmented the confidence the people repose in him. But a better estimate of the man may be gleaned from the epitome of his career which follows.

Mr. McEwen was born in Glasgow, Scotland, on May 10, 1853, his parents being Edward and Jennie (Johnson) McEwen. He grew to early manhood in his native city, receiving a common school education. Coming to America in 1869, he first settled in Canada, where he followed farming for a short time. Coming thence to New Jersey, he resided in that state for about eight years. In 1879 he came to San Francisco, but a short time later we find him in The Dalles, Oregon, where he had his first experience in the transfer business, it being his duty to bear a part in the work of the Overland Stage Company, operating between The Dalles and Baker City. For two years he drove stage for them, then he purchased the Canyon line from his former employers and gave inception to his very successful career as a liveryman and stage operator. He now operates between Sumpter and Canyon City and sends daily stages to the Red Boy, Bourne and Granite mining camps, one hundred miles of route in all, and in this business he employs about one hundred head of horses. Indeed Mr. McEwen does most of the transfer business of this entire region.

The town of McEwen takes its name from our subject, who was the first hotel man therein. He, with Mr. Tabor, of the Red Boy, platted forty acres for the embryo city, and also gave the land on which the school building is located and the sites of the different churches.

Like many others in Baker county, our subject has realized very considerable sums of money out of mining ventures. He sold one of his properties in the Cracker creek district, the one adjoining the North Pole, to

21

the Barring Brothers, of London, who are owners of the North Pole, for fourteen thousand dollars. He was one of the three owners of the Belle of Baker, which one year ago sold for ten thousand dollars, and he has promoted many other valuable properties. He still owns three promising claims adjoining the Badger group at Susanville. Mr. McEwen is likewise the owner of six hundred and twenty acres of land in the Sumpter valley, and considerable valuable property in Sumpter and McEwen. It was he who built the Capital hotel, the Healey building and numerous other houses in Sumpter. Indeed, it may truthfully be said that he has done more building than any other man in that town.

Active in almost every other line, he has borne his part also in the political affairs of the county and state, and more than once he has been honored by his party. In 1896 he was the nominee of the Republicans for sheriff, and notwithstanding the overwhelming fusion landslide of that year, he was defeated by only eighty votes. For the past twelve years his voice has been heard in the state conventions of his party, and in 1900 he was a delegate to the national convention, and had opportunity to assist in the nomination of McKinley and Roosevelt.

Fraternally he is affiliated with the Freemasons, practically all of the degrees of which have been taken by him. He is a past master of Prairie City Lodge, No. 60, and has served as delegate to the grand lodge. He affiliates, likewise, with the B. P. O. E., the A. O. U. W. and the W. of W.. His marriage was solemnized in Baker City, on August 23, 1894, when Miss Minnie Fox, a daughter of old and respected pioneer parents, became his wife.

WILLIAM P. ARBLE.—Of all the pioneer occupations which sturdy mankind have followed there is none that gives greater opportunity for exploration and contact with nature in the rough, and genuine thrilling experiences, than does mining. The subject of this sketch is one of those hardy, intrepid and noble specimens of our race that has ever been on the frontier clearing the path for less experienced feet to follow, searching from the hidden depths of nature's treasure house the precious metals and bravely and faithfully doing his part in the development of the country.

Mr. Arble was born on June 7, 1825, in Altoona, Pennsylvania, being the son of Frederick and Rebecca (Fairfax) Arble, who were natives respectively of Pennsylvania and Virginia. Their marriage occurred in Pennsylvania, where the father was engaged in the iron works, and also operated as a contractor. In 1834 the father died, and in 1860 the mother also departed this life. In his native place our subject was reared and received his education in the common schools. In 1850 he left the parental roof and began life's work for himself, coming, via the Isthmus, to California, where he at once engaged in mining, continuing therein in that locality until 1865, when he removed to Nevada. After some time spent in that territory he repaired to Utah, and thence he went to Montana, always engaged in his chosen work, mining. From Montana he went to the British possessions, and from there he came to Oregon, settling first in Canyon City, in 1868, where he mined for three years and then came to Sparta. Thirty years ago he sought out a place in this locality and at the present time he is still living in Sparta. During his many years of travel and frontier life he has endured many hardships and passed through many thrilling experiences, which would be very interesting to detail had we the space. At one time he was snowed in on the mountains for three months in the dead of winter and only managed to subsist by getting elk meat, his only article of diet for all of these weary weeks.

Mr. Arble has never chosen a partner to share his pleasures and stand with him during the shades of life, and to-day is passing the golden years of his life in the quietness of celibacy. He owns considerable property and among it may be mentioned the Blue Cloud mine, a property of great promise.

JOHN S. LOCKE.—The population of Baker county have always been noted for their push and enterprise and forwardness in developing the resources that nature has so bountifully bestowed within the county's precincts, and among the leaders, even in this active number, we are compelled by force of right to mention the well known and prominent citizen whose name heads this article, and whose capabilities and excellent business operations have placed him in his present enviable position.

The birth of 'Mr. Locke took place in the Granite state in 1848, March 10, at Manchester, he being the son of Levi and Nancy M. (Durgin) Locke. The father died in 1893, and the mother is still living on the old home place at Concord, New Hampshire. When our subject was still a child he removed with his parents to the city of Concord and there received his education in the common schools until he was sixteen years of age. At that time he entered the employ of the United States and Canada Express Company, continuing with them for seven years. Following this he went into business for himself, handling fuel and ice, in which he was prospered until 1879, when he sold all and migrated to Baker county, locating first in Rye valley. Here he operated as superintendent of mines and later furnished all the timber for the Snake river bridge that was constructed by the O. S L. Co. He spent some time in this line of contracting and then turned his attention to stock farming, handling cattle and horses. He built and operated the first livery stable that was in Huntington, which he sold three years since. At the present time he resides in Huntington, having a handsome home there, besides a farm of eight hundred acres some ten miles west of the city; he is also interested in the Vaughan mines and other valuable properties.

Mr. Locke and Miss Charlotte A., daughter of Newell D. and Eliza A. (Averill) Foster, were married in Franklin, New Hampshire, on October 11, 1868, and to them have been born three children: Hattie A., wife of Daniel Padrick, of Portland, Oregon; Jennie B., deceased; Grover F., attending school in Huntington. Mr. and Mrs. Locke are members of the Congregational church in Huntington, and take especial interest in its support and welfare. Mrs. Locke's parents are both dead. Mr. Locke is associated with and is past noble grand of the I. O. O. F., Burnt River Lodge, No. 86, and has been the representative to the grand lodge nearly every year for the past sixteen years; he is also a member of Rathbone Lodge, No. 32, Knights of Pythias, and is past master workman in the Huntington Lodge, No. 19, A. O. U. W., and is a member of the Maccabees. He was for several years sheriff of Merrimac county, New Hampshire.

HON. ISRAEL D. HAINES.—It is ever a pleasure to take under review the life history of one who has wrought valiantly and well in the business of life, combining with sterling integrity and worth a degree of native ability enabling him to occupy a place of leadership and prominence among his fellows. The man whose career is now our theme was such an one. A pioneer of the pioneers, he knew well the topography and understood well the genius of the west, facts which caused him to become distinguished in the counsels of the state, during the decade spent in the Oregon Legislature. As a lawyer, also, his standing was such as to win him a reputation more than state wide, and to bring to his office many distinguished clients, but the qualities which chiefly rendered him esteemed were sincerity, benevolence and a broad minded interest in the general welfare. With this general preface we must attempt to present a specific outline of his career.

Mr. Haines was born in Xenia, Ohio, on December 7, 1827. When he arrived at the age of nineteen he set out across plain and mountain to the wild and unknown Pacific. On the way both he and his brother were stricken with cholera, but both survived, being in this respect more fortunate than many of their fellow tourists. Arriving, after a journey beset with many dangers, in the state of California, he piloted the first boat that crossed the bay to Jacksonville, where he and his brother Robert were for a time engaged in the mercantile business. Later he went to California and engaged in the search for hidden treasure, but eventually he returned to Oregon, Jackson county, where he read law under Judge Primm. In 1864, he was admitted to the bar, and he thereupon went to Silver City, Idaho, and opened a law office. He soon won distinction in practice, and it fell to his lot to be of counsel in the Poor Man case and in many other celebrated trials. He spent the winter of 1865-6 in San Francisco, in the company of Binger Hermann, Thomas H. Brents and others who have won like renown. In the spring of 1856, he started back to Idaho, but while passing through eastern Oregon, he found Colonel Loring, his old commander in the expedition, made by the Rifle regiment in 1849, also other old friends and comrades. By these he was persuaded to remain in Baker county, so he located at Auburn and engaged in mining and the practice of law, beginning his career of success and usefulness as a lawyer and political leader. He soon won the esteem and confidence of his own profession and the state generally. For ten years, he represented the people of Baker county in one branch or the other of the state legislature, as he had done those of Jackson county in 1862. He was one of those who took an active and prominent part in securing the removal of the county seat of Baker county from Auburn to Baker City.

Mr. Haines became the owner of large landed interests and great herds of sheep in the Powder River valley, also of much valuable realty in Baker City. He also founded the town of Haines, the site of which is still owned by his heirs, he having died on June 19, 1892.

Fraternally, Mr. Haines was affiliated with the I. O. O. F., his name being on the charter of the Baker City lodge. In the metropolis of the county, on November 23, 1817, he married Miss Sarah M. Dorsett, a daughter of James A. and Sarah M. Dorsett, who crossed the plains to Auburn in 1864. To this union five children were born, four of whom still live, namely: Stella M., wife of Judge Messick; Robert W., of Haines, Oregon; Amy C., teacher in the public schools of Baker City; J. David, a printer, and Elsie, deceased.

A. J. TONEY.—This industrious and enterprising stockman, farmer, and dealer in horses is deserving of rank among the leading citizens in the vicinity of Haines. He is thrifty in his business and possesses a liberal public spirit which causes him to take an active interest in the affairs of his community and county, while his standing as a man and member of society is of the highest. It is therefore a pleasure to accord him representation in this portion of our volume.

Mr. Toney was born in Jefferson county, Illinois, on July 7, 1845, his parents being John and Martha (Hudson) Toney. He resided under the shelter of the parental roof until he became eighteen years old, acquiring a good common school education. When the time arrived for him to sever family ties and to begin life's battle on his own account, he removed to Virginia City, Montana, where he followed mining and teaming for two years, coming then to Baker county, in 1866. Soon he had acquired a start in the stock business, and to that he has given the major portion of his time and energy since, though he does some general farming, owning a fine farm of two hundred acres. In 1892, he drove a band of four hundred horses to South Dakota and exchanged them for a valuable farm there, which he still owns. He is quite extensively engaged in the business of raising and shipping horses, and is achieving a very enviable success therein.

On December 3, 1871, our subject married Miss Hannah R., daughter of A. J. and Martha Ann Brown, who crossed the plains in 1864, and to their union ten children have been born, namely: Effie B., wife of A. J. Willis; Ida E., wife of I. G. Young; Etta E., now Mrs. Joseph Carter; Daisy E., wife of John R. Long; Eva G., a dressmaker in Baker City; Alta R.; Edna A.; Carlie; and Ocie and Emmit, twins.

ALONZO LONG.—For many years one of the progressive farmers of the county and at present an enterprising grain dealer in Haines, the subject of this review is deserving of rank among the forceful factors in the county's development and it is but fitting that due representation as such should be accorded him in this portion of our volume.

Mr. Long is a native of Mercer county, Illinois, born July 31, 1847, his parents being Lewis and Sarah Ann Long. In 1854 he crossed the plains with his parents, making the journey by the aid of the slow moving oxen, as the custom of the time was. Eventually they settled in Linn county, Oregon, where our subject devoted himself to the basic art of agriculture until 1872, during which year he came to Baker county. In due time he settled on Muddy creek and engaged in the business of farming and raising cattle. As above stated, he was for many years a leader in this dual industry in the county, and he still owns his original home and superintends the operation thereof, but at present he is himself engaged in managing his grain handling establishment in Haines and has been since 1899. As a business man he is energetic and progressive, possessed of the good judgment and foresight essential to success in commercial pursuits, and as a citizen and member of society he enjoys a very enviable standing.

In Linn county, Oregon, on May 13, 1869, our subject married Miss Julia Ann Taylor, a daughter of James and Elizabeth, and a native of Oregon. They have ten children: Ida Belle, wife of William Jackson, living west of Haines; Charles Denino, married to Ida Hodges, a native of Arkansas, and living on the home place; Clara May, wife of William J. Welch, of Haines; John R., living on the home place and married to Daisy E., daughter of A. J. Toney; Viola Ann, wife of R. P. Anderson, a resident of Haines; William Oscar; Lee Cleveland; Archie Jackson; Lora Ellen; Rosa Odelia.

DOW F. SHEPARDSON.—The industrious and enterprising merchant and business man whose life's career it is now our pleasant duty to epitomize is one of those men that are able to adapt themselves to the country in which they are, and to make the resources of their region respond with the reward of wealth for the labor put forth. To such that take the lead into new sections and patiently open the way for others to follow there is much credit due, and in the business ventures of our subject we see that sagacity and progressiveness manifested that may well characterize the real leader.

Born on October 4, 1857, at Mongo, Indiana, to Edmund G. and Catherine (Wilson) Shepardson, he was there educated in the public schools, and also received a fine training from his father in the commercial establishment that he owned. At the age of twenty-three he came, by way of Kelton, Utah, to Baker City, and there was engaged in various enterprises until June, 1901, when he saw an opening at Unity for a general store, and he immediately put in a stock of goods, and is now operating a good concern there, having in the meantime, by careful attention to busi-

ness and uniform geniality and uprightness, secured a fine patronage, which is steadily increasing. He is already increasing his stock, and the outlook is that in the near future he will have to enlarge his capacities for the transaction of business.

Mr. Shepardson and Miss Lillie Horfield, the daughter of Mrs. A. B. Swift, were married on October 12, 1898, and to them have been born two children: Iva and Roy.

BURTON MILLER.—Any compilation purporting to give a review of the leading citizens of Baker county would be sadly incomplete were there failure to mention prominently the leading business man and stanch and worthy citizen of the bright village of Whitney, whose name introduces this article and whose untiring efforts in the upbuilding of his native town and in the promotion of its welfare are well known to all, as well as his excellent business capabilities in the prosecution of his private enterprises.

Mr. Miller was born in Attleboro, Massachusetts, on February 15, 1865, being the son of John and Elizabeth (Stevens) Miller, and in his native place he received the educational discipline to be had in the common schools. As early as fifteen years of age he started in life's battles for himself, migrating first to Deming, New Mexico, and thence to Alma, in the same territory, where he occupied himself in stock-raising until 1888, at which time he came to Pocatello, Idaho, and embarked on the mercantile sea. For a decade he carried on a successful business in that place and then sold out and came to Sumpter and took up prospecting for a time. On October 10, 1900, he took the first load of lumber into what is now Whitney and built a store and again commenced operations in the commercial realm. His energies and ability have been directed into the channel of upbuilding and extending his trade, and he has been eminently successful, for today his customers are counted in large numbers and come from all adjacent points. He is considered one of the brightest and most enterprising citizens of the town, and on February 16, 1901, after Whitney was incorporated, he was chosen the first mayor, thus being the recipient of the highest honors that his fellows had to bestow. In this capacity he has rendered efficient service, and is faithful in the care of the interests of all.

Fraternally, Mr. Miller is affiliated with the A. O. U. W., Lodge No. 122, of Whitney, and holds the position of master workman; he also belongs to the W. of W., in Pocatello. The quiet joys of celibacy have heretofore claimed Mr. Miller, having never chosen the responsibilities of matrimonial life.

CHARLEY J. AKINS.—Among those to whom specific mention is granted in this volume, there is none of whom it gives us more pleasure to speak than the gentleman, whose name initiates this paragraph; and an epitome of his interesting career is matter that will be pleasant reading to many in this county, since his name is familar to a large circle and his integrity and ability, coupled with genuine affableness and broad public spirit have made him generally beloved and esteemed by all.

Charles J. Akins is the son of Dennis and Triphena (Sanders) Akins and was born on October 1, 1854, in Trumbull county, Ohio, whence he was removed by his parents, at the age of eight years to Iona county, Michigan. In 1865, they removed to Polk county, Iowa, and three years later they crossed the plains to Idaho Springs, Idaho. While the advantages in early life were few for Mr. Akins to gain educational training, still he so improved what were available and also carefully occupied his spare moments with profitable reading so that he became a well informed citizen and in some lines he chose later in life, a leader, thus demonstrating what perseverance and pluck can accomplish. In 1871, he left the parental roof and went to Wyoming, engaging with the Union Pacific Company as fireman on a locomotive, where he remained until he had mastered the intricacies of locomotive engineering. Following this, we find him in California and Oregon operating in the mines and making himself master of placer mining and other parts of the art as well. Then he went to Las Vegas, New Mexico, engaging as engineer on the Santa Fe road from 1879 to 1882, then returned to Montpelier, Idaho, and took an engine on the Oregon Short Line. After the road was completed to Huntington, he took

a passenger engine run from there, serving from 1885 until 1897. At the above date, Mr. Akins determined to leave the service of the company and accordingly took charge of the works of the Huntington Placer Mining Company, which incorporation was instituted under the laws of Nebraska. He is a practical placer miner, having operated in many places since he came west. He is a heavy share owner in the company. Their property is located at the mouth of Connor creek, about eighteen miles below Huntington, and is considered one of the finest placer propositions in the state of Oregon.

The marriage of Mr. Akins and Miss Kate O'Hara, a native of Nebraska, was solemnized on August 29, 1879, and to them have been born seven children, four of whom are still living: John L., a graduate of the Huntington high school, and at the age of nineteen a graduate also of the law department of Drake University, of Des Moines, Iowa; Charley E., who finished the high school course at the age of fifteen years; Jessie E. and Myrtle, attending school in Huntington. Mr. Akins affiliates with the Masonic fraternity. His father was a veteran of the Civil war, enlisting in 1861 in Company C, of Light Artillery, Ohio Volunteers, and participated in a number of battles, but was discharged in 1863, on account of disability, which in 1879 caused his death while in the state of Colorado.

EDWARD WILKINSON.—This enterprising merchant and prominent citizen of Pine has lived a life of great activity and adventure, traveling over almost the entire globe. He is quite an early pioneer of Baker county, which has greatly profited by his living within its borders, and it is but consistent with our plan that a brief review of his career be given place in our volume.

Mr. Wilkinson was born in Westmoreland county, England, in 1846, the son of Edward and Elizabeth (Atkinson) Wilkinson, natives of the same place. He remained at home until fifteen years old, acquiring a common school education, then yielded to the promptings of his adventurous nature, and went to the coast of Africa. He traveled quite widely over the Conger river region, then visited the Cape

Verde islands, the island of St. Helena, Ascension island and many more in the region, and when they had explored the country sufficiently to satisfy him he set sail for Rio de Janeiro, thence to the Falkland islands and through the strait of Magellan to the Pacific ocean. He went to Honolulu, thence to Portland and thence to San Francisco, arriving at the latter point in 1867.

Soon he was engaged in mining in the Golden state, but apparently not finding conditions to his liking, he came north to Portland, and thence to the Boise basin, where he was engaged in placer mining for about eighteen months. At the end of that period he entered the Malheur district, in which he spent a couple of years, eventually coming to Sparta. For about three years he followed mining and the general merchandise business there, and for three years more he followed like pursuits in the upper end of Pine Valley He then came to Pine postoffice and embarked in the general merchandise business with S. S. Pindle, whom he afterward bought out, that he might enter into partnership with his brother, Robert A. The two are in business together at present and are building up a very extensive and thriving trade, the natural result of their business sagacity and fair dealing.

Our subject is the owner of a couple of Galena claims in Idaho, some realty at Sparta, and fruit ranches at Eagle, Bridgeport and Pine.

Mr. Wilkinson states that he has never had any personal difficulties with the Indians, though he participated in the Joseph war. It is of interest to record at this juncture that he met Captain Semmes, of the Alabama, at Luzon island, and that he saw the Kearsage and was on board her a short time before she fought the Alabama.

JAMES SUMNERS.—While we are not in possession of enough material concerning the gentleman whose name gives caption to this article to give a connected outline of his life, his popularity in Baker county, and his standing among its pioneer citizens, was such that we cannot omit all mention of him. Coming here from his home in Kentucky when twenty-two years old, he was identified with Baker county from that time until, at the age of fifty-three years, he passed to the great beyond. During the early Indian wars he acted as a scout, and he was in all other respects a typical frontiersman. While he possessed the daring, hardihood, patience and resourcefulness which characterize the true pioneer, he possessed also a warm, tender heart, which ever inclined him to espouse the cause of the unfortunate and the oppressed. Without relatives in this section of the country, he had friends by the hundreds, and his demise was a cause of mourning in many a household. He was buried close to the Galena mine, which was discovered by him, his pick and shovel, which had been his companions on many a journey among the hills being placed beside him in the tomb. May he rest in peace.

ALBERT GEISER.—Among the great captains of industry who have figured in the development of Baker county, none stands more permanently conspicuous than he whose name appears above. Successful in winning from the earth its wealth of hidden treasure, in the banking business and in farming, as also in numerous other lines of endeavor, he has become one of the wealthiest men in the Inland Empire, and what is of more importance to the general public, he is employing his riches in such a way as to contribute immeasurably toward the general forward march. Nothing therefore, could be more fitting than that a review of his life should be given due place in a volume of this character.

Mr. Geiser is a son of John and Elizabeth (Briebach) Geiser, both natives of Germany. He was born in the vicinity of Denver, Colorado, on the 10th of February, 1863, and in 1870 he accompanied his parents thence to Nevada, from which state they later journeyed to Utah and thence to California. Our subject's father, who was a veteran of the Mexican war, and one of the originial Gilpin county miners, was engaged for several years in the Golden state in endeavoring to win from Mother Earth her hidden treasure.

In that state Mr. Geiser completed his education, which had been begun in Colorado, graduating from the high school in Oakland. He then joined his father in the mining pursuit, continuing in the same in that state until 1881, when he came to Baker county, resolved to try his fortune in the rich gold fields of this region. He worked several quartz mines in the section, and eventually, with his mother and sisters, became interested in the Bonanza mine. His progress since coming to the county has been uninterrupted, and he is now an owner or part owner of several dividend-paying mines, among them the Brazos, situated southeast of Baker City, over the company owning which, he presides; the Keystone Bell and the Gold Boy, with headquarters at Pittsburg, Pennsylvania; the Pyx, in the Bonanza district, with a five-stamp mill; and the Greenbow or Worley mine. He is also a director in the Baker City Gas & Electric Company; also owns the Geiser Grand hotel and other valuable property in the city. Though interested in so many other lines of activity, he is one of the most prominent large contractors in eastern Oregon.

In fraternal connection, our subject is a leading Mason, belonging to all the degrees of that order except the thirty-third, and he likewise belongs to the K. of P. and the B. P. O. E. He was married, in Baker county, on December 19, 1894, to Miss Bernice Dodson, daughter of Henry Dodson, who at one time was school superintendent of Grant county. They have two children, Annie and Edward. One of the leading achievements of Mr. Geiser, in the county, has been the developing and bringing out of the Bonanza mine, which he operated from 1891 to 1898, when he sold it.

HENRY LOENNIG.—The enterprising agriculturist whose career it is now our pleasant task to trace a brief outline of, is the son of Arnst and Marie Loennig, who crossed the plains with ox teams to Baker county in 1863, locating on Willow creek shortly after their arrival. Our subject, who was born near Quincy, Hancock county, Illinois, on July 8, 1860, was brought by them over the trail of many moons, and his home continued to be the parental hearthstone on Willow creek until 1881, when he bought a place about five miles west of Haines post office, where he has ever since lived. By dint of hard work and assiduous application he has brought his place to an excellent state of cultivation, improving it by the building of fences and the erection of a good house, barn and other structures.

Public-spirited and vitally interested in everything which promises to promote the general welfare and tends toward tht development and progress of his neighborhood and the county, Mr. Loennig is especially solicitous for the cause of education, his interest therein finding manifestation in the faithfulness and ability with which for six years he has discharged the duties of school director of his district.

In religious persuasion our subject is a Catholic and his membership at present is in the church of that denomination at Baker City. He was married on December 1, 1881, the lady being Miss Celestine Agatha, a daughter of Michael and Elizabeth Relling, and a native of Minnesota. They have seven children: Ernest, attending school at Mount Angel, Oregon; George, attending the Muddy creek high school; Barbara; Joseph; Ralph; Agnes; and Emma Agatha.

OLE DIDRIKSON.—A typical frontiersman and possessed of that dauntless courage and intrepidity, coupled with a frame of iron strength, that are so necessary to the successful prosecution of the pioneer life, the subject of this sketch has passed an interesting career, and it is a matter of regret that we are not enabled to grant more space to the details of his experiences.

Born in Denmark, to Nelson and Coskasine (Kreston) Didrikson, natives of that kingdom, and passing their entire lives near Kolden, our subject early learned the thrifty ways of the people of his country, and was engaged variously, from 1843, seven years after his birth, until 1864, the time of his advent into the United States. Driving stage, farming, serving as soldier, and other occupations kept him busy until the last date mentioned. His first night in this country was spent in Castle Garden, and the next day he was the subject of some very shrewd tricks on the part of the United States recruiting officers, who sought for two weeks to entrap him into enlisting in the army. Finally the consul of his native land was called in and he was sent on his way to Wisconsin, his journey's destination. By some mishap he was switched onto the wrong train, and was fast being carried to the seat of war but was enabled finally to get transferred to a train going to Oshkosh. At one dinner stop the accustomed hurry of a late train was interfering with dinner, when our subject seized a roast chicken, some bread and other things from the table and made the train, amid the merriment of the passengers and the discomfiture of the host. For a few years Mr. Didrikson was employed on a farm, in the woods on Lake Superior, in Chicago, in Minnesota, and finally, in 1868, crossed the plains with ox teams. His same adventurous spirit led the way to the mines at Helena, on Peace river, even to Lawson, Alaska, then to Walla Walla, afterward to Colorado, and then to Baker county, with a bunch of stock. While on this last trip he was so taken with the view of the Pine valley as seen from the tops of the mountains that he immediately came thither and secured a homestead, only two families being in the valley at the time. Quietly and industriously pursuing the life of the agriculturist and stockman, he has passed the intervening years on this ranch, until the present, but now he has sold and again is embarking in mining near the Iron Dick, on Snake river. His properties are rich in copper.

The life of Mr. Didrikson has always been that of the celibate, he preferring the freedom of that career to the cares of domesticity.

M. WILSON WHAM.—Four miles north from Unity, on the south fork of Burnt river, we find located one of the most substantial and enterprising of Baker county's stockmen, M. W. Wham, who by his industry and sagacity has accumulated a fine large holding in both real estate and cattle and horses, while his quiet and faithful demeanor in all his life has won for him the esteem of his fellows and made him the center of a large circle of admiring friends.

The birth of Mr. Wham occurred in Fayetteville, Arkansas, on October 26, 1848, his parents being John and Elizabeth Wham. In his native state he received the educational discipline to be had from the common schools, and there continued until he had arrived to the age of manhood. It was in 1869, that with others he made the weary journey from his eastern home to Clackamas county by the means of ox teams. For three years he remained there and then came to the east side of the Cascades and settltd on Willow creek. Two years later, in 1874, he came to his present place and located. He has a fine stock farm and abundance of water. He has continuously been engaged in raising stock since the date of his settlement, except the time that was spent in the Indian wars in the late seventies, where he did some good service.

Mr. Wham was married to Miss Frances, daughter of William and Lucretia Hill, in Baker county, on June 20, 1883. They have been blessed by the advent of the following children: Roy, Belle, Eddie P., Melvin, Irene and John. While Mr. Wham is not solicitous for political preferment of any kind, still he takes the part of the good citizen in all matters of local interest and political import, ever putting himself on record for that which is for the advancement of all and the upbuilding of the community and its interests. He is one of those quiet, substantial men that form the boast of any well regulated community and are the real stanch part of this strong republic.

JUDGE JOHN B. MESSICK.—Prominent among the young professional men of Baker county is the public-spirited political leader and successful attorney whose name gives caption to this review, and it is with pleasure that we accord him due representation here as a man who has already proven himself a forceful factor in the community, and who promises to be still more influential in the years to come.

Judge Messick was born in Nicholasville, Kentucky, on the 14th of July, 1862, his parents being Richard M. and Mary B. (Tomlinson) Messick. The family removed to Missouri in 1870, and there our subject grew up and received his educational discipline, the same consisting of a public school training and a course in the William Jewell College, at Liberty. Upon completing his preliminary training he returned to the Bluegrass state and engaged in the mercantile business, a line which he followed until 1885, when he returned to Missouri and engaged in school teaching. A year later he came to Oregon, locating in the Willamette valley, where he practiced the pedagogical profesion until 1890. He then came to eastern Oregon and taught in somes of the schools at Union and Baker counties for a time, but he had been devoting his spare moments for years to the study of law, and in 1892 he was admitted to the bar. He opened an office in Baker City, and here has ever since been engaged in the practice of the law, winning an enviable success, his ability and devotion to the interests of his duties having won his a large patronage. Indeed he is considered one of the ablest attorneys in the city. In the spring of 1900 he was elected to serve a two years' term as justice of the peace, a post for which his professional skill and his natural disposition toward absolute fairness have eminently fitted him.

In fraternal affiliations, our subject is identified with the Woodmen of the World, in Queen City Camp, No. 48, of which he has served as counsel commander. On April 3, 1895, he and Miss Haines were married and they now have one daughter, Minerva Bell. Mrs. Messick is a daughter of the noted Judge Haines, of whom more particular mention has been made in another part of this volume.

JOHN ERICKSON.—To the energetic farmer and stockraiser whose career we must now essay to outline, belongs the honor of having wrought his own way in the world from a very early age, and he has the independence of character and resourcefulness which result from such early struggles with conditions. Born in Arboga, Sweden, in 1829, he was left fatherless in early infancy, so had to be cared for by persons not related to him. Naturally, under those circumstances, he felt it incumbent upon him to attempt for himself the battle of life as soon as possible, so when he became fifteen engaged in farm work independently of all supervision by guardians. He was thus employed for about half a decade, going then to Stockholm, where for a few years he was in the service of a sugar refinery. He next worked in a gas factory, then in a machine shop, learning a trade in the latter place. In 1864 he emigrated to Quebec, Canada, and proceeding thence to Lake Superior, he there wrought for a time in the copper and iron mines. In 1867 he removed to Illinois, in which state and

in Kansas he farmed until 1877, when he came to Union county, Oregon. Eventually, he came thence into Pine valley, where he purchased a quarter section of land, and to the cultivation and improvement of this he has devoted his time and energies ever since. He is a diversified farmer, producing almost all kinds of crops suitable to the soil and climate, as well as cattle and horses. He is a thrifty, energetic man and a good citizen.

Politically, Mr. Erickson is a Republican, and he takes the interest everyone should in the general welfare of the community, county and state. In 1867 he married Miss Martha Johnson, a native of Sweden, and to their union have been born two children, John J. and August, both at home.

WILLIAM J. LACHNER.—The prominent young attorney and influential political leader whose name appears at the beginning of this article is one of the most promising young men in Baker county. A most excellent public speaker and blest with a genius for leadership among his fellows such as few possess, he has already risen to distinction, and the historian of the future will doubtless accord him rank among the greatest men of a great state.

Mr. Lachner was born in Canyon City, Grant county, Oregon, on November 30, 1869, the son of J. M. and Walburg W. Lachner, natives of Germany and pioneers of Baker county of 1862. When he was but two years old he was taken to Baker City, where he received a public school education, which was afterward supplemented by a course at the St. Joseph College. He then studied law with the late T. Calvin Hyde, of his home town, afterward entering the law department of the University of Michigan, from which he was graduated in 1896. Most persons who achieve such success as he in college work are assisted financially by their parents, but we have here an instance where one not only works his own way through college and the law school, but actually assists his parents all the time he is so doing. Upon receiving his degree, he at once began practice, and success has been crowning his efforts ever since. He has been in political life since he reached his majority and twice he has been chairman and once secretary of the

Republican County Central Committee. In 1898 he was offered the nomination of his party for the office of representative, but refused. He was, however, nominated for prosecuting attorney, much against his wishes, but the ticket was defeated, and that particular office secured by Samuel White. When McKinley was first a candidate for the presidency Baker county gave his opponent a majority of 956. In the last election this majority was reduced to one hundred and fifty, this very radical change in the sentiment and political complexion of the county being due in large measure to the efforts of our subject, who was serving as chairman of the county committee.

In fraternal circles, also, our subject is quite a prominent figure, his affiliations being with the A. O. U. W. and the B. P. O. E He was married, on November 30, 1898, to Miss Ida M Tibolet, a native of Upper Sandusky, Ohio.

WILBER J. SELBY.—This prominent young merchant and respected citizen of Baker City is a native of Kirksville, Missouri, born October 19, 1867, the son of Joshua and Harriet (Howerton) Selby. He grew to manhood there, receiving unusually good educational advantages, the same consisting of a course in the local common and high schools and in the State Normal school. In 1888 he went to Utah, where he taught successfully for the ensuing decade; then he moved to Colorado, and was there engaged in the mercantile business for a period of one year, after which he came to Baker county. He was employed here by P. Basche for a short time, but soon he had purchased an interest in the Baker City Mercantile Company, an establishment doing business in the Geiser Grand building, carrying a full line of fancy and staple groceries, queensware, feed, etc. He is manager of the business and the other members of the firm are M. and L. B. Miller. Theirs is one of the leading mercantile establishments of the city and does credit to the men whose energy and business ability have built it up.

Our subject is a public-spirited man and has ever taken an active interest in the affairs of communities in which he has lived, as he is doing in the politics and welfare of Baker City.

He once served on the city council of Ophir, Colorado.

In Kirksville, Missouri, on October 17, 1900, Mr. Selby married Miss Alice, daughter of Solomon and Fannie (Tinsman) Otto, of that city. Both she and our subject are members of, and prominent workers in, the Methodist Episcopal church here located. They reside in a pleasant home, No. 2314 Fifth street.

JOHN POWELL.—Oregon is well known as a stock raising state, and within its boundaries are some of the largest and most skillful stockmen that are to be found in the United States, and it is our pleasure at the present time to give the epitome of the career of one of the largest owners of thoroughbred Shorthorn cattle in the state, and it is largely due to his skill and enterprise that the standard is placed so high in his state in regard to registered stock, for he has produced some of the finest specimens and owns today some excellent animals.

Mr. Powell was born on April 1, 1834, in Genesee county, New York, his parents being Milo and Lucina (Gardner) Powell. While yet a child he was removed by his parents to Cass county, Michigan, there remained until he had gained manhood's estate, receiving meanwhile a good training in the public schools and in assisting his father on the latter's farm. When he was twenty-two years of age he started to the Eldorado of the west, California, via New York and the Panama Isthmus; landing in Amador county, he at once engaged in mining, and in 1858 went to Virginia City, Nevada, and there was among the first discoverers of the mines in that vicinity, and made a fine stake. During the summer of 1860 he returned to his home in Michigan, and for one year was taken up with seeing old friends and visiting his relatives. Following this pleasant trip he returned, by stage from St. Joseph, Missouri, to Virginia City, where he owned considerable mining property, among which were the claims now owned by J. W. Mackey, and known as the consolidated Virginia. In 1861 we find him in the forefront of the gold excitement in Florence, Idaho, with what success we are not told, and then later he went to Vancouver, Washington, and engaged in butchering, which he followed until 1873, then came to Baker county. From this date until 1879 he was engaged in hunting and prospecting, and during these years he was a veritable Daniel Boone. In 1879 he determined to change his occupation, and accordingly located a ranch where he lives at the present time, three miles northwest from Unity, on the south fork of the Burnt river. From one quarter section at the beginning, he has increased his holdings to the mammoth proportions of six hundred acres. His estate is well improved, and he has a large herd of excellent thoroughbred Shorthorn cattle, being one of the largest owners of pure bred stock in the state. He has three registered bulls that will weigh about twenty-three hundred pounds a piece.

The marriage of Mr. Powell and Miss M. Ella, daughter of James and Rose Moore, was solemnized in Baker county on July 4, 1894, and to them have been born three children: Adell Adalade, Margery Lucina and John Leland A. Mr. Powell is highly esteemed by all the community, and his life of uprightness has given him the meed of the admiration and confidence of all, while his thrift is rewarded by a generous competence.

JAMES MOORE.—Among the representative citizens of Baker county and the substantial property owners, mention must be made of the esteemed gentleman whose name forms the heading of this article, and to whom there is great credit due for his praiseworthy efforts and achievements in this county and in other places, ever laboring for the advancement of the interests of the community and the good of all, while he has been eminently successful in his private business operations.

Mr. Moore was born near Terre Haute, Indiana, on May 23, 1846. There he worked on the farm with his father, and also attended school during the school seasons until he was eleven years of age, when the family removed to near Marysville, Missouri, where they lived during the Civil war, and they experienced some stirring times and thrilling adventures. In 1869 they emigrated to Wilson county, Kansas, and continued there farming until 1881, when he came with mule teams across the plains and located twelve miles north from Baker City, buying a ranch and remaining there until 1889. Then he located his present ranch, five miles northwest from Unity, where he has resided since, giving himself to the improvement of the same and general farming and stockraising. He has now a very comfortable home and a goodly holding in various other property.

The marriage of Mr. Moore and Miss Rosina S., daughter of William and Mary Stingley, was celebrated at Whiteville, Missouri, on October 15, 1867, and they have become the parents of six children: Hester A., wife of Franklin McCullough; John W.; Thomas E.; Ella, wife of John Powell; Lettie J.; Bessie R. Mrs. Moore was called from the scenes of life to the world beyond on May 1, 1900, and her demise was universally mourned.

Mr. Moore's father was a soldier in the Civil war, enlisting in the Missouri Volunteers, in 1861, and saw much service in battles and skirmishes. He was honorably discharged at the close of the war, and then moved to Elk county, Kansas, where he died in 1881. The mother is still living in the old home place in Kansas.

ZENO DENNEY.—It is now our pleasant task to present in brief outline the life history of the successful young farmer and stockman whose name appears above. He is one of the enterprising citizens residing in the vicinity of Pine. and though he has not been on his present place long enough to have greatly improved it, he is energetically at work, and will no doubt soon have a pleasant and comfortable home. He was born in Lake county, California, in 1868, his parents being James P. and Sarah (Jones) Denney, natives respectively of Arkansas and Kentucky, and both at present residing in Dry creek valley.

Our subject remained under the parental vine and fig tree until twenty-five years old, then took a homestead not far from his present place of abode and engaged in farming. After about two years experience in the basic art he resolved to try his hand in commercial pursuits, so engaged in business at Homestead, on the Snake river. He busied himself in the development of his trade for about four months, then embarked in numerous other enterprises, but about a year ago he purchased land seven miles northeast of Pine post office and again engaged in tilling the soil. He owns a fine place of one hundred and sixty acres, and is raising all varieties of crops which are suited to soil and climate.

On September 9, 1895, Mr. Denney married Miss Clara A., daughter of Joseph and Lyda (Hughes) Ludiker, residents of Pine valley. Their union has been blest by the advent of two children: Nadie and Noel Z., both at home. Mr. Denney handles considerable stock in connection with his agricultural pursuits.

———◆◆◆———

L. S. KELSEY.—This extensive real estate owner and prosperous, progressive agriculturist and stockraiser, of the vicinity of Haines is to be counted among the leaders in his line of enterprise in Baker county to the development and general progress of which he has very materially contributed and of which he has long been an esteemed and honored citizen. Mr. Kelsey was born in Tooele county, Utah, on January 21, 1855. He resided there until the fall of 1879, receiving his education in the local public schools and developing his bodily powers by hard and invigorating exercise on the farm. In the year mentioned he came to Baker county and settled on the North Powder river, seven miles north of where Haines now is, and to his original homestead he has kept adding betimes, as means came as a reward of his well directed efforts, until he is now the owner of a princely domain of two thousand acres. He is the owner of a fine band of graded Shorthorn cattle, consisting of about two hundred head, likewise is interested in the production of many different kinds of agricultural products, especially hay. He also owns some very promising mining properties.

Honored for his forcefulness and ability in business, Mr. Kelsey is no less honored as a worthy member of society, his unvarying integrity and many other good qualities as a man rendering him trusted and esteemed.

Fraternally our subject is affiliated with North Powder Lodge No. 109, W. of W. His marriage was solemnized on August 5, 1875, in Tooele county, Utah, the lady being Miss Susan Tanner, who some years later died, leaving three children: Violet, wife of Henry

Parder resides at home; Laura, now Mrs. Lane Goff, and a resident of Baker county; Letta, wife of H. H. Wilson, living on Beard creek. In the fall of 1883 our subject again married, the lady of his choice being Miss Grace, daughter of James B. and Jane Wilson, of Union county and to this union four children have been born: Edna, Maude, Nellie and Ethel, all at home.

———◆◆◆———

JAMES P. DENNEY.—Among the earliest pioneers of the coast is he whose name appears above, and as he is also quite an early settler of the political division with which our volume is concerned, it is but fitting that he should be granted representation herein. It is always a pleasure to review the lives of those who have assisted in the herculean task of founding and building the west, and such pleasure is ours in outlining the career of Mr. Denney.

Our subject was born in Illinois on November 17, 1832 his parents being John and Martha (Llewellyn) Denney, natives of Tennessee. He accompanied them to Arkansas when quite young, and in that commonwealth he grew to manhood and received his educational discipline. When twenty-three years old he began the battle of life independently of parental guidance, and in 1856 he set out over the untrammeled highway of the prairie, and through the fastness of the mountains, to the Pacific coast. He came to a halt at a mining camp called Jamieson creek, in California, and in 1857 he went thence to the Sacramento valley, where the ensuing twenty-one years of his life were passed, his principal occupation being farming. At the end of that extended period he emigrated to southern Oregon, but not finding conditions there exactly to his liking, he soon came to Pine valley, arriving in 1880. Locating on a homestead about seven and a quarter miles northeast of Pine post office, he engaged in farming here, and to the cultivation and improvement of his land he has given his best energies ever since, compelling it by judicious tillage to yield the abundant harvests of which it is capable. He is a man who stands well in his community, being of unquestioned integrity and unusual force of character.

On October 6, 1852, our subject married

Miss Sarah Ann, daughter of John W. and Katie (Caudel) Jones, natives of Kentucky, and to this union seven children have been born, as follows: John; Martha L., wife of J. B. Whelock; George W.; Catherine, wife of James W. Cann, of Melrose, Oregon; Charles; Mary F., who died in 1897; and Zeno.

IRA B. BOWEN.—It is now our task to present in brief and necessarily incomplete outline the life history of one of the most prominent newspaper men and most potent factors in Democratic politics in Baker county. Mr. Bowen, now editor of the well-known journal, the *Morning Democrat*, is a son of the old and respected pioneers, I. B. and Ann Bowen, and was born near Chicago, in Cook county, Illinois, on November 28, 1858. He is, however, practically a product of the west, his parents having brought him across the plains in 1862. The family located in Auburn, where the father started a saw mill, the first ever operated in eastern Oregon.

Our subject attended the first school ever organized in Baker county, but completed his educational discipline in Salem, Oregon. For the half decade succeeding the year 1875 he was engaged in serving an apprenticeship in the office of George H. Himes, then the leading book and job printer in the state. Upon completing his handicraft he returned to Baker City and engaged in the publication of the *Bedrock Democrat*, which had been established in 1870, the second oldest paper in eastern Oregon, and the oldest in Baker county. He was engaged on that paper in one capacity or another, much of the time until 1887, when he and George B. Small purchased the plant, and ever since that date our subject has been editor and publisher of the *Daily Morning Democrat* and the *Bedrock Weekly Democrat*. Thanks to his energy and ability, his paper has always taken the lead in the county, and it now has a larger circulation than any of its rivals. It belongs to the Associated Press, hence is able to give to its readers the benefit of the dispatches secured by that powerful organization. It is also the county official paper.

As before stated, Mr. Bowen is very active in the counsels of the Democratic party, and several times he has been called upon to serve as chairman of its county central committee, the duties of which office he invariably discharged with great faithfulness and ability, materially strengthening the Democratic plurality in the community. Like most of the prominent men, he is interested in fraternal organizations, his membership being in the B. P. O. E., the A. O. U. W., and the Fraternal Union. He was married on October 16, 1895, the lady being Miss Mary E., daughter of P. and B. Burke, pioneers of the county. They have two children, J. B., Jr., and Anna Marie. Mrs. Bowen's father is one of the large and successful stockmen of the county.

FRANK HARDMAN.—The stockmen and farmers of Baker county have done no small part in redeeming the wilds of nature to be wealth producing regions and making the property estimate of this county to be largely increased, while their labors and wisdom have added much to the improvements of the country and the comfort of all. One of these worthy citizens is named above, and we now endeavor to chronicle in brief outline the salient points in his career.

Mr. Hardman is a native of the Web-foot state, being born in Linn county on May 24, 1866, to Joseph and Barbara (Ritter) Hardman. The parents crossed the plains in 1850 with ox teams and settled in the same year in Linn county; the father died in 1897, and the mother in 1899, each being in the seventieth year at the time of death. When our subject was three years of age he came with his parents to the John Day country, settling first at Prairie City. In 1892 he bought the land where he resides at the present time, eight miles south of Whitney, on the Burnt river. Here he has a fine estate, well improved, which produces many tons of fine timothy hay each year, and in addition he owns a goodly herd of excellent blooded cattle.

The marriage of Mr. Hardman and Miss Lillie, daughter of H. M. and Martha (Wilcox) Craig, was solemnized on April 4, 1888, and to them have been born the following children: George H., Thomas, Grace, deceased, April 9, 1894, and Hazel. Mrs. Hardman's parents live near Prairie City, this state. Mr. Hardman is affiliated with the Modern Woodmen of America, Unity Lodge, No. 7977. He is also one of the directors of the school district where he lives, and takes a lively interest in political matters and local affairs. He is considered one of the most substantial citizens of the community, and is one of those worthy men that form the boast and foundation of any well regulated district.

ANCELL COOK.—It is now our pleasant duty to briefly review the life of one of the most substantial and prominent men of his section, having been instrumental in assisting materially the advancement of the interests of the county and aiding in its progress and development since his domicile within its precincts was acquired; and whose capabilities and stanch integrity and intrinsic worth have been a source of both pleasure and profit to all that have been associated with him in these years.

Mr. Cook was born in Hickory county, near Quincy, Missouri, on October 7, 1846. The educational advantages of that time and place were very limited, but the industry and application of our subject largely made up for that by careful reading and investigation as opportunity afforded. When thirteen years of age he took the long and weary journey across the plains with ox teams to California, and settled six miles from Chico, on the Sacramento river, and engaged in raising stock until 1882. At this date he came to Baker county and bought the place where he now resides one and three-fourths miles southeast from McEwen, on the Baker City road. Here he owns one of the finest farms in the county; while it is not as large as some, still its productiveness is most marked, and an abundance of fine water adds greatly to its general fertility. He gathers annually bountiful harvests of good timothy hay and other crops. He owns a large herd of good cattle, and his ranch is well improved, having one of the most handsome and commodious residences in the valley. In every particular pertaining to the home and business of Mr. Cook there is an air of thrift and careful attention that gives rest and comfort to his rural abode.

In 1873 the marriage of Mr. Cook and Miss Anna E. daughter of Eli and Caroline Brewen, was celebrated in Contra Costa county, California. They have become the parents of six children: Della G., wife of Mark Boyce, living near Baker City; Walter; Carrie M.; Sylvia P., wife of Ervin Spencer, of Sumpter; Jessie M.; Frank. In educational matters Mr. Cook is quite active, and has been instrumental in assisting the cause of education materially in the valley. He and his wife are very active in church work, and are affiliated with that body in McEwen, where he is widely and favorably known.

By way of reminiscence it is interesting to note that while en route to California, although Mr. Cook had several hard struggles with the Indians, and he himself but young in years, he was victorious at every onset and escaped uninjured, although they determined to take his life. This speaks highly both of his courage and his intrepidity as well as of his physical activity.

ISAAC McMULLEN, one of the leading farmers and most respected citizens of the vicinity of Pine post office was born in Goderich, Ontario, in 1846. He lived with his parents, William H. and Elizabeth (Hall) McMullen, natives of Ireland, until he became eighteen years old, acquiring a common school education and learning the trade of a shoemaker. Upon giving inception to his independent career he set out for Chicago and from that time until 1866 he traveled quite extensively, going as far south as Kentucky. In 1866 he came out to Nebraska City, and thence along the Union Pacific railroad, as a member of different construction crews.

In January, 1869, our subject landed in the northern part of Eagle valley, Baker county, and he lived where the premises of W. Tobin now are, for a year or two, coming then to Pine valley, where he took a homestead of one hundred and sixty acres and engaged in farming and stockraising. To this dual occupation he has given his best energies ever since, with good success. He has a pleasant home, comfortably environed, and a place well supplied with buildings and equipments. Though vitally interested in the welfare of his community, county and state, he has never been himself a candidate for political preferment, and never has sought personal aggrandizement. He has, however, done his share for the cause of education by serving as director of his district.

In 1878 Mr. McMullen married Betty K., daughter of Joseph and Susan (West) Bragg, natives of Missouri, and they have three children: Joseph W., Maud M., and Bessie M., all at home.

Mr. McMullen's father was a veteran of the war of 1812, being a boy of sixteen at the time hostilities commenced.

◆•◆

DANIEL GRANT, M. D.—Prominent alike in his profession and in mining circles, the subject of this review is to be congratulated most fervently upon the success which has attended him thus far, as well as upon the bright prospects for future usefulness and reputation which are his. He was born in Nova Scotia, on November 24, 1874, his parents being Alexander R. and Margaret Grant, natives respectively of Nova Scotia and Scotland. Having completed the course offered by the excellent public schools of his native province, our subject entered McGill University of Montreal, and from the medical department of that famous institution he graduated in 1896. He then practiced for two years in the state of New Hampshire, after which he came to Baker City, Oregon, where he practiced a year, thereupon being appointed physician and surgeon to the E. & E., Columbia, Golconda, North Pole, Venus and Mountain View mines. He also enjoys a very enviable patronage outside of his mining practice, this coming to him as a reward of his painstaking care and conscientiousness in the discharge of his professional duties.

Fraternally our subject is affiliated with the Knights of Pythias, at Sumpter, Oregon, and the Pioneers of the Pacific, being examining physician for the last named order. He also affiliates with the very ancient K. A. E. O. He belongs to the British Medical Society, and the New Hampshire Medical Association, and while in Baker City he was on the staff of physicians of St. Elizabeth hospital.

Dr. Grant has achieved a very enviable success in his mining ventures, having been half owner of the Porcupine group, which sold a short time since for fifteen thousand dollars. He also has interests in other valuable properties in the district.

CHARLES O. STEWART, one of the leading agriculturists and general farmers in the vicinity of Pine post office, was born in Eola, Polk county, Oregon, on January 3, 1858. His parents, Francis M. and Anna C. (Strain) Stewart, were natives respectively of Illinois and Indiana, and were married in Polk county, Oregon, in 1855, the Rev. Mr. Waller officiating. After their marriage they lived about six years in that county, then removed to a point about eighteen miles above Seattle, in Washington, that city being at the time their nearest postoffice. They hewed out a home in the forest, and for about six years succeeded as well as could be expected, but in 1867 Mrs. Stewart died, and at the time of her death Mr. Stewart was absent in Seattle. About the same time also all the household belongings of the family, in fact everything except the house in which they lived, were destroyed by flood, the water rising much higher that year than it has ever done since. These misfortunes discouraged our subject's father, so he sold out, moved to Portland and engaged in the carpenter trade. Two years later he came to Union county, Oregon, where he lived with his brother about a year, moving then to Pine valley, of which he was a pioneer. Locating on land about a mile north of Pine, he lived there until September 7, 1895, when death put an end to his earthly pilgrimage. Both he and his wife were lifelong members of, and workers in, the Methodist church. In his earlier years the old gentleman was a Democrat, but he had been a consistent and active Republican ever since the Civil war.

Our subject was born in Eola, Oregon, on January 3, 1858. He remained under the parental roof until the death of his mother, then lived a while with an aunt in Portland, but when his father moved to Union county he also came along. At the age of sixteen he struck out for himself, going to Colorado with a herd of cattle. He passed the winter of 1876-77 there, returning the next spring to Pine valley. Soon, however, he removed to Boise, but in a year's time he was again a resident of Pine valley, and located on a quarter section of land on Dry creek. Of this, however, he afterwards disposed, investing a portion of the proceeds in an eighty-acre tract one and a half miles north of Pine, where he has ever since lived, engaged in improving his

DANIEL GRANT, M. D.

place and in general farming and stockraising. He ranks among the leading farmers of his neighborhood, while his integrity and uprightness of character, together with his many neighborly qualities, have rendered him trusted and respected.

Mr. Stewart was married, at Furman Station, Oregon, on September 25, 1882, the lady being Miss Fannie, daughter of John and Anna (Clark) Furman. To their union nine children have been born: Fannie A.; Marion P., wife of J. H. Haney, of Halfway; Robert C.; Harrison P., died January 17, 1900; Lilah C.; an infant that died unnamed, February 23, 1893; Anna B.; Edith, died October 27, 1898; Vada,

Mrs. Stewart's parents were natives, the mother of Ohio, the father of New York. Both emigrated to the west, and they met and married in Oregon, where for a number of years they followed farming. The father was afterward a partner in the first livery stable in Baker City, but is now living on Boundary creek, Alberta province, Northwest Territory. His wife died in Baker City in 1869.

Mr. Stewart has a herd of seven hundred fine sheep, which he handles in addition to his other enterprises.

———◆◆◆———

ROBERT T. GEORGE.—It is with pleasure that we present here a brief outline review of the life history of the prominent farmer and stock raiser and energetic, forceful man whose name appears above, as we realize that in his long career as an agriculturist and freighter he has, while working out his own destiny, concomitantly contributed very materially to the development of the county in which his home has been.

Mr. George was born in Boone county, Missouri, on July 14, 1858, his parents being A. and Ann Eliza George. In 1865 the family crossed the plains to Baker county, and on the paternal farm on Willow creek our subject lived until he had completed his education and grown to early manhood. In 1874, though only eighteen years old, he essayed the task of fighting life's battles on his own account, going to Rock creek and there engaging in agricultural pursuits. He continued in the same place until about ten years ago, and then moved to a point six miles southwest

22

of Haines, where he now has a fine farm of three hundred and twenty acres. Faithful, assiduous toil has brought it to an excellent state of cultivation and many improvements in the way of substantial buildings, fences, etc., bear testimony to the thrift of its owner.

For several years Mr. George was extensively engaged in freighting, operating with seven six-horse outfits, and transporting goods to many parts of eastern Oregon and Idaho. About six months ago, however, he sold out, and he has since been giving his entire attention to his farm and stock.

On December 18, 1889, in Pocahontas, Baker county, our subject married Miss Etta, a daughter of James and Eliza Ingraham, and a native of Arkansas, and their union has been blessed by the advent of three children: Bertha, Leona and Rosa.

———◆◆◆———

ANDREW P. GREENER.—No volume which has to do with the leading and public spirited citizens of Baker county could escape the charge of incompleteness and inconsistency did it fail to incorporate a brief review of the Civil war veteran and representative man whose name appears above. Ever an active worker in his business and in the promotion of the public good, he has contributed his share toward urging on the forward march in Baker county, and in substituting light for darkness, cosmos for chaos.

Our subject is a native of Shelby, Illinois, born in 1841, his parents being John J. and M. J. (Savage) Greener, natives respectively of Bavaria and Indiana. He continued to reside under the parental roof until the outbreak of the Civil war, when he enlisted in Company B, Fifty-seventh Illinois Infantry, and he did not lay down his arms until the last disloyal gun had been silenced, never more to awake the echoes. He was wounded twice, the first battle scar being received at Pittsburg Landing, the second at Corinth.

When his services as a soldier were no longer required he went to Kansas and engaged in school teaching. For nine consecutive years he wrought for the educational amelioration of the youth of Jefferson and Linn counties, but in 1875 he came out to Grande Ronde valley, Oregon. For two years he followed his profession there. In 1877 he came to Eagle valley, and after teaching a term took a claim of one hundred and sixty acres a mile and three-quarters north of the present Pine postoffice and turned his energies to farming and stock raising, a line of endeavor in which he has been engaged ever since. He is an energetic man, and has highly improved his premises by the erection of good buildings, fences, etc., and by judicious cultivation of the soil.

In politics Mr. Greener takes quite a leading interest, being a stanch Republican, and an active worker in the conventions of his party. For two years he served as county assessor, and to him belongs the honor of having secured the establishment of the post office at Pine, and of having acted as its first postmaster.

In April, 1873, our subject married Miss Amanda, daughter of Josiah and Mariah (Long) Brooks, natives respectively of Pennsylvania and Delaware, and to their union seven children have been born: Birch, deceased; Elmer; Edward, Ola and Eva, at home; Orville, who died in 1900, and Norvall, at home, the last two being twins. Mr. Greener is a member of Phil Kearney Post, No. 66, G. A. R.

MARION A. BUTLER.—A leader in political circles, a good public speaker and a lawyer of distinguished ability, the man whose name gives caption to this article is to be ranked among the foremost citizens of the county with which our volume is concerned, and it is therefore fitting that he be given due representation among the men who have built up and are building up this section of the great Inland Empire. Our subject is yet a young man and the achievements of his past life are such that much may be expected from him in the future, so that indications must prove false if he fails to make a record for himself which will place him among the noted men of the state of Oregon.

Mr. Butler was born in Douglas county, this state, on May 21, 1865, the son of Benjamin and Lydia (Beard) Butler, natives of Ohio, who crossed the plains in 1853. They spent the first winter in Clackamas county, then took a donation land claim five miles southeast of Oakland, where they resided until 1871,

moving then to Olympia, Washington, in which town their home was until 1878. Our subject attended the common schools wherever the family resided, finishing his common school training in Pomeroy. He then took a two years' course in Whitman college, and finally graduated from Lewis Collegiate Institute at Lewiston, Idaho. Upon receiving his diploma he engaged in teaching school in Idaho, but later he went to Farmington, where he spent a period of two years in the drug business. Going thence to Spokane he followed real estate brokerage until 1892, in which year he located at Pendleton, Oregon, and began the practice of law. In 1899 he came to Baker City, where he has built up a very lucrative and flattering practice. He is the law partner of the well known Senator John H. Mitchell.

Our subject has contributed his share toward the mining development of this section since coming here, and has at present some valuable properties. He formerly held a controlling interest in the Virginia mine.

As before intimated, Mr. Butler is a very enthusiastic politician, his party affiliations being with the Republicans, for whose success he has wrought very faithfully, making many campaign speeches. His fraternal connections are with the K. of P., Gauntlet Lodge, No. 8, of which he is a past chancellor, and with the W. of W.

On July 13, 1885, our subject married Miss Alice, daughter of David S. and Acena A. Trescott, natives of Ohio, but residents, at present, of Asotin county, Washington. The issue of this union is two children, Harold R. and Ella May. The family reside at 1940 Seventh street, Baker City.

GEORGE B. SMALL.—This prominent editor, publisher, and political leader was born in Butte county, California, on January 14, 1864, the son of S. H. and Frances E. Small, natives of Missouri, who crossed the plains with ox teams to California in 1860. When eight years old our subject accompanied the remainder of the family to Baker county, in the public schools of which county he received his common school education. He then attended for three years Blue Mountain university at La Grande, working during vacations in the Democrat office, learning the printer's trade. When he retired from college he assumed editorial management of the paper in the office of which he had acquired his technical skill and to this work he gave himself uninterruptedly for several years.

In May, 1887, our subject and I. B. Bowen purchased the Democrat, and they now have, it is said, the finest and largest newspaper and job printing plant in the state of Oregon. Mr. Small attended the national editorial association at Chicago in 1893 as a delegate from this state, also the one at Asbury Park, New Jersey in 1894. He is also past president of the Oregon press association.

Prominent in the journalistic profession, our subject is no less famed as a political leader His voice has been many times heard in Democratic state conventions and more than once he has served as chairman of the county central committee.

Like many other prominent men in Baker county, Mr. Small is interested in mining properties, and he is also the owner of some very desirable city realty, including his fine residence on the corner of Seventh and Washington streets.

Fraternally our subject is affiliated with the B. P. O. E., of which he is a past exalted ruler, and with the K. of P., in which he is a past chancellor. He attended the grand lodge of the Elks at St. Louis in 1899 as a delegate, and he has also twice attended the grand lodge of the K. of P. He was married on January 20, 1887, the lady of his choice being Miss Nea B. Hazeltine, a daughter of old and respected pioneer parents. They have had three children, namely: Eva B., deceased; Nea Hazel, and Frederick Irving.

DOUGLAS M. NICHOLS.—No class of men have aided more in the development of the resources of the country and in bringing civilization within our bounds than have the stockmen and agriculturists, of whom Baker county has a large quota of progressive and capable devotees, and among this enterprising class there is to be given especial mention of our subject, since he has wrought in the west for many years and has been one of those substantial citizens who form the very bone and

sinew of any community and whose stability and integrity have been displayed in a manner worthy of emulation in his long years of faithful service.

The son of Luther R. and Adelia (Woodbridge) Nichols, being born on December 12, 1844, in Kenosha, Illinois, he was removed by his parents to Yreka, California, in 1852. They crossed the plains with horse teams, the train being led by Judge Tolman, who is now in Jacksonville, Oregon. The first venture of the father on the Pacific coast was in the hotel business for two years, and then at Canal Gulch, and later at Shasta bridge, he operated in the mercantile realm. Following this he took a homestead and tilled it for six years, or until the death of the mother, and then the father and our subject came to Portland. When Douglas M. arrived at the age of twenty-one he migrated to Idaho City, engaging in dairying. Two years later we find him at Falks Store postoffice in the stock business, then in Eagle valley in 1880, whence, three years later, he removed to his present place one mile northeast of Bridgeport, where he took a homestead and has since added by purchase four hundred and eighty acres more. His farm is very valuable, being supplied with an abundance of water, and produces bountiful crops of hay. He has improved it in good shape, having comfortable buildings, a good orchard and other essentials to a thrifty and first class ranch. He handles many cattle and has some very fine specimens of registered Shorthorn animals.

The marriage of Mr. Nichols and Mrs. Rufina (Sawings) Paddock was celebrated in 1869 at Falks Store postoffice, Rev. Ford, of the Methodist Episcopal church, officiating. Five children were born to this union, as follows: Ernest, who at four years of age fell a victim of a sad accident and was burned to death; Arthur E., married to Zetta Vanburen; Cora, wife of Charles Vanburen; Wilbert E.; and Ira. On April 22, 1900, Mrs. Nichols was called to pass the river of death; she was a noble woman, loving mother and faithful wife and her demise was universally mourned.

Mr. Nichols contracted a second marriage April 8, 1901, Mrs. Nina Ahlhauser, of the vicinity of Salem, becoming his wife at that time. Mrs. Nichols is a native of Canada, and by her former marriage has one daughter, Grace Ahlhauser. Her parents, Job and Mary (Heath) Denyer, were natives of England and immigrants to the United States, the mother dying in Turner, Oregon, where the father still lives.

Mr. Nichols' father was a volunteer in the Rogue river war with the Indians, and on October 4, 1901, he died at Salem, aged eighty-four.

* * *

ANDREW DEWAR.—Born in Perthshire, Scotland, on January 31, 1836, the subject of this review possesses his full share of the thrift and forcefulness of character which have made his race famous the world over, and which have made them such worthy citizens of the United States. While Mr. Dewar has not been characterized by any ambition for personal aggrandizement, and has never, so far as we know, been a candidate for any office, he takes the interest every good citizen should in the affairs of his county and state. He belongs to the great class of men whose names are not on everybody's tongue, but who nevertheless form the real sinew of any community.

Mr. Dewar received his education in the excellent public schools of his native land, and remained there until 1872, when he resolved to enjoy the larger advantages to be had in the new world. Accordingly he set sail for America. During the first two years he traveled considerably, seeking a suitable location, and when he finally came to a halt it was that he might try his fortunes in the rich mining region of which Sumpter, Oregon, is the center. He soon acquired an interest in various properties which have since became famous, among them the Ibex, which sold two years ago for sixty-five thousand dollars. This property was discovered and located in 1895 by our subject, with Joseph Michael, Edgar Main and James Fain as associates. Mr. Dewar was also interested in the Amazon mine, which was sold in 1898 to Mr. English for five thousand dollars.

It is of interest to note that when Mr. Dewar came to Baker county Sumpter was merely a placer camp, and that the quartz mines which have made it famous have all been of more recent discovery. There was only one house and a few small shacks in the town when first seen by our subject, and at that time lumber had to be hauled from Auburn, where also all the Sumpter people got their mail. Other provisions had to be conveyed from Umatilla by pack train.

Mr. Dewar has therefore enjoyed the opportunity of seeing the place develop from a primitive mining camp to a first class center, and he no doubt also enjoys the consciousness that he has been in a very considerable measure a contributor to this progress and development.

* * *

TABOR M. REED.—In the character now before us we have one of those sturdy men of courageous spirit and dauntless intrepidity who so nobly did the praiseworthy work of opening the frontier regions to the march of civilization, and whose life has been filled with stirring adventures and interesting incidents. Much more is due this worthy class of pioneers than ever the citizens of the now wealthy county of Baker will ever be able to pay, both as a debt of gratitude and for commendable effort that has resulted in opening up to the settlers that followed later the rich territory now embraced in our county.

On September 16, 1838, near Muncie, Indiana, the subject of this sketch was born, and he was reared on a farm, attending the public schools during the winter season. At the age of seventeen he went to Holt county, Missouri, and thence to Fremont county, Iowa. In December, 1859, he migrated, via New York and the Isthmus, to California, going direct from San Francisco to the mines in Shasta county, in February, 1860. He continued in mining there until the spring of 1862, when he came to Auburn, in Baker county, thence to Canyon City, returning to Auburn and then going to Clark's creek, being the first white man in that section, which afterward proved the best placer camp in eastern Oregon. Following this he took a trip to California and Nevada, which was a very dangerous undertaking at that time, as the Piute Indians were at that time on the war path. In the spring of 1863 he returned and at once engaged in mining in different parts of Baker county until 1872, when he located the ranch where he now lives, five and one-half miles east of Hereford. At this place he owns three hundred and twenty acres of fine land, well watered, and that produces abundant crops of hay. He has added many valuable improvements and his is a comfortable and valuable home place. He also owns large herds of cattle and horses and engages in mining in addition to his stock and agricultural interests. In political matters he is active and prominent in his vicinity, having been justice of the peace for a number of terms.

In 1871 the marriage of Mr. Reed and Miss Frances, daughter of Belta and Sarah Dragoo, was solemnized at Muncie, Indiana. To them have been born the following children: Daisy M., wife of John Wallace, of Lagrande, Oregon; L. Belle, who has been instructor in the high school at Express for some time; Mary R.; Birdie A.; Nellie P.

It is of note that the father of Mr. Reed's grandfather was a soldier in the Revolution, and the stanch characteristics of his ancestors have been commendably displayed in the subject before us who bears the worthy name. During the Indian trouble of 1878 Mr. Reed removed his family to a place of safety in the fort at Clarksville. Once, in 1868, Mr. Reed's uncle was lost in the mountains, and became so badly frozen that the services of a surgeon were required. Our subject went to Boise, Idaho, for one and in the trip very nearly lost his own life by freezing, but finally pulled through.

RIEUBEN REED, an enterprising farmer and mining man, residing in the vicinity of Halfway postoffice is deserving of mention among the builders and benefactors of the county with which our volume is concerned, and it affords us pleasure to accord him such. He was born in Union county, Ohio, in 1836, and was taken thence to Clayton county, Iowa, by his parents, John and Malinda (Asher) Reed. In that state he was deprived of his father by the icy hand of death, and in 1859 he brought his mother and the remainder of the family to Colorado. He mined there a couple of years, then embarked in cattle raising, an industry which continued to engage his energies uninterruptedly for thirteen or fourteen years. In 1882, however, he sold out and came to Pine valley, Baker county, homesteaded one hundred and twenty acres of land

a mile and a half north of Halfway postoffice, and engaged in diversified farming, although he has also given some attention to mining and prospecting and is the owner of interests in various properties at Cornucopia and Snake river. He has been an energetic man in his endeavors to secure a competency, and at the same time contribute toward the development of his section, and is richly deserving of whatever success has been his. His integrity and worth of character have secured him the confidence and esteem of those who know him, giving him an enviable standing in his community.

Mr. Reed was married in Clayton county, Iowa, in 1862, to Sarah A. Zimmerman, a native of Richfield, Pennsylvania, and daughter of Jacob G. and Catherine Zimmerman, and to them have been born eleven children: John, Ida, Katie, who died in 1888; Charlotte M., Ella, Melinda, Effie, Charles, Delmer, Myrtle and Cleveland. Most of the children are now married and doing for themselves, but Charles, Delmer, Myrtle and Cleveland are still at home. Mr. Reed's father was a soldier in the war of 1812, and his mother died in Colorado. Her mother died in Pennsylvania when this daughter was seven years of age, and her father died in Iowa in 1884.

JOSEPH L. SAVAGE.—Active for many years in the processes of bread-stuff production, as well as in stock raising and horticulture, a man of great energy and activity and one who easily overcomes difficulties which would overwhelm a less resolute person, the honored gentleman whose name forms the caption of this article has certainly earned the right to be considered among the builders of Baker county, and it affords us pleasure to accord him representation as such herein.

Our subject was born in Cook county, Illinois, near Plainfield, on January 19, 1843. He resided with his parents, Americus and Mary Savage, at their home in Peolia, Illinois, until 1851, when he accompanied the remainder of the family across the plains to Linn county, Oregon, where he lived until he was seventeen years old. He then went to California, where he worked at mining for about three years, thereupon returning to Linn county. He farmed until 1872, which year is the date of his advent in Baker county. His first home was on Rock creek, but in 1876 he moved to his present place of abode six miles west of Haines, where he has lived ever since. For a number of years he ran a blacksmith shop in addition to his other industries, then he invested in a threshing outfit, which made the seasons for twelve years. In 1900 he sold this, and last fall he operated an outfit owned by himself, in conjunction with several other farmers. He has a fine, well improved place, supplied with machinery, implements, buildings, fences, and in fact almost everything requisite to a well regulated ranch.

Fraternally our subject is affiliated with Haines Lodge, No. 11, A. O. U. W. He was married in Linn county, Oregon, October 22, 1864, to Melinda, daughter of James and Elizabeth Taylor, and a native of Illinois, and to this union have been born eleven children, namely: Minnie, wife of Bayard Angell, now deceased; William, deceased; Dean, residing near his father's home; Guy, at home; Ollie, wife of W. N. Gardner, of North Powder; Edward, at Laclede mine; Nora, wife of Samuel Lang; Lulu, wife of W. M. Cavin; Ivy, deceased; Joseph; Ira.

_____

ISAAC McCLANAHAN.—The stock men of Baker county are well known for their progressiveness and the commanding position that they have held for some time, and they have been instrumental in materially advancing the interests of their county and in enhancing the wealth of the same, as well as developing the resources of the eastern part of Oregon. A worthy representative of this thrifty class is mentioned at the head of this article, and without doubt he is one of the most skillful and successful stockmen of the county, although there are others, perhaps, that may own herds that will outnumber his.

The son of Isaac and Sarah McClanahan, born on March 4, 1833, near Muncie, Indiana, he spent his early years on the farm with his father, also attending school a portion of each year. When he had attained the age of nineteen he was allured by the tales of the fertile Willamette valley to cross the plains with an ox team to Portland, this state. The following spring he went with pack horses to

Yreka, California, thence to Redding's diggings in Shasta county, and took up mining there until 1858, when he went to the Fraser river region, also in quest of nature's hidden treasures, but what success attended his efforts we are not told; but soon after we find him in Portland, and until 1862 he tilled the soil on a farm near that city. At that date he went to Tillamook bay, and in the following summer he went to the Clark's creek mines near Bridgeport, where he mined and kept hotel until 1867, then sold his property. In 1871 he bought the property where he now lives, about one mile southeast from Hereford, and his thrift and industry have enabled him to add to its acreage until he has one section of fine hay land that is well watered and forms one of the finest stock ranches in the whole county. He is very skillful in handling it, having it well improved and gaining sufficient hay therefrom to support a large herd of cattle.

The marriage of Mr. McClanahan and Miss Annis, daughter of John and Catherine (Bonett) Butt, was solemnized in Washington county, Oregon, November 13, 1859.

It is of note that in the Indian war of 1878 Mr. McClanahan, with some of his friends, stood guard on a prominent point to keep the Indians from stealing their stock in the valley. The wily savages were too shrewd, however, for the white men and succeeded in making quite a haul.

_____

W. W. FELIX.—This respected citizen of Sumpter and esteemed member of society, familiarly known as Judge Felix, has, during all the years of his active life been deeply interested in the cause of education and in the promotion of humanity's welfare in other ways, and it affords us pleasure to mention him here as one whose benevolent disposition has made him a useful and honored man in other states, and will doubtless result likewise in the town where he now lives. Our subject was born in Wayne county, Illinois, the son of David K. and Susan E. Felix, natives of Kentucky. He received a public school and academic education, then, though only seventeen years old, began teaching. He followed that profession in Mississippi, Kentucky and Illinois for half a decade then engaged in the commission business in St. Louis, Missouri, continuing therein until 1889, when he came to Tacoma, Washington. For two years he was engaged in real estate brokerage there, after which he embarked in the fruit business in Los Angeles, California. For about four years he was engaged mostly in buying fruit for different wholesale houses, but becoming inspired with the hope that perhaps he might make money more rapidly in mining, he made a two years' prospecting tour into the desert. Returning he came to Baker county, arriving here in 1898. He prospected in this section for a short time, then moved to Lagrande, where he wrought as a bookkeeper for a time, returning then to Sumpter and turning his attention to contracting. He was engaged in this line of activity and in bookkeeping until June 14, 1900, when he was elected justice of the peace on the Democratic ticket. He is discharging his duties as such with fairness and impartiality and in a manner to commend himself to the confidence and esteem of the public.

As above indicated our subject has taken an active interest in public affairs wherever he has lived. For two years he served as assistant superintendent of schools of Wayne county, Illinois, and in 1885 he was proposed to the legislature of his state for the office of doorkeeper.

Fraternally Mr. Felix is affiliated with the Ancient Order of Red Men, Eagan Tribe No. 20, of Sumpter, and in religion he holds to the Baptist faith.

Mr. Felix is interested with A. H. Huntington and Thomas Barbee in two mining claims, the St. Charles and the Queen Esther, in Grant county, near the Baker county line, both of which, it is expected, will be shipping ore in the course of a year.

THOMAS R. IRWIN.—We must now essay to present in brief outline the life history of the prominent and enterprising farmer and mining man whose name appears above. He is a very early settler of Baker county, in the development of which he has been a potent factor, adding to its wealth by assisting in the conquest of its agricultural resources and the discovery of its mineral treasures.

Like many other citizens who have distinguished themselves in the industrial upbuilding of this section, our subject is a native of Ireland, his birthplace being Newtown-Limavady, Derry county, and the date 1839. In 1849 he accompanied his parents, Thomas and Hannah (Ramsey) Irwin, to the United States. For a number of years afterward he remained under the parental roof, but in 1864 he, his father and three brothers came west to Montana, where they remained two years. Our subject then came on to Portland, Oregon, the others returning east. For the ensuing three years he worked for wages, hauling lumber to Oregon City, on contract for a portion of the time, then removed to southern Oregon, where he lived about eighteen months. He then went to Central City, Nebraska, farming in the vicinity of that town for another period of a year and a half, after which he came again to Oregon, halting first in Union, but soon coming to Pine valley. In 1881 he pre-empted one hundred and sixty acres of land four and a half miles northwest of the Pine postoffice, where he has been engaged in general farming and stock raising ever since. His energies are, however, too great to be confined to farming, and for the past fifteen or sixteen years he has also been engaged in mining. He has five or six ledges on Snake river, and most of the mines now being worked at Cornucopia were discovered by him, twenty-four mines in that locality being located in one year. Thus by energy and resourcefulness he has been enabled to add very materially to the wealth and prosperity of Baker county and earned the right to be considered one of its benefactors.

In Portland, Oregon, in the year 1873, Mr. Irwin married Mrs. George Coggan, daughter of Ezra and Fannie (Robinson) Stone, natives of Ohio, and they have one child, Ira at home.

At one time our subject had a white horse stolen from his barn, and it may be of interest to record his experiences in pursuing the thief. The horse was taken in Silver City, Idaho, and the thief at once struck out toward the Nevada line, whither he was followed by Mr. Irwin, who was guided by the tracks of the horse. The day before he came upon his man Mr. Irwin was set upon by seven Indians, whom he motioned back. The reds paid no attention, so he got off of his horse and shot two of their ponies, whereupon they concluded to go, though they followed him at a distance all day. The next day Mr. Irwin saw the thief going down towards the Humboldt, got ahead of him, met him, got the drop on him, and secured his prisoner and his horse.

CHARLES FLEETWOOD.—The region with which our volume is primarily concerned is the home of many men of marked ability, who have migrated hither from various states, and also there is coming to the front to take the places of these pioneer business men and developers of the county a class of younger men, some of whom are immigrants, and some of whom are native born, and among this latter number may be placed the subject of this sketch, who ranks high in the capabilities that make a successful business man, in uprightness and unswerving integrity, having demonstrated what energy, guided by masterful wisdom, is able to accomplish in at least two lines of industry within the boundaries of our county.

Charles Fleetwood is the son of Asa and Elizabeth (Johnston) Fleetwood, and was born in Bridgeport, Baker county, on September 28, 1870. He was reared on his father's farm, from early youth displaying energy and industry in the assistance that he rendered in the duties of the farm, and gaining from the common schools his educational training, which has been greatly increased by careful and constant reading. When he had reached his majority he entered the business realm of life on his own account, taking up first the raising of stock. This he has continued ever since and is making a marked success in that line. In 1893 he bought the store at Hereford and in a most successful manner has operated it since that time. He has manifested marked ability in handling his commercial interests and has built up a flourishing trade that is constantly increasing. He carries a well assorted and full line of general merchandise that is fitted for his surrounding country and is one of the leading rural merchants of the county. In addition to the duties that are incumbent upon him in these lines, he has also been postmaster since entering the store and has discharged the duties of that office in a satisfactory manner. Mr. Fleetwood has spent his entire life in the neighborhood where he now resides and is a son of the county in which his native country may well take pride.

The marriage of Mr. Fleetwood and Miss Maggie A., daughter of John R. and Sarah J. (Duff) Vancil, was celebrated on September 7, 1891, and to them has been born one child, Maud Ethel, who is attending school at Hereford. Mrs. Fleetwood's parents live near Union, this state. Mr. Fleetwood is a member of the Modern Woodmen of America, where he holds the position of venerable counsel. Mr. Fleetwood's father lives about two miles west from Hereford, but his mother died on March 20, 1899. Although just beginning a career of business activity, Mr Fleetwood has displayed such integrity and uprightness that he has won the confidence of all and the outlook for his future success is very flattering.

LEMUEL D. KING.—While Baker county has produced millions of wealth from her mines, she is nevertheless distinctively a stock country as well as rich in mineral treasure, and many of the most prominent citizens have been quick to perceive the rich bestowals of nature in these associated lines and have allied their efforts in following the course pointed out by the natural resources of the country. Among the progressive ones that have wrought a gratifying success in these industries may be mentioned the prominent citizen whose life's career it is now our pleasant privilege to epitomize in a brief review.

Born in the greatest mining state of the Union, California, in Siskiyou county, on November 3, 1861, and at three years of age removed with his parents to Grant county, equally famed with her sister political organization in the production of the minerals, he has been associated with the great industry of producing the minerals from the native soil since his earliest remembrance; using his own words, he was "Raised in the mines, and educated in the public schools." His parents were Flavius J. and Nancy C. (Fancher) King, natives respectively of Arkansas and Alabama, who crossed the plains with ox teams in 1859 and wrought on the Pacific coast for many years in the development of its resources and the advancement of its interests. The father was

MRS. L. D. KING.   LEMUEL D. KING.

LEMUEL M. BARNETT.   JOSEPH SHEPARD.

a cabinet maker and designer. He passed from the scenes of life in Washington, on December 18, 1897, and the mother departed this life at Susanville, Grant county, in 1883.

The immediate subject of this sketch began the battle of life on his own account when he was eighteen years of age and mining was the work that he first took up, and more or less he has continued at that occupation since. He also raised stock in connection with the former, Susanville being his headquarters until 1883, at which time he sold his cattle and repaired to the John Day valley and occupied himself with farming and teaming until 1887. In that year he migrated to Baker county and acquired land where he is living at the present time, eight miles southeast of Whitney. He continued the mining industry and stock raising and added farming. He formed a partnership with his uncle, Lemuel Barnett, and together they own three hundred and twenty acres of land and handle one hundred and twenty-five head of cattle. They are progressive and prosperous and are among the most substantial citizens of the entire county. In addition to the property already mentioned, Mr. King is equally interested with his uncle in the Phœnix and other mines which give great promise of value and richness.

At Prairie City, Grant county, on July 18, 1882, Mr. King and Hattie J., daughter of Joseph C. and Sarah J. (Dimmick) Gillenwater, and a native of Grant county, were married, and they have become the parents of the following children: H. Pearl, married to Joseph B. Hardman, and is living near by; Lemuel J.; William C. and Mary Z., twins; Audry M. Mrs. King's parents were among the first settlers of Grant county, and the father is a native of Tennessee, and the mother of Illinois. Mr. King is affiliated with the Modern Woodmen of America. He is a man respected and esteemed by all and has made a record for faithfulness and enterprising accomplishment that is both worthy and commendable, while his integrity and uprightness are manifest to all who have to do with him.

LEMUEL M. BARNETT.—To one who has ever been in the vanguard of civilization's march and has continuously wrought with energy and wisdom for the development of the country and the welfare of his fellows, as has the intrepid veteran and hardy pioneer and esteemed citizen, Lemuel M. Barnett, it is a pleasure to grant a representation in this volume that purports to epitomize the careers of the leading citizens of Baker and Grant counties.

Mr. Barnett was born in McMinn county, Tennessee, on February 13, 1830, being the son of Lemuel and Cecilia (White) Barnett. He was reared on a farm and at the early age of twelve years started into the realties of life for himself, migrating first to Georgia, and then, four years later, returned to his native state, whence he went to Arkansas, and on June 7, 1847, enlisted in Company C, Twelfth Volunteer Infantry, for service in the Mexican war. He was soon sent to the City of Mexico, and was there transferred to Company A, and participated in many skirmishes. In August, 1848, he was honorably discharged and returned to Arkansas, whence, in 1854, he started across the plains with ox teams for Yreka, California. In that place he mined for a decade, and then came to Canyon City, this state, where he continued the search for nature's hidden treasures until 1889, when he added farming and stock raising to his other employment. He is in partnership with his nephew, Lemuel D. King, and they own three hundred and twenty acres of fine land, well watered, that produces an abundance of hay, and which is situated at the mouth of China creek, about eight miles below Whitney. They also have a large herd of cattle and some very valuable mining property—one-fourth interest in the Phœnix mine, located in the Greenhorn district in Baker county.

The marriage of Mr. Barnett and Miss Mary J. King was celebrated at Mount Vernon, Arkansas, on January 8, 1851. For thirty-eight years Mr. Barnett has been a master Mason. During his long residence in this county he has conducted himself with such uprightness and integrity that he has won the confidence and admiration of all that have the pleasure of his acquaintance. Mr. Barnett's grandfather fought in the Revolutionary war, and his father served under Jackson in the Creek war.

JOSEPH SHEPARD.—A very early pioneer of the west and a prominent mining man and agriculturist, the man whose name appears above has done his full share toward the development of Baker county and eastern Oregon, and it is but fitting that representation be accorded him in this volume as one of the builders of the section.

Mr. Shepard was born in Tazewell county, Illinois, in 1843. He lived with his parents there until his majority was attained, going with them to Kansas. In 1864 he set out across the plains with mule teams for Boise, Idaho, where he was engaged in mining for four years, going then to the Feather river country, on the headwaters of the Boise, where he prospected all summer, returning to Boise in the fall. The next spring he prospected on Cedar creek, and the next he went into the Boise basin, where he worked for two years, going then to Walla Walla. Early in the spring he went to Cedar creek, in the British possessions, and after prospecting all summer he returned to Walla Walla, wintering there. The next season was spent in the Spokane country and in the Cœur d'Alene region, and the next in the Eldorado country, not far from Baker City. During the summer, fall and winter of 1870 he was engaged in rocking on the Snake river bars, and the ensuing quadrennium was spent in the country around Sparta, where he wrought at placer mining. In 1875 he purchased a farm of one hundred and sixty acres in Pine valley, and turned his attention to farming and cattle raising, a line of activity in which he has been engaged ever since. He brings the same enthusiasm and vigor to his efforts in this direction which formerly characterized his search for earth's hidden treasures, and is regarded as one of the leading farmers of his section.

On December 22, 1891, our subject married Miss Elizabeth Gosen, and to them have been born six children, namely: Harry E., Louis, Delbert, Violet, Lillia, and one that died in infancy.

We should not forget to record the interesting reminiscence that Mr. Shepard was one of the five men who were attacked by twenty Indians on Big Camas prairie in the fall of 1864. In the fight thirteen of the redskins were killed, but fortunately none of the whites were injured. The battle occurred at daybreak.

———◆◆———

RICHARD T. LANGRELL.—This enterprising merchant and leading citizen of the vicinity of Carson is, like many other thrifty and progressive men who have found homes in the west, a native of Canada. He was born in Alfred, Ontario, July 27, 1844, the son of Joseph and Mary (FitzGerald) Langrell, natives of Ireland, who came to the American shores at a very early date and spent their lives in Canada. He remained under the parental roof until his majority had been attained, then removed to Minneapolis, Minnesota, and engaged in the lumbering industry. In 1873 he emigrated to Puget Sound, and in the conversion to lumber of the mammoth timber abounding in that region he busied himself for a couple of years, going then to Nevada and into the search for earth's hidden mineral wealth. He mined over different parts of Nevada and California, coming from the latter state to Baker City in 1881. Here he resumed sawmilling and followed it for a year, coming then to Pine valley. In 1883 he located on a quarter section of land two miles from Carson, but was not yet ready to give up lumbering, so he ran a saw mill on his own account in different parts of the valley, combining this with farming. Eventually he sold his mill to G. W. Brown and engaged in general merchandising, erecting a store on his own premises. The same energy and foresight which characterized his operations in the lumber business are enabling him to succeed in his present endeavors and he is building up and extending his trade steadily.

Politically Mr. Langrell is a Republican. He takes an active interest in affairs of general concern, and for four years served with efficiency and faithfulness as county commissioner of Union county. Fraternally he is identified with the subordinate lodge of Masons at Baker City, and with Pine Camp, No. 7579, Modern Woodmen of American at Langrell hall.

At Baker City, on December 22, 1881, our subject married Miss Clara, daughter of

Charles and Maggie (Bohna) Schellworth, and they have seven children: Nellie, Etta, Maud, Charley, Richard, Willie and Albert.

LESTER L. HOLCOMB.—This prominent farmer, mining man and political leader of the vicinity of Richland was born in Rollersville, Ohio, on July 7, 1846. His parents, James T. and Amanda (Loomis) Holcomb, natives respectively of Connecticut and Ohio, were engaged in farming there and he lived with them until about twenty-two years of age, being absent, however, for four months during the Civil war as a member of Company H, One Hundred and Sixty-ninth Ohio. When he became twenty-two he gave inception to his independent career, engaging first in farming in the commonwealth of his nativity. Later he moved to Central county, Kansas, where he farmed about seven years, thereupon crossing the plains with horse teams to Eagle valley, in Baker county. He made his advent into the country during the Bannock war, when travel was exceedingly dangerous, but though the trains ahead and behind his suffered losses in the conflicts with the Indians, his train escaped uninjured.

For the first year Mr. Holcomb lived in the upper end of the valley. He then took one hundred and twenty acres of land one and one-fourth miles east of Richland postoffice, where he has ever since lived, engaged in general farming and stock raising, at the same time giving some attention to mining ventures. He owns several placer and quartz mines on Snake river.

Fraternally our subject is identified with Phil Kearney Post, No. 66, G. A. R., of Pine valley. In politics he is an ardent Republican, and in the councils of his party he is quite active. He was one of the first justices of the peace in Eagle valley, being elected first in 1880, and again two years later, while his interest in the cause of education has made him prominent in the affairs of the local school district.

On October 15, 1868, Mr. Holcomb married Miss Candace, daughter of Joseph H. and Eleanor (Evans) Jennings, natives of the state of Ohio. To this union six children have been born: Donna M., now Mrs. Strayer; Alta M., now Mrs. Reynolds; James T, deceased; Addie, Noval and Linn, at home.

Mrs Holcomb's father was a prominent man in the politics of his state, and in the Civil war he did valiant service, first as a member of Company A, One Hundred and Eleventh Ohio, and later as captain of Company G, One Hundred and Sixty-ninth Ohio.

DANIEL F. MOORE.—A man of great inherent energy, the subject of this review has lived a life of intense activity, leaving home when only twelve years old and traveling extensively. He is a pioneer of the Pacific coast of 1856 and has for many years been identified with Baker county, to whose development he has contributed not a little. His interest in all things pertaining to the general good bespeaks broad-minded public spirit, and his standing as a citizen and member of society is an enviable one.

Mr. Moore was born in Candia, New Hampshire in 1836, the son of Daniel and Mary (Brown) Moore, both natives of New Hampshire, and both of whom died in Lowell, Massachusetts. As above stated, he started in life for himself when only twelve years old, going to sea at first for two years. At the end of that period he returned home and visited for three or four months, but as soon as the gold excitement broke out in Australia his love of adventure again asserted itself and in 1850 he landed on that far-away island. For more than half a decade he sought for the precious metals in that distant land, but with what success we are unable to say. Early in 1856 he embarked for Massachusetts, coming via England, over which country he traveled extensively. After another visit of three months we find him en route for California, coming via the Isthmus despite the terrible massacre which occurred there just previous. Arriving at Redwood City, California, he again took up the search for the key to nature's vaults, and his search led him all over the state. He likewise spent two years in the shingle business in California.

In 1862 he came to Baker county, Oregon, being one of the first to search for gold in this famous region, his first place of abode being Auburn. He remained there and in different parts of the county until 1869, when he settled in Sparta and engaged in the hotel business and in mining ventures, remaining until 1874. He then went to Union county and engaged in hotel keeping again, building the Centennial hotel, which was so named on account of its being completed July 4, 1876. The year 1885 found him again in Pine valley, where he located a homestead and engaged in farming, stock raising and market gardening, not, however, to the entire neglect of the old and much-beloved occupation, mining. He states that when he first saw the valley in 1873 it had but five settlers.

Fraternally our subject was affiliated with the Union lodge of Red Men, which was instituted in 1876, and in politics he is an ardent Republican. His marriage was solemnized in 1865, in Auburn, Miss Emmaretta, a native of Ohio and a daughter of Henry and Mary (Davis) Moffett, then becoming his wife.

AUGUSTUS MASTERS.—A very early pioneer of the Pacific coast and of Baker county and a forceful factor in the industrial development of both, the man whose name appears above is deserving of rank among the prominent and representative citizens of the section in which he lives, and it is but fitting and consistent that a brief resumé of his career be given place in our volume.

Mr. Masters is a native of Ithaca, Tompkins county, New York, born May 3, 1836. He grew to manhood in the city of his nativity, or rather on a farm just adjoining it but in 1863 he set out across the plains to the west, making the trip with mule teams. In due course of time he arrived in Yam Hill county, Oregon, whence, in 1865, he came to Baker county. For a number of years after his arrival here he was engaged in placer mining, and contributed not a little in that way to the wealth of the region, but in 1872 he located on a farm thirteen miles northwest of Baker City, where he now lives, and where he has two hundred and eighty acres of excellent land. This has been brought to a high state of cultivation and has been improved by the erection of outbuildings, fences, etc., until it reflects great credit upon the energy and well directed efforts of the man who owns it.

In Baker City, on November 3, 1880, our subject married Miss Hulda Coyle, a native of Ohio, and their union has been blessed by the advent of two children, Samuel E. and Augusta, both at home, and two children, Lanina and an infant, are deceased.

Mr. Masters did good work in the defense of the settlers during the Indian wars of 1867, serving under Captain H. W. Estes.

ALVA P. FLEETWOOD.—Among the substantial and thrifty stockmen and agriculturists of Baker county mention must be made of the young and capable gentleman and esteemed citizen whose name initiates this paragraph and who has wrought with commendable zeal and sagacity in the prosecution of his business enterprises for the time that he has been meeting the battles of life on his own account.

The parents of our subject, John and Ann (Johnston) Fleetwood, came to this county and settled on the Burnt river in 1886. The father was born on February 18, 1829, in Indiana, and the mother was born on February 5, 1833, and they were married on April 1, 1852, in Bloomington, Illinois. They were both devoted members of the Christian church, and faithful in their lives to exemplify the principles of their Divine Master. On March 28, 1895, the mother, and two days later the father, was called from the walks of this life to the rewards of that which is beyond, and their demise was universally mourned, they being noble and true Christians who had won the love of their fellows.

The subject of this sketch was born in Bloomington, Illinois, on July 31, 1874, and there spent the first twelve years of his life in assisting his father on the latter's farm and in attending the public schools. In 1886 he came with his parents to this county and attended the public schools and continued with his father on the farm until he was twenty years of age, and then he took up the realities of life for himself, embarking in farming and stock raising. He lives at the present time a half mile west of Hereford.

The marriage of Mr. Fleetwood and Miss Lou F., daughter of Andrew J. and Patsy G. (Lockett) Eblen, was solemnized at Baker City on March 15, 1896, the Rev. Bell, of the

Presbyterian church, officiating. To them have been born two children, Bruce Leondis and Cecil Lockett. Mrs. Fleetwood's father was born in Nashville, Tennessee, on May 18, 1829, and the mother was born on May 14, 1840, in Henderson county, Kentucky. They emigrated to Dell postoffice on Willow creek in this state, via Kelton, Utah. On April 7, 1900, the father died in Baker City, but the mother is still living in Ontario, Malheur county, this state. It is pleasant to be able to state that the subject of this sketch is one of the most thrifty and respected of the younger class of business men that are in his section of the county and his uprightness and integrity and uniform geniality have won him hosts of friends and the confidence and esteem of all the community, and a bright future seems to stretch before him and his.

ARTHUR W. ELLIS.—Among the wealthy and prominent business men of Sumpter must be numbered the public spirited citizen whose name appears as the caption of this review. Formerly owner of the entire town site, he still retains large interests in its real estate, while he also has some very valuable mining properties, and is principal owner in the Columbia Brewing and Malting Company of Sumpter. Inquiry into the antecedents and former life of Mr. Ellis develops the fact that he is a native of Michigan, born November 22, 1865. His mother died when he was but three years old, and at seventeen the hand of an assassin left him fatherless also. He was privileged to enjoy but meager educational advantages, and whatever intellectual discipline he has has been acquired in the large school of life, and in the hard, practical battles thereof.

He was engaged in various enterprises in different states until 1894, when he came out to Sumpter and purchased the town site, also the Ellis placer mines. For a time he operated the latter, reaping a rich reward for his labor, then he leased them to other parties and gave his attention to the lumber business. In course of time he sold his mill to Stoddard & McEwen, afterward investing a portion of the proceeds in a half interest in J. B. Stoddard's plant. In the fall of 1899 he sold this also, and since that time he has devoted his attention mainly to his mining and real estate in-

terests, though in the spring of 1900 he bought a share in the brewery, of which he became manager the ensuing fall.

Mr. Ellis was active in incorporating the town of Sumpter, of which he has ever since been a councilman, and in many other ways he has manifested his interest in the promotion of the general welfare and the upbuilding of his section of the county.

Fraternally our subject affiliates with the W. of W., the Red Men and the Elks. He was married in Baker City, December 31, 1894, the lady being Miss Maude Spaulding, and to their union three children have been born: George A., deceased; Madge E., and Edwin E.

H. W. B. SMITH.—Among the men who are occupying leading positions in the grand forward march of Baker county's mining interests the man whose name appears above is certainly to be given a prominent place. 'Tis a well known fact that though the mineral resources of this section have been in course of development since the early 'sixties, the period of discovery is as yet only begun, so that there is still much room for the genius and energy of such a man as our subject to find abundant operation. It is to be hoped that his push and courage in endeavoring to develop new mines and produce an augmentation of Baker county's wealth will find their well earned meed.

Mr. Smith was born in Portland, Oregon, on May 5, 1866, his parents being George R. and Catherine J. (Morrison) Smith, natives respectively of Maine and New Brunswick, and pioneers of this great commonwealth of 1861. He received a common school education in the public schools of Portland, then for three years followed the transfer business, after which he tried his fortune for two years in a retail cigar and confectionery store, his own venture. The ensuing three years were devoted to traveling as a salesman for the J. N. Matschek Candy Company, and the four years succeeding the expiration of that period to the grocery business at Long Beach, Washington. Having eventually disposed of this last mentioned business, he again became a traveling salesman, representing various wholesale confectionery firms until 1896, when he entered the employ of the American Biscuit

Company, for whom he traveled over eastern Washington, Oregon and Idaho until July, 1900, when he resigned to accept the general managership of the Cracker-Summit property, situated at Bourne, Oregon, in the famous Cracker creek district. This property consists of nine claims adjoining the well known Eureka, Excelsior and North Pole properties on the west and the Columbia on the north, so that our subject and his company entertain not unreasonable hopes that sufficient development will bring to light another wealth producer. Mr. Smith has a force of men at work at present, and is pushing developments with all vigor.

Our subject is also interested in numerous other promising properties, among them the Cyclone, in the famous Virtue district, near Baker City, of which he is a half owner, likewise he has some city property in Sumpter. He is a very energetic man and is justly regarded as one of Baker county's most valuable citizens.

The marriage of our subject was solemnized in Waitsburg, Washington, October 7, 1899, when Miss Sophia M., daughter of Duncan and Marion (Mason) Ingraham, became his wife.

JACOB H. ROBBINS.—No compilation which has to do with any section of the great state of Oregon and the men who built it could escape the charge of incompleteness did it fail to grant due representation to the energetic and forceful citizen whose name appears as the caption of this article. A native of this great commonwealth and the son of pioneer parents, he has, by his energy and distinguished ability as an operator in the commercial world, reflected credit upon both his state and his family. But without further introductory remarks we shall present here a brief summary of his life and allow the reader to judge for himself.

Mr. Robbins was born May 12, 1859, in Salem, Oregon. In 1862 the family removed to Umatilla Landing, where our subject's father organized several big pack trains wherewith to transport supplies to Boise City and various other mining camps in Idaho. In 1864 they went to Granite, the older Mr. Robbins taking the first wagon into that region, cutting

his own wagon road. Later he went into the merchandise business, establishing trading post throughout the entire country, and in company with Joe D. Young opening the first trading post on the ground where Sumpter now stands.

Our subject received his early intellectual discipline in the public schools of this and neighboring counties, and his initial training in business in his father's trading establishments. It was afterward his good fortune to enjoy the advantages of Baker City Academy and the Portland Business College, graduating from the latter institution in the spring of 1879. After returning from school he remained with his parents about a year, then went to Umatilla county, where he was engaged in merchandising until 1886. In that year he moved to Pendleton and engaged in real estate brokerage. Two years later he was called by the franchises of the people to the post of county treasurer, and for the ensuing two terms he retained this office. During the same time he was appointed assistant cashier of the Pendleton Savings Bank. In 1893 he retired from the service of this institution to accept a position as receiver of the United States land office at Lagrande, and for the next half decade he busied himself with "Uncle Sam's" business, during the latter part of this period becoming also interested in the Farmers and Traders National Bank at that point, of which he is still vice-president and a director. He was also engaged in the merchandise business there for a time.

In 1899 Mr. Robbins came to Sumpter. Shortly after his arrival he with others had organized the first bank of Sumpter, with our subject as president, J. W. Scriber vice-president, J. W. Mead cashier and director. They have a very fine brick building. Mr. Robbins is also quite extensively engaged in mining ventures in this district, among his properties being the Concord, adjoining the famous Red Boy, looked upon as one of the coming mines.

Our subject has ever manifested an active and public-spirited interest in affairs of general concern, doing all in his power to conserve and promote the welfare of town, county and state. In 1901 he was elected mayor of Sumpter, the duties of which office are being discharged by him with faithfulness and good judgment.

' In fraternal circles Mr. Robbins is well known. He belongs to all the degrees of Masonry up to and including the Knight Templar, also to the A. O. U. W., the W. of W., the United Artisans, the Pioneers of the Pacific, and numerous other orders. He formerly served as the grand officer in the last named fraternity. The marriage of our subject was solemnized in Portland, Oregon, February 1, 1882, the lady being Miss Edith V., a daughter of F. C. and Caroline (Thomas) Carr. Their union has been blessed by the advent of three children: J. Franklin, clerking in a drug store in Sumpter; Charles H. and one that died in infancy.

ERIC P. BERGMAN.—A very early pioneer in the west, an energetic and successful business man of Sumpter, and a public spirited citizen, vitally interested in the welfare of the town, county and state, the subject of this review is certainly deserving of representation in a work of this character, and it is with pleasure that we are enabled to accord him a place herein. He is withal a self-made man and entitled to the respect instinctively paid to men who possess the conquering spirit to such a degree that they are able to overcome all obstacles and win for themselves success in their own chosen line of activity in spite of poverty or any other disadvantage.

Mr. Bergman is a native of Sweden, born February 21, 1867. He grew to early manhood there, receiving a public school education, but when he arrived at the age of nineteen years he emigrated to Seattle, Washington, and for a number of years he wrought as a laborer in logging camps and on farms in the vicinity of that city. He saved his money, contrary to the usual custom of men among that class, and in 1888 engaged in a produce business in Seattle. A year later he went to Sumner, Washington, and embarked in general merchandising, in which he continued to employ his energies for a period of three years. He then sold out and went to Portland. Here he was in the grocery business continuously for eight years, after which he removed to Sumpter, where we now find him. He is now manager of the E. P. Bergman company, the leading grocers of the town, whose place of business is on Mill street. They carry a stock valued at about fifteen thousand dollars and are doing a large business and enjoying a very profitable and rapidly extending trade.

Mr. Bergman also has some very good mining properties, among the number being the Gypsy King, the Intermountain, the Buffalo and the St. Louis, and he owns a nice residence on Auburn street. He is certainly to be congratulated on the success with which he has climbed to his present exalted position in the commercial world despite the many obstacles which beset his pathway when he first arrived from Europe, without money, without influential friends, and without even a knowledge of the language. His thriftiness and natural business ability are to be credited in large measure to the decided change in his standing and condition in life.

Fraternally our subject is affiliated with the Masons, the K of P., and the Odd Fellows. His marriage was solemnized in Sumner, Washington, in April, 1893, Miss Nellie M. Seaman then becoming his wife, and their union has been blessed by the advent of one child, Beth Edell.

Mrs. Bergman's father crossed the plains to California in 1849, and came thence to the Sound before Tacoma was started, becoming one of the oldest pioneers of the state of Washington.

DAVID S. BERRYHILL.—A veritable pioneer of the pioneers, and a man that has had wide experience in all of the leading mining camps of an early day in the west, ever manifesting a sturdiness of character and an intrepidity and uprightness that made him a stanch supporter of the right, the subject of this sketch is eminently deserving of a place in any volume that purports to give mention of the representative men and leading citizens of this section, it is with pleasure, therefore, that we are enabled to give here an epitome of his career.

Mr. Berryhill is the son of Alexander and Elizabeth (Smalley) Berryhill, and was born in Miami county, Ohio, on February 13, 1827. He was reared on a farm and acquired during the years of his minority, his educational discipline in the public schools of his native place. When he arrived at eighteen years of age he embarked on the career of life's realities for himself and remained in his native country until 1852, then the siren of fortune's fields beckoned him to the regions of golden store and he embarked thither, via the New York and Isthmus route, landing in San Francisco on January 9, 1852. He immediately sought the mines and for one complete decade he wrought faithfully in the various camps of the state of California, then came to Auburn, in Baker county, in the spring of 1862, continuing mining there and in various other camps in eastern Oregon, and then repaired to Montana, where he spent two years in his favorite occupation, mining. Following this he rivaled the hero of Mark Twain's novel by making a trip down the Missouri in an open boat, landing at Sioux City safe and sound. After a short stay there he crossed the plains in a stage to Helena, Montana, whence, after a short stay he came to Powder river valley, near Baker City.

There he bought a farm and turned his attention to tilling the soil until 1877, at which time he bought his present place, three miles west of Hereford, and embarked in raising stock, cattle and horses. He has a valuable ranch that produces plenty of hay, and he has improved it in a fitting manner.

Enjoying the legacy of the bachelor's quiet comfort and freedom from the responsibilities that attend the domestic life of connubiality, Mr. Berryhill is passing the golden years of his adventurous and stirring career in the quiet of his rural retreat, where he directs his estate and herds.

---◆•◆---

LEWIS T. BROCK, M. D.—Baker county, so fortunate in the spirit and enterprise of the business and mining men who have made their homes within its borders, is likewise to be congratulated on the superior scholarship and skill of its professional classes, especially those who minister to the sick. Not the least prominent among its excellent staff of medical practitioners is he whose name appears as the caption of this article, and in presenting here a brief review of his career it is ours to enjoy the pleasure always attending upon the consideration of the biographical history of one who has fought life's early battles faithfully and achieved remarkable success in any line of scientific accomplishment.

Dr. Brock was born in Woodsfield, Ohio,

April 11, 1855, his parents being Dr. Jacob and Annie (Brock) Brock, pioneers of Ohio. His father died when he was yet in his infancy, and his mother moved to Illinois, where she married again, and where our subject grew to early manhood, receiving a public school education. He then graduated from the pharmaceutical department of the state university of Illinois, from which, however, he received no diploma, being too young at the time of graduation. He next went to California and there entered a San Francisco drug store as a clerk, remaining three years. In 1875 he moved to Boise, Idaho, where for the ensuing half decade he was engaged in the drug business in company with Dr. J. B. Wright, then the firm started a branch store in Bellevue, Idaho, of which our subject had charge until 1884. In that year he went to Seattle, and engaged again in the practice of pharmacy, continuing therein until 1888, when he went to South America. After making an extensive tour of that continent he returned to Portland, where he again engaged in the drug business, at the same time studying in the medical department of the university of Oregon, from which he graduated in 1897. He acted as surgeon for the Southern Pacific Railroad Company for a time, then as surgeon for the Spreckles Sugar Company, during the construction of their factory at Salinas, California. He then came, in 1898, to Sumpter, where his abilities as a physician speedily received recognition and soon he found himself in possession of a pleasant and lucrative practice. He is considered one of the finest physicians and surgeons in the county, his standing being an enviable one, both among the people and his fellow practitioners. He was elected city physician shortly after coming here, and in that capacity he has acted ever since. He is also surgeon for the Sumpter Valley Railroad Company and examiner for the Equitable, the Mutual, the Pacific Mutual, the State Life and other insurance companies.

In his fraternal affiliations he is identified with the Royal Arch of the Masonic fraternity, the W. of W., the M. W. A., the Pioneers of the Pacific and the I. O. O. F. His marriage was solemnized in Bellevue, Idaho, on November 15, 1882, when Miss Ada A. Worswick became his wife, and they have one child, Jessie. The family live in a very pleasant home on Granite street.

WILLIAM J. ROGERS, one of the enterprising farmers and stock-raisers of the county and a popular hotel man, is a native of Westville, Franklin county, New York, born January 5, 1825. He remained under the shelter of the parental roof until about of age, then engaging in farming, and he was numbered among the leading agriculturists of the Empire state until 1871, when he came to Grant county, Oregon, and embarked in placer mining. Early in 1873 he came to Baker county, and located on a quarter section of land on Dooley mountains, twelve miles south of Baker City, where he has ever since lived, and where he has a very fine stock farm of one hundred and sixty acres. Hay is his principal crop.

Mr. Rogers is also proprietor of what is widely known as the Mountain House, a hostelry in which all guests receive a warm welcome and hospitable treatment.

In Westville, New York, on May 8, 1862, our subject married Miss Hannah Brown, and to their union was born one child, which died in infancy.

L. C. EDWARDS.—Gifted with all the qualities which go to win success for a man in commercial pursuits, and possessed of an intimate knowledge of his profession, the man whose career we shall now attempt to outline has won an enviable place among business men and pharmacists in Baker county and it is with pleasure that we are able to present here a brief review of his life as one who has contributed largely in his own way to the general progress. While he does not seem to be specially ambitious for political preferment (though he has been the candidate of his party for some high offices of trust) he ever manifests a deep and abiding interest in the welfare of his locality and his state, and deserves to be counted among broad-minded, public-spirited, and benevolently disposed men.

Mr. Edwards was born in McMinnville, Tennessee, on March 2, 1860, and there he grew to manhood, receiving a public school education. Later he graduated from the Walters and Walling College, and in 1881, shortly after receiving his degree, he came west to Arlington, Oregon. He engaged in the drug business, and to that he gave his best energies

23

for about thirteen years, thereupon coming to Sumpter, where he has succeeded in building up the finest trade enjoyed by any drug store in the county. He owns his building and carries a full line of drugs, chemicals, notions, etc., in fact, everything usually to be found in a thoroughly equipped and well stocked pharmacy.

For a number of years Mr. Edwards acted as mayor of Arlington, and once he was candidate from the district in which that town is located for the office of representative in the state legislature. Fraternally he is affiliated with the Masonic order. He was married in the Willamette valley in 1885, to Miss Mattie Simon, a daughter of old and esteemed pioneer parents, and to their union one child has been born, namely, Jesse E.

JAMES MILLS, an old and esteemed pioneer of Pine valley, and a man who has always enjoyed an enviable standing among his neighbors, by whom he is trusted and respected, is a native of Ballygawley, Ireland, born in 1836, the son of James and Ester (Laughran) Mills, likewise natives of that place. He remained under the shelter of the parental roof until fifteen years old, then began for himself the battle of life. Believing the new world contained excellent opportunities for an energetic, ambitious youth like himself, he took passage in 1852 for the United States. His first home on this side of the Atlantic was in Warren, Ohio, where he worked two years, going then to the lead mines of Grant county, Wisconsin, where the ensuing three years of his life were passed. The fall of 1856, found him in the then highly agitated state of Kansas, there he continued to reside until the spring of 1859, when he started for Pike's Peak, Colorado. The ensuing sixteen or seventeen years of his life were devoted to farming in that commonwealth, but in 1877, he determined to try his fortune further west so came to the state of Oregon. Purchasing a place six miles north of Union, he remained here three or four years, but 1881 witnessed his entrance to Pine valley. He settled upon a farm of eighty acres two and a half miles north of Pine postoffice, and to the cultivation and improvement of this he has devoted some portion of his time and energy since, though he has also been engaged for years in the search for hidden treasure, and has a very promising mine at Cornucopia.

Mr. Mills has always fully sustained the good name his countrymen have for industry, frugality, and thrift, and is one of those whom all good citizens are glad to welcome to our shores.

In Weld county, Colorado, in 1861, our subject married Miss Cornelia, daughter of Eli and Jane (Bird) Phelps, and to their union have been born nine children: William E., Edward, Minnie, Alice, Ester, Nora, Patrick H., Andrew J., and an infant that died in Colorado in 1864.

Mrs. Mills' father is a native of Canada and was twice sheriff of Buchanan county, Iowa.

HENRY BARNES.—We are pleased to grant to the subject of this sketch a representation in this volume of the chronicles of Baker county, since he has wrought here with an assiduity and energy, coupled with keen foresight and dominated by commendable sagacity, that have made him the recipient of gratifying success and given him the meed of the confidence and esteem of his fellows, while his unswerving integrity and uniform geniality have won him hosts of friends.

Mr. Barnes was born in Millford, Connecticut, on November 25, 1831, being the son of Harry and Laura (Root) Barnes. His father was a hatter, and in assisting him in this trade and attending the public schools of the city where he lived, Henry spent the earlier years of his life. When he arrived at the age of manhood his adventurous spirit led him to the realms of the unexplored west, coming to California via New York and Panama. He landed at San Francisco and later was at Marysville, but he soon bought a ranch near San Jose and continued in the culture of the same until 1862, the year that he came to the Grande Ronde valley in this state. In that valley he bought a farm, and there lived until 1873, when he went to Eldorado, near where Malheur is now situated, and kept hotel and operated a livery and feed stable. In 1878 he took a homestead where he now lives, three and one-half miles southwest from Hereford, and here he has re-

sided since. His time has been occupied with stock-raising and culture of the soil, and he has been favored with a very gratifying success in these enterprises. His farm is a valuable producer of hay, being well watered and well improved, and he has a fine herd of cattle and some horses.

The marriage of Mr. Barnes and Miss Mary M., daughter of Jacob and Julia (Shaver) Conner, was solemnized on October 2, 1878. The golden years of this worthy citizen are being spent in the quiet enjoyment of the competence that his skill and industry have provided, and he is one of the substantial members of society and an active worker in the realm of good government.

E. A. CASE.—This esteemed citizen and enterprising furniture dealer of Sumpter was born in Essex, Vermont, January 16, 1849, his parents being Lyman and Mary A. Case, natives likewise of Vermont. When Mr. Case became six years old he was taken by his parents to Marine City, Michigan; then known as Newport, and about two years later he accompanied them to Minnesota, where he grew up and received th major portion of his education. Coming to Walla Walla in 1876, he spent the next two and a half years in the wood business there, going then to Asotin county, where he followed his trade, carpentering, for about three and a half years. He then went to Puget sound and embarked quite extensively in the manufacture of lumber, building several saw mills in different parts of that country. In 1896 he came to Sumpter and resumed his contracting and building, erecting some very imposing edifices, among them the public school house. In 1897 he embarked in the furniture business in the town, conducting it alone until 1899, when he incorporated a company of which he is president and manager, Clark Snyde vice-president, and H. S. Durgan secretary and treasurer. Theirs is the only furniture store in town, and it enjoys a large and increasing business. The company own the building in which they are doing business, and carry a stock valued at about fourteen thousand dollars, including besides furniture proper, carpets, wall paper, etc. The company also do an undertaking business and own the Blue

Mountain cemetery. Their building is practically three stories high, and is supplied with a basement twenty-five by one hundred feet. The company also owns a large warehouse. Mr. Case is personally the owner of some valuable town property, including a fine residence at the head of Center street, and is interested in mining.

Our subject has, by his business enterprise, added much to the development of the town, but he is not satisfied with this, and is striving in other ways to build it up and promote its welfare. Its political interests find in him a jealous guardian, and its first city council profited by his presence and the wisdom of his suggestions, he being a member of that body, and on December 3, 1901, he was again chosen by the people as councilman for the city.

On January 1, 1891, in Tacoma, Washington, Mr. Case married Mrs. Louis Mullett, of Delmar, Iowa, and they have one child, Earl L.

ALEXANDER A. BUCHANAN.—This pioneer settler and enterprising farmer and stock-raiser of the vicinity of Pine was born in Middlebrook, Virginia, in 1833, his parents being James and Margaret Buchanan, likewise natives of Virginia. He continued one of the circle around the parental hearthstone until eighteen years old, and received such educational advantages as were to be had in the local schools, then engaged in the pursuit of the carpenter's trade in different places in the south. In 1852 he moved to western Iowa, and after two years more had been devoted to carpenter work and building in that locality, he set out across the plains and through the mountains to Placerville, California. Three years were there devoted to mining, then he moved to Jackson county, Oregon, where for half a decade he busied himself as a teamster. Returning then to the Golden state, he spent there eight years more, this time engaged in farming, then he farmed six years in his former place of abode, Jackson county, afterward coming to Pine valley, Baker county.

In 1870 he located on a homestead five miles northeast of Pine postoffice and engaged in the dual occupation of diversified farming and cattle raising, in which kindred industries he has been occupied ever since, achieving such success as properly belongs to well directed, long continued effort and judicious management.

In Stockton, California, in 1861, our subject married Nancy J., daughter of Marion and Emily (Million) Taylor, natives of Missouri, both of whom died in Oregon. To their union eight children have been born, William, John, Thomas, Jennie, Robert, George, Margaret and one that died in infancy.

C. M. PEARCE, M. D.—Though a very young man, the subject of this review has already achieved much in the difficult profession he has chosen for his own, and he certainly gives great promise of becoming one of the leading physicians and surgeons in the west. A graduate of one of the most famous medical colleges in the United States, and gifted with great natural ability, he seems to have come into prominence all at once, without undergoing the novitiate so trying to young professional men, and already he and his partner are in possession of a large and lucrative practice.

Dr. Pearce is a son of Thomas M. and Laura M. (Carter) Pearce, natives respectively of Iowa and Illinois. The father crossed the plains to the Willamette valley in 1850, and ten years later came to Clark's creek in eastern Oregon to engage in mining and in operating with a pack train between Umatilla Landing and Boise. The mother came with her parents via New York and Panama to California, and thence they removed to Oregon in 1861. In 1874 their marriage was solemnized, and on February 16, 1876, our subject was born. He received the advantages offered by the common schools of the county and by Baker City high school, and with this preparation entered Jefferson Medical College, of Philadelphia, from which he graduated in 1899. He then took a course in the Jefferson Medical College hospital and three months' training in the Philadelphia sanitarium for children, thereupon coming to Sumpter, Oregon, where he and Dr. Tape started the Sumpter general hospital. Dr. Tape later sold out to Dr. Anderson, our subject's present partner. They have a large practice, the natural result of their skill and care, for they are counted as among the leading physicians of the county.

In fraternal affiliations Dr. Pearce is identified with the B. P. O. E. of Baker City; he also belongs to the W. W. Keen Surgical Society, of Philadelphia. In Philadelphia, on September 19, 1899, Dr. Pearce married Miss Janette, daughter of James and Elizabeth Hurley, of that city. Mrs. Pearce is a graduate nurse of Jefferson Medical College hospital of Philadelphia, and renders her husband very material assistance in the supervision and management of his hospital.

HIRAM B. GRIFFIN.—Among the most esteemed and respected of the leading citizens of Sumpter is the prominent hotel and mining man whose career it is now our task to present in brief resume. Perhaps no class of men contribute more to the development and prosperity of a town than they who cater to the material necessities of its visitors and transients, and Mr. Griffin certainly understands how to make his hostelry a place of comfort and a place at which commercial travelers will delight to make their temporary abode.

Mr. Griffin is a native of Warren county, New York, born December 2, 1833, the son of Jonathan and Sybil (Seely) Griffin. His educational advantages were such as the common schools afforded, and as soon as he had completed his intellectual discipline he engaged in the lumbering industry, at first in his native state and later in Canada, where he spent about four years. Returning eventually to New York, he followed the livery business there for a period of eleven years, thereupon coming to California, where he gave inception to his career as a hotel man. Coming to Oregon, he took up land in Umatilla county, and there he farmed for a few years, ultimately going to Caldwell, Idaho, where he again engaged in the hotel business, remaining until 1898. In that year he came to Sumpter, purchased the property on the corner of Mill and Auburn streets, enlarged the same to accommodate fifty guests, and engaged in the hotel business in good earnest.

Mr. Griffin also has some very valuable mining claims in Baker county, among them the Eureka and the Grey Eagle in the famous Cracker creek district, and among his realty holdings is some valuable city property.

A public-spirited man, our subject has ever manifested a deep interest in the promotion of the public good wherever he has lived, taking an active part in the upbuilding of his town and county. At present he is doing what he can for the promotion of the cause of good government in Sumpter by serving with faithfulness and good judgment in the city council. In fraternal affiliations he is a Mason. His marriage was solemnized in July, 1855, in New York state, when Miss Mary F., daughter of Mr. and Mrs. Crandall, became his wife. The issue of their union is five children: Mary, widow of Mr. Brink; Helen, wife of Dr. J. C. Epperson, of Illinois; Sybil, wife of Frank B. Clopton, of Pendleton, Oregon; Ruth, wife of L. S. Carter, of Portland; and Hiram B., Jr. On March 31, 1900, Mrs. Griffin was called away by death, leaving a mourning household and many friends, being highly esteemed and beloved by all.

CALEB K. ROSWELL.—The enterprising business man whose name forms the caption of this brief biographical review has for years belonged to that adventurous and daring class of men now almost passed from the face of the earth, being supplanted by the railroads, which have proven so useful, so indispensable in the development of remote regions. We refer to the stage drivers. Our subject's line of activity has kept him on the frontier almost all his life, and in him are fully developed the daring, independence of character and resourcefulness for which pathfinders of the wilderness and pioneers of new and uncivilized sections are renowned.

Mr. Roswell entered upon the stage of this life in Atlanta, Georgia, on May 28, 1836. His parents, N. C. and Rachel Roswell, moved to Missouri when he was fifteen years of age, their children, of course, accompanying them, and it was in that state that our subject received the major portion of his education, which was confined to a common school course. When he became eighteen years old his love of adventure could no longer be restrained and he removed to Mexico to give inception to his career as a frontiersman. Before the year was over we find him in an emigrant train and bound for the Pacific states. He settled in Santa Fe, New Mexico, where for four years he was employed as a stage driver, then, in 1859, he went to Pike's Peak, Colorado, and for two years devoted himself to mining. He thereupon removed to Idaho, locating in Boise, where for twenty-five years he was engaged in the stage business. During his long career as a stage operator he had occasion to travel extensively over the western part of the United States, and the topography of this vast region is quite thoroughly known to him.

In 1895 Mr. Roswell came to Sumpter, Oregon, and again engaged in the stage business, operating between that city and Bourne and the mines in that vicinity. He continued to busy himself thus until 1897, when he opened what is known as the Pioneer Feed Store, on the corner of Mill and Auburn streets, and to the upbuilding and extending of this establishment he has devoted his energies assiduously since. His enterprise is meeting with deserved success and his trade is increasing rapidly.

———◆◆◆———

ALEX. McPHERSON.—This energetic and progressive farmer and stock-raiser of the vicinity of Bridgeport is a native of Ontario, Canada, and he possesses in a full measure the thrift, resourcefulness and other qualities of good citizenship for which the sons of that province are noted. An early pioneer of Baker county, he has, during all the years of his residence here, so conducted himself as to win the confidence and good will of the people with whom he has been thrown in contact, and his standing in the community in which he lives is certainly a very enviable one.

Mr. McPherson grew to man's estate on the farm of his parents, Donald and Catherine McPherson, but as soon as his legal majority had been attained he came out to Baker county and began seeking his fortune in the mining regions of this section. After two years' experience he began dividing his time between that search and farming, and he carried on this dual occupation in different parts of the county until 1881, when he settled on a three-hundred-and-twenty-acre farm three miles west of Bridgeport. To the cultivation and improvement of this he has given himself assiduously since, and as the meed of his hard and painstaking labor he now has a very excellent place, with fine home and comfortable environs. He has a large herd of very choice graded Shorthorn cattle, and also a drove of horses.

In fraternal affiliations our subject is a member of Malheur City Lodge, No. 111, of the W. of W., and of the Baker City lodge of the Knights of Pythias, and he formerly belonged to the lodge of Odd Fellows at Malheur City, which surrendered its charter. On January 1, 1889, he married Miss Euphea, daughter of Andrew Eblen, and a native of Kentucky, and to their union three children have been born, Donald, Alexander and Catherine G.

———◆◆◆———

JOHN N. DOANE.—Surely our volume, purporting, as it does, to give in brief review the biographies of the leading men of this county, would be seriously incomplete were there failure to mention the career of the substantial mining man and estimable citizen that has for many years wrought within the precincts of Baker county and who has ever maintained a position of esteem and respect in the communities where he has labored, and whose name heads this article.

Mr. Doane was born at Springfield, Pennsylvania, on September 24, 1845, being the son of Joseph C. and Mariah (Scranton) Doane. He was taken by his parents while a child to Clinton, Connecticut, and at the age of thirteen years commenced work on a farm. After this he attended the high school and then later again sought to the basic art of agriculture, after which he clerked in various mercantile establishments, among them the large house of C. H. Oakes & Company in New Haven. Following this he came to Iron Ridge, Wisconsin, and thence to Jacksonville, Illinois, at which latter place he was commissioner of the insane asylum for two years. After this he visited various cities and counties in the interest of a stock company, finally coming to St. Louis and engaging on the street railway as conductor. Later he was traveling salesman for a St. Louis house and then returned to the railway company and eventually went to Denver and took up mining. After some years spent at this he came across the plains on horseback, accompanying a government supply train, and also took part in the Bannock Indian war in 1878. Following this he purchased a farm near Baker City and turned his attention to tilling the soil until 1889, when he sold out and removed to Sumpter valley and in 1896 to Sumpter. He owns a good house and lot in the city of Sumpter and also some very promising mining property in the regions adjacent to that place.

The marriage of Mr. Doane and Miss Mary A., daughter of John and Ellen Weatherford, of Briton Station, in Baker county, occurred on February 5, 1885, and to them have been born the following named children: Leslie L., Roscoe B., Earl N., Annie L., John L., Alice M. Mr. Doane is a member of the Fraternal Union of America, in Sumpter.

ALBERT VAUGHAN. — Among the young men of whose industry and achievements Baker county has reason to be proud, the gentleman whose name initiates this paragraph must be given a conspicuous place. Though less than a quarter of a century old, he has already achieved fame and wealth by discovering one of the most remarkable mines in the region, and his strength of character and mental equipoise are demonstrated by the fact that notwithstanding his good fortune he is still active in lines of endeavor which will still further add to the wealth of the county.

Mr. Vaughan was born at Elko, Nevada, in 1877, his parents being Henry C. and Lois (McCarthy) Vaughan. He remained with the remainder of the family in the old parental home until his parents passed away, his business being mining. After he began life's struggle on his own account he still continued to search for mineral wealth. In 1897, in company with his brother, Jake P., he discovered what is now extensively known as the Irondyke mine. The two were searching for iron used in fluxing in smelters, and while so engaged they discovered a very rich copper mine, which they named the Irondyke, commemorative of the search in which they were engaged at the time. They retained the claim about six months, at the end of which time they had ten thousand tons of ore in sight. They then bonded their mine for two years, the consideration to be forty thousand dollars. Immediately upon negotiating this sale our subject engaged in the cattle business and in general farming, purchasing a quarter section of land two and a half miles northeast of Pine

postoffice, but it is needless to state that he is still interested in mining. He owns some promising claims at Sumpter and Homestead.

In politics Mr. Vaughan is an active Democrat. He was married at Baker City on February 18, 1900, the lady being Amy A., daughter of Emsley and Martha (Whitley) Ridenour, natives respectively of Illinois and Oregon and residents at present of Pine valley.

JOSEPH SCHWARTZ.—This enterprising merchant of Sumpter, Oregon, is a native of Germany, born June 16, 1868. He received the advantages of the excellent public school system which has made his native country famous, and a year later, or, in other words, when he was fifteen years old, came to the United States. He settled in Lincoln, Nebraska, where for the ensuing five and a half years he wrought assiduously as a clerk in a store, gaining that excellent knowledge of commercial pursuits which has stood him in such good stead since. He then went to Omaha, and clerked four years longer, going then to Sioux City, Iowa, where he embarked in the grocery business, continuing in the same for about three and a half years. Eventually selling out, he came to Oregon, settled in Oregon City, and engaged in the clothing business. He was numbered among the enterprising merchants of that town for two years, but in 1899 he sold his business and holdings and went east on a visit. Returning the following year, he started in business in Sumpter, Oregon, and though the establishment of his enterprise, known as the Hub Clothing Store, has been so recent, he has already built up a large trade, and his business is extending and ramifying more and more widely as time goes on.

Mr. Schwartz's experience is an exemplification of the statement that "concentration is the secret of success." He has devoted himself diligently and uninterruptedly to mercantile pursuits, gaining an intimate knowledge of business methods, and this, coupled with his natural sagacity, foresight and good judgment, has enabled him to achieve a success in the commercial world seldom reached by one of his years. But though our subject attends strictly to business, he is not so exclusive but that he can take the interest becoming every good citizen in public affairs, and he has ever manifested a public-spirited solicitude for the advancement and the welfare of his town and county.

Fraternally Mr. Schwartz is affiliated with the W. of W. and the K. O. T. M. In Iowa, on October 28, 1896, he married Miss Rosa Ginsberg, also a native of Germany.

ELLIS L. LEAP, one of the leading citizens and prosperous farmers of Pine valley, is a product of the sunny south, his birthplace being the vicinity of Wheeling, West Virginia. He remained with his parents, John and Sarah (Wise) Leap, until about twenty-two years old, then, in 1866, went north to Indiana. Two years later we find him again in Virginia and engaged in the oil works there and in mercantile pursuits. A quadrennium was thus passed at the end of which time he built what is known as a trading boat, which he ran up and down the various rivers of the system existing near his home for a number of years, eventually selling and moving to Missouri, whither his father and the remainder of the family had gone. He farmed in that state two years, then went to Texas and spent four years on the railroad, after which he bought cattle and drove them over the trail to Missouri, then returned to Texas, later crossing the plains to Oregon. He spent the first winter, that of 1875, in the Grande Ronde valley, coming the next spring to Pine valley, Baker county, taking a homestead of one hundred and sixty acres, now increased to two hundred and twenty acres, a half mile north of Halfway postoffice, where he is now to be found. He has been ever since engaged in general farming and cattle raising, a business in which he has achieved a very enviable success. He has a pleasant home and surroundings and his premises bear testimony to his thrift, energy, and progressiveness. As a man and citizen his standing in the community in which he has passed so many years is of the highest.

While in Missouri, our subject married Miss Anna Fortune, a native of Missouri, who died while crossing the plains in 1875, and was buried at Laramie. She left one infant child, which died upon reaching the Grande Ronde valley. In 1878, at Brown Lee ferry,

in Idaho, Mr. Leap again married, the lady being Miss Anna Bragg, who died in Pine valley in 1879, leaving one daughter, Anna B., at home with her father.

Mr. Leap tells that when he came to Pine valley, there were any number of bears, deer, elk, and antelope in the country, and that while the settlers were stockaded up for fourteen days during the Indian troubles the bears wrought great depredations among their hogs and other domestic animals. Apropos of the fort, he says that it was built about a quarter of a mile from Halfway, and was constructed in this wise. A trench three feet deep around a one hundred feet square was dug and into it were inserted the butts of fourteen foot pine trees, stood side by side, the smallest being two feet through. At each corner a semicircle of logs was made to shoot from, and a lining of logs was constructed inside of the inclosure as high as the portholes. Inside of this stockade a block house was built with roof about two feet higher than the outside palisade, with portholes near the top.

ALVIN P. JONES.—Among those who have wrought for the material advancement and substantial progress of Baker county and have ever been manifesting a praiseworthy interest in the welfare of all, the subject of this sketch stands high. He is one that has devoted much time and energy to the search for valuable prospects and also in developing them to the time of producing, taking rank with the leading men engaged in the business of mining in this section.

Mr. Jones was born in Gage county, Nebraska, on October 10, 1859, being the son of Samuel and Rebecca (Pethond) Jones. His early life was spent on the farm receiving the invigorating exercise incident to the agriculturist's art, and also attending the public schools of his place. When he had attained the age of eighteen years, his desire and ambition was toward the west and accordingly he turned thither and made the journey in the methods of former years, driving horse teams the entire distance. He settled at Junction City, Lane county, and in the following spring came to Pendleton. That was the time of trouble with the Indians and he experienced much difficulty with them. In 1879, he migrated to Malheur and engaged in raising stock which occupied his attention until 1891 being attended with good success. At the last date, he disposed of the homestead he had taken meanwhile and came to McEwen in Baker county and engaged in mining. It was in 1897 that he came to Sumpter, where he now owns a fine home and considerable other property adjacent. He owns one-fourth interest in the Magnolia mine in the Granite district about eighteen miles west from Sumpter which is considered a very valuable property, he also owns a half interest in the Rising Sun, which is known as the Lucky Boy. In addition to these valuable properties he has various others and is a substantial mining man of the county.

The marriage of Mr. Jones and Miss Addie L., daughter of Samuel B. and Josephine (Sanborn) Reeves, was celebrated at Malheur and to them have been born two children as follows, James D. and Frank J. Mr. Jones is affiliated with the A. O. U. W., Lodge, No. 100, at Baker City. He is a respected member of society and has so demeaned himself in all of his associations that his reputation is of the best and the confidence of the entire community is his to enjoy.

RICHARD M. GARRETT.—It is with pleasure that we essay the task of outlining the career of the venerable frontiersman whose name appears above. For nearly forty years he has been identified with the development of the Pacific coast states, most of that time being spent in Oregon, and in all that period he has shown himself willing to do his share for the advancement of the general good; has participated in the Indian wars; and in many ways manifested an enlightened public spirit.

Born in Sheridan county, Missouri, on June 10, 1834, he grew to early manhood there, acquiring a common school education. When he became nineteen he yielded to the promptings of his ambitious and daring spirit, which were summoning him westward, and came out to Oregon. The next year he journeyed southward to California, where he was engaged in freighting and packing into various mining camps in the mountains for the ensuing eleven years, and during that time he participated

in the Modoc war, serving under General Crosby as a member of Captain Ballard's company. In 1864 he returned to Oregon and engaged in packing from Umatilla landing to various points in Idaho and Montana. In 1868 he settled on Powder river, where for a period of two years he followed trapping and hunting, afterward taking a quarter section of land, about ten miles south of Baker City, and engaging in farming and stock raising. To this dual occupation he has devoted his energies assiduously ever since, though his present home consists of a quarter section other than that on which he first settled, but close to it. He carries hay and vegetables, and keeps about forty head of cattle and sixty head of horses.

In Baker county, on April 2, 1876, our subject married Miss Louisa Hart, a native of England.

During the Modoc war, above referred to, Mr. Garrett endured many hardships, and his company sustained severe losses in several of the engagements in which it participated.

W. H. BENTLEY.—It now becomes our pleasant task to outline in brief the career of the estimable gentleman and well known pioneer and leading business man whose name heads this paragraph and whose life of wise achievement has been potent in the development of this and adjacent counties, while his uprightness and stanch principles have ever displayed an integrity and stability that have commended him to the entire community.

He was born in Licking county, Ohio, on March 24, 1831, and while still a child was removed to Richmond, Indiana, with the other members of the family, later to Greenfield, the same state, and then to Putnam county, Missouri, and finally, in 1846, they came to Iowa, where our subject attended school in a log house and acquired the discipline of birch and literary research there to be obtained. In 1849 he removed to Illinois, and in 1852 turned toward the occident and threaded the dreary and dangerous plains with ox teams for four months and ten days until he reached the land "where rolls the Oregon" and selected a home on one of its tributaries in Yam Hill county, there occupying himself in

RICHARD M. GARRETT.

W. H. BENTLEY.

HENRY H. ALBERT.

WILLIAM McKINNELL.

carpentering and operating a saw mill. After some time he was attracted to Florence, Idaho, and spent one summer in searching for the hidden treasure of that region; he also went to Boise basin, where he continued the search for a brief period After this he repaired to Umatilla for the winter and the following spring was engaged as superintendent on the Indian reservation, his duties being to instruct the aborigines in the art of agriculture. It was as early as 1865 that he made a permanent settlement in Baker county, although he had frequently been in its territory previous to that date. At that time he bought state land and occupied himself in its culture and in teaming for a short time, when he again turned to mining in Burnt basin, near the Express ranch. In 1868 he came to this valley and followed farming and carpentering until 1886, when he removed into Baker City, there also prosecuting his handicraft for a time and then was elected justice of the peace, discharging the duties of that office with such ability and faithfulness for four years that he was called by the people to accept the position of police judge, auditor and clerk for the municipality of Baker City, and in the fulfillment of the functions of this incumbency we find him at the present time, being re-elected to the same office on November 4, 1901. His life has been one constant expression of the faithful performance of duty that devolved upon him and the faithfulness and integrity thus manifested have won for him the entire confidence of the people, while he is also held in marked esteem and distinction by all who have the pleasure of his acquaintance. In fraternal affiliations the Judge is with the I. O. O. F., and the Redmen, being a popular associate in both orders, as well as generally throughout the county.

HENRY H. ALBERT.—One of the substantial stockmen and agriculturists of that thrifty and enterprising class in Baker county, the subject of this sketch, is here accorded representation, since it is very fitting that in a volume purporting to review the lives of the prominent men of the county, he should have a leading place, having spent his life in great activity, displaying an adaptability that made him successful in many lines of enterprise and

gave him experience wide and enjoyable. Also it is to be recorded to his credit that at a time when this nation called for her sons to rally to the rescue of our beloved institutions he quickly responded and freely gave his services to face the cannon of the enemy, and if need so require, give his blood for his country.

Henry H. was born in Newark, New Jersey, on January 1, 1848, being the son of Frederick and Johannah Albert. There he attended the schools of the city until he was twelve years of age, and then learned the tinsmith's trade, at which he continued until the spring of 1863, when the call came for one hundred day men, and he promptly responded, enlisting in Company F, Thirty-fifth New Jersey. At the end of his service he was honorably discharged and returned home and took up his trade until 1867, then he determined to satisfy his desire for travel and accordingly made the circuit of the east and south, working at his trade at intervals, and in 1870 we find him in Texas, later in New Mexico, and he also visited Arizona, where he turned to driving cattle in 1873. Two years after this he was in the mines in Arizona, and with what success we are not told, and then he came to California, and finally to Portland, whence he went to the Waterford cannery and took charge of the tinning department of the same. In 1878 he came to Baker City and took up mining until 1884, when he deemed it time to settle down in life, and accordingly took a homestead where he now resides, five miles west from Bridgeport. His property is valuable and well improved and he owns a large herd of fine cattle and some horses, his time being occupied in stock raising and agriculture. He has accumulated ten thousand dollars and more and is one of the most substantial stockmen of the county. Politically he formerly held with the Democratic party, but since the free silver issue he has taken his stand with the Republicans. As yet Mr. Albert has preferred the quieter joys of the single life with its freedom and repose, rather than the cares of conjugal relations and the responsibilities of domesticity.

WILLIAM McKINNELL.—Perhaps no country in Europe is so widely noted for the sturdy character and sterling integrity of its

sons as is old Scotland, the country which has
sent so many men to our shores who have afterward become noted for thrift and assiduity
in business and loyalty to the principles for
which our government stands. It is now our
pleasure to accord brief mention to one of these
sturdy sons of Caledonia, who has distinguished himself in Baker county as a mining
man and merchant, and who formerly distinguished himself when opportunity offered as
a valiant defender of the Union and the flag.

Mr. McKinnell was born in Dumfriesshire,
in September, 1845, the son of David and
Violet (Wilson) McKinnell, likewise natives
of Scotland. His mother died in 1854, and
three years later his father came to Markham, Canada. Our subject lived in the home
of a paternal uncle from the time of his mother's demise until sixteen years of age, then
started for America, the date of his departure
from Europe being likewise the date of the
firing on Fort Sumter. Naturally he went to
Markham, where his father was, but about
eighteen months later he moved to Chicago,
and from that time until November, 1864, he
traveled around considerably. During this interval he assisted Edwards, a directory man,
to compile a directory of Chicago, and a ga-
zetteer of Wisconsin, the latter being done in
1863. In November, 1864, he enlisted in Company K, Ninth Illinois Cavalry, and for the
ensuing year he did service as a soldier, being
also quartermaster's clerk a short time. At
the close of hostilities he returned to Canada,
but three months later was in Chicago again,
where he entered the employ of R. M. & O. S.
Hough, packers, for whom he worked during
the next eight years as shipping clerk.

The panic of 1873 determined him to try
his fortune in Oregon, and in 1874 he reached
the Willamette valley. After a short residence
in that famous basin he came to Sparta, where
he mined, but though he was in Pine valley
at about that time, he did not permanently
settle there until 1882, when he took up land
and started farming. Prior to that date he
was engaged in mining almost wholly, and in
that industry he has never lost his interest.
He owned claims in the Copper creek country.
He owns a mine on the hill above Carson,
and also has a quarter section of land at Halfway. At present Mr. McKinnell has charge
of the estate of S. S. Pindell, deceased, which

includes the store at Carson, in which he is
now carrying on business, having been admini-
istrator since 1900. For four years Mr. Mc-
Kinnell has served as notary public. In fraternal affiliations he is identified with Phil
Kearny Post, No. 66, G. A. R., of which he
served as adjutant for several years. It is of
note that the great grandmother of Mr. Mc-
Kinnell, Mary Paul, was a sister of the noted
admiral John Paul Jones, of world-wide fame.

<hr />

STEPHEN S. PINDELL, deceased.—It
is very fitting that we accord to the estimable
gentleman whose name is at the head of that
article a representation in the history of Baker
county, since he took such a prominent part
in its industries and by his upright life and
fine qualities won as friends all who had the
pleasure of his acquaintance.

Mr. Pindell was born near Marathon, Cler-
mont county, Ohio, in February, 1834, and
there passed his boyhood days. In 1852 he
came to the coast, via the Isthmus, and immediately took up mining in Yreka and at Scott's
Bar until 1860, and after that date he was
in most of the prominent camps of the entire
northwest, having spent two years in the Kootenai district with his brother, Reason Pindell, and there he owned a large ditch and
did much active mining on good claims. In
1871 he wintered in Walla Walla, being occupied in the commercial establishment of the
Adams Brothers, and the following year he
came to Sparta, Union county, now Baker
county, and after mining for several years in
Maiden Gulch he formed a partnership with
Edward Wilkinson, and for four years thereafter they conducted a general store at Sparta.
In the spring of 1883 the firm sold their entire
interests at Sparta and Mr. Pindell moved to
Pine valley, and there started the first general
store in the place. Later he took as partner
Robert A. Wilkinson, and soon thereafter he
also took into the firm Edward Wilkinson,
brother of Robert, and the three operated the
establishment for ten years, and then the firm
dissolved. They had one of the best trades in
that part of the county and were generally
esteemed and confided in by the people. Soon
after this event Mr. Pindell repaired to a place
that is now named Carson and there opened a

general mercantile house and in the operation of the interests of this business he was constantly found thereafter. He did a good business, and best of all he had the love and confidence of every one in the community. His patrons were only limited by the population. On February 12, 1900, the messenger of death came to Mr. Pindell and summoned him from the scenes of his home and the cares of his business to the realities of another world than this. No man in the community was more esteemed and beloved than was this worthy character. Upon the day of the funeral the weather was exceedingly inclement, and at that time there had been a smallpox scare that had scattered every public meeting for some time, but these things could not hold back the throng of loving and mourning friends from assembling in a great concourse and paying their respects to the memory of the deceased. Surely no man of the county was ever followed to his tomb by more or sincerer friends.

WILLIAM H. WELLINGTON.—While the man whose career we shall now attempt to present in outline was not one of those whose names are especially familiar in political circles and the ambition for personal aggrandizement never controlled in his life, he belonged, during his lifetime, to that great class which forms the real strength and boast of any community, the class which goes assiduously about the work in hand and in a quiet way contributes immeasurably toward the general progress and development. It must not be understood, however, that our subject was lacking in public spirit. He always manifested a deep interest in the affairs of county and state, and his concern for the cause of popular education found expression in faithful service for several years as school director of his district. He also served for eight years as postmaster of Keating postoffice. Mr. Wellington will long be remembered by those who knew him as a faithful, honest, industrious man and a good neighbor and citizen.

But to be more specific in our remarks— our subject was a native of Cornwall county, England, born June 6, 1849, his parents being Thomas and Ann Wellington. He ac-

quired his educational discipline in the excellent public schools of his native land, then learned the trade of a stone mason. When he arrived at the age of twenty he executed a determination previously formed of trying his fortune in the new world. Accordingly he came out to San Francisco, California, where for the ensuing nine years he was engaged assiduously in the pursuit of his handicraft. He then followed mining in California, Oregon and Idaho until 1887, when he purchased a quarter section of land in the lower Powder river valley and embarked in farming and stock raising, an industry which continued to engage his energies until August 27, 1896, when he passed to the unknown beyond. His interest in public affairs has been already adverted to, and it is only necessary to add that his standing in the community in which he resided for so many years was such as can only be enjoyed by a sincere man and a good citizen.

In Baker county, Oregon, on October 29, 1881, our subject married Miss Grace Crews, daughter of Wiley and Maria (Cushman) Crews, and their union was blessed by the advent of seven children: William H., A. Vivian, Phila H., M. Irene, Geneva G., Jonathan C. and Thomas G. Mrs. Wellington still owns the old home place and she has increased the holdings bequeathed by her husband to six hundred acres, upon which, at present, she keeps one hundred head of cattle. She has a very pleasant home at 1405 Fifth street, Baker City, where she now lives, having moved into town that her children might enjoy the superior school advantages.

HENRY S. MORRISON.—Few men in Baker county have a better right to be called public-spirited than he whose name gives caption to this article. The county has many citizens who take a deep interest in the promotion of the general welfare, but Mr. Morrison is always working zealously in various ways for the good of his town, county and State, and it affords us pleasure to pay a slight tribute to his wealth of worth and to his broad-minded patriotism.

Our subject was born in Statesville, North Carolina, on August 21, 1859, the son of

James B. and Elizabeth A. (Summerland) Morrison, likewise natives of North Carolina, but of Scotch-Irish descent. He grew to manhood in the state of his nativity, receiving a common school education, then a course in Taylorsville College, where he studied medicine for a year and a half. A protracted fever and consequent impairment of his health necessitated his giving up all thought of professional career, so he engaged in the merchandise business in Taylorsville, following the same until 1886, when he came west. Locating in Mitchell, Oregon, he accepted a position there as head clerk for the firm of Sargent & Company. After serving in this capacity for a period of two years he took a trip back to his home in the east, and upon his return to the occident he started in business for himself in Spokane. Soon, however, he went to Portland, where he served first as a clerk in the school clerk's office, then in a large grocery establishment. In 1891 he became city salesman and collector for the firm of Northup & Sturgis, the duties of which position were discharged by him until May, 1900, when he went to Cape Nome, Alaska, with intent to try the mercantile business there. This he did and with very fair success, but in January, 1901, he sold out, came to Bourne and embarked in the grocery business in that town. He carries a full line of staple and fancy groceries and enjoys a large and constantly extending trade. As a business man he has, perhaps, no superior in the county. Possessed of a liberal education, he has added to that and to his natural endowments a wide and varied experience in the line in which he is now engaged, while his foresight and caution have enabled him to avoid failure and bankruptcy, so frequently the lot of business men, at every stage of his career.

As above stated, Mr. Morrison is characterized by a broad-minded interest in public affairs. He is a leader in every project for the upbuilding of his town, which was incorporated chiefly as a result of his endeavors, and of whose first council he was a member. At present he is making strenuous efforts to secure water works in the town.

In military affairs, also, our subject has ever taken an active part. He was first sergeant of Company A, First Regiment, O. N. G., the members of which were all six feet or over, and which was widely known as the six-foot company of Oregon. Of this, also, he was twice elected captain, but both times resigned on account of the pressure of other business. When the Spanish-American war broke out he organized the first volunteer company of the state, but the membership being all new recruits and there being too many militiamen in the state already, their services were not accepted.

Fraternally our subject is affiliated with the W. of W. and the Pioneers of the Pacific, being commander of the latter order, of which also he was an organizer. His marriage was solemnized in North Carolina, in September, 1887, when Miss Mamie I., daughter of Julius P. and Margaret (Sharpe) Douglas, became his wife. They now have two children, Ada E. and Dwight D.

Like most of the other leading men of Baker county, Mr. Morrison is interested in the mining development of the region, and is himself the owner of some promising properties.

JERE J. DOOLEY.—It is with pleasure that we here present a brief review of the venerable pioneer of the state and esteemed citizen of Baker county, whose name appears above. He has held some important positions of trust here and elsewhere, ever proving faithful, and in all respects so ordering his life as to win esteem and confidence. Born in Albany, New York, on April 25, 1834, he grew up in Utica receiving there a good education and early learning the principles which govern all commercial transactions, having begun life's battle as a clerk in a dry goods store. His father, Mark Dooley, died when Jere was a child. In Utica, New York, also, occurred the marriage of Mr. Dooley and Miss Christiana Thomas, a native of Ohio, the wedding taking place on March 24, 1856. Leaving the home of his mother, Honora Dooley, in 1857, he removed to Chicago, Illinois, where for five years he was employed first as brakeman and later as conductor on the railway between Freeport and Chicago In 1862, he crossed the plains to Auburn, Baker county, which honored him with the election to the office of city treasurer, he being the first to serve in that capacity. While there he was clerk also for Brooks &

Cranston, who maintained a general merchandise store. In 1863, he went to Idaho City, where he remained for eight years, the first three of which were devoted to mercantile pursuits and the remaining five to the duties incident upon his appointment as United States revenue assessor. The year 1871 found him again in Baker county, this time running a general merchandise store on Clark's creek and giving a portion of his time and attention to placer mining. He also had charge of the postoffice there established. In 1886, he moved his stock to Bridgeport, of which he has the only store and of which he is postmaster. Fair dealing and correct business principles have secured for him a very enviable trade, while his integrity and magnanimity have won him respect and esteem from those with whom he is associated. It is worthy of note that he has served Uncle Sam as postmaster for twenty-four years of his life.

Fraternally he was affiliated with the local lodge of I. O. O. F. at Malheur City, which has surrendered its charter.

Mr. Dooley is notary public and was for many years justice of the peace, also acting as school director, in all of which capacities his characteristic faithfulness and attention to business have been displayed. Mrs. Dooley is known throughout the entire community as one whose aid in sickness is never solicited without a kindly response, and her benevolence and goodness have won her a place in the hearts of the people, which she justly merits.

GEORGE W. BROWN.—It is with no little pleasure that we are enabled to incorporate here a brief review of the career of the energetic lumberman and farmer, whose name initiates this paragraph. A leader in business enterprises, he is likewise a leader in the promotion of the general welfare and in local politics, fairly deserving to rank among the representative men of his section.

Born in Jasper county, Iowa, in 1849, Mr. Brown passed there the initial fifteen years of his life, residing at the home of his parents, A. J. and Martha A. (Harp) Brown. In 1869, he went to Nevada, where for more than a decade he followed teaming, but in 1881 he went to Oregon, and spent a year in the vicin-

ity of Powder river, coming then to Pine valley, where he took a homestead northwest of Pine and engaged in farming. He has recently purchased another farm of one hundred and sixty acres, in the west end of the valley and still handles both farms. He busied himself entirely in agricultural pursuits and stock-raising until about six years ago, when he bought saw mills, and turned his attention to the manufacture of lumber. He operated his mills in different parts of the section, one being at Sparta, bought in 1896, and one at Carson, bought in 1898. At present he is devoting most of his attention to the lumber industry.

The esteem and confidence in which he is held by the people of his county found expression in 1900, when he was elected county commissioner. At that time the territory in which Mr. Brown lives was in Union county, but recently it has been transferred to Baker county, that act taking place while he was an incumbent of that office, and he ceased to act as soon as the real transfer was made. Mr. Brown is highly esteemed in the sections where he is known and deserves great credit for the skill and enterprise manifested in the industrial and business world.

WILLIAM WIEGAND.—An active man in the public affairs of his town and county and a leader in commercial pursuits, the subject of this review is a forceful factor in the development of his community, and as such it is but fitting that he should receive credit in this portion of our volume, the purport of which is to give due representation to the founders and builders of Baker county.

Mr. Wiegand is a native of Allegan county, Michigan, born May 8, 1866, his parents being John and Ann Wiegand, natives respectively of Germany and England. He passed his early youth in the commonwealth of his nativity, receiving a common school education, then engaged in the lumbering industry, continuing in the same until 1893, when he came out west and turned his attention to mining. He was in this line of endeavor but a short time, however, when misfortune overtook him; he met with an accident which rendered it impossible for him to continue in that pursuit and with true resourcefulness and versatility, he embarked in merchandising, buying out the dry goods store of Kear & Edwards, in Bourne, and establishing the Wiegand Wonder Store. He carries a full line of dry goods, notions, tobacco, cigars, and confectionery, owns the building in which he is now located, and has a large and constantly increasing trade. Mr. Wiegand is also the owner of some other buildings in the town and of many mining interests in the vicinity. Thus has he brought success and prosperity out of an accident which would have crushed and ruined a less resolute and resourceful man. Our subject is treasurer of his town and agent of the Express and Telephone Companies. Fraternally he is a Pioneer of the Pacific, of which order, also, he is treasurer.

The marriage of Mr. Wiegand and Miss Annie, daughter of J. A. and Annie Zerlant, was celebrated in Bourne, on October 16, 1901, and they are highly esteemed members of society.

————◆◆————

JOHN C. TRAVILLION.—To the gentleman of whom we speak, there is much credit due for the enterprising and excellent manner in which he took hold of the resources found in Baker county and wrought therefrom advancement of the county's interest and wealth for himself. Farsighted in business matters, and possessed of good judgment and ability in handling both finances and the products of the country, he has distinguished himself in at least two distinct lines of industry; and a success such as he has attained in either one of which is sufficient to stamp a man as both capable and prominent in our county.

Mr. Travillion was born to Thomas M. and Ann E. (Williams) Travillion on August 1, 1852 in Otterville, Missouri, where he was reared on a farm and secured his educational training in the public schools. In 1873, he left the home nest and turned toward the west for exploration and to seek a home for himself. He came by rail to Kelton, Utah, and thence by stage to Baker City, where he at once went into the operations of mining, which he prosecuted with vigor until 1878, then took government land on Powder river, about sixteen miles north of Baker City. He gave himself to farming and stockraising, most of his time being occupied in handling cattle and sheep, and uninterruptedly he has continued that industry since. He has gained an enviable success in this work because of his wisdom in handling affairs and because of his tireless energy in caring for detail in every department of his business. His real estate holdings have grown from the government piece to an estate of one thousand acres of good land all fenced and improved in an up-to-date manner with all the buildings and conveniences needed for the transaction of his business. In 1892, Mr. Travillion entered into partnership with Mr. Kelsey and Mr. Gorham in the milling business in North Powder. They erected a good mill of fifty barrels capacity per day in that city and equipped it with modern and complete machinery. The power for operating it is taken from the Powder river it being a water power plant. The business has been handled with sagacity and deferential treatment of its patrons until at the present time they enjoy a trade as large as the plant can handle and have the entire confidence of the community. In 1898, Mr. Kelsey sold out his interests and Mr. Travillion, in company with Mr. Gorham, owns the entire plant. In 1892 Mr. Travillion removed his family from the stock farm to North Powder and there resided until 1898, when he erected a modern ten-room residence at 2208 Clark street, Baker City, elegant and tasty, where his home is made at the present time, although he spends much time in personal supervision of the plant at North Powder.

On September 7, 1879, Mr. Travillion and Miss Fannie J., daughter of Captain Edward M. and Nancy M. White, were married and the fruit of the union is three children, Lillie A., Harry C., and Nettie J. Mr. Travillion is a past grand in the I. O. O. F., Lodge No. 88, in North Powder, and is also a member of the W. of W., Camp No. 109, in the same town, and in Baker City he belongs to the Fraternal Union. The parents of our subject came to Baker City in 1883, the father was retired from business and his demise occurred in 1894, but the mother is still living in Baker City. He has one brother in the Willamet valley and one, County Judge Travillion, in Baker City. Mr. Travillion is at this day one of the most prominent business men of the county and has ever manifested a worthy conduct that has won for him the esteem of all and the entire confidence of the business world where he operates. While never pressing forward for personal preferment in the political world, nevertheless he has taken the interested part of the good citizen and forms one of that number of substantial men who are the bone and sinew of the community and of the political world are the very foundation.

RICHARD W. MAKINSON,

an energetic and prosperous farmer of Pine valley, of which he is a representative citizen, is a native of Missouri, born in 1848, the son of Evans and Hannah (Armstrong) Makinson, natives of England. When but two years old, he was left an orphan, and for the ensuing eight years he made his home with a brother-in-law named Solomon Townsend. When ten years old, he began life's struggles on his own account, though he lived with his brother about two years thereafter. He followed whatever he could get to do in Iowa until 1862, then removed to Missouri. He was at this time too young to enlist, but showed his willingness to fight the battles of the republic by following the army from place to place, and he was present at the battle of Shiloh. When he became nineteen, he removed to Kansas, and after exploring some portions of that state, he started for the Black Hills. Changing his course, however, he came to Cheyenne, Wyoming, and thence, in 1876, to Union county, Oregon. In the fall of that year he moved to Pine. The next year he bought land where Halfway now stands, but for some reason, sold this again soon, and moving to Eagle valley, purchased some land there. After seven years had been devoted to agricultural pursuits in that neighborhood, he sold out, investing a portion of the proceeds in a half section, upon a portion of which the village of Pine has been built. He is farming this and a quarter section on the reservation, which is known as the Pendle ranch. In addition to his fine farm, Mr. Makinson owns some valuable realty in Richland, where he makes his home at present. He is a self-made man, having, as has been said, started in life without educational advantages, without a dollar and without a friend of any influence, and to him belongs a share of the honor bestowed upon those who possess within them the energy and force needed to conquer overwhelming adverse circumstances.

In Linn county, Kansas, in 1872, our subject married Sarah, daughter of Josiah and Mariah (Long) Brooks, and to them have been born six children, Fred; Alberta, wife of Oscar Kendall, postmaster at Pine; Robert; Mary, now Mrs. H. Moody; Charley; and Josiah .

With Mr. Makinson in the trip to the Black Hills above referred to was just one companion, a man named Smith, and their worldly wealth consisted of but little more than a mule team apiece. When they reached Green river, three other men joined them, one of whom was Jacob Rainwater, who laid out the town of Dayton. Another, whose surname was Green, died en route, being buried at Boise, Idaho, falling a victim of a fever, caused by exposure in the attempt to cross a swollen stream with the wagon box as ferry boat.

GEORGE W. KERNS.—

This prominent mining man and stage operator of Bourne has the honor of being an early pioneer of the west, almost all parts of which have been visited by him. The place of his nativity is the vicinity of Bloomington, Illinois, and the date August 8, 1863. His parents, Samuel and Jane (Wallace) Kerns, moved with their children to Kansas when he was but a small boy, and there he grew up and received a public school education. In 1881 he removed to Colorado, where he remained for one year engaged in railroading, a line of endeavor which he also pursued in Idaho for a time. Eventually, however, he went to Butte, Montana, and turned his attention to mining. In the spring of 1883, he returned to Idaho and with his brother, John, engaged in stage operating, but two years afterward he sold out, and from that time until 1892, he traveled quite extensively, visiting almost all the western states. In 1892 he began mining in the Baker City region and in 1895 he came to Bourne, still engaged in the quest for mineral wealth. He continued the search until the summer of the current year, in fact he has never given it up as he still owns some promising claims, but a few months ago he embarked in the stage business, operating between his home town and Sumpter. A register of his mining properties would include the Monday, the Oregon, the Golden Crest, the New York, and others.

Our subject was married in Union county, Oregon, on August 18, 1890, to Miss Emma, a daughter of Israel and Jane (Wallace) Todd, natives of Illinois, and to their union three children have been born, Margaret J., Ruby M., and Georgie.

HENRY J. BAKER, one of the prominent agriculturists of the vicinity of Pine postoffice and one of the substantial and respected citizens of Baker county, was born in Iowa, being the first white child born in Dallas county and was raised in the great Empire state, his parents, George and Charlotte (Crouch) Baker, being natives respectively of New York and England. He obtained his education in the schools of Rochester, New York, and when seventeen years old, began for himself the battle of life, his parents having both died previous to that time. He first went to Missouri, where he embarked in the general merchandise business in the town then known as Waterville, which was afterwards called Bakerville, and has recently experienced another change of name. After a residence of about four years in Missouri, our subject came, in 1878, to North Powder, Baker county, Oregon, where he assisted in the construction of the first store and where he remained for three years. Coming then to Pine valley, he engaged in farming and the stock business, at first on rented land and afterward on a two hundred and forty-acre tract five miles northeast of Pine postoffice, which his thrift and frugality enabled him to purchase. He is also engaged in the mercantile business at that place, dealing especially in farm produce, which he buys and sells. His integrity and fair dealing have won him the confidence of the rural population in his vicinity, and as a natural result his trade is increasing and extending.

Fraternally, Mr. Baker is identified with the time-honored order of Free Masons, his membership at present being in Union Lodge. His marriage was solemnized at Union in 1883, Miss Hester, daughter of Frederick and Sarah (Myers) Shoemaker, then becoming his wife. To their union eight children were born, John H., Mollie, Walter T., Maggie L., Louis J., Hallis C., Hettie and an infant. Mrs. Baker's parents were among the earliest settlers of Grande Ronde valley, where their remains have been laid to rest. Her father was widely known on account of his activity in church work. Mr. Baker was census enumerator in 1900, and has held numerous government positions in the revenue department, in civil service, and other branches, and is a capable and efficient man dominated with sagacity and faithfulness.

JAMES RICHARDSON, one of the most successful cattlemen in Baker county, is, like many others who have achieved a conspicuous success in different lines of enterprise, a native of Ireland. He comes, too, from that thriftiest portion of the Emerald Isle, the northern part, his birthplace being Belfast, and the date of his advent into life August 12, 1839. He received his educational discipline in the land of his nativity and resided there for some years after he became a man, but in 1869, he set out for the new world. He came direct to Baker county, settled on Clark's creek and engaged in mining, an enterprise which continued to busy him for the ensuing decade. He then purchased a quarter section of land a mile north of Bridgeport postoffice, and embarked in the cattle raising business. Success crowned his efforts from the start and his herds grew until he now has an average of two hundred head. He was a member of the old Malheur lodge of the I. O. O. F., but has never been identified with any local organization of that fraternity since the charter of his first lodge-home was given up. He has never exchanged the freedom of celibacy for the pleasures supposed to belong to the married state.

SANFORD RUSK.—It is with pleasure that we are able to incorporate here a brief biographical review of the honored citizen of Bourne whose name appears above. An industrious, active, energetic man he has wrought his way to success in several different lines of enterprise, and well-directed effort in mining has enabled him to win a competency. Nature gave him the ability to perceive his opportunity and when the tide which taken at the flood leads on to fortune came to him he took it and success in commercial affairs was the result.

Mr. Rusk is a native of Montgomery

county, Indiana, born August 14, 1842. After receiving a common school education, he engaged in farming, continuing a devotee of the basic art until 1870, when he embarked in the drug business in Fort Wayne, Indiana. He divided his energies between this and mercantile pursuits until 1873, when he removed to Roswell, Illinois, and turned his attention to operating a meat market. Two years were thus spent. In 1878, he crossed the plains with mule teams to the Grande Ronde valley, where he accepted a position as foreman on the right of way for the O. R. & N. Company, who at that time were constructing their road. Upon leaving their employ he engaged in hotel keeping in Orodell, but after a year's experience in this, he sold out and moved back to Kansas. There he spent another period of two years in the drug business. Returning then to Lagrande, he once more engaged in hotel keeping, and for two years also discharged his duties as town marshal. In 1890, he opened a hotel in Bourne, but soon gave his attention more particularly to dairying and mining, though he ran the E. and E. boarding house, for about eight months, serving at the same time as watchman of their mill. In 1896 he located the Silver Dick, which he afterwards sold for $27,000. He owns quite a herd of neat cattle and some horses, also some realty of value in the town of Bourne.

Fraternally, Mr. Rusk is an Odd Fellow. His first marriage was solemnized in Indiana on March 12, 1863, Miss Ellen, daughter of John and Elizabeth Sloan, then becoming his wife. To their union were born four children, two of whom are living, namely, John, and Effie, now Mrs. Fred Budde. Mrs. Rusk died on October 1, 1872, and on March 4, 1873, our subject married Miss Nellie, daughter of Lorenza D. and Martha E. Hayes, and to them were born four children, Burton S., Loui R., Walter W., and Mabel B.

———◆◆◆———

CHARLES ZIEGLER, a representative of the versatile French race, and an old and honored pioneer of the coast, at present an enterprising farmer in the vicinity of Newbridge, was born at Puttalange, France, in 1831, the son of John and Nanette (Field) Ziegler, likewise natives of Europe's greatest republic. He
24

remained with his parents until eighteen years old, then yielded to the impulses of his adventurous nature, which were urging him to seek larger opportunities, and came to America. Landing in New Orleans, he made his way thence up the Mississippi and across the plains to California, where for the nine years following 1850, he sought assiduously for hidden treasure. He then went to farming in Mendocino county, which he helped to organize, and after busying himself in agricultural pursuits for about eight years, he spent a year in the southern part of the state. Returning again to Mendocino county at the expiration of the twelve months, he farmed near his old home for a full decade, thereupon coming to Oregon. Until four years ago his home was in Harney valley, but in 1897, he removed to Eagle valley and purchased eighty acres a mile and a half north of Newbridge postoffice, where he has lived and farmed ever since, making a very pleasant home for himself and family.

In 1865, our subject married Miss Zarrisia Babcock, and to their union six children have been born, Pardon, Charles, Mary, Leonie, Anna, and Louis. Mrs. Ziegler's mother, Elizabeth Rieburn Babcock, who lives at the home of Joseph Beck, is eighty-four years old and has great-great-grandchildren. In 1851 Mr. Ziegler participated in battles against the Indians in California, being under Brigadier General Winn.

———◆◆◆———

JOHN COBB.—To this esteemed citizen and enterprising business man of our county and pioneer of the state, we are pleased to accord representation in this volume, since a compilation of this character would be sadly deficient if there were failure to incorporate his life's career therein, having been a prominent figure in this county for a third of a century.

His father was a sea captain, in command of a vessel, the Connor, carrying on a coast trade on the Atlantic and later on the Pacific. On this vessel, in 1838, Mr. Cobb was born and for eighteen years he was with his parents, learning well the sailor's arts and skill. Following this time, he was engaged as seaman on board a United States revenue cutter plying between San Francisco and the Sound ports.

Two years spent on this vessel, The Shoe-brick, gave him much experience in this line of business. In 1863, he left San Francisco for Portland, thence to Canyon City and later to Auburn, engaging in mining which he also followed later at Granite creek, and also at Robinson's mill. He has traveled well over the county and over the adjacent counties of this and other states. From mining he took up the life of the surveyor and has followed it continuously since. He was one that was prominently connected with the laying of the northern boundary line of the county. During his life he has ever manifested that integrity and uprightness that are so praiseworthy and becoming the citizen of any community and his demeanor has been such that he has won the confidence and esteem of all who may have the pleasure of his acquaintance. His life has been active and adventurous, but still he has never ventured on the matrimonial sea, choosing rather the freedom and quietness attendant upon the life of a celibate than the cares and responsibilities of domesticity.

RANDLE L. TURNER.—Of all the leading and representative citizens of Bourne none is more universally esteemed and respected than the successful mining man whose name gives caption to this review. The popularity of the man found expression as soon as the town was incorporated, he being the unanimous choice of the people for the highest office in their gift, that of mayor. Integrity and force of character, combined with a liberal public spirit, are the traits which have won him his enviable standing in the community in which he lives, while careful application and absolute trustworthiness have enabled him to win success in business.

Mr. Turner is a native of Dubuque, Iowa, born August 3, 1864, the son of Richard and Rosana E. (Miles) Turner, natives of England. His parents took him to Kansas when he was but six years old, and there he received some educational discipline, but when he arrived at the age of twelve, he took upon himself the struggle of life, severing home ties and going to Texas. There he rode the plains herding cattle until 1881, when he went to Idaho and engaged in freighting. After hav-

ing devoted two and a half years to that he removed to Union county, Oregon, where for a short time he followed freighting and lumbering, but the major portion of his attention and energy has been devoted to mining since he arrived in Oregon. He is an assayer by profession and has mined in Idaho and Montana as well as in this state, everywhere achieving success on account of his carelessness and skill. He has acted as foreman of the East Eagle in Union county, and since coming to Bourne, in 1898 has wrought as a skilled miner in the Columbia, much of the time. In the beginning of 1902, Mr. Turner was appointed superintendent of the Mammoth Gold Mining Company's properties, a position which he is filling with credit to himself and profit to his company. He is the owner of several mining claims in the district of which his home town is the center, and likewise of realty of much value both in Bourne and in Baker City. At one time he had title to the Blue Bird on Wind creek and an interest in the Porcupine group, which latter property was sold for fifteen thousand dollars.

As previously stated, Mr. Turner is mayor of the town and an active worker for its development and for the substantial progress of the same. Fraternally, he affiliates with the North Powder organization of the I. O. O. F., all the chairs of which have been occupied by him. His marriage was solemnized on December 1, 1897, the lady being Miss Ada B. Powers, whose parents, William B. and Adaline (Barclay) Powers, were among the earliest pioneers of California and of his state. They were natives of Kentucky and Virginia, respectively.

JOHN WOOD.—This enterprising farmer and market gardener of the vicinity of Baker City was born in Rochester, New York, on November 11, 1875, his parents being John and Isabella (Cotchfer) Wood, natives of England. He continued to reside under the parental roof until sixteen years old, receiving such educational advantages as the public schools afforded, but he then determined to give inception to his independent career, so came out to Oregon. Soon he settled upon land seven miles south of Baker City, a tract of swale or bottom land, well suited to the production of hay and vegetables, and to that kind of farming he has ever since devoted himself, marketing his products in Baker City. He is an enterprising, industrious and progressive young man, belonging to the great and numerous class who work quietly and unostentatiously and who are yet the real strength of a community, the men behind the guns in its battles.

Mr. Wood was married on December 24, 1896, the lady being Miss Lucinda, daughter of George and Lucinda (Bigley) Springer, both of whom are residents of Baker county. Of this union one child, Ben, was born.

DANIEL H. SHAW.—Prominent among the leaders in the farming and stockraising industry in Baker county is the energetic and thrifty gentleman whose name gives caption to this review, and it is with pleasure that we are able to accord him representation here as one of the builders of the political division with which our work is concerned, of which he is an honored pioneer.

Born in Putnam county, Missouri, near the Iowa line, on April 10, 1845, he grew to early manhood there, receiving such educational advantages as were to be had in the local public schools. He in the spring of 1863, and his parents Theophalis and Elizabeth (Leachman) Shaw, in 1865, came over the trail of many moons to Oregon. The engine which pulled his train was an ox team, his coach a prairie schooner, time from Iowa to the coast four months and a half. Eventually they landed in Union county, where the first winter in the new state was spent. From the time of his advent until 1865, our subject busied himself in packing from Umatilla Landing to Silver City and other points in Oregon and Idaho. He then bought a pair of oxen with which he teamed in Silver City for a couple of years. In the fall of 1867 he moved with his parents onto a homestead of one hundred and sixty acres, situated six miles south of Baker City, and upon this he has ever since lived. He has added to his original holdings from time to time, until he now has a fine farm of four hundred acres, all of which has been long since rendered mellow by the plow, and most of which is now producing its annual crop of hay.

He raises each year about three hundred tons of excellent timothy hay, which is fed chiefly to cattle and horses on his own farm. He keeps a fine band of graded Shorthorn and Hereford cattle, such as would delight the eye of any connoisseur in such things. Mr. Shaw also owns some valuable property in Baker City.

Fraternally our subject is affiliated with the A. O. U. W. In Baker City, on March 15, 1879, he married Miss Perlina F., daughter of Alfred G. and Eliza J. McKinney, old pioneers of the county, and to their union were born four children, Daniel A., Samuel T., Mamie B., and Pearl J. Mrs. Shaw passed to the great beyond on March 21 1901, and her remains were laid to rest in the Baker City cemetery. Mr. Shaw's parents died in 1874.

HENRY WENDT.—To the esteemed pioneer and eminent citizen, whose name heads this article, we are constrained to grant this memorial since his was a life that well merits the encomiums of his fellows both for the ability displayed in the private walks of business enterprise and because of the public spirit manifested throughout his entire career.

In March, 1834, in Germany, our subject was born, and the years of his minority were spent in the "Fatherland" where he was well trained in those ways of thrift and enterprise that so characterize his counrymen. At the age of twenty-one years he came to the United Sates and began the life of the agriculturist on the fertile prairies of Illinois, but later the siren of nature's hidden treasures lured him to the frontier and he took up the life of the miner in California, and in 1862 came to Baker county, continuing this occupation in Auburn and then at Clarke's creek until 1871, at which time he settled at Bridgeport and began raising stock. In that place and occupation he was always faithfully pursuing the course of the estimable and industrious citizen until he was called, on May 10, 1898, to lay down the burdens of this life and depart to the realms of another world. He was universally beloved and esteemed and it was with sincere grief that his loved ones and his wide circle of friends and neighbors consigned to their last resting place the remains of the noble pioneer, stanch business man and faithful father and husband.

The marriage of Mr. Wendt occurred in Freeport, Illinois, in 1869, Miss Amelia Brinkman, also a native of Germany, at that time becoming his wife. To them were born the following children: Amelia, deceased; Pauline, now Mrs. N. N. Elliott; Minnie, deceased; Charles, born December 29, 1875; Henry, born June 27, 1878, and married October 23, 1901, to Miss Addie Elliott, a daughter of Daniel and Josie Elliott, and a native of Baker county; William, born December 24, 1881. Mrs. Wendt is still living with her sons on the old place, where they are going on with the stock business that was so well started by their father. The farm is well improved and annually produces many tons of fine hay. An elegant residence, besides other buildings, adds attraction, value and comfort to the place, while their holdings in live stock are large. Five hundred head of fine Durham and Hereford cattle and a large drove of horses, besides small stock, are a part of their quota. The three sons mentioned above are operating the place in partnership and they are considered the finest and most skillful stockmen in their section.

FRANK LENTZ, one of the most thrifty and prosperous farmers and stockmen in the county, of which he has long been an esteemed and honored citizen, is a native of Keokuk county, Iowa, born July 22, 1867, the son of William and Mary (Boyd) Lentz, likewise natives of that state. When about seven years old he accompanied the remainder of the family on the long journey across the wide waste of plain and over the mountain barriers to Baker City, in the vicinity of which his father took up land. He grew to man's estate in the county, receiving his educational discipline at the James schoolhouse. As soon as he became of age he took up three hundred and twenty acres of government land in Sumpter valley, six miles east of Sumpter, and engaged in farming and stock-raising, an industry to which he has devoted the efforts of his life ever since. As a natural result of his assiduity and thrift he has achieved a very enviable success and is now in possession of an excellent farm of generous proportions, well improved and stocked and supplied with all needed buildings and machinery. In 1899 he purchased eighty

acres two miles east of Auburn, where he now lives, controlling operations upon this farm and the one in the valley. He raises hay and grain principally and keeps about fifty head of cattle and some horses.

On October 5, 1890, Mr. Lentz married Miss Mary, daughter of William and Rebecca (Smith) Graham, natives of Missouri, pioneers of this state of 1862 and residents now of Boise, Idaho. To their union has been born one child, Harry F. Mr. Lentz's father lives in Sumpter, but his mother died in 1887.

WILLIAM BENNETT. — Among the prosperous and leading business men of Baker City, mention should be made of him whose name initiates this paragraph, since his enterprise, industry and ability are manifest both in his private business life and in his demeanor as a public-spirited citizen. He is the senior member of the firm of Bennett & Sons, leading lumber merchants and manufacturers of Baker county.

Mr. Bennett is the son of Joel and Sarah (Bird) Bennett, natives of New York and England respectively, and he was born at Williamsport, Pennsylvania, in 1829. He passed his minority in his native place, staying with his parents and receiving a good education in the public schools and Dickson Seminary. In 1860 he started to Pike's Peak, being led thither by the gold excitement at that time. For four years he mined in that vicinity and then went to Montana, on Alder creek, and engaged in freighting to Fort Benton until 1870, when he returned to Pennsylvania and started a sawmill in Sullivan county. For a number of years he followed this occupation and then removed his plant to Klickitat county, Washington, and later to White Salmon. At this last point he added a planing mill, and two years later, in 1886, he removed the whole plant to Baker City, establishing the planing mill in the city and locating his sawmill nine miles out. He has since added another mill thirteen miles south of Baker City, and the combined capacity of his plants is one million feet of lumber for one year. He has always found time to take up the questions of political import and local significance, as well as matters of educational interest, ever manifesting his characteristic wisdom and keen foresight. Several times he has been before the conventions, but his preference is not for political preferment of any kind, and hence he has retired in favor of others.

Mr. Bennett and Miss Elizabeth Berry were married in Pennsylvania in 1856, but on February 14, 1868, Mrs. Bennett was called to pass the river of death, and her remains are buried in the cemetery at Hughsville, Pennsylvania. To this union were born the following children: Milliard F.; Bion, died September, 1898; Thomas E.; Eugene; Elizabeth.

Mr. Bennett contracted a second marriage in 1871, the lady of his choice being Miss Mary J. Watters, a native of Pennsylvania. To them have been born the following children: Cora; Callie; Stella; Mary and Martha, twins; infant, deceased; infant, deceased; and Malcolm.

Mr. Bennett not only deals in lumber and all kinds of planing mill products but also handles implements and is sole agent for the well-known Fish Brothers' wagon.

FREDERICK COLE, at present postmaster of Auburn and a prominent mining man of the county, of which he is a leading and esteemed citizen, is a native of Devonshire, England, born May 21, 1866, his parents being Elias and Eliza Cole. He grew to manhood in his native land, receiving the advantage of the excellent public schools there established, and when he became twenty-two years of age yielded to the ambition which was urging him to seek newer and larger opportunities than are to be had in Europe. He landed in Canada, where for a twelvemonth he was engaged in farm work.

Coming to Baker county, Oregon, in 1889, he settled in Auburn and found employment in the placer mine belonging to David S. Littlefield and Charles Duckworth, the latter of whom was an uncle of his, who had come to Auburn in 1862, and had been a partner of Mr. Littlefield ever since his arrival. When, in August, 1898, Mr. Duckworth died, our subject succeeded him in interest, and he has ever since run the mine in partnership with Mr. Littlefield. It is known as the French Gulch placer mine from its location, and its average annual output at present is $1,500. Mr. Cole also owns a small interest in a quartz

claim which is supposed to be the mother lode of his placer mine, from which the company expect to begin shipping ore in the near future.

Fraternally our subject is affiliated with the Baker City camp of the W. of W. His marriage was solemnized in England in February, 1894, Miss Emily Greenslade then becoming his wife, and to their union two children have been born, Ellen L. and Emily E.

THOMAS E. BENNETT.—The young business men of Baker county have fully merited the encomiums that have been given to them, as also they have in every particular sustained the reputation of the county's prosperous condition gained by the older organizers of commercial enterprise in this section; and as a prominent one among these rising men, we mention the gentleman whose name heads this article, and who is well known throughout the entire county, being at the head of the firm of Bennett & Eickorn, lumber manufacturers and merchants, as well as heavily interested with his brother in mining propositions in the Greenhorn district.

Mr. Bennett was born in Pennsylvania in 1868, being the son of William and Elizabeth Bennett, who are mentioned in another part of the work. In his native place and in Portland and in Baker City business college he received his educational discipline, and in this county he embarked in business for himself. His mill is situated three miles north from Auburn and has a capacity of fifteen thousand feet per day.

The marriage of Mr. Bennett and Miss Grace, daughter of H. H. and Catherine Sparks, was celebrated in 1894, and to them has been born one child, Georgia E. Mr. Bennett also owns a planing mill located on Resort street, and does a general planing business, being prosperous in all his business enterprises.

JOSEPH D. YOUNG.—An old pioneer of the Pacific coast and of Baker county, in the development of which he has very materially aided, the man whose name gives caption to this review is richly deserving of representation in any volume whose purview includes biographical notice of the founders and builders of this section, and it is with pleasure that we accord him such herein. Mr. Young is a native of the sunny south, having first opened his eyes to the light in Independence, Virginia, on July 10, 1832, his parents, Timothy and Elizabeth (Baker) Young, being likewise natives of the state famed as the "mother of presidents." He resided under the shelter of the paternal roof until about twenty-three years old, receiving a rudimentary education, but on March 27, 1855, he stepped on board a ship in New York harbor bound for the "westmost west." In due time he went via Greytown to San Francisco, and on April 22 of the same year he sped through the Golden Gate. His occupation for seven years was in the horticultural line, supplying fruit and vegetables for the markets, and one year he clerked in a store. In 1864 he came to Granite, Grant county, Oregon, and engaged in placer mining. While prosecuting this industry he discovered the rich ground that is now known as Joe Young's bar. In 1871, Mr. Young, in company with Harvey Robbins, opened a general merchandise store and meat market in Sumpter, beginning operations in the spring of that year. This business continued until 1874, when they sold out. Mr. Young also supervised the building of the wagon road from Sumpter to Granite, and he served as the first postmaster of the former place and has the honor of naming the postoffice. The christening was on this wise: In 1862 some prospectors camped on the ground where now stands Sumpter, and they named it Fort Sumter. But when they were casting about for a name for the office Mr. Young suggested Sumpter, which means a pack animal, since all the goods came there by pack trains. And Sumpter it has been since. The first team, which consisted of four horses, was driven by Joe Young and Charles Rimbol to Cable Cove on Silver creek. They built the first sawmill in Sumpter, engaged in general merchandising, operated a hotel, handled freight, did a butchering business, built ditches and sold water to the miners, and added other improvements to the amount of ten thousand dollars or over. Much credit is due to Mr. Young for the efficiency and wisdom with which he wrought for the upbuilding of Sumpter during his residence there and for the liberal contributions made toward its development. He has ever shown himself a public-spirited man, and no enter-

prise of general concern fails to elicit his interest. Mr. Young has always been strictly a temperance man, hence he had no time to waste about the saloons or loafing places of drink, and the result was that many times he was searching over the hills and brought in many trophies of the chase, such as good, fat deer, antelope, elk and bear.

In 1884 Mr. Young married Mrs. Mary A. Flynn, daughter of Edward and Mary Coffey. The following year their only child, Rimbol, was born, being the second white child born in Sumpter. Mrs. Young has by her first husband three children, two boys and one girl, who received the name of their stepfather and have been reared and educated as his own. The daughter is now the wife of Andrew E. Lucas, son of W. W. Lucas, an early pioneer of Oregon. Mr. Young is highly esteemed by his fellows, and he has an unsullied reputation, being a man of unswerving integrity and intrinsic moral worth. At the present time Mr. Young and family are living on his farm, four miles southeast from Sumpter. He has a fine estate, well improved and supplied with all needed buildings and machinery, and it is handled in a skillful manner, his principal crop being timothy hay.

———◆◆◆———

WARREN W. LUCAS.—Hardly could the charge of incompleteness be refuted by the publishers of a volume whose purview includes biographical mention of the leading men in Baker county were there failure to accord due representation to the esteemed pioneer, energetic and successful mining man and public-spirited citizen whose name initiates this paragraph. Mr. Lucas was born in Ashtabula county, Ohio, on August 15, 1833, the son of Thomas and Rachel (Percival) Lucas, natives, respectively, of Vermont and Connecticut. He grew to manhood in the Buckeye state, but on arriving at the age of twenty-two he set out across the plains to the Willamette valley. After consuming six months and four days in making a journey which would now require not more than the four days, he reached his destination, not, however, without a brush or two with Indians, by whom some of the train's stock were stolen.

For the seven years succeeding the date of

his advent in Oregon our subject worked in various lines of endeavor, but in 1862 he caught the gold fever, and came to Auburn, Baker county. He was engaged in mining there and around Granite until 1884, in which year he went to Stien mountain and turned his attention to farming and stock-raising. Three years at that, then he went back to the mines, and his search for earth's treasure was not again renounced until 1898. Then, however, he purchased four hundred and eighty acres of land five and a half miles southeast of Sumpter, and for the second time in life engaged in farming, believing that industry better suited to his advancing years than the more rigorous occupation of mining. He still has, however,

some good quartz claims and some valuable placer diggings in Granite. His realty holdings also include a fine two-hundred-acre farm within twelve miles of Salem, Oregon.

Mr. Lucas married, in the Willamette valley, on August 18, 1859, Miss Adelaide, daughter of Leonard and Emily Williams, pioneers of Oregon of 1847. Their union has been blessed by the advent of two children, Viola A. and Andrew E., who married Libbie M. Young, and they also have two grandchildren, Elsie and Libbie.

Mrs. Lucas died in the Willamette valley on January 17, 1862, and her remains lie buried in the cemetery at Independence, Polk county.

GRANT COUNTY

HISTORY OF GRANT COUNTY.

CHAPTER I.

CURRENT HISTORY, 1862 TO 1885.

The early history of Grant county, like that of almost every other section, must be garnered mostly through interviews with men who assisted in making that history, and as few remember any but the most striking and sensational incidents, a work depending for its material upon the memories of men must of necessity be somewhat fragmentary and incomplete. It is a well known fact also that those who are able to recall accurately events which happened thirty-five or forty years ago are very few, so that the earliest annals of our section can hardly be written as authoritatively as one could wish. We have, however, endeavored to make the best possible use of the means at hand, and when no printed accounts of happenings could be obtained, have verified verbal reports of them as far as possible by consulting others beside the original narrator that "out of the mouth of two or three witnesses every word might be established."

The original Grant county has long been known to white men, though its settlement dates back only about forty years. Its earliest history is a part of the mist-like annals of old Oregon territory, with its trappers and fur traders. Later it figured not inconspicuously in the military arrangements of our government. By an order of the secretary of war,

bearing date September 13, 1858, the old department of the Pacific was subdivided into the departments of Oregon and California. General G. W. Harney, in whose honor the present Harney county was named, was assigned to the command of the Oregon department. Two days after his arrival at his headquarters in Vancouver, namely, on the 31st of October, 1858, he secured the plaudits of the entire population of Oregon by issuing an order opening the Walla Walla valley (which had been remanded to barbarism in 1855 by the interdict of General Wool) to the occupation of white men. Harney proved a better friend of the people than any of his predecessors, though even he was inclined to think lightly of the Indian troubles and to devote his attention mainly to gratifying his passion for establishing military roads. Accordingly in April, 1859, he sent Captain D. H. Wallen to reconnoiter a road from The Dalles to Salt Lake City, ascertaining whether it was practicable to build such a road up the John Day valley, thence over to the headwaters of the Malheur and down that river to the Snake. Wallen met no predatory bands of Indians, and for a good reason. They had eluded him, and when safely in his rear had swooped down upon the Warm Springs reservation, driving away cattle belonging to friendly Indians. The result was a call upon Harney for forces to protect the reservation, to which that general replied by sending rifles and ammunition. Acting upon this hint, the agent in charge organized a company of reservation redskins, which, under command of Dr. Thomas L. Fitch, marched up the John Day in hope of recovering the stolen property. They killed a number of braves, took their women and children prisoners, and secured a few horses, but the immunity purchased by this victory was short-lived. A few months later the Snake Indians again raided the reservation, killing a number of women and children, scaring the whites out of the country and destroying thousands of dollars worth of property.

Meanwhile Wallen pushed his explorations as far as the Harney valley. He proved of inestimable service to the large immigration of 1859, only one company of which was attacked by Indians.

In the spring of 1860 Harney sent Major E. Stein into the region, for the purpose, among other things, of continuing the exploration of the Salt Lake road from the point where Wallen left it onward. This expedition and another sent in company with it under Captain A. J. Smith were resisted by the Indians, so that reinforcements became necessary. When these arrived Stein marched southward to what is now known as Stein mountain, and surprised a small band of Indians there, who fled to the top of the butte. Stein pursued with all his forces over the crest of the mountain and down the opposite slope. The descent was through a narrow and dangerous canyon, but fortune favored the command and it escaped with the loss of a single mule.

In September Colonel Wright, who had succeeded Harney to the command of the department of Oregon, reported to headquarters that the routes of immigration had been rendered safe by the operation of the troops. Even before he made this statement, however,

the horrible Snake river massacre, the details of which are most shocking, had transpired, and soon accounts of it came in, effectually contradicting his report.

Such was the condition of things in southeastern Oregon at the close of the year 1860. Certainly but poor protection was offered to the miner, the prospector or the agriculturist who might wish to seek his fortune in this region. Yet no danger can deter the hardy searcher after gold from going wherever he thinks himself likely to find the precious metal, and even while the country was closed to miners by military orders, parties of men ventured into its bounds prospecting for mineral deposits. The adventures of one of these parties have been narrated at some length in a previous chapter and the foundation of the Auburn camp and of Baker county detailed. We saw that when the expedition which set out from Portland in the fall of 1861 in search of the Blue Bucket diggings was ready to return home it resolved itself into two parties, one of which set out through the John Day country, intending to return over the Barlow trail. In answer to a request by the writer for information concerning this party, D. S. Littlefield, of Baker City, stated that about the 18th of October fourteen men started back from Burnt river by this route, intending to go to Portland or The Dalles, and that the next day five more left. Of the men who constituted this party Mr. Littlefield remembers the names of three, Woodward, Bennet and Lewis, the first named being the captain of the company. The next spring he was informed by Bennet and Lewis, who came over to where he was mining in Griffin's gulch, that this party discovered gold on the north fork of the John Day five or six days after they separated from their companions. They staked out claims for all; then Woodward and most of the company went on to get a supply of provisions, leaving Lewis and Bennet at the claims. These remained upon the river as long as they could but they awaited in vain the return of Woodward. At length their larder became dangerously lean, and they were compelled to strike out for civilization. Upon reaching The Dalles they found that Woodward had been killed by Indians while on his way to Portland. Whatever may have been the merits of the mines discovered by these men, they had little effect upon the history of the county, and the discovery which resulted in the settlement of the region was of a somewhat later date. The earliest settlers on Canyon creek had no knowledge of this discovery, were not induced into the country by it, but were on their way to the Idaho mines when the fortunate find was made which caused them to pause and eventually to give up their design of going on to Florence.

Evidently the first company of gold seekers to reach the site of the present Canyon City arrived on the 8th of June, 1862. William C. Allred, one of the party, states that to his knowledge two or three companies had started ahead of his for the Florence mines, but of their subsequent operations he knows nothing. They must have traveled by some other route, for his company saw no signs of a previous visitation to Canyon creek, and had to make their own trail. They reached the headwaters of this noteworthy stream about the first of June, and about midday on the 8th pitched camp on Little Pine creek, just below the spot on which Marysville now stands, having left Canyon creek at the western foot of Canyon mountain. "When we pitched camp," says Mr. Allred, "the understanding was that we were not to move until the next morning, so several of us took our pans and started off to do some prospecting. I concluded to try the creek we had just descended, so headed my horse westward and soon found myself on the banks of a rushing, roaring stream. At that time the bottom of the canyon was covered with a heavy growth of brush and grass. The most likely place (now known as Hog Point) to try a prospect was across the stream, so

leaving my pan and all needless articles on this side I plunged in, and after quite a struggle reached the other bank. Then I found I had forgotten my handkerchief, in which I purposed to tie up some dirt and gravel. There was nothing else to do but to press my underwear into service, so taking off my drawers I constructed a receptacle out of them, filled it with gravel and returned to the other bank. The result of a few minutes panning was perhaps very nearly four dollars in gold. I hastily mounted my horse and rode for camp to tell the boys what I had found. Imagine my surprise and anger to find that during my absence the company had decided to move on, and had left me. I came up with them on the flat just below the present Prairie Diggings, and reported my find. But it was no use.. They were bound for Florence, and to Florence they would go, so there was nothing for me to do but accompany them.

"When we reached the John Day river it was so high and swift that we could not ford it. Of course that meant the building of a bridge, so we prepared for a few days' stay.. We found a good place to build a bridge just below where the present bridge stands, and set to work with a will to build a rude structure. Macgruder's party was close on our heels, and came up the next day after we arrived. It was here that I became acquainted with this noted leader through an adventure that nearly cost us both our lives. I was down on the river doing some work when he came along and inquired if I thought it would be safe to cross. 'No,' said I, 'it's too deep and the current too strong. Besides, you notice that the bank overlies the water, and if you were once caught in a current and carried under one of those banks you could not save yourself.' He listened to what I said, but announced his intention to try it, anyway, and it was no use to argue with him. Where I failed, however, his horse won, for the animal refused to enter the water. Time after time Macgruder urged him to, but not a step would the animal take. So Macgruder got mad, and riding back a few rods. dug in his spurs and whipped the horse into a run, thinking he would force him to take the water.

"Just as I expected, the horse stopped short right on the edge of the river, sending Macgruder sprawling over his head into the water. Macgruder wore heavy spurs, and in some way they caught in the reins, thus holding him feet uppermost, and strangling him. He struggled frantically, but without avail. I ran to his aid, and climbing out on the horse, which was so frightened it could hardly move, grasped the bridle to pull it off and disentangle it from Macgruder. Just then the horse reared, throwing me into the water. Then Macgruder, strangling and excited, clutched me and began to try to climb up, just as drowning men do. He pulled me down, fighting like a mad man, and to save myself I struck him a blow, causing him to loose his hold, after which I took him by the hair and held him away from me. By this time we had drifted out into the stream, and were being whirled rapidly away under one of those overhanging banks, when I managed to grasp a willow and hold on, yelling all the time for help. Some of the men hurried to the scene, and, throwing us ropes and poles, hauled us out. Macgruder refused to take hold of anything but me, and more dead than alive, we finally reached the shore. It was some time before either of us were in a fit condition to work.

"Well, we crossed a few days later on the bridge we had built, and proceeded on across the Dixie and Burnt river ranges, in due course of time sighting Auburn. When we crossed down into the Powder River Valley several of us determined to proceed no further, having heard discouraging reports of the Idaho mines, and here twenty-six of us left the main company. Of this number eighteen, including myself, elected to return to where I had panned so well in the John Day country. We stayed

at Auburn, which was then a thriving, bustling camp, only long enough to secure more supplies, and then struck westward over the old trail. Arriving at Canyon City, July 3d, we found a camp of several hundred men, and the creek bed down to the John Day taken up as claims. At Prairie Diggings we met a party of eighteen men bound for the Idaho mines, but upon hearing from our company that the outlook at Florence was discouraging, they voted to proceed no further. This was the beginning of the Prairie Diggings camp, for they found gold, organized a company and stayed there."

But during Mr. Allred's absence from Canyon creek important developments were taking place. The next day after the departure of his company another party of California miners came through en route to Auburn and Idaho. They camped on the banks of the creek, and some of their number suggested the idea of prospecting for color. The result was that on what afterwards became known as Whisky flat a good prospect was obtained, so good, indeed, that the idea of proceeding further on their journey was given up. During the next few days the banks of Canyon creek were prospected energetically, and soon the entire creek bottom to the confluence of the stream with the John Day river was divided into mining claims.

The same causes which brought the parties of which we have spoken into the valley were still operative to bring others here. Indeed the spring of 1862 was a season of migrations among the California miners, nomadic as were their habits, and ever ready as they were to take up the line of march whenever a promising discovery was made. David Deitz says that on the road that spring the traveler could look away ahead of his train and see other trains winding up the hillsides like huge serpents, and looking backward could see yet others far in his wake. Most of these emigrants were satisfied with the prospects in Canyon creek and remained, so that before many months the place had a numerous population. By the first of July there were probably three hundred people operating between the site of the present Canyon City and the junction of the creek with the John Day river.

Of course some regulations had to be made for the government of the colony, especially in relation to the different mining claims, and on July 3d the miners convened for the purpose of drafting a code of laws. The regulations adopted were much the same as those which were in vogue in the mining districts of California. George Woodburn was elected recorder of claims. He had distinguished himself in California as a legislator, and is credited with having made a map of eastern Oregon and Idaho remarkable for its approximate accuracy. H. C. Paige had been spoken of for the position, but declined, as he thought Woodburn the proper man. Mr. Paige, who served as secretary of this meeting, tells us that he was also secretary of a similar assembly which convened on Pine creek some time previous. The laws drafted at the meeting were written out *in extenso* and copies posted in conspicuous places on Canyon creek, Little and Big Pine creeks.

So busy were the miners in taking out the gold that they did not spend time to build houses at first, but lived all summer in tents. The first house in the district was erected by Tim Whiting & Company on Rebel Hill, in the early fall of 1862, the material used in its construction being cottonwood logs. It was later torn down to make room for a better building.

There is no disputing the fact that the Canyon creek placer mines were very rich, certainly among the richest that have ever been discovered on the Pacific coast, and if the best machinery could have been brought into operation all at once, fabulous fortunes would have been made in a day. Even with the crude

methods in vogue, large returns were secured for labor, and unlimited prosperity prevailed.

Those who know of the convivial disposition of the California miner need not be told that the institutions which win lucre by taking advantage of the social instincts in our nature were soon on the spot. The saloon was here before gold had been discovered many days, and with it came the gambler, with his deck of cards, ready to try his skill with any poor son of toil who might be willing to "take a hand." Deprived of the restraining influences of the home, the church and settled institutions, and with little of the elevating and purifying atmosphere which refined, virtuous women take with them wherever they go, many a youth strayed from the path of purity and rectitude, who might under more favorable circumstances have always remained a light in his community. It must be remembered, however, that it is not the miners who give any new camp the name of being a rough, lawless place. Labor itself has its own purifying and restraining influence. The toiler may be passionate and have in his blood the fire which may betray him into some crime of violence or impel him to lapses from the highest morality. His passion for the pleasures of society, failing to find pure sources of gratification, may impel his footsteps into forbidden paths; but the toiler is seldom a criminal at heart, or a moral leper, and his failings are chargeable to the force of environment, rather than to a firmly rooted disposition to do wrong. It is that despicable class that flock to the frontier because they cannot thrive in a land where laws are established and enforced, who give the mining camps a bad name. It is that equally reprehensible class, who, too indolent to seize legitimate opportunities for themselves, prey like parasites upon the industry of others, who bring reproach upon mining communities; and Canyon City had an abundant supply of both.

Some of these men were killed in quarrels with each other, but when a bad man met a violent death nobody attempted to bring the slayer to justice. One gambler whose fate is frequently spoken of by old residents was Dan La Follett, better known by the sobriquet of Black Dan. He is described by H. C. Paige as having been a tall, handsome fellow, about thirty years of age, probably a member of an excellent family in the east. "The last time I saw him alive," says Paige, "he was standing in front of Marchand's saloon on a beautiful evening about sundown. I had a ten-cent piece, a rare coin in those days, too small in value for any use, as nothing less than twenty-five cents would purchase anything. Seeing a small crack in a post to the awning, I placed the money in it and remarked to Dan, 'I wonder if anyone will dig that out.' Having business, I went away, and in a few minutes heard a shot."

Dan was not killed instantly, but knew himself to be mortally wounded. He was laid out on a table in a saloon, there to repose until summoned to the "undiscovered country from whose bourne no traveler returns." To beguile the last weary moments of his earthly pilgrimage he had the women of his acquaintance called in, and they sang songs and poured whisky down his and their own throats until the spark of his unprofitable life was quite extinguished.

Meanwhile a man had been sent to dig a grave for Dan, for it was thought proper to give him a decent burial. The task was not an easy one, as the grave had to be dug in hard cement, but at last it was accomplished. Unfortunately, however, for the plans of the funeral managers, another man had been shot in the night, and his body, too, must be laid to rest. A character known as Sailor Jack was selected to dig a grave for the second victim. Jack found the grave already dug for Dan, hastened back after the body for which he was preparing a sepulchre, got it in the grave, oth-

ers assisting, of course, hastily lowered it to the bottom, and returned to Canyon City. In the language of the miner's, Dan's grave was "jumped," and the gamblers who had his body in charge were forced to dig another one for him.

But though little attention was paid to shooting scrapes over card games and the like, miners were always determined that cold-blooded murderers should be made to pay the penalty of their crimes. As Mr. Hiatt says, the most determined mobs which ever undertook to perform acts contrary to law were composed of California miners. Nevertheless, there seems to have been no lynchings if we except the execution of Berry Wey during the early days in Grant county, consequently mistakes costing innocent men their lives (an almost certain accompaniment of mob rule) have never darkened the earlier history of the county.

M. Paige tells a strange incident in which a camp of Californians came near making a serious mistake of this kind. He says that while traveling into the John Day country from Auburn he lost his partner, George Wilcox, somewhere along the trail, owing to the fact that Wilcox would stop and talk to every man he met. Paige continued his journey alone, and soon his troubles commenced. The John Day river had to be crossed. "I made several attempts," says he, "to cross by fording, but it was too deep and rapid. I wanted to keep my clothes dry and save the pick, pan and shovel. At last I made it, ten miles below, but got wet. Night was coming on. I saw smoke; thought it was an Indian camp. Indians or no Indians, I was bound to go to that camp, as a very cold wind was blowing; so hungry and wet, I started to the camp. I had been in wild Indian camps alone many times before with safety, therefore felt that I could take another chance. As god luck would have it, it proved to be a party from California, and by me they were posted of the locality they were in. I

lay down. A little way off all had got together but two, who remained with me. I
thought nothing of it at the time. I slept
between two men, Wallace and Kitchen, from
whom I learned at a later date that the meeting they held was for the purpose of discussing about hanging me, believing I had murdered my partner and was trying to get away.
Only for the pick, shovel and pan, I might
have lost my life, but they reasoned no man
would commit a crime and pack those tools,
without food."

The story illustrates how liable to error is
a company of men disposed to take the reins
of justice into their own hands. Yet resort
to lynching, dangerous and demoralizing
though it is, cannot well be avoided in new
communities where crime is rife, and legally
constituted courts lacking, or so far distant as
to preclude the probability if not the possibility of the law's being enforced. The Grant
county miners had no occasion to deal with a
murderer of the deepest dye until the early
spring of 1863. Then, however, a crime was
committed of a very atrocious nature. It appears that Berry Wey and a man named Gallagher were traveling together with pack animals between Canyon City and The Dalles.
While camped somewhere between Currant
creek and Antelope valley, about eighty miles
this side of the latter point, Wey, as is supposed, killed his partner, and dragging the
body of his victim to a wide-spreading juniper
tree, secreted it there, covering it with a few
boughs. He then continued on his way to
The Dalles with his murdered companion's
money and mules. He purchased goods,
loaded the mules and returned to Canyon City,
where he made the statement, on being questioned regarding Gallagher, that his former
partner had sold him his mules and had gone
to Portland over the Barlow road. Unfortunately for Wey, however, some persons traveling toward Canyon City discovered the body
in its hiding place. Wey was arrested, but

escaped from his guard and struck out over the
mountains. He was followed to Boise City,
captured and brought back to Canyon. Upon
arriving there, he was forcibly taken by a committee of citizens from the custody of Frank
McDaniels, the deputy sheriff in charge. They
purposed to hang him immediately, without
ceremony, and this would doubtless have been
done were it not for the efforts of Ike Hare,
who is described as being a bold, fearless man,
and a fine speaker. He had served as an officer in the Mexican war, and later in the legislative halls of California. Hare mounted a
pile of whip-sawed lumber and made an eloquent plea for calmness and prudence, advising that the man be kept till the next day, then
given a "fair and impartial trial." "Yes, gentlemen," said he, "we will give him a fair and
impartial trial. We know him to be guilty,
and we will hang him, anyway."

Next day a jury of twelve men was selected, counsel was furnished the prisoner and a
trial in somewhat resembling legal form was
had. He was convicted and the day following was taken outside the town and hanged.
The sentence was considered a just one, and
his executioners were never questioned by the
law on account of their acts.

It is related that after Wey's escape from
his custodians, an express rider named Van
Tichner related the circumstance to the people
of Auburn. They were so incensed that when,
a few days later, McDaniels came through
their town following the trail of the murderer,
they were ready to hang him. A strong plea
kept the mob from carrying their threats into
execution. McDaniels proceeded on his journey and soon had his man. The deputy sheriff was so angry at Van Tichner for causing
him this trouble that he threatened to kill the
expressman on sight. He probably had no
intention of doing so, but in time they met;
Van Tichner got the drop on his adversary,
and McDaniels fell at the first fire.

Throughout the whole of the year 1862

25

men were pouring into Grant county from different parts of the west. Many who failed to find what they were looking for in the Auburn camp or elsewhere in what is now Baker county came to the John Day valley, and hundreds of prospectors fresh from California, as well as others disappointed in the Idaho mines, were searching for gold in all the creek bottoms and gulches. The Canyon creek camp was far more important than any other in Grant county, and Canyon City early became a populous, thriving town. During the first few years the banks of the stream from Whisky gulch to the John Day river were covered with shacks and tents. What is now the town of John Day was called lower town and Canyon City, upper town, but while the houses were not arranged in any order there was practically only one community, and that extended over an area more than two miles long. The discovery of gold on Little Pine creek led to the settlement of Marysville, which in 1862 had perhaps two hundred and fifty or three hundred inhabitants. The Prairie Diggings camp, as before stated, was discovered by a party of eighteen Californians, mostly of German descent, who prospected there early in 1862, while en route to Florence, finding some gold, but not enough to cause a permanent halt in their march. On being met by Allred's return party, as heretofore related, and informed of the discouraging reports from Florence, they determined to return and prospect the region more thoroughly. They soon found fair prospects and located eighteen claims. Among the original discoverers of the camp were George Robinson, Bar Smith, A. Lytle, W. Stone and Neil McNulty. Immediately afterward, F. C. Sels, E. J. W. Stemme and three others took six adjoining claims, and a little later several more locations were made, so that the camp soon numbered between thirty and forty men. The original discoverers at once pooled their interests into a joint stock company and began constructing a ditch from a creek, some two miles distant. The ditch was completed early in the summer, and carried about three hundred miner's inches. What water the incorporators could not use was sold to individual claim owners, who thus procured enough water to keep them busy about four hours each day.

The same year (1862) another and much larger ditch was constructed by Marysville and Canyon City miners, conveying some eight hundred inches of water from Indian and Big Pine creeks. This canal was twelve miles long. It belonged to a co-operative miners' company, unincorporated, and in it water rights were secured by the Prairie Diggings miners. At present this ditch and the smaller one are both controlled by the Hoosier Boy Mines Company, and are used to furnish water power for their stamp mills and hydraulics. It has been estimated that the eighteen original owners of the Prairie Diggings cleared $10,000 each during the first year of their operations, and many hundreds of thousands of dollars have been garnered from this natural thesaurus of wealth by the numerous companies which have since owned them.

The first ditch constructed by the Canyon creek miners was known as the Rawhide ditch, because the flumes were built of rawhide, on account of the lack of lumber in the community at the time. The ditch took its water out of Canyon creek, near where the courthouse now stands, and conveyed it about a mile down the west side. Eli Lester and A. P. Riley were its principal owners. It was a very small ditch, its capacity being about two hundred inches, and it was abandoned entirely after having been used a year or two. It did not long antedate the Lone Star ditch, put in by a small party of Texans. It took its waters out of the creek, tapping that stream about a mile above Canyon City. By the close of the year 1862 it was one mile long, and the next year was continued to Blue gulch. For some time the

Lone Star was the principal ditch of the Canyon district and it was used more or less until some nine or ten years ago.

The Humboldt ditch was also begun in 1862. It was so named from the fact that its first owners came from Humboldt county, in California. Like the Lone Star, it was a public ditch, and water could be obtained from it for fifty cents per inch per day of twelve hours. The work on this ditch was done largely by miners owning property under it, who received their pay in water. The ditch is still in use, though it has long since passed out of the ownership of the Sproul Brothers and Kaiser, its original proprietors. It occupies a position on the hillside far above the old Lone Star, so that a breakage anywhere in it was sure to cause like damage to the other ditch, doubling the expense of making repairs. To remedy this, the Humboldt purchased the Lone Star five or six years ago, since which time the latter ditch has remained unused and neglected.

During the early days perhaps nobody in the county had any idea of permanently settling here. The miners purposed to get all the money they could in a few years, then return to the lands whence they came, to enjoy their speedily acquired wealth. Judging by the latitude and the altitude of the place, it was thought that the climate must be very cold, too cold to be endured with any comfort during the winter months. This belief was fostered also by the unusually cold, backward spring of 1862, following, as it did, a winter of extreme severity. Agriculture they considered out of the question entirely, and notwithstanding the abundance of luxuriant bunchgrass covering each hill from base to crest and spreading out profusely over the valleys, even Oregonians thought that stockraising could never be profitably engaged in, owing to the supposed length and severity of the winters. Provisions of all kinds, including potatoes and other vegetables, had to be imported from with-

out, and as freight from The Dalles was 16 to 24 cents per pound, it may be imagined that the price of living was high. The enormous profits to be reaped from the raising of vegetables, should experiments in that direction prove successful, early induced a few men to plant small patches of potatoes and garden vegetables. Mr. Overholt says that for some unknown reason all the first horticultural experiments failed utterly, confirming the general impression that the country was worthless for agriculture. It may be that the planting was done too early. Nevertheless, potatoes were successfully raised during the early 'sixties, for John Herburger states that he got a fine crop at a very early date. He offered them for sale at twenty-five cents a pound, and they were purchased with such avidity that he was forced to limit the sale to any one man to four pounds, so that all might enjoy the taste of the unwonted luxury. He says that not infrequently he got a dollar for four potatoes, a fact which shows that the soil was capable of giving generous proportions to its products. The success of Mr. Herburger and the few early experimenters encouraged others to try, and so agriculture in the John Day valley got its start. The same causes induced the importation of a few cattle and horses, giving inception to the stock industry. The first homesteads were taken by B. C. Trowbridge and William Wilson, on the 16th day of July, 1862. They were situated in the John Day valley, on the opposite side of the river from the mouth of Canyon creek, and were held originally by their locators, in partnership.

At first all lumber used in the construction of flumes and sluices had to be whipsawed. As it sold for three hundred dollars per thousand, an excellent opening was presented to the lumberman, and perceiving this, Sanborn & Roy brought in a little sawmill in the fall of 1862. setting it up on Big Pine creek. It had a capacity of between one thousand and fifteen hundred feet per day. A little later a mill was established on Canyon creek above Canyon City, by a man named Penfield, and the necessity of producing the lumber supply of the colony by the laborious whipsaw method was obviated.

When fall came many of the miners wished to return to their homes for fresh supplies of provisions, and perhaps, too, because they feared the severity of the coming winter. A miners' meeting was therefore called at which it was decided by common consent that claims should be respected until June 15, 1863, though no work should be done on them between the time of the meeting and that date.

Just how many people there were in Grant county in the fall of 1862 we have no means of determining, but conservative men estimate the number at between four and five thousand. Of course, these men could not bring with them provisions enough to last for any considerable length of time, so a base of supplies had to be sought somewhere. Mr. Hiatt tells us that at the Auburn camp there were a great many discouraged and disappointed men who were willing to sell their outfits and provisions for almost any figure and get out of the country, and the same may have been true to a less extent in the John Day mining region. But though the circumstances might lessen the demand for tools and provisions somewhat, a sure base of supplies must be found, and the miners, though they knew not their exact geographical position at first, were sufficiently cognizant of their whereabouts to look toward The Dalles as their nearest supply point. The first pack train to enter the John Day valley was brought from The Dalles by J. J. Cozart and D. N. Luce. It had started for the Salmon river country, but turned aside to Canyon creek, on account of the reports of miners met en route. It arrived some time in July or August, and from its packs the first two stores in Canyon City obtained their stocks of goods, which were duly installed upon shelves sheltered by canvas tents. Later, J. W. Case and

a Frenchman named Wadleigh brought in packs of goods. Nevertheless, provisions were not plentiful in the fall of 1862.

The business of packing provisions into the mining camps on mules was a very lucrative one, and many were engaged in it during the first few years, notwithstanding the terrible gauntlet of highwaymen and Indians which had to be run by the freighters and packers. To accomodate these adventurous knights of primeval transportation, and at the same time to draw trade to their little city, public-spirited merchants of The Dalles had the old trail materially improved. Indeed the first men who went through from Canyon City to The Dalles after provisions were a company made up of two or three members from each party of Californians. They followed the route which looked easiest, guided only by the contour of the country and such inaccurate traders' maps as they possessed. On their return journey they were enabled to make several cut-offs, but the trail they made was far from the best that could be found. To facilitate transportation the citizens of The Dalles straightened out and improved this primitive highway, putting a new bridge across the DesChutes river many miles above the old one. At a later date a company was formed, known as The Dalles Military Road Company, which obtained a grant of land from the general government to remunerate it for building a military highway from The Dalles to Fort Boise. A fair road was built, over which, for many years, vast amounts of freight were conveyed by pack train and wagon.

"For several miles south of Upper Currant creek, and west of a small stream called the Muddy, which comes from the south and strikes Currant creek at right angles, is a large scope of country of peculiar formation," says an Oregonian correspondent, writing in 1886. "The appearance of this locality can best be understood by the name 'Potato Hills,' given to it by the first travelers along the route.

These small grassy knolls were clustered thickly over the expanse, interspersed with scrubby pines and clusters of service berry, wild plum and greasewood bushes. These potato hills increase in size, elevation and ruggedness to the east, a distance of nearly five miles, till the little stream of Muddy is reached, when the hills give place to bluffs of shelving and scale rocks.

"In this locality the Snake Indians made their principal attacks upon trains and travelers in 1862, though the whole distance from this place to Canyon City was subject to their attacks. Down this creek filed a pack train belonging to a man named Nelson, who was on his return from The Dalles with a load of goods. Along the creek were numerous clusters of wild currant bushes, from which the creek received its name, affording excellent shelter for the skulking Indians. The packers were gaily, or otherwise, urging their mules along the gravelly path, and had possibly forgotten that the locality was a dangerous one.

"The train was strung out down the narrow trail, the bell-mare and rider far in the lead. An abrupt, though low, ledge of scale rocks was a few rods to the left of the trail, the creek with its skirting of current bushes close to the right; the packers were busy 'fixing' the packs, and the riding animals were loose on the trail. Suddenly the rider of the bell mare shouted 'Indians!' to those behind, and, clapping spurs to his horse, clattered off down the trail at a keen run. Out from the currant bushes, down from the ledge of rocks, poured the Indians. Some tried to catch the mules, others opened fire with bows and arrows and guns upon the packers, who left their work and hurriedly mounted saddled mules and scampered back on the trail to the rear. The Indians were too numerous to be successfully contended with by the train; two men, armed only with revolvers, could not reasonably hope to cope with fifty or more Indians, all armed, many of them with rifles. The music of the fleeing bell, far in the front, could not be heard, and when the two men had retired to a safe distance, they stopped on an elevation and surveyed the savage horde below, in earnest chase of the fleeing mules. The men all escaped unhurt, but the mules and cargo were lost."

The above incident is only one of a very great number in which Indians robbed pack trains during the early days, sometimes getting the mules without killing their owners, but taking human life whenever they could. The road was also infested in some places with highwaymen, or "road agents," as they styled themselves. These were as unrelenting as the Indians, and almost as much to be feared. They usually accomplished their object without bloodshed, being able to secrete themselves so as to take their victims wholly by surprise, but when resistance was offered they failed not to use their weapons with deadly effect. The Indians were also very troublesome on the road entering Canyon from the south, but the "road agents" confined their operations mostly to the northern route.

Not alone were the routes of travel infested by the thievish and murderous redskins, but the country contiguous to the mines was also overrun by the same scourge. The Indians did not attack the miners in the towns, but contented themselves with hanging around the outskirts and picking up any horses or mules they might find insufficiently guarded, or murdering small companies of prospectors. The residents of Marysville and Canyon creek were accustomed to hire herders to range their horses on the hills during the day time and put them in a large corral at night. On at least one occasion the Indians made a desperate effort to raid this corral at night, but failed.

Late in the fall of 1862 a company of five men were prospecting up the South Fork of the John Day river on a stream since known as Murderer's creek. They made their camp under a projecting rock near the brook, and not far from the road over the Blue mountains. The road was rather infrequently traveled by wagons or pack trains, and as the men knew this, and had seen no signs of Indians, they believed themselves absolutely safe. One evening they retired, as usual, to their beds under the rock, and lay there conversing and smoking. Suddenly, about dusk, the sharp crack of four rifles broke upon their ears, and simultaneously a flight of arrows came from the neighboring rocks, some of which found lodgement in the bodies of the unfortunate men. One of the miners was killed outright, and all the others were wounded. Two struggled to the creek and down its shore half a mile, when one of them could go no farther, having been mortally wounded by a rifle ball. He lay down in a cluster of bushes close to the stream and died. His companion pushed on to Officer's ranch, where he also passed away the next day, after a night of great agony.

The following summer a party of emigrants, with whom was G. I. Hazeltine, were camped near the place where the first victim died. While two of the girls belonging to the party were wandering along the creek one of them found a gold watch near a cluster of bushes. Upon further search they discovered the skeleton of a man, undoubtedly the remains of the murdered miner.

The two other members of this ill-starred prospecting party escaped from their covert under the rocks to a thicket of brush a short distance away, where they paused, that the wounds of the younger man might be bandaged. It was found that he had received a very severe wound in his side, from a rifle ball, also two less serious wounds from arrows. His companion, a man quite far advanced in life, was but slightly injured by an arrow, and considered himself most fortunate in escaping so well, but time proved that the arrow inflicting the apparently trifling wound had been poisoned. When the younger man had been made as comfortable as possible, the

two climbed painfully over the high bluffs on the east side of the South Fork, hoping to make their way to Canyon City. They were afraid to take the trail along the main river, lest the Indians should again attack them, so kept on over the rough, gorge-cut country as best they might. The death of the younger man seemed unavoidable, so he finally prevailed upon his aged companion to leave him and try to save his own life. The old man eventually reached Canyon City, but the poison had permeated his system so completely that he could not live.

Meanwhile his deserted companion struggled slowly onward, stopping at all convenient places to bathe his wounds. He, too, at last reached the town. By careful nursing he recovered sufficiently, after a few months' confinement, to go about again, though he never regained his former vigorous health.

Some time during the year 1864 a man named Middlesworth left his pack train half a mile outside Canyon City and himself came into town to spend a few hours. While he was gone the Indians stampeded the mules, running them over the mountains and into Harney valley. Mr. Middlesworth raised a company of men and set out in an attempt to recover his property. In due time he came upon them in the valley, but his force was so badly outnumbered by Indians that he considered it unwise to make an attack.

During the same fall an attempt was made by Indians to drive away some horses that were feeding on the hills near Canyon City. They were opposed by a superior force of white men and driven back, leaving one of their number apparently dead. His only wound, however, was found to consist of a broken leg. His captors brought him into town, and when he had sufficiently recovered to endure the operation, his limb was removed. Mr. Onsley, the physician of the town, was without a supply of surgical instruments, but succeeded in amputating the wounded member with a knife and a butcher's saw. Chloroform was also lacking, but the stolidity and stoicism of the savage were equal to the occasion. After recovery he traversed the streets at will on crutches, living off the bounty of the men he tried to rob, and apparently enjoying his new environment. For several months he remained in civilized society, but the promptings of his savage nature at last impelled him back to the wilderness. It is said that someone gave him an old horse to get rid of him.

During this and the two or three years succeeding, roving bands infested the stage and immigrant roads, thieving and murdering, terrorizing small settlements and infusing into the everyday life of the miner, the rancher and the traveler an element of unrest and anxiety that was almost unendurable. The details of these raids are not only intensely interesting as stories, but they show the conditions under which life was sustained during this period of the country's history. Stages over the various routes suffered a great deal from Indian attacks and travelers never risked their lives on journeys without being well prepared for defense. An interesting story is told of an attack by the Indians on the Canyon City-Dalles stage, as follows:

H. H. Wheeler, for whom Wheeler county is named, came to The Dalles in 1863 with considerable money realized in the lumber business in California. With this capital he established the first mail and stage line from The Dalles to Canyon City. Commencing in 1864, he took the mail contract for four years, at $12,000 per annum. He ran four-horse coaches, and had eight changes of horses on the route. The coaches held eleven passengers, and the fare was $40 from The Dalles to Canyon City. Besides, Mr. Wheeler had a contract to carry all of Wells, Fargo & Company's express, mostly gold from the famous Canyon City mines. It was a paying business, but the risks were great.

In the fall of 1866 a band of Indians attacked the stage, on which were Mr. Wheeler and Wells, Fargo & Company's messenger, H. C. Paige, about three miles above where the town of Mitchell now is, then in Wasco, now in Wheeler county. The Indians had rifles and commanded the driver to stop, which he did. Paige at once opened fire on the Indians, but without effect. Then a big buck on the hillside shot Mr. Wheeler through the face, the bullet passing through both cheeks, taking the upper gum and teeth away, besides a piece of jaw bone. He hung his whip on the brake, jumped off the stage and unhitched one of the leaders, while Paige unhitched the other. Each then mounted a horse and rode at full speed by to C. W. Myer's station, on Bridge creek, a distance of about six miles. Some of the redskins followed them, while the remainder stayed to plunder the stage. About half way to the station Paige's horse threw him. (Neither horse was broken to ride), and while he held the Indians at bay with his rifle Wheeler caught the horse and helped him (Paige) to mount again. The Indians continued shooting from a distance, but the pursued suffered no further injury. Balked of their human prey, the entire band turned their attention to the stage and its contents. They cut open the mail bags and cut the top off the coach, broke open the express box and took everything they thought of value. Fortunately for the express company, the Indians had never seen paper money, and threw $10,000 in greenbacks contemptuously to one side, which Paige picked up two hours afterward, when he returned to the spot with a posse of armed men. The Indians had by this time fled, so had the wheel horses. Two days afterward Mr. Wheeler went down on the stage to The Dalles to have his mouth treated. During the time Mr. Wheeler was running the stage line the Indians stole eighty-nine head of horses, for which he has had a claim of $20,000 pending before the government for twenty years.

Howard Maupin was a pioneer of 1864,

who settled in Antelope valley, on the Canyon City road. When he came here with his family and stock the Piute Indians held undisputed sway over all the country south of the road leading from The Dalles to the mines on the John Day river, at Canyon City. These Indians were warlike by instinct, and marauders from necessity; they knew no peaceful neighbors; every stranger was an enemy. From time immemorial a Piute Indian, standing in his realm of sage brush, alkali beds and rim rock canyons, could turn his eyes in no direction but he faced a land where dwelt hereditary enemies of his tribe.

When the whites began to pass through his country as immigrants to western Oregon, or in later years, as gold seekers, the Piutes regarded them as but a new enemy come to torment them when in strong parties, and proper victims to kill and plunder when venturing in small ones.

Such were the environments of Antelope valley, when, lured by its luxuriant grass, which covered an almost unlimited scope of free pasturage, Howard Maupin built his cabin. He was not ignorant of the danger that menaced him, for he had spent his youth on the Texan border, and was well schooled in Indian character, learned in many a bloody conflict with Comanches and Apaches. He was a man of gigantic proportions, a Hercules in strength, true to his friends and a terror to his enemies.

One dark July night, while a gentle drizzling rain was pattering on his cabin roof, the stampeding and snorting of the horses in the corral awoke Mrs. Maupin. She heard the swish of the lariat, followed by a wild rush of the horses in the corral. From this she knew that the Indians were endeavoring to steal their horses, and she awakened her husband. Howard Maupin rushed to the corral; all was dark, nor sight nor sign of Indians was to be seen or heard, but the horses were greatly excited.

He waited and listened for some time, but could not hear footfalls of moccasined Indians.

He then returned to the house, put on his clothes and, with gun in hand, started back to the corral. The Indians, on seeing or hearing his first approach, had clambered over the stone wall that formed the enclosure, and squatted in the shadows. During the short time it took Maupin to go to the house and dress, the Indians made a breach in the wall and drove the horses out. Maupin could hear their hoofs clatter as the Indians drove them up a steep, stony hill. The Indians were not mounted, and as Maupin's first appearance had balked their attempts to catch horses to ride, they were attempting to drive off the band afoot, and consequently could not put them at a full run.

Maupin, followed by his twelve-year-old son, gave chase, and in a mile came up to the horses. They saw in the darkness an Indian glide behind a rock. Maupin fired at the shadow. It fell, and then seemed to be endeavoring to crawl off. Another shot made the shadowy phantom lie still. The shots startled the horses, and to fire more was to put the whole herd to flight. As dark shadows of Indians glided among the horses Maupin had hard work to keep his son from shooting. By daylight he and his son had the horses under control, and drove them back to the corral.

After breakfast he and his son went back over the ground again. By the rock where he had shot at the Indian was a great pool of blood and many wads of grass where the wounded Indian's comrades had vainly attempted to staunch the blood by plugging the wound with grass. The Indian had died, however, and his companions had carried him to a stony hillside and covered him with rocks. It was most probably the attention which the Indians were giving their wounded companion that prevented their killing Maupin and his son and making off with the band of horses.

A short time afterwards the Indians made a successful raid upon Maupin's horses and drove off the herd, and it is to recover something from the United States that his widow is now pressing her claim. Maupin always believed that Paulina, the chief, was responsible for his loss. A year or more afterwards he had an opportunity to avenge his loss, and at the same time rid the country of a murderer and robber who had been the scourge of the border.

Frank McBean first came into Grant county in 1863, when miners dug coarse gold out of Canyon creek by sackfuls. He was there when the mail sacks and pack trains ran the gauntlet of ambush by day and swift attack by night, when packers and express riders were left dead by the wayside and a government escort was necessary to safe conduct from The Dalles to Canyon City. About 1865 he joined the United States troops stationed at Camp Watson, and followed the savages into the Beaver creek country, where they were overhauled and engaged in a battle, the details of which are not known. However, the prompt measures taken by the miners and soldiers served to check the hostile raids, and trouble was only intermittent until the murderous old chief, Paulina, was killed.

In 1870 Mr. McBean engaged in the mail service of the United States, his first contract being to transport military mail once a week from Canyon City to Fort Harney, in which service he gained the distinction of being the first mail carrier to enter what is now Harney county. This route was over sixty-eight miles of mountain road, which was traversed on horseback when possible, and at other times on snowshoes. For four years he filled this service, during which his contract was extended to carrying general mail from Canyon City to Camp McDermitt, in Nevada. This service carried him over a route that is unique in the history of the United States mail service in Oregon, for it extended 245 miles south of the initial point, in which distance Fort Harney

and Egan, near Burns, were the only post offices supplied. He carried a camping outfit, and wood, water and grass were the only adjuncts necessary to his stopping places. After leaving Harney and Egan the only inhabitants passed were the pioneer cabins of Todhunter & Devine, at Alvord, and at Camp C. F. Smith.

In August, 1866, a band of about fifty Indians raided the Elk creek and Dixie creek regions, murdering, firing buildings and stealing stock. A temporary camp, named Logan, had been established and garrisoned the previous winter, on the north side of Strawberry Butte, but in the spring the troops were removed, and the country was left practically unprotected from the attack of the savages. This camp was most advantageously located. It guarded the best Indian passes into the John Day valley, and had it been continuously and properly garrisoned settlers in the valley and travelers along the Boise road, from Canyon City to Willow creek, would have been comparatively safe. But for some unexplained reason, and against the earnest protest of the settlers and miners, the camp was never properly garrisoned, and was eventually abandoned. Camp Watson, established in 1865, was sixty miles from Canyon City, on The Dalles road, and therefore no reliance could be placed upon its troops in time of danger. For many months the John Day valley was at the mercy of the Indians, and during this time many miners were killed and their property stolen, cabins were burned, schools in the settlements were abandoned, and business of all kinds was at a standstill. These conditions prevailed, with but little change, until late in the year 1867, when proper consideration was given the demands of the settlers and effectual protection was granted.

From 1865 to 1878 was an alternating period of placer and quartz mining and the development of the agricultural and horticultural resources of the county. While the richer placer mines of Canyon creek had been practically worked out, placer mining near John Day continued into the 'seventies, the work being done by Chinamen on shares.

The first quartz mill was established in the summer of 1867, in connection with J. A. Porter & Company's sawmill at Susanville. The mill was an eight-stamp, two-battery mill, with a capacity of between eight and ten tons a day, and was erected by a joint stock company of mining and business men of the county at a cost of about $5,000. John L. Miller was the first manager. The mill was not a success, however, for the reason that it was poorly constructed, and the ore was not rich enough. It was operated but very little, and in the early 'seventies was purchased by Cabal & Roy, and taken to their mine.

In the meantime a number of ranches had been taken in the valley, at first for the sole purpose of harvesting hay for stock feeding, and cultivating vegetables for home supplies. The B. C. Trowbridge ranch was taken in 1862. A little later the Belshaw ranch was located twenty-two miles further down the river. D. B. Rinehart was also among the early ranchers. In the early 'seventies Nicholas Noble and John Paul settled on Long creek. Their old ranch is now known as the John Randu place. In the south end of the county W. S. Southworth located at Seneca, in 1883. These have been followed by others, until all the arable lands were appropriated. The change from stock ranches to farms was gradual, in fact, it has never become radical, as the stock interests in the county have always been so great, and the facilities for shipping farm products so poor, that there has been no occasion for the ranchman to devote himself exclusively to agricultural pursuits. But the adaptation of the land to agriculture has been thoroughly tested. As early as 1870 there was an overproduction of grain in John Day valley. Much of the surplus found its way over the mountains to Camp Harney. On

the Belshaw, Trowbridge and Rinehart places orchards were planted many years ago, and they now produce, in great abundance, fruits of all varieties and of the finest flavor. It may be of interest to record here the fact that in the early 'sixties oats and barley sold for ten cents per pound, while potatoes brought $20 per hundred pounds.

Following the mining industry, the next to receive the attention of the settlers was the stock industry. Until 1882 the stock men dealt chiefly in cattle and horses. In that and the following year over 30,000 head of cattle were driven from the Grant ranges to those of Harney and Malheur counties. Other thousands were sold and many cattlemen became sheepmen. Herds of cattle gave way to flocks of sheep, principally because of a change in the conditions of the ranges. The first sheep for breeding purposes were brought in by Small and Wolfinger in 1867. Because of the care that has been exercised in breeding, and because of the special adaptation of the ranges to the sheep industry, Grant county has always excelled in the production of wool. The Spanish, American and Delaine Merinos are the breeds that have done best here, and Grant county clips are noted for their long fibre, light shrinkage and freedom from cockleburrs and grease.

Horse breeding was one of the early industries, existent with the raising of cattle. For many years some of the best horses in the state came from the Grant county ranges and ranches. But the industry has degenerated, owing to the fact that it has ceased to be sufficiently remunerative. Thousands of horses roam the ranges now and breed at will, the result being that the most desirable draught horses and roadsters cannot be found here. While there are a few who are giving special attention to the breeding of blooded stock, the industry has practically lost its importance.

A condition of general prosperity prevailed in the late 'sixties. On July 1st, 1869, there were $1,501.97 in the county treasury. On the main John Day river eighty claims had been taken, 9,064 acres were fenced, 3,608 acres were under cultivation. The largest claims fenced contained 400 and 250 acres respectively. Freight rates from The Dalles were from six to ten cents per pound. A comparison of prices prevailing for necessaries in 1869 and in 1888 shows that while in a few instances there was a marked difference, owing to new freight lines and changes in rates, as a rule supply, demand and cost of transportation have maintained equable relations. Some of the prices in 1869 were as follows: Coffee, 26 cents; kerosene, $1.12 to $1.25; beans, 11 to 14 cents; butter, 45 to 50 cents; eggs, 50 cents; soap, per box, $3 to $3.50. In 1888: Coffee, 25 cents; kerosene, $1.00; beans, 12 to 14 cents; butter, 35 cents; eggs, 50 cents; soap, per box, $3. Greenbacks in 1869 were worth only 72 cents on the dollar.

An act passed by Congress in October, 1868, was vastly important in its effect upon the people of Grant county. This was the measure authorizing the construction of The Dalles military road, which ran up the John Day valley, across the divide, and down Willow creek and Malheur river, in Malheur county. By this act the government and the state of Oregon were defrauded of 600,000 acres of land, including large areas of the best ranges and arable tracts of Grant county. This land is now valued at many million dollars, and settlers, instead of being allowed to homestead it, or purchase it from the government at a nominal price, have been compelled to buy it of the Eastern Oregon Land Company, at several dollars per acre. This has worked great hardship to the settlers of Grant county, and it will be many years before the evils resulting from this land steal will disappear. A complete history of the gigantic fraud is given in another chapter.

On the evening of December 18, 1872, there was a slight earthquake in Canyon City

and vicinity. It lasted only a few seconds, but during this inconsiderable space of time its effects were distinctly perceptible. Houses were shaken, glassware, earthenware and tinware clinked together in the shelves, swinging lamps oscillated from side to side, and in other ways the activity of the earth was manifested. The stores were all open, and business men and loungers, noticing the movement of articles over the floor and on the counters and shelves, and experiencing the sensation of rocking, believed at first that they were victims of hallucinations. The violence of the disturbance increasing, however, and finally culminating in a slight though distinct shock, these beliefs were dispelled, and the true nature of the phenomenon became apparent. A few were badly frightened, but no damage whatever was done.

Even before the establishment of schools the influence of the church began to permeate the mining camps and the hastily built settlements. When the first sermon was preached, or where, or by whom, in Grant county, history does not say, but one thing is certain, the gold hunter and the Methodist preacher arrived on Canyon creek just about the same time. The first preachers were men who adapted themselves to the surroundings, working during the week and preaching on Sundays, thus imitating the example of the great apostle to the Gentiles. Services were held in the open air, in tents and in private houses, and later on, in the school houses, also at the court house, and in the Good Templars' hall.

The first society was organized at Canyon City in 1874, Rev. A. J. Joslyn, pastor, and quite a number of the original members of the class are on the church roll yet. The first M. E. church built in the county was begun at Canyon City by Rev. G. W. Grammis in November, 1876, and pushed to completion immediately. Since then three other churches have been erected at the following places: Long Creek, John Day and Prairie City. The churches are well furnished inside and outside. Evidently the old pioneers intended to do the best they could, and spared no expense to have creditable churches. The seating capacity of each church is about 250, except the one at John Day, that being smaller. Although situated so far from a railroad, the annual conference with Bishop Walden held a regular session at the Canyon City church during the regular pastorate of Rev. G. W. Grammis nine years ago. The Long Creek church is situated on a hill out and alone from the rest of the buildings. The cyclone of June, 1894, wrenched the building somewhat, but it was built on a rock, and stands firm, though slightly disfigured.

The Prairie City church has more veteran members than the other three combined, and is well attended.

The early Methodists did not forget the Sunday school, and Frank I. McCallum, of John Day, has the books of the first school ever held in the John Day valley. The records show that a Mr. Dillinger was the first superintendent. The Canyon City Sunday-school has an enviable reputation, and a most serviceable superintendent in the person of Hon. E. S. Penfield, who has been superintendent since the school was organized, over twenty years ago. At present the school has a membership of seventy. Each of the four churches has an Epworth League. There have been seventeen pastors on the Canyon City charge since Rev. A. J. Joslyn began in 1874, several attaining more than local celebrity.

The Episcopal church was established at Canyon City in 1876, with Dr. Nevius as the rector. A handsome church edifice was erected in the same year. Another of the early Episcopal ministers was Arthur N. Wrixon. The Advents have a society at John Day.

For a short time during the summer of 1878 Grant county was greatly disturbed, and intense excitement was created by the sudden appearance of the Indians. When Buffalo Horn announced his intention to lead the Ban-

nocks to war, the aid of the Piutes on the Malheur reservation was sought and given, and early in June, 1878, the redskins appeared several hundred strong on Strawberry range, and the mountains east, General Howard pursuing. Here the Bannocks were joined by the Piutes, and followed the range westward, the troops being in close pursuit. No damage was done by the Indians thus far in Grant county. When about twenty miles south of Canyon City, the inhabitants here took to the abandoned tunnels west of town, most of the people taking clothes and other valuables and preparing to stay until the danger was over. Many did stay several days. At Long Creek a stockade and log fort were built, and into it was taken all stock, goods and the women and children. The Indians passed westward, without attempting to molest the inhabitants of Canyon and John Day, and crossed the valley about ten miles below Canyon creek, where they burned several ranch houses and murdered two sheepherders, nephews of James Small.

While the Indians were passing south of Canyon a scouting party of seven men left the town to watch the Indians' movements. On Murderer's creek, a branch of the south fork, about thirty miles southwest of Canyon City, the scouting party came upon the Indians, and a skirmish ensued, resulting in a man named Aldrich losing his life instantly and another named Schutz being slightly wounded. The rest of the party, William Burnham, Casey Officer, William Colby, Joseph D. Combs and James Clark, escaped unscathed.

From the John Day valley the redskins took a northward course over Fox valley and past Long creek, going by within sight of the fort, but attempting no hostilities. Then, veering eastward, they passed up Butter creek and attempted a junction with the Umatillas, with the result known to history. Having been dispersed, the Piutes came back by way of the Dixie range, crossing the John Day valley at its extreme head. The only atrocities known to have been committed on this return trip were the murders of James Verdaman and a man whose name is unknown. The former was shot dead at his ranch near Susanville, while standing in his doorway, and the latter at his home on Olive creek. The settlers in the valley were under arms during the whole war, and at Prairie City a home guard was organized with J. W. Mack as captain. There was no organization at Canyon City, so far as recorded. Mr. Allred claims that there was a secret organization of one hundred men formed with Robert Lockwood as captain. These men planned to join the army as scouts, but were refused the privilege, it being feared that they would precipitate a battle which Howard was very anxious to avoid. This company was never regularly organized, and never saw service. A more detailed account of this war will be found in another chapter.

The period covered by the years 1879 to 1883, inclusive, was one of general prosperity. All interests advanced. There was a feeling of security from Indian depredations. At no time in the past had the people felt absolutely safe from the attacks of the marauding bands of savages that infested the country. This element of unrest or insecurity had had its influence upon all industries. Perhaps not directly, but indirectly, it acted as a clog on the energies and enterprise of the stockman and ranchman, as well as upon those of the miner and business man. The ventures of all were attended with serious risks and served to prevent their fullest developments. But with the passing of the troublesome Indian question every man's way was clear, and all interests began to forge to the front. In 1882 the assessor's records showed a net gain in real and personal values of several hundred thousand dollars. With the exception of cattle, the number of stock on the ranges had increased enormously. At this time the gross value of all properties was $2,068,353, and the taxable property was valued at $1,603,779. Since

1879 there has been a steady and uninterrupted increase in all values, and many fortunes have been made in the mines and on the ranches.

The spring of 1884 saw a determined effort to remove the county seat from Canyon City to some town in the Harney valley, the promoters of the project contending that the seat of local government ought to be there, in view of the fact that Harney valley was almost equal in extent to that of the Willamette, and that the heaviest taxpayers were resident in it. They argued that the placer mines of Canyon creek, Marysville and Dixie creek were almost all exhausted, and the narrow strip of land along the John Day was already too much impoverished for successful agriculture, and unable to furnish enough cereals, vegetables and beeves for home consumption of the sparse population. "Furthermore," they said, "Harney valley is soon to be connected with the outside world by railroad."

The county commissioners in power were seriously considering the plan of erecting a new court house and jail, in fact had gone so far as to ask for bids, and perhaps their only reason for not proceeding at once with the work was that the plans and specifications submitted to would-be contractors called for too expensive a building. The bids ranged from $20,500 to $34,000, and it was thought that even the smaller of these sums was more than the county's treasury would warrant the commissioners in expending. Tureman and McGowan, candidates for membership in the county court, made the main issue of their campaign opposition to the erection of new county buildings until the voters should have a chance to express their opinion by the ballot as to the permanent location of the county seat. Tureman and McGowan were defeated and the movement failed. It would seem that the project was hardly a wise one, as it was plainly discernable to all that the mammoth empire then included in Grant county could not long remain one political head, and must have a location which would be central to a new county, when such would be formed. It might therefore be necessary to again move the seat of government. The true policy for the residents of Harney valley to pursue would seem to be to endure patiently any inconveniences which their distance from the county seat might entail until such time as they should become strong enough to bear the burdens of independent government, then work for the formation of a new county. This policy was the one which ultimately prevailed.

The administration of the affairs of Grant county at this time seems to have been remarkably efficient and satisfactory. In 1882 the indebtedness was $20,464.99, and in 1884 it had decreased to $12,463.30, a reduction of $8,001.69. This showing is all the more encouraging when it is remembered that during the biennial period referred to more money was expended for the improvement of roads and the building of bridges than in any previous four years of the county's existence, also that the tax for county purposes was lower in the year 1882-83 than ever before, and in 1883-84 was reduced to two-thirds of that of the previous year, or to ten mills.

The reduction in the rates may, however, have been due in part to an increase in the assessment rolls, for the county was enjoying not a little prosperity at the time. The prospects for the cattlemen of eastern Oregon were very bright, as the demand for their product was steady and the price high.

As affording a basis from which the wealth of the county at this time may be roughly estimated, we quote below a summary of the assessment roll for the year 1884. Probably the total there given must needs be multiplied by three or four in order to get the real value of Grant county's assessable property, but the summary referred to makes the following showing:

Number acres of agricultural land, 109,799, valued at $174,822; number of lots, 79, valued at $7,335; value of improvements, $337,922; value of merchandise, $138,516; value of money, notes, etc., $393,453; furniture, $54,875; number of horses and mules, 17,359, value $643,351; number of cattle, 83,602, value, $1,632,415; number of sheep, 172,305, value $387,311; number of swine, 1,721, value $4,123; gross value, $3,774,123.

Considerable disquietude seems to have prevailed throughout this period of the county's history over the existing political divisions. Eastern Oregon counties were inconveniently large. Long distances had to be traversed by citizens in order to reach the different seats of local government, and though this was necessary at the time the counties were formed, owing to the paucity of the settlers and their wide distribution, it was thought that the time had arrived for the amelioration of conditions in this respect. Thus in the fall of 1884 the citizens of Trail Fork precinct, in Grant county, met at the Lost Valley school house and drafted resolutions protesting against the proposed extension of Crook county so as to include quite a large tract of Wasco and Grant counties lying north and east of John Day river, on account of the inaccessibility of Pineville to the section, and because it had no interests in common with Crook county. This meeting also passed resolutions favoring the erection of a new county embracing the eastern portion of Wasco county, beginning at the John Day river; the western part of Umatilla county and all that portion of Grant county lying north of the John Day river. Frank Aholt and W. F. White were appointed a committee to confer with representatives of other portions of the territory directly concerned and draft a memorial to the legislature praying for action in accordance with the resolutions. Like many similar projects, this plan failed to materialize.

CHAPTER II.

CURRENT HISTORY, 1885 TO THE PRESENT.

Perhaps it would be as well to interrupt the current of our narrative to give the reader a bird's-eye view of the general conditions obtaining in Grant county at this time. This we are enabled the better to accomplish on account of an excellent article on the subject which appeared in the issue of the West Shore of February 15, 1885.

"The largest and agriculturally least developed county of Oregon," says the article referred to, "is Grant, lying just east of the Cascade mountains, and extending from Umatilla county to the Nevada line. It is nearly a rectangle in shape, about two hundred miles long from north to south, and ninety miles from east to west, and contains a superficial area of 13,000 square miles, equal to the combined area of the states of Massachusetts, Rhode Island and Connecticut. It is one of the 'cow counties' so often spoken of; in fact, it stands at the head of the stock industry in Oregon. Its population (some six thousand) is engaged chiefly in mining and stock raising. The reason why it has not been settled by an agricultural population is its isolation from navigable rivers or railroads, and a misapprehension by the people of the quantity and quality of its arable land. The construction of the Oregon Railway & Navigation Company's line through Baker county has greatly reduced the distance from the center of population in Grant county to a railroad outlet. For this reason, and because it contains a large portion of desirable vacant government land, unincumbered by railroad grants, the county offers inducements which should receive the careful consideration of emigrants."

The great trouble with the country at the time, according to the statement of this writer, was that a few wealthy men had monopolized the valleys and hills and covered them with vast bands of stock, to the exclusion of the small farmer. These men, he said, had persistently slandered the country, asserting that it had no agricultural value whatever, and was fit only for the grazing of stock in large bands, such as would require many square miles to be under the domination of each cattle owner, while the facts were that there were thousands of acres of arable land, some of it, to be sure, requiring irrigation, which were suitable for farms, where farming and stock raising might be profitably united. "When," says this writer, "these numerous valleys are wrested from the grip of the cattle kings and divided up into homesteads for actual settlers; when they are made to yield the diversified products of which they are capable; when the numerous farmers shall utilize the adjacent hills for the grazing of as many cattle, sheep, etc., as each can properly care for; when the school house shall replace the cowboy's hut and the settler's cabin shall be seen in every nook and corner of these vacant valleys, then the country will multiply its population and wealth, and the era of its real prosperity will dawn. The tendency towards this happy state of affairs is already marked, and the tide sets in stronger every year. Land is too valuable to be devoted exclusively to pastoral pursuits for the benefit of a few fortunate men, while thousands of energetic, intelligent and worthy men are seeking homes for themselves and families. Were the vast bands of cattle grazing within the limits of the county divided among two thousand, instead of two score owners, each with his family ocupying a small, well-cultivated farm, the population and assessable value of property woud be increased tenfold and the region would enjoy a prosperity it has never known. There would then be no need to travel a hundred miles to reach a railroad; railroads would go further than that to seek the county. Then can the great mineral resources of the region be properly developed and made to yield their store to add to the general wealth. There need be no fear that the settlements of those valleys by an agricultural people will be a death blow to the stock industry. It will simply change the system of conducting it, and will place the ownership of cattle in many hands, instead of those of a few. It will, in fact, if the history of other sections may be relied upon as an indication of what may be expected, actually increase the total number of cattle, the value per head and the value per acre of land. The states of Illinois and Iowa, divided up into multitudes of small farms, besides producing their millions of bushels of corn, grain and countless other products, support more cattle, and of a far better quality, than an equal area of the finest cattle ranges of the west. This is because, by cultivation of cereals and tame grasses, each acre, in addition to its other products, is made to yield the nourishment for stock which a dozen acres of purely grazing land will not give. The result is schools, churches, colleges, factories and a dense population enjoying all the comforts and refinements of an advanced civilization."

"In proportion to its total area," says the writer, "the amount of arable land is small, but when the numerous valleys are considered by themselves, and their areas added together, the result carries the total far up into the millions of acres. Put together in one body, it would make a compact arable tract equal in size to some of the best counties in the state."

In 1885 there were a few farms in the John Day valley, one of the principal being the Gundlach farm, a mile and a half west of Canyon City, which gave abundant proof, by its production of wheat, barley, oats, potatoes, alfalfa and fruit, of what the soil of the valley is capable of when properly tilled and irrigated. Fox valley, about fifteen miles north of Canyon City, was nearly all settled; Long creek valley was likewise mostly taken up, and there were a number of small valleys along the Middle Fork, which were appropriated to the uses of the agriculturists, but Haystack and Corncob valleys, in the warmest part of the county, still offered many choice locations to homeseekers. Murderer's creek valley, twelve by five miles in extent, Beaver creek valley, thirty miles long by three to fifteen wide, Rabbit and Paulina valleys, four miles each in diameter, the valley of Twelve-Mile creek, twenty miles long and three wide, and the valley on the south fork of Crooked river, eight by twenty miles, were all ocupied exclusively by cattlemen. The same was true of Bear valley, twenty-five miles long and from seven to ten wide, situated twenty miles south of Canyon City; also of Silvies valley, twenty miles long and an average of about seven wide, and of the valleys of Emigrant and Silver creeks, of Warm Spring valley, the great Harney valley, with its numerous tributary valleys, Diamond, Dunder and Blitzen, Catlow, Warner Lake and many others, some of them small and nameless, some of considerable size.

"Along the eastern edge of the county," says the West Shore, "are numerous tributaries of the middle fork of the Malheur, along which is much desirable bottom land, all occupied by cattlemen. Juniper valley is four by six miles in extent. On White Horse creek is White Horse ranch, the headquarters of Todhunter & Devine, the largest cattle owners in the county. It is the home of Mr. Devine, and shows what this country is capable of agriculturally. The ranch is a model in every respect, producing grain, vegetables, fruits and flowers in abundance. Fowls and domestic animals of the best strains may here be found. The ranch, which occupies the whole valley, is eighteen miles long by six wide. 'P' ranch, headquarters of French & Glenn, is another illustration of the productiveness of this region. Crane Creek valley, tributary to the Malheur, is twenty miles long and two wide, and is occupied by a stock firm. The same is true of Otis valley, a tract four by fifteen miles in extent. On the middle fork of the Maheur there is, within the limits of Grant county, a tract of land eighteen miles long and six wide; also several arms stretching out from the main valley from three to six miles. Below this the river passes into Baker county and flows across it to a junction with the Snake.

"One cannot peruse the foregoing review of the location, size and condition of the numerous valleys of the county without being forcibly impressed with the fact that the stockmen have appropriated the lion's share. This they have been permitted to do because the public has been led to believe that they were fit for nothing else. These men have steadily and persistently asserted that the lands of these valleys could not be successfully cultivated, and this in the very face of the fact that whenever they have found it necessary to cultivate them for their own use—as in the case of the 'P' and White Horse ranches—they have met with the highest success. They have thus far been successful in keeping settlers out and appropriating the whole country to their own use, even completely fencing in many of the valleys and grazing their vast bands of cattle free of expense on the public domain. In this every

26

taxpayer in the county has been wronged. Were these valleys settled, as they should be, the assessable valuation of county property, now $3,300,000, would soon reach five times that amount. The cattlemen are nearly all non-residents; the cattle are sold out of the county and the money used elsewhere; all the benefit the county derives is the presence of the few men needed to care for the stock, and the taxes upon the cattle, greatly undervalued, both in quantity and price. Todhunter & Devine have 40,000 cattle; French & Glenn, 30,000; Thomas Overfelt, 30,000; Riley & Herdin, 25,000; C. G. Alexander, 15,000; Sweetzer Bros., 25,000; George W. Mapes, 10,000; William Hydespath, 6,000. Without counting the many smaller bands, this gives a total of 181,000, and yet the total number assessed for the year 1883-84 was but 74,611, valued at $20 each, at a time when cattle were selling on the ranges, big and little, old and young, for $30, and good beef cattle were worth $50. There are also from 15,000 to 20,000 horses, and from 125,000 to 150,000 sheep. Settlers would keep fully as many cattle, besides adding to the assessment rolls the value of their farms and improvements. Some of the best wheat lands in the Walla Walla region were for years held for free occupation by stockmen by this same plan of decrying their value for agricultural purposes. The truth was finally discovered, and now farms, towns, school houses, churches and millions of dollars worth of property may be seen where were formerly but a few bands of cattle. Good locations for homesteads are becoming harder to find every year, while the number of people seeking them suffers no diminution. In the nature of things these valleys cannot much longer be sequestered. It has been the history of every region that the home-seeker has searched patiently till every desirable spot was found, and so it will be here. The citizens of Grant county are desirous that these valleys shall be filled with an enterprising and industrious population, and they extend to all such who are seeking homes a cordial invitation to come here with their families and settle."

Such was the condition of Grant county in the year 1885, and such some of the sentiments and hopes which animated its population. A small army of placer miners had begun forcing the streams and creek banks to give up their wealth of golden treasure in 1862, and so assiduously did they work, and with such energy, that the cream of nature's bounty had long since been skimmed off. True, numerous valuable quartz ledges had been discovered, the wealth of which could not be so quickly garnered, and copper was known to exist on Dixie creek, galena on Elk creek, limestone and marble on Dog creek, near Canyon City, and coal in various places, but none of these sources of wealth had been developed to any great extent. The agricultural possibilities of the region were likewise lying latent, and cattle raising was far and away the leading industry of the county. It was known that future development must be along two lines, namely, the division of arable lands into small tracts, each held by a *bona fide* settler and cultivated for diversified crops, and the installation of costly and heavy machinery for the economical handling of ores. The mills of the gods are said to grind slowly always, but they grind with especial slowness in a country a hundred miles from railway transportation, and to be reached by wagons only after a tedious climb over forbidding mountain ranges. Seventeen years have elapsed since the West Shore correspondent said he plainly saw forces at work which must eventually produce the highest material and social development of the country, yet has their ultimate result only begun to be accomplished. The development which fully utilizes a section's natural possibilities is yet far in the future in Grant county.

But to take up again the thread of our annals—the closing days of the year 1884 were made memorable by a disgraceful event in Har-

ney valley which quite thoroughly aroused the citizens of Burns and vicinity. Saturday, December 26th, two men named Todd and Vickers set out from Burns to Stofer's cattle ranch, on Crane creek. The next day came the news that two white men had raided an Indian camp in that direction, killing one Indian, breaking another's arm and beating two squaws most shamefully. Todd and Vickers were at once suspected. A mass meeting of the citizens of Burns was called, by which Messrs. Abbott and Hedges were authorized to arrest these men. This task was accomplished without difficulty.

In the meantime a coroner's jury was impaneled to hold an inquest over the body of the murdered brave, but when the men arrived at the scene of the tragedy they found that the Indians had decamped. Todd and Vickers were given a preliminary hearing and bound over. Vickers escaped. His partner was discharged for lack of evidence, and the indignation of the people soon subsided.

At this period Harney valley was developing more rapidly than any other part of the county. The homeseeker had turned his attention in that direction, and there was quite an influx of settlers from Grande Ronde valley, the vicinity of Salem and from California. About one thousand filings were sent out of the valley to the Lakeview land office during the spring of 1885, a fact which encouraged the hope that the day of the non-resident stockman was approaching its close and the day of the settler and home builder was dawning. All the best meadow and bottom lands in the northern portion of the valley, not claimed by the wagon road company, were taken. Considerable grain was sown in the spring of 1885 and opportune rains insured a good crop, so that prospects for this section of the country seemed bright and hopeful.

The precipitation in the northern portion of the county was also copious, but it did not prove an unmixed blessing, and in one instance it assumed a destructive form. Referring to this remarkable phenomenon, which was the second to visit the region down the river from John Day, a less violent one having occurred some four years earlier, the *Grant County News* of July 2, 1885, says:

"The most destructive cloudburst ever known in this county occurred last Monday and extended over a tract of land twelve miles in length. The Dalles stage, which was due here Monday night, did not arrive, owing to the washout. Rocks weighing tons were washed loose on the hills and came down like an avalanche, sweeping away fences, houses and groves; dry gulches were filled to overflowing; the smallest rivulets became roaring torrents. Below the immediate scene of the flood the river rose ten feet, covering meadows and destroying growing crops. No estimate can now be made of the damage sustained by farmers, but it will amount to many thousands of dollars.

"The deluge started back of W. W. Stone's place and extended down to Harvey Field's lower place. The bridge across Birch creek, at Addingtons, and one at Warren Carsner's were swept away, and the gulches washed out from twenty to twenty-five feet in depth. At Carsner's it washed out a cut thirty feet wide and about twenty-five feet deep, and changed the channel of the river from its former course to Mr. Carsner's meadow, almost completely destroying it. The fences from Stone's to James Small's place on the north side of the river were nearly all swept away. The principal sufferer is John Wolfinger, sixty-five bales of wool and some sheep. Harvey Fields has his old Gundlach place almost completely ruined and the house demolished."

Notwithstanding opposition from the southern part of the county, and perhaps from other sections, the county court, during its May term, in 1885, received bids for the erection of a new court house, jail and vault. Butz & Stansell's bid was found to be the lowest and

to them the contract was awarded, the price to be paid being $10,770. At first the intention was to tear down the old building and erect the new one on its site, but it was later decided to put up the new building on a level and sightly tract near Canyon creek. The total cost of the court house and jail was greater by several thousand dollars than the contract price, owing to variations in the plan.

The year 1886 was not fruitful of anything sensational or revolutionary in the section of which we are writing, but the range for stock was good, prices were high, crops fair and the mines were profitably worked, though there were no large transfers, and few new developments. The greatest disaster of the year was a cloudburst just above Canyon City, which did considerable damage to property in that town. It is said to have been more destructive than one which occurred five years previously, in short to have been the worst that had occurred in the memory of white men. Otherwise the year was generally prosperous, though not phenomenal in any respect.

The early months of the year 1887 saw a decided movement inaugurated by residents of Harney valley looking toward the division of Grant county and the creation of Harney county out of the southern portion. Several petitions were signed and forwarded to the legislature and most of the residents of the part of the county it was proposed to segregate became exceedingly anxious for the division. The movement was opposed by the *News* for the reason that Harney valley was as yet but sparsely settled and it would be unwise for new settlers to assume the burdens of separate county government until there was a sufficient number of taxpayers to make the rate of taxation reasonable. The people of Grant realized that a separation must come, but thought it yet too early.

On January 18, 1887, Representative Johnson, of this county, introduced house bill No.

104, providing for the creation of Harney county out of all that portion of Grant county lying south of the fourth standard parallel. The temporary county seat was to be located at Burns, and the two counties, Grant and Harney, were to be represented in the legislature by one representative and one senator. All delinquent taxes assessed from the roll of 1886 within the limits of Harney county were to be payable to the proper officer of Harney county, and within one year of the passage of the bill. Harney county was to pay to Grant a just proportion of the indebtedness of Grant county, after deducting therefrom the value of its public property, such proportion to be determined by the two county judges of said counties. The bill passed the house almost unanimously, but in the senate the committee to which it was referred reported adversely. Thus the measure was killed after it had passed the house by a large majority.

Its defeat was attributed to a petition signed by 226 residents of Harney valley, protesting against the division at this time, and another petition signed by forty-seven persons who claimed to have signed the petition favoring the divison under a misapprehension. The bill was fought by residents of the northern portion of Grant county for three reasons: First, as the value of the public property was upwards of $23,000 and the county debt was far below this figure, Harney would have nothing to pay on Grant's indebtedness and would have something like $15,000 taxes of 1886 in its treasury; second, only a very small amount of the taxes of 1886 had as yet been collected, and therefore nearly the whole tax roll stood at that time as delinquent; and lastly, because the bill was prematurely introduced.

A month later another bill was framed and presented to the senate, the intent of which was to cut off the northwestern part of Grant county and add it to Gilliam, making the north fork of the John Day the boundary line between the two counties. It was defeated by

a majority of four, so the year passed without the loss to Grant of any of its territory, except a small portion which was taken with a section of Baker to form the new county of Malheur.

But though so prolific of division schemes, the year 1887 was not especially productive of anything else. It was not a favorable year for stock or sheepmen, or for the general farmer. During the winter of 1886-87 snow lay on the ground to a great depth for many weeks, with the natural result that heavy losses were sustained, and the summer following was exceedingly dry. Crops were almost a failure on the lower John Day, and were light everywhere. The next year, however, brought abundant crops and a return of prosperity generally.

In July, 1888, the passions of Grant county's citizens were stirred to their profoundest depths by the commission of a most revolting crime in the county jail. At the time there were two prisoners confined in the jail, namely Buccaro Jim, an Indian, charged with killing J. M. Bright, of Harney valley, and Patrick McGinnis, held to answer a charge of horse-stealing. On the evening of July 5th Deputy Sheriff Robert Lockwood failed to return to his home at the usual hour, and when midnight was passed and still he did not come, his family became alarmed. A search was instituted, with the result that about one o'clock the body of Lockwood was found in the jail, pierced by an assassin's bullet. Both the prisoners had escaped. The county court at once offered a reward of five hundred dollars each for their apprehension, and a further reward of two hundred and fifty dollars each was offered by Sheriff Gray, but there can be do doubt that a diligent search would have been made for the fugitives, even without a mercenary motive.

McGinnis was soon found hiding near Alexander Fisher's farm, down the river, and Buccaro Jim near the Indian camps on the Malheur. Both were, of course, returned to the jail.

The appetite of the Irishman for blood was not fully satisfied by his one brutal murder, so he secured some morphine and placed a sufficient quantity of the drug in the Indian's tea to have caused the death of the redskin had the plot not been discovered.

The Indian was released at an examination held later, but McGinnis was convicted at the November term of the circuit court and sentenced to death on January 18, 1889. By dilatory proceedings his attorney managed to prolong the life of the prisoner until the 26th of the following April, when he expiated his crime on the scaffold. This was the second legal execution to take place in the county.

Unfortunately it became necessary to erect a scaffold for the third time before the year was passed, the condemned man in the last instance being one Peter Sullivan, who confessed to having murdered his companion, John Bronkee, who was living with him in a small cabin on Pine creek, a few miles east of Canyon City. Sullivan's execution took place on November 15th.

We have spoken of the failure of numerous county division schemes proposed prior to 1889, among which was one to create Harney county out of the southern portion of Grant. The citizens of Harney valley were too nearly successful in their last attempt to long abstain from further efforts for a new county, indeed the promoters of the scheme worked quietly and persistently in the moulding of public opinion until they created such a sentiment in favor of their project that more than five-sixths of the legal voters signed a petition to the legislature praying for the passage of an enabling act. A bill in harmony with their wishes was introduced by Representative Gilliam at the January session, and it passed practically without opposition, the citizens in the northern part of the county deeming it useless to resist. On February 25th the bill was approved by the governor, and Grant county lost nearly two-thirds of its territory.

According to the provisions of this act, the county judges of the two counties, with the assistance, in case of a disagreement, of one of the judges of the sixth district, were appointed to adjust the proportion of indebtedness to be assumed by Harney county. This commission reported November 25th, as follows: Net debt of Grant county, February 25th, $62,620.80; assessable property, $3,262,080; value of assessable property of Harney county, $1,618,220; proportionate share of net debt to be assumed by Harney county, $31,064.30; deductions by reason of taxes collected, $12,063.66; balance due from Harney county, $19,000.64.

For some reason the year 1890 did not prove a very prosperous one in Grant county, and complaints were made that money was scarce, yet crops were all excellent, with the single exception of fruit; the range was good, and there was plenty of hay, so that the stockmen had no cause for complaint. The assessment roll for 1890 showed a decided increase in the number and value of stock in Grant county, with the exception of sheep, of which there were 240,201 in 1889, against 125,291 a year later. Land values increased nearly $200,000, and town lots nearly $40,000.

The population of Grant county by precincts, according to the official census of 1890, was as follows: Austin, 28; Bear Valley, 188; Canyon City, 382; Fox, 244; Granite, 249; Hamilton, 352; Haystack, 290; John Day, 331; Long Creek, 533; Marysville, 227; Middle, 200; Mountain Creek, 107; North Fork, 179; Olive Creek, 52; Rock Creek, 85; Rosebud, 135; Shoofly, 131; Silvies, 192; Susanville, 52; Union, 760; Warm Springs, 293; Waterman, 41; total, 5,080; Canyon City, 304; Prairie City, 222; John Day, 211; Long Creek, 60.

With the creation of Harney county the seismic disturbances which were threatening to overturn existing institutions in eastern Oregon did not wholly cease. As a general thing, a new county scheme excites but little bitterness in comparison with a proposal to change the seat of local government. Perhaps the most virulent fights that ever occur in any community are over the location of the county seat or for the capture of some other prize promising to give one town the advantage over its nearest rival. The year 1891 brought one of these contests to Grant county. Just before the session of the legislature a petition was framed and signed by citizens of Long Creek asking for the passage of an enabling act providing that the voters of Grant county might express their opinion on the advisability of removing the county seat from Canyon City to Long Creek. The movement gained considerable strength in that part of the county and other towns, especially Prairie City, John Day and Mount Vernon began to count up their chances of capturing the prize.

Naturally counter-petitions were presented by citizens of Canyon City and vicinity, calling the attention of the legislature to the fact that Canyon had been the location for more than twenty years, and that the county property, valued at thirty-four thousand dollars, had been erected in the town, and that this would have to be practically sacrificed, necessitating the expenditure of more than that sum for the erection of new buildings. The petitioners respectfully represented that the county was deeply in debt, and that the expense which would be incurred in removing the county seat and establishing a new one would be an unjust burden upon the taxpayers.

The enabling act was introduced into the house by Representative Dustin, and notwithstanding the strenuous opposition of residents in the John Day valley, passed that branch of the legislature. The senate, however, postponed action indefinitely, thus killing the bill. The people of Long Creek manifested their chagrin and indignation by hanging in effigy Senator Blackman, who strenuously opposed the measure.

Notwithstanding the almost unanimous demand which was made in 1889 for the erection of Harney county, some of the citizens thereof soon tired of their allegiance and, in 1891, petitioned the legislature that the northern part of Harney, including the town of Drewsy and a portion of Silvies river valley should be detached from Harney and annexed to Grant county. Their brethren further south opposed them and the matter was eventually dropped.

On January 8, 1892, another legal execution took place, the victim this time being Ming How, a Chinaman. This is the only instance of a Mongolian's having been convicted of a capital offense within the limits of Grant county. Sheriff Cresap was in charge of the details of this execution.

Residents of Grant county at this time will remember that in 1892 this county was considerably stirred up over the suit instituted by the government against The Dalles Military Road Company and its successors. Although this suit was commenced two years earlier, not much was heard of it outside the courts until this year, when much testimony was taken in the counties affected. In order to make the whole matter of this gigantic swindle clear, however, we will digress from the thread of our narrative here and give the history of the case from its beginning, as no other county was effected more than Grant county in its outcome.

By act of Congress, passed February 25, 1867, there was granted to the state of Oregon by the United States, to aid in the construction of a military wagon road from The Dalles, on the Columbia river, to Fort Boise, on the Snake river, each alternating section of the public lands designated by odd numbers, to the extent of three sections in width on each side of the said road.

By the terms of the act of Congress, the state of Oregon was authorized to dispose of said lands for the purpose of aiding in the construction of the said military road; and in pur-

suance of this authority the legislature passed
an act which was approved by the governor on
the 20th day of October, 1868, granting to The
Dalles Military Road Company, a corporation
duly organized for the purpose of constructing
this road, all of the lands aforesaid.

The act of Congress further provided that
the land should be disposed of in the following
manner, to-wit: "That when the governor of
said state shall certify to the secretary of the
interior that ten contiguous miles of said road
are completed, then the quantity of land hereby
granted, not to exceed thirty sections, may be
sold, and so from time to time until said road
shall be completed."

On June 23, 1869, Governor Woods filed
the following acceptance, which is such an important document that we deem it worth publishing:

"EXECUTIVE OFFICE,
"SALEM, OREGON, June 23d, 1869.

"I, George L. Woods, Governor of the State
of Oregon, do hereby certify that this plat or
map of the Dalles Military Road has been duly
filed in my office by the Dalles Military Road
Company and shows in connection with the
public surveys, as far as said public surveys
are completed, the location of the line of route
as actually surveyed and upon which their road
is constructed in accordance with the requirements of an act of Congress approved February 25th, 1867, entitled 'An Act granting
lands to the State of Oregon to aid in the construction of a military wagon road from Dalles
City on the Columbia River to Fort Boise on
Snake River,' and with the act of the legislative assembly of the State of Oregon approved October 20, 1868, entitled 'An Act
donating certain lands to Dalles Military Road
Company.' I further certify that I have made
a careful examination of said road since its
completion and that the same is built in all respects as required by the said above recited acts
and that said Road is accepted.

"In testimony whereof I have hereunto set

my hand and caused to be affixed the Great
Seal of the State of Oregon.

"Done at Salem, Oregon, June 23d, 1869.
"GEO. L. WOODS.
(Seal of the State of Oregon.)
"SAMUEL E. MAY,
"Secretary of State."

On January 12, 1870, the governor issued
a further certificate in like terms and effect as
that of June 23, 1869, certifying to the secretary of the interior the completion of the said
military road throughout its entire length by
The Dalles Military Road Company.

On December 18, 1869, the commissioner
of the general land office of the United States
withdrew from sale the odd numbered sections
of land within three miles on either side of said
road in favor of The Dalles Military Road
Company.

Congress, on June 18, 1874, passed an act
authorizing the issuance of patents for lands
granted to the state of Oregon in certain cases,
which act of Congress, after reciting that Congress had granted to the state of Oregon certain lands to aid in the construction of certain
military wagon roads in said state, and that
there existed no law providing for the issuing
of formal patents for said lands, provided "that
in all cases when the roads, in the aid of construction of which said lands were granted, are
shown by the certificate of the governor of the
state of Oregon, as in said act provided, to
have been constructed and completed, patents
to said lands shall issue in due form to the state
of Oregon as fast as the same shall under said
grant be selected and certified, unless the state
of Oregon shall by public acts have transferred
its interests in said lands to any corporations,
in which case patents shall issue from the general land office to such corporation or corporations."

Under the provisions of this act the road
company selected lands, and May 31, 1876,
conveyed the title to such lands to Edward
Martin, the consideration being given as

$125,000. Then, by sundry mesne convey-
ances, the title became vested in the Eastern
Oregon Land Company.

This was the status in 1885, when public
opinion, calling for an investigation into the
fraud that had been practiced upon the government by this road company, became so
strong that at the session of the legislature that
year a memorial was passed by both houses,
asking Congress to look into the matter and
commence suit for the recovery of the lands.
On March 2, 1889, Congress responded to this
appeal, passing an act authorizing the attorney
general of the United States to bring suit to
procure a decree of forfeiture of all lands
granted by the act of Congress of February 25,
1867, on the ground that the terms of the grant
had not been complied with. This act also
sought a cancellation of all patents therefor,
issued by the United States under the act,
and all conveyances to purchasers under
said patents, and under the act, as well as
a forfeiture of the lands still unpatented. The
bill filed by the attorney general alleged, in
substance, "That the road was never constructed in whole or in part; that through the
fraudulent representations of the officers, stockholders and agents of the corporation, the governor of Oregon was deceived and induced to
issue a certificate in pursuance of the provisions of the act, declaring that he had examined
the road throughout its entire length, and that
it had been constructed and completed in all
respects in accordance with the statute; and
that, relying on this certificate, the patents to
portions of the lands had been issued by the
United States."

Suit was immediately begun in the circuit
court, district of Oregon, before Judge Sawyer, L. L. McArthur appearing as United
States attorney, and James A. Kelley and
Dolph, Bellinger, Mallory & Simpson for the
defendants, The Dalles Military Road Company, et al. The case came up for argument
on February 18, 1890, the defendants filing

two pleas, as follows: That the governor's
certificate was made without fraud; that the
defendants were bona fide purchasers from The
Dalles Military Road Company, without notice of any fraud or defect in the title. In an
opinion rendered February 2, 1890, Judge Sawyer sustained the defendants' pleas and dismissed the case.

From such decision the case was appealed
to the United States circuit court, Ninth district, Justice Blatchford handing down the
opinion, May 25, 1891, which reversed the decision of the district court and remanded the
case for further hearing. The conclusion
reached was that the district court erred in not
permitting the United States to reply to the
pleas and dismissing the bill absolutely. After
the mandate had been filed in the district court
issue was joined on these two pleas, testimony
taken from settlers and others, and on December 7, 1891, a decree was again entered, sustaining the second plea. From this decree an
appeal was taken to the circuit court of appeals,
by which court, on March 10, 1892, that decree was affirmed, and from this decree of af-
firmance the United States appealed to the supreme court of the United States. Assistant
Attorney General Parker appeared for the
United States, and James K. Kelley for The
Dalles Military Road Company. Justice
Brewer handed down an opinion from the supreme court bench, March 6, 1893, which affirmed the decision of the district court and the
court of appeals. Thus the original title of
the road company to these lands has been made
absolute. Several other military road grants,
including that of the Willamette Valley and
Cascade Mountain Wagon Road Company,
whose road passed through what is now Harney county, then Grant, were also in litigation
at this time, and as the basic facts in all were
the same as in the case against The Dalles Road
Company, this case was made a test case and
the cases against the others dropped when
negative decision was rendered against this

company. The main point upon which the defendants rested their case was that by the act of 1867 Congress provided that the only proof of construction required to obtain possession of the lands was the governor's certificate, and when that was given, and proven to have been bona fide, the title to the land was absolute.

The peach crop of 1892 in the John Day valley was a very poor one, but the quantity and quality of all other varieties of fruit were up to the usual standard. The grain crop of the year was much larger than that of 1891, and the price of wool and stock was such as to encourage these industries.

The next year, however, the year that brought panic and distress to the country generally, brought to Grant county its share of depression. The sheepmen, especially, were much discouraged over the gloomy outlook for their business. There was an ominous absence of wool and sheep buyers at The Dalles, Arlington and Heppner, and while the growers were holding their wool for ten cents a pound the dealers were asserting their inability to pay that much. It was claimed that the fear of tariff removal, in accordance with the principles of President Cleveland, was the cause of the depression in the wool market, for the producers of Australia and the Argentine Republic could, were it not for the tariff, lay down their product in the United States at a price which would defy the competition of the western sheepmen. The hay crop in some of the leading valleys was only half the usual average, and the local causes of discouragement, together with the general depression over the country, had a decided effect upon business generally, though no failures were recorded.

Among the noteworthy events of the year was the execution of F. W. Gallin for the murder of A. W. Shaw. The eastern Oregon district fair was held at Prairie City this year. It was a success, notwithstanding the inclement weather, the features of greater interest being the display of fruits and vegetables and the races.

According to the assessment roll for 1893, there were 205,630 acres of assessable land in Grant county, valued at $650,660; improvements, valued at $103,300; money, notes and accounts, $172,370; 8,950 horses and mules, valued at $150,980; 17,631 head of cattle, valued at $209,690; 158,355 sheep, worth $316,-710; and 1,396 swine, valued at $3,060. The reader will note the falling off in the number and value of cattle since 1885, when over seventy thousand head were assessed. This decrease was due in large measure to the formation of Harney county, taking away nearly two-thirds of the territorial area of the original Grant county, but also to the gradual failure of the bunchgrass and the development of other industries. There was an increase in the total valuation of property since the last assessment of $271,150; this, too, in spite of the prevailing hard times.

The year 1894 was a hard year in Grant county. Grain crops were below the average and the price of wheat fell to the phenomenally low figure of twenty-six cents a bushel delivered at the railroad. The general depression was also felt by cattle and sheepmen, and by the business interests generally. But notwithstanding these discouragements another district fair was held at Prairie City, and it proved superior in many respects to that of the previous year. The people were somewhat encouraged by the false hope that perhaps the railroad rumors then afloat might in part, at least, prove trustworthy. It was reported that negotiations were in progress for uniting the Oregon Short Line with the Oregon Pacific, thus giving the Union Pacific a through line to the seaboard at Yaquina. Should this plan be carried out the road, it was thought, would start either from Nyssa or Huntington, and, traveling northward, pass through the John Day valley. However, the era of railroad construction in

Grant county has not yet dawned, though the Sumpter Valley line is gradually extending farther and farther into the interior.

The year 1895 brought little improvement in conditions, as the financial stingency continued and crops were below the average on account of the dry weather prevailing throughout the summer and fall. The hard times were exceedingly oppressive, though not as bad here as in many other parts of the country, for cattle and sheep, cheap though they were, were not as low-priced relatively to the cost of production as wheat, and the people were more self-reliant and versatile than are the residents of manufacturing communities, where there are many employed and few employers. Then, too, the depression and consequent cheap labor rendered it possible to work mines which would not pay the scale of wages obtaining in prosperous seasons, so that a means of obtaining a livelihood was thus furnished to a portion of the population.

In June of this year the northern part of Grant county was swept by a cyclone, which destroyed many thousands of dollars worth of property and resulted in the death of three people and the wounding of several on Long creek. This cyclone entered Grant county from the western portion of Baker county, breaking and twisting off large trees and piling them up like straws, and crossing the mountains struck the edge of the town of Long Creek with tremendous force. Of the buildings which stood in its path not a single trace remained after the storm had passed. An old resident and his wife, Mr. and Mrs. David J. Parrish, were killed in their home, and in the demolition of Dr. and Mrs. Nichol's house their little baby, Blanche, met death. The other members of the family who were in the building at the time miraculously escaped with their lives, though injured to a greater or less extent. C. H. Lee's house was in the path of the storm. All the inmates escaped serious

injury, although one of Mrs. Lee's arms was shattered and nearly wrenched off. Several others were slightly injured. L. W. Solawn was picked up by the wind and carried over the top of Woodall's store. Fortunately he alighted safely on a pile of hay, where N. B. Oliver's barn once stood. In Long Creek eight buildings were swept away, the school house, which cost $5,000, was wrecked, the roller mills of C. L. Williams were badly damaged, making a total loss in property estimated at $25,000. Several families were left homeless and penniless. The people of the town cared tenderly for the injured and loving hands prepared the dead for their long rest. The news was at once communicated to the outside world, and a considerable amount of relief money was raised and forwarded to the sufferers.

The cyclone, after leaving Long Creek, continued its course northward, unroofing two or three dwellings before reaching the middle fork of the John Day river, at which point it seems to have spent its force. Much loss was reported on east Long creek, at the Flood Meadows, on Beach creek, and also in Fox valley, but no further loss of life.

One forward step taken in 1895 was the organization of the Inland Telephone Exchange, with a capital stock of $2,000, divided into shares of ten dollars each. Local men subscribed most of the stock, and the project was heartily supported by residents of this section generally. The purpose of the company was to erect a telephone line connecting the principal towns in Harney county with Canyon City, John Day and Prairie City, where the line would be met by one from Baker City. The organization of this company was not effected, however, and another local company was organized in February, 1896, to build a line between Canyon City and John Day. Nothing was done by this company either, but finally the Blue Mountain Telephone Company constructed the needed lines in Grant and Harney counties and later built a line to Baker City, so that now this country has excellent telephonic communication.

The following statistics made from the assessment rolls for the year 1895 by the *Grant County News* are considered of sufficient importance to merit reproduction here: Number of legal voters, 1,460; males between ten and twenty-one, 567; males under ten, 622; females over eighteen years, 818; females between ten and eighteen, 547; females under ten, 524; wool produced, 2,177,489 pounds; sheep in the county, 119,926; hogs, 2,029; horses, 9,246; mules, 53; cattle, 18,013; wheat produced, 43,575 bushels; oats, 84,999 bushels; barley and rye, 19,128 bushels; corn, 520 bushels; hay, 31,673 tons; butter and cheese, 73,993 pounds; hops, 113 pounds; potatoes, 41,185 bushels; apples, 9,806 bushels; prunes and plums, 12,000 bushels; gold, 4,040 ounces; silver, 30,500 ounces; lumber, 986,000 feet.

The spring of 1896 brought disaster to Canyon City and to many farmers in the lower John Day. Much rain fell in the valleys, while the higher ranges were covered with snow. Toward the last of May the weather turned warmer, and on the afternoon of Friday, May 29th, a heavy thunder shower occurred on Canyon creek, which was followed at once by a downpour almost equal in volume to a cloudburst. The creek was already swollen, and with the torrents pouring into it from all the hills and gulches, it soon outgrew its wonted bounds, breaking over the town levees and sweeping away outbuildings, woodpiles and debris of all kinds. By midnight Canyon City was considered in danger of destruction and the fire bell was rung vigorously to arouse those who might be sleeping in disregard of their peril. Already a large portion of the town was under water, and a change in the creek's channel might occur at any time, which would cause wholesale loss of property and perhaps of life. They went to work with a will, felling and placing timbers so as to

strengthen the frail levees and dam up the critical place. By this means the stream was held in its old channel until early morning, when the weather cooled and the waters began to subside slowly. Of course the same causes produced a like rise in the John Day, with an overflow of its lower valley, occasioning heavy losses of hay, stock and buildings to the ranchmen of that region. But notwithstanding its inauspicious opening, the year 1896 brought large crops of hay, grain and fruit, with better prices, and consequently better times.

Before 1897 had passed prosperity had fully returned to Grant county. The autumn months brought an abundant crop of wheat, which commanded a high price, so high indeed, that many a farmer in the John Day valley and elsewere was enabled to lift the mortgage and pay off all his debts. Beef, wool and mutton also brought high prices, the improvement in the sheep industry being phenomenal. Lambs which could be purchased a year earlier for seventy-five cents a head were held at more than double that figure, and sheep rose in value proportionately. The day had fairly dawned after the long night of financial depression and industry felt the stimulus of the buoyant and hopeful spirit which had taken possession of all.

Big transfers of mining property took place early in March of this year, showing that a revival in the mining industry was beginning. The Western Mining Company, for a consideration of fifty thousand dollars, gained title to some of the most valuable placer claims along the John Day river, and a Mormon company, from Salt Lake, bought up every claim that was for sale along the North Fork. Ditches dug as far back as 1862 were opened for use, and work was renewed on old properties with improved gold saving machines. An impetus was given to development in the Quartzburg district by the proposed erection of a five-ton smelter on Dixie creek.

All these movements and changes presaged

great things for 1898, and indeed that was an exceedingly prosperous year all over Oregon, though it brought some serious disasters to Grant county. Before it had fairly opened the county was thrown into a furor of excitement by remarkable mining developments in the vicinity of Canyon City. During the last week of January Isaac Guker, a well known mining man, who had previously made several small discoveries on Canyon mountain, struck a pocket consisting of decomposed quartz, through which ran innumerable golden wires. The claim was named the Great Northern. In a few days Mr. Guker took out between $700 and $800, and still he had bushels of the precious metal in sight. No costly machinery was available, but it was not needed, for wealth could be garnered quickly enough with a prospector's pan. In this primitive way fully fifteen thousand dollars' worth of gold was taken out by the first of March, the best pan containing $84.75. People flocked over the snow to the discovery, and soon scores of claims were located upon the mountain side. No event of recent years has so profoundly stirred the residents of Grant county. It looked for a while as though a rush would be made from without such as would rival that to the Canyon creek diggings at the time of their first discovery. But it takes more to boom an old camp than a new one, so the people at a distance awaited further developments and the confirmation of reports before setting out for the promising Eldorado, though the whole country was ready for a rush in case other discoveries had been made.

Describing the original find, in its issue of February 10, 1898, the *Grant County News* uses this language:

"An apparently exhaustless seam of gold lies between walls of porphyry, the richness being beyond the wildest dreams of the Klondike argonauts, and the extent of which is yet to be determined. The claim proper embraces two parallel ledges running in a northeasterly and southwesterly direction. On top of the ridge above Pine creek is a three-foot ledge dipping to the northwest. Lower down the mountain is what Mr. Guker calls the mother lode, fourteen feet wide and dipping to the southeast, or in toward the heart of the mountain, and directly toward the other ledge. A spur of copper bearing rock leaves the narrower of the two ledges and runs into the mountain southeasterly, and another spur bearing gold runs in a northwesterly direction, crossing the fourteen-foot ledge just above the place where the rich pockets have been found. A great many seams of stringers of quartz intersect the mother lode, coming in almost north. These seams Mr. Guker followed up last fall before the snow fell, and where they join the mother lode is where the rich pockets have been located. These pockets are merely depressions in the porphyry footwalls, and the gold lies in decomposed quartz and porphyry in seams and crevices, narrowing down and again widening to conform to the contour of their porphyry prison."

The deeper the Great Northern tunnel was driven the richer the ore became, and it certainly seemed that a mine had at last been discovered beside which the cave of Monte Cristo itself would appear commonplace. The mine, however, like almost all which are so wonderfully rich, did not turn out a permanent producer, but it remained the center of local interest a long time, and was much talked of for at least two years after. Smaller veins were opened in the neighborhood, but nothing equaling the original discovery in importance. It is quite probable, however, that rich and permanent mines may yet be discovered on this famous mountain of mineral.

During the year 1898 the Greenhorn mining district began to move forward after a long period of inactivity. Silver is an important product of this region, and the great decline in value of that metal caused a suspension of operations. The revival in the district was not stimulated by any hope of a rise in the market price of silver, but as a result of the return of general prosperity and confidence in the future.

It was during 1898, also, that an initial effort was made to put into operation a project which had been discussed for many years, namely, that of securing with a dredger the gold from the auriferous bed of the John Day river. Long continued and thorough prospecting had proven that very rich deposits exist in the river bed just below the mouth of Canyon creek, and that gold was also plentiful in other parts of the river's course. But it was also known that the wealth of yellow metal could not profitably be secured without a dredger, and local capitalists shrunk from the expense and risk of equipping this, to them, new, and untried kind of machinery.

In August, 1898, however, it was announced that the Urie Mining Machinery Company, of Kansas City, Missouri, would build a dredge on the John Day river, just below the town of John Day, for the purpose of mining the ground from Canyon creek's mouth to some point several miles below. The boat to be constructed was to be eighty feet long by twenty-four wide, and capable of floating at least seventy-five tons of machinery. The plant was to have a capacity of two thousand yards of gravel or sand per day of twenty-four hours. By the middle of November the dredge was completed, but notwithstanding its great size it did not prove equal to the task for which it was designed, and its use in the John Day river has been abandoned. The project was not given up, however.

The martial spirit which spread over the whole United States in a great wave during the spring of 1898 was felt in full force in Grant county, though there were no special demonstrations, owing no doubt to the fact that it was well known that few of the patriotic youth of the section would be given opportunity to show their courage at the battle's front. However, a meeting was held by those of warlike inclinations, and steps taken towards organizing a company of volunteers; but though a call was issued and a roster partially filled out, no company was ever formed, for the simple reason that there was no hope of its being accepted. Doubtless not a few of the young men of Grant county found opportunity to become identified with regiments that were accepted, but the only one whose name we have learned was T. E. Chidsey, of Company C, Idaho Volunteers.

In the early part of October, 1898, occurred the nearest approach to an Indian disturbance that has happened in many years. It created not a little excitement, though no doubt in the early 'sixties, when such things were common, it would hardly have elicited a passing notice. While hunting horses in the vicinity of his home, near Izee, John Hyde, a ranchman, was fired upon by a redskin belonging to a band of roving Columbia river Indians. He immediately informed his neighbors of the circumstance, and a posse was formed forthwith for the purpose of arresting the Indian. The redmen were overtaken the next morning, October 26th, on Deer creek, and a demand was made upon them for the surrender of the offending brave. The Indians refused, and a pitched battle followed, resulting in the killing of the redskin who had been guilty of the offense and the wounding of another. George W. Cutting, of the pursuing force, was likewise wounded so that he died the next day. The Indians fled toward the head of Murderer's creek, where they scattered, some going in an easterly direction and others toward the south fork of the John Day.

Though not so fruitful of events of general interest as its predecessor, the year 1899 was a very important one in Grant county. It witnessed unusual activity in placer and quartz mines, while the cash returns from the cattle and sheep driven out of the county were very large. Grain, hay, vegetables, fruit of all kinds and berries were copious in quantity, excellent in quality, and brought a good price.

All kinds of skilled labor found steady and lucrative employment and the demand for experienced harvest hands during the fall months was far in excess of the supply.

One of the chief animating forces of the year 1900 was the prospect of the speedy building into the John Day country of the Columbia Southern Railway. A large surveying party was in the field running lines along the John Day river, and another was working south from Prineville towards Lakeview, so that appearances justified the hope that the long-looked-for railway transportation was about to be an accomplished fact. That railway builders and promoters were fully awake to the importance of this vast, undeveloped field for railway operations is made evident from an article in the *Railway Age,* which referred most flatteringly to this region "comprising half the state's area, traversed by numerous streams, embracing great stretches of magnificent, irrigable agricultural lands, forests of the finest timber in the northwest, pasture and fruit lands, coal beds, iron and copper deposits, veins of gold and silver bearing ores, the very highest quality of lime and possibly cinnabar, tin and lead ores." It was well known that E. E. Lytle, the moving spirit of the Columbia Southern, projected a railroad from The Dalles to Ontario, through the heart of eastern Oregon, and that he had been working in the promotion of his scheme for three years past. Indeed, the road had already been built to Shaniko, seventy miles out from Biggs, the junction with the O. R. & N., and its speedy extension into the John Day valley was a thing naturally to be expected. Large corporations, however, are notoriously slow in their operations. Complications frequently arise which cause wearisome delays, and complications arose in this case, as a result of which the road has yet failed to make its appearance in the productive valley of the famed John Day, so that the inhabitants of Grant and adjoining counties still "grunt and sweat under a weary load," the load of long freight hauls over bad roads. It is understood, however, that a settlement of the Columbia Southern affairs has been effected, so that again the people may look hopefully in that direction for the solution of the transportation problem. But this railroad is not their only hope. The Nevada, California & Oregon road is headed in this direction, and there is every reason to believe that the Sumpter Valley narrow-gauge will be completed at least as far as Prairie City within the next few years, though that road was primarily designed, and has ever been operated, as an adjunct to the company's lumbering enterprises. Its extension, therefore, will be only as rapid as is necessary to conserve the interests of its proprietors in the timber wealth of this region. But it is not at all improbable that the next few years may witness considerable rivalry between the different roads for the possession and control of this greatest and richest section, yet lacking railway facilities, in the northwest, and some of the towns now greatly circumscribed in their possibilities of growth, by reason of their distance from cheap transportation, may ere long be converted into thriving railway centers.

While the cattle and wool interests of Grant county are still of transcendent importance, forces long at work for the modification of these lines of activity have recently manifested their inevitable trend so plainly that no large stockman can fail to see the handwriting on the wall. Indeed, the cattle kings have long foreseen the denouement now so rapidly taking place, and have endeavored to fortify their interests as well as possible. They have secured, by purchase, pre-emption and homestead all the creek bottoms and water rights within their power. Small settlers have been hedged in and their holdings forced on the market. Some have not hesitated to employ agents to homestead desirable tracts for them, thus securing their desiderata by a species of subornation or perjury. But thanks to the vigilance of the people who have ever closely watched with a jealous eye legislation disposing of the public domain, these men have never been able to fully accomplish their purpose. There were weak places in the fortifications built by the stockmen, through which the settler has gained an entrance, and now nothing can resist the relentless oncoming of the home-seeking hordes, the men and women who want a little ground whereon to plant their vine and fig tree, and from which to obtain a comfortable livelihood. Few places could be found more remote from ordinary courses of travel and less inviting to the superficial observer than Desolation creek, in the northern part of Grant county, yet home-seekers have been pushing into it during the present season in considerable numbers. They are settling upon and fencing the creek bottoms, thus cutting off the stockman from his water supply and conserving the pasturage of the rough hill lands contiguous to their homes for their own little flocks and herds. Other small valleys are likewise being settled and fenced from end to end, narrowing the free range for stock very materially.

But the settlement of the country has indirectly as well as directly, affected the interests of the stock king in Grant county. The Walla Walla country, which now produces its millions of bushels of wheat annually, was formerly a vast stock range. The same was true of the Pendleton country, the Palouse country, in fact, all the old settled communities of the inland empire. Stockmen have retreated before the advance of civilization and their field of operations has ever been narrowing, until now the remaining ranges are greatly overcrowded. Disputes and even feuds have already arisen and the end of the troubles between the different interests cannot be foreseen. Cattle and sheep men encroach upon the rights of the settler or the miner and the result is a damage suit. They encroach upon the supposed or understood rights of one another and disputes are the outcome, too often ending in

the use of firearms either against the unoffending animals or the men who have charge of them. All classes of residents are united in opposition to foreign sheep and cattle, that is, animals which are driven in from adjoining counties to spend the summer in Grant county and eat out its substance without paying any taxes into its exchequer. To remedy the evils and prevent trouble various measures have been introduced in Congress, among them being bills providing for the leasing of public lands to stockmen. The leasing system would undoubtedly do away with disputes by giving to some men rights which all others would be legally compelled to respect, but it has been generally considered as likely to conserve the interests of the large stockmen to the detriment of the farmer and small cattle raiser and the general welfare of the country, hence has been bitterly opposed by the masses. The conclusion of the whole matter is not far to seek. The stockman must himself become a home builder. He must reduce his herds to such numbers as can be supported by his own proper holdings and such public lands of no value for agriculture as lie adjacent to his home and can be controlled by him, through his ownership of water rights. Such land as is arable must be cultivated intensively and such domestic animals as he keeps around him must be improved so as to yield a greater profit per head than did the range stock, valuable only for their hides and flesh. Already many stock-raisers are reducing their herds and the occasion for trouble over ranges must gradually disappear, but during the interim serious complications are almost certain to arise and there is danger of a cattle war of considerable proportions.

While the march of the home builder now fairly taken up may work a hardship upon the large cattle owner, there is no doubt but that it will redound to the general good of the county, bringing in its train the school, the college, the church and all the adjuncts and refinements of an advanced civilization.

CHAPTER III.

POLITICAL.

As before stated, the act creating Grant county was approved October 14, 1864, and on the 7th of the ensuing month the new political division was duly organized. According to the county court journal, the first officers in charge of the county's affairs were: William Lair Hill, judge; Thomas H. Brents, clerk; Edward S. Penfield and William Luce, county commissioners. A provision of the creating act made it incumbent upon these to appoint other officers to fill out the quota, but this duty was not discharged during the first term, the court deeming such action unnecessary at the time.

Aside from the routine business of organization, the first official act of the county court was to refuse to P. T. Sharp a license to sell liquors in small quantities, but this action was evidently not construed as establishing a precedent, for many licenses were granted at a later date; indeed, the major portion of the first volume of the journal is filled with records of petitions for liquor licenses and the actions of the court upon them.

At a meeting held during the fall session, M. P. Berry appeared as sheriff, and on December 6, 1864, M. H. Adams was appointed treasurer; Joseph Tompkins, surveyor; D. B. Rinehart, superintendent of schools, and J. N. Bell, coroner. The first court house was a building known as "Dunker's hall," which on November 9, 1864, the commissioners voted to purchase for twelve hundred dollars. The first deed tendered by the venders was not accepted, but at a later date the building was satisfactorily transferred to the county for $1,114. It was fitted up as well as possible for court room, clerk's office, sheriff's office and jail, and served these purposes, or some of them, until 1870, when it was destroyed by fire.

On Tuesday, December 6, 1864, an order was passed by the court which shows how much more intimately associated with each other were the civil and military branches of the government in the days when the Indian was a power in the land. For the sake of the side light it throws upon the conditions obtaining in eastern Oregon at that time, we quote it in full, as follows:

"Whereas, under a requisition made by the authority of the war department of the United States, the governor of the state of Oregon did, on the 24th day of October, A. D. 1864, issue a call for a regiment of infantry to be raised by the citizens of the state; and, whereas, it appearing that certain expenses will necessarily be incurred by the recruiting officer in making voluntary enlistments to fill the quota apportioned to this county under said call, for which no provision has been made by the law of the United States or otherwise; and it further appearing that it is a matter of great importance to the citizens of this county that such quota should be thus filled.

"It is therefore ordered that an appropriation of $300 be made from the county treasury in favor of such recruiting officer in order to defray such necessary expenses, two

BLUE MOUNTAIN SPRINGS.

OLD HOUSE OF JOAQUIN MILLER, CANYON CITY.

hundred dollars to be paid immediately, the other one hundred at the expiration of one month from this date."

A military poll tax of two dollars was also imposed upon all male residents of the county within certain limits of age, and a poll tax for state and county purposes of two dollars more.

Some time in the fall of 1865, M. H. Adams, the county treasurer, died, and Fred Adams was appointed to fill the vacancy thereby created.

No abstracts of early elections can be found in the clerk's office at present, but as far as may be gleaned from the journal of county court proceedings, the officers elected in June, 1866, were: County judge, C. H. Miller, who afterward became known to fame as Joaquin Miller, the poet of the Sierras; sheriff, Thomas Howard; clerk, Thomas H. Brents; treasurer, F. C. Sels; commissioners, H. H. Hyde and A. P. Riley; school superintendent, D. B. Rinehart; county surveyor, G. W. Kniseley; coroner, G. W. Rosencrans. During the July term of court in the year 1866, J. W. Wood served as commissioner, presumably by appointment. Mr. Rinehart resigned the school superintendency in August and Eli Lester was appointed to fill the vacancy at a salary of two hundred dollars per annum.

The election in 1868 appears by the journal to have resulted as follows: Sheriff, Thomas Howard; commissioners, William Ritchie and H. M. Rice; county treasurer, H. R. Sels; county surveyor, G. A. Stanglen; county assessor, E. W. Webster; county clerk, Thomas W. Poindexter; coroner, F. C. Horsley.

From an old copy of the Baker City Bedrock Democrat, which in 1870 was the official paper of Grant county, we learn the result of the 1870 election in this county as follows: For Congress, Slater, Democrat, majority 51; for governor, Grover, Democrat, 51; for secretary of state, S. F. Chadwick, Democrat, 51; for treasurer, Fleischner, Democrat, 51; for state printer, Patterson, Democrat, 54; for dis-

27

trict judge, McArthur, Democrat, 68; for district attorney, Lasswell, Democrat, 48; for senator, Baldwin, Democrat, 23; for representatives, McCoy, Democrat, 23, and Clark, Democrat, 26; for sheriff, Thomas Howard, Democrat, 49; for clerk, Poindexter, Democrat, 2; for county commissioners, J. J. Cozart and M. D. Cameron, Democrats, 47 and 61 respectively; for assessor, J. G. King, Democrat, 40; for surveyor, Kniseley, Democrat, 52; for school superintendent, Dillinger, Democrat, 23; for coroner, Horsley, Democrat, 57; for county judge, F. C. Sels, Republican, 10; for treasurer, Philip Metschan, Republican, 17.

The total number of votes cast in Grant county in 1872 was 622. These votes were cast in the following precincts: Canyon City, Marysville, Burnt River, North Fork, Rock Creek, Middle, Granite, Elk Creek, John Day City, South Fork, Union and Olive. The result of this election was: For sheriff, William P. Gray, Republican, 326, A. M. Henderson, Democrat, 254; clerk, James Robinson, Republican, 298, William M. Wilson, Democrat, 283; county commissioners, Frank Wallace and T. J. Smith, Democrats, 292 and 285 votes respectively, and William Luce and N. S. Babcock, Republicans, 300 and 282 respectively; treasurer, C. G. Castle, Republican, 317, Joseph Messinger, Democrat, 264; assessor, Samuel French, Republican, 303, J. W. King, Democrat, 279, A. M. Henderson, 5; superintendent of schools, James A. Holmes, Republican, 306, Eli Lester, Democrat, 278; surveyor, J. M. Johnson, Republican, 299, George Kniseley, Democrat, 281.

In 1873 a special election was held in Oregon to choose a member of Congress from this state to fill a vacancy. At this election Grant county's vote was as follows: J. W. Nesmith, Democrat, 170, Hiram Smith, Republican, 129, scattering, 6. This election was held October 13th.

There were three parties in the field in 1874, the two old parties and an independent or "Hayseed" ticket. This independent ticket sprang into existence for the purpose of defeating certain rings which it was claimed existed in the other parties, and was successful in electing its nominees for county judge, county commissioner and treasurer. The vote follows: For sheriff, W. P. Gray, Republican, 301, Cal Farmer, Independent, 234, R. D. Johnson, Democrat, 76; clerk, Phil Metschan, Republican, 204, James Robinson, Democrat, 257, J. F. Cleaver, Independent, 144; county judge, M. Dustin, Independent, 276, J. W. Church, Republican, 217, Eli Lester, Democrat, 106; county commissioners, R. E. Damon, Republican, 255, E. C. Officer, Independent, 244, W. F. Settlemire, Independent, 232, W. S. Southworth, Democrat, 209, Manwaring, Republican, 172; treasurer, A. Hacheney, Independent, 293, I. J. Haguewood, Democrat, 159, D. Saltenstall, Republican, 156; assessor, S. French, Republican, 212, W. B. Davis, Independent, 204, John Motley, Democrat, 191; surveyor, George Kniseley, Democrat, 343, —————, 230; superintendent of schools, W. H. Kelley, Republican, 272, A. J. Joslin, Independent, 255; coroner, F. C. Horsley, Democrat, 260, W. F. Pruden, Democrat, 246.

Another special congressional election occurred October 25, 1875, at which Grant county voters expressed their choice as follows: Harry Warren, Republican, 176, L. F. Lane, Democrat, 147, G. M. Whitney, Independent, 32, G. W. Demick, Prohibitionist, 19.

The June election of 1876 resulted as follows: For sheriff, W. P. Gray, Republican, 256, T. J. Smith, Democrat, 242, G. W. McHaley, Independent, 97; clerk, Phil Metschan, Republican, 309, A. E. Starr, Democrat, 216, G. Gundlach. Independent, 165; commissioners, I. H. Wood, Republican, 326, J. F. Wolfinger, Republican, 268, J. H. Hamilton and T. H. Meador, Democrats, 253 and 172 respectively, F. Perry and P. Thomas, Independents, 214 and 141 respectively; treasurer, J. W. Church, Republican, 274, N. McNulty,

Democrat, 240, T. W. Poindexter, Independent, 160; assessor; S. French, Republican, 351, J. Finnigan, Democrat, 229, J. T. Mael, Independent, 112; surveyor, George Kniseley, Democrat, 293, J. Tompkins, Republican, 206; superintendent of schools, D. B. Rinehart, Republican, 354, W. A. White, Democrat, 280, A. R. McCallum, Independent, 52; coroner, F. C. Horsley, Democrat, 262, G. Sater, Republican, 370.

Two years later, or in 1878, the vote for county officers was as follows: For county judge, George B. Currey, Republican, 428, G. I. Hazeltine, Democrat, 459; sheriff, J. S. Haptonstall, Republican, 378, J. J. Wash, Democrat, 503; clerk, Phil Metschan, Republican, 426, W. S. Southworth, Democrat, 452; treasurer, J. W. Church, Republican, 427, T. W. Poindexter, Democrat, 452; commissioners, B. C. Trowbridge, Republican, 425, H. Hall, Sr., Republican, 462, W. P. Esham, Democrat, 398, J. H. Hamilton, Democrat, 492; assessor, J. B. Johnson, Republican, 448, O. P. Cresap, Democrat, 436; surveyor, James Tompkins, Republican, 420, G. W. McFarland, Democrat, 467; coroner, G. Sater, Republican, 467, F. C. Horsley, Democrat, 7, F. Marnhold, Independent, 2.

Below we give a summary of the election of 1880: For sheriff, I. J. Wash, Democrat, 500, Fred Winegar, Republican, 375; clerk, W. S. Southworth, Democrat, 436, N. Rulison, Republican, 427; treasurer, James Robinson, Democrat, 409, N. H. Boley, Republican, 460; county commissioners, J. H. Hamilton, Democrat, 466, T. H. Meador, Democrat, 408, R. Damon, Republican, 436, H. L. Thompson, Republican, 438; assessor, John Marshall, Democrat, 438, John Luce, Republican, 408; superintendent of schools, J. W. Mack, Democrat, 446, George Ridgen, Republican, ———; surveyor, W. R. McFarland, Democrat, 438, W. H. Kelly, Republican, 430; coroner, W. F. Pruden, Democrat, 390, O. M. Dodson, Republican, 479.

The vote for county officers in 1882 resulted as follows: County judge, W. A. White, Democrat, 355, Phil Metschan, Republican, 512; sheriff, O. P. Cresap, Democrat, 430, W. P. Gray, Republican, 434; clerk, M. Fitzgerald, Democrat, 374, H. C. Jarrell, Republican, 488; treasurer, W. H. Clark, Democrat, 278, A. H. Boley, Republican, 311; assessor, John Marshall, Democrat, 398, W. R. Fisk, Republican, 466; county commissioners, G. W. Shearer, Democrat, 417, C. S. Dustin, Democrat, 388, A. J. Van Horn, Republican, 467, John Laurence, Republican, 479; county school superintendent, J. W. Mack, Democrat, 454, M. N. Bonham, Republican, 419; surveyor, George Kniseley, Democrat, 378, O. Gearhart, Republican, 490; coroner, F. C. Horsley, Democrat, 436, Warren Carsner, Republican, 424. The shrievalty was awarded Cresap in a contest which followed this election.

The Democratic county convention for 1884 assembled April 24th and nominated the following ticket: For representative, J. W. Mack; sheriff, A. C. Dore; clerk, Robert Lockwood; commissioners, George McGowan and Francis Wallace; treasurer, F. C. Horsley; assessor, M. D. Cameron; superintendent of schools, J. T. Mael; surveyor, A. G. Hedges; coroner, Dr. J. W. Ashford. The Republicans met on the 19th and placed their ticket in the field, as follows: For representative, G. W. McHaley; sheriff, James W. Allen; clerk, H. C. Jarrell; treasurer, J. W. Church; commissioners, W. A. Tureman and Charles Frey; assessor, W. R. Fisk; surveyor, P. O. Gearhart; superintendent of schools, M. N. Bonham; coroner, D. J. W. Howard. Both parties expressed themselves as opposed to the erection of permanent county buildings at Canyon City or any other point until such time as the permanent site could be determined by the voters of the county.

Below is a summary of the election in Grant county: Congress, Hermann, Republican, 558, Myers, Democrat, 555; supreme judge, Flinn, Republican, 541, Thayer, Democrat, 572; circuit judge, Olmstead, Republican, 676, Walker, Democrat, 418; prosecuting attorney, Parrish, Republican, 480, Clifford, Democrat, 623; representative, McHaley, Republican, 577, Mack, Democrat, 495; county commissioners, Frey and Tureman, Republicans, 364 and 491 votes respectively, Wallace and McGowan, Democrats, 471 and 606 votes respectively; clerk, Jarrell, Republican, 681, Lockwood, Democrat, 403; sheriff, Allen, Republican, 472, Dore, Democrat, 601; assessor, Fisk, Republican, 530, Cameron, Democrat, 548; treasurer, Church, Republican, 553, Horsley, Democrat, 515; superintendent of schools, Bonham, Republican, 527, Mael, Democrat, 557; surveyor, Gearhart, Republican, 608, Hedges, Democrat, 470; coroner, Howard, Republican, 472, Ashford, Democrat, 598. At the November election, Blaine and Logan received 645 votes and Cleveland and Hendricks 679.

At the January session of the county court, in 1886, Elk Creek, Olive Creek, Monumental and Catalow precincts were abolished, certain other precincts were cut off by the formation of Malheur county, and several new precincts were organized. As reconstructed the precincts were as follows: Canyon City, Rose Bud, Harney, Burns, Camp Curry, Dunder and Blitzen Nos. 1 and 2, Alvord, John Day, Middle, Marysville, South Fork, Union, Granite, Rock Creek, Mountain Creek, Shoo Fly, Haystack, Fox, North Fork, Long Creek, Silvies and Warm Springs.

The Democrats met in county convention April 15, 1886, and made the following nominations: Senator, J. H. Hamilton; representative, M. C. Caldwell: county judge, G. I. Hazeltine; sheriff, A. C. Dore; clerk, J. T. Mael; commissioners, Thomas Meador and T. A. McKinnon; treasurer, O. P. Cresap; superintendent of schools, H. F. Dodson; assessor, M. D. Cameron; surveyor, R. E. Williams;

coroner, F. C. Horsley. Four days later the Republican convention named their standard bearers, as follows: Senator, F. C. Sels; representative, J. B. Johnson; judge, N. R. Maxcy; sheriff, W. Y. King; clerk, G. W. Dart; commissioners, S. J. Gilliam and Max Ramsby; treasurer, Edwin Hall; assessor, W. R. Fisk; superintendent of schools, A. Ladd; surveyor, J. H. Neal; coroner, Dr. Rinearson.

The official vote follows: Governor, Pennoyer, Democrat, 863, Cornelius, Republican, 715, Houston, Prohibitionist, 28; congressman, Hermann, Republican, 795, Butler, Democrat, 794, Miller, Prohibitionist, 15; secretary of state, McBride, Republican, 744, Gibbon, Democrat, 844, Kinney, Prohibitionist, 17; state treasurer, Marston, Republican, 743, Webb, Democrat, 832, Long, Prohibitionist, 19; state printer, Baker, Republican, 752, Nickell, Democrat, 828, Shepard, Prohibitionist, 19; superintendent of public instruction, McElroy, Republican, 769, Bell, Independent Democrat, 196, Lyman, Prohibitionist, 15, Davis, Democrat, 606; supreme judge, Waldo, Republican, 768, Strahan, Democrat, 829; circuit judge, Olmstead, Republican, 821, Ison, Democrat, 752, Balleray, Prohibitionist, 1; prosecuting attorney, Holman, Republican, 628, Clifford, Democrat, 940; senator, Hamilton, Democrat, 802, Sels, Republican, 692; representative, Johnson, Republican, 836, Caldwell, Democrat, 678; county commissioners, Gilliam and Ramsby, Republicans 658 and 681 respectively, Meador and McKinnon, Democrats, 903 and 770-respectively; county judge, Hazeltine, Democrat, 746, Maxcy, Republican, 768; sheriff, King, Republican, 673, Dore, Democrat, 839; clerk, Mael, Democrat, 846, Dart, Republican, 664; treasurer, Hall, Republican, 764, Cresap, Democrat, 743; superintendent of schools, Dodson, Democrat, 841, Ladd, Republican, 670; assessor, Fisk, Republican, 680, Cameron, Democrat, 837; surveyor,

Neal, Republican, 771, Williams, Democrat, 743; coroner, Horsley, Democrat, 805, Rinearson, Republican, 685.

The issues of the election of 1888 were mainly national and resulted in a sweeping victory for the Republicans in Grant county. The two parties placed tickets in the field as follows:

Democrats—Representative, J. F. Morrison; sheriff, J. I. Haguewood; clerk, J. T. Mael; assessor, T. J. Cozad; treasurer, O. P. Cresap; superintendent of schools, J. D. Daly; commissioners, H. H. Davis and T. A. McKinnon; surveyor, George Kniseley; coroner, M. Dustin.

Republicans—Representative, G. W. Gilham; sheriff, W. P. Gray; clerk, John W. Sayer; assessor, Charles Timms; treasurer, N. H. Boley; superintendent of schools, E. Hayes; commissioners, J. H. McHaley and E. Stewart; surveyor, J. H. Neal; coroner, S. Orr.

The result follows: Congressman, Hermann, Republican, 1,116, Gearin, Democrat, 818; supreme judge, Lord, Republican, 1,035, Burnett, Democrat, 904; circuit judge, Fee, Republican, 1,014, Ramsey, Democrat, 906; district attorney, Rand, Republican, 1,018, Crawford, Democrat, 904; representative, Gilham, Republican, 975, Morrison, Democrat, 897; sheriff, Gray, Republican, 997, Haguewood, Democrat, 860; clerk, Sayer, Republican, 767, Mael, Democrat, 1,089; assessor, Timms, Republican, 1,051, Cozad, Democrat, 824; treasurer, Boley, Republican, 982, Cresap, Democrat, 889; superintendent of schools, Hayes, Republican, 939, Daly, Democrat, 931; commissioners, McHaley and Stewart, Republicans, 1,076 and 854 votes respectively, McKinnon and Davis, Democrats, 828 and 971 votes respectively; surveyor, Neal, Republican, 1026, Kniseley, Democrat, 820; coroner, Orr, Republican, 991, Dustin, Democrat, 864. At the national election in November Harrison received 912 votes and Cleveland 892. There were 18 votes cast for the Prohibition candidate.

The Republican county convention in 1890 met April 8th and chose their nominees as follows: For sheriff, John Austin; for clerk, J. W. Waterman; county judge, N. R. Maxcy; for treasurer, N. H. Boley; for assessor, Charles Timms; for superintendent of public schools, M. N. Bonham; for county commissioner, L. D. Palmer; for surveyor, J. M. Fisk; and for coroner, Dr. A. J. Thebido. On the 17th the Democratic convention assembled and nominated: For sheriff, O. P. Cresap; for county judge, G. I. Hazeltine; for clerk, George Shearer; for assessor, James Wallace; for superintendent of the public schools, P. W. McRoberts; for commissioner, W. H. Johnson; for surveyor, J. W. Mack; for coroner, W. A. Fisher.

As in 1888, the campaign was waged on national issues, principal among which was the tariff question. A summary of the votes cast follows: Congressman, Hermann, Republican, 735, Miller, Democrat, 634; governor, Thompson, Republican, 664, Pennoyer, Democrat, 715; secretary of state, McBride, Republican, 720, Townsend, Democrat, 653; state treasurer, Metschan, Republican, 814, Webb, Democrat, 554; supreme judge, Bean, Republican, 717, Bonham, Democrat, 656; superintendent of public instruction, McElroy, Republican, 716, LeRoy, Democrat, 661; state printer, Baker, Republican, 722, O'Brien, Democrat, 660; circuit judge, Eakin, Republican, 586, Clifford, Democrat, 797; district attorney, Rand, Republican, 684, Hyde, Democrat, 677; joint senator, McHaley, Republican, 784, Blackman, Democrat, 574; joint representative, Cardwell, Republican, 637, Dustin, Democrat, 740; county judge, Hazeltine, Democrat, 719, Maxcy, Republican, 613; commissioner, Palmer, Republican, 639, Johnson, Democrat, 698; sheriff, Austin, Republican, 580, Cresap, Democrat, 749; clerk, Waterman, Republican, 664, Shearer, Democrat, 670; treasurer, N. H. Boley, Republican, 762; superintendent of schools, Bonham, Republican, 681, McRoberts, Democrat, 654; assessor, Timms, Republican, 702, Wallace, Democrat, 639; surveyor, Fisk, Republican, 649, Mack, Democrat, 657; coroner, Thebido, Republican, 717, Fisher, Democrat, 603. Henry Blackman was elected joint senator from Morrow, Grant and Harney counties and C. S. Dustin joint representative from Grant and Harney counties.

The Republicans met the latter part of March, 1892, and nominated the following ticket: Sheriff, J. D. Combs; clerk, Marshall Howell; treasurer, N. H. Boley; assessor, Carl N. Wagner; superintendent of schools, M. N. Bonham; surveyor, Charles G. Caspary; coroner, Daniel Morrow; commissioner, Tunis Swick. At the district convention C. A. Richardson received the nomination for joint representative. The Democratic convention was held April 12th, and made the following nominations: Sheriff, O. P. Cresap; clerk, George Shearer; treasurer, Bailey O. Dustin; assessor, Charles H. Utley; superintendent of schools, Thomas Gurnee; commissioner, S. J. Hunt; surveyor, J. W. Mack; coroner, William Wilson. M. R. Biggs was nominated as joint representative. Simultaneously with the organization of the People's party in other portions of Oregon, a county organization was formed here. Friends of the movement met at Mt. Vernon April 21st and adopted the following platform:

"Resolved, That we, as the People's party of Grant county, Oregon, demand the building of bridges over streams on the main and general thoroughfares of the county; we demand that all values bear equal burden of taxation; that our district judges be requested to dispatch business in the interest of the taxpayers instead of prolonging it in the interest of the script ring; that we demand of our county board that a twenty-mill tax levy be a maximum rate and that all needless expense be lopped off."

The following ticket was then nominated: For sheriff, Charles Ballance; for clerk, W. H. Short; for treasurer, John Segerdahl; for assessor, A. A. Dean; for superintendent of schools, George Gilbert; for commissioner, E. C. Officer; and for surveyor, Loren Seward. Mell Fenwick was declared to be the party's choice for joint representative.

The official returns were: Congressman, Bright, Prohibitionist, 13, Ellis, Republican, 593, Luce, Populist, 363, Slater, Democrat, 387; supreme judge, Bennett, Democrat, 496, Moore, Republican, 588, Walker, Populist, 254, Welch, Prohibitionist, 20; attorney general, Chamberlain, Democrat, 596, Webster, Republican, 710; circuit judge, Clifford, Democrat, 710, Kelly, Republican, 413, Green, Populist, 222; prosecuting attorney, Finn, Republican, 522, Hyde, Democrat, 567, Griffin, Populist, 259; member state board of equalization, Hunter, Democrat, 446, Morfitt, Republican, 831; joint representative, Richardson, Republican, 532, Biggs, Democrat, 457, Fenwick, Populist, 352; sheriff, Combs, Republican, 544, Cresap, Democrat, 509, Ballance, Populist, 294; clerk, Shearer, Democrat, 611, Howell, Republican, 499, Short, Populist, 237; treasurer, Boley, Republican, 573, Dustin, Democrat, 565, Segerdahl, Populist, 213; assessor, Wagner, Republican, 613, Utley, Democrat, 448, Dean, Populist, 276; superintendent of public schools, Bonham, Republican, 748, Gurnee, Democrat, 384, Gilbert, Populist, 204; commissioner, Hunt, Democrat, 331, Swick, Republican, 623, Officer, Populist, 368; surveyor, Caspary, Republican, 588, Mack, Democrat, 491, Seward, Populist, 244; coroner, Morrow, Republican, 705, Hodson, Populist, 472. Richardson was elected joint representative by a majority of 28, but resigned shortly afterward, necessitating a special election in November. This special election resulted in the election of A. W. Gowan by the following vote: Gowan, Republican, 478, W. C. Byrd, Democrat, 439, Mell Fenwick, Populist, 288.

The vote on national candidates was: Cleveland, 437, Harrison, 573, Populist candidate, 283, Prohibition candidate, 13.

The political campaign of 1894 in Grant county was marked by a complete and overwhelming Republican victory. The agitation of the tariff question had aroused the wool growers of this region and the result on election day showed that they had taken an active part in the campaign. The Republicans convened April 3d and nominated the following: For sheriff, J. D. Combs; county judge, N. H, Boley; clerk, J. A. Powell; treasurer, M. E. Stansell; assessor, Robert Deardorff; superintendent of schools, M. N. Bonham; commissioner, P. Thomas; surveyor, Clarence Johnson; coroner, Frank White. The district convention nominated Orin L. Patterson for joint representative, and A. W. Gowan for joint senator. The Democratic convention nominated G. I. Hazeltine for county judge; Patsy Daly for sheriff; F. P. Horsley for clerk; O. P. Cresap for treasurer; J. A. Taylor for assessor; W. F. Loder for superintendent of schools; Samuel Capenter for commissioner; and J. W. Mack for surveyor. F. Kellogg was nominated for joint senator and J. A. Steach for joint representative. The People's party met at Mt. Vernon the same day that the Democratic convention assembled at Canyon City, and chose their candidates as follows: County judge, W. H. Gates; sheriff, Newton Livingston; clerk, J. B. Eddington; treasurer, John Segerdahl; assessor, Joseph Putnam; commissioner, Terry Kimzey; superintendent of schools, Thomas Gurnee; surveyor, C. G. Caspary; coroner, J. F. Hodson. C. S. Dustin was nominated for joint representative and W. H. Gilbert for joint senator.

The official vote was as follows: Governor, Lord, Republican, 763, Pierce, Populist, 416, Galloway, Democrat, 336, Kennedy, Prohibitionist, 21; secretary of state, Kincaid, Republican, 762, Wakefield, Populist, 394; Nickell, Democrat, 355, McKercher, Prohibitionist, 16; state treasurer, Metschan, Republican, 862, Caldwell, Populist, 346, Davidson, Democrat, 285, Richardson, Prohibitionist, 27; supreme judge, Wolverton, Republican, 769, Bennett, Democrat, 391, Boise, Populist, 351, Hackleman, Prohibitionist, 18; attorney general, Idleman, Republican, 733, Olmstead, Populist, 408, Holmes, Democrat, 363, Bright, Prohibitionist, 10; superintendent of public instruction, Irwin, Republican, 740, Reid, Democrat, 386, Jory, Populist, 363, Hartford, Prohibitionist, 34; state printer, Leeds, Republican, 768, Orton, Populist, 374, O'Brien, Democrat, 362, McKibben, Prohibitionist, 15; congressman, Ellis, Republican, 784, Raley, Democrat, 390, Waldrop, Populist, 353, Miller, Prohibitionist, 8; circuit judge, Fee, Republican, 1,062, Hudson, Populist, 375; prosecuting attorney, Rand, Republican, 809, Parsons, Populist, 353, Carroll, Democrat, 339; joint senator, Gowan, Republican, 722, Kellogg, Democrat, 392, Gilbert, Populist, 372; joint representative, Patterson, Republican, 758, Dustin, Populist, 451, Steach, Democrat, 282; county judge. Boley, Republican, 643, Hazeltine, Democrat, 506, Gates, Populist, 341; sheriff, Combs, Republican, 681, Livingston, Populist, 446, Daly, Democrat, 370; clerk, Powell, Republican, 752, Horsley, Democrat, 419. Eddington, Populist, 319, assessor, Deardorff. Republican, 749, Taylor, Democrat, 403, Putnam, Populist, 338; treasurer, Stansell, Republican, 619, Cresap, Democrat, 507, Segerdahl, Populist, 350; superintendent of schools, Bonham, Republican, 725, Loder, Democrat, 505, Gurnee, Populist, 252; commissioner, Thomas, Republican, 674, Carpenter, Democrat, 455, Kimzey, Populist, 357; surveyor, Johnson, Republican, 732, Mack, Democrat, 377, Caspary, Populist, 367; coroner, White, Republican, 842, Hodson, Populist, 511. The Republican candidates for joint senator and joint representative were both elected.

The campaign of 1896 raged fully as fierce-

ly in Grant county as in other parts of eastern Oregon, though, in strong contrast to other eastern Oregon counties, Grant county went partly Republican. One reason advanced for this in a mining community is that the large stock interests in this section were favorable to a high protective tariff, and consequently gave more attention to this phase of the campaign than to the monetary side. The Populists were first in the field with their ticket, holding their convention March 5th, with the following result: For sheriff, Newton Livingston; clerk, Lincoln D. Luce; commissioner, Charles Ballance; treasurer, John Segerdahl; assessor, William Collins; superintendent of schools, W. L. O'Hara; surveyor, C. G. Caspary; coroner, Joseph F. Hodson. C. S. Dustin was nominated for joint representative. The Republican convention was held at Canyon City March 28th. Its nominees were as follows: Sheriff, J. B. Johnson; clerk, J. A. Powell; treasurer, N. R. Maxcy; assessor, J. D. Titus; superintendent of schools, A. R. Cobb; commissioner, Al. Porter; surveyor, W. F. White; coroner, Daniel Morrow. For joint representative E. Hall was nominated. Following is the ticket nominated by the Democratic county convention held at Canyon City, April 15th: For sheriff, W. B. Cowne; for clerk, W. A. May; for treasurer, G. I. Hazeltine; for assessor, Scott Hyde; for commissioner, Sol Taylor; for superintendent of county schools, R. D. Williams; for surveyor, George Kniseley; and for coroner, J. W. Greenwell. The nomination for joint representative was left vacant.

The vote in Grant county was as follows: For supreme judge, Bean, Republican, 722, Gaston, Populist, 417, Burnett, Democrat, 361; for congressman, Ellis, Republican, 591, Quinn, Populist, 414, Bennett, Democrat, 339, Northrup, Independent, 163, McKercher, Prohibitionist, 14; district attorney, Dustin, Independent, 648, Parrish, Republican, 514, Buse, Independent Populist, 168, Sweek, Democrat,

138; member of state board of equalization, Holland, Republican, 763, Pierce, Populist, 540; joint representative, Dustin, Populist, 740, Hall, Republican, 641; sheriff, Livingston, Populist, 670, Johnson, Republican, 580, Cowne, Democrat, 251; clerk, Powell, Republican, 640, May, Democrat, 539, Luce, Populist, 319; treasurer, Hazeltine, Democrat, 598, Maxcy, Republican, 519, Segerdahl, Populist, 356; assessor, Titus, Republican, 666, Hyde, Democrat, 453, Collins, Populist, 351; superintendent of schools, Williams, Democrat, 657, Cobbs, Republican, 587, O'Hara, Populist, 206: commissioner, Taylor, Democrat, 432, Ballance, Populist, 391, Porter, Republican, 349, Rader, Independent, 295; surveyor, White, Republican, 600, Kniseley, Democrat, 424, Caspary, Populist, 374; coroner, Morrow, Republican, 707, Hodson, Populist, 398, Greenwell, Democrat, 316. Dustin was elected joint representative. Bryan carried the county by a majority of 129 over McKinley, in November, he receiving 867 votes, McKinley 738, and other candidates 42.

In 1898 the Democrats and Populists fused, nominating the following ticket at a joint county convention held at John Day April 23d: County judge, C. S. Dustin; sheriff, Newton Livingston; commissioner, E. E. Thornburg, silver Republican; assessor, J. T. Berry; treasurer, T. F. Hall; superintendent of schools, R. D. Williams; surveyor, C. G. Caspary; coroner, J. P. Hodson. At the district convention J. W. Morrow was nominated for joint senator; G. D. Hagey for joint representative from Grant and Harney counties; M. D. Clifford for circuit judge of the newly created Ninth judicial district; and E. Hicks as prosecuting attorney for the district.

The Republicans met at Canyon City March 29th and selected their nominees as follows: Sheriff, J. D. Combs; clerk, R. R. McHaley; county judge, John A. Laycock; treasurer, Zach Martin; assessor, J. D. Titus; superintendent of schools, J. F. Slaughter;

commissioner, Daniel Dimmick; surveyor, W. F. White; coroner, W. H. Kelly. The district nominations were as follows: For joint senator, A. W. Gowan; for joint representative, R. N. Donnelly; for circuit judge, C. W. Parrish; for prosecuting attorney, William Miller.

The official vote cast was as follows: Governor, Geer, Republican, 973, King, Fusionist, 678, Luce, Populist, 112, Clinton, Prohibitionist, 25; secretary of state, Dunbar, Republican, 961, Kincaid, Fusionist, 704, Wakefield, Populist, 85, Davis, Prohibitionist, 27; state treasurer, Moore, Republican,.959, Booth, Fusionist, 651, Sears, Populist, 115, Votaw, Prohibitionist, 30; superintendent of public instruction, Ackerman, Republican, 934, Lyman, Fusionist, 644, Hosmer, Populist, 100, Emerick, Prohibitionist, 30; state printer, Leeds, Republican, 923, Fitch, Fusionist, 615, Grace, Populist, 136, McDaniel, Prohibitionist, 25; supreme judge, Moore, Republican, 932, Ramsey, Fusionist, 722, Hackleman, Prohibitionist, 36; attorney general, Blackburn, Republican, 909, Story, Fusionist, 705, Bright, Prohibitionist, 45; Congress, Moody, Republican, 908, Donaldson, Fusionist, 668, Courtney, Populist, 96, Ingalls, Prohibitionist, 45; circuit judge, Clifford, Fusionist, 771, Parrish, Republican, 752, Williams, Independent, 179; district attorney, Miller, Republican, 881, Hicks, Fusionist, 784; member state board of equalization, Hall, Independent-Republican, 937, Gregg, Fusionist, 675; joint senator, Gowan, Republican, 910, Morrow, Fusionist, 754; joint representative, Donnelly, Republican, 944, Hagey, Fusionist, 679; sheriff, Livingston, Fusionist, 921, Combs, Republican, 796; clerk, McHaley, Republican, 884; May, Fusionist, 771; county judge, Laycock, Republican, 993, Dustin, Fusionist, 666; treasurer, Martin, Republican, 865, Hall, Fusionist, 764; assessor, Titus, Republican, 954, Berry, Fusionist, 685; superintendent of schools, Williams, Fusionist, 865, Slaughter,

Republican, 771; commissioner, Dimmick, Republican, 868, Thornburg, Fusionist, 470, Rader, Independent, 283; surveyor, White, Republican, 921, Caspary, Fusionist, 652; coroner, Kelly, Republican, 961, Hodson, Fusionist, 616. Clifford, the Democratic candidate, was elected circuit judge, and Miller, the Republican candidate, received a majority of the votes cast for district attorney. Morrow and Donnelly were elected joint senator and joint representative, respectively.

The Republican county convention met March 24th, 1900, placing their ticket in the field as follows: For sheriff, D. P. King; for clerk, R. R. McHaley; treasurer, Z. J. Martin; commissioner, M. W. Bailey; assessor, Peter Kuhl; superintendent of schools, W. N. Bonham; surveyor, W. F. White; coroner, Dan Morrow. The district convention placed William Miller in nomination for a second term as district attorney, and W. W. Steiwer was nominated for joint senator from Gilliam, Grant, Sherman, Wasco and Wheeler counties. For these same counties three candidates for the post of joint representative were named, George Cattanach, of Grant, George A. Barrett, also of Grant, and George Miller, of Arlington. In the county platform adopted especial stress was laid on Grant county's deplorable financial condition.

The Democrats did not convene until April 16th. The county's financial condition was referred to in the platform adopted, and attention was called to the evils existing in the offices of those to whom is entrusted the assessing and collecting of taxes. E. P. Laurance was nominated for sheriff; William Byram for clerk; W. H. Bowman for commissioner; T. M. Ray for assessor; H. C. Mack for superintendent of schools; and George Kniseley for surveyor. For joint senator V. G. Cozad was nominated, and W. J. Edwards, of Gilliam, T. R. Coon, of Wasco, and Robert Misener were chosen as the party's nominees for joint

representatives. William R. King received the nomination for district attorney.

Official summary: Supreme judge, Charles E. Wolverton, Republican, 779, Thomas G. Greene, Democrat, 550, C. J. Bright, Prohibitionist, 77; state dairy and food commissioner, J. W. Bailey, Republican, 633, W. Schulmerich, Democrat-Populist, 400, P. L. Kenady, Prohibitionist, 54; congressman, Malcolm A. Moody, Republican, 829, William Smith, Democrat-Populist, 498, J. E. Simmons, Independent Democrat, 177, Leslie Butler, Prohibitionist, 48; district attorney, William Miller, Republican, 869, William R. King, Democrat-Populist, 702; joint senator, V. G. Cozad, Democrat, 758, W. W. Steiwer, Republican, 753; joint representatives, George J. Barrett, George H. Cattanach and George Miller, Republicans, 866, 766 and 742 votes, respectively, T. R. Coon, W. J. Edwards and Robert Misener, Democrat-Populists, 538, 525 and 508 votes, respectively; sheriff, King, Republican, 764, Laurance, Democrat, 787; clerk, McHaley, Republican, 939, Byram, Democrat, 643; treasurer, Martin, Republican, 1,256; commissioner, Bailey, Republican, 698, Bowman, Democrat, 625, Barnard, Populist, 195; assessor, Ray, Democrat, 764, Kuhl, Republican, 749; superintendent of schools, Mack, Democrat, 945, Bonham, Republican, 596; surveyor, White, Republican, 641, Kniseley, Democrat, 569, Caspary, Independent, 305; coroner, Morrow, Republican, 1,163. The Republican candidates for joint representatives and joint senator and for prosecuting attorney were elected. At the November election there were 914 votes cast for McKinley, 613 for Bryan, 15 for the Prohibitionist candidate, 26 for the Social Democratic nominee and 6 for the People's party candidate.

The campaign of 1902 is still fresh in the minds of our readers, so we need not dwell on the issues presented. Suffice it is to say that they were mainly along national lines, though the parties took opposite sides on the question of establishing a high school in this county. The Republican convention was held March 26th, and resulted as follows: County judge, R. R. McHaley; sheriff, J. D. Combs; clerk, G. W. Dart; treasurer, Z. J. Martin; assessor, A. O. Mosier; surveyor, W. F. White; commissioners, James A. Pope and P. P. Kilbourne; coroner, D. W. Morrow. The district convention nominated C. P. Johnson, of Grant, W. F. Danneman, of Gilliam,

and R. S. Ginn, of Sherman county, for joint representatives. The Democratic convention assembled April 10th and placed the following in nomination: County judge, Sol Taylor; sheriff, E. P. Laurance; clerk, Neil Niven; assessor, Mack Ray; commissioners, P. Noyer and Walter Brown; surveyor, William Reese; coroner, J. W. Ashford. E. G. Stevenson, of Grant, E. P. Weir, of Gilliam, and P. G. Hanson, of Wasco, were nominated for joint representatives.

CHAPTER IV.

SCHOOLS.

In no way, perhaps, is America's progressiveness better shown than by its superior school system. Europe, it is true, boasts older halls of learning and until recent times was the acknowledged center of the educational world, but as "the star of empire westward takes its way," so it has affected the educational orbit and drawn its center toward the Occident until today our universities and colleges rank with those of Europe and our public school system is the peer if not the superior of any. Our excellent school system has not sprung up in an instant, however; rather it has been the growth of three of the world's most enlightened centuries, and into its development has been inculcated the profound learning and experience of Europe, coupled with the energy and genius of America.

The first step in this great educational system is the little log schoolhouse, the old district school so dear to the heart of the American schoolboy, which has in many instances laid the foundation for some of the world's most brilliant statesmen, profoundest scholars

and greatest merchant princes. Within its rough walls that sturdy spirit of independence and liberty was fostered; its crude pine tables and benches were an incentive to better things and awoke a spirit of ambition that would not down; and the rudimentary principles of education expounded by the zealous and sincere, if not always profound, schoolmaster, added the finishing touches to the mould in which has been cast the American citizen—the leader of the race. Hardly does the courageous pioneer penetrate the forests primeval and erect a home before the district schoolhouse makes its appearance and the education of the young is begun. Everywhere the schoolhouse has followed closely upon the heels of emigrant and settlement.

This being true, it is not strange that the schoolhouse early made its appearance among the pioneer gold seekers of Grant county. The first comers, being adventurers without families, there was no need of schools, consequently nothing was done in this direction the first year. The following summer, 1863, the first immigrant trains arrived from California, forming the nucleus of a permanent settlement. The county was organized at the session of the legislature in 1864, and in December of that year D. B. Rhinehart was appointed superintendent of county schools by the county court. At that time Grant county was considerably larger than the state of Maryland.

His first act was to organize the county into three school districts, which he did December 15th, as follows: No. 1, Canon City (as it was then spelled) ; No. 2, Marysville; No. 3, John Day. On January 2, 1865, district No. 4, or Union district, was organized at the request of several petitioners. A. J. Adams, Joseph Gilbert, A. R. McCallum, directors, and Noble A. Trowbridge, clerk, comprised the first school officers of district No. 1; Joseph Gillenwater, Sr., Samuel Larrison, Joseph Harer, directors, and J. B. Spaulding, clerk, constituted the board of district No. 2; and that of district No. 3 was composed of A. G. Mulkey, N. W. Fiske, Wilson Harer, directors, and W. F. Vinegard, clerk. The records, which are unusually well preserved, show that out of ninety-three children of school age, fifteen boys and fourteen girls attended the first school in district No. 1, which was held in a small rented building. The only other school maintained the first year was at Marysville, twenty-one pupils attending. B. E. Hunt and Miss Elizabeth E. Chope, who were granted teacher's certificates December 16, 1864, have the distinction of being the first to preside over Grant county school rooms, Mr. Hunt teaching at Canon City, and Miss Chope at Marysville. For the sake of recalling pleasant memories (or perhaps unpleasant, as the case may be) to those who attended the first schools in Grant county, we reproduce a list of the principal text books used: McGuffey's series of readers, Thompson, Ray and Colburn's arithmetic, Smith's grammar, Webster's speller and dictionary, Monteith's geography, Cornell's geography, Cornell's outline maps, Sander's primer, Davies' arithmetic, Sander's spellers and Willard's history of the United States.

In his first annual report to the state superintendent, Mr. Rhinehart says, regarding school funds:

"Our school fund, as your Honor may perceive, is very limited, not being sufficient to support one fashionable Pedant for a term of three months in this isolated and expensive section. Canon City district very wisely made an effort to levy a tax for school purposes, but the meeting was annoyed so much by the rabble that it was found impossible even to organize, and consequently adjourned *sine die*. In consideration of the great necessity of upholding our common schools, and our bounden duty to the rising generation, we respectfully submit the following suggestion:

"An amendment to section 7 of an act relating to common schools, substituting five mills on a dollar, or one-half of one per cent, instead of two mills on a dollar, as it now stands. Our object in offering the above suggestion is for the increase of school funds without resorting to district tax, which is next to an impossibility in a mining community. Merchants and miners are almost unanimously opposed to this tax, and will vote it down whenever occasion offers. We hold that it is more essential, financially and morally, to tax the people for the support of the common schools than it is for the support of state prisons and county jails."

This extract gives us a partial insight into the difficulties with which the early supporters of education had to contend and this same special difficulty was not peculiar to this section. There is an element in every community which is so grasping and selfish that it cannot bear to see money expended unless direct personal benefit is received by them, and this class is especially large in a mining district, as so great a proportion are unmarried men with but one object—gold. The public lands were yet unsurveyed, and remained in this condition until

1870, thus depriving the schools of considerable money that should have been derived from the sale of school sections. The state in no way assisted in their maintenance, and the path to knowledge was indeed rocky and uncertain. But one term, lasting three months, was held in Canon City and Marysville, owing to the lack of funds, the two other districts failing even to establish schools the first year. The total amount expended in district No. 1 was $180.50, and in district No. 2, $97.34. The more progressive element of the population triumphed, however, and the schools were maintained and their number increased.

In 1866 Elk Creek district was organized as district No. 5, and schools were conducted at Canon City, Marysville, Union and a summer school at John Day. Owing to an unusually large amount of money received in fines this year, a seven months' school was maintained at Canon City and one quarter each at Union and Marysville. That we may still better understand conditions as they existed then, we again quote from Superintendent Rhinehart's report as follows:

"Union school district is composed of agriculturists, some of them living remote from the school room, in the upper portion of John Day valley, exposed to hostile bands of prowling savages, who would ruthlessly murder or carry into captivity any children who wander from parental protection, on their way either to or from school. Even while at home families are in jeopardy of their lives and property, and many of them contemplate leaving as soon as practicable unless protection is speedily rendered by the proper authorities. Under the above circumstances we cannot reasonably expect a community to be pecuniarily, much less educationally, prosperous. The district has had, however, a three months' winter school, with an average attendance of 13¼. Her citizens seem anxious to continue school, even at their own expense, but on account of the above considerations deem it unsafe at present."

Of school rooms he says: "Our school rooms are too small; not appropriately supplied with furniture and destitute of globes, maps, objects and libraries; all of which are indispensable to a high grade of instruction. They are well ventilated, however, and as comfortable as circumstances will permit."

Of finances he writes: "Our funds are still inadequate for the support of our public schools, although much larger than last year. Canon City district received, per apportionment, $321.56. 3— coin and $684.89 legal tender, which, with an excess of last year, constituted a fund sufficient to support a public school of eight months. Marysville school district received $117.64, 4— coin and $250.59 legal tender. John Day district, No. 3, received, as per apportionment, $164.71 coin, and $350.79 legal tender, being an amount sufficient to pay teacher's salary, with a balance to the credit of the district. Union district is still in arrears to its teacher, the amount apportioned being $86.27, 3— coin and $183.75, legal tender. The total amount of money apportioned to the district was $690.19 coin and $1,470 legal tender. Of the above amount only $685.19 was received from county taxes, the balance being from fines, etc."

"Our school districts," he says further along, "are composed of people from different nations, the children being unequal in intellect, temperament and domestic education; yet I have never witnessed as much unanimity existing between those directly interested in our schools as I have witnessed in Grant county. Our teachers are gentlemen of high moral worth and unconditionally loyal to the government of the United States. It requires no stretch of conscience with them to take the oath of qualification for their responsible positions."

At this time the teachers were: District No. 1, B. E. Hunt and A. B. Power; district No. 2, D. B. Rhinehart; district No. 3, N. A. Trowbridge; district No. 4, A. G. Mulkey. There were fifty-nine scholars in attendance in the first district; twenty-one in the second; nineteen in the third; and twenty-four in the fourth. During the winter of 1867 a private school was taught on Elk creek by W. S. Southworth.

Conditions did not improve during the interim between the second and third annual reports. School funds were low, in fact so low that but one quarter was taught in districts Nos. 1, 2, and 3, and no school at all was maintained in the two other districts. The failure of the government to survey the public lands created a serious deficiency in school funds. Says Eli Lester, superintendent at this time, 1868: "The insecurity of life and property in this county from Indian depredations has been so great that many families have— and much property has been—removed to safer localities."

The superintendent's report for the year ending March 1, 1869, shows only $1,140.44 expended in the maintenance of the county's schools, $631.22 in coin and $509.22 in legal tender. Schools were taught in districts Nos. 1, 2, 3 and 4, with respective attendances as follows: Forty-six, fourteen, forty-eight and forty-six pupils. District No. 1 was the only district in which more than one term was taught, two quarters being held in Canyon City. There was no school maintained at Elk creek this year. Barely enough money was secured to support even these small schools, and the state had thus far failed to aid in their support. Only by private subscriptions and special entertainments could the teachers be paid and progress was impossible.

Between 1870 and 1872 districts No. 6, Mt. Vernon, No. 7, Dayville, No. 8, North Fork, No. 9, Strawberry, and No. 10, Meadows, were created. By 1877 there were fourteen districts organized and reporting, and 379 pupils enrolled out of 678 children of school age. Thirteen women were employed as teachers, and one man, holding five first-

grade and seven second-grade certificates among them. The value of school buildings, furniture, etc., was estimated at $7,100, and $6,485.81 is given as the cost of conducting the schools during the previous year, 1871-72. Sixty-two pupils were enrolled in private schools.

A letter written to Hon. L. J. Powell, state superintendent of public instruction, by J. W. Mack, superintendent of the county schools in 1878, says:

"Hon. L. J. Powell,

"Salem, Oregon.

"Sir: It is a matter of regret that the county has made such a poor showing in educational matters for the past year. Some of our districts were partially or wholly burned out by Indians, and the people are in such a state of expectation and trepidation that nearly all schools were broken up. In Harney valley every dwelling and schoolhouse was burned to the ground. In Blitzen district, Happy valley, every house but the school house was destroyed. Other districts suffered, but not so severely. For months nearly all the families in the county were huddled together in forts, submitting to many inconveniences and neglect of crops, stock and school in the struggle for self-preservation. If the excitement cooled down so that some of the bolder went home, fresh news of approaching hostilities would send them crowding back again, and in Canyon City, the county seat, nearly, if not all, the families spent their nights in the tunnels for some time, and occasionally went for them in a rush during the day.

"Many of the districts are newly organized and have as yet no schools. In consideration of all the circumstances and the scattered condition of our people, and the excitement and suffering of the past year, I am astonished that the schools have done as well as they have.

"If the 'noble red man' will behave himself during the coming summer and let his white brother repose in peace, this county will make a much better report the coming year.

"J. W. MACK,
"Superintendent of the Public Schools of Grant County."

In 1885 the fourteen districts had grown to thirty-four, of which, however, only twenty-seven maintained schools. According to the school census, there were 1,558 children between the ages of four and twenty-one. The annual report for the year 1890 was encouraging to educational workers. There were forty districts, all except one reporting, in which forty-one teachers were employed in teaching 1,104 pupils. Four months and a half was the average length of the term taught.

Thus very briefly have we traced the growth of Grant county's educational system up to the present. The path to knowledge is generally conceded to be among the roughest of paths and it has been only by the hardest work that this path in Grant county has been cleared of the obstacles of financial difficulties, apathy or lack of interest and natural impediments to be found and expected in a new and sparsely settled country, and the public school system placed on a firm footing. But progress has triumphed, as it ever will.

Superintendent H. C. Mack, in his report for 1901, gives us the following resume of the present condition of the schools of the county: Number of children of school age, 876 male, 821 female; number registered, 558 male, 522 female; number under six years of age, 35 male, 33 female; teachers, 28 male, 40 female, holding certificates as follows: State certificates, 17, first-grade, 17, second-grade, 13, third-grade, 8, primary-grade, 1. The county is divided into forty-three districts, all reporting, in which there are forty-one school houses, valued at $25,244.50. The average school year is stated as four and one-half months. Teachers' wages amounted to $11,039.15, the total expenditure for school purposes being $15,364.59. The high grade certificates held by the teachers speak volumes for the standard of the staff, and from an examination of the records the writer is satisfied of the excellence of the work done by the pupils. Professor Mack gained his school education in the schools over which he is now superintendent, and his success is a credit to himself and a living testimonial to those pioneer teachers who fought the early battles of education here. With time, improvement has come, and will come, sometimes slowly, it is true, but always surely.

As yet Grant county has no higher institutions of learning, but the necessity of establishing a county high school is becoming more apparent every year, and the agitation bids fair to result successfully at an early date. District high schools have been established at different times, and this winter Canyon City will have one. Progress is the watchword all along the line.

CHAPTER V.

CANYON CITY.

The first impression the traveler receives of this delightful little mountain town, as he alights from the stage, is that he is in one of the most uniquely located villages in Oregon. The town nestles cozily and peacefully in the bed of a deep canyon at the western base of Canyon mountain, protected from the stormy elements by high green hills and hidden from the gaze of the curious world by its remoteness from thoroughfares of travel. The nearest railroad point is forty-five miles away, and it is two miles down the canyon to the John Day valley. To the southeast towers the Strawberry range, and Canyon mountain, one of the loftiest peaks of this range, has often been termed "Gold Mountain," because of the incalculable wealth of mineral that is believed to be hidden away in its depths, while Canyon creek, of mining fame, dashes angrily through the town on its course to the John Day river. The gold taken from the auriferous bed of this creek alone would have built a city second in wealth to none in the state, and if equally distributed among the present inhabitants would make Canyon City a city of magnificent fortunes.

Owing to its peculiar location the number of its streets may be counted upon one's fingers, the three principal ones running north and south. As is usually the case in smaller towns and cities, the business of the place is conducted on one main street, which here is probaby half a mile long. In early days the stores were lo-cated on Canyon street, a narrow thoroughfare running parallel with, and close to, the creek. At this time it is said that the streets were so narrow that a team could not be turned around in them. In fact, this condition existed until the late fire, when one street was abandoned and the additional space given to the main street. The diverging gulches and adjacent level bench lands have all been utilized for building purposes, and even the creek's waters have been narrowed down to as small a channel as possible by enterprising citizens. Forty years ago the creek's course was through what is now Washington street, but it was turned aside into its present bed by miners anxious to wash its gravel and utilize the ground for building purposes. Every foot of available ground has been used, until now the further growth of the town is limited by the hills, unless one is content to live on their steep slopes or high summits. The business buildings are substantial frame and stone structures and house business enterprises that would be a credit to a much larger city, because of the complete stocks carried and their up-to-date methods of handling trade. Among them are the large general stores of Hazeltine & Company, Begg & Mason, Cunningham & Lyon and R. K. Chambers; the large hardware store of the Interior Mercantile Company, Incorporated; W. C. Thompson's drug store; Mrs. Elizabeth Robinson, millinery; N. Rulison, furniture; John Turner, meat market; the Canyon City

Brewery, F. C. Sels, proprietor; the Canyon City Soda Works, H. B. Guernsey, proprietor; McBean & Haguewood and Alexander Mc-Kinney, livery stables; H. Putzien, photograph gallery; A. J. Stephens, barber shop; J. A. Waterbury, jewelry store; William S. Howie and William Worth, blacksmith shops; the Elkhorn Hotel, Samuel Bauer, proprietor; Mark Rulison, builder; A. Hupprich, boots and shoes; and three saloons. W. S. Southworth operates a sash and door factory. The only banking institution in Grant county is located in Canyon City, the Grant County Bank. This bank has a capital stock of $25,000, and though it has been in existence only a very short time, the most optimistic hopes of its projectors have been realized. Its officers are: W. H. Johnson, president; Clarence Johnson, vice-president; A. P. Goss, cashier. J. W. Ashford is the only physician in Canyon City. W. F. White is a United States mineral surveyor, and the legal profession is represented by Stillman, Leedy & Pierce, Hicks & Davis, Cattanach & Wood, M. Dustin, V. G. Cozad and J. E. Marks. Mrs. Elizabeth Gray is the present postmistress.

Canyon City is fortunate in possessing two such excellent newspapers as the *Grant County News* and the *Blue Mountain Eagle,* published by Glenn & Chandler and Patterson & Ward, respectively. Both are bright, newsy, well edited weeklies, and each strives to outdo the other in working for the advancement of the city's and county's interests. Neither is hampered by blind party devotion, and because of this independence they are able to wield a more powerful influence than they might otherwise. The *News* was established here in 1879, and the *Eagle* was established at Long Creek in 1886 and removed to Canyon City two years ago.

The people of Canyon City are justly proud of their home, and while they do not claim for it all of the conveniences and complex activities of a railroad town, they are well satisfied

with steady and substantial progression, content to await the impetus which the opening of the vast mineral wealth surrounding it will give. At present there is a daily stage between Canyon City and Whitney, the terminus of the Sumpter Valley Railroad, a daily stage to Heppner, also a daily stage to Mitchell, and tri-weekly stages between here and Burns and Izee, so that the city is blessed with unusually good transportation facilities for an inland town.

Soon after the discovery of the mines here, on June 8th and 9th, by Californians journeying to the Idaho mines, a city of tents rose, and the construction of more durable quarters was begun by a few, which resulted in several log cabins and rude shacks with canvas roofs and sides being built, the latter mode of construction leading to the nickname of "Bracetown" for a time. There were no attempts made in a mercantile way until about the first of July, when Charles Becker and Peter Zimmerman opened a small store in a log cabin on Rebel hill. This store was a very small one and the goods were originally intended for sale in the Idaho gold fields. Then Thomas H. Brentz and his partner, Nelson by name, erected a small building for use as an express office, Brentz taking the first letters to The Dalles from this camp. In rapid succession Powers, Shuman & Wadleigh and Luce, Cozad & Stone brought in pack trains from The Dalles, loaded with groceries, whisky and tobacco, and opened establishments in temporary quarters. As might be natural to suppose, a saloon was among the first business establishments, the liquor being dispensed from a canvas structure on a sloping tract of bench land just above the present town, whence the name "Whisky Flat." The business houses next to follow were a bakery, opened by Hall Brothers, and a restaurant, conducted by Louie Hadlich, near where the City brewery now stands. Later this was sold to George A. Bieson, who built an addition and opened the first hotel, the City House. In 1863 a

Frenchman, Fleurette by name, erected a frame building for hotel purposes, which superseded the old City House.

At first no attempt was made towards grouping the tents and cabins, as each miner erected his temporary abode as near his claim as possible. However, when pack trains began to arrive and stores were opened, the necessity of forming a town became apparent to all, and at a meeting held July 20th a rude town site was laid off, Messrs. Mulkey and Cooper taking the lead in this movement. The creek was already known as Canyon creek, and the town was named Canyon City. The Spanish spelling of canyon was first used, but subsequently this was anglicized by inserting a "y." For some time a portion of the town stood on Whisky Flat, but as this site was altogether too inconvenient for those who worked on the creek this settlement was gradually moved down by the stream in the bed of the canyon, where several buildings had been erected, and where the town now lies. There was only one street, Canyon street, which ran parallel with the creek, and adjacent to it on the east side. The principal object of the builders being to get as close as possible to the creek, where the claims were being worked by thousands of men, but little attention was paid to symmetry or fine effects, and consequently the buildings were crowded together as closely as possible so as not to occupy valuable "pay" ground. The street was a mere alley, and the buildings one story high and of the simplest and rudest construction. During July and August of the year 1862 several new stores and some ten or twelve saloons commenced operations. Thus the town grew, numbering probably between twelve and fifteen hundred people when the winter of 1862-63 set in.

At that time the creek bed was a little to the east of the stream's present course, and through what is now the business center of the town. So rapidly was the ground worked,

however, that in the spring of 1863 claim owners along the creek for perhaps three hundred yards through the town decided to attempt to flume the creek that they might get at the gravel in its bed. Accordingly, an immense flume was constructed through Canyon street and the water turned into it. The attempt was successful, and for several weeks Canyon creek was kept within its timber bonds. However, high water caused a flood, and the stream was turned into its old bed, but not until most of the ground had been worked. The construction of the Lone Star and Humboldt ditches, in 1863 and 1864, aided the business of the town quite materially, as many men were given employment on these works in addition to the hundreds at work in the surrounding country. Canyon City was the only town of importance within a radius of a hundred miles, and consequently handled the major portion of the county's trade for many years.

For a mining town, Canyon City seems to have been remarkably free from those law-breaking, bloody affairs which characterized most mining camps in the 'fifties and 'sixties, though the town was by no means a model community. There were the usual number of small affrays, fights and robberies, but murders were infrequent, and the reputation of this eastern Oregon mining camp is unstained by records of lynchings. The miners, as a class, were law-abiding, and only dealt harshly with those who attempted to interfere with their peaceful pursuits. The creek was settled by Californians and Oregonians of the better class, and this fact undoubtedly assisted materially in giving a higher tone to the community. Even at the present day one will hardly find a more peaceful, law-abiding and contented class of people than live in Canyon City, while their cordiality, hospitality and culture are noticed at once by the stranger. Until as late as 1870 prowling Indian bands occasionally managed to steal a few horses on the nearby ranges and commit

28

smaller depredations, but no very serious losses were experienced by the townspeople from this source.

R. H. J. Comer, writing in his paper, the *Canyon City Journal*, in 1868, says: The first death in this camp was that of a man whose name has escaped our memory, on Pine creek. He died of consumption. The second was that of James K. Knox, killed by W. Blevins on the 23d of November, 1862, at which time our too well filled graveyard was picked out and dedicated. The first persons joined in the holy bonds of wedlock were James Adams and Jenette Hunter."

When the first miners came to Canyon City the banks of Canyon creek were covered by a heavy growth of cottonwood and pine timber, and before bedrock could be reached it was necessary to clear the land. This undertaking required many months to complete, and when finished greatly changed the appearance of the canyon. Bunch grass grew knee high and vegetation bloomed luxuriantly everywhere, affording the finest grazing imaginable for the few head of stock which were brought in by the earliest settlers. The first train to arrive came in from California in July, 1863, the size of this train being given by Mr. Comer as consisting of thirty-two wagons, one hundred and five men, fourteen women and several children. This immigration added substantially to the permanent population of the place.

Slowly but steadily Canyon City added to its population and size. A road was opened to The Dalles in 1864, and the current of traffic between these two centers set in, ever growing stronger and building up the business interests of these communities. In this year Grant county was organized and Canyon City took on the dignity of county seatship. In later years other towns, believing themselves to be better located and fitted to maintain the seat of county government, sought to wrest this honor from Canyon City, but without avail. With the establishment of the county offices

here the permanency of the town was assured and many drawn within its limits who otherwise might have settled elsewhere.

The pioneer court house stood on Main street, just east of Washington street, and was built in 1864. This building was destroyed by the fire of 1870. A new court house was immediately constructed in its stead, which was used until 1885, when the present handsome county building was erected at a cost of about $22,000. The grounds are beautifully situated on a level tract of land on the western bank of Canyon creek, and occupy an entire block.

The first very serious setback was given the city by a disastrous fire, which occurred August 12, 1870, by which the entire business section and many private residences were destroyed. The damage was estimated at $278,000, in round numbers, with $40,000 insurance. D. B. Rhinehart, at that time correspondent of the *Oregonian* in this county, writing in that paper under date of September, 1870, gives the following graphic account of this fire

"What a world of smoke, ashes and ruin! Canyon City remains only in name. Nearly all that was once lovely or valuable of our favored county seat has passed away. The city having been composed almost entirely of wooden buildings, save a few bank fire-proofs, and everything as dry as powder, you may well imagine the quick destruction that followed. The fire is said to have originated from the kitchen stovepipe of the International hotel, George Bieson proprietor. The day was calm and lovely. A quiet breeze was perceptible from the north, but was quickly fanned into greater activity by the first burst of flame from the hotel roof. Men, women and children hurried to and fro in wild excitement as the devouring elements spread with increased fury northward, southward, eastward and westward. The flames, like infuriated demons, bent on destruction, leaped from roof to roof, and from attic to base, causing the frail structures to disappear 'like leaves before a driving storm.' There was little hope from the first of saving any buildings in the business portion of the town, but many heroic and successful efforts were made to save human lives, precious relics, public documents and valuable property. Several persons were confined to their beds at the time, and were the first to claim the attention of their friends. By immediate and vigorous action they were rescued just in time to escape most horrible deaths. A decrepit Chinaman, however, fell a victim to the flames and was burnt to a cinder. It is said that he was in the act of secreting some stolen goods when the flames closed him in forever.

"We need only mention a few cases of hairbreadth escapes in which heroism was exhibited. Mrs. Day, wife of the United States deputy marshal for this county, while in a daring attempt to secure her husband's public and private papers from burning in the International hotel, was twice carried from the surrounding flames and falling timbers. Still undaunted, in the spirit of a devoted wife and true heroine, she was about to make her last desperate effort when the papers were secured and she carried them off in triumph, to the joy of many witnesses. We next find her in the storeroom of George B. Fearing & Company, engaged in packing goods into the underground fire-proof, and when informed that the fire was upon them, and that she had better flee for her life, she firmly replied, 'We can save a few more things,' until Mr. Fearing closed the iron door against her and forced her from the burning building. There were also several other ladies who might be honorably mentioned in this connection for their daring perseverance. F. C. Sels, our present county judge, came near losing his life through over-exertion and copious inhalation of heat and smoke. He is still confined to his bed and in a rather critical condition.

"Every business house and many private dwellings have been destroyed. The follow-

ing is a list of the losses as obtained in person from the parties themselves:

"George B. Fearing & Company, storehouse and goods, $7,500; Rhinehart & Overholt, storehouse and goods, $8,000; Dr. F. C. Horseley, drug store, $8,000; Neal McNulty, saloon, $3,000; George Bieson, hotel, $3,000, insurance, $2,000; McCollough & Hellman, storehouse and goods, $100,000, insurance, $10,000; Drs. Tierney & Keler, drug store, $3,000; Dr. Tierney, private property, $4,000; Mary St. Clair, saloon and contents, $20,000; Overholt & Pellett, wagon shop, $2,500; Gundlach Brothers, storehouse and goods, $14,000, insurance, $10,000; Bradley office building, $1,200; Hyatt, saloon, $1,500; Foster, watchmaker, $1,000; Phil. Metschan, meat market, $1,000; M. P. Berger, storehouse, $1,000; Mr. Fleurette and lady, French hotel, $10,000, partly insured; Haguewood & McBean, saloon, $5,000, insurance, $1,500; Haguewood, private property, $1,500; Thomas Poindexter, private dwelling, $1,000; Coffman & Messenger, storehouse and goods, $20,000, insurance, $8,500; Sels & Stemme, storehouse and goods, $7,000, insurance, $3,000; F. C. Sels, brewery, $7,000; B. J. Beesley, blacksmith shop, $1,000; Krause, barber, $500; L. B. Trowbridge, dwelling, $1,500; Fred Marhoe, $1,000; I. O. O. F. building and contents, $8,000, insurance, $2,400; Masonic loss, $1,500; H. Cole, blacksmith, $2,000; I. O. G. T. loss, $1,500; county court house and jail, $40,000." These figures are given as only approximate, and doubtless the real loss was far below that given above.

With characteristic enterprise and energy the citizens went bravely to work repairing the damage done by the fire's ravages, and within a short time new and better buildings arose out of the ruins and cosmos was again evolved from chaos.

Eight years later Canyon City was visited by an Indian scare of considerable proportions. General Howard, in close pursuit of Chief Egan and his warring redskins, drove them east out of Harney valley, passing within twenty miles of Canyon City on the south. When it was learned that the Indians were coming in this direction, steps were at once taken to insure protection for the women and children, and every able bodied man and boy was placed under arms. A requisition was made for more arms, and a consignment of one hundred rifles, with ammunition, was sent from The Dalles.

The mining tunnels west of town were transformed into places of refuge, and here were gathered most of the women and children and valuables; many families moving their furniture, bedding, kitchen utensils, etc., into these temporary forts. The city took on a martial air, scouting parties were organized, sentinels posted and every precaution possible taken to guard against an attack. Steps were taken toward the formation of a military company, but, as the sequel proved, its services were not needed, and it was never formally organized. The citizens remained under arms for several days, or until the Indians had fled through Fox valley, up Long creek and northward out of striking distance. During this time the city was visited several times by detachments of soldiers, sometimes after supplies, sometimes after information, so that the place was well protected at all times and ready to stoutly defend itself.

Not much of particular interest occurred in Canyon City during the next few years. The town grew slowly and was prosperous in proportion to the general prosperity of the mining and stock industries of the county. During the 'seventies many Chinamen secured control of the old creek claims, which had not been thoroughly worked in the eager haste of their early owners, and scores of the Mongolians were employed in sifting the gravel in search of the yellow metal. Thus a Mongolian town grew up on the outskirts of the city. A fire broke out in this district February 6, 1885, and in a short time totally destroyed it. For a

time it was feared that the whole town was endangered, but fortunately the fire was checked before it had progressed far enough to obtain a firm foothold in the business section. The Chinese were not allowed to build on the old site, and the majority of them moved to John Day. The fire department at this time, consisting of sixty persons, was in an efficient condition. Water was obtained from four hydrants of immense pressure, and there were four hundred feet of serviceable hose.

About half past three o'clock on the afternoon of Saturday, May 29, 1886, a cloudburst occurred just above town, which did considerabe damage to business houses and private dwellings generally. The creek became a roaring torrent, rolling large boulders, trees and debris into the roads and streets, flooding cellars, carrying away flumes, filling tunnels, destroying goods, filling stores and shops with mud and gravel, twisting sidewalks and destroying the county bridge across the creek. George Gundlach & Brother were the principal losers, their cellar being flooded and goods damaged to the extent of several hundred dollars. This was a greater storm than the one five years previously, but not so much damage was done, as the water kept a more direct course towards the creek. Old residents give it as their opinion that this storm was the severest which ever occurred in this section. The total damage amounted to several hundred dollars.

Telephone agitation, which had been going on for some time, took a more definite form in April, 1895, when the Inland Telephone Exchange was organized with a capital stock of $2,000. Local capitalists were behind the enterprise and hearty support was given the project by residents of this section. The company purposed to erect a line between the principal towns in Grant and Harney counties, and the line to Prairie City was to be met there by one extending from Baker City. The organization of this company did not materialize, however, and another local company was organized in February, 1895, to build a line between Canyon City and John Day. A portion of the equipment was purchased and preparations made to proceed with the construction work, but in the case of this company, too, nothing was done. Finally the Blue Mountain Telephone Company constructed a line to Canyon City, John Day, Prairie City and Burns from Heppner, and later a line was built from Baker City to Prairie City, giving the country excellent telephonic communication with the outside world. The telegraph will come with the advent of the iron horse.

The spring of 1896 was a rainy one and while rain deluged the valleys, snow fell to a considerable depth in the high altitudes, causing the streams to rise much above their usual height. On May 29th a heavy thunder shower occurred on Canyon creek, and by ten o'clock that evening this quiet stream had become a roaring, raging torrent, and had risen to the danger point, sweeping away outbuildings, woodpiles and loose debris. At midnight the fire bell apprised the sleeping inhabitants of the danger that threatened their city, and at once preparations were instituted on a much larger scale to further protect the town. A large part of the city was already under water, and it was feared that the treacherous stream would shift its channel and sweep everything before it. Families in greatest peril were removed to residences on the hillside, and the frail levees were strengthened by trees and numerous dams, constructed at weak points. It was a night of bustle and anxiety, as the destroying waters did not recede sufficiently to afford a feeling of safety until well towards daylight. The loss amounted to approximately $1,400, the principal losers being W. R. Cunnington, A. Hinsch and Byram & Stansell, wood; Dennis McAuliffe, barn; Robert Ray, a young orchard; and O. P. Cresap, outbuildings and windmill. It was many days before the roads leading into Canyon City were in

condition for travel, and a new county bridge could be built to take the place of the one washed away.

Little did the inhabitants of Canyon City dream, when they retired to rest on that ill-omened Friday night, November 11, 1898, that ere another sunrise their peaceful little city would be all but blotted out of existence by the dread fire fiend, and that many of them would be homeless and not a few penniless. Little did they imagine the awful destruction that was to fall upon them and the fierce struggle that was to ensue to save even a remnant of their homes. Great calamities come when least expected, and in this the catastrophe which befell Canyon City was no exception, although it is true that since the founding of the place its inhabitants had realized that its destruction by a sweeping fire was a possible if not a probable occurrence. The very nature of conditions, the way in which the town was built and its situation in the draught of a narrow canyon, were favorable to such a calamity, and as if to make the circumstances still more favorable, the city's fire system was in a deplorable condition.

So when the clang of the fire bell rang out upon the still night air this clear wintry evening, giving warning to the citizens to prepare for battle, all realized that the fight was to be a hard one. A strong wind from up the canyon fanned the flames, and unfortunately the reservoir above town, which furnished the water supply, was unusually low. It required only an instant to sum up the situation, but, notwithstanding the discouraging circumstances, the fight began.

Away up in the second story of the Elkhorn hotel the tiny flames first burst through into the air, about half past ten o'clock, and as if in response to a preconcerted signal it seemed only a moment until the hotel was grasped by a hundred forked tongues of fire and enshrouded in clouds of tell-tale smoke. Just across the street stood the old City hotel, and without an effort the leaping flames crossed the narrow street and penetrated its dry wooden walls, devouring them as if they were made of paper, and extending its ever reaching destruction to the north and to the south. To the south of the Elkhorn hotel the tide of flame then rolled, and the crackling, snapping and crashing soon told that the buildings in its path in that direction were doomed. Then to the north and west, and the fire fiend was conquering everywhere and melting within its furnace the accumulations of years of hard work and toil, whilst it seemed as if no human power could check the complete destruction of the city.

Meanwhile the fire apparatus had been hurried into service and willing hands lent aid. Bucket. brigades were formed, corps of men, women and children set to work saving what property could be snatched from burning buildings and removing it to places of safety, and an heroic effort, in which all joined, was made to check the conflagration. Everything that even savored of hope was tried, and if energy and tireless effort could have saved, Canyon City would have met with small loss. But early in the night the water supply gave out, and with a strong wind lending life to the flames and the close proximity to one another of the dry wooden buildings, the fight was an unequal one. Straight down Washington street the fire took its course, razing everything destructible in its path. It finally ended its course in that direction by burning the dwelling of Robert Hines. Its progress southward was not so rapid, owing to more unfavorable circumstances, and at the residence of O. P. Cresap the flames were stayed. The Episcopal church, just across the street, was also saved. The creek proved an impassible barrier on the west and that portion of the town across the creek and lying south of the Cresap residence escaped unscathed.

It was a dreary, desolate scene the morning dawned upon. Canyon City's business center

and the greater portion of its residence section were smouldering heaps of ruins; the heart of the city was laid in waste; the winter was close at hand and want and penury stared scores in the face. The picture was of most sombre coloring and it required brave hearts to face the prospect without flinching. One-half the population was homeless; the greater portion of a winter's supplies had been destroyed, a serious loss at this season of the year, and lumber was not to be obtained at any price.

The monetary loss was appalling, footing up into the hundreds of thousands of dollars and practically uncovered by insurance, as, in the majority of cases, insurance companies refused risks at any price and when rates were made they were so high as to preclude the idea of carrying any reasonable amount. Among the principal losses were: Canyon City brewery, $30,000; Elkhorn hotel, $5,000; City or Valade hotel, $5,000; Odd Fellows' hall, $5,000; A. Hinch, $12,000; Cunnington & Horsley, $20,000; R. A. Hines, $3,000; Dr. J. W. Ashford, $4,000; N. Rulison, $2,000; A. L. Markham, $3,000 in United States bonds; Mrs. L. Robinson, $2,000; Methodist church, $2,500; Thompson Drug Company, $3,000; Col. D. I. Asbury, $3,000; Guernsey & Clark, $3,000; I. J. Haguewood, $2,000; Brown & Simpson, $1,000; McBean & Miller, $1,500; Clay Todhunter, $1,000; Frank Fleishman, $1,000; and W. H. Kelly, $1,000. These losses were the principal ones, besides which there were many smaller ones by other business houses and residents. The contents of the postoffice were saved.

No time was lost in mourning, however. The situation was too pressing. The court house was at once thrown open to the homeless and those more fortunate generously extended their hospitality to others. The Grant County News, whose office had been the one business house to escape the fire, was at once offered to place before the outside public news of the dire calamity that had befallen Canyon

City and solicit aid. As soon as the extent of the loss became apparent Editor Chandler and his force commenced work, and by nine o'clock the next morning several hundred copies of the News were on their way to neighboring towns.

The greatest need was building material with which to rebuild the destroyed homes. Many tents were utilized and the surrounding sawmills were notified that a large supply of lumber would be needed at once. Mayor Cresap appointed as a fire relief committee, P. F. Chandler, editor of the News, chairman, Mrs. Frank Sels, Mrs. J. W. Ashford, Walter Brown and E. S. Penfield. Long Creek was the first town to respond to the appeal sent out, the residents of that town sending a subscription of $55. Then Baker City's relief fund was received. It amounted to $202, besides many large private subscriptions. Prairie City, Heppner, John Day, Portland and other towns and mining camps of Oregon contributed generously, in all, something over $3,000 being realized, which, needless to say, was used to the best possible advantage.

Hardly had the last smouldering ember died out before the click of the hammer and the song of the saw were heard, and as rapidly as it was possible to procure lumber and other necessary building material new business and residential structures arose over the ashes. However, it was slow work, this rebuilding, and many months elapsed before the burnt district again assumed the life and appearance of a city.

Canyon City profited by the fire in several ways, the most important being that larger and more substantial structures were reared. Formerly there were three streets running north and south, and in no one was it possible for a team to turn around, the streets being so narrow. At a citizens' meeting held directly after the fire it was voted to do away with one of these streets and widen the business portion of Washington street to sixty feet, the additional width being taken from the western side. Pro-

vision was made for a change in the charter, allowing the council jurisdiction over the streets, that the change might be made legally, and meanwhile it was mutually agreed by property owners to comply with this desire. The street thus abandoned, Canyon street, was at one time the main thoroughfare of the city. The new Canyon City was an improvement in many ways over the old town, and, best of all, was the confidence in the future of the city which the rapid and costly rebuilding instilled in the people.

The most terrific hail storm that ever visited this region passed over the city May 11, 1901, at half past three o'clock, lasting half an hour. Hail measuring one and a half inches fell, breaking windows, tearing off roofs, stripping fruit trees and doing other damage. Teams hitched on the street broke their fastenings and dashed wildly through the city, seeking to escape the storm of missiles. A deluge of water down Town gulch followed the storm, flooding the streets and cellars and doing considerable damage. Temporary levees were hastily constructed to keep the water from rushing down side streets, and by this means the damage was confined as much as possible.

Until 1891 the inhabitants of Canyon City did not possess the privilege of living within the limits of an incorporated town, though in importance and population it had been entitled to that dignity many years before, but at the session of the legislature that year a bill was introduced and passed incorporating Canyon City, Prairie City and Long Creek. Under the provisions of this charter, the first election was held here in March, 1891, which resulted in the following officers being chosen: Mayor, C. W. Parrish; recorder, N. Rulison; treasurer, John Muldrick; councilmen, D. G. Overholt, M. V. Thompson, N. H. Boley, A. Hupprich, Frank McBean; marshal, W. R. Cunnington. The last municipal election was held in April, 1902, when the following corps of officers were elected to administer the city's affairs during the ensuing year: Mayor, William Mason; recorder, Z. G. Martin, treasurer, G. I. Hazeltine; marshal, George Fugit; councilmen, A. Jackson Chambers, V. G. Cozad, Robert Glen, J. F. Turner and George F. Ward.

The city has never had adequate fire protection. Had there been a fairly good system of water works in 1870 and again in 1898 the city might have been saved the appalling losses suffered by fire on those memorable occasions. The present system was installed several years ago and consists of two small reservoirs, with an aggregate capacity of 12,000 gallons, situated on the hill east of the town and fed by springs. With two streams playing at the same time, it is estimated that this supply of water would last but little over an hour, and considerable time is required to refill these reservoirs. Water mains convey this water to different parts of the city, several hydrants being in use. The city boasts a well organized department, there being two companies of fourteen members each. At no time has the city been so well protected from fire as at present, and with the erection of stone and brick buildings from time to time, each year the danger of a repetition of the conflagrations of 1870 and 1898 becomes less. Since the rebuilding of the city the last time the different insurance companies have decided to assume risks, whereas before that it was impossible to obtain any insurance on business houses.

In no way, perhaps, does Canyon City show its progressiveness better than by its excellent school. The Canyon City school is in charge of Professor C. J. McIntosh, assisted by J. M. Montgomery and Miss Olive Conlee. There are about ninety scholars in the school and this year a high school branch will be instituted. The writer witnessed the first annual graduation exercises of the Canyon City public school last May, when a class of ten bright young men and women were granted diplomas, and by word and action they acquitted themselves well. The preceding evening the younger scholars gave a school exhibition and sang the operetta "Red Riding Hood," and it is keeping within the bounds of truth to say that it was the peer of any like entertainment we have ever seen given by children of their age.

There are two churches here, the Methodist, presided over by Rev. P. F. Chandler, and the Episcopal, under the rectorship of the Rev. M. J. Goodheart. Both edifices are a credit to the religious inclinations of the people and each draws to its altar large congregations when services are conducted, every other Sunday in the Methodist and every Sunday in the Episcopal church.

Canyon City might aptly be termed the "City of Lodges," for in no city of its size in Oregon are there more fraternal organizations and societies. In 1899 a handsome stone fraternal hall was erected by the different lodges in the city, at a cost of six thousand dollars, and in this building the different orders meet. The Masons are represented by Blue Mountain Chapter, No. 7, R. A. M., Canyon City Lodge, No. 34, A. F. & A. M., and Julia Chapter, O. E. S. The Odd Fellows have two lodges, Excelsior Encampment, No. 3, and Hobah Lodge, No. 22, besides Hebron Lodge, No. 6, Daughters of Rebekah. Vernon Lodge, No. 43, K. of P., Canyon City Camp, No. 218, Woodmen of the World, Blue Mountain Circle, No. 222, Women of Woodcraft, Homer Lodge, No. 78, A. O. U. W., Maggie Barker Lodge, No. 63, D. of H., D. W. Jenkins Cabin, No. 23, Native Sons of Oregon, Elizabeth Gray Cabin, No. 21, Native Daughters of Oregon, and Evergreen Lodge, No. 57, I. O. O. Lions, recently organized, complete the list of fraternal societies in the city. All have thriving lodges and their influence is apparent in the community.

We have traced in the foregoing pages as best we could the growth of Canyon City from its inception to the present. It has had vicissitudes of fortune to which mining camps are usually subject, has bravely endured the

CANYON CITY.

CASTLE ROCK.

storms of financial depression and discouragement which at times beset the growth of a village, and as a city, looks hopefully forward to the future. At one time it was the center of one of the richest placer mining districts in the world and beneath the mountain forests of the Strawberry range lies an incalculable wealth of quartz, which, when properly developed, cannot but enrich the country and may build a metropolis on Canyon creek.

CHAPTER VI.

JOHN DAY, PRAIRIE CITY AND OTHER TOWNS.

JOHN DAY.

John Day is the second town in population and importance in Grant county, and if its present rapid growth continues it will not be long until Canyon City, the present metropolis, will have to share honors equally with its neighbor. ·Even at the present time it would be impossible to say which of these two thriving towns transacts the most business, so evenly is the trade of this section divided. Both have a population of between four and five hundred, and if a miracle were to be wrought and these two centers combined, the city thus formed would be the equal of any in Oregon of its size. From the border of one town to the border of the other the distance is only about a mile and a half, an excellent highway connecting the two places. Perhaps the day will come, it is not an improbability, when the wealth garnered from the depths of Canyon mountain, the sands of the John Day and the mineralized section which lies between the two, from the fruit and agricultural industries of the John Day valley and the stock-raising interests of the outlying ranges, will build a city on Canyon creek which will extend from Canyon City to John Day and include both these towns.

John Day was founded under the same circumstances, at the same time, by the same class of settlers, grew up under the same influences and is now sustained by practically the same industries that sustain Canyon City. Quite naturally the business of this mining district had a tendency to concentrate in one place, and as the latter named settlement was nearest the center of the mines, it grew more rapidly and became the principal town. The story of the discovery of the Canyon creek and Marysville mines in April, 1862, has been narrated at length elsewhere—of how the creek bed from Whisky Flat to the mouth of the creek was taken up in claims within a few weeks after the arrival of the first miners. Mining was the sole support of the community then; and agriculture was as yet but a misty dream of the future and the fertile John Day valley in its virgin condition.

Among those prominently identified with the discovery and operation of the first mines at the mouth of Canyon creek may be mentioned G. I. Hazeltine, P. V. Middlesworth and C. B. Cobb. A town was unthought of then. The following year, 1863, the numerous population of this district demanded a nearer trading point than the settlement up the creek, and so Captain E. B. Fearing erected a small store near where Main and Canyon streets now intersect. A saloon was also opened. The natural advantages of this place as a commercial center were soon recognized and this same summer a small hotel was opened. In 1864 A. R. McCallum and G. I. Hazeltine, with keen foresight, recognized in the richness and extent of the mines and the thousands of acres of fertile agricultural land in the valley the factors that would result in a permanent settlement here, and, with commendable enterprise, they built a small flouring mill in the little settlement near the mouth of Canyon creek. At that time a few settlers had taken up agricultural land and these promised to sow wheat if a mill were started. Flour then sold at twenty-five dollars per fifty-pound sack. McCallum & Hazeltine paid from ten to fifteen cents a pound for getting the machinery in, nearly all of it having to be packed in on horses from The Dalles, two hundred miles away. Although this mill was a small one, it proved a financial success and assisted in no small way in firmly establishing the agricultural industry here. This mill was used until the 'eighties, when it was remodeled and enlarged. Power is furnished by water taken from the John Day river. The mill is now owned by H. M. Basford.

In 1864, also, another small store was opened and two saloons were doing business, one kept by a man named Hiatt, the other by a man familiarly known as "Shorty." E. Mosier was another pioneer of John Day, having built a blacksmith shop there in 1865. At this time, as heretofore stated, miners were scattered along the creek, and while the upper settlement was known as Canyon City, that at the mouth of the canyon was always referred to as the "Lower Town." About this time, however, the inhabitants of this section christened their business center "John Day," after the famed stream which flows through the valley and gives it its name.

In those days there was much lawlessness in this region. Robberies occurred in the community almost nightly; weapons were carried by every one and petty crimes were frequent. In short, the Canyon Creek camp was typical of most mining centers of the rugged west, and yet, in comparison with some of the early Nevada, Colorado and California camps, the wickedness of this camp was never great.

During the latter 'sixties the population here began to scatter, the placer mines giving out, and all through the 'seventies the Chinese were about the only miners who considered the tailings on Canyon creek worth re-working. The transition period between the passing of the great placer mines and the rise into first importance of stock-raising and agriculture lies in the 'seventies. Stock-raising was the first to relegate the mining industry to secondary importance and it gained very rapidly after the first few years. The John Day valley was quickly divided into small holdings of land, the tributary valleys were populated, immense herds of cattle and horses and bands of sheep occupied the ranges and very slowly, but with ever increasing momentum, the county forged to the front as one of the permanent and rich agricultural and stock-raising communities of the state.

Prairie City and Long Creek sprang into existence and Canyon City and John Day were lifted into greater importance by this rising tide of prosperity. In 1878 John Day was designated as a post office and Frank I. McCallum was appointed the first postmaster. The rapid settlement of the valley around there brought about this action. Until this time the small hamlet here could hardly be called a town, and its inhabitants considered its existence as temporary, though its excellent geographical location was apparent. When, in 1876, Anton Hacheney decided to open a general store at this point and for that purpose erected what was probably the first stone building built in Grant county, there were between forty and fifty people living there. A small variety store was kept by a man named Sloss and there were two other small tobacco stores or stands. The next year, 1877, Miss Metschan built a stone building across the street from Mr. Hacheney's place, but this was not occupied as a store until the following year, when Haptonstall, Dart & Company opened a store here. Earlier in 1878 Frank I. McCallum built a small frame building on Main street and also opened a store. E. A. McCoy afterward became a partner of Mr. McCallum. Haptonstall, Dart & Company continued in business until 1896, when G. W. Dart bought out the remaining interests, also the remnant of Mr. Hacheney's stock, he having gone out of business in that year. Among other pioneer business men here we may mention William Davis, who kept a saloon known as the "Mt. Hood" saloon until his death in a street fight about 1868; Charles B. Cobb, who conducted a hotel about 1880; and Daniel A. Reamer, a blacksmith of this same period.

In November, 1881, according to a correspondent of the Bedrock Democrat, John Day possessed two general stores, two small hotels, two livery barns, a harness shop, a flouring mill, a blacksmith shop, a meat market, a good school, one church (the Methodist), one saloon and three secret orders. From 1883 to 1893 the town grew quite rapidly, and appears to have received more benefit from the growing industries of sheep, cattle and horse-raising and farming than did Canyon City. This period was one of great prosperity and John Day received its full share. After the destruction of the Chinese portion of Canyon City by fire in 1885, and the subsequent refusal of residents of that place to allow the Chinese to rebuild, the Mongolians removed to John Day and added their numbers to the Chinese settlement already there. Thus quite a large Chinese town grew up, which at one time numbered between five and six hundred inhabitants. At present there are perhaps a hundred Chinamen in John Day. They have their own stores,

three in number, and the community is apart from the main town. The inhabitants of this quaint settlement are orderly and apparently contented, and while, as is their way, they do not mingle with Americans nor do they adopt American manners and customs, they are not considered a detriment to the town.

During the hard times which prevailed throughout the country between 1893 and 1897 John Day was at a standstill, going backward if moving at all. But with the dawn of prosperity which has flooded the country with its penetrating and warming rays of progress, happiness and peace since then, the present John Day takes its beginning. The past five or six years marks the greatest and most substantial development of the town, and especially the past three years. From a small hamlet it has attained to the population and importance of a large town—and it is still growing.

From a geographical point of view, John Day is the natural commercial center of the county. Situated at the mouth of Canyon creek, it is the gateway to all that territory which lies on Canyon creek and south of Canyon mountain; the only road through the John Day valley passes through the town; while it is connected with Long Creek and the northern and western portions of the county by excellent roads. John Day is a natural terminus for all these highways. At the present time the different stage lines terminate at Canyon City, but, with the exception of the Burns and Izee stages, all pass through John Day.

The town lies at the mouth of the creek canyon and on a rolling tract of land. Formerly this was all occupied as mining claims and most of it has been worked for the gold deposited in the soil. Until June 1, 1880, the town site might be spoken of as government land, as by that time the mines had been abandoned and the claims had thus reverted to the government. However, William H. Kelly, an old settler, took up forty acres of this land as a homestead during the latter part of the 'seventies, and on June 1, 1880, was granted a United States patent by President Garfield. On this land most of the town is situated.

John Day possesses several fine avenues. The town is fairly embowered in magnificent groves of poplars and other shade trees, which fringe the streets and roads leading into the place, giving it a very pretty and cozy appearance. Like the majority of mining towns, however, its streets are very irregularly laid out, the most important being Main street, on which the business houses are situated, and Canyon street, leading up the canyon to Canyon City. Many beautiful homes and yards lend beauty and attractiveness to the town, while its business structures are buildings of which many larger towns in eastern Oregon might well feel proud. Several are built of stone, a number are frame buildings of recent construction, while the most substantial and commodious building in the county is now being erected by Clarence and William H. Johnson. This is being built of brick with stone trimmings, will be two stories high, with an eight-foot stone basement, and its ground dimensions are sixty-four by seventy-four feet. When completed it will be occupied by a hardware store, a dry goods establishment and a bank, besides which there will be a spacious hall in the second story. T. T. Kelly, of Sumpter, is the contractor, and it is estimated that the aggregate cost of the building will approximate $10,000.

At this point the John Day valley is about a mile wide. On the north side it terminates in rocky bluffs several hundred feet high, while on the south the valley rises into the foothills which farther southward become the Strawberry range of mountains. Between these foothills and bluffs the main John Day river flows, just touching the northern outskirts of the town, and the narrow valley thus formed is not without the impressive beauty usually found in such places. The Trowbridge ranch, which bounds the town on the north, occupies

the whole valley here. This ranch is the oldest ranch in the county, having been taken up in 1862, and is also one of the most highly cultivated and most productive. The location of the town is high and dry and therefore a healthy one, and with congenial people and pleasant surroundings, John Day is unusually attractive as a residence town.

The Prairie Diggings mine, which operates a twenty-five stamp mill and when running full force employs between thirty and forty men, is situated about three miles east of John Day, and three-quarters of a mile below the town is the great Pomeroy mining dredger, recently built and equipped at a cost of over one hundred thousand dollars. This gigantic machine daily sifts hundreds of tons of sand and gravel scooped from the river bed, and with human-like intelligence and skill extracts and saves the smallest grain of gold in this apparently worthless ground. Between fifteen and twenty men are employed, and as the payroll at the present time amounts to about $3,000 a month, this industry means much in a business way to John Day.

John Day was incorporated three years ago by the legislature, the following officers being appointed to act until the election of 1900: Mayor, E. J. Bayley; recorder, J. W. McCulloch; treasurer, F. C. Hacheney; councilmen, Frank I. McCallum, William Geiger, H. M. Basford, C. P. Johnson, Edward Hall and Charles Timms; marshal, Charles Angel. At present Anthony Hacheney is mayor; N. H. Boley, recorder; Frank C. Hacheney, treasurer; H. M. Basford, B. M. Burton, J. T. Berry. Clarence Johnson, G. W. Dart and J. H. Fell, councilmen; and T. B. Hall, marshal.

But few towns have been as fortunate as has John Day in escaping the disasters of fire, flood and wind, which generally overtake communities at some time during their existence. During the nearly two score years John Day has been in existence it has never experienced a fire of any great consequence, nor has it ever been damaged by destructive floods or winds. Its life has been marked by no unusual events and its people have seldom been disturbed out of the serenity surrounding them. The town has received no serious setbacks nor have boom periods been inflicted upon it. Its growth has been steady and in response to the demands of a growing and prosperous community.

The town is well protected from fire by an excellent water system, owned by Anton Hacheney. Just south of town, on the hillside, is a stone reservoir with a capacity of 13,000 gallons. This is filled by a pipe conveying the waters of a large spring, situated between John Day and Canyon City and taken up by Mr. Hacheney twenty years ago. Four-inch mains carry the water from the reservoir into town, where it is distributed by several small mains and hydrants. The pressure thus obtained is excellent, being a fall of 120 feet. A large supply of hose and other fire extinguishing apparatus is owned by the town.

In the eastern part of the town are situated the John Day Roller Mills, owned by H. M. Basford. These mills grind considerable of the flour used in Grant county and use thousands of bushels of grain each year. They occupy the site of the old McCallum & Hazeltine mill.

There are three large general stores here, McCallum & Bayley, established in 1890, Albert Hinsch, established in 1898, and B. M. Burton, established two years ago. Johnson (C. P.) & Parrish (J. L.) conduct a large dry goods and furnishing establishment in what was the old Hacheney store. Clarence Johnson opened a hardware store here in 1889, and this business, together with the dry goods business of his brother William, will occupy the new brick building now under construction and before mentioned. The old Hall hotel is now under the management of R. W. Floyd. M. W. Myers has a furniture store, managed by Winfield Allen. Other business houses here are:

A drug store, recently opened by P. A. Snyder; meat market, Berry & Holloway, proprietors; blacksmith shop, T. P. Morgan; tannery, G. Lucas; confectionery and fruit store, S. F. Ottman; restaurant, Edward Hanna; livery stables, Harvey Middlesworth and Frank Wallace; barber shop, Jacob Bosler; shoemaking shop, Frank Wiseman; millinery and dressmaking parlors, Mrs. P. V. Middlesworth; boarding house, Mrs. E. F. Foren. Besides these business houses there is a new steam laundry, now being built, a Chinese laundry and three saloons. There are two physicians, Dr. J. H. Fell and Dr. William Lewis. The legal profession is unrepresented here because of the town's proximity to the county seat. John Johnson is the present postmaster. Wilkins Lodge, No. 105, A. O. U. W., and Margaret E. Lodge, No. 64, Degree of Honor, are the only fraternal organizations, the remaining orders having combined with those at Canyon City.

There are two churches here, both of which own commodious houses of worship, the Methodist, which is the oldest, and the Advent. The Rev. Perry F. Chandler ministers to the people from the Methodist pulpit every other Sunday, while regular services are held in the Advent church by its pastor, F. W. Brampton.

John Day has excellent schools and its people have always been found standing shoulder to shoulder on all problems affecting the advancement of the educational interests of the town. This school district was established by Superintendent Rhinehart on January 2, 1865, and was known as district No. 3, which number it still retains. The first session of school was held in the summer of 1866. The pioneer board of this district was composed of A. G. Mulkey, N. W. Fiske, Wilson Harer, directors, and W. F. Vinegard, clerk. School has been maintained regularly since then, and at present about one hundred pupils are enrolled. This summer a new four-room schoolhouse, costing $3,400, was completed, which is now in charge of Professor H. L. Mack and wife and F. S. Ottman. The school board is composed of Clarence Johnson, C. H. Timms and G. W. Porter, directors, and E. J. Bayley, clerk.

Blessed with an excellent location, naturally and geographically, a healthy climate, an abundance of pure water, substantial business houses and enterprising and industrious citizens, John Day has much for which to be thankful and may look forward to a bright future. When a railroad enters the John Day valley, and this time is not far distant now, this town will be one of the most important business centers in this part of the state. As the agricultural and stockraising industries grow in importance and extent by thousands, instead of hundreds being employed in these two important branches of business, John Day will grow commercially. In no other town in the county is prosperity more prevalent than in John Day and none is making rapider strides forward.

PRAIRIE CITY.

It is not difficult to discover the reason why the founders of Prairie City chose that name to designate their little settlement, for before it the valley of the John Day river spreads out in all its beauty, one of the prettiest bits of mountain scenery in the west. From the historic river, winding like a silver ribbon through the valley the undulating, magnificent stretches of emerald prairie rise gradually to the foothills, where they melt away into the more sombre green of the pine-covered Strawberry mountains, which tower abruptly and majestically upwards and paint a picture of rugged snowy beauty against the blue of heaven; a display of color that only the eye can appreciate and a scene of grandeur that would require the pen of an Irving to adequately describe.

The town lies at the base of the foothills of Dixie mountain and at the mouth of Dixie

creek, whose auriferous sands in early days furnished the main support of this lively little mining camp. Like most mining centers, it has had its viscissitudes of fortune; now overflowing with prosperity and then again struggling for an existence. Of late years, however, agriculture has gained much in importance in the valley and now contributes as much as mining to the town's support if not more.

But to correctly and fully tell the story of Prairie City the historian must carry his readers back to the earliest settlement of the county, to the summer of 1862, when the van of the great emigration from California reached eastern Oregon. It was about the middle of June when a party, numbering perhaps fifty or sixty persons and known as the "woman party" from the fact that with it were the first two white women to enter this section of the country, encamped near Dixie creek on their way over Dixie mountain. Two parties, Hopper's and Macgruder's, had already passed over the trail, all having the Salmon river mines in Idaho as their ultimate destination. When the woman party, as we will call it, reached the summit of the divide, the next morning they were met by a portion of Hopper's party returning to Canyon creek. Members of the latter named party told discouraging news of the outlook ahead, whereupon the woman party held a consultation and decided to also return. That evening camp was again pitched on Dixie creek about three and a half miles above its confluence with the John Day, and, as the story goes, the women panned out sufficient gold in the creek to warrant a further investigation. The result was the founding of Dixie town, both the creek and the town being so named because of the southern sympathies of its first settlers. The site of this mining town was closely analagous to that of Canyon City, being upon a slightly elevated bar of the stream.

The nucleus of the settlement thus formed

was rapidly augmented by passing miners on their way to Auburn, and soon a population of between three and four hundred was engaged in extracting the precious metal from the creek bed from far above Dixie town to the John Day. Pack trains brought commodities in as rapidly as possible and soon H. H. Hyde and George Dollina were conducting general stores in rudely constructed structures and two saloons were opened. Then Jules LeBrut erected a livery stable; a butcher shop was opened; a hotel conducted by William Davis, and a man named Clark, better known as "Seven-Up Clark," commenced business, and the place began to assume the air of a business community. The population of the town at this time might be characterized as migratory, since strangers were constantly arriving and miners departing in search of richer diggings. The gravel bar on which this thriving, bustling camp sprung up was really mining ground and all taken up in claims, so that the existence of the town depended entirely on the good will of the claim owners. For this reason no attempt was made to plat Dixie town, but it grew and spread wherever the residents willed and the miners permitted. The creek bed was torn to pieces by the eager miners in search of gold until finally it bore rather the appearance of a glacier-swept canyon than that of a quiet-looking gulch through which the mountain stream wended its way undisturbed to the valley below. In 1865 Perine & Hobson erected a small sawmill several miles up the creek and supplied the townspeople, miners and ranchmen with such small amounts of lumber as they wished. In after years this pioneer mill was removed across the valley to Squaw creek, where it was in operation until a few years ago.

Up to 1868 the water used for mining purposes was taken from Dixie creek and tributary streams, but in that year the Kroppe Company began the construction of a small ditch which should take its water out of the John Day river. The next year another ditch was built by the Starr-Webster Company, and in 1870 a third was constructed by Flageolette & Company, the water for both these ditches being taken from the John Day river and being used principally for mining purposes. These three ditches were the principal water canals then and are still the main dependence of the town for its water supply.

But there was to come a time in the near future when the placer mines on Dixie creek could no longer produce as bountifully as in former years and the miners should demand the ground on which Dixie town was situated. This time arrived ten years after the first discovery of gold on the creek, for in the spring of 1872 the encroaching miners could no longer be restrained and the demolition of Dixie town was begun.

At the mouth of the gulch, on the left bank of the creek, a site on which to build a new town had already been selected. As one might expect, the valley had commenced to be settled by a few hardy pioneers. About 1864 Henderson Harrier located a homestead at the mouth of Dixie creek, but though the miners' claims extended down the creek nearly to this farm, no attempt was made to form a settlement at the lower end of the diggings until 1868, when E. W. Webster and Vinton A. Hartley built a saloon, and A. E. Starr and William Kroppe erected cabins on government land just at the base of the hill. Then, realizing that Dixie town was only a temporary place of abode, those who desired to remain on the creek commenced to remove to this new town. A desire to locate a permanent settlement here having been manifested by those already on the ground, it was decided to employ a surveyor to plat the town. So J. W. King (who died just a short time previous to this writing) was engaged, and to him is given the credit of suggesting the name Prairie City. At all events this name seemed most appropriate and pleasing, and Prairie City the place was christened. The town continued to grow slowly until 1872, when those who had remained at Dixie in the hope that something might yet happen to save the town relinquished all hope and added their numbers to those already at Prairie City, resulting in a fair sized village. Meanwhile the tailings of the old placer claims had been either leased or sold to the Chinese, who continued to work the ground to advantage for many years, thus demonstrating that the claims were not as thoroughly worked as they might have been. To-day the former site of Dixie, at one time the second town in the county in population, is marked by a dilapidated weather-stained shack, the former butcher shop, and as the traveler rides down the hill and past the spot a desolate waste of rock heaps and barren gravel banks meets his gaze and tells the story of a deserted mining camp only too plainly.

The first store in Prairie City was conducted by H. H. Hyde, who, in conjunction with the Odd Fellows, erected a commodious building. Frank Flageolette built a saloon and hotel combined, which in after years became known as the Hartley hotel. A Mrs. Cooley kept a boarding house, and other establishments formerly located at Dixie resumed business here. Among the other pioneer business men was Jules LeBrut, who maintained a livery and carried the mails to Prairie City for many years.

Gradually placer mining declined in importance and those previously engaged in that business either moved away or became interested in stock raising and agriculture. Just when the first quartz mine in this section was discovered we have not been able to find out, but it is quite certain that only in the past few years has quartz mining assumed any great importance. For many years after the placer claims were abandoned the mining interests around Prairie City became subordinate to those of stock raising and agriculture and the town became more of an agricultural than a mining center.

A correspondent of the Baker City Bedrock Democrat, writing in the issue of November 9, 1881, says: "This town (Prairie City), as its name implies, is a prairie town, being situated on a sloping side hill, with the John Day valley spreading out beautifully before it. The town contains business houses as follows John Laurance, Jules LeBrut, W. J. Galbraith and N. Fisk, general stores; Mrs. J. W. Cleaver, ladies' goods; Walter Reynolds, harness shop; E. J. Baldwin, tinshop; N. W. Thornton, William Shaw, William Johnson and D. B. Fisk, blacksmiths; Charles Cooley, J. W. Mack, hotels; Jules LeBrut and A. Cripsal, livery stables; Morehead & Cleaver, flour and feed; Samuel Hough and William Brodie, butchers; L. Flageolette, saloon; A. M. Dodson, physician. A good school is kept in operation, and there are several lodges. Several new houses have been erected this season and the future prospects of the town are bright."

A fire originating in Baldwin's tinshop and Galbraith's store, April 24, 1884, reduced the greater portion of the town to ashes, only two buildings being left standing in the upper side of the town. The business section was nearly all destroyed. Of course this calamity was a severe blow to the town, but notwithstanding their loss, the citizens went energetically to work rebuilding, and in a comparatively short time new and more substantial structures had taken the place of those burned, and Prairie City resumed its progress.

Three years later another destructive fire visited the town, consuming the business portion and most of the buildings south of Main street. The flames were first seen pouring out of the Odd Fellows-Hyde building, and despite the desperate efforts made to confine the damage to that structure, the fire spread with the disastrous results above mentioned.

At the session of the legislature in 1891 an act was passed incorporating Prairie City as a town. The spring election resulted in the selection of the following officers: President,

M. Howell; councilmen, William Wright and S. S. Durkheimer; recorder, J. T. Sullens; treasurer, W. R. Fisk; marshal, Albert Worley. The charter bears date February 18, 1891. Ten years later, or in 1901, proceedings were instituted by J. W. Mack, on behalf of the citizens, to secure a clear title from the government to the upper portion of the town site. As heretofore mentioned, the old town was located on government land, title to which had never been obtained, owing to some inexplicable oversight. No one had ever questioned the rights of property owners to the land in that section of the town, but in order that no embarrassing complications might result from this neglect, application for the land was made in the name of Marvin Kilbourn. He had purchased Mr. Harrier's homestead about 1876 and platted the northern or upper portion of the land which now forms the main part of the town and consented to the use of his name. The government readily granted a patent upon the application being filed, and deeds of transfer were then made out to the present property owners.

This same year the legislature granted the town a new charter, giving Prairie City the rights and privileges of a city, under which charter the municipal government is now carried on. At the last election the following officers were elected: Mayor, Marshall Howell; treasurer, William Donaldson; recorder, B. M. Carrier; councilmen, J. B. Dixon, J. H. Blinn, A. L. Babcock and T. M. Ray.

The severest loss which Prairie City has ever sustained was that by fire, May 6th, last, when one-half of the business section of the town was destroyed. Twice before the fire-fiend had wreaked its fury on the struggling village, and now it was to meet with a third and more disastrous loss, just as an era of prosperity had dawned upon it. Within four years the business interests of Grant county's two most important towns have been all but destroyed by the flames.

The fire originated in the Prairie City ho-
29

tel, catching from a defective flue in the kitchen, and in a few minutes the building was enveloped in clouds of flame and smoke. The fire department responded quickly, but for some reason the chemical engine refused to work, and as the town has no water system, the fire fighters had to resort to the old-time bucket brigade. The flames made slow progress at first, however, and had there been even a small water system their progress could easily have been stayed. As it was, the fire spread quickly to Miller's drug store and Durkheimer's general store. From there the fiery element swept westward, devouring the entire business block, including the store and warehouse of Isham Laurance, valued at $25,-000. On the north the residence of S. I. Belknap had caught fire, and in a comparatively short time William Shellabarger's harness and saddle establishment and Kight & McHaley's butcher shop had furnished feed for the flames. Within an hour from the first tap of the alarm the entire business block west of Main street and north of Fifth street was a smouldering heap of charred timbers and ashes, representing a loss of $60,000. Five thousand dollars would probably cover the amount of insurance carried. Besides these business buildings many residences were destroyed and private losses sustained which are not included in the above amount. The citizens, men, women and children, fought heroically to save their town, and many were the acts of daring performed by the fire fighters. Had the wind veered to the southward the whole town would undoubtedly have been destroyed, as conditions were highly favorable for such a calamity. One human life was sacrificed, George Jones, a resident of Prineville, who had come to the city the day previous. He was in his room at the hotel sleeping when the fire broke out, and it is supposed awoke too late to escape from the burning building.

Following is a summary of the losses sustained:

Isham Laurance, general merchandise and

buildings, $25,000; R. T. McHaley, large interests in property, $10,000; Prairie City hotel, $5,000; William M. Shellabarger, harness shop, $3,000; Frank Miller, drug store, $2,500; C. C. Thomas, saloon, $1,700; livery stable, $1,800; P. Basche, office buildings and warehouse, $1,500; Mrs. A. R. Bachus, hotel supplies and household goods, $1,200; Kight & McHaley, butcher shop, $1,000; Sig Durkheimer, store building and household goods, $1,000; Vinton A. Hartley, building, $1,000; Mrs. William Olp, residence and household goods, $800; S. I. Belknap, household goods, $800; Dr. V. C. Belknap, building, $600; H. N. Crain, jewelry store, $500; B. N. Carrier, law office, $300; Prairie City Miner, material and stock, $250; Chamberlain & Long, blacksmith shop, $200; and Levi Anderson, hay and grain, $200.

As rapidly as possible the burnt district was rebuilt, and once again the town resumed its progress with renewed impetus and courage. Fortunately there was no suffering from the cold experienced, as was the case at Canyon City's last fire, and lumber and other necessary building materials were easily secured. More substantial and commodious buildings are being erected and other improvements made which give the place a superiority over its old condition.

Early data regarding the establishment of the first school at Prairie City is almost impossible to obtain. No school whatever was ever maintained at Dixie for the reason that there were very few children in the community, not enough to support a school. The first school of which there is any record was established at Prairie City in the winter of 1876-77, and was taught by a man named White. The school was in session only a few weeks and was held in a small building in the southern portion of the town. The next year, 1877, J. W. Mack, who had just arrived in the country, was engaged to conduct the school, which he did, the session lasting three months. The

desks were of primitive pine board character, and long boards, supported at each end, served for seats. Mr. Mack says there were ninety-seven pupils under him, of all ages and sizes. In 1885 this school house was sold to the Methodist church society and a new frame building of commodious size erected to accommodate the growing school. This building, together with the furniture and apparatus, valued at $3,500, was destroyed by fire Monday, December 16, 1901. Preparations for erecting a new school house are now being made.

Prairie City is the third largest town in Grant county, and Union precinct, in which it is situated, is the largest voting precinct. As the distributing point for the upper John Day valley and the famous Quartzburg, Susanville, Dixie Meadows, Oregon Wonder and Prairie Diggings mining districts, Prairie City is a commercial center of importance, and many predict that it will some day become the metropolis of the county. Its growth has been gradual and substantial and it has grown in response to the country's needs rather than forced into an unnatural existence, as are so many western towns. Its business men are progressive and energetic, and its citizens alive to the needs of their city.

Just above the city are the Prairie City Roller Mills owned by Taylor Brothers. This flouring mill has a capacity of between forty and fifty barrels a day and furnishes considerable of the valley's supply of flour.

The Prairie City Miner is a weekly newspaper published here by W. W. Watson, an experienced newspaper man. The Miner was founded in 1900 and during its two years existence has proven a very valuable aid and potent factor in the upbuilding of the city.

The fraternal societies of the city are represented by flourishing lodges of the A. F. & A. M., organized February 20, 1873; the Grange, organized in 1872; the I. O. O. F., established in 1871; the A. O. U. W., Modern ·

Woodmen, and several auxiliary lodges. There is only one church represented here, the Methodist, and this society owns a commodious building.

At present the population of Prairie City is between three hundred and four hundred people, and growing, and within the past year or two the city has made rapid strides in a business way. The mining industry has had new life infused into it by the introduction of capital and energy, and already a thirty-ton smelter has been erected and is in operation in the Quartzburg district, while preparations are being made to do extensive work in other surrounding districts this year. The Sumpter valley railway has been surveyed across Burnt river and Dixie mountains and down Dixie creek to Prairie City, and all feel confident that this country does not purpose to allow this rich section to be without railway transportation much longer. The vast agricultural possibilities of the John Day valley, with its thousands of acres of the most fertile land in eastern Oregon, are beginning to be appreciated, and with development and progress along mining and agricultural lines, which will follow the advent of a railway, Prairie City cannot help but reap a benefit and attain to high rank as one of the most prosperous, healthy and beautiful small cities in the state.

LONGCREEK.

From a scenic and sanitary point of view the town of Longcreek is delightfully situated at the head of a valley, several miles in extent. The approach to the town, either from the north, south or east, is a long and steep descent, and for miles it is plainly visible—a scattered settlement—on the slope of the foothills far below. Longcreek is one of the older, and perhaps the largest, of the outlying villages of Grant county.

Joseph W. Keeney opened a general store here about 1879. Three or four years later Edward Allen purchased the stock and continued the business. A water power roller-

mill was erected in 1885 by Williams & Blackman. These were the first steps in the building of the town which has grown to one of considerable importance. There are now two general stores, a grocery and a drug store, a jewelry store, the Monumental hotel, a livery stable, two blacksmith shops, a meat market, a harness and saddle store, a newspaper (The Longcreek Ranger). There are two physicians. Two churches and a good school building have been erected. In 1891 the town was incorporated. Its present officers are: Mayor, G. M. Roberts; recorder, George Rinehart; treasurer, Frank Kahler; marshal, J. M. Shields. The postmaster is Frank Kahler. A stock and agriculturil region is tributary to the town, and its prospects for substantial growth are good.

OTHER SETTLEMENTS.

There is a number of minor settlements and postoffices variously located as follows: Mt. Vernon, in the central part of the county on the John Day river; Beach Creek Station, on the creek of the same name; Hamilton, an inland point fourteen miles northwest of Longcreek; Monument, in the northwest corner of the county near North Fork; Fox, in the west central part on Fox creek; Dayville, in the west, near South Fork; Suplee, in the southwest corner; Duncanville, a few miles northwest of Soda Springs; Marysville, directly east of Canyon City; Seneca and Izee, south of the Strawberry mountains; Margaret, twenty-five miles east of John Day, south of the river; Comer, at the head of Dixie creek; Alamo and Lawton, mining towns in the northeast.

Susanville is an old mining camp in the northeastern part of the county—the site of the oldest quartz mining camp in the county. In 1900 it had a population of fifty-one. In the extreme northeastern part of the county is Granite, a prosperous mining town of three hundred inhabitants. Susanville and Granite are in what is known as the Greenhorn mining district.

HON. HENRY HALL.

BIOGRAPHICAL.

HON. HENRY HALL.—There can be no doubt but that Grant county, and the entire state of Oregon as well, owe much to the ability and labors of the prominent citizen of whom we now speak and to whom we desire to grant representation in this volume. A pioneer of the earliest days, acquainted with the county from the time the first white men trod its soil, experienced in all the hardships and toil of a pioneer's career, a man that has ever been ready to put his shoulder to the wheel to assist in the progress of the country and that has ever manifested his public spirit through wise acts and worthy achievements, Mr. Hall is eminently fitted to sustain the honors which have come justly to him and to fill the leading position where his fellows have rightly placed him.

Born in Dorset, England, in 1836, he there spent the years of his life until 1856, gaining the excellent training to be had in the schools of his land and acquiring the skill of the husbandman and horticulturist. In 1859 he came to the United States, filled with buoyant hopes and fired by a spirit of progression and energy. His first occupation was operating a dairy for J. Taylor in Polk county, where he continued for two years, and then in company with his brother, William, bought the outfit and removed it to Walla Walla in the fall of 1861. In the hard winter of 1861-62 they lost all their stock, and the spring bringing tidings of the new diggings on Powder river, in company with his brother, Thomas Brentz and Napoleon Nelson, Mr. Hall determined to seek his fortune there, and soon was on the ground. He went on to Canyon City, and there commenced mining, which occupied him until 1864. Thomas Brentz and Mr. Hall were the builders of the first log cabin in Grant county,

is the opinion of Mr. Hall. After the time in mining, as stated, Mr. Hall and his brother bought the farm where he is living at the present time, four miles west from Prairie City. Their farm contained eight hundred acres, but has been increased to two thousand five hundred acres and is well improved and stocked. In company with his brother, Mr. Hall is still raising cattle and tilling the soil, prosperity having attended his efforts from the beginning. In political matters he has ever been active, and holds with the Republican party. In 1880 the people of the county called him to the office of county commissioner and with satisfaction to all he discharged the functions of that office. From 1882 to 1885 he was state senator and did excellent service in that capacity, holding the chairmanship of the important committee on education, and was also a potent factor in passing the Hygiene bill and the bill against prize fighting. Fraternally Mr. Hall is affiliated with the I. O. O. F., Lodge No. 33, of Prairie City.

Mr. Hall was married in 1870, and has three children, John, Jennie and Egbert. It is interesting that Mr. Hall's sons have, unaided, constructed an electric plant that supplies the house with light, which, even in these days of advanced engineering, is a feat that is very praiseworthy. Mr. Hall believes that Napoleon Nelson was the first man to make a trip to The Dalles with gold dust from the new camp.

GEORGE P. MULCAHY.—While much is due to the hardy prospector that endures the grief incident to finding the veins of nature's hidden wealth, still there largely devolves upon the promoter of these prospects a responsibility that is second to none in the entire operation of mining, from outfitting the prospertor to conducting the full-fledged producer. The successful promoter has to be a skilled prospector, a good geologist, a judge of ores, a mechanical engineer, and capable of judging water powers and landscapes, as well as a first class business man and always filled with that enthusiasm that will interest the capitalist. He also should be able to judge of veins, which in itself is a profession. The gentleman whose name is at the head of this article has gained real distinction in a number of lines in his business life, but as a promoter of mines he is one of the leading figures, not only of our county, but of the entire northwest, having gained a valuable reputation as wide as is the knowledge of the famous camps west of the Rockies.

George P. was born in Ireland, of American parents, on November 10, 1864, and the following year was brought to Toledo, Ohio, with the rest of the family. There and in Michigan he received his education, learning also telegraphy and becoming an expert operator. At the age of eighteen he came to the Cœur d'Alene mining section and at once took part in that business. Later he entered the employ of the Northern Pacific Railway Company as a train dispatcher at Sprague, then managed the same office in conjunction with the Western Union at Ellensburg. While in that city he organized the development company that discovered the iron mines on the Teenaway. At the time of the opening of the Okanagan reservation he went thither and participated in the early times of stirring interest there enacted, both in mining affairs and in county organization. He was nominated for the county treasurership and doubtless would have been elected to that office had not a bitter fight as to the location of the county seat been precipitated. He was not yet of age when that nomination was made. He was connected with some of the first mining locations on Palmer mountain. From here he entered the employ of the O. R. & N. Company in eastern Oregon, and served in several responsible positions. After this he opened a real estate and mining office in Spokane and began the operations that have made his name well known in all this vast mining region and himself famous as one of the most skillful and able promoters

that have ever operated in the west. He helped to build Rossland, British Columbia, has aided in the promotion of many of the finest mines in that section and has induced large amounts of capital to seek investment in the mining camps of the northwest. At the present time he is operating in Grant county and territory adjacent thereto, while his headquarters are in Spokane still. Among the properties that he has promoted may be mentioned the famous Prairie Diggings near Canyon City, as well as many in Idaho and others nearer. Perhaps no other man of the county has been instrumental in assisting materially in the upbuilding of the interests, not only of the county, but of the entire northwest, more largely than has Mr. Mulcahy. His judgment in regard to a prospect has rarely been found to be incorrect. Happy is the prospector when he can succeed in getting Mr. Mulcahy to take hold of his claims.

The marriage of Mr. Mulcahy and Miss Louise Richenberg was solemnized in Ruby, Washington, in 1889, and to them have been born two children, Helen U. and Grace E.

---◆◆◆---

DAVID MAGILL.—There is no class of citizens of our prosperous county that have done more toward the development of its boundless resources and for the advancement of its interests than the stockmen, of which there are not a few domiciled within its borders, and among this number the gentleman whose name initiates this paragraph demands especial mention in this volume of the abiding chronicles of Grant county and the biographing records of its leading citizens, since his sagacity and enterprise have made him prominent in the affairs of the county, besides giving him good success in the private operations of his business.

Brown county, Kansas, is the native place of David, and there he passed the initial four years of his existence after his birth, which occurred in 1860. Then he was taken by his parents to Polk county across the plains with ox teams—thus did the hardy pioneers of the last century brave the dangers and endure the hardships and deprivations of a new country, far from civilization and peopled with savages. His parents were Caleb W. and Nancy

Magill, the father living now in California, and the mother having passed to the rewards of another world, her remains being buried in the Willamette valley. At the age of twenty, our subject came to this county, and soon thereafter took a homestead where he still resides, one mile northwest of Izee. He has added to the original holdings until his estate is now over five hundred acres. This is well improved and he raises the ordinary products of the soil in this region, but his attention is largely devoted to raising cattle. He has some fine herds and prosperity has attended his faithful endeavors.

The marriage of Mr. Magill and Miss Lona, daughter of R. V. Office, was solemnized in 1884, and they have become the parents of two children, Zella and Arthur. Mr. Magill is a member of John Day Lodge, No. 105, A. O. U. W. He is quite prominent in politics, being a potent factor at the conventions. He allies himself with the Democrats, firmly holding the stanch old principles of Jefferson.

CHARLES BALLANCE.—In the person of the subject of this sketch we have one of the most substantial men among Grant county's population of men of both ability and integrity. Mr. Ballance has been one that has labored steadily and with telling wisdom and energy for the welfare of the interests of his chosen section, as well as manifesting commendable sagacity and enterprise in the prosecution of the business interests that are occupying him, and wherein he has been favored with the success that is sure to follow wisely bestowed industry. It is a pleasure to accord to such an one a representation in this volume, and, too, since when the thrilling call came to assemble at the capitol for its defense against the minions of treason and the hordes that would have torn from its proud cupola the star-bedecked banner that had been the light of liberty and the safeguard of the independent citizens of this republic, he was one of the first to offer his services, enlisting in Company E, Second Kansas Infantry. He participated in the battle of Wilson's creek and several skirmishes, serving two months beyond the three for which he had offered himself. After being mustered out he was one of three that were

instrumental in 1862 in forming a company, being Company C, of the Sixteenth Kansas Cavalry, that did excellent service throughout the entire war. He went in as second lieutenant, but was soon promoted to the position of first lieutenant. He was on the plains considerable of the time under Generals Fremont and Curtis, and participated in the battle of Westport, besides many skirmishes. At the close of the war he was mustered out and returned to his home in Kansas and occupied himself with farming until 1874, then came by rail to San Francisco, thence by steamer to Portland, settling in Linn county and taking up farming. Two years later he came to his present place, one mile east of Longcreek, and homesteaded the same where he has devoted himself to farming and stock raising. He owns two hundred and forty acres, well improved and skillfully tilled. He has a good house, barn and orchard, and a band of cattle and horses.

The birth of Mr. Ballance was on November 5, 1840, near Macomb, McDonough county, Illinois, being the son of John and Hannah Ballance. He was reared on a farm and attended the public school. While yet a child his parents removed to Lee county, Iowa, and in 1857 they came to Franklin county, Kansas, where he remained until 1860, going that year to Pike's Peak and returning the following year.

In 1862 he was married to Miss Eliza J. Ricker, of Franklin county, Kansas, and to them were born four children: Charles A. married to Julia Dustin, and living near Susanville; Melvina, wife of Henry A. Murphy, a merchant of Monument; Anna Belle, wife of Orta Walker, of Monument; Effie M., wife of George A. Reinhart, of Longcreek, now deceased. Mrs. Ballance died at her home near Longcreek in 1877.

Mr. Ballance contracted a second marriage on January 16, 1881, the lady of his choice being Sarah J., daughter of S. B. and Berthana (Wright) Carter. They have become the parents of the following children: Robert W., deceased; Bertha; John Carl; Frank O., deceased. Mrs. Carter came to this country from Missouri, bringing her children, her husband having died previously. She is now in her eightieth year, and is living with her children. Mr. Ballance is considered one of the most enterprising and stable citizens of the county, having ever manifested a spirit of uprightness and integrity which has won for him the esteem of his fellows, while they repose generously in him their confidence.

* * *

CLEMENT C. BLACKWELL.—To the esteemed and patriotic citizen whose name initiates this paragraph we are pleased to grant a representation in this volume of the chronicles of Grant county, since he has been a forceful factor in the development of the resources of the county and instrumental in materially augmenting the wealth of the same, while his abilities as a stockman and agriculturist have been marked and manifested in the success that he has enjoyed while he has labored in those industries and his integrity and uprightness are patent to all.

To Joseph and Mary Blackwell, on April 6, 1826, was born Clement C., on Wolf creek, near Centerville, Tennessee, where he was educated in the common schools and worked on a farm with his parents until 1850, when he went to Franklin county, Arkansas; four years later he went to Tarrant county, Texas, and two years following that he removed to Newton county, Arkansas, where he remained until the fifth day of April, 1875, when he started across the plains with teams. The journey was consummated without accident or exceptional incident and their first winter in Oregon was spent in Fox valley, there being but one other family there at that time. He rented a farm near John Day and in the fall of 1877 entered a homestead, on his present ranch three miles east from Longcreek. He bought four hundred and eighty acres more, which he sold subsequently. He set himself to improving his property and raising stock, cattle, sheep and horses. During the Indian trouble of 1878 he lost all of his horses but one, the Indians succeeding in capturing them. His labors continued unremittingly here until 1899, when on account of ill health he sold his stock and retired from more active life. His home place is well improved, being well tilled and having a comfortable house, large barn, and a fine orchard. During the Civil war he offered himself for service in the Union army, but was rejected on account of rheumatism. Later he offered again, and while his

case was pending the war closed and so he did not succeed in gaining the opportunity for fighting for the flag that he loved.

On September 6, 1846, he was married to Jane W., a native of Tennessee, and a daughter of Samuel and Mahala Morris, near Beardstown, Perry county, Tennessee. The following children have been born to them: Jesse A., married to Matilda Hudson, and living in Newton county, Arkansas; James Madison and Thomas Jefferson, twins, deceased; Jeremiah W., married to Mary Parkerson and living in Sparta, Baker county; Samuel B., married to Clara Ethel, living near Glens Ferry, Idaho; Richard S., married to Maggie Cobb, living near Hamilton, Grant county; Nancy E., wife of Samuel F. Branson, near Longcreek; Bernice P., wife of William M. Carter, near Longcreek; Joseph R., married to Sarah, and living at Sumpter; Henry Y., a cattle buyer, of Burns; Mary M., wife of B. O. Dustin, of Sparta, Baker county; Clement W., married to Fannie Shield, living near Walla Walla; James, wife of James Criswell, near Longcreek; John L., living at home; Leona E., wife of Edward Turk, of Sumpter, but now deceased. It is of note that from the time Mr. and Mrs. Blackwell lost their twins until the death of their daughter Leona fifty years had elapsed without a death in the family. It is also interesting to know that the children, grandchildren and great-grandchildren of this worthy and venerable couple now number over one hundred that are living. Mr. Blackwell has been strong and rugged until recently, and Mrs. Blackwell is hale and hearty and active in the duties of the household. They have seen the hardships and deprivations of the pioneers in a number of places and they have reared a family in this community wherein principles of uprightness have been exemplified and their children are all respected members of society. For forty years Mr. Blackwell has been a member of the Masons. He has been a disciple of Nimrod and was very fond of the chase in days of more vigor, claiming many triumphs in large game, as deer, elk, bear, etc. Mrs. Blackwell's father was reared in Maryland and her mother in North Carolina. They removed to Tennessee, and the father died there, while the mother went to Arkansas and remained until the time of her demise.

JOHN HUGHES.—Many of our most esteemed citizens have come from the land whence hails the subject of this sketch, England, and to their credit be it said that no more worthy class of men are supporters of our free institutions than this same number of stanch Englishmen, of whom Mr. Hughes is a noble type. A man of courage, wisdom and ability, coupled with a frame that was capable of enduring hardships, he has spent a goodly time on the frontier stations of our great land and has successfully met and overcome the various obstacles there to be found, as well as passing through the many and thrilling experiences that attend this mode of life.

John H. was born to John H. and Rebecca (Mattox) Hughes, on June 27, 1849, in Liverpool, England. There he attended the public schools and lived with his parents until 1863, when he came across the ocean with his father's brother, landing in New York. For a short time he stayed there, and then came to St. Joseph, Missouri, whence, in June, 1864, he started across the plains in a train composed of twelve mule teams. At Fort Laramie they joined an ox train of sixty-two teams, and another mule train of twelve teams. A short time after leaving Fort Laramie the second mule train became delayed and were separated some distance from the others. The Indians attacked this unfortunate number and killed thirteen men and took one woman captive. The only other woman of that train wrapped herself so well in blankets that the Indians did not discover her. The reds burned the wagons and went away with their booty. The following season they released the captive. The remainder of the trains went on their journey and without serious attack from the savages, except some skirmishes. When the train arrived at Salt Lake Mr. Hughes left it and stayed in Salt Lake City for one winter. In the spring he went to prospecting and until 1878 he was working at this line of industry in all the leading camps of Nevada and Utah. In 1878 he came to Baker City, and shortly afterward on to Granite, where he stayed until 1881, then went to Susanville, where he has been actively engaged and interested in mining since. He was the original owner of the famous Badger mine, now one of the most valuable mines in this region. He sold this property in 1897, but still has some valuable

claims in the vicinity among which is the noted Big Nugget. He owns the Monumental hotel in Longcreek, which he operated until recently, now leasing the same. He owns a good store building, which is well stocked with general merchandise, and here he does a flourishing business, having entered the commercial world three years since. He also has a branch store at Susanville, and is doing a fine business there. He has an elegant residence in Longcreek and several other residence buildings that he rents. He also has eighty acres well improved that join the town, besides other property in various places.

The marriage of Mr. Hughes and Mrs. Ella Walch was celebrated in January, 1892, and to them have been born two children: John, deceased, and Emily Ruth. Mr. Hughes' parents came to this country ten years later than he did and located at Boise, but afterward went to the coast, where they now live. Mr. Hughes is a member of the A. F. & A. M., and is highly esteemed throughout the entire community, having the confidence of the people.

THOMAS H. C. BRASFIELD.—Among the many prosperous and well-to-do stockmen and agriculturists of Grant county there must not be failure to mention the distinguished gentleman and enterprising citizen of whom we now have the pleasure of speaking, since he has wrought within the precincts of this county for a number of years and has demonstrated himself to have capabilities and sagacity that are worthy of commendable recognition, having achieved a visible success in the material affairs of this world and carved a name for himself in the esteem and confidence of his fellows.

In Smithville, Missouri, he was born in 1858, being the son of a prominent business man of that place. His early years were spent in acquiring the needed educational discipline and in operating in his father's general merchandise store. When he had arrived at the age for independent action he came to Denver, Colorado, where he remained for fifteen months and then continued his journey to Linn county, this state, remaining there until 1885, the date of his advent to this county, and after due investigation of its resources, he bought a right to a quarter section, where he now lives, adjoining Izee, and there commenced the related industries of stock raising and tilling the soil. He has added to his estate until now it is one of the generous proportions of two hundred and eighty-seven acres, besides forty acres of desert land that he has recently filed on. He has gained a gratifying success in these occupations and is one of the prosperous and leading stockmen of his section.

Mr. Brasfield and Miss Ida M., daughter of D. P. Porter, of Linn county, Oregon, and a native of Ohio, were married in 1898, and they have become the parents of one child, Thomas W. R., who died in infancy. Mr. Brasfield is affiliated with the A. F. & A. M., Lodge No. 438, of Smithville, Missouri. Mrs. Brasfield is greatly interested in the educational affairs of her section and is occupied frequently in teaching school and is considered one of the leading educators of the county. Mr. Brasfield has always taken an active interest in political matters and is especially interested in school affairs, being one that is constantly endeavoring to better the educational facilities of the county.

ANDREW ANDERSON:—In the person of Mr. Anderson we have one of Grant county's progressive and industrious stockmen and agriculturists, and one also that has wrought in this capacity for nearly one-third of a century on the place that he now occupies, having come here in a very early day when the first pioneers were making their way into this favored region. Substantial, capable and upright, he has ever manifested unswerving integrity and good principles in all his demeanor and dealings.

Born December 1, 1830, in Sweden, he remained there until 1858, and then came to this land of the free. He followed a seafaring life and before 1864 he had served two years in the American navy. His skill and ability were so manifest that in this time he was one of the gunners and gained distinction in this responsible position. On April 10, 1864, he landed in San Francisco and then went to The Dalles in a few months, where he remained until the spring of 1865, when he came to this region and engaged in mining. For three years he

was occupied with this industry and then took his ranch where he lives, six miles northeast from Mount Vernon, on Beach creek. He went to raising cattle and sheep, and at this work he has since continued, while prosperity has smiled upon him. In political matters he is ever active, and he firmly holds to the principles of the grand old party that has piloted the nation safely through crises when other advocates have failed. He has always been a stanch Republican, and has the courage of his convictions. Mr. Anderson has never taken unto himself a wife, preferring the quieter joys of bachelorhood to the responsibilities and cares incident to connubial bliss.

THOMAS B. KEENEY.—It is with pleasure that we accord to the enterprising stockman and esteemed citizen of Grant county whose name is at the head of this article a representation in this volume, since his life of activity and wisdom in operation have justly entitled him to be ranked with the leading stockmen of the county and with its most substantial citizens, having ever manifested stanch principles of uprightness and an unswerving integrity that is but commensurate with his other qualities of worth.

Thomas B. is the son of Jonathan and Mary A. Keeney, having been born on September 10, 1852, in Jasper county, Missouri, whence in 1857 his parents came across the plains with ox teams, the family consisting of five children and the father and mother at the start and the father and mother and six children at the close, when they landed in Sonoma county, California, having consumed six months on the road. In the spring of 1858 the family came to Linn county, Oregon, and a little later went to Lane county, near Eugene. It was in the spring of 1861 that they moved east of the mountains to Umatilla county, where the father entered into the industry of raising sheep. Our subject received his education in the various schools at the places where the family resided. He remained at the home place, assisting his father in raising cattle and sheep until 1874, when he and his brother, Marshall S., came to the vicinity of Longcreek and entered into partnership in the stock business. They have been attended with prosperity from the beginning, a sure result of care, wisdom and industry such as they have manifested. The estate of the firm consists of one thousand acres, well improved and all fenced. Mr. Keeney has a good residence, barn and orchard, and other improvements of value and comfort. Formerly they were operating in sheep, but these were sold and they now give their attention to cattle, of which they have large herds. During the time of trouble with the Indians they suffered heavy losses from these savages, but since they have been uniformly successful in their enterprises.

Mr. Keeney and Miss Nancy E., daughter of Huse and Eliza Snodderly, of Prineville, occurred in 1882, on December 1. To them were born the following children: Elsie Fay, Dora Dott and James Crittenden, the last one deceased. In 1899 Mrs. Keeney was called from the duties and walks of this life to the world beyond, leaving her husband and little ones to mourn her sad demise. Mr. Keeney's father was a prominent wool grower of Umatilla county and a man highly esteemed. His death occurred in 1884, and the mother was called the next year to follow her companion.

DANIEL C. COHOE.—In the person of the estimable gentleman whose name initiates this paragraph we have a character that is full of interest and a sturdy citizen who has wrought in the experiences of the typical frontiersman throughout its entire gamut. A unique character that no other country has ever been able to produce is the typical westerner, of which Mr. Cohoe is a perfect specimen. Fearless, yet gently courageous but careful, moderately educated in books, but possessed of deep erudition in all of those qualities that make up genuine manhood, and intimately acquainted with the face of nature and her ways in this grandest of all regions, the Rockies and their adjacent territory to the Pacific, well acquainted with the savage foe and the fierce hardships which nature binds relentlessly on those who first invade her domains, yet generous and open-hearted as the boundless country where he has spent his days, we feel that Grant county is to be congratulated in the possession of this veteran of pioneer exploration and we are well pleased to grant him a representation in our volume.

To Daniel and Mary Cohoe, on October 24, 1836, near Altoona, Blair county, Pennsylvania, was born the subject of this sketch. Working the farm and attending school in a log house on the present site of Altoona, his childhood days were spent, but when budding majority came he pushed to the west and settled for a year near the young town of Davenport, Iowa, then journeyed on to Leavenworth, Kansas, where he entered the employ of the government as assistant on a surveying expedition into Wyoming. In 1859 he went to Pike's Peak, then returned to Kansas, and finally to his old home in Pennsylvania. In the spring of 1861 he started with mule teams across the plains and completed his journey at Chico, California, where he mined for two years and then went to the Humboldt mines, where he operated for a time, and then, on account of the hostility of the Indians, came to the Owyhee mines, whence in 1869 he came to Boise City, and the folowing year found him at the Eldorado mines in Baker county. In 1872 he visited the Olive mines near Granite and in 1874 came to Prairie City and lived there until 1884. He assisted to build the first stamp mills in the Dixie mining camp. In 1884 he located on his present home place, two miles south from Monument, where he has lived and occupied himself in raising sheep and cattle, the latter taking the place of the sheep in 1898. He has one half section in his home place, which is well improved and wisely laid out, having a handsome residence, good barns and other necessary appliances for a first class ranch, as orchard, fences, utensils and so forth. He also owns three hundred and twenty acres in Fox valley, well improved.

The marriage of Mr. Cohoe and Miss Anna Elizabeth, daughter of Jacob and Mary Rhoades, of Altoona, Pennsylvania, was solemnized on April 4, 1861. They have become the parents of the following children: James C. died in infancy; Willliam H., a farmer living near Hamilton; Nevada, wife of G. V. McHaley, a merchant and stockman of Hamilton; George A., married to Daisy Davidson and living near Hamilton; Celina, wife of Emil Scharff, a stockman of Monument; Charles W., married to Maggie Titus; Mary F., deceased; Dora A., recently deceased; John E.; Alice, deceased; Rodney. In political matters Mr. Cohoe is with the Republicans and is active in the interests of what he firmly believes to be for the welfare of the country and its people. To this esteemed and highly respected couple we are glad to render the tribute of a representation in this volume, and it is but right to say that perhaps no man in the county today has had a more adventurous life and has been dominated by keener wisdom than has Mr. Cohoe, who won his way on the frontier wrested from nature's vaults a rich share of her stores, generously bestowed it with an unstinted hand, fought frequently the savage Indians, and now, after faithfully and wisely consummating it all is quietly spending the golden years of his life in the spot he has chosen for home while he enjoys the competence that his thrift and care have produced.

WILLIAM ARMSTRONG.—No more worthy class of men ever walked the free land of the United States than those who left the comforts of home and civilization to brave the terrors of the desert, the dangers of hostile savages, the hardships of the pilgrim's life and the want and suffering incident to those who are thus isolated. To them is the honor of opening a new realm to the ingress of the thousands that were crowded out of eastern sections of congestion, who have come to the broad fields of the west and made for themselves homes and names and carved out fortunes from the boundless resources of nature's lavish display in these favored regions. Not least among these intrepid and sturdy ones is the gentleman whose name is at the head of this article, and who has wrought well and successfully in the furthering of the development of this country.

In 1830, in the mother country, he first saw the light and for twenty-nine years he labored and studied in his native country and then led by an adventurous spirit he migrated to the new land, settling first in Grant county, Wisconsin, where he remained for a few years, then came direct to Oregon, arriving in Canyon City as early as 1864. His attention was turned to mining here until 1870, when he purchased the old military road ranch, where he is now living, two miles north from Mount Vernon, at the Mount Vernon warm springs. Here he gave himself to stock raising and the

improvement of his property, and the success that has attended his efforts has given him a good competence and a comfortable home. His is a well kept ranch, bearing evidence of thrift and industry in every particular. His improvements are tasty and substantial and he has been satisfied to take a medium sized ranch and improve it well rather than to have a great quantity of land that is half cultivated.

The marriage of Mr. Armstrong and Miss Hannah Stonehouse, a native of England, was solemnized in 1862 and to them have been born three children: Robert E., Lizzie, deceased, and William C.

HON. FRANCIS C. SELS.—If a man is to be judged by the accomplishments of his life and his success is to be measured by the consummation of his achievements, surely then we are to accord to the prominent citizen whose name is at the head of this article a place of leadership in the annals of Grant county, since he has been one of the potent factors in the government of the same and in its proper representation in the state as well as a very material force in the advancement of its progress and the development of its resources since the early day in which he first domiciled within its borders.

Like so many of our most thrifty and enterprising citizens, Mr. Sels was born of good old German stock in Westphalia, his native town being Meschede, and the date of his nativity 1837. At the age of seventeen the attractions of the "Fatherland" were left behind, farewells were spoken to the friends and relatives, and young Sels turned his face to the Mecca of the world's advancement, America, and opened a career that was destined to be fraught with stirring activities, crowded with events and crowned with becoming success. On December 31, 1854, he reached California, and on July 1, 1862, he set foot in what is now Canyon City. That summer was spent in mining in the Prairie diggings, four miles northeast from Prairie City, and the following spring he opened a general merchandise establishment in Canyon, his partner being E. J. W. Stemme, who had been his companion on his journeys hitherto. In this business Mr. Sels continued until 1866, when he sold out to his brother,

HON. FRANCIS C. SELS.

Il. R. Sels. From 1864 to 1866 he was justice of the peace, and the last year of that time was also postmaster, which he resigned to accept the treasurership of the county, having been elected to that position in 1866. Two years later he was chosen state senator, de defeating his opponent, John Driblesby, by a majority of five votes, he being the only Republican candidate that was elected. Driblesby carried the matter to the senate in contest and secured his seat because Mr. Sels had an undecided contest on his hands with L. O. Stearns from the election of 1866. In 1869 he took a pleasure trip back to his native land, and upon returning to Canyon City in 1870 was elected county judge, which position he held for four years. In 1870 Mr. Sels bought the brewery in Canyon City, and two weeks later it was destroyed by fire. Immediately he rebuilt fireproof buildings and gave his attention to the prosecution of this business, which he has successfully operated since, in addition to the varied and numerous public positions that he has faithfully and efficiently filled.

It is of note that when he was in The Dalles in 1863 buying goods, that his train was attacked by the Indians when fifteen miles out from Canyon City. Again, the next year, the attack was repeated, but in both cases the savages were repulsed. During the long and interesting career of our subject he has never entered the matrimonial state, choosing rather the quietness of celebacy than the cares and responsibilities of domesticity. And now in the golden time of life, with the pleasures of a goodly competence that his sagacity and enterprise have accumulated, Mr. Sels is enjoying to the utmost his portion, being also favored with the respect, esteem and confidence of all that are numbered in his acquaintanceship.

FRANK McGIRR.—The prominest citizen and esteemed gentleman whose name is at the head of this article is one of the leading stockmen and stock dealers in eastern Oregon and has wrought with herculean efforts in this county for the advancement of its welfare and for the development of its resources, as well as being eminently successful in the achievements of his private business enterprises. As a pioneer to the region where he

now resides, he commenced at the bottom of the ladder and it is largely due to his efforts that Fox valley owes its prosperity, since he was instrumental in bringing the resources with which it is blessed to the attention of others that the way should be opened for the ingress of civilization.

Mr. McGirr's father was a native of Ireland and came to the United States when a lad of thirteen, locating in Missouri, where later he married Miss Elizabeth Haskins and they became the parents of five children, four of them being in Grant county, and the other is deceased. In 1852 the family came across the plains and experienced much trouble with the Indians en route, losing one man and nearly fifty head of stock in the many battles that occurred on the Humboldt river. They settled near Stockton, California, and later moved to Nevada, where the father died, and in 1899 the mother died in this county. Referring more particularly to Mr. Frank McGirr, the subject of this sketch, we may say that his birth occurred in Stockton, California, on January 23, 1860, but while still a child he went with his parents to Austin, Nevada, where he was raised on a farm and in giving attention to the herds his father owned. Here also he received his education in the public schools. At an early age he commenced the life of the cowboy and rode for several years in Nevada. It was in 1879 that he came to the north in company with thirty-five others who were detailed to bring ten thousand head of cattle from Sterns mountain to Wyoming for a Mr. Davis. The cattle were divided into three bands, and twelve men were the number with each band. Before completing the journey Mr. McGirr resigned his place and came through this valley en route to Walla Walla. In the following spring he returned to this place and took up a pre-emption and then a homestead, where he now lives, at Fox postoffice. He has added until his estate is nearly twelve hundred acres, and it is all fenced and improved. He gives his attention to farming and raising stock and also to buying and selling, being one of the heaviest dealers in this section. He has some very fine specimens of thoroughbred cattle and takes a great interest in improving the stock throughout the valley.

The marriage of Mr. McGirr and Miss Henrietta, daughter of Harice and Marguerite

Hart, late of prescott, Washington, was consummated on March 21, 1880, and to this happy union there have been born the following children: Rhoda E., deceased; Nora May, deceased; Albert; Frank B.; Ettie E.; Nellie M.; Cash E., deceased; Bertha N.; and Mabel Irene. In addition to the stock ranch Mr. McGirr owns a fine home in John Day, where the family reside during the school season, that the children may have the advantage of the better schools. It is of note that Mr. McGirr was the first man to bring a family into the valley and since his settlement here he has been a power for the advancement of all that is for the welfare of the people and the interests of the community. At the present writing he is feeding two hundred young steers on the John Day and is one of the leading stockmen of this entire region.

GEORGE W. PORTER.—Among the progressive and thrifty population of Grant county that give their attention to the art of agriculture and raising stock are found many of the most substantial and worthy citizens, and the gentleman of whom we now have the pleasure of writing is one whose industry, energy and wisdom are manifested to all and who has wrought with faithfulness in the good work of developing the resources of the county and advancing its substantial interests, while in his personal demeanor there has ever been manifested a stanch uprightness and unswerving integrity that are both attractive and commendable.

Mr. Porter was born in Dixmount, Maine, in 1832, and when but three years of age his mother died and he spent his childhood and youth in the home of relatives. When he arrived at the age of twenty his attention and time were turned to teaching school, and for a series of years he was numbered with the active and progressive educators of his native place. Following this he learned the wagonmaker's trade and wrought at it for ten years, then turned to farming for a time, and in 1870 he migrated to this section of the west. For a period he was occupied in farming near to John Day and then took a homestead in Malheur, but subsequently he bought the place where he now lives two miles west from John

Day. Here he owns and cultivates three hundred and twenty acres of land and is counted one of the leading stockmen and agriculturists of the county. His place is well improved and an air of neatness and thrift characterize everything about his premises, and he has added many things that make rural life attractive and comfortable, while his care and ability as a farmer are manifested in every department. Mr. Porter also owns the ranch that he secured in Malheur and considerable other property, being a substantial representative of the property interests of his region. His herds are extensive and his skill in handling them gives him the best of returns from his investments.

The marriage of Mr. Porter and Miss Caroline Prentice was celebrated in Maine in the year 1856. To them have been born four children: Francis, Edith, Lesley and Mary, all of whom are married. In fraternal affiliations Mr. Porter is identified with the Masons, Archon Lodge, in Dixmount, Maine. In politics he is a stanch Republican and has always been an upholder of their platform. He has a goodly prominence in local affairs, having served as justice of the peace for two terms in succession, and is always wide awake in matters that pertain to the welfare of the state and education.

ZACHARIAH J. MARTIN.—Among the worthy representatives of Grant county there cannot be failure to mention the esteemed gentleman whose name heads this article, unless there should be serious incompleteness in our volume, for his life of faithful endeavor and commendable achievement as an educator for a decade and also in administering the law in a judicial capacity have been marked and faithful, while his walk has ever been such as to win the confidence and command the respect of all the people.

Mr. Martin was born in April, 1869, in the Golden State, being the son of P. C. and Phoebe (Davis) Martin, natives respectively of Indiana and Missouri, the father having crossed the plains in 1854, and the mother in the previous year, both having had the experience of riding the entire distance behind ox teams. Their marriage occurred in March 1862, and in 1869 they came to Oregon. Zachariah J. received his education in this state and at the age of nineteen years began teaching school in Gilliam and Grant counties and continued in that capacity with undisturbed and excellent success for ten years. From 1890 to 1897 he was justice of the peace in the Haystack precinct and his decisions and administration of the law were marked with ability and integrity. In 1898 the people of Grant county called him to act as county treasurer, he having run on the Republican ticket. In this capacity he is acting at the present time, and it is with credit to himself and advantage to his constituency. In fraternal affiliations he is associated with the W. of W., Lodge No. 222, Canyon City. Mr. Martin is universally beloved and esteemed, being possessed of those qualities that are the admiration of all and displaying geniality, ability and integrity always.

MARTIN C. LESLEY.—It now becomes our pleasant task to give in brief review the salient points of the interesting career of the esteemed gentleman and enterprising agriculturist whose name initiates this paragraph and who has wrought assiduously for the advancement of the interests of Grant county, as well as making a successful battle in the private business operations that he has prosecuted with vigor and sagacity while domiciled here.

Martin C. was born in Pike county, Kentucky, on October 25, 1831, being the son of Amos and Lucinda Lesley, who removed with their son to Edgar county, Illinois, in 1837. It was the lot of our subject to have the invigorating and wholesome exercise of assisting his father on the latter's farm during his growing days, and also he attended the district school during the proper seasons. In 1848 he was called to mourn that deepest loss to a boy's heart, the death of his father. Four years subsequent to this sad occurrence he turned from the associations of childhood and began the long journey across deserts and mountains to the land of the setting sun, where he has since wrought in various capacities that have been brought before him in the walks of life. The journey hither was consummated by the ox team of that day and landing in Clackamas county he turned his attention to farming. Subsequent to this work he was occupied in assisting to repel the attacks of the savages in their outbreak that brought on the Bogue river war of 1855-56, wherein he served with faithfulness. Later he was engaged in mining in southern Oregon and in California. In 1876 he came to Monument mountain and settled on the Heppner road and took up farming and stock raising, continuing in the same until 1882. At this date he located the home where he now lives, one and one-half miles north from Monument. On this place he has made a specialty of farming, and success has crowned his efforts in a very gratifying degree. He owns sufficient stock to carry on the farm in good shape and his place is well improved, being now of the generous proportions of two hundred acres.

The marriage of Mr. Lesley and Mrs. Clara C. Minkler was solemnized in Clackamas county in October, 1853, and to them have been born two children: Jasper Newton, living in Tillamook county, this state; Ida, wife of Mr. Dunnaway, of Portland, recently died. By her former marriage Mrs. Lesley has four children, Barney, Sarah, Julia and Clarissa. In political circles Mr. Lesley has been quite prominent and for one term he served the county by acting in the important office of commissioner, where he did faithful and efficient work. During the Indian war of 1878, Mr. Lesley and one other man in the community stayed on their ranches and experienced no difficulty with the savages.

JAMES SMALL.—There are few that come to our shores from the mother country that are not men of stanch character, good ability, thrifty and industrious, and one among that number that ranks high in the possession of these cardinal virtues, and has displayed commendable enterprise and especial capabilities since arriving here in the prosecution of the varied occupations that have laid claims on his time is the respected citizen and substantial representative of free government whose name heads this article. Mr. Small has won much honor in the raising of sheep, being the pioneer representative of that industry within the precincts of Grant county and a leader in it from the outset.

In 1824 he was born in England, and at

the tender age of ten shipped for a seafaring life, knowing the hardships of the craft from cabin boy to the top. In 1844 he landed in Baltimore, and from there made his way to Washington, D. C., and being of an adaptive turn of mind, found that market gardening was a paying business and immediately embarked therein. Four years later he shipped on the "W. P. Sable" for an exploration trip in the southern Pacific ocean. On November 14, 1849, in the midst of the unparalleled excitement of that memorable year, he landed in San Francisco, and for eight years he searched for the hidden treasure with diligence and much labor and hardship. In 1857 he commenced to ranch in Shasta county and this occupied his attention until 1862, the date of his advent into Canyon City, which then consisted of a few houses and two stores, was the spring of 1863, and here he immediately took up mining and followed it closely for two years. Then it was his happy lot to take a pleasure trip to the east for one year, after which he again came to Canyon City and commenced the raising of sheep, which he has followed ever since, being attended with a very gratifying success. He was the first one that raised sheep in Grant county, and to-day he is one of the leaders, having one section of land and many of these profitable animals, besides a number of horses. In political matters he is a prominent figure in the county, pulling ever with the Republican party, where his wisdom and keen foresight are particularly useful and acceptable to the good of his party. Fraternally he is a member of the Masons and the I. O. O. F., having passed all the chairs of these institutions. The charms of the celibate's quiet life of comfort and good cheer are his, having never been lured therefrom to try matrimony's sea of uncertainty and career of cares and responsibilities.

ALEXANDER McKENNA.—There are many in the precincts of Grant county who have done valiant service in reclaiming the wilds of nature, the only heritage that fell to their lot; and let it be said to their credit that they have left a legacy to the civilization that is following richer by far than ever can be paid to them; and a most worthy member of this patriotic and intrepid band, it is now our pleas-

ant privilege to outline in brief review of his life, granting a place in these chronicles of the county's history commensurate with his valued achievements of development and production here.

Practically a product of the west since when six months of age, he was brought from his native country, Ireland, by his parents, William and Sarah McKenna. September 23, 1847, was the time when he first saw the light, and California was the destination of the first trip from Ireland. In Humboldt county they finally settled and remained until 1863, at which time Mr. McKenna struck out into the activities of life for himself. He came to Canyon City at that time, and engaged in a hotel for a period, and then went to work in a sawmill on Pine creek, remaining in this last employment for six years. At that time he bought the mill, and for twelve years he was busied with the manufacture of lumber, achieving a very gratifying success. Selling the mill then, he turned his attention to agriculture, purchasing a farm about eight miles from Canyon City. In this occupation he was engaged continuously from that time until 1899, and then he sold his ranch and bought the livery and feed stable in Canyon City, where he is doing a good business at the present time, being one of the most progressive and leading citizens of the town. He is one of the city councilmen at the present time, and has ever demeaned himself with wisdom and a marked display of integrity.

The marriage of Mr. McKenna and Miss Lucetta, daughter of J. C. and Sarah (Demick) Gillingswater, was celebrated in Grant county. Three children were the fruit of this union: William, who died in infancy; Sarah, wife of C. Darrity; and Milton. Mrs. McKenna died on October 7, 1880.

Mr. McKenna contracted a second marriage, the lady of his choice this time being Miss Alice Jenkins, and to them have been born eight children: Anna, the wife of C. Ingle; David; Dora; Emma; Velma; Charley; Edward; Hazel.

GRANT THORNBURG.—It is with pleasure that we are enabled to grant to the leading and enterprising gentleman whose name initiates this paragraph consideration in the history of Grant county, since his labors

GRANT THORNBURG.

have been productive of so much development and in adding so much wealth to this county, besides being a man of geniality and affability, with a dominating sense of honor and uprightness and commensurate business ability.

Mr. Thornburg was born in Indiana, on February 10, 1865, the son of Joseph and Sarah (Wall) Thornburg, natives, respectively, of Indiana and Illinois. In 1865 the family came to Iowa, where our subject was educated and grew to manhood. In 1882 the family went thence to Missouri, and there Grant engaged in farming until 1889, in which year they came to the ground now occupied by the thrifty town of Granite. But one house graced the site at that time. He built the first hotel on the site of Granite, and with the exception of two years, he has been in the business since that time. He now handles the Grand hotel, a house of good reputation, and one in which the comfort of the guests is attended to with an untiring care that bespeaks enjoyment to the traveling public. In addition to the duties of host, Mr. Thornburg has attended to mining, and has made a very commendable showing in that line. He sold the Cougar to its present owners, and in company with his brother, sold the Thornburg placers. At the present time he has some fine properties and devotes much attention to mining. Mr. Thornburg is one of the principal owners of the town site and he takes a very active part in political matters in general, being one of the leading men of the town and county.

The marriage of Mr. Thornburg and Miss Mary M. Gutridge was solemnized in Missouri, in 1885, and they have two children living, Odessa and Harry A., and one deceased. Fraternally Mr. Thornburg is affiliated with the B. P. O. E., of Baker City, and the K. of P., in Sumpter. Since the incorporation of the town Mr. Thornburg has been mayor, and at his own expense he has established a town water works system. It was in 1899 that the town of Granite was incorporated and it has been known as a center of a very rich mining region for a number of years.

Mr. Thornburg is deserving of much credit for his untiring labors, not only for the town, but for the development of the mineral resources of the surrounding country, which has been instrumental in bringing so much wealth to this section.

30

HENRY WORKINS.—A pioneer of the pioneers, capable, vigorous and enterprising, the subject of this sketch has done much for the development of Grant county, and his experience, both in the early days and later, has been varied and extensive. Being a man thus closely allied with the interests of the county, and also of uprightness and integrity, he is justly entitled to a representation in this volume of the county history, asd we gladly accord him such.

Mr. Workins was born in Holmes county, Ohio, in 1839, and received his education in a German school, the same being thorough and well grounded. At the age of ten he was brought by his parents to Indiana, where they lived until 1854, and in October of that year they removed to Jackson county, Missouri. In May, 1857, Henry left Iidependence, Missouri, to make the trip across the plains to California, receiving as compensation for his services while en route fifty cents per day, and the time consumed was four months and seventeen days. Landing in Santa Rosa, he made rails for three dollars per hundred, herded cattle, worked in a blacksmith shop, drove stage between Cloverdale and Petaluma, then in 1859 turned his attention to farming, which he continued until May 1, 1863, when he sold a span of horses for five hundred dollars to secure money to pay the expenses of a trip to Canyon City, and on June 13, 1863, he reached the desired destination and immediately set to work for a Frenchman for five dollars per day operating in the mines. He soon bought some claims above the town for three hundred dollars and the following March sold them for nine hundred dollars. On the first day of March, 1864, he bought a one-third interest in a claim just above the court house, and one month later sold it to John Brown for nine hundred dollars. Following this he went to Silver City and bought claims and worked them until August, then returned to Canyon City, on August 13, 1864. He at once bought a claim above town and after five days' work on it sold it for ten thousand dollars. He then went up the creek to Dead Sheep flat and purchased the Conrad claims and some property in the Greenhorn district, paying for the latter three thousand three hundred dollars. On some of these claims his partner worked until he had taken out one thousand ounces of gold and then left. Mr. Workins secured machinery and built a ditch to the claims and in the spring of 1867, when the ditch was finished, he was three thousand dollars in debt, but on March 26 he returned to the claims on John Day flat from a time of sickness, and in thirty days he had paid this amount and five hundred dollars besides. He worked on these claims until July 4, 1867, and at this time he met the lady who afterward, in February, 1868, became his wife, she being Katie Mosier, daughter of E. Mosier, a pioneer of 1864. To this union were born two children: William Pope, of Canyon City; Harry E., married to Carrie Fry. On April 7, 1875, Mr. Workins was called to mourn the death of his beloved companion. She was a woman beloved and esteemed by all and her memory is dear to all who had the pleasure of her acquaintance.

In 1888 Mr. Workins married again. He has been a member of the I. O. O. F. since 1870, and also of the A. O. U. W. Mr. Workins has had much experience in mining, farming and stock raising, but he has now sold all these properties and is enjoying the golden years of his life in quiet retirement, having wrought well and faithfully in all the industries where he has been found. He is a respected and highly esteemed resident of the county.

SAMUEL P. MORGAN.—While Grant county is so well supplied with the talent and brawn necessary to carry forward successfully the various avocations that are incident to human existence, it may be especially congratulated on its possession of men of ability to handle the mechanical work that is needed, and not least among the efficient corps of machinists and followers of that king of all trades, the blacksmith's, may be numbered the gentleman whose name initiates this paragraph and whose capabilities and integrity has won for him an enviable place in the thrifty community and in the esteem and confidence of his fellows.

Mr. Morgan was born in Belmont county, Ohio, on February 29, 1840, being the son of E. S. and Rosana (Palmer) Morgan, and there on his father's farm he spent the early days of his life, also attending school a portion of each year in the district schools. In 1850

he came with his parents to Iowa City, Iowa, and in the following year he was left alone by the untimely death of both father and mother. A few years subsequent to this sad event he went to Council Grove, Morris county, Kansas and the next occupation that engaged him was driving stage from Independence, Missouri, to Santa Fe, New Mexico. It was during the times of Indian outbreaks, and many were the encounters that he had with the savages. During the years of 1861-63 he was acting in the capacity of government scout in eastern Kansas and adjacent territory and later was constable and then deputy sheriff of Morris county. In 1864 he was captured with the desire for western exploration that then was sweeping over the country, and he migrated to the Pacific coast with a wagon train, settling in Salem. The following year he had charge of seventy-five men in the construction of the new road into the Santiam mines, and then came to the John Day mining camp in Grant county and engaged in the search for gold. Five years later he left that business and was occupied with freighting for twelve years, then sold out and took up the life of a tobacconist and dealer in liquors for five years. His next venture was the purchase of the stage line from John Day to Monument, and a year later he sold this and took up stock raising. In 1895 he sold the entire interests that he had accumulated and opened a blacksmith shop in John Day. He has a fine, well equipped shop and a comfortable home and is doing a good business.

Mr. Morgan was married in November, 1882, to Mrs. Mary C. Stone, of John Day, to them have been born the following children: Maud A. and Leah M. By her former husband Mrs. Morgan had three children, Bert A., Nellie and Arthur. Fraternally Mr. Morgan is affiliated with the Masonic Lodge, No. 36, in Canyon City.

TUNIS SWICK.—We are gratified to have the privilege to grant to the gentleman whose name heads this article an epitome of his interesting and active career, having been a frontiersman for many years and doing much for the advancement of the interests of the section where he has lived and labored and having wrought in Grant county with an assiduity and sagacity that have brought their sure reward, a competence, and a place among the leading stockmen of his section.

Mr. Swick was born in New York state in 1832, being the son of Minor and Louisa (Latourette) Swick, natives of New York. The next year succeeding his birth our subject was brought by his parents to Michigan, and there he received his education and grew to manhood. In 1853 the family came across the plains and our subject drove a team of oxen the entire distance, and he has the distinction of having made the trip in his bare feet. When at Council Bluffs he saw a man hung, and after leaving the Missouri river until they landed in the Willamette valley they saw no house. The parents located in Marion county and our subject spent his first winter in Portland, then but a village. The following year he went to the Siskon mines and for two years wrought there, and then the time until 1875 was spent in various places. At this last date he came to Grant county, locating at Longcreek and taking up the stock business. About 1880 he repaired to The Dalles and there engaged in farming, whence, five years later, he removed to Grant county again, locating at his present place, taking up a homestead and pre-emption, nine miles southwest from Hamilton. At the present time he and his son are proprietors of a fine domain of two thousand and four hundred acres. They are engaged in raising stock, mostly sheep, and they are numbered among the heaviest stockmen of their section. Mr. Swick has always evinced an interest in the affairs of politics and he has labored steadily and faithfully for the welfare of the county, having served in the important office of county commissioner.

In 1861 Mr. Swick married Miss Margaret, a native of Missouri, and daughter of Samuel Madison and Martha Ann (Stevenson) Gilmore, who came to Oregon in 1843. The wedding occurred in June and the following children have been born to them: Yyman D., living about twelve miles northeast from Monument, married to Annie Cochran and the father of two children, Howard and Dewey; William, residing four miles west from Hamilton, and married to Elsie Franklin, one child having been born to them; Martha, wife of

Charles Gentry, on Cottonwood creek, and they have one daughter, Mericle. Mr. Gilmore was in the territorial legislature and was also sheriff of Buchanan county, Missouri, in an early day. He died in The Dalles in 1895, but the mother is still living near that city. Mr. Swick's parents died in Yam Hill county, Oregon. Our subject and his family were here during the time of the Bannock and Piute Indian outbreak, in 1878 and while they were safe from the savages in the fortifications at Longcreek still the Indians burned his improvements, killed his cattle and stole his horses.

* * *

CHARLES R. DAVIS.—As one of Grant county's most thrifty and enterprising stockmen and agriculturists the estimable gentleman whose name initiates this paragraph is well known, being as upright and exemplary citizen and successful business man, but as proprietor of the famous summer resort known as McDuffee's hot springs, he is widely known throughout eastern Oregon and the adjoining states, the springs in question being equal to the celebrated hot springs in Arkansas, as stated by some of the leading physicians who have investigated the subject.

Mr. Davis was born on April 7, 1860, near Mount Vernon, St. Lawrence county, Missouri, whence, in 1861, he was removed by his parents, T. J. and Mary A. (Gentry) Davis, to Susanville, Lassen county, California, crossing the plains and traveling the entire distance with ox teams. His father was a dealer in stock and a farmer, and in assisting in these occupations, as well as in attending the public schools of his home place, the early years of Charles R. were passed. During the years of his minority the family removed to the Pitt river country, and in 1884 the subject of this sketch stepped out into the world for himself, his first venture being to migrate to the Fox valley, in this county. Two years later, after due investigation, he took a homestead a short distance from where he now lives and gave his attention to farming and stock raising. Success attended his efforts and in 1895 he sold that farm and bought the place of his residence, at Ritter postoffice. On this farm are the springs mentioned above, and which are justly attracting attention both from the medical world and from those who are suffering from rheumatism and skin diseases, as well as other maladies. The water from the springs is 110 degrees Fahrenheit, with medical and healing properties that have made the springs sought after each year by hundreds of patients. Mr. Davis has provided his springs with a fine and commodious bath house, while a good hotel store, postoffice, feed and livery stable, are at hand, making it a desirable place to spend an outing and recruit from the maladies to which our race is heir. The surrounding county is also very attractive, both in picturesque beauty and on account of its adjacency to one of the richest mining regions in the northwest. Under the skillful management of their generous and public-spirited owner the springs are rapidly becoming a very popular resort and bid fair to make one of the leading institutions of our state. In addition to this valuable property Mr. Davis owns one half section of land near by that is well improved and also bands of cattle and horses. During the summer season not only those who partake of the good cheer of the hotel from the quota of the guests, but camping grounds are provided for those who desire the outing and it is a very pleasant sight to see from one to two hundred persons camped about, while the grounds of the genial proprietor are thrown open to guests and his herds and gardens supply abundance of good things for the table and the many horses are at hand for trips through the adjacent hills.

Mr. Davis was married on October 2, 1894, Miss Mary, a native of Oregon, and a daughter of William M. and Pernice Carter, who live near Longcreek. They have become the parents of three children, James M., Elijah and Mildred. In 1886 Mr. Davis' parents migrated hither from California and took a homestead and began stock raising but later they sold out and removed to Longcreek, where they live at the present time.

JAMES WICKISER.—In the person of Mr. Wickiser we have one of the typical frontiersmen who were so instrumental in opening up our western territories for the settlement that subsequently came from the more populous states of the east. His life has been filled with incident and adventure that are at-

tended upon this rugged existence and an unstinted amount of credit is due to him for his worthy efforts in blazing the way into the savage regions and in working faithfully and unremittingly for their development and advancement.

In 1828, in the state of Ohio, he was born, and there passed the first twelve years of his life. He then came with his parents to Missouri, later to Iowa, and then to Illinois, in which latter state his parents remained until the time of their death. In 1853 James was led by the glowing accounts from the Golden state region to come hither for the search that many were prosecuting so successfully. He landed at American valley and there mined for twelve years, and then came to Umpqua valley, Oregon, and took up a homestead, where he was engaged in farming for ten years. Leaving this pursuit then he went to what was at that time Cook county and again took up mining and followed it uninterruptedly until sixteen years since. He then sold his ranch and all his other property and came to Izee and retired from active service. His golden years are being spent in the quiet retreat of this retired region and it is his to enjoy the goodly competence that his industry and wisdom have gathered during the years of his toil. Mr. Wickiser has never contracted a matrimonial alliance, being disposed to prefer the quieter joys of the celibatarian. He is highly esteemed by all and enjoys the confidence of the entire community, while his friends are numbered among all the residents of the place and wherever he has sojourned in his pilgrimage career.

◆◆◆

JOSEPH F. HODSON is one of the earliest pioneers of Grant county and has been a constant resident here since his advent in 1861, laboring steadily for its development and for the welfare of all, having displayed in this long time a character of sterling worth and principles that are sound, while his achievements have been praiseworthy and wisely wrought out and to-day he enjoys the esteem and confidence of all who are acquainted with him, being counted one of the wisest and most substantial citizens of the county.

In 1840, in Wayne county, Indiana, Joseph

JOSEPH F HODSON.

F. was born, and while still young, his parents removed to Fairfield, Iowa, and later migrated to Emporia, Kansas. In 1859, with ox teams, they crossed the plains and settled in Douglas county, this state, our subject accompanying them on this arduous journey, and after he saw them well settled departed, in 1860, to Jackson county and engaged in mining for one year. The following year, 1861, he came to John Day, and operated in the mines and at packing for a number of years. Observing the agricultural possibilities of the county, he selected a pre-emption where he now resides, two miles east from Mount Vernon. In addition to the original amount taken he has added much grazing land and is now engaged in the stock business. He is one of the substantial men in that industry and skill and energy are manifested in all his endeavors.

It is of note that during the time when he was in Kansas there were in action the various forces that contended for the supremacy in the state over the question of slavery, and some thrilling adventures were experienced by him in his boyhood days. At one time he participated in a pitched battle, called the battle of Blackjack, while it was his duty to carry dispatches to the captain of Fort Scott. It is worthy of note that in those days the neighbors congregated in companies of twenty or thirty and thus took their grists to the mills to be ground. On one occasion they found three men gagged and bound to trees. Two of the unfortunate victims were already dead, and the other nearly so.

———————

HON. CHARLES S. DUSTIN.—Distinguished in a number of commendable lines, as a pioneer of the west, a veteran of the early Indian wars, where he did faithful and brave service in the military, later by his success in the agricultural and stock raising industries, and then especially in the halls of legislation, where he has twice been sent by a discriminating people, and in which capacity he has left a record that is worthy and gratifying, while throughout he has ever maintained a mien that manifests both sagacity and integrity in connection with capabilities that are recognized as far above the average, the subject of this sketch is properly granted representation in this volume.

Charles S. is the son of Dudley B. and Catherine (Slosson) Dustin, and was born on Ferbruary 23, 1840, near Cincinnati, Ohio. Thence, in the same year, the father removed with his family to Muscatine county, Iowa, whence in 1850 he came across the plains with ox teams to Portland, Oregon, which was at that time but a small village. After exploration they settled in Washington county. When Charles S. Dustin had reached the age of sixteen years he enlisted in the Washington Territory Volunteers under Captain Hamilton J. G. Maxon to fight the Indians who were making trouble at that time. He enlisted at Vancouver and from there the company went to the Sound and from thence across the Natchez pass in the Cascades to the Yakima country, then to Walla Walla, and finally on to the Grande Ronde country, where they had a severe conflict with the savages, three men being killed and a number wounded, while many horses were shot. The company of soldiers numbered eighty, while the Indians were two hundred strong. After this they returned to Vancouver, and he was mustered out. Then he went to Forest Grove and attended college for two years, when, in 1862, he came with a company of men to the Elk City mines in Idaho, and for nineteen days after reaching that famous camp he industriously mined, and found at the end of that time that he was twenty-one dollars in debt. Here his actual experience in digging for gold ended. He turned to freighting, packing goods into Oro Fino, Elk City, Warren, Silver City, Boise Basin, and even to Blackfoot, Montana, and Kootenai, British Columbia. This occupation was followed by him until June, 1868, and then he returned to the Willamette valley, where he was married to Mrs. Rufina Smith, daughter of the Hon. Bart Curl, formerly member of the state legislature from Linn county. The nuptials occurred on December 18, 1868, and the fruit of the union was the following children: Rufina L., wife of William Coy, of Red Bluff, Montana; Julia E., wife of Albert Ballance, of Susanville; Charles B.; Kate, wife of D. S. Flynn, of Ritter. On March 20, 1880, Mrs. Dustin was called from her family and home by death.

On June 25, 1891, Mr. Dustin was a second time married, the lady of his choice being Mrs. Gearhart, daughter of J. F. Miller, of

Prineville, and they have two children, Ruth S. and Hannah.

In August, 1869, Mr. Dustin removed from the Willamette valley to Mount Vernon, on the John Day river, and there followed ranching and stock raising until December, 1878, at which time he removed to Longcreek, and lived on the present site of that village. Later he bought the present large estate of eight hundred acres, three miles northeast from Longcreek. His farm is all fenced and well improved and he has a comfortable residence and gives his attention to the agricultural art and raising various kinds of stock. He has been notary public and justice of the peace and twice was elected to the legislature from Grant and Harney counties, and recently he has given considerable attention to the practice of law. Mr. Dustin descends from English forefathers, among whom was the noted "Hannah Dustin" and on his mother's side he traces back to the Dutch from the Mohawk valley in New York. Mr. Dustin is a man of ability and uprightness and has successfully wrought in the county for one-third of a century and is one of the substantial and worthy citizens of today that has the respect and esteem of all.

FRANCIS M. PEARSON.—Truly the west has reason to be proud of her sons, and one of the most enterprising and wide awake business men among them is the estimable gentleman whose name is at the beginning of this article, and it is with pleasure that we are constrained to grant him a representation in this volume of chronicles of the leading men of Grant county. A son of the occident, and one worthy of the boundless west, he has found here the scenes of his labors and the place of his home, believing in its unlimited resources and the conditions of prosperity that nature has so lavishly bestowed for the hand of man.

Yam Hill county is the native place of Francis M., and his birth occurred in 1860, being the son of Joseph and Ella (Eads) Pearson. The father was a native of St. Joseph, Missouri, whence he came across the plains in 1850 to Yam Hill county, which was the native place of the mother. This worthy couple were among the sturdy pioneers of that time and the father now lies buried at Palouse, Washington,

and the aged mother is still living at Fletcher, Idaho. At the age of twenty-four our subject stepped from under the parental roof and began the voyage of life as captain of his own craft. The first venture that was to attract his attention was buying and selling horses, wherein he was successful, and also in the art of agriculture, that he took up at the same time. In 1886 he took a government quarter where he now resides, twenty miles south from Canyon City, near Seneca, and gave his attention to subduing and improving the same, and also to raising sheep. In addition to these industries he has operated a dairy which demonstrates his business ability to handle successfully a number of enterprises, and it is but right to say that Mr. Pearson is one of the leading business men of this section, being recognized as such by all.

Mr. Pearson and Miss Delia, daughter of Samuel S. Smith, of Pilot Rock, were married at Pilot Rock, and they have become the parents of five children: Austa, Olney, Ada, Edna and Fred. Mr. Pearson's fine practical knowledge and his capabilities were brought into play for the benefit of his fellows recently, he being chosen stock inspector, and so successful was he in this line that he was chosen as his own successor. Fraternally he is affiliated with the I. O. O. F., at Canyon City, and is held in high esteem there as well as in all his walk among his fellows. It is of note that Mr. Pearson, senior, was one of the active participants in the Cayuse Indian war, and there rendered faithful and valiant service. Our subject was a volunteer in the Bannock and Piute war of 1878 and did good work in the battle of Beasley's mill, near Pilot Rock.

WILLIAM NEAL.—One of the earliest pioneers to the state of Oregon, as well as to this county, and one of the oldest men in the county today, the subject of this sketch rightly deserves a place in the chronicles of Grant county, where he has labored for the advancement of the interests of all, as well as faithfully prosecuting the business enterprises that have been his occupation while domiciled here. A man of uprightness and integrity, he has shown also a broadmindedness and public spirit that have won for him the warm approval of the people and the confidence of his fellows.

On April 3, 1815, William Neal was born to Louis and Millie Neal, in the state of Indiana, in Bartholomew county, being the second white child born in that state. He was reared on a farm, and at the age of twenty-two came to Illinois, and there followed the same occupation until 1844, at which time he migrated to Andrew county, Missouri, remaining there until the spring of 1850. At that time he was moved by the reports from the west and came with a wagon train of eight outfits to the Willamette valley, where he settled in Marion county. The trip consumed six months, and was without unusual event, save that at the crossing of the Platte river the wagon capsized and the provisions were lost, and then on the Snake there occurred a skirmish with the Indians. He took a donation claim in Marion county and gave his attention to farming and stock raising until 1868, when he came east of the mountains. From Heppner to his present residence, six miles west from Monument, he drove the first wagon that had been brought into these regions. He took up government land and went to raising stock and farming. Prosperity has attended his efforts and he has today one-half section of land there besides four hundred and forty acres in the Willamette valley. His home place is well improved, having a good house, barn and out buildings, besides the necessary fence and other things indispensable on a well regulated farm. During the Indian trouble in 1878 he endured much hardship and lost heavily, as did many other settlers. In political matters he is with the Republican party and is active in advocating just government, white in educational matters he is ever at the front. Energetic, enterprising, and dominated by a sagacity that is able to discern the best investments and methods, he has made an unbounded success.

The marriage of Mr. Neal and Miss Mahala M. Parker was solemnized in Indiana and to them have been born the following children: Louis, married to Matilda Cox, and living in Wallowa county; Julatha, wife of John Thask, of Marion county, now deceased; Minerva M., married to A. C. Christman of Linn county; John, married to Esther Wagner, of Marion county; Marguerette, wife of John Mc-Culley of Lake county; Napoleon B., married

to Lizzie Munkers, and living on the home place; Martha A., wife of Joseph Putnam, near Monument. Mrs. Neal was born in Indiana, Bartholomew county, on May 19, 1813, and was the first child born to white parents in that state. On May 18, 1901, she was called from the scenes and cares of life to the world beyond, having lived on this earth for eighty-eight years, lacking one day. Mr. Neal is spending the golden years of his life in the home that his skill and industry wrought out for him from the wilds of nature, and here he is highly respected by all and is one of the substantial and leading citizens of the county.

◆◆◆

PETER KUHL.—At least in two different lines of industry the gentleman whose name initiates this article has gained distinction since he has been in the region now embraced in Grant county. From an early day he has been in the vanguard of the developers and advancers of the county and has wrought here with a display of energy, industry and wisdom that are commendable in a high degree.

Like many of the most industrious and substantial of our citizens, Mr. Kuhl was born in Germany, and there was educated and learned his trade, blacksmithing, gaining both in it and in educational discipline the advantage to be sought after and that is found in the older countries where a great premium is placed on thoroughness rather than on skimming over things. The date of his birth was 1847, and at the age of twenty he was ready to bid "good by" to the fatherland and try his fortunes in the land of the free, and indeed to one so full of energy and guided by wisdom and well fortified for the battles of life in the mechanical line as Mr. Kuhl nothing short of the best success could await him. So it proved, for from the beginning he has steadily increased in the goods of this world and also has gained the esteem and confidence of his fellows in an unstinted measure. He settled first in Davenport, Iowa, and wrought at the forge for one year, and then migrated to Grand Island for a one year's stay, whence he set out in 1868 on the long trip overland with ox teams that ended successfully in the regions of the coast, and in 1870 was at Canyon City, where he immediately established a shop, and also in connection therewith a feed store. These he successfully operated and in the meantime settled on a government claim where he now lives, twelve miles east from Canyon City. He has steadily added to his estate until he has now the generous domain of twelve hundred acres. For eighteen years he gave his first attention to the shop, stocking up the farm as occasion provided, and in about 1890 he removed from town to the estate and has since been actively engaged in the raising of cattle and practicing the art of the agriculturist.

Mr. Kuhl and Miss Julia Sels, the daughter of H. I. Sels, an old pioneer who has passed away, were married in 1878, and to gladden their happy union there have been born four children: Henry, Ernest, Hermon and Philip. In fraternal circles Mr. Kuhl is prominent, being identified with the I. O. O. F., Canyon City Lodge, No. 22, and the A. O. U. W., of the same place. In his long career here Mr. Kuhl has maintained a dignity and uprightness that have won for him the encomiums of his fellows and that justly entitles him to the position he holds as one of the most substantial citizens of our population.

WILLIAM HALL is one of the leading stockmen and agriculturists of Grant county, having come here before there were any improvements made by the hand of the white man, and being identified with the county from the incipiency of political organization, he has steadily allied himself with its development and labored for its advancement and progress, as well as prosecuting his own private business with a vigor and sagacity that have brought the wealth of prosperity, its well earned meed.

Mr. Hall was born in Dorset, England, in 1840, and came to America with his brother, Henry, in 1858, remaining in Guelph, Canada, for three years, engaged on a farm, after which he went to Salem, this state, to join his brother, who had preceded him thither. In 1861, in company with his brother, he bought a herd of dairy cows and took them to Walla Walla, and in the winter following was unfortunate enough to lose them all in the unusually cold weather. In the spring of 1862 he was induced by the rumors from the new

diggings in the Powder river region to come thither. He pressed on into the Canyon City district and was occupied in mining until 1864, and then in company with his brother bought the farm where they now live, two miles west from Prairie City. Here he has operated in company with his brother and has given his attention to raising stock and tilling the soil. Prosperity, because of his energy and wise methods of procedure, has attended his efforts and he justly ranks at the head among the stockmen of eastern Oregon. In 1867 he made a trip to England for pleasure, and again in 1872, at which time he was married to his cousin, Miss Elizabeth Hall, a native of Ashmore, Dorset county, England. To them were born three children, William, Sarah and George. Mrs. Hall was taken by the hand of death from her family and husband and her remains lie buried in the cemetery at Prairie City. Her demise was universally mourned. Mr. Hall is a member of the I. O. O. F., Prairie City Lodge, No. 33. In political matters he is with the Republican party and is an ardent supporter of their principles. In 1886 he was a member of the state tax commission. It is of note that Mr. Hall and his brother were the first men to start a bakery in the county, which they operated for some time with success attending their efforts. Mr. Hall is one of the leaders in the county and is a man possessed of a broad public spirit, keen discernment, and a geniality that is manifest to all. Being a fine conversationalist and well informed, he is looked up to as one that is rightly placed in the position of leader among his fellows, and it is gratifying that he is always arrayed on the side of sound principles and uprightness.

WILLIAM T. McKERN.—Among the leading stockmen and agriculturists who have wrought in faithfulness for the development of this county and for the advancement of the interests of all, while he has prosecuted his own private business with a success that bespeaks both his capabilities and attention in the lines of business we mention the subject of this article, whose integrity and sound principles commend him to the confidence and esteem of all.

WILLIAM HALL.

Eighteen hundred and fifty-five was the date of the birth of Mr. McKern and both of his parents died when he was very small. At the age of nineteen he apprenticed himself to a carpenter to learn that trade, but an accident occurred that changed his mind and he entered the business of raising cattle and sheep and tilling the soil. In 1883 he bought the place where he now lives, one and a half miles west from Mount Vernon. His first purchase was one quarter, but his industry and thrift have enabled him to add by purchase until his estate is of the generous proportions of eight hundred acres. He has some fine herds of cattle and sheep and is counted one of the most skillful sheepmen in the county, which is evidenced by his gratifying success.

The marriage of Mr. McKern and Miss Edna, daughter of W. W. and Eva (Allen) Stone, was solemnized in 1887, and to them have been born four children, Salina, Jay E., Enid and Valene. Mr. McKern is a member of the Workingmen's order, No. 105, at John Day, and is quite prominent in the People's party, allying himself with that as more nearly embracing the principles that he believes to be for the welfare of the country.

MARSHALL S. KEENEY.—In the person of the estimable gentleman and successful business man whose name appears above we have one of Grant county's most successful stockmen, a keen business man possessed of excellent foreight and talents that have demonstrated him one of the best handlers of finance in the county, while his principles of uprightness and uniform straightforwardness have made him respected by all and a worthy promoter of the interests of the county, having also materially augmented its wealth by his good judgment and wise procedue and thrift.

Marshall S. is the son of Jonathan and Mary A. Keeney, and was born on October 1, 1850, in Lawrence county, Missouri. Seven years later, in the spring, the family started across the plains, being composed of five children and the parents. When they landed in Healdsburgh, Sonoma county, California, six months later, there was another child, it having been born on the way. In the spring of 1858 they came to Linn county, Oregon, and soon

removed to Lane county, settling near Eugene. Our subject remained there until 1865, having assisted his father on the farm and in the stock business. Then he came across the mountains with a band of sheep to Umatilla county. In 1868 he went to San Joaquin valley, California; later he went again to Lane county, Oregon, and in 1870 came to Birch creek, Umatilla county, whence two years later he went to the Owyhee river in Idaho with a herd of cattle. In 1873 he went to Wallowa county, and from there returned to his home in Umatilla county. From there, in company with his brother he went again to the San Joaquin valley, this time for a herd of horses, with which they returned the same year to Grant county and settled on their present place. He is in partnership with his brother, Thomas B., and together they own one thousand acres of good land, that is all fenced and well improved. Formerly they were handling sheep, but these were replaced with cattle, of which stock they at the present time own large herds. Mr. Keeney has a good home and all the accessory improvements that make the rural life both profitable and comfortable.

The marriage of Mr. Keeney and Miss Carrie, daughter of Enoch and Permelia Conger, living near Longcreek, was solemnized on December 25, 1882. To them were born two children, Bertha A. and Hubert C., who is deceased, having passed away on March 12, 1889. Mrs. Keeney died in November, 1889. Mr. Keeney's father, one of the prominent citizens of Umatilla county, died in 1884, and the mother one year later.

JOHN A. LAYCOCK.—As one of the leading stockmen and tillers of the soil, the subject of this sketch is and has been well and favorably known in Grant county, but as a county officer he has gained more prominence than in any other line, since he has manifested an ability and integrity in the discharge of the duties incumbent upon him as county judge, which has gained for him the encomiums of the people and won their esteem and approval.

On August 27, 1847, John A. was born to Peter and Susanna Laycock, in Hancock county, Illinois, whither his parents had come in 1842 from their native land, England. While still a child he was taken to St. Louis, Missouri, and four years later his father determined to make the journey overland to California. Sending the teams on to Council Bluffs, he embarked with his family on a steamer for the same place. Before they arrived at their destination the boat sunk and all the freight on board was lost, but Mr. Laycock escaped with his family and then secured a team for the completion of the journey to Council Bluffs. Arriving there he established his family temporarily and then returned to St. Joseph, Missouri, to purchase a new outfit. This done he embarked again for Council Bluffs, and before the steamer arrived at its destination he succumbed to the ravages of cholera, as had nearly all of the other passengers on the boat. Our subject was the oldest son, and to his lot fell the hard burdens of assisting his mother in the stern duties of life. Until 1856 they remained in Council Bluffs, and then sold all and undertook the journey to California. At the age of sixteen years Mr. Laycock went to the gold mines of Washoe, Nevada, where he continued for two years and then returned to Napa City, California and took a course in the Napa College. Following this we find him in Canyon City, landing there on November 20, 1865. Here he was occupied with mining for six years and during that time was superintendent of the Prairie Diggings and was one of a company that erected the first quartz mill in this region. After this extended period of activity in the mining industry he turned his attention to farming and stock raising. He purchased two hundred and forty acres where he now lives, four miles west from John Day, and has steadily added by purchase until he owns a broad estate of twelve hundred acres, all of which is utilized in crops and in handling his herds. In addition to this he also owns eight hundred and eighty acres in the Bear valley, which is used for a stock ranch. Mr. Laycock is one of the heaviest property owners in the county and one of the most successful stockmen. In political matters he is allied with the Republican party and is stanch and unswerving in his stand for sound principles. In 1898 he was placed in nomination for county judge, and it is demanded that we remark that in all that canvass he spent no money for liquor and simply waited for the manifesto of

the people at the polls, where he was called into that office with an overwhelming majority, far in excess of his ticket. The ability and sagacity and impartiality and vigorous stand for duty and right that have been evinced in his discharge of duties are powerful in allying to him more than ever the affections of the people.

The marriage of Mr. Laycock and Miss Josephine, daughter of E. C. and Sarah (Howard) Officer, natives respectively of Missouri and Tennessee, was celebrated on December 21, 1871, and to them have been born the following children: William C., married; John A., married; Mary A.; Guy H. Fraternally Mr. Laycock is affiliated with the Masons, having joined Canyon City Lodge, No. 34' A. F. & A. M., in 1868, and he has served his lodge as deacon, warden and worshipful master for several years; also he joined Blue Mount Chapter, No. 7, R. A. M., in 1868, and later the Order of Priesthood, and Washington Council, No. 3 of Portland, Oregon, Royal and Select Masters, and Julia Chapter, No. 56, O. E. S., of Canyon City. Mr. Laycock is strictly a temperance man, both in precept and practice and would encourage younger men to adopt those principles.

GEORGE SOLLINGER.—It is ever with pleasure that we hail an opportunity to add our mite to the tribute to the memory of the worthy life that so many of our sons of freedom experienced in the trying times between 1860 and 1866, when "to the front" was the cry that rose from all loyal lips and the sturdy and intrepid lads that wore the blue rallied with quick step to its stirring tones and with its never-ending cadence ringing in their ears hurried on to the seat of fierce war. One of those brave fellows that flung themselves before the cannons of the enemy and fought with desperate valor until the last attack on the stars and stripes had been forever repulsed is named above and we heartily grant to him the representation in this volume that places him as one of the leading citizens of this county where he has wrought for a third of a century in successful efforts for the development of the resources that nature has so bountifully placed within our borders and the advancement of the interests of all.

Mr. Sollinger came from stanch German stock, being born in the fatherland in 1839, and three years later migrated with his father to this country, settling in Rochester, New York. At the age of six he went to live with his grandfather, where he continued until he was fourteen years old, when he went to Wisconsin and settled in Beaver Dam until the war broke out, and then at the first call he offered his services, enlisting in Company F, Forty-third Wisconsin, under General Thomas. He rendered excellent service until the close of the war and received honorable discharge on May 22, 1866. He immediately returned to his home in Wisconsin and two years later came to Canyon City. For the first year here he worked on a ranch and then went to mining, but later took a ranch for himself, where he now resides, one mile west of Canyon City. To the cultivation and improvement of this property he has devoted himself with energy since, also carrying on a dairy business and raising stock. For twenty-six years he was devoted to dairying, but recently he dropped that branch and handles stock exclusively with his farm products.

His marriage occurred in 1861, Miss Catherine Hubenger becoming his bride at that time. To them have been born the following children: John, Caroline, George, Albert, Frank, and Ella and Elmer, twins. Mr. Sollinger is a member of that distinguished body, the G. A. R., where he is held in high esteem, as he also is by all that know him, for his intrinsic worth and unswerving integrity and good, substantial qualities.

JAMES F. ALLEN—is at the present time operating one of the important commercial establishments of Grant county, and it is due to his excellent ability and uniform uprightness and geniality that he enjoys a good patronage, having labored assiduously to this end since his advent into the realms of trade. Mr. Allen is a man that is universally respected and esteemed by his fellows, and it is especially pleasant to be able to note that in every respect he justly merits the confidence that is so unhesitatingly reposed in him, while his labors for the welfare of all are praiseworthy and commendable.

The birth of James F. occurred in Richmond, McHenry county, Illinois, on February 4, 1855, and his early life was spent on a farm. At the age of four he was taken by his parents to Minnesota, and when he had arrived at the fourteenth mile post in his career he went with his parents to Bates county, Missouri, where he remained until he was twenty years of age. At that time he migrated to California, and in 1880 came to Heppner, engaging as salesman in a mercantile establishment. After a time spent at this work he embarked in the livery business and in 1886 he came to Longcreek in this county, whence in 1890 he removed to his present place in Fox valley and engaged in the general merchandise business. He has a fine trade and carries a good stock of goods. He owns the building in which his store is kept, and also his dwelling, and is universally attended with prosperity. In addition to the duties of his business he has been postmaster at Fox since October 11, 1890, and it is to his credit that he has given universal satisfaction in the discharge of these duties.

The marriage of Mr. Allen and Miss Indial, daughter of John and Sarah Ledgerwood, of Fox valley and a native of Missouri, was celebrated on July 7, 1896, and to them have been born four children, Grace, Doris, Ruby and Theodore E. Mr. Allen is one of the leading men of his community and influential throughout the county, while his integrity and sound principles make him one of Grant's most substantial men.

RICE R. McHALEY.—One of the most enterprising citizens of the county and well known throughout its precincts is the man of whom we now have the privilege of speaking, and who has wrought faithfully and with wisdom during the years of his residence in this region, and who has augmented materially the development and progress of the county and the interests of good government and the welfare of all.

Born in Marion county, Oregon, in 1865, being the son of G. W. and Mary (Jackson) McHaley our subject received his educational training in this state and at the age of twenty-one years entered the stock business, where he was very successful for a period, having his headquarters at Prairie City. In 1890 he was appointed postmaster under Harrison, in the Prairie City office, and for five years he discharged the trying and arduous duties of this position. During this time he was also engaged in the butcher business and following the time when he laid down the duties of his office, he again embarked in raising stock, also engaged in blacksmithing until he was elected county clerk on the Republican ticket in 1898. Following his term of faithful service he was re-elected and is at the present time discharging the duties of this office. He owns a farm of one hundred and sixty acres, three miles north of Prairie City, besides considerable other property.

The marriage of Mr. McHaley and Miss Lizzie, daughter of Nathan and Mattie (Carpenter) Hubbard, was celebrated in Prairie City in 1887. Mrs. McHaley's parents were old pioneers of the state. Mr. McHaley's father was a member of the state legislature, being elected in the spring of 1882. Mr. McHaley is a man of stanch principles and unswerving integrity, and has manifested fine ability and keen foresight in his career, while his geniality and upright conduct have won him hosts of friends from every part of the county and given him the respect and esteem of all.

JAMES W. TABOR.—A native of Grant county, with which our volume is primarily concerned, one who has labored here constantly since his birth for the upbuilding of the county and the development of its resources, a man of uprightness and integrity, possessed of good ability and sound principles, the subject of this sketch is deserving of mention in any volume that deals with this section, and it is with pleasure that we grant him consideration here.

Mr. Albert G. Tabor came to the place now occupied by Canyon City on July 4, 1862, being one of the very first white men to set foot on that soil, and he continued there and in the vicinity of old Granite, and also in other sections of the county in mining until the time of his death, which occurred on July 4, 1893. He was a prominent man of Grant county, a leader in progression and among the councils for the political welfare and industrial development of the county. He married Miss Mary J. McCousland, a native of Indiana, he himself being native to New York, and to them were born three children, William J., living near Union, Oregon; Mattie M., wife of Oscar O. Benton, one of the owners of the Red Boy mine, and residing in Portland; and the subject of this sketch, he being born December 31, 1865. The mother is still living in Portland, Oregon. Our subject grew to manhood and was educated in this county, and at once took up the industry, then the leading one in the county, and doubtless to be so for some time to come, that of mining. He operated at placers until ten years since, and now he is working at quartz mining. He is at present in company with Messrs. Thornburg and Benson, the firm being owner of the Rialto mine. Our subject owns the Stevens addition to Granite besides other property, and is one of the leading men of the town.

The marriage of Mr. Tabor and Miss Margaret McNulty, a native of Canyon City, was solemnized at the Monumental mine, in Grant county, July 9, 1892, and to them have been born the following children: Helen E., Albert C., and Alice. Mrs. Tabor's parents were early pioneers of Canyon City. Mr. Tabor is fraternally affiliated as follows, being a member of the K. of P., Lewiston Lodge, No. 83, and of the A. O. U. W. of Granite, Lodge No. 117. Mr. Tabor has been interested in some of the important mining properties in the county, such as the Red Boy, at its discovery, and he owned one-half interest in the Concord and was the discoverer and locater of the Ibex.

HENRY A. CUPPER.—It is beyond doubt that some of the most thrifty and industrious agriculturists of our land are those who migrated hither from the mother land of the colonies, England. Not least among that worthy class is the gentleman of whom we now have the pleasure of speaking in presenting an epitome of his career, which has been fraught with enterprise and activity and dominated by a sagacity that has settled successfully all of the questions of intricacy that arise in the stockman's life of varied activities.

Henry A. is the son of Henry A. and Mary (Clark) Cupper, and was born in the village

JAMES W. TABOR.

of Benhall, Suffolk county, England, on April 1, 1845. From the excellent schools of that land he gained his training and in assisting his father on the farm he became skilled in the art of agriculture and in handling stock. His father was a prominent man of the county and was occupied largely with public duties in addition to managing his estates. At the age of twenty-four years he commenced the battle of life on his own resources. Soon thereafter his good judgment prompted him to take a helpmeet, which he did on October 1, 1872, the lady of his choice being Miss Cordelia H., daughter of Charles and Harriet (Cockerell) Capon. Mrs. Cupper is a native of Framlingham, Suffolk county, and her father was one of the prominent stockmen of that county and was instrumental in producing some of the leading specimens of the noted Suffolk horses. To Mr. and Mrs. Cupper have been born the following children: Harry C., deceased; Frederick W., married to Laura Gardner, of Drain, Douglas county; Ethel C.; Nora A., deceased; an infant deceased; Percy A.; Norton C.

In 1877 Mr. Cupper disposed of his interests in the home land and accompanied by his family sought the land of his choice, landing in New York, whence he came direct to Oregon, arriving in February, of that year. From that time until July, 1878, he spent in looking the country over and finally bought the place where he now lives, seven miles northwest from Monument. Here he owns about three thousand acres of land and large bands of stock, especially sheep. During his first year on the new place Mr. Cupper was called to demonstrate of what stuff he was made by the outbreak of the Indians, and it was with credit to himself that he was found right at the front. He assisted in building a fort in Monument, and was also captain of the night guards of Heppner. In 1887 he took his family to visit the old home in England, and while there he bought a trio of the well known Suffolk horses, which he brought to this country. He had the misfortune to lose the two stallions, but still owns the mare. Mr. Cupper has gained an enviable distinction as a successful stockman in the quarter of a century in which he has wrought in this county, and it is with pleasure that we are able to state that he is one of the leading men in that industry in all this region. Politically he is a stanch Republican and has the courage of his convictions. Fraternally he is affiliated with the A. F. & A. M., at Monument. Mr. and Mrs. Cupper are prominent members of society and they enjoy the confidence and esteem of all who may have the pleasure of their acquaintance.

LAWRENCE SWEEK.—In a work that purports to give the careers of the leading citizens of this county there would be serious failure were there omission of the gentleman whose name is at the head of this paragraph and who has wrought here for twenty years with an energy and perseverance that are worthy of especial mention. In the course of his endeavors in this county he has met with reverses that would have overwhelmed a less resolute and energetic man, but with every rising difficulty there has been developed in him a determination and fixed purpose to surmount it and come off victorious, which it is pleasant to relate, has been the case in all of his undertakings, for despite the obstacles that have been in his path he has become one of the leading and most successful stockmen of the county.

A native of the occident, being born to John and Maria (Beard) Sweek on February 26, 1857, in the Willamette valley, about ten miles south of Portland, he has ever cast his lot in the west and here he has met and conquered in the battle of life's way. His early life was spent on his father's farm and in attending the common schools of the place and when the time of his majority came he commenced in the basic art of agriculture for himself, continuing therein until the spring of 1880, the date of his advent into this county. Two years were spent in Prairie City, and then he came to Hamilton and took a band of sheep on shares. Success was attending his faithful efforts, but the severe winter of 1887-88 swept off nearly the entire number and the balance he turned over to the ones from whom he rented. In 1890 he bought a band and moved to his present place, four miles south of Monument. Four years later he sold the entire band, realizing ninety cents for ewes and seventy-five cents for lambs, per head. Then he turned his attention to freighting for two years, and in 1896 determined to again try his fortune with sheep, and accordingly bought a band of two thousand for one dollar per head, getting time for the payment and being backed by the First National Bank of Heppner. In three years he was enabled to pay out, and now he has a farm of eleven hundred and twenty acres, all fenced, with a good proportion of tillable land, and his flocks are numbered to about three thousand head. Prosperity has attended his efforts and he is at the present time one of the most substantial stockmen of the county.

Mr. Sweek and Miss Emily L., daughter of Benjamin and Mary Harding, of Washington county, this state, were married on February 17, 1879, and they have become the parents of eight children, as follows: Fay, wife of W. W. Flemming, of Monument; Rex L.; Ona; Bel; Calvin L.; Blanch; Ruth; Gladys. Mr. Sweek is a member of the Masonic lodge in Monument, and also of the Woodmen of the World, Lodge No. 378, of the same place. He is active in the realm of politics and displays his characteristic sagacity and vigor there.

W. D. INGLE.—It is with pleasure that we are enabled to grant to the esteemed gentleman whose name is at the head of this article a representation in this volume of the history of Grant county, since he has labored here for years and has done much toward the upbuilding of the county and the advancement of its interests, having manifested, meanwhile, commendable zeal and ability, coupled with which are displayed an uprightness and integrity that stamp him as a true man and faithful citizen.

The birth of Mr. Ingle occurred in South Carolina in the year 1837, and at an early age he was taken by his father to Darke county, Ohio. His parents were Daniel and Annie (Sharpe) Ingle. natives, respectively, of Kentucky and South Carolina. In Ohio his boyhood days were passed and there he received the education that fortified him for the battle of life. In 1846 he went to Illinois and there engaged in farming and stock raising for four years. Eighteen hundred and fifty-nine was the date that he crossed the plains by horse teams to California, the entire train having the misfortune to lose their horses. The In-

dians stole about four hundred of these animals, leaving only enough to haul the bare wagons, while many of the men were forced to walk the rest of the way. After spending some time in California he repaired to Grant county, and there took up farming and raising stock. At first he homesteaded land, then sold, and later bought school land one-half mile west from Mount Vernon, where he now has the fine estate of five hundred and sixty acres and is devoting his attention to handling cattle and horses and is one of the substantial stockmen of the county.

In Knoxville, Illinois, in 1854, Mr. Ingle married Miss Julia Bibler, a native of Ohio, and seven children have been born to them, Laura L., May, Clara, Stella, Benton, Claude and Omertis. Mr. Ingle formerly was affiliated with the I. O. O. F., and he is highly esteemed in this section and enjoys the good will and confidence of his fellows.

M. M. BRIERLEY.—To the prominent and capable gentleman whose name heads this paragraph we are constrained to grant a representation in the history of Grant county, since he is at the present time one of the potent factors in its population, and since he has wrought here and in other places on the frontier for many years with a display of the true pioneer spirit, and since his personal qualities of morality and ability are excellent and he is highly esteemed by his fellows.

Mr. Brierley was born in Lee county, Iowa, on April 2, 1842, being the son of Samuel and Sophia Brierley, and in 1853 the family came across the plains with ox teams, and while en route they had two pitched battles with the Indians, but in due time they made their way to California, settling in Amador county. The mother died in Oakland and in 1859 the father and our subject came back across the trail with a pack train, the son having the distinction of riding a Spanish mule the entire distance from the Pacific coast to Missouri. In 1875 our subject returned to California, locating in Stockton, where he engaged in farming for a decade. The year 1885 was when he came to Burns, engaging in sheep raising and freighting for five years. Following this period he removed to Hamilton, where he continued in the same business until 1899, when he sold out and removed to Monument. Here he has served as justice of the peace for eight years, and in 1895 he was appointed stock inspector for Grant county and served for one year.

In Buchanan county, Missouri, Mr. Brierley married Miss Barbara Goodman, a native of Missouri, and to them have been born the following children: Samuel, in California; George D., of Canyon City; Lee Annie, wife of John Garrett, of Pendleton; Thomas, of Ione; Bernice, wife of Frank Bowman, of Monument; Eliza, wife of William Bowman, of Monument; Rosa, wife of J. Boyce, of Grant county.

On September 22, 1861, Mr. Brierley enlisted in the second battalion, Missouri State Troops, and in February, 1862, he enlisted in Company A, Fifth Missouri Cavalry, and in that capacity he served until the close of the war, participating in the battles of Lone Jack, Prairie Grove, the expedition on the Red river, besides numerous other battles and skirmishes, making an enviable record as a brave and faithful soldier, intrepid and courageous, and loyal to the banner of freedom. Mr. Brierley is a prominent member of the G. A. R., and he organized the Post, No. 48, at Burns, for two years holding the position of commander; he also organized the Blue Mountain Post, No. 72, at Hamilton, and was commander there for two years. Mr. Brierley is one of the well known and esteemed citizens of this county and he has the entire confidence of his fellows.

JOHN L. MILLER.—It is gratifying to note that in the subject of this sketch we have displayed the praiseworthy qualities of stability and endurance coupled with energy and wisdom that have enabled their possessor to meet, with the calmness that is born of assurance of final success, the greatest obstacles, and in spite of difficulty overcome in a measure that is most praiseworthy, winning every inch of the ground of success by dint of exertion perseverance and determination that would have done credit to a cause of more extended notice and men of great public mention.

The birth of Mr. Miller was in Lane county in 1856 and his parents were David and Maggie (Douglass) Miller the former a na-

tive of Illinois and the latter of Iowa. His father crossed the plains in an early day being in the first train of settlers, and he made his way from The Dalles to the Willamette valley on a raft. He first settled on French Prairie, but later moved to Lane county, and there he lived until death took him from the scenes of life's activities. His remains lie buried at Creswell, in that county, while the mother sleeps at Gresham. John L. was only three years of age when the death of his parents occurred and he then went to California, and there he remained until the spring of 1881. At that date he came to Grant county, locating at Canyon City and engaging in the livery business. In addition to this activity he took up stock raising and farming, giving, however, his personal attention to the livery. At the time of the great fire in that town he lost everything, and was thus obliged to start again in the business world. He moved to Izee and began dealing in general merchandise in a small way, gradually increasing his stock and operating a wagon through the country until he secured sufficient funds to carry a large stock, and now he enjoys a lucrative trade, having purchased the store at Izee postoffice recently. He has anticipated the wants of the people and been so faithful in supplying them that he has won for himself a large trade and the confidence of the entire community. Mrs. Miller is the postmistress at Izee.

The marriage of Mr. Miller and Miss Lillie, daughter of William H. Chambers of Bates county, Missouri, was solemnized in 1895, and they have become the parents of two children, Eugene and Arthur Lyle. Mr. Miller is a member of the Masonic fraternity in Canyon City, and also of the W. of W. in the same place, while his wife is a member of the Eastern Star.

JOHN W. CONGER.—Among the many industries that have employed the hand of man none are more ancient, more widely followed, and more necessary for the sustenance of the race than those of raising stock and farming. Grant county has a wide awake, progressive and intelligent company of patriotic citizens who have given themselves to the prosecution of these industries and prominent among them is the gentleman of whom we now have the pleasure of writing and who has been instrumental in assisting materially in the development of the resources of the county and its substantial progress, as well as demonstrating his ability and good financiering in handling his own private affairs.

Mr. Conger was born in Lane county, Oregon, on March 7, 1861, being the son of Enoch and Permelia (Hall) Conger, who migrated to that county the year previous from the state of Iowa, whither they had come from their native state, Indiana. Remaining with his parents, in working on the farm and in attendance upon the public schools, the minority of John W. was passed, and in 1879 he came direct to this valley and settled on his present place, which is six miles north from Longcreek. He took a pre-emption and also a homestead, and then bought one hundred and sixty acres more, which gives him the generous estate of four hundred and eighty acres. To the improvement and cultivation of this land he has given his careful attention since and the result is that unbounded success has been the meed of his endeavors. In addition to this he handled sheep for two years immediately succeeding his advent here, then in company with his brother they handled them on share for eight years, wherein he has prospered continuously, owing to his vigilance in every detail and his sagacity, and executive ability in manipulating the enterprise. After the close of this time he sold the entire bands and alone bought cattle, which he has been handling since with his accustomed success and prosperity. His fine farm is well improved, having a comfortable house and large barn and other accessories.

The marriage of Mr. Conger and Miss Olive E., daughter of John P. and Harriet V. Baird, of Sumpter, occurred in October, 1888, and they have become the parents of three children, Willard M., deceased; Addie B., deceased; Sadie Marie. In 1881 Mr. Conger's parents removed from their donation claim in the Willamette valley to Longcreek where the mother is still living, but the father died in 1895. Mr. Conger is a member of the Modern Woodmen of America, at Longcreek. He is one of the substantial and successful men of the county and actively interested in public matters, ever manifesting uprightness and integrity.

DAVID G. OVERHOLT.—If there is one quality more than another that is commendable in the human breast and that calls out the praise of one's fellows, it is that of continuity of purpose and ability to rally in the face of defeat. In the life of the esteemed pioneer and enterprising business man that we have the pleasure of epitomizing at the present time, there has been set forth the exemplification of those qualities of the highest order, and while to others of more timidity and less resolute purpose the barriers thrown across his path would have been entirely unsurmountable, still, in the case of Mr. Overholt, the rising obstacle but produced rising strength to scale its loftiest pinnacle and sickening misfortune but strengthened an irrepressible will to call forth a fund of self-reliance and a wealth of personal resource that could bid defiance to all attacks and rally victory out of defeat.

Bucks county, Pennsylvania, is his native place, and 1830 the date of his birth, his parents being Samuel and Barbara Overholt, both natives of Pennsylvania. The old home place was twenty-four miles out from Philadelphia, and there young Overholt remained until he was nineteen years of age, acquiring a good education, and also becoming skilled as a wheelwright. When manhood's budding years began to approach he turned his way toward the west and settled in Ohio. Rowsburg, and there wrought at this trade until 1852, when the siren of the setting sun again beckoned him forward, and he set out on the perilous and weary journey toward California across the plains. The journey was in this wise: Messrs. Rows and Landis had been to California in 1850, crossing the plains and returning in 1851 by water. They reported the land fine, the country good, the gold plenty, but the Indians thick and hostile on the plains. They raised a company of one hundred and twenty-five men, each of whom was to pay one hundred and twenty-five dollars, and assist in handling the teams across the plains. The money thus raised was expended by the enterprising proprietors of the scheme in buying teams, outfits, provisions and so forth, and the men were set to work to take the train across the plains. Our subject was one of these men, and he drove an ox team all the way to California and stood guard one-half of every other night during the trip. Arriving at the sink of the

DAVID G. OVERHOLT.

Humboldt, they took the Trukee route and arrived in due time at the mouth of the Nelson on the Feather river, that being the first settlement, and it composed of miners. A big flume was being built and fifty dollars per day was offered to men to stop, and our subject took advantage of the offer and worked until fall, the ordinary wages being sixteen dollars per day. He went later to Napa, and there carved out honest enterprise at the bench.

On April 7, 1863, he came to Canyon City, where he was destined to play a prominent part in the commercial destiny of the embryonic town. He assisted to build some among the first lumber houses now in Canyon City, and for five years he wrought industriously and with abundant success and then turned back to his native state in 1868. There, in the same year, he married Miss Sebella, daughter of Martin and Elizabeth (Anglemyer) Tyson, natives of Pennsylvania. The following children were born to them: Mary E., married to D. I. Asburg, at McMinnville; Lillie Jane, at home; William E., in the mine owned by himself and father.

In the spring of 1869 he returned to Canyon City and entered the mercantile business. It was but a short time until he had secured a large and lucrative patronage, but the demon of fire sprang out and reduced his store and stock to ashes. No insurance covered his loss and such a blow would have laid to the ground the ordinary business man, but not so with the subject of this sketch. With courage and enterprise and resolution that would brook no defeat he gathered the remnants together and before the smoke of his sacrificed goods ceased to ascend, ground was broken for another and better establishment. Here he was even more successful than before, and soon he was on the topmost wave of prosperity, when again he fell a prey to the ravages of fire. This time, as before, the loss was practically total, as no insurance covered his goods and buildings. Now there seemed no possibility that recovery could be gained, and friend and foe alike prophesied the total defeat of his business career. The genius and courage of Mr. Overholt were equal to the occasion and again he brought out of the ashes of his calamity a more brilliant success than had hitherto been his to enjoy. His achievements were the wonder of all that knew the severity of the blow,

but to the credit of Mr. Overholt let it be stated that at no time of his struggle has he ever for one moment considered the advisability of retrenchment. His vocabulary os business knows but one word, "Onward to success." It was his motto and it led the way. From this last event of misfortune until the date of the sale of his entire business Mr. Overholt was destined to enjoy one continuous round of success, not, however without having to meet and overcome the trying obstacles connected with commercial life. On March 15, 1901, the time came when it was deemed best to retire from the activities of business life, and so the business was sold and now, free from the cares of active affairs, he is enjoying the retirement that he has so well earned and is ministered to by the competence that his own pluck and skill wrought out for himself and his son.

Fraternally he is connected with the Masons, Lodge No. 34, Chapter No. 7.; I. O. O. F., Lodge No. 22, Excelsior Encampment, No. 6, and Julia Chapter, No. 56, of the Eastern Star, the last having been named from Julia Abrams, of Portland. He is a stanch Republican and has always been actively interested in politics, as also in school and local affairs. It is of note that Mr. Overholt was one of four that walked from The Dalles to Canyon City, packing provisions. At supper time they would eat and then slip away four or five miles and crawl into the bush to sleep for fear of the Indians. His oldest daughter was on the stage the first time it was robbed on the way from Baker City.

* * *

ALLEN P. SNYDER.—One of the intrepid pioneers of early days and a man of stanch qualities and worth is the subject of this article, and an industrious and esteemed citizen whose career has given him the confidence of the entire community, he stands today as one of those substantial characters who make the strength and boast of the leading communities of our fair land.

Allen P. was born in Pennsylvania and when eight years of age came with his father to Missouri, where they remained for a few years, and then came to California, crossing the plains with mule teams. For six months after arriving in the Golden State our subject was occupied in mining and then went to Silver City, Nevada, where he continued that occupation until 1864. In the fall of that year he again tried the soil of California, operating in Plumas county, but later went to ranching in Sonoma county. From this he again went to Silver City and then after some time in the mines turned his attention to freighting until he came to Oregon in 1867. He teamed here for the government forts—Harney, Warner and Camp Winthrop, in eastern Oregon—until 1870, when he took up land where he lives at the present time, one-half mile west from Dayville, and entered the ranks of Oregon's stockmen. He now owns one half section and is attended with prosperity, his chief stock being cattle and horses.

Mr. Snyder and Miss Missouri Officer were married at Canyon City in 1876, and they have become the parents of six children, Jessie, Della, Dora, Ada, Alice, and also one, Frankie, who is deceased. The last mentioned was the second born, but the stern-visaged monster stepped in while she was but a child and claimed Frankie for his own. It was a severe blow to the parents, but she waits in the other land, where sorrow comes not, nor pain can despoil the rest of its inhabitants. Mr. and Mrs. Snyder are highly respected in the community and are exemplary in their life and demeanor to all.

━━━━━ ◆◆◆ ━━━━━

HENRY HALL, Jr. Many of our most esteemed and enterprising citizens came from across the waters, especially from England. As one who fully sustains the reputation of his countrymen for industry and wise management of business affairs the subject of this sketch is mentioned and his life of worthy achievement since coming to this county has placed him in the front ranks of prominent and substantial citizens.

Dorsetshire, England, is his place of birth, and May 24, 1844, the date thereof. It is of note that he was born on the anniversary of the queen's birth. In his native city he was trained in the public schools, but at an early age, fifteen, he was destined to meet the battles of life alone. He first took up the work of an architect and surveyor, which he followed for a decade and more, then turned from

the land of his birth to this of newer institutions and wider prospects. Eighteen hundred and sixty-eight was the year in which he landed in Grant county, and after a proper time spent in investigating its resources, he settled ten miles east from Canyon City, and for eleven years he was occupied in the industry of stock raising. In 1880 he bought the place where he now resides, eleven miles east from Canyon City, and hundred and sixty acres being the amount of his first purchase. By careful attention to business and the details of his affairs he was soon enabled to add to this land and the amount of his estate is at the present time ten hundred and forty acres. This fine domain is well improved and stocked with cattle and he is one of the leading men in that industry in the county. Mr. Hall's father was very prominent in church work in the home land. He was instrumental in organizing and firmly establishing the Wesleyan chapel and denomination, where he labored, and in 1860 he was called to the rewards of his labors. The mother passed away in 1871, and they both lie buried in the yard of one of the chapels that the father was instrumental in building.

Our subject is not affiliated with an denomination, but is a man of strict uprightness and of unswerving integrity, while his reputation is unsullied and his demeanor is such that he has won the confidence and respect of all his fellows. Being partial to the quieter joys of celibacy, Mr. Hall has never contracted a marriage and is thus relieved of the greater responsibilities and cares of the marital relation.

━━━━━ ◆◆◆ ━━━━━

MILAS ROACH.—A veritable pioneer of the pioneers, Mr. Roach stands as an exemplary character in that worthy and never-to-be-forgotten band that has done such wonders for these western sections, and he has been through all the experiences and hardships that attend the one that presses into the new regions of nature's fastnesses but to his credit it is said that in all of these trying scenes and in every capacity in which he has walked in the pioneer's life he has never flinched from duty nor swerved from the frank honesty that is so refreshing and necessary in the make-up of institutions that remain, as well as in individuals who would be crowned with honor and success.

On January 17, 1831, in Pickens county, South Carolina, Milas Roach was born to William and Mary (Crooks) Roach. His early life was spent on a farm with his parents and at the age of nineteen he accompanied them to Jackson county Arkansas, but soon after they arrived there the mother died, and a few days later the father also, and one brother. The mother passed away on June 24, 1851, and the father on July 24, 1851. In 1854 Mr. Roach went to Lavaca county, Texas, and one year later came via New Orleans and the Isthmus to San Francisco. He soon went to the Sierra Nevada mines and followed placer mining until 1860, then went to the Palmyra mines in Nevada and two years later came to Granite creek in this county. Following a short stay here he went to Tillamook county, this state, where he remained for a short time inspecting the country. Then followed a trip to the Florence mines in Idaho, where he continued for two years washing out the nuggets of nature's wealth. From there he went to Portland and in 1865 came again to this county and continued at mining in the different camps until 1869, when he located three hundred and twenty acres where he now lives, seven miles west from Monument. He took up stock raising and farming and has continued steadily in this ever since. His farm has increased by purchase until he now owns the generous domain of two thousand acres, which is well improved, with house, barn, orchards, fencing, and so forth. Mr. Roach enjoys the distinction of being one of the first settlers on the north fork of the John Day in the vicinity of Monument and he has wrought well and wisely for the development of the county. Success has attended his efforts and he is today one of the leading men of substantiality and uprightness in this section. He enjoys in unstinted measure the confidence and esteem of all his neighbors and numbers among his friends all the early pioneers of the county. Connubial bliss has never attracted Mr. Roach from the quieter charms of the celibatarian's life and his golden years are being spent in that peaceful retreat that he has wrought out by his industry and careful and wise manipulation of the resources that nature placed in his hands.

JOHN F. FAULKENBERRY.—Many men have wrought well in the arduous undertaking of developing and bringing to the front the resources of Grant county, and their efforts have been universally crowned with success and it is with pleasure that we give here mention of one who has manifested both ability and integrity, coupled with enterprise and thrift in this praiseworthy project since he has been domiciled in the county.

The son of Hugh and Sarah (Estes) Faulkenberry, born on June 19, 1852, in Saline county, Arkansas, Mr. Paulkenberry is, however, really a product of the west, for when he was one year of age his parents started over the plains with ox teams for the far and famed land of the Willamette valley. The train had reached a point in Colorado when the father was taken sick with a fever and soon succumbed to the messenger of death and his remains are buried by the great emigrant road in Colorado. The heart-broken widow with her five children could but proceed on the journey to the expected home in the land of the west and reached Polk county without further incident of note. On the donation claim there secured the subject of this sketch grew to manhood, and there received his education in the common schools. Until he was twenty-five years of age he remained on the farm assisting his step-father and then started in the battle of life for himself, taking up farming. It was in 1892 that he came to his present home in Grant county, which is nine and one-half miles north of Long-creek postoffice. Here, in company with his half-brother, George W. Sebring, he bought the W. H. Ward farm of one-half section. Since that time they have added the J. O. Williams farm by purchase, making their estate four hundred and eighty acres at the present time. Mr. Sebring is still in partnership with his half-brother, and is one of the substantial citizens of the county, being a man of marked enterprise and thrift, ever assisting in those undertakings that are for the upbuilding of the county and its interests. He has demeaned himself with such wisdom and manifestation of upright principles that he has won the esteem and confidence of his fellows. The estate of these gentlemen is well improved and is a very valuable hay producing farm, as well as first class for cereals. They harvest annually from one to two hundred tons of hay in addition to their other crops, while they handle a fine herd of cattle.

The marriage of Mr. Faulkenberry and Miss Daisy, daughter William and Jennie (Hooker) Lanceford was celebrated on August 20 1898, and they have been rejoiced by the birth of two children, Roy F., a bright and promising heir of two years past, and the baby, who is not yet named.

JOHN HYDE.—Under the stars of the occident, where he has remained since, was born the subject of this sketch, and faithfully has he wrought to augment the wealth of the county and has earned a place for himself among the leading stockmen of the county, since he has displayed an unswerving integrity and intrinsic worth that can but commend him to the esteem and draw forth the encomiums of his fellows, and it would be serious incompleteness in our volume were there failure to incorporate in its pages a resume of the salient points of his interesting career.

In 1854 John Hyde was born in Jackson county, this state, being the son of Perry and Eliza (Tyler) Hyde. The parents came across the plains in 1852 with ox teams from Missouri and lived at Harrisburg, in Linn county. When our subject had attained the years of his majority he embarked in the industry of raising cattle, and therein continued, near Prineville, this state, for some time, about six years in all. From that place he came direct to Grant county and selected a homestead near Izee, where he lives at the present time. His place has been increased by the purchase of one hundred and sixty acres and his estate lies two miles northwest from Izee. Cattle raising has occupied his attention since settling here and he has been attended with gratifying success in his endeavors.

In 1878 Miss Mary, daughter of William and Julia (Humgate) Bunton, became the wife of Mr. Hyde, and to them have been born the following children: Maude, Perry, Ollie and Nellie.

An interesting reminiscence that occurred on the journey of his parents across the plains is worthy of mention here. There was in the train one young man of a very aggressive and boastful disposition. It was his delight to constantly affirm, despite the reprovals of his elders, that he was determined to shoot the first redskin that he should see, whether it were man or woman. One luckless day the foolish bravado spied a harmless and innocent Indian woman, and in cold blood he shot her down. Not long after an overwhelming force of redskins equipped for war, surrounded the train. A hasty corral was formed and the women and children protected as well as possible. A messenger from the Indians announced that no harm would be done to the train if the murderer of the Indian woman was delivered to them. Justice demanded that the young man be delivered, and accordingly it was done. The enraged savages chained him to a tree and burned him to a crisp.

DAVID W. JENKINS.—"Render honor to whom honor is due" is one of the old and tried sayings and following this we are constrained to give to the distinguished and estimable gentleman whose name initiates this paragraph prominent representation in this work that endeavors to give proper biographical mention to the leading citizens of Grant county. A pioneer in many senses of the word, and descended from the strong blood that subdued and held, in spite of the world, Scotia's hills, he has demonstrated in a life full of bright achievement and stirring adventure on the frontier of the foremost nation of the globe that he is possessed of the same stanch qualities and commendable characteristics that made his ancestors famous.

Born in Scotland, on August 22, 1811, he enjoys the distinction of being the oldest man in the county of Grant, and perhaps in eastern Oregon. When he had attained his majority his adventurous spirit led him from the fold of his native land to the rising and progressive republic on the west of the Atlantic. Landing in New York, he at once engaged in the Brooklyn navy yards, and until 1844 did continuous and faithful service there. Then he went to Galveston, Texas, and entered the navy yards there for two years, then on to Mexico in the same occupation. At this latter place he suffered the misfortune of being nearly killed by the Mexicans and he repaired to the Golden

Gate in 1848, where he built a vessel and also erected the first buildings in that place, which has become the metropolis of the Pacific coast, his wages for this work being eleven dollars per day.

In the fall of 1848 he went to Stockton, and mined for five months, then returned to San Francisco. In partnership with three others, he bought a vessel to go whaling, but was diverted from that purpose by a reported new diggings, whither they went, they being on what had been named Trinity river; coming up the coast from here, they entered a place named Trinidad, but were attacked by the Indians and driven out. Later in San Francisco they met a captain that wished to find a little bay for starting a town, and they piloted him thither and established a town called Eureka, which is Humboldt today. Later Mr. Jenkins went to the head of the bay and established a town which was named Arcadia. Turning from this occupation he went to packing to the mines, and in 1863 came to what is now Grant county. Here he prospected this and adjacent territory, having traversed all the surrounding country long before there was any Baker City. In 1864 he pre-empted and homesteaded two hundred and forty acres where he now lives, seven and one-half miles west from John Day, and these holdings have increased to one-quarter of section 23 and one-half of section 35. His attention is devoted to raising stock and tilling the soil, and he has been attended by prosperity in his efforts. He is highly respected by all in the community and wherever he is known, and his industry and thrift have wrought out for him a fine legacy to leave to his family when it comes his time to depart from the scenes of earth. At the age of ninety he is hale and hearty and full of life and vigor and writes and handles the affairs of life as steadily as many men in the prime of life. During boyhood days Mr. Jenkins was denied the advantages of education to any extended degree and it was by continuous effort of reading and personal research that he was enabled to store his mind with practical information.

The marriage of Mr. Jenkins and Miss Anna Riley was consummated in 1861, and to them have been born three children: Alice, wife of Alex McKenna, of Canyon City; two infants that died before they received a name.

It is with great pleasure that we are enabled to say that of all the old pioneers, who are a highly esteemed and respected class of citizens, there is none among them that stands higher in the minds of their fellows than Mr. Jenkins, and in point of age he is the senior of them all, which together with his other qualifications of merit, justly entitles him to the place of leadership. Mr. Jenkins affiliates with the I. O. O. F., Hobah Lodge, No. 22, of Canyon City.

GEORGE RADER.—A pioneer that has known the early life of the Pacific from California to Grant county, and a man to whom nature has given liberally of those qualities which make the typical frontiersman, the substantial citizen and the noble representative of our race, the subject of this sketch is today one of the prominent citizens of Grant county and a prosperous and successful stockman that has added materially to the wealth of the county and to the interests of all by the manifestation of an enterprising public spirit and by carefully prosecuting a career of private business undertakings with wisdom and energy.

The son of George and Emily Rader, he was born near Rockville, Park county, Indiana, on August 12, 1840, and when eleven years of age was removed by his parents to Monroe county, Iowa, where he remained until nineteen years of age and worked on the farm with his father until the latter's death, in 1858, and then two years longer he remained with his mother. But on the morning of May 21, 1860, he turned the ox teams that he had provided toward the setting sun and began the long journey that ended in Shasta county, California, on Saturday evening before the election of Abraham Lincoln. He engaged in farming and working for wages until May 22, 1862, at which time he went with a pack train for the Salmon river, but turned aside and stopped in Canyon City on July 4, of the same year. He turned his attention to mining until August, 1865, then went to Susanville, following the same occupation until December, 1876, at which time he located his present place at Longcreek postoffice. He bought the right of a settler with his improvements and then filed on a homestead and commenced the occupation of the stockman and agriculturist. Prosperity has attended his wisely directed efforts and tireless thrift and today he is the owner of large tracts of land and numerous herds of cattle and sheep and is counted as one of the most substantial stockmen of the county. At one time he and seven others, among whom was the noted Jim Cummings, captured thirty-six horses from the Indians after an exciting conflict.

On July 3, 1877, the marriage of Mr. Rader and Miss Frances E., daughter of James F. and Julia Miller, was celebrated, and they have become the parents of four children: Maud O., deceased; Harvey, deceased; Frederick W.; Helen E. Mr. Rader is a man that is highly respected by all and has won the confidence and esteem of those who know him, having demeaned himself in a commendable manner, ever manifesting principles of truth and uprightness.

JAMES ROBINSON, deceased. Any compilation that purports to give the history of Grant county would be incomplete were there failure to mention in connection therewith the capable gentleman whose name is at the head of this paragraph, since he was closely connected with its development and progress during a long life of commendable activity here, and it is with pleasure that we grant to his memory this article, being assured that he is one of the deserving citizens of this section.

St. Johns, New Brunswick, was the spot of his birth, and 1834 the date, his parents being William and Annie Robinson. In that country he was educated and in 1863 started out in the activities of life for himself, coming, via the Isthmus, to California, where he remained until 1855, then returned to his home in the east. The following year he came back to California, and from that time until 1864, he was engaged in the mines in Yreka, California, at which time he came to Canyon City, and there worked at mining. He was soon elected justice of the peace, and for four years he continued in that office, discharging the duties incumbent upon him with efficiency and impartiality. About 1872 he was selected by the people to act in the capacity of county clerk, and in these relations he ac-

quitted himself with distinction. Following this period, wherein he had performed the duties of this important office with an ability and cleverness that gave general satisfaction, Mr. Robinson was often reinstated in the office of justice of the peace, and throughout it all he was characterized with the same sagacity and straightforwardness in dispensing justice.

In 1871 at Canyon City, Mr. Robinson married Miss Lizzie, daughter of Thomas and Jane (Blake) Abrams, natives of England and pioneers to California in 1854, and to this happy union there were born three children, as follows: James S., deceased; Elnora S., deceased, and Edith May.

On March 15, 1901, the angel of death came for Mr. Robinson and he stepped forth into the realities of another world. He was beloved and esteemed by all, and one of Grant county's capable and faithful citizens was then taken, for whom all sincerely mourned. Mrs. Robinson is taking up the burdens of life alone since that sad event, manifesting a brave and good spirit, and nobly she is handling the affairs of life thus resting upon her. She has a good business in Canyon City, in the mercantile line, and also handles the express office, and she is highly esteemed by all.

ROBERT E. DAMON.—It is with pleasure that we embrace the opportunity to chronicle the salient points in the interesting career of the gentleman whose name heads this article, and who has been a potent factor in the affairs of Grant county for one-third of a century, having in that lengthened period manifested those principles of uprightness that commend one to the confidence and esteem of his fellows, while he has wrought with energy and wisdom in all of his enterprises, achieving that success which is the meed of those who are the faithful disciples of wisdom, energy and industry.

On November 25, 1828, at Scituate, Massachusetts, Robert E. was born and there he passed the years of his minority. About the time of the memorable "49" he was stirred by the rumors from the far west and he migrated thither, landing in San Francisco on January 1, 1854. Thence he went to Yreka, where he remained for six years and in 1860 went back

JAMES ROBINSON.

to Massachusetts on a visit and then came to Oregon, settling at Jacksonville, and farmed there for two years. In 1862 he went to Florence, Idaho, where he sought the treasures of nature for two years and then returned to San Francisco for the winter, after which he repaired to Jackson and commenced to buy cattle and drive them to Grant county. He made three trips at this employment and in 1870 came to the county and settled where his ranch is at the present time three miles west from Mount Vernon. He first took one hundred and sixty acres but has added by purchase since until he owns seven hundred acres of fine land, which is well stocked with sheep, cattle and horses. He is personally attending to a feed stable in Mount Vernon. In political matters he is a stanch Republican and has served as county commissioner, being prominent in the county. Fraternally he is affiliated with the Masons, Lodge No. 34, at Canyon City.

In 1870 Mr. Damon and Miss Anna, daughter of William and Ellen (Allen) Stedman, were united in the holy bonds of matrimony, and the fruit of the union has been as follows: Walter H., Sarah E., Catherine, John, Edward and Emily. Mrs. Damon's parents came to this country from Australia and her birth occurred while they were en route. Mr. Damon is now verging into the golden years of his life, and although his industrious career dominated with wisdom, has given him a competence, and even far beyond that, still he is active and prefers to be busied with the oversight and care of his interests than to remain in quietness. He is beloved by all and is one of those substantial men that form the real life and solidity of any community.

<hr/>

PRIOR S. WILSON, deceased. To the memory of the esteemed gentleman, and intrepid pioneer, whose name is at the head of this article, we are constrained to grant this memorial, since to his labors, Grant county is much indebted for development and augmenting its quota of wealth, while his life of uprightness and display of sound principles were a worthy example to those who are left to follow.

Mr. Wilson was the son of John and Ma-

hala Wilson and was born in Holt county, Missouri, on April 25, 1845. There he passed his early life and then came to Linn county with his parents, where he completed his education. It was about 1860 that he came to Umatilla county with his parents, who settled there and opened a dairy and also operated a pack train from Umatilla to Baker City. Much of their packing was done at night, as the burdens were largely composed of butter. Later he engaged in stock business and it was as early as 1870 that he came to Grant county. He wrought with wisdom and energy and his labors and victories were crowned with success. On July 20, 1899, he was called from the scenes of his labors and victories to the world beyond the veil. He was universally beloved and respected. His remains lie buried in the Monument cemetery. His widow, Mrs. Sarah J. Wilson, and four children were left to mourn his demise. He was a prominent member of the A. F. & A. M., and was always active in politics, being a real leader in that realm.

Mrs. Wilson's marriage with the deceased occurred on October 6, 1881, and the names of her children are as follows: Mahala, wife of Thomas Brirly, of Ione; Eppa; Chancey; Lottie C. Previous to this last marriage Mrs. Wilson was the wife of Isaac Violett and by that marriage she had four children: Endora, wife of James Anderson, formerly of Harney county, but now living in Monument; Mary M., wife of Edward Keeney, of Harney county; Homer, deceased: Helen, wife of Joseph Woolery, of Ione, a merchant. Her marriage to Isaac Violett occurred in Linn county, Oregon, in 1862, and soon following this they removed to Wasco county and took up general merchandising there until October 6, 1870, when they removed to Grant county and engaged in the stock business, in which they were laboring when the death of Mr. Violett occurred in 1874. Mrs. Wilson's parents were Daniel and Clarissa (Perry) Minkler, and natives of Indiana and New York, respectively. Mrs. Wilson is living in Monument and is well esteemed by all. She has an elegant residence, owned the land on which the village was built, owns the leading hotel of the town, which is rented, also a livery and feed stable which she is operating, and three large farms near by. Her land is well improved and the one adjoining the town is very valuable. She displays marked wisdom in managing her large interests and is to be commended upon both her ability as a financier and keen foresight coupled with excellent executive force. She has large bands of stock and is counted as one of the most successful operators in that line in the county. When a child, she accompanied her parents across the plains, making the entire distance with ox teams. They settled in Clackamas county in 1849, where the father was engaged in farming until the time of his death a few years later. The aged mother is still living in Monument.

*　*　*

WILLIAM T. HAMILTON.—Among the representative men of this section and one of the leading citizens of Grant county is the gentleman of whom we now have the pleasure of writing. He has gained distinction in at least two different lines of industry in the county and today stands as one of its leading merchants as well as a successful agriculturist and stockman, having been enabled by his ability and faithful dealing to build up a fine trade in the town of Hamilton, where he resides.

Mr. Hamilton was born in Multnomah county, this state, on October 20, 1867, being the son of John H. and Mary J. Hamilton. From near Oregon City, the place of his birth, the parents moved to the place where our subject is now living, in 1872, and here he spent the early years of his life in looking after the stock of his father. He was enabled to attend school but little on account of the school being distant four miles, and also because his eyes were not sufficiently strong to allow him to study. Thus his early education was limited, but by careful observation and treasuring up with an excellent memory what he has dug out by himself in odd times, he has come to be well informed and is thoroughly drilled in the business of which he has shown himself master. His parents were the first settlers in Indian valley on Deer creek and the town of Hamilton was named after them. Mr. Hamilton now owns three hundred and forty acres of good land, which is well improved and carefully looked after; he also has a large band of cattle and horses. In 1897 he erected a store building in Hamilton and occupied it with a stock of general merchandise. His careful attention to the wants of his customers and uprightness in dealing have won for him a fine trade that is constantly increasing. He has a beautiful modern residence in the town and a good barn and orchard in addition to his store building.

The marriage of Mr. Hamilton and Miss Ella, daughter of D. D. and Mamie Hinton, of Hamilton, was celebrated on November 1, 1896, and to them have been born one son, Criss. Mr. Hamilton is a member of the W. of W., Lodge No. 581, in Hamilton. He is deeply interested in educational matters and has been instrumental in forwarding the cause much in his district, having acted as clerk, and always being interested in any movement that will advance the cause. He has won the esteem and confidence of the entire community and is highly respected by all.

*　*　*

JOHN C. LUCE.—In the person of the gentleman whose name appears at the head of this article we have one of the most prominent citizens of the county and one that has been a leader since his advent here in 1862, thus being one of the first white men that settled within the borders of Grant county. In political matters, as well as in the realm of stock raiser and agriculturist, Mr. Luce has been a distinguished figure before the people for some time and his influence has been felt to the remotest corners of the state, having been so prominent in the political arena that he has been in contest for the supreme office of the state.

John C. was born September 20, 1843, in Iowa, and at the age of nine years was brought by his parents across the plains with ox teams to the Willamette valley, where they settled near Eugene until 1859, when he removed to California. It was as early as July 17, 1862, that Mr. Luce made his way into this section and engaged in mining and packing to Canyon City from The Dalles. He discerned the future of the country and accordingly took a preemption claim, where he still lives, three miles west from John Day. This was one of the first pieces of government land taken for farming in the county. To this he has added until he has a fine estate of five hundred acres, which is used in handling his large herds of cattle. He gained his first start in cattle by buying in

JOHN C. LUCE.

the Willamette valley and driving to this section. Prosperity has followed his efforts, because of his thrift and his ceaseless efforts in attention to and wise handling of his cattle, and he has become one among the wealthy stockmen of the county. Care and thrift are manifested in all his enterprises and his place is a model of comfort and neatness. Mr. Luce has by no means confined his efforts to raising stock, but has gained distinction in a number of lines in the county, notably among which is the newspaper realm. During 1893 and 1894 he conducted successfully a sheet of merit in John Day, and was one of the most powerful men in politics in the county. He was instrumental in organizing the first Farmers' Alliance in this and Harney counties and has been a leader in it since. He was a candidate for Congress against Judge W. R. Ellis, and also was in the field for gubernatorial honors against Geer, and made a very commendable race in both cases.

The marriage of Mr. Luce and Miss Cynthia A., daughter of J. F. Hodson, was celebrated in 1868, and to them were born the following children: Lincoln B.; Chauncey M., deceased; Ruhama B.; Frederick O., deceased; James E., deceased; William A.; Charles F.; Bertha E. In 1889 Mrs. Luce was taken from her family by death and her remains were interred in the Canyon City cemetery. She was aged thirty-six years at the time of her demise.

HIRAM C. MACK.—If to one class of people more than to another belongs the privilege of shaping the state and upon whom rests the responsibility of instilling right principles in the rising generation, that honor pre-eminently reverts to the educators of this land; and it is only just to them to say that no class of people are deserving of more credit both for unselfish and painstaking labor and constant care along these lines than are the teachers of our land, and true it is to-day that for the value of the services rendered there is no class that is so stinted in the remuneration received from a generally generous public. Among those who have wrought in these western countries to properly train the youth, to raise a higher standard of educational qualification, to form the plastic forces of an embryonic state

into molds of stanch statesmanship and sound principles, the esteemed citizen whose name heads this article, stands high and as a veritable leader he has been manifested in the years of his toils in this line in Grant and adjoining counties.

Mr. Mack was born in the Willamette valley in 1871, being the son of J. W. and Helen M. (Duston) Mack, natives of New York and Ohio, respectively. In 1852 they crossed the plains to the Willamette valley and settled on a ranch there and in 1877 came thence to Grant county. In the schools of Prairie City the foundation of his education was laid. Afterwards, by hard work and strict economy, he was enabled to spend a term at the State University at Eugene. After leaving the university, he began the career of the educator and it was evident from the beginning that nature had given him those qualifications that marked him as one to whom pre-eminent success would come as the result of his painstaking and arduous labors and careful and constant using of the rich talents with which he had been endowed. It was to be expected then, that he would do soon what he did in fact accomplish, take leading place among the educators of eastern Oregon. His ability for this position was quickly manifest to all and the unbounded enthusiasm in this work and love for the same that were constant companions with him wrought powerfully in the circle of educators of this region, producing more ardent effort and enterprising activities in their various duties, giving withal an inspiration that resulted in untold good to the schools of Grant and other counties where he labored.

Two years ago, he was allured into the field of commercial business, and what educator has not felt the same desire to lay down the seemingly thankless and bitter tasks of training stubborn minds and free himself by loading on his shoulders the cares of commercial life, assuredly knowing that the burdens taken up would be but rest compared with those laid down? Fort two years he reveled in the delights of his freedom while he carried on the drug business, but fortune was not thus disposed to lose an ardent disciple of Socrates and Agassiz, and so insisted by the vote of the people that he should leave the drug business and come back to the higher, though correspondingly harder and weightier duties of superintending the county schools. He immediately responded with the fitting repentence as he again took up life with his first love and the people of Grant county are to be congratulated that they have secured his services in this capacity and also that they rescued from the petrefaction of the commercial world and its strife of competition one who is so well qualified to carry on with unbounded success the calling of the true educator. In political matters, as is usual with the students of the land, he is allied with the Democratic party and is a force in real politics, and it was on this ticket that he was elected to his present position. It is with a bright outlook for the future that the young educator is thus again pressed into the harness and unless every prognostication of past fact in his career is a patent perverter of the truth, the future has in store some rich work and excellent achievement for this student, whose heart is thoroughly in the greatest of all human callings and professions, that of the educator.

VANDEVER L. COFFEY.—Among the leading agriculturists of Grant county, it is fitting to make mention of the gentleman whose name heads this article, and although he has not been domiciled within the county as long as some, still his life has been connected with the interests of eastern Oregon for a long time and with the state for nearly half a century and in this lengthened period he has ever manifested those sterling qualities that are the pride and boast of any well regulated community and which characterize him to this day.

Mr. Coffey was born to John and Nancy Coffey, in Gallatin county, Illinois, on October 26, 1833. In his native county, he worked on a farm and attended school during the proper seasons until the spring of 1853. Then his adventurous spirit was ready for the long trip across the weary deserts to the land of promise near the Pacific. Oregon City was his first stop and soon he was in the mines in Port Orford, where he wrought until 1855, the date of his enlistment in Captain John Craton's company of minute men, a portion of the state volunteers that were led out to quell the uprising of the savages, which conflict continued until the close of 1856. He did faithful military service and

participated in many skirmishes and some battles, among which may be mentioned one at the mouth of the Coquille river in which there were seventeen of the savages slain but not one of the soldiers. Following the retreating red skins, they captured seventy-five of their number and delivered them to the Indian agent and this completed the war. For some time subsequent to this, he was engaged in various places and in different occupations and then came to Weston and embarked in the furniture business and later in a livery stable. The latter burned down and left him penniless. It was in 1884 that he entered a homestead near Heppner and there he gave his attention to farming until the spring of 1901, when he sold the entire property and bought where he now resides, eighteen miles west from John Day. He is postmaster at Beach Creek and also has a long distance telephone station. His farm is well improved, having fine buildings and other accessories to a first-class estate. In addition to the enterprises mentioned, he is operating a hotel and feed stable and is one of the well-to-do and prosperous citizens of the county.

The marriage of Mr. Coffey and Miss Rebecca J. Wright occurred on January 5, 1871, in Marion county, Oregon. Mr. Coffey is a member of the Masonic fraternity and has been for thirty-five years. He and his wife are prominent members of the Methodist church, South, where they take great interest in both church and Sunday-school work.

JOHN C. SILVERS.—It is the pleasant task that has fallen to our lot to write, in brief review, an epitome of the career of the estimable and progressive gentleman whose name heads this article and who is classed as one of the leading agriculturists and stockmen of Grant county, having been one of that worthy class that pressed into this section at an early day and opened it up for the advent of civilization's institutions, undergoing much hardship and putting forth very commendable efforts in this praiseworthy achievement. It is a source of great pleasure to see domiciled in the rich valleys of our county the hardy and brave men that wrought so faithfully in opening up the frontier, and it speaks well of the resources of this county that so many of the early ones remained here.

Mr. Silvers was born on January 22, 1846, on St. George Island, in the far away East Indies, but at the age of nineteen years came to this land of the free, where he has made his home since. He landed at Boston, and soon was enroute to the Golden state, via the Isthmus, and the following year he came to Canyon City. For eight years he was engaged in mining and then took up ranch work for twelve years, and four· years since he purchased the estate where he now resides, one mile west from John Day, which consists of two hundred acres. It is a valuable farm and skillfully handled by its owner. Every department is looked after with a discerning care and thrift, and neatness and dispatch are everywhere in evidence on the estate. It is well improved and all the accessories that add comfort and convenience to rural life are found in place.

The marriage of Mr. Silvers and Miss Jessie Maura, a native of Maria Island, which is close to St. George, was celebrated in 1888 and to this happy union have been born the following children: Mary; Anna, deceased; Manvel; Jessie; John; one infant, deceased. It is very pleasing to see in this worthy couple resting thus under the benign influence of our free American institutions an exemplification of genuine democracy and stanch and fervent love for the flag that waves over a nation antipodal to the sea girt islands of their nativity. It is the blending of such noble pioneer characters that has made the American republic the foremost nation on the earth to-day.

HON. MORTON D. CLIFFORD.—While every true American rejoices in the grand freedom that our matchless democratic institutions furnish to the law-abiding citizens, there is no less comfort and satisfaction in the strong bulwark of law that with its stern hand renders possible the proper enjoyment of true freedom while it holds in check that foul counterfeit, license, that strives to checkmate and absorb the benign influence of the salutary restraints that wise legislators have placed about our firesides and political creations. With courage and spirit never overmastered, with hardy endurance and continuity unparalleled, our forefathers asked for, and then fought until they obtained the birthright of self government and then demonstrated to an amazed world of spectators their deep sagacity as modern Solons by creating in the midst of the throes of a desperate struggle of death, the solid constitutional foundation, and rearing thereupon the magnificent superstructure of statute law, the most brilliant, wise, and practical that had hitherto been wrought in words by human beings. To such a legacy have the American people fallen heirs and it requires no less erudition and probity coupled with a masterful executive power to properly expound, apply, and execute these sound principles of justice and equity than was displayed at their marvelous inception and codification. However, let it be mentioned to the praise of this free nation, that there has never been wanting a son of freedom to rest in the seat of our distinguished ancestors who could and did with honor to his predecessor carry out the spirit of the wisdom manifested in the primary expression of these wise principles. Mighty statesmen and eminent jurists have been in the number from the supreme bench to the remotest parts of the great domain and it is with great pleasure that we are enabled to state, that although not yet in a federal position so marked by exaltation as some enjoy, yet none the less distinguished by his depth of wisdom and sound principles and sterling qualities, coupled with unswerving integrity and unstained honor, stands the faithful expounder of the laws whose name initiates this paragraph and to whom we are desirous of granting this slight mention.

Morton D. Clifford was born May 24, 1859, in Iowa, being the son of Harmon and Jane (Mahon) Clifford. In 1870 he accompanied his mother to Oregon and settled at Canyon City, living first on a ranch and securing what school privileges he was enabled to, but constantly giving himself to good reading and investigation. His stock of information was so thorough and full that he was warranted in beginning the practice of law at The Dalles when he was twenty years of age, doing his initiative work in the office of Hill & Mayes, of that place, where also he continued for two years and then was admitted to the bar of the state. Following his admission, he came to Canyon City, and set up the practice of law. Two years later, he had risen so rapidly and displayed such a breadth of information and depth of legal understanding that the people asked him to accept the position of district attorney of the sixth judicial district. This position was filled faithfully and with manifestation of ability until the expiration of his term in 1888, when he again resumed the practice of law. In 1890 he was appointed by the governor to fill the unexpired term of L. B. Ison as judge of the same district, serving for two years, then he was elected to a six years' term of the same position and at its expiration he was elected to a six years' term of judge of the ninth judicial district, this having been formed from the old sixth. At the present time he is holding his position, and it is with credit to his whole district, for his universal fairness and marked skill and deep knowledge of both the law and the spirit of equity have justly made him renowned.

Judge Clifford and Miss Edith, daughter of Judge G. I. and Emiline (McCullum) Hazeltine, were married in August, 1885, at Canyon City and to them have been born two children, Harold and Emma. In political matters the Judge is associated with the Democrats. Fraternally, he is affiliated with the Masonic lodge No. 60, at Prairie City, and in 1883 he received the degree of Royal Arch in Chapter No. 7, Canyon City, where he held the position of high priest; he also is a member of the Washington Council, No. 3, of royal and select masters, and of the high priesthood in the state commandery, No. 1, Walla Walla; also received the thirty-second degree of Scottish rite at Portland and was elected junior grandwarden of the grand lodge of Oregon in 1891 and senior grand warden in 1892, deputy grand master in 1893, and grand master in 1895; he also belongs to the I. O. O. F., Lodge No. 22, of Canyon City.

ALVA C. DORE.—What thrilling days were those when the fleet and hardy steeds bore their more intrepid riders from post to post in the dispatch of important business in the never-to-be-forgotten pony express! Deeds of daring and bravery that well might stir the spirit of the reader were of frequent occurrence, and hardships were too common to dwell upon. These times are gone, the prairie schooner has been brushed aside for the chariot of steel, the harnessed lightning darts o'er the course where the hoofbeats of the flying pony express are heard no more and it is not without a tear of regret that we glance back at the past while we embrace the new. How acceptable then it is to sit and listen to one who comes as an actual participant from those daring times and relates to us the tales of interest. All hail to the opportunity to chronicle the deeds of those sturdy and noble pioneers that are all too soon passing away from us. The subject of this humble sketch is one who has passed through much of this life and has been instrumental in inaugurating civilization's reign with her aids and inventions, while he brings items of the past as it were from a new land.

Alva C. Dore was born in Penobscot county, Maine, on February 28, 1840, being the son of Serles and Lucinda Dore. He was reared on his father's farm and remained until he was nineteen years of age and then came to the new west, going at once to the Rocky mountains and engaging as a rider on the pony express line that was so famous in those early days. He rode across the mountains until the telegraph line was put up, then was express messenger for Ben Haliday until 1862 and then quit and went to San Francisco, and thence by steamer to Portland, when he made his way to Albany, and operated a sawmill for three years. At the end of this period he went to Walla Walla and operated a mill there for two years and then came to Canyon City and engaged in the same business here, in which he has constantly been occupied since, adding mining also. He came to his present place in 1890. It is located twelve and one-half miles south from Canyon City, on Canyon creek, and here he owns a good mill and one half section of valuable timber and farming land. He has a good house and other improvements.

In 1874 the marriage of Mr. Dore and Miss Emma, daughter of Emanuel and Sarah Mosier, of John Day, was celebrated, and to them was born one child, Alva S., now married to Bertha Voley, of John Day. In 1878 Mrs. Dore was summoned hence by death.

Mr. Dore was married a second time and the lady of his choice was Mrs. Amy Westfall, who was called to pass the river of death in 1888. There were born to this second union triplets, one of whom died in infancy, one died at the age of three years, being named Amy,

ALVA C. DORE.

and the other, named Helen, is still living. Mr. Dore is a charter member of the A. O. U. W. lodge in Canyon City. He takes an active part in politics and is ever working for the advancement of the interests of the county. In 1886 the people summoned him to the service of the county as sheriff, and after a term of faithful and efficient work in that capacity he was re-elected and served two years more. His public career, as his private, has been dominated by wisdom and the manifestation of ability that give him the confidence of his fellows and the respect of all. During his last term of service as sheriff he collected all the taxes of the county, an occurrence which was never duplicated before or since,

---

HON. MEL DUSTIN.—It is inherent in mankind to manifest approval to those who have amidst difficulties and in the face of towering obstacles wrought out a success that is worthy, and among the many sturdy pioneers that have been rightly placed in this class, mention must be made of the esteemed citizen whose name initiates this paragraph, since he has been a conspicuous example of those who by their own efforts have carved a place in the annals of time for their names.

He was born in Iowa, in 1842, of Dudley P. and Harriet A. (Slausen), natives respectively of New Hampshire and Ohio. He is a descendant of the famous Thomas and Hannah Dustin, of Haverhill. In 1850, he crossed the plains with his parents and that winter he attended the first school taught in Portland, the teacher being Mr. Outhouse. Mr. Dustin has been a person of energy and enterprise from the beginning to the present time. He remained with his parents until twelve years of age and then joined the list of trappers and hunters that were prominent in those days and until eighteen years of age he was assiduously following that occupation, becoming skilled in all its interesting lore and experiencing many thrilling and intensely exciting incidents. When he arrived at eighteen years of age, his mind had been sufficiently satiated with those adventures that are so acceptable to younger days of boyhood, and he began to see the need of an education in order to do justice to the name he bore in the battles of life. To see the

need was for young Dustin to supply the same, and so earnestly and wisely did he set to the task of gaining educational discipline that two years later he was the proud bearer of a state certificate granted by Governor Pennoyer. For one decade he gave himself to the worthy art of teaching, but finding a desire for larger fields, he set himself to the greater task of preparing for the practice of law. This also he successfully accomplished and in 1869, he was admitted to the bar in Washington and in 1875 received the same honor from the state of Oregon. From that time he has steadily pursued the practice, perfecting himself in every department that was of practical service in his varied and large clientage. In 1874 he was selected county judge for Grant county, and in 1880 he was nominated for the state senate, running on the Democratic ticket. His practice in Canyon City has been long and successful and his standing in the county and among his associates at the bar has been and is of the highest order.

The marriage of Mr. Dustin and Miss Emma, daughter of Samuel and Wealthy (Lowe) Markee, was celebrated in 1868 and to them have been born six children as follows: Bailey C.; Effie, wife of John Brandt, of Portland; Celia, wife of Frank Foster, of John Day; Hiram E.; Rosa; Mel G. With natural acumen and acquired lore, gathered during a long and studious career of constant experience, dominated by sagacity and probity that are the willing servants of a powerful mind and an indomitable purpose, Mr. Dustin properly holds rank as one of the leading attorneys of eastern Oregon.

DR. L. B. TROWBRIDGE.—It is with pleasure that we are called upon to briefly epitomize the interesting career of the esteemed citizen and early pioneer, whose familiar name is at the head of this article, since he is by force of right classed among the leading citizens of this county and one that has wrought with assiduity and display of sagacity here for the development and progress of the county, and his efforts have been very potent in bringing good to his fellows as well as displaying the latent powers of which he is possessed so richly.

The Doctor was born in Broome county, New York, in 1834, and at the age of twelve years was taken by his parents to Lee county, Illinois, in which place the parents made their home until the time of their death. At the budding age of eighteen years, L. B. commenced the activeness of life for himself, taking up the carpenter trade, and utilizing carefully all of his spare time in the study of medicine. Seven years later he came to Yreka, California, and there engaged in mining until the spring of 1862, at which time he came to where Canyon City now stands. Here he built the first house in the limits of what is now the town, the building occupying the site now utilized by the Masonic hall. For three years subsequent to this he was occupied in mining and buying and selling stock. In 1868 he took up hotel keeping and successfully operated the Western, a popular house in those days, but the fire of 1870 left him penniless. With his accustomed pluck and enterprise, he was soon in business trim again and the mercantile world was the scene of his activities for four years. During these years he was giving his spare time to the medical works that were so dear to him. During the years of 1874-6 he was in the Willamette villey and there he gave himself entirely to the prosecution of these studies. Following this period he was in California pursuing the same line of study and in beginning the practice of medicine. In 1878 he returned to Salem and there commenced in real earnest the practice of his profession and it was his to enjoy unbounded success. Soon he was in Portland and for fifteen years he practiced there, gaining a reputation for skill and sagacity in his profession that was very commendable. Later he went to Harney and from there again to California, where he spent four years in practice, returning again to Portland and then in the last of December, 1898, he came to Canyon City, the scene of his early labors. A few months later he came to Isee and purchased a farm five miles out and desired to rest from the more arduous duties of practice. He is held in high esteem in his community and is sought after from many homes. The Doctor is a man of marked natural ability and his mind is well stored by deep research and continued study while his experience has been over a very wide range, while his travels have given him possibilities for observation and accumulation of knowledge and skill that have rendered him not only a physician of deep erudition but have given him a fund of valuable information on a wide range of topics that is both gratifying and praiseworthy. Doctor Trowbridge is interested in the Mammoth copper mine and the Gold Hill mine, all of which are properties of great promise. Fraternally he is affiliated with the I. O. O. F.

———◆◆◆———

JOSEPH N. DITMARS.—In the person of the subject of this sketch we have one of the doughty and intrepid pioneers of the entire northwest and a man of great and varied experiences, which have given him a breadth of comprehension, which, augmented by his natural keenness and executive force, make hime one of the strong men of Grant county. Joseph N. was born in Clinton county, Ohio, in March, 1846, being the son of Abraham and Jennie (Perkins) Ditmars, natives of Ohio and Kentucky, respectively. In 1849 the family came to Clinton county, Missouri, where our subject was reared on a farm and educated. In 1861 he enlisted in Price's army and fought at Corinth, after which he went to Virginia and served until the close of the war, being wounded once. At that time he went to Texas for a time and then returned to Missouri, where he remained until 1867. We next see him in Nevada, mining, and in the fall of 1868 he went to Fraser river, in British Columbia, and in the following year he went to Bena river, in Alaska, but the guide died and the party were lost, and spent the winter at Fort Sill, subsisting on rabbits. In 1870, he returned to Nevada, going the entire distance afoot, arriving there late in the summer. He was occupied there mining, with good success until 1881, when he went to Fresno, California, and there mined and built mills until August, 1887, at which time he went to China, being engaged by that government as mining engineer in the Ping To gold mines. On account of failing health, after two years he returned to the United States, and came to Oregon with the intention of going into the stock business. Arriving at the Greenhorn district he was so impressed with the mineral wealth of that section that he abandoned the stock business and went to keeping store with Neal Niren in Granite. The firm was known as Niren & Ditmars for eight years and then they sold out, after which he spent two years in the lumber business and now our subject devotes his entire time to the care of his property in Granite, and mining and building mills, being an expert in both of these lines. Mr. Ditmars owns the hotel Granite, one store building, and several residences in Granite.

Fraternally Mr. Ditmars is affiliated with the A. F. & A. M., Lodge No. 47, of Baker City, and he is one of the prominent men of this portion of Grant county, being one of the progressive and enterprising spirits of the county, and is held in high esteem and respect by all.

———◆◆◆———

JOHN G. NEALEN.—Among the sturdy pioneers, who early pressed into these regions held by the wilds of nature and nature's savages, there is none living in the county to-day better known and more highly respected than the estimable gentleman whose name initiates this paragraph. A worthy representative of that indomitable race, whose little island home is become famous the world over for the energy, stanch qualities and intrinsic worth of its inhabitants, Mr. Nealen possesses in a generous proportion the force of character, strength of purpose, keenness of wit, open hearted public spirit, so characteristic of the true Irishman, and these excellent qualities together with his commendable demeanor in his walk in our midst have made him universally beloved and esteemed by his fellow citizens.

Killogeary township, in Mayo county, Ireland, is the place of his birth, and April 20, 1839, the date. His father was a stockman and the years of minority of John G. were spent in handling cattle on the farm and in market, while he also gained his education from the common schools. With the budding years of manhood's estate came the rising spirit of adventure that has pressed the world's darkness back before the onward march of civilization's forces, and Mr. Nealen found himself a captive to its siren voice and soon bade farewell to home and its loved ones and sailed away to New York. On May 10, 1860, he stepped from the Adriatic to the wharves of

the new world's metropolis, made his way to Scranton, Pennsylvania, and there listened to the memorable call of Abraham Lincoln for men to save the Union, which so stirred his young blood that he hastily signed the enlisting roll and seized a musket in defense of the country he had chosen for his home. In the Twenty-first Pennsylvania Volunteer Infantry he served the term of his enlistment as one of the ninety-day men, received his honorable discharge and turned again to the quieter walks of industrial life. In the fall of 1861 he migrated via New York and Aspinwall to San Francisco, whence he went on the steamer to Victoria, where he wintered, then went with the influx to the famous Cariboo mines on the Fraser river. A short time was spent there and he returned down the river to Vancouver and there spent some time in the service of the government making hay, and in the fall of 1862 came to Canyon City, where he went at once to mining. He secured some valuable placer claims, which he worked with very gratifying success until the fall of 1870, when he sold his mining interests and went to the Big Basin country in this county and engaged in stock raising. He owned fine stock farms in different parts of the country and in 1880 he moved onto one near Monument, where he made his home and headquarters. In 1898 he began to sell his stock and real estate holdings, desiring to retire from the more weighty cares and responsibilities of active business. He was attended with fine success in handling stock and at the present time he holds securities in many places through the county and in adjacent counties, while he is also one of a rich company that has promoted a salmon cannery in Alaska, on Dundas Bay. He obtained a patent from the government for a large portion of the bay and erected buildings and put the enterprise in active operation. In the spring of 1901 he made a visit of four months to this property and is much enthused with its favorable outlook. Mr. Nealen carries two heavy policies in two of the old line companies.

It is of note that during the Indian scare Mr. Nealen offered twenty dollars per day for men to assist him in putting up hay for his stock, but was unable to secure hands and so did the work himself alone at great risk. During his long career on the frontier he has met all sorts of hardships and dangers and has faced many trying ordeals, in all of which there has been the true Irish force of character to outride them all and to-day he is well and favorably known to almost every resident of the county, having maintained a faithful walk among his fellow citizens, and a strong adherence to the principles of patriotism and freedom and the beloved institutions of our government, for which he fought with valor and intrepid courage. During his career Mr. Nealen has always been partial to the quiet joys of the celibatarian and has never ventured on the uncertain sea of connubial relations. Now as the golden years begin to draw apace, with the consolation of a well spent career in the past, enjoying the plenty that his thrift and sagacity have accumulated, while his geniality has won him friends on every hand, Mr. Nealen is passing the days of the best years of his life in quietness and peace amid the good wishes and hearty good cheer of all who know him.

———— •♦• ————

OLIVER ·P. ·CRESAP.—What an air of interest clings to the early pioneers of this land that immediately catches the desires and awakens the spirit of investigation in each one of us. This is not without adequate cause, because we are all more or less acquainted with the stirring adventures and dangers encountered by these heroes of the plains as well as the arduous labors endured and mining excitements of the day. The dreary trip across the plains, enlivened by the ferocious attacks of the savages; the restfulness experienced at the end of the journey; the exhilaration of new scenes and ways; the exciting stories of fortunes made in a few days in the mines; the rise of ambition to "try his luck" that fired every young American who entered the domain of the west; the toils, the hardships of the search, the sickening drop of spirits at failure, the buoyant exuberance of joy when a strike was made; the weary trip from camp to camp—all this is only part of what each one lived day by day, and which combined ·to make a distinct type of humanity in the real pioneer of the early days. Genial, kind, patient under hardships and deprivations, ever expectant, never showing a sign of desire to quit the struggle—the sturdy representatives of those unique days carry about

with them a winning something of interest in their life that causes us to halt and bring out the reminiscences of past days in entertaining conversation with the worthy characters. What words could equal these, for the subject of this sketch, that he is a typical representative of the pioneer days, possessed of capabilities and integrity that do credit to even that worthy class. His career began early in this line and he has traveled the complete gamut of experience.

Born in Alleghany county, Maryland, on August 23, 1840, the son of Daniel H. and Eliza Cresap, Oliver P. spent the early days of his life in work on the farm of his father and in attending school. His mother died when he was eight years of age and in 1856 he came with his father to Bonaparte, Iowa, where he remained until 1860. The real spirit of adventure and exploration for his fortune in the west took possession of him at that time and he started across the plains in company with others, driving a band of horses. After passing Salt Lake City the Indians succeeded in stealing the entire bunch, and the unfortunate owners were obliged to walk the rest of the distance to the coast, eleven hundred miles. Ashland, Jackson county, Oregon, was their landing place, and for two years Mr. Cresap was occupied with various kinds of work, then started to Oro Fino, but was turned from this purpose and stopped at Canyon City in June, 1862. He located the second claim of the county, it being situated at the mouth of Whisky Gulch. Two years he followed placer mining and then packed from The Dalles for four years, then went to Susanville, in this county, and followed placer mining for thirteen years with good success.

In this county on June 16, 1880, the marriage of Mr. Cresap and Miss Oregon H. Douthit, a native of Indiana, was solemnized and to them have been born the following children: Helen M., Clara M., Henry O., Wilbur D., Minnie E., Elsworth W. Mrs. Cresap crossed the plains in 1853 with her parents.

In 1882 Mr. Cresap was called by the people to act as sheriff and his service in that capacity was efficient and satisfactory. In 1892 he was again elected to the same office. Under Cleveland's first administration he was postmaster in Canyon City. From 1883 to·

OLIVER P. CRESAP.

1895 he was engaged in mercantile business and at the last date he sold that business and again turned his attention to mining. He now has some very valuable properties in the Marysville district, and also some others in different places. He owns a fine home in Canyon City and some other property. It is of note that many times in the early days Mr. Cresap was frequently shot at by the Indians while in conflict with them, and he was the guide for General Howard during the war of 1878, was in the Birch creek fight and the north fork of the John Day fight. Fraternally he is affiliated with the I. O. O. F., and with the Encampment, and with the A. O. U. W., and with the K. of P. He is past grand of the I. O. O. F. and past workman in the A. O. U. W.

DAVID KEERINS.—What a debt of gratitude does our country owe to the gallant and sturdy sons of the Emerald Isle for the prominent part that they have played in the development of the resources of this wealthy land and for the interest taken by them in the promotion of the welfare of all. Not least among this distinguished number may be mentioned David Keerins, who has allied himself with this, his foster land, leaving behind the scenes and associations of the home country, to carve for himself a fortune in the boundless region of our western territory, and the success that has attended his efforts, speaks strongly of the thrift and industry, dominated by wisdom and keen foresight that are characteristic of him, the evidences of which are manifested everywhere in his handiwork. In 1861 was the date of his birth and Ireland the country and there he spent the first nineteen years of his existence. At the time when manhood's estate began to dawn on him his ideas and adventurous spirit led him to the realms of the new world and thither he came, landing in New York in 1880. From that place he came to California and there was engaged in farming for six years, after which he came direct to Grant county and took a homestead eight miles northwest from Izee. Here, in company with his brothers, Joseph and Owen, he has been engaged in the stock business. Cattle and sheep are the kinds that they raise, with sufficient horses to handle the

business. Their estate has been increased betimes until they are now the proprietors of two thousand acres of good land, which is well improved for their business. Mr. Keerins has so demeaned himself in the walks of life that he has won the confidence of his fellows and the high regard of all. Mr. Keerins has never ventured on the sea of matrimony, preferring to associate himself with quieter joys of the celibatarian's life, where the responsibilities and cares of connubial relations are not found.

BALLARD P. TARTER.—A man who has the courage of his convictions is entitled to respect, and it is well to say that no man ever walked in pioneer shoes who was lacking in that quality. It took men of courage to face the hardships of the west and operate here. Among this number we are constrained to mention the gentleman, whose name is at the head of this article, for he has been a potent factor in the material advancement of Grant county and in its substantial development for a goodly number of years.

His birth occurred in Hawkins county, Tennessee, on June 29, 1842. Scarce out of his swaddling clothes, he was left fatherless, and the widowed mother removed with her little ones to Wythe county, Virginia, where Ballard P. was reared and educated. When the dogs of war became active he enlisted in the cause that lay nearest his heart and took up arms in Company E, Fiftieth Virginia, in Floyd's Brigade in June, 1861. His service was valiant and faithful until laid low by disease and when sufficiently recovered he was transferred to the quartermaster's department where he continued until the close of the conflict. He participated in many skirmishes and witnessed some of the large battles of the war. It was his lot, to use his own words, to see "Dixie bloom and fall." Subsequent to the war he went to Garrard county, Kentucky, and worked at the carpenter trade and from there he migrated to Springfield, Missouri, and in September, 1873, he came to Polk county in this state. He came via San Francisco, and from that city to Portland he went on the steamer, George M. Elder. Through Oregon, California, and Arizona, he followed his trade until 1887, when he came to Grant county and took a homestead nine and one half miles north from Longcreek. Here he resides at the present time and is giving his attention to the art of agriculture and fruit raising. He has been exceedingly successful as an orchardist and possesses one of the finest orchards in the county.

Mr. Tarter is one of the celibatarians of the county and is enjoying the quiets of that life rather than the cares and responsibilities of the connubial relation. He is highly respect by all and is secure in the esteem and confidence of his fellows.

EDWARD S. PENFIELD.—It were impossible to compose a volume that had to do with the biographical part of Grant county without giving a prominent place to the estemed gentleman and worthy pioneer whose name heads this article, and who has been a leading and distinguished figure about Canyon City and in this region for about forty years, being especially active in church work and in the advancement of those things that are for the good of all.

Mr. Penfield was born in Greene county, New York, in 1819, thence, being still a young man, he accompanied his parents to New York City. In 1849 his adventurous spirit was not contented to remain in the realms of civilization, and, accordingly, he came via the Isthmus to California, landing first in San Francisco, and immediately he engaged in mining, continuing the same for one year, and then returned to New York City. He remained in the east for a time, but the attractions of the west were decidedly too strong for a long stay there and accordingly he came again to San Francisco and opened a mercantile establishment at the foot of Sacramento street, where he had purchased a building. After one year there in business he repaired to Santa Cruz, continuing in the same business. In the early fifties he came to Oregon and opened a mercantile establishment in Portland; later he removed to The Dalles, and when the gold excitement broke out in eastern Oregon he came to Canyon City, expecting to soon return, but the years rolled by and he is still a resident of our beautiful county. He mined for some time after arriving here and then erected a

sawmill, it being about the first that was built in this region. One year after he built it he sold out and went down on the John Day river and took up a ranch and commenced to raise stock and till the soil, and this occupation has engaged him constantly until a few years since, when he sold out entirely and retired from the more arduous activities of life. He is at the present time acting as agent for some of the leading insurance companies, and is one of the highly esteemed and respected business men of the city. In church work Mr. Penfield enjoys the distinction of being the real pioneer of the county, having been instrumental in organizing the first church in the county, the Methodist, which he formed in 1864. From the beginning Mr. Penfield gave liberally of his means and of his time and talent to push forward the work that was so dear to his heart. He has stood by it in all the years that have intervened and many times he has assumed the responsibilities of the pulpit, being especially favored in this line as an interesting and fervent speaker of the gospel that has given cheer to his own life of over four score years. Mr. Penfield is deserving of much credit for his valuable and self-sacrificing labors in this work.

NEWTON LIVINGSTON.—Any compilation purporting to mention the leading citizens of Grant county which failed to include the name of the gentleman of whom we now speak would be seriously incomplete, inasmuch as he has wrought with an energy and assiduity in the prosecution of the private enterprises at his hand, which have marked him both as prominent and capable, while in the affairs of the county at large he has been and is both popular and active in bringing about the welfare of its citizens by assisting in the execution of wholesome principles in government and placing in power such men as would be both upright and capable.

In Andrew county, Missouri, on April 7, 1850, he was born to Thomas and Elizabeth (Higgins) Livingston, and one year after this event he accompanied them to the Pacific coast, the entire journey being accomplished by means of ox teams. While en route the train was several times attacked by the savages, who succeeding in capturing a portion of the

EDWARD S. PENFIELD.

NEWTON LIVINGSTON.

MRS. NEWTON LIVINGSTON.

stock, and also in killing several of the emigrants. The parents settled near Roseburg, Douglas county, and took up farming and stock raising, in which the son assisted until he was twenty-five years of age. Like many of the pioneer lads, his opportunity for educational discipline was rather limited, which, however, he supplemented by more careful attention to personal investigation and reading. In 1875 he commenced to farm for himself in the same county and continued in the successful prosecution of this industry until 1886, when he migrated to his present place in Grant county, which is fourteen miles north from Longcreek, on the middle fork of the John Day river. Here he at first took a homestead, and has since bought until he now has the fine estate of nine hundred acres, which is all well fenced and improved, having a good large house, substantial barn, fine orchard, and so forth. He raises horses and cattle and has been favored with the most gratifying prosperity, owing to his tireless attention to details and wise handling of his herds and farms. In the year 1896 he was called by the people from the private walks of life to assume the responsible and arduous duties of sheriff of Grant county, and at the close of his term of faithful and efficient service he was asked by the voters to continue for one term more, which he did to the entire satisfaction of all concerned. He is affiliated with the Hobak Lodge, No. 22, I. O. O. F., of Canyon City, also with the K. of P., Lodge No. 42, of Longcreek.

Mr. Livingston was married to Miss Mattie E., daughter of John and Catherine (Bonebrake) Newman, in Douglas county, in October, 1875, and the fruit of this union has been the following children: Emma E., wife of I. P. Remington, of Comstock, Douglas county, Oregon; Katie E., wife of J. W. Quinn, of Wallace, Idaho; John N., deceased; Marguerette, deceased; Myrtle; Francis G., deceased; Georgia Arvilla. Mr. Livingston's father died in Douglas county in 1885, and the mother also passed the river of death in 1896. Our subject is one of the most substantial and enterprising men of the county, always governed by principles of truth and uprightness and has ever manifested unswerving integrity and intrinsic worth of character in the walks of life, which has made him highly esteemed and respected by all.

HENRY H. DAVIS.—It is ever pleasant to have the privilege to recount some of the salient points in the career of an old timer and pioneer of these hills and valleys and especially so is it enjoyable to speak of those that came here at an early date and have labored faithfully and steadily shoulder to shoulder for the development of the resources of nature and for the advancement of the interests of the county generally, while individual industry has been rewarded by the competence that is so pleasant to enjoy in the later years of life. Such an one is the esteemed gentleman, whose life's record we are about to give in epitome. Patriotic, capable, and upright he has manifested both ability and integrity in a very commendable manner in the days of the years of his pilgrimage in Grant county.

Williamson county, Illinois, was the place of his birth and February 3, 1832, the date.

He worked on a farm until he was twenty-seven years of age and then went to New Orleans, Cuba and across the isthmus to San Francisco, whence he soon made his way to the mines in Siskiyou county, where he sought for the treasures of nature until 1863, then came to Canyon City and followed the same occupation until 1868. At this date he spent some time in looking over the country on a trip of exploration and finally settled at the mouth of Beech creek and took up stock raising and farming until 1878 when he sold out and bought a ranch near Longcreek and continued in the same occupations. He was followed with good success and in 1899, he was enabled to retire with a goodly share of this world's goods for the years of the time of life that are spent in retrospective meditations together with the brightness of the light of hope. He sold the farm and at the present time owns some property in Longcreek, where he is living. After the sale of his farm in 1899, he returned once more to the scenes of childhood, having been absent therefrom for forty-one years. Old scenes brought familiar memories and once again he lived over the times of the bright days of school and farm when he was a boy, and anew were formed the acquaintances that were fresh when he turned to the west in the fifties. Time had relentlessly chiseled over the familiar features, but hearty welcomes remained for the bronzed westerner and warm hearts made glad the day when he again was in their midst. The west is relentless, when once it enfolds a soul, and soon he was longing for his home amid the scenes of Grant county.

Mr. Davis is well and favorably known throughout the county, having served as county commissioner for four years succeeding 1888. He is clerk of the school district and councilman of Longcreek having also been constable for the same venue. Fraternally he is affiliated with the Masons, joining that body in Canyon City in 1864 and when the lodge was formed in Longcreek he became a charter member. His experiences on the frontier have been thrilling and numerous and trying, having endured much in the endeavors to open up the country and subdue the forces that nature arrays against the pioneers. He was in partnership with George Rader of Loongcreek for a number of years and in 1864, he was with the noted Joaquin Miller in combats with the Indians in the Steen mountains.   Politically, Mr. Davis is a stanch Democrat of the Jeffersonian type and is a man of courage equal to his convictions.

HIEL A. HYDE.—As one of the veterans of the Civil war, the subject of this sketch is deserving of especial mention in addition to the fact that he is one of the substantial and worthy citizens of this county. When the call came for help to defend the flag, young Hyde was ready to go to the front and there he did valiant service until his physical system succumbed to the trying ordeal and he sickened and then was honorably discharged to return to the more quiet walks of private life.

Mr. Hyde was born in Franklin county, New York, in 1841, being the son of Alfred and Margaret (Rodgers) Hide. He was with his parents on the farm until 1871 when they came to Oregon and settled where he lives at the present time, seven miles east from Prairie City. They took a homestead and commenced to raise garden vegetables and some grain, and in 1889 his father died, his mother dying two years previous to that time. He does a good market gardening business and raises stock. In 1861, he enlisted in Company E, Ninety-Eighth New York Volunteer Infantry where he did fine service for nine months and then was discharged on account of disability.

In 1887, the marriage of Mr. Hyde and Miss Sarah, daughter of J. G. Barkley, was solemnized and they have become the parents of the following children, Lida M., Josephine L., Mary J., Joseph E., William A., Hiel A., Buel J. Mr. Hyde is affiliated with the I. O. O. F., Prairie City Lodge, No. 33. He is also very prominent among the temperance workers of the county and has done efficient service in that cause, both by bright personal example and careful precept, at opportune times and fitting occasions. He has been a leading spirit in the Good Templar movement for some years and he was instrumental in organizing a blue ribbon club in April, 1901, and at the present time, November, 1901, its membership has increased to over one hundred. Mr. Hyde is highly respected and his life of uprightness is a living example for all.

JOHN D. TITUS.—It is a matter of universal commendation when a man achieves a good success in any one line of honorable industry, but in the person of the subject of this sketch we have a gentleman whose adaptability and breadth of capabilities have enabled him to win the laurels of success from the hands of Dame Fortune in number of different undertakings, some widely divergent, while in all of his career he has ever maintained a reputation untarnished and a walk displaying both integrity and upright principles.

In the sister land of Canada we find the birthplace of Mr. Titus, it being Norwich, Ontario, while his parents were Israel D. and Marguerette Titus, and the date of his nativity April 27, 1842. His early days were spent in the healthful and invigorating exercise of assisting his father on the farm, while he gained a good education from the justly famous schools of the province of Ontario. When he had arrived at the age of seventeen he launched on the sea of life's conflicts for himself and at once came to Painsville, Lake county, Ohio, where he learned the trade of the jeweler. In 1860, during the days of thrilling deeds and intense suffering in some of the southern and western states, he migrated to Lockhart, Caldwell county, Texas, where he remained until 1863. After this period he went to Monterey, Mexico, following his trade there. In the next

JOHN D. TITUS.   MRS. JOHN D. TITUS.   OTIS GUERNSEY.

JOHN ZEPH.   HENRY A. MURPHY.

year he came via Mazatlan, Mexico, to San
Francisco on the steamer and remained in different parts of California and engaged in various enterprises until 1870, when he came to Albany, Oregon, and took up the jewelry business
again, this time in company with his brother.
There they operated successfully until 1881,
when they embarked in the stock business near
the mouth of Pine creek in Wheeler county.
Later they established a horse market in Tacoma, and some time following this they dissolved partnership and our subject came to his
present place in Fox valley, two miles west from
Beech Creek postoffice, in 1893. He owns six
hundred and forty acres of land, all fenced and
well improved, with good house, barn and orchard. He handles horses and cattle and is
one of the successful stockmen of the county.
In 1895 the people called him to public life
as assessor of the county, and at the expiration
of a two-year term re-elected him to the same
office, on the Republican ticket. During his
stay in Albany he was city treasurer for one
term also. In all his public service he has
given entire satisfaction and left a record for
efficiency and faithfulness.

Mr. Titus married Miss Elizabeth, daughter of William C. and Marguerrette Baird, of
Brownsville, Oregon, in October, 1873, and
they have one child, Marguerette, wife, of
Charles E. Cohoe, of Fox valley.

OTIS GUERNSEY.—There are few men
who have had their lives so crowded with continued activities and thrilling adventures,
coupled with hardships and frontier experiences
from every quarter, and in every department
of that eventful and rugged existence, as has
the intrepid and enterprising gentleman of
whom we now have the pleasure to write, in
giving the salient points of his interesting career, which, were it written in full, would make
a very lively volume, full of information of
our western plains and mountains and conflicts
with Indians and search for gold that would do
credit to a ready writer in the pages of American history.

Montpelier, Vermont, is his birthplace, and
September 14, 1833, the date of his advent
into life, being the son of H. B. and Sovia J.
Guernsey, who went to Canada while their son
was an infant. When Otis had reached the

age of eight years the family removed to Valparaiso, Indiana, and there he worked on a
farm with his father until 1853. Then, in
company with two uncles, he undertook the
long journey over plains and mountains to
the Pacific coast. The train was composed
of twenty-five outfits drawn by oxen. The
captain was an uncle to our subject. Several
times they were attacked by the Indians; once
three of their number being killed, and once
one was killed. Their provisions began to get
very low and for two weeks they existed on
half rations, but the government officers hearing of their distress, aid was sent and they
reached their destination, Jacksonville, Oregon, in seven months from the date of starting.
From those that sent aid the train was named
the Miller and Conder train. When Mr. Guernsey reached Oregon he was just in time to meet
the uprising of the Rogue Indians and enlisted
to fight them, being in Captain Love's company. Later on he fell in with the noted Kit
Carson and went with him into Fort Hall, Salt
Lake, to the Colorado river, and on through
Arizona to Los Angeles, California. During
this time he participated in a number of severe
battles and was the subject of some thrilling
adventures. At Los Angeles he separated company with the noted scout and turned to San
Francisco and from there into the mines in different portions of the state. Afterward he was
at Stockton, whence he went to Sonoma county and farmed for two years and then repaired
to Healdsburg, where he engaged in the livery
business in connection with the wholesale liquor
trade. He did a thriving business until
1865. At that date he fitted conveyances
and went back across the plains to Missouri with his family and in that state and
in Iowa he lived until 1880, and then removed
to Colorado, living there for four years, then
crossed the plains again with wagons to Canyon City, arriving there on August 9, 1884.
He at once perceived an opening in the lumber business and was quick to take advantage
of it, erecting a sawmill, and in operating that
he has been continuously engaged since. His
home and mill are eight miles south from Canyon City and he has a fine property, consisting
of sawmill, residence, stock ranch of three hundred and twenty acres and a section of timber
and grazing land, besides interests in some
valuable mining properties.

The marriage of Mr. Guernsey and Miss Nancy J. Fisher, of Stockton, California, was celebrated December 25, 1856, and to them have been born the following children: Hosea B., married to Maggie Solinger, of Canyon City; Lena R., wife of William Lincoln, of Canyon City; Charles O., married to Minnie Hopprich, near Canyon City; Mary S., wife of Enos Trefry, now deceased; and three that died in infancy. Mr. Guernsey is a member of the I. O. O. F., in Canyon City, and politically he is with the Republican party. He is a citizen that always takes an active interest in the affairs of government and is dominated by a wisdom and prudence that have made him both successful in his business enterprises and highly respected by his fellow men. It is of note that the ancestors of our subject were natives of Guernsey Islands, and doubtless gave the name in early days to the islands.

JOHN ZEPH.—It is with a feeling of inability to properly portray the life of thrilling incidents of the subject of this sketch that we make the attempt. Having passed a military career that is seldom exceeded by any man in the United States, being entirely through the war of the Rebellion and in nearly all of the main Indian conflicts on the frontier, and experiencing all the strange and trying adventures that are incident to pioneering, Mr. Zeph could relate incidents and accounts of actual experience that would fill a volume with pleasant and intensely interesting reading.

The grand little republic across the waters that could produce a William Tell is the native land of Mr. Zeph, and 1838 was the date of his birth. When seven years of age he came to this country with his parents, who settled in New York. At the tender age of thirteen years John joined Company I, First Regular Cavalry, as bugler, and for twenty-two years he served continuously in military duty, finally being honorably discharged with the rank of sergeant. He is the oldest white man now living that stepped into the territory that is embraced in Grant county, having come through it in 1853. His company was assigned to the west, being stationed at Boise, to meet the savages in their raids and to quell them, and here he was em-

ployed in various parts of the frontier and in the arduous and dangerous conflicts with the redskins until the breaking out of the Rebellion. He was at the Cascades in one battle with the Indians, and there received an arrow wound in the hand; this was at about the time of the Whitman massacre. When the Civil war broke in its fury upon our fair land Mr. Zeph was ordered with his company to the seat of war, and in the army of the Potomac he served until the last gun was silenced. Seven times he was wounded in this conflict and few men have seen harder service and suffered more pain and hardship for their country than he. Following the Rebellion he was sent to Camp Watson in Oregon, and finally in the centennial year he received an honorable discharge. He then came to Canyon City and commenced to operate as a miner, and later took up gardening. He has a fine and comfortable home in Canyon City and is one of the leading citizens of the county.

In 1886 Mr. Zeph was married to Catherine Rebhorn, but the following year she was taken from him by death.

Mr. Zeph was married a second time, to Catherine (Steele) Powers. After a life of such vigorous activity and such commendable achievement Mr. Zeph is now enjoying the fruits of his labors and has the esteem and confidence of all who know him. Mr. Zeph can read and write English, German, French and Italian, thus being a fine linguist, in which study he excels.

HENRY A. MURPHY is the senior member of the Monument Mercantile Company, and it is very interesting to trace the career of this leading merchant and prominent citizen of Monument, since his has been a life of varied scenes and filled with the manifestation of energy and activity that have wrought out a very satisfactory success, and which mark him as possessed of abilities far above the average, while his integrity and uprightness are entirely commensurate with the display of capability in his business endeavors.

Born in Bremer county, Iowa, on July 19, 1864, he was early taken by his parents, James and Mary (Buckmaster) Murphy, to Aurora, Missouri, whence, after a short residence, they went to Cherokee county, Kansas. When he was nine years of age another move was made, this time to Sipe Springs, Comanche county, Texas, his parents being among the first white families that settled in that county. The Indians were hostile, and their stay there was beset with many dangers from them, and finally, in 1881, they pulled up stakes and came overland to Walla Walla, using teams to cover the entire distance. The following summer they removed to Fox valley, and it was on the birthday of our subject, July 18, that they arrived. According to his report of the state of his exchequer at that time his assets were an Indian pony and $2.50 in cash. But young Murphy was possessed of plenty of courage and he immediately showed the blood of which he came by taking a position on the work that was being prosecuted by the citizens of Canyon City and John Day in constructing a road from Fox valley to Canyon City; the same road is to-day used by the mail carriers from Heppner to Canyon City. He carefully economized his earnings and saved every cent possible, and the result was that in a few years he had sufficient funds to purchase a band of horses, and in 1889 he embarked in raising horses. He followed this several years with excellent success and then on account of the hard riding that was injuring his health, he sold the entire band and opened a store in Monument. He built the first business building on the town site. Here he to-day is operating a first class general merchandise establishment, that is known for many miles in every direction. His stock is complete and well selected. At first he started in the venture with a small stock, purchasing largely from Minor, of Heppner, but to-day he is at the head of a large establishment. His trade is large and constantly increasing and the goods from his shelves and warehouses are found in distant portions of the adjacent county. He operates on the cash plan exclusively, thus being enabled to handle goods at a smaller margin and giving the benefit to his customers, an item that they are quick to take advantage of.

The marriage of Mr. Murphy and Miss Vina A., daughter of Charles and Eliza (Ricker) Ballance, of Longcreek, was solemnized on April 22, 1888, and to gladden the happy union there have been born four children, Stella M., Lera, Florence M., Gladys D. Mr. Murphy is a member of the W. of W., and also of

the Maccabees. Mr. Murphy's father was a native of Tippecanoe county, Indiana, and later moved to Illinois, and then to Iowa, where he enlisted in Company D, Sixteenth Iowa Infantry, and was with General Sherman in the memorable march to the sea. On account of sickness he was honorably discharged to return to the quieter walks of life. He was a member of the G. A. R. and died in Portland in 1898 and was buried in Fox valley. The mother is still living in Monument. Mr. Murphy owns a fine residence in the town of Monument and it is just to state that he enjoys in the fullest measure the confidence and respect of all of his townsmen and those who have the pleasure of his acquaintance.

Since writing the above, on January 1, 1902, Mr. Murphy sold one-half of his mammoth business to J. H. Anderson and together they have bought all the general merchandise business in the town and the firm is known as the Monument Mercantile Company, and they do a thriving business and are representative business men.

EMMET COCHRAN.—There are few stockmen in Grant county that are more industrious and progressive than the capable gentleman of whom it is now our pleasant privilege to speak and whose successful and wisely directed efforts in rearing the ruminants have been instrumental not only in giving him prominence as a leader in his line, but have given him the substantial rewards of competence and materially increased the wealth of the county, while his public spirit and upright principles have ever led him in the interests of all in his walk in public life.

A native of the occident, being born in Clackamas county, near Oregon City, on February 6, 1869, its stars have been the beacon light of his endeavors since. His parents, William W. and Sarah M. (Moody) Cochran, natives of Boone county, Missouri, removed, while he was still an infant, to California, and soon after that trip returned to Missouri on a visit and then went to The Dalles, whence they migrated to this county and settled on what is now known as the Cochran homestead, five miles below Monument, the date of that settlement being the fall of 1870. Sixteen years later the father died at that place. Our subject was educated in the schools of the various places where he spent his early days, and in 1889 he bought the ranch where he now lives, ten miles west of, or below, Monument, at the mouth of the north fork of the John Day river. His original purchase was one thousand acres, but he has added since until his estate is now two thousand acres. It is well improved and all fenced and contains some very fine land. He has good buildings and orchards and is up-to-date in all his efforts. He raised cattle until 1892, and then disposed of them and took up sheep, which he has successfully handled since, having now large bands. Of late years he has been adding some cattle and operates a few head at the present time.

On December 6, 1889, Miss Emma C., daughter of William G. and Catherine Allen, and a native of Oregon, living near Monument, became the wife of Mr. Cochran, and they have become the parents of one child, Benjamin. Mrs. Cochran's father died in May, 1901, but the mother still resides in Monument. Fraternally Mr. Cochran is identified with the Masons at Monument, and with the Woodmen of the World. Wisdom, uprightness and industry characterize the subject of this sketch and prosperity has attended him constantly in his endeavors, while his integrity and intrinsic worth have made him a worthy member of society and respected and esteemed by all.

WILLIAM S. SOUTHWORTH. — A pioneer of the early days, possessed of energy and wisdom, coupled with excellent ability to grapple with the problems of life in the west, while his walk has been commendable in displaying both integrity and upright principles in all his career, the subject of this brief sketch is one of the substantial and worthy citizens of the county that has well earned his good standing and has wrought out in different lines of industry as well as in faithful and efficient public service a success that is both enviable and praiseworthy.

From the Green Mountain state came the adventurous and energetic young American that has fought his way through all the trying scenes of the rugged frontier, displaying the same spirit that characterized the native sons of that state in their daring and courageous conflict for liberty. He was born near Bradford, Orange county, on November 23, 1834, being the son of E. and Phoebe Southworth. Passing the years of his minority on the farm with his father, he also acquired the discipline to be had in the public schools and then at the age of nineteen years same to the west, locating in Kane county, Illinois, where he remained until 1859, when he took the memorable journey of crossing the plains with ox teams. Landing in Shasta county, California, he at once took up mining and followed it with success until 1863, when he came direct to Canyon City and engaged in the same industry in the gulch near the present town site. For eight years he worked in these placer diggings and then sold out. During this time he had also operated a saw mill and to this he then gave his entire attention until 1883, when he located his present home at Seneca, which is at the lower end of Bear valley on the Burns road. He took up a homestead and pre-emption and commenced to raise stock. His land is all fenced and well improved. At his place a post-office was established in 1895 and Mrs. Southworth is the postmistress. He owns a planing mill in Canyon City and gives a portion of his time to the operation of this, while his sons handle the stock and farm. In 1878 the people elected him county clerk of Grant county and at the close of his term rewarded him with re-election. His service in this office was satisfactory to all and very efficient. He also served as deputy sheriff under O. P. Cresap from 1890 to 1892. He has been a member of the I. O. O. F. since 1864 and is past grand.

On October 13, 1874, the marriage of Mr. Southworth and Miss Minnie Hannas, of Kane county, was solmenized and they have become the parents of four children as follows: George, deceased; Edward I.; Webster S. and Florence. Mr. Southworth sold his saw mill in 1898 and since 1883 has been operating successfully the planing mill and sash and door factory above mentioned. Mr. Southworth is one of the successful and substantial business men of the county and has always taken an active interest in the politics of the county and state. He is highly esteemed by all and is a potent factor in the advancement of the county and the upbuilding of its interests.

CHARLES BELSHAW.— How richly were endowed the early pioneers of this country not only in the cardinal virtues that make up stanch manhood but also in the abilities that have led the way to the gratifying development of the resources of nature and the bringing out of the latent talents of their fellows and stirring to a flame the desires for the pursuit of knowledge and the acquisition of that perfection in the arts and sciences,—how richly, I say, were the early pioneers endowed in all this talent can now be plainly seen in the results of their labor, which are manifest in an educated and enlightened population and in the institutions of learning that have been established and maintained by them and their offspring. Well distinguished among this worthy class stands the subject of this sketch as he has been a leading figure in striving for years for the betterment of his fellows and in bringing to practical use the knowledge that he possessed.

March 9, 1833, in the substantial land of England, Charles Belshaw was born and in 1834 came with nine brothers and sisters to the United States, accompanied by his parents, who settled in Indiana. In 1853 with his parents and three brothers, he came to Eugene, in Lane county, this state, and there the parents died. One of the brothers was killed by the Indians in 1855. Mr. Belshaw entered the ranks of the agriculturists and also went to California on a trip of exploration and later came to Canyon City, his arrival here being in the fall of 1862. Late in the same fall he returned to Eugene and in 1864 brought his family to this section, and then engaged in farming and fruit raising, at which he has been eminently successful. He has been the originator of a variety of prune, known as the Belshaw, that is a real addition to the realm of fruit, growing to the great size of six to one pound. He has the reputation of being the leading orchardist of the county, and surely his skill and energy in that line have been of untold benefit to the people of eastern Oregon. In addition to the labors of his hands, Mr. Belshaw has gained real distinction as a teacher of music. When he first landed in the Willamette valley, his abilities in that line were manifested and brought into active service and he has been prosecuting this art for many years, giving many successful benefit concerts for different churches. Sometimes he has given his whole attention to it. Thus in at least two different lines, he has been beneficial to his fellow men and led the way for them.

Mr. Belshaw and Miss Jane Luce, a native of Kentucky, were married in 1859, and to them have been born the following children, Lincoln, Grant, Hattie, Edith, Johnny, the last one deceased. Mr. Belshaw is now passing the riper years of the golden age that is his to enjoy in the quieter retirement from more active service, in the comfortable home that his thrift and industry have wrought for him, being now sixty-nine years of age. He is the only surviving member of the family of ten children that crossed the Atlantic in 1834. George Belshaw, one of that family who died at Farmington, about nine years since, was one of the most successful wheat growers of the world. He received many premiums from the state fairs and also the award of superiority at the Philadelphia exposition and the same in the great fair in Chicago. Our subject has had many disappointments in the course of his pioneer career on this coast and many times suffered the loss of his stock by Indians. But notwithstanding it all, he is still joyful and contented with his lot in this land and is one of our most genial and amiable citizens.

————◆◆◆————

McCLELLAN STOCKDALE and ROBERT J. STOCKDALE.—To swell the army of stockmen and tillers of the soil in Grant county, there have come from every portion of our great Republic, men and women of intrinsic worth and stanch integrity who had capabilities to form from the wilds of the fields of nature domains and estates that smile beneath the harvests of plenty since their wise husbandry has been brought to bear. The estemed citizens and capable gentlemen, whose names are at the head of this article, are two among that number, whose efforts for development and progress have met with proper reward in the prosperity that has followed and in the esteem and encomiums that have been theirs from appreciative fellows.

They are the sons of Allen and Nancy (Price) Stockdale, natives of Pennsylvania, who removed from the Keystone state and settled in Missouri and then later migrated to

California, settling in the San Joaquin valley, where they are living at the present time, eight miles east from Fresno, and are occupied with fruit raising. McClellan was born on November 22, 1862, in Washington county, Pennsylvania, and at the age of twenty-three years came to John Day and engaged in ranch work until he bought, in company with his brother, their present place, one-fourth of a mile east from Mt. Vernon. Here they own in partnership a fine ranch of one hundred and sixty-seven acres and are occupied in raising stock, cattle and horses, and in tilling the soil. He was married on October 4, 1896, to Miss Arba daughter of H. M. and Martha (Webb) Moore, and to them has been born one child, Alva B.

Robert J. was born on November 18, 1864, in Pennsylvania, and at the age of twenty-two years came to Oregon and took a homestead seven miles north of Daysville, which he sold later, that he might purchase, in company with his brother, the farm where htey now live. In 1894, the marriage of Robert J. and Miss Ellen, daughter of R. and Anna (Cardwell) Damon, was solemnized and the fruit of the union has been one child, Elbert.

WILLIAM B. CARPENTER.—What more noble and worthy undertaking has ever fallen to the lot of man than to press forward into the wilderness of nature and clear the path for the onward march of his fellows to bring in the comforts and advantages of civilization; and perhaps no class of people have been more instrumental in this activity than the early miners of our Pacific slope. Conspicuous among them, is the gentleman and enterprising citizen whose name heads this article, and who has been in the front ranks of the vanguard of pioneers from the time that he arrived to man's estate.

Born in Monroe county, Missouri, to Samuel and Elizabeth (McCullom) Carpenter, on November 20, 1830, he early began to learn the hardships of life on account of the death of his mother, which was instrumental in forcing him out into the world at a tender age. His opportunity for gaining an education was very limited and had it not been for his careful reading and constant research, he would have been left without scarcely any book training.

But as it proved, his extra effort in acquiring his training in educational lines has made him to appreciate the lore of knowledge more than those to whom it came easily, and so we have in Mr. Carpenter a very energetic advocate of good schools, and he has been instrumental in materially urging forward that commendable part of our government. For a number of years, at various times, he has been chosen on the school boards and his acceptance of office has universally been with great advantage to the school and district resulting from his energy and wisdom in these lines.

When he first started on his own resources he commenced to till the soil and as early as 1860 he came to California and entered the business of mining, which he has continuously followed since, making it a real business that has drawn out his energies and capabilities. In 1863 he came to Grant county, settling at Canyon City, and he has been connected, more or less, with every prominent mining camp in the entire region adjacent.

The marriage of Mr. Carpenter and Miss Lucy Wilkinson was celebrated in 1849, and to them were born the following children: Elizabeth, Matilda, Eliza, Thomas and James, all of whom are deceased. Mrs. Carpenter also has passed to the other world.

In October, 1874, Mr. Carpenter contracted a second marriage, the lady then becoming his wife was Sarah J., daughter of James and Jane (Cook) Armstrong. They raised two orphan children, Mary, wife of M. K. Young, and Roy, single.

BRADFORD C. TROWBRIDGE.—Among the many prosperous and well-to-do farmers and stock raisers of the region that is so richly favored of nature in the inland empire, we are constrained to give especial mention to the gentleman whose name initiates this paragraph, and whose life of worthy achievement has been spent for forty years in this county, where he has wrought with manifestation of ability and sagacity, acquiring, meanwhile, as the meed of his endeavor and thrift, an excellent holding of real estate and much other property.

Mr. Trowbridge was born in New York and when ten years of age was removed by his parents to Illinois, where he was raised on a farm. At the age of eighteen years he embarked in life's activities on his own responsibility and became one of the thrifty agriculturists of the famed state of agriculture. In 1859 he started for the then famous Pike's Peak, but hearing bad reports while enroute, he turned aside and came to Yreka, California. In that section he mined for two years and then started to the Powder river country, but was allured by the promising country around Canyon City to remain there. The spring of 1862 was the time that he arrived where Canyon City now is and for one year he gave himself to mining, then took up a ranch, where he now lives one-fourth of a mile from John Day on the John Day river. This was the first ranch taken in the territory now embraced in Grant county, and from the spring of 1863 Mr. Trowbridge has been tilling it and adding from time to time to its acreage until he now has the magnificent estate of one thousand acres, which yields him handsome returns annually in bountiful crops. He practices the diversified plan of farming, handling large herds of stock, planting many acres to hay and grain, and also raises much fruit.

The marriage of Mr. Trowbridge and Miss Margery Milliney was celebrated in 1888, and to them have been born the following children: Clara, deceased; Charles; one infant, deceased. Mr. Trowbridge is a leading citizen, progressive and public spirited and actively interested in school matters and political affairs, and enjoys the respect and esteem of the entire community.

---◆◆◆---

JAMES M. SHIELDS is deserving of mention in our volume, not only because he has fought the battle of life with success and with the manifestation of vigor and sagacity and is to-day one of the well-to-do citizens of Grant county, being a successful and enterprising stockman and agriculturist, but also because in the time of trouble when our glorious banner was suffering from the hands of unwise and treasonable sons of the Republic, and dismemberment of the Union and destruction to our beloved institutions of freedom seemed imminent, he stepped forward and offered himself to assist in stemming the tide of destruction and in beating back the champions of re-

bellion. In 1863, he enlisted in Company A, Second Arkansas Infantry, and the fortunes of war were his until the close of the memorable strife that forever wiped out Rebellion's minions and left to us the legacy of a country and a home. He participated in the battle of Saline Crossing and in many skirmishes, being in the western Division under General Steele. When the war closed, he was honorably discharged and returned to the old home place in Johnson county, Arkansas, and followed successfully the pursuits of the agriculturist until 1877, when he came across the plains with horse teams direct to Grant county. He located first where the village of Longcreek is now situated and enjoyed the distinction of being the first settler. Selling out here, he went to handling sheep on shares, but after two years in this industry, he sold out and took a homestead, which he also sold later and bought the farm which he now owns. It is situated eleven miles north of Longcreek post-office and is well improved, being embellished with house and barn and other necessaries for its successful culture. In addition, he owns some cattle and sheep. At the present time Mr. Shields is living in Longcreek.

Mr. Shields was first married in March, 1852, Sarah Martin, native of Georgia, becoming his wife at that time. One child, John Q., was born to them and since he has died. On August 6, 1856, death stole from the happy home the wife and mother and her remains sleep in Arkansas. Later he took to himself another wife, as follows. The marriage of Mr. Shields and Miss Sarah A. McWhorter of Walker county was solemnized on December 10, 1856, and to them have been born eleven children: Samuel M., married to Sarah Morris and living near Longcreek; Julia A., deceased; Martha A., wife of William H. Stirritt, a stockman of Dayville; Lenora F., wife of C. W. Blackwell, of Walla Walla; William, deceased; James A., deceased; Mary C., wife of Augustus Paine on Cottonwood creek; Florence E., wife of Lest Paine of Cottonwood creek; Julius M., married to Anna Blackwell of Longcreek; Elmer A.; Cora M. The birth of Mr. Shields occurred in Jackson county, Georgia, on January 21, 1831, being the son of John S. and Charlotte Shields. He was raised on a farm and in 1859 moved to Franklin county, Arkansas, and a little later to Johnson county, in which place began his military career which has been outlined. He is a member of the G. A. R. post of Hamilton and is highly respected by all.

* * *

ROBERT G. POWELL.—The esteemed gentleman whose name forms the caption of this article is one of Grant county's enterprising and successful agriculturists and stockmen and a worthy citizen of the republic and commonwealth that he has chosen for his home, having manifested a public spirit and patriotism quite commensurate with the sterling qualities of worth with which he is endowed, while his career here has been dominated with a sagacity and display of integrity that have made him both successful and highly respected in all his relations.

The son of Henry and Catherine (McCutchin) Powell, he was born March 15, 1852, near London, in the province of Ontario, in Canada. His early life was spent on a farm and it was his good fortune to be educated in the justly famous common schools of Ontario, which rightly take the lead as being the finest known to civilization. He remained with his parents until he was twenty-three years of age and then opened an account with the world on his own credit. Until 1875 he remained in his native county and then was lured by the tempting offers of advantages to the United States, coming first to Esmeraldo county, working on a farm and then later for one year in the Northern Bell mine. In 1879 he came to Mammouth City, Mono county, California, where he was married on May 1 of the same year, Miss Bell F., daughter of Millet and Mehetabel W. (Baker) Smith, and natives of Maine. They have one child, Ernest Glen, born May 5, 1890, and a bright lad that is now attending the graded school at Longcreek. Mrs. Powell's father was a native of New Hampshire and her mother of Massachusetts, but both died in the state of Wisconsin.

In January, 1881, they removed to Corvallis, Oregon, remaining until 1885, when they came to Heppner and the following year settled on their present place, which is eleven miles from Longcreek. Here he has one thousand acres of land under fence and well improved, with good house, commodious barn, fine orchard, and other accessories for the carrying on of a first-class ranch. He has large herds of cattle and gives his attention mostly to raising them. In 1882 Mr. Powell's parents came from Canada to this county and settled in Heppner, where the mother died in 1890. The father was born November 23, 1822, and has been a preacher in the Methodist church for fifty years. At the present time he is living in Montana. Mr. Powell is one of those men that have never been covetous of political preferment but still is interested in having the best men at the helm of state, while his life of exemplification of those virtues that make the citizen and the noble man has been a light in the community and he is the recipient of the confidence of the entire populace. On September 5, 1898, in a serious runaway accident, Mrs. Powell received an injury that at one time threatened her life. She has, however, gradually recovered from the effects, although she had a very narrow escape from death.

* * *

MARTIN V. THOMPSON.—When nature's wilds were yet unbroken and all the stern and rugged beauty that mingles with the wilderness rested in its pristine grandeur, the subject of this brief sketch found his way into the region that is now comprised in Grant county, being a typical representative of that sturdy class of noble men that unclasped the fastnesses of the forests and blazed the way for men of less intrepidity and daring to follow. Here he explored the hitherto unknown vaults of treasure and was among the very first that broke the virgin soil in their quest.

Born in Machiasport, Maine, on December 9, 1836, being the son of Elijah R. and Sarah (Cole) Thompson, both natives of the Pine Tree state, Martin V. remained there until he had arrived at man's estate. In 1858, his father having preceded him, he went to the Utopia of the west via the Isthmus and landed first in San Francisco. For one year he explored the new land and then returned to the eastern home and took unto himself a wife, who accompanied him on his second trip to the Golden Gate, where he rented his father's farm that comprised the land that is now in the suburbs

MRS. ROBERT G. POWELL. ROBERT G. POWELL. MARTIN V. THOMPSON.

NAPOLEON B. NEAL. NELSON RULISON.

WILLIAM M. CARTER. MRS. W. M. CARTER MARTI

of the metropolis of the Pacific coast. After a time spent in this occupation he took up stock raising on Russian river, California, and then came to where Canyon City now stands. He was one of the second crowd of men that reached the gold fields of this region, the first having staked ground and taken water rights and departed again for provisions. The date of his arrival was June 20, 1862, he being in company with Fouts and Eastman and four others, and they were just two weeks later than the first number. He immediately commenced mining on Rich Gulch and around Marysville and continued in that line for eighteen years, in that time visiting all of the leading camps in this entire region, also doing hydraulic placer mining around Canyon City. It is of note that the second cabin that was built in Grant county was erected by Fouts and is standing to-day. The camp of Marysville was named from the wife of the man who built the first cabin in that memorable town, her name being Mary. This was Mr. Thebeau. In 1880 Mr. Thompson bought the city hotel of Canyon City and gave his attention to the duties of a host until 1885, when he bought the ranch that he now owns at Blue Mountain Springs, twenty-five miles from Canyon City at the head of the John Day valley. There he owns three hundred and twenty acres in partnership with A. H. Groth. In 1887 he sold out his hotel and mines and gave his entire attention to raising stock and building up the health resort at the hot springs on his estate.

Mr. Thompson and Miss Charlotte A., daughter of Matthias and Elnora (Berry) Finney, were married in November, 1859. Mr. Thompson is a member of the Masonic fraternity at Prairie City, and also of the I. O. O. F., at Canyon City. He has taken great interest in the summer and health resort that is on his estate and it is an institution that justly merits commendable mention, having been endowed richly by nature's preparation and also beautifully and comfortably arranged by the improvements that he has from time to time added and to any one that wishes to enjoy the wildness of beautiful scenery in close proximity to the rugged mountains and health-giving ozone that is bountifully provided in the clear atmosphere of those regions, it is worth while to make the trip to the resort. And also it is to be mentioned that in connection with all these advantages, one is enabled to also enjoy the comforts and pleasure of a first-class hotel, while the health-giving properties of the beautiful springs are evidenced by the scores of suffering humanity that have been benefited and cured in their waters.

———◆———

NAPOLEON B. NEAL.—Among the many stockmen and agriculturists that are making the hills of Grant county yield wealth to their skill in rearing stock and tilling the soil, mention should be made in these chronicles of the enterprising and industrious gentleman, whose name initiates this paragraph. A native of the occident, he has steadily pursued his course here considering that the boundless resources of the west were more favorable for advancement than the congested centers of the east.

In Marion county, on April 21, 1856, he was born to William and Mahala (Parker) Neal, and in that county he passed the first years of his childhood and there and in Grant county he received his education from the public schools. He assisted his father on the farm, and when the family moved here in 1868 and settled six miles west from Monument, he came also and here has constantly been in operation with his father in the stock business. Uniform success has attained his efforts and he is one of the well-to-do stockmen of the county to-day.

On November 19, 1876, he was married to Miss Lizzie Munkers, who is the daughter of Benjamin Munkers, of Linn county. Mr. Munkers was a pioneer of Linn county, Oregon, of 1846, where he still resides, but the mother, Marzella (Hester) Munkers, is now deceased. To bless the union, four children have been born as follows: Frederick M., Leo G., Delman R. and Bessie F.

———◆———

NELSON RULISON.—As a prominent member of society, and one that has been active in the welfare of the interests of all, while prosecuting his private enterprises with successful outcome, the subject of this brief review is deserving of more extended mention than our limited space allows, since his integrity, sagacity and good intrinsic qualities of worth have given him the meed of the esteem and confidence of all that have the pleasure of his acquaintance.

The birth of Mr. Rulison occurred in Oswego county, New York, on December 2, 1832, being the son of Samuel and Sarah (Ray) Rulison, natives respectively of New York and Connecticut. In 1853 Mr. Rulison turned toward the Eldorado of the west and sought his fortune in its mines. On American river, he labored until 1856 and then went to Uba county and in 1862, came to the Cariboo district and a few months later landed in Portland. Following this, he spent some time in carpentering and contracting, being the builder of the first bridge across mill creek. On January 29, 1863, he landed in Canyon City and commenced mining, which he followed until 1870. Then he went to carpenter work again and the next year he accepted a position as wheelwright in Camp Harney as operator for the government, where he remained for seven years and then returned to Canyon City and operated a hotel for two years. Selling this property, he commenced the industry of sheep raising in partnership with Mr. Birge and continued until 1882 and then sold that also and took a pleasure trip to the east. Later he started the milk business in Chicago and for some time we find him enjoying prosperity there, but the west was too attractive and he disposed of his interests and came again to Canyon City, where he has remained since. In 1888 he was elected justice of the peace on the Republican ticket and for ten years he has served in that capacity, having given universal satisfaction.

The marriage of Mr. Rulison and Mrs. Mary Birge was solemnized in Canyon City in 1887, and they have become the parents of the following children: Pearl; an infant, deceased; Mark, in business with his father; Minnie, deceased; Dora. Fraternally Mr. Rulison is affiliated with the Masons, Blue. Mt. Lodge, No. 34, of Canyon City; the I. O. O. F., Lodge No. 22, and Excelsior No. 33, in which latter ones he has passed all of the chairs.

Mr. Rulison and son are among the leading business men of Canyon City, handling a stock of paints, oils, wall paper, and so forth, while they do an undertaking business.

WILLIAM M. CARTER.—Among the prosperous and progressive stockmen and agriculturists that have wrought with assiduity and energy in the worthy enterprise of subduing the wilds of the frontier and augmenting the wealth of Grant county while they have carved for themselves homes and names in this substantial community of wide-awake and leading citizens, especial mention should be made of the gentleman whose name initiates this paragraph and who has manifested both industry and integrity in the battle of life, wherein he has been eminently successful and has set forth an exemplary line of conduct.

In Polk county, Tennessee, on October 1, 1844, there was born to S. B. and Barthenia Carter, the subject of this sketch, William M. Carter. At the age of seven years he went with his parents to Montgomery county, Arkansas, and worked on a farm with his father until the spring of 1863. Then came the call of patriotism, for his heart was with the cause, and he enlisted in Company G, Fourth Arkansas Cavalry, volunteers, under Colonel Moore and General Runnels. His fate was to be called to and fro largely in the state of Arkansas, where he participated in many skirmishes and endured all the hardships of war with its suffering and danger. At the close of hostilities he was mustered out at Little Rock and is now a member of the G. A. R., at Hamilton. From the military ranks he went to Newton county, Arkansas, and entered the ranks of its agricultural population, where he continued until 1875, when he prepared teams and crossed the plains to Grant county, settling at Canyon City, where he remained until 1878 and then removed to his present place, which is three miles east from Longcreek, and took up farming and stock-raising. Success has attended his efforts from the beginning and he is now the proprietor of seven hundred acres of good land, well improved. He has a comfortable home and good barns and orchards, while the ranch is in a high state of cultivation.

In 1867, Mr. Carter and Miss Eliza Hudson were married and to them were born three children: Benjamin A., living in the Willamette valley; Sarah E., wife of Dudley Curl, near Sumpter; James S., near Burns, Harney county. In Newton county, Arkansas, in 1872, Mrs. Carter was taken from her family and husband by death.

On December 11, 1873, Mr. Carter and Miss Pernice P., daughter of C. C. and Jennie Blackwell, were married and to them have been born ten children: Mary M., wife of C. R. Davis; Cora Maud, wife of Iven Slone, of Longcreek; Samuel B., married to Martha Harriman; Charles; Carrie A., wife of James M. Scroggins; John L.; William; Leona Dell; Nellie; Jennie Esther. Mr. Carter's mother moved with her younger children, after the war, to Barry county, Missouri, the father having died before the war. Shortly after the son came to this county, the mother removed hither and took a farm in the Fox valley, but recently she has sold this property and lives with her children. She is now in her eightieth year. Mr. Carter is one of the most successful and enterprising stockmen of the county and is respected and esteemed by all, having ever displayed those characterictics that are the associates of typical manhood and the bulwarks of substantial citizenship.

MARTIN A. LUCAS.—No pen will ever be able to record the deeds of valor and bravery that were enacted in the awful conflict that rent this fair land of freedom in twain during the last century; yet when it is possible to place on paper the career of one of the valiant boys that wore the blue, the opportunity is seized with a keen relish, although it must be said that it can only be in a fragmentary way that these deeds of daring are chronicled. As a typical son of the Emerald Isle, whose whole heart and soul entered into the struggles of his foster land, the subject of this sketch made for himself a record in the Civil war that is seldom surpassed and he generously bought the title that distinguishes him as a defender of his country.

In 1845 he was born in Ireland and in 1856 came to the United States with his parents, settling in Boston. When he started for himself it was to go to the cities of Vermont, where he learned the carpenter, harness, and trunk making trades. In this capacity he was serving when the call came for troops and as one of the first he enlisted for the three months' service, all that then was deemed necessary, and participated in the first conflict that was precipitated. At the close of his three months

he promptly re-listed in Company A, Second Vermont Infantry, for three years. He served through the entire war, taking part in the struggle on thirteen distinct battle fields, including the seven days' campaign under McClellan, where he was wounded. After the three years were ended, he again enlisted in the regular army and came west in 1864 with the First Regulars to San Francisco and ten days later came to Vancouver and from there to fort Steilacoom and one year later to camp Watson, where his time expired on September 18, 1867. He immediately engaged in carpentering there and at camp Harney and at the latter place his oldest daughter was born, being the first white child born in that section. From here he went to The Dallas for one year and then operated with a saw mill in Grant county until 1872. Then he took up carpentering for eight years, after which he gave his attention to raising stock in Bear valley. There he owns one half section of land but at the present time he is living seven and one half miles west from Mount Vernon.

The marriage of Mr. Lucas and Miss Anna Walker, a native of Ireland, who came to the United States in 1856, occured in 1864 and to them have been born the following children; Eliza June, now Mrs. W. S. Fields; Thomas William; Annie Etta; Myrtle; Florence.

NEWTON ROBERTSON.—Among the many stockmen and agriculturists that are making Grant county wealthy, mention should be made of the esteemed gentleman whose name is at the head of this article, and who has wrought since his advent into the county in a very successful manner in the prosecution of his business, manifesting a sagacity and enterprise that have won for him the meed that is properly attached to them—the prosperity that is so gratifying to members of our race. Steadily pursuing the business that first occupied him, he has been enabled to overcome the obstacles that have swamped other less wise manipulators and to gain a holding that is very commendable, while his uprightness and intrinsic worth are constant companions to his commendable achievements.

October 11, 1852, was the date that Newton Robertson was born to Charles and Annie

Robertson in Champaign county, Illinois. His early life was spent in the invigorating exercise of assisting his father on the farm and also in attending the public schools of his place. In 1884 he came across the plains direct to Grant county and soon after arriving here he embarked in the sheep industry and continuously he has operated in that line since and he enjoys great prosperity. He now has a large ranch where he resides, eight miles southwest from Monument, and it is well stocked with horses and cattle besides several thousand sheep. Fraternally he is affiliated with the Masonic lodge and in politics he is a stanch Republican and is very active in the affairs of county and state, while he is a very potent factor in the party in the county. Mr. Robertson's father is still living in Kansas, but his mother has passed to the other side. Mr. Robertson is highly esteemed in the county and enjoys to the fullest extent the confidence of his fellows and is one of the leading figures in the county, as well as one of the most substantial.

JOHN H. HAMILTON.—Among the sturdy bands of men and women that left the comforts and quiet of their eastern homes to endure the hardships of the weary trip across the plains, and to suffer from the frequent attacks of the savages while they were making their way to the unexplored and wild regions of the west, where they put forth herculean efforts in their endeavors to subdue the wilderness and bring from the new ground sustenance for themselves and their little ones, we are bound to mention the gentleman whose name initiates this paragraph and who stands as a worthy specimen of this valiant number.

Mr. Hamilton was born in Kentucky, to James and Julia Hamilton, on April 5, 1826, and while still a child was removed by his parents to Decatur county, Indiana. He spent the years of his minority on a farm and in 1851 came to Randolph county, Missouri, where he spent but one winter, starting across the plains the next spring. That dread disease, cholera, came in the train and one night three of his sisters were taken. The next day their bodies were laid in one grave, where they sleep beside the weary trail of many years ago. Mr. Hamilton came on to the Willamette valley and

located near Oregon City, where he took up a half section and went at the task of opening a farm in the midst of the forests. That was the scene of his labors until the spring of 1872, when he came to Grant county and settled near where the town of Hamilton is now located. He was the first settler in this section and the town was named after him. He took a homestead and increased his holdings to one thousand acres of good land and prosperity seemed to smile on him, but as the golden years came on he was unfairly dealt with and his property was largely taken from him unjustly, so that now he has but a small amount compared with the princely estate and stocks that he had accumulated by his care and thrift.

On October 9, 1848, the marriage of Mr. Hamilton and Miss Mary J., daughter of Nathaniel and Nancy Robins, of Greensburg, Indiana, was celebrated and to them have been born the following children: John Milton, married to Lettie Fuller, but he was killed in the mines in Fox Valley; James N., of Burns, Harney county; Arthur J., married to Mary Chapel and living near Portland; Sebastian E., in Portland; Jacob W., married to Emma Shirts and living near Hamilton; Lewis H., married to Mary Wills, near Prineville; William, married to Ella Hinton and living in Hamilton; Edith, deceased; Nancy C., wife of John Hinton, of Sumpter; Permelia J., wife of George Baker, of Sumpter. On May 4, 1900, Mrs. Hamilton was called from the walks of earth to the home beyond, and her demise was mourned by all. Mr. Hamilton is one of the most highly respected and esteemed of the old pioneers, having ever been faithful in the walks of life.

WILLIAM W. HINTON.—Pen and ink can never portray and printed page will never tell half of the hardships endured, the ability displayed, the victories won by the worthy pioneers who took their lives in their hands and faced every danger that man is heir to in the herculean efforts to bring within the pale of civilization the regions that are now placidly owned and richly enjoyed by the citizens of this county and adjoining sections of this and other states on the coast. A work of the character that we are endeavoring to make for the people would be sadly deficient were there failure to incorporate therein a review of the career of the gentleman whose name heads this article and whose life has been an inspiration throughout the entire eastern part of our state by his achievements in the practical industries, by his wise counsels and enterprising progression, coupled with patient and continuous effort in the lines of industry that he allied himself with in the incipiency of his career on the frontier region. Thus, and thus only, is wrought out for the use of generations to follow the facts and knowledge that is beneficial in the practical walks of life, that is not all mere theory and unsubstantial vision. Thus, by patient continuence in the lines of his endeavor he has acquired knowledge more valuable than theory and has demonstrated by carefully conducted experiments, facts that are indispensably coupled to the successful prosecution of the stock and other leading industries of this unique region, while his unbounded personal success in practical demonstration of this valuable information has made him one of the leading men of wealth in his community and throughout all eastern Oregon, where he has operated.

Our subject's parents, Job and Henrietta Hinton, crossed the plains in 1852, the father being captain of a train of fifty-two wagons, which, be it said to his credit, he piloted safely through without the loss of a single person, although they were frequently attacked by Indians. Some of the stock was sacrificed, but human life was preserved intact. The train was headed for California, but for reasons that have not been stated, they turned toward the western part of Oregon and settled in Lane county. Here the wisdom and courage of the father were manifested and very helpful in the solution of the many vexing questions that stand across the way of the early settler, and in meeting the many dangers that faced them on every hand. He was looked up to and beloved by all. Their confidence and affection were manifest in choosing him to positions of leadership and of trust almost continuously during his life time. His death was inexpressibly sad, he being shot in the prime of his life by his own son, who accidentally discharged a firearm with that awful effect, being one of those accidents that human wisdom can never compass, only bow to. With sorrow and general mourning throughout the entire section where his life was cast, the remains of the good and really great man were laid to rest until the day when the future shall be opened to us all and the scenes of life shall have explanation in the boundless wisdom of eternity itself. Many, many pioneers are reposing in the final sleep of life beneath the sod where rolls the Willamette, while nature weeps in silent sadness as she enfolds their mossy monuments and wraps them about with the gentle draperies of the morning mist; but none among that distinguished band e'er wrought with firmer hand or gave wiser counsel, tempered with his great love and sympathy, than the father of our subject, Job Hinton. Following this event of sorrow, the mother came to eastern Oregon to live with the son of whom we now speak, and who had preceded her to this region as early as 1864. She, too, has since been called to the realms of the life beyond.

After spending five years in mining about Boise City, in Idaho, Mr. Hinton came to Wasco county, which is said at that time to have embraced a large portion of eastern Oregon, and engaged in raising sheep. He was one of the pioneers in this industry and from that time until the present he has followed it with the success that he justly deserves for his energy and faithfulness displayed. He owns land in various parts of eastern Oregon, but his headquarters are at John Day, in Grant county. In 1888 he was chosen stock inspector and in this position he rendered excellent and valuable service for three years, being eminently fitted for its duties by his life of practical touch with every department of the business.

In 1866, at Franklin, Lane county, the marriage of Mr. Hinton and Miss Frances Jones was solemnized. To bless this union, seven children have been born, as follows: Hannah H., wife of D. G. Slavens, but since deceased; Clayton B.; William W.; Martha B.; Emma M.; Thomas C.; Lottie. Fraternally Mr. Hinton is affiliated with the K. of P., Lodge No. 40, of Longcreek.

It is of note that the brother of our subject, Clayton B. Hinton, was killed in a battle with the Indians at Hungry Hill. For four days the settlers fought the savages and during that time there was no chance to partake of food, and hence the name of the hill. Mr.

33

Hinton is one of the most substantial men of the county and the stanch qualities that characterized his ancestors are exemplified in his career in a very commendable manner, and now surrounded with a loving family, he is passing the golden days of the years of his life in quiet enjoyment of the competence that his skill and industry have gathered, while he directs his large interests and is content in the crowning joy that the memories of past days show well spent hours.

* * *

EMIL M. SCHARFF.—The sunny land of France has contributed many noble and liberty loving citizens to this country, who are faithful in upholding the free institutions that have been fostered here, and one among that devoted band is the pleasant gentleman of whom we have the privilege of speaking, and who has contributed materially to the advancement of the county where he is now domiciled, having wrought faithfully here both for the good of the public and the augmenting of his private exchequer, being attended meanwhile with the most gratifying success.

As suggested above, Mr. Scharff was born in France, the province of Loraine, in the eastern part, being the place and June 12, 1860, the date. His early life was passed on a farm and he gained the educational training to be had in the public schools. On October 12, 1873, his mother died, and two years later the father, with his four children, emigrated to the United States, settling near Galena, Jo Daviess county, Illinois, being near the birthplace of General Grant. For two years there he worked with his father on the farm and then his adventurous spirit longed for the scenes of the west and thither he came, alert for the fortune that awaited him. One year was spent in freighting from Denver to Leadville, and then

he went to Laramie City and spent a short time on the range. At this place he heard of the Indian war then going on in eastern Oregon and desiring to take part in the same he came thither via Winnemucca, landing in Harney county, but was too late to participate in the conflict. The following spring he came to John Day and engaged to Berge Edington to herd sheep and one year later he purchased a band of sheep for himself. He remained three years in the vicinity of John Day with his flocks and then in 1883 came to the region of Monument and a little later bought the place where he now lives, one-fourth of a mile southeast from Monument. The estate is of the generous proportions of four thousand acres. The town of Monument is partly situated on what was a portion of his farm. Mr. Scharff's flocks are numbered by thousands and his estate is well improved with all necessary utensils and fences and buildings, as a good barn and a fine residence and other things that make it valuable and comfortable. He also has a good orchard and some cattle and horses.

On July 22, 1897, the marriage of Mr. Scharff and Miss Celina, daughter of Daniel C. and Anna Cohoe, took place and to them have been born three children: Bertha D., Cedric C. and John. Mr. and Mrs. Cohoe live near Monument. Mr. Scharff's father had poor health in this country and so went to France in 1884, and in 1888 he passed to the world beyond. Mr. Scharff is affiliated with the I. O. O. F., at Heppner, and the K. of P., Lodge No. 40, at Longcreek. In political matters he is a Republican and holds firmly to the tenets of that party, believing that the principles laid down there are for the welfare of the country. Mr. Scharff is a man of ability and sound judgment and is one of the most substantial of Grant county's population, having ever manifested both sagacity and unswerving integrity.

MALHEUR COUNTY

MALHEUR BUTTE.

HISTORY OF MALHEUR COUNTY.

CHAPTER I.

SETTLEMENT AND PASSING EVENTS.

Traditional Oregon was an inaccessible region, a wild wilderness of wood, mountain and plain, habitable only by preying beasts and prowling savages. When, after his memorable and hazardous ride across the plains, in the winter of 1842-43, Marcus Whitman presented himself to President Tyler and Secretary Webster at Washington, robed in the skin of the mountain lion, shod with moccasins and crowned with fur, his skin red-hued like an Indian brave's, and roughened by the winds of the arid desert and the bleak mountains, his disheveled locks falling over his broad shoulders, it required all the eloquence of his intensely fervid nature to impress with the stamp of truthfulness his strangely fascinating story of Oregon and its wonderful possibilities. The personality of the man, the convincing force of his language eventually won the confidence of President and people and gave credence to his story. The daring spirit of man has never sought for more than a mere excuse to justify exploitation. The Whitman story furnished far more than an excuse. In it there was an eloquent appeal and a promise of great reward. What more was needed to lift the tide-gate and pour out upon the plains the flood of immigration that flowed across the Oregon borders in succeeding years? But, while Oregon was the Mecca, in the popular mind the name

stood only for sheltered valleys, where broad streams flow, where, without consuming strife, may be gathered the wealth of soil and river. The current was swift in the earlier streams of immigration and there was no pausing on the borders of the new territory. But a less impetuous band would hardly have halted when the superficial aspect of the country was so cheerless and uninviting. The repellant features of the desert behind them were stamped upon it. Its sun-parched plains generated a sense of desolation in the hearts of the most venturesome. Extreme eastern Oregon was not yet ripe for settlement. It must await another day and another generation—a people impelled by other influences, actuated by other motives. It so long remained fettered by external appearances and by natural disadvantages that its very name was once a synonym for desolation and loneliness. But the days of its disrepute were numbered and the season of its redemption came at last. Those who braved the adverse conditions existing in the early 'sixties were fearless men whose stout hearts never quailed when facing the privations and dangers of pioneer life. In those days southeastern Oregon was coveted by no man as a place of residence, as a fair, propitious land in which to grow his vine and fig tree. But in various ways men became residents here. They drifted in, sometimes agents of the government erecting forts, sometimes as prospectors, or, again, as squatters along the trails providing food and forage for caravans and overland stages. Through force of circumstances many of these remained. In a sense they became discoverers. Through them a knowledge of the possibilities of the soil was gained and something became known of the character and extent of mineral deposits. Wrong theories concerning climatic conditions and effects were exploded and the peculiar advantages, destined to accomplish so much for later generations, received proper rating in hitherto incredulous minds.

For reasons which may be discerned from a study of the facts and conditions briefly outlined above, the usual order of things has been reversed in the settlement of Oregon. It has developed from the west to east (from the valley of the Willamette to that of the Snake river) instead of from east to west. The territory at present embraced within the boundaries of Malheur county was almost the last within the state to give way before the onward march of civilization. Comparatively speaking, only a few years have elapsed since the war whoop of the Bannock and Piute savages fell upon the ears of the stage driver or the express rider in his wild flight for the protecting walls of the fort or for the camp of the caravan. It was not until the year 1878 that old Chief Winnemucca, of the Piutes, and Buffalo Horn, of the Bannocks, with their murderouse bands were driven from Jordan valley and even later life and property were in jeopardy in some parts of Malheur county.

Some squatter rights were held in various parts of the county very early in the 'sixties, but many years intervened between the period of exploration and that of permanent settlement. There is no authentic account of explorations made in southeastern Oregon prior to the year 1860. Probably the first white men to penetrate this portion of the state were the trappers and hunters employed by the Northwestern Fur and Hudson's Bay companies. These nomads, seeking only for furs, and such valuables as they might obtain from the Indians, traversed the entire northwest annually in their numerous expeditions, and undoubtedly often had occasion to pass through the territory now embraced by Malheur county. In fact, Old Fort Boise, a Hudson's Bay Company post, stood at the mouth of the Boise river, on the Idaho side of the Snake, for many years. This famous old outpost, situated hundreds of miles from the border settlements, and inhabited by a few white men who had braved the perils of the wilderness for the purpose of trading with the Indians, was not abandoned until 1852, and during its long existence served as a beacon light to guide hundreds of emigrants on their westward voyage.

It is quite probable that the name which this county bears was given the river of the same name by a party of French trappers attached to this old trading post. Tradition relates that some time during the fore part of the nineteenth century a party of French trappers and traders ascended this stream to its headwaters in search of furs. The trip was an unsuccessful one, they were attacked by the Indians, several of the party were wounded, others were killed, and still others fell sick. So it was quite natural that this long train of misfortune should cause them to name the river "Mal (bad or unfortunate) heur (hour of time," or, translating freely, the "unhappy" river.

The old emigrant road, if a road it might properly be termed, leading to the far northwest, divided into two forks at old Fort Hall, Idaho, near the present city of Pocatello. One branch crossed the Snake river at the fort and proceeded up the northern side of the river, the other ran along the Owyhee and then up the western bank of the Snake to a point opposite to Fort Boise. From this point the latter road continued north through what is now Malheur county, crossing the Malheur river about fifteen miles above its mouth, following the course of what is now Willow creek for several miles, thence leaving this section by way of Tub Springs and the Burnt river canyon. Seeking wealth, health and happiness in the land of fair promise beyond were scores of immigrants, on foot, or horse, or in the historic prairie schooner, wending their way in all seasons over this old road. Little did these wanderers dream that the day would come, and, too, in the not far distant future, when beautiful, prosperous ranches and happy homes would gladden the vision of later travelers along this highway. Little did they dream that the land which they had passed by as worthless would some day surpass in value many of their own homes on the western slope.

The immigration of 1845 (William Morfitt, a pioneer of 1847, seriously doubts if a single expedition reached the coast that year) probably traveled over this route. Be that as it may, however, we know that the immigration of 1847 used this trail to the Willamette valley, as did also the expeditions made in the 'fifties. Soon after the fame of the newly discovered Eldorados on the Powder river, in Oregon, and Wood river, in Idaho, had spread abroad in 1862 a steady stream of travel passed over this old road. Some went north to Powder river; others south to Wood river.

Prior to its legal formation in 1887 the history of Malheur county is contained in that of the early settlements within its present boundaries. One of the first of these, in fact the first of real importance, was made in the northern part of the county in Mormon Basin, which came into prominence early in the history of the Auburn camp. These placer diggings were discovered immediately following the rush to this region and the camp attained considerable importance and population. The nearby camp of Eldorado sprang into existence in 1865, and five years later Malheur City was founded, lying just a mile from Eldorado. Although the population of this district has risen and ebbed with the varying fortunes of the gold seekers, several hundred being in the district at one time, still there has always been a considerable permanent settlement there. Only recently these old camps have been stirred with new life by rich quartz discoveries, which bid fair to produce larger and more permanent camps than those of the 'sixties. At present Malheur City is a thriving town, while Mormon Basin is inhabited principally by Chinamen.

As soon as travel over the old emigrant road began to increase to large proportions stations were established along the route. So, we are told by L. B. Rinehart, the well known pioneer of eastern Oregon, that during the winter of 1863-64 Jonathan Keeney built a small cabin at the Malheur river crossing, near the present town of Vale. This cabin was constructed of willow logs and poles, obtained from the sparse growth along the river at that time, plastered over with adobe mud. Here this pioneer innkeeper attended the wants of those who cared to tarry and rest and refresh the weary body after the toilsome day's journey. Mr. Keeney had several sons, one of whom, James, conducted this station alone from 1868 to 1870.

About the time this cabin was built the Silver City mines, in Idaho, were discovered. This camp, which is still one of importance, lies just across the state line and only a few miles from Jordan valley. In 1863 what is known as "Ruby Ranch"' was opened in Jordan valley. It is located in the upper valley, contains three thousand acres, and was first owned by "Doc" Inskip. The property now belongs to W. P. Beers. At the same time in the middle valley of Jordan creek, "Sheep Ranch" was opened by a man named McWilliams. This contained eleven hundred acres, and is now the property of J. P. Merrill and John Milky. These ranches are well remembered by all travelers over the old Winnemucca stage road. These stages made stops at each place. United States troops were frequently quartered here, and during the Indian troubles a government telegraph station was kept in operation at Sheep Ranch.

In those days the country was infested by the several Indian tribes living in this section of the state, the Piutes and the Bannocks being the strongest. Small predatory bands of these redskins haunted the emigrant roads and trails, and many a lonely prospector or traveler suddenly disappeared from sight. His bleaching bones, and beside them two or three arrows, found perhaps months afterward under the foliage of a clump of sage brush, only too plainly told the story of his life. These murders were not infrequent during the 'sixties, nor did they entirely cease until the Indian war of 1878 thoroughly subdued the savages.

In 1869 the government made a treaty with the Piutes, and this tribe was established on the Malheur reservation, a large tract of land lying on the north fork of the Malheur river in the extreme northwestern corner of the county. Although constantly causing trouble and necessitating eternal vigilance to keep them on the reservation, the government managed to hold them fairly in check until the outbreak of 1878, when they were removed to the Yakima valley. The following year, 1879, the agency farm and buildings were sold to the Pacific Live Stock Company, and the rest of the valley lands to settlers.

Previous to the establishment of this reservation, however, many small raids were made by the Piutes on the settlements. During the early spring of 1868 they raided the small settlement on Clark's creek and drove off a large number of horses. The settlers raised a company of seven and followed the redskins, trailing them to a point near the Grant county line. There the Indians ambushed the party, killing a young man named Belknap. The rest retreated, and the next day a much stronger party returned to the scene of the attack and buried the body of young Belknap. One night a short time afterward another band of Piutes stole into the Amelia settlement, six miles east of Eldorado, and tearing down a large cottonwood corral there, drove off forty or fifty head of stock. The next morning the settlers, to the number of five, including the Sutherlands, father and son, and James Roland, started in pursuit. For twenty miles beyond Malheur City they tracked the fleeing Indians up Willow creek. They then stopped in a small cove to eat their midday lunch. While eating several rifles cracked on the summit of the hill overlooking the camp, and young Sutherland fell dead. The rest of the party very fortunately escaped and succeeded in reaching Eldorado without further loss.

In 1867 or 1868 Egan, the noted Piute chief, with a party of Piutes and Bannocks, fell upon forty Chinamen en route from Winnemucca to the Silver City mines, and slew all but one. The Chinamen were entrapped near the state line, and after being surrounded by a superior force of redskins, were commanded to surrender. The Mongolians, trusting to Egan's promises of mercy, gave up their arms without resistance. Then, as is usually the case in such instances, the Indians turned the captured weapons upon their defenseless owners and commenced a wholesale slaughter. After many had been shot to death the chief ordered the Indians to save the ammunition and beat the remainder of their victims to death. Despite the shrieks and yells for mercy and the groans and curses of the wounded and dying, the carnival of crime was continued. Only one Chinaman escaped to tell the horrible tale. Notwithstanding the desperate efforts made by the miners and officials to apprehend and punish the guilty Indians, no certain proof could be found against any, and the matter was finally dropped. Years afterward Egan told the story of this affair to an intimate white friend of his in such a way as to leave but little doubt of its truthfulness and as to the identity of the perpetrators.

Until the treaty made with the Piutes in 1869, however, settlement in this portion of Baker county was confined practically to the mining districts, as roving bands of Indians were too numerous to permit isolation. But after the Indians were placed on their reservation the land was opened to settlement, and during that and the following year quite a settlement was made on Willow creek. The valley is divided into two sections, the upper and lower, and being situated close to the mining camp of Eldorado was the first portion of the county to be extensively settled by ranchmen and farmers. In 1865, S. B. Reeves located a claim, now known as the Norwood place, in the lower valley, where the old emigrant road crosses the creek, and the same summer George Derby and a man named Shoemaker took up ranches six miles above the Reeves place. These were the only ranches in the lower valley until 1868. William Morfitt, an emigrant of 1847, and one of the oldest Oregonians living, located the first ranch in upper Willow creek valley in March, 1868. This claim lies about two miles south of Eldorado.

In 1868 L. B. Rinehart, another pioneer Oregonian of whom we have spoken, turned loose at the Washoe ferry on the Snake river the first band of cattle ever ranged in Baker county, south of that point. Two years later, in 1870, Mr. Rinehart purchased the Keeney station and land rights and in 1872 built a stone house on the land and established his home there. This old landmark, known throughout the country as the "old stone house," is still standing. For years it was the only hostelry in this portion of the country, and as such became known to all who traveled through the region.

From Mr. Morfitt and Mr. Rinehart we have been able to secure a partial list of those who settled in Malheur county previous to and including the year 1872. Many names

are doubtles lacking, but Mnemosyne is a poor historian at the best. The list follows:

Jonathan Keeney, James Keeney, 1864; S. B. Reeves, George Derby, —— Shoemaker, Samuel Colt, —— Colt, Thomas Littig, Daniel Bruner, 1865; Henry Barnes, James Delaney, James Lynn, 1867; William Morfitt, L. B. Rinehart, George Drinnon, Archie Turner, Hank Edwards, Thomas Welch, Baltimore Howard, Chauncey H. Eaton, J. L. Cole, Joseph Stevenson, George Coggans, Charles Goodnough, —— Kirkpatrick, 1868; J. H. Rose, B. F. Sargent, 1869; George Collins, Mary Collins (Richardson), John Collins, C. F. Locey, George Phillips, Joseph Moreton, Samuel Lake, William Glenn, William O'Brien, R. W. Worsham, A. LeBard, 1870; John Thomson, William G. Thomson, Samuel McDowell, Hammer & Fuqua, A. W. Turner, Ed Imbler, Silas Imbler, J. C. Phipps, John Tillson, James Thomson, William L. Logan, —— Price, William Emison, Peter Keeney, Thomas Glenn, William Kennedy, Levi Westfall, 1872.

During the year 1872 Levi Westfall initiated a settlement on Bully creek, and Peter Keeney and Thomas Glenn took up ranches on the Owyhee river. In the fall of 1873 J. D. Osborn settled at the grove on the Malheur river about ten miles above the old stone house, and the year following James McMahan led the vanguard of settlers into the Harper valley.

One cause worked greatly to the detriment of the early settlers of this region, and is still working to that end, viz., the gift by the government of thousands of acres of the best land in the county to the two military road companies whose roads passed through this region. The Dalles military road entered the county near the Ironside mountain, following the north fork of the Malheur river down to Willow creek, thence down Willow creek and the course of the old emigrant road. The Willamette valley and Cascade military road enters the county by one of the forks of the Malheur river, and follows the course of the main river to its mouth. By act of Congress, passed in 1866, and of the Oregon legislature, passed in 1868, these two companies were granted each alternate section of land on each side of the road within a limit of three miles. The consequence of this was that hundreds of settlers in this county alone were crowded out or compelled to purchase land at high prices. Not only was valuable land thus donated to these corporations to build roads that were not needed and could have been built at much less cost, but the roads were never built. At the best these alleged highways were but trails; streams were forded instead of being bridged, and in the case of The Dalles road a wagon was simply driven over the course. Several years ago these frauds were investigated and the matter carried to the supreme court of the United States, but owing to a technicality the government was not allowed to prove fraud. By the terms of the acts passed by Congress, the governor's affidavit certifying to the completion of the roads according to contract was the only proof of compliance required, and as Governor Woods made affidavit to this effect, the provisions of the grant were fully carried out and the company could not be held. A fuller history of this case will be found in the history of Grant county.

Until only a few years ago Malheur county possessed an unexcelled stock range and one of immense proportions. In the northern portion the Malheur river valley, with its numerous tributaries, furnished a fine winter range, the streams being lined with a heavy growth of willows and rye grass, and the sage brush and prairie grasses furnishing excellent feed. During the summer thousands of head of cattle, horses and sheep were driven southward among the foothills and valleys of the upper country, where the bunchgrass grew abundantly, even luxuriantly. But with the increasing population and settlement of the county the range gradually failed to support the stock grazing upon it and stock raising lost much of its prestige. However, farming was not yet to assume an important place among the industries of this county, not until the early 'eighties.

The winter of 1873-74 was a severe one, and as stock in those days was simply turned loose on the range during the winter as well as the summer, large numbers perished from the cold. The loss is estimated at between ten and fifteen per cent.

During the later 'sixties and the early 'seventies the Canyon City placer mines were at their zenith, and there was considerable travel to the John Day country from the southern portion of the state and Idaho. So it was quite natural that a stage line should be established between Canyon City and Boise. This pioneer stage line utilized the emigrant road as far as possible and passed the old stone house at the Malheur river crossing. From the meager records we have of this line it is only possible to say further that Charles Moore drove the stage and was its probable owner, and that it was in operation for several years.

Some time in the summer of 1876 a tragedy occurred in the Malheur river settlement which shocked the whole community and cast a deep shadow of gloom over the entire region. This sad affair was the drowning of Florence Moreton, a daughter of Mr. and Mrs. Joseph Moreton, who lived on the Gillerman place, near the confluence of Bully creek and the Malheur river. This young girl was in bathing at the river with another young lady who lived in the neighborhood, and venturing too far into the current was swept off her feet and whirled away into deep water. She could not swim, and struggling frantically to reach the shore, she sank from view within sight of her companion, who was powerless to aid her. Parents and neighbors hastened to the scene as soon as possible and willing hands searched the shores and explored the waters for the body, but it was not until after midnight that two of the searchers, L. B. Rinehart and Jep D. Osborn, were successful. Meanwhile neighbors and friends came in from the country for several miles around until the whole Malheur river settlement was congregated at the Moreton place. Though over a quarter of a century has sped since this sad affair occurred, the story of that weird and ghostly midnight search is still graphically imprinted on the memories of those who participated.

As is well known, eastern Oregon was the scene of a bloody Indian war in 1878. The Bannocks, under Buffalo Horn, left the Fort Hall reservation, in Southern Idaho, in the early part of June and proceeded westward along the Snake river, scattering death and destruction in their path. They crossed the Snake into Oregon at Henderson's ferry, and then taking more of a northward course, struck directly for the Piute reservation in the northwestern part of Malheur county. Here they were joined by the Piutes, under Egan, and under these two merciless warriors the Indians made their famous campaign into Grant and Umatilla counties. The course of the Bannocks led through an uninhabited portion of this county, very fortunately, and with the exception of a small loss of stock and the murder of one or two settlers in the extreme southern portion of the county, and one living near Westfall, no serious injury was inflicted upon this region. Scouting parties were sent out from the Willow creek, Malheur river and Malheur City settlements, who kept watch of the redskins' movements and were ready at an instant's notice to warn the settlers. General Howard passed through Malheur City with two companies of infantry in pursuit of the Indians and several scouts joined the army at this point. The subsequent history of this memorable campaign is fully told in another chapter of this work.

A hard winter, similar in many respects to that of 1873-74, prevailed throughout this section in 1879-80, the stock losses being about

fifteen per cent. This was the last winter of such severity as to entail heavy loss upon stockmen here. One lesson thoroughly learned as the result of this heavy loss was that better covering and feed must be given stock during severe weather.

With the dawn of the next decade, that of 1880-1890, agriculture began to assume an important place among the industries of the county, and several irrigation projects began to create considerable interest among the settlers, who realized that water alone is needed to give life to the fertile valley lands, and that stock raising must go hand in hand with agriculture. In 1880 William Morfitt built the first gristmill in Baker county, south of the Burnt river mountains. This mill was a small water power mill, using the burr process, and was erected on Mr. Morfitt's ranch on Willow creek. For several years he ground all the grain raised in this region, but the abandonment of the mill was finally made necessary by the use of the creek's waters for irrigating purposes. The operation of this little mill greatly stimulated grain production in the Willow creek valley.

In 1883 two important irrigating canals were projected and their construction commenced, the Owyhee and the Nevada. The former was taken out of the Owyhee river and was expected to water that valley; the latter was taken out of the Malheur river and was intended to irrigate the lower Malheur valley. Besides these large canals many smaller ones were undertaken and all tended to enhance the importance of agriculture in its numerous branches. The importance and general effect of this important canal construction during the early and middle 'eighties on the growth and interests of the county at large can hardly be overestimated. By undertaking these works the settlers showed a substantial token of their faith in the country, and by their completion the permanence of the settlement is assured long after the stock industry shall have passed into minor importance by the reclamation of the range.

But perhaps to the Oregon Short Line railroad more than to any other influence is Malheur county indebted for the progress of the past ten or fifteen years. In building down the Snake river in 1873 the company found it convenient to cross the river from Idaho to the Oregon side near Nyssa, a station ten miles south of Ontario. About twelve miles of this line is in Malheur county, crossing its eastern extremity. Up to this time Baker City had the trade of all this section of the state. When a station was established at Ontario in 1884 it at once sprang into importance as a shipping point. Being ninety miles southeast of Baker City, it is more accessible from the ranges of Malheur and Harney counties, and portions of Grant county. The establishment of this trade center made the development of agricultural and other resources not only possible, but highly profitable, while at the same time it greatly enhanced land and ditch values and brought the ranges within easy reach of the markets. In April, 1900, the Oregon Short line purchased eighty acres of land adjoining Ontario and built thereon the most extensive stockyards in eastern Oregon. This step was necessitated because of the heavy live stock shipments, cattle, horses and sheep being driven here from the ranges of Malheur, Harney, Grant and Crook counties. Previous to 1884 all this business had been done at Baker City. But each year following witnessed an increase of shipments at Ontario. A radical change was gradually taking place, in which Baker City was losing and Ontario was gaining as a shipping point. The creation of this new commercial center led eventually to the agitation of the question of the organization of a new political division in the southern half of Baker county. There was but little opposition to the measure and by the year 1887 matters had so shaped themselves that those most directly interested believed the time had arrived

for action. I. D. Haines represented this senatorial district in the state legislature. R. A. Lockett of Willow Creek and R. H. Holland, of Vale, were representatives from Baker county. In February, 1887, they secured the passage of an act dividing Baker county and creating out of its southern portion the county of Malheur. For the new county Governor Pennoyer appointed the following officers: County judge, F. K. Froman; sheriff, Henry C. Murray; clerk, Edward H. Test; treasurer, T. A. Levey; assessor, William Ritchie; school superintendent, Thomas Alves; commissioners, John F. Lackey and C. T. Locey. The organization took effect and the county commenced its official existence April 3, 1887, with an inherited debt from Baker county of $30,-000. Taxable property in the county was at this time valued at $859,624. The territory included in the new county was at that time described as offering exceptional advantages to the stockman, the miner, the manufacturer and the agriculturist. Subsequent advancement and the general progress of the county since its organization have proven that its advantages have never been overestimated. For the information of the citizens and for the purpose of reference we print herein the full text of the act under which the county was organized.

AN ACT

To Create the County of Malheur, in the State of Oregon, and to fix the Salaries of County Judge and Treasurer of said County.

Be it enacted by the Legislative assembly of the State of Oregon:

Section 1. That all that portion of the state of Oregon embraced within the following boundaries be, and the same is hereby created and organized into a separate county and body politic by the name of Malheur, viz.:

Beginning at a point on the boundary line between the state of Oregon and Nevada, which is at the southeast corner of Grant county, in the state of Oregon; thence north on the line between Grant county and Baker county to the first angle corner in the east line of said Grant county; thence north on range line between ranges 36 and 37 east to the summit of the Burnt River mountains, in township 15 south of range 36 east; thence easterly and following the summit of said Burnt River mountains to the intersection of the sounth boundary line of township 14 south of range 43 east; thence east on the said south boundary line of township 14 to the middle channel of Snake river, between the state of Oregon and the territory of Idaho; thence up the meanderings of said Snake river on the line between Oregon and Idaho to the mouth of the Owyhee river on said line; thence south on the line between Oregon and Idaho to the north line of the state of Nevada; thence west on the north line of Nevada to the place of beginning.

Section 2. The territory embraced within said boundary lines shall compose a county for all civil and military purposes, and shall be subject to the same laws and restrictions and be entitled to elect the same officers as other counties in this state: *Provided,* That it shall be the duty of the Governor, as soon as it may become convenient, after this act shall have become a law, to appoint for Malheur county and from among its resident citizens, the several county officers allowed by law to other counties of this state, which said officers, after duly qualifying according to law, shall be entitled to hold their respective offices until their successors are duly elected at the general state election of 1888, and have duly qualified according to law.

Section 3. The temporary seat of Malheur county shall be located at Vale, in said county, until a permanent seat is adopted. At the general state election of 1888 the question of a location of the county seat shall be submitted to the legal voters of said county and the place, if any, which shall receive a majority of all the votes cast at said election shall be the

county seat of said county; but if no place shall receive a majority of all the votes cast, the question shall be again submitted to the legal voters of said county between the two places having the highest number of votes at said election at the next general state election, and the place receiving the highest number of votes at such election shall be the county seat of said county.

Section 4. The legal electors of Malheur county shall be entitled to elect at the general state election of 1888, and thereafter, until otherwise provided by law, one member of the house of representatives, while Baker county shall be entitled to elect one, and said county shall for senatorial purposes be annexed to the twentieth senatorial district and be entitled with said district to one senator, until otherwise provided by law.

Section 5. The county clerk of Baker county shall send to the county clerk of Malheur county within thirty days after this act becomes a law a certified transcript of all delinquent taxes, including school taxes, from the assessment roll of 1886 that were assessed within the limits of Malheur county; also a certified transcript of the assessment of persons and property within the limits of Malheur county for 1886, and the said taxes shall be payable to the proper officer of Malheur county and retained by that county, save and except that the county treasurer of Malheur county shall, out of the first moneys collected for taxes, pay over to the treasurer of Baker county the full amount of state tax on the assessment roll of 1886 due from citizens of Malheur county; the said clerk of Baker county shall also make out and send to the clerk of Malheur county, within the time above limited, a transcript of all cases pending in the county and circuit courts of Baker county between parties residing in Malheur county, including all papers relating to the unsettled estates of deceased persons formerly residing in the territory embraced within Malheur county, and transfer all original papers in said cases to be tried in Malheur county. The expense of all transcripts furnished to Malheur county shall be borne by that county.

Section 6. The said county of Malheur is hereby attached to the sixth judicial district of the state of Oregon for judicial purposes, and the terms of the circuit court for said county shall be held at its county seat on the fourth Monday in June and the fourth Monday in November of each year.

Section 7. The county court of Malheur county shall be held at the county seat of said county on the first Monday of every alternate month, beginning on the first Monday of the month next after the appointment by the Governor of the county officers as provided in this act.

Section 8. Until otherwise provided, the county judge of Malheur county shall receive an annual salary of four hundred dollars.

Section 9. Until otherwise provided, the county treasurer of Malheur county shall receive an annual salary of one hundred dollars.

Section 10. The county of Malheur, within one year after its organization by the appointment of its officers as herein provided, shall assume and pay to the county of Baker a just proportion of the indebtedness of Baker county after deducting therefrom the value of the public property of Baker county, and M. D. Wilson, Ed. Test and L. O. Ison, of Baker county, are hereby appointed a board to determine the value of such property and the amount of indebtedness to be assumed by said Malheur county; said persons shall meet at the county seat of Baker county on the first Monday in April, 1887, or within ten days thereafter, and take and subscribe to an oath before the clerk Baker county faithfully to discharge their duties; thereupon said board shall proceed with said work, and at the same time said board shall compute the amount of the school fund in the treasury of Baker county and the amount derived from taxation and from fines, forfeit-

ures, etc., within the limits of Malheur county and make an award for such proportionate amount to said Malheur; when said board shall have completed its duties it shall file a report of its conclusion, that affecting the school fund separate and distinct from the other, in duplicate with the clerks of Baker and Malheur counties; within thirty days from the filing of such report in Malheur county either county may take an appeal from the decision of said board to the circuit court for Baker county by serving a notice of appeal upon the clerk of the other county; upon perfecting the issues in said circuit court either county may demand a change of the place of trial to any other county of the sixth judicial district which may be agreed upon by said counties, or, in the event of their disagreement, which may be designated by the judge of said district; the trial may be by jury and the judgment rendered may be enforced as other judgments against counties; if the county appealing fails to recover a more favorable judgment than the finding of said board by at least five hundred dollars it shall pay the expense of the trial. If no appeal is taken by either county within the thirty days above provided the finding of said board shall be conclusive, and thereafter the treasurer of Baker county shall pay to the treasurer of Malheur county upon the presentation of a copy of the finding and award of said board as to the school fund above mentioned, certified by the clerk of Baker county, the amount of the award made and such copy shall stand to the treasurer of Baker county in lieu of the warrant of the school superintendent of said county, and the receipt of the treasurer of Malheur county shall be accepted by the school superintendent of Baker county as a full acquittance of the moneys therein represented in the next succeeding settlement between such superintendent and treasurer of Baker county. The persons constituting the board above provided for shall receive for their services the sum of five dollars per day each for every day actually consumed in the work for which they are appointed and mileage at the rate of ten cents a mile for every mile actually traveled in going to and returning from the said county seat of Baker county and such expense shall be borne equally by Baker and Malheur counties.

Section 11. The county judge of Malheur county shall let by contract to the lowest responsible and efficient bidder the work of transcribing all records of Baker county affecting real estate situated in Malheur county, and when completed they shall be examined and certified to by the clerk of Baker county and shall thereafter be recognized and acknowledged as official records of Malheur county: *Provided,* That the clerk of Malheur county shall be allowed to bid on said work.

Section 12. No expenditure exceeding the sum of forty-five hundred dollars shall be made toward the erection or purchase of public buildings within Malheur county until after the location of a permanent county seat.

Section 13. Inasmuch as the early formation of Malheur county is much desired, this act shall take effect and be in force from and after the first day of April, 1887.

Approved February 17, 1887.

Commencing its official existence with a property valuation of $859,624, in ten years, according to the assessment of 1897, this valuation increased to $1,235,920, a gain of $376,296 during this period. In 1897 it was the fifth smallest county in the state in point of wealth. According to the assessment summary for 1901, the gross value of all property was placed at $1,589,760, a gain of $353,840 in the four years between 1897 and 1901. In area it is the second largest in the state. It is nearly as large as the states of Massachusetts and Connecticut combined, having an area of 9,784 square miles. Harney county exceeds this by 202 square miles.

Ever since the passage of the act creating the county an earnest rivalry has existed between Vale and Ontario for county seat honors. The recent action on the part of the citizens of Vale in erecting a court house, which they propose to donate to the county, is possibly the final step in the contest, although there are as yet but few outward indications of surrender in the city of Ontario. The contest having extended over a period of fifteen years, it is fitting that the various acts of the contesting parties should be recorded in this work.

In 1887 section three of the creating act named Vale as the county seat. This selection was ratified by the people of the county at the general elections in 1888, and also in 1890. In new counties, as a rule, the county seat war rages indefinitely, and this statement is true concerning the fight in Malheur county. By some of the citizens it is not yet thought to be definitely settled. Ontario, the metropolis and commercial center of the county, continues to be a vigorous aspirant for county seat honors and at nearly every session of the legislature an effort is made by her citizens and by residents of this portion of the county, to secure the passage of an enabling act, and thus again get the county seat question before the people. In the latter part of December, 1898, petitions were circulated asking the legislature to pass an enabling act at the regular session opening in January, 1899, that would allow the voters of Malheur to select a county seat at the next general election. Ontario was understood to be responsible for this petition, which was signed by 700 voters. A counter petition was also circulated, which obtained 400 signatures. As a result of this agitation House Bill No. 311 was introduced January 24, 1899, by Representative J. R. Blackaby, and was passed January 31st by a vote of forty-five to six. In the meantime the opposition was not idle and a strong influence was brought to bear upon the members of the upper house that evidently had great weight when that body came to vote upon the passage of the bill. The bill was introduced in the senate by Senator Smith and was reported back favorably by the committee on counties, but when it reached a vote it was defeated. There were thirteen for and thirteen against its passage, four members being absent.

In December, 1900, another effort was made to get the matter before the people. A meeting of the citizens of Ontario was held in the opera house. At this meeting David Wilson, who owns a great deal of real estate in the city, proposed to donate grounds and to erect thereon a brick court house, which would include court room, offices, vault, jail and all necessary fixtures. The structure was to cost $8,000, according to specifications and plans submitted by architect W. A. Samms, of Baker City, which described a building fifty by seventy feet, two stories high, with thirty-foot walls. Mr. Wilson proposed to furnish $5,000 of the building fund, provided the citizens of Ontario would subscribe the remaining $3,000. He also offered to Malheur county a $15,000 bond, with prominent citizens of Ontario as security, to insure the fulfillment of his contract, the erection of the court house and its final transfer to the county. A committee of citizens was appointed to proceed in the matter. This committee consisted of E. H. Test, chairman; J. J. Cortwright, secretary; J. A. Lackey, J. M. Babcock, J. T. Clement, C. W. Platt and L. Adam. The $3,000 was subscribed by citizens, who also agreed to bear the expenses of the election. Following these steps a petition was circulated again asking the legislature to pass an enabling act, and a bond was offered by the city to insure the erection of the building and the defraying of election expenses should the act be passed. The petition received 874 signatures.

In the meantime the citizens of Vale were also perfecting plans for the erection of a court house by private subscriptions, the building, when completed, to be given to the county. County Judge J. F. Stevens, Sheriff J. D. Locey and Clerk A. G. King were appointed as

a committee from the county to act with a committee of citizens in securing funds and directing the construction of a court house. The citizens' committee consisted of D. C. Wells, M. G. Hope, J. C. Kelley, Findley McDonald and J. L. Cole. These committees secured subscriptions of $10,000 as a building fund. The final plans for the court house provided for a two-story stone structure, sixty by eighty feet, with court room, jury rooms, offices, vault and jail.

Ontario's petition for an enabling act was again defeated in the legislature, and shortly afterward work was commenced on the building at Vale. L. B. Rinehart donated grounds, and the building contract was awarded to James Patten and Edward Warner. The court house is nearing completion and when finished will be the most modern and in all particulars the finest of any of the eastern Oregon counties. The completion of this building will possibly settle for all time the county seat question and will make it possible for the two contesting cities to unite their energies in efforts for the general advancement of the county's interests.

Malheur county has passed through periods of financial distress, but the suffering from such causes has not been extreme nor of long duration. In 1893 the only interests that had attained an exceptional degree of development were those of the cattle and sheep men, and it is a well known fact that stockmen suffered less from the financial troubles than almost any other class. The burden fell rather upon the mercantile companies through whom the stockmen conducted their transactions, and these companies being strong in financial resources, weathered the storm without serious losses.

The stock interests in the county suffered somewhat during the winter of 1897-98. In the latter part of that winter many range cattle perished. The loss was not attributed to disease, epidemic nor to cold. Until late in the winter stock was forced to subsist upon the scant forage grasses of the plains and hills,

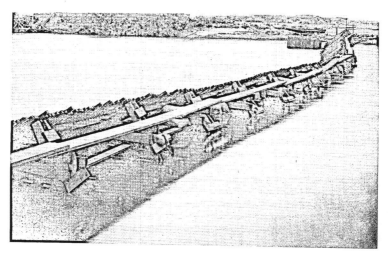

SALMON FISH HATCHERY, NEAR ONTARIO, OREGON, ON SNAKE RIVER.

and it is believed by some that the stockmen delayed the feeding season too long, and the cattle becoming weak and emaciated were rendered incapable of enduring the rigors of the later months of the winter, even when put upon the regular rations of alfalfa. In succeeding years stock losses have been immaterial, stockmen having learned from experience, dearly bought, that it is wise economy to open the feeding season early in the winter.

It has seldom occurred that feed for stock could not be obtained at a fair price, although the prevalence of unusual conditions has at rare intervals made stock feeding somewhat expensive. This was the case in the winter of 1898-99.

In Malheur county alfalfa hay has always found a ready market at four dollars per ton in the stack. It has never sold for less, but has frequently brought much more. The condition of the ranges and the number of stock to be wintered has invariably regulated the price of forage. During the fall and winter of 1898 especially high prices prevailed for all kinds of stock feed. Alfalfa brought one dollar more than usual in the stack, and before the grass on the ranges was ready for the herds in the spring it sold as high as eight and nine dollars per ton in the bale. The summer of 1898 was exceptionally hot, and the ranges were practically dried out by the middle of August. The hay crop was short in comparison with that of former years and these conditions naturally operated in favor of the hay producers, who reaped a rich harvest from their alfalfa fields.

In anticipation of a hard winter and in consideration of the prevailing high price of hay, farmers and stockmen sold a great many cattle and horses. They were further influenced in these sales by the excellent prices offered in the stock market. For cattle buyers paid $18 and $20 for yearlings, $26 for two-year-olds and $33 for three-year-olds. Horses also sold comparatively well, and taking the season

34

through, both the stockmen and the hay producers received excellent returns from their investments.

As was the case in all other stock sections of eastern Oregon in 1899, a great deal of feeling was manifested concerning the proposal of the government to lease to stock raising companies extensive ranges for their exclusive use. As elsewhere, it was a matter of vital importance to ranch and stockmen in Malheur county, most of the range plains and hills still belonging to the government. On October 8th, of this year, a mass meeting of stock and ranchmen was held at Vale for the purpose of formulating a protest against the proposed legislation of Congress. Resolutions condemning such legislation were drawn up and passed. Petitions were also formulated and afterward circulated throughout the voting precincts of the county. The resolutions passed at this meeting were given publicity, and, with the petitions, numerously signed, were forwarded to the proper representatives at Washington. These, with the petitions and resolutions that went forward almost simultaneously from all over eastern Oregon, evidently had the proper effect on the national legislators, and the scheme to build up the larger at the expense of the smaller stock interests was justly defeated.

That the people of Malheur county are patriotic and ever ready to unite on any national or international question that affects their relations to existing governmental institutions was evidenced during the Spanish troubles of 1898. While no special organizations were sent from the county down to the firing line, quite a number of her citizens went to the front and served faithfully while the war lasted. Throughout the county sentiment ran high and nowhere were heard stronger expressions of devotion to flag and country than among the settlers on the plains and in the mining camps of Malheur.

The last six years have witnessed a wonderful increase in population in Malheur county. On good authority we are informed that in 1897, when the population was about 6,000, not fifty foreigners were permanent residents of the county. In this particular a decided change has taken place. During the spring and summer of 1898 the population of the county increased rapidly. Settlers of nearly every nationality, and from all points of the compass traversed the plains and valleys in search of homes. Nearly all came with more or less capital and many with abundant resources. They have proven themselves a very desirable class of citizens. Some bought farms, others bought stock, and a few rented farm lands. All have since been busily and energetically engaged in building for themselves and families permanent homes. They have cleared away large areas of sage brush, set out orchards of fruit and groves of shade trees, planted shrubbery and flowers, built neat and commodious farm houses, and in many other ways added to the beauty and value of their holdings. By their investments and labor the value of farm lands the county over has been greatly enhanced. The immigration of 1898 was not all foreign, but to the foreigners who came, as well as to the native born Americans, is Malheur indebted for the progress and general improvement of conditions that have followed their coming.

The history of Malheur county is unusually free from records of lawlessness. In all border settlements are to be found lawless characters, and records of bank and stage robberies, murders and similar crimes form a part of the history of nearly all new communities. In the earlier years of its settlement Indian raids were of frequent occurrence, but since the Piutes and Bannocks were subdued crimes have been exceptionally few.

In July, 1895, robbers broke into the store of Hope Brothers, at Vale, blew open the safe and secured $1,300 in cash. Efforts to trace and capture the criminals were ineffectual.

Suspicion pointed to certain individuals of lawless propensities, but evidence sufficient to warrant their arrest and trial was unobtainable. The pursuit at last ceased and the matter was allowed to drop.

About ten o'clock Friday evening, December 30, 1898, a masked man entered the store of Scott & Skelton, of Westfall. Exhibiting a revolver, he demanded the postoffice money of John Skelton, who was postmaster, and who was alone in the store. When informed and convinced that this money had been sent to the postmaster at Boise by the last stage, he ordered Mr. Skelton to open the store safe, which was done. Here he secured $70, unintentionally allowing a twenty-dollar gold piece to remain in the cash drawer. The robber, having marched Mr. Skelton out of the store, mounted his horse and fled. The alarm was at once given and William Hart started in pursuit. He overtook the criminal after a furious ride of about three miles and engaged him in a pistol duel. No harm resulted to either from the exchange of shots, but in the excitement of the chase the robber dropped a mitten containing $55 of the stolen money. By practicing a little deception while the robber was in the store Mr. Skelton succeeded in saving $700 of the firm's money which was stored in another place in the safe. For this crime no one was ever apprehended.

In August of the following year a robbery was attempted at Jordan Valley. The affair was managed by a woman living near Jordan Valley and known as "Calamity Jane." She owned a stock ranch and was fairly well-to-do. "Calamity Jane" owed the firm of Blackaby & Parks the sum of $450. August 3, 1899, she drove in from her ranch a small bunch of cattle and disposed of them to a local buyer. She received a check for the sum due her, which, instead of taking to the parties to whom she was indebted, she cashed at another place. She then appeared at the store of her creditors and paid her indebtedness in bills. While in the store she conducted herself in a peculiar and unusual manner, and her actions at last aroused the suspicions of Messrs. Blackaby and Park. When evening came they concealed armed men in various positions in and about the store and awaited developments. About nine o'clock Joseph Lawton, a notorious character who had for some time made Jordan Valley his headquarters, and a man named Jensen entered the store. Lawton was in the lead, and he at once opened fire on the clerk. The concealed watchmen immediately brought their guns into action and Lawton fell dead before he had time to fire a second shot at the clerk. Jensen attempted to escape and ran out of the store. In the doorway he was met by one of the outside watch, at whom he discharged his revolver. The shot fortunately did not take effect and the watchman in turn emptied his shot gun at the fleeing robber. Although badly wounded, Jensen effected his escape. Shortly afterward, however, he was captured and punished. Evidence was not strong enough to convict "Calamity Jane" of instigating the crime and she escaped punishment.

The only attempt at stage robbery in Malheur county of which there is any record was made Saturday night, September 29, 1900. The Ontario-Burns stage had just left the Fopian ranch en route for Burns when from the darkness a shot was fired across the road in front of the horses. At the word of command from the highwayman the driver drew rein and threw out all the mail sacks. There was one passenger on board, but he was not molested. When the mail sacks were thrown out the driver was ordered to go ahead. It was about five hours' drive to the first settlement. There the hold-up was reported and pursuit of the highwayman organized. He was never captured and his identity was never established. He obtained nothing of consequence from the mail sacks, there being but one registered package, containing merchandise.

On the night of August 8, 1902, six unknown parties raided a settlement of Chinese miners at Mormon Basin in the northern part of the county. Thirteen dwellings, one storehouse, two cellars, one barn, one slaughter house and one wood house were burned. Other depredations were committed and the Chinamen driven out of the settlement. Information of the outrage was communicated to the Chinese embassy at Washington. The embassy filed a formal complaint with the government and the department of state at once took the matter up with Governor Geer. Through a misunderstanding concerning the location of the attack, the district attorney at Baker City was instructed to proceed in the matter and to take such action as the facts in the case warranted. When it was learned that the crime was not committed in Baker, but in Malheur county, instructions were at once issued by the governor to District Attorney William Miller, of Ontario, to commence investigations and to proceed against the criminals. The following letter from Mr. Miller, addressed to Governor Geer, explains the situation at the present writing and shows the attitude taken by the authorities of Malheur county toward the criminals:

"Ontario, Oregon, Sept. 2.—Dear Sir:— Last evening Thomas B. Littig, accompanied by one Charley Wing, a Chinaman, called on me and made formal complaint against six parties, whose names are unknown, charging them with the crime of arson in the burning of thirteen dwellings, one storehouse, two cellars, one barn, one slaughter house and one woodhouse, on the night of August 8th, last, at what is known as Mormon Basin, a mining camp in Malheur county, state of Oregon. I have drawn up three separate informations or affidavits and filed same with G. L. King, justice of the peace for this district, and warrants have been issued for the arrest of the guilty parties. I assure you that the authorities here will do all in their power to ascertain who the parties are, and if possible place them under arrest. Mr.

Littig informs me that it will require some detective work to secure evidence, but this can be done."

When this village was destroyed and the occupants driven out the Chinamen were engaged in working the Mormon Basin mines on shares for the owners. Thus far it has been impossible to learn the real object of the raid, and the names of the perpetrators of the act are still unknown.

Malheur county has a past history the important events of which we have attempted to chronicle. But she has a future history of far greater moment to make. The conditions are most favorable for rapid progress and high achievement. There is room on her hills and plains and in her valleys for half a million of prosperous people. There is wealth untold in her soil and in her metal mountains that will yield readily to patient industry. Men and women of moral and intellectual strength have acquainted themselves with her possibilities, have been identified with her past and will identify themselves with her future. When the miner and manufacturer, the capitalist, the husbandman and the stockman shall have expended their best efforts in the development of her wonderful resources, Malheur county will attain an intellectual, a financial and a political greatness the equal of any commonwealth in the great northwest. Indications point to an early realization of these predictions.

CHAPTER II.

POLITICAL.

Until the winter of 1887 the thousands of square miles now embraced in Malheur county constituted the southern portion of Baker county. At that session of the legislature this county was created, and on February 17th, 1887, Governor Pennoyer approved the act. Under the provisions of that act the governor was empowered to appoint the required corps of county officers, who were to hold office until the general election to be held in 1888. Governor Pennoyer appointed the following citizens the first officers of Malheur county: F. K. Froman, county judge; John F. Lackey and C. T. Locey, county commissioners; E. H. Test, county clerk; Henry C. Murray, sheriff; L. A. Sevey, county treasurer; William Richie, assessor; W. G. Thomson, superintendent of schools; E. L. Bradley, surveyor.

The county court held its first meeting on Thursday, April 7, 1887, at Vale, the temporary county seat, the full court being present. The first business transacted, after the officers had been sworn in, was the passage of a resolution authorizing the county clerk to correspond with some firm regarding the construction of a county jail, the Baker county jail to be used meanwhile. Then the matter of a court house was taken up and bids were solicited for furnishing a building suitable for a court house, said building to be situated at Vale.

At the regular meeting of the court, May 2nd, the following road districts and election precincts were created, the boundaries of precinct and district being identical: Ontario, Vale, Stone, Mormon Basin, Malheur, Carlisle,

Castle Rock, Bully, Three Forks and Jordan Valley. At this session bids were received and accepted for the erection of a jail to cost $4,500 and a vault to cost $125. No bids having been received for furnishing a court house, the county judge and the clerk were instructed to contract for the erection of a court house, which was completed that summer, L. B. Rinehart donating the site. This building cost $1,400.

Robert Boswell was appointed stock inspector for this county at the July term of court, and at this term the first county road was ordered and subsequently accepted. This road was built along the Malheur river between the county bridge at Vale and the Tom Glenn ford, several miles up the river. In October the court levied a county tax of 22 mills, the rate deemed necessary to raise $21,186, the amount estimated as required to pay the first year's expenses in the new county. A school tax of 5 mills was also levied.

The first term of circuit court held in the newly created county was convened by Judge L. B. Ison, at Vale, June 27th. Morton D. Clifford was present as district attorney and A. Sicord served the court as bailiff. Principally for the sake of preserving a partial list of those who were in the county at the time, we herewith present the first panel of jurors drawn in the county: W. G. Pennington, G. W. Pierce, W. L. Logan, Joseph A. Madden, Isaac McCumsey, H. F. Norton, George W. Brumm, J. D. Locey, W. C. Johnson, F. P. Smith, M. Crisman, Charles Becker, J. B. McLaughlin, J. L. Yantis, J. G. Lamberton, H. M. Plummer, John McMahon, William Shelby, L. Faulkner, W. L. Boston, J. S. Hunter, James Lynn, A. S. Moss, Emory Cale and William J. Kane. The first grand jury was constituted as follows: J. S. Hunter, foreman; W. L. Logan, Charles Becker, William Shelby, M. Crisman, W. G. Pennington and Isaac McCumsey.

The grand jury brought in five true bills in all, only one of which was disposed of,

that of the state vs. Marquis Stewart, indicted jointly with Frederick Yangen for horse stealing. Stewart pleaded guilty and was sentenced to a three years' term in the penitentiary. Court was in session five days.

As before stated, until 1887 Malheur county was a part of Baker county. Therefore its political history up to that time is identical with that of the latter named county and will be found in that chapter. The first election held in this county took place November 8, 1887, and was a special one, several amendments to the state constitution being voted upon. In Malheur county the prohibition amendment received 149 affirmative and 226 negative votes; that relating to the salaries of state officers received 105 affirmative and 242 negative votes; that relating to changing the time of holding the general elections, 290 affirmative and 57 negative votes.

Of course the permanent location of the county seat was the all absorbing issue at the first general election, held June 4, 1888. There were several strong contestants for the honor, Vale, Jordan Valley, Ontario, Paris (a town site laid out by enterprising ranchmen on the upper Malheur river), Grove City (another embryo town recently surveyed) and Baxterville (likewise a point selected by an ambitious settlement). However, the prize fell to Vale by the following vote: Vale, 215; Jordan Valley, 202; Ontario, 163; Paris, 146; Grove City, 30; Baxterville, 2.

From a party standpoint the first election resulted in an overwheming Democratic victory, as will be seen from the following vote taken from the official records: For congressman, Binger Hermann, Republican, 387, John M. Gearin, Democrat, 396, G. M. Miller, Prohibitionist, 3; supreme judge, John Burnett, Democrat, 407, W. P. Lord, Republican, 377; circuit judge, W. M. Ramsey, Democrat, 417, J. A. Fee, Republican, 362; district attorney, T. H. Crawford, Democrat, 445, J. L. Rand, Republican, 334; representative to the legislature,

H. P. Napton, Democrat, 401, I. H. Holland, Republican, 366; sheriff, H. C. Murray, Democrat, 351, C. E. Boswell, Republican, 256, Thomas Dryden, Independent, 162; clerk, E. H. Test, Democrat, 489, J. M. Harbour, Republican, 283; commissioners, Conrad Ryan and J. C. Skelton, Democrats, 678 and 418, respectively, C. T. Locey and W. G. Pennington, Republicans, 395 and 114, respectively; county judge, J. T. Clement, Democrat, 419, A. W. Kime, Republican, 347; treasurer, L. A. Sevey, Democrat, 478, A. J. Newman, Republican, 259; assessor, W. S. Lawrence, Democrat, 391, T. W. Halliday, Republican, 377; superintendent of schools, Frank Moore, Republican, 411, William Gribble, Democrat, 359; surveyor, Henry Hedges, Democrat, 4—, John E. Johnson, Republican, 360; coroner, Larry Faulkner, Democrat, 414, J. H. Kime, Republican, 357.

At the November election the Republican candidate for President received 330 votes, the Democratic candidate 303 and the Prohibitionist candidate 14.

By the terms of the creating act, unless one town received a majority of all the votes cast for the county seat at the first election, the two receiving the highest number should again be candidates for the honor at the second general election, or that of 1890. So at the June election of 1890 Vale and Jordan Valley again came before the voters as aspirants for the county seat, the former winning by an overwhelming majority, the vote being as follows: Vale, 459; Jordan Valley, 138. This settled the county seat question, as the legislature has never granted the county another opportunity to again vote on this matter.

The official vote for Malheur county at this election follows: For governor, H. S. Pennoyer, Democrat, 362, Thompson, Republican, 337; secretary of state, W. M. Townsend, Democrat, 358, G. W. McBride, Republican, 343; state treasurer, G. W. Webb, Democrat, 356, Philip Metschan, Republican, 343; su-

perintendent of public instruction, A. Leroy, Democrat, 352, E. B. McElroy, Republican, 351; state printer, John O'Brien, Democrat, 361, F. C. Baker, Republican, 342; supreme judge, B. F. Bonham, Democrat, 364, R. S. Bean, Republican, 339; circuit judge, sixth judicial district, M. D. Clifford, Democrat, 364, Robert Eakin, Republican, 331; district attorney, Charles F. Hyde, Democrat, 362, John L. Rand, Republican, 329; congressman, R. A. Miller, Democrat, 355, Binger Hermann, Republican, 348; joint state senator, Dodson, Republican, 354, Chandler, Democrat, 340; state representative, Thomas B. Littig, Republican, 384, Henry Elms, Democrat, 299; sheriff, J. N. Fell, Democrat, 390, L. Cole, Republican, 298; clerk, E. H. Test, Democrat, 430, J. S. Edwards, Republican, 258; assessor, W. C. Carleton, Republican, 377, R. W. Worsham, Democrat, 310; treasurer, J. W. Sevey, Democrat, 346, A. W. Kime, Republican, 340; commissioners, William Cowgill, Republican, 403, A. W. Turner, Democrat, 282; superintendent of schools, J. D. Denman, Republican, 371, William Thomson, Democrat, 319; surveyor, John E. Johnson, Republican, 348, John R. Johnson, Democrat, 324; coroner, no vote recorded.

Although the Populists appeared strong in numbers throughout eastern Oregon in 1892, for some reason they did not become strong enough in this county to nominate a ticket until two years later. As between the Democrat and Republican parties, the county election of 1892 was about evenly divided.

The vote in Malheur county follows: For congressman, J. H. Slater, Democrat, 295, W. R. Ellis, Republican, 240, J. C. Lude, Populist, 54, C. J. Bright, Prohibitionist, 30; supreme judge, A. S. Bennett, Democrat, 297, F. A. Moore, Republican, 257, W. H. Walker, Populist, 43, B. I. Welch, Prohibitionist, 25; attorney general, G. E. Chamberlain, Democrat, 331, L. R. Webster, Republican, 304; circuit judge, M. D. Clifford, Democrat, 325, Harrison Kelley, Republican, 265, William Green, Populist, 33; district attorney, C. F. Hyde, Democrat, 319, C. H. Finn, Republican, 259, G. Griffin, Populist, 40; member state board of equalization, W. G. Hunter, Democrat, 320, William Morfitt, Republican, 308; state representative, W. R. King, Democrat, 370, T. B. Littig, Republican, 257; sheriff, J. N. Fell, Democrat, 571, seven scattering votes; clerk, E. H. Test, Democrat, 365, S. L. Payne, Republican, 270; county judge, C. H. Brown, Republican, 322, H. C. Murray, Democrat, 313; commissioner, Webb Anderston, Republican, 341, M. W. Hart, Democrat, 293; treasurer, A. W. Kime, Republican, 394, J. W. Sevey, Democrat, 237; assessor, C. W. Platt, Republican, 332, L. B. Boyle, Democrat, 299; superintendent of schools, J. D. Denman, Republican, 394, W. C. Hoseason, Democrat, 240; surveyor, L. A. Pickler, Democrat, 539, no opposition; coroner, Dr. G. A. Pogue, 120, James Mahan, 42, several scattering.

In November Harrison received 246 votes, Cleveland 265, Weaver 95 and the Prohibition candidate for President 19.

The official returns for the election held June 4, 1894, follow:

For governor, W. P. Lord, Republican, 313, William Galloway, Democrat, 241, Nathan Pierce, Populist, 238, James Kennedy, Prohibitionist, 17; secretary of state, H. R. Kincaid, Republican, 323, Charles Nickell, Democrat, 234, Ira Wakefield, Populist, 230, F. M. Kercher, Prohibitionist, 14; state treasurer, Phil Metschan, Republican, 323, T. L. Davidson, Democrat, 239, R. P. Caldwell, Populist, 220; Isaac N. Richardson, Prohibitionist, 18; superintendent of public instruction, G. M. Irwin, Republican, 298, D. V. S. Reid, Democrat, 252, T. C. Jory, Populist, 208, Helen M. Harford, Prohibitionist, 24; state printer, W. H. Leeds, Republican, 314, John O'Brien, Democrat, 232, George M. Orton, Populist, 225, James H. McKibben, Prohibitionist, 16; supreme judge, Charles E. Wolver-

ton, Republican, 316, A. S. Bennett, Democrat, 253, R. P. Boise, Populist, 219, T. P. Hackleman, Prohibitionist, 17; attorney general, C. M. Idleman, Republican, 303, M. L. Olmstead, Populist, 233, W. H. Holmes, Democrat, 226, C. J. Bright, Prohibitionist, 20; circuit judge, James A. Fee, Republican, 555, J. N. Hudson, Populist, 211; district attorney, John L. Rand, Republican, 337; J. M. Corrall, Democrat, 212, William Parsons, Populist, 197; joint senator, Baker and Malheur counties, Will R. King, Populist, 434, C. A. Johns, Republican, 321; Representative, I. W. Hope, Republican, 386, R. A. Lockett, Democrat, 374; congressman, W. R. Ellis, Republican, 321, James H. Raley, Democrat, 245, Joseph Waldrop, Populist, 210, A. F. Miller, Prohibitionist, 15; sheriff, T. W. Halliday, Republican, 306, James M. Duncan, Democrat, 298, W. S. Lawrence, Populist, 183; clerk, C. W. Platt, Republican, 342, B. L. Milligan, Democrat, 294, J. C. Skelton, Populist, 150; commissioner, Dennis Dyer, Republican, 331, G. B. Glover, Democrat, 241, Joseph Whiteley, Populist, 209; assessor, F. G. Wilson, Republican, 290, C. T. Yantis, Democrat, 241, W. G. Pogue, Populist, 238; treasurer, James Weaver, Republican, 371, J. W. Sevey, Democrat, 224, E. F. Allen, Populist, 177; superintendent of schools, Susie W. Moore, Republican, 320, Mrs. R. G. Wheeler, Populist, 252, Theresa Keenan, Democrat, 199; surveyor, L. A. Pickler, Democrat, 635, no opposition; coroner, Benjamin McDonald, Populist, 407, James Mahan, Democrat, 221.

The now famous campaign of 1896 was fully as exciting in Malheur county as in other portions of eastern Oregon and the country generally. Curiously enough, however, while the Republicans were given the largest vote at the June election and succeeded in electing nearly all their candidates for county offices, at the presidential election Bryan received more than twice the number of votes McKinley did, or 654 votes to McKinley's 312. Each of the three parties had tickets in the county field, but without going into details we present the vote as cast: For congressman, W. R. Ellis, Republican, 310, Martin Quinn, Populist, 260, A. S. Bennett, Democrat, 230, H. H. Northrup, Independent Republican, 61, F. McKercher, Prohibitionist, 18; supreme judge, R. S. Bean, Republican, 344, Joseph Gaston, Populist, 278, John Burnett, Democrat, 217; district attorney, ninth judicial district, C. W. Parrish, Republican, 390, O. F. Buse, Populist, 236, C. A. Sweek, Democrat, 223, M. Dustin, Independent, 34; member state board of equalization, I. H. Holland, Republican, 422, G. W. Pierce, Populist, 392; state representative, I. W. Hope, Republican, 441, M. N. Fegtly, Populist, 387; county judge, J. G. Lamberson, Populist, 351, B. C. Richardson, Democrat, 345, C. H. Brown, Republican, 196; sheriff, Charles E. Boswell, Republican, 310, J. N. Fell, Democrat, 293, J. D. Locey, Populist, 295; clerk, C. W. Platt, Republican, 422, E. C. Bunch, Democrat 313, W. C. Carleton, Populist, 162; commissioner, James Morfitt, Republican, 424, Sidney Knight, Democrat, 289, G. J. Gray, Populist, 81; treasurer, J. M. Weaver, Republican, 407, J. W. Sevey, Democrat, 266, John Doran, Populist, 198; assessor, A. G. King, Democrat, 321, John Ward, Republican, 303, J. Henry Wilson, Populist, 251; superintendent of schools, F. J. Stanton, Republican, 340, W. J. Calloway, Democrat, 268, William Lemon, Populist, 260; surveyor, J. S. Millikin, Populist, 389, L. A. Pickler, Democrat, 356; coroner, F. K. Froman, Democrat, 365, R. N. Linebarger, Populist, 348.

As is well known, Malheur county furnished the Fusionists with their candidate for governor in 1898, and this may account to some extent for the failure of a single Republican candidate, with the exception of two, Dr. H. T. Hoople, candidate for coroner, and William Miller, candidate for district attorney, to receive a majority of votes cast for any office. Mr. King resides at Ontario, where he enjoys a lucrative law practice. The Democrats and Populists joined their forces in this county as well as in the state.

The vote cast in this county was: For governor, Will R. King, Fusionist, 555, T. T. Geer, Republican, 387, J. C. Luce, Populist, 27, H. M. Clinton, Prohibitionist, 25; secretary of state, H. R. Kincaid, Fusionist, 497, F. I. Dunbar, Republican, 405, Ira Wakefield, Populist, 39, H. C. Davis, Prohibitionist, 28; state treasurer, J. O. Booth, Fusionist, 476, C. S. Moore, Republican, 405, J. K. Sears, Populist, 60, Moses Votaw, Prohibitionist, 19; superintendent of public instruction, H. S. Lyman, Fusionist, 473, J. H. Ackerman, Republican, 408, J. E. Hosmer, Populist, 59, B. E. Emerick, Prohibitionist, 24; state printer, C. A. Fitch, Fusionist, 449, W. H. Leeds, Republican, 376, D. L. Grace, Populist, 53, T. S. McDaniel, Prohibitionist, 19; supreme judge, W. M. Ramsey, Fusionist, 481, Frank A. Moore, Republican, 381, T. P. Hackleman, Prohibitionist, 28; attorney general, J. L. Story, Fusionist, 480, D. R. N. Blackburn, Republican, 389, C. G. Bright, Prohibitionist, 25; congressman, C. N. Donaldson, Fusionist, 482, M. A. Moody, Republican, 392, H. E. Courtney, Populist, 54, G. W. Ingalls, Prohibitionist, 25; representative, J. R. Blackaby, Fusionist, 528, W. A. Sisson, Republican, 343, G. L. King, Silver Republican, 61; circuit judge, ninth district, M. D. Clifford, Fusionist, 548, C. W. Parrish, Republican, 376, Thornton Williams, Independent, 13; district attorney, William Miller, Republican, 458, Errett Hicks, Fusionist, 421; member state board of equalization, J. R. Gregg, Fusionist, 492, William Hall, Republican, 374; joint senator with Baker county, William Smith, Fusionist, 526, J. H. Aitkin, Republican, 402; sheriff, Julian D. Locey, Fusionist, 517, Charles E. Boswell, Republican, 427; clerk, Almer G. King, Fusionist, 498, C. W. Platt, Republican, 345, J. W. Haworth, Silver Republican, 102; treasurer, E. R. Murray, Democrat, 441, James M. Weaver, Republican, 438, T. F. Olk, Silver Republican, 103;

commissioner, G. W. Blanton, Fusionist, 447, R. H. Hart, Republican, 424; assessor, J. H. Wilson, Fusionist, 438, S. L. Payne, Republican, 438; superintendent of schools, B. S. Milligan, Fusionist, 470, F. J. Stanton, Republican, 420; surveyor, J. S. Millikin, Fusionist, 558; coroner, H. T. Hoople, Republican, 486, John Doran, Fusionist, 376. The tie vote between Payne and Wilson was decided by drawing slips from an envelope, according to the law provided for the adjustment of such cases. Dame Fortune smiled upon Mr. Wilson as the lucky candidate.

During the interim between the campaigns of 1898 and 1900 political sentiment in Malheur county, which was growing very rapidly during that period, experienced a decisive change. Whereas in 1898 the Fusionists were in control, in 1900 the Republicans were generally victorious and at the presidential election in November Bryan received only three votes more than McKinley, the figures being, Bryan, 481, McKinley 478.

The vote in Malheur county follows: For representative, Harney and Malheur counties jointly, I. S. Geer, Republican, 472, W. D. Baker, Fusionist, 363, John L. Sitz, Independent, 73; congressman, M. A. Moody, Republican, 400, William Smith, Fusionist, 344, J. E. Simmons, Populist, 101, Leslie Butler, Prohibitionist, 38; supreme judge, C. E. Wolverton, Republican, 427, Thomas G. Greene, Fusionist, 410, C. J. Bright, Prohibitionist, 46; food commissioner, J. W. Bailey, Republican, 375, W. Schulmerich, Fusionist, 364, P. S. Kenady, Prohibitionist, 42; county judge, J. F. Stevens, Republican, 493, J. G. Lamberson, Fusionist, 428; sheriff, J. D. Locey, Fusionist, 646, J. A. Newton, Republican, 296; clerk, A. G. King, Fusionist, 569, S. L. Payne, Republican, 364; treasurer, J. C. Kelley, Republican, 525, William Plughoff, Fusionist, 406; assessor, W. H. Pullen, Republican, 498, M. N. Fegtly, Fusionist, 390; commissioner, T. A. Barton, Republican, 449, James G. Gartin, Fusionist, 441;

superintendent of schools, B. L. Milligan, Fusionist, 662, no opposition; surveyor, J. S. Millikin, Fusionist, 614, no opposition; coroner, H. T. Hoople, Republican, 652, no opposition.

The last campaign is too recent to require any resumé of party platforms. With the campaign of 1900 the Populist party went out of existence after its meteoric career, though traces of its belief are to be found in the platforms of both the old parties. It would be impossible to say truthfully whether the dominant political party in this county at the present time is Republican or Democratic, so evenly is the populace divided. As in all new counties the struggle for supremacy between the leading towns has entered greatly into the political activities here and has more than once resulted in bitter factional contests between members of the same party.

The official vote at the election of 1902 was as follows: For governor, George E. Chamberlain, Democrat, 549, W. J. Furnish, Republican, 543, A. J. Hunsaker, Prohibitionist, 20, R. R. Ryan, Socialist, 18; secretary of state, F. I. Dunbar, Republican, 564, D. W. Sears, Democrat, 474, C. W. Barzee, Socialist, 37, N. A. Davis, Prohibitionist, 35; state treasurer, Charles Moore, Republican, 552, Henry Blackman, Democrat, 477, T. S. McDaniel, Prohibitionist, 36, W. W. Myers, Socialist, 28; superintendent of public instruction, J. H. Ackerman, Republican, 513, W. A. Wann, Democrat, 457, R. W. Kelsey, Prohibitionist, 31; attorney general, A. M. Crawford, Republican, 526, J. H. Raley, Democrat, 438, T. H. Goyne, Prohibitionist, 25; state printer, J. R. Whitney, Republican, 503, James E. Godfrey, Democrat, 428, W. W. Brooks, Prohibitionist, 31, J. E. Hosmer, Socialist, 22; member of Congress, J. N. Williamson, Republican, 600, W. F. Butcher, Democrat, 447, Dietrich T. Gerdes, Socialist, 24, F. R. Spaulding, Prohibitionist, 21; United States senator, T. T. Geer, Republican, 518, C. E. S. Woods, Democrat, 407; joint state senator with Baker county, John L. Rand, Republican, 561, William Smith, Democrat, 520; joint representative with Harney county, E. H. Test, Democrat, 600, Fred J. Palmer, Republican 511; sheriff, James E. Lawrence, Democrat, 625, A. L. Sproul, Republican, 484; clerk, W. G. Thomson, Democrat, 549, J. D. Fairman, Republican, 496; treasurer, J. C. Kelley, Republican, 673, H. B. Donahey, Democrat, 402; assessor, W. H. Pullen, Republican, 565, Thomas J. Goodyear, Democrat, 464, Z. G. Wilson, Populist, 79; commissioner, G. W. Blanton, Democrat, 489, Sanford Emison, Independent, 371, Cassius H. Brown, Republican, 254; surveyor, J. R. Evans, Republican, 576, John S. Millikin, Democrat, 499; coroner, H. T. Hoople, Republican, 542, R. O. Payne, Democrat, 500.

CHAPTER III.

SCHOOLS.

The establishment of schools in a stock raising community is usually a slow and difficult task. The reason for this condition of affairs is to be found, not in the apathy or indifference of these people in educational matters, for the love of knowledge is inherent in the whole American people, but rather in a lack of opportunity. Settlers in these regions are generally widely separated, often many miles apart, and because of this it is almost impossible to gather enough pupils to form a school. The difficulty in organizing schools in mining communities is also well known. Here the reason is not due to lack of population, but to the fact that there are usually few, if any, families in new mining camps and the nature of the work is so exciting and exhilarating that the finer things in life are relegated to the background for the time being in the rush for wealth.

As soon as such settlements as we have mentioned begin to grow and assume permanency, however, the little district school is established at the earliest possible opportunity, and from thence on the general progress of the community may be accurately judged by a reference to the condition of its educational institutions. Then, as settlement gradually continues and the industries become more staple, school houses dot the land and higher educational facilities are provided by the establishment of high schools, academies and colleges.

Malheur county was settled by the two classes of people heretofore named, miners and stockmen. The former settled the mining districts in the extreme northern portion of the county as early as 1862 and 1863; the latter turned the first stock loose over this range a few years afterward. Such was the sparseness of population and the slow growth of the region, however, that the first public school of which we have any authentic record was not opened until the year 1869. This district embraced all of that portion of Baker county lying south of Eldorado. William Morfitt was active in securing its formation, and served as clerk of the board for several years. The school house was a little frame building and stood in the old town of Eldorado. The first term was held in 1869 and was taught by Terry Tuttle, who it is interesting to note was the first superintendent of schools of Union county. Mr. Morfitt says this first term lasted three months. The next term was taught by a teacher named Ison. Mattie Smith and Belle Small were other teachers of this first school. Soon after the founding of Malheur City this district was abandoned and a new one created at the latter place, to which the Eldorado school was transferred. This, perhaps, accounts for the fact that there is no official record of this district on the books of the superintendent, the first school district being given there as the one known now as District No. 1.

This district embraced the settlement on Willow creek, and the school house stood about two miles south of where Dell is now situated. On the school records of Baker county it was known as district No. 12, and the date of its organization is given as January 25, 1875. William G. Thomson, the first superintendent of schools of Malheur county, and at present county clerk, taught this pioneer school.

"The school house was a small frame structure," he says, "rudely fitted up, and I had probably twenty-five scholars of all ages, sizes and dispositions. I guess we had in our little school every text book ever issued from the press, as I could not begin to name the different authors. Wilson's, McGuffey's and Towne's readers were among the books we used. I taught this school during the first term and held four months, for which the directors paid me $60 a month."

District No. 18, of Baker county, was organized December 10, 1877, on Sucker creek, and is now known as district No. 2, of Malheur county. The fourth district school to be established within the confines of this county was organized in Jordan Valley on January 3, 1878, and is now known as district No. 3. The records fail to give the dates of the organizing of Nos. 4 and 5, but this took place some time

between 1878 and 1881. These schools were situated on the Malheur river near Vale and at Ironside. District No. 6 was first known as No. 23, of Baker county, and was organized at Westfall in 1881. District No. 7 is now abandoned, having been consolidated with No. 24 and was organized March 10, 1882, in the settlement above Vale. Ontario was the next community to establish a school, this district coming into existence September 15, 1883, as district No. 30, of Baker county. Then district No. 32, now No. 9, was organized, being located in the extreme southern portion of the county. No. 10 is situated on Willow creek, near Dell, and the records give the date of its formation as March 5, 1885. No. 11 was organized at Beulah, December 20, 1885; Nos. 12 and 13, in 1886; and No. 14, January 20, 1887.

Thus we have traced briefly the history of the Malheur county schools up to the formation of the county in 1887. As will be seen, there were fourteen districts cut off from Baker county. William G. Thomson was appointed superintendent of schools by Governor Pennoyer and served in that capacity faithfully until the first general election, in 1886, when Frank Moore was elected to that position. It is to be regretted that the earliest detailed report of the county's schools to be found in the superintendent's office is for the year 1895. From a comparative table given in one of the late publications issued by the state superintendent's office, however, we learn that the enrollment in the Malheur schools in 1887 was 278, or an average of nearly twenty pupils to each district. In 1895 the fourteen districts had become twenty-three and there were over 1,000 persons of school age in the county, most of whom were enrolled.

In order that the growth of the schools during these early years may be the more easily traced we will give a summary of the report of Superintendent F. J. Stanton for the year ending in the spring of 1897. By this report we see that there were at that time 1,129 persons of school age in the county, of whom 756 were enrolled, 390 male and 366 female pupils. Thirty-one teachers were employed, twenty-two women and nine men, of whom nine held state certificates; seven, first grade; six second grade; and six, third grade. The men drew average salaries of $51, and the women eight dollars less. The average school year taught was four months. The value of school grounds and buildings in 1897 was $15,425; furniture, $2,778; and apparatus, $1,168. Four school houses were built during the year, costing in all $2,615, making a total of seventeen in the county. To maintain these schools required $9,998.54, of which $5,446 went to the teachers.

When the present superintendent, B. L. Milligan, assumed charge of the county's educational affairs in July, 1898, there were thirty-four numerical districts, or more than twice the number there were in 1887. Some of these, however, had been abandoned or consolidated, so that really there were not thirty-four active districts. During Mr. Milligan's occupancy of the office eight new districts have been created, making a total of forty-two, six of which do not maintain schools.

From Mr. Milligan's last report to the state superintendent, that for the year ending in March, 1902, we find there are 1,556 persons of school age in the county, 815 male and 741 female, and that of this number 1,061, or nearly seventy per cent., are enrolled as pupils. The average daily attendance for the past year has been 748. Forty-two teachers, twelve men and thirty women, are employed to teach in the thirty-six public schools maintained in the county, and that the standard of the teachers is high may be seen from the fact that of these forty-two teachers, twelve hold state certificates; nine first grade; six second grade; and five, third grade. Thirty of these teachers are enough interested in their work to be readers of educational journals, thereby keeping

abreast of the latest and best methods employed by the highest skilled teachers in the country. Two new school houses were built during the year, so that there are now thirty-two schoolhouses, in which an average term of six and a quarter months is taught. Besides these public schools there are four private ones, attended by thirty-two pupils. There are no parochial schools or private academies in the county.

Financially the county schools are in excellent condition, there being a balance of several thousand dollars in the treasury. The estimated value of school property is $23,000. Last year $23,600 were collected for school purposes and $15,752 expended, the teachers receiving $12,791 of this latter amount. Nine of the districts levied a special district tax averaging nine and one-sixth mills each.

Comfortable and commodious schoolhouses are ever a necessary adjunct to good schools, and in possessing both of these Malheur county is indeed fortunate. There is but one log schoolhouse in the county, that in district No. 9, on the Nevada state line, while Ontario now possesses an $11,000 brick building, and Vale one of the two stone schoolhouses in the state. Nyssa, Malheur City and Jordan Valley each have provided very comfortable buildings, which are soon to be enlarged.

At the present there is no county high school in the county, but there are two district high schools, one at Ontario and one at Vale, established during the past summer, while the school at Malheur City has been doing advanced grade work for some time. With these two regularly established high schools, this county is unusually well equipped for educational work and nothing augurs so well for a bright future of the county's schools and better illustrates the interest taken by citizens here in the work. The establishement of these higher institutions of learning means that the youth of this county need not go beyond their home for a higher education than that afforded by the public schools and is a strong inducement for the boys and girls to take up this advanced work.

Superintendent Milligan is an experienced and able teacher and to his deep personal interest in the schools and his energy and enthusiasm in building up the system, much credit is due for the present excellent standard maintained in this county. The schools must ever lead the van of progress and all that works for modern civilization.

CHAPTER IV.

MALHEUR'S BUSINESS CENTERS.

ONTARIO.

First impressions of the general character of a county or state are not infrequently formed through a more intimate acquaintance with its larger towns and cities. In a general way a knowledge of the climatic conditions which prevail in surrounding areas, the scenic features of the country, the character of its people, the nature and productiveness of the soil, is gained through intercourse with the merchants and professional men of the business centers. The restless spirit of man impels him to board the transcontinental fast express at some station in the overcrowded east. His thoughts have for a long time followed the "Star of Empire" in its westward course. He has gained some knowledge of the west and his ideas, although crude, are picturesque and fascinating. He believes that its climate, soil and business advantages will combine their greatest possibilities that he may quickly come into possession of a goodly inheritance, when he may rest from the more active efforts of life and enjoy its sweeter, better and more elevating gifts. The startling speed of the fast express is in harmony with his thoughts. His impatience brooks no delay and when at length the "valley-plains" of the Mississippi and the rough range of the Rockies have been left far to the eastward and he stands on the railroad platform of some western town which by pre-arrangement he has selected as his initial point of venture, there is no abatement of urgency. The areas of the west that are peculiarly adapted to the wants of the homeseeker are so vast in extent that but few men can undertake to familiarize themselves, by personal inspection, with the special features of more than a comparatively small division of the whole. The new arrival makes the village or town which marks the first stop in his long journey, his base of operations. He looks it over and is favorably or unfavorably impressed as the case may be. He meets the business and professional men in his quest for information and the locality gains or loses in his estimation as he is greeted cordially or with indifference. A town, though small, with neat homes, with attractive stores, and well kept streets, whose citizens in general and whose business and professional men in particular are cordial and companionable, appeals, as no other influence can, to the better class of people who come from from the eastern states in search of newer fields, better homes and more congenial surroundings. Under these influences the home seeker gains favorable impressions, his store of information grows rapidly, his interest heightens, his faith in the future of the country is established and in natural sequence he forms attachments which eventually result in its becoming his permanent abiding place.

In none of the business centers of southeastern Oregon will the travel-stained tourist who is seeking a western home, find more to interest and to please than at Ontario, the metropolis of Malheur county. One can only be favorably impressed with the general appearance of the town. Evidences of thrift and enterprise are on all sides. Its citizens are affable and enthusiastic in their devotion to local and surrounding interests. In 1900 there was a population of 445. In July, 1902, this had increased to about 700. All lines of business are well represented. Some of the most successful men in mercantile pursuits in eastern Oregon are located here and an enormous volume of business is yearly transacted over their counters and in their offices. In professional circles talented and capable men are found with a fund of interesting lore which is graciously imparted to the solicitous stranger. In social circles are entertainment and instruction of a very high order. A superior tone of moral sentiment is evidenced in the people one meets. The fraternal spirit permeates all circles. Insignia of numerous fraternal organizations are visible when one mingles with the populace at public functions. The following are the chartered lodge organizations having good membership rolls: Arcadia Lodge, No. 116, A. F. and A. M.; Ontario Lodge, No. 90, I. O. O. F.; Armour Lodge, No. 69, K. of P.; Alvin P. Ovry Post, No. 21, G. A. R.; Arcadia Camp, No. 364, W. of W.; Malheur Lodge, No. 97, A. O. U. W.; Beatrice Lodge, No. 82, Daughters of Rebekah; Star Chapter, No. 69, Eastern Star. There is also a Chapter of the Rathbone Sisters.

Ontario is also to be credited with an aggressive interest in religious progress and all who contemplate future residence in the city may feel assured of finding here advantages in this direction equal to those of a great many larger places. There is an organization of the Methodist Episcopal church, whose efficient pastor is Rev. John W. Harvey. This society occupies a commodious and comfortable house of worship, which was erected in 1897. It is pleasantly situated in the southern part of town and in size is 46 by 24 feet, with a lecture room whose dimensions are 24 by 16 feet. The Baptists are also organized. The Rev. Thomas Spight ministers to their spiritual desires. He is an earnest worker, a pleasing and forceful speaker. Under his care the church is growing and its influence has become one of the positive factors in establishing for the town a high moral standard. . The Baptists have not as yet erected a place of worship, but the building is one of the possibilities of the near future. They are at present using the Congregational church. This house was built a number of years ago, but at present the Congregationalists are without a pastor. The organization is kept up, however, and though not very strong at present, it will undoubtedly grow and maintain its present standing as one of the agencies whose mission is to elevate the moral sentiment of the community. The Adventists have quite a numerous following and have built a church edifice that is a credit to the town. To its church membership Ontario is very largely indebted for those influences which have proven so effective in attracting here the more intelligent and progressive class of home builders.

As is universally the case in pioneer settlements in America, the church has followed the school at Ontario. It is an interesting fact of history that in the gradual development of the country, from the Alleghany mountains to the Pacific coast, the first subject to secure the consideration of new communities is that of educational facilities. In 1894, six years before the city was incorporated, and when there were only about fifty persons of school age in the district of which the town formed a part, bonds to the amount of $5,000 (which was five per cent. of the taxable property of this district) were issued for the purpose of erecting a schoolhouse. In 1902 additional bonds aggregating $6,000 were issued and the school building was doubled in size. The structure is of brick and, standing on a commanding site west of the town's center, presents an imposing and enduring appearance. The building and furniture represent an investment of $12,500. The patrons of the district may surely be commended for their efforts in furthering the intellectual progress of the younger generation and the building is decidedly a credit to all, epitomizing, as it does, the advanced ideas and the progressive sentiment of the people. The district was formed in 1883, when Malheur was a portion of Baker county. At its organization in 1887, the entire school population of Malheur county was but 287. At the present time in this district alone there are 262 persons of school age. Great care has always been taken in selection of instructors to be placed in charge of the schools and to this wise precaution is due much of the success that has invariably attended their management. During the school year of 1902-03 Professor W. J. Peddicord will be in charge as principal. He will be assisted in the various grades by Miss Minnie Smith, Mrs. Retta Payne, Miss Emma J. Wade, and Miss Mary B. Locey. A movement is in progress looking to the establishment of a district high school, with every indication pointing to an early consummation of the people's intent. Such an institution will greatly enhance the educational advantages and when it is established, Ontario will become still more inviting as a fixed abiding place, from a homeseeker's point of view.

Co-essential with the public schools in all communities, as educational agencies and as factors in the general progress, are the newspapers. Of these there are two published at Ontario—the Ontario Argus, which is most ably edited by Don Carlos Boyd and Judge James T. Clement, and the Ontario Democrat, whose popular and competent editor is William R. King. The influence for good which is exercised by these publications, the effectual support contributed to all worthy movements of a public nature, the real benefits accruing to the city by reason of the good name they give it throughout the country, cannot well be estimated.

The men of energy and force of character who have brought to successful consummation all public enterprises, who have organized the fraternal orders, who have built the churches and who constitute the membership of the various religious organizations, who have made the schools what they are to-day, and who stand ever ready to give moral and material support to any measure promising the general advancement of the people's interests, are found in all the walks of the city's life; in the shop and in the store, in the counting room, in the bank, in the office of the merchant and that of the professional man, where intelligence, integrity, enterprise, mental and physical activity are absolute essentials. Beside the clergymen already mentioned, the roll of professional men includes the names of William Miller, William R. King, W. E. Lees, John Michel and A. W. Soliss, attorneys at law; G. A. Pogue and Rolla O. Payne, physicians and surgeons; M. Pefferle, dentist. A real estate agency is maintained by W. E. Lees, an insurance and real estate agency by J. J. Cortright. Other real estate firms are those of Kennedy and Millikin, and Butler and Lackey. G. L. King is agent for several insurance companies; he is also the agent of the Burns-Ontario stage line, which operates daily stages between these two points by way of Vale, Westfall and Drewsey, carrying mail, passengers and express. The line is owned and operated by S. S. Williams. Two telephone lines afford easy communication with all points. The Malheur Company's lines run from Ontario to Westfall, while the Bell Telephone Company's long distance lines bring the remote cities and towns within call. Mrs. J. E. Olliver manages the central offices of both lines. Two east bound and two west bound passenger, mail and express trains, stop at Ontario each day on the Oregon Short Line railroad. The numerous connections which this line makes with other roads render the town easily accessible from all parts of the country. E. P. Shaw has charge of the company's affairs at this point, having been installed as agent January 1, 1902. There are two ferryboats operated on Snake river; one south and one east of town, each about one and one-half miles distant from the business center. All mails are handled by A. L. Sproul, postmaster. A very considerable amount of matter passes through this office and the business of the office is on the increase, as will be learned by reference to Mr. Sproul's comparative statement issued February 13, 1901. The receipts for the year 1894 footed $618.75, while those for 1900 were $1,634.71, showing a gain of $1,015.96 in annual receipts after a lapse of six years.

The Ontario hotel is conducted by Frank Smith and Mrs. Etta Stephenson. This is an imposing and modern structure with thirty rooms besides a large parlor, dining room, office and billiard room. It is a much larger hotel than is usually found in towns of this size and is one of its live institutions, adding much to the substantial appearance of the city. The Brown hotel is managed by Thomas Fiser. There is also a handsome two-story brick rooming house owned by J. M. Brown. The accommodations afforded by these houses are excellent and the traveling public has only words of praise for the management. A Chinaman named Jim Roaa conducts a restaurant and is well patronized. Hung Chung is a Chinese laundryman. Mrs. Mary Lackey has a confec-

tionery and bakery. Confections are also sold by J. J. Cortright and at the Ontario confectionery, owned by F. M. Gibler, who has, in addition, a large stock of notions. In other lines there is a photograph studio, where excellent work is done by J. P. Kidd; R. Bolan is a scenic painter and taxidermist; John Babcock and J. A. Draper are contractors and builders; John Landingham is proprietor of the Ontario Transfer line; Noe and Utley, and D. T. Wilkerson have neat barber shops; house painting and paper hanging are done by Robert Turner; he also carries a stock of wall paper.

The Oregon Forwarding Company, of which Fred J. Keisel is president and E. A. Rieger is manager, handles general merchandise and implements. It has four warehouses and its business transactions amount to $150,000 annually. In 1900 it handled 1,500,000 pounds of wool. E. A. Fraser and H. T. Husted, of the Malheur Mercantile Company, handle general merchandise and farming implements, E. A. Fraser is manager of the company. Boyer Brothers & Company handle general merchandise. Griffin and Staples are clothing merchants. The Ontario pharmacy is conducted by Snyder and Newman. The R. J. Stone Drug Company was established in 1901. The Cash Racket store, conducted by George H. Shearer, contains a large assortment of notions. F. M. Gibler is also a notion dealer. There is a furniture store owned and managed by A. Zimmerman. Lumber yards are owned by L. Adam and by J. M. Babcock. James Farley runs the Ontario stables and Carter and Johnson are also doing a good livery business. Harness and saddles are sold by William Shelby; jewelry by W. E. Loomis; meats by C. E. Belding; coal by Madden Brothers; George W. Lyells & Son, I. H. Moore and George Chambers are blacksmiths. Two millinery establishments have been opened, one by Miss Carrie Newman, and the other—the Chicago Millinery parlors—by Simpson and Westrope. Brick are manufactured by David Wilson, whose yard is one and a half miles east of town, and by William R. Shimp, who is located one and one-half miles to the northeast.

The Bank of Ontario was established in 1899. Its capital stock is $40,000. June 10, 1901, its undivided profits were $2,159.93 and deposits, $107,106.75. Stephen Carver was the founder of this bank and is now president. J. R. Blackaby is vice president and C. W. Platt, cashier. Directors are J. L. Cole, L. Adam, Robert Van Gilse, T. J. Brosnan. The volume of business transacted by this institution is clearly indicated by the figures quoted above. The bank enjoys the confidence of the people and has a promising future.

The First National Bank was established June 6, 1901. The capital stock is $25,000. July 16, 1902, the undivided profits were $501.28; deposits, $181,165.25. During the first three days of its existence over $30,000 were received on deposit. The officers of the bank are as follows: John D. Daly, president; M. Alexander, vice-president; E. H. Test, cashier; E. M. Clark, assistant cashier. Stockholders are John D. Daly, M. Alexander, E. H. Test, N. U. Carpenter, William Jones, Abner Robbins's estate, William Miller, Frank R. Coffin, B. F. Olden, Thomas Turnbull. Although but recently established, the bank is already doing an immense business, its officers and stockholders are men of integrity and worth, well known and highly respected, and it is destined to become one of the permanent institutions of southeastern Oregon.

The city officers of Ontario are as follows: Mayor, William Miller; recorder, J. P. Kidd; treasurer, C. A. Martin; justice, G. L. King; marshal, J. M. Bevel; councilmen, L. Adam, A. L. Sproul, V. B. Staples, J. A. Draper, J. M. Brown, D. B. Purcell.

Ontario was so named at the request of James W. Virtue, one of its founders, who wished thus to honor the place of his nativity —Ontario, Canada. In 1883 William Morfitt, Daniel Smith, James W. Virtue and Mrs.

Mary Richardson, all of Baker City, exercised desert land rights under United States laws and took up four adjoining sections of desert land. Filings were made June 11, 1883, at Baker City. The description of the section taken by James W. Virtue, on a portion of which the town of Ontario has been built, is as follows: N. E. Quarter of section nine, S. E. Quarter of section four, S. W. Quarter of section three, N. W. Quarter of section ten; Township No. 18 South of Range No. 47, East of Willamette Meridian. The east two-thirds of this section was subsequently deeded to the Idaho-Oregon Land Improvement Company, of which Abraham Caldwell was president. This was done in order to locate a railroad station on the land, Mr. Caldwell having been granted certain concessions by the Oregon Short Line, which vested in him the authority to establish stations along the line of that road. The five individuals who are named above were all participants in the act of locating, platting and thus founding the city of Ontario. Later the territory which had been deeded to the Idaho-Oregon Land Improvement Company was purchased by David Wilson, who is now one of the most extensive real estate owners in the city. In 1884 William Morfitt concluded a contract with the Nevada Ditch Company by which water was brought onto the land described, and from this source the city is still supplied with water for irrigating purposes.

The period of development dates from 1884, when William Morfitt erected the frame building now occupied by the R. J. Stone Drug Company. This building was originally 25 by 60 feet, and in it Mr. Morfit resided for a time and also carried a small stock of general merchandise. A postoffice was secured the same year and Mr. Morfitt was appointed postmaster. The next to build was James Richardson, also in 1884. The pioneer business firm was that of T. T. Danilson and S. H. Oliver, who commenced operations in 1884.

35

They dealt in general merchandise and for a time occupied a tent near the present site of the depot. A store building was soon erected, however, into which they moved their stock before the close of the year. About the same time a lumber yard was opened by James T. Clement. The Scott House was opened on Thanksgiving day. This was made the occasion of a general gathering and a great celebration. The Caldwell brass band was present, accompanied by a large delegation of citizens from that town. Besides these there were present several hundred people from Malheur, Upper Willow, Weiser, Huntington, Payette and the surrounding country, to dedicate the border railroad town's hostelry, some coming a distance of fifty miles. The festivities closed with a grand ball and supper.

Among the earlier business men were A. W. Porter, who established a drug store, William Shelby, who sold harness and saddles, and A. L. Sproul, who erected the first livery stable. The first blacksmith shop was built by Joseph Durr. Having completed the building, Mr. Durr descended a ladder from the roof, sat down upon the lower round and died. The shop was afterwards occupied by Robert Visel. Among others who located here in early days were James T. Clement, first county judge, and E. H. Test, who came in 1884; R. S. Rutherford and Mrs. Mary Welch in 1885; H. T. Husted in 1886; E. A. Fraser and Josiah Carter in 1888.

The Oregon Short Line was built from Granger to Huntington in 1883. A station was established here in the winter of 1884-85 and G. L. King came from Soda Springs, Wyoming, to take charge. Here are established the largest stock yards on the O. S. L. R. R. Nearly all the stock and wool shipments made from Harney and Malheur counties are forwarded by the O. S. L. from Ontario. In June, 1899, the average of the daily shipments of cattle alone was valued at $25,000, a total of $750,000 for the month. The railroad was

short five hundred cars on its cattle orders. Two or three trainloads were forwarded daily and cattle came from as far inland as Crook county. This month's record may be taken as a fair indication of the stock shipments made here every year.

In 1885 Fred J. Keisel established a general store with E. H. Test as manager, in a building which still stands, an old land mark, on the east side of Main street. In 1886 the stock came into possession of William L. Geary & Company, Mr. Keisel retaining an interest and Mr. Test continuing as manager. Another change took place in 1890, when the Keisel, Shilling & Danilson Company was formed. The business was conducted under this firm name until 1896, when there was a reorganization and it became the Oregon Forwarding Company, Fred J. Keisel, president, and E. H. Test, manager. The R. D. Greer Mercantile Company was organized in 1896. In 1900 this became the Malheur Mercantile Company. E. A. Fraser and H. T. Husted are proprietors. Mr. Fraser is business manager. These two firms do an immense business and to them is very largely due the credit of making Ontario the center of a very extensive trade. Some idea of the extent of the transactions of these two firms may be learned from a statement of the fact that as long ago as May, 1897, their aggregate receipts for the month were something over 900,000 pounds of freight. Another of the earlier business houses which has a very large trade is that of Boyer Brothers & Company, established in 1895. The Hotel Ontario was built by David Wilson, its present owner, in 1895, but was not opened until July, 1897, when C. E. Belding, of Portland, took charge. The year 1894 was a building era; several brick stores and a number of residences were erected. The year 1899 witnessed another building boom. During this year David Wilson constructed several brick store buildings and an opera house.

Ontario has fortunately suffered but little from fires. The livery barn of Morfitt & Cole was destroyed in 1897 and in 1899 seven store buildings were destroyed, entailing a total loss to property owners of $12,050. In November, 1901, Ed Ashley and Company, of Weiser, under contract with the city sunk a drill 1,100 feet at a point on Main street near the Hotel Ontario. The citizens were in quest of artesian water, but instead found oil and natural gas. No practical use has been made of this well, but it is believed by experienced oil and gas men that if it were properly piped natural gas would flow in sufficient quantities to light the streets, business houses and residences of the city.

Ontario was incorporated February 11, 1899. Since 1896 improvements made have cost about $50,000. It is located on a rich sage brush plain in the forks of the Snake and Malheur rivers, the latter river flowing into the former two miles below the city. The foothills of distant mountain ranges are outlined on all sides. The elevation is 2,157 feet. A rich agricultural and stock country, with a radius of 150 miles is directly tributary to the town as a shipping and supply point. All the essentials necessary to permanence and substantial growth are established conditions. As has been previously stated, the town is in many respects a very desirable place of residence. In 1897 the authorities purchased trees enough to plant each side of Main street and the citizens turned out and planted them. These trees now make of the principal business thoroughfare an avenue of shade, and add greatly to general appearances. The summer's heat is not intense and the winter's cold is not severe. Climatic conditions are most favorable. Tributary interests cannot be excelled. Shipping facilities are excellent. The citizens are a unit in support of all public measures bearing the impress of excellence. Men of mettle, sound judgment, strict integrity and keen foresight have put their shoulders to the wheel and it is a foregone conclusion that Ontario must eventually become one of the most enterprising and populous cities of eastern Oregon.

VALE.

To one who is accustomed to the green timber and grass of the eastern states, the sage brush covered hills and plains of southeastern Oregon are not particularly inviting, but to those who have lived in Colorado and Utah and who have watched these arid regions blossom and bloom with luxuriant vegetation at the magic touch of water, to them the Malheur river valley and its numerous tributaries present an unexcelled field for the production of wealth and beauty. All is ready for the wizard's touch and wherever his liquid hand is laid, there will spring up the richest and loveliest of verdure. Gradually this wonderful transformation is taking place and it requires but ordinary vision to foresee what the near future has in store for this fertile region.

Here, nestling peacefully in this valley, about fifteen miles above the confluence of the Snake and Malheur rivers, and on the banks of the latter, is situated Vale, the thriving county seat of the prosperous county of Malheur. The high bluffs of the river rise protectingly to the southeast of the town, while on the north is a low range of hills forming the divide between the Malheur river and Willow creek. The valley makes a slight bend here to the southward, spreading out far to the east and west and traversed throughout its entire length by life dispensing irrigating canals, whose banks on either side are brightened by prosperous and highly cultivated farms.

Of this excellent territory Vale is the commercial center. While possessing probably not more than two hundred inhabitants, the town does a large business and as the surrounding country grows in population and wealth, so must Vale. Ontario is the nearest railroad point, fifteen miles eastward, but the Ontario-Burns stage line passes through the town, the company running two stages daily over this route, one westward and one eastward. Here, also, is located the only flouring mill in the county. This mill was erected in 1897 by the Vale Milling Company at a cost of $12,000, and has a capacity of fifty barrels a day. A large canal taken from the Malheur river furnishes the operating power.

The settlement at Vale is one of the oldest in the county, the mining camps in the northern portion alone laying claim to pioneership. Just which is the oldest we are unable to say but probably it is Mormon Basin. However, as early as 1864, Jonathan Keeney had erected a small house on the bank of the Malheur river just south of the present site of Vale, for the accommodation of passing emigrants and miners on their way to the Powder river and Boise mines. This historic old emigrant road, forming one link in the line of travel to the far northwest, entered the county near the mouth of the Boise river, crossed the Malheur river at Keeney's place and left the county by way of Willow creek and Tub Springs.

Keeney maintained this rude and primitive hostelry until 1870, when L. B. Rinehart, a cattleman who had recently come to this region, purchased the place and the squatter rights of Keeney. Two years later Mr. Rinehart built what has since been known as the "old stone house." This is a substantial stone structure of commodious size and served both the purpose of a home for the Rinehart family and as a resting place for travelers over this route. A grand New Year's ball, given January 1, 1873, marked the occupation of this house, which is still standing and used as the Hotel Vale. The Dalles and the Willamette valley and Cascade mountain wagon roads also intersected at this point and as considerable travel passed over them during the 'seventies, Mr. Rinehart's home became an important station.

Until 1883 the old stone house occupied the site of the future town in solitary peace, but in the spring of the year, Henry C. Murray opened a small store in connection with the old inn, then in his charge. Mr. Rinehart had, during the first years of his occupancy, attempted to maintain a trading post, an effort which failed, however, for lack of sufficient patronage. Mr. Murray kept the store only a few months, selling in the fall to R. N. Linebarger, who in turn disposed of his interests to L. A. Sevey and I. H. Holland the following year. This same year, 1884, also witnessed the establishment of a postoffice here, the name Vale being bestowed upon the settlement by reason of its natural location in the valley. H. C. Murray was appointed the first postmaster.

The country was now settling very rapidly and it soon became apparent that this portion of Baker county would in the near future be cut off and organized as a new county. In 1887 the growing desire of the inhabitants of this region for county division was acceded to by the legislature and Vale was designated as the temporary county seat. Meanwhile the Malheur river, Willow and Bully creek valleys, all tributary to Vale, had become well settled and the little hamlet had grown to be an important trading center. The impetus given the town by its selection as the county seat was of course considerable and many new business enterprises were added to the nucleus already formed. The selection of Vale as the permanent county seat by the general elections of 1888 and 1890 not only the more strongly established the permanency of the town, but also strengthened it commercially. Its growth since then has been steady and substantial, though slow.

The town site of Vale was, until 1887, unpatented government land, the title to the ground being in dispute between L. B. Rinehart and the Willamette Valley and Cascade Mountain Wagon Road Company. Mr. Rinehart claimed the land by right of priority of settlement, he having held it by squatter's rights until the government survey in the early 'seventies, when he filed a pre-emption claim. By act of Congress, the Road Company was entitled to all alternate sections of land lying within three miles of each side of the road. This claim is described in the surveyor's minutes as the N. W. ¼ of section 29, town 18 south, range 45 East Willamette Meridian, and would, therefore, under the road company's grant, belong to that corporation. However, after a period of litigation covering several years, the apparent conflict of the law was solved by the United States allowing the state of Oregon to select this claim as indemnity school land and as such it was sold to Mrs. Rinehart. The state deed bears date December 22, 1887. Eldridge's addition has since been added to the town plat.

In 1887 temporary county buildings were erected at Vale, which have since been occupied by the county officers, owing to the failure of the county to provide more suitable quarters. The continual agitation of the county seat question has also had much to do toward retarding such action. In 1900, however, the citizens of Vale and the surrounding country determined to present the county with the much needed court house and accordingly J. C. Kelley, D. C. Wells, M. G. Hope, J. L. Cole and Finley McDonald were appointed as a committee to raise funds and take charge of the erection of the building. This structure will be completed this fall and will, when finished, have cost between $8,000 and $10,000. It is built of Malheur county dressed stone, is sixty by eighty feet in ground dimensions and two stories high, and besides a vault and jail will contain a court house, two jury rooms and five offices. This will be as fine a court house as there is in this portion of Oregon and one of which the county and especially the citizens of Vale can justly feel proud. James Patten and Edward Warner are the con-

tractors. L. B. Rinehart generously donated the block of land on which the building stands.

The Malheur Gazette, the oldest newspaper in the county, was established at Vale in August, 1888, by S. H. Shepherd. At present this journal is owned by J. D. McCulloch and is an active and ever willing advocate of the best interests of the town and county.

The First Bank of Vale, the only bank in Vale, is only a little over a year old, but during that time has made a fine business record and reflects well the prosperity of the community. This institution was organized August 10, 1901, as a state bank, with a capital stock of $50,000, one-half paid up, the incorporators being J. L. Cole, M. G. Hope, F. O'Neill and Elmer A. Clark. At present its officers are: president, J. L. Cole; vice-president, T. W. Halliday; cashier, Elmer A. Clark; directors, J. L. Cole, T. W. Halliday, E. A. Clark, William Quinn, Thomas Turnbull, J. C. Kelley, and R. A. Lockett. The bank owns and occupies a handsome stone building, costing $5,000.

The first school maintained in Vale was opened in 1887 and was held in a small frame school house. In 1895 the district issued $2,000 in bonds, with which a fine stone schoolhouse was built in the southwestern portion of the town. Mr. and Mrs. O. H. Byland constitute the present corps of instructors and 51 pupils are enrolled. There is only one church in the town, the Methodist, which was erected two years ago. At present the church is without a pastor.

At the last election the following city officers were chosen: mayor, Charles E. Boswell; recorder, John Boswell, treasurer, T. F. Olk; councilmen, I. W. Hope, Walter Glenn, J. A. Newton and B. C. Richardson.

Among the business enterprises and professions of Vale, besides those already mentioned, are the following: general stores, Vale Commercial Company, Charles E. Boswell, I. F. S. Diven; hotels, the Hotel Vale, M. E. Taggart, proprietor; the Hess house, S. V. Hess, proprietor; drug store, John Boswell; livery barns, Henry Eldredge, Nicholas Olk; butcher shops, L. B. Teter and E. R. Murray, harness store and saddlery, Joseph C. Kelley; barber shop, Charles Tillotson; blacksmith shop, Henry Eldredge; real estate, P. E. Phelps; physician, H. T. Hoople; lawyers, R. G. Wheeler, J. W. McCulloch; contractors, James Nurse, T. A. Barton; several saloons. J. A. Newton is postmaster and Phoebe Newton, his deputy.

Just outside the city limits are several wells, from which streams of hot water flow, some of them shooting up into the air several feet. These waters possess highly valuable medicinal properties, and have been pronounced by chemists and specialists at Hot Springs, Arkansas, as the equal, if not the superior of any mineral water on the Pacific coast. The owners of these wells now purpose combining and erecting suitable buildings here for the accommodation of those who wish to avail themselves of the water for medical treatment. The wells were sunk in 1897-98 for the purpose of tapping the great oil region which is supposed to underlie this section of the state.

REMOTE SETTLEMENTS.

For a number of seasons the people of Malheur county cannot yet be said to be a unit, either in sentiment or action. Comparatively speaking the county has only been organized a few years and no questions permitting union of sentiment or action have been before the people. The county embraces a very large territory and the settlements are remote from each other. Jordan Valley is about eighty-five miles from Ontario and Vale and about 150 miles from Malheur City and Mormon Basin. Jordan Valley is almost exclusively a stockraising settlement, Malheur City a mining community, Vale is an agricultural center and Ontario is the metropolis and the only shipping point.

Each settlement has a history peculiarly its own, which in no respect resembles that of any of the other localities. For these reasons the history of the county, after, as well as prior to its organization, may perhaps be obtained in better detail by a perusal of the history of its various communities, rather than by that of general records. The history of its railroad town and metropolis, and of the county seat, has been written. We will now proceed with the record of the smaller settlements. These are records of important events which are intimately associated with the gradual development of the county as a whole, and they carry us back to the period of gold discoveries and the location of stock ranches.

JORDAN VALLEY.

This period dates back about forty years. In 1863 we find McWilliams and Inskip on extensive stock ranches in Jordan Valley. These men and others who followed them and made permanent homes in the valley, came from California mining regions and may be said to have been the pioneer stockmen of the county. Although Jordan Valley is on one of the first established stage routes in the country, it was in the old days far removed from mining camps or other centers and its permanence as a settlement was probably owing to the establishment of forts in its vicinity. For a number of years Camp Three Forks and Camp Lyon were garrisoned by United States troops stationed here for the protection of the whites from the Indians. These forts proved a source of revenue to the first settlers and were an inducement to others to make permanent locations. We learn that J. P. Merrill, who bought "Sheep Ranch" of McWilliams in 1865, put up $2,000 worth of hay for the government in the summer of 1866. Troubles with the Indians continued in this part of the country until late in the 'seventies and during all this time hay and other supplies were in demand by the troops at the forts. At intervals efforts have been made to farm the valley lands, but they have not been crowned with special success. It is pre-eminently a stockman's land. Many have grown rich here in the stock business and all the desirable lands are now occupied. A village numbering one hundred and fifty people has grown up about the postoffice of Jordan Valley. This office was established in 1870. John Baxter is now postmaster. There are two stores, a blacksmith shop, a livery barn and a hotel. In the precinct are polled about seventy-five votes. Among the pioneer settlers, besides those already mentioned, we may name Sherman Castle, William and D. D. Monger, Clarence A. Goodrich, Franklin Cable, T. C. Fletcher, Bert Hooker, Alexander Canter, Joe Tuttle, Al. Carp and Jack Bowden. The last three named were scouts, stage drivers and noted characters, whose exploits would form an interesting chapter in the earlier history of the northwest.

ELDORADO AND MALHEUR CITY.

Although gold was discovered in and about the present site of Malheur City as early as 1864 and development work commenced soon after, no permanent settlements were made until 1870. In the meantime a camp had been made at Eldorado. In 1865 miners began placer work here and three years later a town was started. Charles Goodnough, Kirkpatrick, and Stephenson Brothers each erected store buildings. S. B. Reeves built a hotel. Eldorado continued a thriving camp until 1870. The famous Eldorado ditch, which had been brought from a point on Burnt river over 100 miles away for the express purpose of making these diggings profitable, ran a mile south of the camp. In 1870 the office of the ditch company was removed from the camp to quarters near the ditch. The business houses, hotel and residences were at once removed to locations along the ditch and Eldorado was abandoned.

The new camp was named Malheur City. Of the new buildings erected, the store of Lake Brothers was first. Another was built by George and Mary Collins and still another by William Glenn. A second hotel was put up by W. J. Leatherwood and in a remarkably short space of time Malheur City assumed the appearance of a well founded town. And so indeed it proved to be, as it is still a prosperous village having a population of about 200. There are no indications that the mines will be exhausted in the next half century and Malheur City has therefore good future prospects. It is near the heads of Quartz, Feasta, Cottonwood and Rich gulches and on the Burnt river and Willow creek divide. The placer gold in these gulches has been almost worked out, but extensive and rich quartz ledges have been found and the indications are that some of the most profitable mines in the Blue mountains will be developed here in the near future. In the rock formations of this region, lava, granite and slate are found freely mixed, the gold lying between the granite and slate walls. As on Willow creek, lava is sometimes found here in veins forty feet thick. Under it lie the strata of granite and slate. Of the several mines in operation, the largest are the Red, White and Blue and the Golden Eagle. Several mills are being built and a large number of men is kept constantly at work.

In recent years several rich mines have been opened on First creek, which empties into Willow creek about four miles below Malheur City. A 20-stamp mill is now being put up here. While herding cattle on this creek in 1898, John Ennor picked up some quartz which proved to be very rich in gold. In 1899 he returned and discovered the mines known as the Sunset group, consisting of the Tenderfoot, Johnnie and Sunsetquartz claims. Last year Mr. Ennor worked through nineteen tons of ore from the Johnnie claim which yielded $35 per ton. One-half mile south of the Sunset group is the Uncle Sam group owned by

Thomas Anderson. In this group are the Uncle Sam, Daisy and Idaho claims. Ore from these claims has shown assays from a trace to $900 in gold per ton. Anderson and Ennor have been untiring in their efforts to develop this new Eldorado and these efforts are being crowned with success. These camps are directly tributary to Malheur City and from them it derives considerable revenue from the sale of supplies. Among the merchants are Morfitt Brothers and Robert Boswell, who have general stores. Robert Morfitt is the village blacksmith and Judson Hill, the postmaster. There is also a drug store and a livery stable. A schoolhouse has been built at a cost of $800. Fifty-seven pupils are enrolled. Odd Fellows and Woodmen of the World have lodges here. There is an organization of the Methodist Episcopal church which conducts services in the schoolhouse. The town is not incorporated.

NYSSA.

In contrast with Malheur City, which derives its support mainly from the mining camps is the town of Nyssa, a product of stock and farming interests along the Snake river and the Owyhee ditch. The location was not chosen in answer to the demands of any industrial interests, but was selected by the Oregon Short Line railroad as a convenient point at which to establish a station, being ten miles from Ontario and eight miles from Parma, in Idaho. Subsequent development of the surrounding country, however, has proven that the railroad made a fortunate selection and Nyssa, although for several years it served only as a watering station, has recently grown into a trading center of some importance. Settlers on adjacent lands along the river and along the Owyhee ditch, which is but a mile away, make this a trading and a shipping point. A section house was built here in 1883, about the time of the completion of the railroad. In the same

year Lennox B. Boyle, a trader who followed the construction train of the Oregon Short Line, put up a small building at Nyssa and established a trading post, at the same time taking up a claim. All the surrounding country being directly under the Owyhee ditch, the lands were soon occupied by settlers and Mr. Boyle's post was well patronized. For many years he was the sole occupant of the present town site. A postoffice was established about 1885, but it was not until 1894 that other permanent settlers came to dwell beside him. Shortly afterward Mr. Boyle died and Holiver Megordan, having previously purchased some land from him, put up a building and opened a store. Mr. Megordan was followed the next year by Sanford N. and Charles Emison (sons of pioneer William Emison), who erected another building and opened a large stock of general merchandise. A third store was soon afterward opened by J. L. Lee & Company. From that time to the present Nyssa has continued a prosperous trading point. The district has erected a schoolhouse at a cost of $1,000. This is a substantial and well equipped building and stands about midway between the town and the Owyhee ditch. An addition to the building is contemplated, as the school population is increasing and the present structure is proving inadequate. There are now sixty-six persons of school age in the district, and the average daily attendance last year was forty-five. Emison Brothers now conduct a general store and lumber yard. They also have a large warehouse, over which is a hall or opera house, which is fitted with stage and scenery. J. L. Lee & Company also do a good general business, and A. Peer has opened a hotel. The lands surrounding Nyssa are rich and productive, the settlers are industrious and progressive and its merchants must of necessity continue to be prosperous. The town has become necessary to the farmers and stockmen and will grow in extent and importance.

ARCADIA.

What is known as the K. S. & D. fruit
farm was located about 1890. In 1897 the K.
S. & D. Fruit and Land Company was incorporated by Fred J. Keisel, Watson N. Shilling
and Theodore T. Danilson. The property held
under these articles of incorporation is now
owned by F. J. Keisel and J. W. Metcalf and
is valued at $75,000. It consists of 1,320
acres of land, all under the Owyhee ditch. On
this farm there are sowed to alfalfa 390 acres.
One hundred and thirty-five acres are in orchards, in which there are 12,000 bearing fruit
trees. Twenty-seven thousand shade trees have
been planted. Along the county road, which
passes through the farm, is an avenue of tall
poplars two miles long. Thirteen acres are
occupied by a town site, on which twelve families are now located in neat cottages. The
town has been named Arcadia, a postoffice has
been established and a good school house built,
in which regular terms of school are taught
each year. The O. S. L. railroad has built a
station house on the main line just east of the
farm and a side track has been constructed into
the midst of the orchard lands. Immense
quantities of fresh and evaporated fruits are
shipped from Arcadia annually. A steam
evaporator has been in use for some time, and
in connection with it has been erected a storage
warehouse. Arcadia is an object lesson, showing in detail the wonderful effects of irrigation
on otherwise arid sage brush plains. It is a
vast garden spot, where are seen green hay
fields and ripening grain fields, the shade of
orchard and forest tree, fruits and flowers,
flocks and herds, and where may be heard at
all times the musical hum of an active and
prosperous community. When it is remembered that large sections of Malheur county
lands are just such sage brush plains as were
those upon which was located the K. S. & D.
ranch, some idea may be had of the magical
effects that may be produced by the use of the

grubbing hoe and the waters of the irrigating
ditches, and of the increased values that attach
to these barren lands when brought under cultivation. In no other industry in the northwest
will capital find better opportunities for safe
and remunerative investment than in the work
of reclaiming the barren areas of Malheur
county.

Beulah, on the Malheur river, in the extreme western part of the county, is the postoffice of a number of families engaged in stock
raising. Here is a small tract of valley land,
easily watered, and on it the ranchmen have established peaceful homes near the ranges.

Ironsides is a postoffice in the extreme
northwestern corner of the county, near the
headwaters of Willow creek. The surrounding
country is sparsely settled by miners and
stockmen.

Dell is located at Cole's ranch further
down on Willow creek. It is simply a postoffice, which shifts from one ranch to another
as the postmasters die or resign, or the national administration changes. In this portion
of Willow creek valley are located some of
the oldest and best hay and grain ranches in
the county.

Westfall is a postoffice and small trading
point twenty-five miles directly west of Vale.
It is in the valley of Cottonwood creek, a tributary of Malheur river. This creek furnishes
considerable water and here there is a number
of farms and ranches well stocked and improved. Westfall is in a prosperous community and will doubtless grow in importance
as surrounding lands become occupied and are
placed under cultivation.

Besides these settlements there are several
postoffices of less importance, to which mails
are delivered at irregular intervals, viz.: Cord,
in the southwestern part of the county; Riverside and Juntura, in the upper Malheur river
region; Mosquite, in the northeastern part on
the Snake river; Owyhee, near the mouth of
the Owyhee river, and Watson, near Mahogany

mountain, on the same stream; Carter, on Sucker creek, and Sheaville, on Cow creek; the last four named being on the east side of the county.

All these outlying post offices and settle-ments are advantageously located and will one day, when the county becomes more thickly settled and more fully developed, grew into thrifty villages and towns.

ARCHIBALD W. TURNER.

BIOGRAPHICAL.

ARCHIBALD W. TURNER.—The subject of this sketch is one of Malheur county's heaviest property owners, having an estate of eleven hundred and sixty acres of fine soil and very valuable as a hay producer. He is one of the prominent men of the country, a man of fine capabilities, and highly respected and esteemed by all. Mr. Turner was born in Boone county, Missouri, on February 1, 1827, being the son of James and Sarah Turner. He was reared on a farm, gained his education in the primitive log school house of the time and at the native place on October 7, 1848, he was married to Miss Nancy March, a native of the same place. In the spring of 1851 he started with his wife and one child to San Francisco, going via New Orleans and Nicaragua. While on the sailing vessel from the Isthmus, the little one sickened and died and was buried in the ocean. Owing to tedious delays he did not arrive at San Francisco until March, 1852, and then went direct to Yuba county, near Marysville, where he procured a farm and went to raising the fruits of the field. He also raised stock and continued there until 1862, at which time he came to Walla Walla and then to the Salmon river mines. He returned to The Dalles to winter and in the spring of 1863 went to Idaho City, where he followed mining until 1866. After that date he came to Old Eldorado, near Malheur, and engaged in lumbering, where he spent three years and then in 1869, Mr. Turner came to the vicinity of his present estate and took up a homestead, and there turned his attention to raising sheep. Later he sold his sheep and raised cattle. He now has, as mentioned above, one of the finest estates in the county, being three miles southeast from Dell. He handles much stock and many tons of hay each year. He has a large, two-story, ten-room house, fitted up tastily, and a large barn and all the buildings, equipments, orchards and stock to make rural life both comfortable, enjoyable and interesting. In politics Mr. Turner is a stanch Democrat of the Jeffersonian type and a man with the courage of his convictions. To Mr. Turner and his estimable wife there have been born six children, as follows: Kelton, deceased; Samuel C., deceased; John B., married to Elizabeth Allen and living near Dell; Ellen, wife of M. Grimes, of The Dalles; Laura, deceased; Martha, wife of J. Barrett, of The Dalles. On June 16, 1863, Mr. Turner was called upon to mourn the death of his faithful wife, and on the same day the daughter died, and they two sleep in one grave. Mr. Turner is now enjoying the golden days of his career amid the comforts of his large estate; the kindness of friends and the esteem of the entire community and he is one of the capable and wise men of the region.

WILLIAM H. PULLEN is one of the prominent men of Malheur county, being both a successful business man and property owner and popular county official. He was born in Illinois, on March 1, 1845, being the son of William and Mary (Wells) Pullen, natives respectively of Pennsylvania and Liverpool. When thirteen, he went with his parents to Texas, remaining there until 1867, and then returned to Illinois, where he engaged in farming until 1872. At that date a move was made to Pawnee county, Nebraska, and that was his home until 1880. He next located in Coos county, Oregon, where two years were spent and another move was made to Jackson county, whence one year later he returned to Coos bay and remained there five years. We next see Mr. Pullen in Wallowa county where he engaged in the mercantile pursuit at Lostine. Four years after this venture, he sold out and went to the lumbering business in Paradise, the same county. It was 1897, when Mr. Pullen came to Malheur county and bought one hundred and twenty acres of fertile land one-fourth of a mile from Owyhee. He has also eighty acres in Idaho and his land is well improved. In 1900 he was called by the people to act as county assessor, his name appearing on the Republican ticket and in the spring of 1902 he was renominated.

The marriage of Mr. Pullen and Miss Harriet J. Cross, a native of Illinois was solemnized in Texas in 1866 and the following named children were born to them, Henry, in Coos county; Mary J., wife of Daniel Barklow, of Coos county; Elizabeth, wife of Irmir Miller, of Curry county; John E., of Malheur county; Ella, wife of Walter Applegate, of Malheur county; Richard, in Malheur county; Dora, wife of Robert Minton. In Coos county, on January 21, 1881, Mrs. Pullen died. On October 14, 1881, Mr. Pullen married a second time, the lady being Lucinda Whetstone, a native of Indiana, and the nuptials occurred in Jackson county, and three children have been born to them, Jesse W., Thomas J., and Eva L. Mrs. Pullen's parents came to Oregon in 1871. Mr. Pullen is affiliated with the I. O. O. F., Lodge No. 90, of Ontario and he is one of the well known and highly respected men of our county.

ALVIN S. MOSS.—This enterprising and substantial stockman and farmer of Malheur county is located nine miles northwest from Rockville, Idaho, and is one of the pioneers of this section and has labored with assiduity and sagacity here since the early eighties and is now rewarded with abundant prosperity and a goodly showing, gained by his thrift and careful labors. Mr. Moss was born in Illinois, on September 10, 1857, the son of Sardus B. and Ceria E. Moss. At the age of eight years he went with the balance of the family to southeastern Kansas and there grew up. He gained his education there and labored on the farm

with his father. In 1879, he came to Colorado and two years later, he came thence to Malheur county, locating where his estate now is. He has one half section of good land and over one hundred head of cattle, besides many horses. His estate is well improved and he is counted one of the wealthy and substantial men of his section.

In political matters, Mr. Moss is always active, taking great interest in the affairs of the county and state, while in educational affairs he is found in the place of the intelligent citizen. It has never been among the ventures made by our subject that he should embark on the matrimonial sea, choosing rather the quieter joys and walks of the celibate.

WILLIAM PARKS.—One of the oldest pioneers of Malheur county and a man of excellent capabilities, being possessed of practical ability and judgment, and a keen discrimination that have made him a very successful business man and one of the leaders in the realm of finance in this section, the subject of this article is abundantly worthy of recognition and especial mention among the prominent men of Malheur county and this portion of Oregon, being also a man of worth and personal virtues.

Mr. Parks was born in Brooklyn, New York, on June 7, 1845, being the son of Abraham and Jane Eliza (Vanderhoof) Parks. He was deprived of his mother when an infant, but received his education and grew to manhood in his native place. It was in 1859 that he crossed the plains to California, locating in Eldorado county, where he engaged in farming until 1864. Then he came to Silver City, Idaho, and there took up mining until 1871, when he made his way to Jordan valley, now in Malheur county. He at once took a homestead and gave his attention to farming and stock raising. He was successful in that line and now he owns four hundred acres of fine, well improved and irrigated land adjoining the town of Jordan Valley. He has fine buildings and a large band of cattle. In 1895 Mr. Parks engaged in the mercantile business, and as in his other undertakings, so in this, he was blessed with abundant success, because of his untiring efforts and wise management and careful business methods. He operated in company with J. R. Blackoby and in 1901 he sold out and is now interested in the Jordan Valley Mercantile Company. Mr. Parks is one of the real builders of the county, both in an industrial and commercial line, being one of the leading financiers of the county to-day. He has an interest in the Ontario Bank and is also interested in various other places.

The marriage of Mr. Parks and Miss Julia West was solemnized in Jordan Valley in 1879, and they have become the parents of five children: George, a member of the Jordan Valley Mercantile Company; James W.; Hollister; Guy; Mona. Mr. Parks has seen all the hardships incident to frontier life, being here and open to the dangers of the Indian outbreak in 1878, as also in other lines and times he has braved the dangers and encountered the hardships, but in all he has triumphed and is one of the most substantial, well respected men of the county, being looked up to by all and holding an enviable position of prestige.

RICHARD H. HART.—This capable and enterprising stockman and farmer of the vicinity of Jordan Valley is one of the substantial men of Malheur county, and is numbered with the earliest pioneers who broke sod in this section, and it is to his credit that he has constantly labored for the welfare of the country and its upbuilding in a worthy manner ever since that time. Mr. Hart was born in Indiana, on April 18, 1849, the son of John K. and Eliza Hart. When he was one year of age, his parents removed to Iowa and there he received his education and remained until he had reached his majority. 1871 was the date when he came to Malheur county and located a pre-emption where his estate is now located, being one-half mile west from the village of Jordan Valley. He now has one of the fine estates of the county, well improved and producing abundant dividends annually. In addition to this generous holding, he has eight hundred and forty acres of land on Cow creek. Mr. Hart has two hundred horses, and as many cattle and is one of the leaders in the realm of raising stock, being both expert and progressive in this work. He was here during the Indian outbreak in 1878 and rendered ex-

cellent service for the country, acting as scout and bearer of messages. Also in the time of the robbery, he was efficient in aiding the officers.

The marriage of Mr. Hart and Miss Harriett Luella Moore, a native of Iowa, was solemnized in Indianola, Iowa, in February, 1879, and they have three children, Gertrude, Ruth, and Ethelyn. Mr. Hart always evinces an intelligent interest in the affairs of the state and county and is a patriotic and capable citizen who stands well with his fellows and has done a large amount for the advancement of the county.

JAMES C. FORD.—This well known and enterprising stockman has been a man of frontier life, spending his days since a lad in the various pursuits incident to pioneering, and especially has he been occupied in raising and handling stock, being one of the best posted and most skillful stock men in this county of stock men, and abundant success has been his since he has inaugurated action for himself.

Mr. Ford was born in Arkansas, October 15, 1856, being the son of William Ford. His mother died when he was an infant and he was taken by his father to Tennessee and when the war broke out, the father sent this son to friends in Illinois and joined the ranks to fight for the Union. At the close of the war the father died and our subject was left an orphan. He was filled with determination and courage and soon we find him in Texas, riding the range and becoming familiar with the hardships of the cowboy and all the lore of handling and breeding cattle successfully. He worked for the noted Chisum Company and made several drives from Texas and Mexico to the north. It was 1879 when he came to this country. He was engaged first with Ryan & Lang, driving cattle for three years to Montana, after which he made a drive for Mayberry, from The Dalles to Wyoming. He next operated for Con Shea, being foreman for him for three years and then he retired from riding the range and went into business for himself. He now has a fine ranch of five hundred and sixty acres of fertile land on Sucker creek, six miles west from Rockville. He has good buildings, the estate well improved, raises hay, grain and alfalfa, and also has a fine herd of Hereford and Shorthorn cattle. Being an experienced stockman, Mr. Ford understands the value of raising the best and doing so in a skillful manner.

On November 25, 1888, Mr. Ford married Miss Fannie, daughter of Charles and Mary (Wilson) Smith, who are mentioned in this volume. Mrs Ford is a native of Salem, Oregon, and she is a woman of many virtues and graces and presides over the comfortable rural home with becoming dignity, while this worthy couple are valuable members of society, being esteemed by all.

ALBERT J. SHEA.—While the older members of the pioneer staff are retiring one by one, it is pleasant to note that there are younger men of courage and enterprise to take up the worthy labors of these estimable men, who opened this country for settlement, and to prosecute them with an untiring zeal and a sagacity that is sure to win in the battle of life. Among this wide awake class, we are constrained to mention the subject of this article, who has made a name and place for himself in the ranks of the leading stockmen of Malheur county, being justly entitled to the position he holds, because of his merit and worth, and because of his brilliant achievements.

Albert Shea was born in Owyhee county, Idaho, on February 4, 1872, being the son of Cornelius Shea, the well and widely known stockman of this country. The senior Mr. Shea was one of the heaviest stock owners west of the Rockies and one of the keenest and most energetic operators that ever handled cattle. He sold out his immense herds in 1897, and is now living with his family in San Francisco. He is a native of Canada and came to this section in 1867. Reverting more particularly to our subject, we note that he was educated in San Francisco and also on the farm and in the saddle in Eastern Oregon and Southern Idaho. He knows the cattle business from the ground to the completion, and is making a commendable showing as a worthy son of a wise father. At the present time, Mr. Shea is living on his estate of three hundred and sixty acres of fertile land, in the Jordan Valley, where he operates his herds of cattle and bands of horses. He is one of the wide-awake men of the county and is well known and esteemed by all.

The marriage of Mr. Shea and Miss Celia Cornners, a native of Owyhee county, Idaho, was solemnized in Portland, Oregon, on December 12, 1896, and they have one daughter, Genevieve.

JAMES T. DAVIS.—One of the worthy pioneers of this county, a man of ability and executive force and unswerving integrity, the subject of this sketch is now one of the leading citizens of Nyssa, and a prominent man in Malheur county. He lives one mile northwest from the town of Nyssa, having a farm of one hundred and twenty acres, well improved and handled in a skillful manner, which is a good dividend producer.

James T. was born in Unionville, Putnam county, Missouri, on October 25, 1850, being the son of Hamilton and Saline Davis. In 1862, the father and the oldest son came across the plains with ox teams and in 1865, our subject and his mother came the same journey with horse teams. They both made the trip without serious accident and when the mother arrived in Boise, the father was there to meet them and the reunited family made their way to the Willamette valley where they settled in Polk county. Four years later, they removed from that place to Umatilla county and in 1874, our subject went from the home in that county to Boise valley, Idaho, and later returned to his people, who had in the meantime migrated to Baker City. The reports which he brought from the Boise valley caused all to move there and engage in raising stock. Our subject went thence to Emmett, Idaho, and there married Miss Lulu Brinnon in May, 1881. In 1895, Mrs. Davis was called away by death. In 1885, Mr. Davis came from Idaho to Ontario and there engaged in the livery business, handling also and shipping many horses to various markets. Later he located an island just below the Riverside ferry as mining land, selling the same at a good advantage. Then he bought the land where his home is at the present time and this has been transformed into a valuable farm. Among other productions, he raises much alfalfa hay and has a comfortable home.

Mr. Davis contracted a second marriage,

the lady becoming his wife at this time being Miss Laura, daughter of Mrs. A. J. Lewis, who makes her home with them at the present time. The date of this wedding was February, 1898. Mr. Davis takes an active part in politics, being allied with the Democratic party and he is a good citizen and a well respected and upright gentleman.

GEORGE NICHOLS.—No more worthy class of people ever stepped beneath the folds of the stars and stripes than the doughty, courageous, intelligent, capable and sturdy pioneers, who braved dangers, endured hardships, performed the arduous labors incident to their lot, and wended their way into the wilds of this western country, to beat back the savages and make here the abodes of civilized men. As a worthy one among this illustrious number, we are pleased to mention the subject of this sketch, who is now one of the substantial and enterprising citizens of Malheur county.

Mr. Nichols was born in New York, on October 22, 1841, being the son of Asa and Mary Nichols, who brought their son at the age of five to Kalamazoo, Michigan. There George was educated, grew to manhood and on May 10, 1861, he responded to the cry of patriotism then sounding through the land, by offering himself as one to fight for his country. He was enrolled in Company K, Second Michigan, under Capt. Charles S. May. He was in the battle of Bull Run, at the siege of Yorktown, fought at Fair Oaks and several other engagements, and was wounded at Fair Oaks. On account of disabilities resulting from this, he was discharged on February 3, 1863. He returned to his home, and soon after he was in the west. He assisted to build the U. P. R. R. in Nebraska and in Utah, in 1868 he went to White Pine, Nevada. Teaming and mining occupied him there and then he went to Paradise Valley, then came through this country to British Columbia on a prospecting tour. In 1879 he went to the Wood river country, in Idaho, then in 1894 he came to his present place, which is located seven miles east of Jordan Valley. He has a fine ranch, all irrigated and well improved and which returns abundant crops to his skillful husbandry. Mr. Nichols is a prominent member of the G. A. R., in

Hailey, Idaho, Post No. 61, and he is secure in the esteem and confidence of his fellows. Mr. Nichols has never embarked on the matrimonial sea, and is content in the quiet joys of the celibatarian's life.

CORNELIUS G. MOREHEAD.—A native of the Web-foot State, the son of about the earliest pioneers of this state, raised amid its environments, both eastern and western Oregon, the subject of this article is thoroughly an Oregonian and a typical representative of its energetic and progressive citizens. Cornelius G. was born in Linn county, Oregon, on June 26, 1865, being the son of Robert M. and Martha (Curl) Morehead. The parents came with ox teams to Oregon in 1848 and settled in the Willamette valley and the father being a millwright, built the first mill of the state. It was located at Salem and was built in 1849. In 1869, the family removed to Jackson county, Oregon, and in 1872, they came to Prairie City, Grant county, this state. There the father erected the Strawberry flour mills and in 1879 sold out and went to Weiser, Idaho. He built a mill there and in 1887 he returned to the Willamette valley, where he died in 1890. Mrs. Morehead is still living in Douglas county, this state. Our subject was educated in the schools of the various places where he lived and in 1884 he started for himself. He raised stock in Idaho until 1888, then sold out and came to Malheur county and engaged with the Oregon Horse and Land Company, where he wrought for a number of years. During this time, he made several trips to different markets with stock. In 1901 he purchased his present place, a farm of eighty acres, one and one-fourth miles west from Nyssa. His farm is well improved, produces abundance of alfalfa hay, and other fruits of the field. He has a comfortable residence and a young orchard and is fast making his place an abode of rural comfort and attractiveness. In addition to his property, Mr. Morehead has a good bunch of cattle and devotes considerable attention to handling them.

The marriage of Mr. Morehead and Miss Elizabeth, daughter of David R. and Jane Ehrgood, was solemnized on April 21, 1899, and two children have been born to them, Alma

Pearl and Ruby Edna. In political matters, Mr. Morehead is allied with the Republican party and manifests an intelligent activity and interest in the affairs of the county and state.

WILLIAM MORFITT.—To this worthy veteran of many a struggle with the savages on the frontier, as well as in many of the battles of life in the wild country, being a pioneer of the state of Oregon, and having led a life of activity in the forefront of the progress of civilization, having done well his part. in all this good work, we are pleased to grant a consideration in this volume of Malheur county's history, both because of this prominent part that he has taken in the county and in its leading industries and developments, as well as for his worth as a man and citizen.

Mr. Morfitt was born in Yorkshire, England, on April 17, 1838, being the son of James and Susana Morfitt. In 1842 the father brought his family to the United States, landing in New York and thence to the site of Chicago, where he located the first foundry of that now famous city. In 1847 he came with his family across the plains to Oregon. Enroute they were attacked by the Indians several times, once on the Rogue river, where four savages were killed, but no loss of life among the immigrants. Before that, in the Modoc country, they lost half of their cattle by the redskins. At the mouth of the Yam Hill river, the stock was left and the father came to Oregon City in a canoe. There he located, it being a village of few people, and there he opened a foundry, the very first that was ever erected in the territory of Oregon. Our subject received a good education from the schools of the various places where he resided, perfecting himself as a civil engineer. In 1849 he, with his father, went with the rush of the gold miners to San Francisco in a sail boat and in the spring of 1850, he returned to Oregon. In 1855 our subject enlisted in the Clackamas county company to fight the Indians in the Yakima war. After that he followed farming until 1867, when he removed to Grant county and thence to Boise, Idaho. In company with a Mr. Libby, Mr. Morfitt built the first bridge across the Boise river at Boise. Eighteen hundred and sixty-eight marks the

date when Mr. Morfitt came to upper Willow creek and located the first ranch there. He farmed and raised stock there until 1883, when he came to the site of the present Ontario, and in company with Messrs. Virtue, Smith and Richardson, located the town of Ontario, he surveying the land. He still owns one hundred and twenty acres of this land. His home place is located one and one-half miles southwest from Ontario and consists of forty acres. He has the finest farm house in the county and barns and outbuildings and all tasty improvements to match. His place is well supplied with water and has a fine orchard. It is a model of thrift and beauty in every respect. Mr. Morfitt is vice-president of the Owyhee ditch company and stockholder in the same and also a stockholder and director in the Nevada ditch company.

In politics Mr. Morfitt is a Democrat and takes an enthusiastic part in the advancement of educational interests. The marriage of Mr. Morfitt and Miss Juliette Worsham occurred in Clackamas county, on March 11, 1858, and they became the parents of six children, as follows: James, Robert, William L., Cyrus W., Charles H. and Iona. In 1893 Mrs. Morfitt died. In 1899 Mr. Morfitt was married a second time, the lady becoming his wife at this time being Elizabeth M. Carlisle, a native of what is now Malheur county, and they have been blessed by the advent of two children, Julian and Ashton. Mr. Morfitt served as scout for General Howard during the Bannock war.

WILLIAM C. CARLTON.—This worthy gentleman is one of the substantial citizens of Malheur county and one of the thrifty stockmen and farmers of the vicinty of Rockville, his estate of two hundred and twenty acres of good land lying seven miles west from that place. Mr. Carlton was born in Maine in 1834, beng the son of Amos and Mary Carlton. He received his education from the schools of his native state and there remained until 1854, when he came via Panama to San Francisco, and thence to Indian valley in Sierra county, where he at once engaged in the fascinating labor of mining. In 1860 we find him in Oregon, and then in Walla Walla, whence he returned to The Dalles and then

WILLIAM MORFITT.

visited his home in Maine. Returning again to California, he went to Los Angeles county, and thence to Boise, Idaho, where he engaged in wagon building until 1882, at which time he located his present home place as a homestead. Mr. Carlton has devoted his time and energies to raising stock, cattle and horses, and to general farming, from that time until the present, having achieved a good success in these endeavors. In addition to these labors, Mr. Carlton has also operated a blacksmith shop, gaining a good trade from the surrounding neighborhood. He has the prospects of a fine coal mine on his lands, which will make them exceedingly valuable.

The marriage of Mr. Carlton and Mrs. Phoebe Basil, a native of Iowa, was solemnized in Boise, Idaho, in 1871, and they have six children, William A.; Laura M., wife of John Howard, of Pleasant valley; Alice, wife of Frank Beech, of Owyhee county, Idaho; Charles; Oliver; Robert. Mr. Carlton is a member of the A. F. & A. M., of Boise. For one term, Mr. Carlton served as county assessor and discharged the important duties of that office to the satisfaction of all. He is always interested in the affairs of the county and takes an active part in politics, being allied with the Republican party. For two and one-half years, he has been postmaster of Carter postoffice and he is a man in whom his fellows have confidence and is highly esteemed by all.

＊＊＊

R. D. GREER.—It is with pleasure that we are enabled to grant consideration in this volume of the history of Malheur county to the estimable gentleman whose name is at the head of this article, since he is one who partakes of the real spirit cf the pioneer and since he is a man of excellent qualities and since he has wrought in this vicinity for the substantial progress and upbuilding of the same for many years.

Mr. Greer was born in Ohio, on September 28, 1850, being the son of Guin and Elizabeth Greer. In 1866 he came with his parents to Lancaster county, Nebraska, and there he received the completion of his education and gave his attention to farming. He first came to Malheur county in 1875, then two years later returned to Nebraska, only to come west

again in 1880. Settlement was made at Emmett, Idaho, and twelve years he labored there, then removed to Weiser, where he operated in the lumbering industry and then moved to Ontario, and there embarked on the mercantile sea. He continued in a successful business there until 1900, when he sold his interests and came to his present place, one mile southeast from Owyhee postoffice. He has one quarter section, well irrigated and improved and productive of good dividends annually. Mr. Greer is active in the affairs of the county and has ever been allied on the side of progress and enterprise.

The marriage of Mr. Greer and Mrs. Alice L. Conley, a native of Michigan, was solemnized in 1872, at Lincoln, Nebraska, and they have one daughter, Myrtle. By her former husband, Mrs. Greer has one daughter, now the wife of Frank Davis, of this county. Mr. Greer is one of the leaders in the establishment of the Owyhee ditch and has always been dominated by a keen foresight and perception which has given him abundant success in his endeavors. Fraternally, he affiliates with the W. of W., in Ontario.

＊＊＊

JOSEPH M. DINWIDDIE.—This well known pioneer and responsible and leading business man and stockman of Malheur county, is one of the prominent citizens of the town of Jordan Valley and is a man of sterling qualities of worth and integrity, being possessed of excellent capabilities which have wrought with a winning hand in the business and financial realm of our county for many years.

Joseph M. was born in Indiana, on September 1, 1851, being the son of Daniel and Elsie Dinwiddie. In 1853 his parents came with the noble band of pioneers who crossed the plains in those days, and located in Linn county, Oregon. That was their home until the time of their death. There also our subject received his education and grew to manhood's estate. It was in 1875, that he started out for himself, and at once went to Klickitat county, Washington, and engaged in the stock business. He made a success, but in 1881 he determined to try the vicinity of Jordan Valley, and accordingly came hither with his herds and here he has been one of the prominent citizens since that time. He now has a fine estate of one section of fine land adjoining the town of Jordan Valley, and it is well improved with good buildings and all conveniences for handling it in a first class manner Also he owns twelve and one-half acres in the village and operates a first class hotel and livery barn. Mr. Dinwiddie is also one of the leaders in the realm of stock raising, for he has about three hundred and fifty head of horses and a large band of cattle, having been successful in this line and continuing at it constantly since his first residence here.

The marriage of Mr. Dinwiddie and Miss Laura E. King, a native of Walla Walla, Washington, was solemnized in Jordan Valley in 1884, and they have become the parents of four children, Zora, Elsie, Davis, and William Rufus. Mr. Dinwiddie enjoys the distinction of being one of the leaders of the county, a man of substantial qualities and whose labors establish him to be a man of excellent worth and reliability and wisdom.

JOSHUA L. COLE.—As one of the real builders of Malheur county, being a pioneer of the west in a very early day, the subject of this sketch is justly entitled to consideration in the volume of history now being made and it is with pleasure that we are enabled to recount some of the items of a long and useful career, wherein he has always been a prominent figure in the progress of the county, the welfare of his fellows, and in the prosecution of the business in his hand. At the present time Mr. Cole is the president of the first bank of Vale, being an incorporated state bank, with a capital of fifty thousands dollars and half that amount paid up.

Mr. Cole was born in Ripley county, Indiana, on March 29, 1832, being the son of William and Sarah J. (Clark) Cole. The father was a native of Virginia, but was taken to Kentucky in a very early day before even any wagon roads were made in that state. There he was raised and married and his first four children were born there also. He went thence to Indiana, and in 1858 he migrated to Minnesota, in which place he died in 1862. The mother was a native of Maryland and died in Iowa in 1842.

Our subject was reared on a farm, received a common school education in the primitive log school house, and on April 1, 1856, was married to Miss Malinda, daughter of John B. and Nancy (McLaughlin) Wise. To this union there were born three children, as follows: Leonard, married to Hattie Bond, and living in Huntington, Oregon; Emory, married to Barbara Kennedy, living on lower Willow creek; Eldora, wife of James Moody of Huntington. In 1860, Mr. Cole removed to Scott county, Minnesota, and in the spring of 1864, he went thence on the arduous trip across the plains with ox teams, the journey being completed in good time without serious trouble with the Indians, and the landing point was Boise, Idaho. Until 1868 we find Mr. Cole in that section of the country and then a move was made to what is now Malheur county, and four years later he came to lower Willow creek where he embarked in raising stock. Mr. Cole acquired title to one thousand acres of land, which was known as the J. L. Cole ranch throughout the entire country, and there he raised large herds of stock. In addition to the stock, Mr. Cole handled a large apiary, having as many as five hundred swarms of bees at one time. They brought a handsome return as he had large fields of alfalfa. In the spring of 1901 Mr. Cole sold his ranch and stock to his son, Emory, and he removed to Vale where he had a handsome residence. He was instrumental in starting the bank above referred to and as its head and manager, he has made a fine success in this business equal to his unbounded success in his former enterprises. He has a fine two story stone building in a prominent location in the town and handles a large business, having the bank quarters fitted up in fine shape.

On June 18, 1896, Mr. Cole was called upon to mourn the death of his wife. On May 21, 1898, Mr. Cole contracted a second marriage, the lady of his choice at this time being Miss Emily, daughter of William H. and Sarah J. (McLaughlin) Blackwell, of Ripley county, Indiana, and a relative of his first wife. In politics, Mr. Cole is a stanch Republican, and he cast his first vote for John C. Fremont, and has staid with the party since that time. He and his wife are devoted members of the Methodist church, as was also the former wife and the are warm advocates of the faith and supporters of the same. It is of note that when Mr. Cole came to Boise there were no houses there, the town being one of tents and he has always been in the vanguard of the pioneers laboring wisely and faithfully for the advancement of the country and the upbuilding of good industries, while in his walk he has shown forth those qualities of commendable virtue which have made him a light and example in the community, where to-day he is highly esteemed and beloved by all, he and his wife being leading members of society.

CHARLES SMITH.—This worthy pioneer and substantial citizen of Malheur county, is deserving of a place in any compilation that purports to give the history of this section, since his labors have been here for many years toward the development and progress of the country, and since he is a man of ability and has achieved a goodly success as the reward of his labors and thrift.

Mr. Smith was born in Louisville, Kentucky, on October 18, 1835, being the son of John and Susan Smith. At the age of eight he went with his parents to Illinois and there remained until 1854, when he came across the plains with his brothers, in an ox train, to Siskiyou county, California, and there engaged in mining. He made some good discoveries and later, 1858, went to the Cariboo mines at the time of the Fraser river excitement, whence he returned to Portland, then to Salem, and there followed his trade of brick mason. In 1878 he removed to Jackson county and remained three years and then went to Mugginsville, California, where he mined until 1880. The next year he came to Malheur county, and located the place where he now lives as a homestead, ten miles northwest from Rockville, and devoted himself to farming and stock raising. His place is under the irrigating ditch and well improved and he has a good band of stock. Mr. Smith mines some, being interested in several good properties.

The marriage of Mr. Smith and Miss Mary, daughter of John and Frances Ramsey, was solemnized in Salem, on November 9, 1865, and they have become the parents of three children, William W., residing in Malheur county; Fannie, wife of Mr. Ford, a stock-

man of Malheur county; George V. Mrs. Smith's parents crossed the plains in 1863, and her father died in Salem in 1875, but her mother is still living in Malheur county. Mrs. Smith was born on May 11, 1865. She has some fine relics, as gold rings and so forth, the gold of which she pounded out of the rocks with her own hands in California.

WILLIAM P. BEERS.—To the esteemed and distinguished gentleman and worthy pioneer, whose name initiates this paragraph, it is fitting that a consideration be granted in the history of Malheur county, since he, perhaps more than any other one man, has been instrumental in making the county what it is to-day, and also in the development of the other sections adjacent. Mr. Beers has done the lion's share, and in all this excellent labor and the achievements of his brain and hand, there have ever been manifested noble qualities of the typical man, and the courageous and intrepid pioneer, while his masterful ability has always placed him as leader among his fellows and rightly, too, for success has always been the result of his keen perception, sagacity, and assiduity.

William T. Beers was born in Wayne county, Indiana, on August 18, 1842, being the son of enterprising and leading parents. The family came to Burlington, Iowa, when our subject was quite young and eight years later they removed to Scott county, and three years subsequent to that we find him in Decatur county. In these various places William P. was educated and when the call came in 1862 for the loyal hearts to take up the cause of their country, young Beers was one of the first to press to the post of duty and he enlisted in the Thirteenth Missouri Calvary where he fought in many battles and did arduous military duty until the time of his honorable discharge. Four years and five months were spent in this service, and during this time he participated in the battles of Springfield, Blue Mount, and also others among which was one on the plains, his regiment being stationed for a time at Fort Collins, in Wyoming. In 1866, he crossed the plains to Helena, Montana, then went to the Bitter Roots and mined and in 1868 bought a freight outfit and did business between Fort Benton and Carrinne and Virginia City, making also three trips to Fort Hall, and then he came to the Snake and wintered near Idaho City. Then three years were spent in Nevada, and soon thereafter we find him in Silver City, Idaho, and after some more freighting to that city he sold his outfit and bought a portion of his present ranch, in 1874. The next years he assisted to erect a telegraph line from Winnemucca to Silver City, and also bought another freight outfit and moved mining machinery to Silver City, being in partnership with the well known John Catlow. Mr. Beers was here during the Indian outbreaks and his house still shows some of the bullet holes from the savages' rifles.

Mr. Beers owns what is known as the Ruby ranch, which is located fifteen miles west from Jordan Valley, being one of the first stage stations in the country. The ranch consists of three thousand. five hundred acres of fine land, being one of the best ranches in the entire state. Mr. Beers has about eight hundred head of cattle and three hundred head of horses. He used to handle about four thousand cattle but has now a less number and some of the finest specimens in the range. He has one thousand acres of fertile meadow land and is really the stock king of this country. Mr. Beers is actively interested in political matters and always is progressive and aggressive, although dominated by wise caution, and he holds to the principles of the true Jeffersonian Democracy.

The marriage of our subject and Miss Mary E. Annawalt was solemnized on the ranch where they now live in 1877, and they have five children, Ethel E., William E., R. Leone, Nellie B. and Ruby. Mrs. Beers is a native of Kansas City, Missouri.

--- ◆◆◆ ---

CASSIUS H. BROWN.—It is very acceptable to have the privilege of giving in epitome the salient points of the career of the estimable gentleman whose name is at the head of this article. Mr. Brown, familiarly known as Judge Brown, is one of the pioneers of this county and has always been much interested in its welfare, prominent in politics, a leader in the advancement of the cause of education, a prominent citizen and property owner, and a large-hearted, genial, upright, capable, and talented American citizen.

The birth of Cassius H. was on December 27, 1852, in a log cabin in Mt. Hope, McLean county, Illinois, being the son of George W. and Eleanor (Kenyon) Brown. This was in the Mt. Hope colony and the father enlisted in Company A, One Hundred and Seventeenth Illinois Infantry, being second lieutenant under General A. F. Smith. He participated in the battles at Nashville and Belmont and in many skirmishes. But just before Sherman started to the sea, the elder Brown was taken with pneumonia and died at Pulaski, Tennessee. His enlistment was on July 12, 1862. In 1869 our subject, after having gained a good education in the common schools, went to Henry county, Illinois, and in the fall of the following year he went to Iowa, but soon returned to Henry county. In February, 1873, he came to Plumas county, California, following farming and driving stage until the spring of 1879, when he went to Reno, Nevada, and clerked in a store, then went on the coast survey for the United States. In the spring of 1880, he went to Lyon county, Nevada, and in the fall of 1881, he came to his present place, which is nine miles west from Ontario, in the White settlement. He has a fine two hundred and forty acre farm, well irrigated, and improved in a good manner. He owns a large interest in the Nevada ditch and was one of the promoters of that fine institution, having been an officer in it for some time. His party were the first settlers in this vicinity. Judge Brown was one of the very first who advocated the raising of alfalfa and he was one of the first persons, who demonstrated that the Malheur valley was a successful fruit country, having now an elegant twenty acre orchard of all varieties indigenous to his climate.

In 1892, Mr. Brown was elected as county judge on the Republican ticket, being the first incumbent of that office elected by that party. He served with efficiency and satisfaction to the public for four years. Judge Brown was chairman of the Republican county convention in 1896-98 and 1900, and in 1898 and 1900 he was a delegate to the state convention and was a member of the state central committee. His grandfather Kenyon was a candidate for congress against Judge David Davis in Illinois, and in Atlanta, Illinois, our subject had the pleasure of seeing Abraham Lincoln. Fraternally, Judge Brown is popularly affiliated, being a Mason at Beckwith, California, in Hope Lodge, No. 234, and he has served for several years as secretary. In 1880 he was a charter member of the Hope Lodge, No. 22, in Mason Valley in Nevada, and the first master under the charter. He was a member of the Washoe Lodge, No. 28, at Payette, Idaho, when he came hither. In 1898 he became a charter member of Acacia Lodge, No. 118, at Ontario, and he was the first master for two years. He was a charter member of the Eastern Star, Chapter No. 69, of Ontario, and was the first worthy patron which position he is still filling.

Judge Brown has always taken an active interest in school matters and has served as clerk for many years. In addition to his handsome holdings already mentioned, the judge has an interest in the Vale Milling Company, and also is one of the incorporators of the Ontario Cemetery Association.

HON. J. R. BLACKABY.—Malheur county can boast of many distinguished pioneers who have made brilliant success in both the financial world and in the political realm, and one of the prominent men of this influential number is the gentleman whose name is at the head of this article, and who stands as one of the real builders of the county and is also one of the largest general merchandise operators within her borders at the present time, his store being located in Jordan Valley.

Mr. Blackaby was born in Iowa, on April 12, 1861, being the son of Bernard and Emeline Blackaby. There he grew to manhood and there also he received his primary education, completing the same when he graduated from the college in Keokuk, Iowa. That was in 1880, and immediately he came west, locating in this county and engaged in farming and teaching school. Three years were spent in the work of the educator and four as deputy clerk of the county and four years he served as postmaster in Jordan Valley. In 1898 the people recognizing his abilities, rewarded him with a term in the state legislature, where he did excellent work, serving on important committees and taking part in beneficial legislation

for the entire state. Eighteen hundred and ninety-one was the year when he embarked on the mercantile sea and now he has one of the largest stocks of goods in the entire county and he is the recipient of a large patronage, drawn to his stores by his deferential treatment of all customers and his care of the interests of those who trade with him. He carries a well assorted stock and one can get anything that is in the realm of general merchandise and be assured that it is the best; and when once a person becomes a customer of Mr. Blackaby he is sure to remain. Mr. Blackaby is one of the organizers of the Bank of Ontario of Ontario, Oregon, and is now and has been since its establishment its vice-president. He is one of the financiers of the county and has demonstrated his ability in a worthy manner.

The marriage of Mr. Blackaby and Miss Mary J. Bauch, a native of Van Buren county, Iowa, was solemnized in that county on October 11, 1882. They have five children, Otto C., Earl, Larue, William J., Jay R. Mr. Blackaby is a member of the I. O. O. F., Jordan Valley Lodge No. 158, and of the K. O. T. M. Mr. Blackaby, by reason of real worth and the merits of his achievements, is counted one of the most influential and prominent citizens of the county and he is also one of the men always arrayed on the side of advancement and progress.

HERBERT J. WARD.—This capable and progressive gentleman is one of the leading men of this vicinity, being a well-to-do and prominent farmer and was one of the promoters of the valuable Owyhee ditch, being an incorporator and one who led the enterprise to a successful issue. Mr. Ward was born in Quebec, Canada, on April 12, 1856, the son of George P. and Elizabeth (Sherman) Ward. He spent his youthful days in the invigorating exercise of farm work and in gaining a good education from the public schools. At the age of twenty-two he left the parental roof for the world of labor and trial. His first work for himself was fireman on a locomotive and in due time he had mastered the engineer's art and was installed as an engineer of a steam shovel and then handled an engine on the road. In 1880 he came to Oregon, engaging in the sheep business. It was at this time that he began the agitation of the Owyhee ditch proposition and was among the very first who conceived the plan. He has steadily labored and planned for this valuable consummation and now he has a fine quarter section well watered from this canal. It was in 1894 that he settled on the land now his farm, taking it by the homestead act. It is situated two and one-half miles southwest from Nyssa and is one of the fine farms of the country. He has large fields of alfalfa, fine orchards, a valuable residence with barns and outbuildings to match and shade and ornamental trees and tasty grounds. Mr. Ward has added forty acres by purchase, which gives him a very valuable estate. He has several thousand sheep and is one of the leaders in that industry.

The marriage of Mr. Ward to Miss Sylvinia, daughter of James and Sarah McConnell, was solemnized on November 16, 1896, and one child, George P., was born to them on February 16, 1898. Mrs. Ward's parents were formerly of Ontario, Canada, but went to New York and in 1885 the father died. The mother, with eight children, came to Caldwell, Idaho, and is now living at Owyhee. Mr. Ward came to this country with practically no means and he has won the meed of good success and a generous competence for the industry and wise management that he has bestowed here.

◆•◆

CHARLES M. JONES.—It is gratifying to be privileged to put in print an epitome of one of the brave men who fought, as did the subject of this sketch, for the honor of the stars and stripes and the safety of our free institutions when the foul hand of treason sought to deface all and destroy the homes of freedom. In addition, Mr. Jones has always shown himself in the walks of life to be upright and capable and has done a noble part in the advancement and development of the resources of the country.

Speaking more particularly of his personal history, we note that his birth occurred in Hickman county, Tennessee, on August 13, 1836, being the son of Stephen and Jane Jones. He was reared amid the environments of a farm and gained his education from the schools held in the log cabins of the day. Our subject remained at home until he had reached man-

hood's estate, and in October, 1857, he was married to Miss Emily M. Downey in Searcy county, Arkansas, and soon thereafter went to Marion county, in Arkansas. And there, when the war broke out, he offered his services for freedom's cause. The date of his actual enlistment was August 6, 1862, at which time he was mustered into Company C, First Arkansas Cavalry, in the volunteer army. He was under Colonel Harrison and was soon detailed as musician in the regimental band. He participated in many skirmishes and did his share of hard service until August 23, 1865, when he was honorably discharged. He is now a member of the A. P. Hovey Post, G. A. R., at Ontario. Immediately following his discharge, he returned to his home and family and in 1875 he brought his family, having eight children, across the plains with ox teams, to the vicinity of Prairie City, Grant county. Two years later, he came to Ada county, Idaho, and thence to Washington county. It was in 1892 that he came to the vicinity of Ontario and went to farming and in 1899, he purchased his present place of forty acres, one mile west of Nyssa. He has it well improved and raises abundance of alfalfa hay, cutting as high as eight tons to the acre each year. His farm has abundance of water from the Owyhee ditch.

To Mr. and Mrs. Jones there have been born the following children: William A., deceased; David J.; Mrs. Emma Langley, of Santa Cruz, California; Andrew J., of Washington county, Idaho; John R., traveling agent; Mrs. Laura Stacy, near Vale; George W., deceased; Ada, deceased; Erastus E. Mr. Jones is beginning the golden years of his life and he is well entitled, because of his faithful labors, to enjoy in quietness the portion that he has gained, being respected by all.

◆•◆

JEREMIAH SHEA.—One of our early pioneers, whose worthy labors have done much toward the development of the resources and the substantial progress of Malheur county, is named at the head of this article and he is eminently fitted to be accorded consideration in this volume of his county's history, since he is a man of good standing, influential and prominent, has always been a progressive and patriotic citizen, is possessed of integrity and a stanch character and is held in high esteem by all of his fellows.

Mr. Shea was born in Canada on March 31, 1847, and there he was educated and remained until he had arrived at manhood's estate. Then he engaged in lumbering until 1872, at which date he came to this country and engaged with his brother in the stock business. Afterward he went to South Mountain and operated a meat market, then migrated to Silver City, and went into the livery business, and from there he furnished horses to the fleeing settlers at the time of the Indian outbreak in 1878. In 1883 we find him in Wagontown, keeping hotel, where he spent a number of years and soon afterwards he was on Cow creek engaged in the stock business. In 1887 Mr. Shea removed to Jordan creek and bought a ranch and two years later bought his present ranch home three miles east from Jordan Valley. He has four hundred and eighty acres of valuable land and large herds of horses and cattle. Mr. Shea also owns a stage line to De Lamar and Daisy from Jordan Valley, and he has been county assessor for a time.

The marriage of Mr. Shea and Miss Mary Fenwick, a native of California, was celebrated at Wagontown, in 1877, and they have nine children, named as follows: John, Maggie, Sarah, Neal, Agnes, Ellen, Guy, Ilene, and Eugene. Mr. Shea is one of the prominent men of the county, and also one of the heavy property owners and is a stanch, upright and patriotic citizen and esteemed gentleman.

ANDREW McGREGOR.—This doughty and intrepid frontiersman, now one of the leading farmers and stockmen of his vicinity, having a fine estate eight miles west from Ontario, which is the family home, and being a man of prominence and capabilities, has accomplished much in the development of the county and we are pleased to accord to him a representation in the history of Malheur county.

Mr. McGregor was born in Glasgow, Scotland on June 28, 1845, being the son of Duncan and Marguerette (McIntyre) McGregor. The father was born in Inverness, north Scotland, on February 14, 1800, and the mother was born in Edinburgh, Scotland, on August

27, 1805. In 1846 the family came to America in a sailing vessel, being six weeks on the trip. Landing in New York, they made their way to Boston, where the father worked at block printing and dyeing in a calico factory. In 1849 marks the date when they came to the vicinity of Oshkosh, Wisconsin, and there on August 14, 1862, he enlisted in Company K, Twentieth Wisconsin Volunteer Infantry, being mustered in at Camp Randall, Madison, Wisconsin, and went thence to the barracks at St. Louis, and served under General Schofield in the First Brigade, Second Division, Army of the Frontier. He participated in the battle of Prairie Grove, Arkansas, December 7, 1862, was in the third siege of Vicksburg in 1863, took part in the battle of Yazoo, Atchafalga, Fort Morgan, Alabama, Spanish Fort, the siege of Mobile, and many skirmishes and received an honorable discharge on July 14, 1865, at Galveston, Texas. Following the war he returned to this home in Wisconsin, and followed logging for a time, and on July 3, 1869, he was married to Martha M., daughter of James W. and Caroline Davis, who were natives of the state of New York. Our subject then went to Kewaunee county, Wisconsin, and in 1871 removed to Meeker county, Minnesota, and there farmed and lumbered until 1876. In 1877 he drove a team across the plains to Boise and the following year he was with Colonel Green under General Howard, after the Indians, a few of whom they captured on the head waters of the Salmon. At one time, Mr. McGregor owned the site of the Natatorium in Boise. It was 1879 that his wife and four children joined him at Boise, and in 1882 they came to the vicinity of Ontario, and there he paid fifty dollars for a willow cabin and dirt floor for his family. Eighteen hundred and eighty-six marks the date of his removal to his present place, eight miles west from Ontario, as mentioned above. His place is excellently improved with buildings, orchards, fences, shade trees, irrigating ditches, and all things necessary to make a rural place comfortable and profitable. He has another farm two and one-half miles west from Ontario. Mr. McGregor is a member of the A. P. Hovey Post, No. 21, of the G. A. R. at Ontario. He is also a member of the Armor Lodge, No. 69, K. of P., of Ontario.

To this worthy couple, there have been

born ten children, as follows: Isabella, wife of H. T. Husted, of Ontario; Minnie, wife of H. C. Ross of Nyssa; Andrew; Robert; Maggie, deceased; Harry; Martha, wife of A. Wellington of Dell; Eva; James; John. In addition to the property holdings mentioned above Mr. McGregor has a good band of cattle and fifty stand of bees, which provide abundance of honey from the fine alfalfa fields. He is a man of prominence and ability and enjoys the esteem and confidence of the entire community.

ANDREAS L. SPROUL.—The well known representative of business in Ontario, whose name initiates this paragraph is a man of enterprise and intelligence, being at the present time the incumbent of the postoffice, where he has served the interests of the people since March 20, 1899, and has demonstrated, as also in all his career, his ability, faithfulness, and integrity. Mr. Sproul was born in Annapolis county, Nova Scotia, on February 18, 1863, being the son of Samuel and Mary (Litch) Sproul. He was favored with a good education from the common schools and at the age of fourteen went to sea, and at the age of seventeen years he was promoted to the position of captain, his vessel being the David J. Adams, plying between Digby and Boston. Later, he and his brother purchased the same vessel and rechristened it the Annie M. Sproul, having a sister of that name. The brother still owns and operates the vessel. At the age of twenty-three our subject sold his interest in the ship and came west to Grant county, Oregon, arriving there in the spring of 1887. He located near Dayville and went into the sheep and horse business, which he continued uninterruptedly until 1895. At that date he sold his sheep, but still owns a band of horses. He had acquired real estate interests in various places in Malheur county, and has made this county his home since 1892. On March 11, 1893, Mr. Sproul took to himself a wife, the lady being Miss Ella, daughter of Lewis and Martha Dale, of Missouri. Mrs. Sproul was teaching in Caldwell, Idaho, previous to her marriage. In 1894 Mr. Sproul removed with his family to Ontario and there opened the Ontario Livery and Feed Stable, which he successfully operated until 1899, when he sold, being

appointed postmaster at that time. Mr. Sproul was one of the locaters of the Owyhee ditch, being one of the incorporators of the company and filled the office of director until he sold his interests. He owns considerable real estate in Ontario, and also improved property and is one of the prominent men of the town, being always interested and active in political matters. He has served as councilman of the town and at the present time has received the nomination on the Republican ticket as sheriff of the county and he is well liked and highly esteemed wherever he is known. Mr. and Mrs. Sproul have one child, Harold.

GARRISON J. GRAY.—To the prominent and esteemed citizen of Malheur county whose name appears above we grant a representation in the history of the county, since he is to-day one of the leading men domiciled here, has always labored for the upbuilding of the county, is a man of integrity and uprightness, and receives the commendation of his fellows. Mr. Gray's grandfather, John Gray, was said to be the last living soldier from the Revolution. He was a drummer boy at Bunker Hill and saw his father fall, then seized his sire's musket and fought until the struggle closed. He worked for General Washington after the war. He died near Hiramsburg, Noble county, Ohio, in March, 1868, lacking only two months of being one hundred and five years of age. His stepdaughter, Mrs. Nancy Thomas, is now living at the age of ninety years on the farm adjoining that old homestead.

Our subject was born in Noble county, Ohio, February 23, 1830, being the son of Isaac and Elizabeth (Gorby) Gray. When five years of age he was taken with his parents to Athens county, and the following year, 1836, his mother died. In 1839 he went with his father to Jones county, Iowa, thence to Linn county and then to Cedar county, in which last place, at the age of eleven, he attended his first term of school. The next year they removed to Muscatine county and one year thereafter he tied his earthly possessions in a red handkerchief, clad in simple clothes and with a straw hat which he had braided himself, started forth into the wide world to seek his fortune. His first day's travel led him to Mus-

GARRISON J. GRAY.

RESIDENCE OF GARRISON J. GRAY.

catine and the next stop was Bloomington, and there he visited his sister, who was working at the house of Judge Williams, a brother of Judge George Williams, of Portland. Thence he went to his brother, in Jones county, and there attended school. The next spring he carried the mail from Dubuque to Iowa City on horseback, then went to Rock Island, Illinois, and broke prairie sod with oxen. He kept zealously at work with his books and at the age of twenty had a certificate and was back in his native place in Ohio teaching school. In the spring of 1851 he went with a company to Fort Leavenworth, and then paid fifty dollars for the privilege of driving an ox team across the plains to Huntington. Thence our subject, who was a carpenter, John Weston, a clerk, George Cowne, a printer, and Isaac Hamilton, a farmer, each provided with twenty-five pounds of hardtack, made their way afoot to The Dalles in ten days, arriving on August 13, 1851, the very day that the first steamboat made its way to that town, under the direction of Captain Wells. He went to Portland on the Captain's row boat, and in that town refused a job with pay at three dollars per day and town lots at twenty-five dollars each in the heart of Portland as pay. He went to Astoria, saw Major Halleck, Generals Grant and McClellan, then went to Salmon and the winter of 1852-3 attended the university at Salem, known as the Willamette University. He taught school in Oregon and california and followed carpentering in the summer until 1860, when his industry and frugality had gained him a nice little holding of property. In 1863 we find him in the Idaho mines and at Fort Boise he was in charge of the carpenter work of the post and was there when the town was laid out. He kept a stage station seventeen miles below Boise and sold five thousand dollars worth of vegetables from his ranch, and in 1867 he went to Albany, and having made a snug little fortune, he retired. In 1871 he desired more activity and took a large bunch of cattle for the Idaho mines and stopped and took a homestead at lower Willow creek, where he now lives, having a good farm of four hundred and eighty acres, an elegant two-story and one-half ten-room dwelling, with pure spring water piped into it, a finely improved estate, and a large holding of stock. He has also plenty of water for irrigating,

one hundred swarms of bees, a five-acre orchard of choice varieties and is a leading and prosperous citizen. His estate is located three miles southwest from Dell, of which he was the first postmaster, continuing for fifteen years. He received his commission in this office from General Grant.

Mr. Gray and Miss Sarah A. Moore, a native of Ohio, were married on February 1, 1855, and six children have been born to them: Martha A., deceased; Ida I., wife of B. L. Jones, of Vale; Elizabeth E., wife of B. Emmons, of Eugene; Mary B., wife of Dr. O. M. Dodson, of Baker City; David L., deceased; Rosetta, wife of H. C. Bowers, of Baker City. On January 20, 1885, Mrs. Gray was called away by death. On September 6, 1886, Mr. Gray married Miss Sarah I. Wales, of Roodhouse, Greene county, Illinois, and they have three children, Ethel, Elmer Roe and Edith. On June 17, 1899, this lady died. Mr. Gray and both of his wives were members of the M. E. church. He is affiliated with the Masons. In the early times Mr. Gray had difficulties, as had all the settlers, with the Indians and many are the hardships which he and his were called upon to endure. In 1897 Mr. Gray went to his old home in the east and had a joyous time in renewing old acquaintances.

MILTON G. HOPE.—It is with pleasure that we are enabled to incorporate in the volume of the history of the county of Malheur an epitome of the career of the estimable gentleman, careful and capable business man, and sturdy pioneer of this section, since he is a man of ability, has shown commendable zeal in the development of the country, has gained a handsome holding in this county, is a man of sound principles, and well known for integrity and uprightness.

The birth of Mr. Hope occurred in Brookville, Vernon county, Wisconsin, on August 31, 1859, his parents being George W. and Emeline (Williams) Hope. The account of the father's noble service in the war of the rebellion, the mother's moves to Kansas and so forth, are mentioned in another portion of this work and need not be repeated here. Our subject was educated in the common schools and later took a course in the Institute at Atchison,

Kansas. He went with his mother to Kansas, Brown county, in 1870, in 1873, went to Norton county, and in 1880 he went to Colorado, and the following year, his brother, Isaiah, mention of whom is made in this book, came and they went into partnership, in which they have continued since. In 1882 they came to Wood river, Idaho, and the next year they came to Malheur county, each entering a homestead in the vicinity of Vale. In 1887 they started a merchandise establishment with a capital of one hundred dollars, and here was brought out the real metal of the brothers for it was but a short time before their fair and deferential treatment of patrons brought them such a large trade that they had a fine store and about forty thousand dollars' worth of goods. Such is their business record in short and in part. In addition to this commendable showing they have large interests in the First Bank of Vale, own seven hundred acres of land and sixty acres on which are situated the famous hot springs known now as the Hope Geysers, which have heretofore been a landmark since the white men first came to this country. Politically, Mr. Hope is a stanch Republican, casting his first vote for James A. Garfield in Colorado and walking sixteen miles to the polls. He has served on the school board for thirteen years, thus manifesting his untiring zeal for the welfare of the educational interests of the county. He has been mayor of the town for two terms and for eight years he was postmaster. It is of note that in 1887-8 our subject was in business with his older brother, John A., but finding the need of further training in the school he sold out and went to the institute mentioned amove and after that graduated from the Bryant & Chapman Commercial College of St. Joseph, Missouri. Then followed the successful career that has been outlined.

The marriage of Mr. Hope and Miss Emma H., daughter of Francis and Sarah J. High, occurred at Norton, Kansas, and three children have been born to bless the happy household: Leslie L., Elizabeth, and the baby, not yet named. Mr. Hope is past grand of the I. O. O. F., Vale Lodge, No. 100, and was first chief patriarch of Malheur Encampment of Vale. Mr. Hope is to-day one of the men who enjoys the respect and esteem of the population of Malheur county and is entitled to much credit

for the enterprising labors which he has performed here, and the zeal manifested for the welfare of the town, schools, and county in general, while his own large business interests as vice-president of the First Bank, manager of the Vale Milling Company of which he and his brother own one-half interest, and numerous other industries, are attended to with the same care, geniality, keen foresight, and good practical wisdom that have always characterized him in all his walk.

◆◆◆

HON. ISAIAH W. HOPE is one of the most prominent men in Malheur county to-day, and he has been a leader here for many years, having started in the mercantile business with his brother in an early day and building up one of the mammoth establishments of the west, while also in many lines of industry he has brought the fine talent of which he is possessed into play with the gratifying result that he has achieved a genral round of success in the realm of merchant, general developer of the country, organizer of the Vale Commercial Company, promoter of various leading industries of the county, banker, and representative of his county in the state legislature, in which latter position he has the distinction of being the only man who has received a second term at the hands of the people; thus it is seen that Mr. Hope is deserving of a prominent mention in the history of Malheur county, where he stands esteemed by all both for his work and for his own intrinsic worth.

Isaiah W. was born in Brookville, Vernon county, Wisconsin, September 28, 1861, being the son of George W. and Emeline (Williams) Hope. His father was one of the martyrs of the Civil war, enlisting in the Twenty-fifth Wisconsin Volunteers in the spring of 1862. He was under Sherman in the siege of Vicksburg, was sent to the north to fight the Indians in the Minnehaha massacre, returned to go with Sherman to the south, and was taken sick and sent to the hospital at Memphis, Tennessee, where he died in the spring of 1863. In 1870 our subject went with his mother and the rest of the family to Brown county, Kansas, and in 1873, they went to Norton county, where the mother took up a soldier's claim and is living there at the present time. In July,

1881, Mr. Hope came west to Colorado, entering into partnership with his brother, Milton G., with whom he has labored ever since. In 1883 they came to Bellville, Idaho, and the following year they came to Vale. They each entered a homestead and with their bare hands they commenced the work of improvement. In 1887 they started a mercantile establishment with one hundred dollars capital and they have merited the patronage of the people because of fair and honorable treatment, and the patronage came and the result has been that at the present time the Hope Brothers have a stock of from thirty to forty thousand dollars worth of finely assorted merchandise, and a fine large stone store. In 1902 they incorporated under the name of the Vale Commercial Company in which they hold a half interest. They also own an interest in the Vale Milling Company, and have seven hundred acres of land, besides sixty on which are located the famous Hope Springs. They are interested heavily in the First Bank of Vale.

In 1890 Mr. Hope married Miss Lillie B., daughter of Fred and Hannah Gellerman, near Vale, and to them have born the following children: Norma E., Irma D., Mazie. In 1894 Mr. Hope was elected on the Republican ticket to represent this county in the state legislature and at the expiration of his term was promptly re-elected. He is a member of the state central committee, and chairman of the county committee. Mr. Hope is member and past grand of the I. O. O. F., Lodge No. 100, of Vale; is also past chief patriarch of the Malheur Encampment of Vale. He and his wife are member of the Rebekah and she is past grand, while he has served as secretary of the I. O. O. F. for several years. Mr. Hope was educated in the common schools and then has perfected himself in that greatest of all schools, practical business on the American frontier. He and his brother were the original locators of the Malheur Oil Company and hold large interests in that concern. Mr. Hope has forty acres adjoining the town of Vale and intends soon to erect a residence there.

WILLIAM M. MANGIN.—The subject of this article is one of the oldest pioneers of Jordan Valley, a man of ability and worth, one who has wrought here with assiduity and sagacity since the early days, is now recognized as one of the prominent men of the county, has ever maintained an unsullied reputation and manifested a stanch character of uprightness and integrity, and in business circles has won a success that is a credit to any man, therefore he is deserving of a prominent position in the history of his county and it is with pleasure that we accord him such at this time.

William Mangin was born in Boston, Massachusetts, on March 16, 1830, being the son of James and Elizabeth Mangin, natives of Ireland and Nova Scotia respectively. Our subject received his education at his native place and at the early age of sixteen years he embarked on the schooner, Boston, which went to Newfoundland to load with codfish for Gibraltar; thence to Madrid where they loaded with fruit and wine for America. Returning to Boston, he then went to Mobile for a load of cotton, then transferred, after a summer spent on the bay, to another ship, the Dublin, and went with a cargo of cotton to Liverpool. Returning to New York, he made another trip to Liverpool, then made several trips to foreign countries, as West Indies, France, and many others. In 1856 he arrived in San Francisco, sailing on the good ship, Wild Duck, and spent some time on the bay, and then in 1858 came to the timber regions of Puget Sound, whence he went to Fraser river experiencing some exciting times with the Indians. It was as early 1872 when he came to Jordan Valley. He had a brother living here then, who died in 1874. Our subject took a homestead and at once went to farming and raising stock. He has been eminently successful in these lines and now has one of the finest farms in the county of Malheur, it being located one mile east from Jordan Valley, and consisting of four hundred and eighty acres of fine fertile land. He has a large bunch of cattle and is a leader among the stock men. In 1878 when the savages were on the war path, Mr. Mangin was of inestimable service in defending the settlers, and he has always shown the qualities of worth and bravery.

The marriage of Mr. Mangin and Martha Kellog, widow of John Kellog, a pioneer of 1872, was solemnized in 1883. By her former husband, Mrs. Mangin has four boys, Warren J., Joseph M., Edward C., and George A. It is with pleasure that we have reverted to the career of Mr. Mangin during his entire stay in this county, for it has been passed with credit to himself and advantage to all concerned, while he numbers as his friends all who may have the pleasure of his acquaintance.

* * *

HON. RANSOM BEERS is one of the oldest pioneers of this section and a man of enterprise and energy, having wrought in all the arduous and trying occupations of the frontier life, being eminently successful in them all, as well as having done much here for the upbuilding of the county, while his life of uprightness and integrity, with manifestation of sound principles, has commended him to the confidence and esteem of all who have the pleasure of knowing him.

The birth of our subject occurred in Ohio, near Columbus, on March 27, 1831, and his parents were Conrad and Jemima (Zin) Beers. He was reared on a farm and received his education in the primitive log schoolhouse of that section and day. At the early age of ten, his mother died and he knew the sorrows of that sad event mingled with his boyhood days. Until the fall of 1852 he remained with his father, and then he removed to Henry county, Iowa, and the following spring set out across the plains in a train of twelve wagons to California. Four months later he was digging gold in Placerville, having completed the trip without special incident. Eleven years were spent in that section in mining and success crowned his efforts. Then, in the spring of 1864, he went by ship to Portland, and thence to Mormon basin, where he engaged in placer mining until 1872, being also successful in that venture. Mr. Beers rented his mines in that basin and opened a store which occupied his attention until 1874, when he came to his present place, which is five miles southeast from Malheur. Here he owns one-half section of land, well improved and stocked. He has a fine eight-roomed residence, a good barn and a nice bunch of cattle. Mr. Beers took this land from the raw country and has made all these improvement, being one of the most successful farmers and stockmen of the country.

In fraternal relations Mr. Beers has been for thirty-nine years a member of the I. O. O. F., and is one of the charter members of the Baker City Lodge, No. 25. In 1868 the people of the section where he resides called him from the pursuit of his private enterprises, and elected him to represent the county in the state legislature. And in that capacity Mr. Beers manifested the same thoroughness, good judgment, ability, and faithfulness, that have ever characterized him and he filled the office with credit to himself and satisfaction to his constituency. He was elected on the Democratic ticket. We desire to say that Mr. Beers started out in life with no capital except his hands and a good stout heart and he has accumulated a fine property because of his thrift and industry. He still owns the mines in the Mormon Basin. In the time of the famous Centennial, Mr. Beers went to visit the exposition in Philadelphia. In 1900 also he went to the east, but in all his travels Mr. Beers disclaims having found any place which pleases him as well as his western home. He is now spending his golden days in the quiet enjoyment of his portion, which he has wrought out with his own hands, and he is one of the highly esteemed and respected men of the county, being beloved by all. Mr. Beers has always cast his lot with the ways of celibacy, being content to enjoy its quieter walk than the responsibilities of the connubial relations.

* * *

JAMES McCAIN.—The estimable pioneer whose name initiates this paragraph was a man of energy, faithfulness, and integrity, and he wrought here for the development and substantial progress of the county, with a strong hand and with display of wisdom which gave him a brilliant success both in the established confidence of his fellows and in the financial holdings that came to him. It was a sad day when he was called from the walks of life and associations of his family.

James McCain was born in New York in 1833, and there he remained for the first twenty years of his life, and then came to Wisconsin. There on July 24, 1854, occurred his marriage with Miss Eliza Tamson, a native of England, who came at the age of fifteen with her parents to Wisconsin from her native land. In 1866 the young couple crossed the dreary waste of plains and mountains to Boise valley, locating about sixteen miles from Boise. They took up farming and stock raising and later removed to Reynolds creek and four years later went thence to Cow creek, remaining until 1878, when they were driven out by hostile Indians. At this time they lost about seven thousand dollars worth of stock, mostly horses. They then removed to their present place, two miles east from the town of Jordan Valley. At this place they acquired title to two hundred and seventy-three acres of land. Here, on July 11, 1893, occurred the death of Mr. McCain. He left his widow and two children, Ellen, wife of John Huff, of Riverside; James B., a stockman. There was one other child, Thomas, deceased.

Mrs. McCain has married Mr. G. A. McGovern, and they reside on the home place, which is supplied with all necessary improvements and provided with a good stone residence. Mr. McGovern was born in Canada, on April 18, 1854, and is a man of good standing and well respected.

GEORGE E. WARD.—No work that purports to chronicle the careers of the leading citizens of Malheur county would be complete were there omission to mention the estimable gentleman whose name initiates this paragraph, and whose labors have been fruitful of much good to this portion of the county, as well as adjacent vicinities, having been instrumental in originating the famous Owyhee ditch and in furthering the plans for its completion, while also in general development of the country he has done very much. George E. Ward was born in Quebec, Canada, on September 14, 1852, being the son of George P. and Elizabeth (Sherman) Ward. He was reared on a farm and in a hotel and was educated in the common schools of his native place. In 1879 he came to Silver City, Idaho, and there he engaged in the sheep business, remaining in the same for five years. Then he sold out and went to Umatilla county, in this state, bought a band of sheep and brought them to the Owyhee river and since that time he has continuously devoted his attention to the sheep business. He has a stock ranch in Grant county and one on the Owyhee river and is one of the leaders in this important line of industry, having brought to bear in its prosecution a wealth of ability, energy and wisdom that have given him an excellent success. His three brothers were associated with him in the Owyhee ditch project. Four others were brought into the enterprise and later it was incorporated and Mr. Ward has remained in it, giving his wisdom, energy and money to make of it the unbounded success that it is at the present time. In political matters Mr. Ward is allied with the Republicans and has always devoted the proper amount of attention to the affairs of the county and state. He believes implicitly in the principles of protection for the industries and citizens of this republic and always labors for that end. He has now much stock and is esteemed as one of the leaders of the prominent men of the county.

G. B. GLOVER.—The stockmen of Malheur county are the men who have brought the county to the front by their arduous labors and wise manipulation of the resources here found, and as a prominent one of this distinguished class the subject of this article is well known, being also a worthy pioneer, who wrought here with a firm hand and endured the hardships incident to that life, while his keen foresight and enterprise led him to see the value of the country that he was opening.

Mr. Glover was born in Holly Springs, Mississippi, on December 20, 1841, and at the age of fourteen went with his father and the balance of the family to Arkansas, where he remained until the breaking out of the terrible Civil war and then enlisted in the Confederate army, doing valiant military service until the close of the conflict. He then returned to his home, and in 1870 came to Jackson county, Missouri, and thence, five years later, he journeyed to what is now Malheur county. He located where he now lives, eighteen miles northwest from Jordan valley, at Cow Creek lakes, took land, and engaged in farming and stockraising. Success has attended his thrifty and wisely bestowed labors and he now has a valuable estate of eleven hundred and forty acres of land. "The Lakes," as the estate is called, is one of the most beautiful, as well as valuable, in southeastern Oregon. He has it well improved, and it is made a comfortable and attractive rural abode. Mr. Glover has one hundred and fifty cattle and other stock. He is always active in the political matters of the county and state and is an influential and prominent citizen.

The marriage of Mr. Glover and Mrs. Elizabeth (Shea) Keenan was solemnized in Wagontown and they have become the parents of the following children: Wren, deceased, Holmes, Frances, John, Violet and Elaire. Mrs. Glover is a Canadian by birth, and had by her former husband two children, Anna and Theresa. Mr. Glover has always manifested uprightness in his business life, and the manner in which he has managed his business interests reflects credit upon him and demonstrates him to be a man of ability and wisdom.

ROBERT W. WORSHAM.—This enterprising and representative citizen of Malheur county has the distinction of being one of the early pioneers of Oregon, while also he was among the very first in many mining regions where he endured the almost overwhelming hardships there encountered and wrought with a strong hand and courageous heart, doing well his part in the great development of the west. Robert W. was born in Hopkinsville, Christian county, Kentucky, on April 30, 1839, being the son of Robert and Emeline (Elgin) Worsham. He was reared on a farm and in the winter months attended school. In 1852 he came with his parents across the plains and settlement was made in Clackamas county, near Oregon City. The trip was without danger or special incident, except four of their number died with the cholera, although the train was small, consisting of only eighteen wagons. The father had a large family and the first winter in Oregon City was a time of trial. Flour sold for thirty dollars per barrel and potatoes for five dollars per bushel. Of meat they had none except what game they killed. The father took a half section of land and settled down to make a home, and in 1859, our subject went to the Similikameen mines and then on the Thompson river, in British Columbia, whence he went to Fraser river and from there to the Canal river in the Cariboo district. He followed prospecting and mining and many is the fight he had with the In-

dians and finally he was obliged to leave the region on account of their hostilities. In 1860 he bought a farm and settled down near the home place and on April 11, 1861, occurred the happy event of the marriage of Mr. Worsham and Miss Lucy E., daughter of Joseph T. and Hannah E. Wingfield, of Oregon City. In 1862 he went to the Florence mines in Idaho, and later to the Oro Fino mines, being successful in both places. Then he returned home and spent a little time on the farm, after which he opened a butcher business in Oregon City, remaining there until 1877, when he came to Malheur and bought a stock farm of one hundred and sixty acres four miles southeast from Malheur post office. He has added as much more since and now has a well improved estate and finely stocked, having also good house and barns and other buildings. In 1878 it is of note that Mr. Worsham was scout for the government in the Indian troubles which then occurred. He has followed stock-raising and farming and mining since coming here and has some fine quartz properties at the present time. Mr. Worsham has been superintendent for the Eldorado mines for eight years.

The following children have been born to him and his estimable wife: Adelbert, deceased; Florence E., wife of John B. Woodcock; James T. married to Effie E. Craig; Laura, deceased; David K., married to Sadie Bowman; Charles, deceased; Claud R.; Walter N. The married children all live in the vicinity of Malheur. Mr. Worsham has a good home in Malheur and he dwells there at the present time. He and his wife are members of the Methodist church and they are devoted in the support of their faith.

ERWIN A. RIEGER.—The subject of this sketch is one of the younger men who have achieved brilliant success in the business world of the west, being located in Ontario, where he has an important interest in the Oregon Forwarding Company, one of the largest general merchandise establishments of the eastern part of Oregon, which owes much of its unbounded success to the keen business ability and fine executive force of Mr. Rieger. The birth of Erwin A. occurred in Ludwigburg, Germany, on January 28, 1873, being the son of Frederick J. and Mary (Kiesel) Rieger. The father was a leading attorney of his country, and our subject received a good education in the common schools and in the Heilbronn King Carli College, then studied law and was admitted to its practice in his native town at the age of twenty-one. Soon after this important event, he bade the fatherland adieu, took farewell of friends and embarked for the United States. The spring of 1894 marks the date of his landing in New York, having sailed in the steamer Scandia. From the metropolis he came direct to Ogden, then to Parma, Idaho. He visited these places and others for the purpose of getting acquainted with the American people and their ways, and also he devoted some time to farming, then went to Haley, Idaho, and thence to Salt Lake City, where he engaged in mercantile pursuits with his brother. It was in 1896 that he came to Ontario and here in 1902 he entered into partnership with Mr. Beckman, the firm being known as the Oregon Forwarding Company. That name was changed to Beckman and Rieger in January, 1902, and in April of the same year the old name was again assumed. They carry a large and complete line of goods in all of the following lines, gents' furnishing goods, dry goods, groceries, boots and shoes, hardware, farming implements, and crockery and other lines as well, making their establishment one of mammoth proportions. The business is done in a large brick building, being the most commodious in the town, and they also use in storing their goods five large warehouses. The trade of this company reaches in great directions to every point of the compass and they have builded for themselves a patronage and reputation that surpasses, doubtless, that of any competing establishment in the entire country.

On November 27, 1901, Mr. Rieger married Miss Sylvia, daughter of George and Nellie (Stevens) Lyells, early pioneers of Baker City. Fraternally, he is affiliated with the A. F. & A. M., Acacia Lodge, No. 118, of Ontario, being secretary of the same; also of the Eastern Star; and the A. O. U. W., No. 87, of Ontario. Mr. Kiesel, an uncle of our subject, owns a large interest in the company,

but lives at Ogden, Utah. Mr. Rieger has a fine residence in a pleasant portion of the town and with gracious dignity his estimable wife presides there, making it a center of refined hospitality. Mr. Reiger is a man of ability, as his successful work will show. He manifested this first in acquiring, in an exceedingly short time, mastery of the intricate English language, as well as in all of his business operations.

ALMER G. KING.—The subject of this review is one of the well known and representative men of Malheur county and is to-day entrusted with the responsibilities of one of the main county offices and has made a record for himself of faithfulness, integrity, and capabilities, that places him secure in the esteem and respect of the entire population of the county. Almer G. was born in Waverly, Iowa, on December 6, 1866, being the son of George and Littie (Kimball) King. In 1870, the family came west via San Francisco and Portland to a place opposite Fort Vancouver, on the Columbia, where they resided for a time and then removed to Pendleton, afterwards going to The Dalles in 1872 where they remained until 1882. In that place, our subject was educated in the public schools and then took the entire course in the Wasco Independent Academy, but did not graduate as he was detained from passing the examinations. In 1882 he came to Malheur, at that itme a part of Baker county, and engaged to handle cattle for Thomas R. Davidson and fourteen years he remained with him never losing a day, and for the last half of this time he was foreman. In 1892 he went to Payette, Idaho, and conducted a livery stable for one year then went to Westfall, Malheur county, and operated as a farmer for a time. It was in the spring of 1896, that Mr. King was nominated for county assessor on the Democratic ticket and was elected with a handsome majority, being the only one on that ticket who was elected. At the close of a two years' term, he was put in nomination for the office of clerk of the county and was elected and at the expiration of that term he was nominated for a second term and elected, thus demonstrating his popularity in the county and his standing among his fellows. His long term of public service has been characterized by faithfulness, ability, and accommodation to the people and this has given him an enviable prestige throughout the entire county.

The marriage of Mr. King and Miss Alma B., daughter of Joseph A. and Clementine Morten, was celebrated on September 2, 1890. Mrs. King's parents live in the vicinity of Ontario and were early pioneers of the country, coming as soon as the sixties.

ROBERT M. DIVIN.—This venerable citizen and esteemed gentleman and resident of Vale is one of the substantial men of Malheur county and is well and favorably known throughout the precincts of this region, being a man of stanch integrity, and always manifesting those qualities of worth and merit that redound to the good of all. Mr. Divin was born in Lincoln county, Tennessee, on December 17, 1831, being the son of Irbin F. and Hannah Divin. The father died when our subject was two years of age, having removed with the family to Washington county, Arkansas, where the death occurred. There were but few settlers in that section then, and there Robert M. lived and attended school in the rough log houses of the time, gaining a training therefrom which fortified him for the battle of life. He remained with his mother until he had reached the age of manhood, and in 151 he married Miss Mary J. Kellam, a native of Little Rock, Arkansas. He was occupied on a farm until 1860, then removed to the frontier of Texas among the savage Commanche Indians. Here Mr. Divin and his family endured hardships and deprivations and sufferings from the savages that are calculated to dry up the cup of joy from the human breast, but they bravely fought their way through them all, the father for three years being a member of the state home guards for the purpose of protecting the settlers from the devastations of these reprobate savages and in many fights and skirmishes he participated. In 1865 they returned to Arkansas and remained there until 170 when he came west ith his family via Omaha, San Francisco, and Portland to Clackamas county, Oregon. His mother came with him and in 1875, they lo-

cated on upper Willow creek and there engaged in the stock business. Success attended the efforts of Mr. Divin and he had soon a large band of cattle and horses and three hundred acres of land. In the spring of 1897 he sold this property and came to Vale, where he resides at the present time. He owns here one-half block and a couple of fine residences.

To Mr. and Mrs. Divin there have been born ten children, but eight of these have been laid away in the graveyard, four of them passing away in eight days with that dread disease, diphtheria. Those remaining are Irbin F., married to Josephine Wisdom and at present engaged in the mercantile business in Vale; Ambrose S. married to Mollie Wisdom and engaged in the fruit business in Chico, California. Mr. Divin is a member of the Masonic fraternity and has also been active during his life in promoting the cause of education. During the times of Indian trouble here in 1878 he suffered his share with the other hardy settlers on the frontier. At the present time Mr. Divin has retired from the activities of the farm and is enjoying the retreat of his town residence and receiving the ministry of the competence that his thrift and industry have provided.

HON. WILLIAM RUFUS KING.— Among those granted representation in this volume, none is more worthy of notice, than the subject of this sketch. As a public spirited citizen, he enjoys the confidence of the people and has become well and popularly known, not only throughout Malheur and adjoining counties, but throughout the whole state.

On October 3, 1864, near Walla Walla, Washington, David R. King and Elizabeth (Estes) King, became the parents of a boy, whom they named William Rufus. His parents were pioneers of Walla Walla, Washington, arriving from Arkansas in 1860, his father being captain of a large immigrant train, crossing what was known as "the plains"—the journey being through the dangerous Indian countries between the Mississippi and the Pacific coast. At the age of nine years he moved with his parents to Weston, Oregon, and five years later, in 1878, to Jordan Valley, in this county.

HON. WILL R. KING.

MRS. WILL R. KING.

THOMA

M

After receiving his preliminary education in the common schools, he entered the Agricultural College, at Corvallis, Oregon, where he pursued his studies for three years. He returned again to the farm, but in 1889 left it to take up the study of law at the law school in Danville, Indiana.

After graduating with high honors in 1891, he was admitted to practice by the supreme court of Indiana, and entered a law office in the city of Indianapolis. He remained there but a few months, when he returned to this county and opened an office for the practice of law, at Vale, Oregon.

In 1892 Mr. King was elected state representative for Malheur county, on the Democratic ticket. Removing to Baker City in 1893 he was elected, in 1894, state senator for Malheur and Baker counties, receiving a majority of three hundred and eighty over Hon. C. A. Johns, the Republican nominee.

In his services in the legislature he exhibited the same devotion to the interests of the people as he did to his own affairs in private life. His whole legislative career was marked by such honest and fearless aggressiveness, coupled with a keen perception and sound, conservative judgment, that he became a recognized leader of the reform forces in the legislature and throughout the state. The confidence reposed in him was so great that, in 1898, he was chosen by the allied Democratic, Populist and Silver Republican forces, as the nominee against Hon. T. T. Geer, for the governorship of Oregon. Although Mr. King was defeated in his race for governor, he made such a clean, honest, energetic campaign, that he greatly reduced the large Republican majority in Oregon, won many warm friends throughout the state and increased his already enviable reputation as a leader in public affairs

After his removal to Baker City he formed a law partnership with F. M. Saxton, under the firm name of King & Saxton. On account of the large practice this firm soon enjoyed in this and Harney counties, Mr. King decided to return to Malheur county, and in 1899 established himself in Ontario, where he now has one of the finest and best equipped law offices in eastern Oregon, and enjoys a large and lucrative practice.

Fraternally he is a member of the A. F. & A. M., Baker Lodge, No. 47; of the K. of P.,

Lodge No. 46, of Ontario; of the Woodmen of the World; and of the Royal Arcanum.

On December 6, 1892, Mr. King was united in marriage to Miss L. Myrtle King, of Danville, Indiana, to which union two children have been born, Eldon P. King and Myrtle M. King.

THOMAS C. FLETCHER.—One of the earliest pioneers of this region of the country, a man whose life has always been dominated by wisdom, prudence and upright principles, having ever manifested also stanch virtues and a reliability that are becoming a good citizen and faithful man, the subject of this article is one of the leading men of Malheur county, and a prominent resident of Ontario. Thomas C. was born in Mercer county, Kentucky, on October 11, 1841, being the son of Jewett and Elizabeth Fletcher. When our subject was six years of age he had the misfortune to lose his father and he was soon thereafter taken by his mother to Lee county, Iowa, near Ft. Madison, where he was reared on a farm, attending the common schools for his education. In the fall of 1861, when the stirring call came for men to defend the nation's honor and save her from the assault of treason's bands, he promptly enlisted in Company G, Fourth Iowa Cavalry, as bugler, and was under General Curtis. Several skirmishes were participated in in Missouri and then he was transferred to Sherman's army, Sixteenth Corps, being immediately under A. J. Smith. He was in siege of Vicksburg and on account of sickness was sent home on a furlough, but after recovering was soon again in the ranks and took part in the battles of Ripley, Meridian and Guntown, besides many skirmishes. He continued as bugler until December, 1864, being at that time honorably discharged, having never been wounded, although he was in the hottest of the fight many a time. Immediately subsequent to his discharge he went home and remained with his mother until the spring of 1865, when he started across the plains with a train of ox teams, having one hundred men, on account of the hostilities of the Indians. He drove a team to Virginia City, Montana, and then went to ranching, having taken up a piece of land b. this he soon sold, and turned his attention to freighting and working in a saw mill unti

37

1869, at which time he went to the Willamette valley. In the spring of 1870 we find him on Rock creek, Spokane county, Washington, in partnership with Thomas Phillieo in the stock business. In 1874 he sold this business and went to Silver City, Idaho, and in the following spring located in the Jordan valley. Stock business engaged his energies there and he was successful. There, also, he was married on January 13, 1884, Miss Rosa, daughter of Joseph and Martha Merrill, becoming his wife wife at that time. Mrs. Fletcher's parents came via the Panama canal to California in 1856 and thence in 1865 to Jordan valley, engaging in raising stock there. Mr. Merrill was in Baker county in 1864 and he was well known all over this country, having lived from that time for twenty years on the old sheep ranch in Jordan valley. In 1884 Mr. Merrill went to Sonoma county, California, where they remain still. Mr. Fletcher and his wife went thither also in 1884, the hostile Indians in Jordan valley causing this move. But one year later he came back to Malheur county and here he has been since that time. He at once went at the sheep business when he returned here and until 1899, when he sold out, he was one of the leaders in that industry. He is at present living in a fine eight-room house in Ontario, having ample grounds that are fitted with orchards and gardens. In addition Mr. Fletcher owns numerous residences, and some business property in Ontario, which he rents, also has a fine tract of land of forty acres near town that produces abundant returns, being well watered and carefully tilled.

To Mr. and Mrs. Fletcher there have been born three children, Robert E., Birdie E., Sylvina M. Mr. Fletcher is a member of the G. A. R., A. P. Hovey Post, of Ontario. He is a Republican in politics and is active in the interests of good government and improvement of educational facilities. He and his wife are devout member of the Methodist church and are faithful supporters of the faith. Mr. Fletcher was in the Indian war of 1878.

GEORGE A. HICKEY.—This successful and intelligent stockman resides one-fourth of a mile from Juntura, and in company with M. A. Masterson owns a fine quarter of land which they devote to raising hay for cattle, of which

they have one hundred head, besides other stock. In his walk Mr. Hickey has been upright, capable, and always on the side of movements and issues which make for advancement and development of the country, being a capable and worthy man

George A. was born in Arkansas, on March 18, 1864, and there received his education and grew to manhood. It was when he had arrived at the age of twenty that he went west, visiting Colorado first. Thence he migrated to Idaho, and later made his way into the John Day country, in this state. He worked for wages there for some time, and then came to Malheur county. He took a preemption four miles west from where he now lives, and later sold it, and bought the estate mentioned above.

Mr. Hickey takes an active part in politics as occasion leads, and is well esteemed by all and stands high in the community and wherever he is known.

EBENEZER A. TWYCROSS. — This worthy pioneer has always manifested the demeanor of the typical frontiersman and he is deserving of much credit for the arduous labors performed and the dangers encountered and the hardships and deprivations endured in the many years wherein he has devoted himself and his energies to the development of the country and making it fit for the abode of mankind, and therefore it is with pleasure that we accord to him consideration in this volume of his county's history.

Mr. Twycross was born in Massachusetts, in 1836, being the son of Ebenezer and Mary Twycross, natives also of the same state. He was educated in his native place and there remained until he had grown to manhood, when he took up the responsibilities of life for himself and at once engaged in farming, which occupation engrossed his attention until 1870, the year in which he came to the west. He settled first in Silver City, then took a homestead in Pleasant valley, which he sold and came to his present location, five miles west from Jordan Valley. He has a fine estate of four hundred and eighty acres of land well improved and fertile. Mr. Twycross gives his energies to farming and stockraising and is one of the leading men of his section, being progressive and enterprising. During the trying times of

1878, when the savages endeavored to murder the toiling settlers of this vicinity, Mr. Twycross was one who fought bravely to defend the whites and has passed through much trial and hardship. He is of good standing among his fellows and is worthy of the confidence reposed in him.

HENRY P. TIETSORT.—The subject of this article is one of the venerable and capable men of the vicinity of Nyssa, being also a veritable pioneer of the pioneers of the west, having labored with great energy in many portions of the same, and has endured the privations, hardships and suffering incident to this kind of life. Henry P. Tietsort was born in Cass county, Michigan, on October 14, 1829, being the son of John and Angeline (Myers) Tietsort. The parents were natives of Pennsylvania, but his grandparents came from Germany. Our subject was educated in the common schools of his native place and spent the years of his youth in labor on the farm. In 1859 he went to St. Joseph, Missouri, and thence he came across the plains with mule teams, consuming four months in the trip. The train of thirty wagons landed at Red Bluff, California, and he went to freighting for a time and then mined. It was 1864 when he came to Boise basin, Idaho, and he was also in Baker county, now Malheur, near Malheur City. He mined in various localities in the country, being pretty well over the western country, until 1892, when he located his present place of forty-three acres on the banks of the Snake, three miles southwest from Nyssa. Then there were but one or two houses between his place and Ontario. He opened up his farm, labored for the building of the Owyhee ditch and now has a good place, thirty-five acres of alfalfa, a good orchard and comfortable buildings.

The marriage of Mr. Tietsort and Miss Lyda, daughter of Henry H. and Malissa Carman, of Nyssa, was solemnized on October 3, 1880, and they have become the parents of the following children: Mrs. Lizzie Davis, of Okanogan county, Washington; Jay, of Okanogan county, Washington; Orville, Ada, Ray, Roy, Alta. Mrs. Tietsort's parents crossed the plains from Kansas by wagon to Boise in 1880. The mother died in 1899, July 15.

Mr. Tietsort was a participant in the Pitt river and Selay Indian war in California in 1859, serving under General Kibby, and the whites were universally victorious in this conflict. He was also in a fight with the Indians in the Boise basin in 1878, when many of the savages were slain. Mr. Tietsort has seen his share of danger and hardship on the frontier and now he is entitled to the quiet enjoyment of his place, which his labor has provided.

Mr. Tietsort is also interested in a large tract of mining land situated across the river from his home, in Idaho.

JAMES T. HATFIELD.—Three and one-half miles northeast from Owyhee is found the comfortable and valuable farm and home of the subject of this article. The estate is one of eighty acres of fine land, all covered by the Owyhee ditch and well cultivated and productive of abundant returns of hay, fruit and other valuable crops. Mr. Hatfield is one of the originators of the Owyhee ditch, and he labored faithfully on it from the time it was started until it was finished. Reverting to his personal history, we note that James T. was born in Adair county, Missouri, on July 14, 1839, being the son of Andrew and Mary Hatfield. He removed with his parents while still a child to Putnam county, in the same state, and there remained with them until the time of his marriage, which happy event occurred on September 9, 1858, Miss Lucinda Sumpter then becoming his wife. In September, 1861, Mr. Hatfield enlisted in the Confederate army under Price and participated in the battle of Lexington, serving three months. Then he returned home, and, being convinced of the error of the cause of Confederacy, he did what few men would have the courage to do, that was, own his mistake and offer his services on the right side. He enlisted in Company E, Ninth Missouri Volunteers, and served in this capacity until the fall of 1863, being then honorably discharged. It was in the spring of 1864 that he joined a train of emigrants bound for the west with ox teams. Sixty-five wagons and one hundred and thirteen emigrants formed the train, and notwithstanding several attacks from the savages, they arrived in Austin City, Nevada, in due time without the loss of any of their number. He remained there until 1868 and then returned to Missouri on horseback. Missouri was his home then until 1876, at which time he came to Battle Mountain, Nevada, there running a hotel, freighting and doing various other labors until 1888, when he came by wagon to Owyhee and thence to Boise valley, returning to the Owyhee in 1890. He located a homestead and improved the land, which property he sold in 1901. At the same time he purchased the eighty acres where he now lives, and has it improved in good shape. He also owns another farm of forty acres with his son.

To Mr. and Mrs. Hatfield there have been born five children, one of whom is still living, Emanuel Isaiah, who was born January 22, 1874. Mr. Hatfield is a Democrat and always active in the affairs of the county. He and his son have a large band of cattle and horses and are numbered with the leading stockmen of the section.

WILLIAM J. van LIMBURGH, Jr.—It gives us pleasure to speak in this connection of the talented and enterprising young gentleman whose name appears above, and who has come to us from the busy land of Holland to make one of the stanch American citizens, being of the pure Anglo-Saxon blood whence comes the leading men of the day. He is now one of the well-to-do farmers of the vicinity of Arcadia, owning a tract of eighty acres two miles southwest from that place. William J. was born in Rotterdam, Holland, on September 12, 1878, being the son of William J. and Johanna van Limburgh. The father was a very wealthy and prominent citizen of Holland, being president and chief owner of the famous Basalt Mining Company of Rotterdam. The mines are located in Germany and Belgium and produce a fine grade of stone for building and paving. This gentleman made a trip to the United States to visit his son in 1900 and he was very favorably impressed with the country. He also spent one month in Washington, D. C., visiting the ambassador, Baron Gevars. Returning to his native country, Mr. van Limburgh continued in his business until May 9, 1902, when he was taken very suddenly ill and passed away. He was in his fifty-ninth year. The mother is still living on the old homestead in Holland. Our subject grew up in Rotterdam, received

his primary education in the common schools and then attended the high school and subsequently took his degree from the Agricultural College at Wageningen, Holland. Soon following this event he came to the United States, landing at New York, and thence direct to Ontario, arriving here on February 23, 1897. He purchased his present place, and soon went to improving it, and in the good labor of handling it successfully he has been engaged since that time. The land is under the Owyhee ditch and is productive of large crops of alfalfa and fruit. Mr. van Limburgh is a man of much information, having profited much by his privileged course in the institutions of his native land, and he manifests an active interest in the affairs of his chosen country. He has taken his papers for citizenship and his fellows have chosen him for delegate to the county convention. In fraternal relations he is allied with the K. of P., Armour Lodge, No. 69, of Ontario.

The happy event of the marriage of Mr. van Limburgh and Miss Sophia Boode, a native of The Hague, Holland, was celebrated on October 21, 1900, and to them has been born one child, William J.

GEORGE G. BROWN.—This representative agriculturist and patriotic citizen is one of the leading farmers of the vicinity of Nyssa, having a quarter section of good land, which is his family home, two miles west from that town. Mr. Brown was born in Platt county, Missouri, on January 22, 1850, being the son of George and Jemima (Harris) Brown. In March, 1855, the family went to Doniphan county, Kansas, and the father was one of the early settlers of that section. He was a pro-slavery advocate and was through the exciting times of that period. In 1867 they removed to Newton county, Missouri, and in 1869 the father died there. Our subject grew to manhood on a farm, gaining his education as best could be done from the scanty opportunity of the common schools, which, however, was made the most of by our subject.

On March 15, 1874, in Newton county, occurred the marriage of Mr. Brown and Margaret D. Cary. In 1878 they removed to Grayson county, Texas, and there Mr. Brown devoted his energies to farming and stockraising until 1886, at which time he returned to Newton county, Missouri, and two years later came thence to this country across the plains with teams and wagons. He had his wife, four children and mother on the trip and one hundred days were consumed in making it. They arrived at Long valley, Idaho, without serious accident and there Mr. Brown engaged in raising stock. It was in 1891 that Mr. Brown removed his family to his present abode. He entered a homestead and began the toil of making a fertile farm and comfortable home from the wilds of nature. He has succeeded in a good manner and has a valuable place. He secures water from the Owyhee ditch, has the farm well tilled, has a good residence, fine orchard, and secures a good return annually from the abundant crops raised.

Mr. Brown is affiliated with the K. of P., Armour Lodge, No. 69, of Ontario, and in political matters holds with the Democratic party, being active in the interests of the country and laboring always for the advancement and upbuilding of the same. To Mr. and Mrs. Brown have been born the following named children: Carrie B., wife of Ira Rutledge, near Nyssa; Daisy, wife of John Ray, living near Nyssa; Effie, wife of N. Minton, living near Nyssa; William Edward; Francis; Georgia.

FRANK O'NEILL.—The sturdy pioneer, capable gentleman and patriotic citizen whose name heads this article is one of the leading agriculturists and stockmen of his section of Malheur county, being a man who has wrought with great energy and commendable wisdom in his efforts to assist in the upbuilding and advancement of this section of the country. Our subject was born in the County of Antrim, Ulster province, Ireland, on May 10, 1846, being the son of John and Elizabeth O'Neill. He was reared on a farm and remained in his native place until 1866, when he went to Scotland, and four years later was in Liverpool, whence on September 23, 1870, he embarked on the "Harvest Queen," a sailing vessel bound for the United States. After a very rough trip of thirty-eight days he landed in New York, thence to Pittsburg, Pennsylvania, and one year later went to San Francisco. In Sonoma county, at Visalia, and in Mendocino county, in that state, he labored in the lumber

business. In San Francisco, on December 18, 1875, Mr. O'Neill married Mary Mullary, and in 1881 they came to Portland. Thence they journeyed by team to lower Willow creek in Malheur county and located a quarter section, taking up the stock business. Three children were born to this marriage, Mrs. Annie Zahlor, Mrs. Mary Logan and Francis P. In 1882, very soon after landing in Malheur county, Mrs. O'Neill was called away by death.

Mr. O'Neill contracted a second marriage, the date being October 12, 1886, and the lady Mrs. Anna Jackson, who had by her former husband three children, Frank O., Mrs. Mary B. Madden and George W. To this second marriage there have been born two children, Mable E. and Elsie M. Mrs. O'Neill came across the plains with her husband, Stephen Jackson, and three children from the state of Wisconsin in 1882. They located where Mr. and Mrs. O'Neill now live, fifteen miles west from Vale, on the Burns and Ontario stage line, at what is known as the Hot Springs stage station. Mr. Jackson was murdered there, an account of which occurs elsewhere in the volume. Our subject owns his ranch on lower Willow creek, and they own another quarter near where they live, in addition to the family home. They are worthy and capable citizens and are secure in the esteem and favor of their fellows, being upright and possessed of integrity.

GEORGE W. CLINTON.—A veritable pioneer of the pioneers, and a man of sterling qualities of worth and substantiality, while his excellent achievements mark him one possessed of more than ordinary ability for business enterprises, the subject of this article is to be mentioned with the prominent men of Malheur county and is well worthy of the prestige and esteem that he enjoys.

Mr. Clinton was born in New York, in 1837, being the son of Alexander and Margaret (Balfour) Clinton, natives respectively of Maryland and Pennsylvania. In 1844 the family removed to Wisconsin, and in 1859 they took up the arduous journey across the dreary plains beset with great danger and hardship. In due time they arrived at the Sacramento valley and there engaged in farming. In 1864 our subject made his way into the wilds of this country, locating first at Silver City, then coming to the place where Jordan Valley now stands. He located land and went to raising stock and farming. For twenty-four years he labored on and then sold his possessions and for a period afterward his time was equally divided between this place and California. At the time of the Indian outbreak in 1865 he lost heavily, the savages stealing his horses. The parents of our subject both died in California and also all of a family of eight children but George W. At the present time Mr. Clinton is living on his fine estate of twelve hundred acres of fertile land located twelve miles west from the town of Jordan Valley, where he handles large bands of stock, cattle and horses, and is one of the heavy property owners of the county.

DAVID DUNBAR.—In the person of the subject of this sketch we have one of the leading citizens and stockmen of Malheur county, and it is with pleasure that we chronicle the salient points in his interesting and active career, wherein he has ever manifested integrity, ability and industry. David Dunbar was born in Ontario, Canada, near Kingston, on February 5, 1849, being the son of James and Eliza (Laird) Dunbar. He was reared on a farm with his parents and gained his education from the common schools of that province. In July, 1866, he was called to mourn the death of his mother, and in the fall of the same year stepped forth from the parental roof to do battle with the forces of this world alone. He went to New York and thence by steamer to San Francisco, arriving in that city in thirty days. He worked during the winter on the Union Pacific railroad at Truckee, Nevada, then journeyed by steamer from the Golden Gate to Portland and thence to The Dalles. At that city he joined a saddle train and made his way to the Idaho basin. This was in 1867, and he mined for a time and then freighted from Kelton, Utah, to Silver City, Idaho, after which he purchased a band of horses and took them to Montana and sold them, purchasing a band of stock and work cattle. These he brought back to Silver City, selling the cattle for work there, and brought the stock cattle to the vicinity of Ontario. He had wintered previous to that time near where Ontario now

stands. He located his present place of two hundred acres on Snake river, which is now well improved, and also his place where he now lives, six miles west from Ontario. This farm contains one hundred and sixty acres of good land, well improved, and furnished with plenty of irrigating water. He also owns a fine residence of modern design on a block of lots in Ontario, which is the family home during the school season. In 1880 Mr. Dunbar made a trip to Laramie, Wyoming, with a band of cattle, shipping them to Chicago, and thence he went to his old home in Canada, and made a visit to his father, remaining over one winter. In the spring of 1881 we find him again in Oregon, bending his energies to the prosecution of the stock business, which he has followed since that time with the wisdom and thrift that have given him great success. Mr. Dunbar is selling off his range stock, and is devoting himself to breeding thoroughbred Shorthorns, and raising abundance of alfalfa hay for them.

On March 30, 1891, Mr. Dunbar married Miss Elizabeth, daughter of George and Margaret (Calder) Manson. Her parents are deceased. To Mr. and Mrs. Dunbar there have been born three children, named as follows: Margaret, Ralph and Helen.

ELBERT H. CLINTON, deceased.—It is true that the worthy pioneers whose familiar figures were seen among us so many years are now one by one passing from these scenes to the rewards of another world and it is eminently proper that such as the subject of this article should be granted a memorial in the volume that chronicles the history of the country where he labored and endured, manifesting always those pleasant virtues and principles that characterize the true and typical man. Elbert H. Clinton was born in New York, in 1834, and ten years later his father's family came to Wisconsin, whence they went in 1852 to Iowa, and soon thereafter to Sacramento valley, California. Our subject was in all these journeys, and in 1863 he came to Silver City and thence to Jordan Valley, being one of the very first white men who settled in this vicinity. He took land and went to farming and raising stock, and success from the start attended his industry and wise management of his business. This business occupied him until the time for him to depart the cares and labors of earth. This sad event occurred in January, 1900, and with sincere mourning among a very large circle of friends, this worthy pioneer and good man was consigned to his last resting place. He was a man of energy, and always manifested great interest in the affairs of the county, being a leading and influential citizen, respected by all and worthy of the confidence that was reposed in him by the people.

ALVA P. MACK.—This enterprising and intelligent gentleman is one of Malheur county's leading agriculturists, being a man of good ability and possessed of thrift and those talents which make the successful man, which in its full degree he has demonstrated himself to be, for he came to Ontario in 1890 with less than twenty dollars in finances, and by his own endeavors he has amassed a goodly holding of valuable property; his estate of one hundred and twenty acres, which is highly improved and excellently tilled, lies four and one-half miles southwest from Ontario. It is a model rural home, and shows in every detail both the wisdom and the untiring energy and industry of its proprietor. He produces abundance of alfalfa hay each year, has a good band of cattle, a fine orchard, raising also considerable corn, which yields fifty bushels to the acre. The farm has good buildings, including outbuildings, a commodious barn and a residence of modern architectural design of nine rooms and kept in a tasty and beautiful manner. In fact everything about the premises of Mr. Mack indicates a wide-awake, careful, yet vigorous man in charge and he is justly entitled to the position of leader in his line of business, which is accorded to him by his friends.

Reverting more particularly to the personal history of our subject, we note that he was born in the vicinity of Battle Creek, Calhoun county, Michigan, on January 14, 1868, being the son of Edward C. and Sarah (Talmage) Mack. The father was a native of Michigan and served for one year in the Civil war, after which he returned to his home in his native state and lives there still. Our subject was reared on a farm and received his education in the public schools. His home

was with his parents until the spring of 1890, when he was led by a stirring and adventurous spirit to seek for himself a home in the west. Accordingly he came hither, and as said above, when he landed in Ontario less than twenty dollars lined his pockets. He at once sought employment from the Oregon Forwarding Company, and for six years his face and form were familiar as one of the leading salesmen of that mammoth establishment. At the end of that period he had saved enough money to purchase his present valuable estate, which has already been noted.

On July 4, 1891, the marriage of Mr. Mack and Miss Lulu, daughter of Elbridge and Lois E. (Kentfield) Wellington, and a native of Clinton county, Michigan, was solemnized near Ontario. To our subject and his worthy wife there have been born five children, as follows: Lloyd A., Merle E., Ella M., Gerry E. and Lois E. Mr. Mack affiliates with the K. of P., Armour Lodge, No. 69, of Ontario, while he and his wife are faithful members of the Methodist church.

GEORGE .W. SMITH.—Among the substantial and enterprising citizens of Malheur county is to be mentioned the gentleman whose name is at the head of this article. He is a man of uprightness and has labored here with energy and skill for many years in the endeavor to bring this section into a state of development and also to enhance the condition of his own exchequer. Mr. Smith was born in Carter county, Kentucky, on November 16, 1836, being the son of Clayborn and Cloa (Luck) Smith. He went with his parents to Randolph county, Arkansas, and soon removed thence to Lawrence county, in the same state. At this last place they both died, he being but a small child at the time. Thus early left an orphan, he learned some of the hardships of life and lived in various places in the neighborhood, where he attended the district school as he had opportunity. He was in Arkansas during the war and many dangers and not a few hardships were his to endure. In 1869 he went to Grayson county, Texas, and there followed the art of farming until 1879, at which time he went to Salt Lake City and the following spring he continued his journey to the Salmon river mines, where he prospected and mined and cut wood until 1884, when he came to his present place, three miles northwest from Ontario, locating a quarter section there. He settled down to improve the place, building a comfortable residence, outbuildings, planting an orchard, and so forth. He sold eighty acres subsequently, and now makes his home on the other eighty. Mr. Smith has also a number of stands of bees, with sufficient stock for the farm. When he came here there were but a few houses in Ontario, and settlers were far apart, he being one of the early pioneers of this vicinity. When he came to this country he was not blessed with any financial resources, but by careful labor, wise management and thrift he has been able to make a comfortable home and gain a competence. Mr. Smith is a member of the Methodist church and is devoted to the faith, being active in its precepts and manifesting a life of uprightness and integrity.

CHARLES D. DAVIS.—This worthy pioneer and capable citizen of Malheur county is one of the well known farmers of the vicinity of Ontario, having a farm of eighty acres two and one-half miles northwest from Ontario, which is well improved with comfortable buildings, orchards, etc., having also a good supply of water for irrigating. Mr. Davis is a native of Douglas county, Nebraska, being born on November 23, 1855, and the son of Charles B. and Jane (Platt) Davis. The father was a veteran of the Mexican war, participating in many battles and skirmishes and being honorably discharged at its close. He was a native of Ohio, but went into the war from Iowa. Following his discharge, he removed with his family to Nebraska and settled in Douglas county. In 1861 he again pressed to the front and served his country, enlisting for a three-years' period. In 1864 the elder Davis came across the plains with his family, locating in Boise first, when few people were there and bacon cost fifty cents per pound. In 1868 he removed to the vicinity of Malheur City and being a lawyer, he practiced there and in Baker and Eldorado. In Baker City he was called hence by death, in 1875. In 1873 our subject removed to Lower Willow creek and engaged in the stock busi-

ness. In the spring of 1880 he came to the Malheur river and took land and three years later he came to his present place, taking a quarter section, of which he sold half. He produces much alfalfa hay each year. At various times he has also been engaged in mining, as well as the stock business.

On September 3, 1877, occurred the marriage of Mr. Davis and Miss Jane A., a daughter of Joseph A. and Clementine Morton, and they have been blessed by the advent of seven children to their home, as follows: Lillie, wife of C. A. Haygood, of the vicinity of Vale; Kate, wife of Frank Carmen, near Ontario; Charles; Nellie; Nora; George and Adrian. Mrs. Davis' father lives near Ontario. Mr. Davis' mother has passed away, the date being 1886, as also his father, as mentioned above. Mr. Davis is a member of the A. O. U. W., in Ontario. He started in this country with no money and possessed of good health and a resolute will. He has made a commendable showing and has accumulated a good property. It is of note that Mr. Davis says at the time the site of Ontario was surveyed, he assisted to grub the sage brush from the streets.

JOHN S. EDWARDS.—The subject of this article is one of Malheur's foremost men in the realm of stock raising and agricultural pursuits, which are the wealth of our county, and he has labored in the section since an early day, having the distinction of being one of the first pioneers and real builders of the county. John S. was born near Oskaloosa, Iowa, on November 25, 1849, being the son of Thomas D. and Barbara E. (Rinehart) Edwards. In 1854 the parents came with ox teams in a large train to Lane county, Oregon, passing through the territory of what is now Malheur and Harney counties. Some stock was stolen on the road, but no other trouble befell them. In Lane county the father entered government land and settled down to farming. Until the spring of 1871 the subject of this sketch lived with his parents and then came to where Vale now stands, there being but one cabin there then. Two years later he came to the vicinity of his present home and engaged in stock business. Mr. Edwards now has about nine hundred acres of land, four hundred of which is fine bottom

JOHN S. EDWARDS.   MRS JOHN S. EDWARDS.

M R

land and the remainder grazing land. He has the ranch well improved, occupies a fine two-story residence, has good barns and outbuildings, a fine orchard, and also owns a large band of horses and some cattle.

The marriage of Mr. Edwards and Miss Sarah F., daughter of George W. and Rebecca (Lamb) Smith, of Union, Oregon, was celebrated on July 27, 1876, and they have become the parents of the following children: Thomas O., deceased; Nora M., deceased; Pearl E., attending the normal school at Weston; Harry A.; Alma R.; Phil E.; Irma E.; Clarice B.; and Willard R. Mrs. Edwards was born in Monroe county, Iowa, and crossed the plains with her parents in 1864 with ox teams, the family settling near Island City, Union county, Oregon, where the father died on June 7, 1892, but the mother is still living there. Mr. Edwards' mother died on May 19, 1883, at the old home place in Lane county, and his father passed away at Eugene, this state, on October 5, 1894.

In addition to the other enterprises which he is so capably managing, Mr. Edwards has a large interest in the Simmons group of mines, a valuable property at Cornucopia. He is one of the leading men of the county, has ever conducted himself in a commendatory manner, displaying excellent wisdom, integrity and faithfulness, and is now secure in the esteem of his fellows and well known and admired throughout the entire county.

━━━◆◆◆━━━

EMORY COLE.—Among the leading stockmen and agriculturists of Malheur county, and a man of great energy and executive force, the subject of this sketch is properly accorded a place in the volume of our county's history, and since, also, he is one of the principal land owners of the section, and is, withal, a man of good ability, sound principles, and integrity. Emory was born in Scott county, Minnesota, on December 2, 1862, being the son of Joshua L. and Malinda (Wise) Cole. In the spring of 1864 the family crossed the plains with ox teams to Boise consuming six months in the trip and having no serious trouble except the general hardships and deprivations of such an arduous undertaking. Settlement was made

at Boise, which was then but a hamlet of a few cabins, and there they remained until 1868, when another move brought them to the vicinity of Malheur, where mining was the industry followed until 1872. Then a move was made to upper Willow creek and the father took up stock raising, and later the advantages of the present home place of our subject, five miles northwest from Dell, became evident, and accordingly they came there. Our subject continued to work with his father until December 20, 1883, when the happy event of the marriage of Mr. Cole and Miss Elizabeth, daughter of Benjamin F. and Lucy J. (Russell) Kendall, a native of the Grande Ronde valley, Oregon, was celebrated. But on March 23, 1891, death came and took thence the wife, and Mr. Cole was alone.

On December 23, 1895, Mr. Cole contracted a second marriage, Miss Barbara, daughter of William and Isabell (Russell) Kennedy, and a native of Malheur county, then becoming his wife. Two children have been born to them, Ray and Clifford. Mr. Cole now owns the old home place of his father, which originally was two hundred acres, but now is two thousand and forty acres.. This mammoth estate is productive of lucrative returns to its owner. He raises great quantities of alfalfa hay, has an orchard of fine selected fruits of all varieties known to this climate and handles a large band of cattle. In addition Mr. Cole handles about five hundred swarms of bees. The forty acres' orchard and the fields of alfalfa make abundant feeding ground for these honey makers, so that they are a source of revenue. The home is a comfortable residence of eight rooms, while a commodious barn, good outbuildings and tasty and substantial improvements add beauty and comfort to the rural abode. Mr. Cole manifests the part of an intelligent citizen in his activity in the realm of politics, being allied with the Republican party and always laboring for those measures which conserve the best interests of the people. Mr. Cole's mother died in 1896, and the father is now residing in Vale and is president of the First Bank in Vale. Our subject is rightly ranked with the prominent men of the county; and his standing is an enviable one, being held in esteem and admiration by all, both for his worth and real integrity.

WILLIAM FRANKLIN MINTON.—It is with pleasure that we essay the task of epitomizing the salient points in the interesting career of the estimable and enterprising gentleman whose name is at the head of this article, and it is very fitting that such be granted space in the history of Malheur county, since he has labored here for the upbuilding of the county and has wrought with wisdom and energy for this end, while also he has spent much time on the frontier and in other places, always, however, manifesting that same energy and capability in furthering the chariot of progress and building for the generations to come.

Mr. Minton was born in Cape Girardeau county, Missouri, on November 25, 1856, being the son of Willis J. and Martha S. (Coker) Minton. When he was a lad of seven he was taken by his parents to Cedar county, and in 1874 went with his parents to Pueblo, Colorado, and thence he went to Florence, Colorado, and there followed farming for a time. There also he was married on August 14, 1880, Miss Minerva Jackson becoming his wife on that occasion. In 1884 he removed with his family to New Mexico, securing a farm, which he tilled until 1889. In the last year mentioned he came via the Southern Pacific to San Francisco and thence on the steamer "State of California" to Portland. Soon we find him in Walla Walla and then in Spokane, Washington, later in Butte, Montana, whence he went to Tacoma, remaining there until 1891, occupied as foreman for the Tacoma Contracting Company. After this he was in Spokane again, then at Boise, and finally he came to Nyssa, entered land and went to improving it. He, with others, saw the advisability of the ditch and so started the Owyhee ditch, which has added so much to this country. In 1902 Mr. Minton sold his valuable farm, which was covered by that ditch, and he has property in Nyssa; where he is about to build a fine residence. Politically he is a Democrat and is active in the realms of good government and political matters.

To Mr. and Mrs. Minton were born two children, Samuel P., aged eighteen years, and Eskel P., aged sixteen years. On December 14, 1889, Mrs. Minton was called by death from this realm, being in Durango, Colorado, at the time. Mr. Minton is the oldest of nine children, having five sisters and three brothers,

the entire number living in the west. His father was born and reared in the state of Missouri, and his mother was a native of Kentucky, and they were married about 1853. From Colorado they came west and the mother died at Goldendale, Washington, on June 20, 1900, and the father is still living in North Yakima, that state. Our subject has, in addition to the property above mentioned, some fine placer mines in the Dry Buck country, which he is now working.

EDWARD BEAM.—This young and enterprising farmer and stockman of northern Malheur county is one of the men whose life has been largely spent in this section and he is a real product of the west and a credit to his county, both because of his worthy labors which are being crowned with a good success and because of his own intrinsic worth which stamps him a man of ability and uprightness. Edward Beam was born in Missouri, on January 18, 1874, being the son of William W. and Sarah (Lafton) Beam. In the year of his birth the parents came to Lower Willow creek, in this county, crossing the plains. Two years later they went to the Willamette valley, and two years subsequent to that they returned to this county and located where our subject now lives. Here Edward was educated and spent his time in learning the arts of tilling the soil and raising stock. He has been brought up in the county and is familiar with its resources and history and is well known as a young man of sterling qualities and he has the confidence of the people. Mr. Beam has one-half section of fine land, which produces abundant crops annually, among which is two hundred tons of hay. He has fifty head of cattle and also a bunch of horses. Mr. Beam is considered one of the substantial citizens of the county, and the brilliant success that has attended his efforts is abundant proof of both his industry and his ability.

The marriage of Mr. Beam and Miss Eucibia McPherson, a native of California, was solemnized near Vale, on September 18, 1899, and they have two children, Arthur W. and Nettie F. Mr. McPherson was an early pioneer to California and came to the territory now embraced in Malheur county in 1888. Mr. Beam is always active in the welfare of the county and takes a great interest in the politics of the county and state, being ever allied on the side of progress and upbuilding. He is rightly numbered with the leading men of his section and is one whose efforts have aided materially in the making of Malheur county.

JAMES A. WALTER.—About five miles southwest from Ontario, is the farm and home of the subject of this article. It is a place of eighty acres, well improved, skillfully tilled, has fine buildings, good orchards and a vineyard, and in connection with the care of this estate, Mr. Walter is operating a dairy and manufacturing a good quality of butter, which is readily sold in the markets. In person Mr. Walter is a man of sound principles, stands well among his fellows, possesses good ability, and has made a success of his labor, starting with his bare hands and now has a good property accumulated. He was born in Wayne county, Indiana, on February 14, 1854, being the son of Henry and Lovier (Lee) Walter. He grew up on a farm, received a good education from the common schools, and remained with his parents until 1880, having removed with them to Henry county, Indiana, in 1875. When he stepped out for himself, he came by rail to Reno, Nevada, and in the fall of 1881 came across the country with teams from there to Malheur county, locating in Malheur valley, and doing his first work as a wage earner in this new country. The settlers were few then and the country open and he selected a farm near where Yale stands, but later closed out the farm business and for three years he acted as salesman through the country for the Payette nursery. In 1894 he purchased the improvements of a man and filed a homestead on the eighty above described.

On January 16, 1896, occurred the marriage of Mr. Walter and Miss Lillie M. Steele. She is a native of Arkansas, whence she came across the plains with her parents twenty-five years ago, settling in this county. The parents are now deceased. To Mr. and Mrs. Walter there have been born three children, Maud, Ora M. and Orville. Mr. Walter's mother died in the east, and the father came to this country in 1887, and here he died in 1894. Our subject is a member of the K. of

P., Armour Lodge, No. 69. He is a man of integrity and sterling worth of character and has manifested substantial qualities constantly, which have given him a fine prestige among his fellows.

CHARLIE E. AMIDON.—This well known and representative farmer and stockman is a substantial and enterprising citizen of Malheur county, dwelling near Ontario, five and one-half miles southwest, where he has a fine farm of one hundred and eighty acres, well tilled and improved with buildings, orchards, and so forth, in addition to which he owns one hundred acres of land in another place, besides other property. The birth of Mr. Amidon occurred at Glenn, Allegan county, Michigan, in 1860, August 23, being the son of Edson and Electa (Tracy) Amidon. The father enlisted in Company B, Thirteenth Michigan, in October, 1861. He was transferred to Sherman's army and was with that celebrity on the famous march to the sea. Before going, he was home on a furlough, on account of the measles. Upon his return to the army after his furlough he was promoted as corporal and he did valiant service in the battles of Chattanooga, Chickamauga, Atlanta and many others, as well as numerous skirmishes. He served until the last disloyal gun was silenced, and then received his honorable discharge, after four years of war toil.

Our subject was reared on a farm, educated in the common schools and at the age of twelve went with his parents to Grand Island, Nebraska. Two years later the family returned to Wayne county, Michigan, and from there he went to Glenn, his birthplace. He lumbered in the woods and in the spring of 1883 he went to Elgin, Illinois, from which place he returned to his home and prepared for the trip to Baker City, whither he came in 1884. From Baker City he came to Ontario, which was then a side track and two buildings, and worked at different occupations and raised some stock for a time. In the spring of 1892 he filed a desert claim on eighty acres where he lives now.

Mr. Amidon married Miss Martha J., daughter of Thomas and Mary J. Steele, on December 30, 1896, and they have one child, Alva Tracy. Mrs. Amidon's parents crossed the plains in 1877, from Arkansas and settled in Grant county, this state, where they died soon after. Mr. Amidon is a charter member of the A. O. U. W. and is a man of good standing among his fellows and respected by all who know him.

ROSWELL W. CLEMENT.—Among the leading agriculturists of Malheur county is to be mentioned the subject of this sketch, whose life has manifested a worthy record of honest and vigorous endeavor, dominated with sagacity and tempered with prudence and display of affability and genial bearing toward all. In Middleville, Barry county, Michigan, on January 5, 1862, occurred the happy event of the birth of Roswell W. Clement, his parents being Judge James T. and Lucy (Hayes) Clement. The family came to Osage, Iowa, while our subject was a small child, and thence they removed to the vicinity of Lincoln, Nebraska, in 1868. In these various places Roswell W. was reared, receiving a good education from the common schools. 1881 marks the date when they again removed toward the west, this time journeying with teams, one of which our subject drove the entire distance, to Payette, Idaho, making the trip in eighty days. Here on September 11, 1884, Mr. Clement married Miss Harriet, daughter of John and Melissa Neal, and a native of Denver, Colorado. Mr. and Mrs. Neal were early pioneers of the Payette valley, coming thither from Denver, in which town they also were among the first settlers and lived there when flour retailed at fifty dollars per sack. To Mr. and Mrs. Clement there have been born four children, named as follows: Martha Ethel, James R., Walter and Buell J. Mr. Clement came to his present place, which consists of one hundred acres of valuable land six miles southwest from Ontario, in 1895. He purchased the land when it was raw and at once began the work of improvement with the happy result that now he has it producing abundant crops. He harvested as high as three hundred and fifty tons of alfalfa hay in one year, besides much other fruit of the fields. He has plenty of water for irrigating, has good buildings, a fine orchard, and a shade and ornamental grove that adds great

beauty and value to his rural home. It is of note that Mr. Clement came here without financial resources and now he is one of the wealthy men of this section of the county, and he is to be credited with having gained it all by hard labor and wise management of the resources placed in his hands. Politically, he is allied with the Democratic party and takes the interest that becomes an intelligent citizen in the affairs of politics, while in educational matters he is ever zealous and always labors for the advancement of the cause.

Mr. Clement's parents reside in the Payette valley. The father freighted with ox teams from Kelton, Utah, to the Payette valley in early days before the railroad was built.

ROBERT van GILSE.—The capable and educated gentleman, of whom we now have the privilege of writing, is one of the leading fruit men of the entire northwest, being better fitted, doubtless, than most in this industry in the entire country, for in addition to the practical experience in handling nurseries and fruit farms themselves, he has received from some of the leading horticultural schools of Europe the best theoretical and practical training that is now the privilege of a man to secure. It is with great pleasure, therefore, that we grant space here for an epitome of his interesting career. And it would give us gratification if in brief we were privileged to publish for the benefit of the fruitmen of Malheur county, his valuable experience in these lines.

We will revert to the personal history of our subject and we note first that in the pure Anglo-Saxon country of Holland is his birthplace. Middleburg is the spot and June 18, 1873, is the date. His parents were J. A. and Mary van Gilse. The father is editor of one of the most powerful journals of Holland and was a member of the Congressional body of the country, being a leader in those halls as also in the field of journalism. Our subject attended the common school until twelve years of age at Rotterdam, then entered the Horticultural College at Amsterdam in which noted institution he finished with credit a three years' course, graduating with distinction. Immediately succeeding this, he spent two years in practical work in the nurseries in Holland and

England, being conversant with the methods employed in nurseries in both of these countries. 1892 is the date when he landed in New York and immediately he started thence for the west, landing in Payette, where he at once started a nursery. In the skillful and successful prosecution of this enterprise, he was engaged until 1896 when he sold and took a trip to Holland. In the spring of 1897 he returned and bought one hundred and sixty acres southwest from Ontario six miles. He here opened a nursery and also devotes much attention to producing fruit for the market as well as much alfalfa, having sixty-five acres of the latter and as much of the former. He has all kinds of fruit, has improved his farm in a fine manner with all buildings necessary, and has also plenty of water for irrigating. In addition to this, Mr. van Gilse has another quarter section where he is now living, two and one half miles northwest from Nyssa. This farm is newer than the other, but is well improved and has twenty-five acres planted to alfalfa and one hundred and twenty to orchard. This with his other farm makes one of the finest orchards in the entire country. And on account of the time needed in attention to this vast amount of market fruit, Mr. van Gilse has closed out his nursery stock. He is a man of great energy and in addition to this commendable work he has succeeded in bringing to this country a colony of his people and they are fast becoming the most substantial and worthy citizens of the state.

The marriage of Mr. van Gilse and Miss Trien Tenses occurred on April 29, 1900, and one child is the fruit of the union, Mary. Mrs. van Gilse is also a native of Holland. We are glad to note the energy and skill that have been displayed by this worthy citizen in the progress of the interests of our county and truly Malheur county owes much to his arduous and wisely bestowed labors within her precincts. Fraternally, Mr. van Gilse is affiliated with the A. F. & A. M., Acacia Lodge, No. 118, of Ontario, and also with the K. of P., Armour Lodge, No. 69. He is active in the interests of good government, being allied with the Democratic party and is central committeeman of the Nyssa precinct. Our worthy President said recently of a friend, "He is a man who has done things." Such may well be applied to our subject. He has done things and his works proclaim him the man whom men recognize as a benefactor of the country and of his fellow men. Mr. van Gilse was the moving spirit in inaugurating the rural free delivery system.

◆◆◆

EDMUND A. FRASER.—The young and eminently successful gentleman whose name appears above is one of the leading men of Malheur county, being the owner of a controlling interest in the Malheur Mercantile Company, a large general merchandise establishment of Ontario, which does an immense business not only from the country adjacent to Ontario, but also from the interior of Malheur and Harney counties. Our subject was born in Woodstock, Canada, on September 2, 1870, being the son of George and Sarah (Sheperd) Fraser. He attended the common school, and at the age of twelve was ready to enter the Upper Canada College of Toronto, where he graduated in the spring of 1886. His parents came to Indiana and he came, at the age of eighteen years, to Ontario. April, 1888, was the date of his landing here and he soon was in the employ of Kissel, Shilling & Danielson, of the Oregon Forwarding Company, in the capacity of bookkeeper and clerk. In this position, he performed faithful service until 1900, when he purchased the controlling interest in the R. D. Geer Mercantile Company, changing the name to the Malheur Mercantile Company, which is incorporated. Mr. Fraser is manager and secretary of the company, and they carry a large stock of goods in dry goods, groceries, boots and shoes, hardware, gents' furnishings, and in fact in every line which is used in the vast territory, whence comes the many hundreds of patrons that visit their commodious store, one of the finest in this section of the country. In addition to their large store building, they have two spacious warehouses filled with goods. The firm is a very popular one of the country, and our subject is among the very leaders of the business world of eastern Oregon. The fair treatment always extended to patrons, the spirit of accommodation, and the wise business methods used in selecting and purchasing goods, makes this firm one of great prominence and accounts for its unbounded success and the credit for this pleasant state of affairs is largely due to the wisdom and ability of the subject of this sketch. Mr. Fraser is also a director of the Owyhee ditch and one of the directors of the Ontario opera house, having stock in both companies.

The marriage of Mr. Fraser and Miss Ida, daughter of Mr. and Mrs. J. T. Holland, was solemnized on October 4, 1899, and they have been blessed by the advent of one son, Edmund A., Jr. Fraternally Mr. Fraser is identified with the I. O. O. F., being past grand of the order, Lodge No. 90, at Ontario; and is a Master Mason and treasurer of Acacia Lodge, No. 118, A. F. & A. M.

GILBERT L. KING.—It is now our pleasant privilege to recount the items of the career of the prominent and capable gentleman whose name initiates this paragraph, who is to-day one of the leading men in Malheur county, being not only crowned with abundant financial success as the result of his industry and wise management of the resources that came to his hands, but also a man of prominence in educational lines in younger days, and at the present time a fluent public speaker and well informed man of ability and culture.

Gilbert L. was born in Jeffereson county, New York, on February 9, 1848, being the son of Lorenzo D. and Julia Ann (Schryver) King. While a child he came with his parents to Dodge county, Wisconsin, and grew up there on the frontier, gaining his education at first from the common schools and thorough reading. On February 4, 1864, patriotism stirred young King to offer his services in the Third Wisconsin Volunteer Infantry, Company G, being the Twentieth Corps, under Joe Hooker, a part of Sherman's army. He participated in the battle of Resaca and in several skirmishes, being wounded in his leg. In July, 1865, he was honorably discharged and returned to Wisconsin, thence to Mason county, Illinois, where he taught school for a time. In 1869 he went to Webster City, Iowa, and engaged in the grocery business, but sold out in 1870 and repaired to Bloomington, Illinois, where he took a course of two years in the state normal school. He then taught school in McLean county, the same state, and in 1874 he went to work for the Union Pacific

Railroad Company, having also labored for them some previous to 1869. He had mastered telegraphy in his course at the normal and from 1874 until 1897 he was in the service of this company at various places on their line as station agent. He came to Ontario in 1885, being the first agent here, and in this position he remained until 1897, when he resigned and removed on to his farm, a rich tract of land adjoining the town on the west. It is one of the best in the county, has a fine house, twenty-acre orchard of all varieties of fruit indigenous to this section, and supplied with plenty of water for irrigating purposes. Mr. King has a large band of cattle. In 1899 he opened a real estate and insurance office in the town of Ontario, and he does a good business now in these lines, handling a number of the leading companies. He is also secretary and stockholder in the Nevada and Owyhee ditch companies. Mr. King commenced life with no capital in finances, but with good ability and a resolute purpose to succeed, and he has done so in an admirable manner, both in financial enterprise, being possessed of much wealth, and also in maintaining an untarnished reputation throughout his busy career, being also highly respected and esteemed by all who know him.

The marriage of Mr. King and Miss Isabella Easton occurred on September 14, 1875, in Hall county, Nebraska. They have six children: Edward L., Arthur S., Ira N., Edna L., Alice, Homer G. Mr. King is a past master and member of the Acacia Lodge, No. 118, of the A. F. & A. M., of Ontario, and has represented his order in the grand lodge; he also belongs to the Eastern Star. In politics Mr. King is a Republican and often his eloquence is heard on the platform in political contests.

JAMES E. MADDEN.—This well known and representative business man is one of the prominent citizens of Ontario, where he owns and operates a fine, large livery and feed stable, having fine and comfortable rigs and good horses, and manifesting a careful supervision for the comfort and safety of his patrons. Mr. Madden was born in Perry county, Ohio, on May 31, 1849, being the son of Hezekiah and Mary Madden, natives of Ohio, also. While still a child he was brought by his parents to Putnam county, in the native state, and in 1863 they came thence to Mills county, Iowa. He was reared on a farm, having but limited opportunity to gain educational training, but by dint of hard labor and making the best of the log school house privileges, he received his training. In 1874 he came to The Dalles and one year later returned to Iowa, where, in 1876, July 29, he contracted a marriage with Miss L. A. Barnett. They remained there two years on the home place, then bought a farm and tilled it until 1882, in which year he moved to Saunders county, Nebraska, purchased a farm and remained there until 1887. The last year mentioned was the time he migrated to Oregon, locating at Westfall, on Bully creek, Malheur county. He engaged in sheep raising, but later sold them and bought cattle and in the severe winter of 1889 and 1890 he lost nearly all his stock, as did many of the stockmen. He was not to be discouraged, however, and went at the business again until he had regained his losses, and in 1899 sold out and came to Ontario, where he purchased eighty acres of land adjoining the town and began improving it. He has a fine six-room residence, land all fenced, good orchard, barns and outbuildings, and the place is well supplied with water for irrigating. He owns stock in the Owyhee ditch, whence he gets his water supply. In addition to his farm and other property Mr. Madden has a livery and feed stable in Ontario, as stated above, and he does a good business. To Mr. and Mrs. Madden there have been born nine children, as follows: Arthur, deceased, Perry, John H., Charles, Nona, Ethel, Nina, Joseph A., Robert E. and Pleasant. Mr. Madden is deserving of much credit for the faithful and enterprising manner in which he has labored in this county, and it is with pleasure that we have been enabled to grant to him this consideration, since he is highly esteemed by all.

--- ◆◆ ---

JAMES H. FARLEY has led a life of marked activity and filled with enterprising and various labors, during which, also, he has manifested those rare qualities of integrity, uprightness and perseverance, which, together with his wise methods of procedure and industry, have given him the competence of a prosperous business man and owner of real property. James H. was born in Dubuque, Iowa, on October 15, 1858, being the son of Patrick and Catherine Farley, who settled at Dubuque when it was but a small hamlet, being natives of New York state. The father served three years in the Civil war, participating in numerous battles and at the close was honorably discharged. Our subject went with his parents to Kelsey, Massachusetts, and after the war they all removed to St. Louis, where the father went to railroading on the Illinois & St. Louis Railroad. He held the position of road master for nine years and at the time of his death, in 1892, he was general manager of the entire road. Our subject learned railroading, beginning as a fireman, then operated as engineer, and later retired from it and handled a stationary engine in Kansas City. Following that he went to work on a horse ranch near North Platte, Nebraska, remaining there until 1881, then migrated to Granger, Idaho, worked on the railroad a short time and then came to where Ontario now stands. Not liking the country he went to Olds Ferry, operating the same for a time, and then to the Grande Ronde valley in 1882, where he took a timber claim near Elgin and operated a saw mill. Later he sold this property and then we find him in Seattle, whence he went to Walla Walla, and from that point to Ontario. He engaged to run an engine for the mines on Snake river, and in 1900 he purchased the entire property of the Ontario Livery and Feed Stable, consisting of barn and full equipment. He now handles a first-class livery, probably the largest in the entire country, and his rigs are first-class, his horses of the best and an untiring care for the welfare of his patrons is manifested by him constantly. In addition Mr. Farley handles coal, does a general dray and teaming business, and handles a good farm of one-quarter section, five miles southwest from the town. He also owns twenty acres adjoining Ontario.

The marriage of Mr. Farley and Miss Martha, daughter of Jesse and Catherine Darr, was solemnized at Weiser on November 17, 1884, and they have become the parents of five children: Jesse, Kate, Lulu E., James H., deceased, and Opal M. Mr. Farley is affiliated with the I. O. O. F., Ontario Lodge, No.

90, also with the A. F. & A. M., Acacia Lodge, No. 118, and with the K. of P., and the A. O. U. W., while he and his wife are members of the Rebekahs and the Eastern Star.

RICHARD S. RUTHERFORD.

RICHARD S. RUTHERFORD.—As a man among men, possessed of integrity, ability and perseverance; as a soldier, whose steady and constant service in the struggle .for the punishment of treason and the wiping out of the insult to the stars and stripes was valiant and brave; as a business operator, whose wisdom and enterprise have been well manifested; the subject of this sketch stands, and it is fitting that a representation of him be granted space in this volume of Malheur's hostory.

Richard S. was born in Armagh county, near Belfast, Ireland, on February 22, 1840, being the son of Thomas and Amelia (Parks) Rutherford, who emigrated to this country when this son was eighteen months old. They settled in Quebec, Canada, whence in 1848 they came to Niagara county, New York. In 1852 they removed to Tuscola county, Michigan, and four years later our subject started in life for himself. His first move was to Scott county, Missouri, where he lived until the breaking out of the Civil war. At that particular time he was in charge of a plantation. On the tenth day of August, 1861, he offered his services to fight the battles of the nation, enlisting in Company H, Eighth Missouri Volunteer Infantry, being in the Fifteenth Army Corps under General Logan, and in Sherman's Division. He went in as private and helped with good will to fight the battles of Ft. Donelson, Corinth and Shiloh, and then was promoted to the position of head wagon master for the Fifteenth Corps train, with a salary of one hundred and twenty-five dollars per month. Then he participated in the battles of Vicksburg, Jackson, Atlanta, Chattanooga and Lookout Mountain, then on August 20, 1864, he received his honorable discharge at Atlanta. He returned to Michigan and in twenty days was back again to the scene of fighting, and this time was installed as master of the hospital wood train at Nashville, Tennessee, where he received a salary of one hundred and fifty dollars per month. During this time he was appointed as captain of a special company

when Hood surrounded Nashville. He served until the close of the war, then was honorably discharged and returned to Michigan. He was fortunate during the entire service, being in the hospital but one week and that on account of the mumps. Soon after returning to his old home in Michigan he was married to Miss Elizabeth, daughter of Robert and Mary F. Turner, the wedding occurring on June 14, 1866. Mrs. Rutherford is a native of Canada and of English extraction. He operated a hotel for a short time and then, in 1867, went to Georgetown, Colorado, and shortly after started the mining town of Silver Plume. He handled a pack train, and mined until 1876 and then went to California, thence to Nevada, and in 1878 came to Waitsburg, Washington. Eighteen hundred and eighty was the date he removed to Boise, Idaho, and three years later he came to Ontario. He opened the Rutherford, a first class hotel, and operated it until 1892, when it burned down and then he removed on to his farm, which he had taken as a soldier's homestead, and there he remained until January, 1902, when he sold out and retired to Ontario. Here he has a fine residence in the heart of town, with ample grounds and tasty buildings. To Mr. and Mrs. Rutherford there have been born eight children, as follows: Roy S., married to Beulah Arnold; Benjamin F., married to Daisy Henshaw; Charles E., deceased; Ray W., deceased; Adrian A. Also John, Edwin and Clara, the three oldest, who are deceased. Mr. Rutherford is a past grand of the I. O. O. F., Ontario Lodge, No. 90; of the encampment; and of the A. F. & A. M., Acacia Lodge, No. 118; and of the G. A. R., Alvin P. Hovey Post, of which he is past commander. He and his wife are members of the Rebekahs and Eastern Star, and also are allied with the Congregational church, while in political matters Mr. Rutherford is a Republican.

Mrs. Rutherford's parents were Robert and Mary (Franklin) Turner, and Benjamin Franklin is one of her ancestors on her mother's side.

JOSEPH H. TAGUE.

JOSEPH H. TAGUE.—It is with unfeigned pleasure that we are privileged to recount somewhat of the career of the estimable gentleman and patriotic citizen who is mentioned above, since he is a man of good standing, a well-to-do agriculturist and stockman of Malheur county, and has the honorable distinction of being one of the brave men, who hazarded life and limb for the safety of our beloved union and the promotion of good government. He was born in Ripley county, Indiana, on July 13, 141, being the son of Lemuel and Ann (Buchanan) Tague, the mother being a second cousin of James Buchanan, the president of the United States. Our subject remained at the home place until the cruel war of the Rebellion broke out and then he promptly enlisted in the Sixth Indiana Infantry, Company H. This was in the summer of 1861, and he was among the very first of the three years' volunteers. He served under Rosecrans and then under Thomas. He took part in the battle of Lookout Mountain, also that at Green river and in many skirmishes, doing the part of the true and valiant soldier. He received a wound from a bayonet, in his eye that cost him its sight. He served three years, and one year and three months of this time was on a gunboat. He was honorably discharged and is now commander of the Sedgwick Post of the G. A. R., at Huntington, No. 4. Many were the hardships and deprivations that fell to his lot in the army and many times he suffered from hunger in addition to all the other woes of war. Following the war Mr. Tague went to his native place in Indiana. He had two brothers who served in the Third Indiana Cavalry and one was wounded severely.

The marriage of Mr. Tague and Miss Martha E. Wise was celebrated in Ripley county, Indiana, in 1865, and in 1877 they removed to Gibbon, Nebraska, entered government land and settled down to farming. In 1883 he removed to Council Bluffs and then in 1893 he came to the west via train and located at his present home place, where he purchased a quarter section, three-fourths of a mile southeast from Dell. He has a good farm, well irrigated and improved, having comfortable house, barn and other buildings. Politically Mr. Tague is allied with the Republicans and is also very active in the promotion of educational facilities. To Mr. and Mrs. Tague have been born the following children: Nancy A., wife of B. Parks, of Nebraska; Lavina, wife of R. Boswell, of Malheur; Minnie, wife of A. Derrick, of Dell; Rosa, wife of P. Flaherty, of

Omaha; Carrie, wife of E. Kendall, of Huntington; Bertha, wife of H. Lockett, of Dell; Villa, wife of O. McCauley, of Huntington; Joseph H., Charles R. and Emery. Mr. Tague is a man of good standing among his fellows, has made a fine record in the world as a business man, soldier and citizen and is highly esteemed by all.

JOSEPH C. KELLEY, one of the young business men of Malheur county, was born January 3, 1870, at Idaho City, Idaho, his parents being Joseph and Margaret (Thompson) Kelley, pioneers of that state. Joseph Kelley, senior, was a native of Farmington, Iowa, and was among those who in the early fifties sought the golden sands of California. After spending several years in California, in the middle sixties, Mr. Kelley again emigrated, going to Idaho and establishing himself in business as a mechanic at Idaho City. Here, in the closing days of 1870, the silver cord was broken and all that was earthly of the departed pioneer was laid at rest. A little while later the family removed to Oregon, settling near Nyssa, in this county, and in 1877, Mrs. Kelley having meanwhile become the wife of W. K. Stark, the family again chose a new home, this time on Willow creek, where the subject of this sketch grew to manhood's estate. The mother passed into the life beyond in August, 1897. Of the immediate family now living there are but two, Joseph and his brother, Melville D. Kelley, a prosperous ranchman residing on Willow creek.

Mr. Kelley remained at home, engaged in ranching and stock raising, until 1898 when, having learned the saddler's trade, he came to Vale and opened a small harness and saddle store. From a small beginning the business has grown to one of considerable size. He is the sole saddler and harness dealer at the county seat, and his business occupies new and commodious quarters.

In 1900 Mr. Kelley was nominated for the office of county treasurer by the Republican party and was elected over his opponent, William Plughoff, fusionist, by a majority of one hundred and nineteen votes. He was accorded a renomination this year and was victorious a second time, his majority over H. B.

Donahey being two hundred and seventy-one, or nearly double that he received the first time he appeared in the political arena. Mr. Kelley is a member of the strong fraternal organization, the Odd Fellows, belonging to Vale Lodge, No. 100; he is also a Mason, belonging to Acacia Lodge, No. 118, of Ontario. He is a master Mason and also he has served the Vale Lodge of the I. O. O. F. as noble grand. Mr. Kelley is also as yet, a member of that largest, though most unstable of all orders, the Bachelors.

* * *

HENRY S. ELDREDGE.—The subject of this article has done much toward the industrial development of Malheur county, and is one of the prominent business men in the town of Vale at the present time, being owner and operator of the Glen livery barn, where he has fine, large rigs and good stock, taking an especial care for the comfort and welfare of his patrons; he owns and operates the blacksmith shop, having also a large tract of land in the vicinity of the town, while in all these enterprises he manifests a commendable business sagacity, a worthy integrity and maintains an unsullied reputation among his fellows.

Mr. Eldredge was born near Northfield, Minnesota, on Mary 23, 1862, being the son of Charles R. and Cordelia E. (Carter) Eldredge. While still a child he was taken by his parents to Beaver Falls, in his native state, and there the father followed milling. Our subject was educated in the graded schools and in 1882 he came with his father to the west, traveling through by train to Granger and thence by teams to Baker City and passing through this portion of Malheur. In Baker City Henry S. learned the blacksmith trade and more or less during the time from that date until the present he has been engaged in the king of all trades. In various places he has wrought at the forge, has traveled considerably, and at the time of the great fair in Chicago he visited that city. Mr. Eldredge had two hundred and eighty acres of land, but recently sold a portion and bought the livery mentioned above. He has a good trade both in the barn and in the shop, and is considered one of the substantial business men of the town.

The marriage of Mr. Eldredge and Miss

Euphemie F., daughter of William R. and Sophia Shimp, of Ontario, was celebrated on July 1, 1895, and to them was born one child, Opal V. On March 22, 1900, Mr. Eldredge was called upon to mourn the loss of his wife by death. Mr. Eldredge is happily affiliated with the W. of W., Arcadia Camp, No. 364, of Ontario; with the Maccabees, Council Tent, No. 15, of Council, Idaho. It is of note that Mr. Eldredge's father located the land of a portion of the site of Vale. The father died on April 19, 1886, but the mother is still living in Monon, White county, Indiana. Mr. Eldredge is well liked among his fellows, is a man of stability and capabilities, and it is quite fitting that he should be accorded a representation in this volume of our county's history, since he has wrought here faithfully for the advancement of the county's interest.

* * *

EBER L. BRADLEY.—This capable gentleman, better known as Judge Bradley, is one of the prominent men of this county, having been in the vicinity of Malheur, where he now resides, for many years, and taking always a leading part, both in the development of the country and in the manipulation of governmental affairs, in all of which he has discharged faithfully and well the duties devolving upon him, and now as one of the venerable patriarchs, stanch pioneers, and patriotic citizens, he is held in high esteem and admired by all.

Mr. Bradley was born in Butler county, Ohio, on July 31, 1829, being the son of Eber M. and Elsie (Rinearson) Bradley. He went with his parents to Des Moines county, Iowa, in 1843 and in 1851 he came across the plains in a train of thirty wagons drawn by oxen. He passed through the territory now occupied by Baker and Malheur counties and went on to Oregon City. He followed packing for a time and then took up a merchant's life at Jacksonville, Oregon. Later he packed to Yreka and other points, and in 1855 sold out and the following year visited the spot where the city of Spokane now stands. Thence he returned to Umatilla and The Dalles and that fall he enlisted in Company C, of Oregon Volunteers, to fight the Indians. He was under Captain James K. Kelly, afterward colonel and now ex-state and United States Senator. He participated in several skirmishes and was detailed to appraise the government property, being also clerk in the quartermaster's department, and later was honorably discharged. After this he was again on the mercantile sea with Professor Post and also interested in steamboating on the Willamette. In 1860 he closed out this business and went with a pack train to British Columbia, and the following spring he was in Oro Fino and Pierce City merchandising and mining. Here he was robbed of about nineteen hundred dollars. Later he closed out and went to work for Wells Fargo, carrying the express from Lewiston to Florence. In 1863 Mr. Bradley was deputy sheriff under Captain Fisk and in this capacity he had charge of the famous murderers of McGruder, who were finally hung. Later he was in Walla Walla, and in 1864 he was in Boise, and in 1867 he came to Malheur, where he still lives. He at once engaged in mining and has lived here continuously since that time, being always one of the prominent men of the section, as he is today. While in Oro Fino Mr. Bradley was elected the first county clerk of Shoshone county, Idaho, the date being 1863, and he ran on the Republican ticket. In Boise he was deputy sheriff under Pinkham, and in Malheur he has been notary for the past twenty years, serving a number of terms as justice of the peace. He had charge of the Malheur Indian Agency from 1882 to 1886 and also of the Malheur and Camp Harney reservation. In 1880, in 1890 and in 1900 Mr. Bradley acted as census enumerator. Mr. Bradley owns the hotel in Malheur, has several other valuable buildings and also some good mining property on the Mormon Basin creek. He is highly esteemed wherever he is known and is one of the substantial and upright men of the county. Mr. Bradley is one of the veterans of the Indian wars and was always ready to go to the front in time of impending danger.

<hr>

FRANK D. STARK.—This well known and estimable stockman and agriculturist of lower Willow creek, is one of Malheur county's prosperous and enterprising citizens and has a fine estate of two hundred and forty acres one mile southeast from Dell, where the family home is at present. Mr. Stark was born in Franklin county, Kansas, on August 31, 1869, being the son of James S. and Marietta (Cannon) Stark. While a child the family removed to Cherokee county, Kansas, and there he attended the public school, acquiring a good education. In 1880 the father sold his possessions in that country and came across the plains with the family, being one of a train of twenty wagons. There were six children in the family, including our subject, and they came via Kelton and Boise, and the father selected the place where our subject now lives, which is one of the fine places on the creek. Our subject purchased it from his father and now owns two hundred and forty acres of fine land. He has abundance of water for irrigation, a fine seven-room house, good barn, outbuildings and other improvements, such as an orchard, and so forth. Mr. Stark has also a fine band of cattle and horses and a number of swarms of bees. Mr. Stark takes great interest in the educational advancement of the country and labors assiduously for it, as also for all lines of progress.

The marriage of Mr. Stark and Miss Belle, daughter of Mathias and Alice Olk, of Dell, was celebrated on August 30, 1894, and they have been blessed by the advent of three children, Sybil E., Gerald D. and Homer. Mr. Stark is a good specimen of what may be called a wide-awake, progressive and enterprising westerner and demonstrates what can be accomplished here by care, good management, industry and business ability, having accumulated his holdings by his own efforts entirely and has placed himself among the prominent property holders of the county.

<hr>

CYRUS W. MORFITT.—A native of this state and one of the promising and already well-to-do stockmen and farmers of Malheur county, having a fine estate of four hundred and forty acres, three miles southwest from Malheur, the subject of this sketch is deserving of mention in the history of the county, both because of his excellent success in the financial world and because of his own intrinsic worth, as well as for the labors performed in the advancement of the county's interests.

Cyrus W. was born on September 9, 1865, at Oregon City, being the son of William and Juliet E. (Worsham) Morfit. Her father crossed the plains to the Willamette valley in 1847, being a native of England, and having come to the United States when he was five years of age, and now resides near Ontario. The mother of our subject crossed the plains in 1852 and on January 18, 1894, she was called hence by death. In 1867 Cyrus W. was taken to Boise with his parents and the following year they came to the country where he now lives. He attended the common school and remained with his parents until he was eighteen and then with a capital of five dollars and three ponies, he started life's battles for himself. He engaged in the stock business and now has the fine estate mentiond above, which comprises a large tract of fertile bottom land. He has a band of cattle, and a fine six-room residence, two large barns, outbuildings, and all accessories to operate a first class farm and stock ranch. Mr. Morfitt has also given some attention to fruit raising, having a good orchard.

On May 12, 1889, Mr. Morfitt married Miss Alice M., daughter of George W. and Susan D. (Sult) Duncan, and they have been blessed by the advent of the following children: Edith L., Nellie E., Albert W., Cecil M. and Laura T. Mrs. Morfitt's parents came across the plains from Kansas direct to Willow creek in 1881, and in 1893 the father died, but the mother is still living on Willow creek. Mr. Morfitt is a member of the W. of W., Burnt River Camp, No. 111; also of the I. O. O. F., Eldorado Lodge, No. 152. He is past counsel in the former order. Mrs. Morfitt is a member of the Circle, No. 216, as is also her husband, and she holds the office of guardian neighbor. Mr. Morfitt is actively interested in educational matters, having devoted time to the duties of director for three years. He is one of the patriotic citizens, capable business men and prominent stockmen of Malheur county and is esteemed by all who know him.

CYRUS T. LOCEY.—The subject of this sketch has the distinction of being one of the earliest pioneers of the state of Oregon, as well as among the earliest in Malheur county, and he was one of the capable men who assisted in the organization of the county and has labored here for its upbuilding since that time, being

now one of the venerable and highly esteemed citizens. The birth of Cyrus T. occurred on September 18, 1835, at Mineral Point, Wisconsin, being the son of A. R. T. and Alice H. (Howell) Locey, the father having the degree of M. D. While a child he was taken by his parents to Platteville, and then to Lancaster, in his native state, the father being county clerk in the latter place for a series of years, and there also the mother died in 1842. Thence they removed to Galesburg, Illinois, and then on to St. Joseph, Missouri, and in April, 1846, they started with ox teams across the plains, going direct to Oregon City, which place they reached in six months. The father settled on a farm and Mrs. P. H. Hatch, our subject's sister, taught the first school in Oregon City, the same being in 1846-7. In the gold excitement of 1849 the family removed to Coloma, California, and there the father operated a drug store and hospital, that being the place where the gold was first discovered. In the fall of 1850 the family, consisting of the father, stepmother, one sister, one brother and our subject went via the Nicaragua route to New Orleans and thence to the old home in Galesburg, Illinois. These were the first white women that ever traveled that route. In the spring of 1852 they came across the plains again with ox teams to Oregon City, and the following year the father died. For seven years subsequent to this event our subject went to school in the winter and worked at steamboating in the summer on the Willamette. On January 1, 1860, Mr. Locey married Miss Maria, daughter of James and Susana Morfitt. The parents were natives of England and came to the United States in 1841 and crossed the plains from Illinois with ox teams in 1847. For twelve years subsequent to his marriage Mr. Locey followed steamboating and also operated a mule railroad from Canemah to Oregon City, going thus around the falls in the river at that point. He had the distinction of transporting during this time ex-vice-president Colfax and other dignitaries. In 1872 Mr. Locey left the Willamette valley and came to Willow creek, and in 1877 located on his present place, three miles east from Ironsides. He has a fine estate of six hundred and forty acres, which produces abundant crops of hay, and is well improved, having a good residence and commodious barns. Mr. Locey raises much stock, principally cattle and horses. He has been notary public for several years and in 1880 and 1890 he was census enumerator.

To Mr. Locey and his estimable wife there have been born the following children: Clarence T., deceased; Charles W., deceased; Julian D., who was elected sheriff of this county in 1898 and was re-elected in 1900 by a large majority, but died on June 27, 1901, before his term had expired; Addie M., wife of James Lackey, of Ontario, Oregon; Susie C.; Mary B., a teacher in the public schools, being a graduate of Monmouth Normal school; James E., married to Hattie Derrick; Cyrus C., deceased; Frederick E. Mr. and Mrs. Locey are devout followers of the faith of the Scriptures and hold their church fellowship with the Methodists. In educational matters Mr. Locey is active and has discharged the duties of clerk of the school board with credit for several years. When the county was organized Mr. Locey was chosen one of the commissioners, it being a very responsible office at that time.

He has a very distinct recollection of seeing Dr. Marcus Whitman, a noted pioneer and Christian missionary to this country in the earliest days, and who brought the first wagon train over the Rockies. The Doctor stopped with the father of our subject on one occasion and took supper with them.

PERRY E. PHELPS.—This capable and enterprising gentleman, one of Vale's progressive business men, is at the present time operating a real estate office in the town and does a good business and is considered as one of the most valuable residents of the county, being a man of capabilities far above the average, and having the distinction of making a success in at least two different callings in the walks of life. Perry E. was born in Miami county, Kansas, on April 20, 1863, being the son of Mark Y. and Naomi (McDonald) Phelps. The father had crossed the continent from Pennsylvania to California in 1849 to dig gold, and in 1853 he returned to his native place via the isthmus route. A few years later he removed to Kansas and there was married in 1859. In 1861 he enlisted in the Kansas volunteers and was promoted to captaincy of his company. He was in many skirmishes and in 1863, on account of sickness, he was honorably discharged and shortly after we find him with his wife and two children, our subject being then but an infant of two months, en route via the isthmus to California. They finally located on The San Benito river and the father raised stock there until 1870, when he removed the family back to Kansas, where our subject attended school, graduating from the graded department. In 1881, on account of the father's failing health, they removed to the west again, this time to Boise, Idaho. There they farmed and raised stock until 1893, when the father died, but the mother is still living in Boise. In 1894 our subject came to Mountain Home, Idaho, and engaged in the real estate business, where he was blessed with good success. In 1896, feeling it an urgent call, he entered the ministry of the Methodist church, taking charge of the church of that denomination at Salubria, Idaho. On March 6, 1897, occurred the happy event of the marriage of Mr. Phelps and Miss Flora L., daughter of A. J. Gowey, and they have become the parents of three children, Mark Y., Timothy G., and the baby. In September, of the same year of the wedding, Mr. Phelps came to Vale to assume charge of the Methodist church there, and for two years he continued in this good work, and then because of the failure of his voice, he was obliged to retire from the ministry. He purchased a farm near town, but soon sold it. In 1900 he opened a real estate office in Vale and there we find him at the present time doing a good business and establishing himself as one of the bright business men of the county. He owns a fine seven-room residence, and some other property. Mr. Phelps is held in high esteem by all and is worthy of the confidence reposed in him.

HENRY L. ZUTZ.—Although not one of the pioneers of the county, still the subject of this sketch is one of the substantial citizens of to-day in Malheur county, and is a man of enterprise, capable and given to promotion of the cause of education, of the interests of the county and the prosecution of successful business in the line of agriculture and stock raising. Henry L. was born in Manitowoc county, Wisconsin, on March 20, 1854, being the son of Michael and Christina Zutz, natives of Ger-

598   HISTORY OF BAKER, GRANT, MALHEUR AND HARNEY COUNTIES

many and early pioneers of that county. Our subject was reared on a farm and attended the common schools, where he acquired his education. In 1881 he went to Polk county, Minnesota, and there farmed until 1895, at which date he made his way with his family to Malheur county. He has a quarter section of road land, which is well improved and which produces good crops.

On July 3, 1878, occurred the marriage of Mr. Zutz and Miss Mary Porter, and three children were born to this union: Ferdinand, married to Matilda Gellerman; Lillie; Henry, deceased. On April 16, 196, Mr. Zutz was called to mourn the loss of his wife, the death occurring in Ontario.

In 1898 Mr. Zutz contracted a second marriage, the lady of his choice on this occasion being Annie, daughter of N. C. and Elizabeth Long, of the vicinity of Vale, and one child has been born to them, Grace. Mr. Zutz is active in the matter of betterment of the county's interest and enthusiastically champions the cause of advancement along the lines of education, while in his walk, both public and private, he manifests stanch character, uprightness and commendable zeal in the lines of his enterprises, while he enjoys the esteem and confidence of his fellows.

FREDERICK W. STACEY.—The subject of this review was born in Devonshire, England, on May 8, 1863. In 1870 his parents, Simon P. and Martha O. (Daniel) Stacey, emigrated to America, settling in Honesdale, Wayne county, Pennsylvania. Three years later the family moved to Silver City, Idaho. In the common schools Mr. Stacey received his early education. The year 1878 marks the date of their migration to lower willow creek, Malheur county. Here he remained with his parents until four years later, when they made permanent settlement in their present location, which is twelve miles west of Vale, on the south side of the Malheur river. During his school days Mr. Stacey spent his summers in the service of stockmen on the Idaho ranges and this experience gave him much practical knowledge of the stock business. When final settlement was made in Malheur county he naturally drifted into the stock

trade and has gathered about him on his Malheur ranch quite a numerous herd.

In 1882 he began to "ride the range" for Miller & Lux, remaining in their employ for five years. During one of these years he occupied the position of foreman. In 1901 Mr. Stacey and his brother, Harley O., entered into a partnership in the stock business, operating together since that time, the firm being known as Stacey Brothers.

The marriage of Mr. Stacey to Miss Viola, daughter of L. W. and Lucy Goodrich, who were natives of California, and who came to this state in 1890, was hallowed on June 28, 1891. They have become the parents of five children, Harold (deceased), James C., Beatrix E., Vera V., and George F. Mr. Stacey's father, whose family owned an old homestead in England for many generations, died on February 21, 1901, but his mother still lives in Vale.

Mr. Stacey is recognized as one of the leading men of the county. He has an enviable reputation for integrity and executive ability and, although a foreigner by birth, has ever manifested the true pioneer spirit in his patriotic devotion to American institutions.

THOMAS B. FISER.—This esteemed gentleman is one of the well known and representative men of the county of Malheur and one of the business men of Ontario, where he operates the Brown hotel, also handling a tract of thirty acres immediately east from town, where he has a fine orchard and raises many of the fruits of the soil indigenous to this latitude. Thomas B. was born in Weakley county, Tennessee, on April 27, 1854, being the son of Pleasant I. and Elizabeth (Hunt) Fiser. He grew up on the farm, attending the public schools and remained there with his parents until he was twenty-one years of age. At that time he went to Calloway county, Kentucky, and a few years later went to Johnson county, Arkansas, and there on December 27, 1883, occurred his marriage to Miss Mary K., daughter of John M. and Susan Brown. In 1888 Mr. Fiser migrated with his family to Baker City, Oregon, and the following year he went to Juntura, Malheur county, entered government land and devoted his energies to raising stock. He proved up on the land and owns it. Subsequent to proving up on the farm he was foreman on the Otis ranch for Miller & Lux, and in September, 1897, he removed to Ontario, purchased the land above spoken of and settled down. He handles the hotel mentioned, his wife largely attending to that, while he supervises the gardening and fruit on the land adjoining town.

To Mr. and Mrs. Fiser there have been born the following named children: Clarence L., Susan, William H. and Emma E. Mr. Fiser is a member of the I. O. O. F., Ontario Lodge, No. 90, and also of the W. of W. He has manifested much interest in the advancement of the county's welfare, and has always been characterized by enterprise and sagacity in his affairs, having achieved a good success.

JOHN B. McLAUGHLIN, deceased.—
It is quite fitting that a memorial be granted to the esteemed subject of this review, in the history of the county where he labored so long and faithfully and where he was known far and near as one of the capable, substantial and upright men of the county, being a prominent citizen, while his labors were crowned with success in almost every endeavor to which he put his hand. The birth of Mr. McLaughlin occurred in St. Genevieve county, Missouri, on January 13, 1827, being the son of James and Mary McLaughlin. When a child the family removed to the vicinity of Covington, Kentucky, where he was reared on a farm and educated in the country schools. In 1848 he started west with ox teams and the first winter was spent at Fort Laramie, and in the spring of 1849 he came to California, where he mined until 1861 and then came to Walla Walla and thence to the Idaho basin. It was in the spring of 1863 that he came to Riverside, a point on the Snake, and there in company with Jonathan Keeney and John DuVall put in the first ferry boat at the old emigrant crossing. In 1866 this venture was sold and he turned his attention to farming and stock raising. At about this time, or definitely, on November 19, 1865, Mr. McLaughlin and Miss Bethsinah J. Froman were married. Mrs. McLaughlin's parents, Dr. Felix K. and Martha Froman, were natives, respectively, of Kentucky and Virginia, and lived in Ray coun-

ty, Missouri, where Mrs. McLaughlin was born. Thence they removed to Iowa and then crossed the plains in 1864, coming with a train of one hundred wagons, assembling thus large on account of the hostilities of the Indians. Much hardship was endured on the road and six months were consumed in getting to Boise. In the spring of 1878 Mr. McLaughlin removed to lower Willow creek, and in 1880 they came to their present place, which is nine miles west from Vale on the south side of the Malheur river. They were pioneers in this region, there being only two women west from Vale. Mr. McLaughlin secured about the finest place in this part of the country, and now the widow owns five hundred acres of land, under cultivation, with a fine two-story frame residence, commodious barns and substantial outbuildings, and is carrying on the place in a commendable manner. On March 26, 1901, Mr. McLaughlin was very suddenly taken by death, and he was sincerely mourned by a large circle of friends. The Masonic fraternity took charge of his funeral, he having been a member of that body for forty years. Besides his widow Mr. McLaughlin left four children to mourn his demise, John, George, Mabel and Grace. The oldest child, James F., was also deceased.

GEORGE W. BRINNON is one of the real pioneers of the section where Ontario now stands, having passed through here in 1863. He has led a life of stirring activity and done much toward the development of this section of the west. His birth occurred in Wheeling, West Virginia, on April 15, 1838, being the son of William P. and Elizabeth (Preston) Brinnon, who removed with him, while he was still a child, to Champaign county, Ohio, whence they went to Caldwell county, Missouri, then to Davis county, in the same state. George W. attended school in the log school houses when the teachers were paid by subscriptions. At the age of fifteen years he started to drive a team for the government across the plains from Missouri points to the Rockies, and during the last two years he was assistant wagon master and received seventy-five dollars per month. He made his last trip from Denver to Missouri in 1861. In 1863 he went to Madison county, Iowa, and thence on April 5, 1863, he started across the plains to the Idaho mines, in company with his brothers-in-law, Gardner and Ninemire. They arrived at Boise in the fall, the place being a little burg of two or three houses and some tents. He followed mining for a short time and then went to the mouth of the Boise river and engaged in running a ferry on the old emigrant road across the Snake. He had to defend his property from the attacks of the hostile redskins and in 1864 he left and went to Emmett, Idaho. There he married Miss Nancy J. Smith, a native of Harrison county, Missouri, and who had crossed the plains with the same train in which he came. The wedding occurred on October 24, 1864. It was in 1867 that he came to Malheur City and engaged in mining in that vicinity. In 1871 he moved to the mouth of the Malheur river and secured four hundred acres of land and there raised stock until 1887, when he sold out and engaged in mining altogether, in which line of industry he has been successful. In 1898, while Mr. Brinnon was returning from Denver, whither he had gone with ore, he was caught in a terrible wreck at American Falls, in which ten persons were killed outright and twenty were wounded. He was bruised in a terrible manner, both legs being broken, which resulted in the loss of his right leg. He was taken to the hospital in Salt Lake City, and by his Odd Fellow brothers he was well cared for, but the loss of his limb has been a severe blow to him. To him and his estimable wife there have been born eight children: Louisa, deceased; Mary E., wife of Thomas Brosnan; Jonathan M., deceased; Charlotte, wife of William Hall; George Ann, wife of Martin McEndree; Julia, wife of J. B. Percell; Edward, married to Lulu Brison; Frederick E. On May 15, 1887, Mr. Brinnon was called to mourn the death of his beloved companion.

In 1861 Mr. Brinnon enlisted in Company C of the Twelfth Missouri Volunteers in the Confederate army and participated in many battles and skirmishes. He was in Price's army and fought at Wilson creek, Lexington, and Kirksville, the first battle, and was taken prisoner in 1863 and later was paroled.

Fraternally Mr. Brinnon is affiliated with the I. O. O. F., Ontario Lodge, No. 90, being a charter member, and is also a member of the encampment. He is one of the substantial and successful men of the county and is held in high esteem by all.

───◆◆───

GEORGE A. POGUE, M. D.—The genial and affable gentleman whose name initiates this paragraph is not only a man among men possessed of those pleasant qualities mentioned, but as a professional gentleman of ability and skill he ranks with the best physicians of this portion of our commonwealth, having had abundant practice, and is fortified with deep erudition. George A. was born in Fairbanks, Indiana, on June 22, 1856, being the son of Hiram and Rachel (Hunt) Pogue. When a child he was taken by his parents to Shelby county, Illinois, where they reside at the present time. He received a good education and at manhood's estate gave his attention to teaching for a time. Following that period he went to the Kentucky School of Medicine at Louisville, whence he graduated in 1879, and then one year was spent in the Louisville Medical College in post-graduate work. Another year was spent as assistant physician in the free dispensary at that place, when he removed to Firth, Nebraska, practicing medicine for a number of years, then removed to Lincoln, in the same state, in 1886, and in 1889, October 22, he landed in Ontario, and at once he began the practice of his profession and since that time he has been continually on the alert in the care of his large and ever increasing practice, which has ever given him all he could attend to. In addition to his practice the doctor has a fine farm of two hundred and forty acres well improved and watered. He has an orchard of one thousand pear trees and as many more of different varieties, besides abundance of small fruits. In 1901 Dr. Pogue went to Chicago and took a post-graduate course and did considerable hospital work, keeping himself thus abreast of the times in his profession.

In the social world the Doctor is affiliated with the I. O. O. F., having been initiated at Firth, Nebraska, on March 17, 1882, being now a past grand of the Ontario Lodge, No. 90, and also has served as representative to the grand lodge. On the 17th of March, 1902, he became a member of the encampment, Lodge No. 49, of this town. He is also a member of the

GEORGE A. POGUE, M. D.

JAMES E. LAWRENCE.

JAMES M. WEAVER.

A. F. & A. M., Acacia Lodge, No. 118; W. of W., Arcadia Camp, No. 364, of Ontario. Doctor Pogue takes no part in politics, though in sentiment he is a Republican, but gives his energies to the prosecution of his profession. He has twice been elected coroner but refuses to serve.

On July 13, 1880, the marriage of Doctor Pogue and Miss Emily A. Scott, of Shelby county, Illinois, was solemnized and they have become the parents of two children, Mamie, deceased, and Bessie E.

JAMES E. LAWRENCE.—Although the gentleman whose name appears above is not among the oldest pioneers of Malheur county, still his energy, enterprise, and wise conduct here, coupled with his characteristic integrity and uprightness, make him one of our most valued citizens, and it is with pleasure that we are enabled to grant to him this consideration in the history of the county. James E. was born in Washington county, Arkansas, on November 13, 1873, being the son of William S. and Mary D. (Elms) Lawrence. In 1880 the parents brought the family across the plains with teams and settled in Baker county. In the spring of 1884 they removed to upper Willow creek, in the vicinity of Ironsides, and there remained until 1898. Then our subject was appointed deputy sheriff under the well known Julian D. Locey, and at the latter's death in June, 1901, he was made sheriff of Malheur county. Mr. Lawrence enjoys the no small distinction of being the youngest sheriff that ever served in the state of Oregon, and such has been the excellency of his labors in that capacity that he was again nominated by the Democratic party in 1902 and seated by a good majority. Mr. Lawrence has fine band of cattle on the upper Willow creek and he is numbered with the progressive and leading stockmen of the country.

On September 21, 1898, Mr. Lawrence and Miss Louisa, daughter of J. H. and Louisa Rose, were married and to them have been born one child, Mary Louisa. Mr. Lawrence is at present noble grand in the I. O. O. F., Vale Lodge, No. 100, while Mrs. Lawrence is a member of the Rebekahs, Golden Rule Lodge, No. 64. Mr. Lawrence also affiliates with the A. F. & A. M., Acacia Lodge, No.

118, of Ontario. Mr. Lawrence acquired his education in the common schools and has been a close observer and careful student of men and business since those days, and is to-day one of the most enterprising and capable young men of our county, and he is well worthy of the popularity which is his to enjoy, and the esteem in which he is held.

JAMES M. WEAVER.—This intelligent and enterprising citizen of Malheur county is one of our most substantial and faithful men, as has been amply demonstrated in both commendable demeanor in responsible public capacities and in the popularity which he sustains in fraternal relations, as well as in the excellent industry and wisdom manifested in his private business enterprises. James M. was born in Scott county, Minnesota, on September 4, 1860, being the son of James and Elizabeth (Cole) Weaver, who on the fifth day of April, 1864, started with ox teams across the plains to the unbounded west. Six months later, to a day, they landed in Boise, Idaho, and there remained for two years, when another move was made, this time to the Walla Walla valley, where the father died in 1881. There, also, December 25, 1883, James M. Weaver was married to Miss Emma, daughter of William and Margaret Snyder. The following year he removed to the vicinity of Ione, in Morrow county, where he lived for eight years, when in the fall of 1888, he came to Vale, and there entered into the drug business. In 1892, on account of the resignation of the incumbent of that office, Mr. Weaver was appointed treasurer of the county of Malheur. He finished that term, serving one and one-half years, and such was the satisfaction given to the people that he was promptly elected on the Republican ticket to the same position for a term of two years, and then re-elected at its close for another term, giving him a service of five and one-half years as treasurer of the county, doubtless the longest period any incumbent has ever served in the county. In the fall of 1898 he bought his present farm of one-half section, nine miles southwest from Malheur, where he has a fine home and is in the stock business with his brother. He has a valuable ranch and has it well improved.

To Mr. Weaver and his estimable wife have been born the following children, Ralph J., Walter J., Inez E. and Lloyd A. On May 11, 1891, in Vale, Mrs. Weaver was called to depart this life, having been a faithful and capable helpmeet to our subject. Fraternally Mr. Weaver is prominent in the county, being past grand in Eldorado Lodge, No. 152, of the I. O. O. F., of Malheur, also past chief patriarch and a charter member of Malheur Encampment, No. 39, at Vale, and also a charter member of the Rebekahs, Golden Rule Lodge, No. 64, at Vale. He has also served as representative to the grand lodge of Oregon and is also elected for the same position this year; also he has served as district deputy grand master for three terms. Mr. Weaver's mother is still living on lower Willow creek, and it is of note that they camped in 1866 where the town of Vale is now standing.

FRANK A. KIME.—Among the leading stockmen of the western part of Malheur county must be mentioned the Kime brothers, of which firm the subject of this sketch is the senior member. He is a man of ability and enterprise and ranks well with his fellows. Frank A. was born in Sierra county, California, on September 21, 1867, being the son of David and Nancy (Zimmerman) Kime. The father was a carpenter and miner and died on September 21, 1876. He had crossed the plains with ox teams in 1860 from the state of Iowa to California, and in 1865 he returned to the states and in the spring of 1866 he came via Panama with his wife, locating in California until the time of his death. Subsequent to her husband's death Mrs. Kime came to Oregon, locating the present place, where the boys live, a half section of land three miles east from Westfall, on Bully creek. After proving up Mrs. Kime went to dwell in Caldwell, where she has a fine residence, and lives a retired life from the cares of business, while her interests are looked after by her sons. The farm place is mostly meadow, well supplied with water and has good buildings.

The brother of our subject is John M. Kime, born April 13, 1875, in Sierra county, California. He was married on January 20, 1902, to Martha Kincker.

The subject of this article was married August 12, 1900, to Mrs. Margretha (Kucker) Kime. To them has been born one child, David M. By her former husband Mrs. Kime has three children, William H., Harry P. and Albert J. Our subject and his brother are in partnership in the stock business and while they have a fine bunch of large horses, they also make a specialty of cattle, having a goodly herd of them. They are among the enterprising men in this important industry and have manifested enthusiasm and skill that have placed them in the ranks of the leaders, and they are highly esteemed among all who have the pleasure of their acquaintance.

THOMAS J. GOODYEAR.—The prominent citizen, intelligent gentleman and well-to-do stockman of Malheur county having headquarters at the home ranch of one-half section, ten miles northwest from Jordan Valley post-office. He is a man of energy and industry, who has made his entire holding by his wise management and careful industry since coming to this country. Thomas J. was born in Warwickshire, England, on March 8, 1864, being the son of William and Sarah (Burdette) Goodyear. He was well educated in his native country, being a graduate from the high school. In 1879 he came to the United States, landing in New York, whence he came direct to Silver City, Idaho, traveling by train as far as Winnemucca and thence by stage the balance of the distance. He soon was on the range and has continued to ride more or less since that time. In 1880 he came to Jordan Valley, and the following year he started the stock business for himself, and in 1886 he located his present place on Cow creek, described above. His ranch is well improved and produces abundantly from the meadows, while he has a large bunch of cattle. In 1887 Mr. Goodyear took a trip to England to visit his people. His father is now dead, but the mother still lives. Two years subsequent to this trip Mr. Goodyear came to the happy period of his life when he took to himself a wife, the lady being Miss Mary E. B. Jackson, formerly of his native country. The nuptials occurred on December 27, 1889, and since that time Mrs. Goodyear has presided over their pleasant home with

grace and dignity, being a woman of many
virtues. Mr. Goodyear is a member of the
I. O. O. F., Jordan Valley Lodge, and also of
the Modern Woodmen, Camp No. 5486, being
venerable consul of this last order. Mr. Goodyear has always been active in politics, allying himself with the Democratic party, and he
has achieved a good prestige throughout the
county, having demonstrated his capabilities
and worth. Mr. Goodyear, as mentioned above,
came here with little capital and has through
his faithful labors gained his present competence.

JOHN L. SELLS.—This worthy pioneer
of the county of Malheur is to-day one of the
substantial citizens and leading stockmen. For
many years he has wrought here with energy
and assiduity, gaining by industry and careful
conservation of the resources placed in his
hands the competence that is the crown of his
labors now. Mr. Sells was born in Franklin
county, Virginia, in August, 1856, being the
son of John L. and Elizabeth (Akers) Sells.
In 1862 the entire family removed to Montgomery county, Indiana, and there our subject
was reared on a farm, gaining his education
from the common schools of that locality. In
1874 he turned toward the west with an adventurous spirit and a courageous heart. He
went to California and mined in the principal
camps of that state and Oregon, going then to
Silver City, Idaho. In 1880 he came to Baker
county, Malheur being then Baker, and he says
that at that time there was no Ontario, Vale,
and no fences for miles in any direction and
only ocasionally a settler. He devoted his energies at that time to stock raising, leaving
the mining field. He has continued in the
stock business since that time and has gained
a good success therein. He has a half section
of good land, three miles east from Westfall,
part of which he took as a homestead. The
farm is well improved, with a fine seven room
house, good stone barn, plenty of water for
irrigating and produces an abundance of hay.
Mr. Sells has a good bunch of cattle, a fine
business property in Westfall and his home
place is valuable. In political matters he is
allied with the Democratic party and he has
always devoted that attention to political matters that is demanded.

The marriage of Mr. Sells and Miss Frances, daughter of Joseph A. and Clementine-
(Ireland) Martin, was solemnized on December 6, 1895, and they have become the parents.
of the following children: Selma and Martin C.

JOSEPH A. MADDEN.—One of the enterprising citizens and capable business men
of the vicinity of Westfall is named at the
head of this article and it is with pleasure that
we grant to him a representation in this volume, since he is a man of worth and integrity;
since he has labored faithfully here for the
general advancement and welfare; and since
he is one of the real builders of the county. Mr.
Madden was born in Perry county, Ohio, on
March 5, 1837, being the son of Hezekiah
and Mary Madden. He attended the schools
of the day, which were held in log cabins, and
humble ones at that, and thus he gained his
education. At the age of eighteen years he
came to northwestern Ohio, and thence to
Mills county, Iowa, where he engaged in farming, also labored at saw milling. He returned
to Ohio and in 1861 he married Miss Rachel
H. Spencer, and then returned with his young
bride to Iowa. When the memorable call came
for "ninety-day" men he responded promptly
and went to fight for his country. He served
his time and then returned home and after the
war he removed his family to southwestern
Missouri, where he lived for three years, and
then returned to Iowa, whence, in 1874, with
a train of thirteen emigrant cars he came to.
San Francisco, and thence by steamboat to
Portland. Later he came to The Dalles and
there engaged in raising cattle and sheep until 1881, at which time he sold his property
there and came overland to his present place,
which is located about four miles northwest.
from Westfall, and consists of two hundred
and forty acres of especially fertile land. It
is largely cultivated to alfalfa and some grain.
He has the farm well improved, with fine
buildings and a good orchard. He has plenty
of water to irrigate his land and possesses a
goodly bunch of cattle. In addition to handling this farm Mr. Madden and his son,
Charles, have been operating a general merchandise business in Westfall, which they sold
in June, 1901. Mr. Madden has always been

on the frontier, in Ohio, in Iowa, and in Oregon. He has always manifested those qualities of worth and distinction that characterize the true frontiersman and which have done so much in the davancement of the interests of this country. In politics he is a Republican and displays the interest that becomes the intelligent citizen. He has been justice of the peace for several terms. In all his business relations of late Mr. Madden has taken his son as partner, and together they are interested in the farm. Mr. and Mrs. Madden have become the parents of two children, Charles W., who married Mamie Jackson, and has one child, Elden Leslie; and the other is Ida M., wife of James Stingle.

JOSEPH G. LAMBERSON.—Among the pioneers of Malheur county it is eminently fitting that a representation be granted to the estimable gentleman whose name is at the head of this article, both because of the excellent labors which he has accomplished for the general welfare, and because of his own intrinsic worth and uprightness of character. Mr. Lamberson is the son of Lawrence and Mary (Holtz) Lamberson, and was born on July 31, 1852, in Summit county, Ohio. He grew up with his parents on a farm, attended the common school, and later the college at Mount Union, Ohio. In 1869 he left the parental roof and went to Fremont, Nebraska, thence to Bismark, Dakota, and in 1873 on to Helena. Later we find him in Virginia City, Nevada, and there he labored in the mines until 1875, then returned to Nebraska, and in 1879 he came across the plains on horseback. He landed in Union county, this state, having consumed three months on the journey. He labored on the farms at the Cove, Union county, and in 1881 he came to lower Willow creek, and there, on May 25, 1882, he was married to Miss Rosa Kendall, whose father crossed the plains in 1850, and her mother in 1852. They came from Illinois and located in the Willamette valley, and later removed to Union county, where Mrs. Lamberson was born. Eighteen hundred and eighty-nine was the year in which Mr. Lamberson came to Bully creek, his farm of two hundred and ninety acres being one and one-half miles from Westfall. In 1896 the

people called Mr. Lamberson, on the Populist ticket, to act as judge of Malheur county for four years; and to the entire satisfaction of a discriminating public he discharged the duties there incumbent upon him, and since has retired to private life again. The Judge has won many friends in this county and is popular in all parts of the country. Politically he is identified with the Democratic party. He has a fine farm, which is handled in a skillful manner and produces abundantly. Fraternally Judge Lamberson is a member of the A. O. U. W., Lodge No. 120, of Westfall. His father died in 1900, being in his ninety-eighth year. He was a veteran of the Mexican war. To Mr. and Mrs. Lamberson there have been born five children—Lawrence J., Bertha E., Clara L., May E., and Rosa B.

GEORGE W. BLANTON.—The subject of this article was born in Monroe county, Tennessee, on October 28, 1832, being the son of Vinson and Sarah (Marshall) Blanton, farmers of that place. He came when eight years of age with the balance of the family to Morgan county, Kentucky, and there had the privilege of walking four miles each day to attend the school in a log cabin, which had split logs for benches. His education was acquired by dint of hard application and he also labored hard on the farm during the summer seasons. At his home place, on April 25, 1853, Mr. Blanton married Miss Fannie J. Oliver, and in 1856 they journeyed to Coles county, Illinois, where he took up farming. In the spring of 1860 he removed to Linn county, Kansas, and there on July 16, 1862, he was stirred by the call of patriotism and enlisted in Company G, Twelfth Kansas Infantry, being first sergeant, and his regiment was in the Seventh Corps of the Western Division under General Steele. At the battle of Jenkins Ferry, Arkansas, which was a hotly contested struggle, he participated with credit to himself, and in many other severe fights he did faithful duty. Three years after the enlistment the fighting was done, the disloyal guns silenced, the government saved and our subject laid aside the weapons of war and returned to his home, whence he removed the family to Johnson county, Kansas, near Kansas City. In that place he continued to till the soil until the spring of 1881, when he came across the plains with his family, making the trip with mule teams, and consuming three months in the journey. He located his present place of one-quarter section, four miles southwest from Ontario, and began the good labor of building up the county and improving his place. The first land has grown to two hundred and eighty acres, well tilled and watered and improved with comfortable and substantial buildings. When Mr. Blanton settled here the country was wild, covered with sage brush, populated with jack rabbits and an occasional settler amid the waste, and the howling coyotes were his nightly companions. He was a man of keen perception and fearless courage and he saw that it was capable of great development if only one could weather the trying days of pioneering; he has bravely done so, and has labored with a skill, stability and enterprise that have given him the meed of a worthy position among his fellows, 'and a goodly competence. He built the first lumber house in the valley, assisted to erect the first house in Ontario, and has been a leader in conserving the interests of the county and thereby of its citizens, having ever brought to bear the same wisdom and energy in these noble labors that has characterized him in the prosecution of his private business enterprises.

The children born to Mr. and Mrs. Blanton are named as follows: William F., of Johnson county, Kansas; Mrs. Sarah J. Leavitt, of Douglas county, Kansas; Margaret, deceased; Georgian, deceased; Mary J., deceased; James M., near Ontario; John W., near Ontario; Mrs. Emma J. Smith, near Westfall; Mrs. Ida Hulery, near Ontario; George W., near Ontario; Mrs. Dora Herron, of Lind, Washington; Lena Belle. Mr. Blanton is past master of the A. F. & A. M., Acacia Lodge. No. 118, having been a Mason for forty years; and he is also affiliated with the G. A. R., A. P. Hovey Post, No. 21, being past commander of the same. He has always taken an active interest in the advancement of educational interests and the betterment of the facilities of this important branch of our government. Mr. Blanton has also been active in the affairs of the county, as becomes the intelligent citizen, and it has profited much by his wisdom and labors. In 1898 he was elected on the fusion

ticket as commissioner of Malheur county, and for four years he has done creditable service in this office. At the convention in the spring of 1902 he was placed in nomination by the Democratic party for the same position and was elected by a handsome majority. He has done faithful service in this office and has always the interests and welfare of the county at heart. It is readily seen that Mr. Blanton has been a leading figure wherever he has operated, being especially fitted by nature with keen and fine ability for this position, and as a sturdy pioneer, capable man, brave defender of his country and faithful citizen he is esteemed by all.

STOWELL L. PAYNE.—The well known and representative farmer whose name appears above is one of the wealth producers of Malheur county, having been a pioneer of the same, and has labored steadily since for its development and advancement. His ranch, where the family home is located, is six miles. from Westfall, on Bully creek, and is one of the first places located on that creek above Westfall. He has his land all fenced and well improved and cultivated. Has fine buildings and a good orchard, and is one of the leading tillers of the soil in western Malheur.

Speaking more particularly of the personal history of our subject, we note that his birth occurred in Jefferson county, Wisconsin, on December 1, 1852, and his parents were James and Emiline (Woolley) Payne. The father died when Stowell L. was a boy. He attended the public school, and later the Milton college, after which he took a position as bookkeeper, and finding it too confining for his health he went at out-door labor, traveling over the country. In 1872 he came to the west with an emigrant train, landing in Elko county, Nevada, and rode the range for a time, also mining. In 1873 he was in the Grande Ronde valley a short time. Eighteen hundred and seventy-six is the next date when he came to the Grande Ronde valley, and there, on November 28, 1878, occurred the happy event of his marriage with Miss Sarah A., daughter of Benjamin F. and Lucy (Russell) Kendall, whose father crossed the plains with ox teams in 1851, settling in Linn county. Oregon, the birth place of Mrs. Payne. In 1882 Mr. Payne came to Lower Willow creek, then in Baker county, and the following year located his present place.

Fraternally Mr. Payne is identified with the Masons, Acacia Lodge, No. 118, of Ontario. In politics he is active, being a strong Republican, and he has always labored faithfully for the good of the county. He was appointed county assessor, and was also stock inspector for a period, and in 1890 and 1900 he was census enumerator. To Mr. and Mrs. Payne there have been born seven children, named as follows: James, Benjamin, Frederick, Margaret A., Ella E., Carolie L. and Edward. It is of note that Mrs. Payne's father was in the Rogue river Indian war, and was a true pioneer who always kept in mind the progress of the country and the welfare of the people.

SOLOMON L. SPANN.—The well known gentleman of whom we have now the privilege of speaking is one of the substantial and intelligent farmers of Malheur county, having labored here for many years in the upbuilding of the county, and he has ever manifested himself one of the capable and loyal citizens, maintaining a high sense of honor and manifesting unswerving integrity, while he is highly esteemed by his fellows. Solomon L. was born in Pittsfield, Illinois, on August 23, 1842, being the son of Jordan and Mary Spann. He was reared on a farm, received his education from the common schools, held in a log cabin, and when the call came for men, brave and true, to fight for the nation's honor and safety, he enlisted in the Ninety-ninth Illinois Infantry, Company C, in July, 1862. He was in the Thirteenth army corps, under Grant, and participated in the battles of Hartville, Lebanon in Missouri, Fort Gibson, Champion Hills, Raymond, Jackson, Black River, Edward Station, the siege of Vicksburg, Spanish Fort, Blakely, Mobile, and many others, besides many skirmishes. He did faithful service, endured much hardship and deprivation, and in all of his hard fighting he was never wounded nor taken prisoner. On August 23, 1865, he was honorably discharged and returned to his home. There, on October 22, 1867, occurred the happy event of the marriage of Mr. Spann and Miss Mary J. Moore, a native of Rochester, New York. In 1871 they removed to the vicinity of Indianapolis, Indiana, and in 1876 they returned to Pike county. Two years later they removed to Lyon county, Kansas, and he worked in the coal mines until 1880. In that year he went with his family to Georgetown, Colorado, and in 1882 they came thence to American Falls, Idaho. All these trips were made with teams and wagon. In 1884 the journey westward was continued, and the family came to the vicinity of their present home. Stock raising occupied him for a time, and in 1892 settlement was made on the place where Mr. Spann and his family reside at the present time. This is an eighty-acre farm, four and one-half miles south from Ontario. The land is fertile, well tilled, and improved in a becoming manner. Mr. Spann raises much alfalfa hay, plenty of fruit, and does also a dairying business. The products of his dairy, as well as the fruits of the farm, find ready market.

To Mr. and Mrs. Spann one child was born, Laura E., who married James Grant. To that marriage one son, Edward S., was born on February 8, 1891. Mrs. Grant died in 1891, and Mr. Grant followed in 1899, and the little boy now lives with his grandparents, Mr. and Mrs. Spann. Mr. Spann is a past commander of the A. P. Hovey Post, No. 21, of the G. A. R., in Ontario.

JOHN HOFFMAN.—This gentleman is one of the prosperous stockmen of Malheur county and has labored well here for the upbuilding and advancement of the county, while he has acquired fine holdings in real estate and stock, being one of the leading men of his section. His fine ranch of two hundred acres, well improved and skillfully handled, lies about one mile north from Juntura postoffice.

Mr. Hoffman was born in Switzerland on February 7, 1856, being a son of natives of that land, and he was reared on a farm. He received his education in his native land, and in 1884 came to the United States. He settled first in Florida, spending one year in that place, and next we see him in Wasco county, this state, and later in Ellensburg, Washington. All these years he was industriously laboring and gaining a goodly competence to start in the stock business, and in 1893 he made his way into Malheur county and selected his present place, which he bought, and he has devoted his attention mainly to handling sheep since that time. He also raises other stock and does a general farming business At the present time Mr. Hoffman has a number of thousand of fine sheep, besides his real estate holdings and his other stock, such as cattle, horses, hogs, and so forth. Mr. Hoffman has made a success in his venture of handling sheep, which demonstrates his sagacity, painstaking care, and industry in this labor.

In December, 1900, Mr. Hoffman married Mrs. Mosley, a native of Kentucky, and one son has been born to them, named John Francis.

Mrs. Hoffman has three daughters by her former husband, and they are named as follows: Susie, Mattie and Nannie

Mr. Hoffman is a member of the A. O. U. W., and stands well in the community, and is considered one of the substantial stockmen and public-minded citizens of the county of Malheur.

WILLIAM H. ISAAC.

WILLIAM H. ISAAC.—Malheur county has some of the largest stock owners of Oregon, and one among that number is mentioned at the head of this article. Mr. Isaac has shown remarkable wisdom, skill and ability in handling his stock interests in this county, which by no means contains his entire holdings, for he is one of the well known stockmen of the entire northwest, having property and animals in many places. He started at the bottom, and his native pluck, tenacity and keenness have enabled him to climb the ladder of success until he stands at the very top.

Mr. Isaac was born in New York, in October, 1852, being the son of James and Mary Isaac. When he was seven the family came to Minnesota, and there they lived until 1868. The next move was to Walla Walla, Washington, where William H. completed his minority, and also finished his education. The parents died at Pendleton. The first venture of our subject was in the cattle business, and one severe winter swept away all his hard earned stock. Then he entered the employ of William Sturgis, acting as sheep herder. Few men would have taken this move, but Mr. Isaac

was not to be disconcerted, and was determined to win the smiles of Dame Fortune. He displayed his skill and faithfulness, and soon was enabled to purchase an interest in the business with his employer. Success crowned the efforts put forth, because of the untiring care, wise methods and skill employed, and in 1884 it was deemed best to divide their large holdings. In that year Mr. Isaac came with his herds and flocks to Malheur county, making his residence, however, in Caldwell, Idaho. His interests are in Malheur county in many places, and practically this county has a right to claim him, although he has holdings in other Oregon counties. He prospered well in every turn he made, and his sheep increased until at the present time he has twenty-five thousand head. In 1900 he took as partner M. B. Guinn. They have, in addition to the large bands of sheep mentioned, other stock, and ranches in various sections of the country, located convenient for the handling of the stock. This large acreage places our subject as one of the heavy real estate holders as well as one of the leading stockmen, while he has also other business interests.

Mr. Isaac married Miss Ada Miner, a native of Boise county, Idaho, and one daughter was born to them, Ada Narine. Mrs. Isaac was called from her pleasant home and loving family in 1896, and her remains repose in the cemetery in Caldwell.

Mr. Isaac is affiliated with the I. O. O. F., of Caldwell, and is highly esteemed by all who know him, being an influential, capable and upright man.

SYLVESTER F. BUSH.

SYLVESTER F. BUSH.—The subject of this sketch is a pioneer in the real sense of the word, and has tried the various hardships and labors and deprivations of the frontier in many places of the west, displaying always staunch virtues and courage and wisdom, which have given him the meed of success, and an enviable prestige among his fellows. Mr. Bush is a native of Canada, being born on Wolf island, in the St. Lawrence, on April 21, 1837, the son of Eli E. and Mehetable (Hadley) Bush. His father died when he was small, and he came with his mother to Dexter, New York. Both of his grandfathers were members of the body guard of General Washington during the

Revolution, a position of great distinction, while his father fought in the war of 1812. From Dexter our subject went with his mother to Hennepin county, Minnesota, and there he enlisted in Company I, of the Minnesota Volunteer Infantry. Eighteen hundred and sixty-one was the year of his enlistment, and he served throughout the entire war. He was in Sherman's department, and engaged in the battles of Chickamauga, Chattanooga, Missionary Ridge and others. Being honorably discharged at the close of hostilities with the rank of corporal, having enlisted as private, Mr. Bush then soon went to Helena, Montana, with a large emigrant train, and there engaged in mining. In the fall of 1868 he came thence to Mormon basin, in Malheur county, it being then in Baker county. Mining claimed his attention until 1880, then he spent a couple of years in looking the country over for a location, finally deciding upon his present home place as the spot. He filed a homestead right on it on September 14, 1882. It is fourteen miles west from Westfall, on Bully creek, and the estate is now of the generous proportions of two hundred acres. It is well supplied with water, has good buildings and orchards, and is well kept. In addition to this, Mr. Bush has three hundred and twenty acres on Clover creek, which is fenced and partly cultivated.

On June 8, 1874, Mr. Bush married Miss Ella I., daughter of Jeremiah and Eliza M. (Starbird) Jarvis, and four children have been born to them, as follows: Ernest E.; Charles J., a graduate of the College of Idaho, at Caldwell, Idaho; Brian B., attending college at Valparaiso, Indiana; Elfa M. Mr. Jarvis came from Maine around Cape Horn to California in 1849, and engaged in mining. In 1853 his wife came thither via Panama, and they dwelt in Marysville, where Mrs. Bush was born on July 17, 1854. In 1856 the family came to Portland, later to Burnt river, near where Durkee station is now, remaining there until the death of Mrs. Jarvis, in 1885, November 3, when Mr. Jarvis returned to San Francisco, where he died on October 10, 1897. Mr. and Mrs. Bush are capable and intelligent people, entitled to the esteem and confidence of their fellows, which they enjoy to a generous degree, and they are deserving of much credit for their faithful labors here.

JASON S. HUNTER.—The well known gentleman named above is one of the prominent stockmen and land owners in Malheur county, being also a man of integrity and capabilities that have manifested themselves in the bright success that is his to enjoy at the present time. He has a beautiful estate of nine hundred and sixty acres, nine miles north from Beulah, which is the family home, and is one of the finest health resorts of the county. A number of springs furnish plenty of pure water for all purposes, and the place is well improved, and Mr. Hunter has a good bunch of stock.

Reverting to his personal history, we note that Mr. Hunter was born in Gentry county, Missouri, on April 18, 1840, being the son of John T. and Nancy Hunter. The father was a miller, and consequently the son grew up in town until fourteen years of age, when they went on a farm. His education was gained largely from the subscription school held in the log cabin of the day. In 1862 he enlisted in Company E, Missouri State Militia, and served one and one-half years in Colonel Cramer's regiment, being honorably discharged at the end of his service.

The marriage of Mr. Hunter and Miss Eliza Atkinson, was solemnized on April 13, 1860, and eleven children were born to them, five of whom are living: Oscar M., of Jordan, Montana; Mrs. Louisa Gray, of Callahan, California; Leonard, of Miles City, Montana; Malcolm, of Jordan, Montana; Mrs. Annie Carel, of Ontario. In the spring of 1864 Mr. Hunter started across the plains with his family, and drove five yoke of oxen, hauling four thousand pounds of freight the entire distance from Missouri to the Grande Ronde valley, being five months on the road, and enduring much hardship in the journey. He purchased state and school land near Lagrange, and went to raising stock. In 1878 he had some trouble with the Indians, they being on the warpath then. They burned some of his property. He acted as scout, and also handled freight at that time, securing remarkably good remuneration, on account of the danger. On February 18, 1879, Mr. Hunter was called to mourn the death of his wife. He contracted a second marriage on October 16, 1880, Miss Malinda A., daughter of John G. and Mary J. Moore, becoming his wife on this occasion. Mr.

Moore came from the state of Massachusetts, around Cape Horn, to California, in 1849, and located in San Mateo county, where Mrs. Hunter was born, and her parents still live there. Mr. Hunter sold out in the Grande Ronde valley in 1883 and came to his present place and took land under the preemption and homestead, and desert, and timber culture, and timber rights, and this has been his home since that time. Mrs. Hunter also took two hundred and forty acres of desert land. Five children have been born to the second marriage, named as follows: Clarence J., Elmer N., Ralph G., Edith E. and George W. Mr. Hunter has been living in his present home for nineteen years, and the conditions of climate, water, and so forth, are so conducive to health that it has never been necessary to call a physician for the family in all this long period. Mr. Hunter is a true pioneer, having settled in the Grande Ronde valley when few settlers were there, and coming to his present place when it was fresh in the natural state. He has labored faithfully for the advancement of the country, being an adherent of the Democratic party.

THOMAS L. ARNOLD.—The subject of this sketch is well known throughout the western portion of Malheur county, and, in fact, all over the county, having come here as a pioneer and laboring in prominent positions since that time, being now a leading farmer and stockman of the vicinity of Beulah. His farm of two hundred acres lies four miles northeast from Beulah, and is a valuable place, possessing fine improvements, and is productive of handsome dividends annually

Mr. Arnold is a native of Mississippi, being born in Panola county, on February 28, 1842, the son of John and Mary Arnold. The mother died when he was a child, and he grew to manhood with his father on the farm, securing a good education from the common schools. On May 1, 1861, Mr. Arnold enlisted in the Confederate army, in the first Mississippi battery, and from that time until the discharge at Gainsville, Alabama, on May 5, 1865, he was in the regular army, and generally in the hottest of the fights. He participated in the battles of Shiloh, Baton Rouge, Holly Springs, Memphis, Fort Pillow, Nashville, and the siege

39

of Vicksburg, beside many others. He was wounded in the head, in the breast, in the hips and in the leg, all from gunshots, and also received a saber cut on the hand. He was under Bragg, and then with Forrest, and was field sergeant all the time. In 1867 Mr. Arnold's father died, and the following year he removed to Grayson county, Texas, with his family, having been married on January 9, 1861, to Elizabeth Withers. They were schoolmates together, and about the same age. From Texas they journeyed to Colorado Springs in 1873, and in 1878 to Albion, Idaho, and in 1883 he came to his present place. All of these moves were made with teams, and that across the plains with ox teams. His place is known as the agency valley, and he was appointed postmaster in 1884. He continued to act as postmaster until 1897, the office being named from one of his daughters, and when he resigned it was removed to its present location, four miles southwest from the home place. Eighteen hundred and eighty-six was the date when Mr. Arnold bought his present place from the state and school lands. Fraternally he is affiliated with the A. F. & A. M., Acacia Lodge, No. 118, at Ontario. The children born to this worthy couple are named as follows: Mrs. Mary McManus, of Susanville, Grant county, Oregon; Thomas F., near Drewsey; Mrs. Beulah Rutherford, from whom the postoffice was named, now living in Ontario; Oscar; Charles; Hoyt, near Hamilton, Grant county. Mr. Arnold was the first to locate in the valley with a family. He has continued steadily in the good labor of development of the resources of the country, and deserves much credit for it, while he is highly esteemed by his fellows.

JUDGE WILLIAM MILLER.—It is inherent in our race to give plaudits to the man who has achieved success against a fight with adverse circumstances, and especially so when by virtue of his own ability and pluck and worth, he has won against great odds that for which he fought and labored. As an example of this class of men we are constrained to mention the worthy gentleman whose name initiates this paragraph, being one of the leading men of worth and integrity in Malheur county, and also holding his present position of district attorney for this and Grant and Harney counties by virtue of his intrinsic worth, and enjoying a prestige which has been well earned through faithful effort and excellent accomplishment.

Mr. Miller was born in San Francisco, California, on January 8, 1854, being the son of David and Agnes (Irving) Miller. He was educated in the common and high schools, and then went to Stockton and acted as salesman for a number of years, 1877 being the date when he arrived in that city. Eighteen hundred and eighty-two marks the date when he left there and came to Harney valley, in this state. He drove team all the way for J. F. Mahon. In Harney he broke mules, teamed and made posts for the first year; then in 1883 he went into the store of McGowan & Steugars, where he clerked for thirty-three months. In 1886, while acting as deputy clerk for Grant county, he took up the study of law under the direction of Charles Parish, in Canyon City, and in due time was admitted to the practice at the bar. When Harney county was cut off as a separate political division, in 1889, he returned to Burns and selected all the record books for the county, and was the first deputy clerk of the county, under W. E. Grace, being also elected, later, as the first county judge. He was elected on the Democratic ticket and served for four years, being elected in 1890. On account of the failure of his wife's health he was forced to remove from that place, so located in Ontario. In 1898 he was elected district attorney for Malheur, Grant and Harney counties, on the Republican ticket, served two years, and then was promptly re-elected, the term having been then changed to four years.

The marriage of Judge Miller and Miss Eva F., daughter of Thomas and Sarah D. (Howard) Cozad, of Canyon City, early pioneers from Missouri, was solemnized on November 30, 1887, the issue of which was five children, as follows: Irving; Edna, deceased; Emmet, deceased; Lulu; and Agnes. On March 1, 1898, Mrs. Miller was called from her home and family by death. On September 11, 1899, Judge Miller contracted a second marriage, the lady being Mrs. Mattie Blakesley, a daughter of Mrs. Sisson, of Baker City. Mrs. Miller had one daughter by her former marriage, Madge Blakesley. Judge

Miller is a charter member of Acacia Lodge, No. 118, A. F. & A. M.; also a member of the I. O. O. F., Ontario Lodge, No. 90, being also past grand; and is a member of the W. of W. He is possessed of a good library, some property in both the country and town, including a good office building and much other valuable real estate. Judge Miller is one of the most highly esteemed men of the three counties mentioned, and is well worthy of the entire confidence of the people, being a man of integrity and worth, and having wrought out a success in three counties commensurate with his intrinsic qualities, and it is with pleasure that we have been enabled to grant him consideration in this volume of abiding chronicles of these counties. He is a purely self-made man. Judge Miller is mayor of the city of Ontario, Oregon, at this writing.

———◆◆———

JOHN DORAN.—The interesting career of this enterprising and capable gentleman is fraught with activities and commendable undertakings, and is well rounded by a sagacious care and energy which have made him one of the active participants in the building and developing of many places on the frontier, where he has always manifested that unswerving integrity that has held him in the path of temperance and uprightness in both public and private walk. John Doran was born in Liverpool, England, on November 5, 1840 being the son of Felix and Mary (Leonard) Doran. In 1845 he was brought with his parents to America's shores, landing in New Orleans, where the mother died soon after. He remained in New Orleans until 1851, then went to St. Louis, and in 1852, with a train of four ox teams, he came across the plains, assisting to drive two hundred cattle all the way, and walking the entire distance. He had the experience of being a target for Indian bullets on this occasion, and still remembers the thrilling days. In 1853 we find him working in a hotel in Marysville for twenty-five dollars per month and then he lived with Mr. Gray, and later with a Mr. Brumagin, where he worked and attended school, after which he went to Heald's College, in San Francisco. He then taught for one year in that institution, and then, in partnership with one Vinsonhaler, he organized the Union Business College, which he afterwards sold. Next we see him operating a fruit farm at Fruitvale, for Governor J. B. Weller. Three years later he went to San Diego, then to Bear valley, and in one district he taught for three years, after which he had charge of the reform school for a time. Then he went to Virginia City, and engaged in mining; and there, eighteen hundred feet under ground, he was brought a paper containing an "ad;" which his father had put in in search of this son. He immediately went to New York, this being in 1875, and he found his father and brother, whom he had not seen since 1847. The following year he came to California, and in 1879 to Harney county, Oregon, where he taught again for some years, and in 1882 entered land on Indian creek, now in Malheur county. He sold this later to the Müller & Lux land company, then he turned his attention to his first love once more, instructing the young, doing service in the vicinity of Vale. He then located a ranch on Bully creek, afterwards going to Nyssa, having sold this property, and at that place opened another ranch and was one of the organizers of the Owyhee irrigating ditch. Later he sold this and, returning to Bully creek, bought his old ranch again, and in the fall of 1901 he sold out entirely and retired from business. Mr. Doran is a man of temperance, and although he has never entered the matrimonial sea, is one of the affable, capable and talented gentlemen of the county, and has made a commendable record as an educator, a business man, and has had much experience as a traveler. He is the pioneer school teacher of this county.

* * *

JOHN HARDY ROSE.—This leading and representative citizen of Malheur county is one of the men who has taken hold with his hands and wrought out here in our midst a success which might be a fitting crowning to any man in any place, and in addition to this fine display of both ability and industry he has manifested stanch integrity, faithfulness and sound principles, being a man of wisdom and stability.

Mr. Rose was born in Scioto county, Ohio, on October 3, 1835, being the son of Israel and Mary (Payton) Rose. He lived with his parents in that then frontier country and went to school in the log school house of the time, but spending his time in most earnest study, he was enabled to gain a fortification for life that has been of great assistance in subsequent years. In 1856 he came with his parents to Knox county, Illinois, and the following year they went to Putnam county, Missouri, and there he resided on a farm with his parents until the time of his marriage, which happy event was celebrated on April 2, 1862, the lady of his choice being Miss Louisa, daughter of Francis and Caroline Hastings. The following day, April 3, 1862, Mr. Rose took his young bride and started across the plains with a wagon train drawn by oxen. His wagon has seven yoke of cattle, and these pulled the bridal coach to the region of Walla Walla, where the family wintered, and Mr. Rose returned to Auburn, Baker county, through which they had passed en route, and there worked at mining. The parents of our subject came to the west in the same train. In 1864 Mr. Rose removed his family to Auburn, where he was mining, and from there, in 1872, he came to Willow creek and built a small house, then went after his family, and there they settled down to improve the land and raise cattle. Their home place is two miles south from Ironside, and there Mr. Rose has two thousand acres, a large band of cattle, and his place well improved, with a house of fifteen rooms, commodious barns and substantial outbuildings. The entire estate is one of the finest in this section of the country, and there is manifested the wisdom, skill, taste and good judgment of the owner at every turn on the entire premises. In all of this accomplishment Mr. Rose has unavoidably been called upon to pass through great hardships and much deprivation on the frontier, in which his faithful wife has had her portion, and the family now are enjoying the fruits of the wisely bestowed toil of the parents in the excellent competence that they have gained.

The children born to this worthy couple are: Francis, married to Mary F. Gardner, living near Malheur; Charlotte, wife of Edward Coburn, near Ironside; Angeline, wife of Archie J. Murray, near Unity; Israel, married to Edna Whitely, near Ironside; John H., deceased; Louisa, wife of Sheriff James E. Lawrence; Eli. Mr. Rose and his wife are both devout members of the Christian church, and they are highly esteemed throughout the entire community, and they are fully worthy of the great respect and confidence that are generously bestowed upon them.

JEROME S. DERRICK.—The subject of this article is one of the good and substantial citizens of Malheur county, and is eminently deserving of a representation in this work, since he has wrought for the upbuilding of the county while he has also operated a good stock ranch of one-half section two miles north from Ironside, where the family home is now situated. Jerome S. was born in Roane county, east Tennessee, on February 9, 1841, being the son of Andrew and Julia (Brown) Derrick. The family resided in Tennessee until 1860, then came via New York and Panama to San Francisco, remaining in Sonoma county until 1864. Then they removed to the vicinity of Milton, in the Walla Walla valley, and there farmed. There, also, in October, 1867, our subject took unto him as wife, Miss Hester, daughter of James and Elizabeth (Cole) Weaver, and three children were born to them, as follows: Arthur A., married to Minnie Tague, and living on lower Willow creek; Effie E., formerly wife of Lewis Allen, now deceased, and she is now the wife of John Turner; Julia I. and William Allen, of California. On October 22, 1873, death took from his home Mr. Derrick's wife. On April 24, 1875, Mr. Derrick married a second time, the lady of his choice on this occasion being Miss Mary A., daughter of Alfred and Emoline (Enos) Watts. Mr. and Mrs. Watts crossed the plains in 1859 with ox teams, Mrs. Derrick then being three years of age. They came from Cass county, Missouri, direct to the Willamette valley, and in 1870 settled near Weston, Umatilla county, where Mrs. Watts died. Mr. Watts was a minister in the Methodist church. In 1880 our subject removed to Morrow county, and thence, in 1887, to the vicinity of his present place. The following year he went to Baker county, and four years later went to the vicinity of Portland, and then, in 1896, came back to Willow creek, bought a saw mill and operated the same until the fall of 1901, when he sold it and confines his attention now to

handling horses at his home place. He has a good house, barns, outbuildings, and all satisfactory improvements on the ranch. Also, Mr. Derrick has a large bunch of good horses. Mr. and Mrs. Derrick are the parents of the following children: William A.; Hattie J., wife of Ernest Locey; Horace M.; Claude M.; John E.; Merle I.; LeRoy, deceased; Albert and Delbert, twins, the former deceased; Della, deceased; Wallace M. Mr. Derrick takes an active part in the educational advancement of the country, and manifests the zeal and intelligence of the true American citizen. Mr. Derrick's father died at the old home place near Milton, and the mother passed away at the home of her daughter, Mrs. Kate Henderson, wife of a prominent business man in Walla Walla. Mr. Derrick is one of the substantial and stanch men of the community, and is held in esteem and respect.

WILLIAM QUINN.—Among the most enterprising and capable men of Malheur county stands the gentleman of whom we now have the pleasure of speaking, being one of the men who first penetrated this country, carrying his blankets through the fastnesses and wilds of the uncivilized region, and having wrought here with great success both on account of his industry and beacuse of his fine ability and wise methods of procedure. Mr. Quinn comes of good Irish stock, being born in Wicklow county, Ireland, on December 18, 1837, and the son of Philip and Mary (Deley) Quinn. While still a child he lost his father, and when he had arrived at the age of twelve he came with his brother and sister to America. They were eight weeks on an emigrant ship, and finally landed in Philadelphia, remaining in the state until 1853. At that date he came to Missouri, with the intention of crossing the plains, but no opportunity presented itself until 1855, when he started out with a train of thirty-two wagons, and it was nearly nine months later that he arrived in Placerville, California, having encountered trouble with snow on the Sierra Nevadas, and also some trouble with Indians. He labored at mining in different camps of the state until 1861, then came north to Rhodes creek, Idaho, and then to Salmon river, and later to Granite creek, and in 1865 he landed in the vicinity of Malheur, where he mined for twenty years, after which he purchased a stock ranch, and now owns nearly eight hundred acres of land used for this purpose. This fine estate lies ten miles west from Malheur, and is well improved and handled in a commendable manner, making lucrative returns to the owner. Mr. Quinn has a good residence, large barn, and handles a great quantity of hay.

On December 27, 1883, Mr. Quinn married Miss Nancy, daughter of William and Isabella Kennedy, and a native of San Francisco, and to them have been born four children, as follows: Mary I.; Philip, deceased; William; Christopher, deceased. Mr. Quinn was elected to the position of assessor of the county on the Democratic ticket, and it was with credit to himself and satisfaction to his constituents that he discharged these responsible duties. Mr. Quinn has gone through the entire list of hardships, dangers, deprivations and toil incident to a pioneer life, and he is rightly classed as one of the capable and enterprising builders of the county, since he has both wisely planned and executed thoroughly his business enterprises, and also has done faithfully and well the public duties devolving upon him as county officer and as citizen.

* * *

LAFAYETTE W. GOODRICH.— Among the substantial and enterprising citizens of Malheur county mention must be made of the gentleman whose name appears above, because he is one who has labored for the upbuilding of the county and its interests, has made a commendable showing in spite of frequent adversity in his own business enterprises, is a man of sound principles, uprightness, integrity and sagacity. Mr. Goodrich was born in Nashville, Tennessee, on January 6, 1844, being the son of James and Nancy R. (Stone) Goodrich. While still a small child he went with his parents to Missouri, Polk county, and in 1849, the family started across the plains for California, passing the first winter in Fort Leavenworth, whence in the following spring they made their way across the remainder of the weary waste of plains and mountains to California, and in 1861 the father started a hotel in a canvas house at Stockton, then a small burg. In 1854

they removed to Sutter county, and there, in 1864, our subject commenced for himself the battle of life. His first venture was with sheep, and soon we find him in Colusa county, in which latter place on September 26, 1869, he married Miss Lucy J., daughter of Warren and Catharine A. Markham. Mr. and Mrs. Markham came to California overland with ox teams from New York state, crossing the plains in 1852, on which trip, while the parents were in the territory of Utah, our subject's wife was born. They settled in Sacramento. Our subject sold out his sheep interests and removed to Tehama county and took up farming, later again going to Modoc county, where he resumed the raising of sheep. The winter of 1889-90 was so severe that he lost heavily, so he determined to change residence, and came to Vale, and in 1892 came to his present place, where he started anew in the battle of life. He has a good home, has sixty acres of good land, well watered and improved, and a good band of cattle.

The following children have been born to this worthy couple: Viola and Violetta, twins, the former being the wife of F. W. Stacey, and the latter is deceased; Trask E.; May V., wife of W. Wells; Eva V., wife of B. Richardson; Foster A., deceased; Marion E. Fraternally Mr. Goodrich is affiliated with the Masons, Neuville Lodge, No. 205. He is a man of enterprise, and is the recipient of the confidence of his fellows, while he has wrought for the upbuilding, advancement and welfare of the sections where he has been domiciled, being a man of unquestioned integrity, ability and uprightness.

* * *

JOHN PEDERSON, deceased.— As the old pioneers pass away the younger men rise to fill their places in the business world, but the former made a place and name for themselves in the history of the county that is quite proper to mention in this work, and thus we grant to the esteemed gentleman whose name is at the head of this paragraph, since he was one of the stanch supporters of our free institutions, was a real pioneer, a good and kind father and husband, and a noble man. John Pederson was born in Denmark, in August, 1828, there passing his early years until he shiped on the ocean and in that capacity sailed to all parts of the world, and at the age of maturity came with his parents to New York, thence to New Orleans and up the Mississippi, and across the plains to Utah, using ox teams in the latter journey. Eighteen hundred and fifty-eight was the date of landing there, and two years later he went to California, and on July 7, of that year, was married to Mrs. Adelia (Johnson) Riddles. Mrs. Pederson had crossed the plains in 1847 with her parents, coming from Iowa with ox teams. Our subject and his wife lived in Alpine county, California, on a farm until 1863, then came to Willow creek, and two years later to the present homeplace, four miles west from Vale. They took a quarter section as government land and improved it, builded irrigating ditches, erected house, barns, outbuildings and all the conveniences, and made a fine home. At the home place, on May 17, 1899, Mr. Pederson was called to leave his work, his home and his family, and pass the river of death. His demise was a time for mourning among all who knew him, for he was a good man. The children left are as follows: John O., married to Alice Gelleran; George and Nellie, twins, the latter the wife of J. Benning; Samuel; Lizzie, wife of S. Adams; Olive, wife of J. J. Davis; Alda; Ruby; Vesta May. Mrs. Pederson was born June 14, 1845, and her first husband was Richard Riddles, deceased, and by that marriage she has three children, as follows: Martha A., wife of James Crooks, of Seattle; Mary J., wife of E. Henderson, of Sherman county, Oregon; Celia, wife of James Henderson, of Yreka, California. Mrs. Pederson's sons, George and Samuel, are running the place, in company, and it is the family home.

———— ◆◆◆ ————

GEORGE W. PEIRCE.—No compilation purporting to give in review the careers of the leading citizens of Malheur county would be complete were there failure to incorporate an epitome of the esteemed and capable gntleman whose name heads this paragraph, since he has wrought here with a master hand in the development of the county for many years, having a fine farm six miles west from Vale, since he has done much in different frontier districts, since he fought the battles bravely of the cause of the Union, since as a man he is

upright, possessed of great executive force, genial and affable, and highly esteemed by his fellows.

Mr. Peirce was born in Loudoun county, Virginia, on August 30, 1830, being the son of Gainer and Bethsina (McGeth) Peirce. In 1838 the family came to Columbiana county, Ohino, and in 1840 to Caldwell, Missouri, in which place our subject received his education from the subscription schools held in the log school houses. Also he was in different parts of Missouri. In 1849 he drove seven yoke of cattle across the plains to Santa Fe, New Mexico, drawing a cargo of seven thousand, three hundred and thirty-five pounds of black powder. After this he came to Las Vegas and worked in the quartermaster's department, under Lieutenant Buford, until the fall of 1850, when he returned to Missouri, and in the fall of 1852 he married Miss Frances Griffin, and one child was born to them, Louis B., now in Yakima county, Washington. In September, 1854, Mrs. Peirce was called home by death. On December 5, 1855, Mr. Peirce contracted a second marriage, the lady of his choice at this time being Miss Mary, daughter of Robert and Ann Edwards, a native of Kentucky, and the wedding taking place in Buchanan county, Missouri. Eighteen hundred and sixty-two was the date when Mr. Peirce moved to Keokuk county, Iowa, and there he enlisted in the Ninth Iowa Volunteer Infantry. He participated in the battle of Nashville, and did good military duty until August, 1865, having enlisted in the fall of 1864. He is now a member of the G. A. R., Hovey Post of Ontario. Subequent to the war Mr. Peirce removed his family to Platt county, Missouri, and there he followed the blacksmith trade, having learned the same from his father, who was a blacksmith. In 1874 he removed to Paradise valley, Humboldt county, Nevada, and there followed his trade until 1883, when he came by wagon to his present abode, being six miles west from Vale. This land he took as a homestead on August 16, 1883, and here has been the family home since that time. He has good land, well improved, comfortable buildings and plenty of water for irrigating.

To Mr. and Mrs. Peirce there have been born ten children, as follows: Thaddeus W., deceased; Frances A., widow of the late David Coleman, of Paradise, Nevada; Bethsina J., wife of W. G. Pennington; Felix F., deceased; Laura P., deceased; Sarah S., wife of David Cathcart, of Paradise, Nevada; George W., deceased; Isaac L., deceased; Martha E., wife of George Kershner; James F., married to Amy Ashmore. Mr. Peirce is a Mason, and has been for forty-five years, and he affiliates with the Acacia Lodge, No. 118. In the political realm he is identified with the socialistic movement, and in religious persuasion he and his estimable wife are members of the Missionary Baptists. In all his walk, both public and private, Mr. Peirce is an exemplary man, and now in the golden time of his well spent life he has the satisfaction of being in a circle of friends and relatives by whom he is well beloved, and looked up to, and held in great esteem.

FRANK M. RICKER:—About seven miles west and a little south from Vale we come to the pleasant home of F. M. Ricker, who has an estate of two hundred and forty acres of well irrigated and improved land, which is capable, through his skillful husbandry, of producing abundant returns. He is one of the leading stockmen and agriculturists of this section, and although he has not been domiciled here longer than since 1897 he has made a commendable showing, having fine improvements, a comfortable home, and evidently everything is managed with a wise plan and true executive force and enterprise. Mr. Ricker is a native of far away Maine, being born in Somerset county on August 3, 1835, and his parents were Moses and Mary C. (Dame) Ricker. He found his place under the parental roof, assisting on the farm and attending school, until 1857, when he was lured to the west, going first to Minnesota, and thence, two years later, to the famous Pike's Peak to participate in the mining excitement that was then running high. He followed mining and lumbering until the spring of 1861, then returned to Maine, and in the fall came via New York and Panama to California, landing at San Francisco and going direct to Placer county. He mined, logged and freighted in various sections of California until 1867, then deemed it high time to return to his native state and take unto himself the lady who was waiting there to become his wife; and the pleas-

ant ceremony that made Mr. F. M. Ricker and Miss Sarah J., daughter of Elisha and Elizabeth (Martin) Godfrey, husband and wife was performed on January 25, 1868. He settled in the native state until 1875, then determined to again try the west, and accordingly came to Andrew county, Missouri. But being eaten out there by the grasshoppers which infested that country then, he came west in the fall of the same year and settled in Sutter county, California, where he farmed until the fall of 1880, when another move was made, to Ellensburg, Washington. Two years later we find him in Union county, Oregon, near the Medical springs of that county, and thence in 1885, he came to upper Willow creek, near Ironsides. He farmed and raised stock there until 1897, when a final move was made which brought him to his present valuable and pleasant home place. Fraternally Mr. Ricker is affiliated with the Masons, Acacia Lodge, No. 118, of Ontario, and has been a member of that order since 1875. Mr. Ricker always takes the part of the intelligent citizen in political matters, while in the realm of education he is active and enthusiastic in the advancement of good schools and proper facilities for study and instruction. To Mr. and Mrs. Ricker have been born the following children: George Herbert, whose wife, Daisy Long, died April 1, 1902; Alice May, wife of M. Carlile, of Ironsides; Mertie E., wife of J. D. Miles, of Union county, and she is now deceased; one boy who died in infancy; Lizzie Bell; Nettie M.; Frank Emery.

ALONZO PEER.—One of the sturdy men and faithful pioneers who opened this country for the tread of civilization, and whose labors have resulted so well in developing the resources of the land is the subject of this article, and he is deserving of consideration in this volume of our county's history, being also a man of sound principles and integrity. He is proprietor of the Nyssa hotel and feed stable, where he does a good business, having a popularity with the traveling public that insures him a fine patronage. Mr. Peer was born in Morris county, New Jersey, on June 28, 1842, being the son of Ira and Eliza Peer. He grew to manhood's estate in his native place, and there also received his educational discipline. There also he cast his frst vote, and it was for Abraham Lincoln in 1864. About 1868 he went to Jackson county, Michigan, and opened up a farm on the frontier, entailing no small amount of hard labor and trial. Later this property was sold and he journeyed to Salt Lake, Utah, and thence to Arizona and New Mexico, but returned again to Utah, where he contracted a marriage with Mrs. Sarah J. Green, on May 12, 1883. She had crossed the plains with her parents in 1867, starting from Nebraska on March 4, and landing in Lehi, Utah, on August 4, making the trip with ox teams. Her native place is Richland county, Ohio, and her father was Lyman Warren. By her former marriage Mrs. Peer had three children, as follows: George P. Green, of Lewisville, Idaho; Lyman A., near Nyssa; Mrs. Mercy A. Leuck, of Nyssa. In 1885 Mr. Peer came to Idaho Falls with teams over the old emigrant road and then took a claim, and it was with much hardship and arduous labor that he was enabled to open it up. Water was difficult to obtain, and they had to haul it six miles. Many became discouraged and left the country. But Mr. Peer was persevering, and he reaped the rewards of his labors. In 1899 he sold his property and came to Nyssa, and here he purchased lots and erected the hotel and feed stables mentioned above. He has a good trade and is well liked. To Mr. and Mrs. Peer there have been born three children, as follows: Eliza Ann, Martha Ellen and Sadie Irene. Mr. Peer is greatly interested in educational matters, and labors faithfully for the advancement of that good work. He has always been zealous for the welfare of the county, and in him is found both the capable and good man and the patriotic and progressive citizen.

JOHN M. SNIVELY.—As one of Malheur county's promising men, a public official in the responsible position of superintendent of the entire road system in the county, a progressive citizen and a genial and amiable gentleman, we are bound to accord Mr. Snively a representation in the history of his county. He was born in Watsonville, California, on September 17, 1873, being the son of Daniel and Priscilla (Childers) Snively. The

father is a native of Pennsylvania and came across the plains with an ox train, meeting his future wife at the Missouri river and she traveled across the plains in the same train. Soon after reaching California, they were married and after the birth of our subject, they removed to Sacramento and thence to Red Bluffs, Tehama county, where they reside at the present time. Our subject was reared there on a fruit farm and remained with his parents until 1897, when he came to Jordan Valley and located his present homestead, thirty miles west from Jordan Valley postoffice. His place is adapted to raising hay and is surrounded with the best of stock grazing land.

On October 7, 1900, Mr. Snively married Miss Nellie G., daughter of James and Elizabeth (Thompson) Johnson, of Walla Walla, being early pioneers of that region. In January, 1902, Mr. Snively was appointed road master of the entire county and he is at the present time discharging the duties thus incumbent upon him with wisdom and manifestation of sound practical knowledge that bespeaks much to his credit and the profit of the county and the convenience of its residents. He is a member of the I. O. O. F., Jordan Valley Lodge, No. 158, and is secretary of the same. Although not a pioneer of the county, he is nevertheless a real pioneer in spirit and of the section where he now resides, being a man of energy, integrity, and excellent executive force.

GEORGE W. DUNCAN, deceased.— Among the living representatives of Malheur county there should appear an account of him whose name is at the head of this article, as a tribute to his memory, since he was one of the capable and upright men of this county, having ever manifested praiseworthy virtues in his life, being a devout Christian and also one of the noble men who pressed to the front to save the nation in the time of great danger.

George W. Duncan was born on January 29, 1843, in Williamson county, Illinois, being the son of Dudley W. and Elizabeth (Spiller) Duncan. He was reared on a farm and at an early age was deprived of both parents by death. He made his way in the world, encountering the adversities and sorrow of the orphan, but succeeded well in his undertakings.

GEORGE W. DUNCAN. MRS. GEORGE W. DUNCAN. BALTIMORE HOWARD.

WILLIAM L. LOGAN. S. N. EMISON.

On September 17, 1863, he enlisted in Company B, Fifteenth Kansas Cavalry, for three years. His service was largely on the border between Kansas and Missouri and he participated in many trying skirmishes. At the close of the war he was honorably discharged and went to Linn county, Kansas, to take up the duties of civil life. And there, on May 19, 1867, he was united in the holy bonds of matrimony with Susan D., daughter of Jacob and Georgiana (Gleason) Sult. Subsequent to this important event in his life, he removed to Wilson county, Kansas, and there took up government land and gave his attention to farming until 1880. At that date, on account of failing health, Mr. Duncan sold his property and provided rigs and came overland with teams to the present home place. His health was much improved, but still he was not fully restored, and on November 28, 1892, the angel of death summoned him hence. He was fully prepared to go and he passed as the true Christian to the realms beyond.

The children born to this worthy couple are named as follows: Rosetta, wife of the late sheriff, Julian D. Locey; Alice M., wife of Cyrus W. Morfitt; Ninnie, deceased; Albert, deceased; Wiley B. married to Gretta Wisdom; Cora A., deceased; Walter T., Ralph A., Ray R., and Nannie B. Mrs. Duncan has taken up the added burdens of life since her husband's death in a noble and skillful manner and she is now attending to the management of their large estate of eight hundred acres of land, one-half mile northeast from Ironsides, where the family home is. The place is comfortable and carefully improved and provided with all necessary buildings, orchards and conveniences for a first-class farm and stock ranch, and Mrs. Duncan has also a large herd of cattle. She is a member of the Methodist church, as her husband was, also, and she is a faithful supporter of the true faith, being an exemplary woman in her daily walk and characterized by graciousness and hospitality.

BALTIMORE HOWARD.—To the capable and substantial citizen whose name initiates this paragraph we are constrained to grant representation in the history of Malheur county, as he is a man of ability and integrity,

and has wrought with faithfulness for the general good, and has shown commendable wisdom in the manipulation of his affairs. The father of our subject, Jonathan B., was born in Maryland, in 1803, and the mother, Margaret Vinden, was born in Kentucky. Baltimore was born March 3, 1840, in Shelby county, Illinois, and in 1853 he came with his parents across the plains with ox teams, leaving the Missouri river at St. Joseph on May 5, and landing in Oregon City on August 20, which was about the best time that ox teams ever made across the plains. Our subject remained with his parents until 1860, and then took the gold fever and went to British Columbia and operated on the Fraser river for a season and then returned to Willamette valley. In 1861 he went to Oro Fino, Idaho, and returned to the valley in the fall of the same year and enlisted in Company E of the First Oregon Cavalry Volunteers, under Captain George B. Curry, and our subject was the first man to put down his name on the roll of privates. He enlisted for the purpose of going east, but he was detained in the west and for three years he served, fighting Indians. He was honorably discharged and in 1865 came to Walla Walla, and two years later went thence to Boise, Idaho, and in 1868 he came to the vicinity of his present home and engaged in mining and farming. He entered a homestead in 1880, where he now resides, ten miles southwest from Malheur, and here he owns one-half section, well improved and stocked with a large band of cattle. He has commodious barns and outbuildings and a comfortable residence and is one of the leading stockmen of the region.

On December 25, 1876, Mr. Howard married Miss Fannie, daughter of Jerry Ralston, and a native of Lebanon, Oregon, and to them have been born the following children, Clarence Elmer, Charles Oliver, Juliet Myrtle, Floyd Homer, Clara Rose, and Gladys Naomi. Mr. Howard is a Republican in politics, where he takes the part of an intelligent citizen, and in educational matters he is an enthusiastic worker and ever laboring for the progress of each department of the county. It is of note that Mr. Howard commenced with no capital except his hands and he has wrought out his present success, which demonstrates his ability and enterprise.

In 1878 Mr. Howard served as scout under General Howard and went from Malheur to Pendleton with him.

WILLIAM L. LOGAN.—It is with pleasure that we are enabled to give a resumé of the life of the worthy pioneer, capable gentleman, and stanch and patriotic citizen whose name initiates this paragraph, since he has wrought in many places on the frontier for its development, has done a lion's share of the hard work to accomplish this praiseworthy undertaking, has been exposed to the hardships of such a life, the dangers from the storms of the mountains, the dangers from Indians on the warpath, the dangers from wild animals in the forest, and in it all has shown that true courage, stability, and calm and good judgment that so well become the true American citizen. Also in Malheur county Mr. Logan has wrought with a faithful hand and his works are manifest to all.

William L. was born in Nashville, Tennessee, on May 31, 1827, being the son of Thomas and Elizabeth (Owens) Logan. When a child he came with the family to Illinois, thence to Wisconsin, and in 1852 across the plains with ox teams to Placerville, California. En route they had to fight the Indians, and there, as many times since in such conflicts, the savage foe fell at the crack of the trusty rifle of our subject. He mined and dealt in stock in California, traveling all over the state, and Arizona and New Mexico, as well, until 1862, then pulled up from his headquarters at Marysville and Sacramento and came north to Oregon, through the Grande Ronde valley, to Walla Walla, Lewiston, Florence, Idaho Basin and to the vicinity of Weiser, where he settled and went to farming and stock raising and also kept a stage station. In 1869 he came to lower Willow creek, where he now lives, four miles northwest from Dell, entered a homestead and settled down to improve the land and raise stock. He has added by purchase until he has three hundred acres of land, well supplied with water, and improved with good, comfortable house and all needed buildings. He raises as high as eight hundred tons of alfalfa per year and handles a large band of cattle and horses. When Mr. Logan settled here there were two other cabins, his being the third.

On April 18, 1863, Mr. Logan married Miss Nancy J., daughter of James and Lucinda (Malory) Harris, and they have become the parents of the following children: William Weiser, born March 13, 1864, being the first white child born in the vicinity of Weiser, Idaho, and now married to Hattie Denham, recently deceased; John T., married to Minnie O'Neal; James N., deceased; Edward A., married to Edna Logan; Frankie, deceased; Minnie H., deceased; Oscar W.; Arthur; Young P. and David P., twins, the former deceased; Robert L. Mrs. Logan came across the plains with her parents in 1862, making the trip with ox teams from the state of Iowa. She was born in Kane county, Illinois. Mr. Logan is a man of good capabilities, now well on in the golden time of his life, respected by all and esteemed by those who know him and to be highly credited for the noble part that he has done in the pioneer labors of the entire west and also for the prominent work that he has accomplished in this country.

SANFORD N. EMISON.—No man in the vicinity of Nyssa, Malheur county, is better known than the capable and enterprising business man whose name is at the head of this sketch. He is a member of the firm of Emison Brothers, which does a large business in the general merchandise trade, having a spacious and well equipped store in Nyssa, where they carry a complete stock of gents' furnishing goods, dry goods, groceries, hardware, house furnishings, farm implements, lumber, coal, and in fact a line of all kinds of goods that are needed in the wide range of territory whence comes their extensive and lucrative patronage. In addition to their commodious store, the firm owns a large two-story warehouse, where they have a great quantity of goods and the upper part is occupied with the opera house of the town. The firm also handles the Nyssa ferry, and until recently, they have handled a large stock ranch of fifteen hundred acres, well stocked and one of the largest in this section of the country.

Reverting more particularly to the personal history of our subject, we note that he was born in Baker City, Oregon, on July 13, 1872,

RESIDENCE OF JUDGE JAMES T. CLEMENT.

being thus a native of this portion of the state and one of its younger business men. His parents, William and Mary N. (Rice) Emison, came across the plains with ox teams from St. Louis, Missouri, in the early sixties and settled in Baker City, where the father followed mining for a time. Later he removed his family to near the place where Ontario now stands and engaged in stock raising. Our subject was a small child at this time and he grew up amid the environments of a stock ranch, gaining his elementary education from the common schools, and completing the same by a thorough course in the Willamette University at Salem, of which institution he is an alumnus. The father operated near Ontario for a number of years and then sold out and came to the vicinity of Nyssa and purchased fifteen hundred acres, where he continued his labors until April, 1900, when he was taken hence by the angel of death. The mother then purchased a place in Portland and is residing there at the present time. Our subject and his brother, Charles R., formed a partnership in 1896, handling the father's stock business and also a general merchandise establishment in Nyssa. The brother gave especial attention to the stock portion of the business and our subject handled the store. But in the spring of 1901, they disposed of the stock and gave their united attention to the merchandise business, and they have a fine establishment and the confidence and patronage of a large number of people, their trade extending many miles in every direction. Mr. Emison has a large ten-room house of modern architectural design, tastily surrounded and handsomely furnished, which is the family home at the present time.

The marriage of Mr. Emison and Miss Eva Tharp was solemnized on April 19, 1896, and to them have been born two children, Beatrice and Sidney S. Mrs. Emison is a lady of many virtues and graces, and she presides in a becoming manner over their elegant home, which she makes a center of refined hospitality. Mr. Emison is a member of the Modern Woodmen, Nyssa Camp, No. 7489. He is also postmaster of his town, and in this exacting position he has given satisfaction to all, and he is highly esteemed by all and is a business man of talent and executive force. ·

JUDGE JAMES T. CLEMENT.—It is truly gratifying that we are enabled to chronicle the career of this esteemed and prominent gentleman of Malheur county, being a man who wears the crown of success, having been especially prosperous in the affairs of business, one who has the entire confidence of the people, which is properly reposed, has manifested those virtues of manly uprightness and sagacity, coupled with enterprise and keen business discrimination and at this moment enjoys the prestige that talent and virtue produce.

James T. Clement was born in Pulaski township, Jackson county, Michigan, on May 31, 1840, being the son of Theophilus and Cleora (Webster) Clement. His mother was a second cousin to the noted Daniel Webster. Our subject grew up on the farm, received his education from the schools of his native place and on October 24, 1860, was married to Lucy E., daughter of Eli and Anna Hayes, and a native of Ohio. He settled down to farming until 1867, then drove a team Mitchell county, Iowa, and two years later drove on to Lancaster county, Nebraska, and thence in 1881, he came by team to Canyon county, Idaho. He settled near Payette, where he entered government land and now owns a fine farm there of two hundred acres of fertile soil, watered by his own ditch, and improved with orchards, elegant residence, barns, and so forth, which make it an ideal retreat and rural home. Four children were born to Mr. and Mrs. Clement, namely: Roswell W., married to Hattie Neal, near Ontario; J. Buell, deceased, was married to Helen Plummer; Hattie L., wife of Richard Waters, near Waterville, Washington; Edna, wife of D. C. Boyd, of Ontario. In February, 1884, Mrs. Clement died at the farm home in Idaho. In September, of the same year, Mr. Clement moved to Ontario, where his sister kept house for him. She has the distinction of being the second woman in Ontario. Mr. Clement then engaged in the lumber business, having yards at Payette, Ontario, and Weiser. This business occupied him until 1895, when he sold out and afterward engaged in general merchandise business with R. D. Greer & Company. This was likewise sold out and in 1900, the year following, Mr. Clement purchased, in connection with his son-in-law, D. C. Boyd, the Ontario Argus, a weekly Republican newspaper, which they handle with credit to themselves, it being a sheet of distinct vitality and merit and fearless in champion- ing the principles of right and progress. In 1888 Mr. Clement was elcted the first county judge of Malheur county on the Democratic ticket and for four years he served with abil- ity and in such manner that all were satisfied and approved his wise and faithful course. Formerly he had served as justice of the peace. In fraternal relations the Judge is popularly allied, being a member of the I. O. O. F., On- tario Lodge, No. 90, and past grand, also, having been representative to the grand lodge a couple of times and is also elected to the same position for this year; he is also a mem- ber of the Encampment of Ontario, No. 45, and is the present scribe; and is a member of the Rebekahs. The marriage of Judge Clem- ent and Mrs. Emma Hall, the first white child born in Layton, Michigan, was solemnized on December 25, 1884, and the family home is one of the most palatial and comely residences in eastern Oregon, being situated in lovely grounds, which partake of the practical, hav- ing fine gardens and orchards, and also of the beautiful and decorative, being tastily and skillfully laid out and handled. This lovely home is one of refined hospitality, and with graciousness it is presided over by Mrs. Clem- ent. In addition, the Judge has much other valuable property. It would not be fitting to close this brief article without referring to the pleasant fact that Judge Clement is a member of the Congregational church, and for nine years was superintendent of the Sunday-school, and in all that period he missed his accustomed place at the head of the school but nine Sun- days. He is a man of ability, integrity, and is happily possessed of an amiable nature and an affability that have won him hosts of friends from all classes, and he is highly respected.

WILLIAM J. SCOTT.—The doughty pi- oneer of whom we now have the privilege of speaking, is one of the well known and progres- sive stockmen of Malheur county, having his family residence and home place about six miles south from Dell, where he manages a mammoth establishment of hay producing land

and large bands of stock, being the man who enjoys the distinction of sowing the first al- falfa in the entire county, thus being the means of introducing this wealth-producing plant in our midst. Mr. Scott was born in Angels Camp, Calaveras county, California, on Decem- ber 23, 1852, his parents being Oscar W. and Elizabeth (Logan) Scott, who came direct to that place from Greene county, Illinois, mak- ing the trip with ox teams. It is of note that the well known Joaquin Miller was a guest of the father of our subject for some time. In 1857 the family went to Healdsburg, Califor- nia, and the following year they went to Men- docino county on the coast and there they farmed until 1878. There, also, on September 3, 1874, Mr. Scott married Miss Idella Titus. In 1878 Mr. Scott came to this country, taking a portion of his present estate as a homestead and began the good work of improvement and raising stock. He added two hundred acres of land by purchase and now has a farm that produces six hundred tons of alfalfa each year. In addition to introducing alfalfa in 1881 he also at that time stretched the first wire fence in the county. The farm is well supplied with water from Willow creek and in addition to this fine holding, Mr. Scott has several thousand head of sheep, and also cat- tle and horses. He has a good six-room dwell- ing, large barns and good orchard. When he came here he notes his possessions as one horse, one mule, and an old pack saddle. The chil- dren born to Mr. Scott and his first wife are, Mary A., deceased; Florence L., wife of B. Jones; Frederick F., Winfield, Harry H., Russell. On August 12, 1893, Mrs. Scott was called from her home and family by death.

On January 12, 1896, Mr. Scott married a second time, the lady of his choice on this oc- casion being Mrs. Nancy (Bonee) Murphey, who has by her first husband three children, as follows: Harry H. Howard, married to Ber- tha McCabe; George Howard, married to Bessie Rainey; Newell Howard. The second husband of Mrs. Scott died without issue. The first one was named Marshall Howard. Mr. Scott is a member of the I. O. O. F. in On- tario. He is a capable and upright man and has done much for the advancement of the country and is justly entitled to the approval and confidence of his fellows, which he enjoys in unstinted measure.

JOHN A. WARD.—Among the leading citizens of Malheur county is to be placed the name of the subject of this sketch, since he is a man of excellent talent and enterprise; since he is one of the heavy land owners of this irrigated section; and since he is one of the promoters and originators of the Owyhee ditch—which has been of untold benefit to this and surrounding country, making more wealth for Malheur county than almost any other one venture.

John A. was born in the province of Quebec, Canada, on February 15, 1858, being the son of George P. and Elizabeth (Sherman) Ward. He was reared on a farm and gained his education from the common schools. The father was a man of property and handled a hotel in addition to the farm. In 1872 the mother died and in 1881 the father also was called from the scenes of earth. In September of the same year, our subject came by train direct to Winnemucca, Nevada, and thence on horse back to Silver City, Idaho. He worked a short time in a livery stable and then engaged in the mines and later with his brother he went in the sheep business. In 1884 he engaged in the sheep business in Malheur county, folowing the same until 1891. At that time, he sold his sheep and took up a claim of eighty acres on the Owyhee river, which he watered with irrigating ditches and improved well. In 1899 Mr. Ward removed to his present place which consists of two hundred and twenty acres of fine land, three miles southwest from Nyssa. It is a model place, being well watered and having good improvements. Mr. Ward and his three brothers and four others commenced the Owyhee ditch and later they incorporated and he is one of the original stockholders and incorporators. His land is well watered from this ditch.

The marriage of Mr. Ward and Miss Ida B., daughter of Albert B. and Angeletta (Davis) Neathery, of the vicinity of Nyssa, was solemnized on September 9, 1891, and they have become the parents of the following named children: Audrey J., Pearl F., Irl D., Cecil, and Albert W. Mr. Ward is one of the prominent men of this section and deserves much credit for the energetic and enterprising manner in which he has wrought for the advancement of the country and its improvement. He has the esteem and respect and confidence of all.

GEORGE W. LYELLS.—The hearty, genial and jovial gentleman whose name heads this article is one of the best known men in the county of Malheur, having wrought in industrial development in various portions of it, and always maintaining his reputation untarnished and manifesting that uprightness and integrity and industry that are the sterling virtues of typical manhood. He was born in Jonesborough, Illinois, on January 27, 1858, being the son of Richard C. and Sarah (Toney) Lyells. He was reared on a farm and gained his education from the district schools of his native and other places. In 1869 his father took his family, consisting of himself, wife and ten children, our subject the oldest, across the plains to Pueblo county, Colorado. They endured the real pioneer hardships en route, and suffered much from the attacks of the Indians. In 1872 Mr. Lyells started out in life for himself, his first trip being across the plains barefoot, driving six yoke of oxen hauling two wagons from Colorado to Baker City, Oregon. He helped fight the Indians, being attacked several times en route. October 10, 1872, was the glad day when they first saw Baker City. George W. worked on a farm for a time, then went to Rye valley and mined in the placers of that vicinity, after which he returned to Baker City and attended school for a period. After that he went to Idaho and freighted with oxen to the different camps, and in 1875 returned to Baker City, where he entered as an apprentice at the forge, and for nine years he labored in that city. Then he went to Malheur and opened a shop, 1884 being the date. Five years later we find him in Vale beating the anvil to the tune of skillful labor and honest effort, and in 1900 he came to Ontario. Here he has a good shop, owning the building and the lot, and his patronage is such that he is busied all of the time, and then is not able to attend to it all. He enjoys the meed of a good honest reputation earned by hard and skillful labor and an upright life of careful walk. In addition to the blacksmith shop he operates a wagon repair shop.

July 25, 1880, marks the happy date when Mr. Lyells led to the altar his chosen bride, Miss Mary E., daughter of Benjamin and Rosa Stevens. They are the parents of the following children: Edward R., married to Stella M. Craig, and one child, Percy E., has been born to them; Sylvia V., wife of E. A.

Rieger, of Ontario; George F.; Angeline E.; Lillian E.; Syrene B. He is a member of the Ontario Lodge, No. 90, I. O. O. F., while he and his wife are members of the Rebekahs, and his wife of the Cherry Circle of Woodcraft, No. 304. Mr. Lyells carries with becoming dignity the honors of grandfather, although his geniality and affableness are tinged with the life and vigor of twenty-five. Both he and his wife are esteemed by scores of friends from all parts of the county.

- - -

JONATHAN B. BIGELOW.—The capable and enterprising gentleman, whose name is at the head of this article is one of Malheur county's thrifty agriculturists, and has labored here faithfully in the interests of improvement and building himself and family a comfortable home. Mr. Bigelow was born in St. Charles county, Missouri, on September 6, 1851, being the son of Rufus and Henrietta (Eveisman) Bigelow. While he was a child he went with his parents to Saline county, in his native state, and there he was educated in the public schools. There also the family lived when the war broke out, and they were called upon to suffer much hardship and humiliation from the hordes of soldiers, who carried off nearly all the goods from his father's store. Also the famous James and Younger brothers raided the store, thus the father being nearly robbed of all his property. Subsequent to the war Jonathan worked on a farm, and on March 29, 1877, he was married to Miss Neoma Woolard. In 1880, with his wife and two children, Mr. Bigelow started to Paradise, Nevada, Humboldt county, and there they labored until 1889, when he came across the country to the Malheur valley. He returned for stock, and when he landed here he was possessed of less than twenty dollars. The first winter was one of hardship, and he gained his provisions by selling sage brush in Vale, and he experienced the real life of the pioneer, and he has won success by his hard efforts of labor and industry and skillful management. Later Mr. Bigelow moved to the Owyhee, and then again moved to the vicinity of Nyssa, and in the spring of 1901 he came to his present place. He owns one hundred and twenty acres five miles southwest from Nyssa, and forty acres of this is

under the Owyhee ditch. He has a fine field of alfalfa, a thrifty young orchard and a good berry garden and many other improvements. Mr. Bigelow carries a policy in one of the Colorado accident companies, and he is a skillful manager of business affairs.

To Mr. and Mrs. Bigelow there have been born the following children: Mirtle L., who was married to J. I. Hatfield, but is now deceased, leaving two children; Mrs. Cleora Watkins; Lesse R.; Silas B.; Grover; Owen W. Mr. and Mrs. Bigelow are members of the Methodist church, and are exemplary in their walk and faithful in the support of the faith, being people of integrity and uprightness, and are highly esteemed by all who know them.

- - -

FREDERICK GELLERMAN.—One of the real pioneers of this section as also of others heretofore, and a principal builder of Malheur county, is the subject of this sketch, and he is a man who is deserving mention in any compilation that has to do with the history of this section, being a man of enterprise, industry, and capabilities, far above the average, and withal manifesting stanch principles of uprightness, wisdom, and excellent judgment in all of the trying scenes through which he has passed in the course of his frontier experiences.

Mr. Gellerman, as so many of our best citizens, was born in Germany, the spot being Hanover, and the date of this important event being September 4, 1839, and his parents Bernard and Anna Gellerman. In his native land he was educated, learned the blacksmith trade, and remained until 1858, when he left the Fatherland for the opportunities of the new world. Landing at the well-known Castle Garden, he was soon on his way to Greene county, Iowa, where he followed both blacksmithing and farming. On December 4, 1862, occurred the marriage of Mr. Gellerman and Miss Hannah, daughter of Henry and Mary Drodge, who were immigrants from Berlin, coming thence in 1851 and locating in Clayton county, Iowa, where the marriage just mentioned occurred. Mrs. Gellerman was born in Germany on July 12, 1844. In 1862 the adventurous spirit of our subject led him to seek further in the west and so over the plains he came with his newly-wedded wife, having the thrilling experience of nearly losing her in a serious runaway. They settled in Lander county, Nevada, having their near neighbors at a distance of eleven miles, thus demonstrating the true pioneer pluck of the worthy couple. He at once began to mine and later to raise stock and as the range was eaten off he came further north and in 1879 sold his possessions down there and came through to lower Willow creek, Oregon. Deciding that he had found the right place, Mr. Gellerman purchased the raw land where his fine estate is to-day, three miles west from Vale. He at once set to work to improve, and that was no small task, seeing that he had to go to Baker City for provisions and to Emmonsville, forty-five miles distant, for lumber. He steadily plodded along in the work of improvement and raising stock and now has one of the finest places in the vicinity, an excellent house and other buildings, three hundred and forty acres of fine soil and a goodly band of cattle. Of late years Mr. Gellerman has retired from the more active labors of the farm and rents his land and stock. Seven girls were born to this worthy couple, named as follows, Amelia M., wife of F. Scott; Lillie B., wife of I. W. Hope; Alice F., wife of J. Pederson; Hattie, wife of L. Teter; Matilda P., wife of F. Zutz; Vidella, wife of L. Jones; and Lavina. Mr. Gellerman is a charter member of the I. O. O. F., Vale Lodge, No. 100. In politics, Mr. Gellerman is a Republican and is a man of intelligence on the intricate questions of management of the government. While in the various places of the frontier he has had considerable trouble from hostile savages and in that as in the other hardships of this life, he has manifested the bravery, calmness, and steady continuity in the prosecution of the right and fearlessly he has walked in his course and now triumph is his to enjoy.

Mrs. Gellerman's father died of cholera four days after arriving at their destination in this country and the widowed mother was left with her little flock in a strange land. She died in 1890. Mr. Gellerman's parents died in the old country.

By way of reminiscence it is interesting to note some of the hardships of Mr. Gellerman's life and one among them is as follows: He and his hired man went out to explore the country and became lost in a terrible fog and at last they were forced by exhaustion to camp in the snow on the summit of the mountain. They ate their rations in bed, the cold was so intense. The animals had been hobbled to prevent being lost and the next morning the icicles hung from their nostrils to the ground.

JAMES WEAVER, deceased.—Among the worthy pioneers, the fruits of whose labors many of the settlers of eastern Oregon are now enjoying, mention should be made of the esteemed gentleman whose life's career it is now our privilege to outline. Although he has since passed to his reward in another world, still his labors speak and it is eminently fitting that a memorial of him be placed in this volume of history.

James Weaver was born in 1819 in the Blue Grass state. and when five years of age he came with his parents to Indiana, where he was educated and grew to manhood. In 1852 his adventurous spirit led him to the gold fields of California and seven years later he returned to the Indiana home. He went thence to Minnesota and in 1864 he made the arduous and dangerous trip across the plains to Boise valley. Later he went to Umatilla county and thence he was called from his labors of this life in 1881. He was a good man, a faithful laborer for the development of the country, and was sincerely mourned in his death.

The marriage of Mr. Weaver and Miss Elizabeth Cole, a native of Indiana, was solemnized in Indiana in 1846, and they became the parents of the following named children, Mary A., deceased; Hester A., deceased; William, deceased; James, whose life is mentioned in this volume; and John,, a resident of this county. The widow of Mr. Weaver resides near Vale, in this county, being well-to-do and one of the respected and esteemed citizens, as also are her sons, who have wrought here for some years.

JAMES R. KENNEDY.—In the subject of this article we have one of the young and energetic stockmen and agriculturists of Malheur county, who is demonstrating that he has capabilities to take up with credit the work of the early pioneers and carry forward the development of the country while he properly augments his own exchequer in a commendable and worthy manner. Mr. Kennedy was born in the Idaho basin, on December 16, 1873, being the son of William and Isabella (Russell) Kennedy, natives of Ireland. About 1878 the father brought the family to the Malheur river in the vicinity of the Kennedy butte. It was 1885 when they came to lower Willow creek, and there our subject attended the common schools until he was eighteen and then finished his schooling in an institution in Walla Walla. From that time forward he engaged with his father in the stock business, the home place being located on lower Willow creek. They operated together until 1901, when they divided their herds, and our subject is now living five miles south from Dell postoffice, where he has a fine farm of one hundred and sixty acres of bottom land, which produces abundant crops of alfalfa, having about three hundred tons of that each year. He has a comfortable house, good barn, fine orchard and a nice bunch of cattle. It is much to the credit of Mr. Kennedy that when he began life he had no capital, but by good management and industry he has accumulated a very handsome showing, which but demonstrates the mettle and capabilities of the man. In addition to that mentioned above, Mr. Kennedy carries a life insurance policy for three thousand dollars in the New York Mutual.

The happy event of the marriage of Mr. Kennedy and Miss Ettie Stott, of Walla Walla, and a native of Missouri, was celebrated on August 28, 1900. This worthy couple are valuable additions to the society of their section and they are held in high esteem and are capable and substantial members of the commonwealth.

HON. JOHN F. STEVENS.—It is with pleasure that we are enabled to chronicle a review of the career of the worthy and estimable gentleman whose name is at the head of this article and who has walked the path of the pioneer of the west for nearly half a century, displaying meantime those characteristics of patriotism, stability, vigor, integrity, and fine ability with which he is so happily possessed, and ever performing the part of the true man

and stanch citizen in the various places where he has wrought with credit to himself, being at the present time the choice of the people of Malheur county for the responsible position of county judge, in which capacity he is demonstrating the practical ability and sound judgment possessed by him, much to the general satisfaction of the people.

Mr. Stevens was born in Tompkins county, New York, on April 14, 1834, being the son of Edson L., and Abba A. (Tucker) Stevens. The parents remained in New York state and there died, the father in 1888, and the mother in 1899, being in her eighty-fifth year. Our subject remained with his parents until 1859, reciving a common school education and in that year came west to Macon, Missouri, by cars and from there with ox teams across the plains to Denver, Colorado, there being but one house in the town at that time. He followed mining in that section until 1862, then came with mule teams to Walla Walla and on to The Dalles, where he wintered. The following spring he came to Boise and soon after that trip we find him teaming from Umatilla to the mines in Idaho, receiving as high as fifty cents per pound for some freight. During this teaming he passed frequently over the site of Pendleton, there being no houses there then. In 1866 he went to Montana and followed mining until 1868, then went to Mendocino and Humboldt counties, California, and there engaged in the stock business. In 1871 he came back to Umatilla and engaged in raising sheep. This continued until 1874, when he went to the Powder river, near Baker City, and handled cattle. He was county commissioner at the time the line dividing Grant and Baker was surveyed. Eighteen hundred and ninety was the date of the advent of Mr. Stevens into Malheur county, he at that time starting a general merchandise establishment in Malheur City, which business he steadily prosecuted until 1900, when he was called by the people to assume the responsibilities of the office of county judge and in that capacity we find him at this writing, handling the business incumbent upon him in such a creditable manner that he has the approval and confidence of the entire population of the county. Judge Stevens is now residing in Vale, and although not the wealthiest man in the state, he is possessed of a goodly portion of this world's property and is one of the most substantial men of the county. Judge Stevens was elected to his present position on the Republican ticket and he states that the first vote cast by him was for John C. Fremont, and he has steadily in national politics voted that ticket ever since.

The judge has always walked this pilgrimage way alone, never deciding to assume the responsibilities of the matrimonial relation, but preferring the quieter joys and comforts of the celibate's life. In all the days of his pioneer life he has always been among the first in whatever undertaking was at hand, has done much real labor for the upbuilding of the sections where his toil has been bestowed, and in all the hardships of pioneering, as weathering the storms, trudging over the mountains, packing blankets, faring on limited provisions, doing hurculean work, enduring hardships and deprivations constantly, Judge Stevens has had a lion's share, and he is eminently deserving of the confidence and bestowal of honor which is his from a wise and open-hearted people, and no man in Malheur county to-day is more in the hearts of the people.

THOMAS A. BARTON.—The subject of this sketch is a man of enterprise and vigor, as is evinced by his active and energetic career, having travelled all over the United States, visiting every state and territory in its precincts, and being possessed of a keen perception, skillful adaptability, and executive force, we would expect that he would have been in many enterprises, which is a fact. At the present time he is one of the substantial and capable citizens of Malheur county and a hard worker for the benefit of the county and the progress of its interests.

Mr. Barton was born in Fairmount, West Virginia, on May 12, 1849, being the son of Jackson and Malissa Barton, and while a child had the sorrow of losing his mother. Then he came with his father to Wooster, Wayne county, Ohio, received a good common school education, and later went to Oberlin college in that state. Subsequent to this course he served an apprenticeship of five years in the painting art in his town. And then we find him operating at the trade and afterwards learning the carpenter trade. But on account of failing health

40

he migrated to Salt Lake, Utah, in the spring of 1877, and thence in the fall of the same year to San Francisco, where he embarked on board of a steamer and landed in Portland. Later we find him in Seattle and in 1881 he was in Spokane, where he was installed as foreman of the painting department of the N. P. R. R. Early in 1883 he went to Sprague and purchased the Villard house, which soon afterward was destroyed by fire, when he turned his attention to handling lumber in Dayton, Washington. Then he went again to carpentering and later joined a bridge crew and travelled into various portions of the country. It was in 1890 that he determined to settle down and accordingly made his way to Jordan Valley in the southern portion of Malheur county and located. In that place on November 13, 1900, he married Mrs. Martha A. (Dunbar) Castle, a native of New York. They own a residence at Jordan Valley and Mrs. Barton is postmistress of the office at that place. In 1900 on the Republican ticket, Mr. Barton was elected to the important position of county commissioer with a term of four years. He is at present serving in that capacity and has done much for the advancement of the interests of the county, manifesting the same energy and wisdom in handling the affairs of the county as in his private enterprises. Mrs. Barton came to Jordan Valley in 1882. Mr. Barton is a member of the I. O. O. F., Vale Lodge, No. 100. He and his estimable wife are worthy citizens of the county and are well and favorably known, being esteemed and highly respected. Mrs. Barton's first husband, S. J. Castle, was one of the first settlers in Jordan Valley, coming there in 1874 and participating in the Indian troubles.

JEREMIAH BROSNAN.—In the south part of the Emerald Isle, in County Kerry, was born the subject of this article about thirty-seven years ago. Mr. Brosnan was reared on a farm and in 1883 bade farewell to the scenes of childhood and cast his lot with the fortunes of the new world across the sea. He landed in Castle Garden all right, then came direct to the regions of the west, Boise, Idaho, being the first place for operations. Later we find him on lower Willow creek and with true grit and activity he was soon engaged in handling cattle on the range. For some time he continued this work for wages and then rented land for himself and engaged in raising cattle on on his own responsibility. Success attended the wise and industrious efforts put forth on his part, and he soon rose to be one of the prosperous stockmen of Malheur county. In June, 1898, he bought the place where he now resides, ten miles west from Ontario, having a quarter section on the Malheur river. It is well improved, has a good supply of water, is provided with good and comfortable buildings, and is conducted in a skillful manner. Mr. Brosnan raises an abundance of alfalfa for stock purposes and he has a fine band of cattle.

The happy marriage of Mr. Brosnan and Miss Fannie Burns, also a native of Ireland, was celebrated on March 7, 1892, and they have been blessed with the advent of three children, Maggie E., Fannie H., Thomas J. In Mr. Brosnan we have one of the finest exemplifications of what a man of pluck, industry, and ability can do in this country. He landed in Castle Garden with no more than fifty cents and he has made his way from that time to this by his own efforts of enterprise, having gained his present fine holding solely by his own labors, which he has bestowed with wisdom, as the returns show, and have been carried on with untiring zeal for the accomplishment of the good purpose of gaining a competence for himself and his family and he now has not only a fine rural home, but is among the leading stockmen of the county. Mr. Brosnan is also highly thought of by all who know him, being a man dominated by sound principles and wisdom.

HON. ROBERT A. LOCKETT.—This well known and prominent citizen of Malheur county is one of the largest stockmen of the county, a progressive and capable man, a pioneer of the state, a man of broad and stirring experiences, and withal, doubtless the person, more than any other, that laid the foundation and perefected the organization of Malheur county, and it is very fitting that he should be granted especial mention in this volume of his county's history.

Robert A. was born in Henderson county, Kentucky, on November 29, 1838, being the son of Thomas I. and Euphemia (Agnew) Lockett. He was reared on a tobacco farm and assisted his father in the work of the farm and in portions of the year attended school in a log house, the same being furnished with split logs for seats and the virgin ground for floor. Here, young Lockett acquired the discipline in literary lore that fortified him for the walks of life, which, however, has constantly been augumented by a strong and inquiring mind in various lines of research. In 1852 he was called to mourn the death of his mother, and in 1858 he migrated to Clarke county, Missouri, and the following year went to Pike's Peak with ox teams and returned the next fall in the same manner. While at that famous mountain he followed mining and upon his return went to visit his father in the old Kentucky home, remaining there until the spring of 1862, when he pressed to the front and enlisted in Company A, Tenth Kentucky Cavalry, in the Confederate army, in General Morgan's command. He entered as private and at the battle of Murfreesboro, he was promoted to a first lieutenancy, the date being November, 1862. He was wounded at the battle of Stone River, caused by his horse falling on him. He was in many hotly contested skirmishes and in heavy battles and at the close of hostilities, he was discharged and on May 1, 1865, he started across the plains with a train of one hundred wagons, being elected captain. One skirmish with the Indians at Laramie plains resulted in wounding one white man, but no other casualties occurred, but the hardships of the arduous journey were many and serious. At Green river the train disbanded and our subject came on to Salt Lake and later to Boise, arriving at the latter place on October 20, 1865. The following spring he went to Idaho City and followed mining until 1871, then went to Umatilla county, Oregon, and there occurred the happy event of the marriage of Mr. Lockett and Miss Mary E., daughter of Arphaxad and Martha (Pinkerton) Owens, the nuptials taking place on March 22, 1871. In 1872 Mr. Lockett removed to the vicinity of the mouth of the Owyhee river and embarked in stock raising. In 1879 he came to lower Willow creek and has lived here ever since, his present home being one mile north from Dell. He owns about one thousand acres all fenced, and mostly bottom land and he raises great quantities of alfalfa hay, having abundance of water. He has a fine dwelling, good orchard, barns, outbuildings and a large herd of cattle and some horses.

Before Malheur county was cut off from Baker, Mr. Lockett was twice elected to represent Baker county in the state legislature and it was he who dictated the bill which made a county of Malheur, and much credit is due him in his energetic and capable labors to accomplish this wise end. At the present time Mr. Lockett is active in politics and is justice of the peace. He and his estimable wife are parents of the following children: Marshall, married to Dora Stark, living in Portland; Hardin, married to Susie Sawyer; Hickman, married to Bertha Tague; Thomas J., at Ontario; Mattie, Lee, Clyde, Early. Mr. Lockett is a man of distinction both in labors of upbuilding the county and prosecuting private business enterprises, and also in his happy endowments of affability, keen foresight, wise judgment, and stanch integrity and he has won the esteem and confidence of all.

---◆◆◆---

DANIEL R. EHRGOOD.—The subject of this article is one of the enterprising and capable farmers of Malheur county, and has labored long and faithfully here for the accumulation of the handsome property that he now possesses and for the advancement of the country wherein he has displayed great zeal and becoming sagacity and stability in his ways. Daniel R. was born in Berks county, Pennsylvania, on January 26, 1855, being the son of Abraham and Susan (Lebo) Ehrgood. He was reared on a farm and from the common schools he gained the education that fortified him for the labors and trials of life and when he had reached the age of twenty-two he stepped forth from the parental roof to undertake for himself. He was the eighth of a family of nine children. His first move was to Wells county, Indiana, and from there he went to Parker county, Texas, where he followed farming until 1884. There also, on January 22, 1880, he was married to Miss Sarah J., daughter of Joseph and Elizabeth Erwin, a native of Texas. In the spring of 1884 he took his family of wife and one child in wagons, and with mule teams he made the trip across the country to the Owyhee. He was four months on the journey and passed a very pleasant time, having plenty of game and fish enroute. The next fall he located his present home place, taking it under the pre-emption act. Settlers in the valley were few, and but one man resided where Nyssa now stands. Boise was the market at that time and the toil of taking a raw place with no ditches to bring water and make of it a fine farm is not inconsiderable. However, Mr. Ehrgood has succeeded admirably and has an excellent farm to-day. He has one hundred and four acres under the Owyhee ditch, well improved, having proper buildings and orchards and shade trees and so forth to make the rural home both valuable and attractive. Mr. Ehrgood is allied with the Democratic party and labors incessantly for the advancement of the country and its proper development, being also zealous for the betterment of the educational facilities. To this worthy couple there has been one child born, Susan E., wife of Cornelius Morehead of the vicinity of Nyssa. Mrs. Ehrgood's mother is now living in Parker county, Texas. It is of note that Mr. and Mrs. Ehrgood arrived here without a dollar of cash and they have labored wisely and faithfully until they have gained their comfortable home and are now among the leading citizens of this portion of the county.

---◆◆◆---

MELVILLE D. KELLEY.—The subject of this review is a native of the occident, being born in Idaho City, Idaho, on August 31, 1867, and in the west he has labored constantly, demonstrating both his ability in acquiring property and his integrity and sound principles as a patriotic citizen and man of substantiality. Mr. Kelley has a fine farm of one quarter section one mile south from Dell, having there one hundred and forty acres planted to alfalfa, which produce annually five hundred tons of that excellent cattle feed. He has a good dwelling, commodious barns and outbuildings, and a general air of thrift permeates the entire premises, proclaiming the owner a man of care, industry, and wise management. Mr. Kelley has also a herd of fine cattle and he is numbered among the leading stockmen of the country.

Mr. Kelley's parents were Joseph and Margaret (Thompson) Kelley. The father died at Idaho City, Idaho, in 1870, having been an early pioneer to California and thence to Idaho. In 1871 Mrs. Kelley contracted a second marriage and the step-father to our subject was William Stark. Soon after this marriage the family removed to Ontario, this county, and in 1877 they came to the place owned by our subject and described above, it being the old home place. In 1891 Mr. Stark was called to pass the river of death and in 1897 the mother of our subject died. In the early days the family experienced much trouble with the Indians and knew full well the trying hardships and deprivations of the pioneer's lot.

On March 22, 1891, occurred the marriage of Mr. Kelley and Miss Elizabeth, daughter of John and Amanda Taylor, and they have become the parents of six children, as follows, Maggie M., Ruby H., Rosa E., Charles C., Laban, and the baby, still unnamed. Mr. Kelley takes especial interest in the promotion of good schools and the advancement of the cause of education, having rendered efficient service as clerk of the school board of his district for ten years. Mr. Kelley is a man of capabilities that give him a prestige among his fellows and he sustains an unsullied reputation and enjoys the fellowship and esteem of all who have the pleasure of knowing him.

JOSEPH A. MORTON.—This intrepid pioneer and enterprising stockman and farmer of Malheur county stands among the leaders of this section of the country in the stock business, having an excellent band of horses, numbering many hundreds, besides which he owns much real estate in various sections. He is a man of intelligence and in all his varied career, much of which has been spent in the arduous pursuits of the frontier, he has manifested great energy, perseverance, and faithfulness, coupled with a keen discrimination in business affairs. Mr. Morton was born in Preston county, Virginia, on January 5, 1834, being the son of James and Jane (Connor) Morton. In 1843 he went with his parents to Darke county, Ohio, and from there to How-

ard county, Indiana. His education was gained in the log schoolhouses of those days, and he had to walk a long distance to attend school. He was reared on a farm and in 1852 left the old home place and started for himself. Going to Adams county, Iowa, he there operated a sawmill for a time and there also occurred his marriage with Miss Clementine Ireland, in 1856. They went with ox teams to Coffey county, Kansas, entered government land, and in the spring of 1862 went with ox teams thence to the Grande Ronde valley. They were members of a large train and endured much hardship on the route, being six months in making the journey. Indians were troublesome also. Mr. Morton located land in the new country and the following spring went to Eagle creek, to mine, which occupation he followed until 1870. At that date he came to lower Willow creek, near Vale, and engaged in the stock business. In 1872 he removed to Bully creek and two years later to the Snake river near Ontario. In 1895 Mr. Morton sold that property and bought a toll road running from Horse Shoe bend to Placerville and operated this until 1898, then bought a farm two miles west from Ontario, continuing the stock business all the time. He sold that farm and bought nearer the town, which farm he also sold and then bought a place in Snake river, it being an island of about five hundred acres. In the spring of 1902 Mr. Morton bought sixty acres four miles southwest from Ontario, which is the family home at the present time. His place is well improved with buildings and corrals and orchards and provided with water for irrigating.

The children born to Mr. and Mrs. Morton were eleven, but seven are still living, named as follows, Mrs. Jane Davis; Leonard M.; Mrs. Frances Sells; Mrs. Clementine Chambers; Mrs. Alma King, of Vale; Joseph W.; Reuben M. During the Indian war of 1878 Mr. Morton enlisted as scout and did good service. In the spring of 1901 he went to Alaska with a band of horses, which he sold at Nome, and then spent the summer prospecting, returning to his home in the fall. Mr. Morton relates that when he first came to this country the neighbors were few and about eight miles apart, but he has labored faithfully and steadily here and has seen the country develop to its present prosperous condition, aiding materially in this good work. In addition to the other property named, Mr. Morton owns ninety acres adjoining the town of Boise, besides much other property, being one of the substantial and well-to-do men of the country.

JAMES A. LACKEY.—Among the leading stockmen of the entire country must be placed conspicuously the name of the subject of this article since he has charge of the largest horse ranch in the United States, managing the same with great skill and wisdom, and ever manifesting that fine executive force of which he is so richly possessed, while commensurate therewith are the integrity and stanch principles of worth and uprightness that characterize him.

James A. was born in Rockbridge county, Virginia, near the town of Lexington, on May 22, 1858, being the son of Anderson and Elizabeth (Miller) Lackey. He received his education in the district schools of the county and village and remained with his parents until the spring of 1875, when he journeyed to Kern county, California, and engaged in mining for a time and also in the stock business, continuing his efforts there until 1880, at which time he came to Malheur county. He engaged here in stock raising, settling near Malheur City. There were few inhabitants of this land and no railroad and he had to drive his stock across the mountains to Wyoming. He has made many such trips and his energy and vigor surmounted every obstacle and won success in a brilliant measure.

On April 7, 1885, Mr. Lackey married Miss Addie M., daughter of Cyrus T. and Ma-riah Locy, the nuptials being celebrated at Malheur. The fruit of this union is as follows: Mamie, deceased; Chester T., Hazel C., and James Russell. Mrs. Lackey's parents reside near Ironsides at the present time. In 1890 Mr. Lackey sold out his possessions and removed to Seattle, taking land on the sound. While living there he shipped several carloads of horses to New York. In 1892 he transferred his residence to Ontario and here he took charge of the business of the Oregon Horse and Land Company, supposed to be the largest company handling horses in the United States. In this capacity is manifested the real worth of the wisdom, executive ability, and experience of Mr. Lackey. He has charge of many thousands of dollars of property and does a mammoth business. In addition to this he owns in his own right a farm of two hundred acres two miles out from Ontario, a fine residence in Ontario, and much other valuable property in various places. He always manifests great interest in educational matters, having given his services for nine years as clerk of the district. Mr. Lackey is active and zealous in building up the interests of Ontario and has acted as councilman for many years. He is affiliated with Acacia Lodge, No. 118, A. F. & A. M., also with the A. O. U. W., while he and his wife are members of the Eastern Star. Mr. Lackey spends much of his time, perhaps a majority, in Ontario, directing his business from that point, but he also is occupied much in traveling to various parts of the United States and adjacent countries in marketing stock. He is respected by all and his ability is recognized and properly appreciated, although he is too busy to accept public office other than mentioned.

HARNEY COUNTY

HAULING HAY TO STOCK IN HARNEY VALLEY.

HAYING SCENE IN HARNEY VALLEY.

HISTORY OF HARNEY COUNTY.

CHAPTER I.

CURRENT HISTORY, 1865 TO 1892.

Inasmuch as the territory now constituting Harney county was originally a portion of Grant, much of its early history has been noticed in connection with that county. It is, however, necessary that some facts connected with its settlement and development be somewhat more fully treated. Of the experiences of trappers and hunters who visited the region in the days when the Hudson's Bay Company held autocratic power in the northwest, we have little more record, than of the intertribal relations, wars and wanderings of its Indian inhabitants, or of that still older race whose mortars, pestles, arrow heads and other stone implements are found widely diffused over the country. In Charles W. Parrish's collection of curios are some relics of the emigrant train of 1845, which was one of the first expeditions of white people to pass through the Harney country. Their experiences in the desert and in the Harney lake region have been narrated at some length elsewhere in this volume in connection with the discovery of gold in Baker county. There are some white men now living in central and southeastern Oregon who were in Harney valley, en route to the coast during the year 1853, and it is probable that hardly a year passed since then in which white men have not ventured into the region, though not to remain permanently.

During the early 'sixties the Harney country was threaded by quite a large number of expeditions of miners en route to Auburn, Canyon City and the Idaho mines. To protect this migratory class, as well as the westward moving armies of emigrants, military posts were rendered necessary at a very early date. Of these a succinct outline account was furnished to Charles W. Parrish, historian of the local cabin of the Native Sons of Oregon, by the war department in a letter of recent date. From the communication we learn that Camp Alvord, a temporary United States camp, located near Lake Alvord, in what is now Harney county, was established September 5, 1865, by Company G, First Oregon Infantry, and abandoned May 25, 1866; that Camp Curry, a temporary camp on Silver creek, forty-five or fifty miles north from Camp Harney, was established in August, 1865, and abandoned in May, 1866; that Camp C. F. Smith, on White Horse creek, Oregon, was established in May, 1866, and abandoned November 9, 1869; and that Fort Harney at the mouth of Rattlesnake creek, Harney county, was established August 16, 1867, as Camp Steele; that its name was changed September 14, 1867, and that it was abandoned June 14, 1880. The communication does not mention Camp Wright, which was established at what is now known as Wright's Point, in August, 1865, by Captain L. L. Williams, of Company H, First Oregon Infantry. It was named in honor of General Wright, who went down before Crescent City, California, in the vessel "Brother Jonathan," during the fall of the year 1865.

It has been related that during September, 1865, a fight occurred between the Harney valley Piutes and a part of the force under Captain Williams, somewhere between Camp Wright and Harney lake. About the same time Lieutenant Applegate, of Company H, in command of a part of Captains Williams' men, was attacked while traveling from Camp Curry to Camp Wright at a point called in jest Fort Drellinger, on what afterward became Mrs. McGee's ranch. Next morning about eight miles south of the present town of Burns Indians shot from the rimrock near a cove, wounding a soldier named Griffin, who afterward died from the effects of the shot, and another soldier named Smith.

Mrs. Grace, formerly of the Herald, whose investigations resulted in the discovery of the facts just narrated, states that the grave in front of old Camp Wright's site is that of a soldier known among his fellows as "Reddy," from the color of his hair. "Reddy" was shot by the Indians on the Blitzen as he mounted guard one dark night in February, 1866. It is claimed, however, that the grave is not that of a soldier, but of an emigrant named Stewart, who was killed by the Indians some time in the 'fifties.

Of all the military camps located in the Harney country no other was so influential in the civil history of the section as Camp Harney, established, as before stated, in August, 1867. It had a military post office and received regular mail from Canyon City, the mail being carried on horseback by a man named Walker. There were many civilians in and around the camp from the time of its inception, but as these were totally dependent upon the existence of the camp for a livelihood, they cannot be classed as settlers. Just who was the first to establish himself permanently in the country we will not undertake to state. Abner Robbins used to travel around among the Indians of the valley long before any white man established a residence therein, but he did not become a settler till later. Before the establishment of Camp Wright A. H. Robie, to whom probably belongs the honor of having been the pioneer sawmill man of the vast region of which Harney county forms a part, moved a sawmill from Molthrop, Idaho, to the left fork of Coffee Pot creek, but as he had milling interests in different other places, he did not reside in Harney valley permanently and is not classed as a settler. Mr. Robie was a son-in-law of Colonel William Craig, of the Hudson's Bay Company, whose wife was an Indian woman. He furnished lumber and shingles to build Camp Harney. In 1871 Mr. Robie moved cattle from Idaho into the Harney country. His brand was diamond shaped, and from it Diamond valley received its name. In 1872 Mr. Robie sold his interest in the sawmill, which had been moved to a point some twelve miles distant from Camp Harney, for $44,000. Robie, with a man named Snyder, who had been a sutler at several different military posts in northern California and southern Oregon, also with J. N. Clarke and Frank McBean, acquired some kind of an incipient right under the swamp land act to large tracts of land along the Blitzen river. This right, with all Mr. Robie's stock except a few horses, Peter French persuaded Dr. Glenn, of California, to buy, thus laying the foundations of the noted French-Glenn ranch. The purchase price was $36,000. Mr. Robie was gathering up the reserved horses in June, 1878, and so happened to be present at the Diamond ranch on the eventful day when the battle with the Indians took place.

The first plowing in Harney valley was done by E. C. Bulkley for J. J. Cozort, now residing near Prairie City. Mr. Cozort was attempting to get an advantage over his competitors in contracting for the furnishing of supplies to the United States government. He reasoned that if he could raise grain in the valley he could undersell those who had to transport their grain from the John Day country. He therefore employed Mr. Bulkley, in 1867, to plow up forty acres near Camp Harney. The experiment failed. Mr. Cozort tried again, and again he failed. The ground was so loose owing to the decay of successive crops of grasses, that the frosts, which were of much more frequent occurrence at that time than they are now, completely destroyed the growing grain. It is said that even at this date cereals grow much more luxuriantly where there has been an old road, showing that compactness is a great advantage to soil of this character.

In 1869 or 1870 John S. Devine came into the White Horse country with cattle. Some time later he drove a large part of his stock over into Harney valley, where, in 1877, he bought out Venator and Cooksey, establishing his headquarters on the place of the latter, or where now is the Island ranch of the Pacific Live Stock Company. Mr. Devine was one of the progressive men who seized the excellent opportunities afforded by the Harney country in an early day, turned the same to his own advantage and built up a splendid property in the section where his lot was cast. His Alvord place is one of the finest in all Harney county. Mr. Devine has been criticised by many on account of his methods of acquiring lands, but he was a large hearted, generous man and many a poor settler received help in one way or another from his bountiful hand. He died recently.

The actual settlement of Harney valley began in the year 1872, when Stilley Riddle, John Boone, George C. Smyth, with his sons, John T., Darius H., George A. and Presley, and John Chapman came in with stock. The Smyth family settled first at Warm Springs, about five miles from Burns. They remained in that locality until November, 1873, when a remarkable snowfall caused them to move. For four days it snowed and snowed, until the level valley land was covered with a blanket of ermine three feet deep. Becoming alarmed, the Smyths and other settlers gathered up their cattle and set out in search of more kindly conditions. In Happy valley they found the snow only six inches deep, so they resolved to stay there. When the snow went away some of those who had taken their cattle into this well-named region returned, but the Smyths remained, making their home in the valley. It was there that the father and oldest son met such a tragic fate during the Indian war, being killed in their house after a brave defense, and then burned with the building which had sheltered them.

In 1873 came J. S. Miller, J. Cooksey, T. Prather and the Venators, with cattle and horses, and James Sheppard and the Curry family, with cattle only. The advent of Frank McLeod and Maurice FitzGerald, the latter of whom was a soldier, also dates back to that year. In 1874 came P. F. Stenger, Thomas Whiting, and no doubt others.

These settlers were without mail privileges other than the weekly military mail from Canyon City until 1874, when a route was established from Canyon City, via Camp Harney, to Camp McDermitt, Nevada. Over this route the redoubtable G. W. Anderson, familiarly known by his sobriquet of "Doc," made weekly trips. In 1879 a tri-weekly service was established, and in 1880 this gave place to a daily mail. The next year, however, the route was abandoned entirely. It is thought W. W. Johnson was the first postmaster at Camp Harney after the abandonment of the military post in 1880. To Daniel Wheeler is ascribed the honor of having first served as justice of the peace in the valley.

During all these years the only industry of

the valley was stock raising. Everything the cattleman and his employes consumed was imported from without. No one believed that anything could be raised in the country, and in this belief they were confirmed by the failure of Mr. Cozort's scheme. The climate was different then from what it is at present. Rain was of much less frequent occurrence; the snows of winter were deeper, and frost was so common that anything in the line of vegetables or cereals would be destroyed before they had well started to grow.

But there was grass everywhere. No fences disturbed the bands of cattle, sheep and horses. The natural meadows supplied what hay was necessary, though at first it was not the custom to feed range cattle in the winter. The market for beef was generally good and prosperity prevailed.

While many of the blessings of an older civilization were lacking, while the children were denied good school privileges, and churches were unknown, yet there was no lack of sociability among the people and plenty of provision was made for the entertainment of young and old. Throughout the long winters a continual round of dancing parties at the homes of the different ranchmen furnished opportunity for social intercourse and pleasure. No slavery to conventionalities marred the happiness of any; no cliques divided people from each other's society, and all had a merry time.

. The first and only great sensation of the early days occurred in the spring of 1878, when the Bannock and Piute Indians made their raid through Idaho and eastern Oregon. As this has been fully narrated in another place, it must be passed over here with a simple mention.

After the Indian war and the abandonment of Fort Harney there seems to have been a very considerable change in conditions in the Harney country. The statement is frequently made by old residents that at that time the large cattlemen began buying out their less favored

brethren and there was a decided movement in the direction of concentration of wealth. The foundations of several large farms had been laid before this, as has been already noted. The men who had invaded the country from California, Nevada and elsewhere and had engaged extensively in the cattle business were men of great energy. Furthermore they were in many instances connected with wealthy cattlemen in the states from which they had come, so they controlled the funds wherewith to do business. They were enemies of civilization and settlement; were far sighted and experienced enough to know that the supply of natural pasturage would not prove inexhaustible and were animated by a desire to control as much of the country as possible. They saw in the small stockman an obstacle to their plans and used the resources at their command for the double purpose of increasing their own holdings and getting rid of him. As long as this could be done by peaceable purchase all was well, but the country was too large to be controlled by a few. Settlers who left were replaced by others. The would-be monopolists were embarrassed in their efforts to secure title to the whole country in violation of the spirit and sometimes the letter of the law by the sturdy opposition of the redoubtable settler, and a war broke out which has been waged in the press, in the courts and in politics until the present day.

In 1879 began the evolution of the Pacific Live Stock Company, the most powerful cattle corporation operating in southeastern Oregon. Some time in the fall of that year T. M. Overfelt and Frank Sweetser came into southern Grant county and bought the cattle of a man who went by the assumed name of Caleb Ran. Mr. Overfelt then interested the large California cattle firm of Miller & Lux in his enterprise and they, with a man named Mason, a resident of Nevada, formed a co-partnership known as T. M. Overfelt & Company, for the purpose of engaging in the stock business in

Oregon. They were named locally the L. F. Company, from their brand. The partnership continued until June, 1885, when Overfelt was accidentally killed by his team running away. Miller, Lux and Mason purchased the interest of their deceased partner. Later the California firm bought out Mason. They denominated themselves the Pacific Live Stock Company. At one time John Devine's interests were identified with those of Miller & Lux.

During the early 'eighties there came a reaction against the tendency toward centralization above referred to. A considerable number of settlers went into Harney valley at that time, despite the assertions of cattlemen that the country had no agricultural value. Their experiments proved that grain and vegetables might be successfull raised under the climatic conditions then existing, although this fact had been in a measure established by the cattlemen themselves, some of whom had built comfortable homes and made some successful efforts to raise fresh products for their own tables. The influx of settlers in 1883-84-85 resulted in the best government lands not already appropriated by cattlemen being taken, so that later comers must of necessity occupy the less desirable locations, where the means of irrigation were not so close at hand. The scarcity of lands naturally irrigated, so that they would produce wild hay in abundance, or on the banks of streams led to contests with cattlemen for the lands supposed to be illegally held by them under the swamp land act or otherwise, and the warfare between cattlemen and settlers became very bitter. The protracted litigation arising out of this struggle for possession in Harney county will be briefly adverted to again later.

In July, 1885, the first newspaper in southern Grant, the Harney Valley Items, issued from the press, and thereafter that section of the country, had a stanch advocate and friend. Its enterprising proprietor and editor, Horace Dillard, was alone in the journalistic field until the fall of 1887, when D. L. Grace established the East Oregon Herald. Both of these journals have almost complete files, the pages of which have given us great assistance in the preparation of this work.

In 1887 southern Grant county made its first effort to secure political segregation and the organization of a new local government. A bill was introduced into the legislature of that year to create Harney county, but the movement had been opposed from the first by many stockmen and others in the territory affected, who feared that the rate of taxation would be raised too high if a section so sparsely settled should assume the burdens of county organization. As stated in a previous chapter, the measure was opposed by the people of northern Grant, who also considered it premature. Some of those who signed the affirmative petition were afterward induced to join the remonstrators by representations that the new county scheme was projected by a few designing men in Burns. The opposition from within the territory itself and the strenuous efforts of Senator Hamilton caused the defeat of the bill.

One of the most sensational events of the year 1888 was the assassination, on May 5th, of James Bright, a quiet, unassuming young man without any known enemies. The unfortunate affair occurred about twelve miles east of Harney, near the spot where a stage robbery had occurred a twelvemonth before. The motive of this homicide was also robbery. Investigation into the matter resulted in the arrest of Buccaroo Jim, an Indian, whose connection with the jail breaking and murder in Canyon City and final acquittal has been previously adverted to in this volume.

The movement for the erection of Harney county, though defeated in 1887, had never been allowed to drop, and early in 1889 a second bill was presented to the legislature. It was forcibly urged that there could be no real security in a country two days' travel from the machinery of the law and that business could not be expeditiously conducted where land titles could not be examined, mortgages released, contracts or bonds executed and like matters attended to without a long and expensive trip. Those who considered any move in the direction of securing the conveniences of civilization, anything likely to advertise the resources of the country a menace to their pecuniary interests were on hand with their remonstrance again, but their efforts proved unavailing, and on February 26th the bill creating Harney county became a law. According to its provisions, the territory of the new political division should consist of all that portion of Grant county south of a line described as follows:

"Beginning at a point where the west line of Grant county crosses the township line between townships eighteen and nineteen, in said county of Grant, and running thence east on said township line to the west line of the old Malheur Indian reservation in said county of Grant; thence north following the west line of said Indian reservation six miles; thence east to the east line of Grant county."

The original draft of Hon. G. W. Gilham's bill provided that the governor of Oregon should locate the temporary county seat of Harney county, but the enemies of the measure had this provision changed so that Harney was designated as the place to be honored. This was a shrewd play, designed to excite the opposition of the Burns people, but the friends of the measure and of Burns were too sharp to be caught. They continued working zealously for the passage of the bill, notwithstanding this one obnoxious provision, and success crowned their efforts.

Great interest centered around the first election held in Harney county, that of June, 1890, for there was to be decided the question as to where the permanent county seat should be located. Harney had gained an advantage over its chief rival, Burns, in that it was designated

the temporary seat of government. The business men of Burns decided to more than offset this by direct appeal to the pocketbook of every voter. They met together on January 27th, and after a half hour's consultation, donated $2,100 with which to purchase what was known as the Smith & Young building, then in course of erection. They did buy this building and offered to donate the same to Harney county for use as a court house, provided the county seat should be located at Burns. The building was thirty-four by eighty feet, and thirty-one feet high, substantially built and quite well suited for the purpose. Furthermore, they gave a guarantee that should the county seat be located at Burns they would pay all the cost of moving the county property from Harney, in order that the county might not incur a dollar's expense by such removal.

The campaign waxed warm. It would have been a hotly contested election in any event, but it gained additional heat from the fact that it was a battle in an old and bitter war, that between the large cattlemen and the settlers. Burns had always been identified with the interests of the latter class in this conflict and so had incurred the unrelenting enmity of the men who wished to keep the country in barbarism for the benefit of their stock interests. That there was much illegal voting on election day is abundantly proven by the fact that 1,016 votes were cast on the county seat issue, whereas the number of legal voters in the county was known to have been much smaller than that. This vote was divided as follows: For Wright's Point, one; for Silvies City, eighty-four; for Drewsey, four; for Harney, four hundred and fifteen; for Burns, five hundred and twelve. The law required that to be successful any of the towns voted for must receive a majority of all the votes cast. From the foregoing figures it is evident that Burns had a majority of eight votes. But the vote for some of the county officers was considerably larger than on the county seat matter, a small proportion of the ballots having been left blank in part. The Harney people contended that in determining majorities these blanks should be counted. Under their interpretation of the law Burns did not receive the required majority; there was no choice of permanent county seat and the county offices of right still belonged in Harney, the temporary seat of government. The citizens of Burns claimed otherwise, of course, and the matter was taken into the circuit court. The judge interpreted the law in accordance with the contention of Burns and issued a writ of mandamus, commanding the county officers to move all the appurtenances of their respective offices and all the county property to Burns as the legal county seat. The writ was served and the offices moved. Harney, however, took an appeal to the supreme court, which declared the writ null on account of errors.

The county court then passed an order, which, after setting forth the facts as above, recites as follows:

"In view of and respect for the decision of the court of last resort of this state in this matter and the importance to the taxpayers of this county that the business transacted by this court is legally so,

"We do deem it justice to ourselves as officers and the taxpayers of this county, that the only legal place of holding court in Harney county is as by law directed in the town of Harney, the temporary county seat of this county, and that we have a copy of this ordinance published in each of the newspapers published in Burns, this county and state.

"W. E. GRACE, Clerk.
"By order of the Hon. County Court."

But in the decision of the supreme court the writ of mandamus was reversed for error only; the decision did not go to the merits of the case. In fact Judge Lord, of the supreme court, gave it as his opinion that the blanks should not be counted. This, it was contended, made it incumbent upon Harney to establish

beyond doubt its right to the county records, which could only be done by proving the eight votes of Burns's majority illegal. The Burns people were also persuaded that the order of the county court above in part quoted was illegal, as all power in the premises passed from the county authorities on the issue of the mandamus by Judge Clifford, and appeal to the supreme court; that the order must come from Judge Clifford or the supreme court for their removal. In the absence of an order from the proper tribunal, they declared, they would not permit the records to be moved.

It is stated that teams did come from Harney for the county property, but found the people of Burns determined to defend their supposed right to the county seat *vi et armis* if necessary. They wisely decided not to precipitate bloodshed by any show of force, and returned with empty wagons.

It was finally agreed to submit the matter for final adjudication to Judge E. D. Shattock, of Portland. One hundred and ten votes were called in question by Harney as being illegally cast for Burns and one hundred and forty-six by Burns as being illegally cast for Harney. The investigation which followed showed that votes had been cast by persons living in Malheur and Grant counties, by residents of Nevada, and by residents of Harney outside of their own precincts. A number of minors also voted. Judge Shattock simply rejected the votes found by him to be illegal, then decided in accordance with the mathematics of the case. His first decision was in favor of Harney, and there was jubilee in that part of the valley. The rejoicing proved premature, however, for a few days later the judge discovered an error in his arithmetic which necessitated a reversal of his former findings. According to his second decision 956 legal votes were cast, of which Burns received 481, or six majority. The opinion is dated November 12, 1892.

The year 1891 was one of great excitement

in Harney county over the discovery of gold in its northern portion. So rich were the finds at first reported that the Blue Bucket legend was revived. The Harney Press of the time contains this language:

"It is authoritatively stated that the long lost Blue Bucket mine has been discovered in what is known as the Peter Mortimer canyon, northeast of Harney City. It appears that an old prospector named White has been tracing the old emigrant trail through from Snake river and found the grave of the woman who died a little over a day's drive from the famous Blue Bucket discovery. He has been at the work about six months and since finding the grave has made diligent search this way from it. About ten days ago he put a man on the road to California with orders to change horses and make one hundred miles per day. White himself packed his things and started a few days later. The rider told at one of his stopping places that his boss had panned out two ounces of gold from ten pans and had sent him for friends in California. The parties receiving this information at once hastened to Harney City and began hunting for the discovery. On Saturday morning there was a rush for the Peter Mortimer canyon. Gold was discovered there, and it is thought that this is the rich mine. Notices were written and pasted on stones and men on horseback rode a race for the first claims.

"The mountains are full of men. The excitement is spreading and wagon loads of eager men are coming into Harney City daily from distant localities. The wildest rumors are afloat of great banks of gold dust being found. It is with the greatest care that the news gatherer can separate the true from the false reports. The discoveries are rich enough without any exaggeration.

"Gold has been found in paying quantities in three gulches on Salt creek. On the Harney City side eight claims have been located, on Soldier creek, Rattlesnake, Coffee Pot and Cow creeks."

Harney business men were deluged for some time with letters of inquiry by every mail from Boise, The Dalles, Portland and other towns. The boom continued all winter, though, as in most cases, the discoveries did not prove so rich as was anticipated. One great drawback to the development of the mines was a lack of water, there being no stream from which water could be diverted.

One of the important movements of the year 1892 was inaugurated by N. Brown, a business man of Burns, and had for its object the encouragement of wheat raising in the valley. Mr. Brown proposed to erect a roller flouring mill of forty or fifty barrels per diem capacity, providing citizens would subscribe $3,000, all sums advanced by subscribers to be paid back in grinding, flour, etc. After the lapse of several years the mill became an accomplished fact. Though a private enterprise, it is thought to have been one of great public moment under the circumstances, as it encouraged attempts to raise wheat in considerable quantities, thus materially helping to establish an important industry.

Another movement of a similar tendency, though of a vastly different nature, had its inception in 1893, the year of the wide-spread panic and disaster throughout the United States. This consisted in an attempt by the county court to secure artesian water, wherewith to redeem for cultivation the arid lands of the Harney valley. An agreement was entered into September 18th, whereby George W. Kellogg, of Salt Lake City, covenanted to bore a well to the depth of 1,500 feet if so ordered by the county court, the consideration being $2.75 per linear foot for boring and inserting the necessary casing in the well. Mr. Kellogg secured a flow, it is said of thirty gallons per hour, but he thought that by going deeper he could secure a much larger flow.

He did sink the well to a considerably greater depth, then met with an accident to his machinery and the project was given up.

During this year Troop A, O. N. G., was organized at Burns and mustered in, with Albert W. Gowan as captain, Samuel E. Joy, first lieutenant, and Henry E. Thompson, second lieutenant. Its original roster contained fifty-one names besides those mentioned. The old cavalry troop is well remembered by many residents of Harney county, though it has been disbanded for many years, having been mustered out in August, 1896. Its final muster roll shows that A. W. Gowan was still its captain and that the number of officers and enlisted men entitled to honorable mention was thirty-two.

The financial depression of 1893-96 was but little felt in the Harney country. Of course the low price of mutton, beef and wool, of wheat and other farm products obtaining in the general markets of the country could not fail to have its effect on this section, but local supply and demand were not very greatly affected by external conditions. During such times it is certainly an advantage to be away from the railways. Furthermore, it is customary in stock countries for the merchants to grant large credits to cattlemen, enabling them to hold over a season of low prices, and if necessary hold over still another season, or until prices come up again. Naturally the merchant must have large interest for the value thus loaned, but the stockman can well afford to pay for the accommodation. Then, too, in countries where the people get their sustenance directly or practically from the products of soil and herds, there cannot easily be the distress that is found during periods of depression in manufacturing centers where employers are few and the employed are many. It may be asserted with confidence that there never were any hard times in Harney valley between the years 1893 and 1897, and that few if any who desired to find employment were long

41

without an opportunity to labor for fair remuneration.

The year 1897, which witnessed the return of prosperity to the country in general, brought bountiful crops, good prices and good cheer to the residents of Harney county. The price of sheep advanced to $2 and $2.25 per head and lambs went from 75 cents to from $1 to $1.75. The price of cattle rose proportionately. Money began to circulate with freedom and rapidity and drummers found the towns a splendid place in which to display samples and book large orders. The exceedingly high water of the springtime, which washed away many bridges, cut Burns off from any wagon communication with points east, making it necessary to use row boats in places for the transportation of the mails, and made trouble for all persons who were compelled to move from place to place, seems to have had no bad effect upon the main industries of the county and did not in any way hinder the advent of the larger prosperity.

One tragic event of the year deserves notice, namely, the shooting of Peter French, one of the most noted men of the Harney country, and the chief factor in the upbuilding of the well known French-Glenn ranch. Mr. French and several of his employes were rounding up some cattle on the Sod House ranch on the day of the fatal occurrence, December 26th. About two o'clock P. M. one Edward Oliver came toward the cattle. French rode out to meet him and demanded that he turn back, as he had been cautioned many times before to remain off the premises. Oliver refused and an altercation ensued in which French was shot and killed. The author of the homicide made good his escape, but was afterward arrested, and on May 24, 1898, was acquitted by the trial jury.

The year 1898 was not inferior in point of prosperity to its predecessor. It was one of almost unprecedented good times throughout the state and Harney county got its full share of the blessings it brought. In the New Year's edition of the Oregonian Hon. A. W. Gowan gave some statistics which, though only approximately correct, are nevertheless of value as showing the wealth and productive capacity of Harney county at the time. The population is placed at 3,500; the number of acres under cultivation, 1,000; number of bushels of wheat raised, 5,000; of oats, 4,000; of barley and rye, 8,000; tons of hay, 100,000; pounds of butter and cheese produced, 25,000; bushels of potatoes, 5,000; of apples, 300; ounces of gold dust mined, 300; feet of lumber manufactured, 2,000,000; pounds of wool produced, 300,000; number of sheep in county, 72,000; of hogs, 500; of horses and mules, 10,-000; of cattle, 55,000.

Circumstances were such as to give Harney county no direct part in the Spanish-American war, although there was patriotism and chivalry enough within its borders to furnish many as bold, courageous and irresistible as ever bore the Stars and Stripes to victory at Santiago or San Juan Heights. The cavalry troop of the O. N. G. at Burns had been mustered out two years before the outbreak of hostilities, otherwise it might have enjoyed the opportunity to prove its mettle in active warfare. Two sons of Harney county, J. H. Loggan and David Loggan, were accepted as members of Company A, First Nevada Volunteers, and served with General Wheaton in his campaigns, acquitting themselves in all respects like men, and reflecting credit upon the wild free region where their manly powers were developed.

As affording some basis by which the wealth of Harney county in 1899 may be estimated, we quote the summary of assessments for that year, as follows: Acres of tillable land, 55,920, total value. $244,790, average value, $4.37; acres of non-tillable land, 553,-901, total value, $892,500, average value, $1.60; improvements on deeded lands, $75,-815; town and city lots, 694, total value, $25,-905, average value, $36.32; improvements on the same, $34,815; improvements on land not deeded, $15,430; miles of telephone and telegraph, 43, value, $450; merchandise and stock in trade, $35,755; farming implements, etc., $32,415; steamboats, railroad, etc., $10,590; money, $9,900; notes and accounts, $36,-320; shares of stock, 75, value $75; household furniture, etc., $17,165; horses and mules, 10,491, total value, $66,065; average value, $6.20; cattle, 59,195, total value, $830,830, average value, $14; sheep and goats, 51,195, total value, $76,805, average value, $1.50; swine, 481, total value, $1,410, average value, $2.72; gross value of all property, $2,416,755; exemptions, $82,975; total taxable property, $2,233,780; number of polls, 362.

The year 1900 is memorable as the year during which the initial Harney county fair was held. It proved a decided success in every way and not a few, even of those who had most opportunity to know about the resources of the section, were greatly surprised by the excellence of the exhibits. Cattle, horses, sheep, swine, grasses, grains, fruits, vegetables, flowers, needle work, paintings, photography, floral and wax work, and many other products of the range, the farm, the garden and the skillful hand were to be seen in artistic disposition and arrangement. The fair was so successful that its repetition every year since has been a matter of course, though subsequent exhibits have not equaled the first in point of excellence, on account of their failure to elicit sufficient interest among the people.

The prosperity which had been smiling so benignly upon central Oregon for two or three years caused quite a revival in the fall of 1899, in the interest in the region taken by the various railroad companies. Surveyors were running lines in almost every direction. The Sumpter Valley from the east, the Columbia Southern from the north, the Oregon Midland in the southwestern section, the Corvallis & Eastern from the west and the California, Nevada & Oregon from the south, all had engineering parties in one part or another of this great isolated region and the prospects seemed bright that one or more of the roads would penetrate the county in the near future.

The railroad has not yet made its appearance in Harney valley, though its appearance in the near future is still looked forward to with eager anticipation by many, but with anything but pleasure by others so situated as to realize large profits out of the prices prevailing by reason of the freight hauls. Neither will the railroad be welcomed by those who dread the settlement of the country. They have realized large fortunes in the pasturage of public lands, and while these cattle kings have secured title in various ways to large tracts of land, the appropriation of government domain under the homestead and desert laws of the United States is looked upon by them as a menace to their industry. Naturally, then, they seek to discourage railroads, or anything else having a tendency to promote settlement. The history of our country has been that the settler has invariably conquered in the long run, and this history is repeating itself in Harney county.

In several different ways has the United States, acting through the state of Oregon, attempted to assist in the development of this and other sections by the appropriation of public lands in aid of public improvements. The way in which these schemes have almost invariably miscarried is creditable neither to the astuteness of our legislators nor to the general uprightness of human nature. The most notorious of these schemes affecting Harney valley was given effect by act of Congress of July 5, 1866, which reads as follows:

"That there be and hereby is, granted to the state of Oregon, to aid in the construction of a military wagon road from Albany, Oregon, by way of Canyon City and the most feasible pass in the Cascade range of mountains, to the eastern boundary of the state, alternate sections of public lands, designated by odd numbers, three sections per mile, to be selected within six miles of said road: *Provided,* That the lands hereby granted shall be exclusively applied in the construction of said road, and shall be disposed of only as the work progresses; and the same shall be applied to no other purpose whatever; *And provided further,* That any and all lands heretofore reserved to the United States by act of Congress or other competent authority be, and the same are, reserved from the operation of this act, except so far as may be necessary to locate the route of said road through the same, in which case the right of way is granted, subject to the approval of the President of the United States.

"SEC. 2. *And be it further enacted,* That the said lands hereby granted to said state shall be disposed of by the legislature thereof for the purposes aforesaid and for no other, and the said road shall be and remain a public highway for the use of the government of the United States, free from tolls or other charges upon the transportation of any property, troops or mails of the United States.

"SEC. 3. *And be it further enacted,* That said road shall be constructed with such width, gradation and bridges as to permit of its regular use as a wagon road, and in such special manner as the state of Oregon may prescribe.

"SEC. 4. *And be it further enacted,* That the lands hereby granted to said state shall be disposed of only in the following manner—that is to say, that when ten miles of said road shall be completed a quantity of land not exceeding thirty sections for said road, may be sold coterminous to said completed portion of said road, and when the governor of said state shall certify to the secretary of the interior that any ten continuous miles of said road are completed, then another quantity of land hereby granted, not to exceed thirty sections, may be sold coterminous to said completed portion of said road, and so from time to time until said road is completed, and if said road is not completed within five years no further sales shall be made, and the land remaining unsold shall revert to the United States."

On October 24, 1866, the legislature of the state of Oregon conferred said grant on the Willamette Valley and Cascade Mountain Wagon Road Company by the following act:

"SEC. 1. *Be it enacted by the legislative assembly of the state of Oregon,* That there is hereby granted to the Willamette Valley and Cascade Mountain Wagon Road Company all lands, right of way, rights, privileges and immunities heretofore granted or pledged to this state by the act of Congress, in this act heretofore recited, for the purpose of aiding said company in constructing the road mentioned and described in said act of Congress, upon the conditions and limitations therein prescribed.

"SEC. 2. There is also hereby granted and pledged to said company all moneys, lands, rights, privileges and immunities which may be hereby granted to this state to aid in the construction of such road for the purpose and upon the conditions and limitations mentioned in said act of Congress, or which may be mentioned in any further grants of money or lands to aid in constructing such road.

"SEC. 3. Inasmuch as there is no law upon this subject at the present time, this act shall be in force from and after its passage."

On June 25, 1867, the company, by vote of its directors, accepted the grant.

Afterward the route described in the congressional act was changed by act of Congress dated July 15, 1870, as follows:

"*Be it enacted by the Senate and House of Representatives of the United States of America in Congress assembled,* That an act entitled 'An act granting lands to the state of Oregon to aid in the construction of a military road from Albany, Oregon, to the eastern boundary of said state,' be amended so as to strike out the words 'by way of Canyon City,' in the first section of said act, and insert instead thereof the words 'by way of Camp Harney.' "

By the operation of this legislation the Willamette Valley & Cascade Mountain Wagon Road Company secured about 900,000 acres of the public domain. No greater wrong was ever perpetrated upon the general public of Oregon than resulted from these unwise acts of the national and state governments and the perfidy of this company. That the road was not constructed according to requirements of the statutes is as sure as anything can be. In Harney valley, level as a floor, so that a first class road might be constructed almost anywhere for a sum very much less than three sections per mile were worth, even at the government price of $1.25 per acre, the company did nothing but to set stakes marking out a route. They went ten miles around in order to secure the best lands in the valley and an extra thirty sections of land. Of course what travel there was through the valley would not follow their meanderings, so that the sage brush was never killed out by the hoofs of passing teams and the road never had an existence. Yet, by driving these mile stakes, the company secured thousands of acres of the best lands in Harney county. Litigation over this land formed a part of the great war fought by settlers for the possession of the Harney region. The United States government had lots of land at that time; the state of Oregon was not particularly interested in the matter and the brunt of the battle against this egregious wrong fell upon the poor settler who wished a small portion of this domain for a home. It is probable that had the suits of the settlers been pushed at the proper time and with sufficient vigor, the company would have lost the land, as it should have, but delays operated in favor of the company and its assignees and they held their unearned estates.

As giving a concise and authentic history of this matter we quote in part the decision of

Judge Gilbert, rendered in 1892. After abstracting in brief the conditions of the grant, the opinion says:

"Within the time limited for the construction of the road, the whole line of road from Albany to the state line, 487 miles in all, was certified to have been completed in the manner required by the act, by four several certificates of the governor of the state of Oregon, the first bearing date April 11, 1868, and the last June 24, 1871.

"On June 18, 1874, Congress passed an act recognizing the transfer to the wagon road company, and authorizing the issuance of patents to that corporation for all the lands so granted to the state, with the following proviso: 'This shall not be construed to revive any land grant already expired nor to create any new rights of any kind, except to provide for issuing patents for lands to which the state is already entitled.' On June 19, 1876, under this statute, patents issued to the wagon road company for 107,893 acres of the land.

"On August 19, 1871, the wagon road company sold and conveyed the land grant to H. K. W. Clarke, for a consideration, as recited in the deed, of $75,000, and on September 1st of the same year Clarke conveyed the same to David Cahn in trust for said grantor and for T. Egenton Hogg and Alexander Weill.

"In March, 1878, complaint was made to the secretary of the interior by citizens of Oregon that the road had not been constructed according to the provisions of the original granting act, and two years later a special agent was appointed to investigate and report upon the matter contained in said complaint. In October, 1880, the agent made his report to the effect that the road, and particularly the eastern portion thereof, had not been constructed as required by the act of Congress. His report with the evidence accompanying the same was placed before Congress. In the House of Representatives the matter was re-

ferred to the committee on military affairs, and that committee after investigation, reported that no action be taken.

"Subsequently in February, 1882, further charges and proofs were laid before Congress which, in the House, were referred to the committee on public lands and in the Senate to the committee on military affairs. Both committees reported that no action be taken by Congress, alleging as a reason for that conclusion, 'that the executive department of the government had ample authority in law without any instruction from the legislative department.'

"The secretary of the interior thereupon made an investigation of the matter, and as a result thereof, directed the commission of the general land office to proceed and certify the lands for patent. In October, 1882, patents issued to the wagon road company for 440,856 acres of the lands which had been selected. Since that date no patents have issued for the remaining lands claimed to have been earned by the wagon road company, and 312,691 acres of the same remain unpatented.

"On March 2, 1889, Congress passed an act directing the attorney general to cause a suit to be brought against all claimants of the lands so granted for wagon road construction 'to determine the question of the reasonable and proper completion of said road in accordance with the terms of the granting act, either in whole or in part, and the legal effect of the several certificates of the governor of Oregon of the completion of the road, and to declare forfeited to the United States all land not earned in accordance with said act, saving and reserving the right of all bona fide purchasers of such lands for vaulable consideration,' and providing that said suit or suits should 'be tried and adjudicated in like manner and by the same principles and rules of jurisprudence as other suits in equity therein tried.'

"In pursuance of the authority so conferred upon the attorney general this suit was com-

menced by the United States against the wagon
road company and the subsequent grantees of
the land in question.

"The bill sets forth the facts above enumerated and alleges that no portion of the road
was constructed as required by the act within
the time limited therein, that the certificates
of the governor were fatally defective in form
and were procured by the fraud and misrepre-
sentation of the wagon road company, and
that the present grantees of the land from the
wagon road company purchased the same with
knowledge of said facts.

"To this bill the defendants, Alexander
Weill and David Cahn, make answer setting
forth the following defenses:

"1. That the road was completed in all
respects as required by the granting act and
within the time therein limited.

"2. That the certificates of the governors
of Oregon were by the act made conclusive
evidence of the completion of the road, and
that upon the strength of said certificates the
defendants became bona fide purchasers of the
lands.

"3. That conceding that the road may not
have been completed within the time limited,
nevertheless, and before any declaration of
forfeiture by the United States, the road was
fully completed in the manner required by the
act, and thereby the forfeiture was avoided.

"4. That the defendants after purchasing
said lands, relied upon the action of Congress
in 1874 in directing the issuance of patents to
said land, and upon the result of the investigation made by Congress above referred to, and
the action of the secretary of the interior
after his investigation in 1882, directing the issuance of patents, and in consequence thereof
expended large sums of money in and about
said lands in repairing said road, whereby the
United States have become estopped to claim a
forfeiture."

The judge admits in the opinion from which
this excerpt has been taken that the road was

not completed in the manner contemplated by
the granting act, especially the eastern portion
of it, but on account of the certificates of the
governor, and the appearance of good faith in
the purchasers of the grant, who paid for their
land a price commensurate with its value at the
time, and on account of the delay on the part
of the United States in bringing the matter to
issue and of several of its acts in a measure
confirmatory of the grant, he considered the
government estopped from further action and
decided in favor of the defendants.

The present owners of the land are making
no effort to improve the same, neither are they
disposed to sell it in small tracts to would-be
settlers, so that large areas in Harney county
are thus held back from settlement. Some of
these lands are rented to residents, but the consistent policy of the road land holders has been
and is to spend as little money as possible on
anything from which benefit might inure to
the country and to hold their property indefinitely for the sake of the unearned increment in its value. They thus compel the settler
to reward them for the wrongs they or their
grantors have done him; all of which
they are enabled to accomplish through the
bungling incompetence of men who were sent
to Congress or to the legislative halls on account of their supposed superior wisdom and
statecraft.

Another piece of legislation which has
caused no end of trouble and litigation in Harney county was the grant of all swamp lands to
the state government and the subsequent disposition of the same by the state; howbeit the
evil arising from this policy was not inherent in
the policy itself but grew out of the abuse of it.
It certainly was legitimate enough for the national government to grant to the state for its
use and benefit all lands unfit for cultivation by
reason of their swampy character and it was
legitimate and right that the state should dispose of these lands to any person who would
reclaim them to the uses of man. The wrong

was perpetrated by the land grabber, who attempted to procure under the provisions of the law, thousands of acres which were not swampy in character and if covered with water in the spring time were only rendered the more valuable on that account from the fact that the growth of natural grass was made luxuriant and healthy by this annual inundation. Even had the law been duly respected in letter and spirit it would have enabled large cattle owners to secure title to vast quantities of land, thus defeating the policy of the government, which has generally been, in theory, if not in practice, to prevent the accumulation, by individuals and companies, of large areas. But the intent of the law was not respected. It is claimed that cattlemen in some instances actually created swamp lands artificially by damming up streams and causing overflows. Others undoubtedly secured lands under the swamp land act which were never swampy. It was by making swamp land purchases, legitimate or otherwise, that the foundation for some of the mammoth cattle ranches of Harney county was laid.

In the struggle against the "swamp angels," as these swamp land claimants were called, the settler was again called upon to bear the heat and burden of the battle. The United States was apathetic in the matter and it was to the interest of the state that as much should be "swamped" as possible, as the price paid for such land went into the state coffers. With admirable courage, the settlers took up the gauntlet, filing upon lands which they believed the swamp claimant had no right to and instituting contests in the local land office. The litigation lasted for years, causing bitter feeling and much personal animosity. As each case had to be decided upon its merits, it is impossible in a volume like this to state definitely what was the final result of this protracted contesting in the land offices, before the secretary of the interior, and in the United States courts. It may be stated, however, that the settlers

were generally successful, though of course the swamp claimants got the land in every case where they were able to prove that it was actually swampy in character. They got it also in many instances where the settlers despaired of final success, grew weary of litigation and determined to accept the pittance offered by the "swamp angels" to secure a settlement.

A third cause of bitter protracted litigation in Harney valley was presented by the recession of Lake Malheur, whereby thousands of acres of land, formerly the bed of the lake, were left high and dry, ready for the agriculturist. The causes of the recession have been called in question and it was even intimated by some that the rich cattle companies caused the overflow into Lake Harney by artificial means. It is probable, however, that the lowering of the lake was wholly the result of natural forces. The doughty homeseeker was ready to appropriate this land as soon as the receding of the water made it possible for him to do so. In due time a petition was presented to the department of the interior asking for a survey of the land below the meander line. This precipitated litigation for the large cattle men, who owned thousands of acres on the shore of the lake, and they at once asserted claim to the land as riparian owners. It is an old and well established principle of common law that the property of residents on the banks of a stream or body of water is not considered as grounded as the surveyed line along the shore, but extends at least to the water's edge. The principle has its foundation in justice, being meant to protect property holders, so situated, from being cut off from direct water communication in case the meander line does not mark the exact boundary between the land and the water as is frequently the case. It is ordinarily just, too, and it is certainly law that where the water recedes from its old levels the land thus left uncovered should belong to the man who owns the property contiguous to it. The loss would be his if by erosion or other-

wise the water encroached upon his land and
the gain should be his when from natural
causes the water acts in an opposite way. Under ordinary circumstances the justice of the
rule could hardly be questioned, but in the Malheur lake case it operated to give to wealthy
corporations, who had already acquired by the
bounty of our government thousands of acres
of land for a nominal price, other thousands of
acres of rich and valuable land practically as
a free gift.

When the settlers on the land made application for the survey as above stated, the department of the interior hesitated about ordering
it on account of a then recent decision of the
supreme court of the United States which con-
firms title to an owner adjoining a meander
survey of "lands bounded on a lake or pond,
which is not tidewater and is not navigable, to
the center of the lake or pond, notably with
other riparian proprietors if there be such."
But in 1892 the Hon. Binger Hermann appeared before the department and made an argument in behalf of the settlers, making the
point that as to the status of the land beyond
the meander line, adjoining which there were
no private owners, the title being in the government, the supreme court decision does not refer
and hence that such uncovered and now dry
areas are subject to occupancy under the homestead law. The department decided that as to
such lands covered by lakes or ponds and not
patented or applied for under the general land
laws, when the same should have become dry
and fit for agricultural purposes they should be
surveyed and disposed of as government land.
A survey was accordingly ordered. It is stated
that the local land officers misunderstood the
instructions of the department of the interior
and allowed the survey lands below the meander
line, not alone contiguous to unpatented and
unclaimed government lands, but contiguous
to the lands belonging to the cattle companies.
When the matter was again brought before the
department of the interior it rather arbitrarily,

as it seems to the writer, refused to sustain the
old meander line and ordered the survey of a
new meander line conforming to the boundaries
of the lake as they were at that time. The cattle
companies were therefore compelled to relinquish their claims to the land they had formerly
claimed as riparian owners.

Within a year or two an act has been passed
which promises, if carried out according to its
spirit and intentions, to prove a great blessing
to Harney county. We refer to the Carey act,
the gist of which is that any person, association,
or corporation may enter into contract with
the state land board to reclaim any tract of
desert government land. The applicant must,
at his own expense make a survey of the section to be reclaimed and submit with his application for contract a map and plan of the proposed reclamation project with estimates of first
cost and maintenance, statements of the amount
of water to be rendered available, the area to
be covered, etc. The contract when entered
into by the state land board creates a lien upon
the land for the cost of construction and maintenance which shall be valid against the legal
subdivisions of the land for the amount due
as agreed upon with interest at six per cent.
from date of reclamation. Congress grants
the land to the state under certain conditions
and those conditions must be fulfilled as required by law to the satisfaction of the secretary of the interior before the transfer is fully
completed.

Under this law the Harney Valley Improvement Company, and it may be other corporations and individuals have begun operations. The Harney Valley Improvement
Company purposes to take water from the
Silvies river chiefly, though they also expect
to construct storage reservoirs for emergency
service. They believe that the withdrawal of
water from the river will so reduce the volume
of the stream that it will not overflow and create marsh land about its mouth, and that thus
indirectly, as well as directly, land will be re-

claimed by their scheme. It would seem on the surface that the Carey act could hardly operate otherwise than beneficially, but so many times have such schemes miscarried in the past history of Harney county that many of the people view this one with suspicion. They are inclined to doubt the sincerity of some of those who have undertaken to redeem land under the provisions of this act, believing that their real intention is to secure the free use of the land for pasture for so long a period as possible. They have an extended period in which to complete their operations and it is possible for them to control the lands until the time is nearly or entirely up, by doing very little work.

CHAPTER II.

POLITICAL.

Harney county began its official existence in the spring of 1889 under the following corps of officers, appointed by the governor: County judge, T. J. Shields; county clerk, W. E. Grace; sheriff, P. F. Stenger; commissioners, T. J. Morrison, D. H. Smythe; superintendent of schools, L. B. Baker; surveyor, W. H. Gradon.

In 1890 the following were the successful candidates for office in Harney county: For sheriff, A. A. Cowing, Democrat; for clerk, W. E. Grace, Democrat; for county judge, William Miller, Democrat; for county treasurer, Thomas H. Roberts, Democrat; for assessor, W. E. Alberson, Democrat; for commissioners, William Altnow, Democrat, and N. E. Duncan, Republican; for superintendent of schools, Charles Newell, Republican; for surveyor, T. A. McKinnon, Democrat; for coroner, F. P. Moore, Democrat.

The principal event of the campaign of 1890 was the contest between the different towns for the seat of county government. This struggle for supremacy was very sharp and so close was the vote that it was only by a decision of the courts that Burns was able to maintain its victory over Harney. There were 1,016 votes cast, of which Burns received 512, or a majority of eight over all. Harney contested the election. The detailed story of this contest will be found in the chronological history of the county in another chapter.

The vote in 1892 was as follows: For congressman, C. J. Bright, 19, W. R. Ellis, 257, J. C. Luce, 147, J. H. Slater, 346; for district judge, M. D. Clifford, 272, W. Green, 25, H. Kelley, 483; for prosecuting attorney, sixth district, C. H. Finn, 293, G. Griffin, 157, C. F. Hyde, 329, C. H. Fill, 8; for member board of equalization, W. G. Hunter, 426, W. Morfitt, 339, C. D. Huffman, 1; for joint representative with Grant county, M. R. Biggs, 328, M. Fenwick, 153, C. D. Richardson, 290; for county clerk, H. C. Levens, 365, P. L. Shideler, 396; for sheriff, H. Gittings, 410, P. F. Stenger, 350; for county treasurer, H. Cheatham, 138, J. S. Geer, 249, T. H. Roberts, 154, C. Ziegler, 225, George Huston, 1; for assessor, R. Hendricks, 363, S. W. Miller, 406; for superintendent of schools, D. L. Grace, 302, C. Newell, 465, Peter Martimer, 1, John Vaughn, 1; for county surveyor, F. J. Martin, 328, J. H. Neal, 433; for county commissioner,

R. R. Sitz, 396, T. Walls, 375, Samuel Kings, 1; for coroner, C. F. McKinney was elected by a plurality of 29 over several other candidates.

The official vote at the election which took place two years later resulted: For circuit judge, M. D. Clifford, Democrat, 272, W. Green, Populist, 25, Harrison Kelley, Republican, 483; for prosecuting attorney, C. H. Finn, Republican, 293, G. Griffin, Populist, 157, C. F. Hyde, Democrat, 329; for member of state board of equalization, W. G. Hunter, Democrat 426, W. Morfitt, Republican, 339; for joint representative with Grant, M. R. Biggs, Democrat, 328, Mell Fenwick, Populist, 157, C. D. Richardson, Republican, 290; for county clerk, H. C. Levens, Republican, 365, P. L. Shideler, Democrat, 396; for sheriff, A. Gittings, Republican, 410, P. F. Stenger, Democrat, 350; for county treasurer, H. Cheatham, Populist, 138, I. S. Geer, Republican, 249, T. H. Roberts, Independent, 154, C. Ziegler, Democrat, 222; for county assessor, R. Hendricks, Republican, 333, S. W. Miller, Democrat, 406; for superintendent of schools, D. L. Grace, Democrat, 302, Charles Newell, Republican, 465; for surveyor, E. Martin, Democrat, 328, J. H. Neal, Republican, 433; for coroner, R. R. Sitz, Republican, 396, T. Walls, Democrat, 375.

The famous campaign of 1896 was as closely contested in Harney county as in other parts of eastern Oregon, as will be seen from the official vote herewith presented:

For congressman, second district, A. S. Bennett, 220, W. R. Ellis, 217, F. McKercher, 8, H. H. Northrup, 27, Martin Quinn, 273; for supreme judge, Robert S. Bean, 230, John Burnett, 243, Joseph Gaston, 241; for prosecuting attorney, Charles W. Parrish, 265, O. F. Buse, 118, M. Dustin, 111, C. A. Sweek, 260; for joint representative with Grant, C. S. Dustin, 360, E. Hall, 316; for member state board of equalization, J. H. Holland, 309, G. W. Pierce, 305; for county clerk, E. L. Beede, 163, Harrison Kelley, 315, S. W. Miller, 277; for sheriff, A. Gittings, 236, John Jacque-

min, 200, John McKinnon, 310; for treasurer, W. N. Jorgensen, 137, L. Waldenberg, 198, J. C. Welcome, 391; for assessor, J. O. Cawlfield, 190, Albert A. Reineman, 268, W. S. Waters, 275; for superintendent of schools, W. C. Byrd, 280, Horace A. Dillard, 269, Charles Newell, 192; for sureyor, V. Deffenbaugh, 207, T. A. McKinnon 322, J. A. Neal, 197; for commissioner, Charles Bonnett, 158, George Hagey, 287, W. B. Johnson, 268; for coroner, Lloyd Culp, 242, Austin Goodman, 169, Thomas W. Stephens, 293.

The result of the election in 1898 may be gleaned from the following figures: Circuit judge, M. D. Clifford, Union and Democrat, 474, Charles W. Parrish, Republican, 289, Thornton Williams, Independent, 65; prosecuting attorney, Errett Hicks, Union and Democrat, 435, William Miller, Republican, 335; senator, A. W. Gowan, Republican, 356, J. W. Morrow, Union and Democrat, 440; representative, R. N. Donnelly, Republican, 269, George D. Hagey, Union and Democrat, 457; member state board of equalization, J. R. Gregg, Democrat, 438, William Hall, Republican, 310; county judge, Charles P. Rutherford, Populist, 253, James A. Sparrow, Republican, 345, Thomas Walls, Union and Democrat, 257; clerk, H. A. Dillard, Populist, 290, Harrison Kelley, Republican, 190, Henry Richardson, Union and Democrat, 385; sheriff, E. H. King, Republican, 351, A. J. McKinnon, Union and Democrat, 514; treasurer, H. E. Cheatham, Populist, 137, J. J. Tupker, Union and Democrat, 198, J. C. Welcome, Republican, 522; assessor, J. W. Buchanan, Union and Democrat, 335, J. H. Loggan, Populist, 233, W. S. Waters, Republican, 289; superintendent of schools, W. C. Byrd, Union and Democrat, 475, Charles N. Cochrane, Republican, 326; surveyor, George Whiting, Republican, 523; commissioner, Robert Drinkwater, Populist, 184, Charles R. Peterson, Union and Democrat, 272, A. Venator, Republican, 359; coroner, W. L. Marsden, Republican, 573, S.

B. McPheeters, Union and Democrat, 245.

The vote in 1900: For joint representative, ninth district, W. D. Baker, Democratic-People's candidate, 309, I. S. Geer, Republican, 333, John L. Sitz, Straight Republican, 194; for district attorney, ninth district, Will R. King, Democratic-People's, 402, William Miller, Republican, 388; for county clerk, R. T. Hughet, Republican, 335, Henry Richardson, Democrat, 495; for sheriff, Thomas Allen, Republican, 403, George Shelley, Democrat, 423; for county treasurer, R. C. Angevine, Democrat, 357, R. A. Miller, Republican, 467; for assessor, J. W. Buchanan, Democrat, 470, M. B. Hayes, Republican, 349; for school superintendent, J. C. Bartlett, Democrat, 491, Charles N. Cochrane, Republican, 325; for surveyor, J. R. Johnson, Democrat, 488, Frank M. Jordan, Republican, 327; for commissioner, Thomas Bain, Republican, 292, R. J. Williams, Democrat, 485; for coroner, W. L. Marsden, Republican, 637.

The result of the last campaign, that of 1902, in Harney county was as follows: For congressman, W. F. Butcher, Democrat, 382, D. T. Gerdes, Socialist, 45, F. R. Spalding, Prohibitionist, 12, J. N. Williamson, Republican, 470; for joint senator, 25th district, John L. Rand, Republican, 472, William E. Smith, Democrat, 427; for joint representative, 27th district, Fred J. Palmer, Republican, 348, E. H. Test, Democrat, 516; for county judge, W. C. Byrd, Democrat, 443, H. C. Levens, Republican, 507; for county clerk, R. T. Hughet, Republican, 390, Frank S. Reider, Democrat, 556; for sheriff, Thomas Allen, Republican, 540, George Shelley, Democrat, 409; for assessor, W. E. Alberson, Democrat, 413, J. E. Loggan, Republican, 530; for treasurer, James M. Dalton, Democrat, 450, R. A. Miller, Republican, 488; for commissioner, Edward J. Catlow, Democrat, 410, C. F. Miller, Republican, 515; for coroner. W. L. Marsden, Republican, 712; for surveyor, John H. Neal, 24, F. M. Jordan, 62.

CHAPTER III.

TOWNS OF HARNEY COUNTY.

BURNS.

While the thriving little city of Burns has been a town for but little more than a decade and a half, he who would trace its history from the first must go back to the year 1878. Not long after the Indian war of that date had been brought to a close a man named Jonas, so an old settler informs us, bought a quantity of merchandise and put up a small store on the spot afterward occupied by the City hotel, of Burns. The Fitz Gerald Brothers, of Lakeview, brought in and installed in the same building a couple of barrels of whisky, which found a ready sale among the thirsty cowboys and cattlemen. In the spring of 1879 so much of Mr. Jonas's stock as remained on his shelves was purchased by William Curry and removed to a place called Egan. During 1881 P. M. Curry dispensed whisky for twenty-five cents a drink in a small log cabin about two miles from the present Burns, and his place became a sort of rendezvous and headquarters of the cattlemen who spent the winter in the valley. The nearest postoffice at this time was Camp Harney, which was visited once each week by a mounted mail carrier from Canyon City. The following year Mc-Gowan & Martin opened a general merchandise store at Egan, with the result that a postoffice was established there, a new mail route granted and the town given a fair start.

About the same time, however, A. O. Bedell started a small store on the site on which P. F. Stenger's residence was afterward erected. Later Robertson & Johnson put up a building in the same locality, forming the nucleus of another town. The usual rivalry resulted, but fortunately was of short duration, for Bedell sold his stock to P. F. Stenger, who formed a partnership with Mr. McGowan, of Egan, uniting the two mercantile establishments. With this bond of union drawing them together, weak as they both were, their consolidation in May, 1883, was a natural consequence. The postoffice was removed from Egan. Its name was changed to Burns, in honor of the celebrated Scottish poet, and the foundations of the metropolis of Harney valley and county were fairly laid.

At this period an influx of population set in toward Harney valley. Would-be settlers began disputing the claims of stockmen that the country was of no value for agricultural purposes and contending with them for a foothold in the broad unsettled region. The result was that Burns grew quite rapidly. In 1885 it had so far progressed as to justify the establishment of a newspaper, and Horace Dillard came in with a small plant and began the publication of a four-page six-column patent outside sheet, known as the Harney Valley Items. On November 23, 1887, volume No. 1, of the East Oregon Herald, made its debut, announcing that in politics it would be straight-out Democratic and that its purpose should always be to promote the in-

terests of its home town and county in every way, holding itself strictly independent of any corporation control or class domination of whatsoever nature. D. I. Grace was its first editor and proprietor. Under date of May 16, 1888, this publication gives a register of the business of Burns, from which we learn that P. S. Early was then engaged in blacksmithing and wagon making; that J. C. Welcome carried a stock of harness and saddles; that W. C. Byrd was proprietor of the Red Front livery barn; that T. Sillman was engaged in the saloon business; that N. Brown was building a flouring mill near the town; that W. E. Grace had a drug store; George McGowan a hardware, P. F. Stenger a general merchandise store, Charles Sampson a jewelry store, and that J. W. Sawyer, of the firm of Sawyer & Dore, was the proprietor of the best equipped saw mill in the valley, situated near Burns. The town at this time, so the paper states, was forging ahead at a rapid pace. The influx of settlers had continued for three years pervious, exerting a marked effect upon the development and upbuilding of the principal trading point of the country. But notwithstanding this healthy condition of things, the ignorance obtaining on the outside with regard to Burns and eastern Oregon generally was very dense, as is strikingly illustrated by the fact that the Oregon State Board of Agriculture stated in one of its publications that this rising star of the interior of eastern Oregon was the county seat of Malheur county. The same statement was also made in the Pacific States Newspaper Directory.

Although Burns was not in Malheur county and had no desire to leave its own most favorable location, even at the behest of the board of agriculture or the newspaper directory, and though it was not ambitious to contest with Vale and Ontario for the honor of being the political center of Oregon's newest governmental division, it was ambitious both for county seatship and for segregation from the county of which it then formed a part. It had led in the movement for the formation of Harney county in 1887. Though defeated in its purpose it was not disheartened, and in 1889 it was again before the Oregon legislature with its new county proposition, determined to win. It did win.

Its next effort was in the direction of securing to itself the prestige and advantage always attending the location within the borders of a town of county buildings, and all the machinery of county organization. In the legislature its rival, Harney, had secured a decided advantage by getting itself designated as the temporary county seat, but Burns went to work with a will to carry the ensuing election. Its business men showed their energy and public spirit by purchasing a new and suitable building and pledging themselves to convey the same to Harney county by warranty deed in case the town were chosen as the seat of government. Burns had already secured the location within its limits of a United States land office. Its two newspapers were not slow in pointing out this advantage and also that it was the terminus of all stage lines, and the center of public highways, that it had a daily mail and the only distributing postoffice in the valley, the only money order and postal note office, the largest number of private residences, the only harness and saddlery store, the only jewelry establishment, the only boot and shoe shop, the only brewery, the only flouring mill, the only tin shop, the only drug store, the only public bath house, the only photograph gallery, and the only church building. Persons wishing to transact certain lines of business or make certain purchases must, therefore, of necessity come to Burns, and to such location of the county seat in that town must be a great convenience. Mention was also frequently made of new enterprises under way, such as the fine central school building, a large and complete saw mill, a furniture manufactory, a bank building and a modern hotel.

These and other arguments must have had their weight with the voters, for the official count gave Burns a small majority. The contest which followed has been sufficiently treated of in other parts of this work. It is sufficient here to state that Burns held and still holds the county seat and that it still holds the lead among the rising towns of Harney valley.

In January, 1891, Burns secured from the legislature of Oregon a charter permitting it to organize and maintain a city government, and in accordance with the powers therein granted, it elected as its first officers: Captain Kelley, mayor; J. C. Welcome, recorder; Irwin Geer, treasurer; Peter Stenger, Lee Caldwell, L. M. Brown and Dr. J. W. Ashford, councilmen.

The city of Burns has enjoyed a steady, substantial and almost uninterrupted growth, though it has never had a boom. Not even during the period of financial depression did it cease to forge ahead, and since the advent of prosperity it has been steadily building up and assuming a more solid and substantial aspect. It is the center of a large area of rich country, and wares from the shelves of its merchants find their way into the homes of families living many miles distant. The stock raisers and farmers who make Burns their base of supplies have for the last few years been realizing good prices for their products, while the seasons have been favorable for abundant yields and large increase. The prosperity resulting has been shared by the merchants and business men of the towns to such an extent that it may with truth be asserted that there is not a single commercial establishment in the place which is not realizing excellent profits upon the money invested. As soon as the stranger enters Burns he perceives unmistakably that progress and improvement are the watchwords. The services of every man who can handle a mason's trowel are called into requisition, the man known to possess even a little skill in any of the building trades is not only offered employment and good wages, but is importuned to endeavor to arrange his plans so that he may lend a hand in the erection of some of the brick and stone structures in course of construction. Commercial travelers are agreed in classing Burns among the finest business points in the west.

A residence of some weeks in this prosperous inland city has enabled the writer to form a fair estimate of the people of Burns, and he must bear testimony that he has invariably found them genial, approachable, obliging and orderly. Were it not for the long freight trains that are to be seen daily on the streets, the arrival and departure of stages and the conspicuous absence of the locomotive's sonorous whistle, one might easily forget that he was in a frontier town more than a hundred miles from the nearest railroad. The carousing and breaches of the peace which are usually to be found in the commercial centers of cattle countries may have obtained here in times past, but at present the rules of order and decorum seem to be as well respected and when necessary the laws and ordinances as faithfully enforced as in any other city in the west.

A reasonably comprehensive register of the present business of the city would include the following: Five hotels, the Burns, Samuel Bailey, proprietor; the Syme, Mrs. H. B. Syme; the Oregon House, Mesdames Weis and Winters; the French Hotel, Mrs. L. Racine; and the Cottage; one restaurant, of which Tom, the Chinaman, is proprietor; the Harney Valley brewery, owned by L. Woldenberg; Geer & Cummings and Voegtly & Kenyon, hardware and implements; N. Brown & Sons, Lunaberg & Dalton, Miller & Thompson, Schwartz & Budelman, general merchandise; the City drug store, owned by H. W. Welcome & Company; G. W. Waters & Brother and J. W. Jones & Company, dealers in fruits, farm produce, etc.; the Burns Furniture Company, of which W. C. Byrd is manager; John Gemberling's jewelry store; the White Front and Red Front livery stables, both owned by McClain & Biggs, also Jorgensen's and Simon Lewis' barns; Mrs. C. M. Byrd's millinery; three newspapers, the Times-Herald, the Harney Valley Items and the Harney County News; Shelley & Foley, Grant Kesterson's and Joe Tupker's blacksmith shops; five saloons; the harness and saddlery establishments of J. C. Welcome & Son and Hopkins & Hunter; one bank, the Bank of Burns; a United States land office; John McMullan, photographer; James Smith, shoe maker; the meat market of Levens & Mace; G. W. Clevenger's undertaking parlors; several barber shops; Hibbard & Broncton, dentists; Marsden & Geary, and H. Volp, physicians and surgeons; Parrish & Rembold, Biggs & Biggs, Williams & Fitz Gerald, John G. Saxton, George Sizemore, A. W. Gowan, C. S. Sweek and Charles L. Leonard, attorneys.

There are also the flouring mill of Joseph Sturdevant and four saw mills and two shingle mills in the country surrounding the town.

Burns has three churches, the Presbyterian, Baptist and Catholic, all supplied with commodious frame or stone edifices and settled pastors. All the leading fraternal and some of the less known secret orders are represented, some of them by flourishing lodges.

The educational interests of the town are conserved by an excellent public school, employing five teachers, and well attended. There is also a well equipped business college in Burns, maintained by a joint stock company of local business men.

HARNEY.

The old fort from which this pleasantly situated little town received its name has been referred to in the former chapter. It was located about two miles from the site of the Harney of the present, on Rattlesnake creek. The fort has done its work and not a vestige of it remains at this day, for the soldier, whose habitation it once was, has done his work and

SCHOOL HOUSE, HARNEY CITY.

in his place has come the farmer, the stockman and the merchant.

One of the results of this supercession of the military by the civil is the town of Harney, whose first business establishment was instituted the summer of 1885 by Thomas Bain. At this time the land which was to form the site of the town was held by one Robert Ivers, under the pre-emption laws of the United States. Mr. Bain paid him for lots on the property, taking some kind of an obligation that title should be furnished as soon as Ivers received his patent from the government. The same year a saloon was built by Samuel Overlander and Herman Lawen, and a hotel and livery stable by N. Fisk. Several dwellings were also erected, no doubt in the expectation that Mr. Ivers would convey title to the lots whereon they stood as soon as he was able to do so. During the next summer Stewart Brothers put in a flour and feed store, and one other business was established, of a decidedly temporary character, however.

So far all was harmonious, but in 1886 Ben Brown, J. C. Buckland and Jasper Davis determined to build a rival town on a site near by. Brown put in a general merchandise establishment, Davis moved a small stock of goods from Harney and opened a store in the new town and Buckland built a hotel and feed stable. A saloon was started by a man named Coatsworth, in 1887.

Now came a battle for supremacy. Mr. Ivers seems to have decided with the new town, for he conveyed one-third of his own site to Ben Brown and one-third to John Ainsley, retaining the remaining third for himself. This evidently made it possible for the new town to put a stop to the growth of its rival or kill it entirely. But the indignation of the friends of Harney proper was thoroughly aroused by this procedure. They determined to checkmate the adversary if possible and they found their opportunity in the fact that Ivers had violated the law in obligating himself to convey the land

before final proof had been made and patent had issued. Suit was begun, Henry Lyons filing the complaint at the instance of Mr. Bain. The case was carried to the secretary of the interior, who decided against Ivers, holding his title void, and all transfers under it. Mr. Bain then had the land declared a government town site so that any person wishing to settle in the place and erect a building might have two lots for the cost of filing and final proof. To further work the discomfiture of his adversaries, he secured indirectly a third interest in their town site. The result was that the opposition town ceased to grow and soon its business houses were removed to Harney or allowed to stand idle. When the postoffice was removed from old Fort Harney it was established in the lower town, but after Cleveland's election T. B. James was appointed postmaster, and by him the postoffice was taken to the present town.

According to a Burns newspaper, the business men of the town in 1888 were Victor J. Miller, attorney at law; Jasper Davis, general merchant; J. C. Buckland, hotel keeper and liveryman; J. H. Loggan, store keeper for W. J. Snodgrass, and deputy postmaster; Lessing & Coatsworth, saloon men; Van S. Curtis, blacksmith and wagon maker; E. H. King, sawmill man on Rattlesnake creek.

As before stated, Harney was designated as temporary county seat by the act which created Harney county, and it made a desperate struggle to retain the honors and advantages accruing to the county's official center. It failed, however, though many of its citizens still believe in the justice of their cause in that contest and feel that the county seat was not fairly won by Burns.

Since its defeat in the struggle Harney has not grown rapidly, indeed it is hardly as lively a town as it was twelve years ago. It has had several fires which have done considerable damage, but never a general conflagration. In 1894 a lamp exploded in the Pacific Hotel, and

several buildings were destroyed · in· consequence. The next year Waldenberg's and Price
Wither's stores were burned, also Buckland's
and George Tregaskes' saloons and Snodgrass' livery barn. Louis Waldenberg, Jr.,
built a store in the place of his uncle's destroyed one; a saloon was moved on to Buckland's lot, and another was put on the site of
the destroyed livery barn, so that Price Withers's store was the only business not replaced
in some way.

A business register of the town at present
would include the general merchandise stores
of Fred Haines and Seth Bower & Company;
the blacksmith shops of Seth Bower and
Charles Crawford; the Hotel Harney, owned
by William Russell, and the Tremont, owned
by Charles Roper; the carpenter shop of R.
Everett; and the saloon of Charles Rand.

Two years ago a fine city hall was built and
last summer a beautiful and commodious
schoolhouse. These, with the few residences,
constitute about the only developments which
have taken place since the buildings which replaced those destroyed by fire were finished.

An excellent graded school is maintained
in Harney and there is a church building belonging to the Presbyterian denomination, in
which both the Burns preachers hold services.

LAWEN.

This is a small town in the Malheur lake
country. It has several business establishments
and is growing steadily. Its population, according to the last census, was 27. Other villages and settlements, in which postoffices have
been started are Andrews, Crane, Denio, Diamond, Egli, Narrows, Riley, Shirk, Silvies,
Smith, Van and Venator.

DREWSEY.

Situated near the southern boundary of
what was the Malheur Indian reservation, in
the center of a stock raising and agricultural
community of no little importance, is Drewsey,
one of the four chief towns of Harney county.
Its inception is coeval with the opening of the
reservation, and to the influx of people resulting from the removal of the red men its owes
its existence. Messrs. E. E. Perrington and A.
Robbins were the first to take advantage of
the opportunity for profitable trade incident to
the new regime. They opened a general merchandise store in 1883. The same year a postoffice was established, with Mr. Perrington as
postmaster. Next came S. T. Childs, the first
village blacksmith, and in 1884 was established
the first saloon. During the fall of that year
McAfee & Bales built a hotel, a saloon and a
livery stable. They succeeded to the business
interests of the pioneer vendor of liquors, who
shot a man in a quarrel and was compelled to
become a fugitive from justice. Hardly was
the hotel of McAfee & Bales completed when
it fell a victim to the fire demon. Thomas
Howard resolved to avail himself of the opportunity afforded by this accident to establish
a profitable business, so he erected what became known as the Elkhorn hotel. In 1885 a
man named Lessing started another store; Al
Jones became the saloon man of the town in
place of McAfee & Bales, retired, and Joseph
Bales, of this firm, put up another hotel, which,
in 1888, was purchased by Thomas Howard
and moved away.

After the impetus given to the building of
the town by the settlement of the reservation
had spent its force, the growth of Drewsey was at an end until 1897, in which year
A. I. Johnson & Brother built a general
merchandise store, M. M. McDonald and
William Altnow a saloon, and Annie Robertson the City hotel. New structures have
been erected at different times since, among
them the I. O. O. F. hall, built in 1899.
At the time of the writer's visit, in the
fall of 1902, evidences were not wanting
that a healthy development was in progress.

Though there has never been a general conflagration in Drewsey, fire has on several occasions wrought its work of destruction, the last business building to fall before its fury being the old Elkhorn hotel.

A register of the present business houses of the town would include the Bartlett Hotel; the City Hotel, owned by J. W. Ward; general merchandise stores, J. D. Daly and A. I. Johnson & Brother; livery stables, Williams & Drewett and J. A. Bartlett, that of the latter having been erected this summer; saloons, J. A. Weatherly and E. Olson; blacksmith shops, Jesse Brunner and R. B. Johnson; a money order postoffice, H. J. Clark, postmistress. Near

the town is a grist mill, which was built in 1896, and is said to be supplied with good, modern machinery. Though designed for water power, it was run by steam one fall. Owing to some complications about the ditch in which it was intended to convey the water to the mill, the plant has been idle for several years, but the property is thought to have recently passed into the hands of A. W. Gowan, of Burns, who is considering the advisability of putting it in operation again. Should he do so a great impetus will be given to the wheat raising industry of the country contiguous to Drewsey.

JOHN D. DALY.

BIOGRAPHICAL.

JOHN D. DALY.—It is with pleasure that we are permitted to write concerning the talented and enterprising business man whose name appears above, since he is one of those men of honor and stability who form the real strength of any community, and since he is numbered as one of the leading business men of the county of Harney, and has here and elsewhere achieved a success which is very gratifying both in the results to him individually and in the general business world of eastern Oregon, where he has operated.

Mr. Daly was born in Canyon City, Oregon, on May 13, 1866, being the son of Eugene and Mary A. (Donohoe) Daly. His parents were natives of County Cork, Ireland, and came to the United States in 1862, locating in Boston, whence in 1863 they came via Panama, to California, and in 1864 came on to Canyon City. His father died in 1881 and the mother died in 1897. Our subject grew up in Canyon City, gaining a good education from the schools there and at the age of sixteen years started on a course of teaching, wherein he made a commendable record. He gained sufficient money by this labor to pay his way at college, and he attended at Santa Clara, California. In the fall of 1890, he came to Drewsey and in partnership with Abner Robbins started a general merchandise establishment, which has since been one of the leading business houses of the county and is operated under the firm name of Daly & Robbins. They commenced with a small stock of goods, labored hard and have built up a fine trade, because of their wise methods and because of the manifestation of integrity and uprightness in all their ways. They have a large stock of all kinds of goods from dry goods, clothing, furnishings, boots and shoes, crockery, groceries, and feed to lumber, hardware, and machinery and implements. In addition to this fine business, Mr. Daly and his partner are among the leading financiers of the section, being largely interested in the First National Bank of Ontario, and the First National Bank at Burns, Oregon. Our subject is the president of both of these institutions and they are in a flourishing condition and well established. The firm also handles a sawmill, twenty-two miles north from Drewsey, and Mr. Daly has about one-half dozen ranches of value in various parts of the country, and he manages this large amount of business with marked wisdom and discretion, putting into the entire lines energy and vigor which are characteristic of his own personality.

Mr. Daly was married on May 5, 1894, to Daisy O., daughter of Joseph and Emeline (McAtee) Robertson, and three children have been born to them, as follows: Mary E., born June 18, 1895; Eunice M., born July 25, 1897; Abner R., born September 10, 1899. Mr. Robertson was a native of Scotland, came to Illinois, and thence in 1860 to Jackson county, Oregon, crossing the plains with ox teams. They were six months making the trip having to fight the Indians considerably. In 1863 he came to Grant county and to Harney in 1889. Mrs. Daly was born near Canyon City, Oregon, on February 5, 1875.

Fraternally Mr. Daly is affiliated with the A. F. & A. M., Burns Lodge, No. 97, and the A. O. U. W., Drewsey Lodge, No. 119. He dwells in a fine modern residence of nine rooms, over which his estimable wife presides with a graciousness and dignity that are becoming.

JOSEPH P. RECTOR.—Among those who have gained a remarkable success in Harney county we are constrained to mention the gentleman whose name initiates this paragraph, and who has wrought with such wisdom, energy and assiduity that he has gained one of the finest holdings of the county and is numbered among the leading stockmen of this section. This is more to his credit when it is mentioned that he came to the county with no means and has gained his entire property by his thrift and wise management since his advent.

Joseph P. was born in Schenectady county, New York, on August 28, 1844, being the son of Matthew H. and Ruth Rector. He grew up on a farm and gained his education from the adjacent schools. In 1869 he came west as far as the railroad ran and then took wagon transportation to the terminus of the Central Pacific and came to San Francisco. He soon located in Humboldt county and for several years engaged in farming and dairying. Then he transferred his residence to Palisade, Nevada, and engaged in raising stock. In 1880 he came to Harney valley and worked for wages for a time and then located his present place, fifteen miles northeast from Lawen and as many miles southeast from Harney. He devoted his attention to raising stock, cattle and horses, and he has been attended with fine success. He now has one thousand acres of fine land, all fenced and well improved. He has a fine grove, excellent orchard and devotes much of his land to raising hay. His industry and thrift account for the success that he enjoys. His ranch is known all over the country as the Crow Camp ranch. The reason for this is that in the early days a Mr. Rankin Crow, who was herding stock for Todhunter & Devine, discovered the excellent springs located at this point and also the abundance of good grass all about, which resulted from the fertility of the soil and the generous supply of pure water free from alkali, and he made it his headquarters for a long time. Then the soldiers from Camp Harney took their stock to this place. Since that time it has been known as the Crow Camp ranch and it one of the finest stock ranches in this portion of the state. Mr. Rector manifested his excellent judgment in securing it and making it a permanent location. Mr. Rector is esteemed by all and stands well throughout the county. He has always kept within the realm of the celibate, and chooses rather the quiet and comfort of that life to the cares of connubiality.

◆◆◆

MARY A. MILLER, familiarly known by all as "Grandma Miller," is one of the lovable elderly ladies of our county and it is especially gratifying to have the opportunity to append an epitome of her career in this the abiding chronicles of Harney county. She is a woman of many virtues and graces and has done a noble part in the life of the pioneer and she has many friends who admire her real worth of character, her faithful life, and her own rare qualities of intrinsic worth. She is now making her home with her daughter, Mrs. Jane Poujade, who is the wife of one of the leading stockmen of Harney county and whose comfortable and commodious residence is six miles east from Harney, on what is known as Cow creek ranch.

Mrs. Miller was born in Richland county, Ohio, on September 29, 1827, and at the age of eleven went with her parents to Henry county, Iowa. There she married Mr. Isaac H. Jones, on October 26, 1845. They removed to Boone county, Iowa, where Mr. Jones died on June 27, 1860. In 1862 Mr. married William Miller and in 1863, with five children, they started across the plains with ox teams for the Pacific coast. The arduous and trying journey was completed when they landed in Salem. There Mr. Miller engaged in raising stock for three years and then removed to the Rogue river valley, where he continued in raising stock and farming until the time of his death, which sad event occurred on June 6, 1886. Since that time, Mrs. Miller sold the property and has come to reside with her daughter, as mentioned above.

By her first husband there were born to Mrs. Miller, five children, named as follows: Albert J., deceased; Mrs. Elizabeth J. Lu, of Baker City; Mrs. Amy A. McIntyre, deceased; George W., near Portland; Charles W., deceased. By her second marriage she had four children, Mrs. Mary Savage, of Burns; Mrs. Jane Poujade, near Harney; John C., deceased; Frank S., near Burns. Mrs. Miller has always lived on the frontier and she has done a

noble part in the advancement of civilization
into the wilds of the various frontier regions.
She is hearty and well now, and remarks that
she loves to dwell in a new country, thus showing the admirable pluck, courage, and spirit of
which she is possessed. She is beloved by all,
and her pilgrim years have been crowded with
good deeds and now she is enjoying the golden
years of life in comfort and happiness.

MARTIN V. SMITH.—A veritable pio-
neer of the pioneers is Mr. Smith, having come
to the Pacific coast in the early fifties and continued here in worthy labors in various lines
since that time, ever displaying the same courage, capabilities, tenacity of purpose, and integrity, that have made the pioneers such a
noble class of people. Mr. Smith was born in
Kennebec county, Maine, on January 10, 1833,
being the son of James and Hannah Smith,
natives also of Maine, the father being born
near Portland. His death also occurred in that
state. Martin V. received a good schooling
and remained with his parents until 1853, when
he went to New York and stepped aboard of
one of the Vanderbilt ships, that took him to
Nicaragua, whence he went to San Francisco
and soon we see him in the mines delving with
the vigor and strength of young manhood for
the hidden gold. Five years he labored there
and then went to Yuba county and took up
farming and stock raising. The hard winter
of 1861-62 killed all his stock and he went to
freighting from Marysville to various points
in California and Nevada. In 1873 he went
to Butte county and settled on one of Judge O.
C. Pratt's grants and went to farming. His
landlord was the first territorial governor of
California. Mr. Smith was successful in this
venture and continued until 1880, when he
went to the foot hills in Butte county and engaged in gardening and fruit raising until
1884. Then he freighted until 1886 and came
overland to Silver creek, Harney county. He
entered land and took up stock raising until
1892, then traded his ranch for his present
home place, two miles south from Lawen,
which consists of one quarter of fine hay land
and is well improved. He handles cattle
mostly.

On January 28, 1864, Mr. Smith married
Miss Mary E. Kennedy, in Yuba county, and
two children were born to them, Othniel, deceased; Izora, wife of Scott Hayes, near
Lawen. In August, 1867, at Marysville, Mr.
Smith was called to mourn the death of his
wife. On Thanksgiving day, 1876, Mr. Smith
married Sarah (Linn) Gorman in Butte county, California, and two children have been born
to them: Ada L., wife of Charles T. Miller,
near Lawen; Otto V., of Tulare county, California.

It is of note that Mr. Smith was one of the
delegates to the war convention in California,
from Yuba county and the times were exciting
as many were for the south. Mr. Smith was
a stanch Union man. In religious persuasion,
Mr. Smith is allied with the Universalists. In
1900 he was appointed as census enumerator
in Harney county. He is a man of good standing, and now is passing the days of the golden
years of his life in the enjoyment of his portion in peace, being beloved and esteemed by
his associates and acquaintances.

ISADORE L. POUJADE.—This promi-
nent citizen and leading stockman of Harney
county is one of the men who deserves to be
accorded space in the history of the county
because of his worth, because of his uprightness, integrity and probity, and because of the
excellent work that he has accomplished in the
upbuilding and progress of the county.

Mr. Poujade was born in Marion county,
Oregon, on December 8, 1857, being the son of
Andrew and Matilda (Clinger) Poujade. At
the age of fifteen he went to Jackson county
with his parents, with whom he resided until
1880. He gained his education in these places
and also a wealth of excellent training in the
practical walks of life and in raising stock and
in farming. In 1880 he came to Harney valley and engaged as foreman for Todhunter &
Devine. Six years were spent in this responsible position, and then he engaged in partnership with Charles W. Jones, in the stock business. They purchased what is known as the
Cow Creek ranch. This estate consists of
eight hundred acres of fine meadow land, six
miles east from Harney, and is improved with

a fine dwelling of twelve rooms, good shop, barns, corralls, fences and all implements for handling a first-class stock and hay ranch. After the death of Mr. Jones Mr. Poujade purchased all the stock, but owns the ranch in partnership with Mrs. Jones, the widow of his late partner. Mr. Poujade is one of the prosperous stockmen of the county, and has demonstrated his ability to so conduct the affairs of business that a crowning success is his to enjoy.

On May 20, 1888, Mr. Poujade married Miss Jane Miller, and to them have been born five children: Lulu Ivy, Verna Lee, Mary Matilda, Floy Willina and Amy Girtrude. Mr. Poujade stands well among his fellows, has earned the prestige that he enjoys and Harney county is favored to have domiciled within her borders such men of talent, integrity and faithfulness.

MÉLVIN FENWICK.—A true pioneer, a man of exemplary standing and life, possessed of capabilities and qualities of worth, the estimable gentleman of whom we now speak, is entitled to representation in the volume of Harney county's history. His parents, Alexander and Nancy (Long) Fenwick, were natives of Kentucky, and his father crossed the plains to California in 1849. He was a blacksmith and carried his tools on a pack horse and wrought at his trade, shoeing horses, and so forth, all the way. In 1851 he returned via Panama, and with his wife and seven children he came in 1852 to Amador county, California. There our subject was born on May 18, 1855, being the ninth child. The family removed to Napa county in 1858, and in August, 1865, came thence to Lane county, Oregon. There the father remained until his death in 1883. It was in February of that year that Melvin came to the Harney valley. He entered land at his present home place four miles north from Burns, and has engaged in farming and raising stock there since that time, being favored with abundant success on account of his industry and perseverance. He now owns five hundred acres of land, well improved and skillfully tilled. He formerly handled hogs, but is now devoting his attention to cattle mostly. When Mr. Fenwick came here there was but one house where Burns now stands, and settlers were very few in the country. Bacon cost

thirty-five cents per pound and flour ten cents. Mr. Fenwick put up the first barbed wire fence in the valley, the year being 1884 when this was done.

The marriage of Mr. Fenwick and Miss Jennie, daughter of Arthur and Mary Wallace, who were natives of Kentucky and came to Oregon in 1876, was solemnized on September 22, 1889. In political matters Mr. Fenwick was allied with the Democratic party, but at the time of McKinley's election he voted for that worthy man and has since cast his vote with the Republican party. In 1872 and 1873 Mr. Fenwick enlisted to assist in quelling the Modocs, he being in Captain Roger's Company E, of Oregon militia. Mr. Fenwick has quitted himself in all the various relations of the frontiersman in a commendable manner and he stands high among his fellows to-day and is a worthy citizen of our county.

It is not right to close this article without a special mention of one item that has had much bearing on the general history of the county of Harney and in which Mr. Fenwick took a leading part, though it cost him much effort and money to do so. Early in 1887 fifty-eight of the small farmers of the county banded together and formed a corporation known as the Harney Valley Dam and Ditch and Irrigation Company. The purpose was to divert the water from the Silvies river to irrigate their barren lands. Labor and money were freely expended by all these hard working men until the dam and ditches were all completed. At that juncture W. B. Todhunter, one of the cattle kings of Harney county, commenced suit against this company and secured injunctions stopping proceedings of their work and project. The shareholders were poor people and fifty of the fifty-eight threw up their shares and quit the field. Some men's mettle is shown only the better when in the face of desperate opposition, and so in this case. Mr. Fenwick saw the crisis, the wonderful amount depending on the issue and so threw himself into the breach and fought, supported by the other seven, with such desperate and telling force and manifestation of right and demand for justice that after three years of severely contested litigation, Todhunter threw up his case and victory was gained for the common people once more. Twelve thousand dollars and more were spent in the fight of this unreasonable opposition to proper improvement, and it is with great pleasure that we can chron_ icle that this move and worthy stand on Mr. Fenwick's part was entirely successful, and it has materially changed the history of Harney county, and it is the entering of the wedge that will allow Harney county to become one of the leading political divisions of the west, for the sullen and avaricious heel of monopoly can not and shall not forever stay the way of the chariot of progress and development. Mr. Fenwick is now and has been secretary of this company from its incipiency and he is a man of resolution and ability and has nobly cleared the way for further improvement and advnce_ ment.

——◆◆◆——

FRANK BAKER.—This native young Oregonian has demonstrated what pluck and perseverance can do when manipulated with wise management in the things of the financial world, as conditions obtained in this country, having made a brilliant success, as will be noted from the following.

Mr. Baker was born in Lane county, Ore_ gon, on June 20, 1870, being the son of George and Mary (Watson) Baker. His mother died in that county and the father with his children removed to Washington county in 1874. In the fall of 1878 he came with his family to Harney valley, settling where the town of Burns is now located. The children were three boys and two girls. The father went to freighting and soon died, thus leaving the little group orphans in a frontier region. Our sub_ ject had but little opportunity to gain an edu_ cation from schools, but made the best of what he did have and also by careful and diligent re_ search qualified himself for the battle of life. He soon went to riding the range for wages and continued diligently at this occupation un_ til 1894, when he started in for himself, hand_ ling stock. He gained steadily and in 1898 he purchased his present place of one hundred and sixty acres three miles northeast from Burns, which is a well improved ranch, pro_ ducing abundant crops of hay for his stock, which consists mostly of cattle.

The marriage of Mr. Baker and Miss Grace, daughter of Milton and Eliza Riggs, was solemnized on December 15, 1896, and two children have been born to them, Lulu and

Frank. Mr. Riggs was an early pioneer of Oregon and died in Burns in 1895, while his widow still lives there.

Mr. Baker has, unaided, and by his own efforts of industry and skill, gained a fine prop_ erty holding and bids fair to be one of the leading property owners in the county. He has always manifested with these fine quali_ ties mentioned a becoming stability and integ_ rity and he is counted by all as a reliable, up_ right and stanch young man.

——◆◆◆——

WILLIAM L. CLARK.—Among the suc_ cessful business men of Harney county is to be mentioned the gentleman named above, whose well known establishment of general merchan_ dise at Lawen, where he has done business for some time, is one of the prosperous business houses of the county; and in addition to hand_ ling this, Mr. Clark has a hay farm of one hundred and sixty acres, which he attends to and also raises cattle, and also he has been a mail contractor of the interior of Oregon.

William L. was born in Carroll county, In_ diana, on April 3, 1845, being the son of Thomas and Ann (Davidson) Clark. In the spring of 1853, the father started across the plains with his family in an ox train from Car_ roll county, Indiana. They made the trip suc_ cessfully, but the last six weeks they had to live on the flesh of the oxen they killed, without even the luxury of salt. Fresh meat with water for six weeks is not so pleasant as might be imagined. They came through the Harney valley and settled in Lane county, near Eu_ gene. The remaining oxen ate poison weeds in the valley and all died. The father took a donation claim, and, being a miller, wrought at his trade in Eugene as well as handled his farm. He died in Eugene in December, 1896, and the mother died in 1899. On April 6, 1865, William L. enlisted in Company K, First Oregon Volunteers, under Captain A. B. Ingra_ ham, to fight the Piutes and the Snake In_ dians. He was in one battle on the middle fork of the Malheur and one on the south fork of the John Day. He was in the service for one year and did scout duty most of the time. He covered the entire portion of eastern Oregon and did valuable work. Being honorably dis_ charged at the close of the conflict, he went home, and there on February 12, 1867, he married Nancy E., daughter of William and Irene Ogle. The father was a soldier in the Union army and is living in Missouri. Mrs. Clark came across the plains with an uncle in 1864. Mr. Clark learned the wagonmaker's trade at Springfield and wrought at that after his marriage. In 1880 he went to Eagle Point in the Rogue river valley and worked at his trade and then returned to Lane county, where he did the same labor. It was in 1885 that he came to Harney valley and entered a homestead near Lawen. He has it well improved and handles stock and raises hay. In 1898 he took the contract of carrying the mail from Burns to Crane, which ended on July 1, 1902. In 1900 he engaged in the general merchandise business in Lawen, and owns a block of lots with his store buildings and also a residence there. He does a good business and is fast working up a first class patronage.

To Mr. and Mrs. Clark there have been born six children, named as follows: Mrs. Irena A. Way, of Klamath county, Oregon; Mrs. Bertha A. Johnson, near Lawen; Mrs. Viola J. Page, of Coos county, Oregon; George W., Ira B., Thomas R.

———————◆◆◆———————

IRA STUBBLEFIELD.—A man of great adaptability, with vigor to carry him through his various undertakings, and wisdom to guide him in the safe path, and, withal, possessed of executive force to manipulate enterprises with success, the subject of this article is a man to whom we gladly accord representation in this volume of Harney county history. He was born in Blanco county, Texas, on April 28, 1866, being the son of W. K. and Eliza (Lumas) Stubblefield. The father of our subject was born in Tennessee, October 30, 1816, and at the age of fourteen went to Bolivar, Missouri, and in his twentieth year he went to Texas and lived in twenty-three different counties in that state. He was on the frontier all of the time and did much hunting and scouting and fought the Indians continually. He was with the noted cattle king, Bob Tout, and the two doubtless slew more Indians when the savages were on the murderous raids than any other men of the country. At one time eight white men, including Mr. Stubblefield and Bob

Tout, were attacked by Indians, seventeen in number, and all of the whites fled but Stubblefield and Tout and two companions, and they fought the savages to a finish, completely whipping them. Mr. Stubblefield was in many a battle and skirmish with the treacherous savage and always came out victorious. In 1868 he went to Carroll county, Arkansas, and bought a farm and settled down until 1885, when he came to Walla Walla, thence to Portland, then to Lagrande and finally to the Imnaha country, where he raised stock. In 1896 he sold his property and moved to Enterprise and started a livery stable, where he is doing a good business at the present time. He is eighty-six years of age, well preserved and hearty. In his younger days he shouldered and carried five hundred and sixty pounds of iron on a bet of twenty-five dollars. He was always a quiet man but never found any one who could withstand him in a struggle. During his life Mr. Stubblefield married six times, each wife dying a natural death, the last one passing away on the Imnaha. He is the father of twenty-six children, fourteen of whom are living, named as follows: Mrs. Martha Mickle, of Boundary county, Texas; Thomas, in Indian territory; Mrs. Sarah White, of Boone county, Arkansas; Jasper, in Nebraska; Mrs. Christina Blue, in Stone county, Missouri, born on Clear creek, Blanco county, Texas, on January 22, 1864, being a full sister of our subject; Ira, the subject of this sketch, now in Harney county; William and Mickle, in Wallowa county; Mrs. Eliza Newell, of Burns; Haymon, of Wallowa county; Mrs. Lydda Rowley, of Union county; Fancho, Newell and Breman, in Wallowa county.

Returning more particularly to our subject, we note that he came to Wallowa county in 1886 and to Burns in 1888, where he bought and sold stock, taking a band to the Willamette valley. On September 23, 1890, Mr. Stubblefield married Miss Ettie, daughter of Jefferson and Emily (Smith) Byerly. The father came across the plains in 1846, from Illinois, and settled in the Willamette valley, so Mrs. Stubblefield is a native-born Oregonian. Mr. Stubblefield took his young wife to Chico, California, thence to Lagrande, Enterprise, The Dalles, Prineville and Burns, arriving here in 1892. In 1893 he went to Newport, Oregon, and in 1894 to Garfield county, Washington, thence to Whitman county, then to Wallowa county, and in June, 1899, he returned to Burns, having been trading and buying and selling stock, etc., on all these trips, in which he did well. He bought a place near Burns and in the spring of 1902 he sold and bought his present home place, six miles northeast from Burns, where he has a quarter section of good land, well improved, and gives his attention to tilling it and raising stock. He also owns another quarter near by. To Mr. and Mrs. Stubblefield there have been born four children: Christnia died in Wallowa county; Peach, born August 16, 1896, in Colton, Whitman county, Washington; Fancho, born April 1, 1898; Ruth, born February, 1901.

* * *

JAMES P. DICKENSON has gained a good success in material things in Harney county since his advent here and is one of the substantial and leading stockmen and farmers to-day. He and his family have two good hay farms near the Narrows and also three near Lawen. These fine tracts of land return him annually large amounts of hay and give him opportunity to handle many head of stock.

James P. was born in Grayson county, Virginia, on February 18, 1842, being the son of John and Rosa (Hale) Dickenson. He grew up on the farm and gained his education from the common schools, and in the spring of 1861 he enlisted in Company C, Forty-fifth Virginia, as second lieutenant under General John B. Floyd. He was in the battles of Wytheville, Parisburg, Big Sewell Mountain and Carnifax Ferry, besides many skirmishes. At the end of the year for which he enlisted he retired from the army and went home and was chosen tax collector for Grayson county. Eighteen months later he enlisted in the Twenty-second Virginia Cavalry and took part in the battles of Lynchburg and Luray valley, at which last place his horse was shot from under him and he was captured. He languished in the war prison at Point Lookout, Maryland, until the close of the war, July, 1865. The treatment was severe in the prison. He returned to Grayson county, and in February, 1866, he married Miss Laura A. Milton. He engaged in farming and stockraising until 1872, then came via San Francisco and Portland to Linn county.

Oregon. There he farmed until 1888, and then migrated to Crook county, and in 1889 came near to Lawen. He entered a homestead on the Malheur lake and took up raising stock. He has gained title to the land mentioned above and he has a fine band of stock. He resides at Lawen and is a worthy and progressive citizen. Mr. Dickenson is a member of the Stock Association of Harney Valley. To Mr. and Mrs. Dickenson there have been born three children, Mrs. Effie M. Syrne, of Burns; Guy E., at Lawen; Mrs. Rosa C. Kern, of Lawen.

* * *

THOMAS HOWARD.—This substantial and capable gentleman is one of the real builders of the county of Harney, and it is quite proper that he should be accorded representation in its history, being a man greatly respected and worthy of the high esteem given to him. He was born in the city of New York, on May 11, 1833, being the son of Patrick H. and Mary (Ford) Howard. The father was an engineer, operating a stationary engine. Thomas grew to manhood, gaining a good education meanwhile, and part of the time working in the markets, where he learned the butcher trade. In the memorable 'forty-nine he was one of the gold seekers, going from New York on a steamer to Panama and thence to San Francisco on a sailing vessel. The trip was hot and tedious, being two months from Panama to the Golden Gate. He mined for a time and then went at his trade in Marysville and other places in the state. It was in 1859 that he went to Carson and Virginia Cities, Nevada, and there operated at his trade, and also wrought in Esmeraldo. In the spring of 1862 Mr. Howard was hired at a wage of one hundred dollars per month to accompany a herd of cattle belonging to Job Dye to Florence, Idaho. The water around Harney lake being so high that it was impossible to make headway, they were turned aside, not knowing the route they were taking, and came where Canyon City now stands. They discovered the first gold on the creek and their band of cattle were the first cattle that were driven into this section. The first gold that they discovered on Canyon creek went as high as one dollar per pan. Mr. Howard butchered the first beef in Canyon country, and the meat sold at thirty cents per pound.

They went to Auburn and the cattle were left on Powder river and there part of them were butchered and the balance driven to Boise. In 1864 Mr. Howard was nominated for sheriff of Wasco county on the Democratic ticket, but was defeated. However, he carried his portion of the county by a large majority. While stumping the county he was on his way to Rock creek with two men who were going to The Dalles. They had the express, about ten thousand dollars of dust, and Mr. Howard had two hundred ounces of dust with him. They were attacked by Indians, who shot his horse and headed off the express men, who were running away with the mules. All the saddles, canteens, purses, etc., were taken, but the dust was left, the Indians not seeming to know its value. They were shot at a number of times, but the savages seemed poor marksmen. Mr. Howard got a party of men to go back with him and he secured nearly all of his gold.

After Grant county was cut off from Wasco Mr. Howard was elected in 1866 sheriff on the Democratic ticket, being the first incumbent of that office in the county, serving six years, and was nominated for the fourth time but removed from the county before the election.

The marriage of Mr. Howard and Mrs. Shinn, a native of Illinois, was celebrated on April 18, 1865. Mrs. Shinn had been a pioneer of 1861. After leaving Grant county Mr. Howard traveled to various places and then returned to that county, and in 1883 he came to his present place, four and one-half miles west from Drewsey. He entered land and went to the commendable labor of improving and he has been numbered with the leading men of the county since his advent here. Mr. Howard now has a fine estate of one section, and plenty of water for irrigating purposes.

This worthy couple have one son, Edward J., who lives at home.

<hr/>

WILLIAM HENRY CANADAY.—It is fitting that in a work that purports to accord to the leading citizens of Harney county representation there should be special mention of the well known business man whose name heads this article and who has labored in our midst for a number of years, gaining a good success and making for himself a name and standing which are enviable.

Madison Canaday was born in Hillsboro, Highland county, Ohio, on October 21, 1831, and when a boy went with his parents to Illinois and thence to Iowa, whence they crossed the plains with ox teams in 1852. They settled in Douglas county, Oregon, the parents taking a donation claim. Later they removed to Yam Hill county. Miss Sarah E. Abbott was born near Springfield, Missouri, in 1842, and started across the plains with ox teams in 1852, having traveled to Texas and returned to Missouri in 1844. The train was a large one and the dreaded cholera attacked them and her father was the first victim to succumb to that terrible disease, passing away on June 9. Before the journey was completed the mother died also, the date being September 30, and she sleeps near where Baker City now stands. Thus from the happy eastern home this child was left an orphan on the dreary plains. She came on to Yam Hill county, Oregon. There she met and married Madison Canaday, the date of this happy wedding being 1857. In 1860 they went to Douglas county, and in 1862 to Lane county, where our subject was born on May 26, 1863. They still live in that county, near the old homestead place, and are honored and respected citizens. William H. was reared in Eugene, in Lane county, and there received his education. He also learned sawmilling and became head sawyer. In 1883 he went to Weston, Umatilla county, and there learned the art of the photographer. He bought the gallery later and removed it to Heppner, where he did business for a time and then returned to Lane county. He worked at his trade and in a sawmill there for a time. In 1887 he came to Longcreek, in Grant county, and there did business in a gallery, after which he came to Drewsey. He built a gallery there and then came to Burns, where he opened the first gallery in the town. This was in the fall of 1887. He has continued in the county since that time. In addition to his business he entered land, and later sold it, and also has operated at the saw milling business some.

On December 22, 1897, in Portland, Mr. Canaday married Miss Mary C., daughter of Silas W. and Elizabeth McMurphy, natives of Canada and Ohio and born July 6, 1836, and May, 1841, respectively. They were early pioneers from Iowa to California, and in 1885 they came to Harney valley, where they now live. Mrs. Canaday was born in California, on January 26, 1872. To Mr. and Mrs. Canaday two children have been born, Ambrose W., born July 4, 1899; Sylvester M., born June 3, 1901. Mr. Canaday is past grand in the I. O. O. F., Harney Lodge No. 77, of Burns, while he and his wife belong to the Rebekahs.

WALLACE McCLAIN. — This well-known and representative business man and patriotic citizen of Harney county is one of the firm of McClain & Biggs, liverymen and dealers in horses and mules in Burns, where their stables are, being also owners of a fine stock ranch. Our subject was born in Scotland county, Missouri, on September 16, 1854, being the son of Martin and Sarah (Childers) McClain. The father was in the Confederate army and in the battle of Pea Ridge lost his right arm. He served under Price. In 1866 the family removed to Schuyler county and our subject was educated in these two localities and he remained with his parents until 1875, when he went to Waterloo, Iowa, and took up the grocery business. In 1877 he went to Elk City, Kansas, and the next year he came to San Francisco, and thence by steamer, George M. Elder, to Portland and soon he was in Linn county. He was engaged in a flouring mill until 1881 and then came to Summerville, Union county, and freighted from Umatilla to Idaho.   It was 1883 when he came to the Silvies valley, engaging with Lux & Miller, stockmen. He took a train of twenty-one cars of cattle to Chicago and another to Omaha and was foreman of the company until he met with an accident of falling under a wagon, which unfitted him for the arduous labors of a stock foreman. This was 1886, and he went into business in Drewsey and in 1889 Mr. McClain married Mrs. Eva (Robertson) Whittle and then moved to Umatilla county. He took up the business of making and selling ties, took land, operated a store and butcher shop. also ran a butcher shop in Pasco, Washington, continuing in these lines until 1897, when he sold out and came to Burns. He opened a hotel and livery stable and in 1900 he sold the hotel and entered into partnership with John W. Biggs, and they are

now handling a general horse and mule market in addition to their livery business.   They handle more stock than any company in the county and are leaders in their line. They own fine stables and a full quota of rigs and good stock.

Fraternally Mr. McClain is affiliated with the W. of W., being council commander of Harney Valley Camp, No. 381, in Burns. Mr. and Mrs. McClain have one child, Harry Goulden. It is of note that Mr. McClain was special deputy sheriff under W. J. Furnish in Umatilla county and was one of twelve invited to see the hanging of a noted criminal, "Zoon," in Pendleton. Mr. McClain is well known throughout the county and is respected by all and stands high both in business circles and in the social realm.

N. E. DUNCAN.—It is with pleasure that we are enabled to write concerning the estimable gentleman whose name is at the head of this article, since he has been one of the potent factors in the development of Harney county, has manifested wisdom and enterprise in all his ways here, has labored as a true pioneer in many other sections of the country and has always manifested the same unswerving integrity, moral uprightness and sound principles, having sustained a reputation as an exceptionally reliable man, and ever arraigned on the side of right.

Mr. Duncan was born in Williamson county, Illinois, on March 27, 1838, being the son of Dudley W. and Elizabeth Duncan.   On April 16, 1859, Mr. Duncan started to New Orleans on the Panama route to California. He had an adventurous spirit and was ready to grapple with the hard problems of pioneer life and has since proved himself of the right kind of stuff.   He stopped five days on the way, at Havana, and then landed in San Francisco on May 16. He worked for wages until the fall of 1861, then went by steamer to Portland, Oregon.   On April 16, 1863, he started to Auburn, Baker county, arriving there on the 16th of May, and for fifteen years he was numbered with the hardy and worthy miners of that vicinity. It was 1878 that he came to upper Willow creek and took up ranching. In 1884 he came thence to the vicinity of

Drewsey, and there engaged in- farming and stock raising. He took raw land, two hundred and forty acres, and made of it a fine farm, and was successful in raising stock. Later he sold the farm and neat stock and handled sheep and horses exclusively. In 1899 he sold his entire property holdings in this section and retired for a time from active business. He is at present continuing this retired life. Fraternally he is affiliated with the I. O. O. F., Drewsey Lodge, No. 147. Mr. Duncan was nominated 'for county commissioner on the Republican ticket, and notwithstanding his protests he was elected, but refused to qualify. Mr. Duncan has never ventured on the matrimonial sea, but is enjoying the quieter placidity of the celebate. He is a man of unquestioned integrity and stands high in the estimation of the people.

GEORGE W. PAGE.—Among the leading stockmen of the country, the subject of this article also stands with the prominent and substantial citizens of the county of Harney and is one of the real pioneers of this section, being also a westerner by birth. He owns Sonoma county, California, as his native place and February 13, 1858, is the date thereof. His parents were Joseph W. and Nancy (Johnson) Page. In 1867 they all came overland to Lane county, Oregon. The father had been operating a large dairy in California, and in Oregon he devoted his attention to farming, also raised stock. In 1884 our subject came to Harney county and operated a saw mill. After this he roved about in Idaho, Washington, and Oregon and in 1893 came to Harney county and engaged in the sheep business, entering into partnership with G. W. Bartlett. Later he sold out and then went into partnership with James Campbell. They divided up in 1901 and Mr. Page sold one-third interest to his brother, Edward N., and his nephew, Claud Hendricks. They own several thousand head of sheep and are prosperous in this business, being skilled in handling them. Mr. Page is a member of the I. O. O. F., Drewsey Lodge, No. 147. He is a man of public spirit, has always labored for the advancement of the county and is one of the promoters of substantial progress.

JAMES T. SIMMONS.—Among the arrivals in Harney county who have come from native places to identify themselves with this progressive region, we must not fail to mention the gentleman whose name is at the head of this article and who has wrought here with untiring energy and unflagging zeal in the line of stock raising, and in addition now handles the mail and stage line from Diamond to Andrews. Mr. Simmons was born in Berryville, Arkansas, on March 22, 1862, being the son of Isaac and Sarah Simmons. He grew up on a farm and received his education from the public schools and in 1877 went to Millville, California, afterward returning to Arkansas. It was in 1888 that he came to the Harney valley, and here at the Narrows, on January 1, 1893, he married Mrs. Mary A. Burneson, daughter of Albert and Mary Hembree, who are mentioned in this volume. To this happy union there were born two children, Alice Esma and Rose Alliene. By her former marriage Mrs. Simmons had two children, Charles Albert and Ira D. P. Mr. Simmons engaged in raising stock and handles the stage line in addition. His father was a captain in the Union army and died soon after the war was over.

Mr. Simmons is a man of sound principles and has won friends in his walk, being well known and respected by all.

ALBERT HEMBREE.—It is indeed very gratifying to be allowed to epitomize the career of this esteemed pioneer, being, as he is, one of the earliest pilgrims who ever crossed the dreary plains and rugged mountains toward the setting sun; and since that early date he has been identified with the progress and development of the great west, having ever done a worthy share where his lot has been cast. It will be of interest to chronicle some of the more definite details of this life and we note first that Mr. Hembree was born in Tennessee on April 23, 1833, being the son of Joel J. and Sarah Hembree. While a child he came with his parents to Dade county, Missouri, remaining there until the spring of 1843. In that spring they joined the famous train of four hundred wagons led by Captain and Jesse Applegate, and guided by the noted and beloved Dr. Whitman, which wound its way across the plains to the latter's home near Walla Walla. No roads were built and the work had to be done as they progressed. An incident of the journey illustrates the nature and courage of the man to whom, more than to any other single individual, we owe the opening of this vast territory, Dr. Whitman. While crossing the Platte our subject's mother and some other women were in one wagon and the teams became tangled up. Dr. Whitman saw the trouble which threatened death to the women and cried out, "Boys, are you going to let those women drown?" He at once sprang into the water and swam to the teams, straightened them out, and so saved the occupants of the wagon. The train divided in Oregon, our subject's parents going to Dr. Whitman's home, near Walla Walla, and thence to The Dalles and finally to Yam Hill county. There a donation claim was located and the worthy pioneers settled to develop the country. The father operated a store at Lafayette and later at McMinnville, where he died in 1867. The mother died in 1854. The father started across the plains with nine. children; one died en route and one was born on the way. Our subject grew up on the farm and in the store and acquired a good education and then went to teaching school. On December 28, 1854, he married Miss Mary, daughter of Calvin P. and Mary (Aladine) Pell. Mr. and Mrs. Pell were married in Holmes county, Ohio, where Mrs. Hembree was born on April 8, 1839. Mr. Pell moved to Missouri in 1840, and in 1852 came across the plains with a large ox train direct to the Willamette valley. Mr. Pell had two brothers, Gilbert and John, and their father, Nathaniel Pell, served in the Revolution. They descended from English lords.

In 1856 Mr. Hembree removed to Lane county and went to farming and raising stock. In 1886 he brought a band of stock to Harney county, settling on Poison creek. In 1891 he came to the Narrows and took a homestead and sold his cattle and engaged in mercantile business. In 1899 the store was burned, entailing a great loss. Since that time Mr. Hembree has been operating a hotel and livery stable and handling his farm. He also owns

the ranch on Poison creek. Mr. Hembree kept the postoffice for six years at the Narrows. To Mr. and Mrs. Hembree have been born nine children, as follows: Mrs. Mary A. Simmons; Mrs. Annie L. Hamilton; Mrs. Emma D. Moomaw; Mrs. Minnie E. Wooley; Eugene F.; John L., of Portland; Guy L., a merchant at Silver Creek; Mrs. Rose E. McGrath; Loren C. Mr. Hembree's uncle, Abraham Hembree, was a captain in the Indian war of 1855-6. Mr. Hembree and his estimable wife are worthy citizens of this county and have earned and enjoy in generous measure the esteem, confidence, good will and admiration of all who know them, being good people and worthy pioneers.

GEORGE M. STANCLIFT.—Surely the subject of this review has passed the various stages of all kinds of pioneer work, with its hardships, deprivations and dangers, while he has met each point with a calm determination to overcome and make his way through it all, which he has done in a most commendable manner, being now one of the stanch and upright men of Harney and one of its well-to-do citizens, having his home on one of the finest pieces of soil in central Oregon, the same being one hundred and fifty-three acres, one mile north from Burns, which forms the family home and is a good dividend producer.

Mr. Stanclift was born in Erie county, New York, on April 25, 1837, being the son of Reuben and Elvira (Adams) Stanclift. At the age of fifteen he went with the family to Cass county, Michigan, and thence to Berrien county, where his mother died. In February, 1855, he came via New York and Panama to San Francisco, crossing the Isthmus with the first through passenger train. On the sea they encountered great storms that made the passage unpleasant. Upon landing in California he went to the Poor creek country, and thence to Plumas county and mined. Yuba county he later took up mining and dairying together and in the spring of 1860 he went to the vicinity of Virginia City. But the second winter there his partner was killed by the Indians, and all the stock driven off by them, entailing a loss upon Mr. Stanclift of seven thousand dollars. He went to work for wages again and on January 8, 1867, he married Miss Mary C., daughter of Gabriel and Kitty A. Stephens, who were natives of Kentucky, their daughter also being born there; and they had removed to Missouri, where they died. Mrs. Stanclift came across the plains with an elder brother in 1853, the trip being exceptionally tedious. After his marriage Mr. Stanclift came by wagon to Douglas county, Oregon, and took up stock raising, the year being 1871. In 1876 he came to Harney valley with a band of cattle and in 1878 he removed his family over here, it being the year of the Bannock war. He was exposed to much danger and hardship, there being but eight families in the valley. He settled on his present place, and soon he sold his cattle and bought sheep and later sold them and confined himself to farming alone. To Mr. and Mrs. Stanclift have been born three children: Mrs. Etta Horton; Mrs. Laura P. Biggs, of Prineville; Lewis L., of Montana. It is of note that the grandfather of our subject, John Stanclift, fought in the Revolution, and was with Washington's army at Valley Forge.

W. D. MARTIN.—One half mile southeast from Harney is one of the finest small grain farms in the county. It consists of eighty. acres of choice land and is well under cultivation. The improvements are of a quality and kind quite fitting such an estate and its owner is the subject of this article. Mr. Martin was about the first man to try raising grain in this locality and he has made a marked success in this direction. He raised in 1901 the largest crop of any one man in Harney county and he is classed as one of the leading agriculturists of middle Oregon.

W. D. Martin was born in Walla Walla county, Washington, on February 13, 1865, being the son of John and Nancy (Owens) Martin. The parents came from the state of Iowa overland with ox teams direct to Walla Walla and the father took a ranch that joined Oregon, and within one hundred yards of the state line our subject was born. Soon after that event, the family removed to the Oregon side and dwelt in Umatilla county until 1885. W. D. was educated in the common schools

there and grew up on a farm, developing both his mental and physical powers in a becoming manner to a western born son. In 1885 he came to Baker county, near North Powder and on June 8, of that year, he married Miss Leorah, daughter of Jason and Margaret Wyatt, who were pioneers from the state of Indiana to Baker county in 1876. Mrs. Martin was born in Indiana. They removed to Walla Walla county and thence in 1891 to Harney county. He at once engaged in farming here and was one of the very first to raise grain on the fertile face of this county. He succeeded in good shape and in 1895 he took his present place, gaining title by purchase.

To Mr. and Mrs. Martin, five children have been born, named as follows: Earl L., Oran, Christine, deceased, Agnes and Ester, twins. Mr. Martin's parents are living in Walla Walla and are among the prosperous and wealthy residents of that city.

DAVID CARY.—The stockmen and farmers are the ones who have made Harney county what she is at this time, and it is they who have wrought out the wealth here that gives the county a standing among her sisters and to them is due the credit of opening the country and developing its resources in a commendable manner. One of this worthy class is named at the head of this article and it is with pleasure that we grant him consideration in this volume of his county's annals.

Mr. Cary was born in Jackson county, Missouri, on January 16, 1836, being the son of Armenious and Anna Cary. David grew up on a farm in the native country, gaining an education from the primitive schools held in the log cabins. It was 1852 when the father provided the ox team conveyances and undertook the long journey across the plains to the Pacific coast. Six months were consumed on the trip and our subject drove an ox team the entire distance. They arrived at Oregon City on October 22, and settlement was made in Linn county. The train with which these people came was composed of twenty wagons and some deaths occurred from cholera, the grandmother and uncle of our subject being among those who perished. In 1854, David went to California and engaged in mining and the following year he returned to Oregon, and then enlisted in Captain Keeney's company to fight the Indians and he participated in the struggle until the savages were repulsed and then returned to California and in 1860 came again to Oregon. Thence he went to Idaho and wrought in Oro Fino, Florence, Warren, and other camps until 1865, when we see him again in Linn county and on December 26, of that year he married Miss Rebecca A., daughter of Jesse and Anna Barr, pioneers from Iowa in 1853, having made the trip with the ox teams of the day. Our subject took up farming, and also operated at general merchandising and in 1883 he sold out and removed to Harney valley. Here he gave his undivided attention to stock raising. His present home is six miles northwest from Crane postoffice and he owns one thousand six hundred acres of good grazing and meadow land. Mr. Cary pays attention to cattle mostly and has a goodly band. He was one of the first settlers and has always wrought on the frontier and while he started the battle with nothing, he has now a commendable holding and is one of the substantial men of the valley. He is road supervisor, and always active in the advancement of the interests of the country. The following children have been born to Mr. and Mrs. Cary: Mahalie A., wife of George Shelly, ex-sheriff of Harney county; Mrs. Malinda A. Stenffer; Clarence T.; John L.; Gracie. Mr. Cary has always so conducted himself that he has maintained an untarnished reputation, and he stands high among his fellows.

◆◆◆

NATHAN BROWN.—The worthy pioneer and capable business man of whom we now have the privilege of speaking is one of the leaders in the business realm of Burns, being senior member of the firm of N. Brown & Sons, general merchants, who have one of the largest stocks in the county and do a mammoth business, being well established and highly esteemed by all.

Mr. Brown was born in Germany, in January, 1835, and at the age of thirteen years came to America. In 1852 he came via Cape Horn to San Francisco, and thence to Oregon City, where he engaged in business for a few years. We next see him in Walla Walla,

where he took up the business of general merchandising, and in 1866 he returned to San Francisco and there operated at the clothing business until 1883, at which time he sold out his entire business there and came to Burns. It was 1884 when he entered into business here, taking his two sons, Benjamin and Leon M., as partners. They began in a small way and by careful attention to business and deferential treatment of their patrons have increased their trade until it is at present of far reaching and generous proportions, and success in a very brilliant form is theirs to enjoy. In 1896 they erected a large two-story structure, which they occupy at this time, the upper story being rented to the I. O. O. F. lodge of Burns, and the United States land office. They carry a large stock of merchandise and are favorably known all through the country. In addition to the merchandise the firm owns several tracts of land in the county, mostly improved hay and grain land, which is rented. Mr. Brown has a wife and two married daughters and the two sons mentioned, all of whom reside in San Francisco. Mr. Brown is a man of excellent capabilities and has won success, while he is highly esteemed by all, and is a man of unswerving integrity and intrinsic worth of character.

◆◆◆

GEORGE W. CAWLFIELD.—This worthy gentleman is to be numbered with the younger men of Harney county who have attained a good success in the stock business here and who bid fair to gain much better in the future, judging by their faithful and wisely bestowed labors of the past. George W. was born in Johnson county, Kansas, on October 21, 1870, being the son of David A. and Abigil (Evans) Cawlfield. The father was a native of Tennessee, and went across the plains to California in an early day and then returned via Panama, after which for some time he acted as government freighter on the frontiers and finally settled in Kansas. In 1874 the family came overland to Pueblo county, Colorado, and there the father followed stock raising. In 1888 the father, with his wife and ten children, came by covered wagons to Harney and settled on Rye Grass flat, east from Burns, and there engaged in raising stock. Our subject attended school in the various places of his residence, and in 1891 he went to Portland and acted as express messenger and baggageman to different points on the O. R. & N. This continued for two years, and he returned to Harney county, and there, on November 24, 1897, he married Miss Hattie, daughter of Jesse O. and Emma Bunyard. To them have been born two children—Gladys R., born February 3, 1899, and Edna, born July 1, 1901. In 1898 Mr. Cawlfield located a homestead twelve miles north from the Narrows, where he lives now. This he has improved in good shape, having a good six-room house, barns, outbuildings, corralls and all necessary conveniences for a first-class stock ranch. In 1899 he formed a partnership with his father, in the stock business, and they are succeeding well. His parents live with him now. The father also owns a ranch of one-half section on Cram creek. Our subject started in with no capital and now has a large band of cattle, a good home and is prospering well. He has labored faithfully and managed his business interests with excellent wisdom and practical judgment, all of which combine to make him the competence which he now enjoys.

JAMES F. MAHON.—It is especially gratifying to be enabled to chronicle in this volume of the history of Harney county the salient points in the career of the estimable gentleman whose name appears at the head of this sketch, since he has done so much for the development and advancement of this county, has demonstrated his ability as a financier and to handle successfully large interests, of which he is happily possessed at the present time, being doubtless the largest grain farmer in the county and also a leader in raising fine horses and mules; while individually, Mr. Mahon is a man of marked ability and integrity, always dominated by sound principles and possessed of an executive force and practical judgment that array him on the side of success, and his moral virtues and untarnished reputation for honor and uprightness are commensurate with his other qualifications of high order. The account, therefore, of Mr. Mahon's operations in this county would form an important parts of its history,

and it is but right that such giants of achievement, whose labors have wrought such advantage to all, should be granted a position which their sagacious conduct rightly marks as their own.

Reverting more particularly to the personal history of our subject, we note, which accounts for his indefatigable energy and the boundless resources of his personality, which demonstrate him equal to any emergency, that he comes from stanch Irish blood, his parents being natives of the Emerald Isle. He, himself, was born on April 29, 1855, in Syracuse, New York, to Patrick and Catherine Mahon, who had come hither while young. James F. was reared on a farm, gaining his education from the schools of his vicinity, and early he manifested the precocity which later produced the success winning talents which have characterized him in his entire walk. At the budding age of nineteen, James F. started out for himself, and soon we see him in the far west in the vicinity of Stockton, California. He engaged on the farm of Jacob Grundike, as a laborer. The estate of this worthy gentleman consisted of two thousand five hundred acres of land devoted to grain and stock. Mr. Grundike was a man of keen perception and sound judgment and withal of a kind and dissriminating spirit and soon he discovered that in his employee, he had a man of no ordinary ability and trustworthiness, and he did the wise thing both for himself and our subject,—he placed him in the position of superintendent of the entire estate, which was a very responsible incumbency. For two years in that capacity and also as renter of the entire property for five years, Mr. Mahon remained with Mr. Grundike; and the only outcome that could resolve itself to the skill, energy, industry, and excellent judgment of Mr. Mahon was the unbounded success that attended his efforts, both to his own and Mr. Grundike's financial advantage. During these years, Mr. Mahon's father had come to join his son and in 1879 they disposed of their interests in California and came thence to central Oregon, settling in Harney valley. Let it be said to the honor of the kind benefactor of Mr. Mahon, Mr. Grundike, that he willingly placed to the credit of our subject the financial backing necessary to start this young man on a career that has won a most brilliant success. Space forbids the de-

JAMES F. MAHON.

tails of the years since the first settlement in Oregon to the present, but a brief summary of the present will manifest plainly the talent with which Mr. Mahon has wrought. For a time his father remained in partnership with him and then the son bought his interest and now he is one of the heaviest property owners in the state. Coming early, and being a practical farmer, Mr. Mahon secured the choicest farms to be had in Harney county. He has five different well improved ranches in the county. Two of them, aggregating two thousand five hundred acres, make the finest grain farm in the county. The other three amount to four thousand acres, while Mr. Mahon has a number of sections of fine grazing land. His home place is at Steins mountain, and the postoffice was named by Mr. Mahon, Mule, from the fact that he handles so many of these animals. Mr. Mahon makes a specialty of raising horses and mules and is the largest owner of these quadrupeds in the county. On his home place he has twenty-six miles of fencing and utilizes it as the breeding ranch for his entire stock. His horses are all well bred black Percherons and he owns a Dexter Prince stallion, Thomas H., which paces in two-fourteen, and many other horses of fine blood, as Clydesdale, and so forth. Mr. Mahon is a noted nimrod and has some fine animals for the chase consisting of Chesapeake hounds and Blue Dane; and many exciting chases he participates in.

The marriage of Mr. Mahon occurred in 1881 and his wife died in 1886. He contracted a second marriage and has four children by this union, Emily F., a graduate of Oxford; Iva J., attending school in California; Pearl R., and Stella M., deceased. Fraternally he is well connected, being a member of the Masons, the Elks, the I. O. O. F., the K. of P., the A. O. U. W., and the M. W. of A. Politically he is allied with the Democratic party and is active in the interests of good government. Mr Mahon is a fine expert with horses and an admirer of that beautiful animal. He is a leading man in the county, and has done much for the advancement of its interests. From the time his faithful labors attracted the kindly notice of his worthy employer, Mr. Grundike, who promptly placed him on the road to brilliant success, which he has achieved, Mr. Mahon has always been faithful, upright, pro-
43

gressive, dominated by wisdom of a high order, and he has made a name and place for himself among men that is worthy of emulation, and the prestige which he now enjoys is the result of his intrinsic worth wrought into crowning achievements. Mr. Mahon is taking great pains and sparing no expense to grant his children all opportunity to gain a first class educational training. He has recently given his son, Ira J., an interest in the business. The young man is proving his ability and mettle by making a success which is a credit to himself and his father.

JACKSON A. BARTLETT.—This well known and representative business man of the town of Drewsey has a fine hotel, where he does a thriving business and also a large livery and feed stable, being a man of excellent capabilities and one of the prominent figures in this part of Harney county. He was born in Owen county, Indiana, on August 31, 1847, the son of James and Sarah (Alexander) Bartlett. He was reared on a farm and gained his education from the public schools of the vicinity and when he heard the call for troops in the times of fratricidal strife he enlisted in the One Hundred and Forty-ninth Indiana Volunteer Infantry, Company B. He was largely on post duty, being in Louisville, Kentucky; Nashville, Tennessee; and Decatur, Alabama. The date of his enlistment was February 14, 1865, and his honorable discharge occurred in October, 1865. He at once returned to his home in Indiana. In 1868 he migrated to Scotland county, Missouri, and there on December 31, 1870, occurred his marriage with Miss Arminta J., daughter of William and Margaret Myers. He followed farming there until 1887, and then with his family of wife and seven children he made the trip across the country to Union county, Oregon. The following year he came to the agency, in the vicinity of Beulah, Malheur county, entered a homestead, improved it and settled to raising stock. It was in 1896 that he came to Drewsey and bought a hotel and embarked in that business. He did a good business from the start, but in 1899 the entire property was destroyed by fire. He immediately rebuilt a fine two-story structure, fifty-six feet front and forty-four feet deep. He has a nice large office, parlors, dining room, kitchen and twenty sleeping apartments. In 1890 he sold his ranch and stock and devoted his entire attention to the hotel and feed stable.

The following children have been born to Mr. and Mrs. Bartlett: Jesse, near Longcreek, Grant county; James C., who was elected in 1900, on the Democratic ticket, as superintendent of the schools of Harney county; Mrs. Grace Arnold, of Pine creek; Hattie, Hettie, Hugh, triplets, Hugh being deceased; Carl and Stella V.

ROBERT J. McKINNON.—This worthy pioneer is a man of energy, ability and stirring qualities of worth, having wrought with a ready hand and willing heart in the noble work of developing the western wilds and he is now one of the well-todo and respected stockmen and farmers of Harney county, residing about nine miles northwest from Burns, on Curry Garden creek.

Robert J. was born in Hancock county, Indiana, on January 22, 1837, being the son of Thomas D. and Elizabeth McKinnon. He attended school in a log cabin with a mud chimney, and the expenses of the teaching were borne by subscription. In 1853 he removed to Des Moines county, Iowa, and in 1857 the family went to Page county and there on November 7, 1858, our subject married Miss Emily H., daughter of Daniel and Elizabeth Long, who had resided in Indiana, where our subject was born, and these young people had been raised together. In 1861 our subject and his wife removed to Keokuk county, Iowa, and thence to Des Moines county, and in 1863 he came via Panama to California, then to Virginia City, Nevada, and took up mining and lumbering and in 1864 he went to Downing, California, and there did the same work until 1865, when he came back to his Iowa home. In 1869 he removed to Jackson county, Missouri, and in 1875, returned to Page county, Iowa, whence he journeyed to California, settling in Shasta county. He entered government land and also did freighting. In the fall of 1881 he went to Red Bluff, and

in 1886 he came overland to Harney valley. He lived near Burns on a rented farm and did freighting until 1888, when he came to his present place, which is well improved with good house, orchard, shrubbery, and so forth. He handles stock, mostly horses.

To Mr. and Mrs. McKinnon there have been born eleven children, James Edward, of Cornucopia, Baker county; Mrs. Ida M. McCampbell, of Shasta county, California; Robert J., near Burns; Andrew J., of Santa Rosa, California, who was sheriff of this county from 1896 to 1900, being elected both times on the Democratic ticket; Mrs. Lucy J. Baird, of South Dakota; Mrs. Belle Dora Clark, of Harney, her husband being superintendent of the French Glen ranches; Thomas D., of Cornucopia; Hattie Elizabeth, deceased; Mrs. Emma Alice Clark, near Burns; William L., who was killed in Burns in 1898; Mrs. Elsie Alvie Cleveland of this county; Mrs. Essie Geneva Smith, of Burns. Mr. McKinnon owns a half interest in a good mining property in the Virtue district in Baker county. He also took a trip to Alaska in 1900, and also went the next year, prospecting and mining, and made the trip in 1902. He has a good farm of one-quarter section.

UBALD J. COTE.—This enterprising gentleman is one of the worthy citizens of Harney county and is a man who has demonstrated his excellent qualities in the estimable success which he has wrought out here in our midst, as is evidenced by the fact that when he came to this country he tells us that he was somewhat in debt, but now he has a fine estate of six hundred and eighty acres of hay and grazing land, all fenced, a good six-room house, barns and outbuildings, a good blacksmith shop, a band of stock and is well-to-do and prosperous. Mr. Cote is also a man of integrity and sound morals and is esteemed by all. He was born on August 4, 1866, in Champlain county, Canada, being the son of Antoine and Marie Cote, natives of France. In 1871 the family came to Lowell, Massachusetts, and there he attended common school. worked in the cotton factories and at fourteen entered as apprentice to a blacksmith. where he served for three years. He worked there at his trade until he came west in 1886. During this time he took three different trips to Canada and in the date mentioned he came to Winnemucca by train and thence by stage to Burns. He went to work for wages, herding sheep for a number of years, and gained some stock of his own, and in 1895 he entered a homestead where he now lives, about half way between Riley and the Narrows, in Warm Springs valley. He also took a desert claim and commenced to raise cattle. He has improved in good shape and is a man of influence and integrity, which is recognized by all.

The marriage of Mr. Cote and Miss Annie, daughter of John and Emma Bankofier, was solemnized on June 22, 1902. Mr. Bankofier was a native of Germany and his wife of California, to which state he was an early pioneer. Mrs. Cote was born in Nevada county, California, and her father died there in 1882, but her mother, Mrs. John McNulty, lives there still. Mrs. Cote came up from California in 1893 and has followed teaching school in Harney county since that time, being one of the leading educators of the county, and having the confidence and hearty approval in her work of all wherever she taught. Mr. Cote has a good home. He is a member of the I. O. O. F., Harney Lodge, No. 77, of Burns.

CHARLES W. RANN is well known in Harney county, and he has been a great traveller and consequently has gained much experience that gives him prestige and enables him to gain a good success in his labors. He was born in San Francisco on December 14, 1848, being the son of Caleb and Lucinda Rann. He was among the very first white children born in that place. The father was a native of Nova Scotia and came to Maine and thence around Cape Horn to San Francisco in 1846. The mother crossed the plains in 1847 with ox teams from Tennessee. They were married in Santa Clara and removed to San Francisco. The parents removed to various places in the state and finally settled in Peach Tree valley where the home was until 1864. Then they came to Canyon City region and the parents went to raising stock while our subject went to mining and followed it until 1871. We next see him in White Pine county, Nevada,

where he mined for two years. On April 10, 1874, he was in Canyon City again and married on that date to Miss Mattie Harper. Four children were born to this union, Clifford, Frank M., Maggie, and Agnes. In 1880 Mr. Rann went to Butte, Montana, thence to Fort Benton and Walla Walla and in 1882 he settled in Srague, Washington, where he went into business until 1886. Then he came to Canyon City remaining until 1890. From that date until 1900 he was in various places in Idaho, Nevada, Arizona, California, Washington, and Oregon, prospectinig and mining.

On August 8, 1901, Mr. Rann married a second time, the lady then becoming his wife was Mrs. Ione (Whiting) Baker. At present Mr. Rann has a good building in Harney where he operates a retail liquor store, carrying a choice stock of wines, liquors, tobaccos and so forth. He is doing a thriving business. He also owns a good residence in the town. Mr. Rann stands well among the business men and is one of the energetic workers for the welfare of the county.

❖❖❖

WILLIAM B. JOHNSON.—Among the enterprisiing citizens of Harney county we should mentioin the gentleman whose name initiates this paragraph, and who has labored here faithfully and continuously for a long time, being at the present time one of the influential men of his section. Mr. Johnson was born in Crawford county, Arkansas, on September 24, 1852, being the son of John L. and Frances J. (Elliott) Johnson. The father was an orderly sergeant in the Confederate army and died in service. The widow was left with four children and the improvements of the plantation were all destroyed by the ravages of war. Bravely she stood with her little flock and kept them together. Our subject received a primary education from the schools of his native place and in the spring of 1868 came with an uncle to California, assisting to bring a band of cattle. They landed in Merced county and he worked with stock for a time and then attended school for two years, one of which was at the San Joaquin college at Stockton. In 1874 he went to Modoc county and there engaged in farming, stock raising, and dairying. He owned a good farm there, but in 1883 he brought his stock north to Silver Creek, Harney county, and in 1884 he sold his California property, and the year following his family joined him in the Oregon home. They settled first near their present home, but later removed to the place where they now reside, five miles northwest from Riley postoffice. Mr. Johnson has two hundred and forty acres of fine land, well improved with good house, barn and outbuildings, orchard and plenty of water. His stock consists mostly of cattle and he is one of the thrifty men of his section. Politically, Mr. Johnson is allied with the Democratic party and is active in that realm, being now central committeeman for his county, while in educational matters he is zealous for advancement and betterment of school facilities.

On August 3, 1873, Mr. Johnson married Miss Mary E., daughter of John and Martha A. Street, of Merced county, California, and they have become the parents of eight children, Francis A., deceased; Mrs. Martha Dibble, of Silver creek; Alfred J.; Mrs. Elizabeth Garrett, deceased; Lulah; Roxana; Mary E.; Clarissa, deceased.

Mr. Johnson's mother died in Arkansas February 27, 1868. Mrs. Johnson's father died on August 31, 1883, but her mother still resides in California.

CHARLES S. JOHNSON.—This capable and enterprising stockman and agriculturist of Harney county is one of the substantial men who have labored for the upbuilding and material progress of this section of central Oregon for many years, and now holds prominent places as leading citizens. Our subject was born in Winneshiek county, Iowa, on October 20, 1854, being the son of John and Permelia Johnson. In 1864 the family came across the plains with the "prairie schooner" of the day to Honey Lake valley, California, where they stopped for a short time and then made their way to Butte county. Our subject received his education there from the primitive schools of that pioneer day. His parents were pioneers in Iowa and also in California and so the education of our subject was gained with meager advantages. He grew to manhood in Butte county and there on September 18, 1883,

he was married to Miss Sadie E., daughter of Shelby and Darlutha (Daugherty) Simmons. Mr. and Mrs. Simmons were pioneers from Arkansas to that county in 1850, crossing the plains with ox teams. It was 1888 that our subject came to Rockford, in Harney county, and engaged in the stock business. Later, he went to The Narrows and then to the warm springs on the west side of Harney lake. There he entered government land and improved it in good shape. This continued to be the family home until 1900, when he sold out and came to his present place, twenty-four miles west from Drewsey. He has a half section of good land all fenced and improved in an excellent manner, with fine house, barns, orchard, and plenty of water for irrigating purposes. He raises hay for his stock principally.

To Mr. and Mrs. Johnson have been born the following children: Amanda B., Emmett S., Sadie D., Elbert C. Mr. Johnson has always evinced great interest in the betterment of school facilities and labors wisely and zealously for this worthy end, while also he takes the part of the intelligent citizen in general politics.

JASPER DAVIS.—In the work of developing Harney county, Mr. Davis has done a good share and in many other places he has done pioneer work, having spent most of his life on the frontier, and in opening up various sections. He is a man possessed of those qualities so much admired in the pioneer, has always shown himself upright, courageous, and active in the affairs of life. And to-day he is one of the substantial citizens of Harney county and has gained and retains the confidence of the people.

Mr. Davis was born in Van Buren county, Iowa, on April 5, 1840, being the son of David T. and Laurinda (Baker) Davis, natives of Kentucky. Our subject was reared on a farm and gained his education in the various places where the family resided. He commenced school at the age of twelve and continued until nineteen, being familiar with the log cabin schoolhouses of his day. The family came to Davis county, Iowa, while he was young and there on July 31, 1862, he married Miss Mary E., daughter of Adam and Mary A. (Lasley) Miller. In 1865 they went to Wilson county, Kansas, and there farmed and raised stock. Mr. Davis was elected sheriff of that county in 1867. In 1876 he removed to Stafford county and entered government land. In 1879 he was elected justice of the peace. In 1880 he prepared mule teams and with his family of wife and six children started on May 10, for the west. On July 31 they arrived at Union, Union county, Oregon. In 1884 they went to Spokane and he mined some in the Coeur d'Alene country. The same year he came to Camp Harney and soon thereafter came to Harney, where he engaged in mercantile business until 1891, then sold out. The next year he bought his present place, one-fourth of a mile south from Harney. He has a good farm and a comfortable home. Mr. Davis was the first justice of the peace appointed when the county was set off and he has filled that office most of the time since, being at present the incumbent. In political matters, Mr. Davis is a Democrat. To him and his estimable wife there were born ten children, named as follows: Mrs. Laura M. Boyd, of Coos county; Laurinda, deceased; Jasper F., of Harney; Emily Ann, deceased; David P., of Baker City; Alma, at home; Peter, of Baker City; Charles H., Ira, and Dottie Lee, at home. On February 14, 1894, Mrs. Davis was called to pass the river of death. She had been a noble Christian woman, of fine ability and constantly employed in good works. She was a conscientious member of the Church of Jesus Christ of Latter Day Saints, and was always laboring for its advancement. She took especial pains to rear her children carefully and in a Christian manner. She was born on the frontier in Iowa and was always on the frontier and did much hard and self-sacrificing labor.

On June 22, 1900, Mr. Davis married Miss Lucy B., daughter of John W. and Nancy W. Coleman. Mrs. Davis is from Decatur, Illinois. Mr. Davis and his wife are interested in church work and they are highly respected members of society having displayed real worth of character and sound principles.

◆◆◆

JAMES A. WEATHERLY.—The subject of this article is one of the men whose labors have been instrumental in building up the country and bringing it to its present prosper-

ous condition. James A. was born in Fannin county, Texas, on August 12, 1870, the son of Jesse C. and Frances (Williams) Weatherly. In 1877 the family came across the plains with mule teams, coming direct to the Grande Ronde valley, having a tedious journey of nine months. Two years were spent in the Grande Ronde and then another move was made to Wallowa county. There the father took up stock raising and lives at the present time, the mother having passed away on May 22, 1882. Our subject received his education from the common schools and remained with his father until 1890, when he came to central Oregon and went to riding the range for the Pacific Live Stock Company. He was one of the foreman during the last six years of his service and was an efficient stockman. On account of his health failing, he was obliged to retire from the more active duties of handling stock and accordingly he opened a wine and liquor store in Drewsey where he is at the present time. He carries a choice stock of liquors and tobaccos. He owns his own building in the center of town and has it well furnished. He affiliates with the I. O. O. F., Drewsey Lodge, No. 174. He is a man of good standing among his fellows and has done his share for the development of the country.

◆◆◆

PLEASANT M. CHENEY.—Although born in Arkansas, still the subject of this sketch is practically a product of the west since his birth occurred on February 26, 1856, and the spring following his parents came overland with ox teams, settling in Sonoma county, California. The parents, William W. and Martha (Meek) Cheney, soon went to Lake county, thence to San Louis Obispo county, raised stock and later removed to San Bernardino county, and in 1880 went to the vicinity of Los Angeles and engaged in fruit raising and farming there until the death of the father in 1899. The mother died in 1901 and she and her husband were each eighty years of age at the time of death. When Pleasant M. reached the age of sixteen he went to Kern and engaged in riding the range and visited Carson City, Nevada, also went to Texas. He rode after stock on the frontier of Texas and on the Rio Grande for nearly two years, then returned home. After this he visited Arizona and mined there and in thee different states in Mexico and Lower California, returning home after an absence of four years. He was at Tombstone, Arizona, when nine thousand people were there before a house was built, and in his stay in Texas he saw much fighting between the Texas rangers and the Mexicans. It was 1883 that he came to Lake county, Oregon. He worked on the range for Cox & Clark then went to Crook county and rode for Logan & Son for three years and then we find him in the Harney valley in 1887, where he worked for Riley & Hardin for four years, the last three being in the capacity of foreman. In 1891 he entered a homestead on upper Silver creek and engaged in stock raising. He now owns eight hundred acres of hay and grazing land all fenced and improved with comfortable house, outbuildings, and orchard and he has a goodly band of cattle. His estate is located twenty-five miles southeast from Riley.

On January 17, 1895, Mr. Cheney married Lizzie A., daughter of John C. Garrett, of Okanogan county, Washington, and one child, Martha Tillie, has been born to them. Mr. Cheney is a good citizen, an upright man, a first class neighbor, stands well with his fellows, and is one of the substantial property owners of the county.

◆·◆·◆

JAMES M. PARKER.—To detail the active career and stirring adventures of the subject of this sketch would require a volume, so incessantly has he labored and travelled; but space forbids, however much we may wish to give more, that we chronicle more than a review, but it demonstrates the vigor, the true pioneer spirit, the ability and the stirring qualities of our subject when we note how he has wrought and gained success.

James Parker comes from a good stock of patriots, his maternal grandfather fighting in the Revolution, his uncle Zelock Darling, being in the war of 1812, and his father a captain in the regular army. James M. was born on January 24, 1833, in Douglas, Worcester county, Massachusetts, to Abel and Sarah (Darling) Parker. He was educated and stayed on the old homestead until nineteen, and then,

having also had experience in the cotton factory and Hunt's ax factory and machine shop, he came in 1852 to Linn county Iowa, and the next year started across the plains. He was nearly drowned in the Platte and at the sink of the Humboldt, he started a foot toward California, while the train went another way. He was beset with thirst and hunger and great hardship in this journey on foot, going fifty miles once through a desert. He also met the noted Jim Beckwith, a leader of Indians. He finally landed with his companion in Plumas county and went to mining, then repaired to Gibbonville and worked in a hotel, afterwards going to Hopkinville, where he saw the first woman that came to the camp. He mined until the spring of 1855 and then with twelve hundred dollars in his pocket he went via the isthmus to his home in Massachusetts. He engaged in the merchandise business until the father removed to Rockford, Illinois, and then he bought a stock of goods and came to Iowa, with them. He sold them through the country and traded for timber land in Bremer county. Then we see him successively in Boston, New York, Chicago, Rockford, and in the spring of 1857 in St. Louis. Then he went up the Missouri river to Fort Leavenworth and there saw General Harney from whom our county is named; not liking the country, he returned to Lawrence, St. Louis, Rockford, and finally to Bremer county, Iowa. There he married Miss Lyda J. Fletcher, in 1857, she being a native of Maine. In May, 1862, with his family of wife and two children, his own parents, his wife's parents, and others, he started across the plains. One child died at the Platte from scarlet fever. They went to Lassen county, California, and ranched until 1870, then went to various localities and in the spring of 1876 he came from Honey lake country to Clarke county, Washington, and in 1878 went to The Dalles. Leaving his family there until after the Indian war of 1878 was over, he then, in June, 1881, came to Harney valley. There were but eleven families in the entire valley then. Later Mr. Parker went to Sage Hen valley and in the fall of 1882 returned to Honey lake and one year later came back to Silver creek. Then again he went to Sage Hen valley, entering land and taking up stock raising until 1892 when he sold and went to Fall River lake, California, thence to Chico, Red Bluff, and back to Harney, on a visit. In June, 1893, he bought his his present place of one hundred and twenty-six acres, hay land with good house, barn and other improvements. The farm is eight miles northwest from Burns.

To Mr. and Mrs. Parker, thirteen children have been born: Estella, Everett E., Prince A., deceased; Walter B., at Warm Springs; Mrs. Adaline I. Mace, near Burns; Mrs. Augusta Terrill, near Burns; John N., in Sage Hen valley; Mrs. Hattie M. Tyler, of Warm Springs; Chester R., deceased; Carlton E., at home; Lute A., near Burns; Mrs. Rosa Thornburg, near Burns; James M., near Burns.

JUDGE CHARLES P. RUTHERFORD.

—All over Harney county the name of Judge Rutherford is well and favorably known and he stands high with all, being a man of sterling qualities of worth and having demonstrated his ability not only in the business operations of his hands but also in the capacity of public officer, having been judge of the county for four years with manifestation of impartiality and sagacity and faithfulness that have commended him to the intelligent and order loving people.

Charles P. was born in Calhoun county, Illinois, on November 29, 1847, being the son of Robert and Mary (Bolter) Rutherford. The father died on November 29, 1848, and the mother died in 1852, thus the orphan boy was forced to find his home with relatives. In 1853 with his uncle, George Bolter, he came across the prairies with two teams and a small band of cows. They settled in Polk county and had provisions enough to last a year, while the trip was so favorable that they did not stand guard one night and the stock were all in good condition when they reached their destination. Our subject remained with his uncle until 1863 and then went to the Boise basin and mined, and in 1866 came to Umatilla county and took up stock raising. In 1868 we find him packing to the mines and in 1872 he sold his outfit. Then on August 20, 1873, Mr. Rutherford married Miss Malinda F., daughter of W. F. and Nancy J. (Stice) Moffet. Mr. and Mrs. Moffet were pioneers from Missouri and settled on a donation claim in

Clarke county, Washington, later moving to The Dalles, and are now living on the Malheur river in Harney county. The wedding of our subject occurred in Grant county and there he engaged in the cattle business on the middle fork of the John Day river. At the time of the Indian trouble, he was a scout for the settlers. Then he went to Umatilla county and sold his cattle and bought sheep, being thus engaged until 1887. That was the year when he came to Harney county, settling on the Malheur river where he remained until 1899. He had also bought his present place of one hundred and twenty acres, one mile north from Burns. It was well improved, has good water, and is a valuable ranch. Mr. Rutherford had also been in the hotel business in Drewsey for a time. In 1894 the Populists nominated Mr. Rutherford for county judge, and his popularity was so great that although his party was far in the minority, still he was elected by a handsome majority. For four years we find him filling the responsible position of the judicial bench and it is to be said to his credit that in no case did he fail to mete out impartial justice, being a man of integrity. He was renominated but as party lines were drawn so tight by leaders, his popularity could not gain the day.

To Judge Rutherford and his estimable wife there have been born eight children: Mrs. Clara E. Masterson, of Malheur county; Mrs. Mary J. Robertson, or Drewsey; William R., attending school at Monmouth in preparation for the medical profession; Olive and Rose, teaching school; Frances, attending school; Archibald P., and Arland. The Judge is a member of the I. O. O. F., Lodge No. 77, also of the Encampment and the Pioneers of the Pacific Coast, the latter at Pendelton. Judge Rutherford is a man of uprightness, sound principles, and has done in a commendable manner the labor which he has performed.

JOSEPH ROBERTSON.—A real pioneer in every sense of that significant word, and one, too, who has never shirked the responsibilities of that arduous and dangerous position, being also a man whose capabilities and enterprise entitle him to be ranked with the leading men of Harney county, and who has made a record in the various frontier regions where he has wrought which is replete with wise and good acts and display of bravery and courage,—the subject of this article is entitled to especial distinction in the history of Harney county.

Joseph Robertson was born in Renfroshire, Scotland, on August 31, 1833, being the son of Joseph and Mary (McDonald) Robertson. He was educated in the public schools of his native land and there also served an apprenticeship at the tailor's trade. In 1848 he was stirred with a strong desire to travel and see the world, and accordingly embarked on a sailing vessel for New Orleans. Landing there he made his way to Cincinnati and there worked at his trade until the spring of 1851, when he migrated to Lee county, Iowa, remaining there until 1853, at which time he acted as laborer in a train of teams and loose cattle which came to Jackson county, Oregon, consuming six months in the trip. He labored at various callings in the Rogue river valley for a number of years, and then went to raising cattle on his own resources. The hard winter of 1861-2 swept all his cattle off but thirteen head, which he traded for milk cows. In the spring of 1862 he went on a trip to the Salmon river mines but turned aside at Canyon City, because of the reports which they received at Shields bridge. After a short time there he returned and brought his family and settled at Mount Vernon, naming the postoffice. He at once took up the stock business and prospered. It was 1878 that he removed his stock to Malheur valley, bringing his family in 1888, making settlement on Otis creek, where he now lives, six miles northeast from Drewsey. That country was then Indian reservation and as soon as it was opened he filed on his present home. He now has six hundred acres of fine land, well watered, embellished with fine house and commodious barn, and provided with all the necessaries for a first class stock ranch and farm, and he is one of the most prosperous men of the county. Mr. Robertson fought in the Rogue river war and also in the Indian outbreak in 1878. At one time he was with Joaquin Miller and some soldiers for eighteen days, under Lieutenant Waymeyer, on an Indian raid in 1864 and one citizen was killed and four soldiers, and Mr. Robertson has seen much hardship and danger

on the frontier, having ever conducted himself in a becoming manner to a manly man and patriotic citizen.

The marriage of Mr. Robertson and Miss Drucilla E. McAtee, who crossed the plains in an ox train in 1853, was solemnized on May 9, 1859, and they have seven children: John A.; Mrs. Eva McClain, of Burns; Mrs. Eunice L. Thompson, of Barns; William A.; Mrs. Daisy Daly, of Drewsey; Lena, and Gussie. Mr. Robertson is a member of the A. F. & A. M., Royal Arch chapter in Canyon City.

◆◆◆

CHARLES A. HAINES.—A brief outline of the career of this stirring business man will establish the fact beyond a doubt that he is one of the leading men of Harney county and has ability and has achieved a success that will compare favorably with any in the state, considering the material of circumstances, country, inaccessibility, and so forth with which he has worked and contended. He is a man of fine executive ability, keen perception, and sterling worth, having the entire confidence of the populace.

Mr. Haines was born in Ripley county, Indiana, near New Marion, on October 6, 1870, being the son of John A. and Eliza W. (Jennings) Haines. He grew up on a farm, gained a good education, and in the spring of 1892 he came by rail to Ontario, thence to Burns and clerked in his brother's store until July 6, of the same year. The date of his arrival was March 10. His next move was to look up the country adjacent to the Narrows and he decided to locate there. He put up the first building there, a small store building, and brought a small stock of goods. He went at the matter in a business way, laid his plans well ahead and commenced at the bottom. It was soon discovered that no commonplace man had established himself at this point, for the trade that used to go elsewhere was now beginning to be diverted to his store. He was a fine salesman, quick to perceive what goods were needed and as quick to provide them in the quantities called for, and back of it all and pervading his entire dealings there was a manifestation of uprightness and integrity that won the confidence of the people and his trade was in a short time pouring in at a rapid rate

CHARLES A. HAINES.

He now has a fine store building, 22 by 55, a fine stone warehouse, fire proof, about the same size, and a basement, all of which room is well packed with a skillfully selected stock of goods of all kinds that are needed in his trade. He carries everything that is used in this section, from all classes of furnishing goods, groceries, hardware, housefurnishings, to vehicles, farm implements, and supplies for the large ranches. His trade is very large. In addition to this, he does a general banking business and acts as justice of the peace, being held in this latter position by the votes of the people. Since July 3, 1897, he has been postmaster and discharges these duties with strict faithfulness and efficiency. Mr. Haines was instrumental in getting the telephone to the Narrows from Burns, subscribing liberally himself and inviting others to assist. Politically, he is with the Republicans, is active and acts as central committeeman for his precinct.

On February 22, 1896, Mr. Haines married Miss Annie, daughter of Nimrod and Sirilda Comegys, and they have two children, Hazel, born April 10, 1897; Wilbur E., born April 23, 1899. Mr. and Mrs. Comegys were early pioneers of the Willamette valley and have lived in this county for twenty years. Mr. Haines owns a good residence in the Narrows, a quarter section of fertile hay land adjoining the town and is a man of broad public spirit and labors for the upbuilding of the country, being progresive and enterprising.

* * *

EDWARD C. KEENEY.—Although the subject of this sketch has not been so long domiciled in Harney county as some of the pioneers, still he has spent a greater portion of his life in the adjacent territories and thus is justly entitled to a place among the pioneers, having been engaged in labors incident to that worthy life for many years. Edward C. was born in Salt Lake City, Utah, on May 6, 1868, being the son of Joseph B. and Frances M. (White) Keeney. His father was an operator in the stage business and did service over many portions of the west. From Salt Lake City they went to Kelton, Utah, thence to Boise, Idaho, and from there to Walla Walla, Washington. Thence a move was made to Weston, Oregon, then to Pendleton, later on to Gilliam county, in which latter place our subject engaged with his father in the horse business. This was about 1889, and later we find our subject in Heppner, operating the stage from that city to Monument. The next move was to Longcreek, Grant county, where he was engaged in operating a hotel for two years and then we find the active Edward C. Keeney in Umatilla county, on Camas prairie, handling stock and tilling the soil. It was from that place in 1895 that he came to his present abode, twenty-three miles west from Drewsey. He has a farm of one hundred and fifty acres, well improved, having comfortable residence and plenty of water for irrigating. He devotes his time and attention principally to raising cattle.

The marriage of Mr. Keeney and Miss Mary May Vilott, was solemnized on January 1, 1893, at Ione. They have the following children: Juanita B., Chauncey W., Gladys P. Mrs. Keeney's father, Isaac Vilott, was one of the very first settlers of the north fork of the John Day river. Mr. Keeney is a member of the A. O. U. W., Lodge No. 119, of Drewsey. He has served for two years as justice of the peace and his efforts in this line have been with acceptability to the people.

* * *

JOHN E. LOGGAN.—Among the young men of Harney county who have gained distinction, both in the military line as well as in the business enterprises, while also he enjoys the honor of being called to the office of county assessor by the people in the June election in 1902, we are constrained to mention the genial and capable gentleman whose name initiates this paragraph.

John E. was born in Cass county, Nebraska, on August 8, 1870, being the son of John H. and Emily D. Loggan. The parents removed to Washington county, Kansas, when this son was small and in 1879 they came across the plains with teams to Union county, Oregon. John E. attended school there until 1885, when another move was made, this time to Harney valley, and soon thereafter to Harney, where the father engaged in the hardware business. In 1888 our subject went to Philomath College, in Benton county, this state, and graduated from the same in 1891. He came home and entered his father's store where he labored faithfully until 1898 at which time, in company with his uncle, D. M. Loggan, he enlisted in Troop A, First Nevada Volunteer Cavalry, to go to the Philippines. These two were the only ones who went from Harney county. He was in San Francisco a short time and then went to the seat of war at Manila. He served under General Lawton and had his share of the peculiar hardships which the soldiers there were called to endure. He was honorably discharged in the fall of 1899, as corporal, having had part in numerous skirmishes and the battles that were fought. He returned home after the war, and took up the stock business, having a quarter section on Rock creek, this county. As stated above, in the June election, 1902, he was chosen on the Republican ticket to act as assessor for the county and is discharging the duties incumbent upon him there with dispatch and efficiency.

On November 28, 1901, Mr. Loggan married Miss Ella Howser, daughter of Andrew W. and Hannah (Kuster) Howser, near Harney. Mr. Loggan is a young man of great promise, has displayed stanch integrity and intrinsic worth of character, and he has hosts of friends throughout the county.

‹ ♦ ♦ ›

NEWELL HALL.—Among those who have gained a well earned success in Harney county and have turned all opportunities and resources to advantage, must be mentioned the gentleman whose name initiates this paragraph, being a man of boundless energy and courage and withal a man whose life has been well spent in various kinds of labor. When McKinley was assassinated, the governor of New Jersey, an old friend of Mr. Hall, was threatened and Mr. Hall promptly offered his services with those of three friends to come to his assistance which elicited a hearty response of gratitude from the governor.

Newell Hall was born near Freehold, Monmouth county, New Jersey, on August 29, 1849, being the son of Gordon and Susan Hall. The father was educated for a physician but never practiced. At the time of the Civil war he was four years above the limit of age but enlisted nevertheless, and served the term and then re-enlisted and served to the

end of the war. He was through much hard service, and was taken prisoner at the battle of Williamsburg. The Confederates demanded from him the oath of allegiance or he would be shot. Hall calmly replied, "Shoot." He was released and rejoined the army. He was under Generals Sherman and McClellan.

Our subject was educated in the common schools and in Freehold Academy, then served four years in the Burdon iron works in Brooklyn, learning there the machinist's trade. He also acted as locomotive engineer for eight years. In 1881 he went west over the first through train on the Atchison and Topeka line from Deming, New Mexico, to San Francisco. Enroute, they were robbed and the brigands stole Mr. Hall's boots, so he was forced to go into San Francisco barefooted. He went thence to Jackson county, Oregon, and worked for wages and was taken sick and when he left that county for Harney he was owing the doctor three hundred dollars. One year after landing in Harney he had the doctor paid up and a good start. He worked nine years for the V cattle company and during this time purchased his present home place, which consists of five hundred and sixty acres and lies on Peaceful flat, twelve miles southeast from Riley. In 1893 he moved on the ranch and began raising horses and mules, devoting especial attention to mules, of which he has a good band. He is a member and past grand of the I. O. O. F., Paola Lodge, No. 102 Miami county, Kansas, and also he belongs to the Order of Washington, in Portland. Mr. Hall is a man of considerable property, has displayed good energy and ability with uprightness and integrity in his labors here and stands well to-day, being prominent among his fellows.

‹ ♦ ♦ ›

ANDREW W. HOWSER.—It has been many years since this worthy pioneer settled in the territory that is now Harney county, and many years before that he was a pioneer to the Pacific coast, and it is very fitting in a volume that has to do with the old pioneers, that we should grant an epitome of his life, having always been a man whose conduct commends him to the esteem and confidence of his fellows, and having done much hard labor to advance the interests of the country, while also he has always been a champion who has led the way for better school facilities and deeper education of the people.

Andrew W. Howser was born in Warsaw, Benton county, Missouri, on October 19, 1837, being the son of Stephen A. and Sallie P. Howser. He was the first boy born in Warsaw, and it seems to have been his lot since to be among the first ones to open the country in various localities. The father was a farmer but lived in town and in 1850 he started to go to California the land of gold; but fate decreed otherwise and in the vicinity of Carson City, Nevada, he died and was there laid to rest beside the weary trail that led but to his death, and a lone grave on the wide expanse of plains. In 1853 the mother with her five children undertook the same dreary journey and in due time they halted their ox teams in Yuba county, California. While all this was occurring another line of history was forming, which began with the birth of a girl amid the rugged scenes of Switzerland. She was cherished by loving parents and came across the Atlantic with them and their home was in Ohio until 1852, when they came across the wide expanse of dreary plains to California, with ox teams. In due time Mr. Howser met this lass and on June 15, 1861, they were married, the lady being Miss Hannah Kuster. They remained in Yuba county raising stock until 1876, and then they took up the course of the pioneer again and wended their way to near where Burns now stands. Less than one hundred citizens, some estimate it was sixty-five, were then domiciled in the vast territory that is now embraced in Harney county. Few houses were in the country and one must know that many hardships were the lot of those brave and hardy ones who with families would penetrate into this lonely region. Mr. and Mrs. Howser were not of the fainthearted kind and vigorously they went to work to make a home and establish themselves. They took a homestead and went to raising stock and from that time their lives have been identified with Harney county, or the territory that is now embraced in this county. They have seen the growth, have experienced the hardships, have endured the privations, have fought off the savages, and have remained steadfast to the one purpose of making this the abode of civilization. Hand in hand they have trodden the journey and now as the years of the golden time of their lives are dawning, it is with great pleasure that we can add that they are comfortably established in their own home one mile southwest from Harney, where they own two hundred and forty acres of good land and have a fine band of cattle. And also it is gratifying to have the pleasure of placing their names on the pages of history that will be read with interest by the succeeding generations. It was in 1882 that Mr. Howser moved to his present place. To this worthy couple, eight children have been born, named as follows: Lola, wife of Lewis Stenger, of Whatcom, Washington; Mary F., wife of Thomas J. Vickers near Harney; Sarah L., wife of C. C. Kilburn, foreman on the Harper ranch in Malheur county; Emma E., wife of D. R. Meyers, of Toledo, Ohio; Thomas G., married to Rose Loggan, near Harney; Stephen R., at home; Susan B., deceased; Ella, wife of John E. Loggan, near Harney. Mr. Howser is a stanch supporter of the Jeffersonian principles of Democracy and he has been a zealous advocate of educational facilities and good schools, and his efforts have resulted in much good for the schools of Harney county.

———◆◆◆———

JUDGE THOMAS J. SHIELDS.—To this eminent and well known citizen of Harney county it is very fitting that especial mention should be made in his county's history, since he has been prominent here, has ever been forward in develpoment andadvancement, and has manifested himself as an upright and capable man, true to all trusts imposed, and faithful and upright in all relations.

Thomas J. Shields was born in Andrew county, Missouri, on August 17, 1849, being the son of James and Matilda (Crowley) Shields. His father was captain of the state militia for a number of years until 1852, when he came to the Pacific coast with his family of wife and five children. Our subject's uncle, G. W. Crowley, was captain of the train, a large one, and pulled by oxen, and they had some difficulty with the Indians, losing some stock. They came direct to Linn county, and settled on a donation claim and there the father remained until his death in 1890. He was treasurer of Linn county for a number of terms in succession, and when the state was admitted to the Union, he was a member of the body that framed the constitution. He was also justice of the peace for many terms. The mother of our subject was a daughter of Judge Crowley of Andrew county, Missouri. Thomas J. grew up on the old donation claim, attended the common schools and finished his education in the academy at Lebanon. In 1865, he went to Douglas county and took up sheep raising. Later, he sold out and returned to Linn county, attended school and then acted as salesman in a general store. In 1871 he went to Siskiyou county, California, now Modoc county. He assisted to erect the first house in Dorris Bridge, now Alturas, the county seat of Modoc county. He followed the calling of the educator most of the time until 1871, then settled on land and the creek received his name. Later, he went to Lake county, taught school, did carpenter work and painted the first house in Lakeview, the county seat of Lake county. In 1882 Mr. Shields returned to Modoc county and soon came thence to Harney county, bringing a band of cattle. He settled on Silver creek near his present home and engaged in the dairy business, taking his butter to Canyon City. He entered a homestead in 1884 which is the present family home, two miles southeast from Riley. He has a good estate of hay and grain land and pays attention to raising cattle and horses. When Harney county was organized, Mr. Shields was chosen the first county judge and he discharged those important duties in a becoming manner and to the satisfaction of all concerned. Judge Shields brought to bear in his official work not only a fund of great experience among men, but also sterling qualities of integrity, impartiality, justice, and keen perception, which rendered his regime one of excellent administration of justice.

On October 5, 1880, Mr. Shields married Miss Julia A., daughter of John C., and Nancy E. Garrett, of Okanogan county, Washington, and to them have been born six children: Myra E., wife of Joseph W. Vanderpool; James E. Elmer F., deceased; Ruby M., Virgil E., Marie, Judge Shields is a member of Lake Lodge, No. 63, I. O. O. F., of Lakeview; also a member of the Pioneers of the Pacific; and Encampment, No. 71, being worthy commander of the latter. Politically, he is affiliated with the Democrats.

By way of reminiscence, it is fitting to note that Mr. Shields was lieutenant of a company raised to fight the Indians in Modoc county, California, but he did not get into the field with his men on account of the ending of the war.

WILLIAM ALTNOW.—The worthy pioneer whose name appears above is one of the intrepid and sturdy men who fought the battles of the country in the Civil war and has done a lion's share in developing the west in various frontier regions, having been also one of the very first settlers in the region where he is now living, seven and one-half miles northeast of Drewsey, Harney county. It is, therefore, very fitting that consideration be granted him in this volume, which devotes space to the leading and prominent citizens of this and adjacent counties.

Mr. Altnow was born in Moxfelde, Germany, on June 16, 1835, and there was reared, attending school for eight years without a vacation and finally graduating from the high school. In 1855, he bade the fatherland farewell with friends and home and sought the new world for the fortunes that might smile upon his honest endeavors. He landed in New York after a five weeks' voyage on a sailing vessel. Thence he went to Watertown, Wisconsin, and from there to Sibley county, Minnesota. There in June, 1864, he enlisted in Company H, Second Minnesota Volunteers. He first served in Tennessee, then was under Sherman in Georgia and went on the famous march to the sea. He fought in the battles of Jonesborough and Bentonville, and many skirmishes and had but one sick day in the entire service. He was mustered out at Louisville, Kentucky, at the end of the war, having made a fine military record. From Kentucky he returned to his home and there on October 28, 1866, he was married to Miss Matilda Mathia, a native of Germany. In October, 1868, he started with wife and child via New York and Panama, to California, getting to San Francisco in twenty-two days. He went thence to Salem, Oregon, coming to that town on December 11, 1868, whence in the following year he removed to Antelope, in Wasco county. But few people were then settled there and our subject remained until Gilliam county was cut off, thus living in two counties without moving, and had he remained until Wheeler was cut off it would have been three. He was occupied in raising stock and he has always made a success of his business. It was in 1881 that he located his present place. He moved the family first to Canyon City and thence in 1884 to the present home. He has a fine estate of four hundred acres, all fenced and well improved with orchards and buildings, having two very large barns and one of the finest residences in the entire country, it being an eleven room house of modern architectural design and provided with all conveniences. In 1890 the people called Mr. Altnow to act as the first county commissioner of Harney after it was a separate political division. He discharged the responsible duties that devolved upon him in that incumbency with credit to himself and satisfaction to all concerned. Mr. Altnow has steadily and wisely labored for the upbuilding of the entire country and has done much for Harney county. He came here when the nearest neighbors were forty-five miles distant and he has endured much hardship and deprivation to help build up the country and has always shown the true spirit of the pioneer. The following children have been born to Mr. and Mrs. Altnow: Emma, deceased; Willie J., Mrs. Lillie Glen, of Vale; Albert and Mrs. Ina Brittingham.

JAMES J. DONEGAN.—From the Emerald Isle came the ancestors of our subject, and thus he is infused with that patriotic and stirring blood that has made itse'f felt all the world over in the march which the sturdy Irish race has made to every clime and region in the interests of civilization. Patrick Donegan came from western Ireland to New York in 1852, and two years later he went thence via Panama to San Francisco, and then to Jackson county, Oregon. He returned soon to Ireland and married Margaret Lynch and brought his bride to Jackson county. In that place, on August 29, 1872, our subject was born to them. The mother died in 1874. The father was a blacksmith and mechanical engineer, and our subject was brought up in Jacksonville, where the father labored. He was a graduate from the Jacksonville high school and in

1889 came to Burns. Returning to his native place he worked the father's farm until 1894, then came to Burns and tended bar for Mr. Trisch, who is now his partner. They own a fine corner in Burns, with a good building and operate a good orderly saloon, carrying a fine stock of wines and liquors. Mr. Donegan is a member of the Native Sons of Oregon, at Burns, having been its first president. He is also a member of the K. of P., Inland Lodge, No. 70. The former lodge is No. 33, since Oregon was the thirty-third state admitted to the Union. Mr. Donegan was chairman of the Republican county central committee from 1896 to 1898 and at the same time he was a member of the state and congressional committee. He was also a stockholder and secretary of the Citizens Bank of Burns which was sold to the First National Bank in June, 1902. He is also interested in mining in the Pueblo district and has a fine six-room modern dwelling in Burns and is counted one of the progressive and capable business men of the town.

On August 30, 1896, Mr. Donegan married Miss Margaret, daughter of John and Margaret Smyth, pioneers of Harney county, from Douglas county, Oregon. Mr. Smyth was a settler in Diamond valley, this county, and was killed by the Indians in the Bannock war of 1878. Mrs. Smyth is married again and lives in Lagrande. To Mr. and Mrs. Donegan were born three children, Carrnen, Patrick Hugh, and James Donald. Mr. Donegan's father is still living in Jacksonville, Oregon.

ABRAHAM L. VANDERPOOL.—This enterprising stockman is a native son of Oregon, and his life has been such that his state may take commendable pride in him. He was born in Benton county on October 29, 1855, being the son of C. M. and Eliza J. Vanderpool. The father crossed the plains from Missouri in 1858. The mother came from Illinois about the same time. The father has followed farming and raising stock in Benton county ever since his settlement there. He fought in the Indian war for two years and was in many battles and many skirmishes, being on duty actively for the entire two years. Our subject attended the common schools until eighteen and then started out for himself. He went to the Yakima country, thence to Prineville, working with stock in the latter place, and in 1889 he went with a band of horses overland to Colorado. It was in 1890 that he came to the vicinity of his present place. He worked for wages a while and then entered land and took up stock raising. Here he has three hundred and sixty acres, well improved, a good band of cattle, and also some horses.

On November 6, 1892, Mr. Vanderpool married Miss Arlu E., daughter of J. C. and Nancy A. Garrett, of Okanogan county, Wash ington. To this union there have been born four children: Jessie C., Maggie C., Agnes A., Della L. Mr. Vanderpool is a member of the Native Sons of Oregon, at Burns.

SAMUEL B. STEWART.—The pioneer's life is one that demands a strong body, resourceful mind and courageous heart, and we are pleased to state that the subject of this sketch is happily possessed of all the requisites of a true pioneer and in the years that have gone by he has demonstrated repeatedly his capabilities and faithfulness in this line, for in Iowa, Kansas, and in Harney county, he has wrought on the frontier and has done a lion's share in the development of the country. At present Mr. Stewart is dwelling three miles east from Drewsey, on Otis creek, and has a fine farm and well watered with a ditch, and improved in a becoming manner. He handles cattle and horses and raises hay, and is considered one of the prominent men of his section.

Mr. Stewart was born in Otsego county, New York, sixteen miles from Cooperstown lake, on February 15, 1830, being the son of Leeman and Susan Stewart. He grew up with his parents and went with them to Kalamazoo county, Michigan, where they both died, the mother passing away in 1863, and the father in his eighty-third year. The father had been a prominent man in New York, having held the judgeship of the county for twelve years. Also he taught school for a number of years and his son was well educated. In Michigan on December 25, 1854, our subject married Miss Rebecca L. Forrester. Her parents were natives of Pennsylvania and she was born in Erie county, that state, on March 18, 1829.

In 1860, our subject and his wife removed to Cass county, Iowa. When the call came for men to defend the country, Mr. Stewart was quick to respond and in 1862 he enlisted in Company I, Twenty-third Volunteer Infantry of Iowa. He was under Sherman and Grant and fought through the entire war. He did service at the siege of Vicksburg, fought at Champion Hill, and Jackson, and in many other battles. He went to New Orleans and up the Rio Grande and fought in Texas and served throughout without a gun wound, but had his leg broken at New Orleans. He was mustered out at that city in May, 1865, having seen much of the hard life of the soldier under various conditions. He returned home and the family soon removed to Taylor county and thence in 1868 they went to Crawford county, Kansas, and there followed farming until the spring of 1880, when he fitted out covered wagons and made the trip across the plains to Walla Walla. We see him next in Jackson county, Oregon, whence in 1883 he came to near where he now resides and in 1887 he settled on the present home place. He has two hundred acres in this farm and also has an undivided half interest with his son in a quarter section on the north fork of Malheur river. Mr. Stewart is one of the substantial men of the community and expresses his desire to remain in his favored spot until his pilgrim career is done.

To Mr. and Mrs. Stewart there have been born four children: Mrs. Seraphine Gittings, Charles C., Mrs. Lillie E. Gibler of Ontario; Rolla F.

SETH BOWER.—This well known business man and stockman is one of the successful men of Harney county, having gained that enviable distinction both in the stock business and in the mercantile line, both of which, with the assistance of his capable and genial wife, he is carrying on at the present time.

Mr. Bower was born in Trumbull county, Ohio, on September 10, 1840, being the son of Joel and Belsy (Kaler) Bower. He was educated and grew to manhood in his native place and when the war clouds burst on this fair land he was quick to respond, and enlisted in the Fifteenth Ohio Heavy Artillery. He served his time of three years and then promptly re-enlisted and fought clear through to the end of the struggle and saw the last rag of defiance pulled down and the last gun silenced. He was in hard service, participated in numerous battles and skirmishes and was with Sherman on that memorable march to the sea. He received his honorable discharge at the close of the war and on December 3, 1865, he married Miss Mary E., daughter of Elijah and Wealthy (Lamb) Weston. Mrs. Bower was born in Geauga county, Ohio, on October 5, 1844. In 1868 Mr. Bower and his family removed to Mason county, then to Peoria, and later to Logan county. In 1871 he went to Crawford county, Kansas, thence to Butler county, Kansas, where they remained on a farm until 1881. In that year they crossed the plains with teams landing in the Grande Ronde valley, which was their home until 1884. Then another move was made and they settled south from Burns where they took a homestead. They continued there in the stock business until 1897 when Mr. Bower sold his ranch and removed his family to Harney. He at once entered in to the general merchandise business, and he has a good trade now. He carries a good assortment of all kinds of general merchandise and is known as one of the reliable men of the county. In addition, Mr. Bower owns a ranch and some stock to which he devotes considerable of his personal attention, while Mrs. Bower attends to the store. In addition to the store, Mrs. Bower has charge of the stage office, and the telephone office. They own their store building, their residence and considrable other property in Haney, in addition to farm land and cattle.

To Mr. and Mrs. Bower there have been born two children: Herbert S. married Maggie Loggan, and he operates a blacksmith shop in Harney; Alma L., who keeps books in the store. Mr. and Mrs. Bower are reliable and highly esteemed people of the county and they enjoy the confidence of all, being worthy of the same.

JAMES P. GEARHART.—The wealth and prosperity of Harney county are largely due to the enterprising stockmen of its precincts, and prominent among those on the north Malheur is the gentleman whose name is at the head of this article, and whose labors have been bestowed here with wisdom and vigor. James P. was born in Howard county, Missouri, on October 14, 1844, the son of John M. and Catherine (Brown) Gearhart. His mother died in 1851, and the following year the father came, with the balance of the family, across the plains with ox teams to Benton county. The trip was made in the company of a large train, and the end reached in safety. In 1858 the family removed to Josephine county, and in 1862 our subject came to the territory now embraced in Grant county. He landed at Canyon City in the time of the rush, and mined there until 1866, then journeyed to Humboldt county, California, and engaged in the cattle business. We find him there until 1873, when he came with a bunch of cattle to the Goose lake country, in southern Oregon, where he remained until 1882, then came to the Malheur valley, near his present place. He assisted to build the first house erected west of the agency in the Malheur valley, and in 1883 he located at his present place, which is twenty-two miles west from Drewsey. He now owns three hundred and twenty acres of land, all fenced and well improved. He has a comfortable home, good orchard and plenty of water for irrigating purposes. He raises cattle principally.

The marriage of Mr. Gearhart and Miss Margaret A. Davis was solemnized in 1873, and they have become the parents of five children—Mrs. Cora A. Capps, James W., John F., Bessie and Jessie. Mr. Gearhart is a member of the I. O. O. F., Drewsey Lodge, No. 147.

FRED HAINES' success is a fine exemplification of what the thrifty, sagacious and industrious man can do in Harney county. He came here, to use his own words, "with nothing," and now he is one of the heavy property owners of the county, he is a leading business man of eastern Oregon, and he has gained a real prominence in the political field, and withal, he has maintained an untarnished reputation, enjoys an enviable prestige, and is one of the builders and prominent men of the county.

Fred Haines was born in Ripley county, Indiana, on November 20, 1864, being the son of John and Eliza (Jennings) Haines, where he was reared on a farm and gained his education from the public schools. In 1885 Mr. Haines came to Linn county, Oregon, and went to work for wages on a farm. In 1886 he came to Prineville, and went to riding for stock. The next year he came to Lawen, where he labored for two years, and then on to Harney. He used his small capital to open a general merchandise store, and so commenced business. His genial and affable ways soon drew him customers, which his fair and upright dealing have always kept, and it was not long until the people perceived that they could rely on Mr. Haines, both as to his ability to select goods and as to his honesty and integrity in treating them right, and the result was that the trade increased in a most thriving manner. At the present time Mr. Haines has a fine store building thirty-six by seventy feet, filled with a choice selection of all classes of goods needed in his trade, including groceries, gents' furnishings and clothing, crockery, hardware, dry goods, harness, and in fact everything that is required in this section of the country. In addition, he has all kinds of farm machinery and vehicles. He has a large stone fireproof warehouse, twenty-four by sixty-five, packed full of choice stock. Mr. Haines has a branch store in Burns, owns a saloon building in Harney, a fine farm of two hundred acres, five miles east of Harney, a good band of cattle, besides other property. He has a brother in the general merchandise business in the Narrows, who is also making a good success. Mr. Haines is now serving his third term as mayor of Harney, which is done to the general satisfaction of the people. He is an active Republican, and is frequently in the county conventioin, although not striving for personal preferment, and on three different occasions he has been delegate to the state convention. He was appointed postmaster on April 15, 1897, and was the first postmaster appointed in Oregon under McKinley's administration.

On September 7, 1890, Mr. Haines married Miss Julia, daughter of Robert and Permelia Ann Ferguson, early pioneers of Baker county, where Mrs. Haines was born. To this happy union one child was born June 10, 1891, named Ethel Lee. Mr. Haines is a worthy man, a public-minded citizen, who has done much for the welfare of the county, a thorough

and capable business man, and a loyal friend, and he justly deserves the position of trust and the place of honor and prestige that is accorded to him by his fellows.

I. N. HUGHET was born in Linn county, Oregon, on February 15, 1857, being the son of Milton and Sarah E. (McMillan) Hughet. The father came across the plains in an early day and settled in Linn county. His father, Robert R. Hughet, fought in the war of 1812 and took a donation claim in Linn county, where he lived until the time of his death in 1887. Milton Hughet died in Canyon City in 1862. The mother of I. N. came across the plains with an ox train and is now living in Harney county. When this son was seven years old he went with his mother to Humboldt county, California, and there he received his education. He milked cows and broke horses to earn sufficient for his board and clothes while he was studying. And later he invested his earning in calves, which gave him a fine start in the stock business. We wish to mention one of the hard labors and trying undertakings that our subject did when he was but a boy in California. It was carrying mail from Petrolia to the upper Mattole valley over the mountains. Three times a week he made the journey and many times it was necessary to swim the streams. However, for three years he steadily did this labor and in 1884, he sold his stock and came to Harney county. He first located on road land, but later gave this up, as he was not sure of winning in the litigation. In 1886 he went to Rockford, about ten miles southeast from The Narrows, and preempted one hundred and sixty acres, which he sold in 1889. Then he removed to Warm Springs, where he now lives and since that time he has been occupied in raising stock, and handling his large estate of about twelve hunderd acres.

About the time of the county seat fight, Mr. Hughet was the leader in securing the road from Rockford to intersect with the Burns-Silver creek road via The Narrows. Mr. Hughet named the road. The enterprise was opposed by Peter French and others, but through the skillful management of Mr. Hughet the opposition was placated and overcome.

I. N. HUGHET.

In addition to his fine estate, Mr. Hughet has an excellent bunch of cattle, numbering over one hundred and twenty. He has commodious and substantial barns, good house and all other improvements 'needed on his ranch and is one of the leading citizens of the county. Mr. Hughet has always been of a public mind, has labored well for the advancement of the country, and the cause of progression and upbuilding always finds a champion in him. While he was at Rockford, he was in partnership with his brother, who came from California with him, and this arrangement continued until 1891. Some time since, Mr. Hughet unearthed the skeleton of a buffalo, which demonstrates that these noble creatures roamed here as they did on the eastern plains.

In 1891 Mr. Hughet married Miss Lillie, daughter of George and Philiamenia (Hartman) Pfordt, of Pittsburg, Pennsylvania. To this union there have been born the following issue: Glen N., Esther, Mildred, Louis M., Albert, Lee, and an infant unnamed. Mr. Hughet is a member of the Native Sons of Oregon, A. H. Rubie Camp, of Burns. He came to this county with limited means, but has gained a large holding by his wisdom, his industry, and his fine business ability.

SAMUEL N. WILLIAMS.—This prosperous and well known citizen of Harney county lives on a fine ranch about fourteen miles west from Drewsey, where he does a general farming business and raises stock. He is a man of good principles, and has done a noble part in the development of Harney county and other portions in the west.

Samuel N. was born in Henry county, Illinois, on October 9, 1853, and at nine years of age his mother died, and the father passed away three years later. As an orphan he knew the hardships of life, and was early thrown on his own resources. At the age of fifteen he went to Iowa and there worked for wages until 1874. Then he determined to try the west, and accordingly came to Grant county, this state. In that county he did faithful labor for a decade, and then came to Harney county. He located near where he now lives, taking government land and devoting himself to its improvement. He prospered and made a good
44

showing, and in 1901 he sold that property and bought his present home place. It is a quarter section of excellent hay land, well improved and produces fine returns annually. Mr. Williams has about one hundred head of cattle, and devotes considerable attention to this department, being one of the successful and substantial stockmen of this stock country.

In social life Mr. Williams is genial and affable and always has a hearty welcome for all, while he has hosts of warm and loyal friends. He is a member of the I. O. O. F., Lodge No. 147, of Drewsey. Mr. Williams has never seen fit to embark on the matrimonial sea and is one of the quiet participants in the peaceful joys of the celibatarian's life.

AMBROSE M. DIBBLE, deceased.— Harney county lost a fine citizen and his family a devoted father and husband when the subject of this memorial passed away. He was a sturdy pioneer all the days of his life, and did very much for the upbuilding of the various sections where he wrought, and he is deservedly ranked with the leading men of this county.

A. M. Dibble was born in Chenango county, New York, on March 5, 1813, being the son of Reuben and Anna Dibble. His father served seven years in the Revolution under Captain Roberts, in Washington's army. In 1835 our subject went to Hillsdale county, Michigan, and there assisted to survey much of that section. In 1849 he crossed the plains with the train known as the Fayette Rovers, which was accompanied for six weeks in the most dangerous parts by Kit Carson as scout. At Salt Lake they experienced some trouble with the Mormons, who stole their stock. Mr. Dibble visited most of the important camps of the state of California, and finally went to raising stock. During the Indian troubles of 1852-53 he lost about twelve thousand dollars worth of stock. He fought the savages under the noted Captain Lawton, and experienced some thrilling times in this service. Following this Indian war Mr. Dibble went to farming, and in 1854 returned via Panama to Hillsdale county, Michigan, where, on June 19, 1855, he married Miss Clarrissa, daughter of Aaron and Martha Spencer, natives of the state of

New York. To this union there were born four children—N. Adelbert, born March 5, 1856, and married to Rosetta Penick; Herbert A., born October 12, 1858, in Michigan; Carrie A., deceased; Frank C., born February 19, 1871, in California, married to Martha A. Johnson. Mr. Spencer was the first white child born in Canandaigua county, New York, and his daughter, Clarissa, was born there also, on January 13, 1832. In 1835 Mr. Spencer removed his family to Hillsdale county, Michigan. In 1860 Mr. Dibble and his wife crossed the plains with ox teams to Butte county, California, and there engaged in farming until 1883, then came overland to Lewis county, Washington, and in May, 1884. came to Silver creek, Harney county. They live here at the present time, and are engaged in raising stock, being prosperous, and the sons own land in addition to that of the mother. On September 6, 1886, came the summons for Mr. Dibble to depart this realm, and, sincerely mourned, not only by his family, but also by all who knew him, the good man went to his final rest. Since that time the widow has conducted her affairs with commendable wisdom, and is one of the highly respected residents of the county.

JESSE C. DAVIS.—The enterprising and genial gentleman whose life's career it is now our pleasant privilege to outline is one of the substantial men of the Malheur river valley, and has wrought here with an energy and sagacity that have rendered him one of the prosperous and well-to-do stockmen of that section. Jesse C. Davis was born in Carroll county, Missouri, on December 2, 1862, the son of Archibald and Elizabeth Davis. The father was killed in an accident on the railroad while the son was a child. In 1874 the mother came with her children to Reno, Nevada, on the train, and thence by wagon to Lake county, Oregon. In 1882 our subject came to Malheur valley, near his present place, and soon after went to lower Willow creek. and there engaged in the stock business for a time. He returned, however, to the Malheur valley, near his former settlement, and entered land, the same being twenty-one miles west from Drewsey. He has a half section, well improved and partly in meadow grasses. He has a

comfortable home, and is one of the prominent stockmen of his vicinity, handling cattle principally.

The marriage of Mr. Davis and Miss Bertha E. Wintermeier was solemnized on July 16, 1893, and they have become the parents of the following named children: William B., born February 5, 1894; Ethel B., born September 4, 1895; Charles W., born May 6, 1898. On September 22, 1899, Mr. Davis was called upon to mourn the death of his wife. He started in this section with no money, and has labored along with care and enterprise, and now he is in a very prosperous condition and has the privilege of enjoying the recompense of his faithful toil, having been blessed with success in his business ventures.

Mr. Davis has taken to himself a second wife, and the date of this happy marriage was June 8, 1902. The lady then becoming Mrs. Davis was Louisa May Landing, a native of Oregon.

ROBERT J. WILLIAMS.—Three miles east from Riley postoffice, on Silver creek, we come to the estate of the subject of this sketch. It consists of one thousand acres of fine hay and grazing land, fenced and skillfully handled, while its improvements are all that are called for on a modern stock ranch, as Mr. Williams handles a goodly bunch of cattle. He is the son of Frederick and Mary (Davis) Williams, and was born in Sevier county, Arkansas, on July 21, 1861. The father was a soldier in the Confederate army, and was taken prisoner, and as he was never heard of after that it is supposed that he died in prison. In 1865 Robert J. was taken by his mother to Madison county, Arkansas, and he remained there until 1879, at which time he came to Modoc county, California. He worked for wages for a time and then went to raising stock, continuing the same until 1882. At this last date he came with a band of cattle to Silver creek and located his present home place. He has continued here in the stock business since that time with good success, and he is numbered with the substantial and capable and prosperous men in the county, being also a popular man among his fellows, for in 1900 he was elected, on the Democratic ticket, as county commissioner for four years. He was one of the very earliest settlers of his locality, and he knows the hardships of the pioneer, and has done excellent work in the development of the county and bringing out its resources.

On January 2, 1884, in Modoc county, California, Mr. Williams married Miss Emma, daughter of J. C. and Nancy E. Garrett, now of Okanogan county, Washington, and to them have been born six children—Ella, deceased; John Lester; Robert Frederick; James Lee; Harry Amos; William Edgar. Mr. Williams is a member of the A. F. & A. M., Burns Lodge, No. 97, and is also a member of the Pioneers of the Pacific, at Pendleton. Mr. Williams is a man of ability and integrity, and his fellows have confidence in him, since he has always so conducted himself that he is above reproach and has maintained an unsullied reputation and possesses a stanch character of intrinsic worth.

———◆◆◆———

THOMAS HASKELL, deceased.—In outlining the career of this doughty and capable frontiersman it is becoming also that especial mention should be made of his worthy wife, who is still living, and is one of the highly respected citizens of Burns.

Thomas Haskell was born in Auburn, Maine, in February, 1826, being the son of Thomas and Ruth Haskell. He grew to manhood in his native place, and then came via New York and Cape Horn to San Francisco, in 1855. He went to Placer county and mined, and there, on February 7, 1863, he married Mrs. Sarah (Broadhead) McClintock, widow of John McClintock, who died in Iowa in 1861. Mrs. McClintock was born on November 21, 1823, and by her first husband has four children—Thomas; Mrs. Ione Whiting, near Burns; Mrs. May Dalton, deceased; Frank, of Burns. After the death of her first husband Mrs. McClintock started, with her youngest child, via New York and Panama, to San Francisco. On account of the intoxication of the captain and crew the ship was nearly wrecked, and amid the commotion one frightened Irish woman was heard in fervent prayer, and amid other things she exclaimed: "Oh, Lord, if you will only put me on shore, I don't care a d——n if the old ship does go to the bot-

tom." Danger of all going to the bottom was imminent, but the ludicrousness of the scene and words combined was too much, and hearty laughter greeted this ebullition of intercessory zeal. In due time, however, Mrs. McClintock reached San Francisco, and went thence to Tumales bay, and then to Placer county, where she opened a laundry for a time, and then rented a hotel. After her marriage with Mr. Haskell they removed to Alta, and Mr. Haskell engaged to drive fast freight to Cisco. In 1867 Mrs. Haskell bought a hotel on the installment plan, and was successful in the venture. Then she operated the Tule hotel in Winnemucca, Nevada, and in 1869 she was in the same business in Carlin, Nevada, also operating a restaurant. Then a move was made to Long valley, California, and they went to ranching. In March, 1882, Mr. Haskell had his feet frozen, and it was necessary to cut off his toes, but as no surgeon was to be had Mrs. Haskell was forced to do it with the shears. All on one foot and one on the other foot were sacrificed. This shows the stern realities of living on the frontier. On June 5, 1882, Mrs. Haskell, with her crippled husband, started overland with a team for Burns, whither her children had preceded her. The first day an axle was broken, and this heroic woman unloaded the wagon, took it back for repairs and then came on. One week of the journey was spent without seeing a house. Having divided their rations with some starving pilgrims met on the way, it caused our subjects to run short, and the last of the journey was spent without food. Upon arriving in Burns, there being but a house or two, our subjects took a homestead and went to work, their capital being three horses and ten dollars. Mrs. Haskell put up a tent and cooked for the men who were building the first hotel in Burns, then she went to Egan and cooked there. (Egan was a town now extinct.) Then Mrs. Haskell operated the hotel there. Mr. Haskell was engaged in raising stock, but soon a cancer developed in his mouth and he had to go to San Francisco to be doctored, and there he died in 1889.

Since the death of her husband Mrs. Haskell has struggled on alone, and has managed her own affairs, and is now the happy possessor of a good residence in Burns, a well improved ranch, and a goodly competence for her old age, the golden years that now begin to run apace. She is seventy-nine years old, and has good health and is highly respected by all, being a noble and true woman of sterling worth and many virtues.

* * *

LOUIS RACINE.—This worthy gentleman and his estimable wife have the true spirit of the pioneer, and have manifested it in a very becoming manner since coming to Harney county, as they have by dint of hard labor, wise management and careful handling of the resources of the country, come to be among the leaders in the business realm and in stock raising, being also people of integrity, worth and uprightness.

Mr. Racine was born in November, 1854, at St. Hiacinth City, Canada. He grew to manhood there, went to Montreal, and there married Miss Mathilde Giguere on June 24, 1877, she being a native of that city and born March 22, 1861. Mr. Racine was a baker, and operated a store of general merchandise and a bakery, Mrs. Racine managing the store while he baked. In 1882 they removed to Lowell, Massachusetts, and started a grocery and bakery, and in 1886 sold this and came to Burns. They landed here with four small children and but little capital. Mr. Racine could speak English, but his wife knew the French only. Burns was a hamlet of but few houses, and Mr. Racine started a hotel in a small shack, doing the cooking, while his wife managed the business. They did well; supplies being high, the high price of meals offset it, and they made money. Soon they purchased a house and lot on the installment plan, and from that time to this they have been steadily adding to their property. They now have a fine hotel of twenty-five sleeping apartments and other rooms, while the care that is maintained for the comfort of the guests and to make the cuisine the best that skill can do has given the French hotel a very enviable reputation with the traveling public. Mrs. Racine manages this while her husband attends to a large stock ranch which they own, about twenty-five miles from Burns. This ranch is supplied with all necessary improvements and supports a fine band of cattle. Also they have a good ranch of one hundred and sixty acres, the other ranch

being about seven hundred acres, six miles from town. In addition to these ranches, the fine hotel and lots, they have a good seven-room residence and considerable other property.

To this worthy couple there have been born four children, named as follows: Adelord, Wilfrid, Eugenia and Dolaress. The boys are graduates from the Portland Commercial College. The girls are now in the New England Conservatory of Music, at Boston. Miss Racine has finished a classical course and is now devoting her whole attention to the art of music, while Miss Dolaress is pursuing the classical studies in connection with the musical work. They both have displayed great talent in their various studies and are accomplished and gracious ladies. Mr. Racine has his sons with him on the ranch, and they are much interested in raising fine stock. When Mr. Racine and his wife came here they determined to start a French colony, and so paid the way of a number of immigrants here, but they became dissatisfied with the country and returned without paying their transportation, except one who staid and went to work and is now a well-to-do citizen. Mr. Racine and his estimable wife are talented business people, and they are both handling the affairs under their charge with commendable wisdom and skill, and they stand high in the esteem of the people, having many friends wherever they are known.

* * *

GEORGE SHELLEY.—Honest industry, uprightness and integrity with capabilities have placed the subject of this article in an enviable position among his fellows, and it is with pleasure that we are permitted to grant a review of his life's career. His parents, Jeremiah and Martha (Williams) Shelley, were natives of Kentucky, and at Louisville, in that state, they were married, and there, on September 23, 1855, George was born. They went to Daviess county, Missouri, and the father removed them later to Texas, where he was in the stock business. He had previosly been a soldier in the Mexican war. This son stayed with his father in the stock business until the latter' death, and then he came to Colorado Springs, and here attended school. Later he went to Colorado City and learned the blacksmith trade, and after working there for a time, in 1875, he came overland to Boise. where he engaged to ride after stock until 1877. In that year he went with a band of cattle to Wyoming and accompanied the train to Chicago. In the spring of 1878 he was in the Leadville excitement, and in July of that year he enlisted under Captain Maxim to fight the Indians, and he did scout work over eastern Oregon and in Idaho. He was in the battle of Monday Ferry, where one man was killed. He fought until all was done, and then went to the Grande Ronde valley and worked at his trade there until 1884. He next opened a shop in Camp Harney, and in 1887 went to Crane creek, where he operated a shop until 1895, when he came to Burns, where he has been since. In 1897 Mr. Shelley entered into partnership with J. C. Foley, and since that time they have worked together. In 1900 the people called Mr. Shelley to act as sheriff of Harney county, being elected on the Democratic ticket. He rendered good service for his entire term, satisfying the people and leaving a commendable record. On July 1, 1902, he retired from the office and again went to the forge, and is working there at the present time. Mr. Shelley is a member of the K. of P., Inland Lodge, No. 70.

On October 23, 1886, Mr. Shelley married Miss Hallie, daughter of David and Rebecca Carey, of Crane, and to them have been born two children—Frankie and Lenora.

GEORGE W. SHAW.—A successful tiller of the soil in Harney county, a man of stability and uprightness, while also he is a patriotic citizen, the subject of this article is deserving of conspicuous mention in his county's history, which we are gratified to accord to him. Mr. Shaw was born in Oswego county, New York, on December 28, 1847, being the son of Parley and Elizabeth Shaw. When he was eight years old he went to Wapello county, Iowa, with his parents, thence to Kane county, Illinois, and then to DeKalb county, Illinois, and in 1863 they removed to Kankakee county. The father died in 1866, and in 1874 our subject came to Lincoln county, Kansas. His mother accompanied him and they dwelt there until 1883, when they came west to

Canyon City. The following year they came to Harney valley, but returned to Canyon City and operated a hotel there for a time, and then came to Harney valley again. He located first on Poison creek and engaged in raising stock. It was in 1896 that he bought his present place of four hundred and eighty acres, four and a half miles east from Burns. The estate is well fenced, mostly cultivated, provided with good house and outbuildings and a fine young orchard. Mr. Shaw also owns the one hundred and twenty on Poison creek, which is also well improved. He does considerable gardening in addition to general farming and raising stock.

The marriage of Mr. Shaw and Miss Maud, daughter of David and Alice Martin, of Decatur, Illinois, was salemnized on February 25, 1900. Mr. Shaw's mother lived with him until the time of her death, which occurred on January 18, 1901. She was a noble and good woman, and had wrought faithfully in life's battle. Mr. Shaw is considered one of the substantial and leading citizens of his section, and is esteemed and stands well among his fellows.

TOM ALLEN.—In the history of Harney county the name of Tom Allen is inseparably connected with the stock industries, while also he has ever manifested a public spirit and great zeal in the upbuilding of the interests of the county, and thus he should be accorded especial mention in this work, since also the people have entrusted him with the important office of sheriff, having been elected in the June election, in 1902, on the Republican ticket. Mr. Allen was born in Benton county, Oregon, on May 9, 1854, being the son of Jacob and Cynthia A. Allen. The father was a native of Indiana, and came across the plains in 1850 with the ox teams of that day, settling in Benton county. The mother was a native of Kentucky, and in 1851 came from Missouri across the plains with ox teams, landing in Benton county. In 1853 they were married, and our subject is their first child. In 1864 the family removed to Walla Walla, and two years later returned to Benton county. Our subject was reared on a farm and received his education from the district schools. In 1878 Tom Allen came to Silver creek and at once engaged to ride for stock with Cecil Brothers. Four years were spent with them, and he then accepted the foremanship for Hardin & Riley for four years. Then he went to Crook county and engaged in raising horses for himself, which he retired from a few years later and took the foremanship for Hardin & Riley again for three years. Then he was cattle foreman for the Pacific Live Stock Company; then held the same position for William Hanley, and then for the French-Glen Company, where he continued until the first day of July, 1902, when he took the oath of office as sheriff of the county of Harney. Mr. Allen is well known, and it is no experiment to place the responsibilities of this office in his hands. He is at present master of Lodge No. 97, of the A. F. & A. M.

On December 23, 1888, Mr. Allen married Miss Ada, daughter of Isaac and Mariah Thornburg, and they have one child, Fred Bither, born July 26, 1898. Mr. Thornburg died in 1894, but his widow lives with Mr. Allen. In his labors Mr. Allen has been faithful, vigorous and capable; in his walk he has been upright, and always manifests stanch integrity; while as a man, a neighbor and an associate he has the confidence, the approbation and admiration of the people.

It is of note that Mr. Allen's father fought in the Mexican war under General Scott, and participated in the battle of Buena Vista and also did some skirmishing.

CAPTAIN HARRISON KELLEY.— One of the legal fraternity of the state of Oregon, the subject of this sketch, is now allied with the interests of Burns, having been domiciled here for a number of years, in which time he has won hosts of friends in all parts of the county and has shown himself an upright and faithful man, a patriotic citizen and a good business man, being one of the foremost practitioners of the eastern part of the state.

Mr. Kelley was born in St. Joseph county, Michigan, on November 2, 1838, being the son of Harrison and Nancy (Edgar) Kelley, natives, respectively, of Virginia and Kentucky. His great grandfather fought in the Revolution. Our subject attended school in Michigan, then went to the Baptist University at Hillsdale, afterward graduating from the law department of the State University of Michigan at Ann Arbor. This was 1860. He commenced the practice of law in Sturgis, Michigan, and was admitted to the supreme court of the state and the United States courts. Upon the re-organization of the Eleventh Michigan Infantry he enlisted as private in Company A, in March, 1865, and was soon after appointed sergeant major of the regiment. He was afterward given the position of second lieutenant of Company A, in this regiment. He went as far south as Tennessee, southern part, and was commander on detail duty at Chattanooga until the close of the war. Then he returned home, and in 1866 he married and practiced until 1867, when he came via New York, Panama, San Francisco and Crescent City to Jacksonville. He practiced law and took up mining also. In the outbreak of the Modoc Indians in 1872 he organized a company and was commissioned captain by Governor L. F. Govern. He was in the thickest of the fight, with his men, and in the Lava bed battle one of his men was killed beside him, and about fifty killed and wounded in this battle, being every fourth man of the entire command. The captain was shot at many times, but was not seriously hurt. He manifested great bravery, courage and coolness, and this may truly be said of him in all of his military career. After the struggle he returned to his practice and in 1889 was appointed receiver of the United States land office at Burns, and came thither in his own covered conveyance. Five years were spent at this labor, also attending to the practice of law, and in 1896 he was elected to the county clerkship on the Republican ticket, and it may be said that the Captain is a Republican through and through, having voted for Abraham Lincoln and the ticket straight since, and he hurrahed for Fremont. He was the first mayor of Burns and has always been active in politics. While practicing in Jacksonville he was editor of the old Oregon Sentinel, one of the oldest papers in the state. He built the first house on the hill in Burns and dug the first well there, having now a very fine place and a good farm six miles south from town, which is mostly hay land. Mr. Kelley gives considerable attention to raising stock, horses and cattle.

To Mr. and Mrs. Kelley has been born one child, Phoeba L., now in charge of the telephone office in Burns. She graduated from the Commercial College in Portland and has taught, having also been on the board for examining teachers for eight years. The Captain has a good practice, is an upright and honorable man of ability and stands high in the community.

WILLIAM H. CULP.—This well known and good man has been successful in at least two different lines of endeavor in the battle of life, being at the present time engaged in dairying, farming and gardening, while also he raises stock, his home place being about five miles northeast from Burns, where he has a good body of land, well improved and handled in a skillful manner.

William H. Culp was born in Pickaway county, Ohio, on June 15, 1837, his parents being David and Catherine (Cach) Culp. While he was young his parents removed to Schuylkill county, Pennsylvania, but soon returned to Ohio, and thence went to Clark county, Illinois. In 1855 they removed to Tazewell county, Illinois, and then to Woodford county, Illinois. Our subject grew up on a farm and gained his education from the schools of the various places where he lived. On June 18, 1862, he married Miss Rebecca, daughter of John and Sarah A. Culp, then removed to McLean county, Illinois. Mr. Culp had previously mastered the painter's art, and he wrought at this for a few years, and then removed to Linn county, Iowa, continuing his trade there until 1887. In that year he came direct to Harney county, and for four years wrought at his trade in Burns. He then determined to engage in stock raising and farming, so took a homestead, later trying the business on a rented farm, which is now his own. He has a fine herd of milk cows, his farm is provided with good buildings, and he is comfortably and prosperously settled. In Iowa Mr. Culp used frequently to act as justice of the peace, being elected often, and also did the duties of road supervisor for the people.

To Mr. Culp and his estimable wife there have been born four children: Lloyd, near Burns; Mrs. Florence M. Schock, in San Francisco; Austin W., of Harney county; John

H., of Burns. Mr. and Mrs. Culp have been married for forty years, and all of this time they have been treading in the narrow way, being pilgrims of the Christian faith. They are zealous in this cause, as is evidenced in the fact that they have opened their dwelling for the organization of the Christian church of Harney county, and for several years services have been regularly held there on each Lord's Day. His faith and his life, comparable therewith, has been a source of much testimony in the county, and he is esteemed by all as an upright, capable and good man.

FRANK O. JACKSON.—This young man is one of the substantial residents and citizens of Burns, having displayed here the happy and worthy capabilities possessed by him, both in an untarnished life of uprightness and in a successful career in the business world, being of enviable standing and highly respected.

Mr. Jackson was born in Sauk county, Wisconsin, on March 14, 1876, being the son of Stephen and Annie Jackson. The parents came to Wheeler county, Nebraska, while their son was a child, and in 1882 they came across the plains to Warm Springs, Malheur county. The father was engaged in ranching and raising stock, and our subject studied at home, there being no schools near. In 1893 Mr. Jackson came to Burns and spent some time in the schools here and in the business college. He worked for wages while not in school, and in 1896 he went into the wood business. He was very successful from the start, also doing farming. He now owns his wood business, handles his farm, owns three good residences in Burns and forty good lots for residence purposes, while he devotes the major part of his time to clerking in the establishment of Lundberg & Dalton. Mr. Jackson is a member and past grand of the I. O. O. F., Burns Lodge No. 77; also of the K. of P., Lodge No. 70; and of the Encampment; and the Rebekahs. He is also one of the councilmen of Burns.

On September 5, 1885, a stranger came to the home of our subject's father and asked to stay all night. He was granted the favor, and about one o'clock the next morning he went to a haystack, where Frank O. and a Frenchman were sleeping, and killed the

Frencman with an axe and set fire to the stack. He then went to the house, shot Mr. Jackson in the head, killing him instantly, and also shot Mrs. Jackson, but she recovered. The fire was burning the clothes of our subject when he awoke. The supposed object of the murder was money. This will be more fully detailed in another portion of this volume. Mrs. Jackson later married Mr. O'Neil, and they live at the Warm Springs ranch.

Our subject is a man of energy and ability, and has done a commendable work in Burns, being now one of the recognized business leaders and in every way respected and esteemed.

RANSOM DRAKE.—This estimable gentleman and patriotic citizen of Harney county has long been one of the enterprising stockmen and real developers of the country, manifesting the worthy qualities of which he is richly possessed in the labors that he has accomplished. He was born in Michigan on March 24, 1859, the son of Francis and Julia (Wilson) Drake. From the native state they migrated to Green county, Wisconsin. There the father enlisted in Company E, Thirtieth Wisconsin Infantry, the date being August, 1864, and he served on detached duty until the close of the war, being mustered out the last of June, 1865. He returned to his Wisconsin home, and in 1872 went thence to California, and the year following the mother and our subject followed. Settlement was made in Santa Barbara county, and our subject remained there and in Ventura county until 1877, at which date he came to Prineville, this state, then being in Wasco county. He worked for a brother of Joaquin Miller for a time, and then came to Harney county, the date of this last move being 1879. He settled on the Malheur river, taking up land as soon as it was opened for settlement, and turning his attention to raising horses. He was one of the first settlers in this vicinity. He is living at the present time about six miles southeast from Van postoffice, on a rented farm, and he devotes his entire attention to handling stock. His own ranch of one quarter section lies on the Silvies river, and is a good place, well improved.

The marriage of Mr. Drake and Miss Bertha Selle, a native of Minnesota, was cele-brated on December 9, 1894. Mrs. Drake came west with her parents in 1886. They were Christopher and Susie Selle, natives of Germany, but both dead now. Mr. Drake is one of the upright and capable stockmen of his vicinity, and has always made a record that has commended him to his fellows, in whose esteem and confidence he stands high.

CYRUS HAYES, deceased.—The members of the noble band of pioneers who wended their way across the wilds of this region fifty years ago, are going one by one to that bourne whence no traveller returns, and it is very fitting that we should chronicle in this history of Harney county the salient points in the life of one worthy man, Cyrus Hayes, that his memory may be handed down to succeeding generations, since he was a real builder in the great west and a good man.

Cyrus Hayes was born in Guernsey county, Ohio, October 4, 1818, being the son of Bailey and Mary Hayes. He grew to manhood in his native place and then went to Marion county, Iowa. There, on February 15, 1855, he married Miss Julia A., daughter of W. S. and Catherine Duncan. Mr. Duncan was a native of Robinson county, Tennessee, came to Illinois when it was a territory, acted as sheriff of Franklin county for two terms, and also was a member of the legislature for one term while the territory of Illinois existed. Mrs. Duncan was born in Caldwell county, Kentucky, and was married in Franklin county, Illinois, where Mrs. Hayes was born on April 12, 1832. They removed to Iowa, and later were in Warren county, that state. In 1862 Mr. Hayes with his wife and three children started across the plains with ox teams. The train consisted of one hundred and fifty wagons and some trouble was experienced with the Indians. Mrs. Hayes drove the oxen much of the way, which necessitated walking, and she has done very much hard labor which falls to the lot of the pioneer. They wintered in Auburn, Baker county, then went to Boise basin and in the fall following their arrival they went to Lane county. Mr. Hayes entered land and engaged in farming until 1874, when the family came to Lake county. In this latter place they lived until the death of Mr. Hayes,

JULIA A. HAYES.

HARVEY DIXON.

MRS. HARVEY DIXON.

which sad event occurred on September 24, 1887. Mr. Hayes died of heart disease while on the desert with his son, Marcellus B. His remains were buried at Paisley until 1901,when they were removed and now rest in the Silver Lake cemetery. The son, Scott, had come to Harney county and soon after the death of her husband, the mother came hither also and entered land where she now lives, three and one-half miles northwest from Lawen. She has a half section of fine hay land and owns some cattle. To Mr. and Mrs. Hayes there were born five children: Mary C., wife of William T. Hill, near Lawen; George W., married to Annie Alberson, at Burns; Scott, married to Mrs. Izora (Smith) Buck and they have one child, Ora Scott, and live near Lawen; Marcellus B., married to Belle Claypool, near Lawen; Linley Bailey, married to Edith Claypool, near Lawen. Mrs. Hayes has nobly borne the burdens of life since her husband was called hence and she is one of the highly esteemed residents of the county, and is beloved by all.

HARVEY DIXON.—Rightly Mr. Dixon belongs in the list of reliable and sturdy pioneers of the West, for he has been on the frontier for fifty years, laboring in various capacities as is needed in frontier life, and now being one of the real builders and leading men of Harney county. He was born in Illinois on December 25, 1838, being the son of Raphael Dixon. While an infant he was taken with the family to Andrew county, Missouri, where the mother died soon after. In 1852 he came across the plains with his uncle, James Dixon, and he has the distinction of driving from five to nine yoke of oxen all the way, being then but fourteen years of age. They settled in Marion county, and the following spring, the subject of this sketch started on horseback alone to Yreka, California, and he got there, too, in good shape. In that vicinity he mined with good success. In 1855 he enlisted in Captain Bushe's spy company to fight Indians. He was, soon after, the express messenger and was in numerous skirmishes, being also in many tight places where he barely escaped with his life. Following that war, Mr. Dixon settled at the mouth of the Rogue river and engaged in stock business. Later he was at the

mouth of the Klamath, packing for the government. In 1861 he came to Walla Walla and packed to British Columbia to the Cariboo mines; then in 1862 he went to The Dalles and packed to Canyon City, Elk City, Lewiston and other points and mines. He was at the falls of Spokane river when there was not a house in the vicinity.

On January 14, 1868, Mr. Dixon married Miss Mary E. Demeris, who crossed the plains with her parents from Iowa to Walla Walla with oxen in 1863. Mr. Dixon made his home in Walla Walla until 1873, then went to California and later came to Prineville, and finally in 1863 he came to his present place and settled. He has a fine farm of one hundred and sixty acres, well improved, and lying one mile northeast from Burns. Also he owns two hundred and eighty acres twenty miles north from Burns. He has stock, cattle and horses, and is one of the substantial men and property owners of the county.

To Mr. and Mrs. Dixon there have been born two children, Mrs. Susan S. Whiting, and Mrs. Sarah E. Baker.

By way of reminiscence it is interesting to note some of the adventurers of Mr. Dixon. On one occasion, he was prospecting in British Columbia and in company with his partner he made a raft and they attempted to go down the Finley river. The raft was destroyed, their chattels lost, their camp equippage was all lost and they were obliged to ride one hundred and fifty miles bareheaded, with only their underclothes for protection against the weather. They subsisted on Sarvis berries. At the time of the Modoc Indian war, Mr. Dixon was taken prisoner and after three months, he succeeded in making his escape.

CHARLES W. JONES, deceased.—No compilation that has to do with the history of Harney county, or in fact with eastern Oregon, would be complete were there failure to incorporate a review of the active career of the gentleman whose name is mentioned above. We therefore with pleasure grant this memoir to give this worthy man the place which belonged to him, as he was one who labored with great energy and sagacity in the development of the country.

Charles W. Jones was born in Jasper county, Iowa, on January 28, 1858, being the son of Isaac H. and Mary (Garrison) Jones. They crossed the plains in 1863 to the Willamette valley, and afterwards lived in Jackson county. Mr. Jones was reared on a farm and was always marked by his force of character, vigor and excellent qualities. He was educated in the common schools, and in 1878 he came to the Harney valley and engaged to ride after stock for Peter French. He volunteered to fight the Indians soon after coming here, and was in one brush in Diamond valley, when one Chinaman was killed and one white man wounded. After that he went to his labors again, and his worth soon became apparent. It was in 1881 that he was engaged by Todhunter & Devine to have charge of their entire herds. They were the largest stock owners in this country. Afterwards they were known as the L. F. Company. In 1879 he had been appointed as superintendent of the entire holdings of the L. F. Company in eastern Oregon, and in this capacity he continued until 1895. He was noted for his wisdom in handling stock, for his vigor in accomplishing the hard tasks incident to stock raising on the range, and he was equally well known for his executive force and practical judgment in handling men and manipulating large interests. During this long service he, in company with I. L. Poujade, bought the Cow Creek ranch, a fine property of eight hundred acres of valuable land. He operated with his partner in handling much stock, and they were wealthy stock owners. In addition to this fine property, Mr. Jones had several ranches in his own individual right throughout the county. The date of the purchase of the Cow Creek ranch was 1885. This property has a fine twelve-room house, a good blacksmith shop, barns, coralls and other improvements necessary for a first-class stock ranch.

On August 3, 1882, Mr. Jones married Miss Jennie, daughter of George H. and Mary A. Baker. To this happy union there have been born two children—Frankie C., wife of J. C. Welcome, Jr., a druggist of Burns, and they have one child, Charles W. H.; the other child of Mr. and Mrs. Jones being Thomas Allen. On October 29, 1896, came the summons for Mr. Jones to depart the scenes of this life. He was well known over the entire por-

tion of the eastern part of the state and was respected by all, and his friends were numbered by legion. He was laid to rest in the Burns cemetery and all knew that a good man had passed away.

Mrs. Miller, Mr. Jones' mother, is living with the widow. Mrs. Jones has continued the operations of the stock ranches of her husband, handling them in connection with her partner. She has shown great fortitude, and has borne nobly the stroke that left her a widow, and she is recognized as one of the leading business women of the county and is held in high esteem by all.

◆•◆

JOHN ROBINSON.—When the land where Burns now stands was unbroken sod Mr. Robinson came here and, in company with W. W. Johnson, erected a two-story house, which was known as the Burns hotel. In many lines, as well as this, Mr. Robinson has been a leader, and has been in pioneer work almost all of his life and he is deserving of especial mention in the volume that would chronicle his county's history. He was born in Placer county, California, on April 20, 1856, being the son of John and Biddie (Waren) Robinson, natives, respectively, of North Cumberland and Cornwall, England. They were married at Mineral Point, Wisconsin. The father had been a seaman in England, and came to California during the gold excitement of 1849, and the mother came west in 1853. While a child our subject was taken to Nevada county, California, where he remained with his father on the stock farm until thirteen, and then went out into the world for himself. He rode the range and freighted in the coast range and saved money and then attended the Healds business college in San Francisco for one year. Then he farmed in Colusa county, and later farmed and built levees on the Sacramento river. It was in 1880 that he came to Harney county and engaged in raising horses. Eighteen hundred and eighty-two was the year that he erected the first building in Burns, and also he built for others. He conducted the Burns hotel with a bar until 1888, during which time he built the first race track in the county and kept some fast horses. In 1883 he was appointed as deputy sheriff under A. C. Dore, having the southern part of Grant county, which embraces all of Harney. The territory was large and sparsely settled, and he did much riding over this vast territory. During the last of this service the county seat was at Harney, where he made his headquarters. He opened the first barber shop there, and when the county seat came to Burns he came hither and opened the barber shop, which he has continuously operated since. He owns the Robinson building, which is rented, a good residence of seven rooms, being the first building on the hill, his shop, and various other property. Mr. Robinson is a member of the A. O. U. W.

On February 15, 1886, occurred the marriage of Mr. Robinson and Miss Olive, daughter of Henry McDonald and Mary E. (Beckwith) Bland. Mr. and Mrs. Bland were pioneers from the east in the early fifties, settling in Douglas county, where Mrs. Robinson was born on December 22, 1866. The father died in 1874, and the mother still lives in Grant's Pass. To Mr. and Mrs. Robinson have been born five children, named as follows: John Wesley, born November 20, 1887; Jennie Lee, born April 13, 1889, being the first white child born in Harney county after its organization as a separate county; George B., born June 15, 1896, and died March 5, 1897; George Dewey, born April 13, 1898; William Nicholas, born September 25, 1900. Mr. Robinson has always been in the lead in the line of advancement for the county or for the town, and he has done much to assist in progress and building up. He is one of the prominent men of the county, well known and universally liked, and he is an enterprising, public-minded citizen.

GREEN HUDSPEATH.—Few men have seen more of the real life both of hardship on the frontier and arduous service in the military of the United States than the worthy subject of this article. Surely such a veteran is eminently deserving of especial mention in this volume, and with pleasure we attempt to chronicle the salient points of his stirring career.

Green Hudspeath was born in Pickens county, Alabama, on March 20, 1827, being the son of Strickland and Arroda Hudspeath, natives also of Alabama. While a child the

family removed to Winston county, Mississippi; when he was ten they returned to Marion county, Alabama, and soon after went to DeSoto, Mississippi, and in 1846 came to Red River county, Texas. Our subject was reared on a farm and received his education from the primitive schools in log cabins. In the fall of 1847 he enlisted in Company A, First Texas Volunteers, under Captain Henry E. McCullough, and in General Wool's brigade. He was on the frontier all the time, was in several battles and skirmishes and was wounded in the leg, in the back and in the finger. In the spring of 1848, at a skirmish near Eagle Pass, he received a bullet in his left side, just above the heart, that lodged in his back and is there yet. For twelve months he languished in bed, being honorably discharged, and then recovered, but the effect of that bullet is still felt by Mr. Hudspeath. After the war he teamed for the government; when the soldiers were stationed on the border. He had his headquarters at El Paso and served until 1852. Then he went to Independence, Missouri, and carried the mail from that point to Salt Lake City, handling six horses and a passenger coach. One year was spent at this work and he had many a brush with the redskins. On November 5, 1855, Mr. Hudspeath married Miss Julia A. Brady, a native of Ireland, the wedding occurring in Independence, Missouri. Our subject continued at that place until the fall of 1862, when he enlisted in the state militia under Captain W. W. Sage and was attached to the Second Colorado, under the command of Colonel Ford. He was skirmishing against Price and fought all the way through Missouri and Kansas; and in skirmishes with bushwhackers, battles and scouting duty, he was constantly in the harness and in hardships more than can be mentioned until the close of the war. Then he went home, and in 1869 he came to Miami county, Kansas, and engaged in farming there until 1880. He made many trips on the plains to hunt buffalo and many a fine specimen of that noble beast fell before his rifle. It was in the spring of 1880 that he came with his family across the plains to Baker City, and in 1885 came thence to Harney valley. He entered land about five miles south from Burns and went to improving it and raising stock. He has done well at this work and is now retired from the farm and living in

Burns, where he owns a good five-room residence and a block of lots. He removed to Burns in July, 1901. To Mr. Hudspeath and his faithful wife there have been born eight children, named as follows: John, in San Francisco; Robert N., in this county; Thomas H., of Baker City; Julia A., wife of Oscar Hindman, of Baker county; William G.; Joseph, deceased; Sarah A., wife of James McDivett, of Decora, Idaho; Susan E., deceased. Mr. Hudspeath came to Harney with but little property of this world's goods and now has a band of cattle, his farm, his residence in Burns, and is prosperous.

WILLIAM W. JOHNSON.—Hiram A. Johnson was born in 1819, and his wife, Elizabeth J., was born in the same year. In the spring of 1847 they started from Illinois across the plains, and near the site of Fort Hall occurred the birth of their son, the subject of this sketch. This birth was in the covered wagon, and oh May 20, 1847. They came on to Marion county, Oregon, and the father selected a donation claim near Jefferson. That was the scene of William's childhood, and there he was educated and at the age of eighteen apprenticed to Benjamin VanBuren to learn the blacksmith trade. Mrs. Johnson died in 1897, and her husband passed away in 1896. They had removed from the farm to Salem in 1872, and lived in that city at the time of their death.

At Jefferson, on February 25, 1869, William W. married Miss Caroline, daughter of David and Hester Harris. Mr. Harris died at Sweet Home, Oregon, in 1897, and his widow is living in Burns now. Our subject worked at his trade in Jefferson until 1873, then came with a band of his own cattle to the vicinity of Mitchell, Wheeler county. He named the town for ex-Senator Mitchell. Mr. Johnson operated a blacksmith shop and handled his cattle until 1875, then sold out and returned to Marion county. He next accepted a position as agency blacksmith on the Malheur reservation, remaining until 1878. This year marked the outbreak of the Bannocks and Piutes, and Mr. Johnson took his family to Canyon City, but upon his return to the agency all had fled. He returned to Canyon City and accepted a position as blacksmith to shoe the

government horses and accompanied the soldiers in the expeditions. He witnessed some fighting, especially at Castle Rock. Following the war he was engaged as post blacksmith at Camp Harney until that was abandoned in 1882, and then he remained with the buildings until 1883. It was in this year that, in company with John Robinson, Mr. Johnson built the first house in Burns. It was located where the Burns hotel now stands, and was a hotel and bar room. Since that date Mr. Johnson has been identified with the town of Burns and the county of Harney. He is now operating a liquor store, having a fine stock of choice liquors and tobaccos. He has always been progressive, and for two years he was deputy United States marshal under Marshal Barran.

To Mr. and Mrs. Johnson there have been born seven children—Mrs. Ada M. Mothershead, near Seattle, Washington; Charles W., Lloyd L., Eldon E. and Mrs. Hester E. Goodman, all of this county; Lulu J. and Leon M., at home. Mr. Johnson has a good residence in Burns, and he is respected and stands well in the community, being a man of energy, ability and uprightness.

THOMAS BAKER.—We are pleased to append the following review of the salient points of the career of this esteemed and excellent young citizen of Harney county, both because of his intrinsic qualities of worth and because of the good achievements he has accomplished in this county, having been beset with adverse circumstances, yet manifesting a purpose and fortitude that have enabled him to conquer all to the forwarding of his own brilliant success.

Thomas Baker was born in Lane county, Oregon, on October 22, 1868, being the son of early pioneers, George and Mary (Watson) Baker. The mother died in Lane county, leaving five children. The father, a contractor, removed in the fall of 1878 to Harney valley, and there, in January, 1879, he was called away by death, being one of the first ones buried in Burns cemetery. The little group of orphans were cared for by the kind neighbors, there being no property left to them, and at the age of thirteen our subject commenced to work for the stockmen of the valley. He was careful of the money that he earned, and soon had sufficient to purchase a place, and a part of his present home place was then bought, and he added since that time until he has now four hundred and eighty acres of fine grain and hay land, six miles east from Burns. He has a good house, barn and outbuildings, and a fine young orchard, and his estate shows great skill, industry and thrift. Mr. Baker, from the first opportunity, went to acquiring a bunch of stock, and he has been successful in that line also, and he is the owner of much of that valuable property now. His place is admirably situated, having plenty of water for irrigating and also springs in abundance for stock and domestic purposes.

On December 15, 1892, Mr. Baker took a wife, Miss Ettie, daughter of Harvey and Sarah Dixon, of the vicinity of Burns. Three children have been born to them—Mary Ida, Alvin Douglas and Mabel. There is much credit due Mr. Baker for the excellent success that his sagacity and labors have wrought out, and he is one of the most substantial men of the county, being recognized by all as an upright, capable and good citizen, and a fine man of ability.

◆◆◆

JOHN CATLOW, deceased.—Who shall ever tell the hardships endured, the labors wrought, the dangers encountered, the thrilling struggles with savages, the vigils of weary nights and the wearing watchfulness of the pioneer's life in its fullness? In recounting some of the salient points of the career of the esteemed gentleman of whom we now have the pleasure to speak, and to whom we accord this memorial, we tread the sacred ground of the worthy pioneers in the fullest sense of the word, and feel assured that he was one of the notable ones to whom we justly do honor.

John Catlow was born in Yorkshire, England, on November 5, 1824, and at the age of sixteen his adventurous spirit broke the bounds of the civilized east and overleaped the barriers and plunged into the scenes of the west. He landed in New York, went thence to Boston, labored until he had sufficient means to start west and in 1861 we find him threading the dreary plains with an ox train to Modoc county, California. Several skirmishes were fought with the Indians, some of the immi-

grants were killed and some stock lost. He engaged in farming and in 1864 came thence to Silver City, Idaho, and there followed teaming, contracting, and mining. He handled and raised stock and was very successful in his labors. He took part in all the Indian fights that occurred in the various sections where he lived and it is truthfully said of him that he was a man who never knew fear. At one time he was one of thirty-six white men pitted against two thousand Indians, and when they were reinforced, they had but two rounds of ammunition left. He pioneered in Owyhee county, Idaho, and then in 1872 took his stock to Harney county, then Grant county. He entered a valley that was named Catlow valley to this day from him and there he established himself in the stock business. He owned large tracts of land, always was interested in the affairs of the county and labored to assist the early settlers.

The marriage of Mr. Catlow and Miss Margaret Finn, who came around Cape Horn from Boston to San Francisco, occurred in Silver City, and they became the parents of three children: Edwin J., Joseph J., and Mrs. Sarah M. Feour, of Dilley, Oregon. On June 7, 1901, the summons came for Mr. Catlow to depart this life and he passed quietly to the world beyond. By his request his remains were buried on the home place, which is in Pueblo valley, where the widow now resides. Mr. Catlow was a Mason for many years and his labors in this and adjacent counties have done much for the development and advancement of them. Being always a public spirited and generous man and ready to assist his fellows, he left a pleasant memory behind and many over a large region mourned sincerely when the good man passed away.

◆◆◆

HIRAM M. HILL.—Much of the life of the subject of this sketch has been passed in the west, and most of this in the state of Oregon, where he has labored faithfully in the various callings that came to his hand, and he is an upright man of sound principles, and is respected by all. He was born in Whiteside county, Illinois, in January, 1855, being the son of Zachariah and Lyda Ann (Boyer) Hill. The father died in 1856 and soon thereafter the mother married Jesse Hill, a brother of the father. In 1864 the family came across the plains to Lane county, Oregon. They used mule teams in the journey and had some trouble with the Indians. In one battle one of their number was wounded. The spring following their arrival they went to Yuba county, California, and in 1866 came back to Lane county, which continued to be the home until 1874, when they came to Silver lake, in Lake county, this state. They took up stockraising, and in 1886 moved to Prineville, in Cook county. The father and stepfather were natives of North Carolina and the mother was born in Pennsylvania, on June 9, 1832. The stepfather died at Prineville in 1887. The father was an early settler in Illinois and in the time of the gold excitement in California he went thither and returned in 1852, when he got married. The children by this marriage were: Cerilda; W. T., near Lawen; Mrs. Mary Maxwell, of Eugene; Hiram M., our subject. By the second marriage four children were born: Mrs. Elzora Brown, of Linn county; Eliza, deceased; Charles E.; and Albert, of Prineville. Our subject has labored at raising stock and farming much of the time in this section of the west and is a man of much experience in these lines. He carries a three-thousand-dollar policy in the Woodmen of the World, Camp No. 215, of Dufur, Oregon. Mr. Hiram M. Hill married Miss Martha Connery, and to them was born one child, Mrs. Minnie E. Richardson. Mrs. Hill was called hence by death and her remains lie buried at Silver Lake cemetery. Mr. Hill contracted a second marriage, the nuptials taking place in Illinois, at which time Sarah Endsley became his wife. One child was born to them, Phlorie, now deceased.

It is fitting here to note some of the details of the life of the brother of the subject of this article. William T. Hill was born in Whiteside county, Illinois, and in 1864 he crossed the plains with his parents to Lane county, Oregon. In 1865 they went to California and returned to Oregon in 1866. In 1874 a move was made to Lake county and there he engaged in raising stock and farming. In 1880 he moved to Harney county and in 1900 he located where he is now living, seven miles southeast from Harney. He has a fine farm of four hundred

and sixty acres and devotes his attention to raising stock and general farming.

In Lane county, Oregon, on October 13, 1872, Mr. Hill married Miss Mary C., a daughter of Cyrus and Julia Hayes, and a native of Warren county, Iowa. To this happy union there have been born six children: George T., Harriett L., Emory, Ora W., Effie A. and Julia A.

+‑+‑+

JOSEPH A. WILLIAMS.—A man of activity in the labors of the pioneer, the subject of this article is one of whom Harney county may well be proud, on account of the faithful labors that he has bestowed here for the general development and advancement, while he has prosecuted his own business enterprises with a vigor and sagacity that have given him the emoluments of good success. He is a native of Oregon, having been born in Lane county, on January 13, 1861, the son of Elias P. and Almira (Russell) Williams. The parents crossed the plains with ox teams from the state of Ohio in 1853, settling on the old home place in Lane county. The mother died soon after our subject was born, but the father is still living on the old homestead which he settled upon over forty years ago. Joseph A. received his education in the schools of his vicinity and remained with his father on the farm until 1882, when he came to the western part of Harney county, then Grant county. He worked for a salary for a time, and then went to raising horses, later changing to cattle, which stock he still handles. He entered land and improved it, puchasing some also. He remained there until 1900, when he purchased his present place of four hundred and eighty acres, sixteen miles west from Drewsey. The year following he sold his estate in the western part of the county and now devotes his whole attention to handling his stock and caring for the present home place. The farm is well improved, with house and other outbuildings and orchard, and is well watered with four ditches, both from creeks and the Malheur river.

The marriage of Mr. Williams and Miss Ruth A., daughter of Samson McConnel, a pioneer of Lane county in 1852, was solemnized on May 9, 1892, and the fruit of this union has been as follows: Martha Louise and Ira M. Mr. Williams is a member of the M. W. A. and of the I. O. O. F., of Drewsey, and while he was in the western part of the county he was justice of the peace for six years. He has always manifested great zeal and interest in the advancement of educational interests and labors unceasingly in this worthy cause.

CHARLES H. VOEGTLY.—The subject of this sketch is a first class representative of what skill, pluck, and enterprise can do in the business world, for in October, 1891, he started into the hardware business in Burns with a very limited stock of goods, in a small wooden building, and by careful attention to business, deferential treatment of customers, wise buying, and untiring care of every detail, he has grown to be one of the largest dealers in the county, has a stock of all kinds of goods that are handled in the hardware trade, and a fine two-story brick building, twenty-six by ninety, and also some warehouses which he utilizes in his very extensive trade. The new building was erected in 1899, and the upper story is rented for lodge room and offices. On February 1, 1902, Mr. Voegtly took as a partner in this business, Charles E. Kenyon, and they operate under the firm name of Voegtly & Kenyon, being the leading hardware dealers in the county. Mr. Voegtly still owns the building personally, which he rents to the firm.

Reverting more particularly to the personal history of our subject, we note that he was born in Allegheny, Pennsylvania, on January 8, 1861, being the son of Nicholas H. and Mary S. Voegtly, natives also of the Keystone State. Our subject was reared there, learned the machinist trade, and gained his education from the public schools and the Western University of Pittsburg. On April 13, 1886, he was stirred to see the west and accordingly, came to San Francisco, thence to Portland, Oregon, and soon he was in The Dalles. September of the same year found him in Burns and engaged in the stock business. He now has an interest in two hundred and forty acres of good hay land and also a bunch of stock. And we desire to mention that in addition to he complete stock of hardware, paints, oils, stoves, doors, windows, sash, tinware and all

that is handled in the trade, the firm has one of the finest tin and repair shops in the entire community. Mr. Voegtly has also valuable town property in addition to his holdings mentioned.

The marriage of Mr. Voegtly and Miss Mary A. Tupker was solemnized on December 16, 1894, and they were blessed by the advent of two children: Nicholas H., born November 24, 1895, and one daughter, Flora Mary, born February 13, 1900, who died February 27, 1900. Mrs. Voegtly died on March 1, 1900, and on March 21, 1901, Mr. Voegtly married Miss Luella, daughter of M. F. Williams, and one son, Charles Raymond, was born to them, January 11, 1902. Fraternally, Mr. Voegtly is affiliated with A. F. & A. M. Lodge No. 97, of Burns, also with the Royal Arch chapter, Blue Mountain Lodge, No. 7, of Canyon City. He is a charter member of the Eastern Star, and his wife also belongs to that order. Mr. Voegtly is one of the substantial and leading men of the county and has gained the enviable position that he owns by reason of his real worth and the excellence of his achievements.

WILLIAM H. GEARHART.—This sturdy and intrepid pioneer, whose labors have been instrumental in bringing about the development of the country where he now lives as well as various other portions of Oregon, is worthy of representation in any volume that has to do with the history of central and eastern Oregon. William H. was born in Howard county, Missouri, on February 12, 1847, the son of John W. and Catherine (Brown) Gearhart. The mother died soon after his birth and the father started across the plains with the balance of his family in 1852, making the way to Benton county with ox teams, whence soon after they went to Josephine county, where they remained until 1861. The father followed farming and raising stock, but at the date last mentioned sold out and went to California, there taking up the same business. In 1872 he came back to Oregon, this time to Klamath county, and soon after our subject and his brother, James P., engaged in partnership in the stock business and then came on to the Malheur river, near where he resides at the present time, about fourteen and one-half miles west from Drewsey. They built the first house erected west from the agency, making it of juniper logs. Mr. Gearhart now owns four hundred and eighty acres of land in one body fenced and half cultivated to meadow and grain. He handles cattle principally. His place has been comfortably fitted as a home with good improvements.

The marriage of Mr. Gearhart and Miss Agnes Durkee was celebrated on May 6, 1883, and they were the parents of two children, Hannah M., deceased, and William L., deceased. Mr. Gearhart married a second time, Mrs. Eliza E. (Davis) Metcalf, becoming his wife on October 29, 1894. Mrs. Gearhart is a native of Carroll county, Missouri, and emigrated to Oregon in 1874. She had by her former husband the following children: George W., deceased; John A., deceased; Mrs. Mary E. Holebos; Mrs. Dora E. Cranmer; Emma J., wife of William O. Newell; James S. E.; Ida M. Mr. Gearhart is a member of the I. O. O. F., Drewsey Lodge No. 147. He is a prominent man of his section and has always manifested great sagacity and enterprise in his endeavors.

JOHN C. FOLEY.—This well-known and enterprising gentleman is one of Harney county's leading citizens and is a potent factor in the development of the country, having wrought here in two distinct lines, being the substantial stockman and agriculturist and also at the present time handling in partnership with ex-Sheriff George Shelly, one of the leading blacksmith shops of the county. John C. was born in Marquette county, Wisconsin, on January 8, 1858, to James and Mary (McNulty) Foley, natives of the west coast of Ireland. They migrated to the United States in 1847, settling in Vermont, whence in 1855 they came to Wisconsin. The country there was wild and new and the nearest railroad was at Chicago. The father followed farming and remained on the old homestead, where he is living to-day. The mother died there in 1894. Our subject grew up on the farm, received his education from the district schools, and served his apprenticeship in the blacksmith shop. In 1879 he went to Alexandria, Dakota, and there opened the first shop of the place. Two years later he sold out and returned to Wisconsin.

In 1883 he came thence to California, Nevada county, and entered into the stock business. In the fall of the same year he brought a bunch of cattle to Harney county, bought land, and located. He now has four hundred acres of good land, well watered and improved with house, barn, and all necessary conveniences for handling stock and farming. For a time, Mr. Foley retired from his trade and was foreman for the Pacific Live Stock Company, and made some of the principal improvements on their ranches in various parts of the state. He travelled all over the state for eight years in the service of this company, also handling stock for himself. Mr. Foley has been on the frontier all of his life and is well acquainted with its rigorous service and hardships and dangers and he has wrought with a firm hand, and wisdom, and has made a brilliant success of his labors as is evident by his fine holdings. In the political realm, our subject is always active, being a firm Democrat. His name appeared on that ticket for county judge in 1902, but although he made a stirring race he was beaten.

Miss Mary E. Boylan, of Marquette county, Wisconsin, was a schoolmate of our subject and he made a trip to his old home in 1898 and on April 11, of that year, they were married. Two children have been born to them: Charles B., and Agnes J. Mr. Foley and his wife are devout members of the Catholic church and he is one of the substantial and highly esteemed men of the county. In his shop he does a good business, being a fine workman and his affability and skill have brought him patronage from all directions. He has a fine residence in Burns in addition to the other property mentioned.

HON. ALBERT W. GOWAN is a man well known over the entire state of Oregon and has made a record with which the people are familiar and nothing that we could say would add to this or to the success that he has achieved, which are justly his own by reason of his worth and excellent achievements.

Mr. Gowan was born in Allegheny county, New York, on May 16, 1846, being the son of Nathaniel and Rhoda (Putnam) Gowan. His father was grandson of Dr. John Gowan,

HON. ALBERT W. GOWAN.

JAMES SMITH.

JAMES W. SHOWN.

who was an officer in the Revolution, being with George Washington at the crossing of the Delaware. The mother of our subject was a descendant of General Israel Putnam, famous as an Indian fighter and revolutionary soldier. While a child, Albert W. went to Crawford county, Pennsylvania, was educated there and in the fall of 1863 enlisted for three years in Light Battery M, First United States Artillery, and took part in all the manoeuvers of the armies of the James and Potomac, under Benjamin F. Butler, except when he was absent with his command quelling the election riots in New York City in 1864. He fought in Petersburg and Richmond and all the way along until the surrender at Appomattox court house. In June, 1865, he was sent to Texas under General Steele, and served seven months on the Rio Grande; and also he was with his command to quell the Fenian raids at Buffalo, Ogdensburg, New York, and so forth. Upon the expiration of his term of enlistment he was honorably discharged and returned at once to Cambridge, Pennsylvania, and established himself in the grocery business, and on July 14, 1868, was married to Miss Delnora J. Pitcher, whose parents were early pioneers of Wisconsin. In 1871 a move was made to Osborne county, Kansas, and Mr. Gowan took up farming until 1882 when he came across the plains with a large train, being captain and going direct to Union county. He settled in the Wallowa valley and the following year went to Joseph, where he took up in earnest the study of law, having also been studying it before. He was connected with C. H. Finn, now of Lagrande, Oregon, and later formed a partenrship with W. G. Piper, who had formerly been chancery judge in Indiana and district attorney of the third judicial district of Oregon. This partnership was dissolved in 1888 and two years later, our subject left Joseph and came to Burns. He was in 1890 appointed special agent for the abstractor of census and travelled over the entire state and later received the appointment as clerk in the United States land office at Burns, which he held until 1892. From 1880 to 1882 Mr. Gowan was representative for his county in the state legislature in Kansas. In 1892 at a special election he was chosen representative for Grant and Harney counties to the legislature. He was elected on the Republican ticket and in 1894 was chosen

45

joint state senator for Morrow, Grant, and Harney counties. In 1898 he was defeated for the same position by a small majority. During this time Mr. Gowan had been in partnership with A. W. Waters, ex-United States marshal for Oregon. In 1900 this relation was dissolved and Judge N. A. Cornish was partner of Mr. Gowan under the firm name of Gowan & Cornish. April 30, 1902, this partnership was dissolved and Mr. Gowan is now enjoying a large and lucrative practice alone. While in the legislature Mr. Gowan served as chairman of the committee on railways and transportation, also on the committee on public lands and introduced the farmers artesian well bill, which passed both houses without opposition, but was vetoed by the governor. While senator, he was on the committee on military affairs, that of railroads, and that of the judiciary, and in 1897 was also chairman of the latter committee, besides serving on other important committees. Mr. Gowan was admitted to the bar of the supreme court of his state in 1888, and to the United States district and circuit courts in 1901. He has valuable property in Burns and is a man of enviable standing. The following children have been born to him and his estimable wife: Mrs. Cora Shafer, of Hoxie, Kansas; Winfield A., of Burns; Mrs. Lotta Harpers, of the Narrows; Mrs. Nora Kesterson, of Burns; Mable E.; Frank, clerk in Burns; Genet. Mr. Gowan was a member of the Oregon National Guards being first lieutenant of Company I, Third Regiment, and resigned in 1890. Then he was captain of Troop A, Burns, serving until June, 1898. He is a past master Mason of Joseph Lodge, No. 81, and also affiliates with Lodge 97, of Burns, having served both lodges in prominent capacities. He is active in G. A. R. circles and was judge advocate for Oregon in 1895. Judge Gowan is prominent and well liked and maintains a high sense of honor, being of untarnished reputation and established character rightness and integrity, while his ability is recognized by all.

JAMES SMITH.—Among those who came to this country in an early day, we place the name of James Smith, and feel assured that he has worthily performed the labors of the pioneer and is deserving of the esteem and respect which is generously accorded him and also a place among the real builders of Harney county, and his labors have always been for development and progress, while personally he is a gentleman of unswerving integrity and intrinsic worth.

Mr. Smith was born in Hampton, Geauga county, Ohio, on August 13, 1857, being the son of Robert and Elizabeth (Yearger) Smith. The father was a native of Ohio, and the mother of Pennsylvania. The father gave his services at the beginning of the Civil war and fought through to the end. He was in the battle of Gettysburg and in many other battles and also many skirmishes. He was wounded in the knee and was a cripple on account of it until the day of his death, which occurred in 1894. During the war the mother and the children went to Johnstown, Pennsylvania, and thence to Williamsburg. While our subject was growing up, he was educated in the common schools and learned the shoemaker trade from his father. In 1876 he left home and went to Clay county, Missouri, thence to New Orleans the next year, then went to New Mexico, Arizona, Colorado, and the Black Hills, and finally on to the John Day country. He arrived here at the time of the Indian trouble in 1878, and the same year, he went to Cheyenne, Wyoming, through Camas prairie, with a band of cattle to ship to Chicago. He returned to Baker City on horseback and in the spring of 1879, he went to the mines of Granite and then to The Dalles. In the spring of 1881 we find Mr. Smith driving a band of cattle to Eagle creek, Idaho, and two years later he came again to the John Day country. It was 1884 that he came to Burns and entered land and engaged in the stock business. The hard winter of 1889 and 1890 caused him to turn to farming, but in 1895 he shipped three car loads of his horses to Georgia. After selling the horses he went to Pennsylvania and visited with his mother for one year. He then returned to Burns and after a time turned his attention to his trade. He now owns and runs a shop for the manufacture of foot wear and the general repair of the same and is now favored with a good trade. Mr. Smith has never embarked on the matrimonial sea, always preferring the quieter joys of single life. He is esteemed by all and maintains a good standing in the community.

JAMES W. SHOWN.—There are no words of introduction that we could utter that would make the subject of this sketch better known to the people of Harney county than is the case already. He is not only well known, but he is very favorably known and highly respected by all, having always been stanch and upright in the walks of life, has maintained a reputation untarnished, has arrayed himself on the side of morality and good government, and his example has been most favorable. James W. was born in Johnson county, Tennessee, on March 26, 1851, being the son of Peter L. and Mary Shown. He was reared on a farm and gained a good education and as well was thoroughly trained in the school of hardship, as he was in the path of the awful Civil war that swept with besom the fair country for many miles in the south. His father lost all of his property and was terribly abused in the war and soon thereafter died from the exposures and hardships sustained. The mother died when James was a small child. He continued to reside in Tennessee until 1884, then left the scenes of childhood for the regions of the west. He landed at Mitchell, then in Grant county, Oregon, and thence in June, 1886, he came to Harney. He worked for wages for a time and then took a pre-emption in August, 1886, near Harney. When the town of Harney was platted he secured some lots and put up a house, barn, and made other improvements. He now owns eighty acres adjoining the lots and also the pre-emption and a good ranch on the island. The eighty is farmed to grain and the other ranches are used to raise hay.

Mr. Shown has always taken an active part in politics and also in the welfare of Harney. He has served as councilman and mayor and he has also been active in the educational affairs of the town. He taught the first school and he has constantly befriended the cause of education. Mr. Shown is a past grand in the I. O. O. F., Pandora Lodge, No. 74, of Pandora, Tennessee. In 1899 he had the joy of making a trip to the home place and visited there for six months. He has one sister, Mary L. Goodwin, in Tennessee, and three brothers, Landen, Caleb and Peter, all three in Tennessee. Mr. Shown has never ventured on the matrimonial sea, and he is now one of the well-to-do and happy devotees of celebacy and is respected and esteemed by all. Still it may be that the charm of this life may be broken by the invasion of some southern belle.

By way of reminiscence it is well to note that during the troublesome times of the Civil war mentioned, a large bell was to be tapped when danger came, but on one occasion a squad of Confederates were upon the house of our subject's parents without any warning. James saw and quickly recognized the danger and began a parley with the captain, whom he cajoled into tapping the bell to learn the sound and the result was a timely warning. Another time a soldier stole the lad's cap, and, boy though he was, he fought the intruder to a finish. But the cap was demolished. Mr. Shown is a strong supporter of good government and zealous for the prevailing of the right. He is interested in seeing the gospel preached and supports it liberally.

EDWIN J. CATLOW.—The subject of this sketch is one of Harney county's younger men, who are coming forward as the old and worthy pioneers drop, one by one, from the posts which they filled with such credit to themselves and advantage to the country. Edwin J. Catlow was born in San Francisco on May 14, 1870, being the son of John and Margaret (Finn) Catlow, the father one of the leading pioneers of this coast and especially of southern Idaho and central Oregon. Our subject remained in San Francisco and there gained an education while his father was handling stock on the range. He attended the common schools and then graduated from the Sacred Heart College, after which he studied in a law school for a time. He also did bookkeeping and acted as salesman for a number of years and then, in 1895, he came with his mother to their present home in Pueblo valley, ten miles north from Denio. He there engaged in the stock business with his father and brother, Joseph J., and he has prosecuted the same business with vigor and wisdom since that time. He has always taken an active part in political matters and has served as justice of the peace for a number of years.

The marriage of Mr. Catlow and Miss Julia Allen, of Silver City, Idaho, was sol-

emnized on July 20, 1898, and they have two children, Eunice M. and Dolores M. Mr. Catlow is a prominent citizen of his section, has a fine ranch and a large bunch of cattle and is one of the substantial men of the county, well known and highly esteemed.

JUDGE HENRY C. LEVENS.—Eminent among his fellows as a man of ability and intrinsic worth of character and integrity, a worthy successor to the office of county judge, to which the people called him on the Republican ticket in 1902, a leading property owner and stock raiser and agriculturist in Harney county, the subject of this article is especially worthy of a place in his county's history.

Henry C. Levens was born in Galesville, Douglas county, Oregon, on July 10, 1861, being the son of Daniel A. and Fannie I. (Tryon) Levens. His father came from Iowa to California across the plains in 1851, thence to Oregon in 1852. He operated a pack train from Scottsburg to Yreka in the time of the Rogue river Indian war and was among the very first settlers in Douglas county. He had a fort at his stage station which was known as Fort Levens. His station was also called Levens station, and there he remained until the time of his death, October 25, 1889. The mother crossed the plains from Michigan to Douglas county in 1851, and there married Mr. Levens and remained on the old home place till her death on December 26, 1894. Our subject was reared there and gained his education in the common schools and in the business college in Portland, from which he graduated in 1883. He engaged in mercantile business in Canyonville and other places until 1886, then removed to Burns, there being but a few houses here at that time. Previous to this time Mr. Levens had been engaged in the stock business, and had driven into this valley in 1878, 1880 and in 1882. He made a permanent location here in 1886. He bought land close to town and engaged in the stock business. He now has about nine hundred and sixty acres of good land and much stock. He rents as much land as he owns and cuts about one thousand tons of hay each year, besides raising about three thousand bushels of grain. He has his estate well improved with buildings, orchard and so forth and handles many cattle, horses and hogs.

The marriage of Mr. Levens and Miss Maggie M., daughter of Jacob C. and Leona Welcome, who were pioneers from Illinois to California and then to this country in 1888, was solemnized on June 11, 1889. Fraternally Mr. Levens is affiliated with the A. F. & A. M., Burns Lodge, No. 97, while he and his wife are members of the Eastern Star, his wife being past worthy matron of that order. On the Republican ticket, June 2, 1902, Henry C. Levens was elected as county judge and it is without doubt that he will conserve the interests of justice and equity in the service that he will render to his county.

It is also to be mentioned that Mr. Levens has a butcher shop on one of the best business corners in Burns, while he has a residence also in that town.

CHARLES F. McKINNEY.—There are few men in Harney county that do not know Charles F. McKinney, and to know him is to be his friend, for he is one of the enterprising, upright, capable, affable and successful men who have done much to build up the country and develop its resources, being at the present time not only a heavy land owner, but also an operator of a good sawmill and a dealer in timber goods.

Charles F. was born in Fayette county, Ohio, on October 15, 1847, being the son of William S. and Sarah (Adams) McKinney. The mother was a great-granddaughter of John Quincy Adams. In 1849 the family came to Marion county, Iowa, and there our subject grew to manhood, receiving his education. The father enlisted in Company G, Fortieth Iowa Volunteers, and after fighting for a time he was taken sick and died in the hospital at Keokuk. The mother died at the old homestead in the fall of 1901. Until 1872 Charles F. remained with his mother, and then came to Silver City, Idaho, where he mined and wrought at the lumber business. In 1875 he went to Benton, Mono county, California, and thence to Bodie, a thriving mining camp at that time. On account of there being so many bad characters gathered there the phrase originated, "The bad man from Bodie." In 1882 Mr. McKinney was elected sheriff of that

county and in 1884 was re-elected on the Democratic ticket, receiving a handsome majority at both elections. In addition to this public service, faithfully rendered, he followed mining and kept a hotel. It was 1887 when he came to Harney county, and he at once engaged in the sawmilling business. He has a fine plant located twenty miles northeast from Burns and about eight hundred acres of fine timber land. In the spring of 1889 Mr. McKinney entered into partnership with Judge Sparrow, and together they carried on the lumber business until 1898, when Mr. Sparrow was elected judge of the county, then Mr. McKinney bought his interest. Mr. McKinney is interested in various lines in addition to the mill business, and he has one of the finest houses in Burns that is in Harney county, and in fact in eastern Oregon. It is a modern, twelve-room structure, of beautiful architectural design and suitably located. At the time Harney was the county seat our subject and his partner erected a fine county court house, which they rented to the county, and when the county seat went to Burns Mr. McKinney was at his mill and his buildings all took fire and burned up in Harney, without insurance.

The marriage of Mr. McKinney and Miss Emma Wilson, a native of Iowa, was solemnized on February 21, 1867, and they have two children: Cora, wife of E. E. Punington, of Pendleton; William M. Mr. McKinney was made a Mason in 1869, in Iowa, and now belongs to the Burns Lodge, No. 97, and also belongs to the Royal Arch Chapter in Bodie, California, and is a member of the commandery there and of the K. of P., Inland Lodge, No. 70, of Burns.

WILLIAM C. BYRD.—The power of adaptability which has enabled the subject of this article to engage his abilities to the most advantageous way in the affairs of life that have came to his hand is a happy talent and is quite commensurate with his excellent capabilities in the business, literary and educational world, wherein he has wrought with abundant success in each line, and therefore it is with pleasure that we grant him representation in the list of leading men of Harney county.

Mr. Byrd was born in Highland county, Virginia, on May 10, 1843, being the son of James H. and Alice Byrd. He received a good education in the schools of his vicinity and then attended the law school at Charlottesville, Albermarle county. In April, 1861, when the demon of strife was stirred in our fair land, he enlisted promptly where his interests and home lay, being enrolled in the Thirty-first Virginia Infantry, Company B. He entered as corporal, was promoted to a second lieutenancy and fought under the distinguished Stonewall Jackson. He participated in the battles of Phillippi, McDowell, Winchester, Sharpsburg, Cedar Mountain, Petersburg, Gettysburg, and in numerous other engagements, being wounded twice. He fought to the end and then returned home and in May, 1866, he married Miss Amanda R. Bird. The next year he went to Pettis county, Missouri, and in 1883 he migrated to near where Burns now stands, took government land and set to the improvement of it and teaching school. To this latter calling he had devoted considerable time while in the east. Mr. Byrd also operated a livery stable for a number of years. In 1889 he purchased the Times-Herald and was immediately installed as editor. He made the paper one of distinct merit and vitality and it has since been a power in the county. Of later years Mr. Byrd's son has taken immediate charge of the paper, and our subject has turned his attention to handling furniture and house furnishing goods, having the largest store of the kind in the county and carrying a complete line of goods and being favored with an excellent patronage. This last venture was taken up in February, 1901, and his son, Julian, who edits the Times-Herald, is interested in merchandising. Politically Mr. Byrd has always been active and has filled many offices of trust. In the recent election Mr. Byrd was defeated on the Democratic ticket for county judge, but only by a very few votes. He has filled the office of justice of the peace for many years and in 1896 he was elected county superintendent of schools and re-elected in 1898, and has made a very excellent record in this office. In Missouri Mr. Byrd was city clerk for many years. Six children have been born to him and his estimable wife, namely: Charles A., Julian C., Ambrose M., Mrs. Alice King, Mrs. Madge S. Leonard, Mrs. Edith M. Hunter. Fraternally Mr. Byrd is a member of the I. O. O. F., the K. of P., the Encampment and the Rebekahs, being past grand of the first order.

BYRON TERRILL.—As an upright man, a patriotic and public minded citizen and a successful and enterprising stock man and business man the subject of this sketch is mentioned in this connection, and he is personally an affable and genial gentleman who stands well with his fellows, and has wrought with a true pioneer's spirit and hand in the upbuilding of the country. Mr. Terrill was born in Monroe county, Iowa, on March 31, 1856, being the son of Horace J. and Lucy A. (Wilcox) Terrill. In 1867 the family came across the plains with mule teams in four months, making settlement in Linn county. The train with which they journeyed was commanded by Captain Cook and consisted of about thirty wagons. In October, 1868, the father went to Jackson county and bought a donation claim. He devoted his attention to farming and stock raising and the subject of this sketch assisted, also attended school. In 1879 he left the parental roof and came through Harney county on his way to Fort Hall, Idaho. He went from that place to San Francisco, thence by steamer to Portland and then to Jackson county again. In the spring of 1881 Mr. Terrill again passed through this country to Boise, Idaho, and in the fall returned here and worked for wages and then took up merchandising at Silver Creek. Then he located a ranch about eight miles southeast from Burns and on January 1, 1885, he married Miss Augusta, daughter of James M. and Lydia Parker, early pioneers of California and Oregon. Our subject took a homestead about eight miles south from Burns and that was the family home for a time and then a move was made to Burns, where they resided until April, 1902, when M. Terrill purchased his present ranch of one hundred and eighty-four acres of land. This is located seven miles north from Burns and is a very valuable for hay. During most of his time in this county Mr. Terrill has devoted his attention to raising stock and he has some nice bands at the present time. He has also a valuable residence in Burns.

To Mr. Terrill and his worthy wife there have been born five children: Effie A., Nora Blanche, Ina D., Vella V., deceased, and Violet. Mr. Terrill is a member of the W. of W. and of the I. O. O. F., Lodge No. 77, of Burns, and he and his wife are members of the Rebekahs. Of the I. O. O. F. Mr. Terrill is a past grand. During all his life our subject has been on the frontier and he has served faithfully in the development of the country, and there is much credit due him for these worthy labors. For to bring a land from the wilds of savagery to civilization is a herculean task and demands courage, endurance, tenacity and stanch principles, in all of which Mr. Terrill excels. Mr. Terrill's parents are still dwelling in Jackson county.

———◆•◆———

ALEXANDER McKENZIE.—This intrepid and doughty pioneer and successful stockman is one of the prominent property holders of Harney county and a leading citizen, living at the present time one and one-half miles north from the Narrows postoffice, where he has a fine tract of land and is engaged in raising stock.

Mr. McKenzie is a native of Mercer county, Virginia, born on March 16, 1842, the son of Alexander and Barbara McKenzie. He was educated in a log cabin, remained at home until fifteen and then started out for himself. He went to Ray county, Missouri, and in 1859 went across the plains to Fort Laramie, driving a band of cattle for Frank Saner. The next year they went to Santa Clara county, California, and for two years subsequent to this time acted as foreman for Mr. Saner, until that unfortunate man was murdered for his money. Then Mr. McKenzie went to Sonoma county, bought a farm and after working it for a time he went to Idaho City, Idaho, operating a pack train. In 1866 he went to Salem and for a time ran a dray and express outfit, then went into the butcher business until 1875, when he went to Staten for a short time, in the same business. He then went to Douglas county, bought a ranch and raised sheep, which he closed out later and migrated to the Narrows, where he lives now. This was in 1888, and he was the first settler that took land in that vicinity. He went to raising

cattle, horses and mules, and in this he has been very successful, with the exception of the winter of 1889 and 1890, when he lost heavily. He now has several hundred acres of land, good buildings and is considered one of the leading stockmen of the county.

On October 12, 1867, occurred the marriage of Mr. McKenzie and Miss Alice Blue, a native of Salem, Oregon, and to them have been born six children, Charles, William, Mrs. Olive Cummins, Marshall, Josephine L. and Julia, twins. It is of note that in 1862 Mr. McKenzie volunteered to fight the Indians in Nevada, being under Captain Armsby, with a company of one hundred and forty-six men. He was in one fight near Reno, where all the company, including the captain, was killed with the exception of nineteen. Our subject survived, but carried three wounds in his head, one in his knee and one in his knee. For two months he was unable for active service, then fought under General Crooks at Pyramid lake, when they killed fifteen hundred of the savages, which practically ended the war. These were the Piutes. Mr. McZenzie is a substantial man and possessed of unswerving integrity and uprightness.

———◆•◆———

HENRY C. RICHARDSON.—No compilation that has to do with the leading men of Harney county would be complete were there failure to mention the esteemed gentleman and public minded citizen whose name initiates this paragraph, since he has labored long and faithfully and successfully here for the upbuiding of the county's interests and has always maintained an untarnished reputation, being a man of excellent capabilities and keen and practical business judgment.

Mr. Richardson was born in Benton county, Oregon, on October 8, 1869, being the son of Madison G. and Savanah (Cox) Richardson. The father was born in Lane county, Oregon, in 1847, and his mother came across the plains from the state of Missouri in 1863, with her parents, in an ox train. Our subject went with his parents to Silver City, Idaho, in 1874 and thence to Malheur City, Baker county, in 1877. Then they went to Weiser, Idaho, where Henry C. finished his education. The parents live there still. In 1884 our subject came to Burns and engaged in the butcher business for three years, then operated the Burns hotel from 1892 to 1898, owning the same which is the largest and best one in the county. The structure contains twenty-four sleeping apartments upstairs and two below, besides the office, barroom, kitchen and dining apartments below. Mr. Richardson still owns a one-half interest in the hotel, which is rented In 1898 the people called Mr. Richardson to act as county clerk and two years later they re-elected him to the same position, thus demonstrating their approval of his faithful services. Mr. Richardson owns about five hundred acres of hay land twenty-five miles southwest from Burns, which is well improved with buildings and necessary corralls and he handles a band of cattle. In Burns, he had a modern seven-room house in a desirable locality and a half block of lots.

The marriage of Mr. Richardson and Miss Nora, daughter of William K. Goodman, a pioneer to this county in 1882, from Kansas, was solemnized on January 17, 1893, and two children have been born to them, James T. and Henrietta. Fraternally, Mr. Richardson is affiliated with the K. of P., Lodge No. 70, and also with the Native Sons of Oregon. Mr. Richardson is a man of honor, capable in business, faithful in trusts, affable and genial, and has hosts of friends in all parts of the county.

CHAUNCEY CUMMINS.—In at least two lines of human endeavor the subject of this article has gained distinction and he stands to-day one of the leading business men of central Oregon, being of the firm of Cummins & Geer, hardware merchants and implement dealers of Burns, Oregon, where their mammoth store is situated. Chauncey was born in Steuben county, Indiana, on January 20, 1844, being the son of William and Almira (Clark) Cummins, who brought their family across the plains in 1853, coming with ox teams and consuming six months in the journey. Settlement was made in Lane county and there our subject grew to manhood, assisting on the farm and gaining his education from the common schools. In 1870 he went to Douglas county and there engaged in raising sheep, and two years later he removed his stock to the

Harney valley and the next year sold out and returned to Lane county. There he farmed until 1882, when he repaired to Paisley, in Lake county, and engaged again in the sheep industry, and in 1885 he removed from that location to the Steins mountain country, then in Grant county. He prosecuted his labors with success, adding cattle to the sheep raising, and in 1900 he sold his sheep and came to Burns. He has a fine residence here and still owns his farm of about six hundred acres of hay land in the Steins mountain country with his cattle, which his two sons are handling, being in partnership with him. At the time Mr. Cummins came hither, he entered into partnership with I. S. Geer, cousin of ex-governor Geer, and they started a hardware store. They have a fine two-story structure built of stone and brick and carry the largest stock of hardware in the county. In addition to hardware, they have crockery, glassware, farm implements, and so forth. They have a fine patronage and the goods from their shelves find their way all over the interior of Oregon.

The marriage of Mr. Cummins and Miss Margaret A., daughter of George C. and Margaret Smith, was solemnized on November 9, 1866, and they have become the parents of four children, Horace, deceased; Dora, wife of I. Bubbington, of this county; George W. and Francis W., on the farm. Mrs. Cummins' father was murdered by the Indians in the Bannock war. He was a pioneer of 1853, crossing the plains with ox teams and settling in Lane county. Mr. Cummins is affiliated with the A. F. & A. M., Lodge No. 97, at Burns, and in political matters he is with the Republicans and in March, 1902, the people chose him as chief executive of the town of Burns.

SAMUEL T. MOTHERSHEAD.— While there are some who have been residents of Harney county longer than the subject of this sketch, still he stands among the leaders in the county to-day and is a young man of untarnished reputation and good ability, and has gained a place in the esteem and confidence of the people that is enviable and of which he is worthy on account of his uprightness and sound principles. Samuel T. was born in Jefferson county, Missouri, on September 23,

1872, being the son of Willis T. and Malissa (Wiley) Mothershead. They were natives of Kentucky and came to Jefferson county in an early day. The mother died there but the father is still living on the old homestead and has always taken an active part in politics with the Democratic party. Our subject grew up on the farm and attended school, graduating from the Desoto high school in 1890. The next year he came to Burns and worked for one and one-half years on the Items newspaper, having charge of the same. In 1895, in company with Ben Brown, he started the Burns Times which they sold one year later to the East Oregon Herald, which is now the Times Herald. Subsequently to this, Mr. Mothershead accepted a position with the sheriff as deputy, serving four years under A. J. McKinnan and for two years under George Shelly. Mr. Mothershead has always been active in politics, being a firm Democrat.

On September 26, 1897, occurred the marriage of Mr. Mothershead and Miss Ella, daughter of A. S. and Elizabeth Swain, early pioneers to the Grande Ronde valley, from Iowa, and coming to this county in 1889, where they settled at Lawen. To Mr. and Mrs. Mothershead has been born one child, Mildred. Our subject is a member of the I. O. O. F., Harney Lodge, No. 77, a charter member of the K. of P., Inland Lodge, No. 70, and he and his wife are members of the Rebekahs. He has represented his lodge in the grand lodge and is past chancellor. Mr. Mothershead has a fine six room house on one of the fine corners of the town which was biult in 1897, being the first plastered house in Burns.

JESSE O. BUNYARD.—A noble portion of the pioneer's work has been done by the estimable gentleman and patriotic citizen, whose life's career it is now our pleasant privilege to outline, since he has spent most of his days on the frontier and has always been in the harness for advancement, and progress, while the trying scenes incident to a pioneer's life have all been undergone by him.

Mr. Bunyard is a native of Mercer county, Missouri, being born on October 2, 1843, the son of James B. and Eliza Bunyard. In 1849 the father crossed the dreary plains with ox teams to California in search of the mining treasures of that land. In 1854 the mother with her six children, three boys and three girls, crossed the plains to Lane county, Oregon, where the father joined them from California. The trip across the plains with ox teams for this little family was a serious undertaking and they suffered much on the road. For three weeks they were without flour and were forced to kill one of the oxen for food. In the spring of 1854 they all went to Jackson county and the father took land near where Ashland now stands. They were pioneers of the county and labored faithfully to make a good home and open a farm. The mother died in 1863 and the father died in 1886. Our subject gained his education in the little log school house, grew up on a farm and in 1866 came to Walla Walla with nine yokes of oxen and wintered on Wildhorse creek. He sold his cattle the following spring and went to Silver City and engaged in freighting from Umatilla landing. Later he sold his outfit and went to mining and in 1868 he was in Eldorado, and acted as foreman on the rock work of the Eldorado ditch. After this he went to Lane county and farmed and there on July 24, 1870, he married Miss Emma, daughter of G. C. and Louisa Duncan, who crossed the plains in 1854 from Iowa to Lane county. In 1874 Mr. Bunyard removed to Jackson county and worked his fathers farm for a time, then came to Silver Lake valley in 1876. His youngest son was the first white child born ther and Mr. Bunyard sowed the first grain in that favored spot. In 1866 he sold there and came to this county, settling in the Cow creek country. He raised stock and handled his land to hay mostly. In June, 1901, he bought his present home place of one hundred and sixty acres of good land, seven miles northeast from Harney. He has good buildings, a fine orchard and handles many cattle and horses. To Mr. and Mrs. Bunyard there have been born six children, Mrs. Arvilla Thrash, of West Virginia; Frank M., of Harney county; Elva, deceased; Mrs. Hattie Cawlfield, LeRoy, and James B., all of Harney county. Mr. Bunyard has been in many fights with the Indians and his prowess as a marksman has saved his life in different encounters with them. He has worthily filled his position as frontiersman and real pioneer and builder of this county and is highly esteemed by his fellows.

HON. IRWIN S. GEER.—As one of the substantial and capable citizens of Harney county, whose life has always been allied on the side of right, and whose efforts in this county in the business realm have given him need of brilliant success and the entire confidence of the people, while in a political line he has been active and rewarded by the people with the highest honors they have to give, we are pleased to accord to Mr. Geer representation in this volume of his county's history as both a pioneer and a prominent and distinguished man.

A native of the occident, Mr. Geer was born on February 28, 1864, Marion county being the spot. His parents, Cal and Ellen S. Geer, came across the plains in 1847 and 1852, respectively, both making the journey with ox teams. Our subject was reared on the farm and received a common-school education, finishing the same with a course in the business college at Portland. It was 1890, that he started for himself, coming direct to Burns where he opened a hardware store, starting on a small scale and increasing as the trade demanded until he has become the largest dealer in these goods in the county of Harney. In 1900 he took as partner, C. Cummins, and they have a mammoth trade extending many miles in every direction. They handle a full line of hardware, sporting goods, crockery, stoves and tinware with farm implements and tools. In 1892, Mr. Geer was in partnership with his brother, R. C. Geer, and they erected a fine large two-story brick and stone structure, which is the store to-day.

Politically Mr. Geer is among the leaders, having the confidence of the people both as to his ability and integrity. In 1900 he was elected as representative of Malheur and Harney counties, and did good service in the house. In 1891 he was selected as city treasurer and in 1892 he was called to be treasurer of the county, being re-elected in 1894. He ran on the Republican ticket each time. Fraternally Mr. Geer is affiliated with the K. of P. and the I. O. O. F., Lodge No. 77, of Burns; and also with the Masons, being both past grand chancellor and past grand; and he is a member of the encampment. The marriage of Mr. Geer and Miss Belle Erb was solemnized on August 4, 1889, and they have four children, Juanita A., Waldo G., Henry C., and Ellen M. Mr. Geer is a man of good standing, is always active for the interests of his county, is upright and stable, and has the confidence of all.

PETER CLEMENS.—The well known gentleman whose name heads this article is one of the prominent men of Harney county, a heavy property owner, a leading stockman, and withal a gentleman of ability, and who has wrought out his present large holding by reason of his industry, thrift, and wise management in the affairs of business. Mr. Clemens was born in Loraine, France, on July 5, 1850, being the son of Nicholas and Margaret Clemens. In 1855 the family came to America and located in Canada, then moved to Menominee county, Michigan. It was 1865, that our subject came via Chicago, New York, and Cape Horn to San Francisco, making the ocean trip in a trading vessel, which was a very tedious journey. In California he labored at various callings and learned the brick mason's trade. In 1869, he went to British Columbia and Alaska and mined successfully for three years. Next we see him in Seattle and in 1872 he went to Manataron, South America, and went into the employ of his uncle, who operated a bakery. The next year he came back to San Francisco, and the following year went to Seattle and there built the Wharton and Dexter bank. In the spring of 1875 he was in the Black Hills, Dakota, where he mined a year and then went to Tuscarora and in 1877 to Eureka, Nevada. In this latter place he followed freighting to White Pine. The next year he went to Paradise valley to build a stamp mill and in 1879 Mr. Clemens came to Steins mountain, in Harney county. He had a pack and saddle horse and went to work for wages. He built the large store on the White Horse ranch and did various other work in the country and in the fall of 1882 he located on his present place, six miles north from Burns. He pre-empted and then homesteaded and went to raising stock. He has been eminently successful, for at the present time he has in fifteen hundred acres of fine land, a good house, barn, corrals, and all the improvements needed on a first class stock and hay ranch, besides large bunches of cattle and horses. He has some fine specimens of thoroughbred Durham cattle.

The marriage of Mr. Clemens was celebrated on December 7, 1882, Mrs. Jennie Thomas then becoming his wife, and they have three children, Thomas, Peter Clay, and Glen. Mr. Clemens is a member of the A. F. & A. M., at Burns. He is general road master for the county of Harney.

CYRUS A. SWEEK.—To the leading and capable attorneys of a county and state very much credit is due for the excellent institutions that are brought out as the result of salutary and wise laws which they have framed and caused to be placed on the books. As one of the worthy gentlemen of that important profession we mention the patriotic and public minded citizen, mentioned above, who is now at the head of his profession in Harney county, being a man of broad and comprehensive views, given to an impartial judgment of matters, with a well stored mind and a keen perception and dominated with an unswerving integrity that controls his acts and places him as one of the most reliable and substantial men of the country.

Mr. Sweek was born in Washington county, Oregon, on August 5, 1853, being the son of John and Maria (Beard) Sweek. His parents were married on February 29, 1852, and the same spring they came across the plains with ox teams to Oregon, from St. Genevieve county, Missouri. The father had started across in 1849, but at the Rockies he heard of the death of his parents and returned and came as stated. He was one of the very first settlers in Washington county, took a donation claim and there wrought until his death on February 26, 1890. The mother is still living at the old home place. They raised a family of six children, all living, of whom our subject is the eldest. Cyrus A. grew up on the farm and learned his primary lessons in the primitive country school and then attended the Pacific University at Forest Grove, and immediately after his course there he went into the study of the law with W. Lair Hill, of Portland. For three years Mr. Sweek pursued this course and on January 7, 1880, he was admitted to the bar, and on January 11, 1880, he married Miss Ella S., daughter of John P. and Missouri A. Gage, of Clackamas

county, Oregon, being pioneers from Missouri to Oregon in 1872. Mr. and Mrs. Sweek then came to Prairie City, Grant county, and there they taught school for a time and in the spring of 1881 he commenced the practice of law in Canyon City. He was admitted to the United States district and circuit courts in 1888. In the spring of 1889 they removed to Harney, then the county seat of Harney county. In 1890 they came thence to Burns, and here Mr. Sweek has practiced since with the gratifying success of gaining a large patronage from the county, and he now has one of the finest residences in Burns and three hundred acres of fertile meadow land adjoining the town of Burns, besides other property. Mr. Sweek is a charter member and was the first master of the A. F. & A. M., Burns Lodge, No. 97, joining the order in Canyon City in 1885. To Mr. Sweek and his noble wife there have been born ten children: John M.; Earl L., attending the Corvallis College; Agnes, also attending the same institution; Alice; Ella; Dorcas; Cyrus A.; Lois; Esther and Alexander D. Mrs. Sweek is a descendant of General Gage of Revolutionary fame. Mr. Sweek is one of the leading citizens of the county and has many warm friends in all parts, being a man of real worth and his walk has always been with dignity and uprightness.

ANDREW SPANGENBERG. — The well known and respected gentleman of whom we now have the pleasure of speaking is one of the well-to-do stockmen of Harney county and is worthy of especial mention because of his pioneer labors and the manner in which he has always wrought for the advancement of the country and its substantial progress. He was born in Denmark, whence come so many of our most substantial and thrifty citizens, the date of his advent into life being February 14, 1838. He grew up there and received a common school education and at the age of twenty-one was married to Miss Kate Wolfe, and the fruit of the union was two children, Peter and Adolph. Mr. Spangenberg was called to mourn the death of his wife and then he determined to leave the native land and accordingly came thence to the United States in 1867. He was engaged in various sections until 1872, when he came to Carson, Nevada, and in 1875 went to Modoc county, California, thence to Chico, and finally in 1883 he made his way to Harney county. He settled in Catlow valley, thirty miles west from Andrew postoffice, on the south side of the valley. From that time to the present he has steadily pursued the way of the stockman, and he has been well prospered. He has now a fine estate of eight hundred acres of land and a fine band of cattle. He was one of the early pioneers of the valley and has done the work of the frontiersman in a commendable manner. Fraternally Mr. Spangenberg is affiliated with the Red Men at Penn and he is popular in the social realm, as in all of his ways he is highly esteemed, being a man governed by sagacity, integrity and sound principles, and highly honored by all who know him.

JOHN W. GEARY, M. D.—It is a matter of congratulation that Harney county is so well provided with professional talent, as that fraternity is well to the front; one of the leaders of this distinguished class of men is the subject of this sketch, being a man of unsullied reputation, with a strong personality, characterized by stanch qualities of worth and firmness, possessed of excellent capabilities, which have been exceptionally well trained in the medical lore, Dr. Geary is calculated to stand high in his profession and we are not disappointed at the prestige that he enjoys and the high regard in which he is held by the people.

John W. Geary was born in Fredericksburgh, Ohio, on November 16, 1850, being the son of Edward R., D. D., and Nancy M. (Woodbridge) Geary. About the time of his birth his parents came via New York, Panama and San Francisco to Portland and on to Yam Hill county, Oregon, settling at La Fayette, and in 1857 removing thence to Linn county. The father was a clergyman in the Presbyterian church and was one of the founders of the Collegiate Institute at Albany, being the moving spirit in it and teaching there for a number of years. He removed to Eugene later and was one of the regents of the state university there until the time of his death, in 1887, having been there fourteen years. Our subject received his primary education in the

public schools, and completed the training at an academy at Homer, New York, and at Lafayette College. In 1871 he went to work for the Northern Pacific in the civil engineer corps and also spent some time as a salesman and clerk, and in 1879 he laid aside all these various employments and gave himself to the study of medicine, at the Willamette University at Portland, graduating from that institution in 1883. He immediately began the practice at Halsey, Oregon, and three years later went to the Polyclinic school at New York City, taking a post-graduate course and then returned to Hasley, remaining there until 1894. Then he located at Harrisburg and later was at Junction City and in August, 1899, he made his advent in Burns. He immediately entered partnership with Dr. Marsden, the firm being known as Marsden & Geary.

Fraternally the Doctor is affiliated with the A. F. & A. M., Lodge No. 97, at Burns, and with the I. O. O. F., at Junction City, being both past master and past grand. Also belongs to the Encampment at Harrisburg, Oregon, the W. of W. and the A. O. U. W. Doctor Geary stands well with his colleagues, being recognized as a talented practitioner and a very skillful physician. He is a member of the Oregon State Medical Society and the American Medical Association. The Doctor is highly esteemed by all who know him and has a very extensive practice.

JOSEPH W. BUCHANAN is one of Harney county's reliable and enterprising citizens. He is a man of energy and has labored with assiduity and sagacity in the improvement of his fine estate of six hundred acres of good land on Rock creek, thirteen miles east from Harney, while also he conserves the interest of the county in his faithful service in the assessor's office, where he has served for nearly one term. Mr. Buchanan was born in Tama county, Iowa, on April 19, 1860, being the son of William D. and Helen J. (Cullen) Buchanan. The parents are now both in their seventy-fourth year, being married when they were twenty. They live at their pleasant homestead, twelve miles east from Burns, and are accredited with being the oldest couple in the county. In 1865 they came across the plains with ox teams from Iowa to Lagrande. They fought frequently with the savages, but did not lose any of their number. Five months of this weary journeying brought them to their destination and the father took land and engaged in farming. Union county was the scene of our subject's childhood, and there he received his education. There also, on May 12, 1884, he married Miss Hattie E., daughter of William P. and Eliza A. Gates, pioneers from Vernon county, Missouri, to Union county in 1879. Our subject came to Harney county in 1885 and selected a homestead where his home estate is now located. He gave his attention industriously to raising stock and improving his place and he has a good residence, barns

and so forth. It was in 1898 that Mr. Buchanan was elected county assessor on the Democratic ticket, being re-elected in 1900. Fraternally Mr. Buchanan is a member of the I. O. O. F., Harney Lodge, No. 77. To our subject and his worthy wife there have been born four children: Warren, deceased; Eliza E.; Albert Leo and William Monroe.

Mr. Buchanan successfully handles his line of business, as he has shown his capabilities to judiciously and in a becoming manner discharge the public duties entrusted to him by the franchises of his fellows. In addition to the other property mentioned, Mr. Buchanan has a modern six-room residence in one of the best portions of Burns.

DESCRIPTIVE AND GENERAL.

CHAPTER I.

TOPOGRAPHY, RESOURCES, ETC., OF BAKER, GRANT, MALHEUR AND HARNEY COUNTIES.

"No menace, now, the desert's mood of sand;
Still westward lies a green and golden land."

"For, at the magic touch of water, blooms
The wilderness, and where of yore the yoke
Tortured the toilers into dateless tombs,
Lo! brightsome fruits to feed a mighty folk."

"After all there is no desert," says a recent writer, after quoting Emerson's well known aphorism, "To science there is no poison; to botany no weed; to chemistry no dirt." Certainly to the present generation there are no "waste places" in the severe sense of the term. But many are living to-day who in youth were schooled in a knowledge of the "Great American Desert" west of the Mississippi. The borders of this vast wilderness were not definitely outlined either on the maps or in the minds of those who had undertaken its exploration, but it was believed to include large portions of what are now Kansas, Nebraska, Oklahoma, Texas, New Mexico, Arizona, California, Colorado, Nevada, Wyoming, Utah, Idaho and Oregon, an almost illimitable territory. Descriptions that found their way into print, telling of its vastness, its repellent visage, its blazing heat, its deadly simoon, its sun scorched plains and its dark canyons, its rushing torrents and its dry river beds, its savage beasts and its equally savage men, excited intense interest in the credulous eastern mind. And these stories were not overdrawn. The most imaginative and sensational writer could scarcely have pictured in too vivid language the gloomy grandeur and utter desolation of this arid empire. Withal it was not without beauty of a startling barbaric sort. In its midst was the great dividing wall of the Rocky mountains and the gray sands of the plains were relieved by the browns of the mountain slopes and the snows of the mountain peaks. There is beauty in majesty and the desert was majestic in its portrayal of the titanic forces of nature. There is beauty in grandeur and the desert was grand in its passion of storm and flood. But it was no less a desert and for many years only stout hearts and fearless souls dared venture into its midst or attempt to traverse its cheerless wastes.

But stout hearts came; at first, in bands of two or three, later in companies of a score or more and, later still, in armies a thousand strong. Forty years ago these armies began their encroachments; the "Great Desert" boundaries became, year by year, less and less distinct; year by year its area was diminished, until now it exists only in the memory of the sturdy pioneer who weathered its rigors in those old heroic days.

Much of the territory of eastern Oregon was once classed with the desert lands of the west, but at last the miner, the stockman and the agriculturist forged into the region. They subdued the savage and drove him within the reservation confines. They braved the frown of nature and forced ajar the door of her treasure house. Nature, with all her powerful forces, was arrayed against them, but they were men of mental vigor as well as men of might, and they marched on to victory. Now, lo!—

Where once was sombre gray, are richest shades of green,
And yellow gold of ripening grain on plain and vale is seen.

And on the mountains' slope and by the river's flow,
Where savage Piutes' council fire blazed forth in angry glow,

There roam a thousand flocks and herds, in wood and wold,
O'er countless miles of bunchgrass range—"Oregon's check for gold."

Far up the rocky gulch where lair of beast was laid,
Are spread the tents of miners' camps. With pick and pan and spade

Now delves the miner deep in rock and sand and soil
And gathers stores of shining gold—reward for patient toil.

And over all the land—once sombre-hued and gray,— Is spread the sky of light and peace, undimmed the livelong day.

BAKER COUNTY.

In the transformation from desert plain to farm, orchard and garden, with their verdure and beauty and bloom, with their wealth of comfort for man and beast, Baker county has had a goodly share. The black sage brush soil of its valleys was early found to be productive, when supplied with a greater abundance of water than parsimonious Nature was

willing to afford, and though the valley was much less favorable to agriculture in 1862 than it is in 1902, the earliest efforts to court the favor of Ceres were by no means unavailing. We have mentioned these first experiments in former chapters. Their success and the demand for farm produce incident to the operation of the placer mines soon resulted in a considerable development of the agricultural resources of the county and the work of home building and soil subjugation has progressed steadily, if somewhat slowly, ever since. As if to reward the farmer for his faith and perseverance, the climate of Baker county and eastern Oregon generally has become much more mild and equable than it was when the region was first visited by white men; frosts are less frequent and severe and the rainfall has shown a tendency to increase with the tilling of the soil.

To the proper appreciation of the agricultural and other resources of Baker county, a general understanding of its topography, elevation, etc., is necessary. The area of the county is given by Rand, McNally & Company's maps as 2,275 square miles, but the Panhandle of Union county has since been added, so that the present area would be expressed by figures considerably larger than these. Its western boundary follows for the most part the summit of the axis of the Blue mountain range; its northern boundary may be said to be formed by the Powder River mountains and from these spurs are sent out extending far into its interior. The ranges referred to reach a maximum altitude of nearly 9,000 feet above the sea and are from 4,000 to 6,000 feet higher than the general level of the valleys. "Snow remains on the highest peaks throughout the year, and, with the exception of a short period during the heated season, these mighty monuments are dressed in the white liveries of angels and point in marble-like majesty to heaven's azure vault as if directing, in their virgin purity, that the happy inhabitants of this region should ever be thankful for the privilege of enjoying a life well worth living in one of the most resourceful, fertile and healthful counties to be found anywhere in all our peerless republic." The eastern boundary is formed by the swift and treacherous Snake river, into which all the drainage of the county eventually makes its way. The principal water courses are Burnt and Powder rivers, though there are several small creeks which flow directly to the Snake, never mingling their waters with the currents of these major streams.

The largest valley in the county is that of Powder river, which is approximately thirty miles in length and up to twenty in width. It was the first to be blessed by the permanent presence of white men, for the mines which attracted settlement to the county were discovered within its confines. The valley is for the most part a level, sage covered area, not beautiful in itself, but surrounded by majestic mountain uplifts, always varying in sympathy with the seasons and faithfully reflecting the changing climatic conditions of the upper air into which their crests extend, yet ever retaining their own characteristic beauty, grandeur and granitic ruggedness. The valley below might take on all the beauty it could desire, might clothe itself in garments of deepest verdure bejewelled with the most brilliant of gems, were the elements of its soil but fertilized by the one element lacking to give them vitality, nature's universal solvent—water. The rainfall is not sufficient for this purpose. The currents which course through the valley on their way to the bosom of the ocean are not strong enough during the growing season to accomplish it. Art must come to their assistance and store the flood waters of winter and spring if all the dry ground of Powder river valley is to be made to blossom as the rose. This storage of water for irrigation is deemed feasible by engineers and the initial steps have been taken in the past looking toward the com-

plete reclamation of the valley in this way, but as yet no such project has been carried to a successful issue.

It must not be assumed, however, that Powder river valley is entirely a desert at this time. Streams have been halted in their courses and made to transform sagebrush plains into fertile farms, which pour into the garners of the husbandman an abundant reward for well directed toil. Bonanza farming is not in vogue in the valley. Most of the agriculturalists are devotees of diversified industry, raising hay, grain, fruit, cattle, hogs and horses. The natural fertility of the soil enables them to secure crops of wheat averaging sometimes as high as fifty bushels per acre, perhaps even higher, and of oats up to 105 bushels. The usual crop is, of course, far below this.

Climatic and other conditions are favorable to the live stock industry. Loss from disease is inconsiderable. Horses have the strength of limb, spirit and soundness of constitution so much desired by breeders. Cattle produce a juicy, palatable and wholesome beef, and the sheep of the country are noted for their large production of superior wool and for the excellence of the mutton they yield.

On the line of the Sumpter Valley railroad, about twelve miles up Powder river from Baker City, one enters a beautiful elevated valley, which takes its name from the thriving mining town of Sumpter at its upper end. The valley does not attain a great width in any part of its extent and in places is very narrow. Its soil is a rich alluvium, capable of producing any of the farm products in great abundance, but owing to its elevation of 4,000 feet it is unsuited to fruit raising or horticulture. At present its chief product is hay, which is fed to cattle or shipped to Sumpter and sold to the mining companies and freighters. The valley lands are surrounded by gentle sloping, forested benches, whose wealth of timber, in part, induced the building of the Sumpter Valley railroad. From Sumpter this road climbs over Powder River mountain, passing through forests all the way, until it reaches the small valley in which the terminal town of Whitney is situated.

Southeast of Whitney, down the north fork of Burnt river, is the Upper Burnt river valley, the lowest elevation of which is given by Lindgren as 4,100. It is nearly circular in shape, having a diameter of about five miles, and surrounding it are gently sloping ridges rising to an elevation of 6,000 feet. The timber surrounding it is excellent yellow pine. In the valley is a considerable settlement of farmers and stockmen. After passing through a narrow canyon fifteen miles long the river emerges upon a remarkable valley about twenty miles in length, having an elevation at its upper end of 3,900 feet and at its lower of 500 feet less. This lower Burnt river valley is very narrow in places and is perhaps not much over a mile wide anywhere. The soil is alluvial nearest the river and is covered with meadows of alfalfa and other grasses. Hereford is the principal settlement of the upper end of the valley and Bridgeport of the lower. To these villages the latest United States census ascribes populations of 32 and 18, respectively. The valley is so sheltered as to form a huge natural hot house, in which all the more delicate fruits of the temperate zone, such as peaches, grapes, etc., and such tender vegetables as cantaloupes and water melons may be produced in great perfection. Much attention is given also to the culture of apples, pears, plums, prunes and berries, and the valley, already noted locally as a fruit region, will experience in future such a development in the industry as will win it a much wider fame. Stock raising and general farming are not neglected and many thousand head of sheep are owned by the residents.

Rye valley in southeastern Baker county is noted more for its rich placers and promising quartz claims than for farming, though there is in it a small area of alluvial soil, exceedingly

fertile, upon which some comfortable homes have been established.

Some of the most beautiful and productive of the valleys of Baker county are in the Panhandle country, recently annexed. Eagle valley, in this neighborhood, lies fifteen miles south of the Eagle mountains and perhaps thirty-six miles in an air line from Baker City. It is traversed in its southern end by Powder river and through its entire length passes Eagle creek, which rises in the Eagle mountains. The valley proper is perhaps four by seven miles in area, but with the benches watered by irrigating ditches, it is much larger, possibly ten miles long by up to ten miles wide. It is a very beautiful valley, surrounded by rolling foothills furnishing an abundance of range for stock. Water for irrgation purposes is plentiful; the climate is mild owing to the sheltering foothills and mountain ranges surrounding; the soil is as fertile as a garden and all conditions combine to make it a pleasant place in which to live and an easy place in which to accumulate a competence or even a small fortune. Three heavy crops of lucerne may be raised annually. The hay crops are mostly utilized in the rearing of sheep, cattle and horses. All the other products of the farm, orchard and garden find a ready market among the miners in the neighboring mountains and plateaus. Peaches, apples, apricots, prunes, grapes, plums, cherries, strawberries, raspberries, blackberries, gooseberries, currants and all garden vegetables, as well as the cereals, are produced here in abundance and perfection. The mild climate of the valley, said to be the best in eastern Oregon, gives it special adaptation to fruit raising. Its products carried away seventeen premiums out of thirty-two at the World's Fair. Favored indeed are the people who have found homes in Eagle valley, but they have in their isolation one great drawback to contend with. Should the proposed Oregon & Idaho Central railroad be built, this difficulty will be overcome.

Twelve miles northeast of Eagle is Pine valley, situated at the base of the Powder River mountains. It is similar to the region last described in many respects, but is somewhat larger and has an elevation greater by 300 feet. Its soil is a rich clay loam, producing from twenty-five to thirty bushels of wheat per acre. It is a fine grain raising section, but is also noted for its fruit of all kinds. Its peaches possess a delicacy and richness of flavor not found in the products of other sections less favored in soil and climate. Stock raising receives much attention here also. The valley and creek were named from the heavy pine forests which abound in the vicinity. The villages of the valley are Pine, Halfway and Carson.

The above described valleys constitute the principal agricultural districts of the county. Their aggregate area is small compared with that of the entire county, but it must not be assumed that the non-tillable lands are a waste. They produce annually a wealth of pasturage, upon which thousands of head of livestock feed during a large part of the year, and the timber upon the mountain sides will some day be worked up and exchanged for great riches, to say nothing of the valuable mineral deposits which are at present the chief source of revenue of the county. About the only source of information we have regarding the number of cattle, horses and sheep which find pasture on hillside and mountain slope is in the assessment roll for the year 1901, which shows the horses and mules to number 4,782 head; the cattle, 20,697; the sheep and goats, 75,078; and the swine, 1,932. The value of these animals is placed at $430,636, but as it is a custom among assessors in Oregon to place the valuations as somewhere about one-fourth or one-fifth of the actual to avoid paying an unjust amount of state tax, the real value of live stock in Baker county is probably between $1,700,000 and $2,000,000, figures which show that the cattle and sheep industries in this section are still of great importance.

46

The vast treasures of timber wealth in the county bring in hundreds of thousands of dollars annually and there are many millions of feet which can not yet be utilized on account of the lack of transportation facilities. It is said by the promoters of the Oregon & Idaho Central railroad that from their proposed line through the Goose creek farming country it is intended to build a branch to tap a timber belt estimated to contain one billion, two hundred and fifty million feet of lumber, which has seldom echoed back the sound of an axe. A great impetus was given to lumbering by the construction of the Sumpter Valley railway, which has been pushing farther and farther into the timber belt to the west and southwest of Baker City. The Oregon Lumber Company, whose stockholders are in reality the owners of the railroad, have a large mill just outside the limits of Baker City, the daily capacity of which is 80,000 feet. Among the other lumbering firms of the county, the Stoddard Brothers, at McEwen, whose mill has a capacity of 35,000 feet, and McMurren & Shockley and Bennet & Company, of Baker City, and the Sumpter Lumber Company, of the vicinity of Sumpter, are prominent.

Of such transcendent import are the mines of Baker county that we have reserved them for treatment in a chapter especially devoted to that industry. If the opinions of experts and the teachings of experience are to be credited, the mining districts have before them possibilities of development almost unbounded. Their development will lend encouragement and aid to that of all the other industries, and in the converting to the uses of mankind of the vast unelaborated, unsubdued sources of wealth many will find the means of establishing homes of comfort in this favored section of our commonwealth.

GRANT COUNTY.

"An epic quest it was of elder years,
Through strange, scarred hills, for good red gold,
The trail men strove in iron days of old."

While this description has to do chiefly with conditions as we find them to-day, it is an appropriate place for brief retrospection. Doctor Thomas Condon, Professor of Geology in the state university at Eugene, has recently written a book which he has entitled "The Two Islands and What Came of Them." No more fascinating story was ever told than that related by Doctor Condon of the physical life of the present state of Oregon. In his own words let us read the history of the first formative epoch:

"The geological history of the Pacific coast consists chiefly in the description of the low elevation of successive belts, of the bed of the ocean into dry land, and the progressive addition of these to the western border of North America. These belts of ocean bed have not only been elevated into dry land, but in varying degrees hardened into rock, though retaining through all these changes the clearest evidence of their former sea-bed condition. The floor of the sea from which these beds were lifted, was in favored places strewn then, as such places are strewn to-day, with shells, fragments of corals, or of bones, all bearing record of the life of the period in which they were covered by the ocean sediment.

"So carefully have the results of geological studies been formulated that it is entirely practicable to tell what portion of any country were first above the seas, and often to trace the successive additions to the land until its outline is recognized as the present continent. Following this method in deciphering the geological history of Oregon, one is carried back to a time when this region, which we now call our home, was covered by the ocean.

"In the natural world the evident results of violent upthrusts of portions of the earth crust are now accepted as among the trustworthy records of many lands. These disturbances were sometimes accompanied by great heat, often by violent earthquakes and the outflow of melted rock, and sometimes only by heat enough to change the materials without melting them. Oregon's geological history had its origin in just such a violent crumpling of its ancient sea bed, and when the disturbance that caused this ceased, and quiet was restored to the region, there was left, as a result, two islands off the western coast of North America. It was these two islands that grew into Oregon. Of these islands, one occupied the eastern portion of what is now the Blue mountain region, the other extending over what is now the southwest corner of the state of Oregon, together with a portion of northern California, occupying what is now the Siskiyou mountain region."

Doctor Condon states that these islands were set in the ancient Pacific, three hundred miles apart, with the waters of the ocean flowing between. The western he has designated as the Siskiyou Island, and the eastern as the Shoshone Island. At a later period a colossal sea dyke slowly arose from the bed of the ocean, midway between the islands. In process of time this dyke, with the sea bed on either side, reached an altitude above that of the two islands and the waters receding, left lofty mountain barriers between what afterward became "Siskiyou Region" and "Shoshone Region."

Geologically speaking, eastern Oregon is in the Shoshone Island region. In a work of this character, it is not possible to enter minutely into the results of geological research. This region has had a wonderful history, which is intensely interesting in its details, but, having recited the bare facts of the first period of its physical life, we must leave to the student the search of minutiae and proceed to the description of superficial areas in which the present generation is more directly concerned.

In the 'fifties and 'sixties men came to eastern Oregon from the agricultural districts of the east, influenced chiefly by the desire to accumulate wealth. Some came in quest of newer, better lands on which former pursuits might be followed under more propitious skies, and others came with but one purpose—to possess themselves of the gold in the mountains. This state, which has been termed the "Keystone State of the Pacific coast and the fairest of all lands," offered to both classes unparalleled inducements and almost limitless territory in which to conduct operations. California on the south is too dry and too warm to be an ideal country. Washington on the north has an atmosphere too cool and damp. The desirable medium of conditions is to be found in Oregon and especially in the eastern part. It has a climate unsurpassed; valleys of productiveness and beauty watered by clearest rivers and streams; mountains among the grandest on the face of the earth, whose mineral deposits are rich and inexhaustible. It is a country that has rarely disappointed. Many a pioneer recalls his emotion, when, his tiresome journey ended, he reached a summit on the eastern boundary and gazed westward over grassy plains and wooded hillsides. Forgotten were the terrors of the desert; with hope revived and courage strengthened, he pressed forward with renewed energies and, wherever he pitched his tent, the water, the sunshine, and the soil combined to crown his every effort with success.

Grant county was not invaded under the inspiration of the rallying cry—Westward, Ho! Some of her pioneers had visited the Pacific coast of California and others, leaving Grant far to the south on their western pilgrimage, and journeyed to the Willamette valley and the extreme western part of Oregon. But in the farther west the spirit of unrest had not left them nor had their toilsome efforts met with satisfying reward. Turning their faces eastward fortune's star became their guide. It led them a torturous way, but proved a faithful guide, directing their footsteps at length into the beautiful valley of the John Day river.

The incidents associated with the settlement of this valley having been related in another chapter, we proceed with its description. On a grander scale Grant county has been fashioned like the old Roman amphitheatre, the John Day valley representing the arena. This valley is rapidly becoming the field of action where will be expended the energies of future generations in furthering the progress of the county.

The John Day river rises on the eastern side of the county, some of its minor sources in the Strawberry range and others in a spur of the Blue mountains, along the summit of which is traced the eastern boundary line. The course of the river is almost due west for ninety miles, when it makes a sharp curve to the north, crossing the county line in a northwesterly direction at a point twenty-five miles south of the county's northern limits. Here its waters are joined by those of the North Fork. While numerous creeks and small streams join the John Day in its course down the valley, the most important of which are Dixie creek from the north and Canyon creek from the south, the first stream of considerable size to effect a junction with the main river is the South Fork, which enters its channel about fifty miles below the town of John Day. The northwest is famed for its beautiful valleys, and among the most charming is that of the John Day. It is about seventy miles long and varies in width from one to six miles. The elevation in the upper portion is 3,500 feet and in the extreme lower end slightly over 2,000 feet. On either side are foothills and mountain ranges towering to elevations of from five to seven thousand feet. On the north these higher altitudes are painted with the green of the pine, fir and tamarack; on the south the hills are barren and rocky. The undulating lands of the valley are arable throughout its entire length and well adapted to agriculture, while the slopes and bench-lands on its borders are the natural homes of the fruit and forest tree.

There are more than two hundred square

miles of tillable land in this valley, making it vastly the most important in the county, but a number of others are worthy of mention. The South Fork rises on the west slope of the Strawberry mountains, its general course being directly north. In its central portion is a fertile valley some fifteen miles in length and averaging one and a half miles in width. In elevation it is slightly higher than its larger neighbor, but it is similar in its adaptations. There is an extensive valley region on the north side of the county, where, although the altitude is greater, the climate is milder than elsewhere and the winters less rigorous. Along the Middle Fork, whose headwaters are near those of the main river, there are several small valleys whose combined areas would make a tract of considerable extent. The course of the stream is northwest across the county and in length it is fully sixty miles. It empties into the North Fork near the north county line. Its main tributary is Long creek, which courses for forty miles in the same direction between low ranges of mountains in the north central portion of the county. The valley of this stream is six by seven miles in extent and is occupied by prosperous ranchers and agriculturists. Fox valley is fifteen miles north of Canyon City and is drained by Fox creek, a small tributary which flows west into the John Day river. It is one of the most fertile valleys in the county and contains eight square miles. Haystack and Corncob are miniature valleys on the Middle Fork in the north, noted for picturesque surroundings and warm climate. One of the sources of Crooked river, a Crook county stream, is in the extreme southwest corner of Grant, on the divide between North Fork and some of the Harney county streams.

Silvies river, which empties into Malheur lake in Harney county, rises on the south side of the Strawberry mountains and for fifteen miles flows through Grant county territory. The valley of this river is twenty-five by ten

miles in area, a small portion of it lying within the limits of this county. It is occupied principally by stock ranches. Bear valley is twenty miles south of Canyon City, near the source of Silvies river. This valley extends for twenty-five miles along the Strawberry mountains and has a width averaging eight miles. The altitude here is more than 4,000 feet, making it almost exclusiely a stock region. It is abundantly supplied with water by numerous streams and wild grasses grow luxuriantly. Soda Springs, flowing water impregnated with medicinal properties, is located at the upper end of this valley. Farther west, along Murderer's creek (a tributary of South Fork), is a valley twelve miles long and half as wide, occupied almost exclusively by stockmen, its elevation unfitting it for the production of other than forage grasses. Besides these named there are several other valleys in various parts of the county which, although not occupying any considerable extent of territory, are abundantly watered from surrounding mountains and are very productive, cereal grains and fruits yielding rich harvests.

There are no extensive plains in Grant county. It is a region of lofty mountain ranges dwindling into foothills which cast their shadows across fertile valleys below. Strawberry Butte, in the southeast, has an elevation of 8,600 feet; Greenhorn peak, in the northeast, an elevation of 8,100 feet; Dixie Butte, on the east side, an elevation of 7,700 feet. Olive lake, in the northeast part of the county, is at an altitude of 5,950 feet. In its course around the county the boundary line, on the east, north and south, remains at an altitude but little below 5,000 feet at any point. At some points the elevation is over 7,000 feet. On the west side in the valley of the John Day, the altitude is slightly over 2,000 feet. But, even on the west, except for a short distance on either side of the river, the boundary line traverses high altitudes. The county is practically hedged in by the bordering mountain ranges.

No railroad has as yet crossed its borders. The physical barriers interposed are many and they are not easily surmountable. But this is, perhaps, not the only cause for the absence of the railroad and the consequent isolation of the region. In its present stage of development the county does not offer inducements sufficiently great to warrant its invasion. Its need of railroads is, however, very great; in fact, its future development will depend largely upon its success in securing easy means of transportation to outside markets.

Several stage lines cross the county and all points are thus connected. There is a daily stage service between Whitney and Canyon City. Six times each week the stage runs from Canyon City to Heppner; three times each week from Canyon City to Burns. The mining regions about Susanville and in the Greenhorn districts have direct stage connections with Whitney and with points west and south. Other lines reach outlying postoffices of lesser importance, and stages visit these places at regular intervals. All settlements of importance are connected, and have communication with the outside world by telephone.

A ride over the stage lines of Grant county is a most interesting and delightful experience. There are but few easy grades. The routes cross directly over the successive ranges of mountains, and wind through intervening valleys or canyons. From the mountain summits many of the views are matchless in beauty and grandeur. On leaving the John Day valley at Prairie City enroute to Whitney the road climbs over steep grades to the summit of a spur of the Blue mountains, a distance of nine miles. Progress is necessarily slow and the summit goal seems to recede rather than to advance. At the start it is apparently just ahead—half an hour's drive. But distances are proverbially deceptive in the mountains as well as on the plains. When the first stage in the journey is accomplished and the elevation of the foothills is reached, the mountain heights have seemingly been lifted to greater altitudes and removed still farther from our immediate presence. In front and to the left the ranges expand in broken outline, revealing dark reaches of wooded knobs that stretch away in dim outline to the northwest until they are blended with the mists of the horizon. Bald and rocky summits are here and there projected above the timber line; castellated promontories frown at us from distant heights, while on every hand are dark mysterious alcoves in which haze and shadow lie engulfed. Dixie Butte and Greenhorn peak lift their barren rocky crowns in bold profile against the sky, thousands of feet above their neighbors. While our thoughts have been engrossed with the beauty and magnificence of the view before us, the region behind has arranged its wonders for our inspection. The peaceful valley lies far below us, its upper portion rounded against the dark hills, its lower portion narrowed into canyon confines. There are ranches outlined by rows of tall poplars, squares of crimsoning orchard and shade trees and fields of green and gold with their charm of color, of light and shade. The river winds, at times, close to the bordering hills under the shadow of the pines. Again it crosses the valley or follows an irregular course in its midst, finally disappearing in the gorge at the lower end. To the south of the valley the foothills and the Strawberry range form a receding terrace which culminates forty miles away in an altitude of 8,600 feet on the summit of Strawberry Butte. The mountain range is outlined in jagged profile in the distant south. Its massive ridges rise majesically above the intervening hills, streaked and columned with snow, broken and serrated with projecting rocks. Shadowy canyons zigzag among the hills and through the further range. The scene is one of weird mystery and wild beauty. The scenery throughout the John Day valley is much the same and yet there is nothing like monotony. The valley itself widens and narrows many times as the hills recede from the river or crowd close upon its channel. There are always hills in the foreground and always mountains in the background. But there is endless variety in form and color and the river pursues a wayward course in harmony with the ever changing contour on either side.

But while the valley of the John Day river is one of the most beautiful in eastern Oregon, Grant county furnishes many other views of rare beauty and attractiveness. These may be found along any of the stage lines which trail through its hill and mountain regions. These stage roads pass over some of the highest ridges in the county. They traverse the valleys and wind up the canyons, sometimes close by the waters of a rushing mountain stream and again high up on the mountain side. Each turn in the road brings some change of scene; now a village miles away and thousands of feet below, the houses huddled together between the precipitous walls of a canyon or scattered about on a gentle slope at the head of a valley; now tremendous uplifts of stratified rocks, bent and crumpled under prodigious pressure, curiously weathered, broken and worn until they are only colossal fragments of the original upheaval; or again, buildings and stacks of the prosperous ranchmen, clustered in a miniature valley—a gem of beauty rough-set in nature's mightier works.

Although the greater portion of the county is extremely rough and mountainous, the level, tillable areas are comparatively small, yet it is by no means a desert waste. In another chapter will be found reference to the products of its mines. Everywhere its mountains are abundantly stored with minerals. In the Canyon City region development work has proceeded for many years and enormous values have been taken from the surrounding mines. Canyon mountain is called locally "Gold Mountain" because of the immense quantities of the precious metal that have been taken from it and that are believed to be still stored in it.

Other regions famous for gold deposits are what is known as the Prairie Diggings, a few miles east of Canyon City; the Quartzburg district, at the head of Dixie creek; the Dixie creek region; Spanish Gulch, a few miles east; along Ruby creek, a tributary of Middle Fork; the Susanville district on Middle Fork; the Greenhorn mountain district; the country about Granite, in the northeast and the bed of the John Day river below the city of John Day. A map of the gold belt of eastern Oregon, recently published by the United States Geological survey, includes all of the eastern half of Granite, in the northeast and the bed of the the Strawberry mountains.

The John Day valley is famous for the geological records contained in its rock formations and in its bed of fossil remains. Of these Doctor Condon, of the State University, says:

There are many residents of the Pacific slope who will remember having journeyed from The Dalles, on the Columbia river, to Canyon City, among the Blue mountains. For sixty miles or more the road passes over volcanic materials which have drifted there from the Cascade range. Twenty miles further and this outflow thins out into a mere capping of basalt on the hilltops. The hills themselves, and the foundations on which they stand, are here found to be sedimentary rock, wonderfully filled with the abundant records of former animal and vegetable life. Oldest of all in sight is the old ocean bed of the Cretaceous period, with its teeming thousands of marine shells, as perfect to-day in their rocky bed as those of our recent sea shores, their cavities often filled with calcareous spar or chalcedony as if to compensate for the loss of their own proper marine hues. Next in ascending order come the fresh water deposits of the earlier Tertiaries, so full of the leaf prints of the grand old tropical forests which during that age of semi-tropical climate covered those lake shores. The marine rocks form the outer rim or shore-line of what was in those early times a lake of irregular outline, extending from Kern Creek hill on the west to Canyon City on the east, and from the hills north of the John Day river to the Crooked river valley on the south. Within this lake depression, whose former muddy sediment is now elevated into chalky hills, so despised for their alkaline waters and unproductive soils, the geologist feels at home. How strangely out of place a score of palm trees, a hundred yew trees, or even a bank of ferns, would seem here now, and yet here these once lived and died and were buried, and beautiful beyond description are their fossil remains even now as they are unburied.

Seen from the summit of Kern Creek hill, its west-ern border, this vast ampitheatre of lesser hills presents a wild, wonderful grouping of varied outlines and colors. A spur of the Blue mountains—its nearest point forty miles away—covered with a dense forest, forms the dark background of the view. The varying shades of brown that characterize the older marine rocks rise in vast border masses, almost treeless and shrubless, in an inner, irregular circle, while the lighter shades that fill the deeper depressions of the central portion mark the later sedimentary deposits; and then, like vast ink blots on a painting, one sees, here and there, a protruding mass of dark colored trap. Through the heart of this wild region winds the John Day river, running westward until it passes the middle ground of the picture, and then turning northward to join the Columbia. This stream, so insignificant in appearance, has done wonderful work among these hills. The river itself was in the olden times merely a series of connecting links between a chain of lakes that extended from the Blue mountains to the Cascades of the Columbia. It has for unnumbered ages gone on excavating vast gorges and canyons as all other streams in central Oregon have done, till lake after lake was drained off and their beds changed to a treeless desert. The deep excavations that resulted could hardly fail to lay bare important records of the past, cutting as they do through the whole extent of the Tertiary period. In a deep canyon, through which runs a branch of Kern creek, may be found the remains of a beautiful fern, a gem of its kind, which no thoughtful mind can see without wonder and admiration. In another ravine are seen in great numbers the remains of a yew, or yew-like tree, that sheds annually not its leaflets but its branchlets; for in this form they are found of almost uniform length and structure imbedded in the rocks. This tree was evidently abundant upon those ancient shores, for it can be found at almost every spot where a little stream washed its miniature delta into the lake. Oaks, too, and occasionally a fine impression of an acorn, or acorn-cup, are found at intervals from this place to the Blue mountains.

But the great geological importance of that old lake depression does not arise from the fossil remains of its forests, beautiful, varied and abundant as they are, but from its finely preserved fossil bones. Two species of rhinoceros lived their quiet, indolent lives among the reeds that line the old lake shore. A little beyond the southern spur of that distant mountain there evidently emptied a stream of some size, for its delta is strewn with fragments of silicified bones. Among these the bones of the rhinoceros are frequent, but the remains of an extinct animal, allied in some respects to the camel, in others to the tapir family, are most abundant. Mute historians are they of the far distant past, uniting with hundreds of others to tell strange stories of the wonderful wealth of forest, field and lake shore of that period. A tapir-like animal to which

the name of Lophiodon has been given lived here too. His remains indicate an animal the size of the living tapir. Not far from the last were found some bones of a fossil peccary of large size. Another of the denizens of these ancient lake shores bore some resemblance to the horse. The remains of this animal, the Anchitherium, were first discovered in the Tertiary rocks of France a few years ago; more recently they were found in the "bad lands" of Nebraska, and later in the John Day valley. But the richest chapters in the history of the horse in Oregon are not from those rocks of the lower valley, for another and a later record in the upper part of the valley contains these.

Doubtless both portions of the valley were once continuous and formed one lake, but a stream of lava from the Blue mountains seems to have run into it near the present site of Camp Watson, dividing it into an upper and a lower lake. The lower one seems to have drained off first, the upper one remaining a lake into the later Tertiary period, and receiving into its archives the remains of the animal types of a later age. The river was apparently turned northward by that outpouring of volcanic materials, and cutting for itself a new channel in the deep canyon thirty miles or more away formed a great bend, and excavated an immense basin in these nearer and lighter colored Tertiary rocks. Above that bend, that canyon and that volcanic outflow, the valley opens again, and there, extending from Cottonwood creek to Canyon City, are the remains of the upper lake depression of the John Day valley. This later lake depression received into its sediment a larger amount of volcanic ashes and cinders than the lower one did. Several of its strata are pure volcanic ashes, rough to the touch as ground pumice stone, which must have fallen on that lake in vast quantities. The purest was evidently that which had fallen directly into the lake, the less pure that which, first falling on the surrounding hills, had subsequently drifted from them by the action of the winds and waters and had become part of the lake sediment.

Upon the hills that overlooked these lake shores there lived three or four different species of the horse family. Their remains are easily distinguished, for the teeth are well preserved and the teeth of the horse are well marked. Almost as well marked as these equine remains were some teeth that apparently represented a member of the camel family found there, too, in a fine specimen of a lower jaw silicified completely and in solid rock. Fossil remains of other species also giving a wide range of life record were found.

But the most remarkable thing about this upper lake record is that which reveals the way in which its history of this period was brought to a close. The last rock of the series fills the place of a cover to the volume. Never was cover better defined nor more distinctly separated from the well written and well illustrated pages it serves to protect. The cover itself, too, has a history worth reading. It extends for miles, varying but slightly in thickness, which amounts to twenty or twenty-five feet, and is throughout so entirely volcanic as to leave no room for mistake. Its materials are volcanic ashes and cinders, the cinders ranging from an inch across downward to the minuteness of the ashes. Volcanic showers fell here certainly over hundreds of square miles and in such vast bulk that, pressed by the hydraulic force of later masses above it into a solid plate of rock, it now in this form measures from twenty to twenty-five feet through. No wonder it closed one of the finest life records of that remote period, and with the record that volume, becoming at once the proximate cause of the changes that followed, and the upper cover of the volume it sealed.

Mineral and warm springs are numerous over the county, Soda Springs, on the south of Strawberry mountains, have been mentioned. In the mountains on the north side of the county are several hot springs, all possesing, to a greater or less degree, medicinal properties. The most noted warm springs are near Reynold creek, a tributary of the John Day, about twenty-five miles east of Canyon City. The location has become the summer resort of the county. Bath houses have been constructed for the use of visitors. It is an ideal camping ground, the surroundings are picturesque, the streams afford good fishing and the mountains on the south abound in game.

The forests of Grant county are extensive on the east and north. Fir, pine and tamarack are the leading lumber varieties of timber. Saw mills are scattered here and there over the country, supplying the local demand for lumber. Citizens of Grant county are now petitioning the President in opposition to a proposed forest reserve which would include over half of its territory and all of its timbered areas. The future development of the county will depend largely upon the settlement of the forest reserve question, which is now pending.

Mining, stock raising and agriculture are the principal industries of Grant. Stock raising has been in the past and must continue to be a leading pursuit. At one time the stockman's investments were almost entirely in cattle, but in recent years the range has not fur-

nished grass in quantity and quality suited to the highest development of this industry, and the cattle herds have given way to sheep. In 1897 there were about 200,000 sheep in the county, valued at $300,000. The annual wool sales return over $200,000 to the producers.

The soil of the arable lands of Grant county is rich and highly productive. It is a black silt deposit from the waters of the prehistoric lake that covered the entire surface of eastern Oregon. For ages it has been washing down from the mountain sides and accumulating in the valleys and it has been wrought by the alchemy of time into a soil of rare productive qualities. It is well suited to the production of all the cereals, but no effort has been made to excel in the quantities produced, only the local demand for wheat, oats, barley and rye being given consideration. In 1897 30,000 bushels of wheat were raised in the upper John Day valley. Alfalfa and other hay grasses grow luxuriantly and there is each year a larger acreage sown to these than to any other ranch product. In the warmer valleys in the northern part of the county, some corn is raised, but it is not a leading product, elevation and consequent cool nights interfering materially with the proper maturing of the grain.

Considerable attention has been given to fruit raising, apples, pears, cherries and plums doing exceedingly well. Berries of all kinds are easily raised. During the early mining days vegetables were raised by a few. It was many years before the supply was equal to the demand and the pioneer miners were glad to get potatoes at 33 1-3 cents per pound. A bunch of three or four green onions brought fifty cents and other vegetables sold for proportionately high prices. Fruit growing received no attention until about the year 1865. Joaquin Miller,—"the "Poet of the Sierras,"— who at that time resided in Canyon City, is credited with being the first to experiment with fruit trees. It was purely an experiment, but was in all respects a success. An orchard of apple, plum, pear and cherry trees was set out about his home in 1865. By the year 1872 every tree was in full bearing, the yield was abundant and the flavor of the fruit excellent. This orchard demonstrated the fact that horticulture might easily be made a leading industry in Grant county. Although Mr. Miller's orchard has of late year been neglected, many of the trees are yet living and yielding their yearly crop.

For several years after the first settlements were made, fruits were freighted to Canyon City over the mountainous road from The Dalles, a distance of two hundred miles. Apples sold for five dollars a box, or, by retail for twenty-five cents per pound. But these conditions were doomed to radical and speedy change. Climatic and soil conditions were peculiarly favorable for the production of fruit. During the years 1867 and 1868 large orchards were planted by B. C. Trowbridge, Fisk and Rhinehart, J. J. Cozart and Luce Brothers. These were the pioneer horticulturists. Following them, each year has witnessed a material growth of the industry, until now every farmer or ranchman in the county has an orchard of greater or less extent. The home market can not consume the supply, a portion of which finds its way over rough mountain roads to the cities and towns of bordering counties. D. B. Rhinehart's orchard, containing forty acres, is the largest orchard in the county and is a credit both to the possibilities of the soil and to the energy and industry of its owner. The full development of this industry only awaits the coming of the railroad.

The mining, agricultural and horticultural possibilities of Grant county can not be accurately estimated until transportation agencies afford the proper incentives to full development of all her resources. Her boundaries enclose an area of 4,560 square miles. Her natural advantages are equal to those of any and superior to those of some of her neighboring counties. Union, Umatilla and Morrow counties form her northern boundary; Wheeler and Crook counties are on the west; Harney is on the south; Malheur and Baker are on the east. In many particulars her interests will in time become successful competitors with those of her bordering counties.

The mercury ranges between seventy and one hundred degrees from June 1st to October 1st, rarely passing the one hundred mark. The atmosphere is light and dry during these months and nights are invariably cool. The winters are not severe. It is seldom that the mercury falls below ten degrees and sometimes rises to seventy-five degrees in January. Snow fall in the higher altitudes in sufficient quantities to furnish an abundance of water through out the year for stock and for irrigation on the table lands and in the valleys. Every plateau and every valley is webbed with ditches and water is everywhere to be had for the beautifying and fructifying of the land. Many of the streams over the county and some of the irrigating ditches flow sufficient quantities of water and have sufficient fall to operate mills and factories, and these are building up in response to a demand that is growing as all other interests advance.

In a great many ways Grant county is fast becoming a desirable location for the business man in any commercial pursuit. Despite its isolation it has made progress after its own fashion, and in the face of great difficulties has achieved a prosperity, of which many regions of more fortunate opportunities may well be envious. In lighter mood it has a charm all its own. The touch with nature is close, and to those who love the soughing of the forest, and the solitudes of its shadows; to those to whom the rush of clear waters and the melody of their song are gladness; to all who find joy in the larger moods of nature, here is a land of abounding and perpetual charm.

MALHEUR COUNTY.

It may be said without extravagance that

Malheur county is a term applied to southeastern Oregon. The eastern boundary of Oregon is about 290 miles in extent and of this distance Malheur county occupies 174 miles, or about two-thirds. The county is about fifty-seven miles in width, and is credited with an area of 9,784 square miles. The total area of the state is 94,560 square miles. Over one-tenth of this area, then, is included within Malheur's boundaries. As there are thirty-three counties in the state, it will be readily seen that Malheur has the lion's share of the territory. Baker county is on the north, Grant and Harney are on the west, Nevada is on the south, and Idaho and the Snake river are on the east.

The north and northwest boundaries pass over the Burnt River mountains region. The divide between Malheur and Baker counties is at an elevation of 5,000 feet. Between Malheur and Grant counties it reaches an altitude of 7,000 feet. There is a gradual slope from this region east and south to the basins of the Malheur and Snake rivers. The western boundary traverses the slope in the higher altitudes of which are the headwaters of the Malheur river, and in the extreme south the sources of some of the western tributaries of the Owyhee river. The summit of the divide from which these waters come is farther west in Harney county. Along the western side the elevation varies from 7,000 feet in the north and in the extreme south, to about 3,000 feet in the central portion. The surface in this region has four distinct slopes. Beginning at the north, there is a downward slope following the north and middle forks of Malheur river, which take a southeasterly course toward the main stream. From the point where the boundary line crosses the Malheur river there is a southern upward slope to the summit of the divide between Crooked creek in Malheur and Dunder and Blitzen river in Harney county. From here the country falls again toward the south and the waters of Crooked creek, and from this stream rises to the higher elevations

on the southern state boundary. Along the southern boundary is an elevated region in which are the numerous sources of the Owyhee river and of some small streams that enter the state of Nevada. About three-fourths of the eastern boundary line runs along the divide between the Snake and the Owyhee rivers. The elevation drops from 7,000 feet in the extreme south to 4,000 feet at Jordan valley, and to about 2,500 feet at the mouth of the Owyhee river, where the line enters the Snake river. The slope of this entire section is northwest, following the course of the streams tributary to the Owyhee. On the northeast the county line centers the waters of Snake river, and this portion of the county has very gradual slopes toward the valleys of that river and of the Malheur. Elevations along the Snake river are as follows: Huntington, in Baker county, has an elevation of 2,110 feet; Weiser, Idaho, 2,123 feet; Payette, Idaho, 2,150 feet; and Ontario, Malheur county, 2,157 feet, showing a fall of but forty-seven feet from Ontario to Huntington, a distance of forty miles.

The Malheur county side of the Burnt river divide, in the north end of the county, is drained by Willow creek, a stream that heads in the Ironsides mountains. Willow creek is about seventy-five miles in length and pursues a southeasterly course, emptying into Malheur river a few miles below Vale and about fifteen miles above the rivers' mouth. In the upper Willow creek region the stream flows down narrow gulches and canyons. There are no lowlands along its banks and its waters are used by prospectors and miners on the adjacent hillsides. Farther down the creek the valley widens, and hay and grain ranches have been located at intervals along its course. Both hill and valley lands are covered with a heavy growth of sage brush. There is but little timber here and the sharp contrasts in color from the gray of the sage brush plain to the green hay fields and groves on the ranches and the many-hued rocks and slags of the mountain sides make a picture that is impressed indelibly upon the memory. Six miles southeast of Malheur City and about the same distance south of the north county line, is situated what is known as Cow valley. Its altitude is 6,000 feet. It is a level tract of land but little below the mountain tops, several miles in extent and about two miles wide. No stream courses this valley except in the spring and early summer, when the snow melts into torrents. Wild grass grows here abundantly and the valley forms an immense pasture where cattle and sheep range the summer through. Both this valley and the lower Willow creek valley are deeply rutted by the spring floods from the mountains. At this season the volume of water and the momentum it attains in its downward course are so great that these gulches have been washed out in places fifteen to twenty feet deep. When the flood is on they are as impassable as are the deep, broad rivers of the lower valleys.

Ten miles west of Willow creek valley is that of Bully creek. The sources of this stream are on the east slope of the Ironsides mountains. Its tributaries are Cottonwood, Clover and Indian creeks. Bully creek joins the Malheur river a short distance above Vale. These streams flow through a broken stock range country, but in many places along their banks are small tracts of irrigable land which are occupied by ranchmen and sown to grain and grasses.

Across the northern part of the county, trending slightly north of east, flows the Malheur river, emptying into the Snake about two miles below Ontario. It courses through a valley of varying width, nowhere exceeding two miles. This stream has quite a number of tributaries, the largest of which is Willow creek, which we have just described. The south and middle forks form a junction near the western line of the county, while the north fork enters the main stream about ten miles below this junction. This latter tributary receives the water from Warm Springs creek,

which heads on the south slope of the Ironsides mountains. The middle fork is fed by Otis creek and Round Valley creek, which rise in the old Malheur Indian reservation, in northeast Harney county. Tributaries of the south fork are Coyote creek, Carman creek, Crane creek and Camp creek, all Harney streams. The forks of Malheur river and their numerous feeders drain a timbered region along the west side of the county. This is the only timbered section in the county, and the area within its boundaries is comparatively small, the greater portion of the belt lying across the line in Harney. The growth includes pine, fir, tamarack and juniper. The only sawmill in the county is at Ironsides, in the extreme northwest corner. It supplies a limited local demand for lumber. On the south the lower Malheur valley rises almost imperceptibly to the level of the central plains of the county. In the lower valley on the north is an extensive level tract known as Dead Ox Flat. Farther up the ascent from water level is more abrupt to the high divide between Willow creek and Snake river.

This divide apparently terminates in what is known as Malheur Butte. It is also called Kennedy Butte, in honor of a pioneer of that name whose homestead was at its base. It is the most prominent landmark in the county and is located about seven miles west of Ontario. It is set down in the midst of a perfectly level plain and has the appearance of an immense dump of refuse or screenings from a coal mine, although the volcanic scoria which forms its exterior distinguishes it from coal slack by the varied colors which are reflected from its slopes. It rises at an acute angle to a height of a thousand feet and immense, ragged multiformed rocks project from its apex and at intervals from its sides. Both from the east and from the west it is visible for many miles, and altogether it is one of the most wonderful formations in the northwest.

The northern half of the county is drained

by the Owyhee river and its numerous tributaries. Jordan creek is the most important of these feeders. Of the others we may name Soldier creek, the North, Middle and South forks of the Owyhee, Antelope and Rattlesnake creeks, Crooked creek and Twelve Mile creek. Cow creek rises in Idaho and flows into Jordan creek at a point about fifteen miles west of the state line. Jordan creek rises in Idaho, but for twenty-five miles its course lies westward through Malheur county. The three forks of the Owyhee also rise in Idaho. The main stream of the Owyhee forms a junction with the Snake river about fifteen miles south of Ontario, on the state line. This portion of the county has an elevation of from four to seven thousand feet. It is exceedingly rough and mountainous. In their upper regions the streams flow precipitately down wild, deep canyons. The general character of this section is rough and broken, an irregular tableland, which extends across the county from east to west. In the lower portions of Jordan creek and of Owyhee river there is considerable valley land suited to the growth of grain, hay and vegetables, but the hill country further south is strictly a stock raising region. Along Jordan creek there are three valleys at different altitudes and separated by a narrowing of the canyon. Every available tract of land is occupied by a ranch, the most extensive being Ruby ranch in the middle valley, in which there are 3,000 acres. Along lower Owyhee river are located some of the finest ranches in the county. There is much in this portion of Malheur that is of interest. There is a fascination about life in a region so remote from the active centers of the west. There are no extensive forests, but the hills and mountains are bold and picturesque and the valleys are beautiful in their contrasting characteristics. The streams are abundantly stocked with fish and in the hills is plenty of game. The stockman will search in vain for a country better adapted to the business of his life.

Near Jordan valley along the creek are extensive fossil beds. Here are found the fossil remains of many extinct species of the animal and reptile kingdoms, as well as those of fishes and vegetable growths, which geologists have classed with the deposits of the pliocene period. Near these fossil beds are evidences that this was once the home of a prehistoric people. These evidences consist of numerous ruins along the rocky hillsides, smooth-hewed caverns and pillars, where are found scrolls, figures, pictures and hieroglyphics cut into the stone. Scientific research has not yet reached this section and conjecture is a poor substitute, hence we will not attempt to enlighten the reader concerning the character, customs and civilization of this ancient folk, who have left naught to tell of their life work but the unintelligible scroll on the broken door post or the cavern wall. There is interesting and exhaustive work here for the student, and the field will no doubt engage his attention at no distant day.

For about fifty miles the Snake river courses along the northeast line of the county. At this point the Snake is a broad, deep stream with but little fall, and consequently with a comparatively slow current. The fall from Nyssa to Huntington is less than ninety feet. But this is of course sufficient for purposes of irrigation, the surface outline of this portion of the county sloping as the river runs, to the north. The lands adjacent to this stream on the Oregon side are very rich. The elevation is but little above 2,100 feet and the whole area is well adapted to the production of all farm crops, vegetables, fruits, berries, etc. Here the rolling sage brush plains are unrelieved by hill or mountain except in distant outline. In its wild state the country possesses no engaging features, but "at the magic touch of water" trees and grasses flourish in wanton luxuriance and there is everywhere the "mute, mute comfort of the green things growing." Water is the crying need of the Snake river valley, and when, by the ingenuity of man, it shall be drawn from the river bed and spread over the land this will become a region of rare beauty and unequaled productiveness.

The soil of the cultivable areas of Malheur county is of recent formation, speaking geologically. It is the light alluvial soil common to all arid districts. The top layer varies in depth from six inches to eight feet. Underlying this layer is a stratum of hard-pan, from three to fifteen inches in thickness. Beneath the hard-pan is a gravelly loam, rich in plant food, but not available by reason of the fact that plant and tree roots do not penetrate the stratum above. The most successful horticulturists have in recent years adopted the plan of dynamiting the hard-pan below the trees, thus enabling their roots to reach the rich loam. Concerning the alkali soils of the west, W. S. Harwood, writing in the June issue of Scribner's magazine, says: "Investigations at the United States agricultural experiment station of California demonstrated that the salts of the soils of alkali lands, injurious to grains, grasses, fruits and forests, bear no relation to the salt of the sea, the alkali land being wholly different from coast marsh lands deriving their salts from the ocean waters; that the salts of the alkali lands are native to the soil, their presence being largely due to the absence of rainfall (the salts staying in the soil because they are not leached out and carried away by the rain) ; that the salts rise to the surface after heavy rainfalls, as oil rises in the wick of a lamp; that when the land is flooded with water by sudden rainfall or by over-irrigation, so that the salts rise to the surface and destroy vegetation, it is only necessary to resort to under-drainage, a reversal of the usual process; that the salts in the soil have a way of running up and down in the upper four or five feet of soil, following the movement of moisture. It was proven, also, that the evil in the soil called black alkali—stretches of dark, barren regions unfit for agriculture—may be neutralized by spreading over the black earth a coating of gypsum."

As is well known, alluvial soils are of virgin character and are composed of disintegrated rocks, volcanic ash, and similar elements. These soils, being fresh from nature, have never been exhausted by the varied processes of vegetable life and are hence much more enduring and fruitful than the soils of earlier geological periods.

There are rarely more than three or four weeks of real winter, and during this short season the thermometer seldom falls lower than ten or twelve degrees below zero. Even when the zero mark is reached the dry atmosphere tempers the severity of the weather. Farm work frequently continues through every month in the year. The heat of the summer is not oppressive, the nights are always cool, and altogether the climate is conducive to physical health and to the rapid and perfect maturing of all vegetable life.

Canal building is practically in its infancy in Malheur county, although a number of ditches have been constructed, others are under contemplation and a great deal of capital is already invested in the work.

Necessity has long been recognized as the mother of invention ; but while she may be credited with much of the wonderful progress of recent years in mechanics as well as in other fields of action, it should also be remembered that the civilization and development of new territories have many times resulted from discoveries made in the effort to meet the demands or supply the necessities of the hour with elements and conditions new and untried. It was with the greatest difficulty that the densely populated mining camps of the 'sixties were supplied with some of the necessities of life. Points of supplies were many miles away and during the greater part of the year the trails were next to impassable. Such conditions led to experiments in the raising of vegetables and other products of the soil. It was not, however, until 1874 that any determined effort was made to farm the soil of Malheur county, although there were vegetable gardens in Jordan valley as early as 1864. In 1874 J. L. Cole and Alfred Loftin began the cultivation of grains and vegetables near the mining camps on Willow creek. They were very successful and were soon followed by others. In some locations irrigation from ditches was necessary, but in many places sub-irrigation from the creek and from surrounding hills and mountains was sufficient to produce excellent crops.

But it is upon her vast sage brush plains that Malheur county must ever depend for prosperity. These desolate looking plains are fast disappearing and in their stead may now be seen in many parts of the county fields of grains and grasses, groves of trees, extensive orchards and gardens of small fruits, flowers and vegetables. The reclamation of the sage brush lands has been gradual since the year 1879. About this time a few families located along the larger streams, grazed stock in adjacent territory and incidentally cultivated patches of land near the water. In 1881 or 1882 it became evident that a line of railroad would be built down the Snake river, and consequently numerous claims were taken along the streams. From Nevada and from other sections where crops are raised by irrigation came a large number of families who understood this method of cultivating arid lands. The Nevada families located on Malheur river, about ten miles above its junction with the Snake. Going five miles farther up the river, they commenced the construction of a ditch which was intended to convey water to their ranches. This ditch was completed in 1884. It accomplished all for the farmers that was expected of it, and in the territory watered are now many beautiful and highly productive farms. This is known as the Nevada ditch. It has first right to 2,000 inches of water from Malheur river, measured under six inches pressure. It was incorporated in 1887, and the

stock, valued at $40,000, is all owned by farmers directly benefited by the ditch.

When the results of experimental farming on Willow creek and of the more extensive operations under the Nevada ditch became known ditch building and farming in Malheur began in earnest.

What is known as the Owyhee ditch was the next to engage the energies of the farmers. Construction work commenced in 1883, and it reached completion in 1896. The estimated cost was $150,000. About 30,000 acres of land are under this ditch, although but ten thousand acres are at present under cultivation. It was opened on the Owyhee river about ten miles from the river's mouth and has first right to 30,000 inches of water. For the first twelve miles it is twenty feet wide on the bottom, tapering afterward to an eight-foot ditch. It is tweny-six miles long, with a fall of twenty inches per mile, running from the Owyhee river to the Malheur, into which it empties a short distance above Ontario. The ditch was started as a private canal by A. Matheson, C. O. Wilson, M. H. Dryden, D. T. Rigsby, Perry Kriss, T. C. Fletcher, J. A. Ward, Otto and Gustav Schweiser. Articles of incorporation were taken out in 1888. In order to complete it, bonds to the amount of $50,000 were issued at the time of incorporation. The stock of the company is at present valued at $250,000. The officers are E. W. Metcalf, president; C. E. Hunt, vice-president, and G. L. King, secretary.

The Malheur Farmers Irrigating Ditch Company has constructed an eight-foot canal seven miles long, starting from the Malheur river at the head of the lower valley and carrying 3,000 inches of water. This ditch was completd in 1885 and was promoted by W. G. Thompson, E. R. Gruwell and T. W. Pierce.

The Pacific Live Stock Company has a twelve-foot ditch carrying 1,000 inches of water, which has been taken from Warm Springs creek in the upper Malheur country.

It is used exclusively to water the company's immense ranch on the old Malheur Indian reservation.

A short distance above Vale another eight-foot ditch leaves the Malheur river, carrying 1,000 inches of water. It was built by Giller-man and Froman.

The Wilson ditch was taken from the Snake river a few miles above Ontario in 1894. It is ten feet wide and thirteen miles long, entering the Malheur below the mouth of Owyhee ditch. It carries 1,000 inches of water and was constructed by David Wilson at a cost of $8,000.

Sand Hollow ditch, taken from the Malheur, is six feet wide and carries 500 inches of water. The McLaughlin ditch, from the same stream, is five feet wide and flows 400 inches of water. Besides these named there are numerous small ditches in Jordan valley and along Willow creek, which water small tracts of hay, grain and garden land.

The latest ditching enterprise has in contemplation a high ditch from the upper Owyhee river to the Halliday place on the Malheur river, a distance of about forty miles. C. M. Foster has completed a survey which provides for a dam and two large reservoirs in the Owyhee canyon. The route courses along high slopes in the Cedar mountain region and when completed the canal will be at a considerable elevation above the plain level of the country. Land that cannot be reached by water from any of the ditches now constructed could be easily watered from this one. One of the main objects in the construction of this high ditch is to flume water across the Malheur onto what is known as Dead Ox Flat, an extensive plain north of this river. The local promoters of the enterprise are E. H. Test, William Miller and Thomas Jones. The cost of canal, dam and reservoirs is estimated at $280,000 and an effort is now being made to interest capitalists in the work.

Stimulated by the construction of these necessary adjuncts to successful farming in Malheur county, agriculture and horticulture have made wonderful strides in the last decade. The ditches have also both directly and indirectly advanced the stock interests. In many localities they furnish water for stock, but what is of greater importance, they have made possible the production of vast quantities of alfalfa and other hay grasses, upon which the stockman must depend for winter feeding.

That the reader may have accurate knowledge of the extent of the various industries of the county, we give below the output sales of 1897. In bushels there were produced that year, of wheat, 10,000, oats 20,000, barley 40,-000, corn 3,000, potatoes 20,000, apples 1,000, prunes and plums 100, wool 800,000 pounds, butter and cheese, 20,000, fish 5,000, sheep sold 50,000, cattle 20,000, horses 5,000, hogs 500, lumber 500,000 feet, gold mined $100,000, tons of hay 35,000. The assessment summary for 1901 shows values of stock then in the county as follows: Horses and mules $80,975, cattle $312,605, sheep $201,870, hogs $970.

In 1886 there were 673 cars of live stock shipped from Ontario, and two train loads of wool. In 1896 were shipped 1,039 cars of live stock, valued at $750,000. In 1897 1,982 cars were forwarded. In 1899, during a period of six weeks, $1,500,000 worth of cattle alone went forward from Ontario. These comparative figures show the rapid growth of the stock industry. Farming has kept pace with stock raising and the culture of fruit and berries is every year receiving more attention. The lower Snake river valley is especially suited to the culture of fruits. All the varieties are grown here, and in size and flavor the ripe fruit is unsurpassed. In another chapter considerable space has been devoted to a description of the Arcadia farm, which is an object lesson on fruit culture in this valley.

The annual wool sales' day is one of the important events in the calendar of the Malheur county sheep man. On this day he learns exactly what his income for the year is to be. He collects his money, pays his indebtedness, estimates his expenses for the coming year, deposits his surplus in the bank and looks up opportunities for further investment in sheep. All sheep men do not wait for the annual sales' day, but small sales are for various reasons often consummated earlier in the season. In 1902 there were but few early sales. The big strike down east in the mills of the American Woolen Company, where is consumed half the wool product of the United States, kept prices low and the May wool market very quiet. There were but few buyers on the market and May sales were considerably below the average. The regular annual wool sales for 1902 were made at Ontario, Monday, June 23rd. By this date circumstances had grown favorable both to buyers and sellers and all were fairly well satisfied. The sheep men received from ten to twelve and a half cents per pound for their clips. June 30th there had been received at and shipped from Ontario about 1,000,000 pounds and it was estimated that this was about two-thirds of the clip for the year.

Reports of the discovery of coal in various parts of the county have been made at intervals during the past few years, but investigation has proven that as yet no coal beds of real commercial value have been found. On Sucker creek in 1897 quite an extensive deposit was located, which it was thought at first would prove to be valuable fuel coal. In this, however, the discoverers were doomed to disappointment. Some of the more important elemental substances found in first class fuel coal were absent. It was not solid and heavy, but very light and porous, resembling charcoal in these particulars. It was not deficient in oils and gases, lighting readily and burning rapidly. These latter qualities condemned it, as it was consumed so rapidly that it was found to be impossible to maintain with it a lasting and intense fire. No effort has thus far been made to de-

velop these mines and the coal has been put to no practical use.

In October, 1899, while boring for artesian water at Mosquite, in the northeastern part of the county, at a depth of 1,024 feet the drill entered a cavity charged with gas. The flow was considerable for a time and created a great deal of excitement. Again in November, 1901, while drilling for artesian water at Ontario, Ed. Ashley, of Weiser, working under contract with the city authorities of Ontario, struck oil and gas at a depth of 1,100 feet. The purpose for which the well was drilled was not accomplished and no effort has been made by the city to develop the oil and gas prospects. The well was abandoned, but, although there are over a thousand feet of water and debris in the pipe, the gas makes its way to the surface and burns when lighted. It is believed by those experienced in gas prospecting that practical use could be made of the gas from both these wells if they were properly cleaned and piped. An inexhaustible supply of natural gas would be of inestimable value to the people of this section, where there are neither coal deposits nor timbered areas and where in many localities reliance is placed by the poorer classes upon the sage brush of the plains for fuel.

A great many are firmly of the belief that portions of Malheur county are underlaid with stores of coal, oil, and gas. In 1901, Hope Brothers and Keady and Moore, of Vale, in connection with a number of Portland capitalists, located about 12,000 acres of oil land twenty miles northwest of Vale. The land has been tested and found to be perfect in all its indications of oil. Another company has also made locations in the same vicinity. While some preliminary prospecting has been done, the actual work of developing has not yet commenced. Should the field prove to be as rich in oil and gas as indications promise, the building of a railroad across the county will be assured and, together, the oil fields and railroad will speedily solve many troublesome problems for the people of Malheur.

At present the O. S. L. is the only railroad that touches the county. All points are connected by stage and freight lines. There is also good connection by telephone between the more important towns and outside localities.

The history of the gold mines in the Malheur and Mormon Basin district has been written in another chapter of this work. It is estimated that at least a million dollars have been taken from this section and it is believed that there are other millions yet to be mined.

In 1860 men hurried along the lonely trails of Malheur county loathe to tarry even for a day in the midst of her seeming desolation. She afforded no rest for the weary emigrant, offered no hand of welcome to the traveler, held out no promise of better things to the homeseeker. It was indeed a country of *mal heur* (misfortune). But, during the forty-two years that have elapsed since 1860, what wonderful tranformations have taken place! Now there is promise in every sunrise and hope in every sunset. Grains grow and fruits ripen and roses bloom where once stretched arid plains—

"Then, desert land—now, gardens of delight."

HARNEY COUNTY.

The Harney country is one of the few large, rich regions in the United States still unpenetrated by the iron horse. Strange it may seem that in a section so progressive as the northwest, so inviting a field should remain this long open, but such is the fact, nevertheless, and if we would explore this wondrous region we must enter it by stage or private conveyance. There are two routes from the railroad by which ingress may be had, the Canyon City route and the Ontario-Burns route. He who takes the former must traverse the Sumpter Valley line from its beginning in Baker City to its terminus at Whit-

47

ney, going thence by stage, forty-five miles to Canyon City, and thence by a second stage line over another spur of the Blue mountains to his destination. The visitor who chooses the other alternative leaves the O. R. & N. at Ontario. A ride continued day and night without intermission for thirty-six hours will bring him to Burns, the county seat and metropolis of Harney county. Except for the first few miles the journey is dreary enough. Sand, sagebrush and alkali dust there are in great abundance. The farmers who have homes in the country through which the route leads us are remote from the road, and only at long intervals can human habitations be seen. The view which greets one when, after many hours of such cheerless travel, he emerges upon the outskirts of Harney valley, is therefore all the more impressive. The most striking characteristic of the scene is its wonderful expansiveness, for the visitor is beholding the second largest valley in Oregon. To the superficial observer it seems level as the floor, and in vain does he attempt to catch a glimpse of its utmost bounds. Its magnitude may be judged from the fact that it contains about 2,500 square miles, an area greater than that of some of the smaller eastern states. Add to it the small valleys and the mountain areas which are included in Harney county and we have an empire larger than Massachusetts by 1,671 square miles.

When we first enter this mammoth domain, we are still in the sagebrush. The experienced eye will perceive, however, that this desert shrub is here a healthy plant, showing that its mother earth is rich in nutritive powers, a fact further evidenced by the blackness of the surface soil. The visitor is likely to experience a feeling of genuine regret that a land so abundantly capable as this evidently is, so level and convenient for the agriculturist, is lying almost totally idle. The reason is found in the lack of capital wherewith to bring into use the needed water for irrigation purposes. Water in unlimited quantities is found a few feet below the surface, proving that the country must be especially well adapted for the raising of alfalfa, could a system of surface irrigation be installed which would enable the grass to live and thrive until its roots could sink down and bathe themselves in this underground reservoir. Let the waters of the adjoining mountains be stored and applied to the irrigation of these broad stretches of level land and the beauty and verdure of the growing lucerne will speedily replace the unsightly sagebrush.

A few miles further and we enter one of the finest meadows of natural grass to be found anywhere. The numerous large stacks of hay which dot its surface give us an idea of its productiveness and an insight into the occupation of the people who have found homes upon it. Travel over the valley in almost any direction during the fall season and you will see large stacks of wild hay in great profusion. This is natural enough when we remember that the great master industry of the valley is stock raising, that the wondrous expanse of level land in which we are, is more than 4,000 feet above the sea, hence has some of the climatic characteristics of great elevations, and that during the winter months hundreds of tons per day must be fed to the immense herds, which at other seasons find sustenance in the succulent bunchgrass that constitutes nature's richest gift to the inhabitants of eastern Oregon. Here and there are to be seen fields of golden grain. The area devoted to this industry is relatively small. It must needs be so, for wheat will not pay the cost of transportation to the railroad, hence its production must be limited by local demand, but the health and luxuriance of the crops give prophecy of great things to be accomplished in the development of this industry, when the modern gladiators of commerce shall have pushed their way into this last unoccupied field in the western states.

However much the magnitude of the scene may impress one upon his first entrance into Harney valley, the largeness of things in the region will grow upon him as he becomes better acquainted with existing conditions. Catching the spirit of their surroundings, some of the earliest settlers of the country embarked in their chosen pursuits on a mammoth scale, laying the foundations of the immense cattle farms which now form the distinguishing characteristic of Harney county. It has been claimed that Harney county contains the largest single ranch and the largest combination of ranches in the world; that the Pacific Live Stock Company's combination of ranches is the greatest on the face of the earth and the French-Glenn the most extensive single ranch. This may be an exaggeration, but certainly these and other farms in the section are empire-like in their extent. They are empire-like also in many of their appointments and in the completeness and system of their government and operation. On its various farms the Pacific Live Stock Company employs a large number of men, who are managed with as much system as are the employes of a well regulated railway company. There are general managers, assistant general managers, local managers and assistants, foremen for the different departments, and subordinates of various grades down to the common haymaker and cook's assistant. "When the head superintendent comes," writes a newspaper correspondent, "there is awe among the underlings for fear that everything will not please, and when the owner comes it is like the coming of a king." The center of this system of ranches is the White Horse ranch, so called because the superintendents ride and drive white horses. It contains about thirty thousand acres.

The French-Glenn ranch is said to cover more than 120,000 acres under fence. It is situated at the base of Stein's mountain. Upon its are many thousand head of cattle, horses and mules, and from its meadows are cut from 8,000 to 10,000 tons of hay per annum. "It is an empire within itself—fine buildings, fish streams, broad meadows, groves of timber, deer and elk and everything that is wild and grand."

Besides these there are the Alvord ranch of John Devine, upon which are a number of elk and large herds of deer; the Riley ranch, containing between 12,000 and 15,000 acres; the Shirk ranch, in Catlow valley, containing 5,000 to 6,000 acres, noted as being one of the prettiest places in the county; the Sissen ranch of 12,000 acres deeded land, and hundreds of others smaller than those mentioned, but still large enough to elicit surprise and wonder, if situated in a locality less habituated to the gigantic.

The manner of stacking hay on both the larger and the smaller farms is worthy of passing notice. Hayracks, wagons and pitchforks are dispensed with in the field, being replaced by a labor saving implement known as a "buck." This is a huge rake borne upon wheels, so designed as to gather the bunches of hay when drawn through the field. A load secured, the teamster heads for the stack, and upon reaching it, he deposits his load upon a net, which is hoisted by derrick to the desired place. The meadows furnish fall pasture for the herds that are gathered at that season from the surrounding ranges and the hay is fed to them during the winter months.

While wool growing is secondary in importance to cattle raising, it is nevertheless an industry of great wealth producing power. Wool is the only product of the county, aside from live stock that is exported, and the revenue derived from it and from the sale of sheep and lambs adds very materially to the enormous annual income which makes its way into the pockets of the farmers and the stockmen.

As already noted, the production of wheat, fruit, potatoes and vegetables of all kinds must needs be limited to the capacity of the county for home consumption. The few who are engaged in the cultivation of the cereals must realize large profits from their business, as the yield is as great as in the most favored portions of the state, while the price is two or three times as high as is secured in railroad points. But this is an elevated region and wheat is sometimes so injured by frost as to be rendered unfit for milling purposes. The testimony given by residents as to the feasibility of raising fruits, vegetables, garden produce and the like is not altogether harmonious. That those products are raised is too palpably true to be disputed. It is maintained, however, that even the hardier vegetables can not be successfully cultivated in all parts of the different valleys and that fruit raising is practical only in favored spots. Some succeed in raising enough for their own use by building fires in their orchards during the dangerous seasons, a scheme which obviously has its limitations.

Extensive in their combined areas as are the numerous valleys within the confines of Harney county, Harney, Diamond, Catlow, Dunder-und-Blitzen, Sage Hen, Happy, Warm Springs, etc., etc., a large part of the county is made up of mountain ranges and the foothills extending away from their bases. Besides the wealth of pasturage which these produce, they are known to possess much wealth of timber and give great promise of proving rich, also, in wealth of buried treasure. Many years will doubtless pass before the buzz of the saw mill will be heard in the more remote forests of the Blue mountains of Harney county. The action of our government in creating the Blue mountain forest reserve, if the temporary withdrawal proves permanent, will delay developments in this direction indefinitely. The lack of transportation has rendered the sawmilling industry totally dependent upon the local demand, and the business is still limited in its possibilities of development by the circumscribed character of the field to be supplied. There are, however, five sawmills in the county ranging in per diem capacity from six or eight thousand feet to twenty-five thousand feet. Lumber and shingles from these mills are utilized in the construction of buildings as many as a hundred miles away, notwithstanding the fact that they must be transported by wagon over the entire distance. It is said that the best equipped shingle mill in the county is that in connection with the saw mill of E. H. King. There the shingles arrive at the mill in logs which are cut out by the lumber saw into what are called "cants." These pass on to the cut-off saw, which converts them into bolts, and these in turn, by the operation of two shingle saws, are converted into the finished product.

Although Harney county has been known for many years to contain precious metals, comparatively little attention has been paid to mining, owing largely to the fact that the people have been too deeply interested in the surer pursuits of agriculture and stock raising. In two regions, however, considerable progress has been made in the development of promising mines. These are the Trout creek, or Idol City, and the Pueblo camps, the former twenty miles northeast of Burns, and the latter not far from the Nevada line.

The Trout creek camp has been one of slow development, but thanks to the perseverance and unwavering faith of Charles Ingraham, Samuel Roach, O. J. Darst and others, work has progressed steadily. While the prospecting period is not yet passed, developments thus far have encouraged the hope and expectation that time and labor spent and to be spent will eventually find an abundant reward.

The Pueblo region, in the southern part of Harney county, is likewise too superficially developed to furnish any producing mines, but it ranks among the most promising undeveloped districts of eastern Oregon. Unless indications and the result of work already done are altogether unreliable and misleading, it must some day become a large producer of rich gold, silver, copper and nickel ores.

It is stated that the existence of mineral wealth in the Pueblo region has been known for many years, but the first white men who invaded the country were driven out by hostile Indians, resulting in the abandonment of operations. The region then lay undisturbed by the pick of the miner until a few years ago, when C. P. Rutherford and Maurice Fitz Gerald, both of Burns, took claims in two distinct portions of the district, some ten miles apart. In the Fitz Gerald country, W. H. Welcome, Thornton Williams, William Wylie, Frank Hindman, Ben Brown, H. C. Levens, J. C. Welcome and several others have taken claims. In the vicinity of Mr. Rutherford's camp, Ben Brown, John Cupid, Thomas Davidson, Richmond L. Neill, Thomas Dunphy, William Davidson, Joseph E. Reed, J. W. Biggs and others have found prospects sufficiently promising to induce them to locate claims. It is claimed by Mr. Fitz Gerald, who has watched the returns from assays closely, that Pueblo ore averages 10 to 40 per cent. copper.

While briefly treating the mining interests of the county we must not overlook the borax industry, which has been developed by the Rose Valley Borax Company. Their plant is situated about twenty-five miles south of Burns, where the Trout Creek and Wild Horse valleys merge into each other. Several hot springs boil up in this region and as their waters run through the valleys along their natural courses, they deposit a white substance. For years the residents in the vicinity and travelers supposed this to be alkali, but a few years ago a borax expert discovered the mistake. He made known his find to certain capitalists, who took advantage of its owners' ignorance of its value to purchase the property for a reputed sum of $7,000. The company instituted a costly plant and in due time began operations. They gather and refine from 80,000 to 100,-

ooo pounds of the white mineral every year, which is transported by mule teams to Winnemucca, Nevada, and sold for more than double the cost of production.

From the foregoing review of the developed and undeveloped resources of Harney county, brief and incomplete though it be, the reader may gain some idea of what has been accomplished and form some conception of the great things the future most certainly has in store. The men who, in company with those who have already planted here their vine and fig tree, are to work out this development will find this country by no means lacking in those ulterior attractions which add so much to the pleasure of living. The climate is not ideal, but it is healthful and generally pleasant. It is said that in some places high winds are of common occurrence, though cyclones and tornadoes are unknown here, as elsewhere in the west. The springs are frequently rather dreary and backward. The summers and falls are grand, the heat of midday never being oppressive and the nights being invariably cool and conducive to refreshing slumber. Some stormy weather in winter there certainly is. Sometimes the thermometer indicator plays around a point far below the zero mark, but severe cold is of short duration, owing to the influence of the balmy chinook, which seldom delays its coming long. In its topographical features the country is varied and pleasing. Even the sage brush plains have an attraction of their own, and a few hours ride will bring him who has grown tired of the stretches of arid, semi-arid, or marshy prairies, to regions where the tall mountain peaks rear their crests far skyward, where the dark forests give forth gentle music in response to the technique of the breezes, the crystal streams sing mournful lullabies and the calm, clear lakes mirror their beautiful environs with vividness and fidelity.

While no attempt can be made to describe the topography of the country in detail, some special features are deserving of a passing notice. Two large lakes, Harney and Malheur, cover an area in Harney valley aggregating about 150 square miles. They are connected by a channel some twenty yards wide and two hundred long. It cannot with truth be said that these lakes are beautiful, for there is nothing especially attractive about either their brackish, shallow waters or the country stretching away in any direction from their shores. They are, however, the delight of thousands of ducks, geese, swans and numerous other varieties of water fowl, and hence the delight of the sportsman. The country in their vicinity, though not favored with topographical beauty, is rendered attractive by the fact that there Nature frequently vouchsafes to manifest one of her strangest and least understood phenomena. The hour of sunrise, always possessed of a sweet, inexplicable charm, is usually attended during the summer months by a delightful mirage. Towns, houses, mountain peaks, herds of peacefully grazing cattle or sheep rise up from the ground by magic and are pictured on the atmosphere with great distinctness of outline. It is said that distant objects are so vividly mirrored that persons several miles from home have identified without difficulty the different members of their families as they went about their work. Mirages are not confined to the lake region, but are also seen, though less frequently, in other parts of the Harney country.

One of the greatest natural attractions of this region is what is known as Malheur Cave, situated on a sage brush plain about a mile from the place where the south fork of the Malheur river heads. G. C. Duncan, to whom we believe the honor of being its first explorer belongs, has described this marvel in the following language:

"The cave is twenty feet wide and six feet high at its entrance, and has an incline downward for the first two hundred feet. It then turns to the northeast and runs very nearly straight to the water, a distance of one-half mile from its mouth. It will average fifty feet wide and twenty feet high and is very uniform in its structure the walls running up about six feet on either side, and then commencing to arch over, forming certainly the finest arch ever discovered in the whole family of caves.

"It is grand almost beyond description, and rivals the great Mammoth Cave in its smoothness of character and uniformity. For the first 250 yards the bottom is as smooth as a floor; then are found piles of rubbish or debris that have accumulated by falling from the ceiling above, one hundred yards or so apart, the last one being something over one hundred yards from the water.

"There is no difficulty in reaching the water; it runs back on either side in a trough from the main pool. a distance of 100 feet, settling down on either side leaving the floor crowning.

"The water is remarkably clear; one can see the sand in the bottom at a depth of four feet, and it appears to have no outlet, as it is perfectly still and quiet; it is good drinking water.

"This wonderful curiosity has to be seen to be appreciated. It is truly of basalt formation and is quarternary. The walls are honeycombed in many places. The wall on the south side sits on a horizontal basement of eruptive rocks.

"This magnificent cave has evidently been used in time by the Indians as a fortification; the entrance has been walled up with stone, and there are also two walls or breastworks on the inside, running from each corner of the entrance diagonally near the center some fifty feet long; this was for the second defense in case they were driven back from the mouth. Around and about the mouth of the cave there are considerable fine chippings, where the aborigines have sharpened their stone implements, made of obsidian or volcanic glass.

"I think that water exists in the end of the cave, but cannot tell without further exploring. I was informed by two parties that

fish have been caught in the cave that were of blue color and eyeless."

Of still greater interest, especially to those who take pleasure in the study of antiquities or prehistoric man, are the curious caves described as existing in the southeastern part of Harney county. As far as the writer knows, the only person who has given them any attention is O. M. Rosendale, a mining engineer, who about two years ago described them and the circumstances attending their discovery in a Portland newspaper as follows:

"I had occasion to visit Harney county last week and have every reason to believe that I discovered traces of cliff dwellers. I was alone on horseback, traveling through the southeastern portion of Harney county, when I made the discovery.

"The spot was a peculiar one. Cliffs of black basaltic formation, without a vestige of vegetation, rose abruptly from the desert and formed a narrow defile. After passing through the defile and leading my wornout horse, I proceeded to scale a hill for the purpose of getting my bearings, as I had evidently lost them for the past six hours. Turning on one point of the hillside, which was half filled with sand-blown crevices, a strange sight was presented to me. There before me were about sixty-five cliff dwellers' habitations, deserted, of course, but in a fair state of preservation. The clear and unclouded sky was looking upon a picture of queer and very strangely formed small buildings, roofless, bound together with no material whatsoever, but hewn with all the skill of the ancient craftsmen.

"In the middle of the place was an upright stone, resembling the famous altar stones of the ancient Aztecs of old Mexico. Most probably on this stone the bloody rites of human sacrifice were once performed by an extinct race. As I was already much delayed in my journey, time did not permit a thorough examination of the locality, nor an exploration of the caves; yet I am thoroughly convinced that the caves served at one time as the habitations of what are commonly known as cliff dwellers.

"In 1893 I had the honor to be one of a party of Smithsonians sent into the almost inaccessible regions of New Mexico, the Goronda del Muerto, or, translated, the Journey of Death, for the purpose of examining the extensive cliff dwellers' ruins in that country. We were also to obtain measurements for the reproduction of the habitations of the cliff dwellers to exhibit at the World's Fair. The caves were reproduced at the fair, and are now a part of the Field museum in Chicago. Outside the fact that the trip of last week was in Oregon, one might have felt himself transferred to the wilds of New Mexico again.

"The interior of southeastern Oregon affords a great field for the mineralogist, the explorer, the entomologist and the admirer of grand and weird scenery.

"These are the first traces of cliff dwellers that have been found above the 42nd degree."

So isolated is the Harney country of Oregon from all the usual courses of travel, and so non-communicative have been the stockmen and prospectors who alone have penetrated to its most remote regions, that its topography, its mineral wealth and its scientific wonders are comparatively unknown to the general public. The day is already dawning when ignorance shall be completely dispelled. Knowledge and the building of railroads will bring an influx of people to take advantage of its natural resources, and the result will be development along many different lines, such as few even dimly foresee.

CHAPTER II.

THE INDIAN WAR OF 1878.

The most exciting event in the history of eastern Oregon since its settlement by the whites was the Bannock and Piute war of 1878. Nearly every county of eastern Oregon was embraced in the field of operations, and every section was affected either directly or indirectly. While the results of this final struggle of the Indians for supremacy in the northwest were not as serious as they might have been had the plans of the leaders been carried out, the results were serious enough. The war caused the death of hundreds of settlers and the destruction of thousands of dollars worth of property, besides seriously disturbing the existing prosperity of the country. Settlers coming from the east had just begun to appreciate the advantages offered by this region to homeseekers and after the news of this war had been heralded abroad this influx was almost stopped for a time. Western Oregon took advantage of this misfortune to decry the eastern portion of the state and it was many years before this region fully recovered from the effects of this influence alone.

Speaking of the causes of this war, Col. William Parsons, of Pendleton, says nothing could be further from the fact than Gilbert's surmise when he says in his history:

"Buffalo Horn was a celebrated warrior, who had the year before aided the government against Chief Joseph and his hostile band of Nez Perces. His reward for such service was not in keeping with his estimate of its value and importance. He saw Chief Joseph honored and made the recipient of presents and flattering attentions, while the great Buffalo Horn was practically ignored. His philosophical mind at once led him to the conclusion that more favors could be wrung from the government by hostility than in fighting its battles."

"With the exception of the Utes," says Colonel Parsons, "the Bannocks are the meanest, most treacherous, most savage and most bloodthirsty of all the Indians west of the Mississippi river. From time immemorial they have been the hereditary enemies of the Oregon and Idaho Indians, including the Cayuses, Umatillas, Walla Wallas and Nez Perces, and more than once they crossed the Blue mountains and inflicted bitter injuries upon the Cayuses and their allies. Therefore, when Chief Joseph and his band of non-treaty Nez Perces, took up arms in 1877, rather than surrender the Wallowa country to the whites, and began their famous retreat through the Lolo pass and the Yellowstone park to the British possessions, the Bannocks, under command of Captain Samuel G. Fisher, a white man, furnished nearly a hundred warriors to harrass the fleeing Nez Perces. They saw the whole of that remarkable campaign; they saw Joseph, with less than four hundred warriors, and encumbered with one thousand women and children, carry on a running fight for one thousand and four hundred miles, defeating General Howard again and again, recapturing his camp at Big Hole Basin from General Gibbon and pursuing the latter so fiercely that nothing but his reserve artillery saved his force from annihilation, and finally surrendering with the honors of war to General Miles at Bear Paw mountain, near the British line; he saw Joseph captured, but not disgraced, and he became jealous of the Nez Perces chieftain's military fame; he also realized, when it was too late, that he had made a serious mistake in joining his forces to that of the whites in the pursuit and capture of

the brave Nez Perces, and that in gratifying a tribal grudge he had dealt a deadly blow at the Indian race; he saw the whites crowding into Montana and Idaho, his people ordered within the confines of the Fort Hall reservation, and it finally dawned upon his benighted mind that the same chains which had been fastened to the ankles of Joseph were already forged for his, and were about to be riveted on them. Buffalo Horn was something of a statesman, but no general; Joseph was, in the opinion of General Miles, the ablest strategist and general of the Indian race, from the time of King Philip to the present. Buffalo Horn came to the conclusion that if he could unite all the Indians west of the Missouri into a confederacy, the whites could be whipped out. Thereupon, he visited the various bands of the Utes, the Shoshones, the Umatillas, Cayuses, and Walla Wallas, and sent runners to the Columbias, Spokanes, Chief Moses and other northern Indians, requesting them to unite with him in a final effort to drive the whites out of the Inland Empire. His overtures were received with favor.

"The plan was to move west and north from Pocatello, past Boise, until a junction could be formed with the Umatillas, Cayuses, Walla Wallas and Columbias, on the Umatilla reservation, then, devastating the country, to move north, uniting with the Spokanes and other Indians in northern Washington, there to make a stand. If too hard pressed the Indians were then to retire across the line within the limits of British Columbia. The plan was well conceived and could have easily been executed had the Indians been possessed of a general with the ability of Chief Joseph of the Nez Perces.'

During the latter part of May the execution of the plan outlined above was begun by the Bannocks, starting from the Fort Hall under the leadership of Chief Buffalo Horn. The Indians numbered about two hundred braves, besides their squaws and children. After the attempted slaughter of two white men on Big Camas prairie, Idaho, who fortunately escaped with their lives in time to warn the settlers of the outbreak, the Indians encamped in the lava beds between the Big Camas prairie and Snake river and from there commenced their murderous and pillaging expeditions.

Two weeks previously Buffalo Horn had ridden into Boise one day with a small escort and, under the guise of being friendly and loyal to the whites, had finally obtained an order from Governor Brayman authorizing the sale of firearms and ammunition to him. This was in plain violation of a standing order from the President, forbidding the gift or sale of ammunition and firearms to Indians.

So, well supplied with the means of carrying on warfare, Buffalo Horn immediately placed himself at the head of his formidable band and proceeded to his bloody work. He told the settlers that they must leave the prairie or be killed, then without much delay, commenced the work of massacring the whites and destroying property. Payne's ferry, near Rattlesnake station, was their first objective point, and there they killed a man and a woman, pillaged houses and stole several head of stock. The first force sent against them was entirely too small, consisting of ninety mounted troopers under command of Major Collins, so practically unresisted the Indians pushed their way westward and northward.

But the redskins had overlooked one very important point in this campaign—the telegraph—for hardly had they started from Fort Hall before the news was communicated to all important military stations in the northwest. Troops were hurried from Salt Lake City, Camp Harney; Camp Halleck, California; Carson City, Nevada; Corrine, Utah; Portland, Boise and other points.

The Indians crossed into Oregon near Silver City, Idaho, and then proceeded in a northwesterly direction, meeting the Piutes under Chief Egan, on the Warm Spring reservation in what is now Malheur county, or it may be in Barren valley. During the trip of the Bannocks through the southern portion of Baker county a few depredations were committed by the Indians, but only one or two lives were lost and the property loss was very small. In Barren valley, on the present Malheur-Harney county line, the first habitation of white men in Grant (now Harney) county was visited. Green Crowley and James, his son, lived here. Old Chief Winnemucca, uncle of the noted Sarah Winnemucca, and Natchez, her brother, were friendly Indians. They interceded with the hostiles to spare these men and with success, for the Indians left them unharmed. When the redskins had passed out of sight Winnemucca and Natchez returned and advised the Crowleys to leave. They mounted fleet horses and at once started for the Alvord ranch, which they reached, going thence to the White Horse ranch. A small band of redskins pursued them some distance but could not overtake them. At White Horse ranch the settlers had constructed a small fort, built of juniper posts, and were prepared to defend themselves. The Indians did not molest them, however, but they did return to the Crowley place and burned the inside of the house and roof, leaving nothing but bare stone walls standing.

From Barren valley the hostiles advanced in a northwesterly direction up Indian creek and through Anderson valley, on the northern slope of Stein mountain. Here they burned G. W. Anderson's house. From Anderson valley the Indians passed on to Happy valley, where, about the middle of June, they attacked George C. Smith and his son, John, who took refuge in the home of the father. There the white men made a stand and for a day and a half successfully resisted the Indians, but they were finally overpowered and killed. The house with the bodies was burned, as also the barn. The redskins also burned the

house of John Smith, situated within a mile
and a half of the place in which he and his father were massacred, and that of Stilley Riddle.

About this time Sylvester (Coon) Smith
was journeying to Happy valley on his way
from the Willamette, and arriving at the top
of the divide between Diamond and Happy
valleys, he saw Indians and horses below him
and suspected that something was wrong. He
returned to Diamond, but there was laughed
at for his fear. Thus spurred on he again
started for Happy valley. This time the Indians caught sight of him and chased him to
the ranch where Messrs. French and Robie,
assisted by sixteen men, were rounding up
horses. When French saw them coming he
gathered his men around him and with only
one rifle and sixteen rounds of ammunition,
the company charged the Indians. The Indians waited until the cowboys were close and
then dropped off their horses in the sagebrush
for cover. French called a retreat back to the
ranch buildings. As the Indians rounded a
point, he mounted a board fence, fired one shot
and missed. The Indians returned the fire,
one of the bullets striking the post astride of
which French stood. Meanwhile the horses
had been turned loose and French now ordered
a retreat to the "P" ranch. A running fight
ensued. The Chinese cook was riding bareback and fell behind in the race up the rimrock.
Finally he jumped off and attempted to hide
under a little bridge, crossing a gully. The
Indians dragged him out and killed him.
"Coon" Smith tried to catch the Chinaman's
horse and narrowly escaped being shot. An
Indian aimed at him but was too slow, as
French, who had gained the summit of the
hill on the north side of McCoy creek, shot
and killed the redskin before the latter could
fire at Smith. Meanwhile John Wetzel, one of
the party, had gained the same hill and dismounted to cinch his saddle. As he remounted, a rifle ball struck him in the thigh, wound-

ing the horse, also. The faithful animal carried Wetzel half a mile and then fell dead. On
the hillside, also, was a friendly Rogue River
Indian, who had camped at the Diamond ranch.
A ball struck the stock of his rifle, splintering
it and driving a large splinter into one of his
hands, making a very painful wound. The rest
of the party escaped uninjured. Wetzel rode
behind another man to Krumbo. From Krumbo all went to the "P" ranch, twenty-five miles
further, where fresh horses were obtained and
the party rode to Camp Harney, arriving the
next afternoon about two o'clock. A man
named Dixon and an employe came to Harney,
also, but later returned to Krumbo, where they
had abandoned their wagons in their hasty
flight for safety. While on the return trip
Dixon and his companion were killed by the
Piutes.

While these events were transpiring, Howard's command was pursuing the Indians, and
on Silver creek the first battle took place. Colonel Bernard, with four companies of cavalry,
his own, Whipple's, McGregor's and Perry's,
under Bomus, aided by the scouts under Colonel Robbins, were in the van of the army,
and on Sunday, June 23d, overtook the Indians
and surprised and charged their camp. A second charge was made, but the hostiles, who
greatly outnumbered the troops, rallied and
the soldiers were compelled to withdraw. The
redskins then strongly entrenched themselves
and the troops withdrew to await reinforcements. This fight occurred near Curry creek,
forty-five miles from Harney. In this battle
Buffalo Horn was killed, during one of the
charges. Colonel Robbins and Chief Egan
fought a personal duel, in which Egan was
twice shot, his left arm being crippled and his
well known buckskin war horse captured.
Egan was dragged from the field by his young
warriors and the severe wound he received in
this action made his subsequent capture easy.
Colonel Robbins had his horse shot from under
him and was rescued by Peter French, who

took him on his horse. Two soldiers were killed on the battlefield, also a scout, named Myers. Another trooper was mortally wounded. After the escape of French and Robie from the ranch near Happy valley, and their subsequent ride to Camp Harney, they went to the front with Bernard's command and participated in the Silver creek fight. From here Robie took dispatches from Colonel Bernard to Camp Harney and upon his arrival there, volunteered to carry dispatches to Boise, which was his home. This gallant old pioneer never recovered from the effects of the long, arduous trip, and shortly after he reached home, passed away.

This fight is graphically described by a correspondent of the Baker City Bedrock Democrat at the time, as follows:

"At midnight, June 21st, Colonel Bernard's First cavalry, with four companies and 168 scouts, left Camp Harney to attack the hostile Indians, who were known to be in large force in the vicinity of Silver creek. The command camped at a burnt ranch the following night. Scouts sent out reported Indians close at hand, but large trails, which plainly indicated between 1,200 and 1,500 warriors on the rampage.

"Early the next morning the advance scouts under Colonel Robbins sighted the Indians on a creek known as Silver creek, about sixty miles south of Camp Harney. It was evident that the red men were unaware of the approach of the troops, for their stock was unguarded.

"Colonel Bernard quickly formed his men in line, as follows: Company F in advance under Lieutenant Bomus; Company G next, under Lieutenant Ward; Company A in the rear, under Captain McGregor; and Company L to guard the supplies, under Colonel Whipple.

"Then after a speech by the Colonel encouraging the men to do their best, the little company of troops singing, 'Scouts to the Front,' and determined on either victory or death,

rode on an enemy at least six times their number. When within about 600 yards the charge was sounded and with a yell, the men dug in their spurs and charged. The Indians left their village and took to a fortified position on the bluffs to the left and in front where it was impossible for the cavalry to follow. The village was situated on the creek, which was covered with dense willows. The battle raged fiercely for a time, two charges being made. Personal encounters were numerous. One of especial interest was that between Sergeant George H. Richards, of McGregor's company, and Bear Skin, a noted Bannock chief. A good shot finally ended the struggle, leaving the Indian stretched out on the ground. When it was found that nothing could be gained from charging the positions on the bluff, the command withdrew temporarily.

"Companies A and G coming up, the attack was renewed with the old vigor, Company L being deployed as skirmishers on a small hill to the left of that held by Colonel Bernard, to prevent a flank movement. The fighting, at times fierce and again desultory, was kept up on both sides until far into the night, great gallantry being displayed by our troopers. Between midnight and two o'clock, however, the hostiles left, closely pursued by Colonel Bernard for a distance of ten miles, when the Indians rallied and made another stand. Troops then awaited the arrival of General Howard.

"Much property in the Indian camp was destroyed, also considerable money and ammunition was captured."

After the fight on Silver creek and the subsequent retreat of the hostiles up this creek, the redskins crossed the Strawberry range and went down Murderer's creek to the south fork of the John Day river and thence down into and across the John Day valley, ravaging and pillaging farms and ranches whenever in their path and occasionally killing herders and ranchmen. While descending into the valley the redskins were met by a small scouting party under command of James N. Clark, an old pioneer freighter. This company was organized at Canyon City for the purpose of keeping watch of the movements of the Indians. The little company was immediately attacked and defended itself with great heroism. A young man named Aldrich was killed and Clark's horse was shot under him, falling upon his leg. Another member of the company named Burnham pulled the horse off and he and Clark escaped to the willows fringing the bank of the South Fork, from which they finally found their way in safety to the settlements. One of the party received a bullet in the heel of his boot. Another squad of citizens left John Day a little later, among them being Emil Schutz. This expedition was also organized for the purpose of scouting. At the Cummings ranch, twenty miles west of Canyon City, the Indians fell upon this little company, wounding Schutz and driving them back to the settlements.

At Canyon City preparations were made for the defense of the town. Many stockmen and ranchmen living in outlying districts came into the place with their families and during the period of greatest danger, when the Indians were crossing the mountains several miles south of the town, the abandoned mining tunnels west of town were converted into temporary places of refuge and were occupied by many. Had there been any real danger, the citizens of the town were prepared to resist to their utmost, but the redskins were wise enough to make a wide circuit of the place and cross the valley where it was less thickly settled, so that the citizens of Canyon City and John Day were spared the necessity of shedding blood. At Prairie City a volunteer company was organized with J. W. Mack as captain. This company never saw service, however.

Considerable property in the John Day valley was destroyed by the Indians while crossing it and two nephews of James Small

were killed while herding sheep. Pursued by Bernard the fleeing redskins then took a northeastward course through Fox valley and across Long creek to the Middle Fork of the John Day river. At Long Creek a small log fort had been built and in this the settlers were congregated in force, ready to protect their families and themselves in case the Indians attacked them. The Indians sent a small party to the fort under the protection of a flag of truce and this party sought to entice the defenders outside for a conference, intending to fall upon them and massacre them and those inside the fort. The Indians pretended that they were friendly and sought in several ways to gain entrance. But the settlers were too experienced and cautious to be so easily deceived and finally the Indians gave up their plan and went by within six hundred yards of the stockade.

In this region the Bannocks and Piutes were joined by a large number of renegades known as Columbia river Indians, stragglers from tribes recognizing no reservation as home. These Indians were formerly from Priest Rapids. Many Umatillas also joined the war party about this time. Crossing the Middle and North Forks the Indians went down Birch creek toward the Umatilla reservation.

In the territory now embraced in Baker county there were no hostilities. The proximity of the hostiles during their march to the Columbia river was sufficient, however, to arouse the inhabitants of this section to a sense of their danger and precautions were taken to insure the safety of all. Those living in outlying districts left their homes and ranches and congregated in Baker City for defense. Reports coming in from nearby points to the effect that the Indians were approaching, gave a martial stir and bustle to the town and several contingents of troops going to the front stopped there. For a time, in July, Baker City was division headquarters for the army and thus became an important military station, though no actual hostilities occurred within the confines of the present county. Preparations were made to repel the Indians should they appear, but fortunately they did not, and Baker county was saved from the ravages of an Indian raid.

The story of the war in Umatilla county, the battles of Willow Springs, of Birch and Butter creeks, of the defense of Pendleton and the subsequent defeat and dispersal of the redskins is told by Col. Parsons in one of the publisher's former works, and believing that this account will enhance the value of this narrative, the substance of it is given herewith.

The first definite information received at Pendleton of the approach of the Indians was brought in by Narcisse A. Cornoyer on the second of July, who reported that while out on the John Day river with a hunting party, he had struck the hostiles. The consternation can hardly be described. In wagons, on horseback and on foot, the settlers hastened to the nearest towns for protection. Pendleton, Umatilla, Wallula, Weston, Milton and Walla Walla were crowded with refugees. Homes were abandoned so hastily that neither provisions nor extra clothing were provided. All settlements within reach of a warning voice were deserted in a day. Cattle and sheepmen in the mountains were in a precarious situation, and many were killed before they could reach places of safety. Major Cornoyer, the Indian agent, gathered in all the Indians possible, including the non-combatant Columbia river and Warm Spring Indians, amounting to about two thousand, the loyalty of many of whom was seriously doubted.

But while most of the settlers escaped to the towns, it must not be forgotten that the towns themselves were scarcely able to make any defense. Pendleton had not more than one hundred and fifty inhabitants, but with the refugees it had perhaps three hundred, of whom perhaps seventy-five were capable of bearing arms. Heppner, Wallula, Weston and Milton were mere hamlets. They were widely separated—

too far for support—and fifteen hundred savage warriors were supposed to be about to fall upon them. Pendleton was to receive the first assault. That the result would be the complete destruction of Pendleton and its outlying settlements was believed by many, while the most sanguine felt but little confidence. Buffalo Horn, the Bannock leader, having been killed the command of the allied forces of Snakes and Piutes devolved upon Egan, who was totally unfit for so heavy a responsibility, and was also incapacitated in a measure from wounds. His army arrived in and had possession of Camas prairie on July 4th, and if he had marched at once upon Pendleton, he would have met no effective resistence, could have followed the Umatilla down to the Columbia, and in spite of the two or three armed steamboats patroling the river, made a successful crossing. That accomplished, he could have gathered up the northern Indians, and with augmented forces, could fight or retreat across the British line, as seemed most advisable; but he hesitated, and delay was fatal to his enterprise. Compare Egan's imbecility with Chief Joseph's masterly strategy when he emerged from the Lolo trail near Missoula, Montana, the previous year, and found himself confronted with a strong force, behind an impregnable fortification of logs, while General Howard was thundering in his rear. Joseph called for a parley with the whites in his front and tried to get permission to pass, under promise to commit no depredations. Failing in that, he notified the enemy that he would force a passage the next morning; and then he opened fire on the disputed passage with a thin line of skirmishers, and while the whites were thus occupied, he led his whole party of nearly fifteen hundred people, mostly non-combatants, by a devious route through the timber and almost impassible canyons, to the rear of the fort, effecting his escape without the loss of a man.

It was fortunate for the people of eastern Oregon that they did not have a man of Joseph's ability as a commanding officer to cope with on that momentous fourth day of July, 1878, but only a blunderer like Egan. Instead of striking a decisive blow and falling upon Pendleton before the troops from Walla Walla, and the volunteers from Weston, Milton and other points, could concentrate, he frittered away the time in killing a few straggling sheepherders and skirmishing with Captain Wilson's handful of thirty men, which had met the Indians near Alba, and finding that the enemy was in force, had retreated to Pendelton with considerable alacrity. So small was the force of the whites at Pendleton, and so badly was it provided with arms and competent officers, to say nothing of its utter demoralization through rumors and reports of the overwhelming strength of the Indians, that men who were present affirm that if one hundred Indians had made a sharp attack, either on the 4th, 5th or 6th of July, the town would have fallen. If Egan's whole force of five hundred warriors had made the assault upon either of those days no effective resistance could have been made, and the valley of the Umatilla from the Blue mountains to the Columbia would have been swept clear of the whites. The Umatilla reservation Indians would have been forced to unite with the hostiles, the Columbias and Washington Indians would have followed the example, and Buffalo Horn's confederacy would have been consummated, to the enormous damage of white interests throughout the whole Inland Empire. Fortunately, it was Egan, not Joseph, who led the hostiles.

Pendleton consisted of about thirty or forty houses, mostly one-story shacks, scattered along Court and Main streets from the Golden Rule hotel to the Pendleton Savings Bank building. Besides the courthouse, there was in the town a three-story frame mill, where the main building of Byers' splendid frame mill now stands, but it was away out of the then town. The houses were in a sort of quadrangle, by no means compact. The first defense erected by the panic stricken inhabitants of Pendleton was a row of wagons stretched across Main street from the Savings Bank building to where the Odd Fellows' building now stands. The women and children were hustled into Byers' mill, and a number of the men went there to guard them. Frank Vincent was made captain of the company organized for the defense of the town.

At Umatilla City similar precautions were taken. J. H. Kunzie was appointed assistant adjutant general by Governor Stephen F. Chadwick and made his headquarters there. That point was selected because it had the nearest telegraph office, and because supplies for troops and volunteers were landed there. Volunteers were organized and armed by Kunzie, and the town was closely guarded. It had a population of about one hundred and fifty at that time. The stone warehouse of J. R. Foster & Company was fitted up for a fort, in which a final stand could be made in case of an attack. Like preparations were made at Heppner, Weston, Milton and other places which were supposed to be in danger.

As soon as Captain Wilson's company had straggled in from Camas prairie with the information that the hostiles were in force in that region, and that some of their number and some sheep-herders had been killed, another company was organized by Sheriff J. L. Sperry, which started July 5th for the front, with a company from Weston under Dr. W. W. Oglesby and another under M. Kirk. At Pilot Rock they received recruits and were then consolidated into a single company.

The next morning they marched from Pilot Rock for Camas prairie, but stopped at Willow Springs for dinner. Willow Springs consisted of a house, a shed and a sheep corral. While at their dinner the volunteers were attacked in force by the Indians, who drove in the pickets so rapidly that it was a close race between the pursuers and the pursued as to which should first announce the assault. At the first alarm, thirteen of the volunteers sprang onto their horses and struck out for Pendleton. The others made a virtue of necessity, tied their horses in the sheep corral, and took refuge in the shed. The position was absolutely indefensible, being commanded by the surrounding hills and rocks. It had one advantage—there was water—but the water was not exactly available so long as the spring was outside the shed and commanded by the rifles of the Indians. The remnant of the company made a stout resistance all the afternoon, but at the last began to suffer severely for water. One of the men refused to stand it, and taking a pail left the shed, against the earnest protestations of his comrades. Strange to say he walked through the zone of Indian fire, filled his pail and returned unscathed to his companions. The shed was riddled with bullets, and several casualties resulted. William Lamar, a school teacher, who was engaged to be married to a daughter of Dr. W. C. McKay, was killed and S. I. Lansdon, A. Crisfield, S. Rothschild afterward a prominent merchant of Pendleton, G. W. Titsworth, C. R. Henderson, Frank Hannah, Jacob Frazer, J. W. Salisbury and H. H. Howell were wounded, Salisbury twice and Hannah seven times.

Realizing that they were in a trap, the volunters decided to abandon their position during the night and try to escape to Pendleton. Loading their wounded upon a wagon (it was a curious thing that all of them were shot in the leg) they started for Pendleton, the men being instructed to fall prostrate the instant a gun was fired. They had gone but a few hundred yards when the flash of a gun caused them to throw themselves upon the ground just in time to escape a destructive volley from the hostiles. Harrison Hale, too slow in falling prostrate, was shot dead. The rest of them returned the fire and the Indians gave way after discharging a few scattering shots. The retreat began at midnight and before daylight the fugitives were attacked four times.

The return of this shattered company added to the demoralization of the defenders of Pendleton, and they were in very bad case for a fight had the Indians followed up their advantage. Luckily the defeat of Sperry's company was covered by the arrival from Walla Walla of Major Throckmorton's regulars on the eveninig of the 6th, and the next day other troops arrived from Lapwai, making Throckmorton's force one hundred and fifty men. Upon the arrival at Pendleton of the thirteen men who had fled from Willow Springs at the beginning of the action, Throckmorton instantly started to the relief of the party under Sheriff Sperry, and they met the retreating volunteers, soon after daylight, about four miles north of Pilot Rock. They escorted them back to Pendleton, where that remnant of an unfortunate company all arrived in safety.

And now the real defense of Pendleton began. A line of rifle pits was constructed from Foster's mill down to the mouth of Tutawilla, and manned by the regulars, and all the soldiers were fully supplied with ammunition. Captain Vincent's company of volunteers had general charge of the northern defenses of the town, but even then the line was not well maintained. The women and children were concentrated in Byers' mill, but there were no outposts to protect it, and the line along the Umatilla river to the north was without any adequate defense. At this stage of affairs, James H. Turner, a lawyer, suggested the idea that the noncombatants in the mill were at the mercy of the Indians if the latter should attempt to fire that building. Thereupon Lot Livermore, Turner and James Drake, who had seen service in the Civil war, organized a company of twelve men, who under Drake as captain, took possessions of a fence east of Byers' mill, determined to hold it. The line along the river north of Court street was held by Captain William Martin and a dozen other volunteers, so that no Indians could cross the river from the north. In this shape Pendleton was defended until July 7th, when General Howard and Major Throckmorton formed a junction of their forces at Pilot Rock, and proceeded to make an attack, in force, on the Indians, who were reported to be encamped at the head of Butter and Birch creeks. The situation in Pendleton during these fateful days was terrifying, and yet very amusing, to one who looks back upon the excitement in the light of subsequent events.

Sunday, July 7th, Howard's forces, coming from the east, united with Throckmorton's regulars at Pilot Rock, and the next morning assailed the Indian camp at the head of Butter and Birch creeks. The forces thus combined were much more than a match for the Indians and Egan's chances of victory were gone. According to Gilbert,

The command moved in two columns, two companies of artillery, one of infantry and a few volunteers under Throckmorton, seven companies of cavalry and twenty of Robbins' scouts, under Captain Bernard, accompanied by Howard in person. The Indians were encountered and driven with considerable loss from their strong positions, and finally fled in the direction of Grande Ronde valley.

Meanwhile events were happening along the Columbia. Governor Ferry hastened to Walla Walla on the 7th and raised a company of forty volunteers under Captain W. C. Painter, that proceeded to Wallula and embarked the next morning on the steamer Spokane under command of Major Kress.

Captain Wilkinson had the Northwest with twelve soldiers and twenty volunteers. These boats, armed with howitzers and Gatling guns, patroled the river. This was the day that Howard drove the Indians back into the mountains, thus heading them off if they had any designs of crossing the river.

There were several hundred Indians that had never lived on the reservation and they were considered non-treaty Indians. They belonged chiefly to the Umatilla and Walla Walla tribes, lived in the vicinity of Wallula and Umatilla and were known as the Columbia River Indians. When Major Cornoyer gathered in the scattered bands, many of these refused to go and were looked upon as sympathizing with the hostiles and were supposed to have joined them. The morning of the day Howard had his fight on Butter and Birch creeks a number of these attempted to cross the river with a quantity of stock. They were intercepted at three points by the Spokane, and, being fired upon, several

Indians and a few horses were wounded and killed. All canoes from Celilo to Wallula were destroyed. Captain Wilkinson on the Northwest fired into a small party in the act of crossing a few miles above Umatilla. Two braves and a squaw were killed.

The death of State Senator C. L. Jewell was ascribed to Columbias by many. He had a large band of sheep in Camas prairie, and went there with Morrisey to look after them. They encountered a number of Indians but succeeded in eluding them and reaching the herders' cabin in safety. Leaving Morrisey there, he returned to Pendleton to secure arms for his men, who had decided to remain and defend themselves. The morning of the 5th he left Pendleton with several needle guns, contrary to the advice of many friends. He was expected at the hut that night but did not come.

The 8th Morrisey started to see if he could be found. Near Nelson's he met Captain Frank Maddock with a company of Volunteers from Heppner, who informed him that two men had been killed there. A search revealed the bodies of Nelson and N. Scully. Morrisey went around Nelson's house, when he saw a piece of shake sticking up in the road, upon which was written the information that Jewell was lying wounded in the brush. Morrisey called out, "Charley!" He received a faint response, and the injured man was found with a severe wound in his left side and his left arm broken.

When Jewell had approached Nelson's place on the night of the 5th he had been fired upon and fell from his horse, but, while the Indians were killing those at the house, he had crawled into the bushes. In the morning he worked his way out into the road, wrote his notice on the shake and crawled back again. For three days he had lain there without food and unable to help himself, when he was found by Morrisey. He was conveyed to Pendleton and carefully nursed, but he died the next Friday.

Meanwhile all was confusion at Pendleton and the agency. The citizens were suspicious of the reservation Indians, fearing they intended to unite with the hostiles. Consequently volunteers would not go to the agency to defend it. Forty families of Columbias slipped out and went into the enemies' camp, and a few young Umatillas started off without permission, probably with a similar intention.

Two of these saw George Coggan, Fred Foster and Al Bunker coming down from Cayuse Station on a course that took them in dangerous proximity to the hostiles. They rode toward the men with the intention of warning them, so they said afterward, and at the same time a third Indian rode up from another direction. The men had seen some deserted wagons a few miles back, where Olney J. P. McCoy, Charles McLaughlin, Thomas Smith and James Myers had been killed. They had also passed a band of Columbias on their way to the hostile camp.

When they saw the Indians dashing toward them from different directions they supposed them to be the ones they had passed, and, concluding that their time had come, began firing at them. The Umatillas suddenly changed their pacific intentions and commenced shooting. Coggan was killed and Bunker wounded. Foster, who had every reason to believe that he was assailed by at least a score of savages, took the wounded man upon his horse and carried him two miles, when Bunker could go no farther. Foster was then compelled to leave him and hastened to Pendleton, where his arrival created a panic. Besides killing the teamsters, the Indians burned Cayuse Station that day.

At this time news was received that Colonel Miles had been informed of Egan's movements, and had determined to take the responsibility of marching to the agency for its protection. To the exertions of Major Cornoyer and those accompanying him that night is due the fact that Colonel Miles arrived in time to defend the agency and avert the evils that would have followed its capture, including the murder of many people and a possible union of reservation Indians with the hostiles.

The troops, upon reaching their destination, proceeded at once to eat breakfast, but before they were through, the Snakes, Bannocks and Piutes, four hundred strong, were seen riding down from their camp. A line was quickly formed across the flat and up the hill, and before the soldiers were all in position the Indians began to fire upon them. Nearly all day a battle was maintained with the soldiers lying in holes they had scooped in the ground to protect themselves.

Finally Miles decided to charge his assailants, although he had but one company of cavalry and would not be able to pursue them. The Cayuses requested permission to join in the fight, and were allowed to do so on condition that they would keep with the soldiers and not get in advance of them. The command to charge was given, and the soldiers sprang from their rifle pits and rushed upon the enemy, vying with their Cayuse allies in the onslaught. The hostiles, fleeing to the mountains, returned no more, and that night found them eighteen miles from the agency, after having finished the destruction of Cayuse Station by burning the barn, and the soldiers returned and went into camp. There were no casualties on the side of the troops and the volunteers.

Before the fight Umapine started out to do a little work on his own account. His father had been killed years before by Egan, who was in command of the hostiles, and he wanted revenge. When the battle was over he told Egan the Cayuses would join him, and persuaded that chief to accompany him the next night to a point twelve miles from the agency to meet the Cayuse chiefs and arrange matters. He then sent word to Major Cornoyer to have forty soldiers stationed at the appointed place to capture or kill Egan when he appeared.

48

Colonel Miles held the same opinion of Umapine's loyalty that the citizens did and refused to send soldiers on such an errand. The Cayuses expressed their disappointment to the agent, and complained of these suspicions. He told them the best way to convince the whites of their loyalty was to go out themselves and capture Egan.

Whirlwind, chief of the Cayuses, acted on this suggestion, and picking out a party of about forty men repaired to the rendezvous, which was between Meacham and Cayuse station. Umapine and Five Crows visited Egan at his camp and asked him to accompany them to a conference with the Umatilla chiefs, near Cayuse station. Egan fell into the trap, and went with them. All were on horseback. When they arrived near the rendezvous Egan began to grow suspicious, sprang off his horse and closed with Five Crows, who was leading his horse. A desperate struggle ensued, but as Egan was crippled in one arm, as a result of the fight with Colonel Robbins a few days previous, he soon fell, shot through the head by Five Crows. Five Crows scalped Egan, and as Egan's sub-chief started to ride off, Umapine shot him also. The firing brought a number of Piute warriors and women to the scene, and a very lively skirmish followed. The Cayuses were supported by the Umatillas, who were in ambush, and the Piutes rallied to the support of Egan. When the battle was over, the Cayuses, with nine scalps and eighteen women and children prisoners, returned in triumph to the agency. The hostiles retired toward Meacham.

A triumphal procession of all Indians on the reservation was formed and passed in review before the troops that were drawn up in line by General Wheaton, that officer having arrived from Walla Walla and taken command. Yatinouits, a sub-chief of the Cayuses, bearing the scalp of Egan on a pole, arrived in front of the commanding officer, and pointing to his bloody trophy, said: "Egan, Egan, we give you." "No, no, keep it, you brave man!" exclaimed the disgusted officer.

[Although it was generally stated that the Indians who captured Egan were responsible for his decapitation, W. W. Johnson, of Burns, who was a blacksmith at the Malheur Indian agency at the time of the outbreak and who subsequently joined the army in that capacity, says the Indians did not commit this outrage, but that an army surgeon cut off Egan's head and a portion of Egan's wounded arm. These two ghastly relics Mr. Johnson believes are now preserved in alcohol in a San Francisco museum. In a conversation with the writer a short time ago, Whirlwind, who was in charge of the Cayuse party that killed Egan, denied that the Indians ever decapitated Egan, claiming that it was done by army surgeons.]

Defeat on the reservation, the death of their leader, the return of the cavalry and the knowledge that the Columbia river could not be crossed, so disheartened the hostiles that they began to break up and return to their own country. Chief Homeli, with eighty picked warriors of the Umatillas, Cayuses and Walla Wallas, joined the troops in pursuit and kept the hostiles constantly on the move. Homeli reached their front the 17th on Camas creek, and when the retreating bands came along, charged into their midst, killing thirty of them without losing a man. He also captured twenty-seven women and children and a number of horses.

After their disastrous defeat on the Umatilla reservation and their retreat into the Blue mountains, the hostiles, being without leaders, broke up into small parties and scattered in every direction, except to the north. Howard, with ten small columns, pursued them energetically, overtook them and finally cornered them in Harney county, forced their surrender and marched the Piutes across to Yakima, where they were placed under charge of Father Wilbur, supported by a strong garrison of troops from Fort Simco.

The effect of the war upon eastern Oregon generally was very bad. Farmers left their homes at a moment's notice, and in some instances were gone for weeks. Stock broke into their fields and damaged the crops. Many of them had their houses and barns burned, and their stock destroyed or driven away. Large bands of sheep and cattle were dispersed in the mountains, where great numbers perished. Settlers that owned nothing but a little stock and a cabin had the one killed or driven off and the other burned. Citizens of Portland subscribed eighteen hundred dollars, which was distributed in small amounts among the destitute to enable them to live until they could get work again. Many stock thieves took advantage of the confused condition of affairs to gather up scattered horses and cattle and run them off.

The 18th of July, Governor Chadwick addressed a letter to Sheriff Sperry, instructing him to arrest all Indians guilty of murder or robbery, to be tried by civil authorities. This was a matter of great difficulty because of lack of witnesses. By appointment a great council was held on the reservation August 26th, at which General Howard, Governor Chadwick and others were present. The chiefs were made to understand that the only way to clear themselves and their tribes from blame was to surrender all that had been guilty of wrongful acts, and hostages were taken to insure their doing so. Some of the Columbia river Indians were arrested, but were afterward released for want of evidence.

By the persistent investigation of Major Cornoyer, the murderers of George Coggan were discovered. Four young Umatillas were arrested. One of them gave evidence at the trial in November and was discharged. White Owl, Quit-a-Tumps and Aps were convicted and sentenced to be hanged. The first two were executed in the jail yard at Pendleton, January 10, 1879, a company of cavalry and one of militia being present as a guard. A week later Aps was hanged at the same place.

CHAPTER III.

THE GOLD FIELDS OF EASTERN OREGON.

No full history of mining in the counties with which our volume is concerned can be attempted here. While such a work would contain much that has the fascination of romance, and many illustrations of the fact that truth is stranger than fiction; while it might do something toward rescuing from complete oblivion the names of many whose heroism and self-sacrifice should be given the credit for material additions to the world's wealth, yet it could not be prepared without many months of arduous investigation, and when prepared, it would fill a volume of no small size. Some of the early history of mining in parts of eastern Oregon is to be found in previous chapters. Later developments have often received incidental mention, but nowhere has the industry been accorded such comprehensive treatment as its importance merits. Neither will it be possible in this chapter to treat the subject comprehensively, but the purpose of the work would fail of its full accomplishment, were not some more complete outline of this industry incorporated herein.

It has not been the writer's privilege to visit all the mining districts, to say nothing of individual mines, and even had it been possible for him to do so, he is not a mining expert and could not trust his own observations. He will therefore be pardoned, perhaps, if he makes Professor Waldemar Lindgren's geological report, prepared under the auspices of the United States government, the basis of this chapter.

Besides the mining region under consideration, there are at least four gold bearing areas in Oregon. Of these the gold fields of the Blue mountains are by far the most important, though they were not discovered until about ten years later than those in the southwestern part of the state.

The beginnings of placer mining have been already adverted to. After the first few years the industry rapidly declined though the output of placer gold in the Blue mountains is still very considerable, perhaps about $200,000 annually. The decline in the production of gold dust has, however, been more than compensated for by the development of quartz mining, a permanent and comparatively staple industry. "We find records," says Lindgren, "of quartz mines being worked in Susanville and at Mormon Basin in 1865 and 1868. One of the first mills was built at Susanville in 1869 and the process used was pan amalgamation. The Virtue mine was discovered soon after 1862, and the Connor creek mine in 1872, when the first prospecting in the vicinity of Cable Cove was begun and La Belleview and Monumental mines were worked. The ore was shipped on horseback for hundreds of miles. Under such conditions the development of quartz mining was necessarily slow. Its active development dates from 1885, when the country was made accessible by the construction of the transcontinental railroad now traversing it. About 1886 valuable discoveries were made in the Eagle Creek mountains near

Cornucopia. From 1889 a rapid increase in the production was noticed. Quartz mines were worked in various parts of the country and some of them produced heavily. A number of mines in the Crocker creek district were then, for the first time, considered worthy of exploitation and soon began to add to the annual production. This quiet development continued until 1899, when public attention was drawn to the extremely gratifying results obtained from the quartz mines in the Sumpter, Granite and Bonanza districts. The west seemed suddenly to become aware that the long neglected gold fields of the Blue mountains had far greater value than was commonly attributed to them. In 1899 and 1900 a strong influx of prospectors and miners from all parts of the west took place, and under the stimulus of this new immigration and the introduction of modern methods of mining the country has rapidly developed."

According to the reports of the director of the mint, Baker county produced $9,542,625 worth of the precious metals during the period between the beginning of the year 1880 and the end of the year 1899, while Grant produced $3,258,197 in the same period. The product of Union county for the two decades is placed at $5,350,648, much of which was mined in territory now belonging to Baker county.

Of the early placer productions no statistics of even approximate accuracy are obtainable. That they poured many millions into the world's treasury, both directly and indirectly, cannot be doubted. The placer deposits are widely distributed over the entire gold fields, being found from the sands of the Snake river to the gravels of the John Day. They were the first discovery of the miner and their effect upon the history of eastern Oregon is incalculable. While their riches have been largely garnered, they are still maintaining a small annual production and it is possible that the introduction of dredging may result in a

very material revival in the placer mining industry. The distribution of the placer mining districts is given by Lindgren as follows:

"On the east the Snake river bars still contribute some fine gold. In the Eagle creek mountains and at Sparta a small but steady production is maintained. Sparta especially was noted for its rich gulch diggings in early times. The belt extending from Connor creek by Weatherby, Chicken creek, Rye valley, Humboldt, Clarks creek and Malheur was formerly the most important gold mining region in the state and still maintains a diminishing production.

"The Virtue placers, near Baker City, were long ago exhausted. West of Baker City is the gold belt of the southern Elkhorn range, with the once celebrated camps of Auburn, Pocahontas, and Minersville. The headwaters of Powder and Burnt rivers, as well as those of Granite creek, including the districts of Sumpter, Granite, Robinsonville, Bonanza, and Gimlet, may be said to form the central placer mining region of the Blue mountains. These placers, while not as extraordinarily rich as some of the others, have maintained a steady though small production, and seem likely to continue to do so for many years. Finally, on the western side are found the isolated districts of Susanville, Dixie creek, and Canyon creek, the latter having the reputation of having been the richest placer camp in the state. Both at Susanville and at Canyon a fairly steady production is maintained. Farther west are the small placers of Fox creek and Spanish gulch, on Crooked river, the latter locality sixty miles southwest of Canyon."

New mining districts are coming into prominence from time to time but among the best known districts are Elkhorn, Pocahontas, Sumpter, Cable Cove, Granite, Alamo, Greenhorn, Robinsonville, Bonanza, and Upper Burnt river, Susanville, Quartzburg, Canyon, Virtue, Copper Butte, Sparta, Cornucopia, Lower Snake River, Connor Creek, Mineral,

Lower Burnt River, Rye Valley and Mormon. As showing how great a variety of mineral deposits occur in the Blue mountains we may state that the geological survey determined the presence in one or more of the districts of the following minerals: gold, silver, platinum, copper, quicksilver, pyrite, marcasite, pyrrhotite, galena, zinc blende, stibmite, cinnabar, argentite, chalcocite, chalcopyrite, cornite, arsenopyrite, tetrahedrite, tetrahedrite mercurial, freibergite, pyragyrite, hessite, sylvanite, quartz, zircon, opal, chalcedony, chromite, cuprite, specularite, magnetite, ilmenite, pyrolusite, limonite, garnet, vesuvianite, epidote, tourmaline, natrolite, erinite, serpentine, fuchsite or mariposite, roscoelite, calcite, dolomite, magnesite, malachite, calciovolborthite, scheelite, gypsum and chalcanthite. Some of these, particularly roscoelite, are of rare occurrence.

Of the principal mining districts of the Blue mountains only brief outlines must here be attempted. The Elkhorn district, situated about twelve miles northwest of Baker City in the Elkhorn range, contains gold, pyrite, zinc blende and chalcopyrite. Its most promising mine, the Baisley-Elkhorn, was discovered in 1882. After being worked by arrastre for five years and later by a mill, it was sold in 1897, to the Eastern Oregon Gold Mining Company for $60,000. Its production since that date has doubtless aggregated several times the original price paid for the mine. The Robbins-Elkhorn is similar in the character of its ore to the Baisley. Credited with a production during its past history of several hundred thousand dollars, it is believed to possess great possibilities of future development. Other mines and prospects of this district are the Hurdy-Gurdy, the Denny group and the Elkhorn Bonanza. The Rock Creek district, two miles west of the Baisley-Elkhorn mine gives promise of furnishing several important producers. Several mines have been worked to a considerable extent, particularly the Maxwell and the Chloride. The ore is said to contain more silver than that found in the Baisley-Elkhorn district.

At the southern end of the Elkhorn range are the Pocahontas, Minersville and Auburn districts, the last named of which has enjoyed such a prominent place in the history of Baker county. Indeed all these districts were more important formerly than at present, for the richest placer deposits have long since been mined out and no very important quartz veins have been discovered to keep up their producing power. The districts, however, maintain small production to the present and the wealth taken from Griffin's gulch, Blue Canyon and the numerous other creek bottoms since the original discovery in 1861 aggregates several hundred thousand dollars.

Less favored in their wealth of placer gold, though vastly richer in quartz veins are the Sumpter and Cracker Creek districts, situated to the west of Baker City. "South of Baker City," says Prof. Lindgren, "Powder river cuts through the basaltic plateau at the southern end of the Elkhorn range in a wide semicircle, and for about twelve miles flows in a narrow canyon. Going up the river, the canyon opens, at an elevation of 4,000 feet, into the wide Sumpter valley, an alluvial bottom flanked by broad gently sloping, forested benches. Beyond these the snowy summits of the Elkhorn range rise abruptly eastward, while toward the west a heavily timbered ridge of moderate elevation separates the valley from the Burnt river drainage basin. A little above Sumpter a canyon again begins. The river forks into Silver creek, Cracker creek, and McCully's fork, all heading among the high ridges leading to Elkhorn range or Mount Baldy."

The placers of the Sumpter district were discovered in 1862 and most of the time since operations have been carried on upon them, mostly by Chinese, however, who invariably decline to give definite information as to the amount of their product.

Near the town of Sumpter are many small veins and indications of minerals, but we must go seven miles above to find the large vein systems. It is thought that there is practically one continuous vein system from the Baisley-Elkhorn mine to Cracker creek. Upon it in the vicinity of Sumpter are the well known North Pole, E. and E., Columbia, Golconda, Amazon and Bunker Hill mines. The North Pole was discovered in 1887, sold to a London man in 1888 for $10,000, operated with more or less activity until 1895, then operated with zeal and earnestness, giving large returns. It is equipped with many thousand dollars worth of machinery, stamp mill, cyniding plant, Huntington mill with concentrators, etc. It is one of the leading producers of the district. The E. and E. mine consists of the Eureka and Excelsior claims on the North Pole vein. A twenty-stamp pan amalgamation mill was erected in 1889 by its owners, the Eureka and Excelsior Consolidated Mining Company, but the mill did not prove suited to the purpose intended and the mine did not give expected returns. J. H. Longmaid leased the property in 1895' put vanners in the mill and in three years took out and milled ore to the value of more than half a million. Lindgren estimates its total production at $800,000, or more than any other new mine in the Sumpter district. It has been idle for the past few years and we believe still is at this writing.

The Columbia mine is an important producer, developed by extensive excavations and supplied with much machinery of different kinds. It is stated that one car of its ore, containing twenty tons, gave returns of about $1,000 per ton. Of the Golconda, Lindgren, writing in 1900, says:

"This part of the North Pole vein was located as the Golconda claim in 1887 and sold for a reported sum of $24,000 in 1897, there being at that time only 250 feet of development. The Golconda Mining Company at present owns, besides this claim, eight oth-

ers adjacent, which are said to cover two parallel veins. The Golconda and the Wide West are located on the North Pole vein. In 1898 a large bromination plant, of a capacity of 100 tons a day, was erected but soon found unsuited to the character of the ore. A twenty-stamp mill and a Bryan roller mill, together with eighteen concentrators were substituted, giving a total capacity of over 100 tons per day. Crushing was begun in January, 1900, and the mine has consequently not as yet any great production to its credit. In the fall of 1899 a rich ore chimney was struck, twenty tons of which yielded $10,000 in the mill. Still richer ore was shipped to the smelting works. In September, 1900, fifteen stamps were running. At present there are 2,500 feet of developments, including a 400-foot double compartment perpendicular shaft and four levels, the opening of the fourth having just begun; also a 650-foot tunnel running southwest on the ledge."

Other important mines of the district, some of which have a considerable production to their credit, are the Mountain Belle, the Ibex, the Bald Mountain, and the Mammoth, also the Amazon, Analulu and Bunker Hill claims.

"The Cable Cove district," says Lindgren, "is situated ten miles in an air line north-northwest of Sumpter on the high backbone which separates the drainage of Powder river from that of the North Fork of the John Day river. The road from Sumpter is along Silver creek, the principal fork of Powder river. For some miles above Sumpter the canyon is narrow but soon widens and assumes the broad U-shaped form characteristic of glaciated valleys. Near Cable Cove the road emerges from the thick timber in the bottom of the valley. The head of the creek appears as a wide amphitheater with steep slopes, sparsely timbered. Westward the ridges of Bald mountain rise with bare, light gray, glaciated outcrops. Eastward a number of sharp and high granite peaks meet the eye in the continuation of the Elkhorn range. The elevation at the California mill is 7,000 feet; the high hill back of it attains 7,900. The gaps east and west of this hill are 7,500 feet in elevation. From the summit long ridges extend northward between the heavily timbered valleys of Big Limber creek, Bull creek and the north fork of the John Day. The summits of Cable Cove culminate a couple of miles southwesterly in Bald mountain (elevation 8,330 feet), so prominently visible from Sumpter. It is a bare granitic ridge, sloping abruptly northward and here enclosing a glacial amphitheater in the center of which is a small lake."

Although the earliest discoveries in the district were made by the Cable brothers in 1872, and some rich ore was shipped, the mines and prospects are not even yet very fully developed. In 1885 there was quite a revival in the district and in recent years still greater activity has characterized development work, but the isolation of the region has been against it. Ore must still be hauled fourteen miles to Sumpter for shipment. The Eagle vein is considered the mother lode of the district and the Imperial and California are the best developed mines, though there are numerous other promising claims.

. The Granite district, above the town of Granite in eastern Grant county, has both quartz veins and placers. The latter, though worked since 1862, have never been found especially rich and their operation has been in large measure given over to the Chinese. Of the quartz mines and claims of the district, the best known and most developed is the Red Boy. Its history is similar to that of many other mines. Slow development at first, intermittent operations and indifferent results, mistakes in the character of machinery installed, etc. Eventually Taber & Godfrey acquired the property, built a Crawford mill and met with excellent success in its operation. A twenty-stamp mill, built in 1898, also proved suitable for the work of ore reduction and the mine became an important producer. With-

out attempting to describe the numerous other mines and claims of the district we may enumerate some of the best known of them as follows: May Queen, the Concord group, Cougar, South Cougar, Magnolia, Blue Ribbon, Buffalo, Monumental and La Belleview.

Four miles from the Red Boy mine is the small mining town of Alamo, the center of the mineral district of the same name. Near Alamo is the confluence of Clear, Olive and Beaver creeks, on all three of which good prospects have been found. Their gravels have undergone the washing process, though ordinarily they have not proved very rich. At present little, if any, placer mining is being done. Probably the most extensively developed quartz claim is the Quebec, which gives great promise. Other claims in the district are Alamo, the Scandia Tunnel and St. Anthony Mining Companies' mines, the Strasburg, the Yellow Stone and Van Anda claims, the Little Giant, etc.

In the Greenhorn district are the Intermountain group, Intrinsic group, or Ordway mines, the Morris, Mountain Consolidated, Potosi, Savage, Ben Harrison, Carbonate, the Ruby, the Chloride, the Tempest and the Ornament. Ore from any of these mines must be hauled thirty-five miles over difficult roads, nevertheless small shipments have been made from many of the claims in the district.

With the once famous placer camp, Robinsonville, as a center, and contiguous to the Greenhorn region, is the historic Robinsonville mining district. Its rich, shallow, gold-bearing gravels have been pretty well robbed of their wealth and only in the McNamee gulch has any placer mining been done during recent years. This gulch once gave up a $14,000 nugget. Even during the early days the existence of auriferous quartz in the region was known and many rich chimneys have been discovered from time to time. The deposits are pockety and uncertain, however, and steady production has never been maintained.

The leading mine in the Bonanza and Upper Burnt river districts is the Bonanza, situated ten miles west of Sumpter. Located in 1877 it was sold for $350 in 1879 to the Bonanza Mining Company, by them in 1892 to the Geiser Brothers, who sold it in 1898 for a reputed sum of $500,000, to a Pittsburg corporation. It was estimated by Lindgren in 1900 that the production of precious metals up to that time must have approximated a million dollars. Extensive developments have been made and capacious and costly machinery is being used in its ore development. It is the only producer in the district but contiguous to it are several mines and prospects of promise, among them the Richmond, the Keystone Belle and the White Elephant. Much placer mining was done in the district during the early days and a production of placer gold is still maintained. It is said that in the Hindman placers a small quantity of platinum is found and that this is the only occurrence of this metal in the Blue mountains.

Susanville mining district on the Middle Fork of the John Day river, twenty-two miles from Austin's stage station, has a great deal of historic as well as present interest. The placer mines of Elk creek, discovered in 1864, were very rich and those of Deep, Onion and Big creeks, though less favored with mineral wealth also contributed not a little to the fame of the district. According to Raymond's report for 1870, the production of gold during the first four years after discovery was not less than $80,000, and the total production is thought to be in the neighborhood of $600,000. Placer mining is being carried on by Chinese even at the present time. The gold is coarse and of a fineness of 865. Prof. Lindgren states that a nugget worth $480 was found on Elk creek, another worth $625 on Deep creek, and one worth $800 in Buck gulch. Prospecting for quartz, it is stated, began in 1869, and at an early date ore from the Monumental vein was worked in Mr. Cabel's pan-

amalgamation mill. For many years afterward little was done, but recently prospecting has been renewed. One condition greatly against the development of the region is its inaccessibility, which causes shipping expenses to be excessive. The Badger mine is the most important of the district. It is on a very old ledge, one that was discovered and worked some as early as 1869. A ten-stamp mill with concentrators was once installed but failed to handle the quality of ore satisfactorily, and only the richest ore is now handled. This is shipped to a smelter. Other claims in the vicinity are the Stockton, the Bull of the Woods group, of which the Otter is one of the principal claims, the Gem vein, etc.

The Dixie creek placers of the Quartzburg district were among the earliest discoveries. They are said to have been very rich at first but early in the 'seventies they were turned over to Chinese miners. At present nothing in the way of placer mining is being done there. Spanish Diggings is another worked out placer mine of the district, but the old placers of Happy camp and Ruby creek are still worked by Chinese or whites and Chinese. The Present Need, located about twelve years ago, is the leading gold quartz mine of the district. It has been worked on a small scale ever since its discovery. The ore is calcined and then treated with an arrastre. A little to the north is the old Keystone and above this is the Colorado. The Standard copper mine, an ancient discovery, and the Copperopolis, of more recent location, promise well, though they have not been developed sufficiently to establish beyond a doubt their value.

The history of early placer mining in the Canyon district has been already treated of in this work. That the Canyon placer deposits were richest in Oregon admits of no doubt, but their exact production during early days is not known. Estimates vary from three to five millions. Raymond estimated that in 1865 the output was $22,000 per week and in 1870 the product had fallen to $300,000 per year. The total production probably exceeds $15,000,000. At present the Humboldt mine is being worked with giants, and operations are being carried on on a small scale in the vicinity of Marysville.

Among the departures in experimental mining in eastern Oregon, or in the entire northwest for that matter, none is more interesting that the great Pomeroy mining dredger, now at work washing the sands of the John Day for the auriferous deposits therein contained. The boat is at work in the main John Day river, just below the mouth of Canyon creek and about a mile from the town of John Day. For ages this mountain stream has been washing down fine golden sands from its headwaters and despositing them along its course. When the best ground had been worked by the old placer miners, the river bed was abandoned and this the dredger owners are content to work for what gold there is still left in it. Although the project is still in its experimental stage, the results attained thus far have been eminently satisfactory.

This immense machine was constructed during the past summer by Portland capitalists, chief among whom are the Pomeroy brothers, and cost over $100,000, all the equipment having been hauled in over forty miles of rough mountain roads. In building the hull alone over 175,000 feet of lumber was used, while ten tons of bolts were utilized in fastening it together. The entire weight of the dredger is stated as 750 tons.

Though so rich in placers, the Canyon district is strangely lacking in quartz mines. Canyon peak, just above the town, is celebrated for its rich pocket veins, but has no steady producers. The discovery of the Great Northern mine in 1898 by Isaac Guker and the consequent excitement have been adverted to previously. The mine's rich pockets have been emptied of thousands of dollars. Mr. Guker hopes that further developments will prove the Great Northern a mine not only rich but permanent; though thus far values have been very irregular.

A few miles east of Canyon City and John Day are the rich Prairie Diggings mines, now owned and operated by the Hoosier Boy Mines Company, Limited. Last season a new twenty-five stamp mill was installed by this company, which has recently purchased the mine, and considerable development work has since been done. Six concentrators are in use. The product of this mine is chiefly free gold and gold bearing concentrates. When in full operation between thirty-five and forty men are employed and under the present careful and energetic management this, the only producing quartz mine in the Canyon district, gives promise of a bright future.

South of Prairie City and high up on Strawberry butte a large number of claims have been located, principal among which is the Oregon Wonder. It is claimed that the ledge taking its name from this prospect promises to prove indeed a wonder. It is miles in length and in places hundreds of feet wide. The ore is low grade on the surface but if values increase with depth, the ledge may prove as marvelous as its name would imply.

Coming back to Baker City from our brief review of the principal mining districts to the west, let us take a bird's eye view of those to north and east. A trip of seven miles will bring us to the western border of the Virtue district, one of the oldest quartz districts in eastern Oregon. The veins of auriferous ore are numerous and the gold free and of a high degree of purity. The leading mine of the district, the Virtue, has long been one of the largest producers in entire Blue mountain region. The details of its discovery have been spoken of heretofore. Developed to a considerable extent in early days, it was worked almost continuously from 1871 to 1878, when it was sold to Grayson & Company, of San Francisco, who operated it intermittently until

1884. From that time until 1893, the mine was idle. Then work was resumed and continued until 1898, when it became the property of a Montreal company. The mine is now being operated, though only a small force is at work. The total production of this mine is estimated at $2,189,000. In the immediate vicinity of the Virture are numerous claims and prospects, none of which have as yet become producers. The Flagstaff, six miles northeast of Baker City, has been quite extensively developed, and ore from its interior, worked in a ten-stamp mill, has yielded good returns.

Three miles southeast of the Virtue is the White Swan mine. It has been worked for more than twelve years and was credited by Lindgren in 1900 with a total production of not less than $200,000. According to the mint reports, its product in 1891 was $72,000 and in 1892, $72,642. At present the mine is being operated with a force of fifteen or twenty men.

The Brazos, two miles south of the White Swan, is a mine of recent development. A ten-stamp mill was erected during the year 1900 for the reduction of its ore. There are numerous prospects and partly developed claims in various parts of the Virtue district. Little placer mining has been done in recent years.

Passing over the promising district in the Farley hills in the vicinity of North Powder and the old, rich Copper Butte district, we come to the consideration of the famous properties of the Panhandle, recently made a part of Baker county. The placers in the gulches of the Sparta district were early traced to well defined quartz veins, many of which were worked in primitive fashion at a very early date. These operations were gradually discontinued and the production declined correspondingly until the late 'eighties, when a revival took place, resulting in a jump of the Union county gold production in 1889 to $576,000, a considerable portion of which was to be credited

to the quartz mines of Sparta. Various conditions have been operative since to cause a decline. In 1900 according to Prof. Lindgren only the Gem mine was being worked on a larger scale than formerly. The placers in the vicinity of Sparta were known to be rich in an early day, but owing to scarcity of water nothing could be done until the completion of the Sparta ditch in 1873, the length of which was twenty-two miles and the capacity 3,000 miner's inches. Great activity followed the advent of the water, but production declined after a few years and at present is inconsiderable.

Northwest of the Sparta district is the Sanger mine, a noted producer. In its vicinity was the old placer camp of Hog 'Em, credited with a production of $500,000. The Summit lode of this mine was discovered in 1870, produced $60,000 in 1874, began to increase its production in 1889, and from that year to 1892 produced $813,000, according to mint reports. It is in operation at present.

In the vicinity of Sanger and in the Eagle creek district are the Basin claims, small producers, the Snowstorm, the Lily White, the Dolly Varden, Miller & Lane, and other claims some of which have produced considerable sums. Placer gold was mined in the district in early days and a small production is still maintained.

In the Eagle Creek range, not far from the head of Pine valley, is Cornucopia, the center of the prosperous and promising mining district of the same name. It occupies the upper end of the famed Pine valley. The mines are of comparatively recent development but in the early eighties began a small and intermittent production. In 1889, however, the district is said to have produced $74,000, the beginning of a steady and continuous output. "The camp has passed through many vicissitudes," says Lindgren, "and much money has been unwisely spent. Even at the present time the industry is not established upon as firm a basis as it ought, for without doubt it is a district of great promise and should yield good returns from capital judiciously invested.

"The producing veins are all situated from two to three miles east to north of the town and at elevations ranging from a few hundred to 3,000 feet above it. Prospects have also been found on Red Mountain, at the head of the west fork of Pine creek, several miles above Cornucopia, but these are not, as yet, much developed. At least five principal veins may be distinguished; one of these is on Simmons mountain, the others west of the creek. The strike is in general north-south, but with directions slightly converging northward. The dip on Simmons Mountain is eastward, while the other veins dip west at moderate angles. The veins are simple, sharply cut fissure veins, with a filling of quartz and sulphurets; the ore is, to a great extent, free milling."

Upon one of the principal veins of the district is located the Union-Champion mine, which, with the Last Chance and the Red Jacket, belongs to J. E. Searles. Before the mine fell into his hands much money was injudiciously spent upon it in inaugurating unsuitable machinery. It was found best by Mr. Searles to send the ore, when partly treated, to the smelter, notwithstanding the heavy freight rates over fifty miles of poor road. The total production of the mine runs into the hundreds of thousands. Other promising mines, some of them with a small output to their credit, are the Robert Emmet, Bryan, Last Chance, Queen of the West, Wild Irishman, etc.

The Snake river canyon is an interesting mining region and merits a more detailed description than be attempted here. The gold in the sand bars of the river is fine and occurs in thin and not very persistent streaks. Many prospectors and individual miners have sought grub stakes by working these sands in primitive fashion, and inventors of new porcesses for catching fine gold have found here opportunity to test their machinery. The experi-

menters have usually met with failure, and the really successful process is yet to be discovered. In recent years dredging has been attempted with some success. The Snake river vicinity has become noted within the last few years for its copper deposits. Iron Dyke, discovered in 1897, is considered very promising; indeed it is thought by some to be richer in copper than any claim in the Seven Devils region in Idaho. It is being developed by the Northwest Copper Company, who contemplate building a railroad from Huntington to tap it. On the Idaho side, half a mile above Ballard's Landing, is the River Queen deposit. The Copper King group is two miles below Ballard's Landing on the Oregon side, and numerous claims have been located around the landing on both sides of the river.

In the lower Snake river canyon, four miles above Huntington, is the largest limestone mass in Oregon, convenient to a railroad. Gypsum is also found near Huntington and is being utilized by the Oregon Plaster Company.

Lower down the Snake river basin on the stream from which it receives its name is the celebrated Connor Creek mine. The vein was discovered in 1871 by Wood and Edelmann. It was worked by a five-stamp mill until 1876, then by a fifteen-stamp mill. In 1884 it was sold to the Connor Creek Mine and Mill Company, who instituted a thirty-five stamp mill. The production of this mine has been estimated as high as nine million dollars, but Lindgren thinks that its production prior to 1900 probably did not exceed two million. It was undoubtedly the source of the placer gold found in Connor creek. The entire gulch of the stream has been repeatedly washed, the result being, it is thought, about $100,000.

Without pausing to speak of the auriferous deposits and fine opals of the Lower Burnt River valley around Durkee, we pass to the Rye valley district. The placers of this region were discovered during the early 'sixties, and have been worked continuously since producing perhaps more than $1,000,000. Water is not available at all seasons, but a steady annual production is nevertheless maintained. Of the quartz mines in the locality, Lindgren says:

"A number of quartz veins containing silver have been found on Pedro mountain and attracted great attention between 1870 and 1880. The Monumental, Green Discovery, Washington, and Rising Sun veins were known in 1872; all of these were very rich in wire silver, chloride and silver glance, besides containing a little gold. In 1875 a five-stamp mill was erected on the Lafayette, a gold-silver vein and a similar pan-amalgamation plant on the Green Discovery. In 1880 the New England and Oregon Mining Company erected a large pan-amalgamation mill, spending $50,000 on the property, evidently with unfavorable results. All these veins are situated high up on Pedro mountain. Green Discovery is said to strike northwest and dip seventy degrees southwest.

"In the canyon of the south fork, leading up to the Mormon Basin, are many quartz prospects containing both gold and silver, tethahedrite is frequently found in them. Seven miles from Rye valley a three-stamp mill has been erected, but was idle in 1900. It was built to treat the oxidized sugary quartz of the Golden Gate, a small, flat vein occurring in granite half a mile north of the road. The contact between granite and metamorphic schist with crystalline limestone is crossed a short distance from the wagon road."

It remains to us only to advert briefly to the famous placer districts between Willow creek and Burnt river in that part of their course where they most nearly approach each other. On the Burnt river slope of the divide are the Clark's creek and Bridgeport districts and on the Willow creek side are Mormon Basin, Amelia, Malheur and Eldorado districts. All have yielded heavily in placer gold, having been discovered and worked during the first period of placer exploration in Baker and ad-

joining counties. Mormon Basin is described as almost circular in shape, about three miles in diameter, with its sloping floor covered by heaps of tailings from placer mines. The gold is coarse and it is said that in 1866 a nugget worth $640 was found. As the water supply is somewhat scant the placer miners of the early day were not able to exhaust the gold and not even to this day has all the wealth of the district been garnered. Quartz veins were discovered as early as 1863 and some work has been done on a small scale toward the reduction of their ores at different times since. A number of promising prospects are being developed intermittently at present, among them The Humboldt group, the Morning Star group, the California, Royal Arch, Sunday Hill, Eagle Head, the Golden Eagle, the Rising Sun, the Atlantic, the Asaler and the Blue Jay.

The placer deposits of Clark's creek were very rich and have been extensively worked, but are now about exhausted. Crossing the divide, one finds below the summit a few hundred feet, the ruins of Eldorado camp, where once was a flourishing town. Between this and Malheur all the gulches have been quite thoroughly worked in years past, producing bountifully. It was for the mining of these deposits that the Eldorado ditch was constructed, which takes water from the upper Burnt river, through Shasta gap to the Willow creek slope. This ditch, 134 miles long, carrying 2,400 miner's inches of water, was the greatest achievement of the early days. On ledges discovered near Malheur are the Red, White and Blue and the Golden Eagle mines, but neither these nor the numerous other quartz claims and prospects of the district have yet gained a place among important producers.

The reader of the foregoing necessarily superficial and incomplete outline of the mining industry in the Blue mountain region cannot fail to be impressed with the fact that though forty-one years have elapsed since the first discovery of pay dirt, the mining indus-

try is still in its infancy. The placers have
been quite thoroughly exhausted, except such
as can only be worked by the dredging process
which is receiving considerable attention at
present, but in place of this unstable species of
mining has come and is coming the scientific
treatment of ores from the rich quartz veins,
an industry incomparably superior in the permanence and stability of its wealth production.
The success attending the efforts of the few
miners and mining companies who have
through cloud and sunshine persistently developed their claims and scientifically treated
their ores, gives earnest of like success to be
achieved in other instances, and it is but reasonable to suppose that the number of producers
in the Blue mountains will be increased many
fold with the flight of future decades.

That the opinion of the writer is confirmed
in the sober judgment of experts and men who
have made a close study of this and other mining regions is attested by numerous utterances
from the lips and pens of such men. In reply
to a request for an opinion as to the future of
the district, a well known mining man handed
us the following communication:

BAKER CITY, October 3, 1902.
Western Historical Publishing Co.

GENTLEMEN :—In speaking of the future mining outlook of Baker county, Oregon, I take pleasure in stating
that I have been in the mining business for over fifteen
years, have been actively engaged in every capacity in
the pursuit of the business in nearly all the leading
camps of the United States, and have given this section
a five years' attention, canvassing the district closely at
intervals.

During the five years that I have spent here it has
been my good fortune to see the mining industry grow
from a few mines, eight in number, in 1896, to some
thirty-seven good producing mines at this time. This I
call excellent, when it is taken into consideration that
Oregon is a long way from the money centers of the
east and that comparatively few people are engaged in
business by the side of the more centrally located districts of Colorado, Montana and Utah. If the same
mining region were located in Colorado I sincerely believe a hundred good producing mines would now dot
the various mineral belts of Baker county.

Developments on every hand conclusively prove that
the mines go down in this section. In every instance

mining properties have marvelously increased in value,
and I think it is impossible at this time to foresee. the
greatness of the mineral development of this section.
Yours very respectfully,
J. D. Voss, M. E.

Similar requests sent out to George Gordon
McNamara and J. N. Esselstyn by the Baker
City Chamber of Commerce in 1900 elicited
the following replies:

BAKER CITY, OREGON, March 23, 1900.
Hon. O. L. Miller,
Sec. Chamber of Commerce.

SIR :—Your letter of the 20th inst., requesting. my
written opinion, as mining engineer, of the different
mineral districts of Baker and adjoining counties, was
received a day or two ago, and I beg to state in answer
that I am pleased to be of service to your Chamber, if
by so doing I can bring the outside world to know the
splendid possibilities that eastern Oregon offers to the
legitimate mining investor.

Although the mineral country adjacent to Baker
City has a great variety of valuable metals and other
products besides gold and silver, viz., nickel, cobalt,.
chromium, copper cinnabar and also sodium and phos-
phates (the latter in the form of apatite ore), I shall,
however, confine my remarks to briefly outlining the
different gold-bearing zones of this and adjacent districts.

To the east of Baker City the gold-bearing belt commences almost at the city limits and extends to the
north and east for a distance of from forty to fifty
miles. In this territory are located such producers as
the Virtue, Collateral, Flagstaff, Carrol B.; and it also
includes the copper-bearing belt known as the Copper
Butte District, which is now giving promise of rivaling
the Lake Superior mines, the ores being of the same
nature and character. It is true that many of these
mines, and also many valuable prospects, are lying idle,
but they are only awaiting capital and intelligent management to be made valuable producers.

To the west of this city lie the mines of the Elkhorn range. The gold-bearing belt commences about
four miles from Baker City, extending to the southeast several miles and to the northwest over twenty
miles. This magnificent and picturesque range, with an
altitude of over ten thousand feet above sea level and
some six thousand feet above the surrounding country,
is creased and furrowed by innumerable gulches, many
of which yielded richly in placer gold to the pioneer of
this section of the country. Even now the bars and
hillsides are being worked successfully by hydraulics.
The gold-bearing veins of quartz commence near the
valley paralleling the mountain and extend to the summit and many miles beyond. The Baisley-Elkhorn,
which has probably produced more money for its own--

ers than any other mine in Oregon, is located in these mountains, as are also the Robbins-Elkhorn, the Baisley Gold Mining Company's group, the Sherman group and many other valuable mines and prospects.

Near the crest of the mountain, and some five miles to the southwest from the Baisley-Elkhorn, is the now famous Cracker Creek District, in which are located the North Pole, Columbia, Eureka and Excelsior, Golconda and many other valuable properties, several of which are paying valuable dividends to their owners.

The limited space you awarded me will not permit me giving any detailed description of the mines near Sumpter, Granite, Canyon City, Prairie City and Susanville, where are located such divident payers as the Bonanza, Red Boy, Cougar, May Queen, Little Giant, Golden Eagle and Magnolia and such well known prospects as the Van Anda, Ibex, South Cougar and Maiden's Dream, all of which have been sufficiently developed to warrant the immediate erection of machinery and are destined to be classed among the producers of this part of eastern Oregon.

The general formation of the above described districts is slate, porphyry and granite, with occasional belts of lime schist and phonolite. The ores, as a rule, are of the free-milling class, though in many instances they merge into sulphurets as depth is obtained. However, in most instances, when this change takes place the gold value of the ore increases very materially. In many cases there are associated with the quartz stringers and bunches of tellurium, silvanite and nagvagite. These last-mentioned ores are in every way similar to the Cripple Creek deposits, and are generally amenable to the cynide treatment.

I have found in my general conversation with prospectors of the above districts that, as a rule, they are willing to give a liberal part of their holdings to parties having sufficient money to develop their claims.

GEORGE GORDON MCNAMARA, E. M.

BAKER CITY, OREGON, March 22, 1900.
Mr. O. L. Miller,
    Sec'y Baker City Chamber of Commerce.

DEAR SIR:—In reply to your favor of recent date, regarding the mineral resources of the districts tributary to Baker City, would say, that while the country tributary to Baker City, and, in fact, the whole of eastern Oregon, has for years been locally recognized as a great mineral belt, yet it is only in the past few years that it has attracted the attention of outside capital; and as a result to-day we find paying mines being operated in any direction we may choose to go from Baker City. While the gold fields in the vicinity of Baker City have attracted the greatest attention, yet we find very rich copper deposits, which are attracting more and more attention every day. The copper deposits of the district are of two distinct classes, namely, copper ores and native copper. The ores are principally the sulphides and oxide of copper, varying somewhat in

their percentages of copper. Some of the most prominent of the copper ore deposits are to be found to the east along Snake river, where large veins of high grade copper ores have been opened; also at Copper Butte, twenty-one miles to the northeast of Baker City, and another large deposit is being developed about twenty miles northwest of Baker City, while in the main range of the Blue mountains, only five miles from Sumpter, a deposit of copper ore has recently been discovered. Also at Copperopolis, south of the Greenhorn mountains, are many well-defined ledges of copper ore. All of the above ores are smelting ores, and in the same districts are found large deposits of limestone and iron ore for fluxing these ores; all of which points to a very prosperous future for the smelter.

Native copper is found about three miles from Granite, along Clear creek; also about eighteen miles northeast of Baker City. This district is of a basaltic formation, with zones of amygdaloid, carrying native copper. These amygdaloidal deposits are the same as the amygdaloidal deposits of the Lake Superior copper region, upon which are located the Quincy, Pewabic, Franklin, Arnold, Wolverine and many other of the famous copper-producing mines of the Lake Superior country. For the year 1899 the Quincy mine stamped 559,164 tons of rock, from which it obtained 25.6 pounds of refined copper per ton of rock, or 1.28 per cent. With this production, the Quincy paid $950,000 in dividends to its stockholders, and spent over $400,000 in the construction of a new stamp mill and other improvements.

The amygdaloidal copper deposits of Baker county will necessarily have to carry a larger percentage of metallic copper than the Lake Superior mines in order to make them a paying proposition, on account of the higher price of labor, fuel, supplies, water supply, freight rates, etc. If the work which is now being carried on in this great copper belt in Baker county will develop an ore body from which can be extracted not less than one thousand tons per day and carrying three per cent. metallic copper, I believe it can be made to pay large dividends, and Oregon will soon be classed among the copper-producing states of the country.

Very truly yours
J. N. ESSELSTYN, E. M.

Dr. Alfred R. C. Selwyn, late director of the geological survey of Canada and the geological survey of Australia, says in part:

Coming to eastern Oregon gold fields, I find here older rocks, generally speaking, than exist on the surface in Australia. The country rock here, almost universally designated as slate, has been metamorphosed and appears to be of different composition than the country rock of Australia, but is substantially the same.

I find in eastern Oregon one of the most interesting and hopeful mineral zones of the globe. The formation, contour, climate, accessibility, timber and water form a combination which tend to reduce the cost of extracting gold to a minimum. And, in addition, I find the ores are less refractory and contain a larger amount of free gold, generally speaking, and besides are softer and less expensive to treat.

. Concerning the quartz ledges, I say unreservedly that I have never been in any mining country which I consider more promising or as having a brighter future than that of eastern Oregon.

The mines, I believe, are more promising than those of Rossland or any in British Columbia that I know of. Values are more uniformly distributed here. Ores are not so hard and can be treated at less expense, and there appears to be more free gold. I find here mines running ten and twenty stamps which could just as well be operating fifty. They would not be able to exhaust the ores during this or the coming generation.

CHAPTER IV.

HISTORY OF THE PRESS.

One who has occasion to study, even super-ficially, the history of newspapers in any section, can hardly escape the conviction that the business is an exceedingly precarious one, perhaps more so than any other in which men commonly engage. Judging from the number of ambitious sheets that have made their appearance in eastern Oregan and have disappeared after a short and checkered career, in the meantime having undergone, it may be, several changes of hands, it would seem that the path of the newspaper man is a stony and dangerous one, with many pitfalls and with few flowers by the roadside. Literary men, from Homer to the author of the latest maga-zine article, have almost invariably failed to realize rewards for their labor in any sense commensurate with the blessings they have bestowed. The newspaper man, whose work is allied to that of the more pretentious writer, is almost as poorly paid. Even where men do reap some measure of success in the business, the question remains as to whether the same energy, the ame executive ability and the same early and late application would not achieve much greater success in some other walk of life.

But Baker county's pioneer paper has with-stood all the storms and vicissitudes of a long career, developing as the country developed, and ever anticipating the wants and the tastes of the people in such a way as to keep them its friends. It was most happy in its choice of a name for perhaps no two words in the English language could better describe the character of this doughty pioneer sheet than the words "Bedrock Democrat." The former gives the idea of strength, sturdiness and solidity, and the latter names the political party which the paper has, for thirty-two years, steadfastly sup-ported in every campaign.

The first issue of this paper bears date May 11, 1870. Abbott and McArthur were the en-terprising men who gave inception to it and their intentions and policy are outlined in their salutatory remarks as follows:

"In accordance with a custom as ancient as journalism itself, we, after making our bow to the generous public, desire to point out our aims and objects in establishing and issuing the Democrat. We propose to join in the very general and laudable effort, which is being put forth by influential citizens in every sec-tion of the state, to furnish the reading public reliable information concerning Oregon. Whilst others are laying before the world its peculiar advantages, both as in agricultural and manufacturing pursuits, which present themselves in the fruitful and almost boundless valley of the Willamette, we shall be assiduously engaged in presenting to our readers all matters which may transpire in eastern Oregon, whose mineral and pastoral resources are today unequalled in wealth, fertility or extent. We shall endeavor so to conduct the Democrat as to make it a welcome visitor to every resident of this portion of the state and a valuable vehicle of information to those who reside elsewhere. So far as politics are concerned it is almost needless to say that this paper will be thoroughly and uncompromisingly Democratic. It will endeavor to be one of the true exponents of the Democratic party in Oregon, and as such strive to support the party. Entertaining the hope that the Democrat will prove a success, both politically and financially, we submit it to the public in whose hands rests the confirmation of our words."

It is safe to assert that all the objects proposed for itself by the Bedrock Democrat have been consistently and energetically pursued. There certainly can be no doubt that the cause of Democracy in Baker county has been greatly strengthened by the unceasing labors of the paper during all these years and, what many men would consider of more importance, that the country has been builded up and its resources widely advertised through this same medium.

In July, 1870, Mr. L. L. McArthur retired from connection with the Bedrock Democrat, having been elected to a judicial position. The paper remained in the charge of Mr. Abbott alone until August 1, 1872, when it passed under the control of J. M. Shepherd, who on May 5, 1875, took into partnership with himself his son, H. C. Shepherd. In 1876 the Bedrock Democrat increased its size considerably, becoming a twenty-eight column paper with the columns three inches longer than they had been formerly. It then ranked equally in size with any other paper in eastern Oregon.

The Democrat was not long permitted to enjoy a journalistic monopoly of Baker county, for, in 1872, the Herald was established.

It suspended in 1876, however, and from that date until 1880, the pioneer journal was without opposition. But in 1880 M. H. Abbott and sons began publication of the Reveille, an independent weekly, of which M. D. Abbott became the full proprietor some two years later. For a few years prior to 1890, he issued a daily edition. In 1892 he sold his plant to the People's Publishing Company, retaining, however, the books and the right to the name "Reveille."

On December 15, 1880, the Bedrock Democrat changed hands, going to J. T. Wisdom. Mr. Shepherd states in his valedictory that during the eight years of his administration of the paper's affairs, its circulation had increased from 320 to 800. Mr. Wisdom continued the former policy of the journal during the four months it remained in his hands. The paper was thereafter issued by the Bedrock Publishing Company, with S. H. Shepherd and J. T. Donnelly as editors. April 1, 1882, it underwent at least a partial change of hands, becoming the property of J. T. Donnelly & Company, who remained the owners and publishers until the 9th of May, 1887. A daily edition of the Democrat appeared April 1, 1884, but it suspended about a month later. The publishers stated that they thought that in starting it they were supplying a long felt want, but they had now discovered their mistake and would undertake no more dailies until sure that the demand existed. For convenience in publishing the daily the time of appearance of the weekly was changed from Wednesday to Monday.

From Donnelly & Company, in 1884, the

Democrat passed to Donnelly, Bowen & Company, and in May, 1887' it became the property of Bowen & Small.·

In the fall of 1883 the Daily Sage Brush was instituted in Baker City, by that veteran journalist, J. M. Shepherd. It was independent in politics and claimed to be entirely uncontrolled by the Democrat, although it used the same office and materials. It has been spoken off as a sprightly little sheet and those who know what a vigorous writer and thinker "Old Shep" was will not doubt the accuracy of the description.

A few months before the Bedrock Democrat passed into the hands of Messrs. Bowen & Small, the Sage Brush was absorbed. and the Morning Democrat started. The firm name of the owners has continued unchanged from that time to the present, though I. B. Bowen succeeded F. A. Bowen as manager in August, 1888.

The Democrat has an excellent plant, supplied with engine, cylinder press, job presses, abundance of type of many varieties, and even that most important of all modern inventions for facilitating the rapid production of newspapers, the linotype. It is a member of the Associated Press and gives its readers the latest news from off the wires. Indeed the Democrat has many of the characteristics of the metropolitan daily, though it has not yet attempted the publication of a large special Sunday edition, with a magazine supplement, etc.

Quite recently the Democrat office was visited by a fire, damaging the plant to the extent of a thousand dollars or more. The loss incident to this misfortune most especially to be regretted, was that of the files, which were partially destroyed. They presented a continuous history of the county and of eastern Oregon generally from May, 1870, to the present and were of incalculable value. Not alone the office but all interested in the past annals of this region deplore the fact that the fire reached this priceless treasury of information.

49

BAKER CITY HERALD.

The prosperous times of 1893 in Baker City, brought forth a new aspirant for honors in the journalistic field, the Weekly Epigram, founded and published by John G. Foster. This terse, newsy sheet made its first appearance October 3d. The Epigram espoused the cause of the People's party, just rising into prominence at this time, and during the campaign of 1894 a daily edition was published in connection with the weekly. L. C. Bell purchased a half interest in the property on November 1, 1894, the firm name then being Foster & Bell. These gentlemen continued as owners and publishers until two years later, when F. A. Bowen, formerly of the Huntington Herald, became proprietor. Mr. Bowen guided the Epigram safely through the treacherous shoals which continually beset the course of a newspaper, for nearly three years, disposing of the property, March 1st, 1900, to Wesley Andrews. Then, for a time, the paper was published by H. F. Cassidy, as lessee. Meanwhile the name was changed to the Baker City Herald. Letson Balliet, of the White Swan Mines Company, Limited, purchased the plant for his company on November 12th, 1900, and it has since remained the property of that well known mining corporation. Mr. Balliet, soon after the paper into his control, determined to publish a daily in connection with the weekly, and April 15, 1900, the evening Herald made its bow to the Baker City public. Its political affiliations are with the Republicans and the Herald has, by its forceful and vigorous interpretation of the principles of that party, gained a place among the leading and most important Republican journals of Oregon. As a newspaper, it was successful from the beginning and its well filled columns of local and state news, its energetic and breezy style and clean typographical appearance have gained recognition for it throughout the state and speak volumes for the men who are devoting their whole strength and enthusiasm to its production. Ever alive to the best interests of the community, the Herald is a real aid in advertising the country's advantages and focusing public attention upon some needed public improvement or existing evil, thus contributing to the betterment of conditions. It devotes much attention to the mines of the surrounding region and its columns are always replete with news of these sources of the country's wealth.

Charles W. Hill is at present the publisher and L. Bush Livermore the editor. The mechanical equipment at present consists of an engine, two modern Cottrell presses, one of which was recently built to order for the special use of the Herald, two jobbing presses, typesetting machines, together with the latest styles and series of job and news type.

THE BLUE MOUNTAIN AMERICAN.

This Sumpter paper was founded in February, 1879, by J. Nat Hudson as the Sumpter News. It was conducted and edited by that well known newspaper man until some time in the year 1899, when it passed into the hands of Edward Everett Young, who is the author of its change of name. In April, 1901, Charles Liebenstein succeeded to the editorship and control of the paper, and under his efficient management it has become one of the leading periodicals of the county. It has forged ahead with great rapidity in the matter of accumulating equipment and now few other papers in a town the size of Sumpter can boast a plant of half the value and completeness. The building is now twenty by fifty feet, but it is expected that by next fall, it will be twenty-five feet longer and that the addition will be a two-story one, the upper room being devoted to illustrating entirely. Its equipment at this writing consists of a thirty-three by forty-eight Cranston cylinder press; a twelve by eight Chandler & Gordon platen

press; also another press of the same make, eight by twelve; a ten by fifteen universal platen press; a paper cutter, wire stitcher and largest assortment of job and book type and high grade printing papers to be found between Portland and Salt Lake City. It is expected that a complete stereotyping plant will be inaugurated forthwith.

The paper is a wide-awake, six column, eight-page weekly. In national politics it is Republican, but in local affairs it is strictly independent.

THE SUMPTER REPORTER.

The history of this enterprising daily is quite unique. Its founder, J. Nat Hudson, was practicing law at the time of its inception and not being burdened with a very extensive and exacting practice, and having a printing outfit on hand, he decided to publish for his own amusement as much as anything, an occasional issue of a small paper. Accordingly on December 5, 1900, the first number of volume one of the Sumpter Reporter made its appearance. It was a four-page sheet in length and width about equal to a duodecimo volume, and sold for one cent a copy. The editor must have sounded the right chord to suit the popular ear, for his venture received encouragement and it was rapidly increased in size until it has become a five-column, four-page daily, giving its readers all the local news and the cream of the Associated Press dispatches.

While the size and value of the paper have increased, the price for which it sells remains unchanged, and the people of Sumpter have the advantage of a daily paper for the phenomenally low price of five cents per week or two dollars and a half per year. It is the policy of the paper to limit its circulation to six or eight hundred as more profit will accrue from a business of that size than if the circulation were larger. The equipment consists of a Campbell book press, two job presses and a full supply of type, paper and other requisites of a progressive periodical. The machinery is operated by water power procured from the city water system.

THE SUMPTER MINER.

This important journal was given inception on the 13th of September, 1899, by Marsh & Connella. January 1, 1902, it became the sole property of the junior partner, J. W. Connella, who has owned and operated it since. As its name implies, the Miner is devoted almost solely to the promotion of the master industry of Baker and Grant counties, but it is a mining newspaper, not a strictly technical journal. In its special line it is regarded as authority, having acquired a reputation for accuracy and fidelity in the portrayal of mining conditions and the progress of the industry in this region. Its plant is valued at $5,000, and that it has an abundant supply of modern equipment is evident to one who scans, even superficially, its twelve neat artistic pages. It is undoubtedly one of the leading mining journals of Oregon and a credit to the community that supports it, as well as to its editor and publishers.

HUNTINGTON HERALD.

The publication of the Herald of Huntington was begun by F. A. Bowen, on the 10th of February, 1891, and on the 1st of November, 1896, passed into the hands of John G. Foster, who sold it on October 1st of the following year to the Herald Publishing Company. Originally the paper was independent in politics but in 1894 it showed a strong leaning toward Populism and in 1896 it gave its hearty support to the cause of that party and the Fusionists. At present it is Republican. The paper at this writing is a seven column folio, patent outside, its editor being C. A. Northrup. Its plant and equipments are valued at $1,000.

The history of journalism in Grant county

has been fraught with all the incidents common to the establishment of the press in all interior regions of the west. The growth of the press has kept pace with the settlement of the county, but as the valleys here are small and as there is so much mountainous land that has never been or never will be settled, the progress of journalism has of course been limited. A newspaper, like any other business, cannot thrive without support and the amount of support given it determines, in a great measure, the standard of the newspaper issued. There are no towns large enough to support a daily but the county is fortunate in having four excellent weeklies, two published at the county seat, one at Prairie City and one at Longcreek. As the range and immense stock farms are cut up into smaller tracts and settlements gradually increase, however, Grant county will be able to support larger and better papers and then the owners of the present journals will doubtless be only too glad to make the desired improvements.

The first newspaper printed in Grant county, of which we have any record, was the "City Journal," published at Canyon City by R. H. J. Comer during the years 1868 and 1869. This pioneer sheet was composed of four pages each three columns wide and about eleven by eight inches in size. In 1868 Captain George B. Fearing was a merchant in Canyon City and, being an enterprising business man, determined to advertise his business by issuing a small bulletin. Accordingly he sent to Portland for a small army press and type and learning that Mr. Comer, a California miner, who had come to the Canyon creek mines in 1862, was a printer, he arranged with him to take charge of the paper. The printing outfit arrived in due course of time and on Christmas day, 1868, the City Journal made its bow to the public. The name was so chosen, Editor Comer tells us, because of the limited supply of large type in the office. The editor announced in this issue that the paper would appear semi-occasionally and true to his promise seven numbers were published at intervals of several weeks, the last one appearing September 6, 1869, in which Mr. Comer states his determination to "return to the pick and shovel for a living." During its rather precarious existence the Journal took up the cause of the settlers against The Dalles Military Road Company and did much good in fostering a spirit of progress in the community. Mr. Comer is still living and is now a resident of Prairie City.

Then for several years, Grant county was unrepresented in the journalistic field. But the country was growing rapidly and the more stable pursuits of agriculture and stock raising were taking the place of mining, so that the field was not left long unoccupied. In 1872 the Canyon City Express was founded and though at times its existence was most uncertain, still it survived the perils continually begetting it and seven years later, or in 1879, S. H. Shepherd purchased the property and established the

GRANT COUNTY NEWS.

The initial number of the News appeared Saturday, April 5, 1879, and was printed on an historic press brought from Baker City by Mr. Shepherd. Of this old press, the News says in its issue of January 6, 1887:

"We are prepared to assert that the first press ever brought to the state of Oregon is at present stored in the junkshop of the Grant County News. It was brought to the coast via Cape Horn sometime during the 'forties by the Methodist missionaries, when it knocked around here and there for awhile until the Oregon Spectator was started with it at Oregon City. After the suspension of that paper the press was taken to Lewiston, Idaho, by the American Board of Foreign Missions, where tracts and pamphlets were printed in the Chinook language for the Nez Perce Indian school at Fort Lapwai. The next trace we find of this press is at Idaho City, then at Boise. Later it was removed to Baker City where the Herald was printed on it and after that the Bedrock Democrat. From Baker City it was removed to Canyon City by S. H. Shepherd, who founded the Grant County News. Here it has since remained until the past summer, when we purchased a cylinder press and placed the old pioneer on the retired list."

Whether or not this press was the first one brought to Oregon it is not certain. The Oregon Historical Society claims to have the pioneer press in its collection at Salem, the date of the arrival of this press being 1839. However, the press by which the News was first given to the world is one of the very oldest, if not the oldest, in the state.

J. H. Neal finally came into possession of the Grant County News during the early 'eighties and in 1884 the News Publishing Company was organized by O. P. Cresap, M. D. Clifford, and W. C. McFadden. This company purchased the News in January, 1884. The following July Editor McFadden severed his connection with the firm and for a time the business was in the hands of Robert Cresap and D. I. Asbury. Then J. T. Donnelly of Baker City and Mr. Asbury assumed full control and a year later, in 1885, the latter became sole proprietor and editor. For twelve years he guided the News through the mazes of country journalism, ever improving the paper and broadening its field, until the Grant County News became one of the strong journals of eastern Oregon. However, the News was destined to again change hands, for on October 29, 1898, Perry E. Chandler, formerly superintendent of the Canyon City schools, and W. E. Overholt acquired possession of the plant. Mr. Overholt has since retired from the firm, his interest passing to Robert Glen, who with Mr. Chandler are the present proprietors and editors. Under their painstaking and energetic management the News has attained to a high reputation among the weeklies of eastern Oregon and bids fair to step still higher. At present the News is a seven column folio, all home print. Its columns teem with news from all portions of the county and state and its advertising columns are well filled, thereby testifying to its recognized popularity and standing in the community. The office is equipped with a cylinder news press, a job press and with all the other auxiliaries necessary to conduct a first-class printing establishment. In politics the News is independent. Both Mr. Chandler and Mr. Glen are possessed of a genial, courteous personality and these qualities, combined with ability, have much to do with the success of the Grant County News.

THE BLUE MOUNTAIN EAGLE,

published by Patterson & Ward, at Canyon City, is one of the leading weeklies in eastern Oregon and is in every way typical of the best there is in country journalism. Its four pages are always well filled with news of the county and state and the business interests of the county are well represented in its advertising columns. The journal occupies its own building, a fine two-story frame structure situated on the main street, and the office is one of the best equipped smaller offices in the state, containing a new Country Campbell news press, a National jobber, and the latest models and faces of type and other necessary equipment. In politics the Eagle is content to be independent, serving the interests of no one party but the people in general.

The Long Creek Eagle was established at Long Creek, November 26, 1886, by Ed. C. Allen, who remained its owner and editor until September 5, 1889, when Orin L. Patterson, one of the present proprietors, purchased the plant. In February, 1896, Mr. Patterson changed the name of the journal to the Blue Mountain Eagle. George F. Ward, the other member of the firm, purchased a half interest

in the business, May 20, 1900. The following August the paper was removed to Canyon City, where it has since been published. Both Mr. Patterson and Mr. Ward are very genial and very successful newspaper men.

THE PRAIRIE CITY MINER,

a journal devoted especially to the interests of Prairie City and the upper end of the John Day valley, made its first appearance May 19, 1900, published by C. H. Marsh, J. W. Connella and Henry Stuart. It was an eight page, four column newspaper, of clean typographical appearance, newsy and bright and well edited, characteristics which it retains to the present day. In the spring of 1901, the Miner Publishing Company succeeded to the ownership of the property and again in the summer of the same year the plant changed hands, this time being purchased by J. L. Hoffman and C. K. Cunningham, who in turn sold to Glen & Chandler of the Grant County News, its present proprietors. They acquired possession of the property, December 26, 1901. W. W. Watson, a veteran Oregon newspaper man, is the present editor and manager, having taken charge of the journal February 6th last.

LONG CREEK RANGER.

The Ranger was established August 17, 1900, by Charles A. Coe, who is its present editor and owner. In size the Ranger is a six column folio patent inside, and is issued Fridays. The office is equipped with a Washington hand press, a Chandler & Price Gordon jobber, and the paper issued is a very neat one. Politically, the Long Creek Ranger is an independent Republican paper.

The John Day Sentinel was founded by W. A. Logue in October, 1896, succeeding the Alliance Publishing Company. The Sentinel was conducted as a Populist organ until January 1, 1898, when the Grant County News purchased the property. Since then there has been no newspaper at John Day, though there is a probability that one will be established there in the near future.

THE TIMES-HERALD.

The East Oregon Herald was the second paper started in Harney county, D. L. Grace began its publication in the fall of 1887, his wife, Mrs. Nellie Grace, assisting in the work at least part of the time. In the spring of 1890 W. C. Byrd & Son acquired the property. They began the issue of a four page, five column, semi-weekly in 1891, and ran the paper as a twice-a-week for a few years, eventually abandoning the plan and changing the paper to a weekly again. July 22, 1896, it consolidated with another paper known as the Times, and became the Times-Herald, under which name it has ever since been published. January 6, 1897, Byrd Brothers took charge of the Times-Herald, vice the firm of W. C. Byrd & Company, and in the spring of the following year Julian Byrd succeeded to the interests of his brother, becoming sole proprietor. The paper has always shown a progressive spirit and has worked faithfully for the upbuilding of its home town during all the years of its existence. Consistently Democratic in politics, it has ever been maintaining, however, an independent and manly spirit, not alone in this, but in all things. It has kept a complete file of all its papers from the very first number. These valuable records the editor very kindly placed at our disposal and to their pages we have been greatly indebted for valuable material.

At present the paper is a four-page, seven column weekly, all home print. It has just purchased a complete modern plant, including a big Cottrell press, a typesetting machine, an engine, a paper cutter, etc., in all weighing something over six. This, with the outfit already in the office, will give the paper the best equipped printing plant in Harney county.

HARNEY COUNTY NEWS.

In the year 1892, some time after he had severed his connection with East Oregon Herald, D. L. Grace instituted and established a paper known as the Harney County News, independent in politics. In 1896 it espoused the cause of Populism and became the organ of the People's party of its home county. Two years later it passed into the hands of the Boyd Brothers and in March, 1899, Mark M. Boyd sold his interest to F. E. Wilmarth, who was thereafter for a short time associated in its publication with D. C. Boyd. On May 15, 1899, Mr. Wilmarth bought his partner out and the plant is now owned and operated by him and Mina Wilmarth, his wife. To them personally and to the files of their paper we must likewise offer acknowledgement for much held rendered in the preparation of this volume. The paper is a bright, ably edited, eight page, four column weekly, all home print. It is Republican in politics.

HARNEY VALLEY ITEMS.

To this journal we are also indebted for valuable assistance in the use of files. It, too, is Republican in its political faith and allegiance and to that party it has constantly adhered for a number of years, though it was nonpartisan at first. Its initial number appeared July, 1885, so that to it belongs the honor of pioneership in Harney county journalism. This pioneer journal was printed upon a Washington hand press and the name at the head of its editorial columns was Horace Dillard. After nearly two years of successful newspaper work Mr. Dillard retired, his successor being J. M. Vaughn, who was its editor and publisher for the ensuing three years. Mr. Dillard then repurchased the plant and again assumed editorial charge of it. For more than a year it was in his hands, but in the fall of 1891 W. Y. King purchased it. In the spring of 1893 a local publishing company bought the plant and gave the editorial management to its former editor, Mr. Dillard.   That fall Charles Newell took the paper.   It has undergone several changes of ownership and been in the hands of several different editors since, its present editorial head being C. N. Cochrane.

MALHEUR GAZETTE.

The Malheur Gazette, published at Vale, is the pioneer newspaper of Malheur county, having been established in 1888. The Gazette was founded at Vale, where it has since remained, by S. H. Shepherd, who continued to act as its publisher and editor for several years, finally disposing of his interests to the Gazette Publishing Company. This company owned and conducted the property until the first of this year, when the present management assumed charge. The Gazette is a seven column folio journal of neat typographical appearance and fully alive to the best interests of Vale and the county in general. The Gazette supports the Republican party now, though it was founded as a Democratic paper.

THE ONTARIO ARGUS.

is the leading newspaper of Malheur county and one of the neatest printed and best edited weeklies in eastern Oregon.   The Argus owns the building it occupies in Ontario and is published in a well equipped office, including a newspaper cylinder press, a job press, a complete assortment of modern display and body type, a new Chandler & Price paper cutter and other auxiliaries usually found in an up-to-date establishment.   Six pages are issued and their well filled advertising and news columns betoken the liberal patronage of an interested reading public.   The Argus is Republican in politics.

Five years ago this journal first appeared, being then known as the District Silver Advocate, and published at Vale.   As the name implies, the newspaper was established to advance the interests of the silver party in this judicial district.   Burt Venable was the first proprietor and John E. Roberts the editor.   The initial number appeared January 6, 1897.   Subsequently Mr. Venable transferred his interests in the enterprise to E. R. Murray, and during the latter part of 1897 the paper appeared for a short time as a daily.   A year later John E. Roberts secured sole control of the newspaper and moved the plant to Ontario, from which place it has since been issued.   On November 28, 1900, the Advocate was purchased by Don Carlos Boyd, who changed the journal's name to the "Ontario Argus" and transferred its political allegiance to the Republican party.   Ex-Judge J. T. Clement became associated in business with Mr. Boyd about a year ago, and under this joint ownership and management, the Argus is at present published.

THE ONTARIO DEMOCRAT

is also one of Malheur county's progressive weekly journals and is owned and edited by Will R. King, one of the best known politicians in Oregon, having been the Fusionist party's candidate for governor in 1898.

The Democrat was first published at Vale as the Malheur County Herald, by William Ugholl and was established in 1898.   Subsequently William Plughoff acquired possession of the property and retained it until March, 1901, when Almer G. King and Paul Delaney purchased the plant.   They moved it to Ontario in February, 1902.   W. R. King was the next to try his fortune in steering the paper through the narrow and treacherous channels which lie in the course of journalism, he having assumed charge May 19th last.   Thus far he has succeeded admirably.   The Democrat office is equipped with modern necessities and conveniences and the four page paper issued bears evidence of excellent workmanship in both the mechanical and editorial departments.

As elsewhere in the United States the newspaper graveyard in Malheur county is filled with graves of many unsuccessful ventures. Some accomplished their mission during their brief existence; some did not reap such a reward. All contributed their ideas and experience toward the enlightenment of mankind so that even of the least successful some good may be said; none were absolute failures.

The Ontario Mattock was founded March 14, 1899, by Edward L. King and after a year's existence was sold to John E. Roberts, who consolidated it with the District Silver Advocate.

The Westfall Independent commenced publication at Westfall in December, 1900, under the management of J. E. Roberts, but survived only a few months.

The Ontario News was one of the pioneer journals of the county, having been established during the campaign of 1892, by W. E. Bowen. The News was conducted first as a Democratic paper and later as a Populist journal. The News lived six years, or until 1898, when the plant was removed from the county.

The first newspaper published in Malheur county was the Ontario Atlas, established in 1886 by a Mountain Home printer. This pioneer journal was printed on an army press and was a newsy and interesting, though small, sheet. After a precarious life of three or four months, the paper was revived by W. G. Cuddy, of Nampa, Idaho, who published it in Ontario until after Vale was chosen as the county seat in 1888, when the plant was taken to that town.

CHAPTER V.

REMINISCENT.

Possibly some ambitious reader of this volume will in the future win fame by making an exhaustive collection of pioneer incidents, presenting them in graphic and fascinating form. Could such a work be properly prepared it would be read with profound interest. The long toilsome journeys across the wide, sky-bordered buffalo range of the prairies and over the towering mountains or through the rugged passes were rich in adventures of the most thrilling nature, while the constant menace of the red man, the intrigue, diplomacy and chicanery resorted to by the immigrants to avoid trouble with them, the frequent forays of these depredators upon cattle, horses and even children, the hot pursuits and the occasional battles throw around the days when the plains were populated with ever advancing prairie schooners a rich glamour of romance.

But the days of adventure were not over when the pioneers safely ran the gauntlet of ten thousand dangers on the plains and in the mountain fastnesses and eventually came to a halt in the far away "westmost west." He was still in the midst of savages, and moreover he was in a new environment and confronted with new conditions, so that it became necessary for him to work out for himself a thousand economic problems. It is probable that could all the adventures of the pioneer peoples of this section be collected and set in order a marvelous array of tragedy, pathos and humor would be the result. The limits and province of this work and the limitations of its authors render an attempt to embody any extensive collection of incidents herein decidedly out of the question, but realizing that a few anecdotes might better preserve the spirit and flavor of early times than pages of descriptive history, we will give a few simple stories of "the brave days of old."

A REMINISCENCE OF THE INDIAN WAR.

O. P. Cresap, one of the earliest pioneers of Grant county and now an esteemed resident of Canyon City, served as a guide to General Howard's army during the Bannock and Piute war of 1878 and in that capacity witnessed much of this campaign in Grant and Umatilla counties. His account of the adventures in which he participated during this war is interesting and is as follows:

Tom Meyers and I left Elk creek on the morning of July 2, 1878, bound for Canyon City. We had no particular object in view except to visit the city and did not know there was an Indian war in progress. We arrived at the old Dribblesby ranch, now known as the Smith ranch, about noon, intending to stop there for dinner. I went up and knocked at the door but could get no answer, so went back of the house to see where the family had gone. But I could find no one and going into the house discovered that things there were undisturbed. I concluded that the occupants were away in the hills. We fed our horses and secured a cold lunch for ourselves, then rode on. At the next ranch I found no one at home; likewise at the next. Then I became suspicious and the more so because I saw a man scouting near us. So I made bold to inquire of him the reason for this condition of affairs and learned for the first time that the Bannocks and Piutes were on the warpath and that he was one of General Howard's scouts. As he was going to Canyon City, we rode along with him

and learned more of the trouble. He said that Howard was south of Canyon City in pursuit of the Indians, who were crossing the range and headed toward Long Creek.

At Canyon City there was a martial stir in the air and all was excitement. Most of the men of the town were under arms and a portion of the women and children had been removed to the mining tunnels west of the town. A shipment of one hundred stands of arms together with ammunition had just been received from The Dalles in response to an appeal from the citizens, who found themselves short of weapons, and every able bodied man and boy in the town was well equipped and ready to give an account of himself, should the redskins appear. As soon as I learned enough of the particulars to convince me that the people at Elk creek were in danger I made preparations for an immediate return. Before midnight I was well on my way accompanied by Tom and two others who joined us. That was one of the darkest nights I have ever seen and we had to walk our horses as soon as we reached the foothills. We reached Elk creek, or Susanville, about nine o'clock the next morning and in a short time the six or seven families there, the Blake, Bison, Mael and other families, had packed what few necessities were required for the trip and with the exception of John Blake, the merchant who offered to stay and keep watch until we could return, the party headed southward.

After we were well on our way, John Austin and I left the company with the intention of reconnoitering and if possible, discover the exact whereabouts of the redskins, who were thought to be over toward Fox valley. We took a northeastward course. We saw no signs of Indians that day and camped that night on Long creek, about eight miles above the town of that name.

The next morning we descended the creek, soon reaching the open country. We passed Thomas Keeney's place but looked in vain for the next ranch house. I knew about where the house was situated and could not account for my failure to see it now. As we came a little nearer we noticed that the chickens were out of their yard and huddled together in the branches of a tree. By this time we were close to where the house had stood and looking again very closely, we easily solved the mystery of its non-appearance, for there lay a pile of ruins still warm. Although we were aware that the the Indians were probably not a great many miles away, we did not believe they were very close to us and rather ascribed the fire to accidental causes than to the redskins. The ruins of the next ranch house were smoldering when we reached it and then it dawned upon that we were probably close to the trail of the redskins. From that on we proceeded with great caution. The next house was burning and afar off we could see the flames leaping skyward and the smoke curling up in great clouds. Here we saw our first Indian, a scout, but evidently he thought that we were advance scouts of the army for he quickly rode out of sight. Little did we think we were so close upon the Indians' heels, but in a few minutes we came in sight of the party of Indians which had passed through Long Creek the day previously and which was now headed toward the Middle Fork of the John Day.

The inhabitants of this town and settlers living nearby had constructed a log fort and stockade here and in it were gathered the population of the town and those who had come in from surrounding ranches. When the Indians reached this place they attempted to send a small force into the fort on the pretext of being friendly Indians. Wisely and fortunately for those in the fort the warriors were refused admission. Further parley followed, the Indians endeavoring to effect an entrance through some ruse and each time meeting with a repulse. Finally when they saw that the whites could not be deceived and that the fort was too strong to be attacked successfully, the war party passed by within two hundred yards of the fort without offering in any way to molest property. Had the redskins succeeded in gaining an entrance to the fort a massacre of the whites would probably have followed.

Of the Indians there were probably between six and seven hundred, mostly Bannocks and Piutes. The old men, women and children formed the van, the fighting men the rear. With the Indians were between two and three thousand head of horses and these were herded and driven by those unable to fight. The wickiups, personal property and plunder were packed on poles which were dragged by the horses. This advance did most of the plundering and pillaging.

Here at Long Creek we met Colonel Bernard, who was the real fighter of the army. He asked me where I had come from and what I had seen of the Indians and I told him all I knew. I told him of conditions at Susanville and he very kindly placed a small detachment of troops at our disposal to guard property at Elk creek. Austin accompanied the soldiers back. With the army were about thirty scouts, recruited mostly from Arizona, and in command of Rube Robbins. While these scouts were well acquainted with Idaho and that portion of Oregon lying near the southern boundary, they were unfamiliar with this region and Colonel Bernard was looking for a man who could pilot them northward through the mountains. He proposed that I go with them and I accepted his offer to act as guide, though no actual enlistment was required of me.

General Howard's plan was to make no attempt to drive the Indians, but rather to follow them closely and keep them headed northward if possible, planning to surround and capture them on the Columbia river. He was afraid that if the Indians were pushed too hard they might make a dash across the Columbia before he could place troops and boats there in sufficient numbers to check them while he cut off their retreat. During the whole time the Indians were marching northward troops had been gathering along the Columbia river, but their movements were very slow. Up to this time but one battle had been fought in this region, the battle of Silver Creek, in which the Indians held their own and might be said to have been victorious. As to General Howard's ability as an Indian fighter, opinions differ, but that he was sincere in his belief that it would be disastrous policy to push the Indians too hard, there is no doubt in my mind. The Indians did not go very far out of their way to commit depredations, but confined themselves strictly to their line of march, evidently wishing to delay hostilities until they were reinforced by their hoped for Umatilla allies.

Thus the army moved slowly, going from Long Creek north across the Middle Fork of the John Day, thence to the North Fork and down on Camas prairie toward Pendelton. Our route was marked on every hand by evidences of destruction and carnage. Some times we found ranch buildings razed to the ground by fire; again simply ransacked, furniture destroyed, clothes, carpets, etc., stolen, windows broken and goods scattered about. Occasionally we found a white man murdered by the savages. At all the ranches the stock had been driven away or killed, and one had only to notice the dead horses and cattle along the road to know that the Indians had passed that way. At one ranch on Birch creek we found a baby carriage drawn out under the arbor leading to the door of the house and in the carriage was placed a dead colt. At another place, evidently a dairy farm, in Camas prairie, our attention was attracted by a huge pile of butter stacked up near the house. From the appearance of it the little Indians had used it as a toboggan slide. As we approached one place we noticed a high white pyramid. At first we could not make out what it was but as we drew nearer we saw that it was composed of dead sheep, several hundred of them. One of the most pitiful and frequent sights was that of a dead

lamb tied between two posts so that it could not move and under its body the ashes of a small fire showing that it had been burned to death. Around these dead lambs were always small moccasin tracks, indicating that this was the work of the children.

Our scouts had frequent skirmishes with the Indians but none of enough consequence to be worth relating. The scouts always moved in front and were followed by the cavalry, the infantry, pack train and artillery bringing up the rear. Next in command after General Howard were Colonel Forsythe and Brevet-Colonel Bernard. When we reached the headwaters of the North Fork there were two courses for the Indians to leave the country, by Butter creek or by the Grande Ronde river. By a little manoeuvering we turned them from the Grande Ronde and they started down Butter creek. Here we fought a battle.

A succession of low hills slopes away westward, forming an ideal place for the Indians to make a stand and they did make a stand. When we came up, the hillside was fairly alive with Indians and they commenced heavy firing in our direction. The scouts fell back, the cavalry was ordered to the front and formed into two lines and the men were then ordered to dismount. Then the gatling gun, the only one with the army, was brought up and in less time than it takes to tell it, was dashing out in front of the army and on its way up the first hill. The redskins were on the second hill, while between the two there was a smaller elevation within two hundred yards of the Indians. Slowly the horses mounted the first hill, reached the summit, and then to the astonishment of all, kept on its way to the smaller elevation. The Indians could not understand such apparently foolhardy actions and they stood thunderstruck, not even offering to fire. Had they not been overcome by the audacity of the act our men would certainly have met death. As the lead horses reached the summit of the elevation they whirled around; the carriage was unlimbered and in an instant a perfect storm of bullets was carrying death and destruction to the ranks of the dusky warriors. The redskins scrambled from their hiding places and rushed pell mell over the summit of the highest hill and into the timber. Our troops came to support the gun, but were not needed. The officers did not allow the soldiers to take full advantage of this victory and the result was that the Indians were pursued only a short distance. George Smith, a soldier was killed in action and several were wounded, though none mortally. After the battle scores of dead horses covered the ground telling plainly of the deadly work of the bullets. This fight took place between the 10th and 15th of July. The casualties among the Indians must have been great, though I never learned just how great. I had followed the gatling gun up the hill and so saw the whole fight very plainly.

The defeated braves, closely pursued by the army, pushed northward and as is well known were defeated in battle by Miles near Pendleton. With the death of their chief and leader, Egan, the Indians lost courage, and executing a flank movement commenced to retreat southward. We followed and came up with them a few days later on Lake creek, which empties into the North Fork. Here the Indians made another and final stand and had they possessed the courage which accompanies success they might have made us pay more dearly for victory.

This time they chose for their battle ground a high table rock covering several acres and with nearly perpendicular sides. From its top they bade defiance to the cavalry and scouts, who were under Colonel Forsythe. The trail over this high plateau led through a small gap which could easily be defended against hundreds by a handful of brave men. The scouts, led by Rube Robbins, were ambushed while attempting to gain the summit of this rock through the gap and as a result suffered the loss of one man killed and several wounded,

among the latter being Robbins himself. Kennedy, the man who was killed, was wounded in the arm and bled to death. I found him on the field and after giving him a drink of water from my canteen, went for the surgeon and informed him of Kennedy's condition. Then I went to look after another wounded man named Campbell. When the surgeon found Kennedy he was dead.

The cavalry were drawn up in line for a charge when Colonel Bernard came up to me and asked if I knew of any way to dislodge the redskins without great loss of life. I pointed to a high steep hill to the west, which overlooked the table rock, and told him if he could gain its summit, it would be an easy matter to take the Indians in the rear. The troopers having ascended the hill in safety soon dislodged the Indians and forced them to retreat.

This last defeat was too much for the Indians and soon after they divided into two bands, one going south by way of the Greenhorn mountains and the other down the Dixie range. The party which returned by way of the Dixie range killed a Frenchman near Robinsonville and Jimmie Varderman on Elk creek. The Indians kept in the mountains as much as possible, however, and destroyed little if any property. The war was now at an end and as I could be of no further service to the army I helped to take Campbell, the wounded man, down Burnt river, after which I returned to my home at Susanville.

THE HAPPY VALLEY MASSACRE.

Brief mention has been made in a former chapter of the death of George C. Smyth and his son John, who were residents of Happy Valley, in Harney county, during the Indian war of 1878. The story is graphically told by a correspondent who signs himself, "J. W. E.," to the Baker City Bedrock Democrat. The facts of the case were all learned from the Indians themselves, as no white men witnessed the massacre, though Darius Smyth, brother of John, at one time looked down into the valley from the surrounding foothills. He saw the Indians around his father's house, but saw no signs of hositilities at that time and thought his father and brother had escáped to the hills. J. W. E.'s story follows:

Under the smiling skies of a bright June day in 1878 the grass-clad and cliff-ribbed heights of the Stein's mountains in southeastern Oregon's great plateau, stood in ghostly silence. As the sun's dying rays left in purple shadow the pretty vale of Happy Valley, wherein a half-dozen hardy pioneer families were conquering out joyous homes from the isolated riches of the wilderness, not a hint was in the peaceful air of the death stalking thitherward with the soulless ferocity of the merciless tiger.

Sixty-five miles away the sunset gun at Fort Harney had marked the lowering of freedom's banner in the post garrisoned by two troops of cavalry. Some thirty miles further, at the Malheur agency, the redmen were on the verge of open revolt. Southward from Happy valley, in the state of Nevada the famous warlike Bannock Indians, under the fiery war chief Egan, he of the many battle scars, were no longer restrained, nor their northern brethren, by the one-time strong force of 1,200 hated bluecoats at Fort Harney.

The sun's level rays bathed in dying splendor the long mounting slopes sweeping above Happy Valley. Here and there upon the mountain ramparts were small clusters of juniper and mountain mahogany trees. But the eyes had a practically unbroken sweep for miles to right and left and upward over the weirdly beautiful heights. Far off, up the slopes and near the crowning cliffs some of the settlers saw a moving speck, which, swiftly moving downward, resolved into an evidently expert horseman, spurring his steed as though pursued by a fiend. Approaching the first ranch house, the vacquero, in the terse sentences of the frontiersman, told how since sunrise he had ridden eighty long miles over parched sage brush plains and pathless mountains; that the pitiless Bannock Indians were having their war and death dance and that the settlers must flee to Fort Harney for their lives.

Hastily rigging their wagons, through the long summer night, with their wives, young folks and helpless little ones, the pioneer men of Happy valley dróve onward in flight to Fort Harney.

A father and son named Smyth had left at their deserted ranches about one hundred head of good horses, and, since they hoped the Indians had swung aside from the little settlement, they concluded to return and endeavor to bring off their horses. With the pioneer's ever firm courage, they had no premonition of their impending fate as at the fort they bade what proved their last farewell to their faithful wives and loving children.

The father and son reached the deserted homes without having seen a single sign of marauding red warriors. That night they slept unmolested in their cabin.

The next day was Sunday. A little Spanish cowboy returned to the headquarters ranch of the Miller. & French Cattle Company, thirty miles from Happy valley, with the information that he had seen a great drove of stock coming down the Stein's mountains to invade his company's ranges. "There must have been more than a thousand of them," said he in broken English, "and the rushing beasts raised a great cloud' of dust." Manager French told the boy that what he had seen were beasts, but that each one had but two legs and that they were more cruel and savage than any four-footed beasts on earth. And the stockman was right. The bright eyes of the Spanish lad had from afar seen the onward march of one thousand Bannock Indians, the men, women and children, each and all on murder bent. The dust cloud was from the beating hoofs of the savages' ponies and the trailing lodge poles. The Indians were en route to join their northern brethren in an Oregon raid of murder and destruction.

Unknown to the advancing savages, the two doomed whites watched their foes approach. There was absolutely no means or way of escape since the treeless foothills of the mountains extended for miles around the valley, and, in the direction of the great Harney valley, which is about seventy-five by forty miles in extent. Hence, expert riflemen and fearless American pioneers that they were, the father and son resolved to make the Indians pay dearly for their barbarity.

At high noon on that dreamy, peaceful day of that long ago June, the redmen entered the head of the little valley and encircled the first ranch. Finding this deserted they fired the buildings, and the two Smyths, one-half mile away, saw the flames rising high in the air. In disorganized marching order, the Indians, led by their chiefs and great warriors, streamed onward toward the Smyth home. As they neared the little cluster of buildings, but the foremost yet nearly a quarter of a mile distant, two sharp reports followed two little puffs of steam-white smoke from the paleface cabin and two Indians fell from their horses, one dead and the other sorely wounded. The ranch cabin was quickly surrounded, and from the cover of rocks and juniper trees the savages kept up a constant fire on their prey. But the unequal battle was with heavy loss to the besiegers. The showing of even so little as a part of a dusky head, a hand or foot seemed to draw an avenging rifle ball.

All through the long afternoon the savages played hideous hide-and-seek in trying to down their partly sheltered human game. As the sun dropped low, fully fifteen warriors, one a great chief, were bloody corpses, and several dozen others of the reds had been more or less hard hit by the rifle balls speeding from one hundred and fifty to two hundred yards. The circle drew near and many crawled, under the sable shades, to within a very few yards of the cabin. Some straw shedding near the cabin, or leaning against it, was fired, and the pioneer home caught. Then the end came swiftly to the dauntless whites. Fighting with the Anglo-Saxon's unquenchable, ice-cool courage, the father and son came from their blazing home to their death. The elder hero had been horribly shot through the hips. He was partly supported by his worthy son. Spartan courage never bore itself more nobly. The fierce firelight shone on a scene worthy the brush of the greatest artist who ever lived. With the world-famed grit of the Yankee at bay, the twain faced their merciless foes. Their rifles spoke not vainly, until they were beaten down and quickly butchered.

A few days later the bluecoats of a cavalry troop found the charred bones of the father and son in the ruins of their pioneer cabin home and reverently laid the remains to rest

SIDELIGHTS ON PIONEER DAYS.

Until after the war of 1878, the Bannock and Piute Indians terrorized the settlers in Jordan valley almost continuously. For several years the government kept troops at Camp Three Forks and Camp Lyons and even the large ranches were at times garrisoned, equipped with stacks of arms, howitzers and other defensive weapons. "Sheep Ranch" was for several months, in 1866 and 1867, headquarters for a detachment of United States troops under command of Lieutenant Koppinger, a son-in-law of James G. Blaine. Sheep Ranch was a station on the old Winnemucca stage road and attacks by the Indians on the stages of this line were of frequent occurrence. During periods of special aggressiveness on the part of the Indians a telegraph station was maintained here, the line reaching Boise and Silver City on the north and Winnemucca on the south. Ernest L. Merrill, a lad of thirteen, who had learned the Morse alphabet in California, was at various times pressed into service by army officers. His several periods spent at the keyboard amounted to a continuous service of almost a year. In perilous times he was indispensable to the officers and through him many lives and

much treasure were saved, and yet the government and its officers whom he so faithfully served have been so forgetful of moral obligations that his labors are to-day still unrewarded.

Journeys over the old stage lines were fraught with great danger. Many brutal murders were committed by the Indians, but it sometimes happened that they were badly worsted in encounters with brave stage drivers and fearless passengers. The pioneers of Jordan valley still residing there tell both laughable and heartrending stories of the troubles that beset the stages in the early days.

In one instance the Silver City stage, Nathan Dixon driving, was surrounded by a howling band of Snake Indians near Summit Springs. In the stage were fifteen men and one woman. All the men had small arms and several had repeating rifles. One man had with him a brace of bull dogs. The savage yells of the Indians struck terror to every man's heart. They fled from the stage and undertook to hide in the sage brush. The stage driver at once opened fire on the savages. The woman passenger seized a rifle from a frightened male companion, called the bull dogs, and jumped from the stage. The dogs obeyed her orders and went after the Indians tooth and toenails. She rested the rifle on a wheel of the stage and began firing. One redskin was killed and another wounded. In the meantime the driver had dropped down among his horses and was doing good execution with his revolvers. In ten minutes the dogs, the woman, and the driver had routed the Indians and sent them out of range. The faint hearts hurriedly gathered in from the sage brush retreats and the balance of the way was pursued in peace and, by the male contingent, in silence. They doubtless reflected that there were more Molly Pitchers than one in the world. Possibly they changed their minds on the woman's rights question. It is said that when the hotel at Silver City was reached they registered under assumed names.

One day in June, 1878, the stage arrived at

Sheep Ranch from Winnemucca. It was known that the Indians were in strong force in the country north and east. The driver telegraphed to Boise for information concerning their whereabouts and for instructions, not knowing whether or not it was safe to proceed. The line manager at Boise, desiring to get the mails through regardless of risk to driver and passengers, misrepresented the state of affairs and wired back that the Indians were camped far to the west of the road and that the stage should proceed to Boise. George McCutcheon was driving and with him was one passenger. When well on their way and far from any point where assistance could be had, they were attacked by the Indians. McCutcheon laid whip to the horses and a furious race began. It was soon discovered that the pursuers were gaining on them and they realized the necessity of loosening the horses, mounting them and leaving the stage. The passenger was the first on the ground. He had unhooked the traces of one horse and was about to mount when McCutcheon said "Don't take that horse, he stumbles." The passenger mounted the other horse and McCutcheon mounted the stumbler. The horses were still fastened together with lines and neck yokes. As they flew madly over the road breast straps and lines were cut with their pocket knives and the horses were separated. They were now lengthening the distance between themselves and the Indians. There was hope of escape. Five minutes later McCutcheon's horse stumbled and fell and looking back, the fleeing passenger saw the Indians circling around him and firing into his prostrate form. The passenger (whose name we have been unable to learn), escaped, reaching Boise in safety. McCutcheon was one of the noted and respected stage drivers of the early days and his death was lamented by all who knew him. His heroic, unselfish act, in himself mounting the untrustworthy horse, speaks volumes in praise of his noble character.

William Hemmingway was another of the well known drivers of those days, who was ambushed and murdered by the Piutes in 1878 near the Owyhee ferry, while enroute without passengers between Sheep Ranch and Silver City. Shortly before his death he and his passengers had an unusual experience with the Indians near Sheep Ranch, while on the down trip. As passengers he had with him Mrs. T. C. Fletcher, of Ontario, then a resident of Jordan Valley, and a lady friend whose name the writer has forgotten. Beside him on the driver's seat was Jack Bowden, Wells Fargo express agent. It was just prior to the battle of South Mountain and the Indians were making their way from the Oregon to the Idaho side of the Snake river. It is related by Mrs. Fletcher that on entering a narrow canyon near Jordan Valley they suddenly came in sight of a large band of Indians, a short distance in front. It was not possible to turn around, there was nothing to do but to drive ahead. The two men drew their revolvers and prepared for a fight while the women resigned themselves to the horrible fate which seemed inevitably in store for them. As soon as the Indians discovered the stage, they halted, an order was given and they formed in two rows, one on either side of the narrow road. Hemmingway drove on. As he neared the lines of savages he noted that their guns were grounded. He drew the horses down to a slow walk and entered the passage way. Every Indian stood erect, hideously daubed with war paint and gazing stoically across the path. Not a move was made nor a word uttered. The stage passed slowly down the line and when the end was reached the Indians closed ranks and marched away without a demonstration of any character. Breathing prayers of thankfulness for their safety but puzzled and bewildered by the strange actions of the redskins, the occupants of the stage rode on, scarcely daring to break the silence until the protection of the fortified ranch was reached. The only explanation offered of the Indians' unusual behavior was that they were massing by previous arrangement to attack the whites, were then on their way to the rendezvous and did not want to arouse the people of Jordan Valley until their plans for concerted action were consummated.

In 1886 J. P. Merrill secured a hay contract from the government. He cut and stacked under this contract two thousands dollars' worth of hay, receiving his pay in government scrip. There was but little money in the country and Mr. Merrill was unable to cash his scrip. Shortly after being paid for the hay his horses were stolen by a band of Indians and he could not secure others in the neighborhood. He must go elsewhere both for cash and horses and The Dalles was the nearest point where he could hope to find either. It was late in the fall, but he borrowed a horse and joined a party of freighters bound for The Dalles. The country was infested by thieving, murderous bands of Indians, and the party was compelled to keep constantly on guard to escape them. It was their custom to travel each day until sundown, then make camp as if for the night, eat their suppers, roll up in blankets and lie down, and about eleven o'clock quietly break camp and move on several miles, secreting themselves as well as they could in some sheltered spot at a distance from the road, where they would camp without fires and rest. The Indian habit of making attacks in the early morning hours made it possible for the travelers to follow this deceiving course successfully. In due time they reached the summit of the Blue mountains near what is now the boundary between Baker and Grant counties. Here they were overtaken by a heavy storm and were effectually snowed in, the snow falling to a depth of fifteen feet. The freighters fortunately had a store of supplies. It was not sufficient for their needs, however, in the event of a long imprisonment and this they were doomed to endure. They were held in the mountains until spring and at times suffered severely from hunger and cold. It was many weeks before they

were able to make excursions to points any distance from camp. There was but little game to be had and no habitations could be reached, but they managed to exist, and as soon as the snow began to go off, they pushed on toward The Dalles, arriving there in March, 1867.

Mr. Merrill succeeded in exchanging his scrip for cash, purchased a stock of supplies and secured four horses. After a two weeks' stay at The Dalles, he started with another party of four freighters on the return trip. They were attacked two or three times by small bands of Indians but had no trouble in beating them off, as the attacks were made during the day. They pursued the same tactics at night that Mr. Merrill and his former party had followed. They were having a comparatively uneventful journey and had reached a point on the Malheur river near its junction with the Snake. Here they were met by a train of emigrants encamped for a few days' rest. The freighters decided to camp with them for a short time as their animals were becoming jaded and worn. Mr. Merrill was anxious concerning his family, to whom he had expected to return months before. On the morning of the second day after their stop he endeavored to persuade the freighters to move on. Failing in this he determined to go ahead alone, and started, against the advice of the campers. For two days he traveled without discovering any signs of Indians and was congratulating himself on the final, successful termination of his journey. He was within half a day's journey of home when night overtook him. He followed the usual plan in making camp for the night. On the morning of the last day out he arose, and while preparing breakfast, discovered signs of the recent presence of deer near the camp. Hastily swallowing his food, he took his gun and struck out on the trail of the deer. He was near home and, as he thought, safe from Indian attacks. He followed the deer tracks for an hour or more, and succeeded in shooting one. It was a small animal and, shouldering it, he started for the camp. When he reached it, judge of his consternation and wrath when he learned that his horses, which he had left securely tied, together with all his packs, were gone. He soon discovered the trail and pursued. After following the trail for five or six miles he sighted a band of fifteen or twenty Indians and in front of them, his horses, which were being driven away with all his supplies. Realizing that he was powerless to contend with such a savage horde, he resolved to hasten home, secure the assistance of soldiers and neighbors and then attempt the recovery of the animals and supplies, and the punishment of the thieves. He eventually reached home, after a toilsome journey lasting six months, poorer than when he started, but gladly welcomed by family and friends, who had long since given him up as dead. A company was at once formed and the pursuit of the Indians commenced but neither Indians nor horses were found.

This is a fair illustration of the trials and hardships to which the pioneers of eastern Oregon were subjected.

THE NAMING OF BURNT RANCH.

Grant County News, Aug. 6, 1885.

Over in Wasco county, on the main John John Day river and near the mouth of Bridge creek, is a ranch and postoffice called Burnt Ranch, and it came to be thus named from the following circumstances:

In 1866 James Clark was occupying the position of a pioneer settler there and had a very comfortable home. Along in the early fall his wife had departed for the Willamette valley to visit her people. One bright September morning Jim and his brother-in-law, George Masterson, forded the John Day river and were cutting up a lot of drift wood on the opposite bars. Suddenly they discovered a band of Indians rushing down the hill from the direction of the Ochoco country. The

50

men had left their rifles at the house and they thought there was a possible show to reach them ahead of the Indians. They unhitched the horses and climbing on bareback, forded the river and raced for the house. But when they saw that the Indians were going to get there first, they swerved to the left and struck up Bridge creek, with the enemy in hot pursuit.

It took but a few miles of hard riding to use up Masterson's work horse and he told Clark to keep on and save himself. Masterson jumped from his horse and struck into the brush. He jumped into the creek and, swimming down stream a little distance, found a deep hole overhung with thick brush, where he "camped." The Indians chased Clark a few miles farther and then returned to finish up Masterson. But he confined himself to his covered haunt, and after hunting all around him the Indians gave him up and returned to the house, where they took everything of any value to them. Clark kept on to the nearest ranch, eight miles distant, where he found a number of packers, with whom he returned to the front. They yelled for Masterson and at last he took chances on their being friends or foes and came out of his hole chilled almost to death.

The party then went on to the ranch, where they found the house smouldering in its ashes and the Indians gone. The raiders had cut open feather beds, taken away the ticking and scattering the feathers everywhere. Another house was built upon the place but ever since the premises have borne the name of Burnt Ranch.

WHY THE GREENHORNS WERE SO NAMED.

The following story is told to account for the naming of the now famous Greenhorn mining camp and mountains:

In the early days an old fellow came out to the camp of Robinsonville, representing himself to be a miner. His experience in mining had been acquired in digging potatoes in Missouri, or prying a wagon from the abyssmal depths of mud on the Pike county highways. He was given employment and sent down a thirty-foot shaft to put in a blast. After considerable time he managed to get a three-cornered hole drilled into the rock and the powder securely tamped therein. He was slow of speech and when everything was ready he sang out that he was ready to be hauled up. He had been given a fifty foot coil of fuse so that he could cut off as much as was required. As the boys at the windlass started to haul him up he drawled out: "Haul me up slowly so I can unwind the fuse." He was going to use it all. This was only one of the long series of like bright thoughts on his part and the nickname of "greenhorn" was saddled onto him and finally, as he worked all over the camp, it came to be applied to the district and to the mountains.

THE GOLD HUNTER.

Among the marked characters in a mining country the gold hunter, or as he is more generally known, the prospector, stands pre-eminent. To describe him and his life is no easy task for the amateur writer, indeed, the subject is worthy the facile pen of a master. The prospector may be short or long, fat or lean,—he cannot conceal his identity from the observation of one used to mining life. His gait, his talk, his every action, become such as are peculiar to the class which he represents. In the early winter he casts about him for a deserted cabin in which to "hole up" until the welcome sunshine comes to dispel the long, dreary winter. Having found such a receptacle for his camp outfit, if he is in funds (and he is not always so fortunate), he stores provisions for the winter, consisting of a plentiful supply of flour, bacon, beans, and tobacco, and settles down to solid comfort. If there is a crowd in winter quarters together, it will be a lively one, for the prospector is no cynic and makes the most of his peculiar style of

life. He has no use for a stove; bakes his bread in a long handled frying pan before the fire, and boils his tea and beans in tin kettles. A tin plate, butcher's knife and sometimes a large spoon constitute his table service. For dessert he takes a contenting smoke drawn from the depths of an immense wooden pipe. When night comes he lays himself on his gray blankets and peacefully sleeps without a single care on his mind. In questions of national importance he takes no interest. It is all one to him whether the currency is legal tender or not; the inter-oceanic canal may be cut across the isthmus and extended on around the world without causing a ripple of trouble in his tranquil mind.

But when the thawing sun begins to shine and the accumulated snows melt and rush out through the mountain streams, the sleepy prospector is suddenly transformed into a different being. The faithful cayuse, the companion of his summer wanderings, is brought forth from his winter quarters, packed, and off they start on their hunt for the precious gold. They seek no traveled road or ready made track, but plunge boldly into the most rugged mountain wilds. He seeks the gulches and bars, sinks his "prospect hole" and sometimes he finds gold, but oftener another winter comes on and finds him without a "color."

The traditional gold hunter seldom becomes wealthy; year after year he travels on and hunts through new lands for something rich. If he finds good pay dirt, he sells out for enough to carry him through another year in the hope of finding something richer; in time he becomes, in truth, the counterpart of the gambler; when he wins a stake, he puts it down in the hope of doubling it, and all is swept away. There is nothing left to do but to try it again. Men often become so attached to this mode of living that they have no desire to change it and luck is often against them so that they could not if they would. It is a life full of hardship and adventure but is made fascinating by the pleasures of hope "that spring eternal in the human heart."

THE COWBOY'S PATROL.

(Grant County News, May 28, 1885.)

A cowboy rode through the driving rain,
To hold his herd on a western plain.
The rain came down in a blinding sheet,
Which the frozen earth soon turned to sleet.

The shivering herd moved with the rain,
Loud crashing lash cannot restrain.
Toward the swollen stream they madly press,
But the rider rode with skill address.

The deadly stream, with its floating ice,
Will swallow the herd unless device
Can mass them round in solid wheel,
Like yarn wound round the spinner's reel.

On dash the herd, but the cowboy knows
Just where to ride and hurl his blows.
They veer, they turn, the leaders find
The outpouring herd around them wind.

The angry flood and the ice floe meet
The high, steep banks of crystal sleet,
But cowboy skill has saved the herd,
Till the morrow's dawn—not a hoof has stirred.

All night he sat in his saddle seat—
His coat-of-mail the glittering sleet;
And the ice-clad herd, he held them there
Till the morrow's sun shone bright and fair.

THE OLD SLUICE BOX.

By Morris Gregory.

Where the rocks are gray and the mountains steep,
And the gulch below looks dark and deep;
Where the gnarled pines in their rugged pride
Look gloomily up on either side;
Where the manzanita is crooked and thick;
Where once was heard the shovel and pick;
Where the shadows lie heavy upon the rocks,
There lies, half buried, the old sluice box.

The idle stream through it lazily glides,
Gently washing its mouldering sides—
Sides that once were muddy and dim
From the yellow dirt that was cast within.
While across the stream on the gravel heaps
The agile squirrel, chattering, leaps,
And the crested quail fluttering drops
For its evening drink from the old sluice box.

Oh, many a day, with a weary hand,
Have I tossed in its bed the glittering sand,
And dreamed as I leaned on its rotting side,
And raked the depths of its turbid tide,
Of father's gray hair and dear mother's smile
And the loved ones at home who were waiting the while
The wanderer's return; but time sneeringly mocks
At the days that I toiled at the old sluice box.

From the moss-grown rock on which I lean
I gaze down into the sluggish stream,
And the face that I see has graver grown,
And the voice, it seems, has a sober tone;
And the wanton winds with my hair at play,
Shows that my locks have all turned gray.
But I love to think of the days gone by,
When my spirits were bright and my hopes were high.
And again I could welcome the rough, hard knocks
To be mining once more with the old sluice box.

MY FRIEND JOE.

By Ex-Governor Gale.

(Published in the Bedrock Democrat, March 17, 1875.)

Joseph Meek, my friend Joe, when we first knew each
      other,
'Twas in the winter of 'thirty-two; 'twas cold and stormy
      weather.
The snow was falling fast, Joe, and the ground was
      covered o'er,
The day we met I'll ne'er forget, now forty years and
      more.

'Twas on that stormy day, Joe, when we were first ac-
      quaint;
Our locks were dark and flowing then, our manly brows
      were bent.
But now our brows are wrinkled, Joe, and our locks are
      frosted o'er
By toil and care and wear and tear of forty years and
      more.

I often sit and think, Joe, of our dangers and our toils,
While fighting with wild Indians, or threading dark de-
      files,
Or having crossed those mountains, Joe, we o'er the des-
      ert strayed,
With hearts of glee and souls as free as the winds that
      'round us played.

Now, Joseph Meek, my friend Joe, we are on top the
      hill;

Of trapping and of hunting, Joe, we both have had our
    fill;
And now we'll hobble down, Joe, come, hand in hand
    we'll go,
As best we may, preparing the way to meet the final
    blow.

Now to conclude our song, Joe, we'll cast our eyes up
    there
Where you and I have hunted, Joe, in the mountains
    wild and drear,
Now pause and lift them lightly, Joe, to yon calm and
    peaceful shore,
Where you and I shall meet in the sky when our last
    hunt shall be o'er.

TO ELKHORN.

Fair mountain! Guardian of the peopled plain,
The outline of the pine against thy cone.
Blending in shadowy whiteness with the blue,
Enchains me to the footsteps of thy throne.

A fleeting cloud upon thy lifted brow
Obscures thee, veil like, from the mourning skies,
The molten glory of the golden west
Makes thee at evening dearer to mine eyes.

Great rivers change their courses; cities grow,
And hide from view some old, historic spot;
The wild rose, by the snow-fed streamlet fades,
But thou, O changeless mountain, changest not.
                         —'02.